Central Mexico City

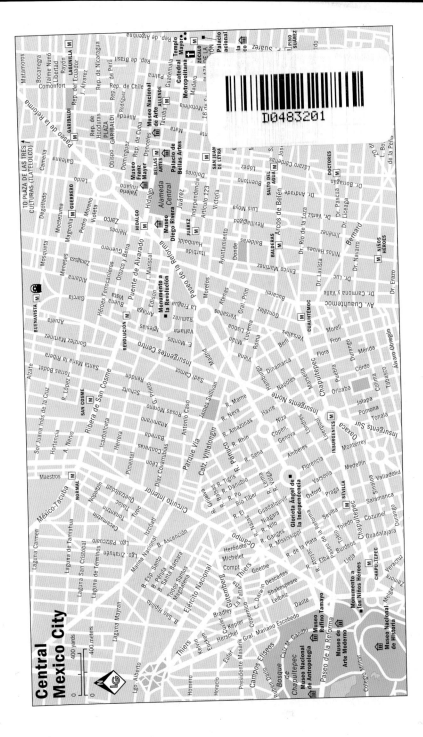

Mexico City Metro

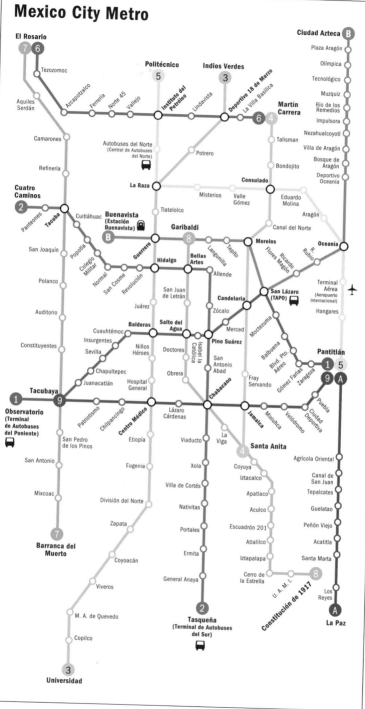

LET'S GO

■ PAGES PACKED WITH ESSENTIAL INFORMATION

"Value-packed, unbeatable, accurate, and comprehensive."

—*The Los Angeles Times*

"The guides are aimed not only at young budget travelers but at the independent traveler; a sort of streetwise cookbook for traveling alone."

—*The New York Times*

"Unbeatable; good sight-seeing advice; up-to-date info on restaurants, hotels, and inns; a commitment to money-saving travel; and a wry style that brightens nearly every page."

—*The Washington Post*

■ THE BEST TRAVEL BARGAINS IN YOUR BUDGET

"All the dirt, dirt cheap."

—*People*

"Let's Go follows the creed that you don't have to toss your life's savings to the wind to travel—unless you want to."

—*The Salt Lake Tribune*

■ REAL ADVICE FOR REAL EXPERIENCES

"The writers seem to have experienced every rooster-packed bus and lunar-surfaced mattress about which they write."

—*The New York Times*

"[Let's Go's] devoted updaters really walk the walk (and thumb the ride, and trek the trail). Learn how to fish, haggle, find work—anywhere."

—*Food & Wine*

"A world-wise traveling companion—always ready with friendly advice and helpful hints, all sprinkled with a bit of wit."

—*The Philadelphia Inquirer*

■ A GUIDE WITH A SPIRIT AND A SOCIAL CONSCIENCE

"Lighthearted and sophisticated, informative and fun to read. [Let's Go] helps the novice traveler navigate like a knowledgeable old hand."

—*Atlanta Journal-Constitution*

"The serious mission at the book's core reveals itself in exhortations to respect the culture and the environment—and, if possible, to visit as a volunteer, a student, or a teacher rather than a tourist."

—*San Francisco Chronicle*

LET'S GO PUBLICATIONS

TRAVEL GUIDES

Australia 9th edition
Austria & Switzerland 12th edition
Brazil 1st edition
Britain 2008
California 10th edition
Central America 9th edition
Chile 2nd edition
China 5th edition
Costa Rica 3rd edition
Eastern Europe 13th edition
Ecuador 1st edition
Egypt 2nd edition
Europe 2008
France 2008
Germany 13th edition
Greece 9th edition
Hawaii 4th edition
India & Nepal 8th edition
Ireland 13th edition
Israel 4th edition
Italy 2008
Japan 1st edition
Mexico 22nd edition
New Zealand 8th edition
Peru 1st edition
Puerto Rico 3rd edition
Southeast Asia 9th edition
Spain & Portugal 2008
Thailand 3rd edition
USA 24th edition
Vietnam 2nd edition
Western Europe 2008

ROADTRIP GUIDE

Roadtripping USA 2nd edition

ADVENTURE GUIDES

Alaska 1st edition
Pacific Northwest 1st edition
Southwest USA 3rd edition

CITY GUIDES

Amsterdam 5th edition
Barcelona 3rd edition
Boston 4th edition
London 16th edition
New York City 16th edition
Paris 14th edition
Rome 12th edition
San Francisco 4th edition
Washington, D.C. 13th edition

POCKET CITY GUIDES

Amsterdam
Berlin
Boston
Chicago
London
New York City
Paris
San Francisco
Venice
Washington, D.C.

LET'S GO

MEXICO

LAURA CAVA NORTHROP EDITOR
DWIGHT L. CURTIS ASSOCIATE EDITOR
NATALIE I. SHERMAN ASSOCIATE EDITOR

RESEARCHER-WRITERS
RAÚL CARRILLO
LIZA COVINGTON
CORA CURRIER
HANNAH SARAH FAICH
RUSSELL RENNIE
JOSEPH TARTAKOFF

ANDREA TSURUMI MAP EDITOR
VICTORIA NORELID MANAGING EDITOR

ST. MARTIN'S PRESS NEW YORK

Maps by David Lindroth copyright © 2008 by St. Martin's Press.

Distributed outside the USA and Canada by Macmillan.

ISBN-13: 978-0-312-37452-5
ISBN-10: 0-312-37452-6
Twenty-second edition
10 9 8 7 6 5 4 3 2 1

Let's Go: Mexico is written by Let's Go Publications, 67 Mount Auburn St., Cambridge, MA 02138, USA.

HOW TO USE THIS BOOK

COVERAGE LAYOUT. *Let's Go: Mexico* begins in **Mexico City,** the country's heart, and follows with a whirling tour through Mexico. From the idyllic **Baja California Peninsula,** cross the Sea of Cortés into **Northwest Mexico,** home of the famed Copper Canyon. Sweep through the mountain villages and cloud forests of the **Northeast** before exploring the colonial heritage of **Central Mexico.** Venture down the **Central Pacific Coast,** continuing into the sun-soaked **Southern Pacific Coast** before descending into the laid-back college towns of the **Gulf Coast** and the jungles of **Chiapas.** Our coverage ends with the archaeological ruins, coral reefs, and tourist-filled nightclubs of the **Yucatán Peninsula.**

TRANSPORTATION INFO. For connections between destinations, information is generally listed under both the arrival and departure cities. Parentheticals usually provide the trip duration followed by the frequency, then the price. For more general information on travel, consult **Essentials** (p. 9).

COVERING THE BASICS. The first chapter, **Discover Mexico** (p. 1), contains highlights of the country, complete with **Suggested Itineraries.** The **Essentials** (p. 9) section contains practical information on planning a budget, making reservations, and other useful tips for traveling in Mexico. Take some time to peruse the **Life and Times** (p. 54) section, a crash course in the history, customs, art, and culture of Mexico. The **Appendix** (p. 700) features climate information, a list of national holidays, measurement conversions, and a glossary. For study abroad, volunteer, and work opportunities in Mexico, **Beyond Tourism** (p. 77) has all the resources you need.

SCHOLARLY ARTICLES. Ph.D. candidate in Latin American history **Isaac Campos** writes on the history of drugs in Mexico, with a focus on the drug trade between the United States and Mexico (p. 76). In **Beyond Tourism,** A.B. candidate Laura Ann Schoenherr recounts her experience working with sustainable health care initiatives in Mexico (p. 78).

PRICE DIVERSITY. Our researchers list establishments in order of value from best to worst, with absolute favorites denoted by the *Let's Go* thumbs-up (🖐). Since the cheapest price does not always mean the best value, we have incorporated a system of price ranges for food and accommodations.

PHONE CODES AND TELEPHONE NUMBERS. Area codes for each region appear opposite the name of the region and are denoted by the ☎ icon. Phone numbers in text are also preceded by the ☎ icon.

UNIQUE AND USEFUL SECTIONS. Our 2008 edition bursts with new listings of **vegetarian** restaurants, **GLBT** establishments, and an expanded **glossary** of useful Spanish terms. Check out our revamped **history** section in the **Life and Times** chapter. We've also expanded our **beaches** and **outdoor activities** sections, bringing you more detailed coverage of **national parks, camping,** and Mexico's **Copper Canyon.**

A NOTE TO OUR READERS. The information for this book was gathered by *Let's Go* researchers from May through August of 2007. Each listing is based on one researcher's opinion, formed during his or her visit at a particular time. Those traveling at other times may have different experiences since prices, dates, hours, and conditions are always subject to change. You are urged to check the facts presented in this book beforehand to avoid inconvenience and surprises.

CONTENTS

VIII

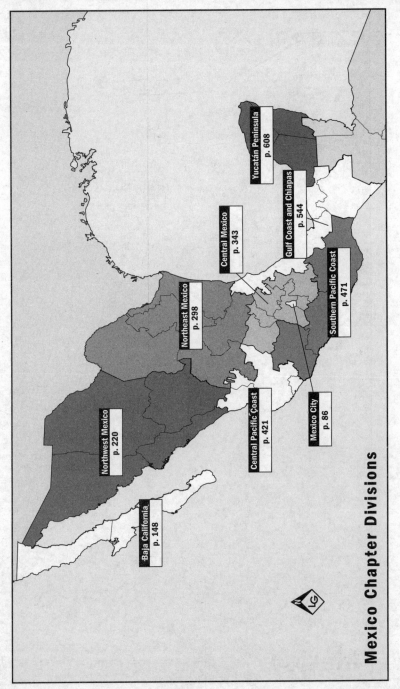

Mexico Chapter Divisions

Baja California
p. 148

Northwest Mexico
p. 220

Central Pacific Coast
p. 421

Mexico City
p. 86

Northeast Mexico
p. 298

Central Mexico
p. 343

Gulf Coast and Chiapas
p. 544

Southern Pacific Coast
p. 471

Yucatán Peninsula
p. 608

Mexico

PACIFIC OCEAN

UNITED

CALIFORNIA
ARIZONA
NEW MEXICO

Tijuana
Yuma
Rosarito
Mexicali
Ensenada
San Quintín
San Felipe
El Rosario

SIERRA SAN PEDRO MÁRTIR

BAJA
CALIFORNIA

Isla
Cedros

Bahía de
Sebastián
Vizcaíno

Guerrero
Negro
San Ignacio
Santa Rosalía
Mulegé

BAJA
CALIFORNIA
SUR

Loreto

Puerto
San Carlos

La Paz

Todos Santos

Cabo San Lucas

San José
del Cabo

Los Barriles

Tucson

Puerto
Peñasco

Nogales

Caborca

SONORA

Isla
Ángel de
la Guardia

Isla
Tiburón

Hermosillo

Bahía Kino

San Carlos
Guaymas

Gulf of California (Sea of Cortés)

Alamos

El Fuerte
Los Mochis

Topolobampo

Culiacán

SINALOA

Mazatlán

Nuevo Casas
Grandes

CHIHUAHUA

El Paso
Ciudad
Juárez

LAS BARRANCAS
DEL COBRE
(COPPER
CANYON)

Chihuahua

Cuauhtémoc

Creel

Hidalgo
del Parral

SIERRA MADRE OCCIDENTAL

COAHUILA

Jiménez

Parras de la
Fuente

Torreón

DURANGO

Durango

ZACATECAS

Real de
Catorce

Zacatecas

AGUAS-
CALIENTES

NAYARIT

Tuxpan

Tepic

Puerto Vallarta

Guadalajara

JALISCO

Bahía
de Navidad
Manzanillo

Colima

COLIMA

Aguas-
calientes

Guanajuato
GUANA-
JUATO

Morelia
Pátzcuaro

Uruapan

MICHOACÁN
DE OCAMPO

GUEF

Zihuatanejo/
Ixtapa

N
LG

0   200 miles
0   200 kilometers

X

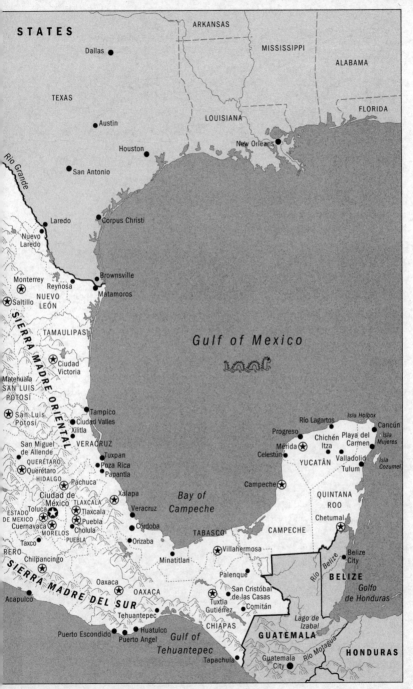

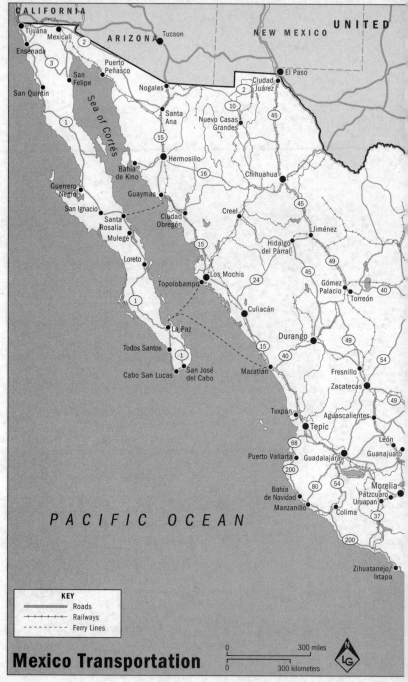

Mexico Transportation

KEY
Roads
Railways
Ferry Lines

0 — 300 miles
0 — 300 kilometers

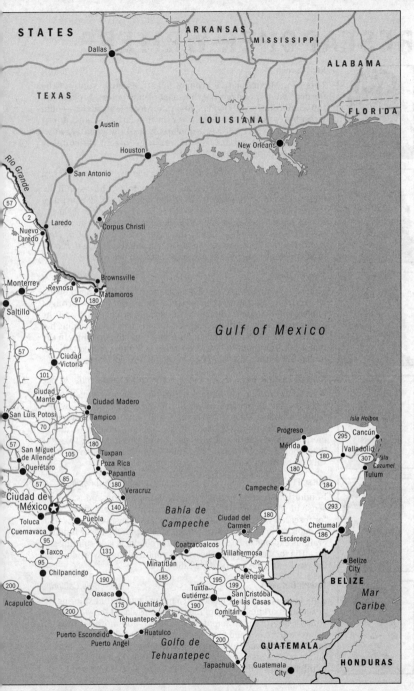

RESEARCHER-WRITERS

Raúl Carrillo
The Northwest

This New Mexico native brought his street-savvy south of the border, where not even the thorniest of obstacles—broken laptops, amorous hostel owners, and runaway rental trucks—could wrest his eyes from the prize. Ever the indefatigable adventurer, *El Animal* expertly traversed nearly half of the country, wowing his Editors with tales of derring-do and thoroughly researched copy all along the way.

Liza Covington
Chiapas and the Yucatán Peninsula

As the ultimate *Let's Go* veteran, Liza Covington has seen it all, done it all, and, fortunately for us, written it all down. Having previously researched for *Let's Go: Central America* and the 2006 edition of *Let's Go: Mexico*, Liza took her can-do enthusiasm back to the Maya Riviera—less than a day after editing *Let's Go: New Zealand 2008*. She blazed across the Yucatán Peninsula in record time, forever earning her a spot in the Let's Go hall of fame.

Cora Currier
The Northeast

This seasoned globetrotter and social activist—she's been everywhere from Bhutan to the Central African Republic—brought unparalleled moxie to the cloud forests and college towns of the Northeast. Cora's spark captivated locals in every town, leading her to the finest cafes, vegetarian fare, and local music joints in the region. Every step of the way, she kept her Editors enchanted with thoughtful writing, Mexican candy, and picture postcards.

Hannah Sarah Faich
Mexico City and Central Mexico

With two homestays in Latin America and a degree tucked under her belt, Hannah Sarah took off for the Mexican heartland, where students, archaeologists, and bouncers alike were won over by her kilowatt smile and new black dress. She consistently turned in meticulous research and professional prose, wangling five-star hotel rooms, climbing a volcano, and celebrating almost every festival Central Mexico had to offer in the process.

Russell Rennie
Central and Southern Pacific Coast

In addition to an unfailingly cheerful disposition and a shrewd sense of whimsy, Russell possessed an almost supernatural talent for research-writing. Whether braving public transportation, would-be captors, or bizarre hostel mates, this superstar never failed to craft his exploits in Pacific Mexico into rollicking, side-splitting stories. His flawless copybatches wryly captured the flavor of life on the road—and the hearts of his Editors.

Joseph Tartakoff
Baja California

Joe's laid-back attitude made him a natural match for exploring the peaceful, sparkling shores of the Baja peninsula. At the wheel of his trusty (albeit temperamental) rental car, Joe motored through gaudy resort cities and meandered past idyllic fishing hamlets, gazing at many a beautiful sunset along the way. Joe's witty, discriminating eye consistently picked out the best and brightest Baja had to offer, a skill reflected in his concise, straaaaightforwarrrdd copy.

ACKNOWLEDGMENTS

TEAM MEX THANKS: Our kick-ass ▨RWs—without your dedication and perseverance, this book could not exist. Victoria and her stellar ME talent. Andrea, the best Map Editor a bookteam could ever hope for. The ME team, who stepped in when the going got rough. SPAM: the winningest pod—so nasty! Evy's iPod. Laura's laugh. Vinnie's spirit. Meghan, for getting the ball rolling. The ▨coffeemaker and the never-ending office-wide bakeoff. The sleepy chair and the "creative" chair. All the lawyers associated with the publication of this book. Last but certainly not least, we'd like to thank Mississippi...jam on.

LAURA THANKS: The RWs, for giving it their all. Cora, Raúl and Russell for hilarious tales from the road. Victoria, Natalie and Dwight, Esq. for all the hard work. Jakub, for unconditional encouragement and support. *Miluji tě.* Lots of love to my understanding, caring family. Meg: the LG adventure started with you & OAXV. Emy: soon it'll be our turn. CM, KS, NJ, AW, NR, JK, DD, KM, and KBS for listening.

DWIGHT THANKS: Laura, Natalie, and Victoria, for editorial expertise. Liza and Joe, for topnotch writing. Boston drivers, for helping me wake up in the morning. Everyone whose couch I've ever slept on. The powers that be, for bringing me on board.

NATALIE THANKS: Mumoo for housing me, feeding me, and putting up with me, Hannah Sarah for her thorough research and prose, Dwight and Laura for their editorial commentary, Victoria for her eagle eyes and patience.

ANDREA THANKS: Thanks to team Mexico for all their hard work, Tom, Maisie, Drew and Joy for a great mapland pod, and Sam and Phil for an awesome summer!

Editor
Laura Cava Northrop
Associate Editor
Dwight L. Curtis
Associate Editor
Natalie I. Sherman
Managing Editor
Victoria Norelid
Map Editor
Andrea Tsurumi
Typesetter
Teresa Elsey

LET'S GO

Publishing Director
Jennifer Q. Wong
Editor-in-Chief
Silvia Gonzalez Killingsworth
Production Manager
Victoria Esquivel-Korsiak
Cartography Manager
Thomas MacDonald Barron
Editorial Managers
Anne Bensson, Calina Ciobanu, Rachel Nolan
Financial Manager
Sara Culver
Business and Marketing Manager
Julie Vodhanel
Personnel Manager
Victoria Norelid
Production Associate
Jansen A. S. Thurmer
Director of E-Commerce & IT
Patrick Carroll
Website Manager
Kathryne A. Bevilacqua
Office Coordinators
Juan L. Peña, Bradley J. Jones

Director of Advertising Sales
Hunter McDonald
Senior Advertising Associate
Daniel Lee

President
William Hauser
General Managers
Bob Rombauer, Jim McKellar

PRICE RANGES
MEXICO

① ② ③ ④ ⑤

Our researchers list establishments in order of value from best to worst; our favorites are denoted by the Let's Go thumbs-up (👍). However, because the best value is not always the cheapest price, we have also incorporated a system of price ranges, based on a rough expectation of what you'll spend. For **accommodations**, we base our range on the cheapest price for which a single traveler can stay for one night. For **restaurants** and other dining establishments, we estimate the average amount a traveler will spend. The table tells you what you'll typically find in Mexico at the corresponding price range; keep in mind that no system can allow for every individual establishment's quirks, and you'll typically get more for your money in larger cities. In other words: expect anything.

ACCOMMODATIONS	RANGE	WHAT YOU'RE LIKELY TO FIND
①	under 170 pesos (under US$16)	Hostels with dorms and communal showers; campsites; basic hotel rooms with very limited amenities; usually does not include private bathroom.
②	170-220 pesos (US$16-20)	Upper-scale hostels with private rooms; simple hotel rooms with more of the basic amenities, including A/C, phone, and TV; expect private bathroom to cost extra.
③	220-270 pesos (US$20-25)	Similar to ②, but includes private bathroom. Some offer Internet access and free continental breakfast. In general, cleaner and more attractive than the previous options.
④	270-325 pesos (US$25-30)	Hotels in tourist and resort locations with all the amenities, including private bathroom. Some places have been recently remodeled. Private *cabanas* in smaller beachside towns.
⑤	over 325 pesos (over US$30)	Luxury hotels in resort destinations; sometimes ③ or ④ quality rooms in smaller towns and border regions that can get away with price hikes.

FOOD	RANGE	WHAT YOU'RE LIKELY TO FIND
①	under 20 pesos (under US$2)	Mostly street-corner stands, *taquerías*, or fast-food joints; usually tacos or *quesadillas*. Rarely ever a sit-down meal.
②	20-35 pesos (US$2-3.25)	Smaller restaurants and cafes; usually serving drinks and sandwiches. Some appetizers and basic entrees, but not a full meal.
③	35-50 pesos (US$3.25-4.50)	Sit-down restaurants with waitstaff; larger plates and meals, usually with sides.
④	50-75 pesos (US$4.50-7)	Nicer eateries serving full meals; elaborate entrees and creative ambience; fresh seafood plates.
⑤	over 75 pesos (over US$7)	High-class establishments; elegant versions of traditional staples. You might have to dress the part.

DISCOVER MEXICO

Built on the ruins of great civilizations, Mexico was born of radical revolution, solidified by the struggle for independence, and is now finding its place in a new era of democracy and global collaboration. Formerly the Aztec capital, Mexico City—one of the world's largest cities—and the D.F. epitomizes the uniquely Mexican mix of past and present. Not far from the buzzing metropolis are sleepy *pueblos* where modern comforts are scarce and residents cling to their ancestral lands and languages. World-famous beach resorts are the playgrounds of the rich, while slums only a few blocks off the touristed path are home to *campesinos*, street vendors, and homeless children living in abject poverty.

This year we've expanded each of our nine regions—the Baja and Yucatán Peninsulas, the Northwest, the Northeast, the Central and South Pacific Coasts, Central Mexico, Mexico City, the Gulf Coast and Chiapas—adding hundreds of new listings and sights. Enjoy entirely fresh coverage on resort cities, beachside getaways, and archaeological wonders alike, including a completely revamped section on Mexico's foremost natural wonder, Copper Canyon. Our team of intrepid adventurers have combed through every square inch of their routes—traversing miles of cobblestones and sand, spending countless hours in transit, and sampling thousands of tacos—while sniffing out the best bargains, cultural treasures, ecotourism, and adrenaline-pumping outdoor activities Mexico has to offer.

Whether you're dreaming of a transformative experience immersed in Mexico's national parks, colonial towns, and ancient ruins, or a tequila-soaked spring break, *Let's Go Mexico* has got you covered from start to finish with quality, budget-friendly coverage. In resort cities and indigenous villages alike, we point you in the direction of the best hikes, hostels, and *horchata* Mexico has to offer—with the hottest nightlife to boot. Savor fiery salsas, succulent meats, and fresh coastal seafood. Marvel at colonial architecture and exotic museum collections. Relax on a sun-soaked Pacific beach. Revel in the eye-popping hues splashed over everything from clothing to churches. Refresh in a city plaza—cold local brew in hand—as roving *mariachis* serenade the streets. Discover Mexico.

FACTS AND FIGURES

MEXICO, DEFINED: Náhuatl word meaning "Bellybutton of the World."

POPULATION: 108 million

LAND MASS: 1,972,550 sq. km

GDP PER PERSON: US$10,700

ANNUAL TORTILLA CONSUMPTION PER PERSON: 270 lbs.

ANNUAL BEER PRODUCTION: Over 6 million liters of brew—the world's fifth largest exporter.

REGULAR CHURCHGOERS: 45 million

REGULAR SOCCER FANS: 31 million

MEXICO CITY METRO: Built for 1968 Olympics, used daily by 9 million riders.

CHICHÉN ITZÁ: Mayan city named one of the "New Seven Wonders of the World" in 2007.

RED SAVINA HABANERO: World's hottest pepper, measuring a scorching 577,000 Scoville units.

WHEN TO GO

Mexico's lush jungles, gleaming beaches, and textured highlands entice visitors year-round. Winters tend to be mild, while summers vary from warm to excruciatingly hot, as **temperatures** soar to upwards of 42°C (108°F). High-altitude regions, such as the Valley of Mexico and the Oaxaca Valley, remain temperate year-round. During the **rainy season** (May-Sept.), the south receives an average of 2-3hr. of rain every afternoon. The best time to hit the beach is during the **dry season** (Oct.-Apr.), when afternoons are sunny, evenings balmy, and nights relatively mosquito-free.

The **peak tourist season** (high season) encompasses December, *Semana Santa* (the week before Easter), and mid-summer. In March and the early part of April— the traditional US spring break—resort towns like Cancún, Cabo San Lucas, and Mazatlán fill with boozing college students. Central Mexico sees the most tourist traffic during July and August, when throngs of students studying abroad hit the books and the trendy cafes. If you travel to Mexico during any of these times, expect to pay slightly higher prices at hotels and restaurants.

WHAT TO DO

Whether climbing age-old Mayan temples, haggling for silver trinkets in colonial open-air markets, diving near coral reefs, or dancing with margarita in hand, visitors head to each region for its individual cultural allure. See the **Highlights of the Region** section at the beginning of each chapter for specific regional attractions.

DIG UP THE PAST

A journey through Mexico is like a whirlwind tour through time. The ancient Olmecs—famous for their colossal carved heads—were the first to call Mexico home, settling the villages of **La Venta** (see p. 580), and **Tres Zapotes** (see p. 571) on the Gulf Coast around 1000 BC. Centuries later, a mighty empire rose in the Valley of Mexico at **Teotihuacán** (see p. 141). Farther south, the Zapotec capital **Monte Albán** (see p. 540) rivaled Teotihuacán from its lofty hillside position overlooking the verdant Oaxaca Valley. To the east, in the lowland jungles of the Yucatán Peninsula, the Maya built grand cities like **Palenque** (see p. 600), where distinct architecture and lush setting continue to dazzle visitors. In central Mexico, the Tlaxcalans drew breathtaking murals at **Cacaxtla** (see p. 401), and the Totonacs carved the Pyramid of Niches at **El Tajín** (see p. 551). After the fall of the Classic civilizations, Post-Classic centers of power—like **Tula** (see p. 370), the birthplace of the feathered serpent-god Quetzalcóatl—advanced Mesoamerican civilization. The Yucatán is also home to the warring Mayan trio of **Chichén Itzá** (see p. 646), **Mayapán** (see p. 628), and **Uxmal** (see p. 634). The last stand of pre-Hispanic Mexico was the Aztec capital of **Tenochtitlán** (in modern-day Mexico City; see p. 55).

SURF AND SPLASH

Mexico's infinite stretches of sparkling golden and white beaches will please even the most discriminating beachgoer. Those who like an audience can strut their stuff in front of the millions of bronzed bodies in **Cancún** (see p. 656) and **Cabo San Lucas** (see p. 207). If the glam tourist scene isn't your style, ramble down the turquoise coast toward **Tulum** (see p. 685), to cavort in the beachside ruins. The shores of **Isla Mujeres** (see p. 668) offer a quiet respite from the insanity, as does **Isla Cozumel** (see p. 679), where coral is king and scuba is queen. The southern Pacific coast harbors the surfing town of **Puerto Escondido** (see p. 513), with formidable waves and scantily clad beach bums. Farther up the coast sprawls the grand old dame of beach resorts, **Acapulco** (see p. 500), complete with cliff-diving men in tiny briefs. The stately duo of **Zihuatanejo** and **Ixtapa** (see p. 493) host droves of sun-worshippers, as do ever-popular **Puerto Vallarta** (see p. 447) and **Mazatlán** (see p. 274), while **San Blas** (p. 422) welcomes hard-core surfers. Off the beaten track to the north are some of the most overlooked and most spectacular beaches in the country. On the calm Sea of Cortés, bask under the stars on the beaches of **San Felipe** (see p. 173), **Bahía de Kino** (see p. 234), or **Bahía de la Concepción** (see p. 191).

CONQUER THE COBBLESTONES

Mexico's colonial past is a white-washed blur of churches, silver mines, and unfair labor practices. To see everything from start to finish all in one place, head to **Mexico City** (see p. 86), where Hernán Cortés first established Spanish imperium by torturing Aztec emperor Cuauhtémoc. Then visit the **Palacio Nacional** (see p. 111), which once housed Spanish viceroys and now holds the Campaña de Dolores (Bell of Dolores) that summoned Mexicans to fight for independence in 1810. When the city starts to swelter, make your way to **Cuernavaca** (see p. 383), once the summer camp of the colonial elite, and now home to wealthy Mexicans and international jetsetters who swarm to the local language schools and lush gardens. Blinded by the bling? Stock up in nearby **Taxco** (see p. 508), a colonial silver town where the winding roads recall visions of Spain. To the south lie the faded limestone streets and lavish temples of **Oaxaca** (see p. 530), the birthplace of Mexico's famous president, *indígeno* Benito Juárez, and its infamous dictator, Porfirio Díaz. Swing by **Morelia** (see p. 475), a state capital packed with cultural centers and rose-colored arcades, then frolic with university students or mummies in the museums of **Guanajuato** (see p. 345). Don't miss artsy **San Miguel de Allende** (see p. 353) before relaxing in the nation's wealthy silver and gold capital **San Luis Potosí** (see p. 330). Head back through steamy **Veracruz** (see p. 559), the port of choice for the country's many invaders (at last count, Spain, France, and the US, twice). Farther inland is **Tlaxcala** (see p. 393), the city-state that collaborated with Cortés to defeat the Aztecs. Neighboring **Puebla** (see p. 403) epitomizes colonial Mexico, exhibiting Renaissance order in its perfectly gridded streets and cobblestone walkways.

TOP 10 FIESTAS

1. Equinox, Chichén Itzá (p. 646): By a trick of light and shadow, the serpent-god Kukulkán appears on the steps of world-famous Mayan ruins. (Mar. 20 and Sept. 20)

2. Cinco de Mayo, Puebla (p. 403): Relive the 1862 victory against the French. (May 5)

3. Día de los Locos, San Miguel de Allende (p. 353): Costumes and cross-dressers galore take to the streets in a parade of expats. (mid-June)

4. Festival de Vainilla, Papantla (p. 548): Vanilla sweets complement performances by the Flying Pole Dancers. (June 18)

5. La Guelaguetza, Oaxaca (p. 539): Dances and ritual gift-giving to 12,000 of your closest friends. (Last 2 Mondays in July)

6. Feria de la Uva, Parras de la Fuente (p. 327): Everyone takes part in the grape-stomping celebration. (August 3-19)

7. Independence Day, Mexico City (p. 111): The *zócalo* erupts when the President rings the famous bell. (Sept. 15-16)

8. Festival Internacional Cervantino, Guanajuato (p. 352): Students honor the author of Don Quixote. (Oct. 3-24)

9. Día de los Muertos, Patzcuaro (p. 481): Cemetery visits and sugar skeletons celebrate human mortality. (Nov. 1-2)

10. Noche de Rábanos, Oaxaca (p. 530): Thousands admire folk art and figurines carved entirely out of radishes. (Dec. 23)

WALK ON THE WILD SIDE

For outdoor adventure enthusiasts, the Baja peninsula boasts a handful of lush natural reserves, including the **Parque Nacional Sierra San Pedro Mártir** (see p. 177), where you can climb the peninsula's highest peak, **Picacho del Diablo** (see p. 178). Back on the mainland, set up camp among the peaks of the **Sierra Madre Occidental** mountain range, hike through the wind-whipped deserts of **Chihuahua** (see p. 251), or traverse one of the many trails along the **Copper Canyon** (see p. 264). The northern state of Sonora, overlooking the Sea of Cortés, is home to **El Pinacate** volcanic preserve (see p. 229), one of the most dramatic biospheres in the world, where you can lay out your sleeping bag in a massive volcanic crater. To the east, in Tamaulipas, Ciudad Victoria provides easy access to **El Cielo Reserva de la Biosfera** (see p. 308), an immense nature reserve brimming with exotic wildlife and plants. Southeast Mexico offers its own riches, in areas like the lagoon at Catemaco (see p. 572), the **Parque Nacional de la Villa Luz** (see p. 582) outside Villahermosa, and the *cenote*-filled jungles surrounding **Tulum** (see p. 685).

▨ LET'S GO PICKS

BEST WAY TO DRINK FOR FREE: On a distillery tour in Tequila (see p. 446), where the town's 16 factories give 3 free shots each.

BEST PLACE TO LOSE YOURSELF IN THE CROWD: On the Metro with **Mexico City's** 22 million residents (see p. 94).

BEST THIGH-MASTER SUBSTITUTE: Climbing up massive pyramids in the ancient cities of **Teotihuacán** (see p. 141) or **Chichén Itzá** (see p. 646).

BEST ONLY-IN-MEXICO ICE CREAM FLAVORS: *Chicharrón* (pork rind), *elote* (corn meal), *aguacate* (avocado), and *cerveza* (beer).

BEST TIME TO BE TOLD YOU'RE GORGEOUS: On the breathtaking CHEPE train, winding through the Northwest's **Copper Canyons** (see p. 264).

BEST ROUTE TO THE UNDERWORLD: Through the longest set of underground caverns in the world, at **Cenote Dos Ojos** (see p. 689).

BEST PLACE TO OBSERVE WILD ANIMALS: In **Tijuana** (see p. 150), where the *americanus bronzus* romps, wearing *sombreros* and downing beers atop zebra-painted donkeys.

BEST ROYAL GATHERING: The annual winter meeting of more than 20 million monarch butterflies in **El Rosario** (see p. 178).

BEST TIME TO BREAK OUT THE SHORT SHORTS: Hurling yourself off a 35m cliff while emulating the famous, loinclothed **Acapulco** (see p. 500) cliff divers.

BEST DEATH: By chocolate in Oaxaca (see p. 535), the Mexican cocoa capital.

BEST PLACE TO PROPOSE: On the shores of **Isla Holbox** (see p. 666), while watching the sunset, dressed in palm fronds, drunk.

BEST PIPELINE: At **Puerto Escondido** (see p. 513), where expert surfers take on world-class waves.

BEST MUMMIFIED REMAINS: In colonial **Guanajuato** (p. 351), where unusual air conditions preserved the aftermath of a cholera outbreak for eternal display.

BEST HEAD: The 33 enormous Olmec sculptures at Parque-Museo La Venta in **Villahermosa** (p. 580).

BEST FEAST FOR CULTURE VULTURES: **Mexico City** (see **p. 125**), by some counts the city with the most museums in the world.

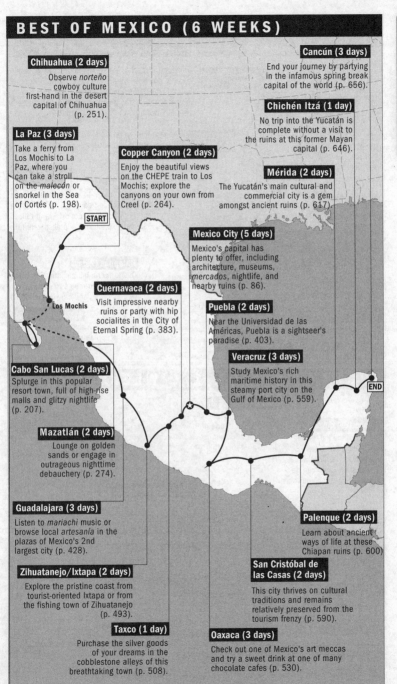

BEST OF MEXICO (6 WEEKS)

DISCOVER

Chihuahua (2 days)

Observe *norteño* cowboy culture first-hand in the desert capital of Chihuahua (p. 251).

La Paz (3 days)

Take a ferry from Los Mochis to La Paz, where you can take a stroll on the *malecón* or snorkel in the Sea of Cortés (p. 198).

Copper Canyon (2 days)

Enjoy the beautiful views on the CHEPE train to Los Mochis; explore the canyons on your own from Creel (p. 264).

START

Los Mochis

Cuernavaca (2 days)

Visit impressive nearby ruins or party with hip socialites in the City of Eternal Spring (p. 383).

Cabo San Lucas (2 days)

Splurge in this popular resort town, full of high-rise malls and glitzy nightlife (p. 207).

Mazatlán (2 days)

Lounge on golden sands or engage in outrageous nighttime debauchery (p. 274).

Guadalajara (3 days)

Listen to *mariachi* music or browse local *artesanía* in the plazas of Mexico's 2nd largest city (p. 428).

Zihuatanejo/Ixtapa (2 days)

Explore the pristine coast from tourist-oriented Ixtapa or from the fishing town of Zihuatanejo (p. 493).

Taxco (1 day)

Purchase the silver goods of your dreams in the cobblestone alleys of this breathtaking town (p. 508).

Cancún (3 days)

End your journey by partying in the infamous spring break capital of the world (p. 656).

Chichén Itzá (1 day)

No trip into the Yucatán is complete without a visit to the ruins at this former Mayan capital (p. 646).

Mérida (2 days)

The Yucatán's main cultural and commercial city is a gem amongst ancient ruins (p. 617).

Mexico City (5 days)

Mexico's capital has plenty to offer, including architecture, museums, *mercados*, nightlife, and nearby ruins (p. 86).

Puebla (2 days)

Near the Universidad de las Américas, Puebla is a sightseer's paradise (p. 403).

Veracruz (3 days)

Study Mexico's rich maritime history in this steamy port city on the Gulf of Mexico (p. 559).

END

Palenque (2 days)

Learn about ancient ways of life at these Chiapan ruins (p. 600)

San Cristóbal de las Casas (2 days)

This city thrives on cultural traditions and remains relatively preserved from the tourism frenzy (p. 590).

Oaxaca (3 days)

Check out one of Mexico's art meccas and try a sweet drink at one of many chocolate cafes (p. 530).

ROUGHING IT: NORTH MEXICO (3 1/2 WEEKS)

START

Puerto Peñasco (3 days)
Finish your trip with an expedition into El Pinacate volcanic preserve, one of the largest and most dramatic biospheres in the world. Gape at El Elegante, one of the nine massive craters in the vast, otherworldly volcanic desert (p. 225).

END

Parque Nacional Sierra San Pedro (3 days)
Camp in one of the breathtaking national parks and climb Picacho del Diablo, the highest peak on the peninsula (p. 177).

Bahía de Kino (2-3 days)
Admire the crystal waters and exotic marine life of Isla Tiburón and Turner's Island (p. 234).

Copper Canyon (5 days)
Hike and camp to your heart's content deep in Mexican canyon country. During the rainy season, cool off with a trek to Basaseachi, Mexico's largest waterfall (p. 264).

Reserva de la Biosfera El Vizcaíno (3-4 days)
Go for a whale watch or check out the hundreds of cave paintings in Latin America's largest nature reserve, while camping at the base of the Tres Vírgenes volcano (p. 183).

Batopilas (2 days)
This former mining center has loads of abandoned mines to explore, as well as caves and canyons (p. 268).

La Paz (2 days)
Relax in the bustling capital of Baja California Sur, and spend lavish days and nights on some of Mexico's most stunning beaches (p. 198).

Mazatlán (2 days)
Make the daytrip to the island oasis Isla de la Piedra. After the sun sets, head to the Zona Dorada for a raucous night of clubbing (p. 274).

SOUTH MEXICO (2 1/2 WEEKS)

Chichén Itzá (1 day)
Visit this world-famous, former Mayan capital recently voted one of the New Seven Wonders of the World in 2007 and see some of the grandest ruins in all of Mexico (p. 646).

Tulum (2 days)
Divers, snorkelers, and hikers alike will be delighted by the numerous *cenotes* surrounding the city (p. 685).

Colima (3-4 days)
Climb Colima's daunting volcanoes. The larger, El Nevado, is dormant while the smaller, El Volcón de Fuego, is startlingly active (p. 465).

Villahermosa (3-4 days)
Skip the oil-fueled inner city bustle and take a trip to the wetlands north of the city, the mountains to the southeast, or the jungle to the southwest (p. 576).

END

Xilitla (2 days)
Explore the complex of caves surrounding this town and marvel at Las Pozas, a world of surrealist architecture and pools built by the eccentric millionaire Edward James (p. 340).

START

Pátzcuaro (1 day)
This small city, nestled in the mountains, is famous for its *artesanía*. Take a boat trip to the island of Janitzio in the center of Lake Pátzcuaro and admire *indígena* crafts (p. 481).

Catemaco (1 day)
Surrounded by a picturesque lagoon, gorgeous Gulf Coast beaches, and an island full of monkeys, Catemaco is a refreshing spot to spend a night (p. 572).

Chetumal (2 days)
Bask in the sun in the 2nd largest lagoon in Mexico, or bring your scuba gear and drop into the Cenote Azul, a 90m deep cave dive (p. 694).

BAJA ROAD TRIP! (4 WEEKS)

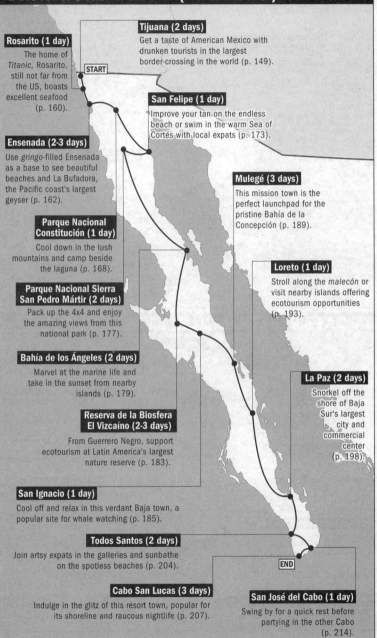

START

Rosarito (1 day)
The home of *Titanic*, Rosarito, still not far from the US, boasts excellent seafood (p. 160).

Tijuana (2 days)
Get a taste of American Mexico with drunken tourists in the largest border-crossing in the world (p. 149).

San Felipe (1 day)
Improve your tan on the endless beach or swim in the warm Sea of Cortés with local expats (p. 173).

Ensenada (2-3 days)
Use *gringo*-filled Ensenada as a base to see beautiful beaches and La Bufadora, the Pacific coast's largest geyser (p. 162).

Mulegé (3 days)
This mission town is the perfect launchpad for the pristine Bahía de la Concepción (p. 189).

Parque Nacional Constitución (1 day)
Cool down in the lush mountains and camp beside the laguna (p. 168).

Loreto (1 day)
Stroll along the *malecón* or visit nearby islands offering ecotourism opportunities (p. 193).

Parque Nacional Sierra San Pedro Mártir (2 days)
Pack up the 4x4 and enjoy the amazing views from this national park (p. 177).

Bahía de los Ángeles (2 days)
Marvel at the marine life and take in the sunset from nearby islands (p. 179).

La Paz (2 days)
Snorkel off the shore of Baja Sur's largest city and commercial center (p. 198).

Reserva de la Biosfera El Vizcaíno (2-3 days)
From Guerrero Negro, support ecotourism at Latin America's largest nature reserve (p. 183).

San Ignacio (1 day)
Cool off and relax in this verdant Baja town, a popular site for whale watching (p. 185).

Todos Santos (2 days)
Join artsy expats in the galleries and sunbathe on the spotless beaches (p. 204).

END

Cabo San Lucas (3 days)
Indulge in the glitz of this resort town, popular for its shoreline and raucous nightlife (p. 207).

San José del Cabo (1 day)
Swing by for a quick rest before partying in the other Cabo (p. 214).

DISCOVER

PLAYAS OF THE PACIFIC (3 WEEKS)

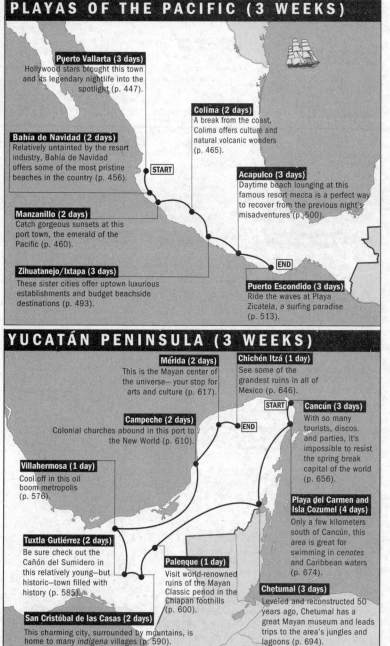

Puerto Vallarta (3 days)
Hollywood stars brought this town and its legendary nightlife into the spotlight (p. 447).

Colima (2 days)
A break from the coast, Colima offers culture and natural volcanic wonders (p. 465).

Bahía de Navidad (2 days)
Relatively untainted by the resort industry, Bahía de Navidad offers some of the most pristine beaches in the country (p. 456).

START

Acapulco (3 days)
Daytime beach lounging at this famous resort mecca is a perfect way to recover from the previous night's misadventures (p. 500).

Manzanillo (2 days)
Catch gorgeous sunsets at this port town, the emerald of the Pacific (p. 460).

END

Zihuatanejo/Ixtapa (3 days)
These sister cities offer uptown luxurious establishments and budget beachside destinations (p. 493).

Puerto Escondido (3 days)
Ride the waves at Playa Zicatela, a surfing paradise (p. 513).

YUCATÁN PENINSULA (3 WEEKS)

Mérida (2 days)
This is the Mayan center of the universe— your stop for arts and culture (p. 617).

Chichén Itzá (1 day)
See some of the grandest ruins in all of Mexico (p. 646).

START

Cancún (3 days)
With so many tourists, discos, and parties, it's impossible to resist the spring break capital of the world (p. 656).

Campeche (2 days)
Colonial churches abound in this port to the New World (p. 610).

END

Villahermosa (1 day)
Cool off in this oil boom metropolis (p. 576).

Playa del Carmen and Isla Cozumel (4 days)
Only a few kilometers south of Cancún, this area is great for swimming in *cenotes* and Caribbean waters (p. 674).

Tuxtla Gutiérrez (2 days)
Be sure check out the Cañón del Sumidero in this relatively young—but historic—town filled with history (p. 585).

Palenque (1 day)
Visit world-renowned ruins of the Mayan Classic period in the Chiapan foothills (p. 600).

Chetumal (3 days)
Leveled and reconstructed 50 years ago, Chetumal has a great Mayan museum and leads trips to the area's jungles and lagoons (p. 694).

San Cristóbal de las Casas (2 days)
This charming city, surrounded by mountains, is home to many *indígena* villages (p. 590).

ESSENTIALS

PLANNING YOUR TRIP

BEFORE YOU GO

Passport (p. 10). Required for citizens of all countries, except the US and Canada. Note that a passport is required to return to the US from Mexico by air. This may be extended to land and sea re-entry in Jan. 2008 as well.

Tourist Card (p. 10). Required for citizens of all countries who plan to venture past border towns and/or stay for more than 3 days. Available at airports and points of entry and can last anywhere from 30 to 180 days depending on country of origin. Included in price of plane ticket or $20 at the border.

Visa (p. 12). Required for visitors from most countries outside of the Americas and Europe. Must be obtained through the Mexican consul before arrival.

Under 18? (p. 12). Any non-Mexican under the age of 18 departing Mexico must carry notarized written permission from any parent or guardian not traveling with the child.

Work Permit (p. 12). Business visas and proof of employment required for all foreigners planning to work in Mexico.

Recommended Vaccinations (p. 23) Hepatitis A, Hepatitis B, Typhoid.

Other Health Concerns: Malaria pills are recommended for those traveling to malaria risk areas (p. 25). If your regular **medical insurance policy** (p. 24) does not cover travel abroad, you may wish to purchase additional coverage.

EMBASSIES AND CONSULATES

MEXICAN CONSULAR SERVICES ABROAD

Australia: 14 Perth Ave., Yarralumla, Canberra, ACT 2600 (☎+61 02 6273 3905; www.sre.gob.mx/australia). Also provides consular services.

Canada: 45 O'Connor St., Ste. 1000, Ottawa, ON K1P 1A4 (☎613-233-8988; www.embamexican.com). **Consulates:** Commerce Court West, 199 Bay St., Ste. 4440, Toronto ON M5L 1E9 (☎416-368-2875; www.consulmex.com); 710-1177 W. Hastings St., Vancouver BC V6E 2K3 (☎604-684-3547; www.consulmexvan.com).

Ireland: 43 Ailesbury Road, Ballsbridge, Dublin 4 (☎+353 1260 0699; www.sre.gob.mx/irlanda). Also provides consular services.

New Zealand: 111 Customhouse Quay, Level 8, Wellington (☎+64 4472 0555). **Consulate:** 88 Shortland St, Private Bag 92 518, Wellesley St, Auckland (☎+64 9977 5041; denis.mcnamara@simpsongrierson.com).

UK: 16 St. George St., Hanover Sq., London W1S 1LX (☎+44 0207 499 85 86; www.sre.gob.mx/reinounido). **Consulate:** 8 Halkin St., London SW1X 7DW (☎020 72 35 63 93).

US: 1911 Pennsylvania Ave., Washington, D.C. 20006 (☎202-728-1600; http://portal.sre.gob.mx/eua). **Consulates:** 20 Park Plaza, Ste. 506 Boston, MA 02116 (☎617-426-4181; http://www.sre.gob.mx/boston); 2401 W. Sixth St., Los Angeles, CA 90057 (☎213-351-6800; fax 389-9249; www.sre.gob.mx/losangeles); 5975 SW

72nd St. Ste. 301-303 Miami, Fl. 33143 (☎786-268-4900; http://www.sre.gob.mx/miami); 27 E. 39th St., New York, NY 10016 (☎212-217-6400; fax 217-6493; www.consulmexny.org).

CONSULAR SERVICES IN MEXICO

Australia: Ruben Dario 55, Col. Polanco, Mexico, D.F., 11580 (☎55 1101 2200; fax 1101 2201; www.mexico.embassy.gov.au). **Honorary Consulate:** Batallon De San Patricio No. 111, Piso 16, Desp. 1602, Condominio Torre Comercial America Col. Valle Ote. 66269 Garza Garcia, Nuevo Leon (☎52 81 8158 0791).

Canada: Schiller 529, Col. Polanco Del. Miguel Hidalgo, Mexico, D.F., 11560 (☎55 5724 7900; www.dfait-maeci.gc.ca/mexico-city). **Consulates:** World Trade Center, Av. Mariano Otero # 1249 Piso 8, Torre Pacífico Col. Rinconada del Bosque Guadalajara, Jalisco 44530 (☎33 3671 4740; guadalajara@canada.org.mx); Edificio Kalos Piso C-1, Local 108-A Zaragoza 1300 Sur y Constitución Monterrey, Nuevo León 64000 (☎81 8344 2753; monterrey@international.gc.ca).

Ireland: Cda. Blvr. Avila Camacho 76-3, Col. Lomas de Chapultepec, Mexico, D.F., 11000 (☎55 5520 5803; embajada@irlanda.org.mx). Also provides consular services.

New Zealand: Jaime Balmes No. 8, 4to piso, Los Morales, Polanco, Mexico, D.F. 11510. (☎55 5283 9460; fkiwimexico@prodigy.net.mx.)

UK: Río Lerma 71, Col. Cuauhtémoc, Mexico, D.F. 06500 (☎55 5242 8500; www.embajadabritanica.com.mx). Also provides consular services.

US: Paseo de la Reforma 305, Col. Cuauhtémoc, 06500 Mexico, D.F. (☎55 5080 2000; mexico.usembassy.gov). **Consulates:** Av. López Mateos 924 Nte., Ciudad Juárez, Mexico (☎656 611 3000; http://ciudadjuarez.usconsulate.gov); Progreso 175, Guadalajara, Jalisco 44100 (☎33 3268 2100; guadalajara.usconsulate.gov); Av. Constitución 411 Pte., Monterrey, Nuevo León 6400 (☎81 8345 2120; monterrey.usconsulate.gov); Tapachula 96, Tijuana, Baja California Norte 22000 (☎664 622 7400; tijuana.usconsulate.gov).

TOURIST OFFICES

Mexico's Tourism Board and Ministry of Tourism (SECTUR) are dedicated to enhancing Mexico as a tourist destination. Most official tourism offices outside North America have consolidated with local consulates while some in Canada and the US still remain open. For more information on tourism, visit the nearest consulate or www.sectur.gob.mx.

DOCUMENTS AND FORMALITIES

PASSPORTS

REQUIREMENTS

Citizens of Australia, Ireland, New Zealand, and the UK need valid passports to enter Mexico and to re-enter their home countries. Citizens of the US and Canada only need some form of valid identification (often more than a driver's license), but a passport is highly recommended. Not only is it a more official document and useful in places like Mexican banks, but the United States also requires a valid passport for re-entry by air. You may also be asked for evidence of a return ticket and sufficient funds. Returning home with an expired passport is illegal and may result in a fine.

NEW PASSPORTS

Citizens of Australia, Canada, Ireland, New Zealand, the UK, and the US can apply for a passport at any passport office or at selected post offices and courts of law. Citizens of these countries may also download passport applications from the official website of their country's government or passport office. Any new passport or renewal applications must be filed well in advance of the departure date, though most passport offices offer rush services for a very steep fee. Note, however, that "rushed" passports still take up to two weeks to arrive.

PASSPORT MAINTENANCE

Photocopy the page of your passport with your photo, as well as your visas, traveler's check serial numbers, and any other important documents. Carry one set of copies in a safe place, apart from the originals, and leave another set at home. Consulates also recommend that you carry an expired passport or an official copy of your birth certificate in a part of your baggage separate from other documents.

If you lose your passport, immediately notify the local police and the nearest embassy or consulate of your home government. To expedite its replacement, you must show ID and proof of citizenship; it also helps to know all information previously recorded in the passport. In some cases, a replacement may take weeks to process, and it may be valid only for a limited time. Any visas stamped in your old passport will be irretrievably lost. In an emergency, ask for immediate temporary traveling papers that will permit you to re-enter your home country. **Consulates in Mexico can issue replacements within seven business days.**

TOURIST CARDS, VISAS, AND WORK PERMITS

TOURIST CARD (FOLLETO DE MIGRACIÓN TURÍSTICA)

All persons, regardless of nationality, must carry a **tourist card (FMT)** in addition to proof of citizenship. Most tourist cards are good for up to 180 days; some, however, are only good for 30 or fewer days. If you need to leave and re-enter Mexico during your trip, make sure your tourist card will enable you to do so; you might have to ask for a multiple-entry permit. Canadian and US citizens don't need the tourist card if they are staying in Mexico for less than 72hr. or intend to stay within the 20-30km US-Mexico border zone (depending on the city). If you are traveling into Mexico by plane, the tourist card fee is included in the airline ticket price (approximately US$20), and the tourist card will be given to you to fill out during your flight. If driving into Mexico, you will be charged the fee at your point of entry. You can avoid any delays by obtaining a card from a Mexican consulate or tourist office before you leave (p. 9).

> ▌V **NEVER LET GO.** Because you may be asked to present your tourist card when leaving Mexico, you must keep it for the duration of your trip. Keep it in a safe place along with your other valuables, and make a copy just in case.

VISAS

As of August 2007, tourist visas are **not necessary** for citizens of Australia, Canada, New Zealand, the UK, the US, and most EU and Latin American countries for stays of up to 180 days; the tourist card is sufficient. Individuals with African, Asian, Eastern European, or Middle Eastern citizenship must procure a tourist visa from a Mexican consulate in your home country before traveling. In order to do so, a valid passport, a valid visa application, three passport photographs, proof of sufficient funds, and evidence of a round-trip ticket are necessary. The consular fee is around US$39, depending on country of origin. Double-check entrance requirements at a Mexican embassy or consulate in your home country (listed under **Mexican Consular Services Abroad,** on p. 9) for up-to-date info before departure. US citizens can also consult http://travel.state.gov. Entering **Mexico** to study for longer than six months requires a special visa. Non-Mexicans under 18 who wish to exit the country must have written permission from their legal guardian(s) in the form of a notarized letter.

WORK PERMITS
Admission as a visitor does not include the right to work, which is authorized only by a work permit. For more information, see the **Beyond Tourism** chapter (p. 77).

IDENTIFICATION
When you travel, always carry at least two forms of identification, including a photo ID; a passport and a driver's license or birth certificate is usually an adequate combination. Never carry all of your IDs together; split them up in case of theft or loss, and keep photocopies of all of them in your luggage and at home.

STUDENT, TEACHER, AND YOUTH IDENTIFICATION
The **International Student Identity Card (ISIC),** a widely accepted form of student ID, provides discounts on some sights, accommodations, food, and transportation; access to a 24hr. emergency helpline; and insurance benefits for US cardholders (see **Insurance,** p. 24). Applicants must be full-time secondary or post-secondary school students at least 12 years of age. Because of the proliferation of fake ISICs, some services (particularly airlines) require additional proof of student identity.

The **International Teacher Identity Card (ITIC)** offers teachers the same insurance coverage as the ISIC and limited discounts. To qualify for the card, teachers must be currently employed and have worked a 18hr. min. per week for at least one school year. For travelers who are under 26 years old but are not students, the **International Youth Travel Card (IYTC)** also offers many of the same benefits as the ISIC.

Each of these identity cards costs US$22. ISICs, ITICS, and IYTCs are valid for one year from the date of issue. To learn more about ISICs, ITICs, and IYTCs, try www.myisic.com. Many student travel agencies (p. 29) issue the cards; for a list of issuing agencies or more information, see the **International Student Travel Confederation (ISTC)** website (www.istc.org).

The **International Student Exchange Card (ISE Card)** is a similar identification card available to students, faculty, and youths aged 12 to 26. The card provides discounts, medical benefits, access to a 24hr. emergency helpline, and the ability to purchase student airfares. An ISE Card costs US$25; call ☎ 800-255-8000 (in North America) or ☎ (480) 951-1177 (from all other continents) for more info, or visit www.isecard.com.

CUSTOMS
Upon entering **Mexico**, you must declare certain items from abroad. Mexican regulations limit the value of goods brought into Mexico by US citizens arriving by air or sea to US$300 per person and by land to US$50 per person. Amounts exceeding the duty-free limit are subject to a 15% tax. Note that goods and gifts purchased at **duty-free** shops abroad are not exempt from duty or sales tax; "duty-free" merely means that you need not pay a tax in the country of purchase. Upon returning home, you must likewise declare all articles acquired abroad and pay a duty on the value of articles in excess of your home country's allowance. In order to expedite your return, make a list of any valuables brought from home, register them with customs before traveling abroad, and be sure to keep receipts for all goods acquired abroad.

ENTERING MEXICO

BY CAR

If you plan on driving into Mexico, you will need to obtain a **vehicle permit** at the border, a local consulate, or at the **Banjercito** website (www.banjercito.com.mx). **Vehicle permits are needed only for travel more than 22km past the border.** To acquire a permit, evidence of citizenship, title for the vehicle, a vehicle registration certificate, a driver's license, and a processing fee are required.

Permits are around US$100 when you pay with a valid debit or credit card. Those without credit cards will have to provide a cash deposit or bond worth US$200-400, depending on the make of the car. Your deposit will be repaid in full when you return across the border, but paying the minimal fee by credit card is strongly advised. To extend a permit beyond its original expiration date and to avoid confiscation, contact the temporary importation department of Mexican customs. The maximum length of stay granted to tourists is six months. A permit is valid only for the person to whom it was issued unless another driver is approved by the federal registry. Violation of this law can result in confiscation of the vehicle or heavy fines. Despite any advice, official or unofficial, to the contrary, vehicle permits cannot be obtained at checkpoints in the interior of Mexico. Travelers should avoid individuals outside vehicle permit offices offering to the permits, even if they appear to be government officials. There have been reports of fraudulent or counterfeit permits being issued adjacent to the vehicle import permit office in Nuevo Laredo and other border areas. Regulations change frequently; for information, contact a consulate or check the Banjercito website.

MONEY

CURRENCY AND EXCHANGE

The currency chart below is based on August 2007 exchange rates between local currency and Australian dollars (AUS$), Canadian dollars (CDN$), European Union euro (EUR€), New Zealand dollars (NZ$), British pounds (UK£), and US dollars (US$). Check the currency converter on websites like www.xe.com or www.bloomberg.com, or a large newspaper for the latest exchange rates.

PESO		
AUS$1 = 9.2546 PESOS	1 PESO = AUS$0.108054
CDN$1 = 10.3892 PESOS	1 PESO = CDN$0.096258
EUR€1 = 15.0078 PESOS	1 PESO = EUR€0.006664
NZ$1 = 8.06601 PESOS	1 PESO = NZ$0.123977
UK£1 = 22.1290 PESOS	1 PESO = UK£ 0.04519
US$1 = 11.0800 PESOS	1 PESO = US$0.09025

As a general rule, it's cheaper to convert money in **Mexico** than at home. While currency exchange will probably be available in your arrival airport, it's wise to bring enough foreign currency to last for the first 24 to 72 hours of your trip.

When changing money abroad, try to go only to banks or *casas de cambio* that have at most a 5% margin between their buy and sell prices. Since you lose money with every transaction, **convert large sums** (unless the currency is depreciating rapidly), but **no more than you'll need.** Keep in mind that banks tend to have better exchange rates than *casas de cambio*.

Store your money in a variety of forms; ideally, at any given time you will be carrying some cash, some traveler's checks, and an ATM and/or credit card. All travelers should also consider carrying some US dollars (about US$50 worth), which are often preferred by local tellers to the euro or other currencies.

ESSENTIALS

TRAVELER'S CHECKS

Traveler's checks are one of the safest and least troublesome means of carrying funds. American Express and Visa are the most recognized brands. Many banks and agencies sell them for a small commission. Check issuers provide refunds if the checks are lost or stolen. Many provide additional services, such as toll-free refund hotlines abroad, emergency message services, and assistance with lost and stolen credit cards or passports. Traveler's checks are readily accepted in larger commercial and urban areas. Purchase checks in US dollars; many *casas de cambio* refuse to change other currencies. Also, it's probably best to buy most of your checks in small denominations (US$20) to minimize your losses at times when you can't avoid a disadvantageous exchange rate. Ask about toll-free refund hotlines and the location of refund centers when purchasing checks, and carry emergency cash.

American Express: Checks available with commission at select banks, at all AmEx offices, and online (www.americanexpress.com; US residents only). American Express cardholders can also purchase checks by phone (☎800-528-4800). American Express also offers the Travelers Cheque Card, a prepaid reloadable card. Cheques for Two can be signed by either of two people traveling together. For purchase locations or more information, contact AmEx's service centers: in Australia ☎+61 29 271 8666, in New Zealand +64 93 67 4567, in the UK +44 12 73 696 933, in the US and Canada 800-221-7282; elsewhere, call the US collect at 1 336 393 1111. Within Mexico, call 01 866 247 6878 for assistance; this line also accepts collect calls.

Travelex: Visa TravelMoney prepaid cash card and Visa traveler's checks available. For information about Thomas Cook MasterCard in Canada and the US call ☎800-223-7373, in the UK 0800 622 101. Within Mexico, call ☎800 123 4823. Elsewhere call

the UK collect at +44 1733 318 950. For information about Interpayment Visa in the US and Canada call ☎800-732-1322, in the UK 0800 515 884. Within Mexico, call ☎800 123 4826. Elsewhere call the UK collect at +44 1733 318 949. For more information, visit www.travelex.com.

Visa: Checks available (generally with commission) at banks worldwide. For the location of the nearest office, call the Visa Travelers Cheque Global Refund and Assistance Center: in the UK ☎0800 895 078, in the US 800-227-6811. Within Mexico, call 01 800 257 3381 for customer service. Elsewhere, call the UK collect at +44 2079 378 091. Visa also offers TravelMoney, a prepaid debit card that can be reloaded online or by phone. For more information on Visa travel services, see http://usa.visa.com/personal/using_visa/travel_with_visa.html.

CREDIT, DEBIT, AND ATM CARDS

Where they are accepted, credit cards often offer superior exchange rates—up to 5% better than the retail rate used by banks and other currency exchange establishments. Credit cards may also offer services such as insurance or emergency help, and are sometimes required to reserve hotel rooms or rental cars. **MasterCard (a.k.a. Cirrus in Mexico)** and **Visa (a.k.a. PLUS)** are the most frequently accepted; **American Express** cards work at some ATMs and at AmEx offices and airports.

ATMs are widespread in Mexico, even in small towns, and can be a convenient way to change money. Depending on the system that your home bank uses, you can most likely access your personal bank account from abroad. ATMs get the same wholesale exchange rate as credit cards, but there is often a limit on the amount of money you can withdraw per day (usually US$500). There is typically also a surcharge of 7.50 pesos to withdraw and 3 pesos to check your balance.

Debit cards are as convenient as credit cards, and can be used wherever its associated credit card company (usually MasterCard or Visa) is accepted, yet the money is withdrawn directly from the holder's checking account. Debit cards often also function as ATM cards and can be used to withdraw cash from associated banks and ATMs throughout Mexico.

The two major international money networks are **MasterCard/Maestro/Cirrus** (for ATM locations ☎800-424-7787 or www.mastercard.com) and **Visa/PLUS** (for ATM locations ☎800-847-2911 or www.visa.com).

GETTING MONEY FROM HOME

If you run out of money while traveling, the easiest and cheapest solution is to have someone back home make a deposit to your bank account. Failing that, consider one of the following options.

WIRING MONEY

It is possible to arrange a **bank money transfer,** which means asking a bank back home to wire money to a bank in Mexico. This is the cheapest way to transfer cash, but it's also the slowest, usually taking several days or more. Note that some banks may only release your funds in local currency, potentially sticking you with a poor exchange rate; inquire about this in advance. Expect transactions to take between one and three days to complete. Money transfer services like **Western Union** are faster and more convenient than bank transfers—but also much pricier. Western Union has many locations worldwide and works with "Dinero en Minutos" in Mexico for wire transfers. To find one, visit www.westernunion.com, or call in Australia ☎+61 1800 173 833, in Canada and the US 800-325-6000, in the UK +44 0800 833 833. To wire money using a credit card (Discover, MasterCard, Visa), call in Canada and the US 800-CALL-CASH, in the UK ☎+44 0800 833 833. Money transfer services are also available to **American Express** cardholders and at selected **Tho-**

TOP 10 WAYS TO SAVE IN MEXICO

Tourism opportunities abound in Mexico—be a savvy spender and get the most for each *peso* with these tried-and-true budget tips.

1. Visit **museums** on weekends when some offer free admission (usually on Sundays).
2. Listen to time-share hawkers at mega resorts like Acapulco and Cancún; most offer coupons on meals and attractions just for hearing their pitch.
3. Use **public transportation** during the day. Most towns will have have routes to major attractions.
4. Buy your **souvenirs** from smaller towns to avoid inflated tourist prices.
5. When appropriate, **bargain!** It's more accepted than most major credit cards.
6. Stock up on beer, bread, fresh fruit, liquor, and vegetables from **local markets.**
7. Visit during the **low season** (usually any time but *Semana Santa*, mid-summer, or December), when prices are lower.
8. Add more **outdoors experiences** to your itinerary—beachfront camping is often free, and Mexico's countless natural wonders offer plenty of budget-friendly adventure!
9. Stay at hostels and hotels that offer **free breakfast.**
10. Round up hostelmates and fellow tourists when visiting local attractions to get **group rate discounts.**

mas **Cook** branches. In Mexico, money transfer services can usually be found at **Banamex** and **Bancomer** banks nationwide.

US STATE DEPARTMENT (US CITIZENS ONLY)

In serious emergencies only, the US State Department will forward money within hours to the nearest consular office, which will then disburse it according to instructions for a US$30 fee. If you wish to use this service, you must contact the Overseas Citizens Service division of the US State Department (☎202-647-5225, toll-free 888-407-4747).

COSTS

The cost of your trip will vary considerably, depending on where you go, how you travel, and where you stay. The most significant expenses will probably be your round-trip (return) **airfare** to Mexico (see **Getting to Mexico: By Plane,** p. 28) and a **bus pass.** Before you go, spend some time calculating a reasonable daily **budget.**

STAYING ON A BUDGET

To give you a general idea, a bare-bones day in Mexico (camping or sleeping in hostels/guesthouses, buying food at supermarkets) would cost about US$15-25 (160-370 pesos); a more comfortable day (sleeping in hostels/guesthouses and the occasional budget hotel, eating one meal per day at a restaurant, going out at night) costs US$30-40 (375 pesos); for a luxurious day, the sky's the limit. Don't forget to factor in emergency reserve funds (at least US$200) when planning how much money you'll need.

TIPS FOR SAVING MONEY

Some simpler ways include searching out opportunities for free entertainment, splitting accommodation and food costs with trustworthy fellow travelers, and buying food in supermarkets rather than eating out. Bring a **sleepsack** (p. 17) to save on sheet charges hostels, and do your **laundry** in the sink (unless you're explicitly prohibited from doing so). Museums often have certain days once a month or once a week when admission is free; plan accordingly. If you are eligible, consider getting an ISIC or an IYTC (p. 12); many sights and museums offer reduced student or youth admission. Drinking at bars and clubs quickly becomes expensive. It's cheaper to buy alcohol at a supermarket and imbibe before going out. Don't go overboard: though staying within your budget is important, don't do so at the expense of your health or a great travel experience.

TIPPING AND BARGAINING

Ah, the age-old question: To tip or not to tip? In Mexico, it can be hard to know what to do. Overly eager tipping can be offensive (never, for example, throw a couple of pesos at someone you just asked for directions), but many people make their livings assisting tourists in exchange for tips. In general, anyone who offers a service and then awkwardly waits around afterward is expecting a tip.

In a restaurant, waiters are tipped based on the quality of service; **good service deserves at least 15%.** Taxi drivers are generally not tipped, as they do not run on meters—when hailing a taxi, settle the price of the ride beforehand, lest you get pegged as a tourist and charged exorbitantly. Regardless of the quality of service, never leave without saying *"gracias."* In Mexico, skillful bargaining separates the savvy budget traveler from the timid tourist. If you're unsure whether bargaining is appropriate, observe locals and follow their lead, especially in markets.

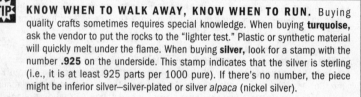

TIP

KNOW WHEN TO WALK AWAY, KNOW WHEN TO RUN. Buying quality crafts sometimes requires special knowledge. When buying **turquoise,** ask the vendor to put the rocks to the "lighter test." Plastic or synthetic material will quickly melt under the flame. When buying **silver,** look for a stamp with the number **.925** on the underside. This stamp indicates that the silver is sterling (i.e., it is at least 925 parts per 1000 pure). If there's no number, the piece might be inferior silver—silver-plated or silver *alpaca* (nickel silver).

PACKING

Pack lightly: Lay out only what you think you absolutely need, then take half the clothes and twice the money. The Travelite FAQ (www.travelite.org) is a good resource for tips on traveling light. The online **Universal Packing List** (http://upl.codeq.info) will generate a customized list of suggested items based on your trip length, the expected climate, your planned activities, and other factors. If you plan to do a lot of hiking, also consult **The Great Outdoors,** p. 44.

Luggage: If you plan to cover most of your itinerary by foot, a sturdy **frame backpack** is unbeatable. (For the basics on buying a pack, see p. 46.) Toting a **suitcase** or **trunk** is fine if you plan to live in one or two cities and explore from there, but not a great idea if you plan to move around frequently. In addition to your main piece of luggage, a **daypack** (a small backpack or courier bag) is useful.

Clothing: No matter when you're traveling, it's a good idea to bring a warm jacket or wool sweater, a rain jacket (Gore-Tex® is both waterproof and breathable), sturdy shoes or hiking boots, and thick socks. Flip-flops or waterproof sandals are must-haves for grubby hostel showers, and extra socks are always a good idea. You may also want one outfit for going out, and maybe a nicer pair of shoes. If you plan to visit religious or cultural sites, remember that you will need modest and respectful dress. Mexican culture values neat and clean appearances, and visitors are recommended to do likewise, especially when dealing with officials at border crossings or military road-blocks. Shorts are rarely worn outside of beach towns and touristy ruins, and bathing suits are only appropriate on the beach.

Sleepsack: Some hostels require that you either provide your own linen or rent sheets from them. Save cash by making your own sleepsack: fold a full-size sheet in half the long way, then sew it closed along the long side and one of the short sides.

ESSENTIALS

Converters and Adapters: In Mexico, electricity is 127 volts AC. 220/240V electrical appliances won't work with a 120/127V current, which will work for any 120V North American appliance; additionally, the electrical outlets in Mexico are shaped the same as those in Canada and the US. Visitors from the UK, Australia and New Zealand should buy an adapter (which changes the shape of the plug; US$5) and a converter (which changes the voltage; US$10-30). Don't make the mistake of using only an adapter (unless appliance instructions explicitly state otherwise). Australians and New Zealanders (who use 230V at home) will need a converter and a set of adapters to use anything electrical. For more on all things adaptable, check out http://kropla.com/electric.htm.

Toiletries: Condoms, deodorant, razors, tampons, and toothbrushes are often available, but it may be difficult to find your preferred brand; bring extras. Contact lenses are likely to be expensive and difficult to find, so bring enough extra pairs and solution for your entire trip. Also bring your glasses and a copy of your prescription in case you need emergency replacements. If you use heat-disinfection, either switch temporarily to a chemical disinfection system (check first to make sure it's safe with your brand of lenses), or buy a 120/127V converter.

First-Aid Kit: For a basic first-aid kit, pack bandages, a pain reliever, antibiotic cream, a thermometer, a multifunction pocketknife, tweezers, moleskin, decongestant, motion-sickness remedy, diarrhea or upset-stomach medication (Pepto Bismol® or Imodium®), an antihistamine, sunscreen, insect repellent, burn ointment, an Epipen® for severe allergies, and a syringe for emergencies (get an explanatory letter from your doctor).

Film: Film and developing in Mexico are expensive, so consider bringing along enough film for your entire trip and developing it at home. If you don't want to bother with film, consider using a digital camera. Although it requires a steep initial investment, a digital camera means you never have to buy film again. Just be sure to bring along a large enough memory card and extra (or rechargeable) batteries. For more info on digital cameras, visit www.shortcourses.com/choosing/contents.htm. Less serious photographers may want to bring a disposable camera or two. Despite disclaimers, airport security X-rays can fog film, so buy a lead-lined pouch at a camera store or ask security to hand-inspect it. Always pack film in your carry-on luggage, since higher-intensity X-rays are used on checked luggage.

Other Useful Items: For safety purposes, you should bring a **money belt** and a small **padlock.** Basic **outdoors equipment** (plastic water bottle, compass, waterproof matches, pocketknife, sunglasses, sunscreen, hat) may also prove useful. **Quick repairs** of torn garments can be done on the road with a needle and thread; also consider bringing electrical tape for patching tears. If you want to do laundry by hand, bring detergent, a small rubber ball to stop up the sink, and string for a makeshift clothes line. Other things you're liable to forget include: an umbrella, sealable **plastic bags** (for damp clothes, soap, food, shampoo, and other spillables), an **alarm clock,** safety pins, rubber bands, a flashlight, earplugs, garbage bags, and a small calculator. A **cell phone** can be a lifesaver (literally) on the road; see p. 38 for information on acquiring one that will work in Mexico.

Important Documents: Don't forget your passport, traveler's checks, ATM and/or credit cards, adequate ID, and photocopies of all of the aforementioned in case these documents are lost or stolen (p. 10). Also check that you have any of the following that might apply to you: a hosteling membership card (p. 41); driver's license (p. 12); travel insurance forms (p. 24); ISIC (p. 12), and bus pass (p. 33).

SAFETY AND HEALTH

GENERAL ADVICE

In any type of crisis situation, the most important thing to do is **stay calm.** Your country's embassy abroad (p. 9) is usually your best resource when things go wrong; registering with that embassy upon arrival in Mexico is often a good idea. The government offices listed in the **Travel Advisories** box (p. 21) can provide information on the services they offer their citizens in case of emergencies abroad.

LOCAL LAWS AND POLICE

Travelers are advised to comply with the Mexican legal codes detailed below, or risk severe penalties. Although the Mexican government is working hard to strengthen its police force, police officers remain infamous for their **corruption.** Remember to exercise caution when approached by individuals identifying themselves as police officers. Some tourists have fallen victim to mistreatment by local officials, including harassment and extortion. Some may try to bribe tourists, generally asking for about US$5, but usually stop when asked to be taken to the police station to speak to higher authorities. Should you encounter an officer, be sure to take their name, badge number, and patrol car number in case you file a complaint. Several larger urban areas maintain a separate **tourist police force;** contact the local tourist office for more information. While in Mexico, visitors should be aware that the Mexican judicial system operates under **Napoleonic law:** offenders are presumed guilty until proven innocent.

DRUGS, ALCOHOL, FIREARMS, AND WILDLIFE

DRUGS. Contrary to international opinion, **Mexico rigorously prosecutes drug cases.** A minimum jail sentence awaits anyone found guilty of possessing any illegal drug, and Mexican law does not distinguish between marijuana and other narcotics. Even if you aren't convicted, getting arrested and tried will be a long and incredibly unpleasant process, and it is not uncommon to be detained for a year before a verdict is reached. Foreigners and suspected drug traffickers are never released on bail. Ignorance of Mexican law is no excuse, and a flimsy "I didn't know it was illegal" won't get you out of jail. If you are arrested, there is little your embassy can do other than inform your relatives and bring care packages to you in jail. (For information on how to address those packages, see **Keeping in Touch,** p. 36.)

Travelers should also exercise caution with **prescription drugs.** The US State Department cautions against bringing large amounts of prescription drugs into the country. Mexican police can arrest you if they feel that your drugs are being abused or exceed the amount needed for personal use. It may be helpful to bring a doctor's letter certifying the drugs' legitimacy. It is also not advisable to buy large amounts of prescription drugs in Mexico—foreigners have been arrested even though they bought drugs legally. Counterfeit drugs are also prevalent, and depending on your home country, importing large amounts of prescription drugs may be illegal.

ALCOHOL. Mexicans get annoyed with foreigners who cross the border for nights of debauchery, so avoid public drunkenness—it is against the law and could land you in jail. Drinking to excess is unsafe for other reasons. The US State Department warns of tourists—almost always traveling alone—at nightclubs or bars who have been drugged or intoxicated and then beaten, robbed, abducted, or raped.

ESSENTIALS

FIREARMS. Transporting firearms across Mexico's borders is illegal. This applies to guns, knives and ammunition. **Under no circumstances should weapons be brought into the country.** Doing so **requires** obtaining permission in advance from Mexican authorities. This law is strictly enforced regardless of whether or not the possessor is licensed to carry a firearm in their native country. Violating this rule may result in fines, arrest, or incarceration.

WILDLIFE AND ARTIFACTS. Mexico prohibits the unauthorized exportation of certain wildlife products, whether as souvenirs or otherwise. These include any native birds, sea-turtle products, black coral jewelry, taxidermied animals, crocodile leather, and furs from spotted cats. The same laws apply to the possession of pre-Hispanic relics.

SPECIFIC CONCERNS

NATURAL DISASTERS

EARTHQUAKES. Mexico is prone to seismic activity, often with devastating consequences. Should an earthquake occur, take cover under a heavy piece of furniture, such as a table or a desk, or a sturdy doorway, and protect your head. If outside, avoid standing near buildings or walls, as debris may begin to fall. Do not stand near windows that may shatter. Listen for radio or television announcements for developing information. Beware of aftershocks.

HURRICANES. Mexico's Gulf and Pacific coasts often fall victim to hurricanes. Tourists should take into consideration the hurricane season (July-Nov.) when traveling. In the event of a hurricane, stay indoors and away from windows. Avoid going outside until the storm has passed, and be wary of the local water supply.

VOLCANOES. Mexico is situated along the Pacific Ocean's Ring of Fire and has its share of volcanoes. While most of these are dormant, some can erupt lava unexpectedly. An active volcano in Colima erupted most recently in 2005, sending ash and lava several kilometers into the sky. If you travel to a volcanic region, be aware of evacuation procedures in the event of an eruption.

DEMONSTRATIONS AND POLITICAL GATHERINGS

From May-Nov. 2006, a massive teachers' strike in Oaxaca City resulted in numerous deaths; since then political gatherings in Oaxaca have escalated into violent demonstrations. Additionally, Mexican presidential elections (the most recent in 2006) tend to be quite turbulent. During election years, expect widespread political protests. It is illegal for foreigners to participate in demonstrations deemed political by officials. Such actions violate tourist cards/visas and can result in arrest, fines, or deportation. Travelers are advised to avoid mass gatherings and keep close tabs on current political conditions.

TERRORISM

There are several insurgent groups operating in Chiapas, Guerrero, and Oaxaca, the most prominent of which are the Zapatistas, the Popular Revolutionary Army, and the Insurgent People's Revolutionary Army. While these groups are not heavily active, they have initiated violent uprisings in the recent past. In addition, the Zapatistas have occasionally been hostile towards foreigners.

OTHER AREAS OF CONCERN

BEACHES. Crime has infiltrated even the most beautiful and pristine parts of the country, and tourists have not escaped attack. **Avoid hidden or secluded beaches** unless they are known to be especially safe. If you are going to the beach, it's a

TRAVEL ADVISORIES. The following government offices provide travel information and advisories by telephone, by fax, or via the web:

Australian Department of Foreign Affairs and Trade: ☎612 6261 1111; www.dfat.gov.au.

Canadian Department of Foreign Affairs and International Trade (DFAIT): Call ☎800-267-8376; www.dfait-maeci.gc.ca. Call for their free booklet, *Bon Voyage...But.*

New Zealand Ministry of Foreign Affairs: ☎044 398 000; www.mfat.govt.nz.

United Kingdom Foreign and Commonwealth Office: ☎020 7008 1500; www.fco.gov.uk.

US Department of State: ☎888-407-4747; http://travel.state.gov. Visit the website to consult *A Safe Trip Abroad.*

good idea to go during daylight hours, when families and visitors are more numerous. Several US citizens have been killed while frolicking alone on beaches; some of these attacks happened during the morning hours. Avoid beaches that have been black-flagged and always exercise caution.

BORDER CITIES. Because of their position along the US border, the narcotics trade has flourished in **Ciudad Juárez, Nuevo Laredo, Tijuana, Nogales, Reynosa** and **Matamoros.** Many foreigners involved in the trade have been kidnapped or murdered, and the violence occasionally affects innocent bystanders. The US State Department urges special caution for those visiting the "entertainment" and red-light districts in these cities.

CANCÚN. This international tourist mecca draws pickpockets and petty thieves from all over the country. Muggings, purse-snatchings, and hotel-room burglaries are on the rise. Use common sense and protect your valuables. Sexual assaults and rapes are known to occur during evening or early morning hours in the Zona Hotelera. Intoxicated clubbers separated from friends are at higher risk of being attacked. Such assaults, while few and far between, are on the rise. There have also been reports of increased harassment and abuse by police officers.

CHIAPAS. Due to recent Zapatista activity, tourists should be especially careful when traveling in Chiapas. While the Mexican government has brought much of the area under control, armed rebels are occasionally active in the highlands north of San Cristóbal de las Casas, Ocosingo, and in the jungles east of Comitán. These rebels have been openly hostile toward foreigners in the past.

GUERRERO AND OAXACA. Due to political unrest in the rural parts of these states, visitors might encounter roadblocks and increased military presence. If your bus or car is pulled over, be prepared to show ID. There is no evidence, however, that the insurgent groups, the Popular Revolutionary Army and the Insurgent People's Revolutionary Army, have targeted tourists. Violent protests in Oaxaca City during May-Nov. 2006 resulted in multiple fatalities. Many of the issues that were the basis for these demonstrations remain unresolved, and travelers are advised to monitor political conditions in Oaxaca City prior to planning a visit.

MEXICO CITY. Mexico City, like most crowded metropolitan areas, has more than its share of crime; in fact, it has the highest crime rate in Mexico. Keep in mind that most crimes against tourists fall under the category of petty street crimes—muggings, pickpocketings, and purse-snatchings. Although the government has prided itself on reducing crime in the city, visitors should still exercise extreme caution, especially on public transportation.

PERSONAL SAFETY

EXPLORING AND TRAVELING

To avoid unwanted attention, try to blend in as much as possible. Respecting local customs (in many cases, dressing more conservatively than you would at home) may placate would-be hecklers. Familiarize yourself with your surroundings before setting out, and carry yourself with confidence. Check maps in shops and restaurants rather than on the street. If you are traveling alone, be sure someone at home knows your itinerary, and never tell anyone you meet that you're by yourself. When walking at night, stick to busy, well-lit streets and avoid dark alleyways. If you ever feel uncomfortable, leave the area as quickly and directly as you can.

There is no sure-fire way to avoid all the threatening situations you might encounter while traveling, but a good **self-defense course** will give you concrete ways to react to unwanted advances. **Impact, Prepare,** and **Model Mugging** can refer you to local self-defense courses in Australia, Canada, Switzerland and the US. Visit the website at www.modelmugging.org for a list of nearby chapters.

If you are using a **car,** learn local driving signals and wear a seatbelt. Children under 40 lbs. should ride only in specially designed carseats, available for a small fee from most car rental agencies. Study route maps before you hit the road, and if you plan on spending a lot of time driving, consider bringing spare parts. For long drives in desolate areas, invest in a cell phone and a roadside assistance program (p. 35). Park your vehicle in a well-traveled area, and use a steering wheel locking device in larger cities. **Sleeping in your car** is the most dangerous way to get your rest, and it's usually illegal. For info on the dangers of **hitchhiking,** see p. 36.

Travelers in Mexico should hail **taxis** from a *sitio* (regulated taxi stand), or telephone a reputable organization ahead of time and make note of the drivers' name and license plate number.

POSSESSIONS AND VALUABLES

Never leave your belongings unattended; crime occurs in even the most safe-looking hostel or hotel. Bring your own padlock for hostel lockers, and don't ever store valuables in a locker. Be particularly careful on **buses** and **trains;** horror stories abound about determined thieves who wait for travelers to fall asleep. Carry your bag or purse in front of you where you can see it. When traveling with others, sleep in alternate shifts. When alone, use good judgment in selecting a train compartment: never stay in an empty one, and use a lock to secure your pack to the luggage rack. Use extra caution if traveling at night or on overnight trains. Try to sleep on top bunks with your luggage stored above you (if not in bed with you), and keep important documents and other valuables on you at all times.

There are a few steps you can take to minimize the financial risk associated with traveling. First, **bring as little with you as possible.** Second, buy a few combination **padlocks** to secure your belongings either in your pack or in a hostel or train station locker. Third, **carry as little cash as possible.** Keep your traveler's checks and ATM/credit cards in a **money belt**—not a "fanny pack"—along with your passport and ID cards. Fourth, **keep a small cash reserve separate from your primary stash.** This should be about US$50 sewn into or stored in the depths of your pack, along with your traveler's check numbers and photocopies of your passport, your birth certificate, and other important documents.

In large cities **con artists** often work in groups and may involve children. Beware of certain classics: sob stories that require money, rolls of bills "found" on the street, mustard spilled (or saliva spit) onto your shoulder to distract you while they snatch your bag. **Never let your passport and your bags out of your sight.** Hostel workers will sometimes stand at bus and train station arrival points to try to recruit tired and disoriented travelers to their hostel; never believe strangers who tell you that theirs is the only hostel open. Beware of **pickpockets** in city crowds, especially on public transportation. Also, be alert in public telephone booths: if you must say your calling card number, do so very quietly; if you punch it in, make sure no one can look over your shoulder.

Travelers in Mexico are reminded to be especially vigilant when using ATMs, as both Mexicans and non-Mexicans alike are sometimes subjected to **express kidnappings** and forced to withdraw large sums of cash. **Avoid street-side ATM machines in favor of protected ones inside commercial buildings.**

If you will be traveling with electronic devices, such as a laptop computer or a PDA, check whether your homeowner's insurance covers loss, theft, or damage when you travel. If not, you might consider purchasing a low-cost separate insurance policy. For US citizens, **Safeware** (☎800-800-1492; www.safeware.com) specializes in covering computers and charges $90 for 90-day comprehensive international travel coverage up to $4000. However, if they are not absolutely necessary, leave these items at home. Using iPods or wearing expensive jewelry and prominently labeled designer clothes in Mexico will make it clear that you are in fact a tourist and therefore a target for theft.

PRE-DEPARTURE HEALTH

In your **passport,** write the names of any people you wish to be contacted in case of a medical emergency, and list any allergies or medical conditions. Matching a prescription to a foreign equivalent is not always easy, safe, or possible, so if you take prescription drugs, consider carrying up-to-date prescriptions or a statement from your doctor stating the medication's trade name, manufacturer, chemical name, and dosage. While traveling, be sure to keep all medication with you in your carry-on luggage. For tips on packing a **first-aid kit** and other health essentials, see p. 18.

DRUG NAME IN ENGLISH	SPANISH TRANSLATION
acetaminophen	*acetaminofén*
antibiotic ointment	*crema antibiótica*
antihistamine	*antihistimíno*
aspirin	*aspirina*
ibuprofen	*ibuprofén*
laxative	*laxativo*
penicillin	*penicilina*

IMMUNIZATIONS AND PRECAUTIONS

Travelers over two years old should make sure that the following vaccines are up to date: MMR (for measles, mumps, and rubella); DTaP or Td (for diphtheria, tetanus, and pertussis); IPV (for polio); Hib (for *Haemophilus influenzae* B); and HepB (for Hepatitis B). **Adults traveling to the developing world on trips longer than four weeks should consider the following additional immunizations: Hepatitis A vaccine and/or immune globulin (IG), typhoid and cholera vaccines, as well as a rabies vaccine and yearly influenza vaccines. While yellow fever is only endemic to parts of South America and sub-Saharan Africa; many countries may deny entrance to travelers arriving from these zones without a certificate of vaccination.** For recommendations on immunizations, consult the Centers for Disease Control and Prevention (CDC; p. 24) in the US or the equivalent in your home country, and check with a doctor for guidance.

> **INOCULATION RECOMMENDATIONS.** Mexico does not require visitors to carry vaccination certificates, nor does it require specific vaccinations for entry. It is advisable, however, to consult your doctor 4-6 weeks before departure. In addition to **booster shots** for **measles, polio, tetanus,** and **varicella,** consider the following vaccines and prescriptions:
> **Malaria Tablets:** Chloroquinine is recommended for those traveling in rural and coastal areas in the southern half of the country.
> **Hepatitis A:** Vaccine or immune globulin (IG).
> **Hepatitis B:** Recommended for those planning long stays, those who might be exposed to blood, and those who plan on being sexually active.
> **Rabies:** Recommended for those who might have contact with animals.
> **Typhoid Fever:** Recommended for all travelers.

INSURANCE

Travel insurance covers four basic areas: medical/health problems, property loss, trip cancellation/interruption, and emergency evacuation. Though regular insurance policies may well extend to travel-related accidents, you may consider purchasing separate travel insurance if the cost of potential trip cancellation, interruption, or emergency medical evacuation is greater than you can absorb. Prices for travel insurance purchased separately generally run about US$50 per week for full coverage, while trip cancellation/interruption may be purchased separately at a rate of US$3-5 per day depending on length of stay.

Medical insurance (especially university policies) often covers costs incurred abroad; check with your provider. **US Medicare** does not cover foreign travel, but in rare circumstances may pay for care in Mexico. **Canadian** provincial health insurance plans increasingly do not cover foreign travel; check with the provincial Ministry of Health or Health Plan Headquarters for details. **Homeowners' insurance** (or your family's coverage) often covers theft during travel and loss of travel documents (passport, plane ticket, railpass, etc.) up to US$500.

ISIC and **ITIC** (p. 12) provide basic insurance benefits to US cardholders, including US$100 per day of in-hospital sickness for up to 100 days and US$10,000 of accident-related medical reimbursement (see www.isicus.com for details). Cardholders have access to a toll-free 24hr. helpline for medical, legal, and financial emergencies overseas. **American Express** (☎800-338-1670) grants most cardholders automatic collision and theft car rental insurance on rentals made with the card.

USEFUL ORGANIZATIONS AND PUBLICATIONS

The American **Centers for Disease Control and Prevention** (**CDC;** ☎877-FYI-TRIP; www.cdc.gov/travel) maintains an international travelers' hotline and an informative website. Consult the appropriate government agency of your home country for consular information sheets on health, entry requirements, and other issues for various countries (see the listings in the box on **Travel Advisories,** p. 21). For quick information on health and other travel warnings, call the **Overseas Citizens Services** (M-F 8am-8pm from US ☎888-407-4747, from overseas 202-501-4444), or contact a passport agency, embassy, or consulate abroad. For information on medical evacuation services and travel insurance firms, see the US government's website at http://travel.state.gov/travel/abroad_health.html or the **British Foreign and Commonwealth Office** (www.fco.gov.uk). For general health information, contact the **American Red Cross** (☎202-303-4498; www.redcross.org).

STAYING HEALTHY

Common sense is the simplest prescription for good health while you travel. Drink lots of fluids to prevent dehydration and constipation, and wear sturdy, broken-in shoes and clean socks.

ONCE IN MEXICO

ENVIRONMENTAL HAZARDS

Heat exhaustion and dehydration: Heat exhaustion leads to nausea, excessive thirst, headaches, and dizziness. Avoid it by drinking plenty of fluids, eating salty foods (e.g., crackers), abstaining from dehydrating beverages (e.g., alcohol and caffeinated beverages), and wearing sunscreen. Continuous heat stress can eventually lead to heatstroke, characterized by a rising temperature, severe headache, delirium and cessation of sweating. Victims should be cooled off with wet towels and taken to a doctor. The risk of heat exhaustion exists all over Mexico, but is greatest in Baja and northern Mexico, where the combination of heat and dryness can result in rapid water loss.

Sunburn: Nowhere in Mexico are you safe from sunburn, and the risk only increases as you travel toward the equator and up in altitude. Always wear sunscreen (SPF 30 or higher) when spending excessive amounts of time outdoors. If you get sunburned, drink more fluids than usual and apply an aloe-based lotion. Severe sunburns can lead to sun poisoning, a condition that can cause fever, chills, nausea, and vomiting. Sun poisoning should always be treated by a doctor.

High Altitude: Many places in mountainous Mexico, including Mexico City, are high enough for altitude sickness to be a concern. Symptoms may include headaches, nausea, dizziness, and sleep disruption. To minimize possible symptoms, avoid rapid increases in elevation, stay well hydrated, and allow your body a couple of days to adjust to less oxygen before exerting yourself. Note that alcohol is more potent and UV rays are stronger at high elevations.

Pollution: Travelers to Mexico City should consider protective measures against pollution. The city is now the most polluted in the world, and its layer of smog can cause problems for contact lens-wearers, the allergic, the elderly, and small children. Travelers may want to bring eye drops or throat spray, and asthmatics would be wise to bring along an extra inhaler. Pollution is particularly bad during the winter, due to "thermal inversion," a phenomenon that occurs when warm air passing above the city traps the colder, polluted air in the Valley of Mexico. The summer rainy season, on the other hand, does wonders for air cleanliness, and from May to October the air is quite breathable. Newspapers and news programs often provide daily pollution indices.

INSECT-BORNE DISEASES

Many diseases are transmitted by insects—mainly mosquitoes, fleas, ticks, and lice. Be aware of insects in wet or forested areas, especially while hiking and camping; wear long pants and long sleeves, tuck your pants into your socks, and use a mosquito net. Use insect repellents such as DEET and soak or spray your gear with permethrin (licensed in the US only for use on clothing). **Mosquitoes**—responsible for malaria, dengue fever, and yellow fever—can be particularly abundant in humid, coastal areas. Travelers should be especially careful in the coastal or rural areas of Campeche, Chiapas, Guerrero, Michoacán, Nayarit, Oaxaca, Quintana Roo, Sinaloa, Tabasco, and Yucatán, and the mountainous northern region of Jalisco.

Malaria: Transmitted by *Anopheles* mosquitoes that bite at night. The incubation period varies anywhere between 10 days and 4 weeks. Early symptoms include fever, chills, aches, and fatigue, followed by high fever and sweating, sometimes with vomiting and

ESSENTIALS

diarrhea. See a doctor for any flu-like sickness that occurs after travel in a risk area. To reduce the risk of contracting malaria, use mosquito repellent, particularly in the evenings and when visiting forested areas. Make sure you see a doctor at least 4-6 weeks before a trip to a high-risk area to get up-to-date malaria prescriptions. A doctor may prescribe pills like **mefloquine** or **doxycycline.** Be aware that mefloquine can have very serious side effects, including paranoia, psychotic behavior, and nightmares.

Dengue fever: A viral infection transmitted by *Aedes* mosquitoes, which bite during the day rather than at night. The incubation period is 3-14 days, usually 4-7 days. Early symptoms include a high fever, severe headaches, swollen lymph nodes, and muscle aches. Many patients also suffer from nausea, vomiting, and a pink rash. If you experience these symptoms, see a doctor immediately, drink plenty of liquids, and take fever-reducing medication such as acetaminophen (Tylenol). *Never take aspirin to treat dengue fever.* There is no vaccine available for dengue fever.

Lyme disease: A bacterial infection carried by ticks and marked by a circular bull's-eye rash of 2 in. or more. Later symptoms include fever, headache, fatigue, and aches and pains. Antibiotics are effective if administered early. Left untreated, Lyme can cause problems in joints, the heart, and the nervous system. If you find a tick attached to your skin, grasp the head with tweezers as close to your skin as possible and apply slow, steady traction. Removing a tick within 24hr. greatly reduces the risk of infection. Do not try to remove ticks with petroleum jelly, nail polish remover, or a hot match. Ticks usually inhabit moist, shaded environments and heavily wooded areas. If you are going to be hiking in these areas, wear long clothes and DEET.

Other insect-borne diseases: Lymphatic filariasis is a roundworm infestation transmitted by mosquitoes. Infection causes enlargement of extremities and has no vaccine. **Leishmaniasis,** a parasite transmitted by sand flies, can occur in Mexico, usually in rural rather than urban areas. Common symptoms are fever, weakness, and swelling of the spleen, as well as skin sores. There is a treatment, but no vaccine. In Mexico, **CHA-GAS disease (American trypanomiasis)** is another relatively common parasite transmitted by the cone nose and kissing bug, which infest mud, adobe, and thatch. Symptoms are fever, heart disease, and an enlarged intestine. There is limited treatment.

FOOD- AND WATER-BORNE DISEASES

Prevention is the best cure: be sure that your food is properly cooked and the water you drink is clean. Don't brush your teeth with tap water, don't rinse your toothbrush under the faucet, and don't keep your mouth open in the shower. Avoid anything including ice cubes and anything washed in tap water, like salad and fresh fruits. Watch out for food from markets or street vendors that may have been cooked in unhygienic conditions. Other culprits are raw shellfish, unpasteurized milk, and sauces containing raw eggs. Buy bottled water, or purify your own water by bringing it to a rolling boil or treating it with **iodine tablets;** note, however, that some parasites such as *giardia* have exteriors that resist iodine treatment, so boiling is more reliable. Always wash your hands before eating or bring a quick-drying purifying liquid hand cleaner.

Traveler's diarrhea: Known in Mexico as *turista*. Results from drinking fecally contaminated water or eating uncooked and contaminated foods. Symptoms include nausea, bloating, and urgency. Try quick-energy, non-sugary foods with protein and carbohydrates to keep your strength up. Over-the-counter anti-diarrheals (e.g., Imodium) may counteract the problem. The most dangerous side effect is dehydration; drink 8 oz. of water with ½ tsp. of sugar or honey and a pinch of salt, try uncaffeinated soft drinks, or eat tortillas and salted crackers. If you develop a fever or your symptoms don't go away after 4-5 days, consult a doctor. Consult a doctor immediately for treatment of diarrhea in children.

Dysentery: Results from an intestinal infection caused by bacteria in contaminated food or water. Common symptoms include bloody diarrhea, fever, and abdominal pain and tenderness. The most common type of dysentery generally only lasts a week, but it is highly contagious. Seek medical help immediately. Dysentery can be treated with the drugs norfloxacin or ciprofloxacin. If you are traveling in high-risk (especially rural) regions, consider obtaining a prescription before you leave home.

Cholera: An intestinal disease caused by bacteria in contaminated food. Symptoms include diarrhea, dehydration, vomiting, and muscle cramps. See a doctor immediately; if left untreated, cholera can be lethal within hours. Antibiotics are available, but the most important treatment is rehydration. No vaccine is available in the US.

Hepatitis A: A viral infection of the liver acquired through contaminated water or shellfish from contaminated water. Symptoms include fatigue, fever, loss of appetite, nausea, dark urine, jaundice, vomiting, aches and pains, and light stools. The risk is highest in rural areas and the countryside, but it is also present in urban areas. Ask your doctor about the Hepatitis A vaccine or an injection of immune globulin.

Giardiasis: Transmitted through parasites and acquired by drinking untreated water from streams or lakes. Symptoms include diarrhea, cramps, bloating, fatigue, weight loss, and nausea. If untreated, it can lead to severe dehydration. Giardiasis occurs worldwide.

Typhoid fever: Caused by the salmonella bacteria; **common in villages and rural areas in Mexico.** While mostly transmitted through contaminated food and water, it may also be acquired by direct contact with another person. Early symptoms include high fever, headaches, fatigue, appetite loss, constipation, and a rash on the abdomen or chest. Antibiotics can treat typhoid, but a vaccination (70-90% effective) is recommended.

Leptospirosis: A bacterial disease caused by exposure to fresh water or soil contaminated by the urine of infected animals. Able to enter the human body through cut skin, mucus membranes, and through ingestion; most common in tropical climates. Symptoms include a high fever, chills, nausea, and vomiting. If left untreated it can lead to liver failure and meningitis. There is no vaccine; consult a doctor for treatment.

OTHER INFECTIOUS DISEASES

The following diseases exist in every part of the world. Travelers should know how to recognize them and what to do if they suspect they have been infected.

Rabies: Transmitted through the saliva of infected animals; fatal if untreated. By the time symptoms (thirst and muscle spasms) appear, the disease is in its terminal stage. If you are bitten, wash the wound, seek immediate medical care, and try to have the animal located. A rabies vaccine, which consists of 3 shots given over a 21-day period, is available and recommended for developing world travel, but is only semi-effective.

Hepatitis B: A viral infection of the liver transmitted via blood or other bodily fluids. Symptoms, which may not surface until years after infection, include jaundice, appetite loss, fever, and joint pain. It is transmitted through unprotected sex and unclean needles. A 3-shot vaccination sequence is recommended for sexually-active travelers and anyone planning to seek medical treatment abroad; it must begin 6 months before traveling.

Hepatitis C: Like Hepatitis B, but the mode of transmission differs. IV drug users, those with occupational exposure to blood, hemodialysis patients, and recipients of blood transfusions are at the highest risk, but the disease can also be spread through sexual contact or sharing items like razors and toothbrushes that may have traces of blood on them. No symptoms are usually exhibited. If untreated, Hep C can lead to liver failure.

AIDS and HIV: For detailed information on Acquired Immune Deficiency Syndrome (AIDS) in Mexico, call the 24hr. National AIDS Hotline at ☎800-342-2437.

Sexually transmitted infections (STIs): Gonorrhea, chlamydia, genital warts, syphilis, herpes, HPV, and other STIs are easier to catch than HIV and can be just as serious. Though condoms may protect you from some STIs, oral or even tactile contact can lead to transmission. If you think you may have contracted an STI, see a doctor immediately.

ESSENTIALS

OTHER HEALTH CONCERNS

MEDICAL CARE ON THE ROAD

The quality of medical care in Mexico often varies with the size of the city or town. The same applies to the availability of English-speaking medical practitioners. Medical care in Mexico City is first-class, while care in more rural areas can be limited. Standards of medical training and patient care vary greatly among beach resorts. Local pharmacies can be invaluable sources of medical help. Most pharmacists are knowledgeable about mild illnesses—particularly those that plague tourists—and can recommend shots or medicines. Wherever possible, *Let's Go* lists 24hr. and late-night pharmacies.

If you are concerned about obtaining medical assistance while traveling, you may wish to employ special support services. The *MedPass* from **GlobalCare, Inc.,** 6875 Shiloh Rd. East, Alpharetta, GA 30005, USA (☎800-860-1111; www.global-care.net), provides 24hr. international medical assistance, support, and medical evacuation resources. The **International Association for Medical Assistance to Travelers (IAMAT;** US ☎716-754-4883, Canada 519-836-0102; www.iamat.org) has free membership, lists English-speaking doctors worldwide, and offers detailed info on immunization requirements and sanitation. If your regular **insurance** policy does not cover travel abroad, you may wish to purchase additional coverage (p. 24).

Those with medical conditions (such as diabetes, allergies to antibiotics, epilepsy, or heart conditions) may want to obtain a **MedicAlert** membership (US$40 per year), which includes among other things a stainless steel ID tag and a 24hr. collect-call number. Contact the MedicAlert Foundation International, 2323 Colorado Ave., Turlock, CA 95382, USA (☎888-633-4298, outside US ☎209-668-3333; www.medicalert.org).

WOMEN'S HEALTH

While **pads** and **sanitary napkins** are plentiful in Mexican pharmacies and supermarkets, **tampons** are harder to come by and, if available at all, come only in regular sizes. It might be wise to bring a supply along, especially if you are traveling to smaller cities. Condoms can be found in most large pharmacies, but other contraceptive devices are difficult to find. Mexico City recently legalized first-trimester **abortion;** elsewhere in the country it is illegal except in cases of rape or to save the woman's life. Women considering an abortion should contact the **Fundación Mexicana para la Planeación Familiar, A.C. (MEXFAM),** Juárez #208, Colonia Tlalpan 14000, Mexico D.F. (☎555 487 0030; www.mexfam.org.mx), for more information.

GETTING TO MEXICO

BY PLANE

When it comes to airfare, a little effort can save you a bundle. Courier fares are the cheapest for those whose plans are flexible enough to deal with the restrictions. Tickets sold by consolidators and standby seating are also good deals, but last-minute specials, airfare wars, and charter flights often beat these fares. The key is to hunt around, be flexible, and ask about discounts. Students, seniors, and those under 26 should never pay full price for a ticket.

AIRFARES

Airfares to Mexico peak in late March/early April and mid-June through August; holidays are also expensive. Midweek (M-Th morning) round-trip flights run US$40-50 cheaper than weekend flights, but they are generally more crowded and less likely to permit frequent-flier upgrades. Not fixing a return date ("open return") or arriving in and departing from different cities ("open-jaw") can be pricier than round-trip flights. Patching one-way flights together is the most expensive way to travel. Flights between Mexico's capitals or regional hubs—Mexico city, Guadalajara, and Cancún—tend to be cheaper.

If Mexico is only one stop on a more extensive globe-hop, consider a round-the-world (RTW) ticket. Tickets usually include at least five stops and are valid for about a year; prices range US$1200-5000. Try **Northwest Airlines/KLM** (☎800-225-2525; www.nwa.com) or **Star Alliance,** a consortium of 16 airlines including United Airlines (www.staralliance.com).

Fares for round-trip flights to Mexico City **from the US or Canadian east coast cost US$500-600, US$400 in the low season; from the US or Canadian west coast US$500/ 300-400; from the UK, UK£800/700; from Australia AUS$4000/3700; from New Zealand NZ$3300/2700.**

BUDGET AND STUDENT TRAVEL AGENCIES

While knowledgeable agents specializing in flights to **Mexico** can make your life easy and help you save, they may not spend the time to find you the lowest possible fare—they get paid on commission. Travelers holding **ISICs** and **IYTCs** (p. 12) qualify for big discounts from student travel agencies.

STA Travel, 5900 Wilshire Blvd., Ste. 900, Los Angeles, CA 90036, USA (24hr. reservations and info ☎800-781-4040; www.statravel.com). A student and youth travel organization with over 150 offices worldwide (check their website for a listing of all their offices), including US offices in Boston, Chicago, Los Angeles, New York, Seattle, San Francisco, and Washington, D.C. Ticket booking, travel insurance, and more. Walk-in offices are located throughout Australia (☎+61 03 9207 5900), New Zealand (☎+64 09 309 9723), and the UK (☎+44 08701 630 026).

Travel CUTS (Canadian Universities Travel Services Limited), 187 College St., Toronto, ON M5T 1P7, Canada (☎888-592-2887; www.travelcuts.com). Offices across Canada and the US including Los Angeles, New York, Seattle, and San Francisco.

USIT, 19-21 Aston Quay, Dublin 2, Ireland (☎01 602 1904; www.usit.ie), Ireland's leading student/budget travel agency has 20 offices throughout Northern Ireland and the Republic of Ireland. Offers programs to work, study, and volunteer worldwide.

✈ **FLIGHT PLANNING ON THE INTERNET.** The Internet may be the budget traveler's dream when it comes to finding and booking bargain fares, but the array of options can be overwhelming. Many airline sites offer special last-minute deals on the Web. Popular Mexican carriers include **Aeroméxico** (www.aeromexico.com), which flies to practically every Mexican city with an airport, and **Mexicana** (www.mexicana.com).

STA (www.statravel.com) and **StudentUniverse** (www.studentuniverse.com) provide quotes on student tickets, while **Orbitz** (www.orbitz.com), **Expedia** (www.expedia.com), and **Travelocity** (www.travelocity.com) offer full travel services. **Priceline** (www.priceline.com) lets you specify a price, and obligates you to buy any ticket that meets or beats it; **Hotwire** (www.hotwire.com) offers bargain fares, but won't reveal the airline or flight times until you buy. Other sites that compile deals include www.bestfares.com, www.flights.com, www.lowestfare.com, www.onetravel.com, and www.travelzoo.com.

SideStep (www.sidestep.com) and **Booking Buddy** (www.bookingbuddy.com) are online tools that can help sift through multiple offers; these two let you enter your trip information once and search multiple sites.

Air Traveler's Handbook (www.faqs.org/faqs/travel/air/handbook) is an indispensable resource on the Internet; it has a comprehensive listing of links to everything you need to know before you board a plane.

COMMERCIAL AIRLINES

The commercial airlines' lowest regular offer is the **APEX** (Advance Purchase Excursion) fare, which provides confirmed reservations and allows "open-jaw" tickets. Generally, reservations must be made seven to 21 days ahead of departure, with seven- to 14-day minimum-stay and up to 90-day maximum-stay restrictions. These fares carry hefty cancellation and change penalties (fees rise in summer). Book peak-season APEX fares early. Use **Expedia** (www.expedia.com) or **Travelocity** (www.travelocity.com) to get an idea of the lowest published fares, then use the resources outlined here to try to beat those fares. Low-season fares should be appreciably cheaper than the **high-season** (mid-June to Aug.) ones listed here.

TRAVELING FROM THE US AND CANADA

Basic round-trip fares to Mexico cost roughly **US$500-600, US$400 in the low season**. Standard commercial carriers like American and United will probably offer the most convenient flights, but they may not be the cheapest, unless you snag a special promotion or airfare war ticket. You will probably find flying one of the following "discount" airlines a better deal, if any of their limited departure points is convenient for you.

JetBlue Airways (☎800-538-2583; www.jetblue.com) Offers cheap flights to a few Mexican cities, including Cancún.

US Airways, 4000 E. Sky Harbor Blvd., Phoenix, AZ 85034 (☎800-428-4322 for 24hr. reservations; www.usairways.com). Discount fares to a number of international cities.

TRAVELING FROM IRELAND AND THE UK

Basic round-trip fares to Mexico cost roughly **US$900-1200, US$800 in the low season**. Standard international carriers like American and Continental will probably offer the most convenient flights.

American Airlines (☎+44 207 365 0777 from London, +44 8457 789 789 from the UK outside London, +353 1602 0550 from Ireland; www.aa.com) Offers international flights to a large number of Mexican cities.

Continental Airlines (☎+44 0845 607 6760 from the UK, +353 1890 925 252 from Ireland; www.continental.com) Offers services similar to American Airlines.

TRAVELING FROM AUSTRALIA AND NEW ZEALAND

Basic round-trip fares to Mexico cost roughly **US$1900-2200, US$1800 in the low season**. Most likely, this trip will require multiple carriers.

Air New Zealand (NZ☎+64 0800 737 000, US☎+01-800-262-1234; www.airnewzealand.co.nz) Offers extensive service within New Zealand and Australia, as well as international service.

Mexicana (☎US+01-800-380-8781, www.mexicana.com) Offers service within Mexico and abroad.

STANDBY FLIGHTS

Traveling standby requires considerable flexibility in arrival and departure dates. Companies dealing in standby flights sell vouchers rather than tickets, along with the promise to get you to your destination (or near your destination) within a certain window of time (typically 1-5 days). You call in before your specific window of time to hear your flight options and the probability that you will be able to board each flight. You can then decide which flights you want to try to catch, show up at the appropriate airport at the appropriate time, present your voucher, and board if space is available.. Vouchers can usually be bought for both one-way and round-trip travel. You may receive a monetary refund only if every available flight within your date range is full; if you opt not to take an available (but perhaps less convenient) flight, you can only get credit toward future travel. Read agreements (and the tricky fine print) with any company offering standby flights with care. To check a company's service record in the US, contact the Better Business Bureau (☎703-276-0100; www.bbb.org). It is difficult to receive refunds, and clients' vouchers will not be honored when an airline fails to receive payment in time.

TICKET CONSOLIDATORS

Ticket consolidators, or **"bucket shops,"** buy unsold tickets in bulk from commercial airlines and sell them at discounted rates. The best place to look is in the Sunday travel section of any major newspaper (such as *The New York Times*), where many bucket shops place tiny ads. Call quickly, as availability is extremely limited. Not all bucket shops are reliable, so insist on a receipt that gives full details of restrictions, refunds, and tickets, and pay by credit card (in spite of the 2-5% fee) so you can stop payment if you never receive your tickets. For more info, see www.travel-library.com/air-travel/consolidators.html.

Some consolidators worth trying are **Rebel** (☎800-732-3588; www.rebel-tours.com), **Cheap Tickets** (www.cheaptickets.com), **Flights.com** (www.flights.com), **TravelHUB** (www.travelhub.com), **Kayak.com** (kayak.com) and **Mobissimmo.com** (mobissimmo.com). *Let's Go* does not endorse any of these agencies. As always, be cautious, and research companies before you hand over your credit card number.

CHARTER FLIGHTS

Tour operators contract charter flights with airlines in order to fly extra loads of passengers during peak season. These flights are far from hassle free. They occur less frequently than major airlines, make refunds particularly difficult, and are almost always fully booked. Their scheduled times may change, and they may be cancelled at the last moment (as late as 48hr. before the trip, and without a full refund). Additionally, check-in, boarding, and baggage claim for these flights are often much slower. They can, however, be much cheaper. Discount clubs and fare brokers offer members savings on last-minute charter and tour deals. Study contracts closely; you don't want to end up with an unwanted overnight layover.

BY BUS OR TRAIN

Greyhound (☎800-231-2222, or for international callers without toll-free access 214-849-8100; www.greyhound.com) serves many US-Mexico border towns, including El Paso (Juárez) and Brownsville (Matamoros) in Texas and San Ysidro (Tijuana) in California. Schedule information is available at any Greyhound terminal, on their website, or by calling their toll-free number. Smaller lines serve other destinations. In the past, buses didn't cross the border, and travelers had to switch to Mexican bus lines at the border. Many bus tours now cross the border, though you can still pick up Mexican bus lines (among them Estrella de Oro, Estrella Blanca, ADO, and Transportes Del Norte) on the other side. Guatemalan bus lines operate at Guatemala-Mexico border towns, including Talismán and La Mesilla. Buses usually stop just short of the border, and you can walk across to Guatemala and pick up a local bus to the nearest town. For more information on entering Guatemala from Chiapas, see p. 607. Buses also operate between Chetumal (p. 695) and the capital of Belize, Belize City.

If you travel by train, your options stop at the border. You can take **Amtrak** (☎800-872-7245; www.amtrak.com) to El Paso, walk across the border to Ciudad Juárez, and continue on with other forms of transportation. Amtrak also serves San Ysidro and Laredo, where you can catch a bus to the border towns of Tijuana and Nuevo Laredo. Train travel is rare in Mexico. Since the system's partial privatization in 1997 Ferromex (☎800-367-3900;www.fer-romex.com.mx) and Ferrosur (☎55 53 876 600;www.ferrosur.com.mx) have become two of the largest companies, but passenger trains are relatively inefficient and have limited reach. Train tickets are either first- or second-class, the latter coming with less services.

BORDER CROSSINGS

There are 24 total overland border crossings to Mexico from **Arizona, California, New Mexico,** and **Texas.** The busiest port of entry by far is that between **San Ysidro, CA** and **Tijuana.** Though currently citizens of Canada and the US do not need a visa to enter the country, they will need to present a valid proof of citizenship (e.g., passport or birth certificate) and photo identification, and will eventually be required to show a passport under the WHTI (p. 10). Other foreign nationals will require a valid passport. If you plan on being in the country for more than 72hr. or venturing beyond the border towns, you will need to obtain a tourist card (p. 11). Though it is done, it is best not to drive into Mexico, as US insurance is not valid in Mexico. The larger border towns have parking lots from which travelers can walk or be bused across the border.

GETTING AROUND MEXICO

BY PLANE

Flying within Mexican borders is a method of transportation typically beyond the reach of budget travelers. That said, time is money. You may want to consider flying when long bus rides (e.g., over 24hr.) cost about the same or are only marginally cheaper than flying. In July 2005, Mexicana launched its budget airline, **Click,** which offers low fares to 16 domestic destinations (www.clickmex.com). For other deals, you can visit the ubiquitous travel agencies. Students and senior citizens should ask about the possibility of discounts or standby seats. You can also check with Mexican airlines directly (p. 30).

BY BUS

From most large cities, it is possible to get almost anywhere in the republic. Several companies run cheaply and efficiently—as efficiently as possible in Mexico, that is. **Autotransportes del Oriente (ADO;** www.ado.com.mx) services Chiapas, the Gulf Coast, Mexico City, Oaxaca state, Puebla, Veracruz state, and the Yucatán. **Grupo Estrella Blanca** (www.estrellablanca.com.mx), which includes **Élite, Flecha Roja, Futura,** and **Transportes del Norte,** services Mexico City, the Pacific Coast, the northeast, and the northwest. **Estrella de Oro** (www.autobus.com.mx) services the Pacific Coast and Mexico City. **Transpais** (www.transpais.com/mx) has routes along the east coast of the country. **ABC** (www.abc.com.mx) services Baja California. Many tickets can be purchased online. The best companies are ADO and Transpais, which have the cleanest buses, timely departures, and security features.

There are several types of bus services. **Servicio ejecutivo** (executive service), also called **de lujo** (deluxe), is fairly rare but provides royal treatment: plush reclining seats, sometimes too-frigid A/C, sandwiches and soda, and movies galore. Less fancy are **primera clase** (first-class) buses, which usually feature second-rate movies and A/C. For both executive and first-class buses, tickets should be purchased in advance at the bus station. **Segunda clase** (second-class) buses are lower in quality. They are usually converted school buses or some variation thereof, and are often overcrowded and uncomfortable. The surest difference is drivers' willingness to pick up people along the road (this service is called **ordinario,** as opposed to **express** and **directo,** which have few or no stops; **sin escalas** is non stop). Tickets for second-class buses can often be purchased on board. When traveling between small towns, second-class buses may be the only available option.

> **❗ THE ROAD LESS TRAVELED BY.** First-class buses are more likely to take toll (*cuota*) roads, while second-class buses often take free (*libre*) highways, which have more reports of hijacking and other crime. To minimize risk, take first-class rather than second-class buses.

Once on a bus—be it local or intercity—keep your wits about you: rumors abound about thieves who wait for travelers to fall asleep. Beware of pickpockets and carry your backpack in front of you where you can see it. Avoid traveling alone if at all possible. It is a good idea to arrange your travel schedule so that any lengthy intercity bus travel is done **during daylight hours,** when there is a lower chance of crime.

Buses are categorized as either *local* or *de paso*. **Locales** originate at the station from which you leave. **De paso** (in passing) buses originate elsewhere and pass through your station. Because *de paso* buses depend on the seating availability when the bus arrives, tickets are not available in advance. Be on the watch for when tickets do go on sale, as buses do not stay in the station long and may fill quickly.

When traveling within a city, take care not to confuse buses labeled "Centro" (referring to the center of town) with those labeled "Central" (referring to the *Central de Autobuses*, or the bus terminal). Also, ask where your stop is, as the bus name (e.g., "Centro") may not be indicative of the final stop.

BY CAR

Mexicans tend to be rowdy on the road. It's not unusual to hear drivers exchange such greetings as *"¡Baboso!"* (Drooling fool!), *"¡Eh, estúpido!"* (Hey, stupid!), and, of course, the ubiquitous *"¿Dónde aprendiste a manejar, menso?"* (Where did you learn how to drive, dummy?). With enough practice, you'll be able to curse with the best Mexican drivers. It's also not unusual for Mexican drivers to overuse their car horns; drive down any busy street and you'll be serenaded by a harmonious chorus of honks. In such a climate, it's best to drive defensively.

In general, avoid freeways *(libres)* and driving at night, when chances of hijacking and other criminal acts are higher. Driving on unpaved side roads can be unsafe and difficult; if you plan to do a lot of driving off major highways, a 4WD car is recommended. The **Association for Safe International Road Travel** (www.asirt.org) is a good resource to learn more about safe car travel while abroad.

FILL 'ER UP. Petróleos Mexicanos, more commonly **PEMEX**, the national oil company, sells two types of unleaded gas: **Magna** (regular) and **Premium** (plus). Prices vary by region, but in most of the country gas is more expensive than in the United States. PEMEX usually only accepts cash and checks.

RENTING

As some of the most beautiful parts of Mexico are off the major highways, a car is definitely advantageous in some regions of the country. Baja California, the Yucatán, and parts of the rural North, where bus stations are more spread out, are areas where you might consider renting a car. As some roads are not paved, having a car whose bottom is farther from the ground (e.g., a pick-up truck) is helpful. 4WD is not necessary, but is certainly recommended if available. You can drive in Mexico with a regular economy car, but keep in mind that cheaper cars tend to be less reliable and harder to handle on difficult terrain. Also note that less expensive 4WD vehicles tend to be more top-heavy, and are more dangerous when navigating particularly bumpy roads.

RENTAL AGENCIES

You can generally make reservations before you leave by calling major international offices in your home country. However, sometimes the price and availability information they give doesn't jive with what the local offices in Mexico will tell you. Try checking with both numbers to make sure you get the best price and the most accurate information possible. Local desk numbers are included in town listings; for home-country numbers, call your toll-free directory.

To rent a car from most establishments in Mexico, you need to be at least 21 years old. Some agencies require renters to be 25, and most charge those 21-24 an additional insurance fee around US$20 per day. Keep in mind that policies and prices vary a lot from agency to agency. Small local operations occasionally rent to people under 21, but be sure to ask about the insurance coverage and deductible, and always check the fine print. The **Mexico Car Rental Guide** (www.mexico-car.net) compares the prices of numerous companies and helps make online bookings. Rental agencies in Mexico include:

Avis: ☎800-311-1212, in Mexico City 555 588 8888; www.avis.com.mx.

Budget: ☎800-700-1700, in Mexico City 55 5566 6800; www.budget.com.mx.

Hertz: ☎800-709-5000, in Mexico City 55 5128 1690; www.hertz.com.mx.

COSTS AND INSURANCE

Rental car prices start at around US$45 a day. Expect to pay more for larger cars and for 4WD. Cars with **automatic transmission** are harder to come by; if available, expect to pay up to US$20 more per day.

Many rental packages offer unlimited kilometers, while others offer a limited number of kilometers per day with a surcharge per kilometer after that. Return the car with a full tank of gasoline (petrol) to avoid high fuel charges at the end. Be sure to ask whether the price includes **insurance** against theft and collision. Remember that if you are driving a conventional rental vehicle on an **unpaved road,** you are almost never covered by insurance; ask about this before leaving the rental agency. Be aware that cars rented on an **American Express** or **Visa/Mas-terCard Gold** or **Platinum** credit card in Mexico might *not* carry the automatic insurance that they would in some other countries; check with your credit card company. Note that Mexican law permits the incarceration of drivers after an accident until they have satisfied their debts to the victim and/or car agency. Many rental companies in Mexico require you to buy a **Collision Damage Waiver (CDW),** which will waive the excess in the case of a collision. **Loss Damage Waivers (LDWs)** do the same in the case of theft or vandalism.

National chains often allow one-way rentals (picking up in one city and dropping off in another). There is usually a minimum hire period and sometimes an extra drop-off charge of several hundred dollars. Full insurance will usually cost around US$10 per day for an economy car.

DRIVING PERMITS AND CAR INSURANCE

INTERNATIONAL DRIVING PERMIT (IDP)

If you plan to drive a car while in **Mexico**, you must have a valid International Driving Permit (IDP), American license, or Canadian license. It may be a good idea to get an IDP anyway, in case you're in a situation (e.g., an accident or stranded in a small town) **where the police do not know English; information on the IDP is printed in 11 languages, including Spanish.**

Your IDP, valid for one year, must be issued in your own country before you depart. An application for an IDP usually requires one or two photos, a current local license, an additional form of identification, and a fee. To apply, contact your home country's automobile association. Be vigilant when purchasing an IDP online or anywhere other than your home automobile association. Many vendors sell permits of questionable legitimacy for higher prices.

CAR INSURANCE

Most credit cards cover standard insurance. **Note that you will need Mexican car insurance if you plan to drive in Mexico.** To avoid being taken into police custody in the event of an accident (as your international liability insurance is most likely invalid in Mexico), purchase Mexican insurance through your car rental agency, at a point of entry, or online at www.drivemex.com or www.bajabound.com.

ON THE ROAD

If possible, avoid driving during the rainy season (June-Oct.), when road conditions deteriorate. If you are planning on driving extensively between cities, check with local authorities or with your nearest consulate for updates on potential dangers. Unless otherwise posted, the speed limit on Mexican highways is 100km per hr. (62mph), but, like most other traffic signs and regulations, it is often ignored. The speed limit in cities and towns is generally 40km per hr. (25mph). Although Mexican police have a reputation for bribery, most cops are honest and helpful. Do not offer a bribe, and if asked for money (usually about 50 pesos, or US$5) when you have not violated the law, stay calm and apologize. If this doesn't work, requesting the officer's badge number, or asking to speak to his chief *(jefe)* may prove effective.

CAR ASSISTANCE

If you're unlucky enough to have a car breakdown on a major toll road between 8am and 8pm, pull completely off the road, raise the hood, stay with your car, and wait for the **Ángeles Verdes** (Green Angels) to come to the rescue. If you have access to a phone, call the Ministry of Tourism's hotline (☎078). These green-and-white emergency trucks, dispatched by radio and staffed by English-speaking mechanics, are equipped to perform common repair jobs, tow cars, change tires, and address minor medical problems. Your green saviors may take a while to show up, but the service— provided by the government—is free (except for gas, parts, and oil). Tipping is optional but a good idea.

BY THUMB

Let's Go never recommends hitchhiking as a safe means of transportation, and none of the information presented here is intended to do so.

Let's Go strongly urges considering the risks before choosing to hitchhike. Hitching means entrusting your life to a stranger and risking assault, sexual harassment, theft, and unsafe driving. For women traveling alone (or even in pairs), hitching is just too dangerous. A man and a woman are a less dangerous combination; two men will have a harder time getting a lift; three men will go nowhere.

KEEPING IN TOUCH

BY EMAIL AND INTERNET

With many Mexican businesses, language schools, and individuals now online, the Internet provides a cheap and accessible alternative to pricey phone calls and slow postal service.

Although in some places it's possible to forge a remote link with your home server, in most cases this is a much slower (and thus more expensive) option than taking advantage of free **web-based email accounts** (e.g., www.gmail.com and www.hotmail.com). **Internet cafes** are listed in the **Practical Information** sections of major cities. These cybercafes can even be found in some of the smaller Mexican towns, with varying quality and speed; expect to pay US$1-8 per hour for access. For lists of additional cybercafes in Mexico, check out cybercaptive.com.

BY TELEPHONE

CALLING HOME FROM MEXICO

You can usually make **direct international calls** from pay phones, but if you aren't using a phone card, you may need to feed the machine regularly. **Prepaid phone cards are a common and relatively inexpensive means of calling abroad.** Each one comes with a Personal Identification Number (PIN) and a toll-free access number. You call the access number and then follow the directions for dialing your PIN. To purchase prepaid phone cards, check online for the best rates; **www.callingcards.com** is a good place to start. Online providers generally send your access number and PIN via email, with no actual "card" involved. You can also call home with prepaid phone cards purchased in Mexico (see **Calling Within Mexico,** p. 38).

 PLACING INTERNATIONAL CALLS. To call Mexico from home or to call home from Mexico, dial:

1. The **international dialing prefix.** To call from **Australia,** dial 0011; **Canada** or the **US,** 011; **Ireland, New Zealand,** the **UK,** 00; Mexico, 00.

2. The **country code** of the country you want to call. To call **Australia,** dial 61; **Canada** or the **US,** 1; **Ireland,** 353; **New Zealand,** 64; the **UK,** 44; **Mexico,** 52.

3. The **city/area code.** *Let's Go* lists the city/area codes for cities and towns in Mexico opposite the city or town name, next to a ☎. If the first digit is a zero (e.g., 020 for London), omit the zero when calling from abroad (e.g., dial 20 from Canada to reach London).

4. The **local number.**

Another option is to purchase a **calling card,** linked to a major national telecommunications service in your home country. Calls are billed collect or to your account. To obtain a calling card, contact the appropriate company listed below. There are often advantages to purchasing calling cards online, including better rates and immediate access to your account. To call home with a calling card, contact the operator for your service provider in Mexico by dialing the appropriate toll-free access number (listed below in the third column).

COMPANY	TO OBTAIN A CARD:	TO CALL ABROAD:
AT&T (US)	800-364-9292 or www.att.com	01-800-288-2872
Canada Direct	800-561-8868 or www.infocanadadirect.com	01-800-123-0200
MCI (US)	800-777-5000 or www.minutepass.com	001-800-888-8000 (US specific)
Telstra Australia	1800 676 638 or www.telstra.com	01-800-123-0261

Placing a **collect call** through an international operator can be expensive, but may be necessary in case of an emergency. You can frequently call collect without even possessing a company's calling card just by calling its access number and following the instructions.

ESSENTIALS

CALLING WITHIN MEXICO

The simplest way to call within the country is to use a coin-operated phone. The **LADATEL phones** that have popped up all over the country have revolutionized the way Mexico calls. To operate one, you'll need a colorful **pre-paid phone card,** available at most *papelerías* (stationery stores) or *tiendas de abarrotes* (general stores)—look for the "De venta aquí LADATEL" signs posted in store windows. Cards come in 30-, 50-, and 100-peso increments. Using a card will usually save time, if not money, in the long run. The computerized phone will tell you how much time, in units, you have left on your card. Phone rates typically tend to be highest in the morning, lower in the evening, and lowest on Sunday and late at night. As of August 2007, phone calls to the US cost 5 pesos per minute, long-distance domestic calls were 4 pesos per minute, and local calls 1 peso per minute.

ON THE LINE. When calling home, you often get more time out of **phone cards** when dialing from a **private line** rather than from a LADATEL, which can cut your time by as much as half. Sweet talk hotel owners into letting you use their phones, and assure them that the card you are using is *prepagada* (prepaid).

CELLULAR PHONES

Some American cell phone companies operate in Mexico, but charge hefty roaming fees. The international standard for cell phones is **Global System for Mobile Communication (GSM).** To make and receive calls in Mexico you will need a **GSM-compatible phone** and a **SIM (Subscriber Identity Module) card,** a country-specific, thumbnail-sized chip that gives you a local phone number and plugs you into the local network. Many SIM cards are **prepaid,** meaning that they come with calling time included and you don't need to sign up for a monthly service plan. When you use up the prepaid time, you can buy additional cards or vouchers (usually available at convenience stores) to "top up" your phone. For more information on GSM phones, check out www.telestial.com, www.orange.co.uk, www.roadpost.com, or www.planetomni.com. Companies like **Cellular Abroad** (www.cellularabroad.com) rent cell phones that work in a variety of destinations around the world, providing a simpler option than picking up a phone in-country.

GSM PHONES. Just having a GSM phone doesn't mean you're necessarily good to go when you travel abroad. The majority of GSM phones sold in the United States operate on a different **frequency** (1900) than international phones (900/1800) and will not work abroad. All three frequencies (900/1800/1900) operate in Mexico, which uses a tri-band system. Additionally, some GSM phones are **SIM-locked** and will only accept SIM cards from a single carrier. You'll need a **SIM-unlocked** phone to use a SIM card from a local carrier when you travel.

TelMex, called TelCel in Mexico, and **Movistar** are the largest cell phone companies in Mexico. Their near-monopoly has resulted in high fees, but the vast majority of the Mexican population still owns cell phones. Prepaid minutes are available in increments of 100, 200, or 500 pesos. A 100 peso card will buy an approximately 10-minute conversation to the United States. It is expensive to receive international phone calls on a cell phone. To cut costs, locals often opt to send text messages in place of phone conversations. In some cases, it may be possible to receive messages from the US for free.

TIME DIFFERENCES

Mexico is divided into 3 time zones and observes Daylight Saving Time. Most of the country—Southern, Central, and Eastern Mexico—is six hours behind Greenwich Mean Time (GMT). Southern Baja, Chihuahua, Nayarit, and Sinaloa are seven hours behind, and northern Baja and Sonora are eight hours behind. A good source for this info is www.worldtimeserver.com.

4AM	5AM	6AM	7AM	8AM	NOON	10PM
Vancouver Seattle San Francisco Los Angeles **TIJUANA**	Denver **CULIACÁN**	Chicago **MEXICO CITY**	New York Toronto	New Brunswick	London	Sydney Canberra Melbourne

BY MAIL

SENDING MAIL HOME FROM MEXICO

Keep in mind that Mexican mail service is painfully slow, even domestically. Airmail from major cities in Mexico to Canada and the US takes anywhere from 10 days to six weeks; to Australia or New Zealand, one month; to Ireland or the UK, three weeks to one month. Add another one or two weeks for mail sent from more rural areas. Sending postcards and letters to the United States via air mail costs approximately 10.90 pesos.

Outgoing mail is picked up infrequently, but the bright plastic orange boxes labeled *Express* that have popped up in large cities are quite reliable and are picked up every morning. Anything important should be sent *registrado* (registered mail) or taken directly to the post office, at the very least. To speed service, it's a good idea to write Spanish abbreviations or names for countries (e.g., E.E.U.U. for the US). Write "airmail," "par avion," or *"por avión"* on the front of the envelope. **Surface mail** is by far the cheapest and slowest way to send mail. It takes one to two months to cross the Atlantic and one to three to cross the Pacific—good for heavy items you won't need for a while, such as souvenirs that you've acquired along the way.

Packages cannot weigh more than 25kg. Keep in mind that all packages are opened and inspected by customs at border crossings; closing boxes with string, instead of tape, is recommended. Sometimes you may have to provide certain information: your tourist card data, the contents, value, and nature of the package ("gift" works best), and your address and return address.

Mexpost, a more expensive, but more reliable, mailing system, guarantees two-day delivery out of state and three-day delivery to major international cities. Despite the promises, expect at least a week for delivery. Mexpost offices are usually found next to regular post offices; if not, the post office staff can usually give you directions to the nearest Mexpost office. Mexpost may not be available in smaller towns.

SENDING MAIL TO MEXICO

To ensure timely delivery, mark envelopes "airmail," "par avion," or *"por avión."* In addition to the standard postage system whose rates are listed below, **Federal Express** (Australia ☎ 13 26 10, Canada and the US 800-463-3339, Ireland 1800 535 800, New Zealand 0800 733 339, the UK 08456 070 809; www.fedex.com) handles express mail services from most countries to Mexico.

There are several ways to arrange pick up of letters sent to you while you are abroad. Mail can be sent via **Poste Restante** (General Delivery; Lista de Correos in

ESSENTIALS

Spanish) to almost any city or town in Mexico with a post office, **but it is not very reliable.** Address *Poste Restante* letters like so:

Gael García BERNAL

Lista de Correos

Street address of post office

City, State, Postal Code

MEXICO

The mail will go to a special desk in the central post office, unless you specify a post office by street address or postal code. It's best to use the largest post office, since mail may be sent there regardless. It is usually safer and quicker, though more expensive, to send mail express or registered. Letters should be marked *"Favor de retener hasta la llegada"* (Please hold until arrival); they will be held for up to 15 days. Bring your passport (or other photo ID) for pick up; there may be a small fee (check in your country). If the clerks insist that there is nothing for you, ask them to check under your first name as well. *Let's Go* lists post offices in the **Practical Information** section for each city and most towns.

American Express's travel offices throughout the world offer a free **Client Letter Service** (mail held up to 30 days and forwarded upon request) for cardholders who contact them in advance. Some offices provide these services to non-cardholders (especially AmEx Travelers Cheque holders), but call ahead to make sure. *Let's Go* lists AmEx locations for most large cities in **Practical Information** sections; for a complete list, call ☎800-528-4800 or visit www.americanexpress.com/travel.

ACCOMMODATIONS

Budget accommodations are not hard to find in Mexico, though things may get pricier in resort towns. All hotels, from luxury resorts in Cancún to rent-by-the-hour joints in Tijuana, are controlled by the government's Secretaria de Turismo (SEC-TUR). This ensures that hotels of similar quality charge similar prices; you should always ask to see an up-to-date official tariff sheet if you doubt the quoted price. Many hotels post their official tariffs somewhere near the reception area. Although hotel prices are regulated, proprietors are not prohibited from charging *less* than the official rate. A little bargaining can work wonders, especially if you stay several days.

HOSTELS

Many hostels are laid out dorm-style, often with large single-sex rooms and bunk beds, although private rooms that sleep two to four are becoming more common. They sometimes have kitchens and utensils for your use, storage areas, transportation to airports, breakfast and other meals, laundry facilities, and Internet access. There can be drawbacks: some hostels close during certain daytime "lockout" hours, have a curfew, don't accept reservations, impose a maximum stay, or, less frequently, require that you do chores. In Mexico, a dorm bed in a hostel will average around 130 pesos (under US$12) and a private room around 170-220 pesos (US$16-21). They are often located within a block or two of a city's *zócalo* and have hot water and private bathrooms but rarely provide amenities such as A/C.

A HOSTELER'S BILL OF RIGHTS. There are certain standard features that we do not include in our hostel listings. Unless we state otherwise, you can expect that every hostel has no lockout, no curfew, free hot showers, some system of secure luggage storage, and no key deposit.

For more information about Mexican hostels, contact the **Hostelling Mexico, A.C.,** Guatemala 4, Colonia Centro, Mexico D.F. (☎55 5518 1726; www.hostellingmexico.com), which is affiliated with Hostelling International.

HOSTELLING INTERNATIONAL

Joining the youth hostel association in your own country (listed below) automatically grants you membership privileges in **Hostelling International (HI),** a federation of national hosteling associations. Non-HI members may be allowed to stay in some hostels, but will have to pay extra to do so. HI hostels are rare in Mexico, though if available, **are typically less expensive than private hostels.** HI's umbrella organization's website (www.hihostels.com), which lists the web addresses and phone numbers of all national associations, can be a great place to begin researching hosteling in a specific region. Other comprehensive hosteling websites include www.hostels.com.

Most HI hostels also honor **guest memberships**—you'll get a blank card with space for six validation stamps. Each night you'll pay a nonmember supplement (one-sixth the membership fee) and earn one guest stamp; get six stamps and you're a member. A new membership benefit is the FreeNites program, which allows hostelers to gain points toward free rooms. Most student travel agencies (p. 29) sell HI cards, as do all of the national hosteling organizations listed below. All prices listed below are valid for **one-year memberships** unless otherwise noted.

> **BOOKING HOSTELS ONLINE.** One of the easiest ways to ensure you've got a bed for the night is by reserving online. Click to the **Hostelworld** booking engine through **www.letsgo.com,** and you'll have access to bargain accommodations from Argentina to Zimbabwe with no added commission.

OTHER TYPES OF ACCOMMODATIONS

YMCAS AND YWCAS

Young Men's Christian Association (YMCA) and **Young Women's Christian Association (YWCA)** lodgings are usually cheaper than a hotel but more expensive than a hostel. Not all locations offer lodging; those that do are often located in urban downtowns. Many YMCAs accept women and families; some will not lodge those under 18 without parental permission. **Fed. de Asociación Cristiana de Jóvenes de la República (FM),** Av. Ejército Nacional #253, Col. Anáhuac, Mexico D.F. 11320 (☎55 5545 0781; www.ymca.org.mx)

HOTELS, GUESTHOUSES, AND PENSIONS

Hotel singles in Mexico cost about 170-250 pesos per night (US$16-20), doubles US$200-600 pesos per night (US$9-55). You'll typically share a hall bathroom; a private bathroom will cost extra, as may hot showers. Some hotels offer "full pension" (all meals) and "half pension" (no lunch). Smaller **guesthouses** and **pensions** are often cheaper than hotels. If you make **reservations** in writing, indicate your night of arrival and the number of nights you plan to stay. The hotel will send you a confirmation and may request payment for the first night. It is often easiest to make reservations over the phone with a credit card.

BED & BREAKFASTS (B&BS)

For a cozy alternative to impersonal hotel rooms, B&Bs (private homes with rooms available to travelers) range from acceptable to sublime. Rooms in B&Bs generally cost **US$75** for a single and **US$100** for a double in **Mexico**. Any number of websites provide listings for B&Bs; check out **Bed & Breakfast Inns Online** (www.bbonline.com), **InnFinder** (www.inncrawler.com), **InnSite** (www.innsite.com), **Bedand-Breakfast.com** (www.bedandbreakfast.com), or **Pamela Lanier's Bed & Breakfast Guide Online** (www.lanierbb.com).

HOME EXCHANGES AND HOSPITALITY CLUBS

Home exchange offers the traveler various types of homes (houses, apartments, condominiums, and villas), plus the opportunity to live like a native and to cut down on accommodation fees. For more information, contact Intervac International Home Exchange (www.intervac.com).

   Hospitality clubs link their members with individuals or families abroad who are willing to host travelers for free or for a small fee to promote cultural exchange and general good karma. In exchange, members usually must be willing to host travelers in their own homes; a small membership fee may also be required. **The Hospitality Club** (www.hospitalityclub.org) is a good place to start. **Servas** (www.servas.org) is an established, more formal, peace-based organization, and requires a fee and an interview to join. An Internet search will find many similar organizations, some of which cater to special interests (e.g., women, GLBT travelers, or members of certain professions). As always, use common sense when planning to stay with or host someone you do not know.

LONG-TERM ACCOMMODATIONS

Travelers planning to stay in Mexico for extended periods of time may find it most cost-effective to rent an **apartment.** A basic one-bedroom (or studio) apartment in Mexico City will range 300-900 pesos per month. Besides the rent itself, prospective tenants usually are also required to front a security deposit (frequently one month's rent). Many websites, including craigslist.org and sublet.com, provide listings of available apartments.

CAMPING

Travelers accustomed to clean and well-maintained campgrounds may be in for a few surprises. By and large, Mexican national parks exist only in theory. The "protected lands" are often indistinguishable from the surrounding countryside or city and may be dirty, unappealing, and overrun with amorous teenagers. Privately owned **trailer parks** are relatively common on major routes—look for signs with a picture of a trailer, or the words *parque de trailer, campamento,* or *remolques.* These places often allow campers to pitch tents or sling up a hammock.

For those budget-minded individuals traveling along the coast, the hammock is the way to go. Most beach towns in Mexico are dotted with **palapas** (palm-tree huts). For a small fee, open-air restaurants double as places to hang your hat and hammock when the sun sets. At beaches and some inland towns frequented by backpackers, **cabañas** (cabins, usually simple thatch-roof huts) are common. For the truly hard-core, camping on the beach can sometimes be an option. Lax permit laws and beach accessibility— every meter of beach in Mexico is public property—offer campers oodles of options. For more information on outdoor activities in Mexico see **The Great Outdoors,** p. 44.

E S S E N T I A L S

THE GREAT OUTDOORS

The **Great Outdoor Recreation Page** (www.gorp.com) provides excellent general information for travelers planning on camping or spending time in the outdoors.

> **LEAVE NO TRACE.** Let's Go encourages travelers to embrace the "Leave No Trace" ethic, minimizing their impact on natural environments and protecting them for future generations. Trekkers and wilderness enthusiasts should set up camp on durable surfaces, use cookstoves instead of campfires, bury human waste away from water supplies, bag trash and carry it out with them, and respect wildlife and natural objects. For more detailed information, contact the **Leave No Trace Center for Outdoor Ethics,** P.O. Box 997, Boulder, CO 80306 (☎ 800-332-4100 or 303-442-8222; www.lnt.org).

USEFUL RESOURCES

For topographical maps of Mexico, write or visit the **Instituto Nacional de Estadísticas, Geografía e Informática (INEGI),** Calle Patriotismo 711, Torre A, Piso 7, Del. Benito Juárez, Col. San Juan Mixcoac, Mexico D.F., 03730 (☎ 01 800 111 46 34; www.inegi.gob.mx).

A variety of publishing companies offer hiking guidebooks to meet the educational needs of novice or expert. For information about camping, hiking, and biking, write or call the publishers listed below to receive a free catalog.

PUBLISHERS

Sierra Club Books, 85 Second St., 2nd fl., San Francisco, CA 94105, USA (☎ 415-977-5500; www.sierraclub.org). Publishes general resource books on hiking and camping.

The Mountaineers Books, 1001 SW Klickitat Way, Ste. 201, Seattle, WA 98134, USA (☎ 206-223-6303; www.mountaineersbooks.org). Over 600 titles on hiking, biking, mountaineering, natural history, and conservation.

Wilderness Press, 1200 5th St., Berkeley, CA 94710, USA (☎ 510-558-1666 or toll free 800-443-7227; www.wildernesspress.com). Carries over 100 hiking guides and maps, mostly for the western US.

BOOKS

Backpacking in Mexico, Tim Burford. Bradt Publishing 1997 (US$17). A guide specifically written about long- and short-distance hiking and volcanoes. Includes important tips and information for travelers.

Mexico: A Hiker's Guide to Mexico's Natural History, Jim Conrad. Mountaineers Books 1995 (US$17). Includes trail tips as well as extensive information on Mexico's geography, vegetation, and wildlife.

Mexico's Copper Canyon Country, John Fayhee. Johnson Books 1994 (US$17). Includes vital tips and details on planning a trip and traveling in the canyon based on the author's own experiences.

Traveler's Guide to Camping Mexico's Baja, Mike and Terri Church. Rolling Home Press 2001 (US$15). Although written with RVers in mind, this guide also includes information on entering Mexico, campgrounds, and recreational activities throughout Baja.

NATIONAL PARKS AND RESERVES

Many of Mexico's lush lands are classified as national parks and biosphere reserves. There are 93 protected areas (encompassing about 6% of the country) controlled by **SINAP** (La Sistema Nacional de Areas Naturales Protegidas; The National System of Protected Natural Areas) and protected by the **INE** (Instituto Nacional de Ecología; National Institute of Ecology). National parks can range from small urban parks to large expanses of land. Volcanoes and most architectural ruins are considered national parks. Biosphere reserves tend to boast high levels of biodiversity, especially those that house endangered species. Conservation and sustainable development are two important goals of the reserves.

In general, it is difficult to explore Mexico's lush wilderness by yourself. Aside from highly visited ruins and parks found in cities, most do not have organized trails. In many places, the safest and most common way to see some of Mexico's beautiful natural areas is to hire a guide.

WILDERNESS SAFETY

Staying **warm, dry,** and **well hydrated** is key to a happy and safe wilderness experience. For any hike, prepare yourself for an emergency by packing a first-aid kit, a reflector, a whistle, high-energy food, extra water, rain gear, a hat, and extra socks. In case of rain, make sure to wear wool or insulating synthetic materials designed for the outdoors. Cotton is a bad choice as it dries painfully slowly.

Check **weather forecasts** often and pay attention to the skies when hiking, as weather patterns can change suddenly. Always let someone—a friend, your hostel, a park ranger, or a local hiking organization—know when and where you are going. Know your physical limits and do not attempt a hike beyond your ability. See **Safety and Health,** p. 19, for information on outdoor medical concerns.

WILDLIFE

MOSQUITOES WILL SAVAGE YOU. Protect yourself from **mosquito bites,** which may transmit diseases like malaria (p. 25). Mosquitoes bite through thin fabric, so cover up as much as possible with thicker materials. **100% DEET** is useful, but the mosquitoes are so ravenous that nothing short of a **mosquito hood** and netting stops every jab.

TICKS. To prevent **tick bites,** exercise the same caution as you would for mosquitoes. When camping, check your site for ticks. Ticks usually bite between your toes, behind your knees or neck, on your head, in your armpits, or around your groin. Damage from ticks can often be prevented by removing them as quickly as possible with a pair of tweezers. Ticks are known to transmit Lyme disease (p. 26). If bitten, seek medical attention immediately.

SNAKES. The **pit viper,** a yellow snake found in the rainforests of southern Mexico, rarely descends from its tree; however, a bite can be fatal, especially if it occurs on the arms or neck. A bite from the **fer-de-lance,** found on farms in southern Mexico, can also be deadly. Its coloration varies from gray to olive to reddish-brown. **Rattlesnakes,** brown in color and known for their rattle-like sound, are found in northern deserts and other dry areas, as well as in southern Mexico. If you are bitten by a snake, go to a hospital immediately. Most bites do not lead to death. Do not ice or otherwise irritate the wound, as this may lead to the need for amputation. Do not try to suck out the venom on your own! Instead, leave the bite untouched and elevate the limb.

LIZARDS. There are some poisonous lizards found in Mexico. The **Gila Monster** in the northwest has dark skin with pink coloration and is 35-45cm long. The **Mexican Beaded Lizard** looks like the Gila and is also poisonous. Never try to

ESSENTIALS

touch or pick up one of these lizards. If bitten, seek medical help immediately. Bites are not usually fatal to humans.

WILD CATTLE AND NON-DOMESTIC ANIMALS. Wild cattle have been known to attack people. This should not be a concern in most tourist areas, but those spending time in more remote places should be aware of the possibility. Note that non-domestic animals may have rabies, and it is best to steer clear and avoid touching stray and wild animals.

CAMPING AND HIKING EQUIPMENT

WHAT TO BUY

Good camping equipment is both sturdy and light. North American suppliers tend to offer the most competitive prices.

Sleeping Bags: Most sleeping bags are rated by season; "summer" means 30-40°F (around 0°C) at night; "four-season" or "winter" often means below 0°F (-17°C). Bags are made of **synthetic** material (heavy, durable, and warm when wet) or **down** (warm and light, but expensive, and miserable when wet). Prices range US$50-250 for a summer synthetic to US$200-300 for a good down winter bag. **Sleeping bag pads** include foam pads (US$10-30), air mattresses (US$15-50), and self-inflating mats (US$30-120). Bring a **stuff sack** to store your bag and keep it dry.

Tents: The best tents are free-standing (with their own frames and suspension systems), set up quickly, and only require staking in high winds. Low-profile dome tents are the best all-around. Worthy 2-person tents start at US$100, 4-person tents start at US$160. Seal your tent's seams with waterproofer, and make sure it has a rain fly. Other useful accessories include a **battery-operated lantern,** a plastic **groundcloth,** and a nylon **tarp.**

Backpacks: Internal-frame packs mold well to your back, keep a lower center of gravity, and flex adequately to allow you to hike difficult trails, while **external-frame packs** are more comfortable for long hikes over even terrain, as they carry weight higher and distribute it more evenly. Make sure your pack has a strong, padded hip-belt to transfer weight to your legs. There are models designed specifically for women. Any serious backpacking requires a pack of at least 4000 cu. in. (16,000cc), plus 500 cu. in. for sleeping bags in internal-frame packs. Sturdy backpacks cost anywhere from US$125-420; your pack is an area where it doesn't pay to economize. On your hunt for the perfect pack, fill up prospective models with something heavy, strap it on correctly, and walk around the store to get a sense of how the model distributes weight. Either buy a **rain cover** (US$10-20) or store all of your belongings in plastic bags inside your pack.

Boots: Be sure to wear hiking boots with good **ankle support.** They should fit snugly and comfortably over 1-2 pairs of **wool socks** and a pair of thin **liner socks.** Break in boots over several weeks before you go to spare yourself blisters.

Other Necessities: Synthetic layers, like those made of polypropylene or polyester, and a pile jacket will keep you warm even when wet. A **space blanket** (US$5-15) will help you to retain body heat and doubles as a groundcloth. Plastic **water bottles** are vital; look for shatter- and leak-resistant models. Carry **water-purification tablets** for when you can't boil water. Although most campgrounds provide campfire sites, you may want to bring a small **metal grate** or **grill.** For those places that forbid fires or the gathering of firewood, you'll need a **camp stove** (the classic Coleman starts at US$50) and a propane-filled **fuel bottle** to operate it. Also bring a **first-aid kit, pocketknife, insect repellent,** and **waterproof matches** or a **lighter.**

WHERE TO BUY IT

The online and mail-order companies listed below offer lower prices than many retail stores. A visit to a local camping or outdoors store will give you a good sense of the look and weight of certain items before you buy.

Campmor, 400 Corporate Dr., PO Box 680, Mahwah, NJ 07430, USA (☎800-525-4784; www.campmor.com).

Cotswold Outdoor, Unit 11 Kemble Business Park, Crudwell, Malmesbury Wiltshire, SN16 9SH, UK (☎+44 8704 427 755; www.cotswoldoutdoor.com).

Discount Camping, 833 Main North Rd., Pooraka, South Australia 5095, Australia (☎+618 8262 3399; www.discountcamping.com.au).

Eastern Mountain Sports (EMS), 1 Vose Farm Rd., Peterborough, 03458 NH, USA (☎888-463-6367; www.ems.com).

Gear-Zone, 8 Burnet Rd., Sweetbriar Rd. Industrial Estate, Norwich, NR3 2BS, UK (☎+44 1603 410 108; www.gear-zone.co.uk).

L.L. Bean, Freeport, ME 04033, USA (US and Canada ☎800-441-5713; UK +44 800 891 297; www.llbean.com).

Mountain Designs, 443a Nudgee Rd., Hendra, Queensland 4011, Australia (☎+617 3114 4300; www.mountaindesigns.com).

Recreational Equipment, Inc. (REI), Sumner, WA 98352, USA (US and Canada ☎800-426-4840, elsewhere 253-891-2500; www.rei.com).

CAMPERS AND RVS

Renting an RV costs more than tenting or hosteling but less than staying in hotels while renting a car (see **Renting,** p. 34). The convenience of having your own bedroom, bathroom, and kitchen makes RVing an attractive option, especially for older travelers and families with children. Mexico's Copper Canyon in the west and the beach towns along Pacific coast have long been popular RV destinations.

Rates vary widely by region, season (July and Aug. are the most expensive months), and type of RV. Rental prices for a standard RV are around 8,600 pesos (US$800) per week.

ORGANIZED ADVENTURE TRIPS

Organized adventure tours offer another way of exploring the wild. Activities include hiking, biking, canoeing, kayaking, rafting, climbing, and archaeological digs. Tourism bureaus often can suggest parks, trails, and outfitters. Organizations that specialize in camping and outdoor equipment like REI and EMS (p. 46) also are good sources for information.

Specialty Travel Index, P.O. Box 458, San Anselmo, CA 94979, USA (☎888-624-4030, elsewhere 415-455-1643; www.specialtytravel.com).

TrekAmerica, P.O. Box 189, Rockaway, NJ 07866, USA (☎800-221-0596 or 973-983 1144, elsewhere +44 870 444 8735; www.trekamerica.com).

SPECIFIC CONCERNS

SUSTAINABLE TRAVEL

As the number of travelers on the road continues to rise, the detrimental effect they can have on natural environments becomes an increasing concern. With this in mind, Let's Go promotes the philosophy of **sustainable travel.** Through a sensitivity to issues of ecology and sustainability, today's travelers can be a powerful force in preserving as well as restoring the places they visit.

Ecotourism, a rising trend in sustainable travel, focuses on the conservation of natural habitats and how to use them to build up the economy without exploitation or overdevelopment. Travelers can make a difference by doing research in advance and by supporting organizations and establishments that pay attention to their impact on their natural surroundings and that strive to be environmentally friendly. For Mexico-specific information on ecotourism, see **Beyond Tourism,** p. 77.

ECOTOURISM RESOURCES. For more information on environmentally responsible tourism, contact one of the organizations below:

Conservation International, 2011 Crystal Dr., Ste. 500, Arlington, VA 22202, USA (☎800-406-2306 or 703-341-2400; www.conservation.org).

Green Globe, Green Globe vof, Verbenalaan 1, 2111 ZL Aerdenhout, The Netherlands (☎31 23 544 0306; www.greenglobe.com).

International Ecotourism Society, 1333 H St. NW, Ste. 300E, Washington, D.C. 20005, USA (☎202-347-9203; www.ecotourism.org).

United Nations Environment Program (UNEP), 39-43 Quai André Citroën, 75739 Paris Cedex 15, France (☎33 1 44 37 14 50; www.uneptie.org/pc/tourism).

RESPONSIBLE TRAVEL

The impact of tourist pesos on the destinations you visit should not be underestimated. The choices you make during your trip can have powerful effects on local communities—for better or for worse. Travelers who care about the destinations and environments they explore should make themselves aware of the social, cultural and political implications of the choices they make when they travel. Simple decisions such as buying local products instead of globally available ones, paying fair prices for products or services, and attempting to say a few words in the local language can have a strong, positive effect on the community.

Community-based tourism aims to channel tourist pesos into the local economy by emphasizing tours and cultural programs that are run by members of the host community and that often benefit disadvantaged groups. This type of tourism also benefits the tourists themselves, as it often takes them beyond the traditional tours of the region. The *Ethical Travel Guide* (UK£13), a project of **Tourism Concern** (☎+44 020 7133 3330; www.tourismconcern.org.uk), is an excellent resource for information on community-based travel with a directory of 300 establishments in 60 countries.

Mexico's inhabitants have been impacted by travel in a variety of ways. Adaptation of Mexican culture to tourist demands, loss of authenticity and commodification of Mexican traditions, and economic inequality between tourists and locals are some of the issues that have been exacerbated by tourism. Showing respect for local traditions and culture is encouraged.

TRAVELING ALONE

There are many benefits to traveling alone, including independence and a greater opportunity to connect with locals. On the other hand, solo travelers are more vulnerable targets of harassment and street theft. If you are traveling alone, look confident, try not to stand out as a tourist, and be especially careful in deserted or very crowded areas. Stay away from areas that are not well lit. If questioned, never admit that you are traveling alone. Maintain regular contact with someone at home who knows your itinerary, and always research your destination before traveling. For more tips, pick up *Traveling Solo* by Eleanor Berman (Globe Pequot Press, US$18), visit www.travelaloneandloveit.com, or subscribe to **Connecting: Solo Travel Network,** 689 Park Rd., Unit 6, Gibsons, BC V0N 1V7, Canada (☎604-886-9099; www.cstn.org; membership US$30-48).

WOMEN TRAVELERS

Women exploring on their own inevitably face some additional safety concerns, but it's easy to be adventurous without taking undue risks. If you are concerned, consider staying in hostels which offer single rooms that lock from the inside or in religious organizations with single-sex rooms. Stick to centrally located accommodations and avoid solitary late-night treks or bus rides.

Always carry extra cash for a phone call, bus, or taxi. **Hitchhiking** is never safe for lone women, or even for two women traveling together. Look as if you know where you're going and approach older women or couples for directions if you're lost or uncomfortable.

Generally, the less you look like a tourist, the better off you'll be. Mexican women seldom travel without the company of men; foreign women who do so often draw attention. Moreover, Mexican men are notorious for their *machismo*, a brand of Latin-American chauvinism accompanied by whistles, catcalls, and stares. Persistent men may insist on joining you and "showing you the sights." If you're fair-skinned or have light-colored hair, you might hear *"güera, güera"* (blonde, blonde). Expect to hear the typical come-on, *"¿Adónde vas, mamacita?"* (Where are you going, babe?). The best answer to verbal harassment is often none at all; feigning deafness, sitting motionless, and staring straight ahead at nothing in particular will do more than reacting to taunts. *Machismo* is usually more annoying than dangerous, but in real emergencies, a firm, loud, and very public "Go away!" *("¡Vete!")* or a yell for help *("¡Socorro!")* might fend off unwanted attention. It might also be a good idea to wear a **whistle.** Be aware, however, that many police officers and uniformed officials are the biggest *machistas* of all. **Local elderly women** or **nuns** often discourage Casanovas simply by their presence.

Awareness of Mexican social standards and dress codes may help to minimize unwanted attention. Mexican women seldom wear shorts, short skirts, tank tops, or halter tops. In many regions, doing so may draw harassment or stares. Shorts and tank tops are appropriate only in beach and resort areas or in towns with a large number of foreign students and tourists. More traditional areas of the country generally require conservative dress; wear a long skirt and sleeved blouses in churches or very religious towns. If you are traveling with a male friend, it may help to pose as a couple; this will make it easier to share rooms and will also chill the blood of Mexican Romeos. Wearing a **wedding band** on your left hand or a **crucifix** around your neck may help discourage unwanted attention. In addition to talking loudly and frequently about their muscular boyfriend *(novio muy fuerte)* or easily angered husband *(esposo muy enojón)*, some savvy women even carry pictures of these "boyfriends" and "husbands," gladly displaying them to prospective suitors. Most importantly, act confidently in potentially dangerous situations.

Memorize the emergency numbers in Mexico (☎ **060**). A self-defense course will both prepare you for a potential attack and raise your awareness level of your surroundings (see **Personal Safety,** p. 22).

GLBT TRAVELERS

Despite Mexico's conservative and Catholic traditions, there is little violence against GBLT travelers in large metropolitan areas. In addition, discrimination by sexual orientation is illegal in Mexico. However, homosexuality is frowned upon at best, and intolerance is especially rampant in more rural areas of the country, where displays of affection may attract harassment. More urban areas are generally more accepting of homosexuality; there are large gay-rights movements in Acapulco, Guadalajara, Mexico City, Monterrey, and Puerto Vallarta. The best rule of thumb is to avoid public displays of affection until you know you are in a safe

ESSENTIALS

and accepting environment, such as one afforded by gay-friendly clubs and establishments (of which there are many). Whenever possible, *Let's Go: Mexico* lists gay- and lesbian-friendly establishments; the best way to find out about the many others that we do not list is to consult organizations, mail-order bookstores, and publishers that offer materials addressing gay and lesbian concerns (see below). **Out and About** (www.planetout.com) is a comprehensive site that offers a weekly newsletter addressing travel concerns. The online newspaper **365gay.com** also has a travel section (www.365gay.com/travel/travelchannel.htm).

Gay México: www.gaymexico.com.mx. All-purpose information in Spanish and English.

Gay's the Word, 66 Marchmont St., London WC1N 1AB, UK (☎+44 020 7278 7654; http://freespace.virgin.net/gays.theword/). The largest gay and lesbian bookshop in the UK, with both fiction and non-fiction titles. Mail-order service available.

Giovanni's Room, 345 South 12th St., Philadelphia, PA 19107, USA (☎215-923-2960; www.giovannisroom.com). An international lesbian and gay bookstore with mail-order service (carries many of the publications listed below).

International Lesbian and Gay Association (ILGA), 17 Rue de la Charité, 1210 Brussels, Belgium (☎322 502 2471; www.ilga.org). Provides political information, such as homosexuality laws of individual countries.

Ser Gay: www.sergay.com.mx. A Mexico City-based site with chat forums and event listings around the country.

ADDITIONAL RESOURCES: GLBT

A Man's Guide to Mexico and Central America, Señor Córdova. Centurion Press 1999 (US$19).

Damron Men's Travel Guide, Damron Road Atlas, Damron Accommodations Guide, Damron City Guide, and *Damron Women's Traveller.* Damron Travel Guides (US$18-24). For info, call ☎800-462-6654 or visit www.damron.com.

Ferrari Guides' Gay Travel A to Z, Ferrari Guides' Men's Travel in Your Pocket, Ferrari Guides' Women's Travel in Your Pocket, and *Ferrari Guides' Inn Places.* Ferrari Publications (US$16-20).

Gay Mexico: The Men of Mexico, Eduardo David. Floating Lotus 1998 (US$22).

The Gay Vacation Guide: The Best Trips and How to Plan Them, Mark Chesnut. Kensington Books (US$15).

TRAVELERS WITH DISABILITIES

Mexico is increasingly accessible to travelers with disabilities, noticeably in Mexico City and popular resort towns like Cancún and Cabo San Lucas. Northern cities closer to the US, such as Monterrey and Saltillo, also tend to be more wheelchair-friendly. Generally, the more you are willing to spend, the less difficult it is to find wheelchair-accessible facilities. Keep in mind, however, that most public and long-distance modes of transportation (e.g., buses) and most of the non-luxury hotels don't accommodate wheelchairs. Though more archaeological sites are becoming wheelchair-accessible, many public bathrooms, ruins, parks, historic buildings, and museums are relatively inaccessible. Still, with some advance planning, an affordable Mexican vacation is possible. Those with disabilities should inform airlines and hotels when making reservations. Call ahead to restaurants, museums, and other facilities to find out if they are wheelchair-accessible. **Guide dog owners** should inquire as to Mexico's quarantine policies.

USEFUL ORGANIZATIONS

Access Abroad, www.umabroad.umn.edu/access. A website devoted to making study abroad available to students with disabilities. Program locales include Cuernavaca and Guanajuato. The site is maintained by Disability Services and the Learning Abroad Center, University of Minnesota, 230 Heller Hall, 271 19th Ave., Minneapolis, MN 55455, USA (☎612-626-9000).

The Guided Tour, Inc., 7900 Old York Rd., Ste. 114B, Elkins Park, PA 19027, USA (☎800-783-5841; www.guidedtour.com). Organizes travel programs for persons with developmental and physical challenges in Mexico, as well as in Canada, Hawaii, Ireland, Italy, Spain, the UK, and the US.

Mobility International USA (MIUSA), P.O. Box 10767, Eugene, OR 97440, USA (☎541-343-1284; www.miusa.org). Provides a variety of books and other publications containing information for travelers with disabilities.

Society for Accessible Travel and Hospitality (SATH), 347 Fifth Ave., Ste. 610, New York, NY 10016, USA (☎212-447-7284; www.sath.org). An advocacy group that publishes free online travel info. Annual membership US$49, students and seniors US$29.

MINORITY TRAVELERS

Nearly all of the Mexican population is white, *indígena* (of indigenous descent), or a combination of the two. This means that many travelers are bound to stick out, particularly when traveling in rural or less touristed parts of the country. In general, the whiter your skin, the better treatment you'll receive. Unfortunately, light-skinned travelers are also viewed as wealthier and therefore are more likely to be the targets of crime. If you are lighter-skinned, take the extra precaution to avoid looking like a tourist and attracting unwanted attention. Travelers of African or Asian ancestry will likely attract attention for their perceived exoticism. East Asians may find themselves called *chinos*, South Asians might be referred to as *indus* or *árabes*, while those of African descent are often called *morenos* or *negros*. None of these words are considered derogatory in Mexico; they are simply descriptive terms. In many rural areas, non-Spanish speakers may also be viewed as a threat. Note that most of Mexico is Catholic—non-Catholics would also be considered a minority.

DIETARY CONCERNS

Vegetarians are rare in Mexico, and vegans are almost unheard of. Expect incredulous stares in many places—sometimes from concerned patrons at nearby tables as well as waiters. *"Soy vegetariano,"* translates into, "I'm vegetarian"; *"Sin carne/puerco/pollo/pescado/animal"* is "Without meat/pork/chicken/fish/animal." If you just ask for your meal "without meat," your waiter may assume that you eat chicken or fish, so be sure to specify what you cannot eat. When pressed, allergies or illness (*"Soy allérgico; voy a vomitar si como mucha carne.* "I'm allergic; I will vomit if I eat lots of meat") make better alibis. With that said, the carnivorous culture of Mexico can make it difficult for **vegetarian tourists,** as almost all meals are prepared using animal products. Some popular vegetarian dishes available in most restaurants include quesadillas (melted cheese between tortillas), *chilaquiles* (strips of fried tortillas baked in tomato sauce with cheese and fresh cream), *molletes* (french bread smothered with refried beans and cheese), *tortas de queso,* and *frijoles* (beans). Be aware that nearly all flour tortillas and many types of beans are prepared with *man-*

teca (lard). **Vegan tourists** will have a harder go at it and may have to subsist on the old standbys of corn tortillas and rice. Wherever possible, *Let's Go* includes vegetarian dining options.

The travel section of the **The Vegetarian Resource Group's** website, at www.vrg.org/travel, has a comprehensive list of organizations and websites geared toward helping vegetarians and vegans traveling abroad. It lists Mexican vegetarian establishments at www.vrg.org/travel/larg.htm. For more information, visit your local bookstore or health food store, and consult *The Vegetarian Traveler: Where to Stay if You're Vegetarian, Vegan, Environmentally Sensitive*, by Jed and Susan Civic (Larson Publications). Some good resources on the web are www.vegdining.com and www.happycow.net.

Despite the increasing number of Jews in Mexico (especially in Mexico City), keeping **kosher** can be difficult. Many large supermarkets sell kosher foods, but travelers will have less luck in restaurants and smaller towns. Those who keep kosher should contact Mexican synagogues for information on kosher restaurants. Your own synagogue or college Hillel should have access to lists of Jewish institutions across Mexico. If you are strict in your observance, you may have to prepare your own food on the road. A good resource is the *Jewish Travel Guide*, edited by Michael Zaidner (Vallentine Mitchell; US$18). Travelers looking for halal restaurants may find www.zabihah.com a useful resource.

OTHER RESOURCES

Let's Go tries to cover all aspects of budget travel, but we can't put *everything* in our guides. Listed below are books and websites that can serve as jumping-off points for your own research.

USEFUL PUBLICATIONS

Living Abroad in Mexico, Ken Luboff. Avalon Travel Publishing, 2005 ($US 17.95). A book with information on Mexican history, advice on starting businesses or moving, and the scoop on popular places for expats.

Mexico Desconocido, www.mexicodesconocido.com. A Mexican magazine that features culture, art, food, and other traditions.

Oaxaca: The Spirit of Mexico, by Matthew Jaffe, Judith Cooper Haden (photographer). Artisan, 2002 ($US 21.90). A great coffee table book.

The People's Guide to Mexico, by Carl Franz. Avalon Travel Publishing, 2002 ($US 16.47). A popular resource with helpful advice and humorous anecdotes.

WORLD WIDE WEB

Almost every aspect of budget travel is accessible via the web. In 10min. at the keyboard, you can make a hostel reservation, get advice on travel hot spots from other travelers, or find out how much a bus from Mexico City to Cancún costs.

Listed here are some regional and travel-related sites to start off your surfing; other relevant websites are listed throughout the book. Because website turnover is high, use search engines (e.g., www.google.com) to strike out on your own.

WWW.LETSGO.COM Our website features extensive content from our guides; a community forum where travelers can connect with each other, ask questions or advice, and share stories and tips; and expanded resources to help you plan your trip. Visit us to browse by destination find information about ordering our titles.

THE ART OF TRAVEL

BootsnAll.com: www.bootsnall.com. Numerous resources for independent travelers, from planning your trip to reporting on it when you get back.

How to See the World: www.artoftravel.com. A compendium of great travel tips, from cheap flights to self defense to interacting with local culture.

Travel Intelligence: www.travelintelligence.net. A large collection of travel writing by distinguished travel writers.

Travel Library: www.travel-library.com. A fantastic set of links for general information and personal travelogues.

World Hum: www.worldhum.com. An independently produced collection of "travel dispatches from a shrinking planet."

INFORMATION ON MEXICO

CIA World Factbook: www.odci.gov/cia/publications/factbook/index.html. Tons of vital statistics on Mexico's geography, government, economy, and people.

Discovering Mexico at nationalgeographic.com: www.nationalgeographic.com/mexico. Travel resources and unique cultural information.

MexOnline.com: www.mexonline.com. An English language resource to travel in Mexico.

TravelPage: www.travelpage.com. Links to official tourist office sites in Mexico.

PlanetRider: www.planetrider.com. A subjective list of links to the "best" websites covering the culture and tourist attractions of Mexico.

US Department of State: http://travel.state.gov/travel/cis_pa_tw/cis/cis_970.html. Consular information sheet, including information on safety, crime, and particular information for US citizens.

World Travel Guide: www.travel-guides.com. Helpful practical info.

LIFE AND TIMES

HISTORY

Over 10,000 ancient ruins pepper the Mexican landscape, testament to some of the world's greatest empires in the period before Christopher Columbus, who "discovered" the New World. After the Spanish conquest, native and European cultures mixed, setting up a neo-feudal system still evident despite years of long and bloody conflict. The country of over 100 million people is incredibly diverse; *indígenas* make up nearly 30 percent of the Mexico's population and over 62 different native languages are still spoken among the different states. In the last two decades, Mexico's economy and its democratic stability have improved, though it is still plagued by severe socio-economic differences and political corruption.

STRAIT CROSSING (14,000-10,000 BC). Relatively little is known about hunter-gatherer societies in Mexico's earliest historic period. Most archeologists hypothesize that the first humans traveled across the **Bering Strait,** arriving in Mexico between 14,000 and 10,000 BC. Historians generally separate Pre-Hispanic history into five periods: Pre-Agricultural (40,000-8000 BC), Archaic (8000-2000 BC), Formative (or Pre-Classic, 2000 BC-AD 200), Classic (200-900), and Post-Classic (or Historical, 900-1521).

900-400 BC: The La Venta **Olmecs** construct a 100-foot pyramid, burying giant masks and mosaics beneath.

THE OLMECS (1700-600 BC). The Olmecs flourished in the warm, humid area that today comprises the states of **Veracruz** (p. 545) and **Tabasco** (p. 576). Though they are most famous for the giant stone heads that were likely portraits of their rulers, by 1350 BC the Olmecs had also developed large-scale public works, hieroglyphic writing, and a long count calendar, which later influenced the Maya. One of the first people to develop farming techniques in Mesoamerica, the Olmecs declined suddenly for unknown reasons.

150 AD: Teotihuacáns complete the **Pyramid of the Sun.**

400 AD: With 125,000 people, **Teotihuacán** is the sixth largest city in the world.

TEOTIHUACÁN (200 BC-AD 750). The return of great Mesoamerican empires was characterized by impressive cultural achievements. From the capital at **Teotihuacán** (p. 141), located near present-day Mexico City, the city-state controlled a region as large as modern-day Belgium. The city's name—given by the Aztecs who were awestruck by the site centuries later—means "Place of the Gods" in Náhuatl. At its peak, it was home to one of world's largest populations—around 200,000 people in AD 600. The empire may have included the **Zapotecs,** who lived in Monte Albán. Teotihuacán left behind a rich cultural legacy; many of their gods, like **Quetzacoatl,** the god of fertility, and **Tlaloc,** the god of rain, were worshipped by the Aztecs many centuries later. Between 600-750 AD, the center was sacked for unknown reasons.

THE MAYA (250-900 AD). The Classic Mayan civilization, based along the Mexican and Gulf coast, is best known for its early advances in astronomy and mathematics. The Maya preceded the Greeks and Romans to understanding the mathematical concept of zero. Their superior stargazing skills—Mayan astronomers predicted the movements of Venus for over 500 years with only a 2hr. margin of error—enabled them to create a sophisticated calendar. Like many tribes in the region, they also practiced human sacrifice. The empire's demise was likely prompted by internal revolts around AD 900. During the post-Classic period, the remaining Maya shifted to new centers on the coast, like **Chichén Itzá** (p. 646), **Mayapán** (p. 628), and **Uxmal** (p. 634). Together these formed the **Mayapán League,** which came to a bloody collapse in 1441.

THE TOLTECS (AD 900-1100). Nomadic warrior societies, like the Toltecs, filled the void left by the fall of the empires of the Classical period. Their rule, which centered in their capital at **Tula** (p. 370), is often remembered as the golden era of the pre-Hispanic period—they were the originators of the central american ball game and the legend predicting the return of the light-skinned god Quetzalcóatl, which would mislead the Aztecs when the Spanish arrived centuries later. Invading tribes and famine brought their civilization to a close.

THE AZTECS (AD 900-1521). In the early 14th century, the Aztecs, known in their native Náhuatl as the Mexica, established **Tenochtitlán** (modern-day Mexico City; p. 86), on an island in the middle of Lake Texcoco. From this watery capital (19 islands, connected by a series of canals and decorated with lush gardens), the Aztecs ruled central Mexico, claiming dominion over more than 25 million people at the time of the Spanish conquest. Organized in a loose federation dependent on tributes from subdued townships, the empire attracted enemies by ruthlessly using conquered tribes for human sacrifice. The rituals—intended to stave off the apocalypse—culminated with the offering of a human heart to patron god Huitzilopochtli.

ENCOUNTER WITH CORTÉS (1519-1521). In 1519, Hernán Cortés landed on the island of Cozumel. Accompanied by 550 Europeans, 16 horses, and a small cannon, Cortés worked his way up the Gulf Coast. During one of these skirmishes he acquired 20 maidens as booty, including **Malintzin** (**Doña Marina** to the Spanish and, later, traitorous **La Malinche** to Mexicans), an enslaved Aztec who would become both his advisor and mistress. The combined language skills of two of his prisoners, Malintzin and Jerónimo de Aguilar, a Spaniard who spoke fluent Mayan, enabled Cortés to overcome the language barrier. The meeting of Aztec emperor **Moctezuma II** (known in the US as Montezuma) and Cortés was initially peaceful, but turned sour when the Spaniards took Moctezuma hostage and began to raid the royal treasury. The Aztecs drove Cortés from Tenochtitlán on July 1, 1520, a night known to the Spanish as **La Noche Triste (Sad Night).** But Cortés regrouped and the Aztecs—weakened by plagues and famine and overwhelmed by guns and steel—were unable to overcome the Spanish. In 1521, the Aztecs were finally defeated at **Tlatelolco.**

909: The Mayan **calendar** lists the civilization's last known ruler.

968: Toltecs found their capital at Tula.

1345: An eagle devours a serpent, an omen prompting the **Aztecs** to settle in Tenochtitlán, bringing their wanderings to an end.

1427: Tenochtitlán becomes an independent state.

1515: Succession struggles in Texcoco splinter the Aztec alliance, and **Moctezuma's** native enemies increase.

1519: Hernán **Cortés** lands just off Veracruz.

1521-1600: The **Aztec Empire** falls. Disease and inhuman labor practices devastate native populations.

LIFE AND TIMES

LIFE AND TIMES

1524: The first **Franciscan missionaries** arrive in Mexico City.

1533: Colonists found the first **university** in the New World.

1534-1558: Spaniards strike **silver** and begin mining their new colony.

1537: Pope Paul III officially defends the idea that **indigenous people are human.**

1618: One family of colonists acquires **over 11 million acres** on the northern frontier.

1810: Miguel **Hidalgo** launches the Mexican revolt with the *Grito de Dolores.*

1824: Mexico's first **constitution** establishes it as a federal republic.

1835: Texas secedes from Mexico, setting the stage for the slaughter at the **Alamo.**

1838: The **French invade** Mexico, to defend the honor of their pastry chef

THE COLONIAL PERIOD (1522-1810). The Spanish quickly were able to gain control of a vast territory by superimposing colonial administration on the Aztec system. Diseases like smallpox and typhoid fever also proved to be a powerful ally of the advancing conquistadors, wiping out whole villages often more effectively than the battles themselves. After being conquered, the *indígenas* were assigned to Spaniards in *encomiendas* (estates). In return, the *encomenderos* (estate owners) were responsible for educating their workers and converting them to Christianity. With little regulation of the system (and few Spaniards who cared), abuse was rampant.

FIGHT FOR INDEPENDENCE (1810-1822). Faced with gross economic and social inequities perpetrated by a powerful landowning class, **Father Miguel Hidalgo y Costilla,** from the small parish of **Dolores** (p. 361), formed a "literary club" that soon turned its thoughts to revolution. On the morning of September 16, 1810, now **Mexican Independence Day,** Hidalgo delivered an electrifying speech, **El Grito de Dolores (The Cry of Dolores),** which called for the end of Spanish rule, equality of races, and a redistribution of the land. The speech launched fighting between Mexican and Spanish forces, but victory did not enter sight until conservatives began to worry about the liberal Spanish Constitution of 1812, and what its promotion of popular sovereignty might mean for the colonies. The most important convert to the cause was **Agustín de Iturbide,** a *criollo* (light-skinned Mexican of European descent) who originally led Spanish troops against Hidalgo. In 1820, he turned thousands of his soldiers to the independence cause, tipping the scales in Mexican favor. In 1821, with the **Treaty of Córdoba,** the country's independence was complete, and the following year the new national congress crowned Iturbide Emperor of Mexico.

A SHAKY START. The victory was bittersweet: a decade of war had left the economy in shambles and anarchy reigned throughout much of the countryside. Over the course of the next 40 years, more than 50 different governments ruled the country, 11 of these headed by **Antonio López de Santa Anna,** who led a military coup against Iturbide's government in November 1822. Alternately liberal and conservative, he was more interested in possessing power than exercising it responsibly, at one point conducting a military coup against his own vice president.

COOKING UP TROUBLE (1838-1839). Debt problems led to a French intervention, dubbed the **Pastry War** in honor of the French pastry chef whose wares had been seized and eaten by rioting Mexican troops. During the Pastry War, Santa Anna's left leg was severely wounded and eventually had to be amputated. Not a man to take a lost limb lightly, Santa Anna had his leg transported to Mexico City where, after an elaborate procession and a formal entombment in an urn atop a pillar, the decayed limb was serenaded and applauded by cabinet members and diplomats. Victory and his famous wound served to bolster Santa Anna's image.

THE LONE STAR REPUBLIC (1836-1845). Santa Anna's image was temporarily damaged during the Texas secession. As US settlers began to outnumber Mexicans in the lands to the north, Yankee-led independence movements mobilized to protest restrictive immigration laws and the abolition of slavery. Santa Anna responded with 6000 troops, which overwhelmed Texan rebels at the **Alamo** in February of 1836, killing all 150 defenders. The Texans ultimately won their independence, capturing Santa Anna and his army on April 21, 1836.

WAR WITH THE STATES (1845-1848). In 1845 the United States annexed the Lone Star Republic, jump starting another war with Mexico over the boundaries of their new state. On March 9, 1847, general Winfield Scott and his 10,000 men launched an attack in Veracruz. After a brutal sack of the city that killed twice as many Mexican civilians as soldiers, the victorious army continued toward Mexico City. By September 7, only the Castle of Chapultepec (p. 118) remained unvanquished. The young cadets defending the castle were revered throughout Mexico for their bravery; and a monument at the castle remembers six teenagers who leapt to their deaths rather than surrender. The war ended in 1848 with the **Treaty of Guadalupe Hidalgo,** which settled the border at the Río Bravo (known in the US as Rio Grande) and ceded California and New Mexico to the US for a paltry US$19 million. Santa Anna resigned in shame, but, back five years later, he agreed to the **Gadsden Purchase,** selling a strip across southern Arizona and New Mexico.

CASTE WAR (1847-1901). Rebellion also hit the Yucatán Peninsula, where ethnic tensions and socioeconomic divisions led to an uprising of the Maya people against the *criollo* rulers. The Maya established an independent state at Chan Santa Cruz, not falling to the Mexican army until more than 50 years later.

REFORM SCHOOL (1854-1876). In 1854, liberals, led by *indígeno* **Benito Juárez,** sent Santa Anna into exile. The move launched the Reform Era (1855-1972), a period of bitter divide between liberal reformers and conservatives, including supporters of the Catholic Church. As president, Juárez introduced the **Ley Juárez,** which abolished clergy and military privileges, and the new **Constitution of 1857,** which established Mexico as a representative democracy. The moves touched off Mexico's bloodiest revolt to date, a three-year conflict known as the **War of the Reform** (1858-1861). Although the liberals repelled the conservatives by 1860, default on debts prompted another foreign intervention.

FOREIGN FOES (1860-1867). While the British and Spanish attempted to resolve the conflict peaceably, imperial ambitions drove the French to invade. Although **Cinco de Mayo** celebrates an 1862 Mexican victory in Puebla, the French eventually forced the Juárez government to flee to the north of the country. Napoleon III chose the Austrian archduke **Ferdinand Maximilian** as emperor. His left-leaning, anti-Catholic policies quickly alienated conservatives and he died by firing squad in

1848: The US wins the **Mexican-American war,** acquiring California and New Mexico.

1853: Mexico agrees to sell the US parts of **present-day** Arizona and New Mexico.

1855: The Yucatán government **prematurely declares victory** over the Maya.

1857: With a new constitution Mexico becomes a **representative** democracy.

1861: Mexico elects **Benito Juárez,** the country's first—and only—indigenous president.

May 5, 1862: The Mexicans defeat the French at Puebla, and celebrate the first **Cinco de Mayo.**

LIFE AND TIMES

1863: Maximilian declared emperor with French backing.

1867: Lack of local support leads to the French emperor's **execution**.

1876: Military dictator **Porfirio Díaz** begins his 34-year rule.

1910: The Mexican Revolution begins, launching the careers of **Emiliano Zapata** and **Pancho Villa**.

1913: The US conspires to put military leader **Victoriano Huerta** in power.

1914: US marines invade the port of Veracruz.

1917: Mexico's new Congress approves **one of the most progressive constitutions in the world.** Carranza begins his presidency.

1920: The number of people of **Chinese** descent in Mexicali outpaces the number of Mexicans.

1867. Juárez returned triumphantly with a program for greater social equity: for the first time, education was free and compulsory. But tensions mounted, eventually prompting General Porfirio Díaz to lead a coup in the name of establishing stability.

THE PORFIRIATO (1876-1910). Porfirio Díaz presided over a period of stability and economic growth, known as the **Porfiriato** or the **Pax Porfiriana.** He introduced a new railroad system, along with institutional and bureaucratic reform, contributing to a new period of economic growth. But the benefits of the reforms remained concentrated in the hands of the small, social elite (the **científicos**) and large foreign investors. Díaz's cronies controlled local politics, enforcing their abuse of the *indígenas* with a new rural police force and the cruel *peonaje* system, which bound peasants to the land. They also worked to destroy the *ejidos*, a system of community farming dating to Aztec times, in the name of more economically efficient privately-owned farms.

THE REVOLUTION (1910). Widespread discontent allowed **Francisco Madero,** a wealthy *hacienda* owner from Coahuila, to run on an anti-reelection platform. Supported by the guerilla forces of **Emiliano Zapata,** an Indian peasant from the state of Morelos, and **Francisco "Pancho" Villa,** a longtime outlaw from the north, the rebels eventually took Ciudad Juárez (p. 243), forcing Díaz into comfortable exile in Paris.

REVOLUTIONARY GOVERNMENTS (1911-1914). The 1911 election ushered Madero and his vice president, José María Pino Suárez, into power. Madero's attempts to govern were challenged by former allies, like Zapata, who saw no indication that he would work to satisfy peasant demands for land redistribution. In 1913, 10 days of violence in the *zócalo* known as the **Decena Trágica** led US ambassador Henry Lane Wilson to convince General Victoriano Huerta to betray Madero and lead a military coup in the name of the conservatives. Huerta's incompetence—in cartoons from the period he is never pictured without a bottle in his hand—only unified the opposition, led by Villa, **Álvaro Obregón,** and **Venustiano Carranza,** who came together under the **Plan de Guadalupe.** Zapata continued to fight independently. The US eventually undermined the dictator with the occupation of Veracruz, and Huerta resigned under pressure in 1914.

VILLA, ZAPATA, AND THE CONSTITUTIONALISTS (1914-1920). The forces of Villa and Zapata met only once in the capital at the end of 1914, and their failure to come to an agreement on a national program created an opportunity for Carranza's **constitucionalistas** (Constitutionalists) to take charge. The **Constitution of 1917,** endorsed by Obregón and Carranza, set out the world's most progressive labor rights and declared that private ownership of land was a privilege, not a right. Its successful passage led to the election of Carranza in 1917. Villa, angered by US recognition of the Carranza government, raided Columbus, New Mexico. This spurred a US invasion by General John Pershing, whose only success was in insulting the newly recognized government. Carranza eliminated his other rival by assassinating Zapata, though the Morelos peasant movement would continue as a political force into the late 20th century.

PARTY PEOPLE (1921-1934). Carranza's decision to seek reelection, which violated the Constitution's one-term-only provision, helped to alienate Obregón. Sensing that the tide had turned, Carranza fled the capital for Veracruz, making off with all the public treasury he could carry (allegedly 20 train cars' worth). He was captured en route to the port city and shot, and Obregón took over, granting amnesty to all parties and pursuing tentative social reforms. He ceded power peacefully in 1924 to his chosen successor, **Plutarco Elías Calles.** As Calles's term came to a close, he sought a way to preserve power while maintaining the trappings of democracy, founding the **Partido Nacional Revolucionario (PNR)** in 1929. Soon known as the **Jefe Máximo** (Highest Chief), Calles ruled behind the scenes from 1929 to 1934, a period of puppet presidents and rigged elections that became known as the **Maximato.** His party and its two descendants would rule Mexico for 71 years.

REDISTRIBUTING POWER (1934-1940). Calles's power came to an end with the election of **Lázaro Cárdenas,** who exiled Calles in 1936. Cárdenas undertook drastic land reform. His single most famous and popular action was the nationalization and consolidation of the oil industry as Petróleos Mexicanos (PEMEX). Cárdenas resigned in 1940, at the end of his six-year term, setting a precedent that has been followed ever since.

THE POST-WAR "MEXICAN MIRACLE" (1940-1968). After Cárdenas, the party's leaders shifted to a more conservative position, emphasizing business and state-led economic growth. In 1946, the new president, **Miguel Alemán,** restructured the party, renaming it the **Partido Revolucionario Institucional (PRI).** Alemán was both the first civilian president since the Revolution and the most conservative. He broke the fiercely independent national unions and undertook massive improvements in infrastructure, including 7500 miles of new highways. He also oversaw the completion of the modern campus of the **Universidad Autónoma Nacional de Mexico,** (**UNAM**; p. 130), though a lack of resources combined with government corruption to leave library shelves empty and facilities in disrepair.

OLYMPIC PROBLEMS (1968-1988). Despite the economic growth (the origin of the "miracle" moniker), rapid population growth and high levels of unemployment, widened the gap between rich and poor and spurred migration to the capital. In the summer of 1968, under the conservative President Gustavo Díaz Ordaz, demonstrations against the corrupt and unresponsive government broke out in the capital. Standoffs between students and the military mounted, reaching crisis levels in the Plaza de las Tres Culturas (p. 123), in the Tlatelolco section of Mexico City, where the army killed an estimated 400 peaceful demonstrators and jailed another 2000 just 10 days before the 1968 Olympics were to open in Mexico City. A campaign of violent repression of political dissenters, known as the **guerra**

1926-7: The government has a shoot-out with 400 Catholics in Guadalajara, part of the pro-Catholic, anti-government Cristero War.

1929: Pres. Plutarco **Calles** founds the **Partido Nacional Revolucionario,** which would run Mexican politics for the next 71 years.

1938: President Lázaro Cárdenas **nationalizes oil** in Mexico.

1942: The US and Mexico test out the first guest worker policy, the so-called **Bracero** Program.

1954: Mexico grants women the **right to vote.**

1968: The government **massacres** 400 peaceful student demonstrators 10 days before Mexico City hosts the Olympic Games.

LIFE AND TIMES

1988: Carlos **Salinas** wins the highly controversial presidential election.

1993: Mexico, the US, and Canada sign **NAFTA.**

1994: In Chiapas, **Zapatistas** revolt in the name of *indígenas*. The year closes with the worst **peso crisis** since 1982.

1996: The Mexican government and the Zapatistas sign the **San Andres Accords,** granting the rebels autonomy and land. The area remains militarized.

2000: Pres. Ernesto **Zedillo** ends the *dedazo* and Vicente **Fox,** from the PAN, wins the presidential election.

2006: In Oaxaca, thousands of teachers go on **strike,** paralyzing the country for months.

2007: Mexico City legalizes first trimester **abortion.**

sucia, followed. A combination of inflation, falling oil prices, and foreign debt brought the miracle to a close. Perhaps the biggest blow was the 1985 Mexico City earthquake, which registered an 8 on the Richter scale and killed thousands.

NAFTA, NO LAFTA (1988-1994). PRI candidate and Harvard PhD **Carlos Salinas de Gortari** won the widely contested 1988 election. Salinas presided over the passage of the **North American Fair Trade Agreement (NAFTA)** in 1993, which lowered trade barriers between the three North American countries. Though they had a broad base of support among Mexico's elite and middle classes, the Salinas reforms left many behind. On January 1, 1994—the day NAFTA went into effect—the **Ejército Zapatista de Liberación Nacional** (**EZLN;** the Zapatista National Liberation Army) captured the city of San Cristóbal de las Casas in a 12-day siege. Over 9000 Mayan peasants followed the eloquent masked guerilla **Subcomandante Marcos** (later revealed to be a university-educated Marxist). The Zapatistas called for a complete government overhaul, extensive land reform, social justice for *indígenas*, and fair elections. Within a year, Salinas's legacy suffered another blow, when members of his inner circle were accused of extreme corruption. Notoriously, Salinas's brother, **Raúl Salinas de Gortari,** was convicted of murdering his former brother-in-law and had alleged ties with drug cartels.

REFORM AND CHANGE (1994-2000). Former Education Minister **Ernesto Zedillo Ponce de Léon** assumed the presidency, only to be confronted with a **devaluation crisis** that was another setback to economic progress. Zedillo changed the political climate, self-consciously distancing himself from the PRI and formally ending the **dedazo**—the president's traditional right to name the next PRI presidential candidate. He personally ushered in the democratic transition, announcing the victory of opposition candidate **Vicente Fox** on national television ahead of the official results.

FOXY BUSINESS (2000-2006). With Fox, Mexico entered the 21st century with a sluggish economy and a growing land shortage, prompting many to immigrate to the US. Soon after gaining a seat on the United Nations Security Council, Fox became the first to allow human rights observers into the country. On the southern front, he honored the **San Andres Accords,** ordering the army out of Zapatista Chiapas.

ELECTING DEMOCRACY (2006-TODAY). The 2006 election was one of Mexico's most competitive yet, pitting **Felipe Calderón,** a former energy commissioner and member of Fox's party, against the leftist mayor of Mexico City, **Manuel López Obrador,** who ran on the ticket of the **Partido Revolucionario Democrático (PRD).** Throughout the campaign, Obrador was dogged by charges that he broke court orders in a land dispute case, which nearly derailed his candidacy. Analysts described the election as a ruling on the free market, with Calderón promising to follow in the footsteps of Fox's free market policies and characterizing Obrador as a dangerous Hugo Chavez in the making. Obrador's championship of the poor also highlighted persistent class cleavages in a country where 10% of the population controls almost half the wealth. In July 2006, Obrador lost to Calderón by less than 1% of the vote, fewer than 243,000 votes out of 41 million cast. He rejected the results and called for a recount, shutting down parts of Mexico City with protests. In September, Mexico's electoral court confirmed Calderón's win. In April 2007, Mexico City legalized abortion during the first three months of pregnancy, a watershed moment for this still largely Catholic country. Moreover, Mexicans have a large stake in the increasingly heated debate about Mexican immigration in the US. In June 2007, the US Congress defeated a bill that included provisions to legalize the status of many illegal immigrants in the US, create a temporary guest worker program, and enhance border security.

LAND

Mexico's distinct geographic curvature makes for a unique topography. These 2,000,000 sq. km of land are home to sun-beaten deserts, jungle rainforests, soaring volcanoes, low coastal lagoons, gorgeous beaches, and red canyons, making Mexico one of the most ecologically striking countries in the world.

GEOGRAPHY AND GEOLOGY

Mexico's Pacific Coast is part of the **Ring of Fire,** an area around the Pacific Ocean characterized by high tectonic and volcanic activity. Over the past millennia, eruptions and earthquakes have shaped Mexico's jagged coastlines, broad mountain ranges, and enclosed valleys. Most spectacular are **Las Barrancas del Cobre** (Copper Canyon; p. 264) in the state of Chihuahua, where multiple canyons converge to form a canyon four times the size of Arizona's Grand Canyon.

The long and narrow strip of land known as the **Baja Peninsula** extends 1330km south from California, dividing the **Sea of Cortés** (Gulf of California) from the Pacific Ocean. Two lofty mountain ranges, the **Sierra Madre Occidental** to the west and the **Sierra Madre Oriental** to the east, cut a V-shape through the heart of the country. The region south of Mexico City at the base of this V, the **Cordillera Neovolcánica,** is the most volcanic in Mexico. Though many of the volcanoes have been dormant since the 1800s, **Popocatépetl** (p. 390) spewed ash over Puebla in 1994, and Colima's **Volcán de Fuego** (Volcano of Fire; p. 469) awoke in 2005. The eruption sent lava and ash 5km into the sky, causing evacuations in nearby villages.

Farther south are the **Southern Highlands,** a series of mountains, plateaus, and valleys in the states of Guerrero and Oaxaca. West of the Sierra Madre Occidental is a dry, flat region of *mesas*. Along the eastern coast of Mexico, a much wetter swampland runs from the Texas border to the Isthmus of Tehuantepec in the Yucatán Peninsula. Northeast of the Isthmus is the **Tabasco Plain,** and southeast are the **Chiapas Highlands,** an area of high mountains surrounding a large rift valley. Northeast of the Highlands, the flat **Yucatán Peninsula** extends into the Caribbean Sea, pockmarked with limestone caverns and **cenotes,** natural fresh-water caves. *Cenotes* once provided Mayan cities with water and served as ceremonial centers; today, divers plunge into their depths to admire the underwater gardens (p. 689). Some scientists believe the unusually high occurrence of *cenotes* in the peninsula is related to the same meteor impact that may have killed the dinosaurs 65 million years ago. In the 1940s, an oil company drilling in the Yucatán uncovered evidence of what is now known as the **Cráter de Chicxulub** (a gigantic terrestrial bowl 180km wide and more than 200km deep. Buried half in land and half under the Gulf of Mexico, most scientists believe that this crater was the site of the meteor impact.

LIFE AND TIMES

WEATHER AND WILDLIFE

Due to its varied climate, Mexico is one of the most biologically diverse countries in the world, hosting an estimated 10% of the world's plant and animal species. Mexico's climate ranges from arid areas in the north to subtropical conditions in the south. The country essentially has two seasons: wet (May-Aug.) and dry (Sept.-Apr.). **Hurricanes** and **tropical storms** sometimes stir up along the southern coasts in August and September, while the north remains relatively dry.

Baja and the northern Pacific Coast are home to a number of large aquatic mammals. Those who want to swim with **dolphins** or snorkel with **sea lions** can easily find an adventure program along the coast (p. 185), while those who prefer to watch sea creatures from a safe distance can do so at various **whale watching** spots (p. 184). Baja also offers ample opportunities to view the mating of rare **elephant seals. Bahía de Sebastián Vizcaíno** (p. 183), near Guerrero Negro, is the best place to see them in action. The beach is on the border of Mexico's largest biosphere reserve, **la Reserva de la Biosfera el Vizcaíno.**

The Sonoran and Chihuahuan deserts meet in the north of Mexico. Together with the Mojave and Great Basin deserts in the US, they comprise one of the world's largest desert regions. Over 250 kinds of cactus grow in the **Chihuahan Desert** (p. 243). Not to be outdone, the **Sonoran Desert** (p. 221) is the only place to find the huge **cardón cactus,** which dominates the parched landscape, and the unique **boojum tree,** a spiky, drought-resistant plant that can reach heights over 15m. At lower elevations (300-1000m), the mountainside is covered in deciduous forest. Flowering plants such as **orchids** and **bromeliads** flourish during summer; at higher altitudes (1000-2000m), the forests are dominated by coniferous pines, junipers, and evergreen oaks. Between the mountain ranges, the Altiplano is covered in grassland, peppered with scrub brush, **prickly-pear cactus,** and mammals including **foxes, mountain lions, and coyotes.**

The states of **Tabasco** and **Campeche,** southwest of the Yucatán Peninsula, contain the only true **rainforests** in Mexico. **Anteaters, jaguars, tapirs, and monkeys** abound, along with endless varieties of birds, lizards, frogs, and insects. At higher elevations, the rainforests give way to **cloud forests,** where moisture from standing clouds continually surrounds the forests. The **Selva Lacandona** (p. 603), home of the Zapatista rebels, is Mexico's largest tropical forest.

Pollution, deforestation, and erosion are serious environmental concerns in Mexico. Mexico City is infamous for its poor air quality, despite recent reforms. In the vast expanses outside the city, logging and deforestation have endangered many rare species and have also contributed to land erosion, causing water pollution and loss of arable land. To minimize your impact on this already-fragile environment, see p. 47 for information about sustainable travel.

PEOPLE

DEMOGRAPHICS

Mexico's heterogeneity finds its roots in history. The Spanish conquest gave rise to the nation's largest ethnic group, **mestizos**—persons of mixed indigenous and European blood—who now comprise 60% of the population. Today, **criollos**—light-skinned Mexicans of pure European descent—make up around 9% of the population, localized in urban areas and in the North. **Indígenas**—sometimes referred to by the politically incorrect appellation **indios**—account for 30% of the population and make up the majority in rural areas, particularly in the southern half of the country.

LANGUAGE

Mexico's official language is *castellano* (standard Spanish), spoken smoothly and without the lisp that characterizes speakers from Spain. More than 50 traditional languages, spoken by over 100,000 people in the country, remain strong links to Mexico's rich cultural past. In the Valley of Mexico, one can often hear the Aztec language, **Náhuatl;** in the Yucatán Peninsula and Chiapas, **Mayan** is frequently spoken in villages and markets; **Zapotec** is still spoken in the Oaxaca Valley.

RELIGION

With 80% of its population identifying as Roman Catholic, Mexico is a country devoted to its faith. Religious traditions and customs permeate the national consciousness, and Catholic imagery—crosses, shrines, rosaries, and candles—decorates every town. Like much of Latin America, Mexico practices a form of Catholicism fused with native traditions that places great significance on the Virgin Mary and the saints. The best example of this syncretism is the **Virgen de Guadalupe,** whose appearance before Juan Diego in the guise of an Aztec princess influenced the conversion of thousands of indigenous people in the 16th century.

Currently, there is a burgeoning interest in native Mexican faiths, spurred in part by new archaeological research and a fresh embrace of Mexican indigenous identity. Synonymous with nationalism and Mexican pride, Aztec symbols such as the famous **Stone of the Sun** can be found on many articles of clothing and jewelry. A recent rise in Protestantism, currently practiced by 6% of the population, may be due to a surge in missionary activity. Another 5% adhere to other faiths such as Judaism and Islam.

CULTURE

THE ARTS

VISUAL ARTS

Mexican art can be classified into three periods: **Pre-Hispanic** (1500 BC-AD 1525), **Colonial** (1525-1810), and **Modern** (1810-present). With the arrival of the Spanish, Mexican art changed dramatically, but its indigenous roots still influence artists today.

THE PRE-HISPANIC ERA

Early Mexican history comes to life in the art and architecture of this period. The pre-Hispanic forms of architecture are often inseparable from the religion that produced them: from pyramids to ritual ball courts, the ruins evoke the vanished traditions of pre-Hispanic Mexico. Despite the differences between the civilizations that made their home here, common architectural elements like the use of **stone** are noticeable across Mexico. The Olmecs (1200-1500 BC) shaped basalt into the famous **colossal heads**. The Toltecs (AD 850-1100) built the **Atlantes columns** out of stone to support the temple that once stood atop the **Pyramid of Tlahuizcalpantecuhtli** at Tula. The Maya (AD 300-900) and Aztecs (AD 1200-1500) used limestone and sandstone as building blocks for palaces, temples, altars, and stelae (upright stone monuments often inscribed with glyphs and reliefs). Capital cities such as Teotihuacán (Mayan), Tula (Toltec), and Tenochtitlán (Aztec) exhibit the use of monumental stone architecture in buildings, carved reliefs, and statuaries.

On a smaller scale, some of the most impressive pieces of pre-Hispanic art are carved **jade** and **ceramic** figurines. Mayan and Aztec gods and nobility were often depicted adorned with massive headdresses replete with feathers, necklaces of egg-sized beads, and bracelets of copper and gold to match the enormous bangles hanging from their earlobes.

Pre-Hispanic peoples also used art to tell stories that were central to their way of life. **Murals**, such as those covering the walls at the Mayan site of **Bonampak** (p. 603), reveal scenes of warfare, sacrifice, and celebration. **Fresco-like paintings** on interior walls of buildings at Teotihuacán depict paradise scenes, floral arrangements, religious rituals, and athletic events. Similarly, scenes painted onto **pottery** depict mythological stories. Other reliefs and objects reveal calendrical events and dates—the **Aztec Stone of the Sun** (p. 118) is a famous example. This prophetic calendar weighs over 20 metric tons and measures nearly four meters in diameter. Its concentric rings contain the four symbols of previous suns (jaguar, wind, rain of fire, and water), each of which represents a different epoch. The Aztecs believed they were living under the fifth and final sun—the arrival of the Spanish conquistadores would later fulfill their prophecy.

COLONIAL ART AND ARCHITECTURE

The Spanish used **colonial art** to facilitate conquest and religious indoctrination of the *indígenas*, erasing local religions by building Catholic churches directly on top of existing temples and pyramids.

Franciscan, Dominican, and **Augustinian** missionaries used distinct styles in building churches and monasteries. The Franciscan style tended to be economic, while the Dominican style was more ascetic and harsh. The Augustinian architects indulged in gratuitous decoration whenever possible. Some remarkable buildings include the **Monastery of St. Augustín of Acolman** near Mexico City and the **Monastery of Actopán** in Hidalgo, where the frescoes exhibit indigenous influences.

The steady growth of the Catholic Church throughout the 17th and 18th centuries necessitated the construction of cathedrals, parochial chapels, and convents. The luxurious **Baroque** facades of the cathedrals in Chihuahua (p. 251) and Zacatecas (p. 287) teem with dynamic images of angels and saints aimed at producing a feeling of awe and respect in the recently converted *indígenas*. Baroque expression is also reflected in the works of artists **Alonso López de Herrera** (c. 1580-1660) and **Baltazar de Echave Orio** (1558-1623). The genre of **portraiture** also became popular in colonial times; one of its most famous artists was **Miguel Cabrera** (1695-1768), whose paintings adorn churches in Querétaro and Taxco.

Luxury, frivolity, and ornamentation became more prevalent in the works of the artists and builders of the 18th century. While the Mexican High Baroque reached its extreme, the **Churrigueresque** style, a Spanish version of the opulent and graceful Rococo style, brought further turns of excess into the world of Mexican architecture. Sculpted rays of light and garlands graced the interiors of Churrigueresque churches, and the intricately decorated *estípites* (pilasters), a hallmark of the style, were installed for looks rather than support. **Neoclassicism** replaced the Rococo style as Spain asserted its dominance over the Mexican colony. With independence from Spain in 1821, Mexican artists began to break away from Spanish artistic traditions and follow the cultural currents of Europe. Although the Neoclassical style persisted in government-sponsored works, foreign travelers soon introduced **Romanticism,** and later **Realism,** styles that allowed artists to explore elements of their indigenous past.

MODERN ART

One of the most important painters of turn-of-the-century Mexico was **José María Velasco** (1840-1912), whose landscapes of the Valle de Mexico anticipated Cubism. On the political front of art, **José Guadalupe Posada's** (1852-1913) famous **calavera** (skeleton) cartoons and engravings criticized the Porfiriato; these later became an inspiration for politicians and artists alike. **Gerardo Murillo** (1875-1964) took on the name **Doctor Atl,** a Náhuatl word meaning water, and is well known for painting volcanoes with "Atl-colors" (pigments dried with resin).

As the Revolution reduced their land to shambles, Mexican artists further rejected European models by developing a national style that better reflected Latin American culture. After the Revolution, Mexican artists became intent on building the concept of Mexico as a nation, and were eager to use art to do so. Using a Mexican art form dating back to the early days of the Spanish conquest, when evangelists used allegorical murals to teach *indígenas* the rudiments of Christian iconography, the Minister of Public Education, **José Vasconcelos** (1882-1959), commissioned *muralistas* to decorate the walls of hospitals, colleges, schools and ministries.

Diego Rivera (1886-1957), the most renowned of the *muralistas,* based his artwork on political themes including land reform, Marxism, and the marginalization of *indígena* life. He used stylized realism to portray the dress, action, and expression of the Mexican people, and natural realism—complete with ugly faces, knotted brows, and angry stances—to represent Spaniards and other oppressors of the *indígenas.* His innovative blend of Mexican history and culture reached a wide audience and embroiled Rivera in international controversy.

Though Rivera is credited as the first to forge the path for *muralistas,* two other artists were vital in defining the art form: **José Clemente Orozco** (1883-1949), whose dark, angular shapes captured the brooding nature of his works' racial themes, and **David Alfaro Siqueiros** (1896-1974), who brought new materials and dramatic revolutionary themes to his murals. The Cubist-influenced artist **Rufino Tamayo** (1899-1991) also adopted the use of murals, but to a less politically charged end than the other muralists who preceded him.

Not all 20th-century Mexican artists exchanged the traditional canvas for walls. By combining abstract art with realism, **Juan Soriano** (1920-2006) forged a name for himself as a painter and sculptor. Surrealist painter **Frida Kahlo** (1907-54) is the only 20th-century Mexican painter with a place in the Louvre. Both Rivera and Kahlo, who shared two turbulent marriages to one another, blended indigenous subject matter with stylistic modernism. Crippled by both polio and a trolley accident that made her infertile, Kahlo was confined to a wheelchair for much of her life and her paintings and self-portraits are icons of pain. In the world of photography, Mexico's master **Manuel Álvarez Bravo** (1902-2002) brought the art of the lens to the fore. A photographer for Sergei Eisenstein's unfinished *¡Qué Viva Mexico!* (p. 68), Álvarez Bravo exhibited at New York's Julien Levy Gallery with Henri Cartier-Bresson and Walker Evans, advancing a new Mexican style of photography characterized by an attention to everyday and indigenous life.

LITERATURE

PRE-HISPANIC WRITING

Research indicates that **Náhuatl** and **Mayan** were the two dominant languages in Mexico before the arrival of the Spaniards. Dating back to 600 BC, the glyphs inscribed at **San José Mogote** and **Monte Albán** (p. 540), are thought to be the earliest examples of Mesoamerican writing. The tumultuous conquest and imposition of the Spanish language resulted in the loss of valuable information relating to *indígena* language and culture. The conquistadors burned Mayan and Aztec **códices** (unbound "books" or manuscripts), considering them an affront to Christianity. Nevertheless, a number of *códices* and a handful of narrative works survived, notably the Mayan **Books of Chilam Balam, Annals of the Cakchiquel,** and **Popul Vuh,** the book of creation. **Rabinal Achí,** the story of a sacrificed Mayan warrior, is considered to be the only surviving example of pre-Hispanic drama.

LIFE AND TIMES

COLONIAL LITERATURE

The Spanish eagerly sent news home about their conquered land and the Mexican way of life. Letters, including Hernán Cortés's (1485-1547) *Cartas de relación* (Letters of Relation), were mainly crown- and church-flattering documents detailing the ongoing efforts to educate and convert *indígenas*. One of Cortés's soldiers, **Bernal Díaz del Castillo** (1495-1584), wrote of the conquistadors' feats in *La conquista de Nueva España* (The Conquest of New Spain), while **Fray Bartolomé de las Casas's** (1474-1566) *Brevísima relación de la destrucción de las Indias* (Short Account of the Destruction of the Indies) is hailed as a humanistic defense of the indigenous people. Also known as the **Florentine codex,** *Historia General de las Cosas de Nueva España* (General History of the Things of New Spain) by **Fray Bernardino de Sahagún** (c. 1500-90) is a compilation of Aztec history and culture in Náhuatl and Spanish.

Poetry also rose to prominence in sixteenth- and seventeenth-century Mexican literary culture. **Sor Juana Inés de la Cruz** (1648-1695), a *criolla* of illegitimate birth who joined a convent in pursuit of an education, became a master lyricist known for her wit. Her most famous works are *"Respuesta a Sor Filotea"* ("Response to Sor Filotea") and *"Hombres necios"* ("Injudicious Men").

STRUGGLING FOR A LITERARY IDENTITY

By the start of the 19th century, the struggle for independence became the central topic in most Mexican texts. In 1816, Mexican journalist **José Fernández de Lizardi** (1776-1827) wrote what is considered the first Latin American novel, *El periquillo sarniento* (The Itching Parrot), a satire of Mexico's social status quo. Using historical themes to mask sweeping indictments of the military and clergy, Mexican novelists such as **Manuel Payno** (1810-94) sought to define a new national identity by glorifying strength, secularism, progress, and education.

Literature during the Porfiriato period (1876-1911) abandoned Romanticism for rational Realism. Most writers, however, avoided critiquing the political regime, since that would most likely lead to incarceration. During the late 19th century, the *modernismo* trend emphasized the value of pure aesthetics and reshaped Mexican literature under the direction of core figures like **Amado Nervo** (1870-1919). Nervo, the famed "monk of poetry," abandoned the clergy to pursue his writing. In addition to his first and most famous work, *El Bachiller* (The Baccalaureate) he produced several collections of introspective and often mystical poetry, notably *Serenidad* (Serenity), *Elevación* (Elevation), and *Plenitud* (Plenitude).

20TH-CENTURY GLOBAL PERSPECTIVES

The desire to reintegrate vestiges of pre-Hispanic culture into the national tradition pervaded post-Revolutionary era Mexican literature. Works produced immediately after the Revolution highlighted social themes, particularly the plight of Mexico's *indígenas*. **Mariano Azuela** (1873-1952), who joined Pancho Villa's forces in 1915, relates first-hand the military exploitation of *indígenas* in *Los de abajo* (The Underdogs). Similar works, such as *El indio* (The Indian) by **Gregorio López y Fuentes** (1895-1966), reinstated the novel as a vehicle of social reform. **Octavio Paz** (1914-1998), the first Mexican writer to win a Nobel Prize, drew on Marxism, Romanticism, and postmodernism in exploring the making and unmaking of a national archetype in such works as *El laberinto de la soledad* (The Labyrinth of Solitude).

The 1960s saw the advent of **Magical Realism,** a literary movement that blends the ordinary and common with fantasy and wonder, resulting in texts that portray a dreamlike and distorted reality. At the forefront of this movement in Mexico stands **Carlos Fuentes** (b.1928), an acclaimed contemporary novelist whose many works include *La región más transparente* (Where the Air is Clear) and *La muerte de Artemio Cruz* (The Death of Artemio Cruz).

The work of female writers, such as **Laura Esquivel** (b.1950), who wrote the fantastical, recipe-laden *Como agua para chocolate* (Like Water for Chocolate; 1989) has been well received both nationally and internationally. In 1991, **Elena Poniatowska** (b.1932) wrote *Tinísima*—a novel recounting the life of activist-photographer **Tina Modotti**. In the past three decades, the **Chicano literary movement** has worked to describe the experiences of Mexican immigrants to the US. **Sandra Cisneros's** (b.1954) *House on Mango Street*—a 1984 novel narrated by an 11-year-old girl who talks about her life on both sides of the Mexican border—has made her one of the most recognized Chicana authors today.

MUSIC

CORRIDOS. Usually sung by guitar-plucking troubadours, these songs remain strongly linked to their folk origins. Based in the oral tradition of storytelling, *corridos* recount the epic deeds of famous, infamous, and occasionally fictional figures from Mexico's past. A *corridista* may also function as a walking newspaper, singing songs about the latest natural disaster, political scandal, or any other decisive event. Controversial *narcorridos*, tales of drug trafficking, have also gained popularity. The outpouring in 2004 of shocked fans in Mexico and the US after *corridista* **Adán "Chalino" Sánchez** died in a car accident at the age of 19 revealed the depth of the genre's appeal.

MARIACHI. Black-and-red-clad men with bells and capes—the same ones that appear in tequila ads around the world—have long been popular images of **mariachis**. The most famous of Mexican musical styles, *mariachi* is lively and light-hearted, with strong guitar and energetic horn sections. Wandering *mariachis* strike up in front of restaurants and play at traditional *fiestas*. The world-famous tradition of women being serenaded by a group of *mariachis* in Mexican garb is a must for any romantic evening. Traditional *mariachi* music may deal with one or several of the following topics: being very drunk, being abandoned by a woman, pondering the fidelity of one's horse, and loving one's gun. In their more somber (or sober) moments, *mariachi* songs have also been known to deal with death, politics, and revolutionary history.

RANCHERAS. Born in a fit of nationalistic fervor following the 1910 Revolution, *rancheras* were originally conceived as "songs of the people," dealing with matters of work, love, and land. Once performed with marimba and flute, *rancheras* are now backed by the guitar and trumpets of *mariachi* bands. The songs are characterized by a passionate, sincere singing style, with long, drawn-out final notes. Like American country-western music, today's *rancheras* are sentimental songs about down-and-out towns, faithful dogs, and love gone wrong. **Norteños** are a type of *ranchera* based in the northwest and strongly influenced by polka. Popular *norteño* bands such as **Los Tigres del Norte** have attracted a number of fans outside of Mexico.

PAN-LATIN INFLUENCES

Mexican music along the east-central coast and continuing into the Yucatán carries a strong dose of Afro-Caribbean **rumba**. In Veracruz and Quintana Roo, drumladen bands often strike up irresistible beats in the evening twilight of central plazas. The style has inspired countless **marimba** bands, whose popularized music can be found blasting in markets throughout Mexico. Imported from Colombia, **cumbia** has joined **salsa** as the dance music of choice across central and southern Mexico.

CONTEMPORARY MUSIC

Mexico has not been immune to the Latin music explosion of the late 20th century. Its own varieties of popular and rock music are gaining international popularity, and Mexico has also served as the springboard for hundreds of other *latino* stars.

ROCANROL. Mexico knows how to rock, since original rock pioneers **Maldita Vecindad** and **El Tri** set the stage during the 1960s. Supergroup **Maná** has been recording music since the 1980s, and their collaboration with Santana on *Corazón Espinado* brought them global acclaim in 1998. They won the Grammy for Best Latin Rock/Alternative Artist in 2002. In 2003, the same award went to **Cafe Tacuba,** who mixes ska, rock, and hip hop with traditional Mexican forms of music. **El Gran Silencio** has also garnered critical acclaim for its innovative blend of *norteño* influences and modern rock, and the indie band **Kinky** has been nominated for three Grammys since 2002. **Caifanes,** a famous band in its own right, later became **Jaguares,** a socially-conscious rock group that has used lyrics to promote human rights in Ciudad Juárez.

POP. Mexican fans may shake it to Colombia's Shakira and Spain's Enrique Iglesias these days, but the land of *rancheras* and *mariachis* has produced many famous artists in its own right. **Selena Quintanilla-Pérez,** of movie fame, won the Grammy for Best Mexican-American Album before tragically being murdered by an employee in 1995. **Luis Miguel,** known for his romantic *boleros* (traditional Spanish dances) and smooth voice, has won a number of Grammys since beginning his career in the 1980s. In the past decade, Tijuana native **Julieta Venegas** has impressed fans with her virtuosity as a singer-songwriter, and **Paulina Rubio** and **Thalía** have progressed from actresses to divas, gaining fans north of the border. The echoes of Mexican folk music also play across the music of **Alejandro Fernández,** who crossed over from *ranchera* to pop.

HIP HOP. Mexican hip hop encompasses hybrid rock-rap forms first conceived by **Calo** in the 1980s. **Molotov** is well-known for songs like "Gimme the Power" and "Frijolero," in which they satirize American power in both English and Spanish. **Control Machete** has been featured in Super Bowl commercials and the *Amores Perros* soundtrack; Control Machete's leader Fermín IV recorded the popular "Siempre Peligroso" with Cypress Hill in 1998. These days, **Plastilina Mosh** reigns supreme in Mexico's hip hop scene. Just north of the border, **Ozomatli** is a hip hop group from Los Angeles that addresses social justice issues with a variety of musical styles ranging from reggae to funk.

FILM AND TELEVISION

Over a century old, the Mexican film industry remains a vital part of Mexican culture. With the 1910 Revolution came a slew of documentaries, notably those of the **Alva brothers**—Carlos, Eduardo, Guillermo, and Salvador. In 1931, Russian filmmaker **Sergei Eisenstein** began shooting ¡*Qué Viva Mexico!* (Long Live Mexico!), a social critique intertwined with panoramic shots of Mexican landscapes; although hailed as a masterpiece, it was never completed. The 1940s ushered in the golden age of Mexican cinema, which began with **Emilio "El Indio" Fernández's** *María Candelaria* (1943), a Cannes honoree, and **Luis Buñuel's** *Los Olvidados* (The Forgotten Ones, 1950), a grisly portrait of the Mexico City *barrio*. Comedian **Mario "Cantinflas" Moreno** (1911-1993), pioneer of Mexican slapstick, earned the moniker of "the Mexican Charlie Chaplin" for his poor *campesino* (peasant) character Cantinflas. In 1960, cinema hit a new high when Mexico received its first Oscar nomination for **Roberto Gavalín's** *Macario*, a film about a starving woodcutter who strikes a deal with Death and gets the gift of healing.

Fox Studios built the first American studio in Mexico in 1996 (p. 162), and a direct-to-video market has flourished alongside increasing Mexican collaboration with Hollywood. **María Novaro** received critical acclaim for her 1991 hit *Danzón*, a film about a Mexico City telephone operator who journeys to Veracruz to find ballroom dance and love. Texan **Robert Rodriguez** gathered a shoestring budget to film

1992's *El Mariachi*, which was later followed by *Desperado* (1995) and *Once Upon a Time in Mexico* (2003). In 1992, director **Alfonso Arau** adapted **Laura Esquivel's** novel *Como agua para chocolate*, which held the title of highest-grossing foreign film released in the US until 1997. In 1999, **Antonio Serrano's** *Sexo, pudor y lágrimas* (Sex, Shame, and Tears) smashed movie records, winning five Ariel awards, the Mexican equivalent of an Oscar.

At the turn of the century, Mexican film cemented its place in American culture with two art-house blockbusters: **Alejandro González Iñárritu's** *Amores perros* (Love's a Bitch; 2000) and **Alfonso Cuarón's** *Y tu mamá también* (And Your Mother; 2001), both starring Mexican heartthrob **Gael García Bernal.** Bernal went on to star in **Carlos Carrera's** *El Crimen del Padre Amaro* (The Crime of Father Amaro; 2003) and numerous Spanish- and English-language films. Iñárritu later filmed *21 Grams* (2003), while Cuarón brought his take on male adolescence to the set of *Harry Potter and the Prisoner of Azkaban* (2004).

Mexican television can, for the most part, be broken down into four different categories: *telenovelas* (soap operas), *comedias* (comedic variety shows), *noticias* (news shows), and imported international TV dubbed into Spanish. Of these, *telenovelas* are second to none and occupy huge chunks of mid-afternoon and prime-time television. Mexico's first globally exported soap opera, the 1979 series *Los Ricos También Lloran* (The Rich Cry Too), drew millions of loyal international viewers. Though sitcoms are not terribly popular, Mexico loves its variety shows, which feature sketch comedy intermixed with musical numbers and audience participation. The long-running sketch comedy show *Chespirito* is so popular that its characters have become cultural icons; it was the inspiration for Bumblebee Man on *The Simpsons*. News and current events shows are popular in the late evenings, but *fútbol* matches dominate airwaves at all hours, especially during the World Cup.

CUSTOMS AND ETIQUETTE

Mexican social interactions revolve around a deep-seated sense of hospitality. The desire to make others feel as welcome as possible influences the way in which Mexicans speak to each other and how they treat tourists and foreigners.

WHO YOU CALLIN' "TÚ"?

Mexicans almost always use formal terms of address when speaking to one another. As in other countries, professional and academic titles convey respectability. Those who have earned a college degree may be addressed as *licenciado* or *licenciada*, and those with doctorates as *doctor* or *doctora*. When introducing yourself, a simple *señor, señora,* or *señorita* (for young or unmarried women) is appropriate.

There are two ways of addressing someone in Spanish: *usted* is formal and indicates respect and distance, while *tú* indicates a closer relationship. Traditionally reserved for people of authority, *usted* and its proper verb conjugations are appropriate for use with strangers. *Tú* and its verb conjugations are used to reflect familiarity and may be used toward tourists to suggest warmth and welcome. Locals use both, depending on location and establishment.

I THOUGHT WE SAID 8 O'CLOCK

Outside of the business world, Mexico is notorious for its relaxed approach to fixed meeting times and schedules. This phenomenon derives not from a Mexican indifference to punctuality, but from a more relaxed attitude toward time and its pressures. So, if you find yourself tapping your foot and staring at the clock expectantly while awaiting the arrival of a friend, it might be more comfortable to pull up a chair.

GRINGO LOVE

Originally reserved for those of European descent, the term *gringo* has recently lost its harsh association and welcomed all English-speaking visitors. Expatriates in Mexico have even taken to referring to themselves as *gringos*. Americans may sometimes find themselves labeled more specifically as *yanquis* (Yankees), and minority travelers may have to put up with racial epithets, but the *gringo* community embraces everyone. Minority travelers should also note that words like *negro* and *chino* are not meant as slurs, but rather as adjectives to describe race or nationality; they do not have the negative connotations that they might in other languages.

FOOD AND DRINK

THE STAPLES

Although regional cuisine varies widely, **tortillas** are popular throughout the country. This millennia-old classic is a flat, round, thin pancake made from either *harina* (wheat flour) or *maíz* (corn flour). In the North, flour tortillas are the norm, while corn rules the South. **Arroz** (rice) and **frijoles** (beans) round out the triumvirate of Mexican staples. *Arroz,* either of the yellow Spanish or white Mexican variety, is prepared with oil, tomato sauce, onions, and garlic. *Frijoles* range from a soupy "baked" variety to a thick "refried" paste. Expect to see this trio accompanying most restaurant meals.

Mexican culinary experts enjoy spicing up a meal with **chiles**, or peppers. Most meals come with red and green hot sauce, and sometimes *chiles curtidos*—jalapeño peppers fermented in vinegar with sliced carrots and onions. Be careful when attempting to bite into any sort of pepper: keep in mind your own tolerance toward spicy food, and don't be fooled by size. A small chile can pack a dangerous punch: measuring less than 6cm, Mexico's native **habanero** pepper is the world's hottest!

Salsas and **moles** (sauces) add zest and flavor to most Mexican dishes. The classic **salsa Mexicana** blends *jitomate* (red tomato), *cilantro* (coriander), and *tomatillo* (green tomato) with copious amounts of onion, garlic, and *chiles*. **Mole poblano** is a thick, simmered-down sauce made with three to four types of chiles, garlic, tomato, cocoa, and a variety of nuts and spices.

DESAYUNO (BREAKFAST)

Breakfast can range from a simple snack to a grand feast rivaling the midday meal. **Huevos** (eggs), prepared in one of countless ways, are the mainstay of most Mexican breakfasts, often served with a side of **café con leche** (coffee with milk) and **pan dulce** (sweetened bread). *Huevos revueltos* (scrambled eggs) are usually prepared with *jamón* (ham), *tocino* (bacon), *machaca* (dried, shredded beef), or *nopales* (cactus). *Huevos rancheros* (fried eggs served on corn tortillas and covered with chunky tomato salsa), *huevos albañil* (scrambled eggs cooked in a spicy sauce), *huevos motuleños* (eggs served on a fried corn tortilla, topped with green sauce and sour cream), *huevos ahogados* (eggs cooked in simmering red sauce), and *huevos borrachos* (fried eggs cooked in beer and served with beans) are other common preparations. In more expensive restaurants, omelettes are offered with any of the common meats or with *camarones* (shrimp) or *langosta* (lobster).

COMIDA (MIDDAY MEAL)

Mexicans eat their main meal of the day—*la comida*—between 2 and 4pm. Both parents and children come home for an hour or two to eat, relax, and perhaps indulge in a *siesta*. Restaurants often offer **comida corrida** (sometimes called *la comida* or *el menú*), a fixed-price meal including **sopa** (soup), **ensalada** (salad), **té** (tea) or **agua fresca** (cold, fresh fruit juice), a **plato fuerte** (main dish), and a **postre** (dessert).

One of the most popular *caldos* (warm soups) is *sopa de tortilla* (or *sopa azteca*), a chicken broth-based soup with strips of fried tortilla, chunks of avocado, and *chipotle* peppers. Other favorites are *caldo tlalpeño*, a smoky blend of chicken broth and vegetables, and *sopa de mariscos*, featuring fish and shellfish. Mexico's strong national pride is evident in **pozole,** a chunky soup with red, white, or green broth. Served with *tostadas* (fried tortillas) and lime wedges, *pozole* is made with large hominy kernels, radishes, lettuce, and meat (usually pork).

The main dish of any *comida* will usually feature some sort of **carne** (meat) platter —usually beef in the country's interior or fish along the coasts—with sides of *frijoles*, tortillas, and *arroz*. Choose from *carne barbacoa* (barbequed), *parrillada* (grilled), or *milanesa* (breaded and fried).

CENA (SUPPER)

Mexicans tend to snack lightly around 9 or 10pm. Dominating nearly every Mexican menu, **antojitos** (little cravings) are equivalent to a large snack or a small meal. Tacos consist of grilled pieces of meat folded in a warm corn tortilla and topped with a row of condiments. **Burritos,** which are especially popular in northern Mexico, are thin flour tortillas usually filled with beans, meat, and cooked vegetables. **Enchiladas** are rolled corn tortillas, filled with cheese and usually meat, baked in a red or green sauce. **Quesadillas** are flat tortillas with cheese melted between them; *quesadillas sincronizadas* (sometimes called *gringas*) are filled with ham or pork. **Tostadas** are crispy, fried tortillas usually topped with meat and vegetables. **Chimichangas** are burritos that have been deep-fried for a rich, crunchy shell. **Flautas** are similar to *chimichangas* but are rolled thin (like a cigar) before being deep-fried, and resemble small flutes, for which they are named. Adventurous eaters can look out for the fried **jumiles** (stinkbugs) or **chapulines** (grasshoppers) sold at roadside snack stands.

DULCES (SWEETS)

Mexicans have an incurable sweet tooth. Beyond the ubiquitous *chocolates* (often flavored with chili powder) and pastries, traditional desserts include **flan,** a vanilla custard cake with a toasted sugar shell, **nieve** (ice cream), and **arroz con leche** (rice pudding). Many of the more traditional Mexican candies rely on fruits and produce, such as coconut, bananas, and sweet potatoes for sweetness, rather than sugar. Puebla (p. 403), the country's candy capital, is full of shops selling **dulce de leche** (a milk-based sweet) and **camotes** (candied sweet potatoes). Morelia and Michoacán specialize in **ates**, sticky sweet blocks of ground and candied fruit concentrate. San Cristóbal de las Casas (p. 590) and parts of Chiapas are renowned for their **cajetas** (fruit pastes) and coconut candies and cookies, while the Yucatán boasts tasty pumpkin marzipan.

BEBIDAS (DRINKS)

Along with the table staples of tortillas, beans, and rice, *cerveza* (beer) ranks high in Mexican specialties. It is impossible to drive through any Mexican town without coming across numerous Tecate and Corona billboards, painted buildings, or roadside beer stands proudly advertising their products. Popular beers in Mexico (listed roughly in order of quality) are **Bohemia** (a world-class lager), **Negra Modelo** (a fine dark beer), **Dos Equis** (a light, smooth lager), **Pacífico, Modelo, Carta Blanca, Superior, Corona Extra,** and **Sol** (watery and light). Mexicans share their love for bargain beer with the world, as demonstrated by Corona Extra's status as a leading export and international chart topper in Australia, Canada, France, Italy, New Zealand, Spain, and many other European markets.

Tequila is the king of Mexican liquor. A more refined version of **mezcal**, tequila is distilled from the maguey cactus, a large, sprawling plant often seen along Mexican highways. **Herradura, Tres Generaciones, Hornitos,** and **Cuervo 1800** are among the more famous, expensive, and quality brands of tequila. *Mezcal*, coarser than tequila, is sometimes served with the worm native to the plant—upon downing the shot, you are expected to ingest the worm. **Pulque,** the fermented juice of the maguey, was the sacred drink of the Aztec nobility. **Ron** (rum), while originally manufactured in the Caribbean, is incredibly popular in Mexico and is manufactured in parts of the Valley of Mexico. Coffee-flavored **Kahlúa** is Mexico's most exported liqueur, but well-made **piña coladas** (pineapple juice, cream of coconut, and light rum), **cocos locos** (coconut milk and tequila served in a coconut), and the ever-popular **margaritas** (tequila blended with ice and fruity mix) are just as tasty. A **michelada**—lemon juice, tabasco sauce and light beer—is a popular way to perk up after overindulging.

Non-alcoholic favorites include **licuados** (fresh fruit smoothies or milk shakes) and **horchata** (a milky, rice-based beverage loaded with cinnamon and sugar). **Atole** is a thick drink made from cornmeal, water, cane sugar and vanilla; the cocoa-based version is known as **champurrado**.

SPORTS

Although more commonly associated with Spain, **bullfighting** is Mexico's national sport. During the summer, *matadores* and their entourages perform in packed bullrings across the country. Mexico City is home to **Plaza de Toros Mexico** (p. 140) the largest bullring in the world. **Jaripeos** (rodeos) are also immensely popular.

While bullfighting is popular, Mexico's heart belongs to **fútbol** (soccer). The Mexican affinity for competitive ball games originated in 1200 BC, when Mesoamerican natives invented the rubber ball. Today, any unused patch of dirt, grass, or concrete is likely to be swarming with young children playing a rowdy pick-up game. In addition to informal street games, Mexico has a popular professional football league with at least one team in each major city. Guadalajara, for example, has arch-enemy teams—Las Chivas and Atlas—complete with rival fan bases. At the international level, the entire country cheers and jeers the **Mexican National Team,** a gang of flashy green-clad young men; life comes to a standstill during important *fútbol* matches. Mexico played host to the World Cup in 1970 and 1986, and hosts other important matches in the **Olympic Stadium** (p. 131) and the enormous **Estadio Azteca** (p. 140) both in Mexico City.

Additionally, **béisbol** (baseball) attracts players and spectators at all levels, and Mexico has had its fair share of world **boxing** champions in the lighter weight divisions. There have been some notable Mexican **marathon runners** in past years, and no discussion of Mexican sports is complete without mention of the country's illustrious record in the Olympic events of **race walking** and **equestrian riding,** two of the few sports in which Mexico has won a gold medal.

HOLIDAYS AND FESTIVALS

Mexico loves to celebrate its rich history, and nearly every month boasts a national holiday. In addition to these official *fiestas*, cities and towns across the country host smaller-scale but lively events to honor patron saints or local traditions. Further information about these frequent celebrations can be found in individual city listings. Sundays are always special; "daily" schedules frequently refer only to Monday through Saturday.

Most Mexican businesses close to observe national holidays, and hotels and sights flood with vacationing families. Advance reservations are absolutely necessary when planning travel during *Semana Santa* and the Christmas holidays. Dates listed below are for 2008 and 2009.

DATE	NAME	DESCRIPTION
January 1	Año Nuevo	New Year's Day
January 6	Día de los Reyes	Mexicans have traditionally honored the historic journey of the Three Wise Men by giving and receiving gifts on this day (rather than on Christmas).
January 17	Día de San Antonio de Abad	Feast of the Blessing of the Animals
February 2	Día de la Candelaria	Candlemas commemorates Mary's purification 40 days after the birth of Jesus.
February 5	Día de la Constitución	Constitution Day
February 24	Día de la Bandera	Flag Day
Jan. 31-Feb. 5 2008 February 19-24 2009	Carnaval	A spectacular week-long festival of indulgences before the 40-day abstinence of Lent. The liveliest celebrations take place in coastal cities such as Mazatlán.
March 21	Día del Nacimiento de Benito Juárez	Birthday of Benito Juárez, 1806 (p. 57)
March 16-23 2008 April 4-19 2009	Semana Santa	Mexico's most popular holiday is marked by colorful processions re-enacting the resurrection of Jesus and highways clogged with vacationing families.
April 30	Día de los Niños	Children's Day
May 1	Día del Trabajo	Labor Day
May 5	Cinco de Mayo	Anniversary of the Mexican victory at the Battle of Puebla, 1862 (p. 57)
May 10	Día de las Madres	Mother's Day
June 1	Día de la Marina	Navy Day
August 15	La Asunción (Feast of the Assumption)	Churches are carpeted with flowers to celebrate the feast day of the Blessed Virgin Mary.
September 16	Día de la Independencia	Anniversary of the Cry of Dolores, 1810 (p. 56)
October 12	Día de la Raza	Day of Race, honoring Mexico's cultural diversity.
November 1-2	Día de Todos Santos and Día de los Muertos	Families honor the souls of their ancestors, who are thought to return to Earth on this day, by visiting cemeteries and creating shrines laden with offerings.
November 20	Día de la Revolución	Anniversary of the Revolution, 1910
December 12	Día de Nuestra Señora de Guadalupe	Feast day of Mexico's patron saint.
December 16-24	Posadas	Candlelit processions that celebrate the voyage of Mary and Joseph to Bethlehem.
December 24	Nochebuena	Christmas Eve
December 25	Navidad	Christmas Day

LIFE AND TIMES

ADDITIONAL RESOURCES

GENERAL

Dancing Alone in Mexico, by Ron Butler (2000). A series of intelligent and entertaining vignettes in which the author's solo wanderings throughout the country come alive.

El laberinto de la soledad (The Labyrinth of Solitude), by Octavio Paz (1950). The classic social critique by Mexico's most acclaimed author and poet.

Mexico: A Higher Vision, by Michael Calderwood (1996). A stunning collection of large format aerial photographs with an introduction by Carlos Fuentes.

On Mexican Time, by Tony Cohan (2001). A chronicle of 15 years in the life of the author, who moved from busy Los Angeles to peaceful San Miguel de Allende.

The Old Gringo, by Carlos Fuentes (1985). The fictionalized tale of the life and love of an American journalist who disappeared in 1913 and may have joined the forces of the Mexican revolution.

HISTORY

The Course of Mexican History, by Michael C. Meyer et al. (2004). Absolutely the most comprehensive and easy-to-read survey of Mexican history from the ancient civilizations to the politics of the PRI.

Mexico: From the Olmecs to the Aztecs, by Michael D. Coe (1994). An engaging and current text that chronicles the history and society of major pre-Hispanic civilizations.

The Mexico Reader, edited by Gilbert M. Joseph and Timothy J. Henderson (2002). A collection of chronicles and creative works from Mexican history.

Zapata and the Mexican Revolution, by John Womack, Jr. (1968). An enthralling account of Emiliano Zapata and his rural followers in the state of Morelos, by one of Harvard University's foremost historians.

POLITICS

¡Basta! Land and the Zapatista Rebellion, by George Allen Collier (1999). Comprehensively studies the reasons and catalysts for the 1994 Zapatista uprising in Chiapas.

Bordering on Chaos: Mexico's Roller Coaster Journey to Prosperity, by Andres Oppenheimer (1998). Examines the collapse of the peso and subsequent economic ups and downs in the aftermath of the political controversy surrounding former president Carlos Salinas de Gortari.

Opening Mexico: The Making of a Democracy, by Samuel Dillon and Julia Preston (2004). The two (married) NYT correspondents combine first-hand journalistic accounts of Mexico in its days after authoritarian rule.

The US and Mexico: The Bear and the Porcupine, by Jeffrey Davidow (2004). Former US ambassador to Mexico Davidow shares a recent recollection of his experiences with Mexico and foreign relations before and after the historic presidential race of 2000.

FICTION

Como agua para chocolate (Like Water for Chocolate), by Laura Esquivel (1989). A piquant, internationally-acclaimed Mexican love story. The 1992 film was nominated for a US Golden Globe.

La muerte de Artemio Cruz (The Death of Artemio Cruz), by Carlos Fuentes (1975). A work of historical fiction dealing with Spain and Latin America, written by one of Mexico's most prominent novelists.

Mexico, by James Michener (1992). The master of historical fiction explores Mexico's evolution from ancient civilization to modern nation, interpreted through the experiences of various period characters.

Pedro Páramo, by Juan Rulfo (1955). A haunting tale of life and death set in rural Mexico; Rulfo's masterpiece (and only novel).

FILM

Amores perros, directed by Alejandro Iñárritu (2000). A widely awarded film centered around the three parties involved in a Mexico City car accident.

Frida, directed by Julie Taymor (2002). A more recent telling of the artist's life and her experiences, starring Salma Hayek.

Y tu mamá también, directed by Oscar Cuarón (2002). A story of adolescence and the sexual awakening of two Mexican teenagers as they travel through their country. The widely acclaimed film is notable for its honest portrayal of Mexican life, albeit with some strong political undercurrents.

LIFE AND TIMES

the never-ending war

a history of drugs and mexico

A CLOSER LOOK

Whether as a destination for tourists seeking altered states, as a primary producer supplying illicit US demand, or as

"rates of American marijuana use skyrocketed, fueling illicit US/Mexico drug trade"

a nation with its own small but important population of drug users, Mexico has played a crucial role in the development of the markets, policies, and ideologies that shape the drug issue throughout North America.

Pre-Hispanic *indígenas* famously consumed native psychotropic plants during spiritual cleanses. In the 1950s, this tradition attracted New York banker and amateur mycologist R. Gordon Wasson and his wife to southern Mexico, where they became the first outsiders to participate in the sacred mushroom rituals of the Mazatec Indians. Wasson's subsequent account of his experiences in Life magazine (where he coined the phrase "magic mushrooms") triggered a steady stream of drug tourism from the US.

As the 60s drew to a close, rates of American marijuana use skyrocketed, fueling illicit US/Mexico drug trade. The Nixon Administration responded with a drug interdiction program that searched cars entering the US from Mexico. Though largely ineffective, Operation Intercept caused enough economic chaos in the border region to drag Mexico into a greater commitment to US Drug War objectives. It has since been revealed that this increased involvement was Nixon's primary objective from the start.

Of course, this "war on drugs" has had few positive results for citizens of either country. Mexico's controversial decision to accede to US demands and begin aerial-born opium and marijuana

crop eradication efforts inspired initial declarations of success, soon tempered by the realization that drug cultivation simply moved elsewhere while Mexican growers adjusted to the new conditions.

The 1980s brought more problems for Mexico as increased US efforts against cocaine smuggling through the Caribbean rerouted traffic through Mexico, where the varied terrain, poorly paid and therefore corruptible-police, and 2000mi. US border have proved nearly impossible to monitor. Thus began an era of unprecedented profits for traffickers, which helped to expand drug cartels and resources available to corrupt officials.

However, the many negative consequences of this "war" have not produced a softening of generally anti-drug attitudes in Mexico. Though many Mexicans still treat their rheumatism by rubbing a tincture of marijuana on their joints, legalization initiatives consis-

"the negative consequences of this 'war' have not softened anti-drug attitudes"

tently sink fast under the weight of deep societal prejudices against the drug. Excluding alcohol, attitudes toward recreational drug use remain overwhelmingly negative, while strong support for prohibition, the sine qua non of the Drug War, endures. Indeed, while Mexico's huge financial commitment to the Drug War can certainly be blamed in part on the need to placate its neighbor to the north, mainstream public attitudes play a crucial role in anchoring what continues to be a costly and failed War on Drugs.

Isaac Campos is a Ph.D. candidate at Harvard University in Latin American history. He is writing a dissertation on Mexican social and cultural history during the Porfiriato and has been funded for research on the rise of prohibitionist ideas on drugs in Mexico.

BEYOND TOURISM

A PHILOSOPHY FOR TRAVELERS

HIGHLIGHTS OF BEYOND TOURISM IN MEXICO
TEACH ENGLISH to schoolchildren in the shanty towns of **Mexico City** (p. 86).
RESCUE baby turtles and their habitat in **Quintana Roo** (p. 656).
FIGHT for reproductive rights in **Oaxaca** (p. 513).
DIG up dirt on the Maya on a research trip in **Yaxunah** (p. 81).

As a tourist, you are always a foreigner. While hostel-hopping and sightseeing can be great fun, you may want to consider going *beyond* tourism. Experiencing a foreign place through studying, volunteering, or working can help reduce that touristy stranger-in-a-strange-land feeling. Furthermore, travelers can make a positive impact on the natural and cultural environments they visit. With this Beyond Tourism chapter, *Let's Go* hopes to promote a better understanding of Mexico and to provide suggestions for those who want to get more than a photo album out of their travels. The "Giving Back" sidebar features (see **The Quick Flipper Fixer Upper**, p. 241; **Party for the Turtle's Sake**, p. 491; **La Ventanilla**, p. 520; **Teach to Tots**, p. 673) also highlights regional Beyond Tourism opportunities.

Mexico offers many opportunities beyond the conventions of traditional tourism. You can play a pivotal role in one of the many organizations that are working to build a better Mexico through conservation, education, and public service. Opportunities for **volunteerism** abound, with both local and international organizations. **Studying** in a new environment can be enlightening, whether through direct enrollment in a local university or in an independent research project. **Working** is a way to immerse yourself in the local culture and finance your travels simultaneously.

As a **volunteer** in Mexico, you can participate in projects from assisting doctors in poverty-stricken areas to tracking endangered turtles, either on a short-term basis or as the main component of your trip. Later in this chapter, we recommend organizations that can help you find the opportunities that best suit your interests, whether you're looking to get involved for a day or for a year.

Studying at a college or in a language program is another option. These schools cluster in Cuernavaca and other university towns. Many programs cater to interest in ancient Mexican ruins, offering the chance to participate in archaeological digs. Opportunities to engage in environmental conservation abound along the coast.

Many travelers structure their trips by the **work** available to them along the way, ranging from odd jobs on the go to full-time, long-term stints. Cities like Oaxaca and Guadalajara are meccas for gringos in search of do-good opportunities.

VOLUNTEERING

Volunteering can be a powerful and fulfilling experience, especially when combined with the thrill of traveling in a new place. The country currently faces significant challenges in terms of education, the environment, public health, and rural development. Be aware that volunteering—particularly in rural areas—will likely mean giving up basic comforts and may involve risks besides travel, including disease, snakes, scorpions, or less accessible health care. It is easy to minimize these

face to face

The summer after my junior year of college, I spent eight weeks in Oaxaca with Child Family Health International (CFHI; p. 80), a nonprofit that sends pre-medical and medical stu-

"Economic disparity permeates every aspect of Mexico's medical services."

dents abroad for service-learning experiences and language study. My experience in Mexico dramatically improved my Spanish, and, more significantly, deepened my understanding of the sociology of medicine, and the problems currently facing Mexico's health care system.

My first rotation was at a government-run neighborhood clinic, where the majority of the patients are diabetic, pregnant, suffering from high blood pressure, or seeking contraceptives. My first day of work took me out of the clinic, as I joined doctors and nurses going door to door in the countryside, teaching residents ways to prevent the spread of dengue fever.

In recent years, dengue infection rates in Mexico have swelled to epidemic proportions. The virus is primarily transmitted by mosquitoes *(Aedes aegypti)*, which thrive in the humid climate. Many of the homes I visited are glorified lean-tos, with dirt floors and fireplaces for stoves. Chickens live alongside humans, and families collect rainwater in jugs for laundry and dishwashing. These open containers of water are prime breeding grounds for deadly mosquitoes.

In one particularly dilapidated house, I saw mosquito larvae as large as tadpoles swimming through the fetid rainwater. Although the nurse accompanying me warned the family of the potential danger and instructed them to throw the water out, she confessed to me she thought it unlikely they would comply. Without this water, there would be none until the next rain. Although families seemed to pay close attention to our well-rehearsed speeches, the doctors and nurses conducting the campaigns rarely notice any improvement. There is only so much medicine can do in the face of the extreme poverty affecting the majority of Mexicans.

Economic disparity permeates every aspect of Mexico's medical services. Upon returning to the clinic, I watched a pregnant woman—already 2cm dilated—experience rapid contractions as she waited to receive the paperwork necessary for a hospital delivery. A colleague of mine described how local pediatricians unnecessarily prescribe penicillin, for fear of being thought bad doctors for letting patients leave untreated. An emergency room intern watched a boy die from cardiac arrest after eating poisonous mushrooms because it took too long to obtain a defibrillator. The highest-ranking professional on duty in the emergency

"I went door to door, teaching residents ways to prevent dengue fever."

room at the time was a resident medical student. Meanwhile, I was shadowing a surgeon in a private clinic as he provided a client with breast implants.

From my perspective, the problem with Mexican health care is not a lack of resources; rather, it's that these resources are not currently being used or distributed effectively. With care and attention, this phenomenon can change. If you can devote a month or two to understanding the problems with modern health care, try an internship with CFHI.

Laura Ann Schoenherr is a member of the Class of 2008 at Harvard University. An A.B. candidate in chemistry, she plans to graduate with a certificate in healthy policy and a language citation in Spanish.

A DIFFERENT PATH

WHY PAY MONEY TO VOLUNTEER?

Many volunteers are surprised to learn that some organizations require large fees or "donations." While this may seem ridiculous at first glance, such fees often keep the organization afloat, in addition to covering airfare, room, board, and administrative expenses for the volunteers. (Other organizations must rely on private donations and government subsidies.) If you're concerned about how a program spends its fees, request an annual report or finance account. A reputable organization won't refuse to inform you of how volunteer money is spent.

Pay-to-volunteer programs might be a good idea for young travelers who are looking for more support and structure (such as pre-arranged transportation and housing), or anyone who would rather not deal with the uncertainty implicit in creating a volunteer experience from scratch.

risks, by doing some background research on the organization you are working with and the region to which you are traveling, and preparing accordingly.

Much of the volunteer work in Mexico relates to economic development or environmental conservation. Most people who volunteer in Mexico do so on a short-term basis, at organizations that make use of drop-in or once-a-week volunteers. The best way to find opportunities that match your interests and schedule may be to check with local or national volunteer centers, some of which are listed below.

Those looking for longer, more intensive volunteer opportunities usually choose to go through a parent organization that takes care of logistical details and often provides a group environment and support system—for a fee. There are two main types of organizations—religious and non-sectarian—although there are rarely restrictions on participation for either.

ENVIRONMENTAL CONSERVATION

The quest for sustainable development is a crucial one in Mexico. On one hand, the exploitation of Mexico's abundant natural resources has been important to economic growth throughout the country's history. On the other, reliance on non-renewable resources has resulted in widespread environmental degradation. Some of the relevant concerns are the disappearing rainforests in Chiapas and the Yucatán Peninsula, destruction of marine habitats in coastal areas, soil erosion in the northern highlands, and dangerous levels of air pollution in large urban areas. The following organizations are some of the many that welcome volunteers to aid in their conservation efforts.

Centro Ecológico Akumal (CEA), Apartado Postal 2, Akumal, Quintana Roo 77760, Mexico (☎984 875 9095; www.ceakumal.org). Founded in 1993, CEA engages in ecological research and direct action, including turtle- and reef-monitoring and teaching. May-Sept.; length of stay negotiable.

Earthwatch, 3 Clocktower Pl., Ste. 100, Box 75, Maynard, MA 01754, USA (☎800-776-0188; www.earthwatch.org). Arranges 1- to 3-week programs promoting ecological conservation and engages volunteers (no special skills needed) in field research. US$700-4000, not including airfare.

Intercultural Center for the Study of Oceans and Deserts (CEDO), Apartado Postal #53, Puerto Peñasco, Sonora 83550, Mexico (☎638 382 0113; www.cedointercultural.org). Volunteers can participate in conservation, education, and science projects. 13-month internships available for those 21+. Eco-adventures US$50-200 (p. 228).

MEDICAL OUTREACH

Mexico offers universal health care to its citizens, but despite this provision good medical services can be hard to find, particularly in the remote, rural areas that house vast numbers of the indigenous population. Corruption within the health industry is also a problem; in 1996 the government arrested the former treasurer of its social security institution, alleging that he had stolen $150 million in public health funds. In larger cities, good care is available, and some North Americans travel South for the less expensive options, like pharmaceuticals and dental care, available just across the border. The organizations below target Mexico's disadvantaged for their help.

Child Family Health International, 995 Market St., Ste. 1104, San Francisco, CA 94103, USA (☎415-957-9000; www.cfhi.org). Sends pre-med and medical students to work with physicians in the developing world. Focuses on working with communities and local organizations as well as learning about health care distribution rather than actually providing medical assistance. Volunteers can also participate in Spanish language classes and homestays. Program fees are around US$2000, not including airfare.

Mar de Jade, PMB 078-344, 827 Union Pacific, Laredo, TX 78045, USA (☎800-257-0532; www.mardejade.com). Accepts volunteers, medical students, and professionals for 2-3 weeks of clinical assistance and Spanish classes. Organized by a resort on Mexico's Pacific coast, the accommodations range from private suites to guest houses.

Projects Abroad, 347 West 36th St. Ste. 903, New York, NY 10018, USA (☎888-839-3535; www.projects-abroad.org). Accepts pre-med and medical students for 1- to 4-month stints volunteering in local hospitals. Run out of Guadalajara. Tuition starts at US$2595 for the first month and includes meals and homestay. Other projects include journalism and conservation.

RURAL DEVELOPMENT

Though Mexico's countryside constitutes more than 80% of Mexico's land and houses nearly 36% of the country's population, it represents just a small share of its economy. Rural areas tend to be poor, with few jobs and less access to government services. A series of organizations, including those listed below, are attempting to bridge the divide between city and country.

The Auris Project, P.O. Box 201731, San Antonio, TX 78220 USA (☎210-462-9032, 866-274-8814; www.aurisproject.org). Development projects with an emphasis on information access. 1- to 2-month volunteer program led by an international journalist in the Altiplano Potosino for US$600 per month. Room and board included.

Habitat for Humanity Mexico, Soria No. 47 Colonia Alamos, Del. Benito Juárez, Mexico D.F. 03400, Mexico (☎55 5519 0113; in the US 229 924 6935; www.habitat.org, www.habitatmexico.org in Spanish). 1-week stays in Mexico to build houses in a host community. Costs range US$1300-2500, not including airfare.

WWOOF Mexico, (in Mexico City ☎55 5437 622, outside Mexico city 045 55 5437 6228; www.argos.net.mx/wwoof). Puts members in contact with organic farms offering work in exchange for room and board. Joint Mexico membership with Costa Rica $20.

SOCIAL ACTIVISM

Mexico has long been dominated by huge disparities between the country's rich and poor. Though the economic growth of the postwar period produced places comparable to parts of Europe, in 2005, 47% of the country's population still lived in poverty. The organizations listed below provide volunteer opportunities, like teaching in youth centers, intended to reduce these problems.

AmeriSpan, 117 S. 17th St., Ste. 1401, Philadelphia, PA 19103, USA (☎215-751-1100, 800-879-6640; www.amerispan.com). Internships and placements in Mexico in education, environmental conservation, public health, and social work.

Global Exchange, 2017 Mission #303, San Francisco, CA 94110, USA (☎415 255 7296, ext. 239; www.globalexchange.org/countries/mexico). Aims to put activists in contact with Mexican grassroots movements, focusing on indigenous rights. Also offers 8- to 9-day "Reality Tours" (US$750-1250) of local life and politics.

Visions in Action, 2710 Ontario Rd. NW, Washington, D.C. 20009, USA (☎202-625-7402; www.visionsinaction.org). Aims to promote social and economic justice through grassroots approach. 4-week or 6- to 12-month programs link volunteers with local NGOs, research institutes, health clinics, media, etc. Must have college degree and proficiency in Spanish. US$5300-7000, not including airfare.

Idealist.org. A comprehensive search-engine run by Action Without Borders listing job and volunteer opportunities domestically and internationally. Specify searches by area of interest as well as by region.

Movimiento de Apoyo a Menores A.C., Montenegro #1786 Col. Barrera, Guadalajara Jalisco, Mexico (☎333 825 2576; www.mama.org.mx). A center for disadvantaged children. Runs after-school program and orphanage.

Voluntarios Internacionales Mexico A.C., Plaza de la Republicano 51, 2 piso despacho-2, Col. Tabacalera, D.F. Mexico 06030 (☎555 566 2774; www.vimex.org.mx). Local search engine for volunteer opportunities.

YOUTH AND THE COMMUNITY

There are opportunities to help in Mexico, even for those still in high school. Many groups, including the ones below, engage high school volunteers in building projects or clean-up in small towns.

American Friends Service Committee, 1501 Cherry St., Philadelphia, PA 19102, USA (US☎215-241-7295; www.afsc.org). This Quaker organization's 2-month summer program focuses on community projects for youth to engage indigenous communities in Xilitla, Querétaro in ecological, political, and economic issues. Emphasis on cultural exchange. US$1350, including homestay and project materials. Scholarships available.

Amigos de las Américas, 5618 Star Ln., Houston, TX 77057, USA (☎713-782-5290; www.amigoslink.org). Sends high school and college students in groups of 2-3 to work in Michoacán, Guanajuato, and Oaxaca for 6- to 7-week public health and environmental education programs. 2 years (or equivalent) Spanish instruction required. Average fee US$3500, including airfare and insurance.

OTHER OPTIONS

With over 10,000 ruins dotting the landscape, Mexico provides some of the most fertile opportunities for archaeological research. This is just one program of many that cater to interest in the nation's history.

MAYA Research Program, 209 W. 2nd St. #295, Fort Worth, TX 76102, USA (☎817-350-4986; www.mayaresearchprogram.org). Runs a 2-week ethnographic field project in the Mayan village of Yaxunah and annual study tours to Mayan sites in Central America. Research program US$110-1450, not including airfare.

STUDYING

VISA INFORMATION. If you're planning to study in Mexico for 6 months or less, there's no need to apply for a visa. If your stay will be longer, you should head to the local consulate. In addition to other documents, you will need the acceptance letter from your school in Mexico to receive a visa. Some countries may be charged US$29 for consular fees.

Study-abroad programs range from basic language and culture courses to college-level classes, often for credit. In order to choose a program that best fits your needs, research as much as you can before making your decision—determine costs and duration, as well as what kind of students participate in the program and what sort of accommodations are provided.

In programs that have large groups of students who speak the same language, there is a trade-off. You may feel more comfortable in the community, but you will not have the same opportunity to practice a foreign language or to befriend other international students. For accommodations, dorm life provides a better opportunity to mingle with fellow students, but there is less of a chance to experience the local scene. If you live with a family, there is a potential to build lifelong friendships with natives and to experience day-to-day life in more depth, but conditions can vary greatly from family to family.

UNIVERSITIES

Most university-level study-abroad programs are conducted in Spanish, although many programs offer classes in English and beginner- and lower-level language courses. Those who are relatively fluent in Spanish may find it cheaper to enroll directly in a university abroad, although getting college credit may be more difficult. You can search **www.studyabroad.com** for various semester-abroad programs that meet your criteria, including your desired location and focus of study. The following is a list of organizations that can help place students in university programs abroad, or have their own branch in Mexico.

AMERICAN PROGRAMS

Augsburg College Center for Global Education, 2211 Riverside Ave., Minneapolis, MN 55454, USA (☎612-330-1159, 800-299-8889; www.augsburg.edu/global). Semester-long programs based in Cuernavaca focus on ecology, economic development, gender, globalization, or human rights. Tuition from $15,500.

Central College Abroad, Office of International Education, 812 University, Pella, IA 50219, USA (☎641-628-5284, 800-831-3629; www.central.edu/abroad). Offers internships and study-abroad programs in Mérida. Courses in English and Spanish. All-inclusive semester- or year-long tuition US$11500/23,000, not including airfare.

Council on International Educational Exchange (CIEE), 7 Custom House St., 3rd fl., Portland, ME 01401, USA (☎800-407-8839; www.ciee.org/study). Sponsors work, volunteer, academic, and internship programs in Mexico.

International Association for the Exchange of Students for Technical Experience (IAESTE), 10400 Little Patuxent Pkwy. Ste. 250, Columbia, MD 21044, USA (☎410-997-3068; www.iaeste.org). Offers 8- to 12-week internships in Mexico for college students who have completed 2 years of technical study.

International Student Exchange Program (ISEP), 1616 P St. NW, Ste. 150, Washington, D.C. 20036, USA (☎202 667 8027; www.isep.org). Places students in 1 of 7 Mexican universities for 1 semester-2 years. Prices vary according to host institution.

School for International Training, College Semester Abroad, Kipling Rd., P.O. Box 676, Brattleboro, VT 05302, USA (☎802-257-7751, 888-272-7881; www.sit.edu/studyabroad). Semester-long programs in Mexico run US$12,900-16,000. Also operates **The Experiment in International Living** (☎800-345-2929; www.usexperiment.org). 3-6 week summer programs offer high-school students cross-cultural homestays, community service, ecological adventures, and language training. US$1900-5000.

MEXICAN PROGRAMS

Applications to Mexican universities are usually due in early spring and require a transcript and a copy of your passport or birth certificate. Short-term language study in Mexico is relatively easy, especially since no visa is required for stays of up to three months. Mexican universities also have flourishing exchange programs with many countries in the world.

Tecnológico de Monterrey, Av. Eugenio Garza Sada 2501 Sur, Monterrey, Nuevo León 64849, Mexico (☎818 358 2000; www.itesm.mx/vi). One of the most prestigious private universities in Mexico, focusing on science, math, and engineering. 8 campuses across the country host their own international program.

Centro de Enseñanza para Extranjeros (CEPE), Apdo. 70-391, Av. Universidad 3002, Ciudad Universitaria, Coyoacán, Mexico, D.F. 04510 (☎555 622 2470; www.cepe.unam.mx). Provides 6-week intensive and 3-week super-intensive programs in Spanish, art, history, and literature. Operated by Universidad Nacional Autónoma de Mexico (UNAM), the largest public university in Mexico, with over 100,000 students. Tuition US$70-300 excludes housing.

Universidad de las Americas (UDLA), Santa Catarina Mártir, Cholula, Puebla 72820, Mexico (☎222 229 2000; http://info.pue.udlap.mx). This private university's extensive international education program is well established. Exchange students can take regular UDLA courses or language and cultural immersion programs.

Universidad Iberoamericana, Paseo de la Reforma No. 880, Lomas de Santa Fe, Mexico D.F. 01210, Mexico (☎555 950 4000; www.uia.mx). "Ibero" for short. A private university that offers semester and summer programs in disciplinary and professional studies, and intensive Spanish instruction. Tuition US$3000-5000 plus application (US$50) and registration fees (US$200) includes room and board for the semester.

LANGUAGE SCHOOLS

Language schools can be independently run international or local organizations or divisions of foreign universities. They rarely offer college credit. They are a good alternative to university study if you desire a deeper focus on the language or a slightly less rigorous course load. These programs are also good for younger high school students who might not feel comfortable with older students in a university program. Some worthwhile programs include:

The Center for Linguistic Multicultural Studies, San Jerónimo 304, Col. San Jerónimo, Cuernavaca, Morelos 62179, Mexico (☎777 317 1087; www.bilingual-center.com). Intensive classes US$300-1250 per week. Offers semester-long language study and special language programs for executives, teachers, and other businesspeople. 5-person classes. Optional homestay. Registration fee US$100.

EXPERIENCIA, Centro de Intercambio Bilingue y Cultural, Av. Leyva 200 Colonia: Las Palmas, Cuernavaca, Morelos 62050, Mexico (☎777 312 6579; www.experienciaspanish.com). Language immersion studies with an emphasis on cultural context. Programs from 1-16 weeks. Individuals US$380 per week, groups US$190 per week. Accommodation in dorms or with host families and meals US$100-200 per week.

Instituto Habla Hispana, Calzada de la Luz 25, Apdo. 689, San Miguel de Allende, Guanajuato 37700, Mexico (☎415 152 1535; www.mexicospanish.com). Intensive month-long Spanish courses for all levels. 10-person classes. Emphasis on improving speaking and listening skills. Optional homestay and cooking classes. Classes US$120 per week.

Cemanahuac Comunidad Educativa, Apdo. 5-21, Cuernavaca, Morelos, Mexico (☎777 318 6407; www.cemanahuac.com). Coordinated by **Language Immersion Institute,** WSB 03D, State University of New York at New Paltz, 1 Hawk Dr., New Paltz, NY 12561, USA (☎845-257-3500; www.newpaltz.edu/lii). 2-week language immersion program around US$1000, not including accommodation.

Spanish Institute of Puebla, 11 Oriente #10, Puebla, Puebla 72000, Mexico (☎222 242 2092; www.sipuebla.com). Intensive classes at all levels with an emphasis on improving communication skills. US$1845 covers registration, tuition, homestay, meals, and excursions. 4-, 8-, 12-, 16-, and 20-week programs available.

WORKING

As with volunteering, work opportunities tend to fall into two categories. Some travelers want long-term jobs that allow them to integrate into a community, while others seek out short-term jobs to finance the next leg of their travels. In Mexico, people who want to work long-term should attempt to make arrangements before they arrive. Otherwise, due to the need for employees with language skills, the tourist industry can be one of the most welcoming to foreigners.

> **VISA INFORMATION.** It is difficult to obtain a general work visa for Mexico, and the government reserves the right to restrict permits to sectors experiencing labor shortages. In order to work, you must be authorized by the **National Immigration Institute,** which will require proof of employment. Instituto Nacional de Migración, Homero 1852; Col. Los Morales Polanco; Delegación Miguel Hidalgo; C.P. 11510, MX, D.F. (☎555 387 2400; www.inami.gob.mx).

LONG-TERM WORK

If you're planning on spending a substantial amount of time (more than 3 months) working in Mexico, search for a job well in advance. International placement agencies are often the easiest way to find employment abroad, especially for those interested in teaching English. Although they are often only available to college students, **internships** are a good way to segue into working abroad; they are often un- or underpaid, but many say the experience is well worth it. Be wary of advertisements for companies claiming to be able get you a job abroad for a fee—often the same listings are available online or in newspapers.

TEACHING ENGLISH

Teaching jobs abroad are rarely well-paid, although some elite private American schools offer competitive salaries. Volunteering as a teacher in lieu of getting paid is a popular option; even then, teachers often receive some sort of a daily stipend to help with living expenses. Expect your salary to match the low cost of living in Mexico. In almost all cases, you must have at least a bachelor's degree to be a full-time teacher, although college undergraduates can often get summer positions teaching or tutoring.

Many schools require teachers to have a **Teaching English as a Foreign Language (TEFL)** certificate. You may still be able to find a teaching job without certification, but certified teachers often find higher-paying jobs. Native English speakers working in private schools are most often hired for English-immersion classrooms where no Spanish is spoken. Those volunteering or teaching in public schools are more likely to be working in both English and Spanish. Placement agencies or university fellowship programs are the best resources for finding teaching jobs. The alternative is to contact schools directly or to try your luck once you arrive in Mexico. If you are going to try the latter, the best time to look is several weeks before the start of the school year. The following organizations are extremely helpful in placing teachers in Mexico.

International Schools Services (ISS), 15 Roszel Rd., P.O. Box 5910, Princeton, NJ 08543, USA (☎609-452-0990; www.iss.edu). Hires teachers for more than 200 overseas schools, including the Colegio Americano de Torreón. Candidates should have experience teaching or with international affairs. 2-year commitment expected.

Office of Overseas Schools, US Department of State, Room H328, SA-1, Washington, D.C. 20522, USA (☎202-261-8200; www.state.gov/m/a/os/). Keeps a list of schools abroad and agencies that arrange placement for Americans to teach abroad.

Teachers Latin America, Río Ebro 31, Ste. 3, Colonia Cuauhtémoc, Mexico City, D.F. 06500, Mexico (☎555 533 1233 or 555 533 1228; www.innovative-english.com). TESS-EFL and TEFL certification, language courses, internships, and job placement services. US$200-1200, including homestay and accommodations. Typical certification program 9-12 weeks for minimum 6-month position.

SHORT-TERM WORK

Traveling for long periods of time can be hard on the finances; therefore, many travelers try their hand at odd jobs for a few weeks at a time to help pay for another month or two of touring around. *Let's Go* lists temporary jobs of this nature whenever possible; look in the **Practical Information** section of larger cities for some of the available short-term jobs in popular destinations.

TOURISM INDUSTRY. Another popular option is to work several hours a day at a **hostel** in exchange for free or discounted room and/or board. The **PocNa Youth Hostel,** Matamoros 15, Isla Mujeres, Quintana Roo (☎877 0090; www.pocna.com.), with a private restaurant and beach, offers this deal. Most often, these short-term jobs are found by word of mouth, or by expressing interest to the owner of a hostel or restaurant. Due to high turnover in the tourism industry, many places are eager for help, even if it is only temporary. High-end resorts in particular look abroad to fill staff positions. These contracts typically last six months.

FURTHER READING ON BEYOND TOURISM

Alternatives to the Peace Corps: A Directory of Third World and U.S. Volunteer Opportunities, by Jennifer S. Willsea. Food First Books, 2005 (US$10).

Back Door Guide to Short-Term Job Adventures: Internships, Extraordinary Experiences, Seasonal Jobs, Volunteering, Working Abroad, by Michael Landes. Ten Speed Press, 2005 (US$22).

Green Volunteers: The World Guide to Voluntary Work in Nature, ed. Fabio Ausenda. Universe, 2007 (US$15).

How to Get a Job in Europe, by Cheryl Matherly and Robert Sanborn. Planning Communications, 2003 (US$23).

How to Live Your Dream of Volunteering Overseas, by Joseph Collins, Stefano DeZerega, and Zahara Heckscher. Penguin Books, 2002 (US$18).

International Job Finder: Where the Jobs Are Worldwide, by Daniel Lauber and Kraig Rice. Planning Communications, 2002 (US$20).

Live and Work Abroad: A Guide for Modern Nomads, by Huw Francis and Michelyne Callan. Vacation-Work Publications, 2001 (US$16).

Overseas Summer Jobs 2002. Peterson's Guides and Vacation Work, 2002 (US$18).

Volunteer Vacations: Short-term Adventures That Will Benefit You and Others, by Doug Cutchins and Anne Geissinger. Chicago Review Press, 2006 (US$18).

Work Abroad: The Complete Guide to Finding a Job Overseas, by Clayton Hubbs. Transitions Abroad Publishing, 2002 (US$16).

Work Your Way Around the World, by Susan Griffith. Vacation-Work Publications, 2007 (US$22).

MEXICO CITY

Mexico City is a feast for the senses. On the sidewalks, bodies jostle to the beat of *norteño* music and the cries of street vendors, mingling their sweat with the scent of freshly fried tortillas. Eight-lane highways run past ancient pyramids, Catholics make pilgrimages to pagan temples, and cacti compete for space with palms. Somehow it all seems to make sense. Composed of 350 *colonias* (neighborhoods), Mexico's capital is one of the world's largest and most exciting cities in the world. Estimates of the city's population vary depending on who's counting and how one determines the urban limits, but most agree that it reaches almost nine million people in the city proper and between 17 and 25 million in the greater Federal District. A contender for the title of most museums and theaters in the world, the city takes in more than 2 million tourists per year. In the city, Mexicans refer to the megalopolis as **el D.F.** (deh-EFF-eh; **Distrito Federal**), but to the rest of the country, it is simply **México,** a testament to its immense size and importance.

First settled in the 13th century by the Aztecs, following divine commands to stop where they saw an eagle devouring a serpent, **Tenochtitlán** became the epicenter of a powerful empire that stretched across the central valley. In 1520, when the Spaniards encountered the Aztec capital—actually a series of garden- and pyramid-filled islands on the surface of Lake Texcoco connected by removable causeways and canals—they were impressed. The "buildings rising from the water, all made of stone, seemed like an enchanted vision ... It was all so wonderful that I do not know how to describe this first glimpse of things never heard of, seen or dreamed before," recalled soldier Bernal Díaz del Castillo in his memoir. After defeating the city, the Spaniards replaced canals with roads and used the rubble to build new *palacios* and cathedrals—many of which are still standing. Despite all the energy devoted to recasting the city, in 1629 a five-year flood nearly wiped it off the map. Great construction projects in the 18th century revitalized the area, linking it via aqueduct to the reservoirs in Chapultepec, and draining the giant underground lake. By the time of Mexico's independence in 1821, the city was Latin America's cultural capital, home to the oldest university in the Americas.

Foreign invasion and internal unrest slowed building stalled during the 19th century, and not until the dictatorship of General Porfirio Díaz (1876-1910) did the city regain stability, embarking on a series of ambitious turn-of-the-century projects. The Revolution (1910-1917) solidified the city's importance, and employment opportunities lured thousands of migrants from the countryside. Between 1950 and 2000, the city's population exploded from 3 million to 18 million. Even as the new arrivals supported a vibrant artistic and intellectual life, they stressed city infrastructure, exposing socio-economic disparities and yielding shanty towns and slums that still line the roads to the capital. In the 1980s and 90s, the city experienced environmental challenges, including a massive earthquake, a volcanic eruption, and dangerously deteriorating air quality. Since the late 1990s, the city has launched new crime fighting initiatives, and began to battle pollution, using educational campaigns and strict controls. The center of Mexican life for centuries, the capital is a dizzying mix of old and new that captivates both tourist and local alike.

HIGHLIGHTS OF MEXICO CITY

SQUARE OFF with centuries of history in Mexico's biggest plaza, the **zócalo** (p. 108).

LOSE yourself in the **Bosque de Chapultepec** (p. 118), the largest urban park in the Americas—it's got everything from panda bears to free concerts to the **Museo Nacional de Antropología** (p. 118), Mexico's biggest and best museum.

FIND your inner muse at the former home of world-renowned painter, the **Museo Frida Kahlo** (p. 125).

GRAB a drink in Plaza Garibaldi, while roving **ranchero** bands strum in the background (p. 134).

PICNIC beneath shady poplars in the **Parque Alameda Central** before enjoying a dazzling show of **Ballet Folklórico** at the Palacio de Bellas Artes (p. 114).

HIT the road; many of Mexico City's most fabulous attractions lie just outside the city. Check out our **daytrips** (p. 140), including the nearby pyramids at **Teotihuacán** (p. 141), the most visited ruins in all of Mexico.

⚔ INTERCITY TRANSPORTATION

All roads lead to Mexico City. Buses, planes, and trains from every town in the republic haul passengers through the smoggy hyperactivity of the city's many temples of transport—the constantly expanding Benito Juárez International Airport, four crowded bus stations, and a network of highways. Airports and stations have information booths, official zone-rated taxi service, and nearby Metro stations.

BY AIR

Benito Juárez International Airport (MEX; ☎ 2482 2400; www.aicm.com.mx) lies 6.5km east of the *zócalo*, the formal city center. The **Circuito Interior,** one of the major roads circling the city, turns into **Blvr. Puerto Aéreo,** which leads straight to the airport.

GETTING TO AND FROM THE AIRPORT

Transportation into the city is simple. The **Metro** (p. 94) is the cheapest route to the city. The airport metro station, **Terminal Aérea,** Line 5, on Puerto Aéreo, is just outside Sala A; signs point the way. Large bags are officially prohibited, but if you avoid rush hour (6-10am and 6-9pm) and can maneuver through the turnstile, a backpack should not pose too much of a problem. Special fixed-rate airport **taxis** (☎ 5571; www.taxisdelaeropuerto.com.mx) and **Transporte Terrestre** (☎ 5786 9358) also run into the city. Windows by the exits to both arrival gates sell tickets. Prices depend on the zone of your destination; taxis to the *zócalo* cost 127 pesos. Give the ticket to one of the cabs waiting outside while avoiding uniformed "taxi supervisors"—porters who will expect a tip.

> **⚑ TIP** **GET OFF HERE.** If traveling to the airport by **Metro,** do not get off at the Aeropuerto stop on Line 1 (also known as Blvr. Aeropuerto). The correct stop is **Terminal Aérea,** on Line 5.

FLIGHT INFORMATION

Flight and General Info Hotline: (☎ 5784 0471). Open M-F 9am-6pm. Specify domestic or international flights.

Terminals: Sala A: Aeroméxico and domestic airlines. **Sala A2:** Mexicana, Aeromar, Aero-California. **Sala B:** Waiting room; all domestic airlines. **Sala C:** Aviasca. **Sala D:** Azteca

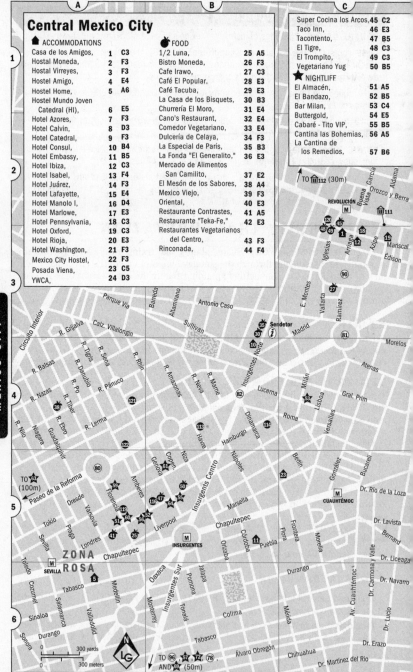

Central Mexico City

🏠 **ACCOMMODATIONS**

Casa de los Amigos,	1	C3
Hostal Moneda,	2	F3
Hostal Virreyes,	3	F3
Hostel Amigo,	4	E4
Hostel Home,	5	A6
Hostel Mundo Joven		
Catedral (HI),	6	E5
Hotel Azores,	7	F3
Hotel Calvin,	8	D3
Hotel Catedral,	9	F3
Hotel Consul,	10	B4
Hotel Embassy,	11	B5
Hotel Ibiza,	12	C3
Hotel Isabel,	13	F4
Hotel Juárez,	14	F3
Hotel Lafayette,	15	E4
Hotel Manolo I,	16	D4
Hotel Marlowe,	17	E3
Hotel Pennsylvania,	18	C3
Hotel Oxford,	19	C3
Hotel Rioja,	20	E3
Hotel Washington,	21	F3
Mexico City Hostel,	22	F3
Posada Viena,	23	C5
YWCA,	24	D3

🍎 **FOOD**

1/2 Luna,	25	A5
Bistro Moneda,	26	F3
Cafe Irawo,	27	C3
Café El Popular,	28	E3
Café Tacuba,	29	E3
La Casa de los Bisquets,	30	B3
Churrería El Moro,	31	E4
Cano's Restaurant,	32	E4
Comedor Vegetariano,	33	A4
Dulcería de Celaya,	34	F3
La Especial de París,	35	B3
La Fonda "El Generalito,"	36	E3
Mercado de Alimentos		
San Camilito,	37	E2
El Mesón de los Sabores,	38	A4
Mexico Viejo,	39	F3
Oriental,	40	E3
Restaurante Contrastes,	41	A5
Restaurante "Teka-Fe,"	42	E3
Restaurantes Vegetarianos		
del Centro,	43	F3
Rinconada,	44	F4

Super Cocina los Arcos,	45	C2
Taco Inn,	46	E3
Tacontento,	47	B5
El Tigre,	48	C3
El Trompito,	49	C3
Vegetariano Yug	50	B5

⭐ **NIGHTLIFE**

El Almacén,	51	A5
El Bandazo,	52	B5
Bar Milan,	53	C4
Buttergold,	54	E5
Cabaré - Tito VIP,	55	B5
Cantina las Bohemias,	56	A5
La Cantina de		
los Remedios,	57	B6

MEXICO CITY

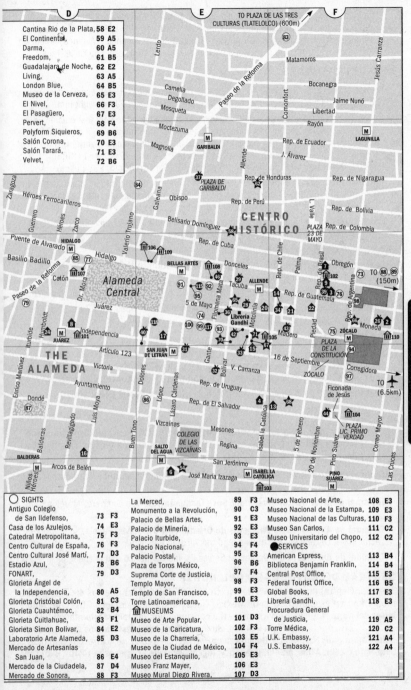

Cantina Rio de la Plata,	58	E2
El Continental,	59	A5
Darma,	60	A5
Freedom,	61	B5
Guadalajara de Noche,	62	E2
Living,	63	A5
London Blue,	64	B5
Museo de la Cerveza,	65	E3
El Nivel,	66	F3
El Pasagüero,	67	E3
Pervert,	68	F4
Polyform Siqueiros,	69	B6
Salón Corona,	70	E3
Salón Tarará,	71	E3
Velvet,	72	B6

TO PLAZA DE LAS TRES
CULTURAS (TLATELOLCO) (600m)

MEXICO CITY

○ SIGHTS		
Antiguo Colegio		
de San Ildefonso,	73	F3
Casa de los Azulejos,	74	F3
Catedral Metropolitana,	75	F3
Centro Cultural de España,	76	F3
Centro Cultural José Martí,	77	D3
Estadio Azul,	78	B6
FONART,	79	D3
Glorieta Ángel de		
la Independencia,	80	A5
Glorieta Cristóbal Colón,	81	C3
Glorieta Cuauhtémoc,	82	B4
Glorieta Cuitlahuac,	83	F1
Glorieta Simón Bolívar,	84	E2
Laboratorio Arte Alameda,	85	D3
Mercado de Artesanías		
San Juan,	86	E4
Mercado de la Ciudadela,	87	D4
Mercado de Sonora,	88	F3

La Merced,	89	F3
Monumento a la Revolución,	90	C3
Palacio de Bellas Artes,	91	E3
Palacio de Minería,	92	E3
Palacio Iturbide,	93	E3
Palacio Nacional,	94	F4
Palacio Postal,	95	E3
Plaza de Toros México,	96	B6
Suprema Corte de Justicia,	97	F4
Templo Mayor,	98	F3
Templo de San Francisco,	99	E3
Torre Latinoamericana,	100	E3
🏛 MUSEUMS		
Museo de Arte Popular,	101	D3
Museo de la Caricatura,	102	F3
Museo de la Charrería,	103	E5
Museo de la Ciudad de México,	104	F4
Museo del Estanquillo,	105	E3
Museo Franz Mayer,	106	E3
Museo Mural Diego Rivera,	107	D3

Museo Nacional de Arte,	108	E3
Museo Nacional de la Estampa,	109	E3
Museo Nacional de las Culturas,	110	F3
Museo San Carlos,	111	C2
Museo Universitario del Chopo,	112	C2
● SERVICES		
American Express,	113	B4
Biblioteca Benjamín Franklin,	114	B4
Central Post Office,	115	E3
Federal Tourist Office,	116	B5
Global Books,	117	E3
Librería Gandhi,	118	E3
Procuraduría General		
de Justicia,	119	A5
Torre Médica,	120	C2
U.K. Embassy,	121	A4
U.S. Embassy,	122	A4

and Magnicharter. **Sala E:** International arrivals. **Sala F1:** Aeroméxico (international), Air France, Argentina, Continental, Copa, Delta, KLM, Northwest, Nova. **Sala F2:** Air Canada, Lufthansa, Mexicana, United, US Airways, Varig. **Sala F3:** American, Avianca, America West, Aviateca, British Airways, Cubana, Iberia, Japan, LAB, Lacsa, Lan Chile, Taca.

AIRPORT SERVICES

Tourist Office: In Sala A (☎5786 9002), with the yellow signs. Hotel reservations available. Open daily 7am-9pm. Information kiosks in Salas A and F have flight info.

Buses: Airport bus service provides direct access to nearby towns from just outside Sala E2. Ticket booth in front of parked buses. Buses go to: **Cuernavaca** on Pullman (34 per day 6:40am-12:30am, 125 pesos); **Pachuca** on Estrella Blanca (every hr. 6:30am-10pm, 125 pesos); **Puebla** on Estrella Roja (42 per day 12:30am-11:50pm, 170 pesos); **Querétaro** on Primera Plus (25 per day 6:15am-10:30pm, 235 pesos).

Currency Exchange: In almost every sala. **ATMs** in Sala A, directly under Sala B, between C and D, and in Salas E and F. *Casas de cambio* have comparable rates to what you'll find throughout the city. Most open daily 6am-9pm, some open 24hr.

Car Rental: In Salas A and E. Companies offer similar rates. Open until about 10:30pm.

Luggage Storage: Corner of Sala A and in Sala E2 (☎5802 8467). 65 pesos per bag per day. Open 24hr.

Lost and Found: Room 102, mezzanine (☎5571 3600, ext. 2289). Open M-F 9am-9pm, Sa-Su 9am-2pm.

Police: In emergencies, go to info booth in Sala E1 or A1; they will direct you to police.

Pharmacy: In Sala C. Open daily 6am-10pm. Also in Sala F. Open daily 7am-10:30pm.

Medical Services: Upstairs from Sala B; follow the Red Cross signs.

Fax Office: Between Salas D, E, and F. Open 24hr.

Internet Access: Servitel, Sala E-2 (☎2599 0541). 12 pesos per 10min. Open daily 6:30am-10:30pm. **Communic@tions, Etc,** Sala E1 (☎2599 0600). 25 pesos per 15 min. Open 24hr. Web kiosks around the airport operate on **LADATEL** phone cards.

Post Office: in Sala A. Open M-F 8am-5pm, Sa 9am-3pm. **Postal Code:** 15620.

BY BUS

Mexico City's four main bus stations correspond to the cardinal directions and serve the corresponding areas of the country. All stations can be reached by Metro, *peseros* (buses), or a fixed-rate taxi service.

Central de Autobuses del Norte: Serves Baja California, northern Veracruz state, Jalisco, and all of northern Mexico.

Terminal Central de Autobuses del Sur (Tasqueña): Serves Guerrero, Morelos, and Oaxaca state.

Terminal de Autobuses de Pasajeros de Oriente (TAPO): Serves Puebla, southern Veracruz state, Oaxaca state, Chiapas, and the Yucatán Peninsula.

Terminal de Autobuses del Poniente: Serves Estado de México and Michoacán.

CENTRAL DE AUTOBUSES DEL NORTE

The vast Central de Autobuses del Norte (☎5587 1552), Cien Metros 4907, is commonly known as Cien Metros or México Norte, and can by reached from **M: Autobuses del Norte** (Line 5). Services near the entrance include: **tourist information** booth (☎5719 1276; open M-Sa 7am-9:30pm, Su 9am-6pm); **hotel reservations** through **Sendetur** (open daily 8am-9pm); **Banco Azteca,** which has a *casa de cambio* (open daily 9am-8pm); **24hr. ATMs;** a **24hr. pharmacy; luggage storage** (15 pesos per 24hr.); and at least one **Sendetel** with **Internet** access (10 pesos per hr.; open daily 6am-10pm). From the **taxi stand**, trips to the *zócalo* or Revolución are 85 pesos.

ADO: (☎5133 2424). To: **Oaxaca** (6½hr., 10 per day 7:30am-11:45pm, 344 pesos); **Papantla** (6hr., 9 per day 12:30am-11:50pm, 198 pesos); **Puebla** (2hr., every 30min. 4am-10pm, 104 pesos); **Tuxpan** (6½hr., 4 per day 6am-10am, 214 pesos); **Veracruz** (5½hr.; 9am, 11:30pm; 292 pesos); **Villahermosa** (12hr., 10 per day 6:30am-11:15pm, 588 pesos); **Xalapa** (5hr.; 12:30, 10:30am, 3pm; 206 pesos).

Élite: (☎5729 0707). The name says it all. To: **Hermosillo** (28½hr., 20 per day 4:30am-11:30pm, 1295 pesos), **Puerto Vallarta** (12½hr., 4 per day 5-10:30pm, 752 pesos), and **San Luis Potosí** (6hr., every hr. 5am-midnight, 321 pesos).

Estrella Blanca/Futura: (☎5729 0707). To: **Acapulco** (5½hr., 16 per day 6am-11:30pm, 315 pesos); **Aguascalientes** (6hr., 17 per day 7:30am-midnight, 392 pesos); **Chihuahua** (20hr., 16 per day 5am-11:30pm, 1052 pesos); **Durango** (12hr., 4 per day 4-9:20pm, 652 pesos); **Matamoros** (14hr.; 5:30, 10:30pm; 715 pesos); **Monterrey** (12hr., 9 per day 7am-midnight, 637 pesos); **Tampico** (8½hr., 24 per day, 288 pesos); **Zacatecas** (7¾hr., 20 per day 5am-11:30pm, 450 pesos).

Flecha Amarilla/Primera Plus: (☎5587 5222, toll-free 800 375 7587; www.primera-plus.com.mx). To: **Guadalajara** (7hr., 27 per day, 357 pesos); **Guanajuato** (5hr., 11 per day 12:30am-11:30pm, 234 pesos); **Morelia** (5½hr., 19 per day, 200 pesos); **Querétaro** (2½hr., 56 per day 4:50am-11:40pm, 138 pesos); **San Miguel de Allende** (4hr.; 7:10, 11:15am, 5:40pm; 173 pesos).

TERMINAL DE AUTOBUSES DE PASAJEROS DE ORIENTE (TAPO)

Follow the indoor walkway from **M: San Lázaro** (Line 1) to General Ignacio Zaragoza 200 (☎5762 5977). Services include **ATMs, pharmacy,** and **luggage storage** at any of the three Guardaplus locations. (☎5133 2700, ext. 5808. 5-12 pesos per hr. Open 24hr.) **Police** booths are scattered throughout the station. **Taxi** booths are near the Metro entrance (to the *zócalo* 65 pesos, to Monumento a la Revolución 70 pesos).

ADO: (☎5542 7192). To: **Cancún** (23hr., 20 per day 7am-12:45am, 1068 pesos); **Córdoba** (4½hr., 28 per day 6:45am-10:15pm, 236 pesos); **Mérida** (19hr., 5 per day 12:30-9:35pm, 1006 pesos); **Oaxaca** (6hr.; 12:30, 12:45am, and every hr. 7am-midnight; 362 pesos); **Palenque** (12hr.; 4, 6pm; 706 pesos); **Veracruz** (5hr., 19 per day 12:30am-midnight, 308 pesos); **Villahermosa** (10½hr., 22 per day 8:30am-12:30am, 618 pesos).

Autobuses Cristóbal Colón: (**OCC;** ☎5133 2433). To: **Oaxaca** (6hr.; 5:30am, 9, 11:30pm; 362 pesos); **Puerto Escondido** (12hr., 5:20pm, 528 pesos); **San Cristóbal de las Casas** (12hr., 7 per day 12:30-9:45pm, 788 pesos); **Tonalá** (13hr., 7 per day 10:45am-10:15pm, 658 pesos); **Tuxtla Gutiérrez** (12hr., 12 per day 12:30am-10pm, 738 pesos).

Autobuses Unidos: (**AU;** ☎5133 2424). To: **Córdoba** (5hr., every hr. 6:30am-1:15am, 210 pesos); **Oaxaca** (9hr., 6 per day 10:30am-midnight, 290 pesos); **San Andrés Tuxtla** (7½hr.; 11:30am, 9pm, 11pm Sa-Su only; 360 pesos); **Veracruz** (7hr., every hr. 7am-2am, 258 pesos); **Villahermosa** (10hr.; 9:30am, 7:30pm, 9:30pm; 550 pesos); **Xalapa** (5hr., every hr. 7am-2am, 192 pesos).

UNO: (☎5133 1100). To: **Oaxaca** (6hr., 5 per day 8:30am-11:45pm, 614 pesos); **Veracruz** (5½hr., 7 per day 9:30am-midnight, 520 pesos); **Villahermosa** (10hr., 9pm, 998 pesos); **Xalapa** (4½hr., 6 per day 9am-midnight, 376 pesos).

TERMINAL DE AUTOBUSES DEL PONIENTE

Follow signs from **Metro: Observatorio** (Line 1) to Central Camionero Pte., Av. Sur 122 (☎5271 4519), at Río Tacubaya. A vendor-lined bridge leads to the terminal. From the terminal to the Metro, walk up the staircase and turn left. The station is built in a "V" shape with the most important services at the converging point. Services include: **tourist info booth,** by the main entrance (☎5272 8816; open daily 9am-2pm and 3-6pm); **pharmacy** (open daily 7am-10pm); **luggage storage** at two locations (2.50 pesos per 4hr.); **Internet** access at **Internet@Poniente** (10 pesos per hr.; open daily 10am-6pm); **fax** service at **Telecomm** (open M-F 9am-8pm, Sa-Su 9am-5pm); and **Western Union.** Buy **taxi** tickets from the authorized stand (☎5277 3752; to the *zócalo* 98 pesos, to the Monumento a la Revolución 80 pesos).

> **ETN:** (☎5273 0305). To: **Guadalajara** (7hr., 7 per day 11am-midnight, 570 pesos); **Morelia** (4hr., 34 per day 3am-1am, 290 pesos); **Toluca** (1hr., M-F and Su every 30min. 7:30am-midnight, 49 pesos); **Uruapan** (5½hr., 10 per day 4:15am-midnight, 405 pesos).

> **Pegasso Plus:** (☎5277 7761). To **Morelia** (4hr., every 30min. 5:30am-1am, 240 pesos) and **Pátzcuaro** (5hr., 11 per day 5:30am-midnight, 270 pesos).

CENTRAL DE AUTOBUSES DEL SUR (TASQUEÑA)

To get to the Tasqueña terminal, Tasqueña 1320 (☎5689 9745), exit **Metro: Tasqueña** from the "Central" exit on the upper level, then go down a staircase on your left. The terminal is across the market, a yellow fence, and a row of trees. Services include: **tourist information,** by the third door (☎5336 2321; open daily 9am-7pm); mini-travel agency, **Sendetur,** for hotel reservations in select cities (☎5549 6378; open M-Sa 9am-7pm); and **Telecomm,** with **fax** and **Western Union** (☎5689 9640; open M-F 8am-5:30pm, Sa-Su 9am-4:30pm). **Taxis** wait at the stand (☎5689 9745; to the *zócalo* 85 pesos, to the Monumento a la Revolución 95 pesos).

> **Estrella Roja:** (☎5549 8749). To: **Puebla, Cuernavaca,** and **Matamoros** via **Cuautla** (1½hr., every 20min. 6:40am-10pm, 74 pesos).

> **Estrella de Oro:** (☎5549 8520). To: **Acapulco** (5hr., 10 per day 2:15am-11:15pm, 315 pesos), **Ixtapa/Zihuatanejo** (9hr.; 12:15am, 7:40pm, 9:30pm; 440 pesos), and **Taxco** (2hr.; 9:40am, 4:40pm; 110 pesos).

> **Futura** and **Turistar:** (☎5628 5738). To: **Acapulco** (5hr., 23 per day, 315 pesos), **Ixtapa/Zihuatanejo** (9hr., 6 per day 6:50am-10:40pm, 440 pesos), and **Taxco** (2hr., every hr. 6am-8pm, 105 pesos).

> **Pullman de Morelos:** (☎5549 3505). To: **Cuernavaca** (1¼hr., every 15min. 6:20am-midnight, 63 pesos).

BY CAR

Few car-related experiences can match the shock of driving into Mexico City. Traffic keeps the city crawling from 8-11am and 3-7pm. Don't expect anyone to drive defensively—residents in a hurry regard stoplights as optional (p. 96). Major roads into the district change names as they intersect the **Circuito Interior,** the route that rings the city. **Mex. 57,** from Querétaro and Tepoztlán, becomes **Manuel Ávila Camacho** just outside the Circuito. **Mex. 15,** from Toluca, turns into **Reforma** as it enters the city. **Mex. 95,** from Cuernavaca and Acapulco, becomes **Insurgentes,** which enters the city from the south side. **Mex. 150,** from Puebla and Texcoco, becomes **Ignacio Zaragoza** on the city's east side. **Mex. 85,** from Pachuca and Teotihuacán, also becomes **Insurgentes** at the northern city limits.

◪ ORIENTATION

Mexico City extends outward from the *centro* roughly 10km to the north, 8km to the east, 20km to the south, and 10km to the west, though there is much debate about where the city actually begins and ends. Few tourists venture past La Basílica de Guadalupe to the north, the airport to the east, San Ángel and the

UNAM to the south, or the Bosque de Chapultepec to the west; this roughly corresponds to the extent of Metro coverage. A rectangular series of routes (the **Circuito Interior**) and a system of thoroughfares **(Ejes Viales)** help make cross-city travel manageable. Of these, the **Eje Central,** commonly known as **Lázaro Cárdenas,** is the central north-south route. At a more local level, the city is difficult to know well; even locals don't have it all down. What's more, many different neighborhoods use the same street names. Still, it is only a matter of cardinal directions and good old-fashioned trial and error before you've mastered the basics of this megalopolis. The most important thing is to know the name of the **colonia** (neighborhood). Mexico City has over 350 such *colonias;* **Col. Polanco, Zona Rosa, Col. Roma,** and **Col. Juárez** are some of the most touristed. Disregard street numbers and orient yourself using nearby monuments, museums, *glorietas* (traffic circles), cathedrals, and skyscrapers. If you are brave enough to drive around the city, a good map of the outer routes is essential. The **Guía Roji Ciudad de México** (170 pesos) is a comprehensive street atlas perfect for those planning to stay in the city for some time.

CIRCUITO INTERIOR AND EJES VIALES

Aside from the large thoroughfares—Insurgentes, Reforma, Chapultepec, and Miguel Alemán—the majority of traffic is routed through the Circuito Interior and via the system of *ejes viales* (axis roads) that run north-south or east-west. *Eje* numbers increase heading away from the *zócalo.* Heavy traffic inhibits fast travel along the *ejes* and Circuito.

CITY CENTER

As huge as Mexico City is, most tourist areas lie within easy reach of the city center. Many attractions are on or just off **Paseo de la Reforma,** the broad concourse that runs southwest-northeast, or **Insurgentes,** which cuts north-south through the city. These two main arteries intersect at **Glorieta Cuauhtémoc.** From Bosque de Chapultepec, Reforma proceeds northeast, punctuated by traffic circles, each with a monument in the center. Some of the more famous ones, in southwest-to-northeast order, include: **Glorieta Ángel de la Independencia, Glorieta Cuauhtémoc, and Glorieta Cristóbal Colón.**

Accommodations and food listings for Mexico City are divided according to the areas of most interest to visitors. Moving northeast on Reforma from Chapultepec, the **Zona Rosa** is followed by the area near the **Monumento a la Revolución,** the **Alameda,** and, east of the Alameda, the **Centro Histórico.**

CENTRO HISTÓRICO. The *centro histórico* contains the *zócalo,* the largest number of historical sights and museums, extensive budget accommodations, and inexpensive restaurants. The area is bounded by República de Perú to the north, Pino Suárez to the east, República de El Salvador to the south, and Lázaro Cárdenas to the west. **M: Allende** (Line 2) for accommodations and the Alameda; **M: Zócalo** (Line 2) for the *centro;* **M: Isabel la Católica** (Line 2); and **M: Pino Suárez** (Lines 1, 2) for sites to the south.

THE ALAMEDA. The Alameda, the central city park and its surroundings, contains many great museums, cheap hotels, and a few restaurants. It is right next to the *centro histórico.* The area is bounded by **Pensador Mexicano** to the north, **Lázaro Cárdenas** to the east, **Arcos de Belén** to the south, and **Eje 1 Pte.** (known as Rosales, Guerrero, and Bucareli) to the west. **Plaza Garibaldi** is approximately 500m northeast of the Alameda. **M: Hidalgo** (Lines 2, 3) and **M: Bellas Artes** (Lines 2, 8) for the park, Palacio de Bellas Artes, Plaza Garibaldi, and the post office; and **M: San Juan de Letrán** (Line 8) for most food and accommodations.

THE DEAL ON WHEELS

A bicycle is still an uncommon sight in this notoriously congested megalopolis of narrow colonial streets and exhaust-fueled smog. Yet Mexico City's progressive mayor, Marcelo Ebrard, has been riding to work on the first Monday of every month since July 2007. The trips are part of his ambitious plan to design a more bike-friendly D.F.

First launched in March 2007, the effort attracted a $100,000 grant from the World Bank, which has gone towards opening hundreds of miles of bike lanes, installing bike racks outside Metro stations and city buildings, initiating an urban bike-loan program, and shutting down the *centro*'s major thoroughfares to cars on the last Sunday of every month (8am-1pm) for family-friendly *ciclismo*. The D.F. is not the first city in Mexico to promote the bicycle: Guadalajara debuted a similar program in September 2004.

Visitors can rent bikes in La Condesa from Taller de Bicicletas Orozco, Av. México 13A, at Sonora. M: Sevilla (☎5286 2582; bike rental 30 pesos per hr., 150 pesos per day with ID and 400 peso deposit; open Tu-Su 10am-8pm; cash only) or from the Cicloestación along the Ciclovía, Av. Paseo de la Reforma y Palmas (Su 10am-5pm. Free, with ID.) Join Bicitekas (www.bicitekas.org) for rides from Monumento a la Independencia (W 9pm) or the zócalo (Su 10am).

NEAR THE MONUMENTO A LA REVOLUCIÓN. The area around Monumento a la Revolución—**Col. Buenavista** and **Col. Tabacalera** on the north and south sides of Puente de Alvarado, respectively—contains a large number of inexpensive hotels and eateries, though considerably fewer glitzy attractions than other neighborhoods. It is bounded by **Mosqueta** to the north, **Reforma** to the south and east, **Insurgentes Centro** to the west. **M: Revolución** (Line 2).

ZONA ROSA. The Zona Rosa is the capital's most touristy commercial district, home to some of the country's most active nightlife and known for its gay-friendly areas. The neighborhood is contained by **Reforma** to the north and west, **Insurgentes** to the east, and **Chapultepec** to the south. A few of the area's listings lie just east of Insurgentes, and a string of clubs snakes south past Chapultepec along Insurgentes Sur. The **Bosque de Chapultepec** sits just west of the Zona Rosa. The mostly residential Colonia Roma lies south of the Zona along Insurgentes; cheaper, laid-back versions of the Zona's entertainment, restaurants, and accommodations spill into here. **M: Insurgentes** (Line 1), right in the middle of the action; **M: Sevilla** (Line 1), toward the Glorieta Ángel de la Independencia.

AWAY FROM THE CENTER

THE NORTHERN DISTRICTS. Approximately 3km north of the *zócalo* is the district of **Tlatelolco**, famous for its archaeological site and Plaza de las Tres Culturas. **Metro: Tlatelolco**, Line 3. Approximately 4km farther north lies **La Villa Basílica**, home to the Basílica de Guadalupe and Tepeyac Hill. **M: La Villa Basílica**, Line 6.

THE SOUTHERN DISTRICTS. Several major southern districts are strung along Insurgentes Sur, 10-15km southwest of the *zócalo*. Southwest to northeast are **Ciudad Universitaria** (**M: Universidad**, Line 3), the suburb **San Ángel** (**M: M. A. Quevedo**, Line 3), and posh **Coyoacán** (**M: Coyoacán**, Line 3). Approximately 20km southeast of the *zócalo* is **Xochimilco** (**M: Tasqueña**, Line 2), where the hustle and bustle of the city invades the once-calm canals.

🄴 LOCAL TRANSPORTATION

BY METRO

Cheap, spotless, and efficient, the Metro never ceases to amaze. Built for the Olympic Games in the late 1960s, it now transports nine million people per day—more than 3 billion per year—to its 175 destinations. Metro tickets (2 pesos, includes transfers) are sold in *taquillas* (ticket booths) at every station. Trains run M-F 5am-12:30am, Sa 6am-1:30am, Su 7am-12:30am. During rush hour (M-F 7:30-9:30am, 2-4pm, and 6-9pm) commuters pack in like sardines; getting on and off can be a daunting and sometimes impossible task.

Theft on the Metro is rampant yet avoidable. It's a good idea to carry bags in front of you or on your lap. The safest place in a crowded car is with your back to the wall and your belongings in front of you. Remember that rear pockets are easy to pick, front pockets are safer, and empty pockets are best. Because of overcrowding, large bags or suitcases are sometimes not allowed on the Metro. If you insist on carrying a big pack, avoid rush hour.

Most transfer stations have information booths with Metro maps, also available at the tourist office. Also helpful are the **Dirección General de Servicio de Transporte Público Individual,** Álvaro Obregón 269 (☎ 5209 9911, ext. 1533; open M-F 9am-3pm and 6-9pm) and the **Sistema de Transporte Colectivo Metro,** Delicias 67 (☎ 5709 1133, ext. 5051; open M-F 8am-9pm). Almost all stations have guards and security offices; all must have a *jefe de la estación* (chief of station) in a marked office to deal with riders' concerns. The **Oficina de Objetos Extraviados,** in **M: Candelaria** (Lines 1, 4), handles lost belongings. (☎ 5542 5397. Open M-F 9am-4pm.)

■ EL METROPOLITÁN. Some Metro stops are sights in their own right. Nearly every transfer station boasts some kind of exhibit, from elementary school drawings of the Metro system to a recreation of a London theater.

Pino Suárez, Lines 1, 2: a small Aztec building at mid-transfer.

La Raza, Lines 3, 5: Túnel de la Ciencia (Tunnel of Science). Nifty fractals glow in the tunnel under a black-lit map of the constellations.

Zócalo, Line 2: models of the *zócalo* as it has appeared throughout history.

Bellas Artes, Lines 2, 8: Aztec statuettes, replicas from the Templo Mayor.

Cien Metros, Line 5: an exhibit of outer space.

Auditorio, Line 7: details the history of Metros world wide.

BY BUS

Peseros, autobuses, trolebuses, and the new Metrobús running up and down Insurgentes compose the city's convenient bus system. *Peseros* (affectionately known as *micros*) are an extremely affordable—if crowded—way to make short, direct trips around town. *Autobuses* are long buses similar to those in Europe and the US. They run on the most popular *pesero* routes, though less often. The fare is anywhere between 2.50 and 5 pesos, depending on your destination, and all destinations cost 5 pesos from 11pm-6am. Destinations are posted on the front window. If you are unsure, ask the driver: "*¿Va a...?*" ("Are you going to...?"). *Trolebuses* (electric buses or "trackless trolleys") are even rarer than *autobuses* and charge 3.50 pesos for the smoothest ride in town. The recently installed and incredibly efficient Metrobús runs up and down Insurgentes 24hr. and charges 5 pesos during the day and 7.50 pesos after 11pm.

In 1997, the city made a great effort to establish set bus stops. Look for the nifty stainless steel bus shelters or the little blue signs with pictures of a *pesero*. The nearest big intersection is probably a designated stop. Note that you must hail buses even from designated stops. Most *peseros* will slow down for anyone with an arm out, even in the middle of a block. To get off, ring the bell (if there is one) or simply shout "*¡La parada, por favor!*" (The stop, please!).

Most *peseros* run until 10pm, but major routes—on Reforma, between Chapultepec and San Ángel, and along Insurgentes—run 24hr. Other *pesero* routes are M: Hidalgo to CU (via Reforma, Bucareli, and Cuauhtémoc); La Villa to

MEXICO CITY

Chapultepec (via Reforma); Reforma to Auditorio (via Reforma and Juárez); *zócalo* to Chapultepec (via 5 de Mayo and Reforma); San Ángel to Izazaga (via 5 de Mayo and Reforma); Bolívar to CU/Coyoacán (via Bolívar in the *centro*); San Ángel to M: Insurgentes (via Av. de la Paz and Insurgentes Sur); and M: Chapultepec to San Ángel, La Merced, and the airport.

BY TAXI

Due to increased hijackings, robberies, and rapes in the 1990s, the US State Department issued a warning against hailing cabs off the street—including the lime-green VW bugs. If you're traveling by taxi, calling a **sitio taxi** (radio taxi) usually ensures a trouble-free ride. Late at night when buses no longer run, *sitios* are worth the cost (about twice as much as regular taxis). Ask at your hotel or check the yellow pages for the best rates; if it comes to it, an overpriced taxi recommended by a nightclub or restaurant is better than nothing. Despite their names, *sitio* companies often don't operate *sitios* (stands). If you can't locate a *sitio* number or a hotel taxi, try **Servi-taxi** (☎ 5271 2560). To get to the airport in a pinch, call **Transporte Terrestre al Aeropuerto** (☎ 5571 9106). Convenient taxi stands at the bus station and airport will give you a fixed rate. Tips aren't required, but they're always accepted. If you insist on using *taxis libres* (cruising taxis), make sure that the picture on the displayed badge matches the driver's face—if it doesn't, or if there isn't one, don't get in. You may want to note the license plate number and driver's name, and avoid riding alone. Alternatively, chat up a taxi driver and get his or her number so that you will have a reliable taxi you can call without having to face the high fares of a *sitio*. Finally, be aware that four-door taxis have easier escape routes than the two-door VW Bugs.

GREEN MEANS GO. When flagging a taxi from the street in the D.F., check the stripes on the license plates—if it has a green or an orange stripe, the taxi is legit. If it has a regular license plate, it's a *pirata* (pirate) taxi, and you should steer clear.

BY CAR

Driving is the most complicated and least economical way to get around, not to mention the easiest way to get lost. The city's drivers are notoriously reckless and aggressive, roads are over-trafficked and confusing, divider lines are frequently absent, pedestrians pounce at any sign of hesitation, and stop signs are planted haphazardly. Red lights are so routinely defied that police often have to direct traffic. If your car breaks down, call the **Asociación Mexicana Automovilística (AMA;** ☎ 5242 0222, toll-free 800 911 026) for assistance. Wait beside your car with a raised hood.

AND ON THE SEVENTH DAY... All vehicles, even those of non-Mexican registration, are subject to Mexico City's strict anti-smog regulations. Restrictions apply Monday-Friday 5am-10pm, and penalties for violations are stiff. Every vehicle must "rest" one day per week and stay off the streets. The last digit of the license plate determines the day. Note that some cars manufactured after 1995 may be exempt from the limitations.
Monday: 5/6. **Tuesday:** 7/8. **Wednesday:** 3/4. **Thursday:** 1/2. **Friday:** 9/0.

Parking within the city is seldom a problem, as garages are everywhere (4-8 pesos per hr.). Be wary of valet parking; cars sometimes wind up with the wrong person. Street parking is difficult to find, and vandalism is common. Police will put an *inmobilizador* (car boot) on your wheels if you park illegally, and in some cases they may just tow your car. If you return to an empty space, locate the nearest police depot (not station) to find out whether your vehicle has been towed—or stolen. If anything is missing from your car and you suspect that the police tampered with it, call the English-speaking **LOCATEL** (☎ 5658 1111).

Car rental rates are exorbitant, driving is a hassle, and the entire process is draining. To rent a car you must be at least 21 years old, have a valid driver's license (from any country), and a passport or tourist card. Prices for rentals at different agencies tend to be similarly high: a small VW or Nissan with insurance, tax (known as IVA), and unlimited km costs about 450-600 pesos per day or 3000-3500 pesos per week. Most agencies have offices at the airport or in the Zona Rosa: **Avis,** at the airport (☎ 5762 3262, call center 5588 8888; www.avis.com.mx; open 24hr.) and at Reforma 308 (☎ 5511 2228; open M-F 9am-2pm and 4-6pm, Sa-Su 9am-4pm); **Budget,** at the airport (☎ 5271 4322; www.budget.com.mx; open 24hr.) and at Hamburgo 68 (☎ 5533 0450; open M-F 7am-9pm, Sa-Su 8am-4pm).

⓴ PRACTICAL INFORMATION

TOURIST AND FINANCIAL SERVICES

Tourist Office: Secretaria de Turismo del Distrito Federal, Nuevo León 56 (☎ 5212 0206, toll-free 800 008 9090; www.mexicocity.gob.mx), in Col. Hipódromo Condesa. A government office that mainly deals with administrative matters. Open M-F 9am-6pm. Tourists are better off visiting one of the 11 **info booths** in the city, which have excellent information as well as city and Metro maps. Booth locations include: the airport, near the Museo de Antropología, Villa Basílica, Bellas Artes, Catedral, Cien Metros, Glorieta Ángel de la Independencia, TAPO, Taxqueña, Templo Mayor, and the Observatorio. Open daily 9am-7pm.

Tourist Card (FMT) Info: Secretaria de Gobernación, Dirección General de Servicios Migratorios, Ejército Nacional 862 (☎ 5387 2646 or 2181 0164), at Periférico in Col. Palanco. M: Polanco. From the station, take an "Instituto Nacional de Migración" *pesero;* get off before you reach Periférico. Office can help extend your FMT or clear up immigration problems. Arrive early to avoid long lines. Open M-F 9am-1pm.

Sendetur, Insurgentes Centro 137 (☎ 5566 5515, ext 118 and 217; toll-free 800 560 9593; www.sendetur.com.mx), in Col. San Rafael. National tourism office. Two other locations, Av. Taxqueña 1320 (☎ 5549 6184), in Col. Campestre Churubusco, and Av. Eje Central 4907 (☎ 5368 5797), in Col. Magdalena de las Salinas.

Embassies: For embassy locations in Mexico City, see p. 9.

Currency Exchange: Exchange rates in the city are generally pretty good. Banks offer one exchange rate and usually charge commission. *Casas de cambio* keep longer hours and give better exchange rates; some are open Su. Among those in the *centro*, along Reforma, and in the Zona Rosa: **Casa de Cambio Tíber,** on Río Tíber 112, at Río Volga, 1 block from the Ángel, behind a Sanborn's (☎ 5208 7688; open M-F 10:30am-5pm); **Casa de Cambio Catorce,** Reforma 122 (☎ 5705 2460; open M-F 9am-5pm). Hotels often exchange currency, but at unfavorable rates.

American Express: Reforma 350 (☎ 5207 7282), in the Torre del Ángel, at Lancaster and the Glorieta del Ángel, in the Zona Rosa. Cashes personal and traveler's checks and accepts customers' mail and money wires. Report lost credit cards and lost traveler's checks here. Open M-F 9am-6pm, Sa 9am-1pm.

LOCAL SERVICES

Luggage Storage: At the airport and bus stations.

English-Language Bookstores: Global Books, Gante 4-A (☎5510 9362; www.global-book.com.mx), off Madero. English textbooks as well as dictionaries and reading material. Open M-Sa 10am-7pm. Also popular is **Librería Gandhi,** Av. Juárez 4 (☎2625 0606; www.gandhi.com.mx), in front of Bellas Artes. Open M-Sa 10am-9pm, Su 11am-8pm. Another at Quevedo 121, near M: M.A. de Quevedo in San Ángel. Open M-F 9am-10pm, Sa-Su 10am-10pm. Another at Madero 32, between Bolívar and Motolinía. M: Allende. Open M-Sa 10am-9pm, Su 11am-8pm.

English-Language Library: Biblioteca Benjamin Franklin, Liverpool 31 (☎5080 2089; www.usembassy-mexico.gov/biblioteca.htm), between Berlin and Dinamarca, behind the wax museum. Books, newspapers, and periodicals. 16+. Open M-F 11am-7pm.

GLBT Resources: Perhaps the best way to find out what's going on in the gay community is through the grapevine. *Tiempo Libre* and the smaller *Ser Gay* (available in gay clubs) provide some info on gay social and political events along with nightlife listings. *Ser Gay's* website (www.sergay.com.mx) contains a wealth of information on gay rights issues, gay-friendly businesses, and medical professionals. **Colectivo Sol,** Cerrada Cuauonchtlill (☎5666 5436 or 5606 7216), in Col. Pueblo Quieto, provides info on upcoming political and social events. Write to: Apdo. 13-320, Av. México 13, D.F. 03500. **LesVoz** (www.lesvoz.org.mx), the literary and political journal for lesbian and bisexual women, is a springboard for community development.

Women's Advocacy: Instituto de las Mujeres del Distrito Federal, Tacuba 76 (☎5512 2831; www.inmujer.df.gob.mx/). Gives legal and psychological advice to women and helps mothers find nurseries for their children. Open M-F 9am-7pm.

Information: ☎040.

EMERGENCY AND COMMUNICATIONS

Emergency: ☎060.

Police: Secretaria de Seguridad Pública (☎060 or 061). **Protección Civil** (☎5683 2838).

Tourist Police: Infotur Seguridad Turística (☎5250 0123, toll-free 800 5903 9200). **Seguridad Publica** (☎5242 5100). **Patrullas de Auxilio Turístico** (☎5250 0123 or 8221). A car service for tourists that deals primarily with accidents, breakdowns, and thefts. **Procuradura General de Justicia,** Av. Niños Héroes 61 (☎5242 6620), in the Col. Doctores. A department of justice catering especially to tourists. Files reports on anything from robberies to lost tourist cards. Open 24hr.

Emergency Shelter: Albergue Centro de Asistencia e Integración Social Coruña, Sur 65-A 3246 (☎5440 2974), between Coruña and Santanita.

LOCATEL: (☎5658 1111). The city's official hotline for missing persons and cars.

Rape Center: Hospital de Traumatología de Balbuena, Cecilio Robelo 103 (☎5552 1602 or 5764 0339), M: Moctezuma (Line 1). Open 24hr.

Legal Advice: Supervisión General de Servicios a la Comunidad, Gabriel Hernández 56 (☎5345 5193), near M: Balderas. Call if you are the victim of a robbery or accident and need legal advice. Open M-F 9am-3pm and 5-7pm.

Red Cross: Ejército Nacional 1032 (☎5557 5757, 5758, or 5759), in Col. Polanco.

Pharmacies: Small *farmacias* can be found on almost every street corner. All **Sanborn's** and supermarkets carry prescription medications.

Medical Services: US Embassy (p. 10) has a list of doctors' addresses and phone numbers. In an emergency, ask for the nearest **IMSS** (Social Security) clinic; there is usually one in each *colonia*.

Secretaria de Salud del Distrito Federal, Xocongo 225 (☎5132 1200), in Col. Transito. Has info on all city hospitals. Open M-F 8am-9pm.

American British Cowdray (ABC) Hospital, Calle Sur 138 (☎5230 8000, emergency 5230 8161), at Observatorio Col. Las Américas. Open 24hr. AmEx/D/MC/V.

Torre Médica, José María Iglesias 21 (☎5705 1820), at Mariscal. M: Revolución (Line 2). Open 24hr.

Courier Services: UPS, Reforma 404 (☎5228 7900), in front of Cine Diana. Open M-F 9am-7pm. **Federal Express,** Reforma 308 (☎5228 9904, toll-free 800 900 1100; www.fedex.com/mx/), in Col. Juárez near Ángel de Independencia. Open M-F 9am-7pm, Sa 9am-2pm.

Internet Access: Internet terminals abound in corner stores and informal cyber cafes.

Central Post Office: (☎5521 1408 or 5518 0508; www.sepomex.gob.mx), on Lázaro Cárdenas at Tacuba, across from the Palacio de Bellas Artes. Open for stamps and *lista de correos* (window 3) M-F 8am-8pm, Sa 8am-4pm, Su 8am-noon. **Mexpost** inside. Open M-F 8am-5pm, Sa 8am-12:30pm. Postal museum upstairs with turn-of-the-century mailboxes and other old equipment. **Postal Code:** 06002.

▐ ACCOMMODATIONS

Mexico City offers over 1000 hotels. Rooms abound in the *centro histórico* and near the Alameda Central. The best budget bargains can be found near the Monumento a la Revolución in the streets around the Plaza de la República. Avoid the sections around the Alameda and anywhere that makes you feel uncomfortable. Beware of any hotel marked "Hotel Garage," where patrons enter rooms directly from the garage for illicit rendezvous. Rooms for 180-250 pesos for one bed and 250-300 pesos for two beds should be clean and have carpeting, a TV, and a telephone. Some budget hotels charge according to the number of beds, not per person, and beds tend to be large enough for two. If you don't mind snuggling (or need an excuse), sharing a bed can save major pesos. Finally, always ask to look at a room before you accept it; this is easier to do after check-out time (noon-3pm).

The shabby neighborhoods by the four bus stations generally offer expensive rooms. If you arrive late at night, it is not safe to walk even the few blocks to your hotel. Both the TAPO and Poniente stations are in especially unsafe neighborhoods. If you arrive at either, take the Metro or a taxi to safer accommodations.

ACCOMMODATIONS BY PRICE

CH Centro Histórico **A** The Alameda **M** Near the Monumento a la Revolución **ZR** Zona Rosa **CO** Coyoacán **S** San Ángel **CT** Near Chapultepec

UNDER 170 PESOS (❶)		Hotel Pensylvania	M
▓Casa de los Amigos	M	▓Hostel Mundo Joven Catedral (HI)	CH
Hotel Oxford	M	**220-270 PESOS (❸)**	
Hostal Amigo	CH	Hotel Calvin	A
Hostal Moneda	CH	Hotel Manolo I	A
Hostal Virreyes	A	Hotel Principal	CH
Hostel Home	ZR	Hotel Rioja	CH
Mexico City Hostel	CH	**270-325 PESOS (❹)**	
YWCA	A	Hotel Azores	CH
		Hostel Embassy	ZR
170-220 PESOS (❷)		Hotel Washington	CH
Hotel Juárez	CH	Posada Viena	ZR
Hotel Consul	M	**OVER 325 PESOS (❺)**	
Hotel Ibiza	M	Hotel Catedral	CH
Hotel Isabel	CH	Hotel Marlow	A
Hotel Lafayette	CH		

CENTRO HISTÓRICO

The accommodations in the *centro histórico* come in all shapes and sizes: busy dorms filled with young internationals, tranquil rooms in historic buildings, and ritzier modernized hotels. Best of all, you're right in the *centro* of things, with many of the city's most spectacular sights within walking distance. Although the quiet streets at night are a huge change from the bustle of the day, nighttime activity is on the rise, and the government has been improving safety conditions at night as well as cleaning up the city. **Metro: Zócalo** (Line 2). Also **Isabel la Católica** (Line 1), **Bellas Artes** (Lines 2, 8), and **Allende** (Line 2).

■ **Hostel Mundo Joven Catedral (HI),** República de Guatemala 4 (☎5518 1726 or 1065; www.hostelcatedral.com), behind the cathedral. Young internationals snack at the cafe/bar in the spacious lobby, surf the web (15 pesos per hr., free Wi-Fi), and hang out after hours at the rooftop bar for the best view in town. Entertainment room, kitchen, washing machine (20 pesos), lockers (padlocks 20 pesos), free luggage storage, purified water, and travel agency inside. Breakfast and walking tour included. Check-out 11am. Brightly lit, immaculate 4-6 bed dorms 145 pesos, with HI or ISIC card 112 pesos; doubles 369 pesos, with bath 389. MC/V. ❷

Hostal Moneda, Moneda 8 (☎5522 5821; www.hostalmoneda.com.mx), between the Palacio Nacional and the Templo Mayor. Friendly, international vibe with a helpful staff. Rooms are not luxurious, but stay includes a walking tour. Great view from rooftop bar and hammocked terrace. Kitchen, some lockers, luggage storage, self-service laundry (35 pesos), Internet, and elevator. Breakfast included. Check-out 11am. Book online for discounts on stay and tour packages. 6-12 bed dorm 115 pesos, 3-5 bed dorm 165 pesos, 1-2 bed room 390 pesos. ❶

Hotel Juárez, Callejón de 5 de Mayo 17 (☎5512 6929 or 0568; hoteljuarez@prodigy.net.mx), in an alley between Isabel la Católica and Palma. Quiet courtyard with fountain provides respite from the bustle of the *zócalo*. Comfortable, carpeted rooms with gleaming bathrooms, TV, and phone; some with balconies. Check-out 1pm. Singles 190 pesos; doubles 250 pesos, 4-person max. Cash only. ❷

Hotel Isabel, Isabel la Católica 63 (☎5518 1213; www.hotel-isabel.com.mx), at Rep. del Salvador. The old Mexico atmosphere, gorgeous atrium, and inner courtyard make this hotel well worth its non-central location. Large rooms with TV, phone, and safe. Rooms without bath are windowless. Internet in lobby. (10 pesos per 20 min.) Elevator. Pricey restaurant and bar attached. Check-out noon. Reservations recommended. Singles 145 pesos, with bath 210 pesos; doubles 210/300 pesos; triples with bath 440 pesos; quads with bath 560 pesos; quints with bath 670 pesos. Cash only. ❷

Hotel Principal, Bolívar 29 (☎5521 1333 or 2032; www.hotelprincipal.com.mx), between 16 de Septiembre and Madero. Tiled hallways stem off a large, plant-filled atrium to well-kept rooms with high ceilings. Rooms have phone, TV and safety boxes. Check-out 2pm. Singles 120 pesos, with bath 225; doubles 315-390 pesos; triples 410-485 pesos; quads 505-540 pesos, each additional person 95 pesos. MC/V. ❸

Hostal Amigo, Isabel la Católica 61 (☎5512 3464; www.hostelamigo.com). Several blocks from the *zócalo*. Laid-back vibes—not lavish rooms—make this a backpackers' mecca. Those with gratuitous curiosity won't miss the writing on the wall. Walking tour, kitchen, lockers, luggage storage, laundry (40 pesos), Internet, and pool table. Breakfast included. Check-out 11am. Book online for discounts on stay and tour packages. 10-12 bed dorm 115 pesos; 6-8 bed dorm 135 pesos; 3-4 bed dorm 150 pesos; double without bath 333 pesos. MC/V. ❶

Hotel Rioja, 5 de Mayo 45 (☎5521 8333 or 8273), 1 block west of the *zócalo*. Clean, comfortable, and centrally located. Rooms with windows facing the street are bright and cool, but noisy. Internet (10 pesos per 20 min.). Check-out noon. Singles 200 pesos, with windows 230; doubles 220-270/250-300 pesos; triples 300/360; quads 340/390. Cash only. ❸

Hotel Washington, 5 de Mayo 54 (☎5512 3502 or 4058). Central location. Cozy rooms with bath, telephone, and complimentary bottled water. Some rooms with balconies. Check-out 1:30pm. Rooms with 1 bed 230-280 pesos; 2 beds 280-320 pesos. Cash only. ❹

Mexico City Hostel, Rep. de Brasil 8 (☎5512 7731 or 5512 3666; www.mexicocityhostel.com). Around the corner from the cathedral. A modern hostel in a renovated colonial building. Less social atmosphere than some other hostels listed. Kitchen, lockers, luggage storage, self-service laundry (40 pesos), Internet (10 pesos per hr.), free Wi-Fi, TV lounge. Breakfast included. Check-out noon. 12-bed dorms 100 pesos; 8-10 bed dorms 130 pesos; double without bath 300 pesos. MC/V. ❶

Hotel Lafayette, Motolinía 40 (☎5521 9640), at 16 de Septiembre. Several blocks from the *zócalo*. Not well-lit at night. Clean rooms with TV, phone, safe, and bath. Rooms facing Motolinía have more light. Check-out 1pm. Prices exclude tax. 1-bed doubles 190 pesos; doubles 260 pesos; triples 340 pesos; quads 420 pesos; each additional person in doubles and triples 50 pesos. Cash only. ❷

Hotel Azores, Rep. de Brasil 25 (☎5521 5220; www.hotelazores.com), less than 2 blocks north of the cathedral. Sleek, business-oriented hotel with attached restaurant and bar. Avoid noise from the street in an interior room facing the solarium. Rooms have TV, phone (free local calls), safe box, hair dryer, and Internet (10 pesos per 20min.). Check-out 1:30pm. Singles 280 pesos; doubles 290; 2-bed doubles 330 pesos, triples 380, quads 400; each additional person 100 pesos. D/MC/V. ❹

Hotel Catedral, Donceles 95 (☎5521 6183; www.hotelcatedral.com.mx), 1 block behind the cathedral. Luxury hotel. Elegant bar and restaurant, rooftop terrace, and elevators. Rooms with phone, cable TV, bath with purified water, and balconies. Wi-Fi and tour agency in lobby. Singles 475-550 pesos; doubles 660 pesos; triples 725 pesos; quads 785 pesos; 3-beds 870 pesos. MC/V. ❺

THE ALAMEDA

Staying in the Alameda means dealing with the construction bombarding the area. You're better off finding a hotel in the *centro* and making the short trip to the sights. The area is being cleaned up and there are still good options in this district, but as with most places in the D.F., remember to be careful at night. **Metro: Juárez** (Line 3), **Balderas** (Line 1), **Salto del Agua** (Line 8), and **San Juan de Letrán** (Line 8).

Hostal Virreyes, Izazaga 8 (☎5521 4180; www.hostalvirreyes.com.mx), on the corner of Cárdenas. M: Salto del Agua. Recently remodeled hostel great for young travelers. Bright, clean, and spacious dorms with interior bath; some with lockers. Entrance with mural and 6th-floor terrace with view. Elevator, common room with TV, kitchen, and restaurant. Internet access 4 pesos per minute; free Wi-Fi. Breakfast included. Some F nights guest DJ plays in lobby. Check-out 2pm. 4- to 8-bed dorms 120 pesos; private rooms 320 pesos. Dorms 10% discount with ISIC. AmEx/MC/V. ❶

Hotel Calvin, José Azueta 33 (☎5521 7952 or 1361; www.hotelcalvin.com), on the corner of Independencia. The closest you'll get to the Alameda Central without parting with too many pesos. Carpeted rooms with phone, room service, and TV; some with hot tub. Singles 190-200 pesos; doubles 190-360 pesos; triples 260-410 pesos; quads 310-510 pesos. MC/V. ❸

YWCA, Humbolt 62 (☎5510 3870; www.ywca.com.mx), between Artículo 123 and Morelos. M: Juárez. Though the view is nothing special, this hostel has neat, clean rooms for both men and women at exceptionally low rates. Ring buzzer at entrance. Elevator, TV room, kitchen, and lockers. Guest discount for activities including spinning, tai-chi, and yoga (30 pesos per class). 2- to 4-bed same-sex dorms 90 pesos. Singles 95 pesos, with bath 110 pesos. Monthly rates available. Cash only. ❶

Hotel Manolo I, Luis Moya 111 (☎5521 3739 or 7709), near Arcos de Belén. Out of the way, but a good choice. An escape from dingy streets. Clean, huge rooms with king-sized bed, phone, TV, and large bath. Elevator. Check-out 2pm. Singles and doubles M-Th and Su 200 pesos, F-Sa 220 pesos. D/MC/V. ❸

Hotel Marlowe, Independencia 17 (☎5521 9540; www.hotelmarlowe.com.mx). Ritzy hotel right by the Alameda. Gym and sauna. Business center with Internet. (10 pesos per 15min. Free Wi-Fi.) Check-out 1pm. Singles 480-550 pesos; doubles 600 pesos; triples 680-740 pesos; quads 770 pesos; suites 600-750 pesos; each additional person 90 pesos. AmEx/MC/V. ❺

NEAR THE MONUMENTO A LA REVOLUCIÓN

Hotels near the Monumento a la Revolución are quieter than their counterparts in the *centro* or the Alameda. It is easy to find a cheap, nice room and, although the area itself does not offer much to do, the location, between the Alameda and the Zona Rosa, is tops. **M: Revolución** (Line 2).

⊠ **Casa de los Amigos,** Mariscal 132 (☎5705 0521 or 0646; www.casadelosamigos.org), between Iglesias and Arriaga. Once the home of painter José Clemente Orozco and now a Quaker house accommodating backpackers, graduate school students, and eco-warriors from around the world. Lounge, kitchen, and Internet available. No drugs or alcohol allowed. Breakfast M-Sa 8-10am (15 pesos). 2-day min. stay; 15-day max. for those not studying in Mexico or volunteering for one of Amigo's service projects. Reception open daily 8am-9:30pm. Check-out noon. Dorms 100 pesos; singles 130-190 pesos; doubles 180-250 pesos, with bath 290 pesos. Cash only. ❶

Hotel Oxford, Mariscal 67 (☎5566 0500), next to the small park behind the Museo San Carlos. Large, comfortable, dark wood rooms with phone, TV, and some with views of the park. At night, the adjoining bar attracts a lively local crowd. Check-out 1pm. Singles 120 pesos; doubles 200 pesos; rooms with king-sized bed 150 pesos; each additional person 50 pesos. Cash only. ❶

Hotel Ibiza, Arriaga 22 (☎5566 8155 or 8398), between Edison and Mariscal. Colorful rooms have small bath, phone, and TV. Rooms on higher floors are quieter. Check-out noon. Singles 150 pesos; doubles 180 pesos. Cash only. ❷

Hotel Pensylvania, Mariscal 101 (☎5592 5250), at Arriaga. Truly beautiful baths compensate for otherwise unmemorable rooms with carpets, TV, and phone. Check-out noon. Singles 130-160 pesos, with king-sized bed 150 pesos; 1-bed doubles 150-190 pesos; 2-bed doubles 230 pesos; triples 270 pesos. Cash only. ❷

Hotel Consul, Insurgentes Centro 133 (☎5705 0975), between Antonio Caso and Sullivan. Three blocks from M: Revolución. Spacious rooms are dark but generally clean, with TV and phone (free local calls). Check-out 2pm. Singles 180 pesos, with king-size bed 190 pesos; doubles 260 pesos; each additional person 60 pesos. Cash only. ❷

NEAR THE ZONA ROSA

Cheap hotel rooms are almost impossible to find; prices become more affordable as you cross Chapultepec and head away from the Zona Rosa. The few affordable rooms in the glamour district, however, should be reserved far in advance.

Hostel Home, Tabasco 303 (☎5511 1683; www.hostelhome.com.mx), between Valladolid and Medellín. M: Insurgentes. From the Metro, walk down Insurgentes Sur for 6 blocks and turn right on Tabasco. 10min. walk from the Zona Rosa. Attractive European building with clean, quiet dorm rooms. No private lockers. Shared kitchen and TV room. Free Internet. Check-out 2pm. 6- to 8-bed dorms 110 pesos. Cash only. ❶

Posada Viena, Marsella 28 (☎5566 0700 or 1-888-698-0690; hotelvie@prodigy.net.mx), at Dinamarca. M: Cuauhtémoc. Gorgeous hacienda-style decor and spacious, well-decorated rooms with TV and enormous baths. Internet 40 pesos per hr. Free Wi-Fi. Breakfast 65 pesos. Check-out noon. Singles and doubles 585 pesos; 3-4 person suite 702 pesos, fifth person 120 pesos. AmEx/MC/V. ❹

Hotel Embassy, Puebla 115 (☎5207 8770 or 5208 0859), between Córdoba and Mérida, 3 blocks east of M: Insurgentes. Despite the less-than-pleasant looks of the fish in the fish tank, luxury rooms have huge bed, pristine bath, carpet, phone, and TV. Check-out 1:30pm. Singles 290 pesos; doubles 340 pesos; triples 380 pesos; quads 420 pesos. D/MC/V. ❹

◘ FOOD

Meal options fall into six basic categories: very cheap (and sometimes risky) vendor stalls scattered about the streets; fast, inexpensive, and generally safe *taquerías;* slightly more formal *cafeterías;* more pricey and decorous Mexican restaurants; locally popular US-style eateries; and expensive international fare. In addition, US fast-food chains mass-produce predictable fare for the timid palate. **VIPs** and **Sanborn's,** popular with middle-class Mexicans, run hundreds of restaurants throughout the capital. Vegetarians will have more to eat here than anywhere else in Mexico: the bright orange chain **Super Soya** has soy versions of many Mexican and US favorites served up in freshly-made waffle cones (15 pesos). Local **supermarkets** have higher prices than *mercados,* but lower prices than corner stores. Except for **Bodega Comercial Mexicana,** Carranza 125, at Correo (☎5510 9758. Open daily 7:30am-10pm.), most are far from the *centro,* at residential Metro stops. **Superama,** Río Balsas 23 at Río Sena, in the Zona Rosa, is directly outside M: Polanco (Line 7). (☎5525 5460. Open daily 7am-11pm.) For fresh produce and meats, try **La Merced** (p. 139), the mother of all markets.

CENTRO HISTÓRICO

If you are wary of eating from street vendors you'll be hard pressed to find true budget options in the *centro.* Locals offset throngs of tourists, keeping prices lower than in Zona Rosa but not as low as near Revolución. After the Zona Rosa, this is the best place for vegetarian fare. **Metro: Zócalo** (Line 2), **Bellas Artes** (Lines 2, 8), **Allende** (Line 2), and **Isabel la Católica** (Line 1).

Cafe Tacuba, Tacuba 28 (☎5518 4950 or 5521 2048). M: Allende. Founded in 1912, this restaurant continues to impress visitors with its vaulted ceilings, stained glass, and *azulejo* tiles. Its storied history includes Diego Rivera's wedding feast and the 1936 murder of a Mexican politician. Anthony Quinn movie buffs may recognize it from *Viva Zapata* as well. Tasty *enchiladas especiales tacuba* (115 pesos) are a restaurant favorite. *Antojitos* 28-79 pesos. Entrees 62-151 pesos. Open daily 8am-11:30pm. AmEx/MC/V. ❹

Cafe El Popular, 5 de Mayo 50 y 52 (☎5518 6081), between Allende and Motolinía. True to its name, this diner packs in locals and tourists alike. Big portions. The *pan dulce* (6 pesos) is a must-try. Eggs 13-34 pesos. *Tamales* 21 pesos. Meat entrees 42-48 pesos. Open 24hr. Cash only. ❷

Restaurantes Vegetarianos del Centro, Madero 56, upstairs (☎5521 6880), between Rep. de Chile and Palma. Another at Filomeno Mata 13 (☎5510 0113), between 5 de

Mayo and Madero, is of lower quality; 3 other locations lie to the south and in Colonia Roma. This all-vegetarian restaurant with colorful walls has an array of meatless takes on traditional Mexican dishes. Choose between *comida corrida* (65 pesos) or specialties like *taquitos compuestos, croquetas de manzana,* or *hamburguesa con papas* (38 pesos each). Open daily 8am-8pm. MC/V. ❸

Bistro Moneda, Moneda 10 (☎5542 0088). This bright local joint serves Mexican delicacies like *chilaquiles con pollo* (34 pesos) as well as American-style burgers (46 pesos). A top pick for tourists on a tight budget. Filling breakfast *paquetes* (46-59 pesos) served until 12:30pm. Open M-Sa 10am-6:30pm. Cash only. ❸

Dulcería de Celaya, 5 de Mayo 39 (☎5521 1787), 2 blocks west of the zócalo. Beyond the visual appeal of candied tropical fruits in the windows, this sweet shop is itself worth a visit: founded in 1874, its mirrored walls and filigreed molding elegantly showcase sugary confections. Traditional Mexican dulces from 6.50 to 300 pesos. Open daily 10:30am-7:30pm. AmEx/MC/V. ❸

Fonda "El Generalito," Filomeno Mata 18-H (☎5518 3711), between Madero and 5 de Mayo. The owner of this small restaurant has added his unique art to the colorful walls and tables. Popular with locals at lunchtime. 2 levels of seating. Rotating *comida corrida* (37 pesos) and breakfast (25-35 pesos). Open daily 8:30am-6pm. Cash only. ❸

Restaurante "Teka-Fe," Motolinía 31-A (☎5521 9728), between Madero and 16 de Septiembre. Plates from Puebla line the walls of this quaint, traditional restaurant. The beef *tampiqueña* (58 pesos) and *pollo en mole poblano* (62 pesos) are sure to please, and the delicious, homemade desserts (24-26 pesos) are a must. Open M-Sa 9am-7pm. Cash only. ❹

Rinconada, Rinconada de Jesús 13 (☎5542 6809 or 3245), facing the Plaza de Jesús at the corner of Pino Suárez and Rep. del Salvador. Located in the courtyard of a beautiful stone building built in 1535 and restored in 1969. Specialties include *steak rinconada* with almonds, pine nuts and raisins (105 pesos), and the *pacholas mixtecas* (75 pesos) served on Th. The friendly staff will gladly transform some dishes into meatless fare. Hearty breakfast (50 pesos) 11am-1pm. Reservations recommended on Th. Piano player serenades 3-5pm. Open M-Sa 11am-6pm. AmEx/MC/V. ❺

Comedor Vegetariano, Motolinía 31 upstairs (☎5512 6515), between Madero and 16 de Septiembre. This homey place has featured original vegetarian variations on Mexican staples since 1936. 4-course *comida corrida* (38 pesos). Fruit and salad buffet 38 pesos, or 12 pesos with the *comida corrida.* Open M-Sa noon-6pm. Cash only. ❸

México Viejo, Tacuba 87 (☎5510 3748) on the northwest corner of the zócalo. Enjoy typical Mexican fare served from an extensive buffet. In the evenings, order dishes like *molcajete* (mixed meats served in a traditional stone bowl; 98 pesos). Breakfast buffet 8am-1pm (70 pesos); lunch buffet 1-6pm (80 pesos). Special prices for groups of 10 or more. Open M-Sa 8am-9pm, Su 8am-6pm. AmEx/MC/V. ❹

THE ALAMEDA

Restaurants are not as abundant here as in the *centro*, but there are some inexpensive choices. For Chinese, go down to Dolores and Independencia. Some restaurants there have better vegetarian options and better deals. The **Parque Alameda,** Juárez 75, next door to the Sheraton Centro Histórico, is a shopping center that has several restaurants as well. **Metro: Hidalgo** (Line 2), **Bellas Artes** (Lines 2 and 8), **Juárez** (Line 3), and **San Juan de Letrán** (Line 8).

▨ **Churrería El Moro,** Cárdenas 42 (☎5512 0896 or 5518 4580). M: San Juan de Letrán (Line 3), between Carranza and 16 de Septiembre. Indulge in *churros* (cinnamon sugar pastry strips) with milk (25 pesos), coffee (27 pesos), or chocolate (33-36 pesos). Choose between 4 types of chocolate: *español* (thick and sweet), *mexicano* (light), *francés* (medium), and *especial* (slightly bitter). Open 24hr. Cash only. ❸

Cano's Restaurant, Carranza 31 (☎5510 2923), between Gante and Bolívar. Enjoy a peaceful and inexpensive lunch in the courtyard of this old building. Hearty breakfast *paquetes* (30 pesos) served 8am-noon. *Comida corrida* 30-40 pesos. Open daily 8am-6pm. Another on Carranza 93 (☎5542 4591). Open daily 10am-6pm. Cash only. ❸

Taco Inn, Tacuba 1 (☎5512 2611), next to the Museo Nacional de Arte. Outdoor seating at this location of the chain places you 50 ft. from the famous Carlos IV statue. Vegetarian options 27-39 pesos. *Fajitas* 47-59 pesos. Open daily 7am-9pm. MC/V. ❸

Oriental, Dolores 27 (☎5521 3093), between Independencia and Artículo 123. Distinguished from other Chinese options by the bronze Buddha at the entrance and paper dragons soaring inside. All the typical dishes, like fried rice with shrimp (66 pesos), and some combination meals (90-135 pesos). Open daily 11am-11pm. AmEx/MC/V. ❺

NEAR THE MONUMENTO A LA REVOLUCIÓN

Without many affluent residents or big tourist draws, this area is dominated by informal cafes, *torterías*, and *taquerías*. This is the spot for hearty portions and low prices. **M: Revolución** (Line 2).

La Casa de los Bisquets, Av. Plaza de la República 4 (☎5546 5225), between the Monumento and Insurgentes. Diner-style restaurant with wide menu of delicious Mexican dishes, a friendly staff, comfy booths, and kids' play area. *Tostadas* 39 pesos. Enchiladas 59-65 pesos. *Menú del día* after 2pm (45 pesos). Open M-F 7am-10pm, Sa 7am-9pm, Su 8am-3pm. D/MC/V. ❸

Cafe Irawo, Insurgentes Centro 121-B and -C (☎5546 5498), between Antonio Caso and Sullivan. Tasty Cuban cuisine and strong coffee satisfy diners in this colorful restaurant decorated with adoring photos of Che Guevara. *Comida corrida* M-F before 6pm 30 pesos; M-F and Sa after 6pm 50 pesos. Cuban *cerveza* (45 pesos) and mojitos (50-70 pesos). F-Sa Karaoke after 9pm. Open M-Th 10:30am-10pm, F 10:30am-2am, Sa 11:30am-4am. Cash only. ❷

Super Cocina los Arcos, Iglesias 26 (☎5535 0525), at Mariscal. Delicious food and quick service lures customers to this small cafeteria. Family-friendly. Most entrees 35-45 pesos. *Comida corrida* 25-40 pesos. Open M-Sa 7am-7pm. Cash only. ❸

La Especial de París, Insurgentes Centro 117 (☎5703 2316). This *nevería* (ice cream parlor) has been in the same family since it started scooping frozen wonders in 1921. 100% natural ingredients, from milkshakes (27 pesos) to delicious dessert crepes (27-29 pesos). Single scoop 16 pesos, double scoop 26 pesos, triple scoop 36 pesos, quadruple scoop 44 pesos. Open daily 11am-9pm. AmEx/D/MC/V. ❷

El Tigre, Mariscal 148 (☎5703 1794), at Iglesias. Home of the *Super Torta Gigante.* Counter seating and friendly cooks enliven this super-typical *lonchería.* Open M-F 9am-10pm, Sa-Su 9am-9pm. Cash only. ❶

ZONA ROSA

With countless restaurants and some of the city's best vegetarian choices, the Zona Rosa has food for all tastes, if not all budgets. *Cafeterías* with fixed menus and *taquerías* cater to the money-conscious. **M: Insurgentes** and **Sevilla** (Line 1).

▨ Vegetariano Yug, Varsovia 3 (☎5533 3296 or 5525 5330; www.lovegetariano.com), between Reforma and Dresde. Also has a cafeteria in the Roma neighborhood. (Puebla 326. ☎5553 5531.) Tasteful Indian-inspired decor and creative "international" vegetable dishes. *Comida corrida* 57-61 pesos. *Paquetes* 49-59 pesos, after 4pm. Upstairs lunch buffet daily 1-5pm; M-F 71 pesos, Sa-Su 76 pesos. Open M-F 7am-9pm, Sa-Su 8:30am-8pm. AmEx/D/MC/V. ❹

El Trompito, Londres 119 (☎5511 1015), between Genova and Amberes. Satisfy your taco cravings at this popular and established joint. Proudly serves the best *tacos de* *pastor* (16 pesos) in the Zona Rosa, garnished with pineapple. 3 tacos 16-31 pesos. *Tortas gigantes* 20-35 pesos. Open M-Sa 1pm-4am, Su 1-9pm. Cash only. ❷

Tacontento, Londres 91-B (☎5514 8073), between Genova and Niza. Festive restaurant with *mariachi* hats and *sarapes* on the walls. Gets especially lively in the evenings when locals stop by for an early beer (20 pesos). Tacos 8-29 pesos. *Tortas* 35-49 pesos. *Comida corrida* M-F 39 pesos. Open M-Th 7pm-midnight, F 7pm-3am, Sa 11am-1am. Cash only. ❸

Restaurante Contrastes, Londres 190-A (☎5511 4222), between Varsovia and Florencia. Colorful paper banners and Mexican-themed murals adorn this conveniently located eatery. Eat in or take out. Tasty *menú del día* 40 pesos. Breakfast 26 pesos. Open M-F 7:30am-5:30pm. Cash only. ❸

1/2 Luna, Florencia 68 (☎5511 2777), between Londres and Liverpool. Small, charming coffee shop with various light food options, along with fresh drinks. Coffee from 12 pesos. Milkshakes 24 pesos. Hamburgers 32-40 pesos. Baguettes 40 pesos. Open M-F 8am-9pm, Sa 10am-6pm. Cash only. ❸

El Mesón de Los Sabores, Ebro 89B (☎5514 4744). Delicious homestyle Mexican cooking in plentiful portions served to a neighborhood crowd. *Menú del día* 40-52 pesos. Open M-F 1-5pm. Cash only. ❸

NEAR CHAPULTEPEC

Food stands inside the Bosque de Chapultepec offer an enormous variety of snacks, but these are always risky for a foreign stomach. The small restaurants cluttered around **M: Chapultepec** (Line 1) are a safer alternative but offer limited food options. For the ritzier tastes, get *antojitos* in the beautiful Colonia Polanco, north of the Museo de Antropología, accessible by **M: Polanco** and **M: Auditorio** (both Line 7).

El Kioskito, Sonora 6 (☎5256 5463; http://kioskito.com.mx), at Chapultepec. Succulent entrees (65-95 pesos) in a lively atmosphere, with tiled fountain and celebrity-photo decor. Most people come for their famous *carnitas* (200 pesos per kilo). You can also eat at the adjoining taco counter (9 pesos per taco). Open M-Sa 8am-9pm, Su 9am-8pm. AmEx/D/MC/V. ❺

Taquería La Pupé, Av. Veracruz 7-101 (☎5211 7028), near M: Chapultepec. Sit-down restaurant offering a diverse menu and satisfying traditional fare. Tacos 5-28 pesos. Breakfasts 15-25 pesos. Specialties 25-40 pesos. Open M-Sa 9am-6:30pm. ❷

Del Bosque, (☎5515 4652 or 5516 4214; www.delbosquerestaurantes.com.mx), at Chapultepec Margen Ote. del Lago Menor, with entrance on Alencastre. Sip fine wine in this classy restaurant jutting over the lake, while you watch kids race toy sailboats. The carp in the water will snap up your leftovers. Del Bosque is the only restaurant in the 2nd section of the park. Fish 115-165 pesos. Meats 150-187 pesos. Sa-Su breakfast buffet 189 pesos, children 130 pesos; lunch buffet 249/130 pesos. Valet parking. Open daily 7am-6pm. AmEx/D/MC/V. ❺

COYOACÁN

If you crave great coffee, cheesecake, or pesto, spend an afternoon at one of the many comparable outdoor cafes surrounding the Jardín Centenario. For local flavor, visit the *taquerías* that line Coyoacán's cobblestone streets. For excellent, inexpensive meals, try the tiny restaurants inside the **market** on Allende, just north of Plaza Hidalgo. (Open M-Sa 9am-9pm.) From **M: Coyoacán** (Line 3), take a *combi* going south on México.

Restaurante Frida, Carrillo Puerto 2 (☎5554 8784), at Ortega. Adjoins a celebrated book and record store on the edge of the Jardín Centenario. Outdoor seating makes for unbeatable people-watching. Entrees (42-88 pesos) include Mexican fare like *enchiladas rancheras* (49 pesos). Open M-F 10am-11pm, Sa-Su 10am-1am. AmEx/D/V. ❸

El Jarocho, Cuauhtémoc 134-G (☎5554 5418), at Allende. Follow the smell of freshly ground coffee to this legendary establishment. Straight from Veracruz, Jarocho has been serving some of the city's best java since 1953. Cappuccino, mocha, and hot chocolate 8.50-11.50 pesos. *Tortas* 12-30 pesos. Open M-Th and Su 6am-1am, F-Sa 6am-2am. Cash only. ❶

VegeTaco, Carrillo Puerto 65 (☎5658 9311 or 5659 7517), at Alberto Zamora, past the other taco joints. Create a meal of faux-meat vegetarian tacos (7 pesos each) or enjoy a *promoción* platter (41 pesos, M-F only). Pomegranate seeds complement their spicy specialty, *chile en nogada* (71 pesos). Open daily 11am-8pm. Cash only. ❷

Manjar, Av. México 215 (☎5658 7998 or 9114), at Madrid. Healthy, delicious dishes and friendly service will win you over. Pick up a refreshing *licuado* (18-29 pesos) from the take-out window on your way to or from the Metro or the Viveros. Crepes 38-58 pesos. Salads 34-50 pesos. Open Tu-Su 8:30am-6pm. D/MC/V. ❸

El Guarache, Jardín Centenario 14-B (☎5554 4506), on the southern end of the Jardín. Bask in the beauty of the coyote fountain from an outdoor table. Entrees 75-108 pesos. *Antojitos* 25-75 pesos. Open M-Th and Su 10am-11pm, F-Sa 10am-2am. Cash only. ❹

Restaurante Rams, Hidalgo 296-G (☎5658 9288), a few steps south of the plaza. A cozy nook ideal for a marine snack. Fried fish (12 pesos each), shrimp *empanadas* (15 pesos), and ceviches (40-80 pesos). Open M and W-Su noon-8:30pm. Cash only. ❷

SAN ÁNGEL

Though some restaurants here are too hip (and too expensive) for their own good, quite a few homey establishments sell solid, reasonably priced food. Great lunch deals can be found in the very stylish **Plaza Jacinto. Metro: M. A. Quevedo** (Line 3).

Restaurante-Bar Carmelas, Arteaga 7 and Frontera 2 (☎5616 3246 and 3247). Quaint views of the plaza from the upper-level dining room pair with traditional Mexican *comida corrida* (45 pesos). Economic options from an otherwise pricey menu include quesadillas (10 pesos) and *sopes* (corn flour patties; 10-15 pesos). Open daily 8am-8pm. AmEx/MC/V. ❸

Taquería Toro, Plaza San Jacinto 12-A (☎5616 2248) on the west end of the plaza. Has something for everyone, including pizzas (34-69 pesos), tacos (6-13 pesos), and Mexican specialties (79-112 pesos). 2-for-1 specials: M burgers, Tu pizza, W *pozole* (traditional stew). Open daily 10:30am-1am. Cash only. ❸

Chucho El Roto, Madero 8 (☎5616 2041), between Plaza San Jacinto and Plaza del Carmen. Oaxacan specialities for good prices in a great location. *Comida corrida* 40 pesos. Open M and Su 8am-7pm, Tu-Sa 8am-8pm. AmEx/MC/V. ❸

La Finca Cafe Solo Dios, Plaza San Jacinto 2-C (☎5550 3302). This hole-in-the-wall coffee stand serves only 100% Mexican-grown beans from Chiapas. Delicious mocha, espresso, and *chocolate* 12-18 pesos. Chiapan coffee beans from 100 pesos per kg. Open daily 7am-10:30pm. Cash only. ❶

Paxia, La Paz 47 (☎5550 8355 or 5616 6964; www.paxia.com.mx). One of the most affordable of San Ángel's many high-end restaurants. Elegant and creative contemporary Mexican cuisine, like *huitlacoche* ravioli (75 pesos) or duck enchiladas in green *mole* sauce (90 pesos). Entrees 75-190 pesos. Open M-Th 1pm-midnight, F-Sa 1pm-1am, Su 1-6pm. AmEx/MC/V. ❺

MEXICO CITY

◎ SIGHTS

Mexico City overflows with history, culture, and entertainment. It is impossible to see everything, and even after the longest trip there always seems to be something that you missed. Most museums are closed on Mondays but free on Sundays. Students and teachers with a valid ID can often get in free or for a reduced fee; however, most archaeological sites and some major museums only offer these discounts to Mexican nationals. There is usually a fee for those who wish to carry cameras or video cameras.

CENTRO HISTÓRICO

To reach the centro histórico by Metro, take Line 2 to M: Zócalo. The station's exit is on the eastern side of the square, in front of Palacio Nacional. Catedral Metropolitana lies to the north, the Federal District offices to the south, and the Suprema Corte de Justicia (Supreme Court) to the southeast. Some sights south of the zócalo can be better accessed by M: Isabel La Católica (Line 1) or M: Pino Suárez (Line 2).

Mexico City spans thousands of kilometers and thousands of years, but it all comes together in the *centro*. On the city's main plaza, known as the **zócalo**, the Aztec **Templo Mayor**, the **Catedral Metropolitana**, and **Palacio Nacional** sit side by side. The people fit the eclectic architecture: along the *zócalo* are street vendors hawking everything from hand-woven bags to batteries, AK-47-sporting soldiers, everpresent political protestors, homeless people, and hordes of picture-snapping tourists. The masses of tourists don't even begin to compare to the number of Mexicans who work in the *centro* every day.

▧ THE ZÓCALO

Officially known as **Plaza de la Constitución,** the *zócalo* is the principal square of Mexico City as well as one of the largest plazas in the world (second only to Moscow's Red Square). Now surrounded by imposing colonial monuments, the plaza was once the nucleus of the Aztec island-capital Tenochtitlán and the center of the entire Aztec empire. Southwest of the Templo Mayor—the Aztecs' principal place of worship (Teocalli in Náhuatl)—was the Aztec marketplace and major square. The space was rebuilt and renamed several times, becoming Plaza de la Constitución in 1812. Dictator Santa Anna supposedly ordered that a monument to Mexican independence be constructed in the center of the square, but only the monument's *zócalo* (pedestal) was in place when the project was abandoned. Local residents began referring to the square as the *zócalo*, a term which has since become the generic name for the central plazas in most cities and towns in Mexico. Today the square is simply adorned with a single Mexican flag, which is raised and lowered daily at 6am and 6pm with great military pomp. Used as a religious center, a venue for social protest, or a performance space, the *zócalo* is definitely worth a visit after the sun sets when all the surrounding buildings are lit up.

▧ CATEDRAL METROPOLITANA.

CATEDRAL METROPOLITANA. The third cathedral built in New Spain was the Metropolitan Cathedral, a mish-mash of architectural styles from three different centuries that somehow turned out beautifully. Originally constructed by Cortés in 1524 over the main Aztec temple, the small church was replaced by a larger cathedral, begun in 1571. The interior was completed in 1667 and famous architect and sculptor Manuel Tolsá (1757-1816) finished the impressive exterior in 1813, adding Neoclassical elements to the facade. Unfortunately, the building's splendor is now partly obscured by high-tension wires and green support structures, designed to alleviate damage from unstable soil and the sinking floor.

The cathedral contains a series of altars and *capillas* (chapels). Highlights include the decadent **Altar de Perdón** (Altar of Forgiveness) at the entrance, and the **Altar de los Reyes** (Altar of Kings) at the far end, and the beautiful murals of dragonslaying and the Virgin's ascension by Juan Correa (1646-1716) that adorn the sac-

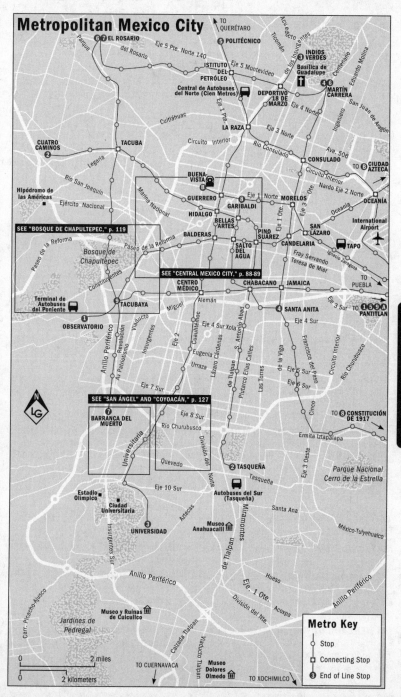

Metropolitan Mexico City

TO QUERÉTARO

67 EL ROSARIO

Parque del Rosario

5 POLITÉCNICO

Eje 5 Pte. Norte 140

Eje 5 Montevideo

ISTITUTO DEL PETRÓLEO

3 INDIOS VERDES

Basílica de Guadalupe

Central de Autobuses del Norte (Cien Metros)

DEPORTIVO 18 DE MARZO

46 MARTÍN CARRERA

Eje 4 Norte

San Juan de Aragón

Cuitláhuac

LA RAZA

Eje 3 Norte

CUATRO CAMINOS **2**

TACUBA

Circuito Interior

Río Consulado

CONSULADO

Ave. 506

TO **B** CIUDAD AZTECA

Legaria

Río San Joaquín

Hipódromo de las Américas

Ejército Nacional

Marina Nacional

BUENA-VISTA **B**

Circuito Interior

Nardo Eje 2 Norte

OCEANÍA

GUERRERO

Eje 1 Norte

MORELOS

HIDALGO

9 GARIBALDI

BELLAS ARTES

SAN LÁZARO

International Airport

SEE "BOSQUE DE CHAPULTEPEC," p. 119

Bosque de Chapultepec

Paseo de la Reforma

BALDERAS

PINO SUÁREZ

SALTO DEL AGUA

CANDELARIA

TAPO

Paseo de la Reforma

Constituyentes

SEE "CENTRAL MEXICO CITY," p. 88-89

Fray Servando Teresa de Mier

TO PUEBLA

Terminal de Autobuses del Poniente

9 TACUBAYA

CENTRO MÉDICO

CHABACANO

JAMAICA

1 OBSERVATORIO

Miguel Alemán

4 SANTA ANITA

Eje 3 Sur

TO **15A** PANTITLÁN

Anillo Periférico

Revolución

Viaducto

Insurgentes

Eje 2

Cuauhtémoc

Eje 4 Sur Xola

S. Antonio Abad

de la Viga

Eje 4 Sur

Francisco del Paso

Circuito Interior

Río Churubusco

Av. Patriotismo

Eugenia

Lázaro Cárdenas

Urraza

Plutarco Elías Calles

Eje 5 Sur

Eje 6 Sur

Eje 7 Sur

Las Torres

Cinco

TO **8** CONSTITUCIÓN DE 1917

SEE "SAN ÁNGEL" AND "COYOACÁN," p. 127

7 BARRANCA DEL MUERTO

Eje 8 Sur

Río Churubusco

División del Norte

Ermita Iztapalapa

Universitaria

Quevedo

2 TASQUEÑA

Tasqueña

Parque Nacional Cerro de la Estrella

Estadio Olímpico

Ciudad Universitaria

Eje 10 Sur

Aztecas

Autobuses del Sur (Tasqueña)

Santa Ana

Insurgentes Sur

3 UNIVERSIDAD

Museo Anahuacalli

de Tlalpan

Miramontes

México-Tulyehualco

Anillo Periférico

Hueso

Anillo Periférico

Carr. Picacho Ajusco

Jardines de Pedregal

Museo y Ruinas de Cuicuilco

Eje 1 Ote. Acoxpa

División del Nte.

0   2 miles
0   2 kilometers

TO CUERNAVACA

Calzada Tlalpan

Viaducto Tlalpan

Museo Dolores Olmedo

TO XOCHIMILCO

Metro Key

○ Stop

□ Connecting Stop

3 End of Line Stop

MEXICO CITY

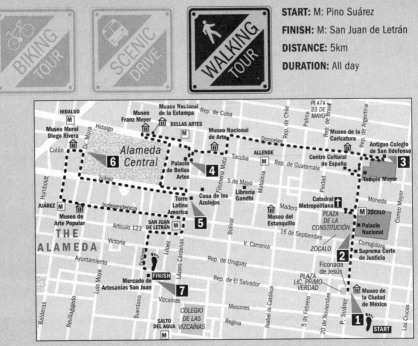

1 MUSEO DE LA CIUDAD. The informative **Museo de la Ciudad** houses a permanent exhibit on the history of Mexico City. Continuing north on Pino Suarez takes you past the **Supreme Court** and the Orozco murals within (p. 113).

2 THE ZÓCALO. The seat of Mexico's government, the **Palacio Nacional** spans two blocks and is diagonally across from the sinking 16th-century **Catedral Metropolitana** (p. 108). To the northeast stand the remains of the main Aztec temple, the **Templo Mayor** (p. 111). The **Centro Cultural de España,** formerly the royal mint, offers a weekly rock concert (p. 112).

3 ANTIGUO COLEGIO DE SAN ILDEFONSO. A right on Doncelos from Rep. de Argentina leads to the mural-filled Jesuit school, the **Antiguo Colegio de San Ildefonso** (p. 112). Nearby, in the courtyard of the **Museo de la Caricatura,** artists will focus on your worst features for a small fee (p. 113). Heading west toward Bellas Artes will take you past the storied **Cafe de Tacuba** (p. 103). Nearby **Taco Inn** is a faster, cheaper option.

4 PALACIO DE BELLAS ARTES. Walking from the **Museo Nacional de Arte,** with Mexico's largest collection of fine art, the magnificent **Palacio de Bellas Artes,** home of Rivera's controversial Rockefeller mural, appears on the left (p. 114). The **Museo Franz Mayer** and **Museo de la Estampa** are further west on Hidalgo (p. 117).

5 TORRE LATINO AMERICA. The ultra-modern **Torre Latino America** offers a view of the distance you've covered and the sprawling vastness you have left to explore.

6 ALAMEDA CENTRAL. The Alameda's central monument honors Benito Juárez. The parks ends opposite the famous **Museo Mural Diego Rivera** (p. 116). To the south, on Independencia and Revillagigedo, is the **Museo de Arte Popular** (p. 116).

7 MERCADO DE ARTESANÍAS. Replenish at **Churreria el Moro** or Sanborn's located in the 16th-century **Casa de los Azulejos,** or detour down to shop at the **Mercado de Artesanías San Juan** (p. 138).

EL CENTRO

110

risty walls. The choir gallery and chapels honoring the Virgen de Guadalupe, near the entrance, also merit a look. *Misa* (mass) takes place daily almost every hour; visitors should take extra care to show respect.

Unauthorized individuals will often try to sell tours outside the entrance of the cathedral, though volunteers give free tours in Spanish (Sa 10:30am-1:30pm). Tours of the sacred *coro* and *sacristía mayor* (chorus and primary sacristy; M-F 11am-2pm, Sa 10:30am-1:30pm; 10 pesos) and the ■**campanaria** (bell tower; M-F 10am-2pm, Sa-Su 10am-6pm; 12 pesos, 20 pesos to be present at the bell-ringing) are available with a 4-person minimum. There are informative plaques in Spanish for each of the altars. *(Plaza de la Constitución. On the left side of the* zócalo *when facing the Palacio Nacional.* ☎ *5510 0440, ext. 123 or 124. Cathedral open daily 7:30am-8pm. Information desk open daily 9am-2pm and 4-6pm. Flash photography prohibited. Free.)*

■**TEMPLO MAYOR.** When Cortés defeated the Aztecs in 1521, one of the first things he did was destroy their main center of worship, the Teocalli, stealing its stones to build his magnificent cathedral across the street. The temple and surrounding plaza were paved over and almost forgotten until 1978, when workers unearthed them while laying wires and piping for the Metro. From 1978 to 1982, the site was extensively excavated, revealing layers of pyramids and artifacts. Today, a catwalk stretches over the outdoor ruins, which include remnants of several pyramids and colonial structures. One of the highlights is the **Great Pyramid,** supposedly located exactly where the Aztecs discovered Huitzilopochtli's snake-eating eagle. It contains the remains of a temple dedicated to Tlaloc (god of rain) and Huitzilopochtli (god of war and patron of the Aztecs) and a *chac-mool.* The **Casa de las Aguilas,** near the end of the path, is one of the better-preserved sections of the temple.

At the back of the site, the **Museo del Templo Mayor,** divided into eight rooms imitating the layout of the original temple, takes you on a tour through the history of Aztec civilization. The artifacts found in the excavation are accompanied by dry museum inscriptions and Spanish translations of excerpts from ancient Aztec texts. The greatest treasure of the museum is the flat, round sculpture of **Coyolxauhqui,** goddess of the moon and mother of Huitzilopochtli. *(Museum at Seminario 8, at Rep. de Guatemala, between the Cathedral and the Palacio Nacional.* ☎ *5542 0606. Signs in both English and Spanish. Audio guides in English 50 pesos, Spanish 40 pesos. Open Tu-Su 9am-5pm. 45 pesos; under 12, students, teachers, and seniors free; Su free.)*

PALACIO NACIONAL. Stretching the entire length of the *zócalo,* the 40,000 sq. m Palacio Nacional has been the site of Mexican government since the time of the Aztecs. The King of Spain granted the land—the site of Moctezuma's palace—to Hernán Cortés in 1521, who constructed himself a spacious home using stones from the original building. In 1562, the King bought back the house from Cortés's illegitimate son to build a palace for the royal viceroys. In 1692 the structure was destroyed by a riotous mob, only to be rebuilt a year later with the same stones. In the 1930s, the palace was restored and a third story was added under the direction of architect Augusto Petrccioli. Today, the *palacio* is the presidential headquarters and houses some other federal agencies. Stern security guards will keep you from going into the courtyard to the right of the entrance, where the most important executive business is conducted.

The **Campana de Dolores (Bell of Dolores),** which came to the capital in 1896 from the village of Dolores Hidalgo (p. 361), hangs over the entrance. Miguel Hidalgo rang this bell on the morning of September 16, 1810, summoning Mexicans to fight for independence. Every year on the 16th, Mexico's Independence Day, the bell is rung as the president repeats Hidalgo's *Grito de Dolores* to a packed *zócalo.*

Most tourists come to the palace for the ■**Diego Rivera murals** that line the main staircase and the western and northern walls. The eight frescoes, painted between 1929 and 1951, trace Mexican history from Aztec civilization through nuclear holocaust and depict Karl Marx, Xochiquetzal, the tattoo-legged Aztec goddess of love, and US forces invading Mexico City in 1847. On the eastern side of the *palacio*'s second floor (turn left at the entrance) is the recently expanded **Museo del Recinto de Homenaje,** dedicated to revered five-term indigenous Mexican president Benito Juárez (1806-1872). The museum occupies the room in which Juárez died and displays a collection of his personal artifacts, described in Spanish. Some of the ruins of Moctezuma's palace are also on display near the entrance to the Juárez museum. The **Museo del Recinto Parlamentario,** on the second floor of the central courtyard, displays political artifacts and a recently restored room that hosted the Parliament (1829-1872) and a meeting of the Constitutional Congress.

Pleasant **gardens** at the back of the palace, straight ahead from the entrance, offer immaculate and well-labeled landscapes with flowers and cacti from all over Mexico. *(Plaza de la Constitución, right of the zócalo when facing the Cathedral. Free guided tours hourly in Spanish, upon request in English. Open daily 9am-5pm. Free. Trade your ID for a turista badge at the entrance. Museums open Tu-F 9am-5pm, Sa-Su 10am-5pm. Free.)*

SUPREMA CORTE DE JUSTICIA. Though the Supreme Court draws some visitors for the spectacle of hand-cuffed foreigners pleading ignorance about the cannabis in their socks, most come to see the four **José Clemente Orozco** murals that cover the second floor walls, where the southern half of Moctezuma's royal palace once stood. The huge, patriotic murals painted in the 1940s represent judicial power and the richness of Mexico's national resources. There are also murals by George Biddle, along with newer additions by Hector Cruz García in honor of the millenium. *(Pino Suárez 2, between Corregidora and Carranza. ☎5522 1500, ext. 2068. Free 40min. audioguide available in Spanish, English and French. Open M-F 8:30am-4:30pm. Bring an ID to leave at the entrance. Free.)*

MUSEO NACIONAL DE LAS CULTURAS. Originally built in 1734 by Spanish architect Juan Peinado to house the Real Casa de la Moneda (royal mint), the building was turned into an anthropology museum by order of Emperor Maximilian in 1865. In 1964, the vast collection of pre-Hispanic artifacts was moved to Chapultepec, and in 1965 the museum was redesigned to promote the understanding of different world cultures. The first floor features ancient civilizations, the second covers the Orient and Oceana, and the third focuses on North America and Africa. A Rufino Tamayo mural can be seen near the entrance. *(Moneda 13, at Correo Mayor. ☎5542 0165 or 0187, ext. 217 or 254. Open Tu-Su 10am-6pm. Call ahead for guided tours in Spanish. Free.)*

ANTIGUO COLEGIO DE SAN ILDEFONSO. In 1922, Diego Rivera painted his first mural, entitled *La Creación,* in the former Jesuit school's amphitheater. The remarkable colonial building has no shortage of other muralists' work: impressive works by José Clemente Orozco line three floors of the museum's interior stairwells; ask to be let into the adjoining UNAM building to see the David Alfaro Siqueiros murals. The museum itself hosts temporary exhibits of Mexican and international contemporary art. *(Justo Sierra 16, 2 blocks north of the Templo Mayor. ☎5702 6378; www.sanildefonso.org.mx. Helpful English mini-guide, available in the bookstore, 6 pesos. Open Tu-Su 10am-6pm. 20 pesos; students, teachers, and seniors 10 pesos; children under 12 free; Tu free.)*

CENTRO CULTURAL DE ESPAÑA. In a beautifully-restored colonial building, the Spanish government treats visitors to temporary exhibitions of contemporary art as well as weekly rock, jazz, and flamenco concerts. *(Rep. de Guatemala 18, behind the Cathedral. ☎5521 1925; www.ccemx.org. Concerts Th-Sa 9pm. Reception open Tu-W 10am-8pm, Th-Sa 10am-11pm, Su 10am-4pm. Free.)*

MUSEO DE LA CARICATURA. The former Antiguo Colegio de Cristo is now a three-room museum dedicated to Mexican political cartoons from 1826-2006. Get your own caricature drawn in the courtyard (daily 11am-5pm; 40-50 pesos). The 1985 earthquake caused some damage to the building, exposing remains of the outer layers of the Templo Mayor, which are now visible from a balcony off the first room. *(Doncelos 99, between Brasil and Argentina. ☎ 5704 0459 or 5702 9256. Open daily 10am-6pm. 20 pesos; children, students, teachers, and seniors 15 pesos.)*

MUSEO DEL ESTANQUILLO. Just two blocks west of the zócalo, this museum is a treasure trove of engravings, sketches, dioramas, maps, newspaper clippings, and paintings honoring the estanquillo (mom-and-pop store), among other icons of Mexican national identity. The personal collection of Carlos Monsiváis, a prominent writer for the Mexican newspaper El Universal, includes over 15,000 pieces, only 500 of which are on display at any time. *(Isabel la Católica 26, at Madero. ☎ 5521 3052; www.museodelestanquillo.com. English brochures 10 pesos. Free guided tours in Spanish Sa-Su at noon. Open M and W-Su 10am-6pm. Free.)*

SOUTH OF THE ZÓCALO

🖾 **MUSEO DE LA CIUDAD DE MÉXICO.** Housed in a beautiful 18th-century palace once home to distant cousins of Cortés, this museum offers an informative and well-curated permanent exhibit on the history of Mexico City, as well as many temporary shows. The former studio of Joaquín Clausell, Mexico's most important impressionist painter, is upstairs. The library holds more than 10,000 volumes and an archive of texts from the Porfiriato (1976-1910). *(Pino Suárez 30, at the corner of Rep. de El Salvador. M: Pino Suárez. ☎ 5542 0083. Tours in Spanish Tu-Su 11am-4pm; call ahead for English. Open Tu-Su 10am-6pm. 20 pesos; students, professors, and seniors 10 pesos; W free.)*

MUSEO DE LA CHARRERÍA. Plaques on the walls of this 1589 convent relate the lifestyles of the *charros* and the development of *charrería* (forerunner to the rodeo) in English, French, and Spanish. Spurs, saddles, and traditional costumes abound. The small museum also houses the Mexican Federation of Charrería, which hosts conferences and special events. *(Isabel la Católica 108, at Izazaga. M: Isabel la Católica. ☎ 5709 5032; fedmexch@prodigy.net.mx. Open M-F 11am-5pm. Free.)*

THE ALAMEDA

The Alameda is serviced by 4 Metro stations: M: Bellas Artes (Lines 2, 8), at Hidalgo and Eje Lázaro Cárdenas; M: San Juan de Letrán (Line 8), 3 blocks from the Torre Latinoamericana; M: Juárez (Line 3), on Balderas 1 block from the park; and M: Hidalgo (Lines 2 and 3), at Hidalgo and Paseo de la Reforma.

With some of the city's best museums, libraries, and historical buildings clustered around its emblematic park (the Alameda Central), the Alameda has several days' worth of sightseeing. After tackling the museums, serious shoppers should head to the city's best crafts market, **La Ciudadela**. Chess addicts can get their fix at Mexico City's most popular chess park in the **Plaza de la Solidaridad**, on the steps near the Museo Mural (vendors usually rent sets). Recently the Alameda has been cleaned up, and emergency call buttons make it much safer.

ALAMEDA CENTRAL

Today's downtown was originally an Aztec marketplace and then the site where heretics were burned during the Inquisition. Viceroy **Don Luis de Velasco II** (1500-1564) created the park in 1592 for the city's elite; it was enlarged in 1769 to its current size. The park takes its name from its rows of shady *álamos* (poplars). Vendors, lovers, and ornately sculpted fountains give this tranquil park just the right dose of activity.

MEXICO CITY

At the center of the Alameda's southern side is the **Monumento a Juárez,** a semi-circular marble monument constructed in 1910 to honor the beloved president on the 100th anniversary of Mexican Independence. A somber-faced Benito Juárez, accompanied by the Angel of Independence and Lady Liberty, sits on a central pedestal among 12 doric columns. On July 19 of each year, a ceremony commemorates the anniversary of Juárez's death.

EAST OF THE ALAMEDA CENTRAL

▨**PALACIO DE BELLAS ARTES.** Construction of this gorgeous art nouveau palace began in 1904 under the direction of the Italian architect Adamo Boari, but work stopped after just nine years due to the Revolution. In 1916, Boari returned to Italy, having completed only the building's exterior. The project was resumed in 1932, and the building was finally inaugurated in 1934. The walls on the second and third floors are covered with works by the who's who of 20th-century Mexican muralists, including **Roberto Montenegro, José Clemente Orozco, Jorge González Camarena, David Alfaro Siqueiros, Rufino Tamayo.** The best-known is a mural on the third floor by **Diego Rivera.** John D. Rockefeller commissioned Rivera to paint a mural depicting "Man at Crossroads, Looking with Hope and High Vision to the Choosing of a New and Better Future" for New York City's Rockefeller Center. Rivera was dismissed from the project when overseers discovered the Soviet flag and a portrait of Lenin in the foreground. The Mexican government asked Rivera to recreate the work here: the result, completed in 1934, was **"El Hombre, Controlador del Universo,"** a Marxist vision that depicts a white man controlling a massive industrial apparatus. Not only did Rivera keep the portrait of Lenin, but he painted in a syphilis-afflicted Rockefeller as well. Plaques describe each of the murals in Spanish. On the top floor is the **Museo Nacional de Arquitectura,** showcasing temporary exhibits on the city's architecture. (☎5512 1410, ext. 227. Open Tu-Su 10am-5:30pm. 20 pesos; students, professors, and seniors free.)

Even if you can't attend a Bellas Artes performance, the elegant *teatro* is worth a visit just to see the **Tiffany's crystal curtain** depicting the volcanoes Popocatépetl and Iztaccíhuatl. The curtain weighs 21,228kg and is said to hold 1 million crystals. (*Free guided tours M-F 1 and 1:30pm.*) The performances of the amazing ▨**Ballet Folklórico de México** integrate *indígena* dancing with more formal aspects of traditional ballet. Orchestral concerts also occur here. The **ticket office** sells tickets for these and other performances throughout the city. An **information booth,** up the stairs next to the ticket booth, has information on shows. Travel agencies snatch up tickets during Christmas, *Semana Santa*, and the summer; check first at Bellas Artes, then try along Reforma or in the Zona Rosa. (*Juárez and Eje Central, by the park; M: Bellas Artes.* ☎5512 2593 or 5521 9251; ext. 152, 153, or 154; www.bellasartes.gob.mx. Open Tu-Su 10am-5:45pm. Ticket booth open daily 11am-7pm. Information booth open daily 10am-6pm. Audio guides available at the info desk 35 pesos. Murals and art exhibits on the upper floors 35 pesos; children under 12, students, teachers, and seniors free. Cash only. Dance performances and concerts at various times throughout the week. No children under 5, no shorts or sport clothing. Prices vary by event and seating. AmEx.)

▨**MUSEO NACIONAL DE ARTE.** Opened in 1982 and thoroughly renovated and expanded in 2000, this museum houses the city's most comprehensive collection of Mexican fine art. Paintings and sculptures from the 16th-20th centuries are organized chronologically and carefully explained in Spanish on the second and third floors. The first floor is home to the museum's temporary exhibits. A number of rooms have hands-on multimedia displays on how art is made, displayed, and interpreted. The elegant building was built from 1904-1911 as part of a Porfiriato public works project to house the Secretary of Communications. The architect, Silvio Contri, took particular care with the impressive central staircase—its

Baroque handrails were crafted by artists in Florence. In front of the museum is the famous equestrian statue of Carlos IV of Spain, *El Caballito*, by Manuel Tolsá. A plaque explains, "Mexico preserves it as a monument of art"—and not in honor of the king. *(Tacuba 8. Half a block from Bellas Artes, between Cárdenas and Filomeno Mata. M: Bellas Artes or Allende. ☎5130 3460; www.munal.com.mx. Open Tu-Su 10:30am-5:30pm. Free Spanish tours noon, 2pm; call ahead for English tours. 30 pesos; students, teachers, children under 13, and disabled persons 15 pesos; Su free. Cash only.)*

PALACIO ITURBIDE. Built in 1780, the grand *palacio* is best known as the home of Mexico's short-lived first Emperor, Agustín Iturbide (1783-1824). Today, it houses wonderful temporary art exhibits on Hispanic art nouveau from the 16th to 19th centuries. The top floor is also home to a permanent exhibit on the palace's complicated history. *(Madero 17, between Bolívar and Gante. ☎1226 0091; www.comentoculturalbanamex.com. Open daily 10am-7pm. Tours M and W-Su at noon, 2, 4pm. Free.)*

CASA DE LOS AZULEJOS. This palace, originally called the *Palacio Azul*, was built in the 16th century. Over the following century, the exterior and much of the interior were covered with gorgeous and expensive *azulejos* (blue and white tiles). According to legend, the son of the Count of Orizaba ordered the redecoration in order to impress his father, who had told him that he would never amount to much. The Sanborn's restaurant chain now occupies the building. You can view the interior for free from the upstairs balcony by ascending the staircase in the main dining room or taking the elevator in the gift shop. Don't miss the Orozco mural over the bathrooms on the staircase landing. *(Madero 4, between Cárdenas and Gante. Sanborn's ☎5512 1331. Open daily 7am-1am. AmEx/MC/V.)*

TORRE LATINOAMERICANA. At 182m and 44 stories high, the *torre* is one of the tallest buildings in the city. The top-floor observatory commands a startling view of the sprawling city, which is even more breathtaking by night. Completed in 1956, this was Mexico City's first earthquake-resistant building taller than 40 stories. In 1957, the tower successfully survived a minor earthquake. The *torre* repeated its performance in the far more devastating quake of 1985, swaying rather than breaking apart. *(Cárdenas 2, at the corner of Madero. M: Bellas Artes. ☎5518 7423. Observatory open daily 9am-10pm. 50 pesos, children 3-11 40 pesos.)*

PALACIO POSTAL (LA QUINTA CASA DE CORREOS). Architect Adamo Boari, of Bellas Artes fame, designed the beautiful central post office in 1907, combining the Spanish Gothic and art nouveau styles. It was restored between 1996 and 2000. The **Museo Postal** is less impressive, with artifacts and history of the Servicio Postal Mexicano. The fifth floor **Museo Histórico Naval** offers plenty of model ships, accompanied by recorded military marches, for maritime aficionados. *(Tacuba 1, on the corner of Tacuba and Lázaro Cárdenas. M: Bellas Artes. ☎5510 2999. Free Spanish tours Tu-F noon, 10-person min. Open Tu-F 10am-5:30pm, Sa-Su 10am-3:30pm. Free.)*

PALACIO DE MINERÍA. This masterpiece of Neoclassical architecture is worth visiting just for the beautiful rooms, which are only accessible through the building tours. You can, however, get up close and personal with the four meteorites on exhibit in the entrance for free. The museum, **Museo Manuel Tolsá**, has a tiny display of 18th-century art from Tolsá's collection. *(Tacuba 5, across from the Museo Nacional de Arte. ☎5623 2929 or 2981; www.palaciomineria.unam.mx. Tours Sa-Su 11am and 1pm, 25 pesos. Museum open W-Su 10am-6pm. 10 pesos. 50% student discount for tours and entrance.)*

TEMPLO DE SAN FRANCISCO. Built in 1524, only four years after the fall of Tenochtitlán, the temple was the first Franciscan convent in the Americas. Its facade is made in the Churrigueresque style of the 18th century. Soon after construction ended, Cortés visited the vast Franciscan complex, which included several churches, a hospital, and a school. In 1838, the church hosted the funeral of Emperor Iturbide. After extensive remodeling in 1716, only the temple and the *capilla* (chapel) remain. *(Madero 7. Next to the Torre Latinoamericana. Open daily 7am-8:30pm. Free.)*

MUSEO DE ARTE POPULAR. Housed in the gleaming Art Deco former fire station, this brand-new museum provides a fresh take on the country's traditional folk arts. Ride the glass elevator up to the fourth floor, and descend downwards through exhibits on daily life, sacred art, *alebrijes* (colorful and fantastic animal-like creations), and Metepec trees of life, reflective of Mexico's cultural diversity. The ground floor hosts temporary expositions of contemporary *artesanías* and an impressive (though expensive) gift shop. *(Revillagigedo 11, at Independencia. ☎5510 2201; www.map.df.gob.mx. Call ahead for free guided tours in English or Spanish. Free children's art classes Sa-Su noon-2pm. Artists' workshops M-F 11am-3pm. Open Tu-W and F-Su 10am-5pm, Th 10am-9pm. 40 pesos; children under 13, students, teachers, and seniors free; Su free.)*

WEST OF THE ALAMEDA CENTRAL

■ **MUSEO MURAL DIEGO RIVERA.** Also known as Museo de la Alameda, this fascinating building holds Diego Rivera's 1947 masterpiece, **"Sueño de una Tarde Dominical en la Alameda Central"** (Sunday Afternoon Dream in the Alameda Central). The mural's key points out, in English and Spanish, the famous figures woven into the work: Hernán Cortés (with his hand covered in blood), Frida Kahlo, and Antonio de Santa Anna, among others. Exhibits on Rivera's life and the cultural climate in which he lived, including a chart listing all of his works and their locations, decorate the walls. One exhibit explains the attack on the painting by university students on June 4, 1948. Mexican philosopher Ignacio Ramírez (1818-1879) was originally depicted holding up the words "God does not exist," a Nietzsche-inspired excerpt from a speech he gave in 1836; students blotted out the entire phrase and drew on Rivera's face in the mural. Rivera eventually allowed the phrase to be left out when it was repaired, and replaced it with *"Conferencia en la Academia de letrás el año de 1836."* Upstairs is a great view of the mural and a temporary exhibit that changes every three months. *(Colón and Balderas, facing the Plaza de la Solidaridad at the end of the Alameda farthest away from Bellas Artes. ☎5512 0759 or 0754; mmdr@correo.inba.gob.mx. Open Tu-Su 10am-6pm. Tours Tu-F 11am, 4pm; Sa-Su 11am, 1, 4, 5pm. 15 pesos, students free; Su free.)*

LABORATORIO ARTE ALAMEDA. This church, begun in 1591, underwent various alterations through the 18th century, including the building of the impressive **Capilla de Dolores.** Today, the building holds unique exhibits of contemporary multimedia art. *(Dr. Mora 7, next to Centro Cultural José Martí. ☎5512 2079 or 5510 2793; www.artealameda.inba.gob.mx. Open Tu-Su 9am-5pm. 15 pesos, students and teachers 7.50 pesos, children under 12 and seniors free; Su free.)*

CENTRO CULTURAL JOSÉ MARTÍ. The poet José Martí, a Cuban independence leader in the late 19th century, warned against foreign imperialism and dreamed of a free and united Latin America led by Mexico. A rainbow-colored mural commemorates his poetry, while a tally sheet in the corner of the mural records British, French, Spanish, and US interventions in Latin America from 1800 to 1969—the grand total is a staggering 784. Temporary exhibits share the space. Movies, concerts, plays, and other cultural events take place in the adjoining theater. *(Dr. Mora 1, at Hidalgo. M: Hidalgo. ☎5521 2115 or 5518 1496; ccjm76@yahoo.com.mx. Open M-Sa 9am-9pm, Su 10am-5pm. Free.)*

ALONG AVENIDA HIDALGO

■ **MUSEO FRANZ MAYER.** In the small, sunken Plaza de Santa Veracruz, the restored Hospital de San Juan de Dios houses a beautiful international collection of applied arts: furniture, textiles, ceramics, tiles, and church ornaments, especially from the *virreinal* (colonial or viceroyal) period. Flyers in English (2 pesos) explain certain works. The upstairs library specializes in decorative arts and rare books. Although anyone can enter the library, only researchers with credentials can use the books. The courtyard cafe alone is worth the price of admission. *(Hidalgo 45, opposite the Alameda, down the steps to the Plaza de Santa Veracruz. ☎5518 2266; www.franzmayer.org.mx. Tours Tu-Su 11am and 2pm, 15 pesos per person. Museum open Tu and Th-Su 10am-5pm, W 10am-7pm. Library open Tu-Sa 10am-5pm. 35 pesos, students 17 pesos, over 60 and children under 12 free; Tu free. Entrance to library and cafe 5 pesos.)*

MUSEO NACIONAL DE LA ESTAMPA. The museum once held the National Institute of Fine Arts' graphic arts and engraving collection but now has only temporary exhibits of engravings by famous artists, both Mexican and international. Highlights have included the work of José Guadalupe Posada, Mexico's foremost engraver and printmaker. His woodcuts depict skeletons dancing, singing, and cavorting in costumes—graphic indictments of the Porfiriato's excesses. *(Hidalgo 39. Next to the Museo Franz Mayer. ☎5521 2244; mne@correo.inba.gob.mx. Call a week ahead to arrange a free guided tour in English or Spanish—and to try your hand at making an engraving. Open Tu-Su 10am-5:45pm. 10 pesos, students and teachers free; Su free.)*

NEAR THE MONUMENTO A LA REVOLUCIÓN

MONUMENTO A LA REVOLUCIÓN/MUSEO NACIONAL DE LA REVOLUCIÓN. In the early 1900s, president Porfirio Díaz planned this site as the seat of Congress, but work halted when revolutionary fighting paralyzed the city streets. Between 1932 and 1938, architect Carlos Obregón Sanacilia tweaked the plans a bit and made a monument to Díaz—and the overthrow of his Congress—instead. Each of the four supporting columns is the tomb of one of Mexico's heroes: Francisco Madero, Plutarco Elías Calles, Lázaro Cárdenas, and Pancho Villa. The museum under the monument takes you through 63 years of Mexican history (1857-1920) and features artifacts such as military uniforms, guns, civilian clothing, and old pesos. Temporary exhibits are often held in the first room, across from the entrance. Sunday is the only day you can climb to the top of the monument. *(At Plaza de la República. ☎5546 2115. Call ahead to arrange a tour. Museum open Tu-Su 9am-5pm. 14 pesos; students, teachers, seniors, and children 7 pesos; Sa-Su free.)*

MUSEO UNIVERSITARIO DEL CHOPO. The modern, relatively tourist-free Chopo (as it is commonly called) hosts temporary exhibits in various media by rising international artists. From mid-June to mid-July, for 12 years running, the museum has proudly hosted *Semana Cultural Lésbica-Gay* (Gay and Lesbian Cultural Week), a show featuring gay- and lesbian-themed photography, sculpture, and painting. The impressive building was first constructed in France and rebuilt here in 1900. *(Dr. Enrique González Martínez 10, off Puente de Alvarado/San Cosme. ☎5546 8490; www.chopo.unam.mx. Call ahead for free guided tours. Open Tu-Su 10am-2pm and 3-7pm. 6 pesos; students, teachers, and children 3 pesos; Tu free. Closed for renovation at time of publication. Call ahead to confirm information.)*

MUSEO SAN CARLOS. The museum, in the old **Palacio Buenavista,** was constructed at the turn of the 19th century by architect Manuel Tolsá for the Count of Buenavista. The building served as a temporary residence for Santa Anna and later

MEXICO CITY

belonged to Emperor Maximilian. It features the impressive former collection of the Academy San Carlos (founded by the King of Spain in 1783), including European art from the 14th to 19th centuries. The museum, which focuses mostly on Spanish contributions, showcases excellent work by minor artists as well as heavyweights such as Cano, Rubens, and Zurbarán. Temporary exhibits on the first floor often highlight themes in modern Spanish art and have featured the work of Picasso and Sorolla. The library contains English and German as well as Spanish documents on European art. *(Puente de Alvarado 50, at Ramos Arizpe.* ☎ *5566 8085 or 8342; www.mnsancarlos.com. Open M and W-Su 10am-6pm. Library open to the public M-F 10am-3pm. 25 pesos; under 13, students, and teachers free; Su free.)*

BOSQUE DE CHAPULTEPEC

The park is divided into 3 sections. To reach the 1st, take the Metro to M: Auditorio (Line 7), by the Auditorio Nacional and the zoo, or M: Chapultepec (Line 1), at the end of the section closer to the Niños Héroes monument and most museums. Alternatively, take any pesero (2.50 pesos) on Reforma to Auditorio or Chapultepec. For the 2nd section, get off at M: Constituyentes (Line 7) and walk toward the blue-tiled building (Museo del Niño). Alternatively, take a "La Feria" or "Papalote" pesero (2.50 pesos) from M: Chapultepec. For the 3rd, by the water parks, take an "El Rollo" pesero from M: Constituyentes or M: Chapultepec. There is an information booth in the 1st section, on Reforma and Gandhi, by the Anthropology Museum. (☎5286 3850. Open daily 9am-6pm.)

Mexico City is a big city that does things in a big way, and the D.F.'s major park and recreational area is no exception. The 2100 acres in the Chapultepec area are home to a slew of fabulous museums, hiking paths, and balloon vendors. The liveliest and most crowded time to visit is on Sunday, when families flock to open-air concerts and take advantage of free admission to the zoo and museums.

The oldest and biggest urban park in the Americas since the Aztec emperor Moctezuma established it in the 15th century, Chapultepec Park is both beautiful and confusing. Dividing it into three sections will make it more manageable. The first section is the busiest, with the most museums, sights, and people. Here you'll find **Chapultepec Castle,** the **zoo,** and Mexico's most famous museum, the **Museo Nacional de Antropología.** The second section, packed with children's attractions, draws fewer tourists and more locals, and is generally less busy on weekdays. There are also great fountains and statues, including Diego Rivera's "Tlaloc" and "Mito del Agua," reproductions of the giant Olmec heads, and a bronze statue of George Washington. The third section has the fewest attractions but features the water parks **Atlantis** and **La Ola.** It is also the most dangerous, with few visitors and hardly any security guards.

SECTION ONE

▨**MUSEO NACIONAL DE ANTROPOLOGÍA.** If you plan to visit all 23 halls in this huge museum, bring your cross-trainers and be prepared to walk 5km. Besides holding Mexico's most impressive archaeological and ethnographic treasures, this museum is the biggest in all of Latin America. Designed by Pedro Ramírez Vázquez, it was built in 1964 out of volcanic rock, wood, and marble. Ancient poems grace the entrances from the main courtyard. At the center of the museum, a tall, column-shaped fountain supports the tremendous weight of an aluminum pavilion that shelters the courtyard.

It would take days to pay proper homage to the entire museum. Upon entering on the right side of the ground floor, you will find a general introduction to anthropology. This first exhibit is followed by a series of chronologically arranged galleries, moving from the right to the left wing of the building, which guide visitors through different pre-Hispanic cultures by region. These galleries trace the histories of many central Mexican groups, from the first migration to America through the Spanish Conquest. In the **Sala México** stands the museum's crown jewel, the

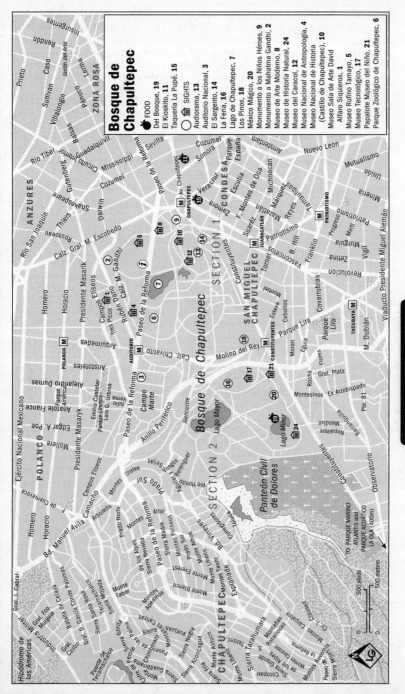

Bosque de Chapultepec

● **FOOD**
Del Bosque, 19
El Kiosckito, 11
Taqueria La Pupé, 15

○ 血 **SIGHTS**
Audiorama, 13
Auditorio Nacional, 3
El Sargento, 14
La Feria, 16
Lago de Chapultepec, 7
Los Pinos, 18
México Mágico, 20
Monumento a los Niños Héroes, 9
Monumento a Mahatma Gandhi, 2
Museo de Arte Moderno, 8
Museo de Historia Natural, 24
Museo del Caracol, 12
Museo Nacional de Antropología, 4
Museo Nacional de Historia
  (Castillo de Chapultepec), 10
Museo Sala de Arte David
  Alfaro Siqueiros, 1
Museo Rufino Tamayo, 5
Museo Tecnológico, 17
Papalote Museo del Niño, 21
Parque Zoológico de Chapultepec, 6

MEXICO CITY

huge Aztec Stone of the Sun. In the center, you can see the god Xiuhtecuhtli sticking out his huge tongue, which doubles as a sacrificial knife and holds two human hearts. Other highlights include Moctezuma's quetzal-feather headdress, colossal stone Olmec heads, and a life-size reproduction of one of the Teotihuacán temples in all its ancient painted glory. Across from the museum's entrance, you can see ▨ **voladores,** who, in true Totonac tradition, climb up a wooden mast and slowly swirl to the ground. *(Paseo de la Reforma and Gandhi. Take an "Auditorio" pesero southwest on Reforma and signal the driver to let you off at the 2nd stop after entering the park; 2.50 pesos. The museum is just east down Reforma. ☎ 5553 6386 or 6381; www.mna.inah.gob.mx. Open Tu-Su 9am-7pm. The museum has a pricey cafeteria (entrees 65-120 pesos) and a large bookshop that sells English guides to archaeological sites around the country. Voladores perform every 10min. Tu-Su 10am-6pm. Free 1½hr. tours for groups of 5 or more; email jorge_ruvalcaba@inah.gob.mx 2 weeks ahead. 45 pesos, after 5pm 150 pesos. Audio tours closely follow signs. English 60 pesos, Spanish 50 pesos.)*

MUSEO NACIONAL DE HISTORIA. Housed in the Castle of Chapultepec, the home of Emperor Maximilian in the 19th century, this museum exhaustively narrates the history of Mexico since the Spanish conquest. The first floor houses a permanent exhibit that guides you through the Mexican Revolution. An immense portrait of Spain's King Ferdinand and Queen Isabella greets visitors in the first room. Galleries along the way contain displays on Mexican society during the War for Independence, the Porfiriato, and the Revolution. The upper level holds mostly temporary exhibits and features a room with Mexican art and dress from the vice-royalty through the early 20th century. Orozco and Siqueiros murals decorate the entryway. Museum admission also includes a peek at some of the castle's interior and access to the most impressive views of the park area. *(Walk a long way up the hill directly behind the Niños Héroes monument to the castle. ☎ 5061 9200. Signs in Spanish. Tours in English after 11am 300 pesos per hr. Open Tu-Su 9am-5pm; tickets sold until 4pm. 45 pesos; under 13, students, teachers, and seniors free; Su free.)*

MONUMENTO A LOS NIÑOS HÉROES. In 1847, during the Mexican-American War, General Winfield Scott led the US invasion of Mexico City. Eventually military academy cadets had to protect the last Mexican stronghold in the capital, Chapultepec Castle. The six white pillars of this monument honor the six teenagers who purportedly wrapped themselves in a Mexican flag and threw themselves from the castle wall rather than surrender. *(On the east side of the park by the entrance to M: Chapultepec; follow the signs or look for the giant white pillars.)*

MUSEO RUFINO TAMAYO. Built by Mexican architects Teodor González de León and Abraham Zabludovsky, this museum won the National Architecture Award in 1981 and is one of the few museums in the city that was actually built to be a museum. The government donated the land in the Bosque after Tamayo, whose abstract style was initially criticized for being insufficiently nationalistic, and his wife, Olga Flores Rivas, offered their international arts collection to the Mexican people. The permanent collection, which is, unfortunately, rarely on display due to lack of space, consists of works by Tamayo, as well as Willem de Kooning, Fernando Botero, and surrealists Joan Miró and Max Ernst—in Tamayo's words, "the most relevant examples of international art of our time." First-rate temporary exhibits more than make up for the missing permanent collection, however, and usually feature contemporary abstract art. Down the steps to the left of the entrance is a multimedia space called the "Cyberlounge," which holds interactive digital video and sound art exhibits by various artists. *(At Reforma and Gandhi. From the Museo Nacional de Antropología, walk straight into the woods across the street. Tamayo is 100m straight ahead. From M: Chapultepec, take the 1st right onto*

Gandhi. Continue walking for 5min.; the museum will be to the left through some trees. ☎5286 6519; www.museotamayo.org. Open Tu-Su 10am-6pm. Guided tours (10 pesos) Tu-F 10am-3pm, Sa 1-3pm; call ahead. Permanent collection partially open several months per year. 15 pesos; students, teachers, and seniors free; Su free.)

PARQUE ZOOLÓGICO DE CHAPULTEPEC. Among the zoo's lions and tigers and bears (oh, my!) are its prized pandas. This excellent and immense zoo has informative signs (in Spanish) about each animal, and a small interactive educational center. Avoid the high-priced chain restaurants inside the zoo by eating from the excellent food stalls west of the entrance. *(Av. Chivatito. Accessible from the entrance on Reforma, east of Chivatito. From M: Auditorio, head away from the National Auditorium. ☎5553 6263; chapulzoo@df.gob.mx. Open Tu-Su 9am-5pm; last entrance 4:30pm. Free.)*

MUSEO DE ARTE MODERNO. This museum, a circular design by Pedro Ramírez Vázquez, houses a fine collection of paintings on the first floor, including works by Kahlo, Orozco, Rivera, and Siqueiros, and excellent temporary exhibits on the second floor showcasing big names in international modern art. It also features an interesting outdoor sculpture garden with benches and views of the park. *(On Reforma and Gandhi, opposite the Museo Rufino Tamayo. Entrance faces the street. ☎5211 8331. Open Tu-Su 10am-6pm. Permanent collection on tour indefinitely. 20 pesos; students, teachers, and under 10 free; Su free.)*

MUSEO DEL CARACOL. Officially the Museo Galería de Historia: la Lucha del Pueblo Mexicano por su Libertad (Gallery Museum of History: The Struggle of the Mexican People for Liberty), the museum is more commonly known as Museo del Caracol (Museum of the Snail) because of its spiral design. It contains 12 halls, where lifelike mini-dioramas divide Mexico's struggle for independence into five periods. The spiral begins with Hidalgo's *Grito de Dolores* and ends with the establishment of democracy. The last room leads into a beautiful, sky-lit hall that holds a handwritten copy of the Constitution of 1917. *(On the road to the castle, turn right at the sign just before the castle. ☎5061 9247. Open Tu-Su 9am-4:15pm. 37 pesos; under 13, students, teachers, and seniors free; Su free.)*

MUSEO SALA DE ARTE PÚBLICO DAVID ALFARO SIQUEIROS. Famed muralist, twice-exiled revolutionary, and would-be Trotsky assassin David Alfaro Siqueiros donated his house and studio to the people of Mexico 25 days before his death in January 1974. The first-floor walls are covered with his murals. Temporary exhibits feature rising artists, and his archive takes up the third floor. *(Tres Picos 29, past Hegel, outside the park. Walk uphill from the Museo Nacional de Antropología to Rubén Darío. Tres Picos forks—follow it for 1 block on the left; the museum is on the right. ☎5203 5888 or 5531 3394; www.conaculta.gob.mx/saps. Call to arrange a free guided tour. Open Tu-Su 10am-6pm. 10 pesos; students, teachers, and seniors free; Su free.)*

OTHER SIGHTS. The **Auditorio Nacional,** on Reforma and Campo Marte, at M: Auditorio, is *the* concert venue in Mexico City, where the hottest music groups in the world come to play. *(☎5280 9250; www.auditorio.com.mx.)* **Los Pinos,** beyond the guard booth at Chivatito and Molino del Rey, is the presidential residence. To see the artwork inside, call or consult the website at least two weeks ahead for an appointment. *(☎2789 1100, ext. 1230; www.lospinos.gob.mx.)* At the heart of Chapultepec is the **Lago de Chapultepec.** Rent rowboats for a romantic experience on the park's green waters. *(Open Tu-Su 9am-4:30pm. Rentals 2 people 60 pesos per hr., 5 people 100 pesos per hr. Paddleboats 2 people 50 pesos per hr., 4 people 80 pesos per hr. Bring a picture ID.)* For an organic connection with pre-Hispanic Mexico, seek out the remains of **El Sargento,** between Audiorama and the Fuente de la Templanza, a 700-year old *ahuehuete* tree over 40m tall and 12.5m in circumference.

SECTION TWO

LA FERIA. The highlight of this awesome theme park is certainly the *montaña rusa*, built in 1964. (☎5230 2121; www.feriachapultepec.com.mx. Aquatic show 20 pesos. Open in high season daily 10am-7pm; in low season Tu-Su 10am-6pm. 125 pesos, selected rides 80 pesos; people under 1.4m, about 4½ ft., 50 pesos.)

"PAPALOTE" MUSEO DEL NIÑO. This children's museum features more than 400 interactive exhibits. It also has the only IMAX theatre in Mexico City. The "Domo-digital," the museum's equivalent of a planetarium, has space-themed projections. Adults take over with live jazz on Th 7-11pm. (Av. Constituyentes 268. The yellow-and-blue building. ☎5237 1773; www.papalote.org.mx. Open M-W and F 9am-6pm, Th 9am-11pm, Sa-Su 10am-7pm. 85 pesos, ages 2-11 and over 60 80 pesos.)

MUSEO TECNOLÓGICO. Another good destination for kids, the large yard in front of the museum holds a planetarium (1 show per hr. 10am-4pm), an impressive heli-copter, train models, electrical plants, and weekend robotics workshops. Inside are exhibits on engines, cars, ships, and more, as well as an Internet room. (Next to Papalote. ☎5516 0964; www.cfe.gob.mx/mutec. Only "experienced users" allowed in Internet room. ID required. Open W-F 9am-4pm. Museum open daily 9am-5pm. Free.)

MÉXICO MÁGICO. Waist-high replicas of the country's key historical locations and a walk-through of canine anatomy educate young visitors while the seat-shaking film simulator and balloon lift draw a more adventuresome crowd. (Between the Museo Tecnológico and the Museo de Historia Natural. ☎5515 9444. Open Tu-F 10am-6pm, Sa-Su and holidays 10am-7pm. 100 pesos, entrance without balloon ride or film sim-ulator 50 pesos, film simulator only 20 pesos.)

MUSEO DE HISTORIA NATURAL. Opened in 1964, this museum has exhibits on topics such as the universe, evolution, and the origin of life. The temporary shows on wildlife often feature live animals. (Follow the signs up the hill from Papalote. ☎5515 2222. Open Tu-Su 10am-5pm. 20 pesos; under 12, students, and teachers 10 pesos; Tu free.)

SECTION THREE

PARQUE MARINO ATLANTIS. Performances feature dolphins, sea lions, and trained birds. The *parque* also has mechanical games for kids and an aquar-ium. Weekend visitors over six years old who have made reservations three months in advance can swim with the dolphins and sea lions. (☎5271 8618 or 5273; www.parqueatlantis.com.mx. Dolphin and seal swims 30min., 9:30am; 10 people max. Open in high season Tu-Su 9:30am-5:30pm; in low season Sa-Su and holidays 10:30am-5:30pm. 55 pesos, plus 24 pesos for tokens.)

PARQUE ACUÁTICO LA OLA. Fun waterslides and the D.F.'s only wave pool are the highlights at this otherwise dilapidated water park. (José María Velasco 130. ☎5515 1285. Open Sa-Su and holidays 10am-6pm. 85 pesos, those 0.9-1.2m, about 3-4 ft., tall 50 pesos, those under 0.9m free.)

TLATELOLCO

M: Tlatelolco (Line 3). Take the González exit. Turn right on González, walk 3 blocks east to Cárdenas, then turn right and walk up 1 block. Tlatelolco Archaeological Site is on your left. Access the church and plaza by turning left before the entrance to the site.

Archaeological work has shown that the Aztec cities of Tlatelolco ("Mound of Sand" in Náhuatl) and Tenochtitlán were born together as "Twin Cities" around 1325. By 1467, the Tlatelolco king, Moquíhuix, had built his city into a busy trading center coveted by the Tenochtitlán ruler, Axayácatl. Tension mounted over terri-torial boundaries, and in 1473 both rulers geared up for attack. The *tenochca* war machine was too powerful for Moquíhuix, and Tlatelolco was absorbed into the huge empire. Despite this loss, once the conquest began, Tlatelolco became the last hope of resistance to the Spanish invasion.

PLAZA DE LAS TRES CULTURAS. The buildings of Tlatelolco's central square, behind the archaeological site at the corner of Lázaro Cárdenas and Ricardo Flores Magón, showcase the bloody past of the three cultures that have occupied it, boasting Aztec ruins, a colonial Spanish church, and modern Mexican buildings. A plaque in the southwest corner of the plaza explains: "On August 13, 1521, heroically defended by Cuauhtémoc, Tlatelolco fell to Hernán Cortés. It was neither a triumph nor a defeat, but the painful birth of the *mestizo* city that is the Mexico of today." More than 400 years after Cortés, the plaza witnessed another bloody event, for which it is most famous: the Tlatelolco Massacre of October 2, 1968. Though the complete story of the massacre has yet to be uncovered, the most common version reports that government forces fired upon student protestors in an attempt to stop alleged plotters of a coup d'etat and to bury social tensions before the upcoming Olympic games. Their shots backfired, and launched Mexico's *guerra sucia* (dirty war), a period of political repression, instead. A memorial on the southern side of the plaza was erected on the 25th anniversary of the attack.

TEMPLO MAYOR DE TLATELOLCO. In front of the plaza lie the well-kept ruins of the Tlatelolco Temple (known as the Templo Mayor) and its ceremonial square. At the time of the conquest, the base of the temple extended from the Eje Central to the Iglesia de Santiago and its summit reached nearly as high as the skyscraper now located just to the south (the Relaciones Exteriores building). For the Aztecs, this spot marked the center of the universe, and the temple was second in importance only to the *zócalo*'s Teocalli. During the Spanish blockade of Tenochtitlán, the Aztecs heaved freshly sacrificed bodies of Cortés's soldiers down the temple steps, within sight of the conquistadors camped to the west at Tacuba. Nearby is the **Templo Calendárico "M,"** an M-shaped building used by the Aztecs to keep time in 52-year cycles. Scores of skeletons, most likely those of sacrificial victims, were discovered near its base. A male and female pair, which can be encased in glass in front of the temple, were found facing each other and have been dubbed "The Lovers of Tlatelolco." *(In front of the plaza on the corner of Cárdenas and Flores Magón. ☎ 5583 0295 or 5582 2240; www.conaculta.gob.mx/templomayor/tlatelolco.html. Open daily 8am-6pm. Free.)*

IGLESIA DE SANTIAGO. On the east side of the plaza is the simple, fortress-like church erected in 1609. Construction of the Franciscan church was commissioned by Cortés in 1524. Its stonework and plain masonry were designed to fit in with the surrounding ruins and their stonework, in contrast to other sights where colonial construction had obliterated pre-existing structures, in order to convince the Mexicans that this was their new Templo Mayor. The mural of San Cristóbal above the entrance is worth a look—it is the only image left uncovered from the church's original interior. Like the rest of the D.F.'s *centro histórico*, the church is sinking an estimated two inches per year. *(On the eastern side of the ruins. Access from the north or south without entering the archeological site. Open daily 7am-1pm and 5-7pm.)*

LA VILLA BASÍLICA

M: La Villa Basílica (Line 6). Pass the vendor stands and turn right on Calzada de Guadalupe. Follow the elevated sidewalk on the left side of the street to the Basílica. Show respect for the area by not sporting hats, shorts, or bare shoulders. Open daily 5am-9pm.

According to legend, in 1531 the Virgin Mary appeared before Juan Diego, a recently converted Aztec, in the shape of an Aztec princess. When he told the bishop what he had seen, the Bishop was skeptical. Juan Diego returned to the hill, an Aztec place sacred for fertility, where the Virgin instructed him to fill his *tilma* (cloak) with flowers, produced miraculously in the wintertime. Returning to the bishop, Juan Diego let the flowers fall. Suddenly Mary's image appeared in the cloth, convincing the bishop of the miracle and establishing the Lady of Guadalupe (where the name Guadalupe originated remains disputed) as the patron saint of Mexico and an icon of the nation's religious syncretism. The famous cloak is now housed in the Basílica de Guadalupe, north of the city center. December 9-12 brings eight million pilgrims who come to venerate her along the shoreline of the ancient Aztec lake.

LA NUEVA BASÍLICA DE GUADALUPE. Designed by Pedro Ramírez Vásquez and finished in 1976 to replace ancient, sinking counterpart, the new *basílica* is an immense, aggressively modern structure. Nonetheless, it is deeply tied to tradition and was the place of Pope John Paul II's mass during his 2002 visit to oversee Juan Diego's canonization. Thousands flock daily to observe the Virgin's miraculous likeness emblazoned in Juan Diego's robe. Visitors crowd around the central altar and impressive organ to step onto the *basílica*'s moving sidewalk, as it allows for easier viewing of Diego's holy cloak. A focal point at the top of the edifice is the gold Byzantine script, which reads *"¿Aquí no estoy yo que soy tu madre?"* (Am I not here, I who am your mother?). *(On the left when you enter the Villa de Guadalupe.* ☎ *5577 6022. Open daily 5:30am-8:30pm; mass held hourly. Free.)*

LA ANTIGUA BASÍLICA DE GUADALUPE. Next to the new *basílica* is the old one, built at the end of the 17th century and remodeled in the 1880s. Religious services and quiet prayers still occur amid gawking visitors and a gift shop. The primary function of the scaffolded *basílica* is to house the **Templo Expiatorio de Cristo Rey.** In the old *sacristía* is the **Museo de la Basílica de Guadalupe.** To get there, walk up the path between the new and old *basílicas*, passing by the Pope-mobile parked on the right. Colonial religious paintings and portraits comprise most of the collection, which pales in comparison to the *ex-votos* (offerings to the Virgin) in the entryway. *(Plaza Hidalgo 1, in the Villa de Guadalupe.* ☎ *5577 5038, ext. 175. Antigua Basílica open daily 8am-8:30pm. Museum open Tu-Su 10am-6pm. 5 pesos, children under 12 free.)*

TEPEYAC HILL. Behind the *basílica*, winding steps lead up the side of a small hill past fountains, crowds of pilgrims, and beautiful flower beds. A small chapel sits on top of the hill at the very spot Juan Diego indicated as the site of the apparition of the Virgin. Murals inside depict the revelation. From the steps beside the church, you can absorb a panoramic view of the smoggy capital framed by the hillsides and distant mountains. Descending the other side of the hill will lead you to the **Jardín de Ofrendas,** past the spouting gargoyles, where statues of Juan Diego and a group of *indígenas* kneel before a gleaming Virgin. *(Open daily 9am-6pm. Free.)* One of the gems of the Tepeyac Hill is this little round chapel, the **Templo del Pocito,** considered the foremost example of the Mexican Baroque style. Built between 1777 and 1791, it has a golden altar and a well inside, as well as blue and white Puebla tiles outside. *(☎ 5577 3844. Open 9am-5pm. Free.)*

COYOACÁN

Take the Metro to M: Coyoacán (Line 3). Then, either take a pesero (2.50 pesos) across the street to the Coyoacán's centro, or walk down Av. México to the Jardín Centenario.

The Toltecs founded **Coyoacán** ("Place of Coyotes" in Náhuatl) between the 10th and 12th centuries. Cortés later established the seat of the colonial government in Coyoacán, torturing Aztec leader, Cuauhtémoc in the hope that he would reveal the hiding place of the legendary Aztec treasure. Well-maintained and peaceful today, Coyoacán—incorporated into Mexico City as recently as 1950—merits a visit for its museums, art galleries and bohemian street vendors, or simply for a stroll in the beautiful **Jardín Centenario,** or nearby **Placita de la Con-**

chita, built by Cortés for La Malinche's (p. 382) daily mass. The neighborhood centers around **Plaza Hidalgo,** which is bound by the cathedral and the **Casa de Cortés.** Calle Carrillo Puerto splits the two parks, running north-south just west of the church. Obtain **tourist information** in the Casa de Cortés, the big yellow building on the north side of the plaza. The office gives free tours of the area in Spanish. (Tours daily 10am, noon, 2pm; English tours only on Sa-Su. Tourist office ☎ 5658 0221. Open daily 9am-3pm and 4-7pm).

SIGHTS NEAR COYOACÁN'S CENTRO

▓**MUSEO FRIDA KAHLO.** Works by Duchamp, Klee, Orozco, and Rivera hang in this restored colonial house, the birthplace and home of Surrealist painter Frida Kahlo (1907-1954). The disturbing work and traumatic life story of Kahlo—the only 20th-century Mexican painter with a place in the Louvre—have achieved international fame since her death; the 2002 Hollywood hit *Frida* (p. 75) further amplified the buzz surrounding Kahlo. Already crippled by polio, Kahlo was impaled at age 18 in a trolley accident, breaking her spine, rendering her infertile, and confining her to a wheelchair for much of her life. Married twice to the celebrated muralist (and philanderer) Diego Rivera, Kahlo was herself notorious for her numerous affairs with both men and women, most famously with Russian communist Leon Trotsky. The "Casa Azul," which today looks just as it did when Kahlo and Rivera lived there between 1929 and 1954, holds some of Kahlo's famous self-portraits, as well as work by Rivera and other contemporaneous artists. Note Kahlo's impressive collection of *ex-votos* (devotional paintings), mounted between the dining room and kitchen. Diary excerpts and letters posted on the walls intimately describe childhood dreams, Rivera's adultery, and the inspiration that fueled her work. The museum also displays family photos and other personal objects from a time capsule opened 50 years after Rivera's death, which coincided with Kahlo's 100th birthday in July 2007. Kahlo's ashes are in a jar in her bedroom. The house is blue, which Kahlo believed would ward off bad spirits, and fronts a gorgeous courtyard decorated with pre-Hispanic artifacts from Rivera's collection. Explanatory labels are sparse; you may want to bring a guidebook in with you. *(Londres 247. ☎ 5554 5999; www.museofridakahlo.org. Guided tours in Spanish or English, 250 pesos; call 2 weeks in advance to schedule. Open Tu-Su 10am-6pm. 45 pesos, students and teachers with ID 20 pesos, under 6 5 pesos.)*

MUSEO CASA DE LEÓN TROTSKY. After Stalin expelled León Trotsky from the USSR in 1929, he wandered in exile until Mexico's president Lázaro Cárdenas granted him political asylum at the suggestion of Trotsky's sympathizers, muralist Diego Rivera and painter Frida Kahlo. Trotsky arrived in 1937 with his wife, and Diego Rivera and Frida Kahlo lent them their house, Casa Azul (now the Museo Frida Kahlo, p. 125), for two years. After falling out with the painterly pair, the Trotskys relocated to this house. Bullet holes riddle the walls of the study, relics of an attack on Trotsky by the muralist David Alfaro Siqueiros on May 24, 1940. Siqueiros and a group of men wildy sprayed the inside of the house with machine-gun fire, wounding Trotsky's grandson in the foot and barely missing Trotsky and his wife. Fearing further violence, this self-proclaimed "man of the people," living in a posh suburban house, installed bullet-proof bathroom doors and hired a team of bodyguards. Despite precautions, Trotsky was assassinated three months later by a Spanish communist posing as a friend of a friend, who buried an ice pick in his skull. The house now offers visitors a trip through the past with old photographs of Trotsky and views of his old rooms, furnished as they were when he lived here. The mausoleum outside, designed by Mexican artist Juan O'Gorman, is also worth a look. *(Churubusco 410. ☎ 5554 0687; museotrotsky@hotmail.com. Call ahead for guided tours. Open Tu-Su 10am-5pm. 30 pesos, students 15 pesos.)*

MUSEO NACIONAL DE LAS CULTURAS POPULARES. The MNCP houses rotating exhibits about contemporary indigenous culture in Mexico. Learn about agriculture, crafts, and art by indigenous children, and peruse the handicrafts sold in tents outside. The museum also holds book readings, concerts, dance performances, and workshops for children and adults. Check the cultural agenda online. *(Hidalgo 289. 2 blocks east of Plaza Hidalgo. ☎9172 8840, ext. 102 or 103; www.culturaspopularesindigenas.conaculta.gob.mx. Open Tu-Th 10am-6pm, F-Su 10am-8pm. Free.)*

CASA DE CORTÉS. Contrary to popular belief, the present-day Casa, built in 1755, never housed Cortés's administration—though an earlier building on this site did, before Cortés moved it to the *zócalo*. Now, Coyoacán's municipal hall honors the past with 1978 murals by Diego Rosales (Diego Rivera's student), which depict scenes from the conquest. A mural by Aurora Reyes, in the Sala de Cabildos, shows the encounter between Cuauhtémoc and Cortés, among other significant events from local history. *(Jardín Hidalgo 1. ☎5658 0221. Open daily 8am-8pm. Free.)*

IGLESIA DE SAN JUAN BAUTISTA. This Dominican church, between Plaza Hidalgo and Jardín Centenario, was begun in 1528 and rebuilt between 1798 and 1804. The interior is elaborately decorated with gold and bronze, while the roof supports five beautiful, recently painted frescoes depicting scenes from the New Testament. *(Open daily 6am-8:30pm.)*

SIGHTS AWAY FROM COYOACÁN'S CENTRO

CONVENTO DE NUESTRA SEÑORA DE LOS ÁNGELES DE CHURUBUSCO. The convent was built on the site of a pyramid dedicated to the Aztec war god Huitzilopochtli, all traces of which vanished after the convent was rebuilt in 1677. On August 20, 1847, led by Generals Manuel Rincón and Pedro Anaya, 800 citizen-soldiers defended the building against 8000 US invaders, surrendering only when the last cartridge had been spent. Today, bullet holes and cannon-ball imprints still mark the front wall, where two cannons used in the defense are kept as memorials. Inside, beyond the well-preserved original convent kitchen, is the **Museo Nacional de las Intervenciones.** Artifacts and an extensive written narrative in Spanish tell the history of the attacks on Mexico perpetrated by British, French, Spanish, and US governments from the late 18th century to 1917. The highlight is the buggy of Benito Juárez, Mexico's first—and only—indigenous president. Pass through the museum to reach the **Acervo Artístico de Churubusco,** where the convent's neck-craningly tiny rooms reveal impressive Mexican religious art from the 17th and 18th centuries. The admission fee is steep and may not merit the price, even for true history buffs. *(20 de Agosto and General Anaya, facing the Plaza Batallón San Patricio. From Coyoacán, walk 4 blocks down Hidalgo and then follow Anaya as it branches left for 4 blocks. M: General Anaya, Line 2, is only 2 blocks east of the convent. The "Gen. Anaya" pesero goes from Plaza Hidalgo to the museum; 2.50 pesos. Take the "Sto. Domingo" back. ☎5604 0699 or 5688 7926. Museum open Tu-Su 9am-6pm. Free guided tours every hour in Spanish only. 37 pesos; Su free. Discounts for Mexican nationals.)*

MUSEO ANAHUACALLI. Designed by Diego Rivera with Aztec and Mayan motifs, the formidable stone building is an exhibit in and of itself. The interior exhibits Rivera's old studio and his huge collection of pre-Hispanic art. Rotating exhibits feature contemporary art. Rivera built the Anahuacalli ("House Near the Valley," in Náhuatl) atop a hill, where it commands an excellent view of the Mexico City valley, including nearby Azteca Stadium. *(Calle Museo 150. To reach the museum from Plaza Hidalgo or Churubusco, take a "Huipulco" or "Huayamilpa" pesero south and get off at Circunvalación; walk 2 blocks and then take a "Cotija" pesero to Calle Museo; keep an eye out—the stop is not immediately visible. Turn right onto Calle Museo. From the Mercado de Coyoacán, take a "División del Norte" pesero and then a "Prepa 5" pesero, which will drop you*

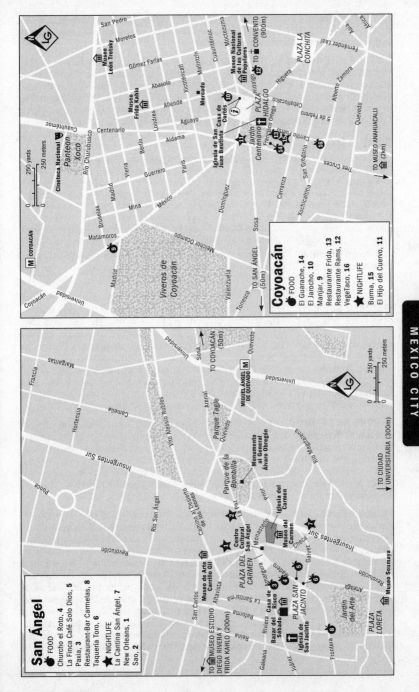

MEXICO CITY

San Ángel

🍴 FOOD
Churcho el Roto, 4
La Finca Café Solo Dios, 5
Paxia, 3
Restaurant-Bar Carmelas, 8
Taquería Toro, 6

🌙 NIGHTLIFE
La Cantina San Ángel, 7
New Orleans, 1
Sao, 2

Coyoacán

🍴 FOOD
El Guarache, 14
El Jarocho, 10
Manjar, 9
Restaurante Frida, 13
Restaurante Rams, 12
VegeTaco, 16

★ NIGHTLIFE
Burma, 15
El Hijo del Cuervo, 11

right on Calle Museo. Alternatively, take a 50-peso taxi from Coyoacán's centro. ☎5617 4310; www.anahuacallimuseo.org. Open Tu-Th and Sa-Su 10am-5pm, F 10am-4pm. 45 pesos, students and teachers 20 pesos, children under 6 free.)

VIVEROS DE COYOACÁN. Wander among rows of saplings and squirrels in this giant nursery, which provides greenery for the D.F.'s public parks. The Viveros's verdant tranquility is enforced by rules prohibiting bicycles, balls, dogs, cameras, and food—though strolling and jogging along its grid-like paths are welcome. *(Five entrances. Principal entrance on Progreso; another on México, between Madrid and Melchor Ocampo. Between M: Coyoacán and Plaza Hidalgo. Open daily 6am-6:30pm. Free.)*

SAN ÁNGEL

To reach San Ángel, 10km south of the centro along Insurgentes, take the Metro to M. A. Quevedo (Line 3), Viveros (Line 3), or Barranca del Muerto (Line 7). From M: M.A. Quevedo, head 3 long blocks west on Quevedo, away from the Santo Domingo bakery; take a left on La Paz and continue along the Parque de la Bombilla. For a more direct route, "San Ángel" buses on Insurgentes will take you straight to the heart of the neighborhood. You can also take the Metrobús on Insurgentes to the Bombilla stop, which will leave you closer to the centro. To get back from San Ángel to points as far north as Buenavista station, take an "Indios Verdes" bus.

San Ángel's beautiful museums and colonial buildings are more upscale than its bohemian neighbor. The area is best visited on Saturday afternoon, when the tiny cobblestone streets burst with BMWs, the weekly Bazar del Sábado takes place, and local artisans sell their work in the Plaza San Jacinto.

▨ MUSEO SOUMAYA. This museum's pride and joy is its vast collection of Rodin sculptures, promoted as the third most important in the world. The Soumaya also countains works from many other European masters, including Pisarro, Renoir, Monet, Miró, and rare Dalí sculptures. On a national level, there is a collection of colonial Mexican art and portraiture from the 18th and 19th centuries. A mural by Tamayo occupies the wall by the exit. *(In Plaza Loreto, a small shopping mall, at Revolución and Río Magdalena. ☎5616 3731 or 3761; www.museosoumaya.com. Open M, W-Th, and Su 10:30am-6:30pm, F-Sa 10:30am-8:30pm. Guided tours in Spanish F-Sa noon, 2, 4, 6pm; Su noon, 4pm. Call 3 weeks ahead for English tours. 10 pesos, students 5 pesos; M and Su free.)*

PARQUE DE LA BOMBILLA. The centerpiece of this park is the **Monumento al General Álvaro Obregón,** which honors one of the revolutionaries who united against Victoriano Huerta, the militaristic dictator who executed Francisco Madero and seized power in 1913. The main statue accurately depicts Obregón, who lost an arm during the Revolution—a separate statue of his severed limb stands on the lower level of the monument. Obregón later became president in 1920, but was assassinated at the restaurant La Bombilla, bordering this park, in 1928.

MUSEO DEL CARMEN. Expropriated under the Reform Laws of 1857, this former Carmelite convent was abandoned in 1861 and restored in the 20th century to house an art and history museum. The collection of colonial art has crucifixes galore, but few labels or explanations. Some of the rooms upstairs have been restored to look as they did when the building was a convent; note the wooden beds and log pillows. Head downstairs to the crypt, where mummies are displayed. The identities of the eerily preserved bodies are a mystery—they were discovered in 1916 by invading Zapatistas, who thought the crypt held treasures. The adjoining church, the **Templo y Ex-Convento de El Carmen,** was designed and built from 1615 to 1626 by Fray Andrés de San Miguel of the Carmelite order; beautiful *azulejos* adorn the inner walls, and the golden altar is stunning. San Ángel fetes the church's namesake, the Virgen del Carmen, with week-long floral festivities in the 400-year-old tradition of **Feria de las Flores** on July 16. *(Av. Revolución 4 y 6, at Monasterio. ☎5616 7477, ext. 104; www.museodeelcarmen.org. Museum open Tu-Su 10am-5pm. 37 pesos; children under 12, students, and teachers free; Su free. Church open daily 4:30-8pm.)*

CASA DE RISCO (CENTRO CULTURAL ISIDRO FABELA). This well-preserved 17th-century house contains an important collection of well-labeled 14th- to 19th-century art. The inner courtyard has a ▨**fountain** made by Spanish missionaries out of shells and ceramics shards (called *riscos*), including Ming dynasty china, Mexican *talavera*, and Moorish tiles. Upstairs in the last room are three small paintings by Mexico's landscape master, José María Velasco (1840-1912). A variety of European portraits, religious paintings, and furnishings form the heart of the collection. The ground floor hosts temporary contemporary art exhibits. *(Plaza San Jacinto 15. ☎5616 2711. Free guided tours W-Su 10am-3pm. Open Tu-Su 10am-5pm. Free.)*

MUSEO DE ARTE CARRILLO GIL. Inside the functionalist building is one of the capital's most interesting collections of art. It includes works by the big 20th-century muralists—José Clemente Orozco, Diego Rivera, and David Alfaro Siqueiros—but only their paintings on canvas, not the famed murals, are there. Siqueiros's renowned **Caín en los Estados Unidos** (1947) depicts the lynching of a black man by a crowd of monstrous whites. The Rivera paintings date from his early years and show heavy influence from Picasso. Other 20th-century artists are also represented. The 1625 pieces in the permanent collection, however, are too plentiful to display all at once, and thus are presented in parts by themed temporary exhibits. The top two floors house traveling exhibits. *(Revolución 1608. M: Barranca or Viveros. ☎5550 3983 or 6260; http://macg.inba.gob.mx. Free guided tours; call 2 days ahead. Open Tu-Su 10am-6pm. Library open Tu-F 10am-6pm, Sa 10am-2pm. 15 pesos, students 9 pesos; Su free.)*

MUSEO ESTUDIO DIEGO RIVERA Y FRIDA KAHLO. These two his-and-hers buildings were the home of Mexican art's royal couple, Frida Kahlo and Diego Rivera, from 1934 to 1940. The pink one houses Rivera's studio, where he did most of his work and lived until his death in 1957. Frida kept her studio in the blue house, which was meant to be their official residence together, until returning to her home in Coyoacán in the early 1940s. Juan O'Gorman designed the two giant blocks, which were among the first houses built in the functionalist style that inspired the public housing structures later popularized all over the Americas and Europe. The museum holds a small collection of Rivera's work and photographs, as well as displays on the artists' lives. On the top floor of the Rivera house, you can see where and how he worked—his leftover paints are still lying around, as well as a significant number of the dolls Frida made each time Diego was unfaithful. The museum also holds temporary exhibits of Kahlo's and Rivera's contemporaries, including Paul Klee, Wassily Kandinsky, and Georges Braque. *(At Altavista and Diego Rivera, 5 blocks up Altavista from Revolución. Look for the pink-and-blue pair with a cactus fence. ☎5616 2679 or 5550 1518, ext 112. Call ahead for tours. Open Tu-Su 10am-6pm. 10 pesos; Su free.)*

OTHER SIGHTS. Across the street from the Iglesia del Carmen is the **Centro Cultural San Ángel,** which borders lovely **Plaza del Carmen.** Besides hosting art exhibits and plays, it is also a good source of information on local happenings, especially at the numerous small performance venues. *(Av. Revolución, at Madero. ☎5616 1254. Free walking tours of San Ángel Sa-Su 11am and 1pm. Open daily 10am-8pm.)* One block up Madero is **Plaza San Jacinto,** at San Francisco and Juárez, which fills on Saturdays with shoppers scoping out pricey arts and crafts at the **Bazar del Sábado** (p. 139). One block past Casa de Risco on Juárez lies the **Iglesia de San Jacinto,** a 16th-century church with a magnificent golden altar and a peaceful courtyard. *(Open daily 8am-8pm.)*

CIUDAD UNIVERSITARIA (CU)

The sheer size of UNAM makes it difficult to navigate by foot. Luckily, M: Universidad lets you off near the free shuttle service, at Salida D or E toward the right at the bottom of the stairs. Shuttles don't run late June-Aug. Always expect a wait. There are 3 principal routes. Route #1 will take you to the heart of campus, the Jardín Central, to the far north of the station. Walk toward the big gray library, away from Insurgentes. Alternatively, if you have a good sense of direction, a few pesos, and are willing to walk a bit, take one of the buses on Insurgentes that runs to driveways leading to both the Jardín Central and the Centro Cultural Universitario. General info ☎ 5565 1344; www.unam.mx. In an emergency, call university security by pressing the button on any security phone throughout the campus. Most UNAM buildings open Jan.-July and Sept.-Dec., when school is in session.

Named a ■UNESCO World Heritage site in June 2007, the **Universidad Nacional Autónoma de México** (National Autonomous University of Mexico), or **UNAM,** is the largest university in Latin America, with a staggering enrollment of over 100,000. Immediately after the new colonial regime was established, the religious orders that arrived in Mexico built elementary and secondary schools to indoctrinate new converts and to educate young Spanish settlers. The original university, the University of Mexico, was established in 1553 in the building at the corner of Moneda and Seminario, just off the *zócalo*, and today it encompasses multiple campuses throughout the city. The Ciudad Universitaria campus was dedicated in 1952. Designed by a number of famous architects, including Félix Candela and Juan O'Gorman, the campus boasts 26km of paved roads, 430,000 sq. m of greenery, and four million planted trees.

CENTRO CULTURAL UNIVERSITARIO (CCU). Films, plays, concerts, and temporary art shows abound in UNAM's modern, beautifully maintained facilities. A big booth in the center of the complex has tons of flyers with information about goings-on at the CCU and all over the city. Most events of interest to tourists take place in the Centro Cultural Universitario (CCU—not to be confused with CU), Insurgentes Sur 3000. This large complex houses the **Teatro Juan Ruiz de Alarcón; the Foro Sor Juana Inés de la Cruz** (☎ 5665 6583; ticket booth open W-Su 5-8pm; tickets 100 pesos, students 50 pesos); the **Sala Miguel Covarrubias,** for dance performances (☎ 5665 6825 or 5622 7137; ticket booth open Tu 10am-2pm, W-Sa 10am-2pm and 4:30-8:30pm, Su 10am-1:30pm); the **Sala Carlos Chavez,** for music performances (☎ 5622 6958; ticket booth open Tu 10am-2pm, W-Sa 10am-2pm and 4:30-8:30pm, Su 10am-1:30pm); the artsy movie theaters **Sala José Revueltas** (☎ 5622 7021) and **Sala Julio Bracho** (☎ 5665 2850; each 30 pesos, students 15 pesos); and the **Sala Netzahualcóyotl,** which regularly hosts big-name concerts and music festivals (☎ 5622 7125; ticket booth open Tu 10am-2pm, W-Sa 10am-2pm and 4:30-8:30pm, Su 10am-1:30pm; 60-150 pesos, student discount 50%). The Sala Netzahualcóyotl is the only section of the center that continues to operate during summer vacation. Also at the CCU is the **Azul y Oro Cafe** and a **bookstore.** (Open 10am-8pm; only Sa-Su in summer.) Check www.musicaunam.net for other events. *(Take Line 3 of the UNAM shuttle.)*

LIBRARY. A huge mosaic by Juan O'Gorman wraps around the library to the left of the Jardín Central. You could spend hours trying to interpret the busy mosaic, which depicts Aztecs, eagles, the Olympic rings, and a huge atom, among other things. Across the grass from the library is the Museo Universitario de Ciencias y Artes (MUCA), which features temporary exhibits. Opposite the museum entrance is the university's administrative building, graced by a David Alfaro Siqueiros mosaic on the south wall that shows students studying at desks supported by society. *(Library ☎ 5622 1625. Open daily 8:30am-9:30pm. Museo de Ciencias ☎ 5622 1659. Open Jan.-June and Sept.-Dec. M-F 10am-6pm, Sa 10am-5pm. Free. Guided tours daily 11am-5pm, 5-person min.)*

ESTADIO OLÍMPICO. The 1968 Olympic stadium, built in 1954, was designed to resemble a volcano with a huge crater. In fact, the ground upon which it is built is coated with real lava. The impressive mosaic over the entrance to the stadium was created by Diego Rivera. It depicts eagles, a little boy, and a man and a woman holding torches. Today, the stadium is home to UNAM's professional *fútbol* team, **Las Pumas;** you'll see their blue-and-gold logo everywhere on campus. *(On the opposite side of Insurgentes Sur from the Jardín Central; cross via the footbridge. ☎ 5622 0495.)*

ESPACIO ESCULTÓRICO. Just outside the CCU is this impressive collection of sculptures from the 1980s. The largest is *Las Serpientes del Pedregal* (1986), by Federico Silva, a long snake crafted from uneven blocks of stone several meters high and separated by narrow spaces. *(Open M-F 8am-6pm.)*

UNIVERSUM (MUSEO DE LAS CIENCIAS). Piet Mondrian sculptures grace the first floor of this natural science museum. Though filled with educational exhibits aimed toward kids, adults can have fun here, too. The building houses 16 permanent exhibition rooms, temporary exhibits, and a theater for shows, forums, and conferences, as well as the world's first interactive quantum mechanics exhibit. All explanations and instructions are in Spanish. A cafeteria is located in the museum. *(In the peach-colored building down the hill from the CCU. ☎ 5622 7287; www.universum.unam.mx. Open M-F 9am-6pm, Sa-Su and holidays 10am-6pm; ticket booth closes at 5pm. 40 pesos; children, teachers, and students 35 pesos.)*

CUICUILCO ARCHAEOLOGICAL ZONE. A bit south of the CCU is the archaeological zone of Cuicuilco ("Place of the Many-Colored Jasper" in Náhuatl). The centerpiece of the eight structures visible today, **El Gran Basamento,** was built between 800 and 150 BC. The area served as a ceremonial center with a population of 20,000-40,000, making it the largest central settlement in Mesoamerica before the rise of Teotihuacán in the early Classic Period. Measuring 110m in diameter and 25m in height, the pyramid was built in at least eight different stages and terminates with equinox-oriented altars at its summit. The area was abandoned near the end of the pre-Classic Period, when the tiny volcano of **Xitle** erupted around AD 100, and coated 8 sq. km of surrounding land in a thick layer of lava. On a clear day, the summit affords a faint view of Xitle to the south and the much larger Popocatépetl to the east, as well as of the modern skyscrapers surrounding the site. A small museum displays artifacts found at the site, including a tomb, with lengthy descriptions in Spanish of the site and the civilization. *(On the southeastern corner at Insurgentes Sur and Anillo Periférico, south of CU. From M: Universidad, Line 3, exit on the side away from campus on salidas A, B, or C, toward the small outdoor market, and take any "Cuicuilco" or "Villa Olímpica" pesero, 2.50 pesos, to the entrance on the western side of Insurgentes Sur, just beyond the Periférico, the big highway overpass. A "Parque Ecoarqueológico Cuicuilco" sign marks the entrance to the site. Peseros will let you off on the other side of Insurgentes, next to the Villa Olímpica housing and business development. To return, take any "CU Metro" pesero. ☎ 5606 9758. Call ahead M-F 9am-1:30pm for free guided tours in Spanish. Open daily 9am-4:30pm. Free.)*

XOCHIMILCO

M: Tasqueña (Line 2). Ride the tren ligero (trolleybus; 2 pesos; follow the "Correspondencia" signs) in the "Embarcadero" direction. For the gardens, get off at the "Xochimilco" stop. For the museum, get off at the "La Noria" stop.

In Xochimilco ("so-she-MIL-co"; Place of the Flower Growing), there are two things to do. First cruise the **floating gardens** of Xochimilco in a hand-poled *trajinera* (boat) along with the rest of the tourists. Then head beyond the crowds to the **Museo Dolores Olmedo,** which houses an impressive Diego Rivera collection and the largest Frida Kahlo collection in Mexico.

■ THE FLOATING GARDENS. The floating gardens of Xochimilco were not built for leisure purposes, but rather as essential elements of the Aztec agricultural system. Settled in the pre-Classic times, the city only became an Aztec territory under the rule of Axayácatl. In the Aztec's brilliantly conceived system, *chinampas* (artificial islands) were made by piling soil and mud onto floating rafts. These rafts were held firm by wooden stakes until the crops planted on top sprouted roots that extended through the base of the canals. They became fertile islands, supporting several crops per year. Though polluted today, the canals still bear the waterborne greenery planted centuries ago.

Multicolored *trajinera* boats crowd the maze of canals, ferrying passengers past a floating market of food, flowers, and music. Families, young people, and couples lounge and listen to the *mariachis* and *marimba* players while downing goodies and booze from the floating taco stands and bars. The canals are especially packed on weekends, when local families arrive in the late morning and spend the entire day feasting and partying on their *trajineras*. Private boats come in two sizes; the smaller is 140 pesos per person, and the larger is 160 pesos per person. A 1hr. trip is just enough to get to the heart of the main canal and make a quick stop at one of the *chinampas*. A shared boat is not much cheaper, with a round-trip at 110 pesos per person (available only weekends and holidays). Beware of vendors who may try to rip travelers off. You should be able to negotiate these prices down by a good amount. *Mariachis* will play for 70 pesos a song, and all the other musicians will do the same for less. Beers are a good deal at 15-20 pesos each, but are cheaper from the stands at the *embarcadero.* Longer, more comprehensive trips, including a 4hr. ride to the Ecological Reserve just beyond the main canal, are also available for a higher price.

Xochimilco also offers two enormous land-bound **markets,** one with the usual food and household items, the other filled with live animals and plants. To reach the marketplace from the trolley bus, turn left on any street within three blocks of the station as you walk away from it. The market lies straight ahead. *(At the "Xochimilco" stop on the tren ligero; numerous "Embarcadero" signs and white-shirted boat owners will direct you. Peseros below the station can also take you; ask to stop at "un embarcadero.")*

■ MUSEO DOLORES OLMEDO. This museum, once the estate of beautiful socialite Dolores Olmedo Patiño, features the art collection she amassed throughout her life. As the long-time lover of Diego Rivera, she is the subject of many of his paintings. The collection holds 146 of these canvases, including a series of 25 sunsets painted from Olmedo's Acapulco home in 1956, the year before Rivera's death. Perhaps even more impressive are the 26 paintings by Frida Kahlo; since much of her work is held abroad or in private collections, this the best Kahlo collection in all of Mexico. A worthwhile room exhibiting popular Mexican art lies at the back of the museum. Temporary exhibits support lesser-known but excellent work by current international and Mexican artists. Take a brief stroll on the museum grounds to appreciate its gorgeous landscaped lawns. **■ Xoloitzcuintles,** hairless Aztec dogs, and **peacocks** patrol the mansion's grounds and boldly approach visitors. *(Av. México 5843. From the "La Noria" stop on the tren ligero, exit to the left, turn left at the corner, turn left again at the next corner, and walk straight ahead to the museum's wooden doors.* ☎ *5555 0891 or 1221; www.museod-oloresolmedo.org. Call ahead to arrange free guided tours, offered Tu-Sa 10am, noon, and 4pm. Open Tu-Su 10am-6pm. 40 pesos, students and teachers 20 pesos, under 6 free; Tu free.)*

♫ ▣ ENTERTAINMENT AND NIGHTLIFE

Whether you want to dance, drink, talk, sing, listen, or watch, you will find your kind of place in the D.F. Clubs offer salsa, rock, house, electronic pop, and everything in between—but there are also laid-back bars, theaters, cinemas, and wild *cantinas*. The options, like the city, are almost limitless.

? **MEXICO CITY PUBLICATIONS.** With Mexico City's everchanging nightlife scene, some printed and online resources may be your best bet at planning your night out on the town.
Tiempo Libre: The best resource for partying in the city. Available at most corner newsstands. Covers movies, galleries, restaurants, performances, museums, and most cultural events. 7 pesos. www.tiempolibre.com.mx.
La Jornada: A top national paper, with news and event listings. 6 pesos.
Ser Gay: Available at most gay bars. Contains a complete listing of gay and lesbian nightlife options. www.sergay.com.mx.
Chilango: Magazine about being a D.F. resident with interesting articles and info about what to do in the city. 19 pesos. www.chilango.com

Cover charges are a necessary evil of the capital's night life. At *discotecas* (dance clubs), called *antros* in the D.F., they range 30-200 pesos for men. Women are often admitted free before a certain hour (usually 11pm or midnight) or at half-price. After this time you will still have to buy drinks—rarely will you be lucky enough to find a *barra libre* (open bar). If drink prices are not listed, ask to avoid exorbitant *gringo* prices. *Bebidas nacionales* (Mexican-made drinks, from Kahlúa to *sangría*) are considerably cheaper than imported ones.

The hours, prices, and popularity of entertainment establishments sometimes change faster than even an annually updated book can track. In the summer of 2001, night owls were stopped in their tracks by mysterious green signs, reading *"Clausurado"* (shut down), placed over the doors of dozens of the city's bars and clubs. The seals explained that the city government had closed the establishments indefinitely, "for violations of the regulatory statutes in effect." Some establishments re-opened within a few weeks, but the future of most is still unclear. The Zona Rosa, the Centro Histórico, and the city's gay nightlife were the hardest hit.

TIP **SOME BACKSEAT DRIVING. Taxis** run all night and are the safest way to get from bar to disco to breakfast to hotel, but—especially after dark—avoid flagging cabs off the street. Remember to get the number of a *sitio* taxi company from your hotel or hostel before you leave, or ask any respectable-looking bartender, bouncer, or waiter to call one for you. For more info, see p. 96.

Women venturing out alone will likely be approached by men offering drinks, dances, and much more. In light of Mexico City's sometimes staggering crime statistics, both men and women should go out in groups.

CENTRO HISTÓRICO
Although the *centro* was once known for being quiet after sundown, the emerging nightlife now offers great spots for both tourists and locals. **M: Zócalo** (Line 2), **Bellas Artes** (Lines 2 and 8), **Allende** (Line 2), and **Isabel la Católica** (Line 1).

Salón Tarará, Madero 39, upstairs (☎5510 8518), at the corner of Madero and Motolinía. This cavernous hot spot has something for everyone. Be prepared for the salsa-dancing big leagues. Beer 20-25 pesos, with occasional 2-for-1 specials. Hard alcohol 35-85 pesos. F latin dance, S electronic or salsa music, Su Mamá Afrika reggae session. Cover varies by event, usually F-Sa 50 pesos, Su 25 pesos. Open F-Sa 10pm-4am, Su 5-11:30pm. Cash only.

El Nivel, Moneda 2 (☎5522 9755 or 6184), just east of the cathedral. The drawings lining the walls in the city's oldest *cantina*—founded in 1855 in a building of the Universidad de Mexico—were left by poor art students as a way to settle their tabs. These days only pesos are accepted. Beer 25 pesos. Open M-Sa noon-midnight. Cash only.

The Chronicle

IN RECENT NEWS

BEACH BUMS?

During *Semana Santa* (Easter vacation) in Mexico City, temperatures typically top 80°F (27°C) and residents flee the heat for seaside resorts. But in 2007, the beach came to Mexico City when Mayor Marcelo Ebrard built four beaches along the lakes and swimming pools in the capital's public parks.

Inspired by Paris Plage and other artificial urban beaches, Ebrard's $200,000 initiative imported nearly 200 tons of white sand from Veracruz, and installed volleyball nets and 'sea breeze' sprayers. Inner-city traffic and the D.F.'s chronic smog made for an unusual setting, but over 5000 visitors flocked to the first Mexico City beach, in a park built for the 1968 Olympics, on opening day.

Ebrard created the downtown retreat for the millions of poor residents in the mega-metropolis who have never seen a beach. Considered frivolous, however, the beaches were met with opposition reflecting Mexico's sharp class divisions: politicians from President Calderon's conservative National Action Party (PAN) said the city, beset by crime and water shortages, had more urgent uses for the money.

The beaches will remain in place indefinitely and, if popular, the city says it will build more.

Beaches are in the public parks of the Tlalpan, Gustavo A. Madero, Iztacalco, and Azcapotzalco delegaciones.

El Pasagüero, Montolinía 33 (☎5521 6112; www.pasaguero.com), between Madero and 16 de Septiembre. Live rock and themed nights attract the D.F.'s young hipsters. Boasts black lights: dress accordingly. Beer 25 pesos, mixed drinks 50-70 pesos. Guest list for special events. Cover up to 100 pesos. Open F-Sa 10pm-4am.

Salón Corona, Bolívar 24 (☎5512 5725 or 9007), between 16 de Septiembre and Madero. You haven't experienced the *centro* until you've stopped by "El Corona." Enjoy a tasty *taco de bacalao* (13 pesos) during the day or grab a beer (22 pesos) and a *taco al pastor* (7 pesos) with the local crowd at night. Open M-W and S 8am-1am, Th-Sa 8am-3am. Cash only.

Cantina Río de la Plata (☎5521 7247), between Allende and Rep. de Cuba. Attracts a younger crowd than most *cantinas*. Its 2 floors fill up on the weekends for cheap beer and good company. Beer 11 pesos. Open M-Sa 10am-2am. Cash only.

Museo de la Cerveza, Bolivar 18-A (☎5510 0951), at 5 de Mayo. This "museum" proudly recounts events in the history of Mexican beer since 1542, when the continent's first *cervecería* was established in Tenochtitlán. Sample a Mexican concoction like the *paisana* (beer with hot sauce; 30 pesos), or *La Querida* (beer with meat sauce; 35 pesos). Read up on the brew's dietary benefits while noshing on nachos and *taquitos* (25 pesos). Menu focuses on Mexico's most famous booze, Corona. Beer 25 pesos. Open M-Th noon-10pm, F-Sa noon-midnight. AmEx/D/MC/V.

Pervert, Rep. Uruguay 70 (☎5510 4433), between 5 de Febrero and Isabel la Católica. House and progressive music mixed by top DJs attract an eclectic crowd at this late night lounge, where rock-hewn walls contrast with mod decor. It may be difficult to make it past the name and the security. Beer 35 pesos, mixed drinks 70-80 pesos. Cover Th 70 pesos for men, F-Sa 100 pesos. Open Th 11pm-3am, F-Sa 11pm-6am. AmEx/MC/V.

◾ PLAZA GARIBALDI

The plaza is at the intersection of Lázaro Cárdenas (Eje Central) and República de Honduras, north of the Alameda. M: Bellas Artes (Lines 2, 8), walk 3 well-lit blocks away from the Palacio de Bellas Artes on Cárdenas; Garibaldi will be on your right. M: Garibaldi (Line 8) plants you 3 blocks away from the plaza. Exit to your left and walk towards the Palacio de Bellas Artes or the zócalo.

Plaza Garibaldi flaunts some of Mexico City's gaudiest and most amusing nightlife. By 5pm, wandering *mariachis* and roving *ranchero* bands begin to play for negotiable prices (60-100 pesos per song). Anybody and everybody—tourists, locals, musicians, vendors, children, and prostitutes—mingle here, enjoying the plaza's alcoholic offerings. Big nightclubs surrounding the plaza aggressively lure crowds. Though they advertise no cover, drink prices are astoundingly high. Your best bet is to find a table at one of the open-air cafes, where you can order cheap beers (15 pesos) or *pulque* (an alcoholic drink made from the maguey cactus, available straight or flavored; 17-69 pesos per liter). If you're hungry, don't miss the **Mercado de Alimentos San Camilito,** on the northwest corner of the plaza. This indoor market contains dozens of small, inexpensive eateries. Most will feed you quite well for around 40 pesos. (Open 24hr.) **Guadalajara de Noche,** República de Honduras 9, is a bar/restaurant that offers nightly folkloric dance and *mariachi* performances. (☎5526 6341. Shows 9, 10:30pm, 1am. Cover Th-Sa 30 pesos. Open daily 8pm-4am.) Exercise caution and avoid wandering beyond the plaza to the back streets, which are considerably less charming. The best time to visit Garibaldi is on Friday or Saturday 8pm-midnight.

TIP

CANTINA CULTURE. The traditional Mexican *cantina* is an endangered species in modern Mexico City, where their numbers have dwindled from 450 a decade ago to just 100 in downtown D.F. today. *Cantinas* were male-only domains until a 1980 law required them to admit women, but even today, women visitors should not go unaccompanied. Visit in the late afternoon to fill up on inexpensive beer and the substantial *botanas* (appetizers) served in return for drinks purchased.

NEAR THE MONUMENTO A LA REVOLUCIÓN

Mexico City's residents fill the inexpensive bars scattered around the monument's flood-lit dome. The dark streets are not particularly safe—it's best to visit these places in groups. **Bar Milan,** Milan 18, all by itself between the monument and Reforma, has established itself as a place for the young and beautiful people to be seen—in T-shirts and jeans or in designer evening wear. Though more relaxed on weekdays, this artsy bar draws the D.F.'s hippest crowd on weekends. Exchange real money for monopoly-like bills to pay for drinks. (☎5592 0031. Beer 35 pesos. Mixed drinks from 45 pesos. Open W 9pm-midnight, Th 9pm-2am, F-Sa 9pm-3am. AmEx.) **M: Revolución** (Line 2).

ZONA ROSA

Home to some of the republic's fanciest discos and highest cover charges, the Zona Rosa can feel like the center of the universe on weekends. Clubs come and go, but a few commercial chains have had the muscle to stay. US sports bar-themed **Yarda's** and **Freedom,** which attract the young and moneyed set. At these and other Zona clubs, you're guaranteed a comfortable environment, large crowds, and minimal flack from bouncers. Mixed among these mainstream establishments are strip clubs (signs say "Table"), and the city's best GLBT nightlife. High covers at most clubs make club-hopping pricey. Sidewalk recruiters will likely try to lure in groups, especially those with high female-to-male ratios; hold out and you might get a deal. Dress codes are not enforced, but you'll feel out of place in sneakers. After a wild night, hop on an all-night Metrobús that runs up and down Insurgentes (3.50 pesos). **M: Insurgentes** (Line 1) and **Sevilla** (Line 1).

Darma, Florencia 32 (☎5514 1406). Gilt bamboo and Hindu gods adorn this dance spot. F live tropical music. Sa DJ plays rock, reggaeton, and *norteño.* Beer 25 pesos. Mixed drinks 100 pesos per liter. Cover 30 pesos. Open F-Sa 9pm-4am. D/MC/V.

El Continental, Florencia 12 (☎5525 6268; www.continentaldjclub.com), near Reforma. Pegged as an "after-hours" place in the Zona Rosa, this popular and exclusive club packs in after 2am. Dance the dawn away with the beautiful and fabulous or people-watch from one of the tables. Cover 200 pesos, W ladies free, Th 10pm-3am no cover. After 4am enter through the back door on Calle Berna. Open W-Sa 10pm-late. AmEx/MC/V.

Afrocaribe, Londres 132 (☎5511 4539). Live salsa and merengue music draws a diverse crowd, mostly couples, to the dance floor amidst larger-than-life jungle decor. 120 pesos min. consumption. Cover Tu-Th 40 pesos, F-Sa 60 pesos. Open Tu-Sa 8pm-4am. AmEx/D/MC/V.

Freedom, Copenhague 25 (☎5207 8456; www.gpofreedom.com.mx), at Hamburgo. 3 floors of throbbing pop lure a lively crowd, despite the half hunting lodge, half sports bar floor-to-ceiling retro decor. Beer 35 pesos. Mixed drinks from 48 pesos. W and Th Live rock music 11pm-midnight. W free drinks for women. Th half-price hard alcohol. Open daily 1pm-3am. AmEx/D/MC/V.

London Blue, Londres 106 (☎5208 7762). Cool blue lights glow from the 2nd-floor windows of this bar. Pool tables (45 pesos), as well as backgammon, dominoes, and darts. No cover. Beer 32-35 pesos, with great deals for groups. Live rock daily. Open T-W 4pm-1am, Th-Sa 4pm-4am. MC/V.

El Bandazo, Londres 148 (☎5208 5060), between Florencia and Amberes. Head upstairs and kick it to live *sinaloense* music (F-Sa) and rowdy *norteño* dancing. Beer 30 pesos, before 8pm 10 beers for 150 pesos. After 8pm cover 40 pesos. Open Th-Sa 6pm-3am. MC/V.

COLONIA ROMA & LA CONDESA

Next to the Zona Rosa, this tranquil residential neighborhood has become a great destination for relaxed nightlife and a growing number of gay clubs and bars. There's no single nightlife cluster, so it's best have a place in mind before heading out. *Tiempo Libre* and *Ser Gay* have especially good listings for this area. **Cafe-Bar Las Hormigas,** upstairs in Casa del Poeta, Álvaro Obregón 73, has ▓live music and spoken word performances in its intimate bar. Call ahead. (☎5533 5456. Domestic beer 20 pesos. Free *botanas* many nights. Cover 50 pesos for shows. Open M-F 2-9pm, Sa 2pm-2am. Cash only.) **M: Insurgentes**. **Mama Rumba,** Querétaro 230, at Medellin, **Zydeca/Pata Negra,** Tamaulipas 30, upstairs, and **Ruta 61,** Baja California 281, are also fun.

NEAR THE WORLD TRADE CENTER

Lining Insurgentes near the World Trade Center skyscraper are a bunch of themed nightlife hot spots. The area has quick turnover, and those that stick around are not the most authentic in the capital, but they can be fun and less expensive than their counterparts in the Zona Rosa and *centro histórico*. The area also has its share of strip clubs, most with male performers. Take the all-night Metrobús (3.50 pesos) on Insurgentes to the Polyforum; most clubs are near this area. If you're coming from San Ángel or Ciudad Universitaria, board an "Indios Verdes" bus.

La Cantina de los Remedios, Insurgentes Sur 744 (☎5687 1037; www.lacantinadelos-remedios.com.mx/). The vast bar will blow you away. Live *mariachi, son,* or rock music daily 3:30pm. 2-for-1 drinks 6-10pm, includes *bebidas nacionales* (37 pesos) and mixed drinks (46 pesos). *Botanas* 37-76 pesos. Entrees 85-190 pesos. Open M-Sa 1:30pm-12:30am. Upstairs club open Th-F 9pm-1am. AmEx/D/MC/V.

Velvet, Insurgentes Sur 878 (☎5523 1153 or 2991; www.velvetmexico.com). Strut down the red carpet into this sleek club, where Mexico City's young and beautiful gyrate to pop amidst strobe lights and fake smoke. Cool off at one of the 4 bars or recline on white couches. Valet parking available. Beer 30 pesos. Mixed drinks 70-120 pesos. Cover 200 pesos for men; women free. Open Th-Sa 10pm-3am. AmEx/D/MC/V.

Polyforum Siqueiros, Insurgentes Sur 701 (☎5536 4520), at Filadelfia. An entire building constructed to display audacious Siqueiros murals. Patrons enjoy a theater, restaurant, and piano bar on the bottom floor at **Restaurante Siqueiros Piano-Bar.** (☎5536 8314. No mixed drinks. Open M-Sa 7pm-3am. D/MC/V.) Next door, the **Dommlite** disco boasts original Joan Miró murals and plays retro and current hits. (☎9115 4502. Beer 35 pesos. Shots 45-60 pesos. Cover 80 pesos; women free 9-11pm. Open F-Sa 9pm-3am. D/MC/V.)

SAN ÁNGEL

The upscale bars along Insurgentes and Revolución cater to an executive crowd, who often arrive in business suits and heels. Cover charges here are low or nonexistent. Although there are no real dance clubs—besides a couple of strip joints on Insurgentes—there's plenty of bar activity, even on a Wednesday night. Jazz bars abound, and several small venues host classical concerts and plays. For information, check at **Centro Cultural San Ángel** (☎5616 1254 or 2097), the big yellow building at Revolución and Madero, before 8pm. Take a "San Ángel" bus or a Metrobús to the Bombilla stop on Insurgentes from points as far north as Buenavista station.

Sao, Av. de la Paz 32 (☎5550 7354), near Insurgentes. This small oxygen bar and lounge with minimalist, classy decor is meant for pure, relaxed socializing. Beer 30 pesos. Mixed drinks from 55 pesos. Oxygen 75 pesos per 15min. Cover on some weekends, 50 pesos. Open Th-Sa 7pm-1am. AmEx/MC/V.

New Orleans, Revolución 1655 (☎5550 1908; www.neworleansjazz.com.mx). The self-proclaimed "Cathedral of Jazz in Mexico," this bar/restaurant features live jazz and blues music. See *Tiempo Libre* for show info. Beer 45 pesos. *Botanas* (tapas-like snacks) for 2 approx. 200 pesos. Live music 8pm; professional bands Tu-Sa, school groups Su. Cover after 9pm Tu-Th 50 pesos, F-Sa 75 pesos, Su 35 pesos. Open Tu-Su 6pm-1am. MC/V.

La Cantina San Ángel, Insurgentes Sur 2146 (☎5661 2292). This upscale bar hosts a variety of live musical acts W-F 4-6pm, but in the evenings the black lights switch on and loud pop and rock entertain a young crowd on top of tables. Beer 37 pesos. Mixed drinks 40-77 pesos. Open M-Th 1pm-midnight, F-Sa 1pm-4am. AmEx/D/MC/V.

COYOACÁN

Plaza Hidalgo, Coyoacán's historic heart, is the place to be. The biggest crowds form on weekends, drawn to free performances by comedians, mimes, and musicians. The colonial buildings nearby often host plays and other performances. (Inquire at Casa de Cortés before 8pm for showtimes.) **Cineteca Nacional,** México-Coyoacán 389, next to the footbridge, screens classic films and recent flops. Check the D.F.'s daily *La Jornada* or *Tiempo Libre* for information on shows. (☎1253 9300; www.cinetecanacional.net. Showtimes vary. Open daily.) Many restaurants host live music, but bars and clubs in the area are sparse: things quiet down by midnight. One option is **El Hijo del Cuervo,** Jardín Centenario 17, on the north side of Jardín, where a diverse crowd listens to live music. (☎5658 7824; www.elhijodelcuervo.com.mx. Drinks from 35 pesos. Tu jazz, W alternative rock. Open M-Tu 4pm-midnight, W 4pm-12:30am, Th 1pm-1:30am, F-Sa 1pm-2:30am, Su 1-11:30pm; music starts at 9pm. D/MC/V.) Or recline on low benches at the hip cafe-bar **Burma,** Carrillo Puerto 14, which offers world music and *shisha* (100 pesos). (☎5658 8594; comentaburma@gmail.com. Cappuchino 12 pesos. Beer 25-27 pesos, Tu-F 3-6pm 2-for-1. Botanas to share 36-90 pesos. Open M 7pm-1am, Tu-Th and Su noon-1am, F-Sa noon-2am. D/MC/V.) **M: Coyoacán** (Line 3).

GLBT NIGHTLIFE

The capital presents a full range of social and cultural activities for gays and lesbians, and an active, fledgling gay rights movement has made its presence known. General tolerance of homosexuality is still very low, and although not illegal, public displays of affection by gay and lesbian couples on the street or on the Metro are sure tickets to harassment, especially by the police. Gay men will have a much easier time finding bars and discos, although more and more venues have begun to welcome lesbians. The free pamphlets *Ser Gay* and *Hot Map* are great sources of information, with listings for gay entertainment, art events, clubs, and bars in the city. Copies are available at many gay clubs in the city, especially in the Zona Rosa. For exclusively lesbian activities, contact one of several Mexico City lesbian groups (p. 98). In June, Mexico's gay pride month, parties, rallies, art exhibits, marches, and *fiestas* occur throughout the city. Gay-friendly establishments are usually marked with a rainbow flag.

▨ **Cabaré-Tito VIP,** Londres 104 (☎5208 2305; www.cabaretito.com), in the Zona Rosa. This laid-back bar-disco draws a gay and lesbian crowd with techno and pop. The attached cafe offers a spot to relax during dance breaks. Beer 2 for 25 pesos until 10pm. Th lesbian night. Cover Th-Sa 70 pesos. Open W-Th 5:30pm-3am, F-Sa 5:30pm-4am, Su 5:30pm-1:30am. 150 peso min. for AmEx/MC/V.

▨ **Living,** Reforma 483 (☎5286 0069; www.living.com.mx), in Col. Cuauhtémoc, near M: Sevilla. Pop and electronic music fill this classy club, and fancy light shows make you feel like the center of attention on the dance floor. Fills up after 2am. Male only. Beer 25 pesos. Mixed drinks from 80 pesos. Cover 170 pesos. Open F-Sa 10pm-3am. MC/V.

Buttergold, Izazaga 9 (☎5761 1861), with a rainbow painted on the outside walls near Cárdenas and M: Salto del Agua (Lines 1, 8). This cavernous dance club fills on weekend nights with a mixed crowd. Great drag shows (Tu-Th 1am, F-Sa midnight and 3am), rock, techno, salsa, merengue, and a relaxed atmosphere make this one of the most fun clubs in the city. Snack bar in the back. Domestic beer 25 pesos. Cover F-Sa 100 pesos, includes 2 beers. Open Tu-Th and Su 9pm-4am, F-Sa 9pm-6am. MC/V.

El Almacén, Florencia 37 and 37A (☎5533 4984; www.eltaller-elalmacen.com.mx). Laid-back video bar with pop dance music. Mostly gay men, but lesbians are welcome. In the basement, construction site decorations and dark alcoves make **El Taller** an intense men-only pickup scene. Beer 30 pesos. Mixed drinks from 40 pesos. Cover W 50 pesos for shows; includes 1 drink. Open daily 7pm-4am. Cash only.

La Cantina del Vaquero, Algeciras 26 (☎5598 2195), in Col. Insurgentes, between Insurgentes and Cádiz. Take the Metrobús on Insurgentes to "Félix Cuevas." The 1st openly gay *cantina* in Mexico has been a favorite for 25 years. Gay men still flock to the bar to watch adult videos or grab a beer and chat. Beer 25 pesos. Mixed drinks from 37 pesos. Videos daily 6-11pm. Cover F-Sa 50 pesos, includes 1 beer. Open W-Su 6pm-2am. Cash only.

▢ SHOPPING

While most Mexican cities rely on one large, central market, Mexico City seems to have one on every corner. Each *colonia* has its own, and the ones downtown rival the size of a small city. Markets are all relatively cheap, but vary widely in quality and content. Shopping throughout the *centro* and the Alameda proceeds thematically: there is a wedding dress street, a lighting fixtures street, a lingerie street, a windowpane street, and even a military surplus street.

▨ **Mercado de la Ciudadela,** Plaza de la Ciudadela 1 y 5 (☎5510 1828), 2 blocks north of M: Balderas (Lines 1, 3) or 3 blocks south of M: Juárez (Line 3). Nonstop tourist traffic flows through the capital's biggest and best *artesanía* market. Traditional clothing at low prices. Open daily 10am-7pm.

Mercado de Artesanías San Juan, Ayuntamiento (☎5512 2790), at Buen Tono, 4 blocks south of Alameda Central, 2 blocks west of Lázaro Cárdenas. M: Salto de Agua (Lines 1, 8). From the station, walk 4 blocks up López and make a left on Ayuntamiento. 3 floors of *artesanía* from all over Mexico, ranging from standard tourist items to exquisite handmade treasures. Prices similar to La Ciudadela, but comparison shopping always helps. Fewer tourists, so you have more bargaining power. Open M-Sa 9am-7pm, Su 9am-4pm.

FONART, Patriotismo 691 (☎5563 4060). Also at Juárez 89 (☎5521 0171; open M-F 10am-7pm, Sa 10am-6pm, Su 10am-4pm) and Reforma 116 (☎5328 5000; open M-F 10am-7pm, Sa 10am-4pm). A national project to protect and market traditional crafts, selling *artesanía* from all over the country. Giant tapestries, rugs, silver jewelry, pottery, and colorful embroidery. Prices are regulated, so are not quite as low as other markets. Open M-F 10am-8pm, Sa 10am-7pm, Su 11am-6pm.

La Merced, Calle Rosario (☎5522 7249) between Anaya and Cabaña, east of the *zócalo*. M: Merced (Line 1). The largest market in the Americas has an enormous selection of fresh produce and more raw meat than your nose can handle—all at rock-bottom prices. Not the safest market in town; tourists are advised to exercise extreme caution if they choose to venture inside. Nearby are **Mercado de Dulces** (Candy Market) and **Mercado de Flores** (Flower Market). All 3 open daily 10am-7pm.

Bazar del Sábado, Plaza San Jacinto, in the center of San Ángel. One of San Ángel's biggest draws. Overflowing onto the plaza, this market tends to be pricey and touristy, but it is one of the few to which contemporary artists bring their work. Open Sa 10am-7pm.

The Zócalo, along Corregidora, the street between the Palacio Nacional and the Supreme Court. This unofficial "market" crowding Mexico's central square has been the subject of much controversy through the years. If you don't mind insanely crowded streets, come here for your non-*artesanía* needs. Vendors overflow from La Merced and clog the street with stands and their brightly colored umbrellas. The persistent vendors have some of the best prices in town on chocolate-covered strawberries, clothing, toys, CDs, and electronics. Open daily 8am-7pm.

Mercado de Sonora (☎5768 2701), on Teresa de Mier and Calzada de la Viga, 2 blocks south of La Merced. Attracts those who enjoy witchcraft, medicinal teas and spices, figurines, and ceremonial images, among others. Search no further for lucky cows' feet, shrunken

THE GOOD FIGHT

Lucha libre, or Mexican wrestling, is not a free-for-all fight as the name would have it, but a series of acrobatic, choreographed moves set to elaborate rules. During the match—typically fixed to pit *rudos* (bad guys who fight dirty) against *tecnicos* (good guys who play by the rules)—fighters wear colorful masks representing an animal, god, or other hero, assuming the mask's identity for the performance. (Some even go so far as to wear them outside of the arena as well.)

Luchadores win a match by pinning their opponent(s) to the mat to the count of three, or knocking him out of the ring for twenty; two out of three matches wins a round. Though frequently and hilariously overlooked by refs, the following moves disqualify a fighter: using an illegal hold, hitting below the belt, attacking the ref, or ripping off an opponent's mask. Depending on the match, losers must shave their heads or be unmasked—a humiliating loss of character.

Visitors to the D.F. can get in on the act at the **Arena Coliseo** or the colossal **Arena México,** which originally opened in 1933 with a capacity for 17,000 spectators. Ticket prices range from 15 pesos in the nosebleed section to over 500 pesos for ring-side seats.

Coliseo: Rep. de Perú 77, between Chile and Brasil; fights Tu 8pm and Su 5pm. México: Dr. Lavista 197, in Col. Doctores. M: Cuauhtémoc; ☎5588 0266; fights F 8pm.

heads, eagle claws, black salt, and powdered skulls (for the domination of one's enemies). Also sells more mundane goods, like household wares, toys, and pets—a very
sad sight. Beware—this is a prime pickpocketing spot. Open daily 6am-7pm.

◎ SPORTS

Whether consumed by their passion for bullfighting, *fútbol* (soccer), *béisbol*
(baseball), or horse racing, Mexican fans share an almost religious devotion to
sports. Although *charrería* (rodeo) may be the official national sport of Mexico,
fútbol is by far the most popular. Soccer fans rejoice—the summer league runs
from January through May, and the winter league runs from July through December. In addition, countless minor and amateur *fútbol* leagues play throughout the
year. Every fourth June, the World Cup takes Mexico by storm—even gas and
water delivery stop as soccer fans throughout the country pack bars and restaurants to watch the games. Whenever Mexico scores a goal, the entire nation
shakes in unison as the word "*GOL!*" rings from every bar, boulevard, business,
and bus. If sweaty discos and endless museums have you craving a change of
pace, follow the sports-loving crowds and prepare yourself for a rowdy good time.

▩ **Estadio Azteca,** Calz. de Tlalpan 3665 (☎5487 3100; www.esmas.com/estadioaz-
teca). Take a *pesero* or *tren ligero* (trolley bus) from M: Tasqueña (Line 2). The proud
home of the *Águilas de America* (Eagles of America), Mexico's largest stadium packs
in 114,000-person crowds for popular *fútbol* matches. Good luck getting tickets; start
with Ticketmaster (☎5325 9000; www.ticketmaster.com.mx). Season runs Jan.-July
and Oct.-Dec. Tickets 50-1500 pesos. If you can't get tickets but still want to see the
stadium, there are guided tours M-W and F-Su (5 per day 10am-5pm) and Th (4,
5pm). 10 pesos, children under 5 free.

▩ **Plaza de Toros México,** Rodin 241 (☎5563 3961). M: San Antonio (Line 7) on Insurgentes Sur. Mexico's principal bullring, the largest in the world, seats 45,000 fans.
July-Nov. *novillada* (novice) fights; Jan.-Feb. and Nov.-Dec. professional fights. Tickets 20-500 pesos, depending on proximity to the ring and *sombra* (shade) or *sol*
(sun). Bullfights Su 4pm. Next door is the big, blue **Estadio Azul,** Indiana 260
(☎5563 9040; www.cruz-azul.com.mx). Home to Mexico City's pro *fútbol* team, Cruz
Azul. Tickets 100-200 pesos.

El Foro del Sol, Av. Viaducto Río Piedad and Río Churrubusco, in the Ciudad Deportiva,
M: Velodromo (Line 9). This "sports city" complex contains volleyball courts, a boxing
ring, an ice-skating rink, soccer fields, and other assorted facilities. The *Foro,* at the
complex's center, hosts home games for Mexico City's 2 professional baseball teams,
the *Diablos Rojos* (Red Devils) and the *Tigres* (Tigers). Sparks fly when the teams face
each other, and local papers have dubbed the match-up the *Guerra Civil* (Civil War).
Tickets (10-80 pesos) are easy to come by and can be purchased at the gate.

Hipódromo de las Américas, Av. Industria Militar (☎5387 0600, ext. 6309;
www.hipodromo.com.mx). From M: Polanco (line 7) take an "Hipódromo" *pesero*.
This compound houses a horse track. Races F-Su 2:30-7:30pm.

◪ DAYTRIPS FROM MEXICO CITY

Even those who have fallen deeply in love with Mexico City need some time away
to maintain a healthy relationship. Fortunately, the capital's central location
makes for easy and painless escape. From small towns to not-so-small towns, from
ruins to volcanoes, all of the following places make convenient daytrips.

TEOTIHUACÁN

Direct bus service from Mexico City is available via Autobuses Teotihuacán (1hr., every 15min. 6am-3pm, 28 pesos), in the Terminal de Autobuses del Norte (☎5587 0501) at Sala 7. Buy tickets for the "Pirámides" bus. There are 5 entrances to the site. Buses drop visitors by Puerta 1, the main entrance. Buses return to Mexico City from Puerta 1, 2, and 3 (last bus 6pm). Puerta 5, the easternmost entrance, is by the Pirámide del Sol. ☎59 4956 0052 and 59 4958 3282. Site open daily 7am-5pm. 45 pesos; national students, teachers, seniors, and under 13 free. Parking 40 pesos, for buses 150 pesos. Videocamera use 35 pesos. At some entrances, booths sell guided tours; sights also have plaques in English, Spanish and Náhuatl. Many hostels also offer 250 peso tours, which include transport, guide, stops at other sites, and lunch, but not the entrance fee.

The massive ruins at Teotihuacán present a perplexing mystery: nobody is quite sure who the Teotihuacanos were. The area was settled in the late pre-Classic period, around 200 BC. Teotihuacán was meticulously planned and split into quadrants, with the Calle de Los Muertos and a now-lost road forming the axes of the city. The city sprawled over an area of 20 sq. km, and controlled the entire Valley of Mexico, with evidence of trade and influence extending as far south as the Mayan cities of Tikal and Copan in Guatemala. The Pirámide del Sol, one of the largest pyramids in the world, was built in the late pre-Classic period, while the newer Pirámide de la Luna was built during the Classic period.

While the reasons for its downfall are far from certain, many speculate that the city eventually collapsed under its own weight, having grown so large and crowded that it could no longer produce enough food to support its 100,000 inhabitants. Overcrowding seems to have led to new buildings built atop old ones, setting the stage for a tremendous fire around AD 800, marked today by layers of blackened stone. By AD 850, few residents remained in the enormous urban complex. When the Aztecs founded Tenochtitlán in the 14th century, Teotihuacán, 50km northeast of their capital, lay abandoned. Impressed by the size and scope of the buildings, the Aztecs adopted the areas as ceremonial grounds, believing that the huge structures were built by gods and that those buried there were superhuman. They called the area Teotihuacán, meaning "Place Where Men Become Gods." When the Spaniards destroyed Tenochtitlán in the 16th century, they were almost certainly unaware of the pyramid's existence, allowing the site to remain astonishingly intact. Porfirio Díaz initiated extensive excavation in 1906 as part of a project to emphasize Mexico's cultural wealth for the centennial of Mexican independence in 1910. The following sites are listed roughly in geographical order.

CALLE DE LOS MUERTOS (STREET OF THE DEAD). This ceremonial center was built along a 4km stretch (only 2 of which are open to tourists) now called Calle de los Muertos, so named because the Aztecs believed ancient kings had been buried alongside it. The northern limit of the street is the Pirámide de la Luna, while the southern boundary remains unexplored. The main structure, the Pirámide del Sol, lies to the east, aligned with the point on the horizon where the sun sets at the summer solstice. An east-west thoroughfare is believed to have bisected the Calle at some point in front of the Ciudadela.

■ CIUDADELA. At the southern end of the site is the expansive Citadel, where priests and government officials once lived. The large plaza was so named because of its resemblance to a military complex, though it actually housed royal residences. On the northern end of the Ciudadela lie four small pyramids. The top of the second one yields a wonderful view of the two nearby pyramids.

MEXICO CITY

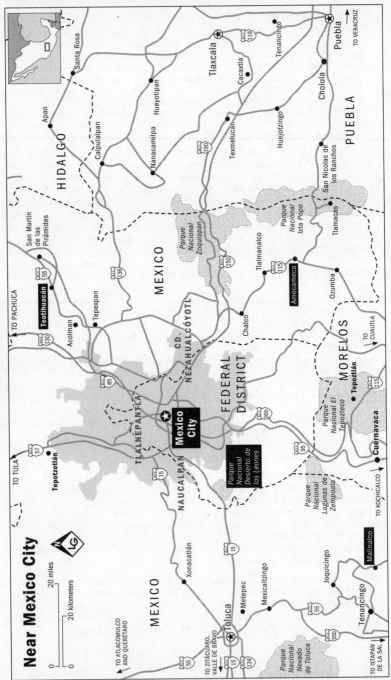

Near Mexico City

TEMPLO DE QUETZALCÓATL. At the center of the Ciudadela is the Templo de Quetzalcóatl, 50m wide at its base and dedicated to the serpent-god. The temple was consecrated during the Miccaotli phase with the sacrifice of over 200 war victims. Enormous carvings depict the sinuous bodies of plumed serpents swimming amongst shells and conches. Along the outer surface, images of Quetzalcóatl alternate with a reptilian image thought to be of the rain god Tlaloc or part of the Aztec creation myth. The still-visible red paint that originally decorated these sculptures was made by smashing the tiny, colorful bugs that burrow into *nopales* (broad, flat cactus leaves).

EDIFICIOS SUPERPUESTOS. Continuing north along Calle de los Muertos, you will cross what was once the San Juan river. On the western side of the street are the remains of two temples, the Edificios Superpuestos, built in two phases (AD 200-400 and AD 500-600) atop older, partially demolished temples. The older buildings were filled in to clear the way for construction—again, unintentionally preserving the temples, which can now be viewed with the aid of metal catwalks. Watch your head on the low doorways, as you descend to visit ancient buildings that the Teotihuacanos living at the time of the city's maximum splendor never knew. Along the sides of the Calle de los Muertos are the **Patio con Pisos de Mica**, the Grupo Viking complex, and the West Plaza and East Plaza complexes. Farther north is the Puma Mural.

■ **PIRÁMIDE DEL SOL.** Farther northeast towers the Pirámide del Sol (Pyramid of the Sun), the single most massive structure in the ceremonial area. The biggest American pyramid of its time, at 222m by 225m, it is second in size only to the pyramid at Cholula. Its volume of about one million cubic meters is comparable to that of Cheops in Egypt. Construction began sometime in the late pre-Classic era, around 200 BC, and completed just before the zenith of Teotihuacano civilization, around AD 150. The inside of the pyramid is filled with rubble and brick, and there is evidence that it was built over the remains of another pyramid. Historical chronicles from the 16th century suggesting that the pyramid was dedicated to the god of the sun may have been off-base. Remnants of a 3m wide moat surrounding the pyramid, child burials at the pyramid's corners, and a cave deep beneath the pyramid all suggest that it was dedicated to Tlaloc, the rain god. At nearly 65m in height, the pyramids afford a breathtaking view of the surrounding valley. A railing helps you up the steepest stretch, and the platforms of the multi-tiered pyramid make convenient rest stops.

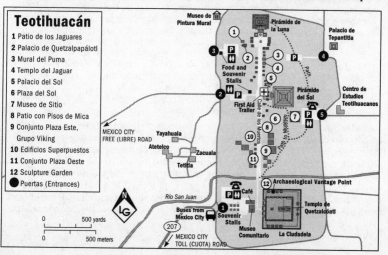

Teotihuacán

1 Patio de los Jaguares
2 Palacio de Quetzalpapálotl
3 Mural del Puma
4 Templo del Jaguar
5 Palacio del Sol
6 Plaza del Sol
7 Museo de Sitio
8 Patio con Pisos de Mica
9 Conjunto Plaza Este, Grupo Viking
10 Edificios Superpuestos
11 Conjunto Plaza Oeste
12 Sculpture Garden
● Puertas (Entrances)

MEXICO CITY

MUSEO DE SITIO. A path just south of the Pirámide del Sol will lead you to the Museo de Sitio. Exhibits focus on the culture and Teotihuacán's stages of construction, with displays of artifacts and graves. In one room, a transparent floor allows you to walk over a model of the ancient layout of the site. *(Open 10am-5pm. Included in Teotihuacán entrance fee.)*

PALACIO DE QUETZALPAPÁLOTL. West of the entrance to the square facing the Pirámide de la Luna is the Palacio de Quetzalpapálotl (Palace of the Quetzal Butterfly). This sumptuous columned palace kept its royal residents far from low-income and student housing. The gorgeous inner patio features colorful frescoes with bird glyphs, which retain much of their intricate detail. On the finely carved, inlaid columns are images of plumed butterflies, which give the Palacio its name.

PATIO DE LOS JAGUARES. Behind the palace and through the short maze of an entrance stands the Patio de los Jaguares and the now-subterranean **Templo de las Conchas Emplumadas** (Temple of the Feathered Seashells), which was buried when the Quetzalpapálotl was built. The patio features several murals of jaguars, which symbolize an ancient creator god that the Olmecs adopted. The Templo, reached via a modern tunnel, has beautifully preserved frescoes depicting green parrots and a four-petaled flower that symbolizes the cardinal directions.

PIRÁMIDE DE LA LUNA. At the northern end of Calle de los Muertos is the stunning Pirámide de la Luna (Pyramid of the Moon). This pyramid also has links to water: a sculpture of Chalchiutlicue, the revered Aztec water goddess, was discovered here. The pyramid was built later than the Pirámide del Sol, most likely around AD 500, and was probably used for public ceremonies. Beyond the five-tiered platform attached to the front, the pyramid's base measures 150m by 130m. Visitors can no longer climb the entirety of the steep, 42m high pyramid, but the view from atop the middle platform is spectacular.

PALACIO DE TEPANTITLA. On the northeastern side of the Pirámide del Sol, if you exit through Puerta 4 and walk 200-300m east, sits the Palacio de Tepantitla, which has some of the best-preserved frescoes in Teotihuacán. Priests with elaborate headdresses and representations of Tlaloc are depicted within the Teotihuacano ideal of a butterfly-filled paradise.

DESIERTO DE LOS LEONES

Bus service to the Desierto is often unreliable. Ruta 43 buses are meant to leave from San Ángel for the ex-convento at M: Viveros (every hr. 8am-5pm). This service is more reliable on weekends. You could also take a "La Marquesa" or "Acopilco" bus (1hr., 5.50 pesos) from M: Chapultepec or M: Tacubaya and ask the driver to drop you off at the Desierto entrance. From there, walk up the path for 4km, or flag down a taxi, which will drive you the rest of the way (30 pesos). Make sure to get a phone number to call for the return trip, or risk a long wait (or a long walk) on weekdays. Colectivos back to San Ángel (approx. every hr.; last bus 5pm) or buses to M: Tacubaya (1hr., 5.50 pesos) leave from the entrance. Free tours Sa-Su every hr. 10:30am-4:30pm (Spanish only). Park open daily 6am-5pm. Convent open Tu-Su 10am-5pm. 10 pesos.

Just outside the city, the Desierto de Los Leones (Desert of the Lions) offers solace and clean air among millions of pines. Hundreds of paths wind through the woods, perfect for hiking, picnicking, walking, or jogging. At the heart of the park sits the pristine **Ex-Convento Santo Desierto,** for which the park is named. Like all barefoot Carmelite convents, this was purposefully built in a desolate area to facilitate the extreme self-abnegation practiced by its sisters. Neither a desert nor inhabited by actual lions, the deserted site got its feline name either from the small pumas found in the area or from the name of the León brothers who founded the convent. The convent was originally built between 1606 and 1611; approximately 100 years later, an earthquake demolished it. The reconstruction finished in 1723, but from 1780 to 1801, due to weather conditions and incessant looting by their indigenous neighbors, the sisters abandoned it for another convent in the Nixcongo mountains. Wander through the immense corridors to catch a glimpse of bedrooms as they were left in 1801. Bring a flashlight or buy a candle (5 pesos) to descend into the *sótanos* (basements), rumored to have been a place of punishment for disobedient nuns. It is pitch black underneath the *ex-convento*, and the winding passages are not for the claustrophobic. The *ex-convento* hosts **concerts** that range from professional symphonies to student choirs. (Sa-Su noon-3pm; shows change weekly. Call the Cuajimalpa tourist office ☎5814 1171 for info. Concerts free with admission.)

AMECAMECA

From TAPO (M: San Lázaro), several bus lines go to Amecameca, the best starting point for volcanoes Popocatépetl and Iztaccíhuatl. Volcanes del Sur (☎5133 2424) has the most frequent service (2hr., every 15min. 5am-11pm; 21 pesos, students 11 pesos). From Amecameca, "Iztaccíhuatl" colectivos (every hr., 40 pesos) will take you to the trailhead. Alternately, take a taxi to the Paso de Cortés trailhead (120 pesos). If you decide to visit Iztaccíhuatl via San Rafael, catch a pesero going to Tlalmanalco (5am-7pm, 3.50 pesos) and get off in front of La Fábrica, a printing press (ask the driver to point it out). From there, another pesero (5 pesos) will take you to the San Rafael trailhead. To return to Mexico City, take a "Volcanes" bus or any "Metro San Lázaro" bus. They stop along at the station 2 blocks behind the Amecameca plaza or on the road labeled "México" in Tlalmanalco (every 30min. 6am-8pm, 21 pesos).

Amecameca is a sleepy, relatively untouristed town with an unbeatable view of its legendary pair of volcanoes. Located 57km southeast of Mexico City, it is the key post for staging an Izta climb. From Amecameca's plaza, admire the red-and-white tiled **Santuario del Sacromonte,** an important pilgrimage site built over a cave by the Franciscan friar Martín de Valencia in 1567 to convert local worshipers of the preHispanic god Tezcaltlipoca, or catch glimpses of the town's other 16th-century churches while cruising in a bicycle taxi. Amecameca goes nuts celebrating the **Feria de la Nuez** in the second week of August, during which many cultural and gastronomical events celebrate the region's walnut production. During the rest of the year, you can find numerous nutty treats in the **mercado** on Hidalgo, facing the plaza. Stock up on sundries for your trek or sit down for a *comida corrida* for 30 pesos. (Most stalls open daily 9am-7pm.)

Amecameca is overshadowed by its main attraction, the two snow-capped volcanoes, **Popocatépetl** (5452m) and **Iztaccíhuatl** (5282m), the 2nd- and 3rd-largest peaks in the country. Aztec legend has it that the warrior Popocatépetl ("Smoking Mountain" in Náhuatl) loved Iztaccíhuatl ("Sleeping Woman"), the emperor's daughter. Once, while Popocatépetl was off at battle, Iztaccíhuatl came to believe that he had been killed, and she subsequently died of grief. When Popo (as he has come to be known) learned of his lover's death, he built the two great mountains. On the northern one he placed her body (which, with a little imagination, you can see on a clear day by looking at Iztaccíhuatl from afar), and on the southern one he stood vigil with a torch. The passage between the two is called *Paso de Cortés* because it is the route the Spanish conqueror took to the valley of Tenochtitlán in 1519; he also used sulphur from Popocatépetl to create gunpowder for his troops.

Pay respect to Iztaccíhuatl on the mountain's snowy summit, as locals have done since pre-Hispanic times. Before your trek, visit the **Parque Nacional Izta-Popo** office, just behind the Santuario in Amecameca, to register your park entrance (20 pesos per person per day). Try to catch a free ride up the mountain in the park rangers' vehicle (8:30am; return 4:30pm). (Plaza de la Constitución 9, inside the Casa de Cultura. ☎978 3829 or 3930; http://iztapopo.conanp.gob.mx. Open daily 8am-5pm.)

Due to its active status, Popocatépetl has been closed to hikers since 1994. Approaching within 12km of the crater is not recommended and visits are presently limited to hikes around the base. Signs pointing to *Rutas de Evacuación* (escape routes) in all nearby towns are reminders of the omnipresent danger. Parts of Iztaccíhuatl can be explored on easy daytrips, but only the seriously seasoned or those with a tour group should attempt the peak. No season is free from rapid weather change; always bring both warm clothes and rain gear. Also, start your hikes in early in the day to avoid afternoon fog or sudden snowstorms. Federación Mexicana de Alpinismo, all Mexican officials, and *Let's Go* strongly advises against making even a daytrip when the **Socorro Alpino** is not nearby. They should be contacted immediately should you have an accident or **medical emergency** in the mountains (Socorro Alpino, Alpine Assistance. Orozco y Berra 26-5, Col. Buenavista, D.F. ☎5392 9299 or 5566 2306, emergency 04455 2698 7557; http://groups.msn.com/socorroalpino). The Socorro Alpino is at **La Joya trailhead** every weekend to provide guidance.

Although Iztaccíhuatl is most easily reached from San Rafael via Tlalmanalco, it is well worth the extra pesos it takes to get to La Joya via Amecameca. If you are planning a longer or non-weekend trip, be certain to register with Socorro Alpino before you go. For general information and contacts of different companies that lead trips to the volcanoes, try the **Asociación Mexicana de Turismo de Aventura y Ecoturismo,** Juan Bautista 450 in Col. La Nopalera Tlahuac, D.F. 13220. (☎5863 3363; www.amtave.org.) Consider staying overnight at a base camp, like the **Albergue Altzomoni ❶** close to Amecameca, before setting out in order to adjust to the higher altitude. (20-30 pesos per night.) From there, guides will take you to the volcanoes.

MALINALCO

From Terminal Poniente (M: Observatorio), Autotransportes Águila (☎5272 9218) runs buses directly to Malinalco (2hr.; 4:20, 5:20, 6:20pm; 50 pesos, students 25 pesos) at inconvenient times. They also run more frequent buses to Chalma (2hr., every 20min. 6:30am-9pm; 62 pesos, students 31 pesos); Malinalco is only a 15min. taxi (20 pesos) or colectivo (7 pesos) ride from there. Return buses directly from Malinalco are equally rare (2hr.; 4:20, 5:20, 6:20am; 50 pesos, students 25 pesos); returning from Chalma is a better option (last bus at 6:30pm). To get to the ruins from the zócalo, follow the blue pyramid signs along Guerrero and go straight. Take a left on Melgar, a right at the next street, and another right at the blue sign that appears to lead into a driveway. From the entrance, it is a long walk up a lot of stairs. Malinalco's tourist office is upstairs in the white municipal building in the park next to the zócalo. (☎147 0152. Open M-F 9am-4pm, Sa 9am-1pm. Kiosk in zócalo open Sa-Su and holidays 9am-4pm.) Site open Tu-Su 9am-5:30pm. 37 pesos; Su free. Free guided tours in Spanish only upon request.

Malinalco is a small, peaceful town with one huge attraction: one of the best-preserved Aztec temples in the country. ◗**El Cuauhcalli,** or the **Templo de la Iniciación,** was cut whole from a nearby mountain and, along with pyramids in India, Jordan, and Egypt, is one of only four monolithic pyramids in the world. The Aztecs conquered Malinalco between 1469 and 1481, and emperor Ahuizotl began the pyramid's construction in 1501. The 1519 arrival of the Spanish interrupted work on the western-most part. Every year on March 21, during the spring equinox, hundreds of people dressed in white pour into Malinalco to climb the pyramid and perform a ceremony that charges them with energy. During the winter equinox, on December 21, visitors witness a ray of light shine through the temple doorway to reveal the image of an eagle on the floor.

The ruins are believed to have been the sacred ground for the rituals that marked the promotion of an Aztec youth into a jaguar or eagle warrior. On the open circular stone platform facing the main temple, prisoners were bound to a pole with only their arms free and forced to wrestle the aspiring warriors. If the prisoner won consecutive bouts with two eagle and two jaguar warriors, followed by a wild-card lefty, he won his freedom. Defeat brought more unpleasant consequences; the small rectangular basin in front of the entrance to the pyramid would hold the prisoner's blood after his ritual sacrifice. Behind the pyramid, the bodies of fallen warriors were burned on the oval bed of rock and their ashes left for the wind to scatter. Climb up the stairs to the right to get a better view of the snake-mouth entrance to the once-polychromatic circular temple. Around the temple are various dwellings, originally plastered in stucco and elaborate murals. The three-story museum, **Museo Universitario de Dr. Luis Mario Schneider,** Calle Amajac at Melgar, houses artifacts from the site and exhibits on Malinalco's traditions. The museum's highlight is the dark, cool replica of the Cuauhcalli temple. (☎ 147 1288; museolms@uaemex.com. Open Tu-Su 10am-6pm. 10 pesos; W free.)

BAJA CALIFORNIA

Cradled between the warm, tranquil Sea of Cortés on the east and the cold, raging Pacific Ocean on the west, the peninsula of Baja California claims one of the most spectacular and diverse landscapes in the world. Sparse expanses of sandy deserts give way to barren mountains jutting into cloudless sky. The high-altitude national parks of northern Baja California are home to evergreens and snow during the winter months. And then, of course, there's the unbelievably blue-green water surrounding Baja California's miles of uninhabited shoreline. Waters flow past coral reefs, encircle rocky coves, and lap at thousands of miles of white sand lining both coasts. Called *"el otro México"* (the other Mexico), Baja California is neither here nor there: not at all California, yet nothing like mainland Mexico. Baja was permanently settled by the Franciscans and Jesuits in the 1600s, who left their legacy in sleepy towns like San Ignacio. Indeed, the peninsula's small Jesuit missions contrast with mainland Mexico's massive Mayan and Zapotec temples.

Until 1973, when the Transpeninsular Highway (Mex. 1) was completed, the only way to reach Baja California's rugged desert terrain was by plane or boat. With the addition of better toll roads and ferry service, Baja has become a popular vacation spot among Arizonans, Californians, and Mexicans, as well as a destination for American expats and retirees. Vacationers range from hardy campers to families that stay in the peninsula's many RV parks. Large resort hotels and condominium complexes are rapidly developing to accommodate human torrents to the south. Cabo San Lucas, the mega-resort haven on the southern tip, and Tijuana, the bawdy border wasteland of **Baja California Norte,** have both embraced the US dollar, leading to two highly Americanized travel destinations at opposite ends of the peninsula. La Paz, the capital of **Baja California Sur,** is a southern beacon of beauty for resort-weary port-seekers. But it is Baja's southern midsection—from the tranquility of Mulegé to the palm-laden oasis town of San Ignacio to the thousands of undisturbed beaches beneath sheer cliffs—that is most pristine and mysterious. Most of Baja California is still somewhat of an undiscovered country, prime for the budget traveler to explore.

HIGHLIGHTS OF BAJA CALIFORNIA

DROP IN on artsy expatriates in the friendly town of **Todos Santos** (p. 204), and then catch the perfect wave at one of the area's pristine surfing beaches.

CAMP on the secluded and beautiful beaches of **Bahía de la Concepción** (p. 191), 48km of turquoise water, powdery sand, bubbly springs, and abundant marine life.

WAVE to a whale during whale watching season in **Puerto San Carlos** (p. 196), **San Ignacio** (p. 185), or **Guerrero Negro** (p. 181).

STROLL down the *malecón* in breezy, beautiful **La Paz** (p. 198), the good-natured capital of Baja Sur, while watching the sun set over the Sea of Cortés.

SNORKEL with sea lions and admire the colorful array of fish near **Isla Espíritu Santo** (p. 202) off La Paz or **Isla Coronado** (p. 195) near Loreto.

SURF the highly acclaimed waves close to the **Corridor** (p. 213), along the road stretching between **San José del Cabo** (p. 214) and **Cabo San Lucas** (p. 207).

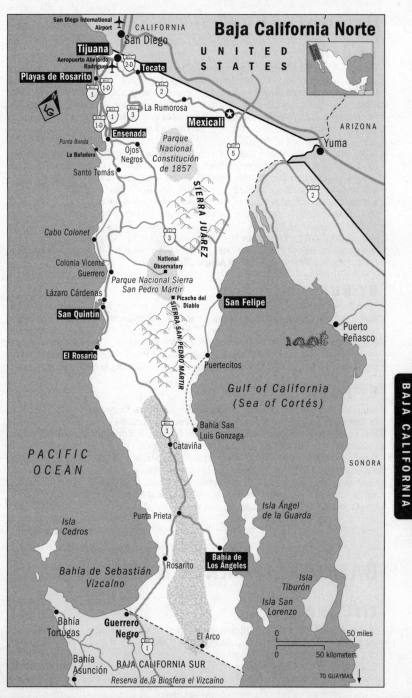

Baja California Norte

San Diego International Airport

CALIFORNIA

San Diego

Tijuana

Aeropuerto Abelardo Rodriguez

Playas de Rosarito

Tecate

La Rumorosa

Mexicali

U N I T E D

S T A T E S

ARIZONA

Yuma

Ensenada

Punta Banda

La Bufadora

Ojos Negros

Santo Tomás

Parque Nacional Constitución de 1857

SIERRA JUAREZ

Cabo Colonet

Colonia Vicente Guerrero

National Observatory

Lázaro Cárdenas

Parque Nacional Sierra San Pedro Mártir

Picacho del Diablo

San Felipe

San Quintín

SIERRA SAN PEDRO MÁRTIR

El Rosario

Puertecitos

Puerto Peñasco

Gulf of California (Sea of Cortés)

PACIFIC OCEAN

Bahía San Luis Gonzaga

Cataviña

SONORA

Isla Cedros

Punta Prieta

Isla Ángel de la Guarda

Bahía de Sebastián Vizcaíno

Rosarito

Bahía de Los Ángeles

Isla Tiburón

Isla San Lorenzo

Bahía Tortugas

Guerrero Negro

El Arco

0   50 miles

0   50 kilometers

Bahía Asunción

BAJA CALIFORNIA SUR

Reserva de la Biosfera el Vizcaíno

TO GUAYMAS

BAJA CALIFORNIA

GETTING AROUND

BY CAR

Highways quickly degrade into pothole-ridden stretches of pavement, making speeds in excess of 80km per hr. dangerous. Livestock on the highways and a lack of guardrails make driving at night impossible—if this warning doesn't convince you, check out the huge number of roadside shrines to the deceased. The intense heat pummels cars, and repair services can be hard to find. Still, a car is the only way to get close to the more scenic and secluded areas of Baja, and the ride is probably one of the most beautiful in Mexico. Drive slowly, never drive at night, and keep your tank full. If you are planning on driving over dirt or sandy roads (there are a lot of them off the highway), you'll be much more comfortable in an 4WD vehicle. The **Ángeles Verdes** (Green Angels; p. 36), who provide roadside assistance, pass along Mex. 1 twice per day. Don't pass a **PEMEX** without filling up, as the central section of the highway does not have many gas stations. If you are driving in from the US, obtain a vehicle permit, which is required south of San Felipe on the Sea of Cortés side and south of Ensenada on the Pacific side. If you will be driving in Baja for more than 72hr., show the vehicle's title and proof of registration for a free permit at the border. For more information on driving in Mexico, see **Getting Around: By Car,** p. 34.

BY BUS

Most buses between Ensenada and La Paz are *de paso*, which means that buses pass through cities, rather than originate or terminate in them. This makes it impossible to reserve seats in advance. You'll have to leave at inconvenient times, fight to procure a ticket, and possibly stand the whole way. It is much more pleasant to buy a reserved seat in Tijuana, Ensenada, La Paz, or Los Cabos, and traverse the peninsula in one trip. For more information, see **Getting Around: By Bus,** p. 33.

BY BOAT

Baja has three different ferry routes: **Santa Rosalía to Guaymas** (10-11hr.), **La Paz to Topolobampo/Los Mochis** (5hr.), and **La Paz to Mazatlán** (17hr.). Ferries from La Paz leave from nearby Pichilingue. The La Paz to Topolobampo/Los Mochis route provides direct access to the CHEPE train (p. 259) from Los Mochis through the Copper Canyon. Ferry tickets, especially for the nicer cabins, are expensive and difficult to find. The bottom-of-the-line *salón* ticket entitles you to a seat in a large room with few communal baths. If you find yourself traveling *salón*-class at night, ditch your seat and stake out a spot on the floor or outside on the deck. Storage is available, but your belongings will be inaccessible until arrival. Those who plan to take their car aboard should make reservations a month in advance. For further ferry information, contact a local **Sematur** office.

BAJA CALIFORNIA NORTE

TIJUANA ☎ 664

In the shadow of swollen, sulfur-spewing factories lies the most notorious specimen of border subculture: Tijuana (pop. 1.2 million). It's hard to say if it's the city's strange charm, its cheap booze, or its sprawling, unapologetic hedonism that attracts 30 million visitors each year. At the time of the Mexican-American War, modest Rancho Tía Juana found itself on the new border between Alta California (US) and Baja California (Mexico). At first, the town grew slowly, but Prohibition gave Tijuana the opportunity to cater to the vices of its northern neighbors. Forbidden industries became deeply ingrained in "TJ." In recent years, officials have made an effort to clean up the city. Sex shops and prostitution have left the *centro*, and Tijuana is now a slightly more family-oriented place. More common are the hollow boasts of debauchery on cheap T-shirts, the chance to have a photograph taken with a donkey painted to look like a zebra, and hats bearing lewd slogans. This is not to say that the city has lost its dirty sheen: catering to the US thirst for illicit substances is a fabulous source of wealth for some in Tijuana, one of the largest ports of entry for illegal drugs.

▐ TRANSPORTATION

INTERCITY TRANSPORTATION

Flights: Gen. Abelardo L. Rodríguez (TIJ; ☎683 1060), east of the *centro* in Mesa de Otay. Serviced by: **Aviacsa** (☎006 2200; www.aviacsa.com); **Aerocalifornia** (☎685 5500); **Mexicana** (☎502 2000; www.mexicana.com); **Aeroméxico** (☎021 4000; www.aeromexico.com). To get to the airport, take the inexpensive "Aeropuerto" bus from Paseo de los Héroes across the street from the Centro Cultural (approx. 15min.). The easiest way to get to the *centro* from the airport is by taxi. Negotiate the hefty prices the taxi drivers will shout out at you, which often run US$15 and up. Your best bet is to avoid dealing with the taxi drivers directly and head to one of the many taxi booths.

Buses: Tijuana has 3 main bus stations, all in different parts of the city, in addition to a separate Mexicoach station.

Downtown Station: The most convenient station, a block from Revolución on Calle Primera. **Élite** (☎688 1979) buses stop here 1hr. before embarking from the Central Camionera for **Mexico City** (46hr., every hr. 7am-8pm, 1128 pesos) via **Hermosillo** (12hr., 417 pesos) and **Guadalajara** (34hr., 981 pesos). **Greyhound** (☎688 1979) also picks up passengers downtown before leaving the Central for **Los Angeles** (3hr., every 2hr. 6am-4am, US$25), where buses connect to other North American cities. **Suburbaja** (☎688 0082) sends buses to **Tecate** (every 20min. 5am-9am, 42 pesos) and **Rosarito** (every 30min. 5am-9am, 14 pesos).

San Ysidro Terminal (☎621 2982), near the main border crossing and a short walk from the *centro*. **Estrellas del Pacífico** (☎683 2938) runs to: **Guadalajara** (32hr., 10 per day 8:30am-10pm, 899 pesos) via **Hermosillo** (12hr., 382 pesos); **Mazatlán** (26hr., 596 pesos); **Mexicali** (2½hr., 150 pesos); **Los Mochis** (19hr., 530 pesos); **Obregón** (17hr., 501 pesos).

Central Camionera: The city's largest terminal, near the airport. **Autotransportes de Baja California** (☎683 5681 or 104 7400) runs to: **Ensenada** (1½hr., 12 per day 9am-11pm, 121 pesos); **La Paz** (22hr.; 8am, 9pm; 1399 pesos) via **Loreto** (17hr., 1147 pesos), **San Ignacio** (13hr., 805 pesos), and **Santa Rosalía** (15hr., 1147 pesos); **Mexicali** (3hr., 11 per day 7am-9pm, 180 pesos); **Puerto Peñasco** (8hr.; 11am, 5:30pm; 392 pesos); **San Felipe** (6hr., 3:30pm, 362 pesos). Station accessible only by overpriced taxi (about US$15, but negotiable) or by blue local bus (30min., 6.50 pesos). To find one of these buses, marked "Centro," go out of the main exit of the terminal, turn left, and walk to the end of the building. Buses will let you off on Calle 3 and Constitución, 1 block west of Revolución; catch the station-bound bus 2 blocks away, at Calle 1 and Constitución. It also stops opposite the San Ysidro terminal near the border.

Mexicoach Station: 1025 Revolución, between Calles 6 and 7. **Mexicoach** (in Tijuana ☎685 1470, in San Diego 619-428-9517; www.mexicoach.com) buses depart for the San Ysidro border crossing (30min., every 30min. 5am-9pm, round-trip US$8). Rosarito beach shuttle also available (1hr., every 2hr. 9am-7pm, round-trip US$16). *Colectivos* to Rosarito 20 pesos.

Car Rental: Budget, Paseo de los Héroes 77 (☎634 3303), next to the Hotel Camino Real. 24+. Open M-F 8am-7pm, Sa 8am-4pm. **Hertz** (☎607 3950), at 9575 Paseo Centenario. 24+. Open M-F 7am-11pm and Sa 9am-2pm. Before driving into Mexico from the US, purchase car insurance for US$10-15 per day in San Ysidro. Prices fall with length of stay in Mexico. Many drive-through insurance companies have offices at Sycamore and Primero, just before the border.

BORDER CROSSING. At the world's largest border crossing, northbound lanes often have backups of more than 150 cars. The best time to cross is during weekday mornings. The southbound ride is almost always smoother, but weekends can be rough in both directions. If you're crossing into Tijuana for a day or so, it's easier to leave your car in a lot on the US side and walk across the border. Remember that a tourist card (roughly US$20) is needed if you plan to stay longer than seven days. Regardless of which way you are crossing, bring proper ID (p. 10) and leave your bushels of fruit, truckloads of livestock, stashes of drugs, and armory of weapons behind.

DRIVING DIRECTIONS:

From **Mexicali:** By car, take Mex. 2 west out of Mexicali (209km, 2½hr), get on *cuota* (toll) road Mex. 2D, and follow the "Aeropuerto" signs west. The airport road turns into Cuauhtémoc and crosses the river before running into Agua Caliente and eventually Revolución (2km).

From **Rosarito:** By car, take Mex. 1 (27km, 30min.), arrive on 16 de Septiembre, head north until the intersection with Agua Caliente, and turn left to reach the *centro*. For the scenic 1D route, take Calle 2A, which continues east to Revolución.

From **San Diego:** Grab a trolley on the blue line and ride to the border. (25min. from downtown.) From there, follow the instructions below for San Ysidro. By car, take US I-5 South or US 805 South (approx. 48km, 25min.). Both lead to the San Ysidro border crossing. "Centro" signs lead to Calle 2a.

From **San Ysidro:** Follow the signs to the *centro* on foot; head for the tall arch at the top of Revolución (15min.). You can also take the red Mexicoach bus (p. 151). If you can't wait, take a taxi (US$3).

LOCAL TRANSPORTATION

Traveling within the city, traditional yellow cabs, which prey almost exclusively on tourists, charge absurd rates. Negotiate a price before getting in, or better yet, avoid them completely. White-and-red *taxis libres* are likely to offer slightly better prices and will go anywhere in the city. Much cheaper communal cabs, otherwise known as *colectivos* or route taxis, are popular with locals and go almost anywhere in the city for under 20 pesos. Operating as small buses, they run circuits of the routes painted above the rear tires and on the windshield, where you'll also see the standard fares written out. Most originate on or around Madero or Constitución between Calles 1 and 5. They go to **Rosarito** (20 pesos, yellow-and-white, originate on Madero around Calle 3), **El Toreo** (10 pesos, red-and-black, originate on Calle 4 and Constitución), and the **Zona Río** (9 pesos, green-and-white, originate on Calle 3 between Constitución and Revolución), among other destinations. At night, it is best to travel by taxi in the *centro*.

🔲🔃 ORIENTATION AND PRACTICAL INFORMATION

To the vast majority of visitors, Tijuana is simply **Avenida Revolución. La Revo,** as it is commonly known, forms the heart of the **Zona Centro.** *Calles* numbered from north to south cross La Revo, while *avenidas* (Constitución is nearest to the west, Madero to the east) run parallel to La Revo. At the intersection of La Revo and Calle Primera (1a), a prominent steel arch marks the northern border of the *centro* and the beginning of Zona Norte. **Avoid the Zona Norte,** notorious for drug-smuggling, prostitution, and border-running. It can be dangerous for tourists. Along the river east of the *centro* is the Zona Río, whose main street is **Paseo de los Héroes.** This zone is home to Tijuana's popular local club, music, and cultural scene.

Tourist Office: (☎685 2210). A small, freestanding booth at Revolución and Calle 3. English-speaking staff with good maps. Open daily 10am-4pm. Branch at the border crossing.

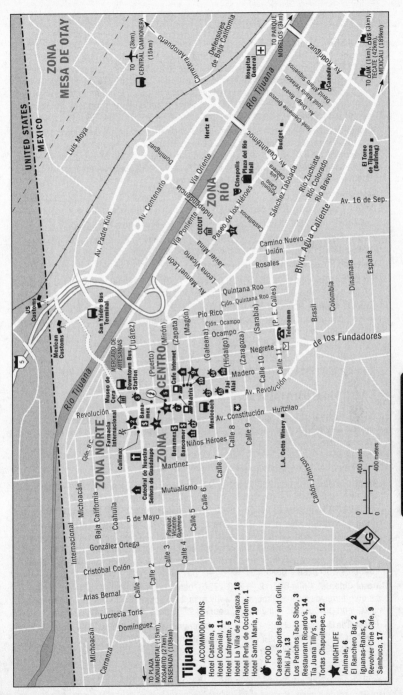

BAJA CALIFORNIA

Tijuana

● ACCOMMODATIONS
Hotel Catalina, 8
Hotel Colonial, 11
Hotel Lafayette, 5
Hotel La Villa de Zaragoza, 16
Hotel Perla de Occidente, 1
Hotel Santa María, 10

● FOOD
Caesar's Sports Bar and Grill, 7
Chiki Jai, 13
Los Panchos Taco Shop, 3
Restaurant Ricardo's, 14
Tía Juana Tilly's, 15
Tortas Chapultepec, 12

★ NIGHTLIFE
Animale, 6
El Ranchero Bar, 2
Iguanas-Ranas, 4
Revolver Cine Cafe, 9
Sambuca, 17

Customs Office: (☎624 2280, www.aduanos.gob.mx), at the border on the Mexican side after crossing the San Ysidro bridge. Sells tourist permits (p. 11). Open 24hr.

Consulates: Canada, Gérman Gedovius 10400-101 (☎684 0461, after-hours emergencies 800 706 2900), in the Zona Río. Open M-F 9am-1pm. **UK,** Salinas 1500 (☎681 8402, after-hours emergencies 686 5320), on Col. Aviación at La Mesa. Open M-F 9am-2pm. **US,** Tapachula Sur 96 (☎622 7400 or 681 8016), in Col. Hipódromo, adjacent to the racetrack southeast of town. In an emergency, call the San Diego office (☎619-692-2154) and leave a message and a phone number; an officer will respond. Open M-F 8am-4pm.

Banks: Banks along Constitución offer similar rates for exchanging currency or traveler's checks. **Banamex** (☎688 0021), on Constitución at Calle 4. Open M-Sa 9am-4pm. **Bancomer** (☎638 4371), on Constitución at Calle 5. Open M-F 8:30am-4pm, Sa 10am-2pm. Both have **24hr. ATMs.** *Casas de cambio* offer better rates but may charge commission or refuse to exchange traveler's checks.

Emergency: ☎066.

Police: Constitución 1616 (☎685 6557, 24hr. tourist helpline ☎078), at Calle 8.

Red Cross: (☎621 7787), on Gamboa at Silvestre, across from Price Club.

Pharmacies: Throughout the Zona Centro. For 24hr. service go to **Farmacia Internacional** (☎685 2790), on the corner of Constitución and Calle 2.

Hospital: Hospital General, Centenario 10851 (☎684 0237 or 0922), in the Zona Río.

Fax Office: Telecomm (☎684 7902; fax 684 7750), on Negrete, to the right of the post office in the same building. Open M-F 7am-7pm, Sa 7am-3:30pm.

Internet Access: Matrix Internet Place (☎688 2273), at Revolución and Calle 5. 16 pesos per hr. Open daily 10am-midnight. **Cafe Internet** (☎290 0508; www.cybertijuana.com), on Calle 5 between Madero and Revolución. 15 pesos per hr., or free with a drink order. Open daily 8am-10pm.

Post Office: (☎684 7950), on Negrete at Calle 11 (Elías Calles). Open M-F 8am-5pm, Sa 9am-1pm. **Postal Code:** 22000.

ACCOMMODATIONS

As a general rule, hotels in Tijuana become less reputable the farther north you go. Avoid any in the Zona Norte. Though crowded during the day, even the Zona Centro can be unsettling at night, especially between Revolución and Constitución close to the Zona Norte. Take a taxi if you need to cross this area at night. Reserve ahead for weekends. Expect to pay in cash.

Hotel Catalina, Madero 2039 (☎685 9748 or 688 1005), on the corner of Calle 5. Friendly staff greets visitors to this homey hotel. Singles are miniature, but other rooms are spacious. Singles 220 pesos; doubles 260 pesos, with TV 320 pesos. Cash only. ❸

Hotel Lafayette, Revolución 325, 2nd fl. (☎685 3940 or 3339), between Calles 3 and 4. Remarkably quiet for being in the middle of Revolución's chaos, though you may still find that your bed throbs to the beat from Iguanas-Ranas across the road. Clean rooms with private bath, fan, phone, and TV. Free Wi-Fi. Singles 295 pesos; doubles 380 pesos. Cash only. ❺

Hotel Colonial, Calle 6 1812 (☎688 1720), between Constitución and Niños Héroes, in a quieter residential neighborhood away from Revolución. Airy rooms with big windows, A/C, and private bath. Singles and doubles 270 pesos. Cash only. ❹

Hotel Santa María (☎685 6160), on Madero between Calles 5 and 6. Offers decent lodging and clean, private bath for reasonable prices. Singles 200 pesos; doubles 320 pesos. Cash only. ❸

Hotel Perla de Occidente, Mutualismo 758 (☎685 1358), between Calles 1 and 2, 4 blocks from Revolución. Dark rooms with private bath and cozy bed around an indoor patio. Singles 150 pesos; doubles 300 pesos. Cash only. ❷

Hotel La Villa de Zaragoza, Madero 1120 (☎685 1832, www.hotellavilla.biz), between Calles 7 and 8. Spacious rooms with king-size bed, phone, and cable TV. Ask for the cheapest room available. Free parking with 24hr. security. Free Wi-Fi. Rooms from 438 pesos. AmEx/MC/V. ❺

🍴 FOOD

Like most things in Tijuana, restaurants are often loud and in-your-face; promoters try to drag tourists into the pricey joints lining Revolución. Sometimes, however, paying a couple of extra pesos can reap delicious benefits. For cheap fast food, try the taco stands in the *centro*. **Calimax** is a supermarket on Calle 2 at Constitución. (☎633 7988. Open daily 6am-midnight.)

Restaurant Chiki Jai (☎685 4955), on Revolución and Calle 7. This Spanish-style restaurant has provided dishes from across the Atlantic since 1947. Large portions of seafood paella (100 pesos). Tapas 30-60 pesos. Open daily 11am-9pm. Cash only. ❹

Los Panchos Taco Shop (☎685 7277), on Revolución at Calle 3. A handy pit stop for hungry clubbers. A large sign in the store says "Say no to drugs. Say yes to tacos." Juicy burritos are filled generously with *carne asada* (13-17 pesos). Open M-Th and Su 8am-midnight, F-Sa 8am-4am. Cash only. ❶

Tortas Chapultepec (☎685 1412), at Constitución and Calle 6. This local favorite turns out tasty *tortas* and breakfasts (25-50 pesos). Open daily 8am-9:45pm. ❸

Restaurant Ricardo's (☎685 3146), at Madero and Calle 7. Deservedly popular, this diner serves some of the best *tortas* in town (32-55 pesos). Try the *super especial* (ham and *carne asada;* 39 pesos). Open 24hr. MC/V. ❸

Tía Juana Tilly's (☎685 6024; www.sdro.com/tillys), on Revolución and Calle 7. Uncommonly good Mexican combo plates US$7.50. Open M-F 9am-10pm, Sa-Su 9am-11pm. MC/V. ❺

Caesar's Sports Bar and Grill (☎685 5608), on Revolución between Calles 4 and 5. In a moment of culinary genius, the Caesar salad was born in this smoky pub in 1924. You can still order the late-night favorite (66 pesos). Open daily 10am-8pm. MC/V. ❹

👁 SIGHTS

While the most entertaining sights in town belong to La Revo, Tijuana's parks and museums offer another side of local culture that is often overlooked. Pay them a visit and you'll go home with a less impressive collection of straw hats but a more balanced sense of the city's culture and heritage.

▓**CENTRO CULTURAL TIJUANA (CECUT).** With its beige sphere, CECUT is Tijuana's most visually striking feature. The main attraction is the **Museo de las Californias,** where a collection of artifacts and models with bilingual descriptions and interactive terminals traces the history of the peninsula from its earliest inhabitants through the Spanish conquest, the Mexican-American War, and the 20th century. Tastefully presented exhibits make for a great introduction to the peninsula's unique cultural heritage. CECUT also hosts temporary science and art exhibitions and showcases Tijuana's cultural vitality with dance performances, concerts, and opera in the **Sala de Espectáculos.** The sphere hosts **Cine Omnimax,** where films are shown on a vast 180° screen every hr. in the afternoon. Occasional interpretive tours and live dance performances are held at the **Jardín Caracol,** a snail-shaped garden with reproductions of pre-Hispanic sculptures. *(CECUT ☎687 9641; www.cecut.gob.mx. Museum open Tu-Su 10am-7pm. 20 pesos, students and children 12 pesos. Cine Omnimax tickets 44 pesos, students and children 25 pesos.)*

BREWERY AND VINEYARD. Since 2000, **Cervecería Tijuana** has been turning out fine European-style gold pilsner. Informative tours of the plant detail the brewing process and end with samples of the best Tijuanan beer. *(Blvr. Fundadores 2951. ☎638 8662 or 2163; www.tjbeer.com. Schedule free tours by phone M-F 10am-noon. Free.)* Family-run **L.A. Cetto Winery,** established by Italian immigrants in 1926, maintains vineyards in the Valle de Guadalupe, northeast of Ensenada. Brief tours of the beautiful California redwood bottling facility are available, but the real draw is the chance to sample and purchase the products at a fraction of their normal shelf prices. *(Cañón Johnson 2108. ☎685 3031; www.cettowines.com. Tours every hr. M-F 10am-1:30pm and 4-6pm, Sa 1-4pm. Free. Wine tasting 80 pesos, includes 4 wines.)*

PARQUE ESTATAL MORELOS. This state-run park is close to the highway but offers walks, boat rides, an open-air theater, and a small zoo with lions, tiger, and ostriches. *(Blvr. de los Insurgentes 16000. Take a green bus from Constitución and Calle 5, 6.50 pesos. ☎625 2469. Open Tu-Su 9am-5pm. Parking 10 pesos. Free.)*

OTHER SIGHTS. If you want to visit a museum in Tijuana without losing sight of La Revo's tackiness, make a beeline for the **Museo de Cera** (wax museum). 86 life-size figures welcome you, organized into Mexican History, International Politics, Stage and Screen, and Horror. Memorable combinations (of which there are several) include President Vicente Fox and Fidel Castro towering over Mother Teresa and Mahatma Gandhi. *(Calle 1 and Madero. ☎688 2478. Open daily 10am-6pm. 15 pesos.)* Tijuana is not known for its architecture, but one building does catch the eye. The distinctive **Jai Alai Palace** on Revolución and Calle 7 was finished in 1947 after 21 years of construction, housing courts for the Basque ball game jai alai. Unfortunately, the sport has not been played there for years, and only the betting shop remains in use. The building, with a central hall that can seat 3000, now hosts concerts, dance performances, and boxing matches. The **Catedral de Nuestra Señora de Guadalupe,** at Calle 2 and Niños Héroes, is also an impressive structure. Finally, the **Monumental Arch,** built in 2000, is a must-see at Revolución and Calle 1.

♪ ENTERTAINMENT

Tijuana is home to two major bullrings. **El Toreo de Tijuana,** 221 Av. Santa Maria, the smaller of the two, is southeast of town just off Agua Caliente. El Toreo hosts the 1st round of fights (May-July alternate Su). Take a red-and-black taxi (10 pesos) from Calle 4 and Constitución to El Toreo. *(☎686 1219; www.bull-fights.org.)* The seaside **Plaza Monumental** hosts the 2nd round (Aug.-Oct.). Mexi-coach sends buses on fight days; alternatively, take the blue-and-white local buses from Calle 3 at Constitución. *(☎680 1808; www.plazamonumental.com.)*

Countless vendors await incoming tourists at the Mexican side of the footbridge from the US. The gaudy shopping scene continues most of the way up Revolución, as far as the intersection with Calle 7. Another spot to browse tourist-oriented wares is the **Mercado de Artesanía,** in the area bordered by Negrete, Ocampo, and Calles 1 and 2. There are also vendors on **Plaza Santa Cecilia,** near the arch on Revolución. Bargaining is a must, as quoted prices are usually well above reasonable.

To catch a flick, head to **Cinepolis,** in the Plaza del Río mall on Paseo de los Héroes, which screens Hollywood blockbusters and Mexican independent films. (☎684 1032. Open daily noon-midnight. Tickets 50 pesos.)

NIGHTLIFE

In the 1920s, the Prohibition ban on alcohol drove US citizens south of the border to revel in the forbidden nectars of cacti, grapes, and hops. The flow of Americans thirsty for booze remains unencumbered, and many take advantage of the low drinking age (18) to circumvent US prohibitions. The price tag, however, has gone up, and a night in TJ is costly, if not memorable. Stroll down **Revolución** after dusk and you'll be bombarded by lights, music and club promoters hawking overpriced two-for-one margaritas. The chaotic mix of pop, reggae, hip hop, and Latin hits spun by DJs sets the tone for all of La Revo. Clubs catering to gays and lesbians cluster in **Plaza Santa Cecilia** between Calles 1 and 2, east of Revolución.

Revolver Cine Cafe (☎685 1233; www.myspace.com/revolvercinecafe), on Madero between Calles 5 and 6, next to Hotel Catalina. Tijuana's young, artsy crowd hangs out at the Revolver, a coffee shop by day that showcases underground movies and bands by night. Open M and Th-Su 10am-10pm, Tu-W 10am-midnight. Cash only.

Sambuca, in the Plaza Fiesta Mall at Paseo de los Héroes and Independencia. Plays Brazilian-influenced dance music. It's best to take a taxi to return to the *centro.* Open M-Th 7pm-2am, F-Sa 7pm-late. Cash only.

Iguanas-Ranas (☎688 3885), on Revolución at Calle 3. A sublimely wacky world of life-size plaster clowns, balloons, and kitschy US pop-culture paraphernalia. Take the opportunity to pound beers (20 pesos) in an authentic yellow school bus high above Revolución. Open M-Th 10am-2am, F-Su 10am-5am. Cash only.

Animale (www.clubanimale.com), on Revolución at Calle 4. The biggest, glitziest, and loudest hedonistic haven of them all. 2 drinks for US$7. Watch out—the similarly named Animale Continental next door is an altogether more "adult" experience. Open daily 10am-4am. Cash only.

El Ranchero Bar (☎685 2800), in front of the fountain in Plaza Santa Cecilia. A popular spot with rainbow-colored parrots and palm trees decorating the long, dimly lit bar. A mellow crowd drinks US$1 beers. Open 10am-6am. Cash only.

TECATE ☎665

Tecate (pop. 100,000), on Mex. 2, between Mexicali and Tijuana, provides a peaceful respite from both of its neighbors. The green Parque Hidalgo is the center of life, where strolling families, vendors, tourists, and even the occasional clown collide. Nearby, a bakery turns out more Mexican pastries than perhaps any other store on the peninsula. Just a few blocks away, a quiet factory produces the town's best-known product—Mexico's unofficial national beer, Tecate. The streets are safe, prices are low, and the people are friendly. Tecate is the perfect place to sit back, relax, and—of course—grab a beer.

TRANSPORTATION

Catch **buses** one block east of the park on Juárez at Rodríguez. **Autotransportes de Baja California** (☎554 1221) sends buses to **Ensenada** (2hr., 10 per day 8am-7pm, 97 pesos), **Tijuana** (1hr., every 20min. 5am-9pm, 42 pesos), and **Mexicali** (2hr., every 30min. 8:30am-9:50pm, 132 pesos). **Transportes Norte de Sonora** (☎654 2343) offers *de paso* buses to: **Ciudad Juárez** (20hr., 5 per day 10:45am-7:30pm, 805 pesos); **Chihuahua** (4 per day 9:30am-7:45pm); **Nogales** (12hr., 4 per day 1:45pm-6:30pm, 930 pesos); **Mexico City** (44hr., 9 per day 10:45am-9:45pm, 1380 pesos). Buses heading to **Mexico City** stop in a number of cities along the way: **Guadalajara** (36hr., 958 pesos); **Guaymas** (14hr., 480 pesos); **Hermosillo** (12hr., 420 pesos); **Mazatlán** (26hr., 750 pesos); **Mexicali** (2hr., 120 pesos).

✳️ 7 ORIENTATION AND PRACTICAL INFORMATION

Tecate lies 42km east of Tijuana and 143km west of Mexicali on **Mex. 2**. The center of social and commercial activity, **Parque Hidalgo**, is bound to the north by the main street **Juárez**, which becomes Mex. 2. To the east, the Parque is bordered by **Ortíz Rubio**, which eventually turns into **Mex. 3** on the southern edge of town. East-west streets parallel the border fence; from north to south, they are: Madero, Revolución, Reforma, Juárez, Libertad, and Hidalgo. Streets named for early 20th-century presidents run north-south perpendicular to Juárez and the border. Starting from the east, they are: Portes Gil, Rodríguez, Ortiz Rubio, Cárdenas, Elías Calles, Obregón, de la Huerta, Carranza, and Aldrete. The **border crossing** and **customs** are much simpler in Tecate than in either Tijuana or Mexicali, busy only Monday mornings and Friday afternoons. (Open daily 6am-midnight.)

Tourist Office: Libertad 1305 (☎654 1095), facing Parque Hidalgo. Provides brochures and maps, including one with a good walking tour of the city. Open M-Sa 8am-8pm.

Banks: Bancomer (☎654 1350), on the corner of Cárdenas and Juárez. Exchanges traveler's checks and has a **24hr. ATM.** Open M-F 8:30am-4pm. **Banamex** (☎654 1188), at Juárez and Obregón. Offers similar services. Open M-F 9am-4pm.

Police: Paseo Morelos 1978 (☎655 1091). Walk east on Juárez out of town; it will become Mex. 2. The station is at the traffic circle, a 10min. walk from Parque Hidalgo.

Emergency: ☎060.

Red Cross: Juárez 411 (☎654 1313).

24hr. Pharmacy: Farmacia Roma, on the corner of Juárez and Aldrete.

Medical Services: IMSS Centro de Salud (☎654 5803), south of town at Juárez and Gil.

Fax Office: Telecomm (☎654 1375), next door to the post office. Open M-F 7am-6pm, Sa 7am-2:30pm.

Internet Access: C-La (☎521 3838), on Hidalgo, immediately east of the Jardín Cerveza Tecate and the Tecate Brewery. Fast connections. 6 pesos per hr. Open M, W-Th, and Su 9am-11pm; Tu and F-Sa 9am-10pm.

Post Office: Ortíz Rubio 146 (☎654 1245), 2 blocks north of Juárez. Open M-F 8am-3pm. **Postal Code:** 21401.

🏠 ACCOMMODATIONS

Tecate has a number of budget hotels, but many are dilapidated. Take a look at a room before you agree to pay for it.

Hotel Tecate (☎654 1116), overlooking Parque Hidalgo on Libertad at Cárdenas. Superb location in the center of town. Simple, mostly clean rooms with private bath and fans. Singles and doubles 300 pesos, with TV 400 pesos. Cash only. ❹

Okakopa Iwa Hotel, Madero 141 (☎654 5230). Large rooms with A/C and TV just steps from the border. Free parking. Singles 380 pesos; doubles 540 pesos. Cash only. ❹

Hotel Frontera, Madero 131 (☎654 1342) between Obregón and Elías Calles. Next door to the Okakopa, Frontera's rooms are cheaper, but the hotel is aging and the staff is less friendly. Singles 250 pesos, with bath, A/C, and TV 300 pesos; doubles with bath, A/C, and TV 400 pesos. Cash only. ❹

Rancho Ojai (☎655 3014; www.rancho-ojai.com), on Mex. 2 east toward Mexicali, 21km outside of Tecate. Outside of town, Ojai is part of a working ranch and offers beautiful vistas, a pool, and mini-golf. Tents US$11, RV with full hookup US$30. 4-bed cabins US$68. MC/V. ❶

🏠 FOOD

The cheapest food in Tecate can be found at the *taquerías* lining Obregón and Juárez, east of the park. The best is popular **Tacos Los Amigos** ❷, at Hidalgo and Ortíz Rubio, where the big, 12-peso tacos are loaded with guacamole. (Open daily 9am-8pm.) **Calimax,** on Juárez between Carranza and Aldrete, sells groceries. (☎654 0039. Open daily 7am-10pm.)

🟦 **El Mejor Pan de Tecate,** Juárez 331 (☎654 0040), between Rodriguez and Portes Gil, a 5 min. walk east of the park. True to its name, this bakery has a huge selection of delicious pastries and bread, most for under 10 pesos. Extremely popular with locals. Open 24hr. Cash only. ❷

La Pena de Losa, Libertad 201 (☎655 7648). Small, friendly restaurant near the park with excellent breakfasts. Pancakes 40 pesos. Open daily 8am-6pm. MC/V. ❷

Restaurant el Mesón, Revolución 261 (☎654 5383), at Ortíz Rubio a couple of blocks from the border. Mexican dishes (20-50 pesos) in an outdoor garden. There's a pleasant view of the city upstairs. Open 24hr. Cash only. ❸

Restaurant Jardín Tecate (☎654 3453), next to the tourist office on the southern end of Parque Hidalgo. Enjoy reasonably priced Mexican food while people-watching in the park. Open daily 8am-8pm. Cash only. ❸

Lolo's Restaurante (☎654 0612), on the park, adjacent to Jardín Tecate. *Chile rellenos* (50 pesos), *tamales* (40 pesos), and other Mexican dishes. Outdoor seating only. Open daily 8:30pm-12am. Cash only. ❸

👁 🎵 SIGHTS AND ENTERTAINMENT

The town's biggest building, the **Tecate Brewery,** on Hidalgo at Obregón, looms over everything in Tecate and attracts thousands of beer-loving visitors throughout the year. Opened in 1944, the brewery, officially known as the Cervecería Cuauhtémoc Moctezuma, now pumps out 39 million liters of beer each month. You can sample one for yourself—on the house—at the 🟦**Jardín Cerveza Tecate,** where locals and tourists sit on plastic chairs in the shade. Should you become a convert to the local brew, the souvenir stall next to the bar will help you become a walking advertisement for Tecate or one of the company's seven other beers: Bohemia, Carta Blanca, Dos Equis, Indio, Sol, Superior, and the Christmastime-only Noche Buena. You can also go on a free tour of the brewery. (No sandals allowed inside. ☎654 9478. At Hidalgo and Oregon. Both open M-F 10am-5pm, Sa 10am-2pm. Tours M-F 11am, noon, 3, 4pm; Sa-Su 10, 11am, noon, 1pm. Free.)

Other than hanging out in the Jardín or strolling through the park, there isn't much by way of entertainment in Tecate. Tecate's **béisbol** (baseball) team, sponsored by the brewery and appropriately called the **Cerveceros,** attracts a small but devoted following whose enthusiasm might be connected to the fact that as the home score goes up, the price of beer in the stands goes down. (Tickets June-Aug. 30-60 pesos. For schedules, contact the tourist office or visit www.cervecerosdetecate.com.)

BAJA CALIFORNIA

PLAYAS DE ROSARITO   ☎ 661

Playas de Rosarito (pop. 76,000) has many selling points, as its tourist promoters have discovered during the city's transformation from elite hideaway to all-out gringo-magnet, but none counts more than its proximity to the US border. Baja's youngest city is just 45min. by car from San Diego, a distance that seems to shrink as Californian weekenders come in flocks to party in Rosarito's clubs and sunbathe on its beaches. The movie *Titanic* was filmed here and Fox Studios now has a tourist park on the site. Most enterprises are geared toward tourists, and the two most widely accepted languages are English and the US dollar. If you're looking for the "real Baja," then this is probably not the place to come, but if the seeping Americanization doesn't bother you, the beaches and clubs are yours to enjoy.

▐ TRANSPORTATION

To get to Rosarito from Tijuana, grab a yellow-and-white **taxi van** (30min., 20 pesos) from Madero around Calle 3. For the return journey, the same vehicles congregate in front of the Rosarito Beach Hotel. You can also flag them down along northbound Juárez, which is also the easiest way to get from one end of Rosarito to the other. Negotiate the price before you get in the van. **Mexicoach** sends buses to **Tijuana** (round-trip US$16) from the Rosarito Beach Hotel. At the intersection of Juárez and Cleofas Arriola is the **ABC bus terminal** (☎613 1151). Buses run to **Ensenada** (1¼hr., 4 per day 7am-4pm, 76 pesos), **Mexicali** (6hr., 3pm, 222 pesos), and **La Paz** (24hr.; 12:30, 6:30pm; 1983 pesos). **Suburbaja** also sends buses from the station to **Tijuana** (every 20min. 5am-9am, 14 pesos).

▟ ▐ ORIENTATION AND PRACTICAL INFORMATION

Rosarito lies roughly 27km south of Tijuana. **Mex. 1** runs straight through Rosarito, becoming the city's main drag, **Juárez**, before continuing south. Coming from the toll road, take the first Rosarito exit to the north end of Juárez, which can be befuddling because of its lack of street signs. Virtually all the businesses in town are on Juárez, with most tourist facilities concentrated at the southern end, between the **PEMEX** station at the corner of Av. Cipres and the Rosarito Beach Hotel. On weekends, hordes of SUV-driving visitors clog up Juárez, making progress painfully slow and parking spaces hard to find.

Tourist Offices: COTUCO (☎612 0396), in the Oceana Plaza, at Juárez and Roble. Open M-F 9am-7pm, Sa-Su 9am-4pm; reduced winter hours. **SECTUR** (☎612 0200), the state tourist office, is on km 28 on Mex. 1, inconveniently located at the very southern end of town. Open M-F 8am-8pm, Sa-Su 8am-1pm.

Currency Exchange: Banamex (☎612 1556), on Juárez at René Ortiz. Exchanges cash and checks. **24hr. ATM.** Open M-Sa 9am-4pm. *Casas de cambio* on Juárez have better rates, though most visitors stick with US$.

Laundromat: Lavamática Estrella, on Juárez near Acacias. Wash and dry 30 pesos. Open M-Tu and Th-Su 8:30am-8:30pm.

Emergency: ☎060.

Police: (☎613 3414; tourist hotline 078), at Juárez and Acacias, next to the post office.

Red Cross: (☎613 1120), on Juárez at René Ortiz, around the corner from the police.

24hr. Pharmacy: Farmacia Roma (☎612 3500), set back from Juárez at Roble in a small shopping strip.

Internet Access: El Tunel.com, Juárez 208 (☎613 1297), near Cárdenas, on the 2nd fl. above a restaurant. US$1.50 per hr. US$1 per 30min. Open M-Sa 9am-9pm.

Post Office: (☎612 1355), on Juárez near Acacias. Open M-F 8am-3pm. **Postal Code:** 22711.

ACCOMMODATIONS

Most budget hotels in Rosarito are cramped or inconveniently situated far from the southern (and more touristy) end of Juárez. Prices soar during spring break, holidays, and summer weekends. If you're going to stay for several days, ask how much you will be paying for each night.

Hotel Palmas Quintero (☎612 1359 or 2347), tucked away on Privada Guadalupe Victoria 26A in a residential neighborhood. To find it, drive up Cárdenas (off Juárez) for 3 blocks and turn left; the hotel is ahead and to the right. Cheap and reasonably close to the center. Large rooms with clean bath and cable TV. Free parking. Rooms M-Th and Su US$25, F-Sa US$35. Cash only. ❹

Hotel el Portal de Rosarito (☎612 0050), at Juárez and Via de las Olas. Cheery Portal de Rosarito offers large rooms with A/C and TV. Free parking. M-Th and Su singles US$27; doubles US$33. F-Sa singles US$45; doubles US$50. Cash only. ❺

Motel Marsella's (☎612 0468), Av. del Mar 75. To get to Marsella's from the south, turn west off Juárez immediately before La Flor de Michoacán restaurant. Close to the beach popular with locals but far from the downtown beach popular with tourists. Rooms are a little dark but come with bath, fan, and TV. M-Th and Su singles US$25; doubles US$30. F-Sa singles US$35; doubles US$40. Cash only. ❹

Alamo Hostel, Calle Alamo 15 (☎613 1179), less than a block from the beach. The hostel, one of the only ones on the entire peninsula, has bunks in 2 crowded dorms. Common area has kitchen facilities. Dorms in summer US$15; in winter US$10. Tent space US$10. Cash only. ❷

FOOD

With pricey restaurants serving international cuisine, Rosarito's culinary scene caters mostly to tourists who consider US$10 cheap. Nevertheless, a good scavenger hunt yields quality budget eateries with simple, yummy food. For lighter fare, check out the city's bakeries. For groceries, try the **Calimax,** at Cárdenas and Juárez. (☎612 0060. Open daily 7am-midnight.)

La Flor de Michoacán, Juárez 291 (☎612 1858), at the north end of town. Another branch on Juárez at Encinas with a broader menu. A carnivore's paradise that has been in business for more than 50 years. Huge *carnitas* (80 pesos) come as either "solid" or "mixed" pork. Solid comprises typical cuts, while mixed includes tongues, stomachs, and all sorts of good stuff. Those with big appetites can order by weight (285 pesos per kg). Open M-Tu and Th-Su 9am-10pm. Cash only. ❺

Spazio Cafe and Crepes, Calle Rene Campay 24 (☎613 0660), on a side street opposite the Banamex parking lot. Good sandwiches on "rustic" bread (40 pesos) and a large selection of crepes (35 pesos). Open M-Th 8am-10pm, F-Sa 8am-midnight, Su noon-10pm. Cash only. ❸

Macho Taco, Juárez 60 (☎613 0630), across from Hotel Festival Plaza. The special combo—2 tacos, rice, beans, and a soda for US$4.50—can't be beat. Attached to the nightclub with the same name. Open daily 8am-2am. Cash only. ❸

Panadería La Espiga, at Juárez and Cárdenas. One of Rosarito's excellent bakeries. Most pastries under 5 pesos. Small but filling loaves of bread 2.50 pesos. Open daily 7am-10pm. Cash only. ❶

D'Angelo's Pizza (☎100 2510), at Juárez and Ebano. This pizza delivery shop offers basic seating and massive combos, which include a 10 in. pizza, a plate of spaghetti, and a drink for 60 pesos. Cash only. ❸

D'Volada (☎612 0682), on Juárez, across from the Rosarito Beach Hotel at the southern end of town. This local branch of a Mexican chain of coffeeshops serves decent coffee (espresso 18 pesos) and delicious smoothies (20 pesos). Open M-F 5:30am-10pm, Sa-Su 7am-10pm. Cash only. ❷

⦿ SIGHTS

Rosarito entices with fancy resorts, beautiful shores, and wild nightlife. The beach itself spans most of Juárez, and there are two distinct parts. Tourists pack the beach near the pier and the town's clubs, which cluster at the southern end of town, between Eucalipto and Nogal. A more local crowd visits the beach on the northern end of town, which is most easily accessible off La Fuente. Horseback riding with a guide is available at both places for US$5-10 per hr.

Rosarito has a proud tradition of hosting vacationing movie stars, but it has taken on new importance in the form of **Fox Studios Baja** and the attached **Foxploration** tourist park, 2km south of Rosarito. Fox's blockbuster *Titanic* was filmed here, and following the film, Fox opened part of the movie set as a tourist park. Unfortunately, with a lack of foresight equal to that of the original designers of the Titanic herself, the studio has dismantled its main attraction—the ship is no longer there. As a result, a visit to Foxploration feels a bit like sitting through a series of film trailers without the feature presentation. (10min. drive on Mex. 1 south of Rosarito at km 32.5. Foxploration ☎614 9444; www.foxploration.com. Open W-F 9am-5:30pm, Sa-Su 10am-6:30pm. US$12, children and seniors US$9.)

⦿ NIGHTLIFE

Rosarito's nightlife revolves around Hotel Festival Plaza, which has a number of bars and clubs of its own. The mega-clubs on the streets behind the hotel are packed with drunken revelers on weekend and summer nights. The clubs are not hard to find. Club hawkers sell drink bracelets valid for an unlimited number of a limited selection of drinks for around US$10. Depending on how hard you party, this can be a good deal. **Iggy's** (☎612 0537; www.clubiggys.com), on Juárez at Hotel Festival Plaza, is a behemoth of a nightspot with its own pool and foam party. With capacity for 6000 partiers, Iggy's offers three adjoining bars with food and all-you-can-drink cocktails. (Cover approx. US$10. Open 11am-3am, later on weekends.) **Macho Taco,** Juárez 60 (☎613 0630), across from Hotel Festival Plaza, is the one über-popular spot on the opposite side of Juárez. (Open daily 10am-2am, as late as 6am on weekends.)

ENSENADA ☎646

With outdoor markets, three history museums, nearby beaches, and a tourist strip that rivals that of Cabos San Lucas, cosmopolitan Ensenada (pop. 370,000) makes the perfect weekend getaway. Not surprisingly, thousands of tourists descend on the city each week, via cruise ship or car. If you don't mind—or can ignore—aggressive salesmen hawking "prescription" medications, bracelets, and *mariachi* songs, Ensenada is worth a visit.

⦿ TRANSPORTATION

Ensenada is 108km south of Tijuana on **Mex. 1.** The 1½hr. drive offers an almost continuous view of the Pacific, and the last 20min. stretch on the Ensenada *cuota* road is especially breathtaking—on a bus, grab a seat on the right-hand side. Car drivers can stop to admire the view from the *mirador* just beyond Bajamar. The

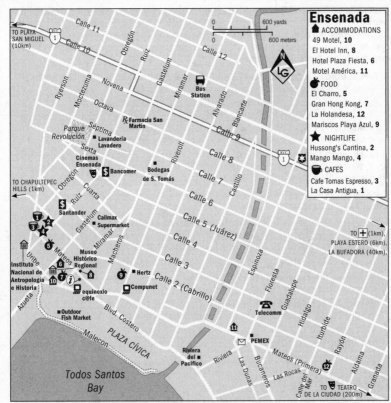

Ensenada

▲ ACCOMMODATIONS
49 Motel, **10**
El Hotel Inn, **8**
Hotel Plaza Fiesta, **6**
Motel América, **11**

● FOOD
El Charro, **5**
Gran Hong Kong, **7**
La Holandesa, **12**
Mariscos Playa Azul, **9**

★ NIGHTLIFE
Hussong's Cantina, **2**
Mango Mango, **4**

◑ CAFES
Cafe Tomas Espresso, **3**
La Casa Antigua, **1**

less scenic Mex. 1 is a poorly maintained highway that parallels the *cuota* road until La Misión, then cuts inland for the remaining 40km. Drive during the day—there are plenty of curves and no streetlights.

Buses: The **Central de Autobuses** is at Calle 11 and Riveroll. To get to the *centro,* turn right as you come out of the station and walk south 10 blocks to Mateos (Primera). **Autotransportes de Baja California** (☎ 178 6680) runs buses south to **La Paz** (20hr., 5 per day 10am-11pm, 1400 pesos), stopping in **Guerrero Negro** (8hr., 614 pesos), **Mulegé** (11hr., 896 pesos), **San Ignacio** (9hr., 759 pesos), and **Santa Rosalía** (12hr., 835 pesos). Buses head north to **Tijuana** (2hr., 12 per day 6:30am-10pm, 185 pesos) and **Mexicali** (4hr., 10 per day 5:30am-8pm). Other buses head to **San Felipe** (4hr.; 8am, 6pm; 248 pesos) and **Puerto Peñasco** (11hr., 8am, 552 pesos).

Car Rental: Hertz (☎ 178 2982), at Calle 2 and Riveroll. From 600 pesos. Open M-F 8am-8pm, Sa 8am-5pm, Su 9am-5pm.

ORIENTATION AND PRACTICAL INFORMATION

Mateos, the main tourist street, is also known as Primera (Calle 1). Numbered *calles,* including **Juárez** (Calle 5), run east-west, approximately parallel to Mateos. Alphabetized *avenidas* run north-south, starting with Alvarado and moving east to Iturbide. If you're driving on Mex. 1 from the north follow signs to downtown

Ensenada or "Centro." These will lead you to **Costero,** which runs along the harbor one block south of Mateos. If you're coming on Mex. 1 from the south, follow signs for the **Tourist District,** which will also bring you to Costero. After sundown, exercise caution in the poorly lit area near the shore and in the region bounded by **Miramar, Macheros, Mateos,** and **Calle 4.**

Tourist Office: Costero 609 (☎178 8578, 24hr. tourist helpline ☎078), near Miramar. Open M-F 8am-8pm, Sa-Su 9am-1pm.

Banks: The main tourist area lacks banks. The closest is **Santander** (☎174 0009), at Ruiz and Calle 3. Open M-F 9am-4pm. Others cluster around Ruiz and Juárez, including **Bancomer** (☎175 1656 or 1657). Open M-F 8:30am-4pm, Sa 10am-2pm. Both exchange dollars and traveler's checks and have **24hr. ATMs.**

Laundromat: Lavandería Lavadero, Obregón 674 (☎178 2737), between Calles 6 and 7, facing Parque Revolución. Small loads 23 pesos, large loads 48 pesos; drying 6 pesos for 5min. Open daily 8am-8pm.

Police: (☎176 4343), on Calle 9 at Espinoza.

Red Cross: (☎174 4545).

Pharmacy: There are at least a dozen "pharmacies" on Mateos advertising heavily discounted Viagra. For a professional pharmacy, though, it's worth walking a few blocks to **Farmacia San Martín,** at Calle 8 and Ruiz (☎178 3530).

Hospital: Hospital General (☎176 7800), on the Transpeninsular at km 111.

Fax Office: Telecomm (☎177 0545), on Floresta between Calles 2 and 4. Open M-F 8am-6pm, Sa 8-11am.

Internet Access: Compunet, Riveroll 143, next to Hertz, is quiet and fast. 15 pesos per hr. Open M-Sa 9:30am-10pm. Friendly **equinoxio c@fe,** Costero 267 (☎174 0455), near Miramar, also serves coffee. 20 pesos per hr. Open M-Sa 9am-10pm, Su 1-10pm.

Post Office: (☎176 1088 or 4050), on Mateos at Espinoza. Open M-F 8am-4pm. Sa 9am-1pm. **Postal Code:** 22801.

ACCOMMODATIONS

Ensenada may be an upscale destination, but there are a number of budget hotels, even in the *centro.*

Motel América (☎176 1333), on Mateos at Espinoza. Quiet rooms with bath, overhead fan, and cable TV; some with kitchen. Parking available. Singles 300 pesos; doubles 400 pesos. Cash only. ❺

El Hotel Inn, Mateos 628 (☎178 3481). Colorful rooms with fan and cable TV in the middle of the Tourist District. Rooms with queen-size bed 350 pesos. Prices rise 50 pesos on the weekends. MC/V. ❺

Hotel Plaza Fiesta, Mateos 542 (☎178 2715). An old hotel in the middle of the *centro.* Large rooms with TV and fan. Singles 350 pesos; doubles 450 pesos. Cash only. ❺

49 Motel, Miramar 6 (☎174 0308). The motel is a cheap, barebones option just 1 block away from the center of Mateos. Rooms US$30. ❹

FOOD

The restaurants on Mateos are prime venues for people-watching and spending money. Nonetheless, there are a few affordable options on the strip, and restaurants become cheaper as you move away from Mateos. For the best deals visit the fish market on the waterfront, north of the huge flag, where *loncherías* serve Ensenada's most famous dish—delicious fish tacos—for under US$1. For grocer-

TIP **CREEPY CRAWLERS.** *Alacranes* (scorpions) frequent Baja, especially mid-peninsula in smaller towns and on the beach. Unless allergic, you won't encounter a slow, painful death—these aren't the fatal buggers found in Asia and Africa—but if stung, expect intense pain for a few days. Ice eases discomfort and locals swear by garlic. The critters like dark, damp places, so shake your shoes and clothing before wearing them. If you wake up to a scorpion crawling on you, don't try to squash it—it will sting.

ies, hit up **Calimax,** on Gastelum at Calle 3, an enormous supermarket with low prices. (☎178 3397. Open daily 7am-11pm.)

La Holandesa (☎177 1965), at Mateos and Rayón. Tasty breakfasts and huge servings in a homey setting. Shrimp omelettes 65 pesos. The restaurant's specialty is its *burrito de machaca* (30 pesos). Tasty cheeseburger with fries 34 pesos. Open M-F 7am-9:30pm, Sa 8am-9:30pm, Su 8am-4:30pm. MC/V. ❸

La Casa Antigua, Obregón 110 (☎175 7320), between Mateos and Calle 2. Awesome sandwiches served in the oldest house in Ensenada. The house was sold for 20 pesos in 1890—now sandwiches (50-55 pesos) cost just a little over twice as much. Open daily 11am-midnight. MC/V. ❹

El Charro (☎178 2114), on Mateos between Ruiz and Gastelum. A budget oasis in the Tourist District. Simple but effective. Enjoy half of a rotisserie chicken grilled right before your eyes (US$7). Open daily M-Tu 10am-9pm, W-Su 10am-11pm. MC/V. ❺

Mariscos Playa Azul, 113 Riveroll (☎174 0622), between Mateos and Calle 2. One of the cheapest seafood restaurants in town, without compromising quality. Fish filet 70 pesos. Open daily 10am-10pm. AmEx/MC/V. ❹

Gran Hong Kong, Miramar 51 (☎178 2368), between Costero and Mateos. A quick, cheap Chinese food restaurant in the *centro*. Big combo plates (40-60 pesos) of fried rice, vegetables or meat, and an egg roll are enough for 2. Open M-T, Th-F, and Su 11am-11pm, W and Sa 10am-11pm. Cash only. ❸

Cafe Tomas Espresso (☎175 7375; www.cafetomas.com), on Mateos, between Ruiz and Ryerson. The excellent tea (chai latte; 24 pesos) and free Wi-Fi attracts a young crowd and the occasional tourist. Open daily 6am-midnight. Cash only. ❹

◉ SIGHTS

With its museums, markets, and *malecón*, Ensenada is a cosmopolitan dream with lots to do by Baja California standards.

RIVIERA DEL PACÍFICO CULTURAL CENTER. Once a roaring casino allegedly financed by Al Capone, today the Riviera del Pacífico hosts the city's **Centro de Cultura.** The buildings have retained many of their original Moorish details, including some elegantly painted walls and ceilings. Tourists can stroll the grounds and well-kept **gardens.** (☎176 4233. On the eastern strip of Costero immediately after the bridge. Open daily 8am-8pm. Free.) **Bar Andaluz**—the casino's original bar—serves inexpensive drinks in an upscale setting. (Beer 15 pesos. Open M-Tu and Su noon-7pm, W 8am-3pm, Th 11am-6pm, F noon-midnight, Sa 7pm-2am). The excellent **Museo de Historia de Ensenada,** in the Riviera del Pacífico complex, takes visitors through the history of the Baja peninsula, portraying each period in an appropriately decorated room. (☎177 0594. Open M-Sa 9am-5pm, Su 10am-5pm. 10 pesos, children under 12 5 pesos.)

MUSEO HISTÓRICO REGIONAL. The **Museo Histórico Regional** also narrates Baja history, but the museum is located in a building that housed the town's jail until 1986. Wealthy prisoners paid money in order to have their own jail cells and were allowed to decorate them. Check out the tiled floors some prisoners installed, along with the beautiful landscapes they painted on the walls. You can also step into the punishment cells, which had openings in their ceilings so that prisoners would have to put up with bad weather and whatever the guards threw down on them. *(On Gastelum, between Mateos and Uribe. Open Tu-Su 9am-5 pm. Free.)*

BODEGAS DE SANTO TOMÁS. The dry, mild climate of Baja's northern coast made it Mexico's prime grape-growing area. The bodegas—the oldest in Baja—have produced wine since 1888. Today, Santo Tomás distills some 80,000 cases of wine each year, although the Ensenada facility itself is mainly a museum. Hourly tours show how the wine is made and conclude with a wine tasting. *(Miramar 666, at Calle 6. ☎ 178 3333. Free tours every hr. 10am-5pm. Optional wine tasting 50 pesos.)*

OTHER SIGHTS. The **Chapultepec hills** offer a stunning view of the bay and the city from a ritzy residential neighborhood northwest of town. *(To reach the top, follow Calle 2 up the steep hill. 15-20min. walk.)* A 3rd museum, located in the **Instituto Nacional de Antropología e Historia** office in an imposing old house, has a small exhibit, usually having do to with Mexican archaeology, which changes twice a year. *(On Ryerson, between Uribe and Mateos. Open M-F 9am-4pm. Free.)*

🎵 🎙 ENTERTAINMENT AND NIGHTLIFE

There are several movie theaters in town, including **Cinemas Ensenada,** on Juárez at Ruiz, which screens recent American hits, including some that are not dubbed. *(☎ 178 8679. Shows daily 3-10pm. 35 pesos.)* The **Teatro de la Ciudad,** a black-and-white striped building out to the east of town on Diamante near Mateos, is a theater that hosts visiting companies from around Mexico and abroad. Mateos is packed with popular cafe/bar/disco establishments, which stuff tourists with overpriced food during the day and overpriced booze at night.

Hussong's Cantina, Ruiz 113 (☎ 178 3210). Hussong's, founded in 1892, tries to replicate its old self, with artificially dusty floors and mounted animals on the walls. But the many, very modern-looking memorabilia stores just around the corner mean that the hype surrounding Baja's supposedly oldest, most famous bar might just a smart marketing scheme to sell Hussong's T-shirts. Beer 28 pesos. Margaritas 30 pesos. Open daily 10am-2am. MC/V.

Mango Mango (☎ 178 3883), at Ruiz and Mateos. Slightly calmer than its neighbor, Mango Mango has outdoor seating perfect for people-watching. No cover charge and Cosmopolitans for 46 pesos. Open daily 10am-1am. MC/V.

⌐ SHOPPING

Watch fishermen bring in the catch of the day at the **fish market** on the west side of the boardwalk, near the Sport Fishing Piers. The **Los Globos Flea Market,** on the other side of town, has a vast array of used goods (and junk), most of it imported from the US. Stores in the area sell used CDs, clothing, paintings, dishware, and furniture, although the market is most active on the weekends. To reach Los Globos from Mateos, walk to Calle 9 and cross Reforma. Walk straight until you reach Morelos. The market begins on your right and extends for a few blocks.

⌐ BEACHES

Ensenada's own shoreline is devoted to shipping and fishing rather than sunbathing, but following the steady stream of daytrippers southwest along the Punta Banda Peninsula leads to a series of beautiful beaches and lovely ocean views known as the Bahía de Todos Santos. Unfortunately, you'll need a car to reach many of these spots. Tijuana and San Diego have the best rental rates (see **Tijuana: Car Rental,** p. 151).

PLAYA ESTERO. Packed with volleyball courts and lobster-colored tourists, Playa Estero is a pleasant, if not especially secluded, place to pass time. The area can get muddy during low tides, when sea lions come ashore. Access is available through the Estero Beach Resort, which houses the **Estero Beach Museum,** with an impressive shell collection and display of Olmec, Aztec, and Mayan art, originally established to give resort-bound tourists a broader view of Mexico. *(From Ensenada, drive south on Mex. 1. Take your first right immediately before a PEMEX station. Drive down the road and take a left at the sign. Parking at the Estero Beach Resort 10 pesos. Alternatively, catch a bus marked "Aeropuerto," "Zorrillo," "Maneadero," or "Chapultepec" from Plaza Cívica. Estero Beach Resort ☎ 177 6230. Museum ☎ 176 6244. Open M and W-Su 9am-5pm. Free.)*

PLAYA EL FARO. Playa el Faro, adjacent to Estero, is similarly rife with volleyball courts and gringos, but has slightly better sand and allows camping right on the beach. Heed warning signs about strong currents. *(☎ 177 4620 or 4630. Parking at the El Faro Beach Motel and Trailer Park 30 pesos. Camping US$10. Full RV hookup US$25.)*

PLAYA SAN MIGUEL. North of the city, this rocky beach isn't of any use to sunbathers or swimmers, but the right pointbreak is an epic hangout for surfers. *(Drive west on Calle 10, which joins Mex. 1, and continue to the toll gate. Don't go through the gate. Make a U-turn and then turn right onto the cobblestone road. Alternatively, catch a "San Miguel" bus departing Gastelum at Costero and flag down your return. Parking 30 pesos. Camping US$12 with electricity 4pm-midnight.)*

TODOS SANTOS ISLAND. Surfers also head out to Todos Santos Island, 45min. from Ensenada by boat. The Big Wave World Championships took place off the island in 1999. Dayboats are available from the captains on the sports fishing pier. *(4-person group US$250, but prices are negotiable.)*

PUNTA BANDA. Punta Banda, the peninsula at the southern end of Bahía de Todos Santos, boasts secluded beaches and Ensenada's best known site, **La Bufadora.** Located at the end of a dramatically curving road along the peninsula, the Pacific coast's largest geyser is announced by large signs—and people trying to charge you for overpriced parking (20 pesos). To reach the geyser, pass the parking attendants and an astounding number of aggres-

THE BIG SPLURGE

RIDING DIRTY

Each fall, hundreds of off-roaders meet in Ensenada for the annual **Baja 1000,** the off-road equivalent of the Indy 500. Mounting ATVs, motorcycles, and dune buggies, riders take just under a day to navigate the rocky and sandy terrain between Ensenada and the finish line in La Paz. Considered one of the most dangerous races in the world, the Baja 1000 was documented in the 2005 adventure film "Dust to Glory." Last year, a team led by Steve Hengeveld, an American motorcyclist, won the race in just over 18hr.

Along the route, spectators gather to watch the drivers zoom by, often scrambling out of the way of oncoming vehicles. The crowds grow in La Paz, where the winners are honored in a ceremony on the *malecón*.

Inspired by the race, plenty of tourists try their hand at off-roading along the dirt roads of Baja, choosing to bump along dirt roads laden with the frames of abandoned cars instead of taking the paved alternatives. 4WD is a necessity on most unpaved roads in Baja, and be aware that if your SUV breaks down along the way, you'll have to wait hours, even days, for the next vehicle to pass by.

Visit www.score-international.com/ baja1000/index.html for information on upcoming routes and dates.

sive trinket sellers and "pharmacies" advertising discounted Viagra and pain-killers. La Bufadora can be weak some days, so all the buildup may end in disappointment. On the other hand, waves sometimes force the water into a natural cave, building up pressure and producing a spurt of up to 40m, accompanied by dramatic snorts. *(From Ensenada, take Mex. 1 south, past the military base and Playa Estero, until you reach the well-marked turnoff for "La Bufadora." Alternatively, taxis will take tourists from López Mateos to La Bufadora for US$10.)*

▶ DAYTRIP FROM ENSENADA

PARQUE NACIONAL CONSTITUCIÓN DE 1857

Follow Mex. 3 from Juárez east toward San Felipe and the town of Ojos Negros. Immediately past the PEMEX station, at km 55, turn left on a paved road that leads to Ojos Negros. In the centro, turn right on the paved road that quickly turns to dirt. After 6km you'll pass through a town, followed 3.5km later by a cattle grid. Ignore the side streets. Another 3.5km on, the road forks twice in quick succession; take the right fork both times, cross another cattle grid, and pass a small community on your left, ignoring a fork to the right. 4km later, a sign points to the park, 24km away; take the left fork here and again 3km later. After 14km take the marked left fork toward the park entrance. High-clearance vehicles are strongly recommended. Be sure to inquire in Ensenada about current conditions before venturing into the wilderness, and to fill your tank before leaving. ☎566 7887.

A thick coniferous forest situated 1650m above sea level, the 5009-hectare Parque Nacional Constitución is unlike anyplace else in Baja. The focal point is **Laguna Hanson,** a small lake frequented by grazing cows, with a number of campsites dotted along its perimeter. The annual rainfall here is low, so the lagoon may be dry if you come in summer. According to locals, the best time to visit is in winter, when snow from the peaks and trees melts to replenish the lake. The towering pines and granite mountains are enticing but guarded by foreboding "Zona Restringida" (Restricted Area) signs. Nevertheless, a few excellent hiking trails are accessible. The **Aventura en el Bosque** (Adventure in the Wood; 2km) is a loop beginning west of Laguna Hanson and opening onto views of the forest. Signs along the trail describe various plants and animals in the park, including coyotes, rattlesnakes, and pumas, which occasionally attack humans. The western side of the park is also home to a series of smooth, granite faces that are increasingly attracting technical rock climbers. If planning to camp in the park, bring warm clothes and a good sleeping bag—temperatures drop dramatically at night. Vehicle registration is required in the log cabin at the southern end of the lake.

MEXICALI ☎686

Hot, polluted, unwalkable, and crowded, Mexicali (pop. 1.2 million) is not a tourist friendly town. Founded in 1903, the city was first populated by laborers from the Colorado River Land Company, many of whom were Chinese. Their vibrant culture continues to form a major part of Mexicali's identity today, particularly in La Chinesca (Chinatown). Unfortunately, La Chinesca also shows Mexicali's other face—that of a run-down border town grappling with crime, drugs, poverty, and prostitution. Mexicali has some intriguing sites, but at times its modern museums and beautiful parks only highlight the stark—and sometimes uncomfortable—contrast with its social problems.

▣ TRANSPORTATION

To get to the **Central de Autobuses** (☎557 2415), take any bus headed south (away from the border) on López Mateos (every 10min., 7.50 pesos). Get off at the intersection with Independencia, two blocks beyond the Plaza de Toros on your

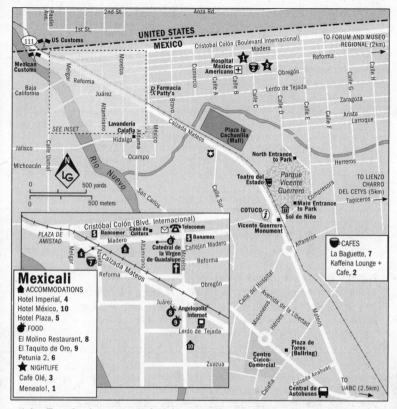

Mexicali

▲ ACCOMMODATIONS
Hotel Imperial, 4
Hotel México, 10
Hotel Plaza, 5

🍴 FOOD
El Molino Restaurant, 8
El Taquito de Oro, 9
Petunia 2, 6

★ NIGHTLIFE
Café Olé, 3
Menealo!, 1

🏷 CAFES
La Baguette, 7
Kaffeina Lounge + Cafe, 2

right. Turn back to your right, almost as if to double back, and walk a block along Independencia; the station is on the left, before the footbridge. To get to the border from the bus station, cross the footbridge just outside the station and hop on a local "Centro" bus (every 10min. 5am-11pm, 7.50 pesos). Get off when the bus goes around the rotary and starts heading the other way on López Mateos; the border is five blocks farther along López Mateos.

Autotransportes de Baja California (**ABC;** ☎557 2440) sends buses to: **Ensenada** (4hr., 6 per day 6am-8pm, 301 pesos); **Puerto Peñasco** (5hr., 7 per day, 2am-8:30pm, 267 pesos); **San Felipe** (2½hr., 5 per day 8am-8pm, 171 pesos); **Tijuana** (2½hr., every hour, 260 pesos). **Élite** (☎557 2450) motors east to: **Ciudad Juárez** (16hr., 3 per day 12:20am-7:15pm, 752 pesos); **Hermosillo** (10hr., every hr., 375 pesos); **Los Mochis** (12hr., every 30min., 572 pesos); **Nogales** (10hr., 11pm, 360 pesos). **Crucero** (☎558 7995), a partner of Greyhound, can take you to **Los Angeles, CA** (4hr., 4 per day 5:30am-12:25pm, US$33) and **Phoenix, AZ** (5hr.; 10:40am, 8:40pm; US$44).

🌐🔧 ORIENTATION AND PRACTICAL INFORMATION

Mexicali stands on the US border 189km inland from Tijuana, just south of Calexico and California's Imperial Valley. The city's streets shouldn't be difficult to navigate, but it's easy to lose your bearings and end up walking in the wrong direction—get a map when you arrive in town. Driving across the border leads straight into the *centro's* main boulevard, **López Mateos.** Mateos heads southeast through **La Chinesca,** past the enormous Plaza la Cachanilla mall, and the civic center. From there it continues past the Central de Autobuses and the ritzy clubs and restaurants of the **Zona Hotelera** before leaving town, where it becomes **Mex. 2.** You'll find the city's liveliest nightlife near the university district, home to the **Universidad Autónoma de Baja California,** east of La Chinesca. The **Río Nuevo** cuts through western Mexicali, spreading its unmistakable odor wherever it goes.

Tourist Office: Comité de Turismo y Convenciones (☎551 9800 or 9801; fax 552 5877; www.cotuco.com.mx). The adobe-colored building on Mateos facing the Vicente Guerrero Monument and park, 3km south of the border. The city's tourism office has loads of brochures, a knowledgeable English-speaking staff, and detailed street maps. Open M-F 8am-6pm. There is also a state tourism office, **SECTUR** (☎566 1116; www.descubrebajacalifornia.com), on Benito Juárez and Montejano. Open M-F 8am-8pm, Sa 9am-1pm. For tourist cards, visit the Mexican customs office in the immigration office at the border. Open 24hr.

Currency Exchange: *Casas de cambio* line Madero, and banks populate La Chinesca. **Bancomer** (☎553 4610), close to the border on Madero at Azueta. Another branch in Plaza la Cachanilla. Open M-F 8:30am-4pm. **Banamex** (☎551 6030), at Morelos and Madero. Open M-F 9am-4pm. Both exchange currency and have **24hr. ATMs.**

Laundromat: Lavandería Calafia (☎552 8416), at Hidalgo and Aldama. Open daily 7am-9pm. Wash 23 pesos; dry 8 pesos per 10min.

Police: ☎060, at Calle Sur and Mateos. 24hr. tourist helpline ☎078.

Red Cross: Cárdenas 1492 (☎552 9275), between Quinta and Durango.

24hr. Pharmacy: Farmacia Patty's (☎552 3423), at Mexico and Obregón.

Hospital: Hospital Mexico-Americano (☎552 2300), Reforma at Calle B, in a district full of clinics and other medical services. Open 24hr.

Fax Office: Telecomm (☎552 2002), Madero 491, next to the post office. Open M-F 7am-6:30pm, Sa-Su 8am-3:30pm.

Internet Access: Angelopolis Internet, 583 Lerdo de Tejada, between Morelos and Mateos. 20 pesos per hr. Open daily 9am-midnight.

Post Office: Madero 491 (☎552 2508), at Morelos. Open M-F 8am-5pm, Sa 9am-1pm. **Postal Code:** 21101.

ACCOMMODATIONS

Some hotels in La Chinesca charge hundreds of pesos a night, and others charge by the hour. Brothels often front as hotels, so be discerning when choosing a place to sleep. Ask to see a room before you pay—it may not be worth your money.

Hotel México, Lerdo 476 (☎554 0669), near Morelos. The best option in La Chinesca. Small rooms with TV and A/C surround a central gated parking lot. Reception doubles as a grocery store. Free parking. Singles and doubles 270 pesos. Cash only. ❹

Hotel Plaza, Madero 366 (☎552 9757), between Altamirano and Azueta. Decent, clean rooms with A/C and TV. Rooms 230 pesos. Cash only. ❺

Hotel Imperial, Madero 222 (☎553 6333). Rooms come with A/C, private bath, comfortable bed, phone, and cable TV. Singles and doubles 370 pesos. Cash only. ❺

FOOD

Mexicali has more Chinese restaurants per capita than any other city in Mexico, and most of these restaurants are concentrated in La Chinesca. If Chinese cuisine isn't your thing, chow down on hearty *tortas de carne asada* (15 pesos) at **sandwich stands** on Madero and Reforma, west of Mateos, or head to the food court in **Plaza la Cachanilla,** where huge combination plates cost less than 35 pesos.

El Molino Restaurant, Juárez 332 (☎552 5210), at Morelos on the circle. A friendly restaurant serving well-prepared Mexican *antojitos*. Excellent *carne asada* with guacamole 60 pesos. Carrot juice 15 pesos. Open daily 8am-10pm. ❸

Petunia 2 (☎552 6951), on Madero between Altamirano and Morelos. Munch tasty *tortas* (30-40 pesos) and tacos (10-15 pesos) at a colorful outdoor counter with bar-style seating. Fruit juice 10 pesos. Open M-Sa 8am-8pm, Su 8am-5pm. Cash only. ❷

El Taquito de Oro, Morelos 334, on the corner with López Mateos. This popular *taquería* serves tasty *tacos de machaca* (shredded beef tacos; 10 pesos). Open daily 7am-10pm. Cash only. ❶

Kaffeina Lounge + Cafe, (☎554 0729), 1080 Reforma at Calle C. Excellent coffee in a hip atmosphere. Small latte 30 pesos. Open M-Th 8am-11pm, F 8am-midnight, Sa-Su 5pm-midnight. Cash only. ❸

La Baguette, at the corner of Azuela and Mateos. A large selection of pastries and breads, most for under 5 pesos. Open 7am-9pm daily. Cash only. ❶

🅖 SIGHTS

Mexicali's pollution means visitors to the city might not realize how spectacular its geographical setting is: the mountains to the west are only dimly visible thanks to the ever-present urban smog. Nevertheless, the tree-lined boulevards that run through the university district offer plenty of respite for the eye, and several places within the city limits provide escape from the fumes. Mexicali's parks are among its most attractive features and, along with its extensive museums, testify to the city's prosperity and pride.

BOSQUE Y ZOOLÓGICO. The Bosque, an enormous park, houses a full zoo complete with lion, jaguars, and two roaring Bengal tigers. Flamingos, pheasants, and a red-tailed hawk live in the recently constructed open aviary nearby. A water park featuring multiple pools and slides, a mini-train (20 pesos) running through the park, and playgrounds galore make the Bosque any child's dream. The park also contains the **Museo de Historia Natural,** which charts the history of life on Earth with a special focus on Baja and houses a complete whale skeleton. It was closed for renovations in summer 2007. *(On Alvarado between San Marcos and Cárdenas, in southwestern Mexicali. Take a southbound black-and-white "Sta. Isabel" bus at the stop on Reforma, near Mateos. Get off at the Bosque's entrance. By car, head south on Azueta over the Río Nuevo. The road becomes Uxmal south of the river; turn left on Independencia, then right on Victoria. ☎558 9080. Open M-F 10am-4pm, Sa-Su 10am-5pm. 20 pesos, children 10 pesos. Water park 50 pesos extra.)*

SOL DE NIÑO. The Sol de Niño "science museum" has a giant slide, a climbing wall, huge bubble blowers, funny mirrors, and a skywalk with views of the city. Thankfully, the museum explains itself with a giant quote on the wall, attributed to Albert Einstein: *"El juego es la forma mas elevada de investigación."* (Playing is the highest form of research.) A must for children and for those who want to act like them. *(The large building on Mateos, next to Parque Vicente Guerrero. ☎554 9595 or 553 8383. Open daily 10am-8pm. May be overrun with marauding schoolchildren during the week. 45 pesos, children 3-12 40 pesos. IMAX theatre 65 pesos.)*

UNIVERSITY MUSEUM. The Universidad Autónoma de Baja California (UABC) runs a museum that traces the history of the northern half of the state. It includes a small display on the influx of American retirees and a much too small display on

BAJA CALIFORNIA

MEXICALI'S BACK DOOR

Border towns have long held a reputation for tawdriness and lewdness and Mexicali is no exception. Prostitution and drug trafficking are on prominent display in the city center, La Chinesca. These businesses, however, is not always as open to public inspection.

Since the era of US Prohibition, the border has been more transparent than many believed, particularly when it came to moving illegal goods. A 1923 fire in Mexicali's La Chinesca revealed the first in a series of tunnels leading to opium dens, brothels, and, surprisingly, Calexico, California.

In recent years, the number of underground tunnels across the international border has jumped, as has the movement of illegal substances. These underground passageways are key parts of the drug trade, but are too numerous and complicated for police to investigate. During routine maintenance work, construction workers and city officials often discover the tunnels. In the first six months of 2005, five were discovered in Mexicali alone, and it seems that the drug flow is not slowing any time soon.

In an effort to curb burrowing, Mexican and US officials have a new plan in the works to install a series of three fences across the Mexicali-Calexico border, complete with underground sensors.

the impact that Chinese immigrants had on Mexicali. Still, some of the exhibits are superbly done. *(On Reforma at Calle L. ☎552 5715 or 554 1977. Exhibits all in Spanish. Open M-F 9am-6pm, Sa-Su 10am-4pm. 15 pesos.)*

🎵 ENTERTAINMENT

The huge **Plaza de Toros Calafia** (☎557 1417 or 3864), on Calafia near the corner of Independencia, hosts regularly scheduled bullfights and wrestling matches. (Tickets 100-400 pesos. Season Feb.-May and Sept.-Nov.) To get there, go to the *centro* stop at Mateos and Reforma and get on a blue-and-white "Centro Cívico" bus headed away from the border (10min., 7.50 pesos). **Lienzo Charro del Cetys,** at the corner of Cetys and Ordente, hosts rodeos in the winter and spring. Check with the tourist office for schedules.

Mexicali boasts two major theaters and a very active **Casa de la Cultura,** on Madero and Altamirano. Hundreds flock to this beautiful Neoclassical building to study sculpture, drawing, painting, theater, dance, and English. The Casa holds rotating displays of very impressive student art and presents plays, concerts, and dance shows. (☎552 9630. Open M-F 9am-5pm. Free.) **UABC,** the university, also presents cultural and theatrical performances in its theater and has artistic displays in the Galeria Universitaria and Sala de Arte on campus. (☎566 4276 for more info.) If you're looking for a major play, symphony, or musical, visit **Teatro del Estado,** on Mateos at the northern end of Parque Vicente Guerrero. (☎554 6419. Box office open 11am-6pm on the day of the event. Tickets 200-400 pesos.)

🍸 NIGHTLIFE

La Chinesca is filled with night clubs that boom all night—and all day—but almost all are strip clubs. For a friendlier strip of clubs, head to the eastern part of town. Public buses stop running at 11pm, so you'll have to either call it an early night or take a taxi (negotiable, around 50 pesos). **Menealo!,** Reforma 1085 (☎555 7144), between Calles B and C, features salsa and merengue dancing; try out one of their free lessons on Wednesday 8-10pm (W and F-Sa live orchestra. Open W-Th 8:30pm-3am, F-Sa 9pm-3am. Cash only.) **Cafe Olé,** Reforma 1150, between Calles C and D, is a hip bar that attracts a young crowd. (F-Sa live rock. Beer US$2. Open daily 6pm-2am. Cash only.)

SAN FELIPE
☎ 686

Set between the desert, the sierra, and the Sea of Cortés, and far from Mex. 1, San Felipe's (pop. 15,000) tranquil bay isn't a place anyone just passes through. With its beautiful beach, gently teased by warm gulf waters, the town has an unhurried, untroubled quality which, along with its proximity to the US, has persuaded a growing number of US citizens to come here for good, taking as their unofficial slogan, "No bad days in San Felipe." The tempo quickens on weekends, when more casual visitors drive into town and the bars and souvenir vendors go into overdrive.

▐ TRANSPORTATION

The **bus station** is at the intersection of Mar Caribe and Mediterraneo. To walk downtown (15min.), turn left upon leaving the station, walk on Mar Caribe, and turn right on Manzanillo. **Autotransportes de Baja California** (☎577 1516) departs from San Felipe to **Tijuana** (5hr., 5 per day 6am-8pm, 362 pesos) via **Mexicali** (2hr., 188 pesos). All buses to Tijuana—except for the 8pm bus—continue on to **Tecate** (308 pesos). Buses also go to **Ensenada** (3hr.; 8am, 6pm; 248 pesos).

◆ ▐ ORIENTATION AND PRACTICAL INFORMATION

San Felipe is 190km south of Mexicali at the end of Mex. 5. About 43km north of San Felipe, this road connects with Mex. 3 from Ensenada, a route whose mountainous sections involve several sharp and poorly signed bends. Los Arcos (a tall, white double arch) marks the town entrance. Chetumal continues straight from the arch toward the sea and is one of the east-west streets named after a Mexican port city. Perpendicular to these are the north-south *avenidas*, including the beachfront *malecón*, and behind it Mar de Cortés, home to hotels, restaurants, and souvenir shops.

Tourist Office: Mar de Cortés 300 (☎577 1155, 24hr. tourist helpline 078), at Manzanillo. Open M-F 8am-7pm, Sa-Su 9am-2pm. Useful information for travelers can also be found on the town's website (www.sanfelipe.com.mx).

Bank: Bancomer (☎577 1090), Mar de Cortés Nte. at Acapulco. **Exchanges currency** and traveler's checks and has a **24hr. ATM.** Open M-F 8:30am-4pm, Sa 10am-2pm.

Laundromat: The Washtub (☎577 2001), on Mar de Cortés, south of the tourist office. Full-service 50 pesos, self-service 20 pesos. Open Jan.-June and Sept.-Dec. M-F 8am-4pm, Sa 8am-2pm; July-Aug. M-Tu and F 8am-4pm, W-Th 8am-2pm.

Emergency: ☎060.

Police: (☎577 1134), on Isla de los Cedros at Mar Negro.

Red Cross: (☎577 1544), located on Mar Bermejo and Peñasco.

24hr. Pharmacy: Hospital San Felipe, Mar Negro 1285 (☎577 0117).

Medical Services: Centro de Salud (☎577 1521), on Mar Bermejo Sur and Ensenada. Open 24hr. **Hospital San Felipe,** Mar Negro 1285 (☎577 0117), is a private hospital, open 24hr.

Internet Access: The Net (☎577 1600), on Mar de Cortés next to the People's Gallery, beyond the tourist office. 27.50 pesos for 1st 15min.; 55 pesos per hr. Open June-Sept. M-F 8am-2pm; Oct.-May M-F 9am-3pm, Sa 10am-1pm. A more affordable option is **Bandido's,** next to the eponymous bar across from the tourist office. 20 pesos per hr. Open daily 9am-9pm.

Post Office: Mar Blanco 187 (☎577 1330), at Ensenada. Open M-F 8am-3pm. **Postal Code:** 21850.

ACCOMMODATIONS

Budget options are limited in San Felipe. Lots of people camp on the main beach, although theft is common. For a bargain, try renting a room in a private home—look for signs that say *"se rentan cuartos"*—although it is sometimes hard to find the owner. Hotels fill up on weekends. Call ahead to make reservations.

Carmencita's, Mar de Cortés 173 (☎577 1831), across from Motel Chapala. A sign on the street offers rooms for rent in a friendly, 4-room guest house. Rooms include powerful A/C, spacious bath, mini-fridges, limited cable TV, and purified water. Singles and doubles 300 pesos. Cash only. ❺

Motel Dona Ramona, Mar Baltico 738 (☎577 0314). A friendly, cheap, and very basic motel, with large rooms and strong A/C, although the bugs might scare some people away. Rooms 300 pesos. Cash only. ❺

Ruben's, Golfo de California 703 (☎577 1442), toward the end of Golfo de California in Playa Norte, a 10min. walk from the *centro*. Camping shelters, some on the beach, are topped with 2-story, open-air bungalows that look like *palapa* tree-forts. Spots in the summer M-Th and Su US$25, F-Sa US$30. Cash only. ❹

Campo San Felipe (☎577 1012; www.camposanfelipe.com), on Mar de Cortés. Fabulous beachfront location near the *centro*. Thatched roofs cover each fully-loaded trailer and tent spot. Sites facing the beach US$25, other sites US$20. Cash only. ❹

RV Park Laura, 333 Mar de Cortés (☎577 1128; www.campoplayadelaura.com), adjacent to Campo San Felipe. Roofs over trailer and tent spots. Site on the beach 275 pesos, other sites 245 pesos. Cash only. ❹

La Posada de Don Jesús Mini Motel, Mar Báltico 186 (☎577 0685). Don Jesús has small trailers for rent, equipped with small bath, electricity, hammock, and kitchenette. 2-person trailers 300 pesos. Cash only. ❺

Hospedaje Turístico Trini, 293 Puerto Peñasco (☎577 4000), is set up like Don Jesús, with small trailers to rent for 500 pesos, although it also has a tidy grass yard where you can put up a tent for only US$8. Clean common bath. Cash only. ❶

FOOD

Unsurprisingly, the real draw in San Felipe is the fresh seafood. As in other cities on the peninsula, the cheapest options are the *taquerías* on the *malecón*, which offer shrimp, fish, or *carne asada* tacos for 8-10 pesos, and the hot dog stands throughout town.

■ **Restaurant el Club** (☎577 1175), on the *malecón* at Acapulco, has cheap, delicious seafood specials. Huge plates of steamed clams cost 45 pesos, while an order of steamed crabs goes for 35 pesos. Open daily 7am-10:30pm. Cash only. ❹

Baja Java Restaurant and Cafe (☎577 2465), at Chetumal and Mar de Cortés, serves great bagel-and-egg sandwiches for breakfast (28-31 pesos) and a variety of sandwiches for lunch (35-53 pesos). The 2nd fl. balcony location also allows you to admire the view, safe from aggressive merchants. Open daily 7am-4pm. Cash only. ❸

Chencho's, 233 Puerto Peñasco (☎577 1058), serves enormous breakfasts popular with locals. *Huevos rancheros* 45 pesos. Open M and W-Su 7am-10pm. Cash only. ❸

Rice and Beans (☎577 1770), on the *malecón* between Acapulco and Zihuatanejo. Tasty burgers (40 pesos) in a restaurant covered with offroad racing memorabilia. Open daily 7am-11pm. MC/V. ❸

Fatboy's Pizza (☎577 4092), on Chetumal and Mar de Cortés. Small American-style pizza 60 pesos. Open daily 9am-11pm. Cash only. ❸

◉ SIGHTS

BEACHES. Each year, more than 250,000 people come to San Felipe to swim in the warm, invitingly green waters of the Sea of Cortés. The main beach follows the *malecón* and changes dramatically with the tide—at high tide, the water can come to within feet of the walkway. It's very popular with tourists and locals, especially on weekends. There's no shortage of people riding banana boats, which are sometimes just floats being pulled by too-fast motorboats (20min., 40 pesos). South of town past the marina, away from the rumbling of boats and cars, clearer water and peaceful beaches provide a better setting for snorkeling or collecting seashells. You can rent ATVs from Motos Carrillo's directly outside Campo San Felipe, although be aware that the roar of ATVs on the beach is always unwelcome. Check out the diagrams of the vehicles' spare parts, with prices attached, before embarking. (☎577 2453. US$20-30 per hr. depending on size.) For breathtaking views of the town, the sparkling blue bay, and the surrounding hills, climb up to the **Capilla de la Virgen de Guadalupe,** on the hill overlooking the beach. *(Walk across the narrow footbridge at the north end of the* malecón *and climb the stairs.)*

VALLE DE LOS GIGANTES. This hidden valley at the foot of the Sierra San Pedro Mártir is home to the world's largest stand of *cardón* cacti, one of which represented Mexico at the 1992 World's Fair in Seville, Spain. That particular cactus was 17m tall, weighed 10 tons, and was more than 1,500 years old. In the valley, towering *cardón* (many nearly 15m tall), thorny orange-tipped *ocotillo*, bearded *abuelo*, and easily provoked jumping *cholla* cacti shelter a community of cows, roadrunners, jackrabbits, coyotes, and other desert-dwellers. **Casey's Place,** on Mar y Sol two blocks south of Campo San Felipe in town, offers comfortable tours of the valley and other destinations in SUVs. (☎577 1431; www.sanfelipe.tv. 3½hr. trips include food. Reserve in advance. US$55 per person. Open daily 8am-8pm.) Alternatively, you can drive to the valley on your own; although you will need a 4WD vehicle. *(To reach the valley, drive up Chetumal away from the sea and turn left at the rotunda toward the airport. Where the airport road splits from the main highway, take the left fork toward Puertecitos along the water. At km 14, take the sign marked "Valle de los Gigantes." After about 20km, take the small dirt road at km 14 on the right marked with a sign for "Sahuaro, Valle de Los Gigantes." Passenger vehicles with partially deflated tires should be able to navigate the sandy terrain as far as the small palapa, where all cars without 4WD should park, though there is a small risk of getting stuck. Local ranchers charge visitors a small entrance fee of 50 pesos.)*

♫ ▣ ENTERTAINMENT AND NIGHTLIFE

San Felipe lures tourists with bars and clubs right on the *malecón*. Saturday nights are much more popular than Friday nights.

Rockodile (☎577 1219), on the *malecón* at Acapulco. Attracts a young crowd to the central volleyball court, outdoor terrace, and loud pop music. Low-key daytime crowd gets pushed out by a sweaty dance party at night. Open Th-Su 11am-3am. Cash only.

Beach Comber, a block down the *malecón* from Rockodile. Sports bar by day and raucous dance party by night. Th-F and Su night karaoke. Happy hour M-Th 4-6pm 2-for-1 margaritas and beer. Open M-Tu 5pm-1am, Th-Su 11am-3am. Cash only.

Bar Miramar (☎577 1192), at the north end of the *malecón*. Seasoned veterans nurse drinks at Miramar. Play a round of pool on the open-air patio overlooking the sea. Free Wi-Fi. Beer 20 pesos. Open M-Th 10am-2am, F-Su 10am-3am.

VALLE DE SAN QUINTÍN   ☎616

On the mid-Pacific coast of northern Baja, the San Quintín Valley is the lifeblood of Baja Californian agriculture. Enclosed by huge barren mountains to the east and the Pacific Ocean to the west, nearly every square inch of land here earns its keep as cropland. The closest thing the region has to an urban center is a collection of services strung out haphazardly along Mex. 1, more or less divided into three discrete towns: San Quintín, Lázaro Cárdenas (distinct from the other Lázaro Cárdenas, 100km to the northeast), and Ejido El Papaloto. The few tourists who visit come for the fishing and surfing in and around the bay to the west, while the rest are simply passing through on their way to the more pristine south. The area may not look like much, but the sleepy towns of the Valle de San Quintín are friendly and cool, making them a fine rest stop, especially for travelers about to venture into nearby Parque Nacional Sierra San Pedro Mártir.

▐ TRANSPORTATION. The one **bus** terminal that serves the area is at the southern end of Cárdenas, on the right-hand side of Mex. 1 from the north. **Public transport within the Valle is limited, however, and it is virtually impossible to travel from here to any of the nearby points of interest except by your own transportation.** All three towns huddle around **Mex. 1.** Streets off the highway lack street signs, and addresses are designated by distance from Ensenada, although kilometer markers are often missing. Beaches, accessible by small dirt roads, are all located to the west of the highway. Coming from the north, **San Quintín** is the first town, **Cárdenas** is next, and **Papalote** rounds out the trio. Directions to all the following locations are given for travelers driving from north to south. All are on Mex. 1 unless otherwise stated. The four street lights and three PEMEX stations are useful landmarks, as well as the bridge in San Quintin.

▐ PRACTICAL INFORMATION. To **exchange currency** or traveler's checks, or for **24hr. ATMs,** head to **HSBC** in Cárdenas behind the PEMEX station, at the second set of street lights after the bridge on the square to the right of the highway. (☎165 2101. Open M-F 8am-7pm, Sa 8am-3pm.) **Bancomer** is on the opposite side of the Transpeninsular, north of the set of street lights (open M-F 8:30am-4pm). These are the last banks before Guerrero Negro. Other services include a number of **laundromats,** including **Lavamática Ángel,** on the right at km 192.5 (wash 20 pesos, dry 25 pesos; open M-Sa 8am-9pm, Su 9am-3pm); **police,** in San Quintín at km 190, off a side street to the left immediately after the PEMEX station (☎165 2034); **Red Cross,** at km 192 in San Quintín on the right (☎166 8621); **Farmacia del Valle,** adjacent to Internet Maria (see below), beyond the PEMEX station after the first set of lights following the bridge (☎107 0343; open M-Sa 9am-11pm), as well as pharmacies on both sides of the road throughout the valley; **IMSS,** at km 193.5 in San Quintín, just beyond the bridge from the north and immediately before the set of lights (☎165 2222 or 3151); **Telecomm fax** service next to the post office (☎165 2269; open M-F 8am-2pm, Sa 8-11am); **Internet** cafes dotting Mex. 1 throughout the valley, including **Internet Maria,** beyond the PEMEX station, after the first set of lights following the bridge (10 pesos per hr., open daily 8am-9pm); and the **post office,** toward the end of Cárdenas on the right, following the second set of lights beyond the bridge (☎165 3646; open M-F 8am-2pm). **Postal Code:** 22920.

▐▌ ACCOMMODATIONS AND FOOD. Hotel rooms in Valle de San Quintín tend to be clean, modern, and reasonably priced. There are several campgrounds along the water at Bahía San Quintín. The best is **Old Mill RV Park ❶,** which has tent sites with superb views. To reach the site from the north, drive past the third PEMEX station after the bridge, take a right at the large green "B. San Quintín" sign, and follow the poorly maintained dirt road for 6km. Sign in at the Old Mill Bait and Tackle Shop on the water. (☎165 6034. 100 pesos with electricity, 100 pesos without. Cash only.) Next door to the RV park, the American-owned **Old Mill Hotel ❺** has the best rooms in the valley. The extremely clean rooms, with purified water, comfortable beds, and fans, are just feet from the water and offer a calm contrast to the traffic-jammed stretch of Mex. 1 in San Quintín. They're especially popular with American surfers and fishermen (☎800-479-7962; www.oldmill-baja.com. Rooms US$30.) If you're not willing to travel down the 6km dirt and stone road to reach the Old Mill Hotel or the Old Mill RV Park, **Motel Chavez ❷**, just before the bridge at the end of San Quintín on the right has clean rooms with fans and satellite TV. (☎165 2005. Singles 240 pesos; doubles 305 pesos. Cash only.) Don't be fooled by the dusty exterior of **Motel Uruapan ❸**, at km 190 in San Quintín. Inside, well-maintained for rooms come with bath and fans. (☎165 2108; fax 166 8186. Singles 200 pesos; doubles 250 pesos. Cash only.)

Fresh local clams, harvested on the bay, claim a spot on every menu in the area. Though pricey for dinner the **Old Mill Restaurant ❹**, adjacent to the hotel and RV park with the same name, dishes out delicious pancakes (30 pesos) and omelettes (55-100 pesos) for breakfast. You can eat outside overlooking the sea and, if you come early enough, your breakfast companions will be American baby boomers preparing for the day's fishing trip. (Open daily 5:30am-10pm.) In San Quintín itself, **Restaurant Bar San Quintín ❸**, on Mex. 1 next to Hotel Chávez, also serves satisfying food. (☎165 2376. Breakfasts 30-45 pesos. Open daily 7am-11pm.) **Restaurant Viejo San Quintín ❷**, past the first two PEMEX stations on the right side of the road, is popular for its cheap and tasty sandwiches for 20 pesos and enchiladas for 44 pesos. (☎165 1651. Open daily 7am-10pm. MC/V.) For cheaper eats, *taquerías* line both sides of Mex. 1 and serve excellent *tacos de pescado* or *carne asada* (around 10 pesos).

◢ **WATERSPORTS.** Tourists who stop in San Quintín for more than a night have likely come for the great fishing or surfing, and they'll probably stop at the Old Mill complex, with its hotel, restaurant, bait shop, RV park, and boat launch on the way to fish or surf. The nearby stretch of protected bays (Bahía San Quintín, Bahía Falsa, and Bahía Santa María) is home to dizzying numbers of cabrilla, corvina, halibut, rock cod, and sea bass year-round. In July and August the open water beyond the bays supports healthy populations of tuna (albacore, bluefin, and yellow), marlin, and other sailfish. Many boats around the Old Mill complex, at the southern end of Cárdenas, offer **fishing tours. Don Eddie's Landing,** right next to the Old Mill, offers daytrips for bottom fishing and tuna fishing. (☎165 6061; www.doneddies.com. US$360 for groups up to 4, includes bait, radio, depth finder, and the services of a captain.) San Quintín also boasts exceptional **surfing** with little competition for amazing waves. Kite surfers head to **Playa Santa Maria** in front of Hotel la Pinta San Quintín or to the beach in front of the Motel Muelle Viejo, a short drive from the Old Mill Complex. To get to other surfing spots, you'll need 4WD and a good map from the tourist office. The best surf is accessible at offshore breaks only by boat. A number of outfitters, including Don Eddie's, will bring surfers to the breaks for about US$360.

▧ PARQUE NACIONAL SIERRA SAN PEDRO MÁRTIR

Most travelers bypass breathtaking Parque Nacional Sierra de San Pedro Mártir, making it one of the least visited of Mexico's national parks. The somber peaks of the Sierra de San Pedro Mártir are visible from San Felipe and San Quintín. Those few intrepid souls who venture up here to the area around the Vallecitos plateau discover a world apart from the surrounding desert, in which comparatively high levels of precipitation sustain verdant forests of pine and juniper. Puma and eagles make their home alongside a hearty population of deer, and ice-cold streams support an endemic population of Nelson rainbow trout.

At 10,154 feet, the jagged double peak of **Picacho del Diablo** (also known as the **Cerro de la Encantada** or **La Providencia**) is the Baja peninsula's highest point and also its greatest challenge to mountaineers—the hike should only be attempted by experienced climbers or those with a reliable guide. Allow 2-3 days to hike to the base from the main road, climb to the summit, and return to the base. Everyone attempting the climb must register at the ranger station. Hikers not brave, skilled, or deluded enough to attempt Picacho del Diablo can take in the view at **Mirador el Altar,** a breathtaking lookout 2880m above sea level. On a clear day, it's sometimes possible to see as far as the Pacific coast to the west and the Sea of Cortés to the east. The trail (2½hr.) to Mirador el Altar is a steep path strewn with loose rocks; look for signs from the main road just east of Vallecitos.

In 1967, the Mexican government took advantage of the park's secluded location, choosing it as the site for the **Observatorio Nacional.** The road to the observatory is clearly marked from Vallecitos; park at the gate and walk along the dirt road to the right. Register at the observatory's office, the large building on the left. The most sizable of the observatory's three gigantic telescopes boasts a lens diameter of 2.12m. The smaller buildings up ahead are the astronomers' private rooms. Friendly scientists are often willing to lead free daytime tours, which can be arranged in advance by calling the observatory (☎ 646 176 4580).

The road leading to the park branches off Mex. 1, 51km north of San Quintín at San Telmo de Abajo, a small village between Camalu and Colonet, and runs east of the highway for 100km. The ride to the entrance (2½hr.) starts on a paved road and continues on a fairly well-marked dirt road (closed during heavy rainfall). This access road becomes the main road inside the park, passing through Vallecitos and ending at the closed observatory gates. 4WD vehicles are recommended. Camping costs 10 pesos per day. If no one is at the ranger station, go ahead and set up camp, and someone will come by to collect your money. Campfires are strictly limited to certain areas. Buy a map of the park before you start your trip, as the maps distributed at the entrance are low-quality. Direct inquiries to the park's main office at km 22.5 on Mex. 2, on the outskirts of Mexicali, in Ejido Sinaloa. (☎ 665 54 4404 or 665 554 5470; spmartir@conanp.gob.mx.)

EL ROSARIO ☎ 616

El Rosario is little more than a bend in the road where the Transpeninsular turns its back on the west coast and starts across Baja's rugged interior. Set up like an extended rest-stop, El Rosario is where you'll find the last PEMEX station for nearly 100 mi. The nearest gas stations to the south are in Bahía de los Ángeles and Guerrero Negro, although people often sell gasoline along the road in Catavina.

El Rosario boasts a number of motels for travelers who need a rest before the long road south. **Las Cabañas ❺,** also known as Mama Espinoza's, adjacent to the restaurant offers simple, though pricey, lodging. (Rooms 350 pesos.) (www.mamaespinozas.com. Cash only.) Next door, **Motel Baja Cactus ❸,** has cheaper rooms, although it's also adjacent to the noisy PEMEX station. (☎ 166 8850. Rooms 250-400 pesos, depending on size and number of beds. MC/V.) The most well-known spot (priced accordingly) is **Mama Espinoza's Place ❹,** on the northern end of town, just beyond the PEMEX station. Since 1930, Mama Espinoza has stuffed Baja trekkers with her famous 145-peso lobster burritos, and she also serves typical Mexican fare for 45-75 pesos. (☎ 165 8770. Open daily 6am-10pm. Cash only). In a yellow building on the opposite side of town to the far south, **Baja's Best Cafe ❸** serves similar—but cheaper—food and promises Starbucks-brand coffee. (Open daily 6am-10pm. Cash only.)

Services include: **police** (☎ 165 8858); **pharmacy** at **Supermercado San José** (☎ 165 8769; open daily 7am-11pm); **Centro de Salud** (open M-F 8am-2pm and 4-6pm, Sa-Su 10am-2pm); and **Internet** access at **Internet,** next door to the Centro de Salud (20 pesos per hr.; open daily 8am-8pm.) **Postal Code:** 22960.

BAHÍA DE LOS ÁNGELES   ☎ 667

After miles and miles of rugged mountains, desert, and dust, the glistening sapphire ocean of Bahía de los Ángeles (pop. 720) is one of Baja's most enchanting sights. The small, undeveloped town has a rich history: originally inhabited by the Cochimi, an indigenous group from central Baja, the town was later used as a mining center for copper, silver, and gold. It served subsequently as the center of Baja's sea turtle industry until the business was outlawed. The sheltered coves and offshore islands of isolated Bahía (as it is known to locals) or "L.A. Bay" (as it is known to the many Americans baby boomers who visit) are a tiny paradise for a wide array of marine species and for visitors who cherish the peace and simplicity of one of the real jewels of the Sea of Cortés.

◪ PRACTICAL INFORMATION. A 66km road leads from Mex. 1 to Bahía de los Ángeles. This access road becomes the town's main street. Two PEMEX stations and a white statue of some sails mark your arrival in town. There are **no addresses** here and very few phones so places can be difficult to find. There is no official office, but for **tourist information,** ask at the Museo de Naturaleza y Cultura. The closest **banks** are in Guerrero Negro, and all local business is conducted in cash—bring all the money you will need with you. Other services include: **police,** at the Delegación Municipal building on the square, near the museum (☎ 124 9111); 24hr. medical services at **Centro de Salud,** just behind the police station (open for consultation M-F 8:30am-2pm and 4-6:30pm, Sa 10am-2pm and 4-6pm, Su 8am-noon). **Restaurant Isla,** a sort of general store across from Restaurante Las Hamacas, has a **pharmacy,** a long-distance **phone,** and **Internet** cafe. (Internet access 25 pesos per hr. Open daily 6am-10pm)

◪◨ ACCOMMODATIONS AND FOOD. A shortage of electricity and fresh water make hotels in Bahía very pricey. Beach camping is the cheapest way to stay here, and the shore breezes provide a welcome respite from the heat. Your best bet is **Daggett's Campground ❶,** a bustling site on the water with spotless bathrooms. To reach Daggett's, turn at the circle with the statue of the two sails in the direction of Punta Griega and follow the signs. (www.campdaggetts.com. Kayak and boat rentals. *Palapas* for tent, US$10 for 1-2 people; each additional person US$5. Cash only.) **Campo Archelón ❶,** on the Punta la Griega road, right before Daggett's, is quieter and more isolated. (*Palapas* for tents 100 pesos. Stone-walled *palapas* with extremely basic cots for those without tents, 50 pesos per person. Bring a pillow and a blanket. Cash only.) The best value hotel in town is **Casa Díaz ❹,** at the far edge of Bahía where the road curves. (☎ 124 9101. Rooms without A/C US$25. Cash only.) **Guillermo's ❺,** on the main road near Casa Díaz, is overpriced and has weak A/C, but has its own beach. (☎ 124 9104. Rooms US$45-65.)

Like lodging, food in Bahía isn't cheap, and restaurant hours may not be reliable. The fish tacos (10 pesos) at **Taquería Carreta ❶,** next to Las Hamacas, have an excellent local reputation. (Open daily 1-9pm. Cash only.) Head to **Restaurante las Hamacas ❹,** in front of the hotel of the same name, if the fish just aren't biting. (Warm, buttery *pescado al mojo de ajo* 70 pesos. Beer 20 pesos. Open daily 6am-8pm. Cash only.) **Palapa Reyna ❹,** on the right at the beginning of town, offers typical Mexican fare in a touristy environment. (*Tacos dorados* 50 pesos. Open daily 6am-11pm. Cash only.) Linger on the rooftop patio of **Restau-**

BAJA CALIFORNIA

rante Isla ❹, across from Las Hamacas, and gaze at the bay while enjoying a delicious breakfast. (Open daily 6am-9pm, though hours may vary. US$10 for MC/V.) **Guillermo's** ❺, adjacent to the hotel with the same name, dishes up excellent burgers (55 pesos) and omelettes (60 pesos) before a spectacular view. (☎124 9104. Open daily 7am-10pm.) Groceries are available at **Restaurante Isla,** on the east side of the road, opposite Las Hamacas.

🖸 **SIGHTS.** The excellent **Museo de Naturaleza y Cultura,** a small building behind the police office, with a whale skeleton and gold mining equipment in its yard, highlights Bahía's diverse history. In addition to newspaper articles on the area and a recreation of a rancher's house, the museum has extensive shell and fossil displays, information on the area's natural history, and a Baja-focused bookstore. (Open daily 9am-noon and 3-5pm. Free.)

The turtle population of Bahía has been recovering slowly since the ban on their capture, thanks in part to the people at **Campo Tortuga,** part of the Mexican government's Comisión Nacional de Areas Naturales Protegidas, located on the dirt road toward Daggett's in the direction of Punta Griega. The project studies the physiology and ecology of the turtles in the bay, which are mostly Pacific green turtles, but also hawksbills and loggerheads. The rehabilitation area provides a chance to get up close and personal (but not too personal—they do bite) with injured turtles that live in a number of large tanks on the site. (Open M-Sa 9am-2pm. US$2 per person).

Imposing islands define the landscape of Bahía de los Ángeles. The federally protected offshore islands, whose colors gradually shift as the light conditions change, are home to a host of rare wildlife, including threatened birds. 95% of the Hermann's gulls in existence come to the 142-acre **Rasa Island,** off of Bahía de los Ángeles, to nest in April each year, along with more than 180,000 elegant terns. In 1979, federal officials prohibited the harvesting of birds' eggs, and the populations of Hermann's gulls and terns have since boomed. (Tourists can see the birds during their nesting season; ask at the Las Islas del Golfo de California office on the main street through town for more information. To visit any of the islands, you need to buy a permit which costs 44 pesos per person. ☎200 124 9106. Open M-F 8am-2pm and 4-6pm, Sa 9am-1pm.)

🖸 **WATERSPORTS.** Bahía's famed fishing is rewarding year-round, and a constant stream of male American baby boomers passes through the town. Expect to hook corvina, dorado, grouper, halibut, and yellowtail from late spring to summer and cabrilla, roosterfish, sailfish, and sierra in winter. Triggerfish swallow bait year-round. Smart fishermen bring their own equipment, as rentals are both expensive and uncommon. Guides, on the other hand, are everywhere. Among them, **Joel's Fishing Tours** (☎200 124 9160; joel_prieto@hotmail.com), opposite the museum in town charges about US$150 for a full-day of fishing and US$120 for a half-day. The **Islas del Golfo de California** office, near the park on the main street in town, has a list of registered fishing guides, along with their contact information. (☎200 124 9106. Open M-F 8am-2pm and 4-6 pm, Sa 9am-1pm.)

The experienced can try **sea kayaking,** but should exercise caution: winds in the bay can pick up without warning, and a few kayakers are lost to the ocean each year. Daggett's Campground rents kayaks. (US$5 per hr. Snorkeling equipment also available.) The beaches in town are not exactly sandy, but broken shells give way to fine, golden-gray sand farther north, along the **Punta la Gringa** peninsula. To get to la Gringa, turn on the paved road at the circle with the statue of the two sails in the direction of Punta Griega and continue straight for 12km, past Daggett's. The small paths leading off the road to the water are usually passable in a passenger car, but flooding can turn them into sticky mud.

BAJA CALIFORNIA SUR

GUERRERO NEGRO   ☎ 615

Guerrero Negro (pop. 10,000) is an industrial town centered around its enormous salt refinery. Most of the town's commercial buildings line an unattractive and traffic-filled main street, which leads to the plant. Still, Guerrero Negro is a useful stopping point for tourists hoping to stock up on gasoline—there are two PEMEX stations here. Year-round, Guerrero's bird refuge draws bird lovers, and between January and April, playful gray whales flock to nearby Laguna Ojo de Liebre, making Guerrero Negro a convenient base for whale watching trips into the Reserva de la Biosfera el Vizcaíno (p. 183).

TRANSPORTATION. The **bus** terminal (☎157 0611) is north of Zapata, two blocks west of the Malarrimo Hotel. Buses head north (5 per day) stopping in **San Quintín** (5hr., 432 pesos), **Ensenada** (7hr., 614 pesos), and **Tijuana** (12hr., 723 pesos). Going south buses (6 per day) go to **Santa Rosalía** (3hr., 220 pesos), **Mulegé** (4hr., 285 pesos), and **La Paz** (10hr., 786 pesos), as well as towns in between. Taxis run frequently on Zapata to both ends of town and to residential areas.

ORIENTATION AND PRACTICAL INFORMATION. Guerrero Negro lies along a 3km strip west of the Transpeninsular Highway. Most businesses are on Zapata, which eventually curves toward the salt plant. A large orange water tank in the middle of the straight section of road is a useful reference point. **Banamex,** on Zapata in front of the salt plant, **exchanges currency** and traveler's checks, and has **24hr. ATMs.** (☎157 0555. Open M-F 9am-4pm.) Travelers continuing south might want to use this opportunity to stock up on cash, as this is the last bank until Santa Rosalía. For those heading north, it's the last bank before San Quintín. Other services include: **laundry** at **Lavamax,** two blocks north of Zapata just beyond the water tank on the eastern side of the street (☎157 0736; wash 12 pesos, dry 15 pesos; open M-Sa 9am-9pm, Su 10am-5pm); **police,** in the Delegación Municipal building, before the salt plant on the left (☎157 0022); **Farmacia San Martín,** the big yellow building on the left of Zapata going into town, close to the bend in the road (☎157 1111; open M-Sa 8am-10pm); **IMSS** on Zapata at Tabasco, past PEMEX (☎157 0303); **Internet** at **Internet Ballenas,** adjacent to Motel Las Ballenas (☎157 2534; open daily 10am-noon and 4-9pm); and the **post office,** on Pino Suárez. To reach the post office, drive down to the end of Zapata and turn left on Baja California; then, turn left on Pino Suárez, a dirt road just before the basketball courts. (☎157 0344. Open M-F 8am-4pm.) **Postal Code:** 23940.

ACCOMMODATIONS AND FOOD. Guerrero Negro has a number of budget motels, and during whale watching season (Jan.-Apr.), rooms fill quickly and reservations are a good idea. If you have a tent, **Motel Malarrimo ❸,** on the right side of the road coming into town from Mex. 1, might be the best option. (☎157 0250; www.malarrimo.com. Wi-Fi. Tent US$12; RV spot US$20; singles US$38; doubles US$45. MC/V.) Also in town, friendly and quiet **Motel Las Ballenas ❸,** a block from Zapata behind Motel el Morro, offers cheap, comfortable rooms with small bath, fan, and TV. (☎157 0116; www.hotellasballenas.com. Singles 240 pesos; doubles 300 pesos. Cash only.) **Motel San Ignacio ❹** has very tidy rooms in a cheerfully painted building (☎157 0270. Singles 250 pesos; doubles 270 pesos; triples 300 pesos. Cash only.) **Motel Gamez ❶,** on Tabasco in front of the IMSS, has basic rooms with fans and private baths. In some rooms, the sink is in the shower. (☎157 0135. Rooms 150 pesos. Cash only.)

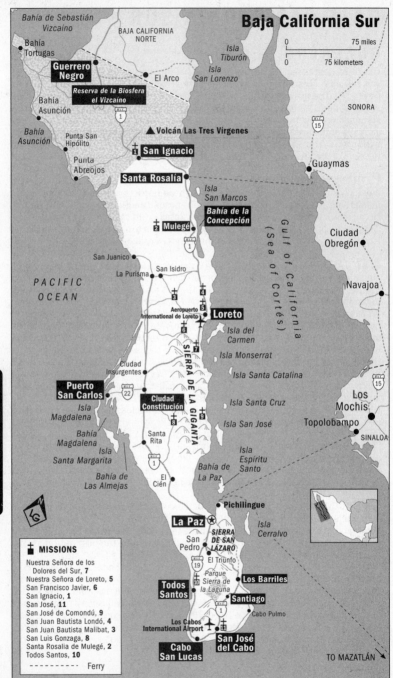

Baja California Sur

Bahía de Sebastián Vizcaíno

BAJA CALIFORNIA NORTE

Isla Tiburón

Isla San Lorenzo

0 75 miles
0 75 kilometers

Bahía Tortugas

Guerrero Negro

El Arco

SONORA

Reserva de la Biosfera el Vizcaíno

Bahía Asunción

15

Bahía Asunción

Punta San Hipólito

▲ **Volcán Las Tres Vírgenes**

Punta Abreojos

✝1 **San Ignacio**

Guaymas

Santa Rosalía

Isla San Marcos

Bahía de la Concepción

✝2 **Mulegé**

Gulf of California (Sea of Cortés)

Ciudad Obregón

San Juanico

1

La Purisma
San Isidro

✝3

✝4

PACIFIC OCEAN

Navajoa

✝5

Aeropuerto International de Loreto

Loreto

✝6

Isla del Carmen

✝7

Isla Monserrat

Ciudad Insurgentes

SIERRA DE LA GIGANTA

Isla Santa Catalina

15

Puerto San Carlos

22

Ciudad Constitución

Isla Santa Cruz

Los Mochis

Isla Magdalena

✝8

Isla San José

Topolobampo

Bahía Magdalena

Santa Rita

SINALOA

Isla Santa Margarita

1

✝9

Isla Espíritu Santo

Bahía de Las Almejas

El Cién

Bahía de La Paz

Pichilingue

Isla Cerralvo

La Paz

San Pedro

SIERRA DE SAN LAZARO

19

El Triunfo

✝11 **MISSIONS**

Nuestra Señora de los Dolores del Sur, **7**
Nuestra Señora de Loreto, **5**
San Francisco Javier, **6**
San Ignacio, **1**
San José, **11**
San José de Comondú, **9**
San Juan Bautista Londó, **4**
San Juan Bautista Malibat, **3**
San Luis Gonzaga, **8**
Santa Rosalia de Mulegé, **2**
Todos Santos, **10**
- - - - - - Ferry

Parque Sierra de la Laguna

✝10

Todos Santos

Santiago

Los Barriles

Cabo Pulmo

Los Cabos International Airport

✝11

Cabo San Lucas

San José del Cabo

TO MAZATLÁN →

BAJA CALIFORNIA

Street-side stands offer the city's cheapest, and perhaps best, food. **Asadero Viva Mexico ❶,** on Zapata, two blocks beyond the water tank, is a traditional *taquería* with outdoor counter seating and indoor tables. (*Carne asada* tacos 10 pesos. Open daily 8am-1am. Cash only.) **El Figon de Sal ❸,** on Zapata, serves inexpensive *comida corrida* for 40 pesos, along with a large selection of soups (25 pesos) in a pleasant indoor setting. (Open daily 7am-10pm. Cash only.) **Maximo's Pizzas & Burger on Zapata ❶,** across from the PEMEX station near the IMSS, has excellent pizza. (Open daily 10am-10pm. 20 pesos per slice.)

🟦 **SIGHTS.** In addition to serving as a base for whale watching trips into the Biosfera el Vizcaíno (p. 183), Guerrero is home to the largest open-evaporation salt refinery in the world. Officially known as **Esportadora de Sal,** or ES, it extends 18km east-west and about 45km north-south. Tours go through an eerie landscape of vast lagoons, and the mountains of salt look oddly like snow, a disconcerting sight in the blistering heat. (Jorge Cachu Ruiz at Internet Ballenas takes tourists on tours of the refinery for 150 pesos per person. ☎ 157 2534.) Another Guerrero Negro highlight is a visit to the **Refugio de Aves** at the end of Zapata. The salt flats near Guerrero Negro are a bird-watcher's mecca, with 120 species of migratory birds visiting between Oct. and March. Even out of season, the *refugio*, a long path surrounded by water, is full of birds and makes for a very pleasant evening stroll. (To reach the *refugio*, drive to the end of Zapata and take a right on the road with signs pointing to "Avistamiento de Aves." There's a small parking area.)

RESERVA DE LA BIOSFERA EL VIZCAÍNO

Both Guerrero Negro and San Ignacio serve as gateways to the stunning Reserva de la Biosfera el Vizcaíno, the largest nature reserve in Latin America—about three times larger than Yellowstone National Park in the US. Boasting many of southern Baja's most extraordinary natural and archaeological treasures, it encompasses the band of the peninsula from the 28th parallel down to the Sierra de San Francisco, and is bounded by the Tres Vírgenes volcanic area in the east and the entire Vizcaíno peninsula to the west. Adding the ocean on either side, the reserve totals more than 6.2 million acres. Within this sparsely populated region, officials are trying to save several endangered species and develop ecotourism as a business, but the reserve is not a park and facilities for tourists are limited. Most parts of the reserve are reachable from either Guerrero Negro (p. 181) to the north or San Ignacio (p. 185) to the south.

> **A WHALE OF A TALE.** Though Guerrero Negro has long held the reputation of being the premier gray whale watching stop, San Ignacio, to the south, makes a much more pleasant jumping off point. It's a bit farther away, but San Ignacio offers a stately mission, freshwater swimming, hikes, and many camping options. There are also fewer tourists: According to the Reserva's 2004 figures, 10,000 tourists visited the lagoon near Guerrero Negro, while only 2,000 to 3,000 visited Laguna de San Ignacio.

🔲❓ TRANSPORTATION AND PRACTICAL INFORMATION

The best source of information on the *reserva* is its main **tourist office** (☎ 157 1777; vizcaino@conanp.gob.mx), on the corner of Caballo Felix and Ruiz Castinez in Guerrero Negro, five blocks into town from the water tank and two blocks to the right. The staff can offer advice on expeditions into the *reserva*, though tours are organized through one of the local tour companies. **Malarrimo Eco-Tours,** in Guerrero Negro on Zapata, on the right as you enter town adjacent to the hotel of the same name, leads a range of tours within the reserve. (☎/fax

THE LOCAL STORY

A WHALE OF A TIME

After being considered extinct in 1970, the **Gray Whale** has reached an estimated population of 25,000, becoming a poster child for the effectiveness of wildlife preservation laws. Their breeding grounds along the coast of Baja California Sur, where the entire population of these whales mates and gives birth, are among the most important protected coastlines in North America. The whales are generally friendly, curious, and playful, and although it's illegal for boats to go closer than 30m from the whales, or for passengers to touch them, some of them may come close enough to welcome you to their habitat. Watch for the following behaviors:

Fluking: Before a deep dive, a whale will arch its back above water and display its tail.

Breaching: A whale will jump out of the water, flip, and enter the water nose-first, often slapping the water with its fluke.

Blowing: As a whale exhales, it will often "spit" water into the air.

Feeding: Although whales usually fast in winter, they've been observed eating in the bay. They'll scoop large mouthfuls of sediment and let the mud and water filter through a series of baleen plates, trapping small crustaceans and edible particles.

Spyhopping: A whale will pop its head out of the water, fix an eye on whatever strikes its fancy, and stare for minutes, often pivoting to survey the area before slipping back into the water.

157 0100; www.malarrimo.com. Make reservations at least 1 day in advance. Open mid-Dec. to early Apr. M-Sa 7am-5pm, during the rest of the year M-Sa 7am-1pm.) In San Ignacio, the local tour co-operative **Kuyima,** on the *zócalo*, offers a similar selection of tours and has its own camping grounds at Laguna San Ignacio. (☎154 0070; www.kuyima.com. Open M-Sa 8am-1pm and 3-8pm.) If you have a particular interest in seeing something that is not covered by the regular tours, such as more remote mission sites or a particular bird, animal, or species of plant, contact the company one or two months in advance to discuss the organization of a specific trip. While some sights in the *reserva* can be visited in a day, others will take more time.

⚡ OUTDOOR ACTIVITIES

WHALE WATCHING. From mid-December to early April more than 50% of the world's gray whale population is born in two lagoons: the **Laguna Ojo de Liebre,** 10km from Guerrero Negro, and the smaller **Laguna de San Ignacio,** near San Ignacio. In 2004, the last year in which a census was taken, more than 2000 gray whales visited Laguna Ojo de Liebre. Tourists in boats can look at—and even touch—the whales. Malarrimo and Kuyima, along with other operators, run popular whale watching trips for about US$45 per person. The whales are shy and sensitive, so private boats are prohibited during mating season. Trained local fishermen can give you a closer look. *(You can also drive yourself to Laguna Ojo de Liebre. The road to the Laguna is 10km south on Mex. 1—watch for a sign with a whale on it. Follow the sandy bumps for 24km until you reach the Laguna's visitor center.)*

DESERT PRONGHORN RESERVE. Sixty kilometers from the town of Vizcaíno, a dirt road peels off to the left toward Bahía Asunción. Another turn to the left about 4km later leads to the **Campamento del Berrendo,** a reserve for the *berrendo* (desert pronghorn), one of North America's most endangered species. These remarkable creatures survive the region's intense heat without drinking water, ingesting moisture from the plants in their diet instead. Moving at speeds up to 100km per hr., they are the fastest animals on the continent and the second fastest animals in the world. Even their tremendous speed, however, has not afforded them protection from hunters, and their territory is shrinking as unfenced cattle run rampant. The Mexican government established the conservation camp in the *reserva* in 1988 and outlawed hunting, in an attempt to save the species, of which there are only an estimated 150 animals living in the wild. Just over 100 pronghorns are kept in large fenced corrals, and a total of about 260 live in the camp. The staff is happy to let visitors have close-up peeks at the animals. *(Ask at the reserve's main office in Guerrero Negro before making a visit. Visits are restricted Jan.-March, when the pronghorns give birth.)*

BAHÍA ASUNCIÓN SEA LION COLONY. Past the Desert Pronghorn Reserve, the bumpy road eventually reaches the coast at Bahía Asunción, an isolated fishing community occasionally visited by American sport fishermen. The village looks out onto a small group of offshore islands, which are home to a large and noisy colony of sea lions. Manuel Arce, who lives near the fishing cooperative building at the far side of the bay, is one of a number of locals who will take enthusiasts out on his boat to watch the sea lions swimming, fighting, playing, and basking in the sun. The Biosphere staff in Guerrero Negro can help you organize a visit as well.

TRES VÍRGENES VOLCANO AND BIG-HORN SHEEP. Standing at 1840m, the Tres Vírgenes volcano, dominates the area of the Biosfera el Vizcaíno east of San Ignacio. Hikers who complete the two-day trek to the summit are rewarded with a view of the Sea of Cortés to one side and the Pacific to the other. The best source of guidance for this trip is the *reserva's* **Campamento Borrego Cimarrón,** which is managed by a local *ejido* (a family that holds land communally). To get there, take Mex. 1, southeast of San Ignacio. At km 32 take a left at the turn-off marked "Campo Geotermaleléctrico las 3 Vírgenes." After about 1km, a short, steep dirt road appears on the left, which will lead you up to the camp. The camp also serves as the base for efforts to protect the *borrego* (big-horn) sheep, about 500 of which live near the volcano. Though the species is endangered, limited hunting is allowed each year. In 2006 park officials determined that six of the animals could be killed and American big game hunters paid US$60,000 for the privilege. Those wishing to enjoy a more peaceful, less pricey experience can take one of the day-long trips led by the friendly rangers at the camp to observe these rare animals. The base also has small *cabañas* and camping spaces for people who wish to explore the area further.

SAN IGNACIO ☎ 615

From a distance, San Ignacio (pop. 3000) seems a cruel illusion—leafy palms, flowering bushes, and broad swaths of lush green appear magically in the blistering desert. Go ahead and pinch yourself—you're not dreaming. The area around San Ignacio is blessed with the most plentiful underground supply of fresh water in Baja California Sur. A prime point of departure for cave painting and whale watching tours, and a delightful place to hike or sample small-town Baja life, San Ignacio, with its intimate atmosphere, nighttime starscapes, and historic mission, has seduced many a traveler.

◧ **TRANSPORTATION.** San Ignacio lies 142km southeast of Guerrero Negro on Mex. 1, and 72km west of Santa Rosalía. A winding road canopied by swaying date palms leads south from the highway and becomes **Luyando** at the *zócalo*. Most activity revolves around the tranquil *zócalo*, bordered by Luyando to the west, **Morelos** to the east, **Juárez** to the north, and **Hidalgo** to the south.

Buses pick up and drop off passengers at the white terminal building adjacent to Mercadito Ravi on Mex. 1. From central San Ignacio, trek north along Luyando and take a left on Mex. 1. Considering the length of the walk, a better bet is to grab a taxi at the *zócalo*. Buses head north to **Tijuana** (14hr., 1 per day, 805 pesos) and **Mexicali** (4 per day 8am-11pm, 972 pesos) via **Ensenada** (13hr., 704 pesos) and **Guerrero Negro** (2hr., 134 pesos). Buses go south to **San José del Cabo** (3 per day 6:30am-

7pm, 769 pesos) and **La Paz** (3 per day 11am-11pm, 594 pesos) via **Santa Rosalía** (1hr., 70 pesos), **Mulegé** (2hr., 129 pesos), and **Loreto** (3hr., 258 pesos).

🛈 PRACTICAL INFORMATION. There is **no official tourist office,** but native English speaker Juaníta Ames at **Casa Lereé,** on Morelos one block from the *zócalo,* has handmade maps of the town and nearby hiking trails, along with other useful information. For laundry, head to **Lavandería,** on an unnamed dirt road. To get there from the *zócalo,* walk past the mission and the museum, following the road as it turns, and take your second right. Look for the red-and-white signs about two blocks in. (Wash 30 pesos, dry 30 pesos. Open M-Sa 8am-8pm, Su 8am-3pm.) Other services include: **police** on Ocampo and Zaragoza in the Delegación Municipal (☎ 154 0147); **Farmacia Ceseña,** Madero 24A, one block back from Juárez (☎ 154 0076; open M-Sa 9am-1pm and 4-7pm, Su 9am-1pm); **Centro de Salud** (pass the mission and the museum, following the road as it curves, and take your first right on Independencia; the Centro is about 3 blocks down; ☎ 154 0001; open M-F 8am-2pm, but emergency 24hr.); **Internet Cafe,** on the *zócalo,* with **fax** service (Internet 20 pesos per hr.; open daily 10am-2pm and 4-10pm); and **post office,** next to the Delegación Municipal on Ocampo and Zaragoza (open M-F 8am-2pm). **Postal code:** 23930.

🛏🍴 ACCOMMODATIONS AND FOOD. San Ignacio's few hotels don't come cheap, and reservations are necessary during *El Día de San Ignacio* (July 31) and *Semana Santa.* If you need to save some pesos, there are several good campsites. Steeped in San Ignacio history and owned by the unofficial town historian Juanita Ames, **🔲Casa Lereé ❺,** one block from the corner of Juárez and Morelos, provides three rooms decorated with the works of local artists and set around a large, well-tended garden. (☎ 154 0158. Rooms 350 pesos; suites 650 pesos. Cash only.) Just outside of town on the entry road, **Ignacio Springs ❺** is a very friendly B&B, where guests stay in riverside cabins and use the hotel's kayaks for free. (☎ 154 0333; www.ignaciosprings.com. Cabins from 580 pesos. MC/V.) **Hotel Posada ❹,** a 5min. walk down Cipris from Hidalgo, is a conventional motel with clean rooms furnished with fans. (☎ 154 0313. Singles and doubles 250 pesos. Cash only.) Camping is available in a shady spot right on the water at **Lakeside RV Park ❶,** next to Ignacio Springs, on the entry road off Mex.1. (Sites 50 pesos.)

    Sport Racing, Bar Restaurant ❶, near Casa Lereé, serves the best *carne asado* tacos (12 pesos) in town and other Mexican specialties in a spot adorned with Baja 1000 off-road racing memorabilia. (Open daily 10am-10pm.) Right next to the water, **Mikasa Cafe ❸,** on the entrance road immediately north of the river crossing, has a simple menu, including *tortas* (25 pesos) and eggs (50 pesos). After your meal, you can rent a kayak from the cafe for 50 pesos or jump into the river to swim. (Open M-Sa 9am-9pm.) The seafood (from 85 pesos) on the menu at **Restaurant-Bar Rene's ❺,** on Hidalgo, is limited to the day's catch, but is always deliciously fresh and cooked to perfection. (On a pond just beyond the *zócalo.* ☎ 154 0196. Open daily 7am-10pm. Cash only.) Family kitchen **Restaurant Chalita ❹,** on Hidalgo at the *zócalo* dishes up traditional *antojitos* for 30-40 pesos. (☎ 154 0082. Open daily 8am-10pm. Cash only.) *Taquerías* and hot dog stands, right on the *zócalo,* are the cheapest options. For groceries, visit **Nuevos Almacenes Meza,** on the corner of Juárez and Luyando, facing the *zócalo.* (☎ 154 0122. Open M-Sa 8am-noon and 2-6pm, Su 8-noon.)

🔆 SIGHTS AND FESTIVALS. La Misión de San Ignacio, on the *zócalo,* was completed in 1786 and is one of the most stately missions on the entire peninsula. It was founded by a Jesuit missionary, Juan Bautista Luyando, in 1728 but was a logistical nightmare to finish because wood had to be hauled from the Guadalupe mission in the Sierras, furniture brought from Mulegé on a four-day mule ride through the desert, and paintings carried by boat from the mainland. Its walls, over 9m thick, are made from blocks of volcanic rock, and the building still has its original imposing wooden doors. Next door to the mission, the **Museo de Pinturas Rupestres** has photos (and a life-size replica) of some of the nearby cave paintings in the Sierra de San Francisco (p. 187). The explanations are in Spanish, but there is a helpful booklet with English translations. (☎ 154 0222. Open May-Oct. M-Sa 8am-5pm; Nov.-Apr. daily 8am-5pm. Free.)

San Ignacio blossoms into a huge *fiesta* complete with singing, dancing, horse races, fireworks, and food during the week-long celebration of **El Día de San Ignacio,** in honor of the town's patron saint. Festivities begin on July 22 and end July 31, coinciding with the harvest celebration (July 30), although the harvest doesn't actually take place until October.

◪ OUTDOOR ACTIVITIES. The **Sierra de San Francisco,** near San Ignacio, contains more than 500 **cave paintings,** estimated to be over 10,000 years old. Anthropologists are unsure who created these paintings or why, but central Baja boasts more rock art than the more famous sites in France and Spain. Located within a 12 sq. km area, most of the paintings are found high (around 10m) above ground. The two most accessible sites are **Cueva el Ratón** and **Santa Marta.** Before heading out on your own, you must register at the Museo de Pinturas Rupestres in San Ignacio. (Visiting permit 34 pesos per person; camera or video camera use 35 pesos.) The staff there will radio ahead to the caves to arrange for an official to meet you and guide you to the sites. To reach Santa Marta, drive 20km east on Mex. 1 and take a left on a marked dirt road. After 37km, you will reach the base and your guide (180 pesos for a group of 3.) It's another 1hr. hike to reach the cave. To reach Cueva el Ratón, drive 40km north on Mex. 1 and take a right on a marked dirt road. Travel on the road for 37km. The caves are a short walk in, making el Ratón a cheaper option (guide 80 pesos for a group of 3). **EcoTurismo Kuyima,** on the *zócalo* in San Ignacio, takes groups on daytrips to both sites. (☎ 154 0070; www.kuyima.com. Groups of 2-3 people US$70 per person. Open M-Sa 8am-1pm and 3-8pm). There are also a number of superb **walks** through the nearby desert that start minutes from the center of San Ignacio. Juanita Ames, at Casa Lereé, has drawn up detailed maps of the trails. One starts right behind Casa Lereé, heading up, then crossing the Mesa de la Cruz that overlooks the town. The path passes an abandoned army barracks and airfield, along with lots of cacti. A second trail starts on a stony road just north of the El Padrino RV Park. It follows a canyon for about 3 mi. past large and seemingly out-of-place pools of water. You can also rent a **kayak** at the **Mikasa Cafe,** immediately north of the river crossing on the entry road to town (open M-Sa 9am-9pm, 50 pesos) and navigate the very calm water to the end of the Arroyo de San Ignacio for about 3km, where you can swim.

SANTA ROSALÍA

☎ 615

Unlike its neighbors, Santa Rosalía (pop.10,500) owes its existence not to the Sea of Cortés but the mountains that frame it. After rich copper deposits were discovered nearby, Mexico's dictator Porfirio Díaz gave the land around Santa Rosalía to French investors, who in 1885 established a company called "El Boleo," to mine the land. They built a town, Santa Rosalía, to house their workers and filled it with French colonial-style buildings, including a church designed by Gustave Eiffel, of Eiffel Tower fame. The French company moved out in 1954 and a Mexican firm took over. The mines finally closed in 1986, and almost all of the French-style buildings still stand.

◰ TRANSPORTATION. The **bus station** (☎ 152 1408), in the same building as the ferry office right off **Mex. 1,** sends buses north to: **Mexicali** (18hr., 4 per day 4am-3:40pm, 1047 pesos); **Tijuana** (15hr., 3 per day 2:30am-5pm, 944 pesos); and **Guerrero**

Negro (3hr., 220 pesos). Heading south, buses go to **La Paz** (8hr., 6 per day 5:40am-12:15am, 566 pesos) via **Mulegé** (1hr., 93 pesos) and **Loreto** (3hr., 203 pesos). Buses also head to **San José del Cabo** (9hr., 3 per day, 700 pesos).

Baja Ferries, on Mex. 1 just south of downtown, sends ferries to **Guaymas.** (☎152 1246; www.ferrysantarosalia.com. 10-11hr.; Tu-W 9am, F and Su 8pm; 650 pesos, round-trip 1080 pesos, children 1-11 540 pesos. Terminal open daily 8am-3pm and 4-7pm.) Due to high demand, tickets should be purchased in advance; during the summer, a day may suffice. Those traveling with cars must purchase tickets further in advance (standard passenger car 2480 pesos) and show a tourist card, registration, and a vehicle permit (available at the border and in La Paz, but not in Santa Rosalía). To get to the *centro* from the ferry or bus station, turn right and walk along the main road until the turn-off to Santa Rosalía.

■✚🔽 **ORIENTATION AND PRACTICAL INFORMATION.** Santa Rosalía lies 555km north of La Paz. Most services in Santa Rosalía are on the two main streets, **Obregón** and **Constitución,** which run east-west. Crossing these, named and numbered streets run north-south. **Mesa Francia** lies up the hill via **Altamirano,** which runs parallel to and north of Obregón before it starts winding its way to the top; pedestrians can also get there by ascending the steps nearby.

Banamex, on Obregón and Calle 5, exchanges traveler's checks and has a **24hr. ATM.** (☎152 0984. Open M-F 9am-4pm.) **Bancomer,** across the street, offers similar services. (Open M-F 8:30am-4pm.) Other services include: **emergency** ☎065; **police,** at Carranza on the plaza (☎152 0651); **Red Cross,** on Calle 2 and Carranza adjacent to the police outpost (☎152 0640); **General Hospital,** at Costeau opposite the museum in Mesa Francia (☎152 0789 or 1336); **fax office** at **Telecomm,** on Constitución across from the post office (☎152 2112; fax 152 0240; open M-F 8am-7pm, Sa 8am-11:30am); **Internet Vision,** on Obregón next to Bancomer (20 pesos per hr.; open daily 10am-10pm); and the **post office,** on Constitución between Calle 2 and Altamirano (☎152 0344; open M-F 8am-4pm). **Postal Code:** 23920.

🔳🔲 **ACCOMMODATIONS AND FOOD.** Santa Rosalía does not have many good accommodations. Most travelers would be better off stopping here for a few hours and then heading west to San Ignacio or south to Mulegé for the night. **Hotel Olvera ❸,** Calle Plaza 14, three blocks from shore on Constitución off the foot bridge, has seen better days but is centrally located. (☎152 2550. Singles 200 pesos, with A/C 250 pesos; doubles 250/350 pesos. Cash only.) Those traveling by car can take advantage of the parking at **Motel San Victor ❷,** Progreso 36, on Calle 9. Bring your own sleeping bag and pillows because the linens here need a good scrub. (☎152 0116. Doubles 150 pesos. Cash only.) **Hotel Francés ❺,** at the far end of Costeau on the Mesa Francia, is worth a visit just to peak in at the grand foyer where the Boleo company once accommodated the unmarried members of its French staff. (☎152 2052. Wi-Fi available. Rooms with A/C and TV 650 pesos.) **Nuevo Mundo Hotel ❺** on Obregón at Calle 2 rents out two rooms with A/C and TV. (☎152 0244. Rooms 300 pesos. Cash only.)

With the exception of its oddly loaf-shaped baguettes, **El Boleo Bakery ❶,** on Obregón at Calle 4, offers a typical selection of Mexican pastries. (☎152 0310. Pastries from 4 pesos. Open M-F 9am-9:30pm, Su 9am-1pm. Cash only.) **Restaurant Don Pedro ❸,** at Calle 5 and Progreso, serves a large selection of eggs for breakfast (35-40 pesos) and typical Mexican fare the rest of the day. (Open daily 7am-midnight.) The air-conditioned **Terco's Pollito ❹,** at Obregón and Playa, dishes up heartier meals. Try the half roast chicken for 55 pesos. (☎152 0075. Open daily 8am-10pm. Cash only.) Homesick expats can try **El Muelle ❹,** on Constitución at the plaza, where the walls are covered in American memorabilia. The spaghetti bolognese (40 pesos) is filling, but the pizza (medium pepperoni 92 pesos) is overpriced. (☎ 152 0931. Open daily 8am-11pm.) **Ángel Cafe ❸**, on Calle 5 and Obregón opposite Bancomer, has good breakfasts (omelettes 40 pesos) and well-priced entrees. (☎ 152 1292. Open daily 9am-6pm. Cash only.) There is a **Mini-Super** on Obregón and Calle Playa. (☎ 152 2851. Open daily 8am-11pm.)

◪ SIGHTS. Santa Rosalía's principal attractions are the French colonial-style buildings, constructed between 1885 and 1954 while the French-owned El Boleo Company operated the nearby copper mines. The town is divided into two parts: the small **Mesa Francia** (where French officers lived) and **Mesa Mexico.** In just a couple of hours, you can take in most of the major buildings here. A good place to start is the Mesa Francia at the Hotel Francés on Cousteau, where some of El Boleo's workers used to live. Walk down Cousteau, which is littered with the company's now-dilapidated railroad cars and lined with French colonial homes, to the company's former offices, now the **Museo Histórico Minero de Santa Rosalía.** In the distance, you can see El Boleo's rusting copper foundry. The museum includes photos of the company's mining operations, a number of old desks, and other miscellaneous company equipment. (☎ 152 2929. Open M-F 8am-3pm, Sa 9am-1pm. Free.) Next, walk down the hill to the **Iglesia Santa Barbara,** at Obregón and Altamirano, designed by Gustave Eiffel. According to a plaque outside the church, the church was shown in Paris, along with the Eiffel tower, at the 1889 World's Fair. The El Boleo Company purchased the church and brought it to Santa Rosalía on the company's sailboat in 1895.

MULEGÉ ☎ 615

Mulegé (pop. 3000) has always drawn in travelers for longer than they expect to stay. Indeed, a number of Americans have moved here permanently. With its thick forest of palms ushering the Río Mulegé into the Sea of Cortés and its proximity to the glistening beaches and opal waters of Bahía de la Concepción, this desert oasis has all the elements of a tropical paradise and rewards divers, archaeologists, beachcombers, and those just looking to relax. Set back from the shoreline, the narrow streets of this small mission town are friendly and Mulegé has not yet bent to the demands of tourists accustomed to a different way of life.

▛ TRANSPORTATION. The **bus station** (☎ 153 0409) is located in Restaurant La Noria, on **Mex. 1** just north of the turn-off for Mulegé. All buses are *de paso.* Arrive 15min. before departure. Buses head north to **Mexicali** (19hr., 3 per day 3am-2pm, 1073 pesos), **Santa Rosalía** (1hr.; 4, 7pm; 59 pesos), and **Tijuana** (16hr., 11pm, 934 pesos). Southbound buses go to **La Paz** (6hr., 6 per day 1am-11pm, 463 pesos) via **Loreto** (2hr., 129 pesos) and **Cabos San Lucas** (8hr., 3 per day 9am-9pm, 573 pesos).

▚▐ ORIENTATION AND PRACTICAL INFORMATION. With its tangle of steep, narrow one-way streets, Mulegé is a fun town to explore on foot. Coming from the north on Mex. 1, there's a turn-off for Mulegé on the left. The road then forks. **Moctezuma** is to the left, and **Martínez** is to the right. If you're driving, one-way traffic will force you onto Martínez. Both streets are crossed a block farther in by **Zaragoza.** Martínez continues east and converges with **Madero,** which follows the north bank of the Río Mulegé for about 4km, ending at the beach, **Playa el Prieto,** and lighthouse. The *zócalo* is on Madero at Zaragoza, a block west of the intersection with Martínez.

Bancomer opened the first bank in Mulegé in December 2006. Located on Zaragoza at Martinez, the bank **exchanges currency** and traveler's checks and also has a **24hr. ATM.** (☎ 153 1029; open M-F 8:30am-4pm.) Other services in Mulegé include: **Lavamática Claudia,** on Zaragoza just downhill from Hotel Terrazas (☎ 153 0057;

wash 19 pesos, dry 7.50 pesos, soap 4 pesos; open daily 8am-6pm); **police,** in the old Pinatel de Educación building on Martínez, near the in-town PEMEX station (☎153 0770); **Farmacia,** at Madero on the plaza (☎153 0042; open M-Sa 9am-2pm and 4-10pm, Su 8am-2pm and 6-10pm); **Centro de Salud,** Madero 28 (☎153 0298; open 24hr.); **Internet** access at **Servicio Internet Minita,** on Madero near the Centro de Salud, as well as fax and photocopying services and Wi-Fi (☎153 0212; Internet 20 pesos per hr.; open M-Sa 9am-9pm); **Fax** services at **Telecomm,** on Moctezuma near Zaragoza (☎153 0133, open M-F 8am-2pm); and the **post office,** in the same building as the police (☎153 0205; open M-F 8am-1pm). **Postal Code: 23900.**

▐▐ ACCOMMODATIONS AND FOOD. Free camping is available on Playa el Farito, a public beach home to noisy weekend parties. (3km from the *centro* at the end of Madero. Camping is only recommended for groups.) Nearby Bahía de la Concepción (p. 191) has much nicer camping. If you'd rather stay in town, Mulegé has a number of well-priced hotels. The best, without a doubt, is **◪Hotel las Casitas ❺,** on Madero near the plaza. Las Casitas offers bright, beautifully decorated rooms around a shady, bird-filled patio. All rooms at Las Casitas have strong A/C. (☎153 0019. Free Wi-Fi. Singles 342 pesos; doubles 393 pesos. MC/V.) **Casa de Huéspedes Manuelita ❹,** on Moctezuma next to Restaurant los Equipales, has basic, small rooms with A/C and baths. (☎153 0175. Rooms 250 pesos. Cash only.) Next door, **Casa de Huéspedes Nacho ❶** has the cheapest rooms in town. The rooms, which are essentially in the backyard of the owner's house, are dark and extremely basic. Rooms come with fan and share two bathrooms with water that comes out of a pipe fixture. (Singles 100 pesos; doubles 200 pesos. Cash only.) **Orchard RV Park ❶** occupies a stretch of Río Mulegé's southern bank, accessible via a well-marked seashell-laden road from km 133 on Mex. 1. Although Orchard suffered extensive damage during a recent flood, the park still has palm-shaded spots. (Tent site US$5. RV site US$18. Cash only.)

For an informal and delicious bite, try **Taquería Doney ❶,** on Moctezuma. One of the nicest *taquerías* in Baja, locals cram the blue checkered tables indoors and the stools outdoors to wolf down 12-peso tacos. (☎153 0095. Open M and W-Sa 7:30am-10pm, Su 8am-10pm. Cash only.) **El Candil Restaurant ❹,** on Zaragoza near Martínez, serves tasty seafood and meat entrees for around 60 pesos. The restaurant mellows out in the evening and service can be slow. (Open M-Sa 9am-10pm, Su 11am-9pm. Cash only.) **Taquería Dany ❶,** at Rubio and Madero, not to be confused with Doney, is a friendly *taquería* that specializes in *carnitas de puerco* (11 pesos), the only dish served on Saturdays.

◙ SIGHTS. There are more than 700 sites with ancient cave paintings and etchings in the mountains and hills near Mulegé. By law, you need a permit to visit them. The easiest way to obtain this permit is by hiring a local guide. Two guides in town will take you to two of the sites, **La Trinidad** and **Cuevas San Borjitas.** Trinidad, which actually is made up of three main caves, is about 1hr. away by car. During the rainy season (Oct.-Dec.) visitors need to swim through a canyon to access the site. Otherwise, it is about a 1 mi. hike. San Borjitas, about 2hr. away by car, consists of five principal caves and is a ½ mi. hike from where you park your car. **Salvador Castro** leads hiking tours to the caves year-round. (☎103 5081. US$40 per person.) **Ciro Cuesta** at Baja Adventure Tours, on Madero near the plaza, also brings tourists to the sites, except during the summer. (☎153 0566 or 0377. US$40 per person.) Since Trinidad is nearer than San Borjitas, both guides also take tourists visiting Trinidad to **Piedras Pintas,** a site with more than 2000 carvings.

Visitors who prefer not to spend 5-6hr. on a tour can visit an impressive array of petroglyphs on their own at **Playa El Burro,** at km 109 on Mex. 1. Park in front of Bertha's restaurant, on the beach. Then, cross the highway. On the side of the road, you will notice a yellow street sign with a left-turning arrow and a smaller "danger" sign. Walk between the two signs. The petroglyphs lie in the gully between the two main hills ahead of you. Follow the gulley (laden with boulders) for about 10min. If you look closely, you will notice that the boulders are covered with carvings of turtles, fish, stars, and even humans. A number of rocks also have flat tops with smaller stones stacked on top of them. These are known as "bell rocks" and, incredibly, if you hit them with the smaller stones, they ring like bells.

The 18th-century **Misión Santa Rosalía de Mulegé** sits on a hill west of town. Walk down Zaragoza away from the *zócalo*, go under the bridge, and turn right on General Emiliano Zapata. The mission is on the hill where the pavement ends. The look-out behind the church provides an impressive view of the town and river.

Museo Comunitario Mulegé is housed in the town's old prison at the top of the hill. To get there, continue up the hill past Hotel Terrazas and turn right. The prison is the large white building around the curve in the road. It was once known as the "prison without doors" for its policy of allowing inmates out into the town during the day and then summoning them back at 6pm by the blowing of a conch shell. Visitors can themselves walk in and out of the prison cells, including one still blackened from the fire a prisoner lit to kill himself after learning that his wife was having an affair. Unfortunately, the cells have recently come under the guard of a belligerent flock of pigeons. The museum includes an assortment of semi-relevant objects, including a piece of a spaceship that allegedly fell to Earth at a *rancho* near Mulegé, rusty dishware, typewriters, a phone, a mini-kitchen set, and a stuffed sea turtle. (Open M-Sa 9am-6pm.)

🎿 **OUTDOOR ACTIVITIES. Cortez Explorers,** Moctezuma 75A, the only dive shop in town, brings divers and snorkelers to Punta la Concepción or the Santa Ines Islands. (☎153 0500; www.cortez-explorer.com. Snorkeling ½-day US$50, full-day US$95. Dive tours US$70. Cortez also rents an array of equipment, including snorkeling gear. MC/V.)

Mulegé is centered around the Río Mulegé, which is flanked on both sides by dirt roads. For a quiet **hike,** follow Madero out of town for 4km as it trails the river and finally reaches **Playa el Prieto.** On the way, you will see a huge array of birds, including flocks of vultures. Playa el Prieto is also home to the town **lighthouse** and if you've still got the energy, you can climb to the top of the lighthouse hill for a view of Bahía de la Concepción. On the way back, **La Casa de Pancha Villa ❶,** on Madero immediately before the beach, has freshly squeezed orange juice for 15 pesos. (Open daily 6am-11pm. Cash only.)

BAHÍA DE LA CONCEPCIÓN

Mex. 1, the highway that connects Loreto and Mulegé, curves around most of the bay, offering dangerously distracting views along with easy access to all of Bahía de la Concepción's beaches. Visiting Bahía de la Concepción without your own car is difficult, since there are no regular public buses. It may be possible to negotiate a fee with drivers on southbound intercity buses from Mulegé to drop you off, but the walk from the highway to the shore can be excruciatingly long. This approach also leaves your return journey unresolved. Though it is common in the area, Let's Go does not recommend hitchhiking. If possible, consider renting a car for a day in Loreto, about 100km away.

Baja's coastline is so endless and often so beautiful that it's possible to take its beaches for granted—but even locals adopt a hushed tone of voice when they mention Bahía de la Concepción. Rocky outcroppings, soft sands, cacti-studded hills, and unearthly opal blue water combine to form a 48km stretch of mesmerizing landscapes, while the distant outline of the bay's opposite shore lends a tantalizing sense of the unknown. Look closely at the serene waters and you'll find that they contain a rich variety of marine life, making for exciting diving and snorkeling. Only at Easter and Christmas is the tranquility disturbed by serious tourist traffic; for most of the year, you might just find that there's almost no one else around to break the spell.

The waters of Bahía de la Concepción are completely sheltered and as calm as a lake, making for easy kayaking and snorkeling, although there are no rentals on any of the beaches. The bay is also a camper's paradise, with *palapa* shelters only feet from the crystal clear water on most beaches. Camping is usually safe, but stick to well-populated beaches and always be on guard. Beaches below are listed from north to south.

> **TIP** **BEACH BUMMERS.** During summer, stingrays mate close to shore, hidden from view underneath the sand. So as not to interrupt and get stung, shuffle your feet as you walk into the water. If they sting you, find the hottest water you can stand, immerse the stung area, and wait out the pain. Locals suggest finding a *garumbillo* ("old man") cactus, distinguishable by the gray hairs growing out of the top of the plant; cut a chunk of it and squeeze a few drops of juice onto the sting to get rid of the pain in seconds. Be sure to cut off all the cactus spines first, or you'll have even more pain on your hands. As the sting is a puncture wound, seek medical attention immediately to prevent infection.

PLAYA LOS NARANJOS. The closest of the bay's beaches to Mulegé, Playa Los Naranjos is a stretch of hard-packed sand, crowded with bungalows, at the end of a dirt road lined with flowering cacti and gigantic piles of seashells. Camping is more expensive than at other nearby beaches (US$10, with *palapa* US$15), although those without a tent can rent bungalows on the beach with two cots and screened windows for US$25 per day. (☎615 155 2542. Reservations recommended.) The family that rents the bungalows also operates the **Playa Los Naranjos Restaurant ❹,** on the beach, which serves standard breakfast fare for 55 pesos and a number of Mexican staples, such as beef enchiladas for 65 pesos. (Open daily 8am-7pm. Cash only.) *(Turn at the sign for Playa los Naranjos and Punta Sueños at km 119. Then, travel 3km down a well-maintained dirt road to the beach.)*

PLAYA SANTISPAC. Crowds are drawn in by Santispac's convenient location, right off Mex. 1 near to Mulegé. The wide beach can feel a bit like a parking lot, and the hard-packed sand behind the motor homes is rougher than asphalt. Nonetheless, the beach remains immensely popular. *(Playa Santispac is just off the highway near km 114. Camping or parking for the day both cost 70 pesos.)*

PLAYA EL BURRO. El Burro's soft sands and quiet atmosphere have enticed a number of Americans to set up semi-permanent *palapa*-style homes right on the beach, often with solar panels, balconies, satellite dishes, and, in at least one case, two stories. There's also a tiny garden set up in memory, presumably, of past residents. A few shelters remain empty, though, for campers willing to pay US$8.50. **Bertha's ❷,** a small bar-restaurant at the far left of the beach from the perspective of Mex. 1, serves egg breakfasts (40 pesos), fried chicken (35 pesos), and lots of cheap beer for as little as 10 pesos. *(Near Mex. 1 at km 109, down a smooth dirt road. Take your 1st left immediately off the highway to reach Bertha's. Restaurant open daily 8am-10pm.)*

▨ PLAYA REQUESÓN. The turquoise water, framed by the beach and a white sandbar, creates one of the most spectacular landscapes of the entire peninsula. Adventurous souls can camp out on the sandbar, but the rising tide may leave them and their gear soaking wet. For more cautious travelers, *palapa* shelters are available for 60 pesos. If you're not going to camp, it's worth taking the short walk to the sandbar just to gaze into the transparent water. *(Down a short dirt road at km 92, marked by a blue sign. Also accessible via a dirt road from adjacent Playa la Perla.)*

PLAYA LA PERLA. Around the corner from Requesón, smaller and lonelier La Perla is tucked between two rocky outcroppings. The *palapa* shelters are more complex here, and camping costs 60 pesos. *(Close to the road at km 91 and marked by a blue sign. Also accessible via a dirt road from adjacent Playa Requesón.)*

LORETO ☎ 613

Loreto (pop. 10,000), set between inhospitable, rugged mountains and the Sea of Cortés, is a tranquil town in a surprising spot. The city was once controlled by Jesuits, who landed on the peninsula in the late 17th century and established the first permanent mission in Baja Sur in 1697, and subsequently by Franciscans, who drove the Jesuits out in 1768. Loreto was the capital of

Loreto

▲▲ ACCOMMODATIONS
Hotel Junípero, **4**
Motel Brenda, **9**
Motel Salvatierra, **10**
El Moro RV Park, **1**
Posada San Martín, **3**

🍴 FOOD
Asadero Don Pepe, **8**
Cafe Olé, **2**
Cesar's Tacos & Beer, **5**
McLulu's, **7**
México Lindo y Qué Rico, **6**

Baja California Sur until the city was abandoned after a catastrophic hurricane in 1829. Today, the city revolves around the tourist trade with a beautifully landscaped historic town center that seems more popular with visitors than locals. The city is a good starting point to explore the Sea of Cortés.

▐ TRANSPORTATION

Buses: Bus terminal (☎ 135 0767), on Salvatierra, about 1km from the *zócalo*. Ticket office open 7am-11:30pm. To get to the *centro* from the bus station, walk down Salvatierra (20 min.) or take a taxi (50 pesos). **Autotransportes Águila** and **Autotransportes de Baja California (ABC)** send buses to: **Guerrero Negro** (7½hr., 2am, 423 pesos) via **San Ignacio** (5hr., 278 pesos); **La Paz** (5hr., 6 per day 12:45am-6pm); **Mexicali** (20hr.; 12:30, 6pm; 1229 pesos); **Santa Rosalía** (4hr., 5pm, 203 pesos); **Tijuana** (17hr., 3 per day 1am-9pm, 1147 pesos).

Car Rental: Budget (☎ 135 1090), on Hidalgo, a block from the water before Pipila. An economy car, such as a Chevy Pop, rents for about US$60 per day, including basic insurance. Must be 24 years old to rent. Open daily 8am-6pm. MC/V.

▟ 🔢 ORIENTATION AND PRACTICAL INFORMATION

Loreto is entirely walkable. There are three main streets: **Hidalgo, Salvatierra,** and **Juárez.** Salvatierra runs east-west from just off **Mex. 1** to the *malecón* (boardwalk). A stretch of Salvatierra, linking the *malecón* to the small *zócalo* to the Misión de

Nuestra Senora de Loreto, is open only to pedestrians and is beautifully landscaped. Juárez runs parallel to Salvatierra all the way to the highway. Hidalgo runs parallel to Salvatierra starting at the *malecón* but then converges with Salvatierra at an intersection known as **Los Cuatro Altos.**

Tourist Information: (☎ 135 0411), in the Palacio Municipal on Madero at the *zócalo*. Maps, brochures, and an English-speaking staff. Open M-F 8am-8pm.

Bank: Bancomer (☎ 135 0315), on Madero at the *zócalo*. The only bank in town. **Exchanges currency** and has a **24hr. ATM.** Open M-F 8:30am-4pm.

Police: (☎ 135 0035).

Red Cross: (☎ 135 1111), on Salvatierra at Deportiva.

Pharmacies: Farmacia Flores (☎ 135 0321), on Salvatierra, between Ayuntamiento and Márquez de León. Every night, a different pharmacy is open 24hr.; check the door at Farmacia Flores for the schedule. Open daily 8am-10pm.

Medical Services: Centro de Salud (☎ 135 0039), on Salvatierra, 1 block from the bus terminal.

Fax Office: Telecomm (☎ 135 0387), on Salvatierra at Deportiva, adjacent to the post office. Open M-F 8am-2pm, Sa 9am-12:30pm.

Internet Access: .Com Internet Cafe (☎ 135 1846), on Madero adjacent to Cafe Olé. 20 pesos per hr. Open M-Sa 9am-5pm.

Laundry: El Remojón Laundry, on Salvatierra, between Independencia and Ayuntamiento. Wash and dry 50 pesos. Open daily 8:30am-8pm. Cash only.

Post Office: (☎ 135 0647), on Salvatierra and Deportiva, behind the Red Cross. Open M-F 8am-4pm. **Postal Code: 23880.**

⌂ ACCOMMODATIONS AND CAMPING

Loreto caters to an affluent crowd. Still, there are a few relatively cheap hotels near the center and more near the bus station.

Posada San Martín (☎ 135 1107), at Juárez and Davis. An incredible deal, Posada San Martin is just 2 blocks from the *zócalo*. Large rooms with fan. The word's out, so reservations are recommended. Rooms 200 pesos, with A/C 250 pesos. Cash only. ❸

Hotel Junípero, on Hidalgo in front of the mission. Not only does Junípero have the best location in town, but the hotel also has large rooms with king-size bed, powerful A/C, and satellite TV. Some rooms overlook the mission. Check-out noon. Singles 350 pesos; doubles 400 pesos; triples 450 pesos. Cash only. ❺

Motel Salvatierra (☎ 135 0021), on Salvatierra near the bus station, across from the PEMEX. Salvatierra has small, basic rooms. The busy road out front can be noisy in the morning. Check-out noon. Singles 270 pesos; doubles 300 pesos. MC/V. ❹

Motel Brenda (☎ 135 0707), on Juárez near Márquez de León. Clean rooms with A/C and TV. Free parking. Singles 270 pesos; doubles 300 pesos. Cash only. ❹

El Moro RV Park, Robles 8 (☎/fax 135 0542), a couple blocks inland off Salvatierra near the center. A big parking lot with minimal shade, extremely hot in the summer. Camping 55 pesos. Trailers US$15. Also has a number of large rooms in an adjacent building. Singles 330 pesos; doubles 385 pesos. Cash only. ❶

♨ FOOD

Most of the restaurants near the *zócalo* are pricey and geared entirely towards tourists. **El Pescador** supermarket, on Salvatierra and Independencia at the Los Cuatro Altos intersection, sells food and household products. (☎ 135 0060. Open daily 7:30am-10:30pm.)

▧ **Cafe Olé,** Madero 14 (☎ 135 0496), just off the *zócalo*. Cheap, tasty burgers (28 pesos), salads (35 pesos), and *huevos rancheros* (39 pesos) attract a touristy crowd. Order at the counter. Open M-Sa 7am-10pm. ❷

McLulu's, on Hidalgo between Independencia and Militar. Friendly, talkative cooks prepare the usual tacos (10 pesos) and quesadillas (13 pesos). Open daily 10am-8pm. Cash only. ❶

México Lindo y Qué Rico (☎ 135 1175), on Hidalgo after Misioneros. An inexpensive sit-down restaurant, México Lindo y Qué Rico serves Baja cuisine like fish ceviche (55 pesos) and fish filet (75 pesos), as well as the staple *hamburguesa* (40 pesos). Open M-Sa 8am-10pm. Cash only. ❸

Cesar's Tacos and Beer, on Hidalgo after Misioneros, across the street from México Lindo y Qué Rico. One of several taco-and-beer places on Hidalgo, Cesar's offers decent beer (22 pesos), hamburgers (50 pesos), and tacos (14 pesos). Open daily 8am-8pm. Cash only. ❸

Asadero Don Pepe, on Hidalgo after Misioneros, across from McLulu's. If you're staying awhile in Baja, you should eat at one of the ubiquitous hot dog stands. This one's good and cheap (10 pesos per hot dog). There's also seating inside. Open daily 10am-10pm. Cash only. ❶

◉ SIGHTS

MISIÓN DE NUESTRA SEÑORA DE LORETO AND MUSEUM. Set in the middle of a pedestrian-only section of Salvatierra, this recently restored mission is an essential stop for anyone interested in Baja's Jesuit history. As the plaque above the door proclaims, this is the mother of all California missions. The church was consecrated in 1697 by Italian-born Jesuit Father Juan María de Salvatierra, made permanent in 1699 and enlarged to its present size by 1752. It echoes the simple lines and plain walls of early Renaissance churches, with semicircular stone arches in perfect proportion to the height of the white-washed nave. Next door, in the monastic complex, the Museo de las Misiones tells the story of Jesuit activity in Baja, although the descriptions are all in Spanish. *(On Salvatierra and Misioneros. Open daily 7am-8pm. Mass M-Sa 7pm, Su 11am, 7pm. Museum ☎ 135 0441. Open Tu-Su 9am-1pm and 1:45-6pm. 34 pesos. Cash only.)*

◪ BEACHES

Loreto is a good base for snorkeling and diving in the Sea of Cortés. In town, the blissful sea views from Loreto's boardwalk make it a popular place to take an evening stroll, or to take a pause on one of the many benches overlooking the waves. The public beach, at the southern end of the *malecón*, has fine gray sand and slightly murky water.

NOPOLÓ. 7km south of town, has cleaner public beaches and excellent snorkeling, but is also the site of a somewhat unsuccessful resort development by FONATUR, the Mexican tourist promotion group responsible for Mazatlán. Vacant lots and preserved dunes contain an 18-hole golf course and well-lit tennis courts. To access Nopoló, drive through the massive Loreto Bay development and park in the Inn at Loreto Bay's parking lot. Walk straight through the foyer and enjoy the clean waters immediately beyond.

ISLA CORONADO. Isla Coronado's wide white beaches are more accessible than Isla del Carmen and host a herd of friendly sea lions who make excellent snorkeling buddies. **Arturo's Sports Fishing Fleet,** half a block from the beach on Hidalgo, offers snorkeling and diving excursions to the island, as well as fishing trips. *(☎ 135 0766. Snorkeling trip 5-6hr.; US$60, includes equipment and lunch. Diving trip 7hr.; US$115, including tanks. Open M-Sa 9am-1pm and 4-7pm. MC/V.)* **Cobadi,** also on Hidalgo, below the Hotel Junípero, guides snorkeling trips for US$60 and diving trips for US$110 with equipment. *(☎ 135 1146. Open M-Sa 8am-8pm. MC/V.)* To learn more about the ecology of Loreto's bay, a national marine park, pay a visit to the tiny natural history museum maintained by the **Grupo Ecologista Antares,** next to México Lindo y Qué Rico on Hidalgo, marked by the large whale signs on the sidewalk. (☎ 135 0086; www.geantares.org.mx. Open M-F 9am-4pm.) Active all over Baja California, GEA monitors the activities of fishermen and sailors in the bay. GEA runs some tours in the winter and can also put you in touch with local fishermen who provide ecotourism opportunities, including boat trips to observe the birds, whales, and dolphins that visit the bay and nearby islands. (5-6hr.; 5-person group approx. US$140.) **Las Parras Tours,** Madero 16, next to Cafe Olé, takes small groups on boat trips around Isla Coronado. The trip includes plenty of time to snorkel or relax on the beautiful beach. Las Parras also offers diving trips (½-day trip US$80-90), mountain bike rentals (US$5 per hr.), kayak rentals (singles US$5 per hr., doubles US$7.50 per hr.), and trips to sights like the mission and village of San Javier. (☎ 135 1010; www.lasparrastours.com. Trips 4-5hr.; US$45 per person, 2-person min. Open M-Sa 9am-1pm and 4-8pm. MC/V.)

CIUDAD CONSTITUCIÓN   ☎ 613

Few travelers spend more time in the transportation hub of Ciudad Constitución (pop. 35,000) than it takes to grab a meal and fill up on gas. Those who do linger will find a busy agricultural center, sparse in the way of attractions, built around the traffic on Mex. 1. As it enters the city, Mex 1 becomes Olachea, Ciudad Constitución's main street. If you must spend the night in Ciudad Constitución, olive-colored **Hotel Conchita ❹,** in the middle of town on Olachea at Hidalgo, offers spartan rooms with A/C and TV. (☎ 132 0266. Singles 240 pesos; doubles 310 pesos.) Olachea is lined with inexpensive *taquerías* serving heaping portions of *antojitos* (10 pesos). There is also a super-size supermarket, **Super Ley,** south of town, on Olachea 217. (☎ 132 6930. Open daily 7am-10pm.) **Coffee Star,** on Olachea between Juárez and Galeana, serves up espresso for 15 pesos and heaping slices of cake for 32 pesos. (☎ 132 7194. Open daily 7am-11pm.)

   Bancomer, on Olachea and Suárez, on the south end of town, exchanges currency and traveler's checks. (☎ 132 3777 or 3779. Open M-F 8:30am-4pm.) **Banamex,** on the north side of Ciudad Constitución, close to one of the several PEMEX stations, offers similar services. (☎ 132 0101 or 1411. Open M-F 9am-4pm.) Both have **24hr. ATMs.** Other services in Constitución include: **police,** on Olachea opposite the turn-off for Puerto San Carlos (☎ 132 1112); **Red Cross,** five blocks off Olachea at Ramírez and Degollado (☎ 132 1111, follow the signs); **Farmacia San Martín,** Olachea at Suárez, has a list of local pharmacies that rotate overnight duties (☎ 132 0124; open M-F 8am-10:30pm, Sa-Su 9am-2pm and 5-10pm; MC/V); and **IMSS** (☎ 132 0388), Olachea 200, at Independencia. **Postal Code:** 23600.

   To travel to and from Ciudad Constitución, **Autotransportes Águila** (☎ 132 0376), at Suárez and Juárez, sends buses to: **San José del Cabo** (7:35, 10:30am, 3pm; 371 pesos) via **Cabo San Lucas** (340 pesos); **La Paz** (3hr., 19 per day 1:30am-8pm, 196 pesos); and **Puerto San Carlos** (1hr.; 11am, 6pm; 52 pesos). Buses also go to: **Guerrero Negro** (midnight, 575 pesos); **Loreto** (2hr., 9pm, 151 pesos); **Mexicali** (2, 10am, 1, 4, 11pm; 1441 pesos); **Santa Rosalía** (midnight, 3pm; 355 pesos); and **Tijuana** (7pm, 1299 pesos) via **Ensenada** (1190 pesos). From the bus station, walk two blocks across the plaza to the corner of Olachea.

PUERTO SAN CARLOS   ☎ 613

Every year at whale watching time, tiny Puerto San Carlos (pop. 3000) undergoes a magical transformation. Beginning in November, hotels dust off their bedposts, tent encampments blossom, and local pilots commandeer every available fishing boat to transport tourists to experience some of the best whale watching in the world, as thousands of gray whales migrate from the Bering Sea through the Pacific to **Bahías Magdalena** and **Almejas.** During peak mating season (mid-Jan. to mid-Mar.), the lovestruck creatures wow crowds with aquatic acrobatics. When the whales and tourists leave in April, the town reverts back to a sleepy fishing village marked by boarded-up restaurants and sand roads.

▤ TRANSPORTATION. Puerto San Carlos is at the end of Mex. 22 and is accessible by car and bus. **Autotransportes Águila** (☎ 136 0453) has a tiny terminal in a storefront on La Paz and Morelos, with only two daily buses that go to Ciudad Constitución (1hr.; 7:30am, 1:45pm; 52 pesos). From there you can catch southbound or northbound buses. (Office opens roughly 1hr. before bus departure.) Coming from Ciudad Constitución (the only route to Puerto San Carlos), Mex. 22 curves around the town to the docks; a rare paved road leads down to the left to become La Paz, the only street in town. All other streets here are sandy tracks that can easily trap the unwary driver; take great care when parking on the side of the road. Street signs are often missing, and of those that exist, many are sun-bleached to the point of illegibility.

▨ PRACTICAL INFORMATION. There are no ATMs, casas de cambio, or credit card connections in town. Make sure to bring cash from the banks in Ciudad Constitución. The **tourist office,** near the docks, is usually only open during whale watching season. If the office is closed, the friendly staff at Hotel Alcatraz (☎ 136 0017), on La Paz, offers plenty of information. The **police** (☎ 136 0694) can be found at La Paz and Callejón Baja California, on the park. The medical services at **IMSS** (☎ 136 0211), at La Paz and México, include a **pharmacy.** (Open M-F 8am-8pm.) **Telecomm,** on Puerto Acapulco at the park, offers fax services (☎ 136 0048; open M-F 8am-2pm) and **Internet** access is available at **Ciber Gimasi,** on La Paz across from the post office (open daily 10am-11pm). The **post office** is located on La Paz between México and Juárez, near the park. (Open M-F 8am-4pm.) **Postal Code:** 23740.

▥▢ ACCOMMODATIONS AND FOOD. Finding budget rooms isn't easy. Puerto San Carlos has only 100 rooms among its few hotels—during whale watching season, they are at a premium. Prices can rise by up to 25% and reservations are a must. The prices given in this section are low-season rates. **Motel las Brisas ❷,** on Puerto Madero right off La Paz, offers the best value in town. Basic rooms around a parking lot have private baths. (☎ 136 0498. Singles 150 pesos; doubles 180 pesos. Cash only.) The rooms at **Hotel Palmar ❹,** on Acapulco and Puerto Vallarta, all have A/C, private bath, and TV. (☎ 136 0035. Singles 250 pesos; doubles 300 pesos. Cash only.) The nicest hotel in San Carlos, **Hotel Alcatraz ❺,** on La Paz near the junction with Mex. 22, has bright, clean rooms with TV and shaded patios. (☎ 136 0017. Parking available. Singles 450 pesos; doubles 600 pesos. Cash only.) **Hotel Brennan ❻,** on La Paz, has a strong Irish theme. Green decor dominates the large rooms, and you'll have to spend plenty of your own green to stay in one. Parking is available, and all rooms have A/C and TV. (☎ 136 0288; www.hotelbrennan.com.mx. Singles 400 pesos; doubles 550 pesos. Cash only.)

Dining in San Carlos is peaceful: a string of restaurants/living rooms along La Paz and Morelos allows you to meet locals while enjoying fresh, local seafood delicacies. **Restaurant la Pasadita ❸** (☎ 136 0129), on La Paz and México, is a town favorite. Enjoy simple, informal dining at the countertop seating or outdoor tables. Platters of *pollo con mole* or grilled fish and generous *tortas* cost 20-35 pesos, while fresh fish goes for 40 pesos. (Open M-F and Su 7am-5pm. Cash only.) Also popular is **Mariscos los Arcos ❹,** La Paz 170. Known for its seafood, los Arcos serves tasty breaded fish (60 pesos), fried crab tacos (55 pesos), and clam ceviche (40 pesos). (☎ 136 0347. Open daily 9am-9pm. Cash only.) **Restaurant/Bar El Patio ❺,** on La Paz in Hotel Alcatraz, is a bit more upscale than the other spots in town. El

BAJA CALIFORNIA

Patio serves a wide selection of Mexican food, including a shrimp omelette with coffee and juice for 110 pesos. (☎136 0017. Open daily 7am-10pm. Cash only.) **Supermercado Falayma,** on La Paz at the park, has a wide selection of groceries and meats for beach barbecues. (☎136 0102. Open daily 7pm-10pm.)

◪ ⊠ BEACHES AND OUTDOOR ACTIVITIES. Both **Bahía Magdalena** and **Bahía Almeja** lie just south of Puerto San Carlos, and veterans insist that the warm climate makes San Carlos a more comfortable place than Guerrero Negro for visitors during the winter. Bahía Magdalena is the source of 65% of Southern Baja's fish yield each year, and more than 75% of the local population are in maritime trades. In addition, extensive mangroves, intertidal sand, mud flats, and seagrass beds make the barrier island's ecosystems as biologically diverse as the bay itself. Among the animals that call the islands home are two colonies of sea lions. Dolphins also swim in the bay. Visitors can explore the bay by boat through ecotours run by local agencies. **Viajes Mar y Arena** (☎136 0599) has an office on Mex. 22 near the docks. The company runs kayaking, fishing, and surfing trips, along with whale watching trips during season. During peak whale watching season, a number of other companies offer whale watching tours for 650 pesos per hr. per person, with a minimum of five people per boat. Ask around town to find a guide. Hotel Alcatraz (p. 197) also rents kayaks for 36 pesos per day.

LA PAZ ☎612

Once home to a thriving pearl industry, La Paz (pop. 200,000) has grown from the small, rustic town depicted in John Steinbeck's 1947 novella *The Pearl* into the bustling, traffic-clogged capital of Baja California Sur. By day, bargain hunters jostle in the municipal market and truck drivers pick up shipments (and later jam the road) at the nearby port in Pichilingue. However, by 8pm each night, La Paz is transformed. From every corner of the city, sea breezes draw the whole town— from schoolchildren and teenage skateboarders to the elderly—out onto the *malecón* lining the Bahía de la Paz to watch the sun set. By far the most charming of the peninsula's major cities, La Paz gives tourists a chance to enjoy the relaxed Mexican lifestyle while exploring the natural wonders of the Sea of Cortés.

⊡ TRANSPORTATION

As the capital and largest city of Baja California Sur, La Paz is also the region's main transportation hub. It is also possible to reach mainland Mexico via the ferry connecting La Paz to Mazatlán and Los Mochis. Most of La Paz is easily walkable.

Flights: West of La Paz, accessible by taxi (200 pesos). Served by **Aeroméxico** (☎122 0091; airport office ☎124 6367), on Obregón between Hidalgo and Morelos. Open M-F 9am-7pm, Sa 9am-4pm; airport office open daily 5:30am-10pm. Also served by **AeroCalifornia** (☎123 9800), on Obregón between Ocampo and Bravo. Open M-F 9am-8pm, Sa-Su 9am-5pm.

Buses: La Paz has 2 bus stations.

La Paz Autotransportes: (☎122 2157), on Degollado at Prieto. Sends buses south to **San José del Cabo** (3hr., 110 pesos) via **Todos Santos** (1½hr., 8 per day 6:45am-7:45pm, 60 pesos) and **Cabo San Lucas** (2½hr., 100 pesos).

Águila Terminal Turística (☎122 7898), on Independencia at Obregón. Sends buses south along 2 different routes. Faster **Vía Corta** buses (14 per day, 6am-9pm) go to **Cabo San Lucas** (2½hr., 155 pesos) and **San José del Cabo** (3hr., 181 pesos) via **Todos Santos** (1½hr., 83 pesos). Longer **Vía Larga** service (7 per day, 10am-5:30pm) is only useful for destinations on the east cape: **Cabo San Lucas** (4hr., 155 pesos) via **Los Barriles** (2hr., 102 pesos), **San José del Cabo** (3½hr., 170 pesos), and **Santiago** (2½hr., 121 pesos). Buses also go to nearby beaches: **El Coromuel** and **Playas el Caimancito** (10min.); **Pichilingue** and **Tesoro** (25min.); **Playas Balandras** and **Tecolote** (35min., 5 per day 10am-5pm, 20 pesos).

Car Rental: Hertz (☎122 0919), on Obregón between Allende and Juárez. About US$60 to rent an economy-sized car. Open daily 7am-7pm. AmEx/MC/V.

La Paz

ACCOMMODATIONS
Hostería El Convento, **14**
Hotel Lorimar, **18**
Hotel Posada del Cortés, **8**
Hotel Posada Luna Sol, **21**
Hotel Quinta Lolita, **20**
Hotel San Carlos, **10**
Hotel Yeneka, **9**
Pensión California, **17**

FOOD
5th Avenue Cafe, **2**
Cafe el Callejón, **11**
Deli's, **12**
La Fonda, **19**
La Fuente, **13**
Los Pargo, **6**
Pa-Pi-Pan, **15**
Restaurant Palapa Adriana, **1**
Restaurante el Quinto Sol, **5**
Taquería Hermanos González, **16**

NIGHTLIFE
La Casa de Villa, **3**
La Paz-Lapa, **7**
Las Varitas, **4**

Ferries: Ferries leave for the mainland from Pichilingue, a 15min. car ride from the *centro*. Águila buses also run between Pichilingue and the downtown Águila Terminal Turística station. **Baja Ferries** (☎800-122-1414; www.bajaferries.com) runs to **Topolobampo,** a suburb of Los Mochis (6hr.; daily 3pm; about 710 pesos, from 1040 pesos per vehicle) and **Mazatlán** (18hr.; daily 3pm; about 800 pesos, from 2150 pesos per vehicle). Tickets available at the dock. If you entered Mexico via Baja California and are bound for the mainland, you will need a **tourist card** (FMT, p. 11). If you drove a car from the US, you will also need a **vehicle permit** (US$29.70). Obtain vehicle permits by showing certification of ownership, major credit card, driver's license, passport, and tourist card at Banjercito, at the ferry station in Pichilingue. (☎122 1116; www.banjercito.com.mx. Open M-F 9am-2pm, Sa-Su 9am-1pm.) Clear all paperwork before purchasing a ferry ticket. Otherwise, Baja Ferries may deny you a spot even if you have reservations.

☀TIP **TICKET TO RIDE.** Getting a ferry ticket isn't as easy as it seems—it requires persistence and determination. To secure a ticket, make reservations several days in advance. Go to the ticket office first thing after arriving into town (preferably right after it opens) and get the ticket in hand as soon as possible. During holidays, competition for tickets is fierce. *Clase salón* (3rd-class) is cheapest, and usually most in demand.

BAJA CALIFORNIA

🔎 PRACTICAL INFORMATION

Tourist Offices: (☎122 5939), on Obregón between Bravo and Rosales on the island. Staffed by the tourist police, this office distributes free maps, an excellent calendar of city-wide events, and plenty of advice. Open M-F 8am-5pm, Sa-Su 8am-3pm; hours sometimes vary.

Immigration Office: Servicios Migratorios, Obregón 2140 (☎122 0429), between Juárez and Allende. Tourist cards (237 pesos) can be obtained here. Open M-F 8am-8pm. After hours, visit the airport post (☎124 6349). Open Sa 9am-1pm. Guards at the airport can assist you Su 7am-7pm.

Currency Exchange: Banks line 16 de Septiembre, a few blocks off the bay. **Bancomer** (☎125 4248), on 16 de Septiembre, is half a block from the water. Open M-F 8:30am-4pm. **Banamex** (☎122 1011), at Esquerro and Arriola. Open M-Sa 9am-4pm. Both have **24hr. ATMs** and **exchange currency** and traveler's checks.

Laundromat: La Paz Lava, Mutualismo 260 (☎122 3112), on Ocampo 1 block up from Obregón in a small shopping strip. Small load wash/dry 48 pesos per kg., large load 85 pesos per kg. Self-service 15/30 pesos per kg. Open daily 8am-9:30pm.

Emergency: ☎066.

Tourist Police: (☎122 5939, 1399, or 6610). The tourist police occupy a small office on Obregón between Bravo and Rosales on the island in the center of the street. Dressed in white outfits, officers stroll, bike, and ATV around the center of the city. Their duties are protection and orientation, but they will also give recommendations about hiking, beaches, hotels, events, restaurants, and barbers.

Red Cross: Reforma 1091 (☎065 or 122 1222), between Católica and Ortega.

24hr. Pharmacy: Farmacia Bravo (☎122 6933), on the corner of Bravo and Verdad, opposite the hospital.

Hospital: Juan Maria de Salvatierra (☎122 1596 or 0166), on Bravo between Dominguez and Verdad.

Fax: Telecomm (☎125 9071; fax 125 0809), upstairs from the post office, on Revolución at Constitución. Open M-F 8am-7:30pm, Sa 9am-4:30pm, Su 9am-12:30pm.

Internet Access: Cafe el Callejón (☎125 4006), on de La Paz just off Obregón. 10 pesos per hr. (10 peso min. charge). Open daily 9am-1am. **5th Avenida Cafe** (☎123 5094), on the corner of Revolución and 5 de Mayo, looking out on Jardín Velasco. Free Wi-Fi. Computers with Internet access 20 pesos per hr. Open daily 7am-11pm.

Post Office: (☎122 0388), on Revolución at Constitución. Open M-F 8am-5pm, Sa 8am-1pm. **Postal Code:** 23000.

🏠 ACCOMMODATIONS

As a large city, with a vibrant business life outside of the tourist trade, La Paz offers a number of budget hotels.

Hotel Yeneka, Madero 1520 (☎125 4688), between 16 de Septiembre and Independencia. A monkey that once roamed this hotel is now stuffed and hangs in a Model-T Ford in the courtyard, and 10 cats now wander the building. Firm beds in large, clean rooms set around a lush courtyard filled with eclectic objects collected over 4 generations. Wi-Fi access. Singles start at 240 pesos. Cash only. ❹

Pensión California, Degollado 209 (☎122 2896), at Madero. While the rooms and bathrooms are very basic, the large courtyard and common area ensure that travelers who stay here will make new friends. Free Internet access. Common kitchen. Singles 170 pesos; doubles 220 pesos; triples 280 pesos. Cash only. ❷

Hostería El Convento (☎122 3508), on Madero between Arriola and Degollado. Same setup as Pensión California without the backpacker crowd. Singles 170; doubles 220; triples 280. Cash only. ❷

Hotel Lorimar, Bravo 110 (☎/fax 125 3822), between Madero and Mutualismo. Half of the rooms at this friendly, family-run hotel near the *malecón* have been renovated. All rooms have A/C. Old singles 230 pesos, renovated singles 345 pesos; doubles 270/385 pesos; triples 310/425 pesos. Cash only. ❺

Hotel Posada del Cortés, 16 de Septiembre 202 (☎/fax 122 8240), between Madero and Domínguez. A good budget hotel, whose pleasant, spacious rooms set around a courtyard come with TV and fan. Singles 200 pesos, with A/C 330; doubles 250/380 pesos. Cash only. ❷

Hotel San Carlos (☎122 0444), on 16 de Septiembre between Revolución de 1910 and Serdán. Rooms range from inner chambers with bed and bath to suites with A/C, TV, and balcony facing the street. Singles and doubles 250 pesos, with A/C 330 pesos. Triples 330/390 pesos. Rooms with balconies are more expensive. Cash only. ❸

Hotel Posada Luna Sol (☎122 7039), on 5 de Febrero between Abasolo and Topete. Although it's slightly out of the way, romantic Luna Sol has a rooftop terrace with views of the nearby water. Excellent for couples. Rooms with A/C and TV US$45. MC/V. ❺

Hotel Quinta Lolita (☎125 3031), on Revolución between Bravo and Rosales. This cozy hotel (reception seems to be run out of the kitchen) offers basic rooms for 300 pesos. Cash only. ❹

◖ FOOD

La Paz has a number of cheap eating options. Along with the *taquerías* and hot dog stands found in other Baja cities, La Paz has a large public market at Degollado and Revolución, where you can join locals eating cheap *tortas* and *antojitos* from clusters of local vendors. The city also places a special emphasis on ice cream, and there are almost as many ice cream shops as pawn shops. La Michoacana alone has 20 shops, most of which are open 10am-10pm. **La Fuente,** on the *malecón*, serves a wide variety of flavors and is a regular evening stop for hordes of local teenagers. (☎119 8587. 18 pesos a scoop. Open daily 9am-midnight.) There is a **market** in Jardín Velasco.

La Fonda (☎125 4700), at Revolución and Bravo. La Fonda serves good, cheap food in the *centro. Comida corrida* or delectable *pescado a la plancha* 40 pesos. Open daily 8am-10:30pm. Cash only. ❸

Taquería Hermanos González, at Madero and Degollado. While the tacos are juicy, it is the huge number of salads and salsas that set this taco stand apart from the others. *Tacos de pescado* 11 pesos. Open daily 8am-8pm. Cash only. ❶

Restaurante el Quinto Sol (☎122 1692), on Domínguez at Independencia. A vegetarian menu includes excellent *licuados* (21-25 pesos) and vegetarian *hamburguesas* (55 pesos). If you're tired of *huevos rancheros* for breakfast, try the muesli and yogurt (48 pesos). Open M-Sa 8am-4pm. Cash only. ❹

Cafe el Callejón (☎125 4006), on de La Paz just off Obregón. Guitar-wielding musicians serenade you as you take in the salty air and munch on traditional Mexican dishes. Generous *antojitos* (50-72 pesos) draw a big crowd. Internet access 10 pesos per hr. Open daily 9am-1am. Cash only. ❸

Restaurant Palapa Adriana (☎ 122 8329), off Obregón at Constitución, on the beach. Although it's slightly pricey, Adriana is practically on the water, with unmatched sunset views. *Pollo con mole* 70 pesos. Open Tu-Su 2-10pm. Cash only. ❹

Deli's (☎ 125 4909), on Esquerro at Callejón La Paz. A good spot for breakfast or a light lunch, Deli's serves baguette sandwiches (35 pesos), mixed salads (35 pesos), and sumptuous chocolate cake (29 pesos). Open daily 7am-11pm. Cash only. ❷

Pa-Pi-Pan, on Degollado, between Revolución and Madero. This bakery offers a mouth-watering selection of pastries, many for the tempting price of 2.5 pesos—perfect to take-along on a stroll along the *malecón*. Open M-Sa 8am-9pm, Su 8am-5pm. Cash only. ❶

5th Avenida Cafe (☎ 123 5094), on the corner of Revolución and 5 de Mayo, looking out on Jardín Velasco. An American-style coffee shop with American coffee (10 pesos) and pastries (7-22 pesos), worth sipping and eating for the computers with Internet access (20 pesos per hr.) and free Wi-Fi. Open daily 7am-11pm. MC/V. ❶

Los Pargo (☎ 123 0707) on Revolución at Reforma. A cheap sit-down restaurant. *Comida corrida* only costs 50 pesos here, although you're likely to be hurried through your meal. Open daily 7am-10pm. Cash only. ❸

👁 SIGHTS

MUSEO REGIONAL DE ANTROPOLOGÍA E HISTORIA. The museum, at 5 de Mayo and Altamirano, has four floors of exhibits covering the entire history of the peninsula, from pre-Hispanic to more modern times. The exhibits feature a number of intriguing artifacts, including ancient tools and colonial guns. (☎ 122 0162; fax 125 6424. Descriptions only in Spanish. Open daily 9am-6pm. Free.)

CATEDRAL DE NUESTRA SEÑORA DEL PILAR DE LA PAZ. La Paz's cathedral was completed in 1865 to replace the original mission, although its most noticeable features, the two towers, were constructed more than 40 years later. The left tower was built in 1910, and the nearly identical tower on the right side was added 10 years later. The Jardín Velasco across the street is perfect for resting and watching the afternoon foot traffic.

🏖 BEACHES

The water around La Paz is turquoise green, the white sand is soft, and the sea is calm. The area's beaches should not be missed. Although there are beaches along the *malecón*, don't expect cleanliness or tranquility—the city's main road runs 20 ft. from the water. If you have half a day to spare, head to the region's jewels: Playas Balandra and Tecolote. *(If you don't have a car, Aguila Autotrans-portes drives 5 buses to the beaches each day. 20 pesos. Tell the driver where you want to be dropped off. The last bus returns at 5pm.)*

🏖**PLAYA BALANDRA.** Balandra is La Paz's most stunning beach. A ring of smooth white sand surrounds a shallow cove and the water is crystal clear. Despite its beauty, Balandra is far less crowded than the beaches closer to the city. *(To reach Balandra by car, drive up Obregón and continue on the road until about km 23. When the road splits, turn left to reach Balandra.)*

🏖**PLAYA TECOLOTE.** Playa Tecolote, or Owl Beach, 25km south of town, is the most popular beach in the area. The white sands here are framed by tall mountains and Isla Espíritu Santo is visible from the shore. There are several restaurants and camping spots. Campsites on the left side of the beach from the parking lot include stone barbecue pits. *(To reach Tecolote by car, drive up Obregón and continue on the road until about km 23. When the road splits, stay straight to reach Tecolote. The paved road reaches a dead end at the beach.)*

PLAYAS EL CORUMUEL, CAIMANCITO, AND PICHILINGUE. These three small beaches are the closest to town. El Corumuel can be reached on foot via a long walk up the *malecón*. Both El Corumuel and adjacent Caimancito tend to be dirty and crowded. About 18km from the city, Playa Pichilingue is cleaner, although near the road and the Pichilingue port. Restaurant Playa Pichilingue (☎122 4565), right on the beach, rents small boats for 100 pesos per hr. *(To reach the beaches by car, drive up Obregón and continue on the road. All of the beaches are marked by signs. The turnoff for Playa Pichilingue is after km 18.)*

DIVING AND SNORKELING. In La Paz, the fun doesn't stop at the shoreline. Jumping into the waters off La Paz is like leaping into a giant saltwater fishtank. It is worth spending at least half a day snorkeling or diving. North of La Paz is the Salvatierra Wreck, a dive spot where a 91m ferry boat sank in 1976. Adorned with sponges and sea fans, the wreck attracts hordes of colorful fish, but strong currents may deter inexperienced divers. Isla Cerralvo, east of La Paz, is more isolated and promises reefs, large fish, giant pacific mantas, and untouched wilderness. Isla Espíritu Santo has hidden caves, pristine beaches, good diving reefs, and excellent snorkeling. Just north of Espíritu Santo, tiny Los Islotes Island is home to more than 350 sea lions. Isla Espíritu Santo and Isla Cerralvo—two of La Paz's best dive spots—are only accessible by boat. For excellent, easily accessible snorkeling, head to San Juan de la Costa, just past Centenario 13km north of La Paz on the Transpeninsular. Nearby on the same road is El Comitán, a beachcomber's paradise of sand and mud flats where tides deposit shells, amethyst, and other semi-precious stones. *(A number of local operators take tourists to dive and snorkel around Espíritu Santo and Cerralvo. The oldest and most established company is Baja Expeditions, 585 Sonora, at the north end of town, which has been leading excursions since 1974. Baja Expeditions charges about US$75 a day per person for a snorkeling trip and about US$120 for a diving trip; both include gear and lunch. ☎800-843-6967; www.bajaex.com. MC/V. Baja Diving & Service, on Obregón between 16 de Septiembre and de la Paz, charges about US$57 for comparable full day snorkeling tours and US$125 for full day diving trips. ☎122 1826; www.clubcantamar.com. Carey has offices in the marina and offers comparable snorkeling trips for US$75 and diving trips for US$115. ☎128 4048; www.carey.com.mx. Azul Tours leads snorkeling trips from Playa Tecolote for US$55. ☎125 2596; www.azultourslapaz.com. Most of these companies can also arrange kayaking tours. Call ahead for reservations to ensure that a snorkeling, diving, or kayaking tour is scheduled for the day of your visit.)*

■ NIGHTLIFE

A stroll down La Paz's *malecón* provides ample early evening entertainment. When the *malecón* dies down, however, a number of clubs and bars—many on the *malecón* itself—open their doors.

   Las Varitas (☎125 2025), Independencia and Domínguez. There's live rock every night, the lighting effects are exciting, and a young crowd kicks up the wood chips that cover the floor. Dancers gradually take over the tabletops. Cover charge F-Sa 30 pesos. Open Tu-Su 10pm-4am.

   La Paz-Lapa (☎122 9290), at Obregón and 16 de Septiembre. La Paz-Lapa, in the same complex as Carlos'n Charlie's, is owned by the same company as El Squid Roe in Cabo San Lucas and tries to put on a similar show: an outdoor booze and Top 40 fest with lots of table dancing. On Tu 9-11pm, women pay no cover and drinks are free. Cover 45 pesos. Open Tu and F-Sa 10pm-4am. MC/V.

La Casa de Villa (☎ 123 2250), at Obregón and 16 de Septiembre, opposite Carlos'n Charlie's, is a high-class club with white leather seating and lime green lights under the open sky. Cover 30 pesos. Open Tu-W 8:30pm-2am, Th-Sa 8:30pm-4am. MC/V.

TODOS SANTOS   ☎ 612

Visitors to Todos Santos (pop. 5000), a town tucked among rolling hills nearby the spectacular surfing beaches on the lonely Pacific coast, often end up staying for good. Expat artists have flocked here in recent years, filling the town with gourmet restaurants, luxurious hotels, art galleries—even the odd ATV and dune buggy. Gentrification has been limited to the more central streets, however, while the rest of the town seems to have been left, sometimes literally, in the dust. The unpaved side streets still retain the flavor of small-town Mexican life, with an abundance of excellent *taquerías* and the quiet afternoon siesta.

▊▊ TRANSPORTATION AND PRACTICAL INFORMATION

The **bus** stop (☎ 145 0289) is on Colegio Militar at Zaragoza. Buses run north to **La Paz** (1hr., 13 per day 7:05am-10:05pm, 67 pesos) and south to **San José del Cabo** (1½hr., 10 per day 7:30am-10pm, 98 pesos) via **Cabo San Lucas** (1hr., 67 pesos).

There are three principal (and paved) streets in town: **Degollado, Juárez,** and **Militar.** Degollado emerges from Mex. 19 as it enters Todos Santos from Cabo San Lucas. Degollado reaches a dead end at Juárez, which runs north-south by the church. Militar runs parallel to Juárez. Grab the monthly bilingual *Calendario de Todos Santos*, which has a useful map and a calendar of events. It's available for free at most tourist-centered shops in town.

Currency Exchange: Banorte (☎ 145 0056), on Juárez at Obregón. The only bank in town. **Exchanges currency** and has a **24hr. ATM.** Open M-F 9am-1pm.

Bookstore: El Tecolote Libros (☎ 145 0295), on the corner of Juárez and Hidalgo. While there is no tourist office in town, El Tecolote sells English-language maps and a large selection of used and new English-language books. Open Nov.-May daily 10am-5pm. Hours vary during low season.

Laundromat: Laundry (☎ 145 0006), on Morelos at Juárez, on the 1st fl. of the Motel Guluarte. Wash and dry 35 pesos per kg. Open daily 8am-8pm.

Police: (☎ 145 0445), in the Delegación Municipal complex at the plaza.

Pharmacy: Super ISSSTE Farmacia (☎ 145 0244), on Juárez between Morelos and Zaragoza. Open M-Sa 8am-8pm, Su 8am-2pm. MC/V.

Hospital: (☎ 145 0095), on Juárez at Degollado. Open 24hr.

Fax Office: Telecomm, at the corner of Hidalgo and Centenario. Open M-F 8am-3pm.

Internet Access: Milagro Real Estate (☎ 145 0219), at Juárez and Topete. 30 pesos per hr. Open M-F 9am-5pm, Sa 9am-1pm.

Post Office: (☎ 145 0330), on Militar at León. Open M-F 8am-3pm. **Postal Code:** 23305.

▛ ACCOMMODATIONS

Todos Santos has plenty of hotels—including a number of outrageously expensive ones—but few budget options exist. Check with the police before staking out a campground and try to stay in groups.

Motel Guluarte (☎ 145 0006), on Morelos at Juárez. Located in the *centro*, Guluarte has clean rooms with powerful A/C or fans, plus TV. Check-out noon. Singles 300 pesos; doubles 400 pesos. Cash only. ❹

Hotel Maria Bonita (☎ 145 0850), at the corner of Militar and Hidalgo. Large, over-priced rooms with A/C, bath, and TV. Rooms 500-600 pesos. MC/V. ❺

Hotel Miramar (☎ 145 0341), on Mutualismo, between Pedrajo and Olachea. Miramar is out of the way, but the price of its simple rooms sings sweetly to the budget traveler. Rooms 300 pesos, with A/C 350 pesos. Cash only. ❸

Santa Rosa Hotel (☎ 145 0394), on Olachea, between Verduzco and Villarino. Large suites with kitchen set around a pool. Singles without A/C US$45, doubles with A/C US$57. MC/V. ❺

El Litro RV Park, on Camino Punto Lobo at Cabrillo. The only RV park in town, El Litro also boasts a number of shaded campsites. Camping spots 80 pesos. RV site US$15. Discounts for longer stays. Cash only. ❶

Pescadero Surf Camp (☎ 130 3032; www.pescaderosurf.com), south of Todos Santos on Mex. 19, near km 64. Surfers should check out Pescadero, which is run by enthusi-astic Americans and offers a pool with a swim-up *palapa* bar. Accommodations vary from *cabañas* to camping spots under *palapas*. Advance reservations of 1-2 weeks rec-ommended; for US holidays, book up to 6 months in advance. Camping US$10 per per-son; *cabañas* US$40, each additional person US$5. MC/V. ❶

FOOD

Food in Todos Santos, like accommodation, comes at a high price. Most plates at sit-down restaurants exceed 100 pesos. For cheap eats, visit the local **Mer-cado Guluarte,** on Morelos between Militar and Juárez. (☎ 145 0006. Open M-Sa 8am-8pm, Su 8am-2pm.)

Barajas Tacos, an outdoor stand on Degollado (Mex. 19) and Cuauhtémoc. Locals are understandably addicted to this outdoor stand—it has the only late-night bites around. By day, the cook serves succulent *carnitas;* after 6pm, the taco stand becomes a lively hot spot. Order food at the taco bar. Open M and W-Su 8am-midnight. Cash only. ❶

Tacos Chilakos, on Juárez near Tecolote Libros. Another beloved local joint. The meat tacos (12 pesos) are superb. Open M-Sa 9am-9pm. Cash only. ❶

Cafe Brown's (☎ 145 0813), at the corner of Militar and Hidalgo. Cafe Brown's serves expensive breakfasts (omelette 80 pesos) and snacks (brownie 55 pesos) but it's worth a trip for the one exception, the delicious "Pancake Brown Bread" (10 pesos). Occasionally hosts live music and poetry readings. Open Nov.-May Tu-Su 7:30am-8pm; Jun.-Oct. W-Su 8am-6pm. ❹

Shut Up Frank's (☎ 145 0707), on Degollado (Mex. 19) and Cuauhtémoc. A full-on American burgers-and-ribs sports bar, decorated with boxing and off-road memorabilia. Juicy burgers with fries 75 pesos. Eggs 55 pesos. Open daily 8am-10pm. Cash only. ❹

SIGHTS

A large number of American artists, mostly from the western US, have moved to Todos Santos to live and paint in what many consider to be the next Santa Fe. The artists have benefited from a booming art market fueled by the construction of mega-mansions between San José del Cabo and Cabo San Lucas. At the **Galería Stewart,** on Obregón at Centenario, you can visit the home and gallery of Todos San-tos's first expat artist, Charles Stewart, who moved permanently to Todos Santos in 1986. Stewart's home itself, constructed in 1810, is a work of art. (☎ 145 0265;

www.charlescstewart.com. Open M-Sa 11am-4pm.) You can get an overview of the art scene at the **Galería de Todos Santos,** on the corner of Legaspi and Topete. Owner and artist Michael Cope displays his own work alongside that of fellow expats, visiting artists, and locals. (☎145 0500. Open June-Sept. M-Sa 11am-1pm and 2-4pm; Oct.-May M-Sa 10am-1pm and 2-5pm.) Cope can sometimes be seen at work at his annex on the corner of Centenario and Hidalgo. Also worth a peek is the **Centro Cultural,** on Juárez at Topete, which houses a rambling collection of local treasures, including murals dating to the Mexican revolution, ancient stone tools and arrowheads, huts replicating a more traditional way of life, and a collection of photographs depicting the history of Todos Santos. (Open M-F 8am-7pm, Su 9am-3pm. Free.)

BEACHES

Todos Santos is surrounded by some of the region's most unspoiled beaches. It's easy to find a sunbathing spot and there's plenty of room to explore or to surf; however, none of the beaches are accessible via paved roads and there are no signs pointing the way. Powerful currents also make swimming unsafe. The isolation may be unsettling, and it's a good idea to always bring a friend and return to town before dark.

> **RIPPIN' TIDES.** Baja is filled with miles of untouched coastline and beaches ripe for exploring, but many of them, particularly on the Pacific coast, have vicious rip tides, fast-moving currents close to shore powerful enough to sweep a person out to sea. If you find yourself in one of these rip tides, try not to panic. Breathe, and let the water move you down the beach until the current is weak enough that you can swim to shore. It is a good idea to bring a buddy to the beach and to remain aware of your surroundings while out in the water.

LA POZA. Vicious undercurrents and waves make romantic La Poza unsuitable for swimming, but there are few better places for solitary beach walks. In the center of the beach is a freshwater lagoon, which is home to a large population of birds. Bring a pair of binoculars. A short drive from the beach, █**Cafe D'licia** ❷ (☎145 0862) serves Mexican-inspired dishes, such as corn tortillas layered with goat cheese (40 pesos) and mango cinnamon toast (25 pesos) in a jungle-like setting complete with a menagerie of talking parrots, dogs, and a tortoise. *(To reach La Poza, follow Topete off Juárez. Take your 4th left down a dirt road called La Cachora. To reach Cafe D'licia, stay on Topete in the direction of Las Playitas. Pass the school and the El Sol 2 market. Follow the signs. Open M and F-Su 8:30am-3pm. Cash only.)*

PLAYA SAN PEDRITO. A quiet beach near the highway, 8km south of town. Most of the beachcombers here are surfers and the water, which is safe for swimming, is filled with large rocks. *(Turn at the sign for San Pedrito RV Park at km 60 and drive down the very bumpy road.)*

PLAYA LOS CERRITOS. At the end of a long, bumpy, and often solitary road across ranchland lies a popular, family-friendly beach. Los Cerritos boasts a restaurant and a number of surf shops. One, **Los Cerritos Surf Shop** (☎142 3701), near the parking lot, offers lessons (US$50), and rents surfboards (US$15 per day) and wetsuits (US$5 per day). Surfers abound in the waters, and while the break is just as big as at the other beaches near Todos Santos, the current is tamer, catering to a diverse group of Mexicans and tourists. Nevertheless, the endless sands are far from crowded. *(Playa los Cerritos lies approx. 14km south of Todos Santos. Coming from the direction of Todos Santos, turn right on the dirt road immediately after Puente El Pescadero, on km 64.)*

🚶 DAYTRIP FROM TODOS SANTOS

SIERRA DE LA LAGUNA

To hire a local guide, ask around in Todos Santos. **Raúl,** *who works at Plaza Comercial Los Faroles (the brick supermarket on Juárez), drives hikers to the trailhead and picks them up later there at a prearranged time. He charges US$80-$100, depending on the number of people in the group.* ☎ *145 0096; Plaza Comercial Los Faroles open M-Sa 8am-8pm, Su 8am-3pm. Raúl can also put hikers in touch with local ranches, including* **Rancho el Salado** *and* **Rancho las Piedritas,** *which loan mules for the trip.* **Todos Santos Eco Adventures** *(☎ 145 0780; www.tosea.net), on Juárez at Topete, offers both 2- and 4-day guided camping trips, complete with food, wine, and warm showers in the mountains. 2-day/1-night trip $175 per person. To get to the trailhead yourself, drive south out of Todos Santos. After passing km 53, you will see the turn-off on the left at the top of a small hill, directing you toward Rancho la Burrera. Drive down this dirt road (4WD recommended) through a fenced-off cattle ranch and bear right at the first unmarked major fork in the road. Follow signs for 40min. until you reach a locked gate and the end of the road. There is a small dirt parking lot. It is unsafe to leave a parked car here overnight.*

Sierra de la Laguna, the mountain range that lines the cape, is visible from virtually any beach around Los Cabos and Todos Santos. Established as a biosphere reserve in 1994, these mountains are home to some of the most exotic flora and fauna in Baja California. Sierra de la Laguna is home to both the only dry jungle and the only pine-oak forest in Baja. The climate of the mountains is completely different from the surrounding coastal areas and can drop below freezing in the winter. La Laguna, the Sierra's most popular hiking destination, is a field of about 4 sq. km perched at an altitude of 1700m amid the rocky peaks of Picacho la Laguna and Cerro las Casitas, the range's tallest points. Once a lake, heavy rainfall eroded the banks of la Laguna until it developed into a grassy meadow. The climb to la Laguna is a grueling 8hr., with steep inclines toward the top. Hikers are rewarded with beautiful vistas along the way; one rest-stop approximately 3hr. into the hike offers a view of the entire width of the peninsula, including both the Sea of Cortés and the Pacific. The trail is well marked and there are several campsites at and around la Laguna.

LOS CABOS

At the end of the long, lonely drive from the US border, you might be forgiven for thinking that the Transpeninsular Highway would peter out at some remote outpost with barely any connection to the rest of civilization. Instead, it swoops down into huge malls and hotels. Los Cabos—the cape region—is a far cry from the sleepy getaway that many Baja veterans remember from the old days, and it gets further away every year as the coastline fills with more resorts, clubs, and golf courses. Yet even though Los Cabos is crammed with *gringos* year-round, it's still possible to escape the crowds and enjoy the southern coast's stunning natural beauty—spectacular rock formations, surf that rivals that of Hawaii, and, of course, glistening white beaches, which are arguably the most stunning in Baja.

CABO SAN LUCAS ☎ 624

The granite cliffs and craggy rock arch that stand at Baja's southern tip are the most famous images of Cabo San Lucas (pop. 50,000). What the postcards don't show is that it's difficult to see those natural wonders without high-rise malls, the glitzy marina, and hordes of sunburned tourists getting in the way. Cabo is the ultimate resort, and probably one of the most expensive places in Mexico. As tourists pour money into its restaurants and clubs, the town can't help but prosper. Nevertheless, Cabo has remained a friendly town, particularly if you move beyond the commercialized *centro*. Cabo's pleasures merit the occasional splurge, and even budget travelers can delight in fabulous fish ceviches, gloriously tacky nightlife, and the nonstop flow of margaritas.

▛ TRANSPORTATION

Buses: Local "Subur Cabos" **buses** run to **San José del Cabo** (30min., every 15min., 23 pesos). Hop on the bus at the stop on Cárdenas between Vicario and Mendoza. There are a few rows of benches under a small shelter outside of the Puerto Paraíso mall. The **Águila station** (☎ 143 7880) is about 2.5km north of town, opposite the PEMEX station, right before the Hotel Oasis. Follow signs to Todos Santos, and the bus station is right after you get on the highway. To get into town from the bus stop, take a local yellow bus (5 pesos) to Blvr. Marina. "Vía Corta" Águila buses go to **La Paz** (3 hrs., 16 per day 6am-9pm) via **Todos Santos** (1hr., 67 pesos). "Vía Larga" services (7 per day 5:15am-5:15pm) take 4hr. to reach La Paz via **San José del Cabo** (30min., 30 pesos). Some of these buses also go to the ferry terminal at **Pichilingue** (3hr.; daily 8, 9, 10am; 150 pesos). Various buses make stops at: **Ciudad Constitución** (6hr., 7 per day, 340 pesos); **Guerrero Negro** (14½hr., 5 per day, 873 pesos); **Ensenada** (23hr., 5 per day, 1443 pesos); **Loreto** (8½hr., 6 per day, 481 pesos); **Mulegé** (10½hr., 5 per day, 610 pesos); **San Ignacio** (12½hr., 5 per day, 739 pesos); **San Quintín** (19hr., 5 per day, 1226 pesos); **Santa Rosalía** (11½hr., 5 per day, 669 pesos); **Tijuana** (26½hr., 5 per day, 1544 pesos).

Car rental is available at **Budget** (☎ 143 5151), on Cárdenas between Guerrero and Hidalgo. Economy cars from US$60 per day. Open daily 9am-6pm. MC/V.

▛ ▜ ORIENTATION AND PRACTICAL INFORMATION

Vicario leads to Mex. 19 and Todos Santos. Restaurants, bars, and most tourist services concentrate on Cárdenas, between Morelos and the western edge of town, and along Blvr. Marina. Cárdenas eventually becomes the four-lane Mex. 1 leading to the Corridor. Plazas are concrete malls or tight conglomerations of shops and follow the curve of the marina.

Tourist Information: The dozens of "Tourist Info" booths located along Blvr. Marina and Cárdenas are simply covers for time-share hawkers.

Currency Exchange: Many hotels and restaurants prefer US$ and exchange them at 10 pesos per US$1 regardless of the going rate. **HSBC,** Blvr. Marina 17 (☎ 143 3888), in Plaza Bonita, exchanges traveler's checks and foreign currency. Open M-F 8am-7pm, Sa 8am-3pm. **Bancomer** (☎ 800-226-2663), on Cárdenas at Paseo de la Marina, offers similar services. Open M-F 8:30am-4pm, Sa 10am-2pm. Both have **24hr. ATMs.**

Laundromat: Lavandería San Lucas, (☎ 122 1093), at Vicario and 20 de Noviembre. Wash and dry 30 pesos. Open daily 8am-10pm.

Emergency: ☎ 066.

Police: (☎ 143 3977), on Cárdenas, 2 blocks north of Morelos.

Red Cross: (☎ 143 3300), on the *carretera* to Todos Santos, near the PEMEX station.

24hr. Pharmacy: Farmacia Express (☎ 143 9333), at Vicario and 20 de Noviembre.

Medical Services: IMSS (☎ 143 1444 or 1445), uphill from the bus station, across the street from the PEMEX station.

Fax Office: Telecomm (☎ 143 1968, fax 143 0231), next to the post office on Cárdenas. **Western Union.** Open M-F 8am-5:30pm, Sa 8am-3:30pm, Su 8-11:30am.

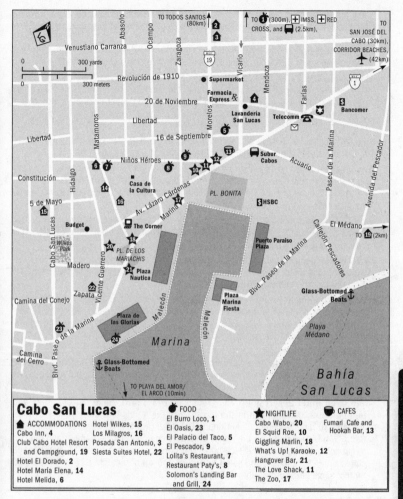

Cabo San Lucas

ACCOMMODATIONS
Cabo Inn, 4
Club Cabo Hotel Resort and Campground, 19
Hotel El Dorado, 2
Hotel María Elena, 14
Hotel Melida, 6
Hotel Wilkes, 15
Los Milagros, 16
Posada San Antonio, 3
Siesta Suites Hotel, 22

FOOD
El Burro Loco, 1
El Oasis, 23
El Palacio del Taco, 5
El Pescador, 9
Lolita's Restaurant, 7
Restaurant Paty's, 8
Solomon's Landing Bar and Grill, 24

NIGHTLIFE
Cabo Wabo, 20
El Squid Roe, 10
Giggling Marlin, 18
What's Up! Karaoke, 12
Hangover Bar, 21
The Love Shack, 11
The Zoo, 17

CAFES
Fumari Cafe and Hookah Bar, 13

BAJA CALIFORNIA

Internet Access: The Corner (☎143 6666), on Cárdenas at Matamoros. Check email while rock music booms in the background—a true Cabo San Lucas experience. 10 pesos per 15min. Open daily 8am-midnight.

Post Office: (☎143 0048) on Cárdenas, next to the police station. Open M-F 9am-5pm. **Postal Code:** 23451.

ACCOMMODATIONS AND CAMPING

Resorts dominate Cabo San Lucas, and even the cheapest hotels will take a bite out of your wallet—they also have a bad habit of continuously hiking their rates. During the winter high season, call ahead and be prepared to shell out 25% more than during the summer months. Some hotels base rates on US$ and not pesos.

Cabo Inn (☎143 0819 or US 619-819-2727; www.caboinnhotel.com), on 20 de Noviembre, near Vicario. Rooms with A/C are set around a lush garden at this community-oriented hotel, where outdoor seating areas and a communal kitchen are only the beginning—there's also a rooftop deck complete with pool and a living room under a *palapa*. Free Wi-Fi, coffee, and purified water. Check-out 11am. Singles US$45; doubles US$50. MC/V. ❺

Hotel Melida (☎143 6564), on Matamoros at Niños Héroes. There are no frills at the Hotel Melida, but it's the cheapest hotel near the *centro*. Rooms, with names like *Amor de un Rato*, have A/C and TV as well as sliding glass doors that open onto a courtyard filled with stones and clotheslines. Reception 24hr. Check-out noon. Singles 350 pesos; doubles 450 pesos. Cash only. ❺

Hotel Wilkes (☎150 2715), on Cabo San Lucas at Cinco de Mayo. Luxurious rooms with A/C and cable TV. Singles US$50; doubles US$65. Cash only. ❺

Los Milagros Hotel (☎143 4566, from US 718-928-6647; www.losmilagros.com.mx), on Matamoros and Cárdenas. Comfortable rooms with A/C, some with kitchenettes, are set around a quiet flower-filled courtyard with a small pool. Reception 8am-8pm. Check-out 11am. Singles 800 pesos; doubles 900 pesos. Cash only. ❺

Hotel El Dorado (☎143 2810), on Morelos between Obregón and Carranza. The rooms have A/C, TV, and large bath. Reception 24hr. Check-out 1pm. Singles 450 pesos; doubles 550 pesos. Cash only. ❺

Hotel María Elena (☎143 3289), on Matamoros between Cárdenas and Niños Héroes. Oversized rooms with A/C and cable TV. Laundromat available on the ground floor. Singles 480 pesos; doubles 550 pesos. Cash only. ❺

Posada San Antonio (☎143 7353), on Morelos between Obregón and Carranza. Standard motel-style rooms in a non-touristy neighborhood. Some rooms do not have windows with outside views. Reception 7am-midnight. Check-out 1pm. Rooms 340 pesos, with A/C and TV 390 pesos. MC/V. ❺

Siesta Suites Hotel (☎143 2773, from US 602-331-1354; www.cabosiesta-suites.com), on Zapata near Guerrero. Recently renovated, Siesta Suites is a smart, well-maintained establishment with pool. Suites include kitchens, TV, and A/C. Internet access US$3 per hour. Singles US$64; 2-bed suites US$69. MC/V. ❺

Club Cabo Hotel Resort and Campground (☎143 3348). Head out Cárdenas and turn on Paseo de la Marina in the direction of the hotels that lie beyond Playa del Medano. Turn on El Medano, continue to Hotel Cascadas, and turn left on a dirt road. Cabo Club is 1km down on the left. A 1-acre campground close to the beach offers a hammock area, hot tub, and ping-pong and pool tables. Also has 10 fully equipped suites with A/C, kitchen, and satellite TV. Full hookup or tent site US$15 per person. Suites: singles US$50; doubles US$60. ❶

▤ FOOD

The dozens of ostentatious restaurants along the water are not geared toward budget travelers, although the restaurants are worth visiting just to watch the cooks throw leftovers to hungry schools of fish in the marina. For better deals on food (and Mexican hats and rugs), head inland along Morelos and its side streets. A supermarket, **Bimbo/Almacenes Grupo Castro,** is located on Morelos at Revolución. (☎143 0566. Open daily 7:30am-11pm.)

El Oasis (☎143 8314), at Blvr. Marina and Cabos San Lucas. An aptly named diner in a desert of overpriced restaurants, El Oasis dishes out *ricas tortas* (sandwiches; 40 pesos) and quesadillas (15 pesos) to locals. Open M-Sa 7am-5pm. Cash only. ❷

El Burro Loco (☎ 143 8980), on Vicario at Alikán. It's out of the way, but you won't find many tourists at this popular local restaurant, which dishes out vast portions. *Comida corrida* 76 pesos. *Alambre de res* 61 pesos. Open M-Sa 7am-9pm. Cash only. ❹

Lolita's Restaurant (☎ 143 1026), at Niños Héroes and Matamoros, is a tiny, casually elegant out-of-doors restaurant. Suitably fiery *fajitas de carne* (82.50 pesos) and chicken *mole* (57 pesos). Open M and W-Sa 7am-7:30pm, Su 6am-2pm. Cash only. ❹

El Pescador (☎ 143 8978), on Niños Héroes and Zaragoza. The man relentlessly hawking this restaurant on the street is right; El Pescador serves delicious seafood. Fabulous ceviches (70 pesos) and shellfish (70 pesos) promise satisfaction. Open daily 10am-10pm. Cash only. ❹

Solomon's Landing Bar and Grille (☎ 143 3050), in Plaza de las Glorias, on the marina. The most inexpensive restaurant facing the water. Watch out for the constant parade of souvenir sellers who will interrupt your meal. Tacos 15-20 pesos. Fish sandwich 60 pesos. Open daily 7am-11pm. MC/V. ❷

Restaurant Paty's, at Niños Héroes and Zaragoza. Serves up a variety of inexpensive Mexican dishes (3 quesadillas for 40 pesos) and costlier American fare (barbecue chicken 100 pesos). Open daily 7am-11pm. Cash only. ❹

El Palacio del Taco, on 16 de Septiembre between Morelos and Vicario. With its wooden chairs and red-and-yellow walls, El Palacio del Taco is classier than its *taquería* competitors. It's also open later at night and has a cheap menu of quesadillas (17 pesos), tacos (12 pesos), *papas rellenos* (60 pesos), and sandwiches (30 pesos). A must after a night out on the town. Open daily 9am-4am. Cash only. ❸

◀ 🗺 BEACHES AND WATERSPORTS

Cabo bills itself as the "marlin capital of the world," and many tourists visit to reel in their share of the millions of huge fish caught each year. Prices for fishing trips are off the hook—nearly all exceed US$200 per day. Most daytime activity in Cabo San Lucas takes place in the pristine waters off the coast. Many head toward the beautiful **Los Cabos Corridor** (p. 213), linking San Lucas and San José, but there are plenty of beaches right in Cabo. Playa del Médano, the best for swimming, reaches east from the marina. The waters here resemble an aquatic zoo, featuring exotic species of parasailers, roaring jet skis, enormous cruise ships, and motorboats full of lobster-red, beer-guzzling vacationers. Fly-by-day operators bombard tourists with beach gear to rent. For a more professional operation, visit **JT Watersports**, in front of the Hacienda Hotel. (☎ 144 4566; www.jtwatersports.com. Waverunners US$45 per 30min. 10min. parasailing US$40. Ocean kayak rentals US$15 per hr. Open daily 9am-5pm. MC/V.) **Baja's ATV's and Watersports** has several locations on the beach, including one adjacent to the Baja Cantina restaurant. (☎ 144 3688; www.bajaswatersports.com. Kayak rentals US$20 per hr. Wave runners US$50 per 30min. Open daily 9am-5pm. MC/V.)

The famous **Arch Rock** of Cabo San Lucas, known as El Arco or Land's End, is a short boat ride from the marina or Playa del Médano (10min.). Here, the tranquil Sea of Cortés meets the rough Pacific. The rocks around the arch are home to about 40 sea lions who hang out and sunbathe. Both JT Watersports and Baja's ATV's and Watersports bring tourists to El Arco from **Playa del Médano** (US$10). Eager, English-speaking boat captains will also take you there and back from the marina. To find them, walk to the far right of the marina, just past Solomon's Bar and Grille. The ubiquitous glass-bottom boats also stop at **Playa del Amor,** a good swimming beach next to El Arco. Beaches crowd easily in

Cabo, so be sure to arrive early. Disembark and head back later on a different boat for no additional charge; switching companies costs 50 pesos. The beach is far from isolated and the many glass-bottom boats continuously dropping off passengers will interrupt your swim. When there's no love, head to **Playa del Divorcio** (Beach of Divorce). Despite its ominous name, this beach—which lies opposite Amor on the Pacific side—offers a much larger and more isolated area to stretch out. The one downside is that dangerous currents and a fierce undertow make swimming unsafe. The rocky area just before Playa del Amor and Playa del Divorcio is a national park and underwater wonderland. **Snorkeling** is the best way to explore the stony recesses packed with coral, urchins, tropical fish, moray eels, stingrays, and octopi. Bring your own gear or rent equipment from your boat captain (boat tour and snorkeling package around US$18-20). You can also rent snorkel gear on Playa del Amor.

For a more adventurous and cheaper way to reach Playa del Amor and Playa del Divorcio, head to Hotel SolMar at the end of the marina on the right side. Walk through the lobby and onto the beach, **Playa SolMar.** Framed by granite cliffs on both ends, SolMar provides a vast and lonely stretch of sand to relax, although, as at Playa del Divorcio, the undertow makes swimming unsafe. Playa SolMar also offers the one way to reach Playa del Amor and Playa del Divorcio via land: Playa del Divorcio is on the other side of the cliff on the left-hand side of the beach. Since there's no designated path, only those with some mountain climbing experience should attempt the 5min. climb.

Constructed on a small rocky hill in the center of the city, **Casa de la Cultura** hosts music and art classes for Cabo San Lucas residents. Although you can't partake in the classes, the Casa de la Cultura offers an incredible vista of all of Cabos San Lucas and the surrounding mountains. The short climb is more than worth the view. (The entrance to the grounds is off Niños Héroes near Abasolo. Open M-F 8am-5pm. Free.)

■ NIGHTLIFE

In Cabo San Lucas, those who play hard pay hard. Drinks are pricey and employees will pressure you to buy drink after drink if you want to remain at a club. Still, clubs usually do not charge cover fees and all offer special deals at least one night a week. Clubs and bars concentrate on Cárdenas and Blvr. Marina, which become a huge laser-lit playground by night, starting after 11pm and winding down at 3 or 4am.

El Squid Roe (☎ 143 0655; www.elsquidroe.com), on Cárdenas at Zaragoza. You can't help but notice the two airplanes whirling overhead as you revel among an excited pickup scene, conga lines, vats of tequila, and short-skirted, shot-peddling girls dancing on any and all surfaces. Beer or mixed drinks 55 pesos. Open daily noon-4am. MC/V.

The Love Shack (☎ 143 5010), on Morelos off Cárdenas, around the corner from Squid Roe. A scaled-down, more intimate version of Cabo's mega-clubs. One small room with a pool table and well-stocked jukebox. Tu night shots US$2. W 9pm-1am women drink free. Open daily 11am-3am. Cash only.

Cabo Wabo (☎ 143 1188; www.cabowabo.com), on Guerrero near Cárdenas. Live rock daily entertains an older crowd; watch for former Van Halen member and club owner Sammy Hagar, who plays here 5 times a year. Hagar memorabilia decorates the club. Beer 44 pesos. Open daily 7:30pm-2am. MC/V.

Giggling Marlin (☎ 143 1182; www.gigglingmarlin.com), across Matamoros from Plaza de los Mariachis. Attracts an older crowd. Patrons can discover the origin of the club's name by being hung upside down like a prize fish. Beer 35 pesos. Mixed drinks 40-45 pesos. Open daily 9am-1am. MC/V.

The Zoo (☎ 143 5500), at the corner of Marina and Zaragoza. Partiers line up behind a cage to get into this zoo-themed club before making their way to the cage on the dance floor. Don't miss the life-size elephant and rhino sculptures. Open daily 8pm-4am. V.

Fumari Cafe and Hookah Bar (☎ 172 0198), on Cárdenas, just beyond Morelos. Smoke hookah (130 pesos) while sitting on a sofa on the outdoor deck and breathe in a much more laid-back Cabo experience. Open M-Th 4-11pm, F-Sa 4pm-2am. Cash only.

What's Up! Karaoke, Bar and Snak (☎ 122 3577), on Cárdenas at Morelos. What's Up! was designed with karaoke in mind. Open daily 8pm-1am. Cash only.

Hangover Bar (☎ 143 7515; www.cabohangoverbar.com), on Marina, on the 2nd fl. of Plaza del Sol, near the Plaza de los Mariachis. Hangover is one of Cabo's only gay clubs and hosts a live DJ every night who presides over an intimate dance floor. Open Tu-Su 7pm-4am. Cash only.

🏃 DAYTRIPS FROM LOS CABOS

THE CORRIDOR

The easiest way to get to the many beaches on the Corridor is by car. All are within 30min. of either Cabo San Lucas or San José del Cabo. "Subur Cabos" buses, which run between San José del Cabo and Cabo San Lucas, will leave you at any of the listed beaches (up to 23 pesos). To get back, flag down a passing bus.

Amazing beaches dot the 30km stretch of coast between Cabo San Lucas and San José del Cabo. Unfortunately, development is creeping in from both sides. The most pristine, undeveloped beaches are those in the middle. The calmest waters and best swimming areas are those closest to Cabo San Lucas. All of the beaches listed below are accessible from the highway; many lie at the end of winding roads, but all are reachable in passenger vehicles if you don't try to drive across the beach itself. Access roads to some are identified by small road signs with the name of the beach. A few are marked simply by dirt roads, and closer to San José it becomes increasingly difficult to locate specific beaches unless you're traveling by bus and can ask the driver for the right stop. The following beaches are listed in geographical order, starting at Cabo San Lucas and moving east along the corridor to San José del Cabo.

PLAYA BARCO VARADO. Barco Varado (Shipwreck) is a scuba-diving paradise, although not recommended for swimmers or sunbathers. Tangled among the rocks is the rusted wreckage of a Japanese freighter, which ran ashore in the 1960s. For non-divers, the studded rocks on the beach create a striking photo opportunity. *(Take the turnoff to the Cabo del Sol complex immediately before km 10; the guards should let you through the gate. Follow the road downhill and turn right; continue as far as the Sheraton Hacienda. A paved road immediately to the left beyond the hotel leads to a small parking area.)*

PLAYA LA VIUDA. Crashing waves and jagged outcroppings shelter quiet, secluded Playa La Viuda (Widow Beach). The winding road that leads to the rocky beach is a good place to spot wildlife, and the ten *palapa* shelters are perfect for picnics. Swimming is not advised. *(Follow the sandy road immediately to the right of the gated entrance to the Twin Dolphin resort at km 11.5.)*

🏖 PLAYA SANTA MARIA. A cove protects the clear waters of this small beach from harsh waves, and swimming is safe year-round. Some of Cabo's best snorkeling can be found here, and you can rent gear from **Servicios Taide,** on the right side of the beach coming from the parking lot. *(Mask and snorkel rental 70 pesos, full snorkeling gear 120 pesos per day. Boogie board 100 pesos per day. Kayak for 2 people 200 pesos per hr. Shade umbrella 100 pesos per day. Open daily 9am-5pm.)* The spectacular hills on either side of the cove are also worth a look. *(Just past Playa Twin Dolphin at km 12. Parking lot open 7am-8pm; supervised parking is free, though tips are appreciated.)*

PLAYA CHILENO. A very popular swimming spot, Chileno has free public showers. Tour operators bring groups here via boat to snorkel, and heavy traffic sometimes spoils the golden sands. *(A large public parking lot lies right off km 14. Open daily 7am-7pm. Free.)*

PLAYA EL TULE. The long, rocky shore is unsuitable for swimming, but surfers fight for waves. You won't find any facilities. *(Leave the road via a sandy track just before Puente del Tule, at around km 15. If you don't have a 4WD, park close to the bridge, since the sand rapidly becomes treacherously thick and the tracks are hard to see.)*

PLAYA PALMILLA. Gentle waves, great swimming, and shady *palapas* attract many families and weekenders. *(From km 26, drive into the Palmilla complex and turn right down the access road. Follow signs to the beach for about 1.5km.)*

PLAYA ACAPULQUITO. Big waves and soft sand make this a popular beach with surfers, swimmers, and sunbathers alike, although the surfing crowd dominates. Locals say Acapulquito is suitable for beginning surfers. *(Park in front of the Cabo Surf Hotel and the 7 Seas Restaurant, at km 27. Walk down the steep flight of stairs through the huge underground pipe, then between the condominiums to the beach.)*

PLAYA COSTA AZUL. Adjacent to Playa Acapulquito, Playa Costa Azul is the best surfing beach in all of Los Cabos. The water is usually filled with expert surfers riding the waves, along with an astonishing number of jumping rays. Those who want to display their skills can rent a board, while wannabes can learn the basics at **Zipper's Surf Rentals,** on the beach to the left of the parking area. Rentals and free surf maps of the cape are available at **Costa Azul Surf Shop,** across the highway from the beach. *(The last beach before San José del Cabo, at km 28 near the Cabo Surf Hotel. Zipper's ☎ 121 4339. Board rentals US$20 per day. Lessons US$50 per hr. Open daily 9am-5pm. Costa Azul ☎ 142 2771. Rentals start at US$20 per day and lessons are US$55 per hr. Open M-Sa 8am-7pm, Su 10am-5pm. MC/V.)*

SAN JOSÉ DEL CABO

With its narrow streets and traditional *zócalo*, San José del Cabo (pop. 50,000) is a gentle complement to its hard-partying neighbor, Cabo San Lucas. While Cabo has embraced the gigantic American-style malls that seem to sprout daily and the American hits blaring from its clubs, San José has preserved its colonial heritage. Still, life is changing quickly here. Already, mega-resorts and condominium complexes have invaded the beaches closest to town, and souvenir stores occupy the antique buildings lining Mijares. Although budget travelers will find San José cheaper than San Lucas, prices are still much higher than on the mainland.

⌐ TRANSPORTATION

Buses: San José del Cabo has one central bus station. A private bus line also transports tourists from the center of the city to **La Paz,** via **Cabo San Lucas.**

Águila/ABC bus station: (☎ 142 1100), on González, 2 blocks from the highway. To get to town, go left from the station, walk 8-10min. down González to Morelos, turn left, walk 6 blocks, and make a right on Zaragoza toward the *zócalo*. Águila and ABC run to **La Paz** (3hr., 17 per day 5:15am-8:15pm, 175 pesos) via **Cabo San Lucas** (30min., 30 pesos) and **Todos Santos** (1½hr., 98 pesos). Of these, the 6:15 and 9:15am go on to **Mexicali** (26hr., 1741 pesos); the

TO ✈ (15km), 🛂, ♨
LOS BARNLES, SANTIAGO

Morelos

Zaragoza

Guerrero

Eco
Lavanderías

Obregón ①

PLAZA
MIJARES

Misión ⓣ

Farmacia
La Moderna

Muñoz

Centro de Salud
✚

Doblado

Green

②

③

℞

⑤

Aramburo
Grocery

Trazzo
Digital

⑥

Mijares

⑧

Municipal Market

⑦

Degollado

Castro

Coronado

Hidalgo

IMSS
✚

Banamex
💲

Margarita de Juárez

Peninsula
Ejecutivo 🚌 ⑨

⑩

Thrifty Car
Rental

TO LA PLAYITA BEACH
(5km)

Tercer Ayuntamiento

Benito Juárez

TO THE CORRIDOR,
CABO SAN LUCAS (25km)

①

5 de Mayo

Red Cross
✚
✉

Estero de
San José

San José del Cabo

🏠 🏕 ACCOMMODATIONS

Hotel Diana, **4**
Hotel Posada Terranova, **5**
Hotel Youth Hostel Nuevo San José, **2**
Yuca Inn, **1**

🍖 FOOD

Correcaminos, **12**
French Riviera, **6**
Habaneros, **11**
San José Cafe, **3**
Taquería Erika, **7**

⭐ NIGHTLIFE

Cactus Jack's, **10**
Escala, **9**
Shooters, **8**

TO BUS STATION
🚌
(2 blocks)

Morelos

Telecomm ☎

Valerio González

Hidalgo

Mijares

MotoSol

Walking Path

Misiones

Blvd. Finisterra

American
Express 💲

Ⓝ
LG

⑪
⑫

Paseo Finisterra

Golf
Course

0 ———— 200 yards
0 ———— 200 meters

Cactimundo

TO BEACH (2km)

TO PLAYA LAS VELAS (1km)

10:15am and 2:15pm go on to **Ciudad Constitución** (6hr., 371 pesos) and **Loreto** (8hr., 512 pesos); the 12:15 and 4:15pm go on to: **Tijuana** (24hr., 1718 pesos) via **Mulegé** (10hr., 640 pesos); **Santa Rosalía** (12hr., 699 pesos); **San Ignacio** (13hr., 769 pesos); **Guerrero Negro** (14hr., 903 pesos); **San Quintín** (15hr., 1296 pesos); **Ensenada** (22hr., 1473 pesos). There are additional services to **La Paz** via the east cape (7 per day 6am-6pm, 175 pesos) that stop at **Santiago** (30min., 49 pesos) and **Los Barriles** (1hr., 72 pesos).

Peninsula Ejecutivo bus stop: (☎ 142 6646) Buses depart from the *centro* at the intersection of Mijares and Juárez. Buses run to **La Paz** (3hr., 7 per day, 239 pesos) via **Cabo San Lucas** (30min., 41 pesos).

Car Rental: Thrifty Car Rental (☎ 142 2380), on Mijares at Juárez. Basic cars cost around US$50 per day. Open daily 8am-2pm and 4-6pm.

🔢 PRACTICAL INFORMATION

Bank: Banamex (☎ 142 3184 or 3219) on Mijares, 3 blocks south of the *zócalo*. Has a **24hr. ATM** and **exchanges currency.** Open M-Sa 9am-4pm.

American Express: (☎ 142 1343) on Mijares, after Paseo Finisterra. Western Union available. Open M-Sa 9am-1pm.

Laundromat: Eco Lavanderías (☎ 142 3086), on Morelos and Obregón. Wash and dry 44 pesos. Ironing 11 pesos. Open M-Sa 8am-9pm, Su 8am-3pm.

Police: (☎ 142 0361), north of town on Mex. 1 near km 33, across from the Soriana supermarket.

Red Cross: (☎ 142 0316), on Mijares adjacent to the post office.

Pharmacy: Farmacia la Moderna (☎ 142 0050), on Zaragoza between Degollado and Guerrero. **24hr. pharmacies** rotate; a schedule is available at the Centro de Salud. Open M-Sa 8am-9pm, Su 9am-2pm.

Medical Services: Centro de Salud, Doblado 39 (☎ 142 0241). Open M-F 8am-7pm. For 24hr. assistance, head to **IMSS** (☎ 142 0180), on Coronado and Hidalgo.

Fax Office: Telecomm (☎ 142 0906), next to the post office. Western Union available. Open M-F 8am-7:30pm, Sa 8am-3:30pm, Su 8am-11:30am.

Internet Access: Trazzo Digital (☎ 142 0303), on Zaragoza between Morelos and Hidalgo. Offers copying, printing, scanning, and sells a small selection of electronic goods, such as USB drives and CDs. Internet access 43 pesos per hr. Open M-F 8am-9pm, Sa 9am-7pm. MC/V.

Post Office: (☎ 142 0911) on Mijares near González, several blocks toward the beach on the right-hand side. Open M-F 8am-5pm. **Postal Code:** 23401.

▐ ACCOMMODATIONS

Room prices in San José del Cabo are high by Mexican standards, especially if you want A/C (a must in the summer). There are still a number of budget accommodations, however, most of which are near Zaragoza.

Yuca Inn, Obregón 1. No longer part of the adjacent Hotel Señor Mañana, Yuca has a friendly staff and brick-walled rooms situated around a garden, with views of the river behind the city. No A/C, although fans keep the rooms fresh. Reception 8am-4pm. Check-out noon. Singles 300 pesos; doubles 350 pesos. Cash only. ❺

Hotel Diana (☎ 142 0490), Zaragoza 30, near the *centro*. Spotless and pleasant, the Diana offers clean and tidy rooms with A/C, small bath, and TV. Check-out 1pm. Singles and doubles 350 pesos. Cash only. ❺

Hotel Youth Hostel Nuevo San José (☎ 113 5773), on Obregón and Guerrero. Great view of the Sierra de Laguna, but check to make sure your room has windows. The backyard, filled with random junk, leaves something to be desired. Singles 200 pesos, with A/C and cable TV 300 pesos. Cash only. ❸

Hotel Posada Terranova (☎ 142 0534; www.hterranova.com.mx), on Degollado and Zaragoza. Mexican art, strong A/C, a huge staff, and a good restaurant make Terranova a comfortable base in the city. Doubles 650 pesos. MC/V. ❺

▐ FOOD

Thanks to the sudden influx of wealthy tourists to Los Cabos, there are few options outside the dirt cheap or extremely high price ranges. To fill your stomach with something other than street-side tacos or filet mignon, head to the well-stocked supermarket **Aramburo Grocery,** at the corner of Guerrero and Zaragoza. (☎ 142 0188, open daily 9am-9pm.) The **municipal market** between Coronado and Castro offers a bountiful selection of fresh food, along with a somewhat smaller variety of souvenirs. (Open M-F 7am-5pm, Sa 7am-3pm, Su 9am-2pm.)

French Riviera (☎142 3350; frenchrivieraloscabos.com), on the corner of Doblado and Hidalgo. A French-style bakery with a menu in flawless English, Riviera sells flaky, buttery croissants (8 pesos), frothy cappuccinos (30 pesos), and ham-and-cheese crepes (60 pesos). Open daily 7am-10:30pm. MC/V. ❷

Taquería Erika (☎142 3928), on Doblado near Mex. 1. Packed with locals, Erika offers inexpensive tacos (10 pesos) and baked potatoes (50 pesos), prepared right in front of your eyes. Open M and F-Su 24hr., Tu-Th 9am-4am. Cash only. ❶

Correcaminos (☎158 2725), adjacent to the American Express office on Mijares. Serves a selection of reasonably priced sandwiches and salads (from 66 pesos), along with a large variety of smoothies (38 pesos). Also has Internet access (1 peso per min.). Open M-Sa 7am-9pm, Su 7am-1pm. Cash only. ❹

Habaneros (☎142 2626), at the shopping center on the corner of Mijares and Paseo Finistierra. Popular among expats, Habaneros has an English-speaking staff that serves well-prepared burgers, quesadillas, and tacos (55-69 pesos), along with delicious desserts like carrot cake (45 pesos). Open M-Sa 10am-10pm. Cash only. ❹

San José Cafe (☎142 6191), at Morelos and Zaragoza, near the *misión*. Serves a variety of salads and sandwiches on a beautiful outside terrace. Veggie sandwich (70 pesos). Pear and apple salad (60 pesos). Open M-Sa 8am-10pm. MC/V. ❹

🌀👁 BEACHES AND SIGHTS

BEACHES. Hurry—even as you read this, new resorts are popping up. **Playa Las Velas,** a stunning beach that runs past the grand hotels at the southern end of San José, can be reached via a path that runs between the Crowne Plaza and Royal Solaris Hotels on Malecón San José; it's a 30min. walk from the *centro*. The undertow makes swimming unwise, although the beach is great for sunbathing and wave-watching. **BajaXplorer Expeditions,** on the beach in front of the Crowne Plaza, runs snorkeling tours at nearby **Chileno Bay** that transport tourists to the bay using waverunners. (☎142 4082; www.bajaxplorer.com. 2½hr., US$150.) A better beach for swimming, **La Playita,** lies 5km east of town in Pueblo La Playa; drive down Juárez and follow the well-marked signs. Adjacent to the brand-new marina, La Playita is popular with local residents. Another way to visit nearby beaches is on horseback or ATV with the English-speaking guides at **MotoSol,** located in the large field on Mijares opposite González. (☎143 9310; www.atvmotosol.com. 1-2hr., US$35 per hr. Dune tours from US$60 for 2½hr. Open daily 8am-6pm.)

MISIÓN DE SAN JOSÉ. Overlooking Plaza Mijares, the mission was founded in 1730 by Father Nicolás Tamaral, a Spanish Jesuit. Only four years after its establishment, though, Tamaral was burned alive in an Indian rebellion. Above the main entrance to the church is a graphic image of three Indians dragging Tamaral to his death. The church was rebuilt in the early 20th century, after the previous building deteriorated. *(On Hidalgo between Obregón and Zaragoza.)*

ESTERO DE SAN JOSÉ. Nature-lovers should visit the Estero de San José, which is home to more than 200 species of birds. A pleasant, shaded path meanders among ducks, birds, and snakes from across the Hotel Presidente Inter-Continental to an outlet in front of the post office on Mijares. Bikes offer a convenient and enjoyable way to enjoy the estuary. *(Find the entrance by heading away from the centro on Mijares and turning left immediately before the beach; the estuary is at the end of the road on the left, near the Hotel Presidente Inter-Continental. It can also be accessed via a small road across from the post office. Tio Sports rents mountain bikes across from the Inter-Continental for US$6 per hr. ☎143 339; www.tiosports.com. Open daily from 8:30am-7pm.)*

BAJA CALIFORNIA

CACTIMUNDO. Established in 2002, Cactimundo already offers an astounding variety of 11,800 densely planted cacti native to Mexico, Argentina, Peru, and Madagascar. The garden claims that it contains "Latin America's biggest collection of cacti and succulents," although anybody who ventures out of town will know that there are a lot of cacti out there too. *(On Mijares, between the American Express office and the beach. Open daily 8am-6pm. 30 pesos.)*

 NIGHTLIFE

San José del Cabo can't compete with wild San Lucas, but a good time isn't hard to find—just kick back, relax, and don't expect conga lines or table dancing.

Shooters (☎ 146 9900), above the Tulip Tree restaurant just off Mijares at Doblado. Free Wi-Fi and laptop-toting patrons make this the most sophisticated locale on the night-time scene, and low drink prices should help keep you and your hardware from over-heating. Enjoy cheap beer (10 pesos before 6pm daily) and 2-for-1 drinks daily before 6pm on a rooftop terrace. Open M and W-Su 11am-midnight.

Escala (☎ 142 5155), on Mijares at Juárez, across from Cactus Jack's. Features karaoke and pool, along with dancing on the weekends. Drink specials may increase your propensity for crooning on the mic. W night beer 15 pesos, Th night 2-for-1 rum. Open M-Sa 10am-4am, Su 7pm-4am.

Cactus Jack's (☎ 142 5601), on Mijares at Juárez. Good food, cheap beer, pool tables—enough said. On W and Th, Pacífico and Corona is 15 pesos all night long. Open M and W 8:30pm-2am, Th and Su 8:30pm-3am, F-Sa 8:30pm-4am.

DAYTRIPS FROM SAN JOSÉ DEL CABO

LOS BARRILES

Águila Malecón "Vía Larga" buses from La Paz to San José del Cabo and Cabo San Lucas (5 per day 10am-5:30pm) stop in Los Barriles (2hr., 69 pesos). A number of Águila/ABC buses heading to La Paz from San José also stop in Los Barriles (1hr., 7 per day 6am-6pm, 72 pesos).

Aficionados insist that windsurfing at the small town of Los Barriles is the best in Baja. Attracted by the claim, large numbers of Americans have moved here in their RVs to surf March through November when the wind is strong, and to fish during the rest of the year. An astounding number of hulking SUVs with California license plates roll down the town's dusty main street, 20 de Noviembre, where more English is spoken than Spanish. The most popular dive spots are near **Cabo Pulmo** and **Los Frailes,** south of Los Barriles, separated by secluded beaches and coves. Aside from diving, San José is a designated fishing zone, as fishing on much of the east cape is prohibited. Off Cabo Pulmo, eight fingers of a living coral reef—thought to be 25,000 years old and one of only three in North America—host hundreds of species of fish, crustaceans, and other creatures, including hammerhead sharks.

SANTIAGO

Santiago is accessible via the same buses that go to Los Barriles, although buses drop visitors about 2km outside of town on Mex. 1.

Rich and famous Americans, such as Dwight Eisenhower and Bing Cosby, used to frequent little Santiago (pop. 4500) to hunt doves. Today, though, the town's largest flock of doves is probably at its remarkable **Parque Zoológico.** Established in 1983, the zoo features a very fat and extremely long python, a Bengal tiger, two lions, an adorable family of raccoons, a trio of gray foxes, and an assortment of other native and non-native animals. Basking under the Baja sun, many of these animals are hungry for attention (or maybe for food) and stare longingly when visitors approach their barred cages. (To reach the zoo, take Misoneros until it ends, turn right onto Guadalupe Victoria, and take a left on Mujica. Open daily 7am-5pm. Free.) In order to visit another of Santiago's attractions, the nearby **hot springs** in **Chorro,** continue past the zoo for 11km on a dirt road until you arrive at the town of **Agua Caliente.** Bear right at the basketball courts and follow this road, keeping to the right at the forks. After 5km, the smell of sulfur welcomes you to the tranquility of the springs. During high season, the springs are diverted into luxurious tubs.

Santiago also boasts the **Palomar Restaurant ❺,** on Misoneros, which serves old-style Mexican food, such as a sea bass dish for 114 pesos. The Palomar also doubles as a hotel, where rooms center around a grove of fruit trees; Sergio can direct visitors to a nearby waterfall. (☎ 130 2019. Open M-Sa 11am-7:30pm. Doubles 450 pesos.) The **police** is located on Independencia, up the hill from the *zócalo* (☎ 130 2028). The **Centro de Salud** is located across from the Mission of Santiago de los Cabos church. (☎ 130 2057. Open M-F 8:30am-2:30pm.)

NORTHWEST MEXICO

Saddle up and make sure you've got that grit in your guts and that spit in your eye, because the Northwest's rugged terrain requires a lot of stamina. Home to aggressive border towns, isolated fishing villages, and some of the most impossibly beautiful scenery in the entire world, this least-touristed corner of Mexico is an area of contrast, extremity, and duress. It's a long trip from the heavy industry and countless shanty towns of the Chihuahuan Desert to the perfect climate and towering waves of the Sea of Cortés. For many, the region serves as an introduction to the country: debaucherous tequila nights, oversized *sombreros*, pack animals, and triple-digit temperatures. As a Mexican rule, things calm down the farther south you go. As time slows to a virtual standstill in the dusty *pueblos*—miles from nowhere—listen to flies buzz, and watch *vaqueros* clad in tight jeans swaggering about. Despite the lack of a tourism infrastructure, the Northwest can be extremely rewarding. Just be ready, and bring a pair of cowboy boots and a *sombrero* of your own—the *noroeste* sun is merciless.

The Sierra Madre Occidental rips through the heart of Northwest Mexico, pushing back the desert and the sandstorms for almost half of the country's length. In this range, one will find Mexico's most beautiful natural wonder—the canyon system known as Las Barrancas del Cobre (Copper Canyon). The chasms stretch down from snow-capped peaks and pines to sub-tropical river valleys and mango trees. Backpackers from all over the world are carted in by the CHEPE train, an engineering marvel often considered the greatest locomotive ride in the entire world. To the far west, the states of **Sonora** and **Sinaloa** open up to endless beach stretches along the Sea of Cortés, where the weather is calm, the locals friendly, and the opportunities limited only by your wallet and watch. Sailing, deep sea fishing, and ecotourism are popular all along the coast.

Although the heat dismays many prospective visitors, intrepid travelers know the two arid states of **Chihuahua** and **Durango,** to the east, are rich in folklore and true-grit adventure. It was from this area that Pancho Villa waged his weary war against the *caudillos* of the Revolution, and in some places he is still worshipped as a Mexican messiah.

Farther south towards the country's heart are **Aguascalientes** and **Zacatecas,** bastions of Mexican patriotism. These major cities—an art lover's dream—remain in 16th-century condition, with towering basilicas, dozens of museums, ornate garden fountains, and even Roman-style aqueducts. The road formerly known as "The Silver Trail" cuts through this region, leading to the riches and wonders of the D.F. and Mexico's core.

HIGHLIGHTS OF NORTHWEST MEXICO

VENTURE into **Copper Canyon** (p. 264), North America's deepest canyon system and home to reclusive Tarahumara natives.

ZIP on cable cars over some of the world's best preserved colonial architecture in 16th-century **Zacatecas** (p. 287).

BREATHE deeply before plunging into the warm waters of **San Carlos** (p. 238)—the scuba diving, spear fishing, and extreme sports adrenaline center of the Sea of Cortés.

TWIRL your fake mustaches as you take photos on the American Western film sets in **Durango** (p. 294).

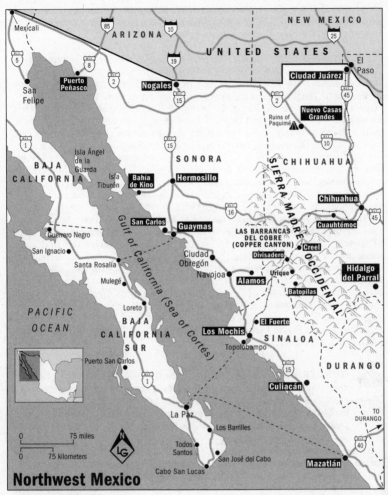

Northwest Mexico

SONORA

NOGALES ☎ 631

An aggressive, restless energy pumps through Nogales (pop. 350,000), dissuading travelers from staying longer than absolutely necessary. Walk toward the border during the day and you can feel tensions increase, as the streets become awash with gaudy souvenir shops all vying for the daytripper's dollar. The first block of the city welcomes many each day, only to see the vast majority move off in a matter of hours or even minutes. It's hard to imagine why anyone would rest their head here: cheaper, cleaner, and safer accommodations can be found in Nogales, AZ and farther down the highway in Hermosillo. Nogales lacks the pleasant parks and *zócalos* that characterize many Mexican cities, and a swelling population combined with competition for dollars have raised crime levels. On weekends, American teenagers often come down to booze it up in the *cantinas* lining Obregón.

⬛ TRANSPORTATION. Nogales can be reached by foot or by car by simply crossing the Arizona border via US 19/Mex. 15. The towns of Nogales, AZ and Nogales, Sonora are divided by an ugly iron fence. Daily crossing fees change depending on the season (or the guards), but are never more than a few dollars. Expect long lines on both sides of the border on weekends. The sleek, modern **bus terminal** (☎313 1603, 5401, or 1703) on Carretera Internacional, 4.5km south of the *centro*, has a **pharmacy** (open 7am-11pm), **luggage storage** (5 pesos per hr.), and call center with **fax**, **copy** and **Internet** facilities (20 pesos per hr.) Next to the pharmacy is the **taxi** kiosk (80 pesos to the *centro*). If you're not in a hurry, white buses marked "Central Camionera" do the journey (6 pesos) until around 7pm. For the return journey, buses line up along López Mateos between Campillo and Ochoa; if in doubt, ask for the bus to "el Central." You can also catch it at any of the blue stops along López Mateos, which merges with Obregón on its way south.

TBA, Estrellas del Pacífico, and **Transportes Norte de Sonora** leave the main station for: **Mexico City** (34hr., 7 per day, 1390 pesos); **Puerto Peñasco** (7hr., 4pm, 270 pesos); **Tijuana** (12hr.; 10am, 1, 7, 8:30pm; 385 pesos) via **San Luis** (8hr.) and **Mexicali** (9hr.); and **Guadalajara** (26hr., 10 per day, 1097 pesos) via **Hermosillo** (4hr.), **Obregón** (8hr.), **Los Mochis** (11hr.), **Culiacán** (15hr.), **Mazatlán** (18hr.), and **Tepic** (22hr.). The last route down the west coast of Sonora is also well served by a number of carriers operating from stations just up the road toward Nogales, such as **Estrellas de Pacífico, Tufesa** (which offers discounts of 25% to students and 50% to those over 60 and children 2-8) and **TBA** (which also offers a 3pm service to **Puerto Peñasco;** 5hr.). You can stock up on provisions for the journey at **Oxxo,** a 24hr. supermarket next to TBA.

> **BORDER CROSSING.** If you plan to travel beyond Nogales, obtain a **tourist card** (US$20; see **Tourist Cards,** p. 11) at the border and have your passport on hand. It's much simpler to get the card here than farther south. After you walk across the border through the arched crossing complex, turn right into the **immigration center,** the last door in the first building on the right.

If you're heading north into Arizona, Greyhound's partner **Crucero** has buses to **Tucson** (1 hr., 8 per day, US$8), though you'll probably find it more convenient to walk across the border, where a Greyhound terminal has departures on the same route (midnight, 3:45, 4:45, 7:15, 8:45am, 1:30, 5:30, 7:45pm). Crucero buses also pass through Nogales on their way to Hermosillo and Ciudad Obregón.

⬛⬛ ORIENTATION AND PRACTICAL INFORMATION. Nogales's small area of interest is stuck between chaotic hillside *barrios*, but the grid of the *primer cuadro* area is fairly easy to navigate. Calle Internacional is the first of the streets running east to west, parallel to the corrugated iron fence which marks the *frontera*. If you come across the border on foot, you'll find yourself walking from north to south on Pesquiera; west of this, Juárez (home to the main concentration of budget hotels), Morelos (a narrow alley for pedestrians and stallholders only), Obregón (the main tourist drag), Hidalgo, and Ingenieros. If you come from Arizona by car, you'll be on López Mateos, which runs at a diagonal angle to the north-south avenues and cuts into the grid, merging with Juárez, Morelos, and, eventually, Obregón.

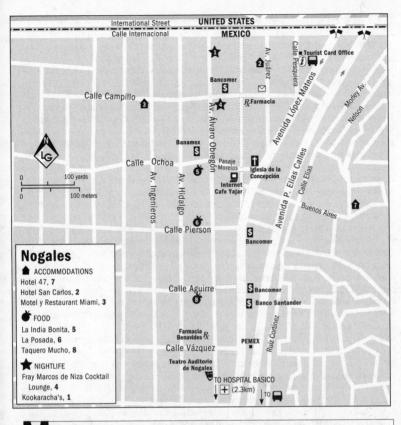

Nogales

🏠 ACCOMMODATIONS
Hotel 47, **7**
Hotel San Carlos, **2**
Motel y Restaurant Miami, **3**

🍅 FOOD
La India Bonita, **5**
La Posada, **6**
Taquero Mucho, **8**

⭐ NIGHTLIFE
Fray Marcos de Niza Cocktail
Lounge, **4**
Kookaracha's, **1**

❗ BARRIO SAVVY. The tourist office cautions that the barrios on both sides of the *primer cuadro* are unsafe, and tourists should remain in the *centro*.

The **Tourist Office** is next to the immigration center, to your left walking in from the US, on the corner of López Mateos and Campillo. The staff is helpful, albeit somewhat surprised if you express any interest in Nogales itself. (☎312 0666. Open W-M 9am-1pm and 2-6pm.) The *primer cuadro* contains several **banks,** which line López Mateos and Obregón. All **exchange currency** and traveler's checks and have **24hr. ATMs.** There is a **Banamex** on Ochoa between Hidalgo and Obregón. (☎312 5505. Open M-F 8:30am-2pm and 4-6:30pm.) Other services include: **emergency** ☎060; **Police** (☎312 1104) at González and Leal; **Red Cross,** at Elías Calles and Providencia (☎312 5808; open 24hr.); **Hospital Básico,** about 3km south of the border on Obregón. (☎313 0794; open 24hr.); a **24hr. Pharmacy, Comercial 3 en 1 Farmacia,** Campillo 73 at Morelos. (☎312 5503; doubles as a liquor store); **Internet** access at **Yajar,** upstairs on the corner of Morelos and Ochoa. (Internet access 20 pesos per hr.; printers also available), and at a bus station (20 pesos per hour); **Telecomm,** has **fax** services above the post office, and the communications booth in the central bus station; and the **post office,** Juárez 52 (☎312 1247; open M-F 8am-4pm, Sa 8am-noon). **Postal Code:** 84000.

▐ ▌ ACCOMMODATIONS AND FOOD. Nogales's position on the border guarantees loads of visitors and high-prices. The most obvious concentration of "budget" hotels is near the border crossing on Juárez; rooms prices often depend on the number of people. **Hotel San Carlos ❺**, Juárez 22 (☎312 1346 or 1409; fax 312 1557), between Internacional and Campillo, rents spacious, clean rooms with glittery-blue mattresses, A/C, cable TV, and phones. Mingle with the ever-present locals watching TV in the lobby. (Reservations recommended. Singles 325-375 pesos; doubles 375-440 pesos. MC/V.) To arrive at the American-owned **Motel y Restaurant Miami ❺**, Ingenieros at Campillo, turn right onto Campillo from the border crossing, cross Juárez, and walk another four short blocks. The large blue-and-white tiled rooms have clean baths, TVs, telephones, and fans. Rooms on the upper floors overlook the town, border fence, and beyond. (☎312 5450. Key deposit 100 pesos. Singles 350 pesos; doubles 380 pesos; each additional person 80 pesos. Cash only.) Visible from the highway, **Hotel 47 ❺**, 47 Buenos Aires, off of Elías Calles, offers spacious rooms with big TVs and windows that provide scenic views of the industrial wonderland that is Nogales. (☎312 7489. Singles 300 pesos; doubles 400 pesos. Open daily 6am to noon. Cash only.)

Nogales is home to several high-priced restaurants catering to daytrippers from the US. If tourist pricing is driving you crazy, head for the **plaza** on López Mateos at Ochoa, where fruits and *tortas*, sold by vendors as rock-bottom prices, entice your taste buds. For a truly economical meal, look no further than the tiny makeshift counters a few steps off Obregón, where local families offer excellent traditional *antojitos* (5-20 pesos). Salty Mexican combos are prepared *para llevar* (to go) at **La India Bonita ❸**, on the corner of Obregón and Ochoa. Try the *gorditas de pollo*, with a side order of *frijoles and arróz* (rice and beans) 35 pesos. (Open daily 24 hr. Cash only.) A small family-run joint, **Taquero Mucho ❸**, 202 Aguirre, off of Obregón, is often populated by gringos chuckling over the clever name while munching on *huevos rancheros*. (Entrees 35-45 pesos. Opening and closing hours at the whim of the owner. Cash only.) **La Posada Restaurante ❹**, Pierson 116, west of Obregón, is a family-run operation, with Rodolfo Monroy greeting the (predominantly male) local regulars who come here for the hearty breakfasts. The dining room is colorfully decorated with Mexican art and handicrafts, and the tart and tasty *huevos con nopales* (prickly pears) are worth the 45 pesos. (☎312 0439. Desserts 25 pesos. Open daily 7:30pm-10pm. Cash only.)

◉ ♫ NIGHTLIFE AND ENTERTAINMENT. Despite the rather half-hearted attempts of the tourist bureau to pass off the statue of Juárez, the industrial park, and even the border crossing itself as attractions, there isn't much in the way of museums or other cultural excitement in Nogales. Most of the Arizonans who come over for the day do so in search of bargain prices on pharmaceuticals and Mexican trinkets, either in the crowded area around Obregón and Morelos, or in the El Greco building on the corner of Obregón and Pierson. Merchandise is priced in anticipation of haggling, so confidence and knowledge of the goods can get you great deals. Shops farther from the border on Obregón are less exclusively aimed at the tourist crowd. If earthenware curios don't set your heart aflame, **Cinemas Gemelos**, Obregón 368 (☎312 5002), between González and Torres, shows recent American films dubbed or subtitled in Spanish (40 pesos). For those seeking a bit of culture, the spacious, modern **Teatro Auditorio de Nogales**, Obregón 286 (☎312 4180), between Vázquez and González, seats just under 1000 and stages theater, music, and dance. Call or visit for show times and prices; the calendar is posted on the door.

If tequila is a must, Nogales's nightlife may have something to offer. Right after lunch, the bars on Obregón open their doors to a mix of locals and tourists by 10pm on weekends. The most popular hang-out (and the most Amero-centric) is

Kookaracha's, Obregón 1. Dance the night away and down tequila shots (US$1), or just chill with a *cerveza* (US$2) on the balcony overlooking the border and the fountain in the Roach's techno-colored courtyard. (☎312 4773. Cover US$10-15. Open W and F-Sa nights.) Kick-back types enjoy mixed drinks and well-dressed company at **Fray Marcos de Niza Cocktail Lounge**, at Obregón and Campillo. (☎312 1112. Beer 20 pesos.Open daily 11am-1am.)

PUERTO PEÑASCO   ☎638

Just over 60 mi. from the border and 212 mi. from Phoenix and Tucson, Puerto Peñasco (pop. 70,000), once a small fishing village, has taken on a new identity as "Arizona's beach." Americans are buying Miami-beach style condos in droves, dollars are preferred to pesos, and the English translation of the city's name, "Rocky Point," is used just as often as Puerto Peñasco. The American invasion is unsurprising considering the city has excellent beaches and is so close to the US. Puerto Peñasco's new residents seem to have established a small Arizonan settlement here, instead of actually adapting to Mexican culture. Long-time Puerto Peñasco residents don't seem to mind so far, although Americans have started taking over much of the land near the beaches, increasingly forcing Mexicans to the town's less-scenic inner streets.

▐ TRANSPORTATION

Puerto Peñasco's main interstate bus terminal is on Constitución, a block away from its intersection with Juárez. **Autotransportes de Baja California** (☎383 1999) goes to **Tijuana** (8hr., 8 per day 1am-11pm, 392 pesos) via **San Luis Río Colorado** (3hr., 218 pesos) and **Mexicali** (5hr., 267 pesos). For travel within Sonora, go to the **Albatros Autobuses bus station** (☎388 0888), several blocks farther out along Juárez past the baseball stadium and across from Hotel Gloria del Mar. Buses go to **Hermosillo** (7hr., 14 per day 1am-12am, 180 pesos) and **Nogales** (5hr., 1:45am-4pm, 205 pesos). **Transporte Mota's Place** (☎383 3640), at the intersection of Calle 24 and Juárez, offers shuttle service to **Phoenix, AZ** (4hr., 5 per day 7:15am-6:30pm, US$35).

▚ ▐ ORIENTATION AND PRACTICAL INFORMATION

Puerto Peñasco is a small town, but its visitor attractions are surprisingly and exhaustingly spread out. It's almost impossible (especially in the blaring sun) to walk from one end of town to the other. Drivers should look carefully at a map before heading out since street signs are often missing or bleached out by the sun.

The labyrinthine **Old Port** area is the smallest and oldest part of town, in Peñasco's southwest corner. On the other side of the harbor is the most concentrated tourist drag, **Calle 13** or **Armada Nacional**, leading out toward **Playa Hermosa**. To the north and east of Calle 13 is the gridded main body of town and the area least frequented by foreigners. Farther along the coast to the east, the exclusive enclave of **Las Conchas** continues to grow. Tying most of these loose ends together is **Benito Juárez** (Mex. 8), which passes through a *centro* of sorts at the intersection with Fremont. South of here the road splits: the branch called **Campeche** drops down towards **Playa Miramar,** a popular spring break spot, while **Juárez** swings round to the west and loops back on itself to lasso the Old Port, briefly becoming the seafront *malecón* in the process.

Tourist Office: Juárez 320 (☎383 6122), at Calle 12 on the shopping strip. Open M-F 9am-4pm.

Banks: Bancomer (☎383 2430), on Juárez and Estrella. *Exchanges currency and traveler's checks.* Open M-F 8:30am-4pm, Sa 9am-2pm. **Banamex** (☎383 4380), on

*Juárez just south of Fremont, provides the same services. Open M-F 9am-4pm, Sa 10am-2pm. Both have **24hr.** ATMs.*

Book Exchange: Rocky Point Times office, 124 Pino Suárez (☎383 6325), off Calle 13.

Laundromat: Lavamática Peñasco (☎*383 6170*), *on Constitución across from Hotel Paraíso del Desierto. Self-service medium wash 25 pesos. 30min. dry 30 pesos. Open M-Sa 8am-8pm, Su 9am-3pm.*

Emergency: ☎060.

Police: (☎383 2626), at Fremont and Juárez.

Red Cross: (☎383 2266 or 065), at Fremont and Chiapas.

Pharmacy: Farmacia La Campana, in the Old Port, between the *malecón* and Estrella. Open M-F 9am-8pm, Sa 9am-8pm, Su 9am-4pm.

Hospital: Hospital Municipal (☎*383 2110*), *Morúa and Juárez.*

Fax Office: Telecomm (☎383 2782), in the same building as the post office. Open M-F 8am-2pm, Sa 8am-3pm, Su 8am-11am.

Internet Access: Ciber Chat (☎*383 5286*), *in the Old Port on Av. 1a de Junio. 10 pesos per hr. Open daily 9am-5pm.*

Post Office: (☎383 2350), hidden around a corner on Chiapas, off Fremont, 2 blocks east of Juárez. Open M-F 8am-3pm. **Postal Code:** 83550.

▌ ACCOMMODATIONS AND CAMPING

As Puerto Peñasco becomes an increasingly popular vacation spot for upper-class Arizonans, budget accommodations are becoming harder to find. Rates rise at many hotels during weekends and American holidays. Camping is permitted northwest of the Playa Boruta Resort on Sandy Beach all the way down to La Choya. Camping at trailer parks is safer, and sleeping on the beach is not recommended unless you're with a large group.

▨ **Posada La Roca,** Primero de Junio 2 (☎383 3199), at the *malecón.* In the middle of the Old Port, this family-run hotel was a favorite of the famous bootlegger Al Capone during prohibition. Rooms with TV and strong A/C. Free Wi-Fi. Rooms US$30, with bath US$40. Cash only. ❺

Motel Alexander, Emiliano Zapata 89 (☎383 3749), just off Calle 13, 3 blocks from the railway crossing. Tidy rooms with A/C and cable TV. Singles 400 pesos; doubles 500 pesos. MC/V. ❺

Motel Playa Azul (☎383 6296), at Calle 13 and Suárez, about 2 blocks from Playa Hermosa. Clean rooms with A/C and cable TV. Singles 400 pesos; doubles 500 pesos. Prices rise 100 pesos on weekends. ❺

Hotel Linda Vista (☎383 1629), on Juárez and Del Agua, on the way to the Old Port. Clean, brightly painted rooms with A/C and cable TV. Rooms 350 pesos. Cash only. ❺

Playa de Oro (☎383 2668; www.playadeoro-rv.com), on Matamoros at Sinaloa, right on Playa Miramar. A huge RV park with 325 spaces. Hook-ups include electricity, satellite TV, and water. Internet, laundry, and movie rental in the office. Regular space US$19, beachfront space US$25. Camping is also allowed. Free Wi-Fi. MC/V. ❸

▌ FOOD

Most food in Puerto Peñasco is expensive, although there are a number of cheaper, American-style cafes. Taco stands line Calle 13. **Super Ley** is a huge supermarket on Av. Constitución between Aldama and Cortinez. (Open daily 7am-9pm.)

Puerto Peñasco

▲▲ 🏕️ ACCOMMODATIONS
Hotel Linda Vista, **8**
Motel Alexander, **2**
Motel Playa Azul, **1**
Playa de Oro RV Park, **12**
Posada La Roca, **6**
🍎 FOOD
Balboa's, **5**
La Curva, **3**
Max's Cafe, **4**
MOAB, **10**
CAFES
Coffee's Haus, **9**
Santana's Coffee, **7**
★ NIGHTLIFE
Manny's Beach Club, **13**
The Pink Cadillac, **11**

Santana's Coffee, on Pescadores in the Old Port, 2 blocks southeast of the church. A cafe with a cool, dark atmosphere and a green logo that screams Starbucks, although the figure in the middle is actually Pancho Villa. Lunch combos with sandwich, drink, and chips US$5. Open M-F 7am-3pm and 7-11pm, Sa-Su 7am-5pm. Cash only. ❸

Coffee's Haus, 216 Juárez (☎388 1065; www.coffeeshaus.com), on the way to the Old Port. A small restaurant that serves beautifully presented and superb-tasting breakfast and lunch dishes. Club sandwich 55 pesos. Banana waffles with sumptuous chocolate sauce 50 pesos. Open Tu-Sa 7:30am-4pm, Su 7:30am-2pm. Cash only. ❹

Max's Cafe (☎383 1011), across from the Peñasco del Sol hotel. A favorite stop near Playa Hermosa, Max's has a large selection of sandwiches (US$6) and omelettes (US$6.50). The menu changes (and the prices increase) at night. 10min. free Internet access for customers. Free Wi-Fi. Open daily 7:30am-10pm. Cash only. ❹

MOAB (☎388 0753; www.motherofallburgers.com), on Matamoros in the Mirador, near Playa Miramar. Delicious 8 oz. burgers US$5.50. For big eaters, try the 12oz. "Mutha" burger (US$8.10). Casual, modern atmosphere. Open daily 11am-9pm. Cash only. ❹

La Curva Bar/Restaurant (☎383 3470), on Kino and Calle 13. Dishes are pricey but you can get a small combination platter with either enchiladas, tacos, *taco rellenos,* or *tamales* with rice and black beans for 50 pesos. Open M-F 7:30am-9:30pm, Sa-Su 7:30am-10:30pm. MC/V. ❹

NORTHWEST MEXICO

Balboa's (☎ 383 5155), at the Naval Marina, on the water off Calle 13. On the water, Balboa's serves a well-priced selection of Mexican dishes, including quesadillas (45 pesos) and chicken *milanesa* (65 pesos). Open M-Tu and Th-Su 7am-9pm. MC/V. ❸

👁 SIGHTS

INTERCULTURAL CENTER FOR THE STUDY OF DESERTS AND OCEANS (CEDO). Super-active CEDO is working to conserve Puerto Peñasco's estuaries from short-sighted, condo-building developers and to educate tourists and schoolchildren about the wonders of the Sea of Cortés and the surrounding desert. The center provides lab space and lodging for researchers trying to learn as much as possible about the local environment. CEDO has a visitor center (constructed partly out of cans and tires) with a gift shop, which stocks a number of books on the flora and fauna of Baja California and Arizona. Researchers also offer **bi-weekly talks** in English on Puerto Peñasco's wildlife, during which they can answer almost any nature-related question you might have (Tu 2pm, Sa 4pm. Free). In addition, CEDO sponsors a number of trips to nearby dunes, estuaries, and tidepools and allows tourists to participate in regular surveys of animals and plants. Call ahead for trip times and reservations. *(CEDO is located in Las Conchas, 7km from the centro. Drive down Fremont, turn south towards Las Conchas, and continue through the guard gate to the Las Conchas development. After 3km, CEDO will be on the right side of the road. ☎ 382 0113, from the US 520-320-5473; www.cedointercultural.org. Open M-Sa 9am-5pm, Su 10am-2pm.)*

CENTER FOR TECHNOLOGICAL SEA STUDIES (CETMAR) AQUARIUM. CET-MAR operates a small, one-room aquarium with flounder, sergeant majors, sea horses, sea turtles, and a rambunctious sea lion named Arthur. Unfortunately, the aquarium is poorly maintained: tanks are dirty and poorly lit. While employees nonchalantly watch television, visitors prod the sea turtles and poke their hands through the bars that surround Arthur's home. CETMAR does provide a rare opportunity to see these creatures up close, but it's debatable whether tourists should reward CETMAR's poor upkeep of the aquarium with the admission fee. *(CETMAR is 4km from the centro on Las Conchas. Take Fremont and turn south towards Las Conchas. The aquarium is on the right side of the road. ☎ 382 0010. Open M-F 10am-3pm, Sa-Su 10am-6pm. US$3, children US$1.)*

🏖 🎣 BEACHES AND WATERSPORTS

BEACHES. Puerto Peñasco's biggest attractions are its many beaches with the warm, turquoise water characteristic of the Sea of Cortés. **Sandy Beach** and **Playa Hermosa** are the best choices for swimming, although Playa Hermosa has been taken over by souvenir and taco vendors. To reach Sandy Beach, head north on Encinas or Juárez until the intersection with Camino a Bahía Choya (2km north of Fremont). Turn left and follow the souvenir shops and bars until you see signs that say "To Sandy Beach." To get to Playa Hermosa, turn west on Calle 13 from Juárez; the beach is five to six blocks straight ahead, but you'll have to veer right around the wall of luxury hotels. The beaches around Miramar and Las Conchas, at the southern end of town, are less crowded and better for snorkeling but also rockier, rougher, and less suited to swimming. True to its name, Las Conchas also has lots of shells. Las Conchas is almost entirely private, so it's difficult to access. Reach the beach through the CETMAR parking lot (p. 228). Head south on Juárez, turn left on Fremont after Bancomer, take a right onto Camino a las Conchas, and follow the rock-slab road for 3km; turn at the signs for CETMAR. Walk straight through the opening in the parking lot gate to the beach. To reach Playa Miramar, head south on Juárez and take a left onto Campeche near the Benito Juárez monument. Continue uphill for three blocks; Playa Miramar is straight ahead.

DIVING AND SNORKELING EXCURSIONS. Several companies take tourists on snorkeling and diving excursions. **Sun n' Fun,** a friendly and well-respected American-run dive shop on Juárez at the entrance to the Old Port, charters boats for diving, snorkeling, and fishing trips (☎383 5450 or 888 381 7720; www.sunandfundivers.com. Open M-Th 8am-6pm, F-Sa 8am-7pm, Su 8am-5pm.) **Santiago's Ocean Services** (☎383 5834; www.santiagosoceanservices.com), south of Keno's Market off Calle 13 near the Naval Marina, offers a similar selection of trips, including fishing trips (US$75 per person), snorkeling trips to nearby Bird Island (US$99 per person, including lunch), and clamming trips to Cholla Bay (2½hr., US$10 per person). Call ahead to both companies for reservations.

🎵 🎭 ENTERTAINMENT AND NIGHTLIFE

Puerto Peñasco was once a favorite spring break destination for US college students, although the town has tried to shed that image, targeting condo-seeking baby boomers instead. At night, the beautiful *malecón* in the Old Port fills with locals and tourists who stop by to watch the sun set over the sea and nearby mountains and admire how dramatically the water level changes with the tides. Nightlife in Puerto Peñasco still livens up in the spring, although it slows down significantly during much of the rest of the year. Calle 13, Campeche, and the *malecón* all host a number of bars, pool halls, and red light establishments. During the week, you may have to settle for exchanging fishing stories with US retirees. The most popular spring break spots are on Playa Miramar. **Manny's Beach Club,** overlooking Playa Miramar, is a favorite among the spring break crowd for chilling by day and partying by night. (☎383 3605. Beer US$3. Margaritas US$3.50. Open M-Th and Su 7am-11pm, F-Sa 7am-3am.) On the same stretch of road just two blocks down, **The Pink Cadillac** is a huge dance club that features foam parties and plays home to weekend revelers, although it shuts down during July and August. (☎383 5880. Beer 18 pesos. Open Th-Su 9pm-late.)

If you don't like the club scene, you could head to the other end of town and catch the **Tiburones,** Peñasco's baseball team, in action. The stadium is on your right as you go up Juárez away from the town center at Calle 25. (Season runs Apr.-Aug./Sept. Games F-Su 8pm. Tickets 30 pesos.)

🔝 DAYTRIP FROM PUERTO PEÑASCO

▨ EL PINACATE VOLCANIC RESERVE

Guides are strongly recommended. For information about tours, ask at the tourist office or call CEDO, which offers day-long tours of the area (p. 228). If you do decide to go it alone, 4WD high-clearance vehicles with partially deflated tires are a must, as are a shovel, a spare tire, a compass, firewood, and plenty of water. Camping is permitted, although spaces are limited and reservations are not taken. Additionally, during much of the year, the temperature makes camping very unpleasant. The ideal time to visit is Nov.-Mar., when temperatures range 15-32°C (59-90°F), as opposed to summer months, when the daytime temperatures can often exceed 47°C (116°F).

Forty-eight kilometers north of Puerto Peñasco on Mex. 8 lies El Pinacate volcanic preserve, one of the largest and most spectacular of its kind in the world. Created in June 1993 to limit rock excavation and protect endangered species, El Pinacate encompasses more than 16,000 sq. km and extends from the Sea of Cortés to the

Arizona border, where it becomes the Cabeza Prieta National Wildlife Refuge and the Organ Pipe National Monument. The landscape incudes vast dunes and nine huge volcanic craters, the most spectacular of which, **El Elegante**, is 1600m across and 250m deep. There's an almost lunar strangeness to the volcanic desert, which is pockmarked with around 400 cinder cones. Visitors are required to register at the Visitors' Center, the group of orange-roofed buildings on the left of Mex. 8 coming from Puerto Peñasco. The staff has maps of the reserve, printed interpretative guides to the major trails, and safety information regarding hazards. There are also videos and exhibits. (Open M-F 9am-5pm.)

HERMOSILLO ☎ 662

Hermosillo (pop. 800,000) is not a typical border town. Businessmen, local families, and intrepid travelers spend their time in "La Ciudad del Sol" chowing on *carne asada* (grilled beef) and *coyotas* (traditional brown sugar pastries), shopping in the dusty *centro*, partying it up with university students, and watching Mexico's winningest baseball team: Los Naranjeros. Summertime temperatures creep up to 120°F in this 120 year-old state capital; luckily, *hermosillenses* have spent the last few years cooling down their city by adding shade trees and water parks, while simultaneously building it up to match their progressive state motto *¡Vamos por Soluciones!*

▐ TRANSPORTATION

Flights: Gen. Pesqueira García Airport (HMO; ☎261 0008), 10km west of town on Transversal toward Bahía Kino. From the bus station, take a small red bus (4 pesos) or a taxi (around 70 pesos). **Aeroméxico** (☎218 0612) goes to **Guadalajara** (2hr., 4 per day), **Mexico City** (2½hr., 8 per day), and **Tijuana** (1hr., 2 per day). **AeroCalifornia** (☎260 2555) goes to **La Paz** (1hr., 1 per day) or **Los Angeles, CA** (1½hr., 1 per day).

Buses: 2km east of the *centro* on Encinas. To get from the station to town, catch a "Centro" bus (every 10min. 5am-8pm, 6 pesos). By **taxi**, you must pre-pay by purchasing a *boleto* for your destination. A trip to the *centro* costs around 70 pesos and takes 10min. To get to the station from the *centro*, wait for a bus at Elías Calles and Matamoros. **Transportes Norte de Sonora** (☎217 1522) goes to: **Chihuahua** (12hr., 540 pesos); **Ciudad Juárez** (11hr., daily 6:30pm, 530 pesos); **Mazatlán** (12hr., 464 pesos); **Mexico City** (31hr., 1127 pesos). **Élite** (☎213 0610) sends buses every hr. to nearby cities including **Caborca** (4hr., 46 pesos), **Guaymas** (2hr., 60 pesos), and **Nogales** (3½hr., 120 pesos).

Car Rental: Budget, Garmendía 46 (☎214 3033), at Tamaulipas. Open M-F 8am-6pm, Sa-Su 8am-3pm. **Hertz,** Blvr. Morales 341 (☎260 1044). Open M-F 8am-6pm, Sa-Su 8am-3pm.

▐ ▐ ORIENTATION AND PRACTICAL INFORMATION

Hermosillo lies 276km south of the border on **Mex. 15**, the main highway connecting the western US and central Mexico. Most of the activity in Hermosillo occurs within the *centro* southeast of the university, the area bordered by **Rosales** on the west, **Juárez** on the east, **Serdán** on the south, and **Encinas Johnson** on the north. Visitors should take note—Hermosillo summers are scorching. In July and August, temperatures may soar as high as 47°C (116.6°F). **Let's Go recommends visitors drink a lot of water.** Staying well hydrated is important, even though most buildings in the *centro* have A/C.

Tourist Office: (☎217 0060, from the US 800-476-6672; www.sonoraturismo.gob.mx), on the 3rd fl. of **Centro de Gobierno** on the corner of Cultura and Comonfort. Walk

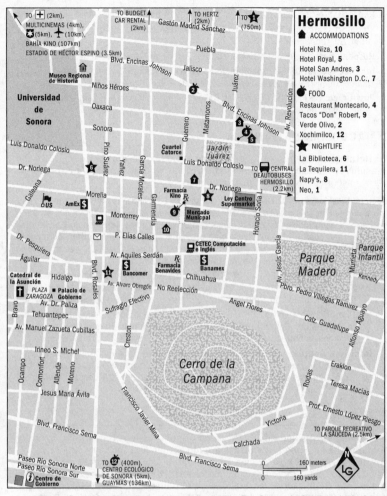

Hermosillo

⌂ ACCOMMODATIONS

Hotel Niza, **10**
Hotel Royal, **5**
Hotel San Andres, **3**
Hotel Washington D.C., **7**

🍴 FOOD

Restaurant Montecarlo, **4**
Tacos "Don" Robert, **9**
Verde Olivo, **2**
Xochimilco, **12**

★ NIGHTLIFE

La Biblioteca, **6**
La Tequilera, **11**
Napy's, **8**
Neo, **1**

south on Comonfort from the *centro* over the bridge. The Centro de Gobierno is the large pink building on your left. Open M-F 8am-3pm.

Consulates: US (☎ 289 2500, 24hr. 217 2375), Monterrey 141 between Galeana and Rosales. Open M-F 8am-4:30pm.

Banks: Banks line Encinas and Serdán. **Banamex** (☎ 214 7615), on Serdán at Matamoros, has a **24hr. ATM.** Open M-F 8:30am-4:30pm, Sa 9am-3:30pm.

American Express: (☎ 213 9371), on Rosales at Monterrey inside Hermex Travel. Open M-F 9am-1pm and 3-6pm, Sa 9am-1pm.

Emergency: ☎ 080 or 066.

Police: (☎ 289 5000), at Juárez and Nuevo León.

Tourist helpline: ☎ 800 716 2555 or 800-903-9200.

Red Cross: (☎065 or 214 0010), on Encinas at 14 de Abril. Open 9am-5pm.

Pharmacy: Farmacia Kino, Morelia 93 at Guerrero (☎260 2040). Open M-Sa 7am-9pm, Su 7am-8pm.

Hospital: Hospital General (☎259 2500 or 2501), on Transversal at Reyes.

Internet Access: CETEC: Computación e ingles, Serdán at Guerrero. Internet 5 pesos per hr. Supplies ethernet cables. Open daily 9am-8pm.

Post Office: (☎212 0011), on Elías Calles at Rosales. Open M-F 8am-6pm, Sa 9am-1pm. **Postal Code:** 83000.

▚ ACCOMMODATIONS

In Hermosillo, low prices tend to come at the expense of cleanliness, as the humidity encourages cockroaches to flourish. As with most cities of El Norte, travelers must often pay a little extra for comfort.

▨ **Hotel Washington D.C.,** Dr. Noriega 68 Pte. (☎213 1183), between Matamoros and Guerrero. The lobby faces the many *zapaterías, mueblerías,* and *heladerías* on Guerrero. At night, guests can hear locals carousing in nearby *cervecerías.* Boasts pristine, tiled rooms with A/C and high-pressure showers. Free coffee, communal refrigerator, and microwave available. Check-out 1pm. Singles 200 pesos; doubles 230 pesos; 20 pesos per additional person. Cash only. ❹

Hotel Niza, Elías Calles 66 (☎217 2028), between Guerrero and Garmendia. A decent bargain if the Washington is full. Maroon rooms with A/C, bath, comfortable bed, and TV. Restaurant open 7am-9pm. Singles 220 pesos; doubles 280 pesos. Cash only. ❹

Hotel Royal, Sonora 15 (☎212 0160). Between P. Horacio Soria L. and Juárez, near the Costa Bus Station. Convenient for those just passing through Hermosillo. Rooms with A/C and private bath. Singles 160 pesos; doubles 210 pesos. Cash only. ❸

Hotel San Andres, Juárez 14 at Oaxaca.(☎217 3099; www.hotelsanandreshermosillo.com). A posh spot in the *centro*. Rooms have private bath and cable TV. A bargain for large parties. Outdoor pool. Singles and doubles 420 pesos. Matrimonial double 450 pesos. Reservations recommended. MC/V. ❺

▐ FOOD

Carne asada (grilled meat), the most popular dish in Hermosillo, is easily found in the taco and *torta* places around Serdán and Guerrero, where *taquitos* and quesadillas cost around 10 pesos and *comida corrida* goes for 20-25 pesos. Don't miss the city's special dessert: *coyotas,* or sweet Seri cookies made from flour, raw sugar, molasses, and boiled milk. On weekdays, sample the different recipes hawked along Av. Obregón. A supermarket, **Ley Centro,** is located on Juárez at Morelia (☎217 3294. Open daily 6:30am-11pm.)

Tacos "Don" Robert, Morelia at Guerrero, outside of Farmacia Kino. Perhaps the most popular taco stand in the *centro,* the DR serves up hot combos: feast on 3 tacos and a quesadilla with beans for 32 pesos. Big gulp of soda 8 pesos. Also serves *tripas* (intestines) cooked in front of your eyes. Open until "Don" Robert gets tired. Cash only. ❷

Xochimilco, Obregón 51 (☎250 4089 or 4052; restaurantxochimilco.tripod.com). Walk down Rosales; after crossing the highway, turn right. Continue past the long, green school building and turn left. The restaurant is 400m ahead on the right. Locals agree that Xochimilco, specializing in every variety of Sonoran *carne asada* since 1949, is the place to go for a taste of Hermosillo. If you've got a hearty appetite, try the *paquete Xochimilco* (280 pesos for 2). Wrap up your meal with a hot *coyota* (20 pesos). Open daily noon-9pm. Reservations recommended on weekends. MC/V. ❺

El Verde Olivo, Niños Héroes 7 (☎213 2881), at Encinas. Attached to the health-food store Jung, the Green Olive is the perfect retreat for vegetarians. Herbivores relax to ambient American music while enjoying vegetarian versions of Mexican favorites. The all-you-can-eat breakfast buffet (105 pesos) is noteworthy, featuring everything from *burritos de hongos* (mushroom burritos) to hotcakes and yogurt parfaits. Open M-Sa 7:30am-10pm, Su 9am-5pm. MC/V. ❺

Restaurante Montecarlo, (☎212 0853), attached to the **Hotel Montecarlo** on the corner of Juárez and Sonora. Air-conditioned with a free, clean water dispenser. Very little sitting room, so arrive early for the eggs, hotcakes, and coffee. Full breakfast 60 pesos. Hamburgers 40 pesos. Fajitas 60 pesos. Open daily 7am-10pm. ❹

👁 🎵 SIGHTS AND ENTERTAINMENT

The Hermosillo municipality has focused on increasing family-friendly activities over the last few years. The brand-new, 100 acre ▧**Parque Recreativo La Sauceda,** on Periférico and Blvr. Serna, has an open-air theater, children's museum, and athletic courts. The park's Acuafantastico section offers wave pools, a slow river, kiddy pools, and a pirate-themed waterslide. (☎212 0509. Open T-Sa 9am to 7pm.)

Hermosillo's two architectural wonders grace opposite sides of the tree-lined Plaza Zaragoza, where children and seniors often enjoy quiet evenings with icy drinks. The yellow, gothic towers of the **Catedral de Asunción** lie on the western side of the plaza, and across is the blue-and-white **Palacio del Gobierno**. A chapel has stood on the site of the cathedral since 1777, but the current cathedral was only completed in 1908. The main attraction of the Palacio, from which the state of Sonora is governed, is a series of murals commissioned in the 1980s depicting key periods in Sonora's history. The **Museo Regional de Historia** is located on Rosales just before Encinas. The first room contains an examination of Sonora's pre-history, including two perfectly-preserved mummies recovered in Yecora. Downstairs and to the right an exhibit narrates Sonora's turbulent 19th century, marked by the Mexican-American war and the Porfiriato days before General José María González Hermosillo brought a revolutionary spirit to the area. (Archaeological exhibit open M-Sa 9am-1pm; 19th-century exhibit open M-Sa 9am-2pm. Free.)

The ▧**Centro Ecológico de Sonora** is a scholastic treasure-house: spending the day here is the best way to learn about Sonora. Loads of time and perhaps a few limbs have been sacrificed to reel in regional flora, fauna, and fish for the education of Sonorans. In the park you will see mostly native Sonoran species: jaguars, pumas, *guacamayas* (macaws), gila monsters, condors, and coatis—and an incredible collection of over 340 species of cacti. (Take a Ruta 6 or 11 bus from the Guerrero and Dr. Noriega stop (20min., 6 pesos) and ask to exit by the Centro Ecológico. Walk down Templo Tlacali to the end of the street. ☎250 1225. Open Tu-Su 8am-6pm. 30 pesos, children 4-12 and students 15 pesos.)

Each May, the capital celebrates the wild **Fiestas del Pitic,** a municipality wide celebration of Hermosillo's founding. From October to December, the Los Naranjeros de Hermosillo show off their 14-time Pacific League champion prowess at **Hector Espino Stadium** on Garcia Morales at Solidaridad. (Ticket prices vary; visit www.naranjeros.com.mx.)

📷 NIGHTLIFE

The area between the University of Sonora (UniSon) and the *centro* lights up on the weekends.

La Tequilera, Suárez 72 (☎217 5337). Formerly El Grito, Hermosillo's most popular watering hole has a new name and new look. Hermosillenses now come to enjoy both the traditional *banda* as well as North American Top 40. Pitcher of beer 200 pesos. Cover charge for men 22 pesos; women free. Open Th-Sa 9pm-2pm. Cash only.

La Biblioteca, on Rosales at Dr. Noriega (☎212 4750.) Many of the college kids shoot pool, watch sports, or surf the Internet. Beer 20 pesos. Tequila shots 30 pesos. Internet access from 15 pesos per hr. Billiards from 25 pesos. Open M-Sa 10am-2am, Su 4pm-2am. Cash only.

Napy's, Matamoros 109 (☎213 2870), between Dr. Noriega and Morelia. Offers more of a club scene. After 9pm, food service stops and the speakers hit maximum volume as couples hit the dance floor, and friends cheer them on with pitchers of Tecate. F-Sa live salsa. Cover 50 pesos for men; women free. Open daily 10am-2am. Cash only.

Club Neo, Juárez 49, between Veracruz and Tamaulipas (☎210 1689) is always bumpin'. On the crazy nights, almost 1,000 students fill-up the club to dance to various Latin and techno. It's a decent walk from the *centro*, so taking a taxi back late at night is a good idea. Cover charge 15 pesos. Open Th-Su 9pm-2am. Cash only.

BAHÍA DE KINO   ☎662

Bahía de Kino (pop. 5,000) is a 20km stretch of glistening sand and brilliant blue water on the Sea of Cortés. The pristine beaches of "La Perla del Mar de Cortés" are often deserted, until the weekend brings daytrippers from Hermosillo. Kino provides an ideal escape from raucous urban desert to *palapa*-shaded serenity. **Kino Viejo,** a dusty, quiet fishing village, lies down the road from **Kino Nuevo,** a tranquil 8km strip of condos owned by full-time residents and *pajaros de nieve* (snowbirds). Bahía de Kino is remarkably underdeveloped for tourism, so outings in Kino require a "do-it-yourself" attitude and a little extra planning. That said, the locals—many of whom speak English—are usually helpful and more than willing to aid the traveler in their outdoor adventures.

■▇ **ORIENTATION AND TRANSPORTATION.** Bahía de Kino is 107km west of Hermosillo, at the end of a newly constructed four-lane highway. **Buses** in Hermosillo leave from the old blue-and-red-striped **Costa Expresso** station on Sonora between Jesús García and Horacio Soria L., near Jardín Juárez. Regular buses stop at several towns along the way (2hr., every hr. 5:30am-8:30pm, 55 pesos) and express buses only stop once before arriving at Kino (7:30, 9:30am, 1:30, 4:30pm; 66 pesos). Buses stop in Kino Viejo before going on to Kino Nuevo. Look for water on your left and get off where you'd like. Early birds can make it a daytrip, but missing the 7pm bus back to Hermosillo means spending the night in expensive Kino. All sites of interest or importance are on Blvr. Kino and Guaymas, which parallels the boulevard. Kino Nuevo has only one paved road, Mar de Cortés, the main thoroughfare. To get from one Kino to the other or back to Hermosillo, flag down the bus (every hr., 6 pesos) on **Mar de Cortés** or on **Bulevar Kino.** Buses are less likely to run on schedule during the week, as they don't expect travelers to be around. Hitchhiking is popular in Kino, although Let's Go discourages it.

⚐ **PRACTICAL INFORMATION.** The **tourist office** is next to the police station. (☎242 0447. No regular hours.) Other sources of information include hotel and RV park managers, as well as the municipal **Comisaría,** in Kino Viejo on Blvr. Kino right before the highway. (☎242 0761; www.sonoraturismo.com. Open M-F 8am-5pm.) There are **public bathrooms** in Kino Viejo at the **Centro de Salud,** at Tampico and Blvr. Kino (bring your own toilet paper) and in Kino Nuevo toward the beginning of the beach, near La Palapa Restaurant. Other services include: **emergency:** ☎080;

police, at Blvr. Kino and Cruz in Viejo or at Santa Catalina and Mar de Cortés in Nuevo (☎242 0032 or 0047); **Red Cross,** at Blvr. Kino and Manzanillo in Viejo, near the post office and police station. also has a **24hr. ATM** and **LADATEL phones; Farmacia San Francisco,** at Blvr. Kino and Topolobambo in Viejo. (☎242 0230; open daily 9am-1pm and 2-9pm); **Internet** access at **Kino Bay RV Park** in Nuevo (20 pesos per 30min.) or **Space Internet Cafe** on Blvr. Kino at Topolobambo, next to the pharmacy in Kino Viejo. (10 pesos per hr. A/C. Open daily 9am-10:30pm.); and the **post office,** next to the police in Viejo. (☎242 1020. Open M-F 8am-3pm.) **Postal Code:** 83348.

█▌█ ACCOMMODATIONS AND FOOD. If you're traveling with family or a group of people, you may want to consider renting a *casita* (bungalow) in Kino Nuevo. *Casitas* can be rented out for a few nights, weeks, or even months. If you've got big wheels, you're in luck—more than 10 RV parks offer beachfront hook-ups. Relatively safe and comfortable lodgings are plentiful on the beachfront—find a free *palapa* and set up camp, but don't leave valuables unattended for long periods of time. Make sure to cover any backpacks or luggage with trash bags to protect them from water, sand, and sea gulls looking to scavenge. **Hotel Saro ❹,** 5685 Mar de Cortés in Nuevo Kino, is right on the beach, and an excellent bargain for two. Gigantic white tiled rooms have kitchenettes and TV. (elsaro1937@hotmail.com. Check-in before 1pm. Singles and doubles 400 pesos. Cash only.) To reach **Islandía Marina ❷,** right on the beach in Viejo, follow Guaymas to the end and make a right; the entrance to Islandía is 100m away on your left. Looks can be deceiving: this place has one of the better locations and rents cabins with bathroom, powerful fans, kitchen and refrigerator. 45 RV hook-ups. (☎242 0081. Quads 380 pesos; each additional person 60 pesos. Cash only.) At the end of Kino Nuevo, **Kino Bay RV Park ❸,** is the largest in the area, offering over 200 full hook-ups. (☎242 0155; www.kinobayrv.com. US$20 per day. Discount for longer stays. Cash only.)

The few restaurants in Kino tend to be expensive; for an economical meal, do as the *hermosillenses* do and pack a lunch to enjoy under a beach *palapa*. In Kino Viejo, *marisco* (seafood) stands near the beach sell frozen coconut (15 pesos) and fresh fish with *mojo de ajo* (garlic sauce; 65 pesos). *Hermosillenses* crave the *pata de mula*, a resident oyster served raw. Be sure to try the *Jaiba* (blue swimming crab)—the local specialty is definitely worth a taste. **La Palapa ❹,** toward the beginning of Nuevo's beach. Homesick *gringos* will like the juicy *hamburguesas* (35 pesos). La Palapa's real attraction is the gorgeous sunset view from its *palapa*-covered balcony. Try fresh fish any way you like it for 65 pesos. (☎242 0210. Alcatraz shrimp (95 pesos) and broiled lobster (300 pesos). Open daily 8am-8pm. MC/V.) **Jorge's Restaurant ❺,** at Mar de Cortés and Alicante toward the end of Kino Nuevo, offers all the *mariscos* your heart might desire. Try *pulpo ranchero* (grilled octopus) for 90 pesos, or the house specialty *camarones empanizados* (breaded shrimp; 75 pesos). (☎242 0049. Public bathrooms 5 pesos. Live music. Open daily 9am-10pm. MC/V.) A supermarket, **Super Kino,** is located in Viejo on the corner of Topolambo and Blvr. Kino across from Space Internet Cafe.

◣▨ BEACHES AND OUTDOOR ACTIVITIES. Kino's primary attraction is its stretch of **beaches,** which are accessible from both Nuevo and Viejo. During the week, the beaches are perfectly deserted. Weekends draw a fair amount of *hermosillenses*, though Kino gets nowhere near as crowded as bigger resort towns. Watch out for sting rays that rest on the sand beds close to shore. Their stings aren't fatal, but they're painful—shuffle your feet in the sand to scare the rays off.

Kino's real treasure is the easy access to the Sea of Cortés, a body of water dubbed "the aquarium of the world" by Jacques Cousteau. The islands in the middle of the gulf boast a wildlife diversity rivaled only by the Galápagos Islands.

NORTHWEST MEXICO

While the soft, sandy bottom off the shores of Bahía Kino often clouds up the water, the waters near **Isla Tiburón** and the other islands are crystal clear—perfect for snorkeling and diving. The largest island in Mexico, the ecological preserve is the property of local Seri natives; Isla Tiburón itself is regularly inaccessible to visitors. Tours of any sort require advance permission from both the nearest Seri village and the municipal government in Hermosillo. For more information visit www.sonoraturismo.com or contact the Seris at their office in Viejo (☎242 0557 or 0556). More accessible is **Isla Alcatraz,** the small island closest to shore, which is home to nine species of endangered birds. Alcatraz can even be reached by kayak, provided you're a strong paddler. Kayaks, bikes, rock-climbing equipment and scuba gear all can be rented at **EcoKino AdvenTours,** in Hotel Saguaro on Mar de Cortés, 100m down from Puerto Peñasco (☎214 4063; www.ecokino.com. **If you do rent a kayak, be careful, as the currents around Kino are very strong.**

Sport fishing is huge year-round in Bahía Kino. In December, sea fishermen come from all around the Western Hemisphere to catch yellowtail. During the summertime, there is an abundance of marlins. Find more information on sport fishing at **Kino Bay Bait and Tackle** at the end of Kino Nuevo near the boat ramp. Owners David and Genia Torres are expert anglers, and speak perfect English. Visit them at www.freewebs.com/kinobayelpescador.

> ▌**CORTÉS COURTESY.** The Sea of Cortés is currently being overfished. Let's Go recommends practicing sustainable fishing practices and catch-and-release.

GUAYMAS ☎622

Nobody is quite sure what "Guaymas" means—the two most popular suggestions are "to shoot arrows at the head" and "tree toad." One thing is for certain: the Heroic Port Town of San José de Laguna de San José de Guaymas (pop. 134,000), birthplace of three Mexican presidents, has long been in the thick of both conflict and celebration. Since its founding by Jesuit missionaries in the 18th century, Guaymas has been invaded by Seri warrior bands, French Imperial troops, northern *villistas*, and waves of budget travelers in search of a base-camp for visiting the nearby beaches. Guaymas is preparing to become a major power destination within the next few years; the Sonoran government, anticipating this, is constructing a brand new marina on the rocky coast.

 TRANSPORTATION. Gen. José M. Yánez Airport (GYM) offers several **flights** per day. **Aeroméxico** (☎222 0123), on Serdán at Calle 16, flies to **Mexico City** (3½ hr., Sa-Su 4:20pm) via **La Paz** (1½hr.); and **Phoenix** (1½hr., Sa-Su 10:55am). (Office open M-F 8:30am-6pm, Sa 9am-2pm.) To reach the airport, catch a "San José" bus along Serdán (10min., every hr., 40 pesos). **Buses** leave from the Transportes Norte de Sonora station on Cuerpo de Bomberos (Calle 14) every 45min. for: **Guadalajara** (20hr., 740 pesos); **Hermosillo** (1½hr., 86 pesos); **Los Mochis** (5hr., 199 pesos); **Mazatlán** (12hr., 520 pesos); **Mexicali** (12hr., 453 pesos); **Nogales** (6hr., 226 pesos); **Tepic** (18hr., 740 pesos); **Tijuana** (13hr., 740 pesos). To get to the main street Serdán, turn right as you exit the bus station. Across the street, **Transportes Baldomero Corral** can take you to **Álamos** (4hr., 4 per day, 126 pesos) or **Navojoa** (4hr., every hr., 96 pesos).

Ferries leave from a small dock on Serdán, about 2km east of the *centro*. To get to the dock, take any local bus headed east on Serdán and ask the driver to let you off at the ferry. A blue-and-white "Sematur Transboradores" sign will be on your right. Passenger ferries only go to **Santa Rosalía** (7hr.; M-Tu, Th and Sa. 8pm; US$55.) Rent **cars** from **Hertz,** Calzada García López 625 (☎222 1000. Open M-F

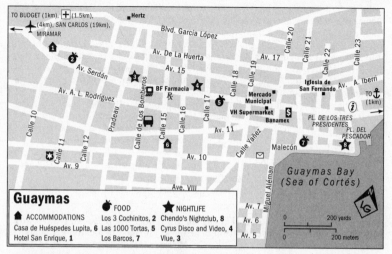

Guaymas

🛏 ACCOMMODATIONS
Casa de Huéspedes Lupita, **6**
Hotel San Enrique, **1**

🍅 FOOD
Los 3 Cochinitos, **2**
Las 1000 Tortas, **5**
Los Barcos, **7**

★ NIGHTLIFE
Chendo's Nightclub, **8**
Cyrus Disco and Video, **4**
Vlue, **3**

8am-6pm, Sa-Su 8am-3pm.) or **Budget,** at Serdán and Calle 4. (☎222 5500; guaymas@rentatur.com. Open M-F 8am-6pm, Sa-Su 8am-3pm.)

🛈 **PRACTICAL INFORMATION.** The **tourist office** is on Av. Serdán between Calle 24 and Calle 25. (☎222 4400. Open daily 9am-6pm, but the booth is only staffed by one person, so hours vary.) **After dark, women should avoid walking alone more than two blocks south of Serdán or east of Calle 25.** Banamex (☎224 1870), on Serdán at Calle 20, **exchanges currency** and has **24hr. ATMs** (Open M-F 8:30am-4:30pm.) **Luggage storage** is available at the Transportes Norte de Sonora bus terminal. (8hr. 15 pesos, each additional hr. 5 pesos. Open 24hr.) Other services include: **emergency** ☎066; **police:** (☎224 0105), on Calle 11 at Av. 9; **Red Cross** (☎222 5555), on México 15, about 1.5km north of the *centro* at km 1980; **24hr. B.F. Farmacia** (☎222 2400) at Calle 15; **Telecomm** (☎222 0292) on Av. 10 and Calle 20, next to the post office (open M-Sa 8am-6pm, Su 9am-12:30pm); **Internet** access at **La Biblioteca,** on Serdán and Cuerpo de Bomberos (10 pesos per hr.; open daily 9am-10pm); and the **post office** (☎222 0104), on Av. 10 between Calle 19 and 20. (Open M-F 8am-4pm, Sa 9am-1pm.) **Postal Code:** 85400.

🛏🍴 **ACCOMMODATIONS AND FOOD.** Guaymas's heat and humidity create the perfect micro-climate for a proliferation of roaches, fleas, gnats, and other vermin, making otherwise adequate budget hotels somewhat uncomfortable. It may be worth your while to pay for A/C, cleanliness, and frequent fumigation, especially during the summer. If you're inclined to avoid both infestation and expense, bring a tent and head to the free, publicly owned beaches of San Carlos, just a 10min. bus ride away. **Casa de Huéspedes Lupita ❷,** 125 Calle 15, two blocks south of Serdán. While not the cleanest, these small rooms come with fans, and a purified water dispenser awaits in the office. (☎222 1945. Key deposit 30 pesos. Towel deposit 30 pesos. Singles 140 pesos, with bath 170; doubles with A/C, bath, and cable TV 250 pesos. Cash only.) **Hotel San Enrique ❺,** Av. Serdán between Calle 9 and Calle 10, offers spotless rooms with A/C, cable, and Wi-Fi in the lobby. (☎224 1919. Singles 350 pesos; doubles 400 pesos. AmEx/MC/V.)

Seafood is Guaymas's specialty. Local favorites include *ostiones* (oysters) in a garlic and chile sauce and *cahuamanta* (manta ray steaks)—not to be confused *cahuama* (sea turtle), which are endangered and illegal to eat. **Restaurant Bar Los Barcos ❺**, on Malecón between Calles 21 and 22, offers the very finest in seafood. Select from 17 different shrimp dishes (100 pesos each) or Mexican surf and turf for 125 pesos. (☎222 7650. Open M-W 11am-10pm, Th-Sa 11am-11pm, Su 11am-1pm. MC/V.) **Las 1000 Tortas ❷**, Serdán 188, between Calles 17 and 18, is not just for *torta* lovers. Try the great sandwiches for 20 pesos, or a large variety of *comida corrida* for 30-40 pesos. (Open daily 8am-11pm. Cash only.) Find **Los 3 Cochinitos ❶**, on Serdán at Calle 11, past the straw-and-stick houses. This joint serves cheap tacos and *tortas* for 9 pesos each. (Open 9am-late. Cash only.) Get fresh produce at the **Mercado Municipal,** on Calle 20 one block from Serdán, or *comida corrida* along Serdán. There is also a **VH Supermarket** on Serdán between Calles 19 and 20. (Open M-Sa 7am-11:30pm and Su 7am-8:30pm.)

> **!** **SEAFOOD SAVVY.** If you're cravin' crustaceans or *camarones* make sure to drift port-side before 11am. The street vendors on Serdán don't have refrigerators and when temperatures rise, the ice melts and the fish spoils.

BEACHES AND NIGHTLIFE. While Guaymas itself doesn't have any beaches, some of the most beautiful beaches in Mexico are located just a short bus ride north in **San Carlos** (p. 238) and **Miramar** (p. 228). Buses marked "San Carlos" or "Miramar" leave from the Colmex on Serdán and Calle 16 (10 min., every 15min. 7am-10:30pm, 9 pesos). The beaches in Miramar are nicer but smaller than those in San Carlos. **Perlas del Mar de Cortés,** (☎221 0136; www.per-las.com.mx), also in Miramar, offers tours of Mexico's most exotic pearl farm. (Free tours every hr. Open M-F 9am-3pm, Sa 9am-11pm.)

Guaymas's nightlife revolves around the many bars of the *centro*. The few clubs with dance floors are crowded with young people on weekends and often stay open until sunrise. **Vlue,** on Serdán and Calle 13, is a favorite with a packed dance floor. (Sa-Su live music from top *norteño* bands. Cover 20 pesos. Th-Su 10pm-3am. Cash only.) **Chendo's Nightclub,** on Malecón and Calle 23, offers more of a lounge scene, but nights are still long and debaucherous. Look for the sign of a drunken cactus holding a flaming beer. (Pool table. Live music. Beer 20 pesos. Open daily 9pm-3am, but crowds don't come until 11pm. Cash only.) **Cyrus Disco and Video** on Serdán at Calle 17, draws a younger student crowd with reggaeton and American hip hop. (☎227 666. Cover 20 pesos, women free F-Su. Beer 20 pesos. Must be age 18-35 to enter. Cash only.)

SAN CARLOS   ☎622

The natural landscape of San Carlos (pop. 2500) is impossibly gorgeous. Located one hour south of Hermosillo between the arid Tetakawi Mountains and the crystalline Sea of Cortés, this tiny town has long been a magnet for snowbirds and outdoor adventure enthusiasts alike. San Carlos is geared to attract elderly wealth—but away from the five-star hotels and yachts, intrepid travelers can find bargain stays and meals, not to mention infinite opportunities to enjoy the outdoors.

TRANSPORTATION

White-striped buses come from downtown **Guaymas** and run down the main road to the Marina Real and Plaza Las Glorias, but don't go all the way to El Mirador Escénico or Playa Los Algodones. (Every 10 min. 7am-10:30pm; to Guaymas 9 pesos, within San Carlos 4.50 pesos.)

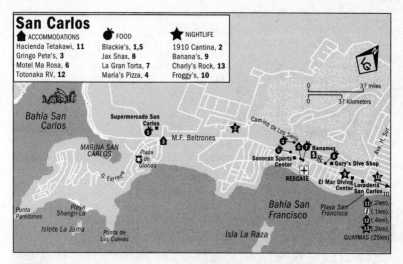

San Carlos

🏠 ACCOMMODATIONS	🍎 FOOD	⭐ NIGHTLIFE
Hacienda Tetakawi, **11**	Blackie's, **1,5**	1910 Cantina, **2**
Gringo Pete's, **3**	Jax Snax, **8**	Banana's, **9**
Motel Ma Rosa, **6**	La Gran Torta, **7**	Charly's Rock, **13**
Totonaka RV, **12**	María's Pizza, **4**	Froggy's, **10**

◼🛈 ORIENTATION AND PRACTICAL INFORMATION

Most restaurants and accommodations lie on Manilo F. Beltrones, which runs east-west. Although easily located, many of these establishments lack permanent addresses. Beltrones spills into Plazas Las Glorias, the most exclusive and expensive part of San Carlos. Most establishments accept credit cards and US dollars.

Tourist office: Near the beginning of San Carlos, across the bridge after Hacienda Tetakawi. Open M-F 9am-7pm, Sa 9am-5pm, Su 9am-1pm.

Bank: Banamex, on Beltrones next to the PEMEX station. **Exchanges currency** and traveler's checks and has a **24hr. ATM.** Open M-F 8:30am-4:30pm.

Laundromat: Lavandería San Carlos (☎226 0013), next to Piccolo Restaurant. Offers full- or self-service as well as hand-wash. Wash 25 pesos, dry 30 pesos. M-Sa 9am-5pm, Su 10:30am-1pm.

Emergency: Rescate (☎226 0097), located across from the PEMEX station. Rescate is funded entirely by donations from San Carlos residents.

Police: (☎226 1400), up the hill on the road to Plaza Las Glorias.

Pharmacy: Farmacia Bahía San Carlos (☎226 0097), across the street from Motel Creston. Open M-Sa 8am-6pm, Su 8am-2pm.

Internet Access: The most reasonably priced connection can be found above Gary's dive shop (☎226 0049), on Beltrones km 10. 30 pesos per hr. Wi-Fi available. Open daily 9:30am-8pm.

Post Office: (☎226 0506), next to Ana Maria's Beauty Shop. Open M-F 8am-6pm, Sa 8am-1pm. **Postal Code:** 85504

◣ ACCOMMODATIONS

Large groups and camping enthusiasts can find cheap stays in San Carlos, but woe upon the penniless loner—budget lodgings are few and far between.

◼ **Motel Ma Rosa,** (☎222 1139) on Beltrones adjacent to the Gran Torta and near Sonoran Sports Center. Offers gigantic rooms for 3-4 people. Rooms include 2 single beds, sofa, kitchenette, carpet, TV, and floor space. Rooms 500-600 pesos per night. Discounts available for extended stays. MC/V. ❸

Gringo Pete's, (☎226 1316). Before Beltrones splits into 3 streets near the Plaza, take the dirt road on your left up the hill. Has the best 2-person deal in San Carlos. Doubles come with A/C, hot showers, TV, and a beautiful view of the bay. Check-out 11am. Rooms US$40. Cash only. ❹

Totonaka RV Park, (☎226 0481; www.totonakarv.com) on Beltrones just before the bridge. If you were wise enough to bump in on the big wheels, Totonaka provides full hookups with cable TV, a swimming pool. Free Wi-Fi. Campsites US$22. MC/V. ❹

Hacienda Tetakawi (☎226 0220 or 0248), on Beltrones at km 9.5 at the beginning of the main strip. The Hacienda itself is run by Best Western, but full RV hookups and tent spaces are available out back. Hookups US$20 per day; tent space 1-2 people US$15 dollars, each additional person US$3. MC/V. ❶

🍴 FOOD

While most restaurants are on the expensive side, budget travelers can still find filling meals for relatively low prices. Vendors toward the western end of Beltrones sell *burritos de carne asada* or fresh *almejas* (clams) eaten raw with salsa and *limón*. Buy groceries at **San Carlos Super Mercado,** in front of the church at the end of the road to Plazas Las Glorias. (☎226 0043. Open daily 7am-9pm.)

Jax Snax (☎226 0270), on Beltrones. Local expats start the day with a fabulous malt (29 pesos) and breakfast (44 pesos). *Comida corrida* 50-70 pesos. M-F lunch specials 32 pesos. Open daily 7:30am-10:30pm. Cash only. ❸

La Gran Torta, on Beltrones next to the Motel Ma Rosa. An out-of-the-way joint that's actually a hot-dog stand, *torta* place, and *pastelería* all rolled into one. *Tortas* 14 pesos. Cash only. ❷

María's Pizza (☎226 2001) on Beltrones in the Plaza Arrecifes. Large pizza 115 pesos. Vegetarian options available. Open T-Su 6am-9pm. Cash only. ❸

Blackie's, (☎226 1525) on Beltrones past the Motel Creston on km 10. Expats and locals alike swear by this place. The menu always features great steaks and seafood. The ribeye (165 pesos) is a house specialty. Open Tu-Su noon-11pm. MC/V. ❺

🏖 🏄 BEACHES AND OUTDOOR ACTIVITIES

Playa San Francisco, which extends parallel to the freeway from Guaymas, is the most easily accessible beach in San Carlos. The sands are rocky, but the water is pleasant. You'll need a car to get to **El Mirador Escénico,** a vista atop a steep road that affords spectacular views of **Tetakawi** and the secluded coves of **Playas Piedras Pintas.** A dirt road near the gate to Costa Del Mar (about 8km past the end of the bus route) leads to 🖼**Playa Los Algodones** (Cotton Beach), named after its especially soft sand. Within walking or biking distance from Beltrones is **Nacapule Canyon,** a tropical eco-reserve smack in the middle of the Sonoran desert. The nature enthusiast can observe iguanas, tree frogs, and many other rare species. (☎224 2672; www.cafenaturarte.com. Guided tours available.)

Adrenaline junkies can get their fix at the 🖼**Sonoran Sports Center,** Edificio Marosa, on Beltrones just west of the Rescate office. SSC is the place to fulfill all your extreme sports fantasies: not only do they have all the gear for snorkeling, mountain biking, kayaking, scuba diving, and spear-fishing; they also offer lessons in kite boarding—the extreme sports world's hottest phenomenon. When the bay winds pick up from October to April, San Carlos offers world-class kite boarding—boarders get up to seven or eight feet of air. SSC has recently registered with the American Sailing Association and provides a boat, a skipper, and lessons for up to 4 people for US$175. The owner, **■Vince Radice,** is both a hardcore spear-fisherman and an excellent source of information about the surrounding area. (☎226 0929; www.sailsancarlos.com. Bike rental US$15 per day. Guided canyon tour US$25, including bike.)

The locally run **El Mar Diving Center,** on Beltrones East, is a professional and affordable water excursion company. They offer guided dives for licensed divers (US$30, not including equipment) and beginners (US$99, equipment included) and boats for snorkeling tours of nearby coves (US$57). **Isla San Pedro Nicolas,** home to large **sea-lion colonies,** is an extremely popular dive site. Other nearby and beginner-accessible dive spots include **Isla Venado, El Choyudo,** and the guano-covered **Isla Pastel.** For an unforgettable experience on the Sea of Cortés, try El Mar's guided kayak tour, which goes through the caves along the imposing cliffs of San Carlos's shore (3-4hr., US$45, 2-person min.) Halfway through the tour, snorkel in **Martini Cove,** host to an impressive array of octopi. (☎226 0404; www.elmar.com. Kayak rental US$30 per day. Open M-Th 8am-6pm, F-Su 7am-6pm.)

For fishing, visit the US-run **Surface Time,** 1 Edificio Villa Marina near the Plaza de las Glorias. Surface Time charters boats and will arrange licenses and equipment for you. (☎226 1888 or US 480-897-2300; surfacetime@cox.net. Full range of diving services available. 1-tank local or night dive US$40 per person with 4 people. Bottom fishing US$70 per hr. for 4 hours. Trolling US$90 per hr. for 6hr. Open daily 7am-7pm. To fish solo, pick up a license (60 pesos per day) at the **Secretaria de Pesca,** on Beltrones, near the tourist office. (Open 9am-3pm). **It is illegal to fish without proper credentials.**

■ NIGHTLIFE

Although a popular beach town, San Carlos doesn't have as wild a nightlife scene as the resorts further south. **■Froggy's,** west of the Super Carnes store, plays popular Mexican music in the evening, and shifts to reggaeton late at night. Patrons rave about Karaoke night and the wood-fire pizzas (55 pesos). (Beer 20 pesos. Open daily 11am-2am. Cash only.) A young and better-dressed crowd can be found at **1910 Cantina,** on Beltrones by the Country Club. The only disco in town, 1910 spins Mexican pop music and serves cold beer (25 pesos). (Open Su 8pm-2am. F-Sa 9pm-2am. MC/V.) **Charly's Rock** chillspot just across from Hacienda Tetakawi. The

GIVING BACK

THE QUICK FLIPPER FIXER UPPER

The Sonoran government's Sea of Cortés Project is a recent multi-million peso attempt to spur ecotourism while educating locals and tourists about marine life. As part of the initiative, the **Delfinario Sonora** center houses four Indo-Pacific bottlenose dolphins trained to interact with Sonoran special-needs children and promote cognitive growth.

Dolphin therapy advocates are still not quite sure how it works. The most-cited guess is that ultrasonic cries alert neurons and improve brain plasticity. Whatever the functional mechanics may be, children with Down syndrome, cerebral palsy, and autism often develop fine motor skills, increase their attention spans, and improve general communication skills at a quicker rate after interacting with dolphins.

At 12,000 pesos for six sessions, dolphin therapy is expensive. Most of the money that the Delfinario uses to subsidize local projects comes from tourists. By attending a water show, purchasing merchandise, or simply making a small donation, budget travelers can give a little back to Sonora.

The Delfinario Sonora (☎662 210 8340; www.delfinariosonora.com.mx) is at km 5.52 between San Carlos and Miramar Beach. Open T - Su. Sea-lion shows 11am, 12:30, 3, 4pm. 60 pesos, children 40 pesos. 400 pesos to swim with the dolphins.

palm-thatched bar is attached to the restaurant offers 2-for-1 happy hour specials for 5 pesos. (Beer 20 pesos. Bar open T- Sa 9pm-2pm. AmEx/MC/V.)
Banana's, on Beltrones near Froggy's, serves food until 1am and has live music on the weekends. (Beer 20 pesos. Open T-Su 7am-2am. Cash only.)

ÁLAMOS ☎ 647

The sleepy town of Álamos (pop. 8000) in the scenic foothills of the Sierra Madre Occidentales, has long been a favorite of colonial architecture enthusiasts. Though founded in 1531, Álamos was relatively ignored until silver was discovered nearby in 1683. For nearly a hundred years, Álamos produced more silver than any area in the world, but when the mines ran dry at the turn of the century, Álamos turned from boomtown into ghost town. Over the last 50 years, wealthy *norteamericanos* have taken an interest in the town. Thanks to their funds, Álamos—called *"la joya del norte"* ("the jewel of the North")—has returned to its glory days—the refurbished *haciendas* and cobblestone streets give the city a historical feel unlike any other in northwest Mexico. Those who are less passionate about touring handsome *haciendas* may wish to spend their time elsewhere.

E TRANSPORTATION. To reach Álamos by **bus,** you can either take a **TBC** bus from **Guaymas** (4hr., 5 per day, 126 pesos) or change buses in **Navojoa,** 53km southwest of Álamos. From the **Transportes Norte de Sonora** and **Elite** bus stations in Navojoa, stand at the corner of Allende and Ferrocarril, looking down Ferrocarril as you face the bus stations. Walk one block to the **Transportes de Pacífico** station and turn left (toward center of town) onto Guerrero. Three blocks down Guerrero is the TBC bus station at **Blvr. No Reelección,** where you can catch a bus to **Álamos** (1hr., every hr. 6am-6:30pm, 40 pesos). From the other stations, ask directions for buses to Álamos. The return trip to Álamos from Navojoa starts from the station at Plaza Alameda (every hr., 40 pesos).

🛈 PRACTICAL INFORMATION. The Álamos **tourist office,** Juárez 6, under Hotel Los Portales on the west side of the Plaza de Armas, offers tours of the town, historical information and maps. (☎428 0450. Open M-F 10am-3pm; Sa-Su hours vary.) **Banorte,** on Madero before the fork in the road, **exchanges currency.** (☎428 0512. Open M-F 9am-2pm.) A **24hr. ATM** is next door. **SuperTito's,** on Madero, operates as a **pharmacy,** grocery store, and liquor store. (☎428 0512. Open daily 7:30am-10:30pm.) The **police** station (☎428 0200), is just off Plaza de Armas on Comercia. Farther from the *centro* on Madero is **Hospital Básico** (☎428 0026). **Internet access** is available at **Ciber-Lucas,** Morelos 39, down Callejón de Beso from the Plaza de Armas. (☎428 1097. 10 pesos per hr. Open daily 8am-10pm.) The **post office** is located in the Palacio Municipal. (Open M-F 8am-3pm.) **Postal Code:** 85760.

🛏🍴 ACCOMMODATIONS AND FOOD. Unless you rediscover silver on your way into town, you'll probably have a hard time finding bargain sleeps in Álamos. **Motel Somar ❺,** Madero 110, has clean rooms with A/C. There is a purified water dispenser in the lobby. (☎428 0195. Singles 350 pesos; doubles 400 pesos. MC/V.) **Hotel Enrique ❸** is a beautiful old building on the west side of the Plaza de Armas. Rooms have fans and simple beds. (Singles 200 pesos, with bath 250 pesos; doubles 250/300 pesos. Cash only.) **Hotel los Portales ❺,** Juárez 8 near Hotel Enrique, is an economical *hacienda*-style hotel. Rooms have A/C. (Doubles 600 pesos. MC/V.)

For cheap food, check out taco stands like **Taquería Blanquita ❶,** in the Madero Municipal by Plaza Alameda. (Tacos 20 pesos. Open daily 7am-10:30pm. Cash only.) Also in the plaza is **La Kazeta ❶,** a two-in-one fast food stand and bazaar. (Hamburgers 125 pesos. Open M-Sa 9am-9pm. Cash only). **Pizza Don Chuy ❶,** Rosales 10, serves large pizzas for 95 pesos and has vegetarian options. (Open daily 9am-11pm. Cash only.) The walk to **Restaurante el Mirador ❷,** on the Mirador overlooking Álamos, is sure to build up an appetite. (*Chimichangas* 28 pesos. Hamburgers 35 pesos. Enchiladas 45 pesos. Open M and W-Su 3-10pm.)

◙ **SIGHTS.** The best reason to visit Álamos is to catch a glimpse of the *haciendas.* **Hotel los Portales** was constructed in 1720 and refinished in the 19th century, when it became the home of José María Almada, owner of one of the world's richest silver mines. Other impressive restored homes can be found in hotels around the **cathedral,** including the Ex-Convento **Casa de los Tesoros, Hotel la Mansión,** and **Casa Encantada.** You can tour the swanky **Hacienda de los Santos,** a series of colonial homes that have been turned into a five-star hotel. (Tours leave from the main entrance on the corner of Molina and Gutierrez. Daily 1pm. 10 pesos.) At the tourist office, ask about Alamos's **ghost tours,** which regale tourists with the local tales of mystery and terror on a late night walk through the old town.

The town's old cathedral, **La Parroquia de la Purísima Concepción,** was completed in 1786 and occupies a commanding position on Plaza de Armas. The Mirador offers an excellent view of the surrounding valley. It can be reached by going east on 5 de Mayo and following the signs. **Museo Costumbrista,** the yellow-and-white building at the northeast corner of Plaza de Armas, has exhibits on Sonora's history. (☎428 0053. Open W-Su July-Aug. 9am-6pm; Sept.-June 9am-3pm. 10 pesos, students and children 5 pesos.) **Museo Casa de María Félix,** Galeana 41, in Barrio la Colorada, occupies the birthplace of the late actress—the "Marilyn Monroe of Mexico"—who hailed from Álamos. (☎428 0929; www.casademariafelix.com. Open daily 10am-4pm. 10 pesos, children 5 pesos.)

Álamos is also the home of the ▨**Mexican jumping bean.** These "beans" are actually the larvae of monarch butterflies and are found hanging from large trees outside the town during the winter, and their "jumps" are muscle spasms. *Brincadores,* as they're called, are also part of a popular gambling game in local bars. **José T. Hurton,** the self-proclaimed "king of the Mexican jumping bean," sells beans at the tourist office. (☎428 1225. Beans 1 peso each. 1000 beans 300 pesos.)

> ᵀᴵᴾ **BUYIN' BRINCADORES.** Follow these steps when purchasing or packaging Mexican jumping beans and you're guaranteed the best bean for your buck.
> 1. Shake 'em. If they rattle the larvae are dead.
> 2. Cut one open. If it's a healthy bean, the inside will be green. The larva inside should seal up the hole quickly.
> 3. Transport in a cool place. Warmth causes the beans to jump vigorously, and extended and exuberant hopping will kill the larvae.

CHIHUAHUA

CIUDAD JUÁREZ ☎656

Long before Juárez became Mexico's fourth largest city (pop. 1.4 million), it was a notorious haven for exiles. *"El Paso del Norte"* got its modern name in 1860, when President Benito Juárez fled here to escape the French intervention and to seek US aid in the overthrow of Habsburg Emperor Maximilian (p. 58). The revolutionary Pancho Villa occupied the city during the beginning of the 20th century. The feeling that something troublesome lies beneath has never quite left the border, and Juárez remains a transitory place. Daytrippers often come from the

Southwestern US for a taste of Mexico and cheaper alternatives for services, ranging from dentistry to the more exotic and less legal. Today, Ciudad Juárez garners global media attention for the continuing disappearances and homicides of *maquiladoras* (factory workers). As of summer 2007, more than 350 women have been found dead and abandoned in the deserts around the city.

CROSSING THE BORDER. The easiest way to cross the border is to walk. From downtown El Paso, the Paso del Norte International (formerly Santa Fe St.) toll bridge is the main border crossing. On the east side is the Chamizal bridge, a toll-free bridge that leads into the commercial ProNaf district. Pedestrian walkways are at the right-hand side of both bridges. Crossing fees are US$0.35 to enter Mexico by foot, US$1.65 by car; 3 pesos to return by foot, 19 pesos by car. If you are planning to venture more than 22km into Mexico's interior, you need a **tourist card** (US$20), available at the Mexican immigration office, directly to your right as you cross the Stanton Ave. (Chamizal) Bridge. Expect to wait an hour or more to drive back into the US. See p. 32 for more information on border crossings.

TRANSPORTATION

Flights: Aeropuerto Internacional Abraham González (CJS; ☎633 0734), 18.5km south, 17km out on Mex. 45 (Carr. Panamericana). Catch the "Juárez/Aeropuerto" bus near the train tracks on V. Guerrero at Francisco Villa (5 pesos). **Aeroméxico** (☎633 1803 or 1804) flies to **Chihuahua, Mexico City, Monterrey,** and nearby US cities.

Buses: Central Camionera, Blvr. Oscar Flores 4010 (☎610 6445 or 613 6037). From the US, take an "Ómnibus de México" bus from the El Paso terminal to Juárez (US$6). From the *centro*, board a "Central Camionera" bus from V. Guerrero at F. Villa. To get to the *centro* from the station, board a "Centro" bus (4 pesos); confirm the destination with the driver. Taxis cost 80 pesos. **Chihuahuenses** (☎629 2229), **Estrella Blanca** (☎629 2229), **Ómnibus de México** (☎610 7297), and others offer service to: **Chihuahua** (7hr., 264 pesos); **Dallas** (US$62); **El Paso** (50min., US$6); **Guadalajara** (22hr., 1120 pesos); **Hermosillo** (10hr., 588 pesos); **Los Angeles** (US$52); **Mazatlán** (24hr., 866 pesos); **Mexico City** (26hr., 1319 pesos); **Monterrey** (800 pesos).

ORIENTATION AND PRACTICAL INFORMATION

The main tourist drag begins at the Santa Fe Bridge and follows Av. Juárez for about a 500m to Vincente Guerrero. Street numbers start in the 800s near the two border bridges and descend to zero at 16 de Septiembre. It's always best to stick to well-lit, active areas and go out in groups at night. West of Av. Juárez is Old Juárez, where streets are often undeveloped and confusing. **Let's Go recommends tourists not venture west of Av. Juárez at night, where the red-light district is located.** The eastern port of entry (Chamizal Bridge) opens into the east-side ProNaf Zone. A decade ago, the ProNaf (Programa Nacional de la Frontera) Zone was the proud host of American tourism and business interests in Ciudad Juárez. Since the devaluation of the peso, many of the foreign firms have abandoned ship, but there are still many shopping and nightlife opportunities in the area. (To get to ProNaf from the *centro*, walk 4km east along 16 de Septiembre or I. Mejía. If you're taking a taxi, agree on a price beforehand, and don't pay more than 80 pesos.)

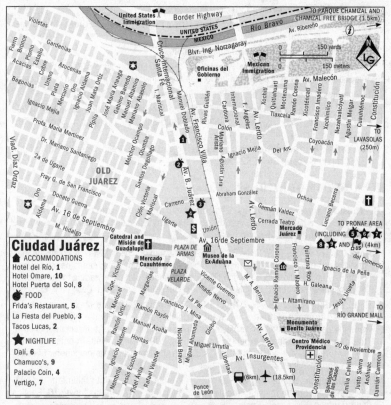

Ciudad Juárez

⌂ ACCOMMODATIONS
Hotel del Río, 1
Hotel Omare, 10
Hotel Puerta del Sol, 8
🍴 FOOD
Frida's Restaurant, 5
La Fiesta del Pueblo, 3
Tacos Lucas, 2

★ NIGHTLIFE
Dalí, 6
Chamuco's, 9
Palacio Coin, 4
Vertigo, 7

Tourist Office: (☎ 611 3174), far from the *centro*, just past the bridge on the western side of the main road, through Chamizal Park. Provides info on Chihuahua state. Open daily 10am-9pm.

US Consulate: López Mateos Nte. 924 (☎ 613 1655, after-hours emergencies ☎ 651 6019; www.ciudadjuarez.usconsulate.gov.), in a nondescript white, concrete building halfway between Hermanos Escobar and Av. Benjamin Franklin, northeast of ProNaf. Open M-F 8am-4:45pm. In an emergency, the El Paso tourist office may be of help (US☎ 915-544-0062).

Currency Exchange: Both pesos and US dollars are accepted throughout Juárez. Pesos can give you the competitive edge when you're driving a hard bargain, and currency money is easily exchanged at any of the *casas de cambio* downtown. Banks line 16 de Septiembre and Av. Juárez, and most have **24hr. ATMs.**

Luggage Storage: At the bus station. 5 pesos per bag per hr.

Laundromat: Lavasolas (☎ 612 5461), at Tlaxcala and 5 de Mayo, 16 blocks east of Av. Juárez. Wash 18 pesos, dry 16 pesos. Open M-Sa 8am-8pm, Su 8am-5pm.

Emergency: ☎ 060.

Police: (☎ 615 1551), at Oro and 16 de Septiembre, 25 blocks southwest of the tourist area. Smaller station (☎ 207 5200) on Gardenias, 4 blocks west of the Santa Fe Bridge. Open 24hr.

Federal Highway Police: ☎ 633 0195.

Red Cross: 4324 Henry Dunant (☎ 611 4330), 2 blocks east of Av. López Mateos near ProNaf. Open 24hr.

Pharmacy: Pharmacies abound on Juárez Avenue.

Medical Service: Centro Médico Providencia, 593 Av. Constitución (☎ 207 3097), at Av. Providencia, just south of the Benito Juárez monument, toward the southern end of the *centro*.

Telephones: LADATELs are plentiful on Av. Juárez and on 16 de Septiembre.

Internet Access: Navega (☎ 613 4756), in the ProNaf Zone inside the Plaza de las Américas Mall. 15 pesos per hr. Open M-Sa 9am-9pm, Su 11am-8pm. Several Internet centers line Av. Juárez.

Post Office: At the southwestern corner of Lerdo and Ignacio Peña. Open M-F 8am-5pm, Sa 9am-1pm. **Postal Code:** 32000.

ACCOMMODATIONS

The most reasonable selections are found near the *centro* and on Av. Juárez and Av. Lerdo. As with traveling, remember that staying west of Av. Juárez, where hotels rent by the hour, is not advisable.

Hotel Omare, Corona 213 Sur (☎ 612 0618), just south of I. de la Peña. This pleasant, bargain hotel 3 blocks east of the main drag has well-furnished, clean rooms painted in eye-poppingly bright colors. Use caution climbing the narrow staircase leading to the lobby at night. Singles 120 pesos; doubles 170 pesos. Open daily 6am-3pm. Cash only. ❷

Hotel del Río, Juárez 488 Nte. (☎ 615 5525) between Colón and Mejía. Pricey, but if you need to crash in Juárez and want to do it in style, this is the place. The hotel recently caught fire after an explosion in the basement *cantina*, but reconstruction of the damaged sections is expected to finish by 2008. Clean, white rooms with fans, homey furniture, and a vigilant staff distinguish this hotel from its neighbors. Check-in before noon. Singles 320 pesos; doubles 370 pesos. ❺

Hotel Burciaga, Ugarte 136 (☎ 615 0059). A large, non-descript building in the middle of the *centro* offers cheap rooms and basic cable TV. All rooms have A/C. Singles and doubles 200 pesos. Cash only. ❶

Hotel Puerta del Sol, Vicente Suárez 421 (☎ 613-5981). Easily the best bargain close to the ProNaf area. Spotless white-tile rooms with cable TV and A/C. Singles 275 pesos; doubles 380 pesos. MC/V. ❺

FOOD

Cheap *cantinas* and taco stands line Av. Juárez and just about every other thoroughfare in the city. For more diverse cuisine options and higher prices, head to Av. Abraham Lincoln in the ProNaf area. The open-air *mercado* behind the cathedral has cheap food stands. **SMART** is a supermarket chain with several locations throughout the city. The one inside the Río Grande Mall, in the southeastern corner of the mall on V. Guerrero at Adolfo de la Huerta (Ruta 8 bus), is brand new, clean, and has lots of free samples. (☎ 613 1398. Open 24hr.) Cheap **Rapidito's Bip Bip!** convenience stores can be found on almost every corner.

Tacos Lucas, (☎ 632 3289), at Av. Juárez and Mejía, a colorful building with Daffy Duck on the entrance sign. In a cavernous room with colorful murals and archways painted like bricks, Tacos Lucas serves its namesake tacos as well as heaping special dishes like *fajitas* and grilled shrimp for 50 pesos. Beer 15 pesos. Jukebox in the corner plays both American and local *banda* hits. Open 24hr. MC/V. ❸

La Fiesta del Pueblo, Av. Juárez 200 (☎615 0404), at the northeastern corner of Gonzales. The festive artwork, wagon-wheel chandeliers, and kitschy Christmas lights are more than just a little geared towards daytrippers. Juicy *tacos de cabrito* (kid tacos) 80 pesos. Margaritas 40 pesos. Open M and W-Su 11am-2am. Cash only. ❷

Frida's, Triunfo de la República 2525 (☎639 0148). A hot spot not only for traditional Mexican cuisine and barbecue, but also for late-night fun. At night, lights dim and the live music or karaoke starts bumpin'. Fantastic murals of famous painter Frida Kahlo's more nationally themed work cover the walls. Entrees 80-180 pesos. Desserts 80 pesos. Open daily 2pm-2am. MC/V. ❹

!Viva Juárez!, Juárez 126, (☎615 9276). This small, eponymous restaurant/bar serves cheap border-fare. 4-taco *barbacoa* 40 pesos. Breakfast buffet 40 pesos. Open daily 8am-8pm. Cash only. ❷

🔘🎵 SIGHTS AND ENTERTAINMENT

The Siberia of Mexico, Juárez historically functioned as a place of escape and exile. By the 20th century, it began to take on a similar role for US citizens fleeing everything from Prohibition to divorce laws. The "Downtown Historic Walking Tour" pamphlet, available at the tourist office, suggests a walking tour through the *centro*, though the route is fairly self-explanatory even without the guide. Just keep an eye out for the placards that demonstrate the suggested route, following Av. Juárez to 16 de Septiembre, where it turns right at the Victorian **Aduana Fronteriza** (customs house). Today, the Aduana Fronteriza houses the **Museo Ex-Aduana de Ciudad Juárez.** One half of the museum is dedicated to the border theater in Pancho Villa's revolution, while the other hosts rotating exhibits. All the placards are in Spanish. (☎612 4707. Open Tu-Su 9:30am-5:30pm. Free.) Turn right at the customs house and down 16 de Septiembre to Mariscal to find a bust commemorating the city's most famous exile, namesake **Benito Juárez,** who hid here during the French coup led by Maximilian in 1865-1866. To the west of Av. Juárez at Av. 16 de Septiembre, is the huge plaza with the outdoor **Mercado Cuauhtémoc,** the thoroughly modern **Catedral,** and next to it the white adobe **Misión de Guadalupe,** built in 1662. (Open daily 7:30am-8:30pm.) The **Mercado Juárez** building, on 16 de Septiembre three blocks east of Av. Juárez, has everything from trinkets to homemade elixirs.

The **Museo de Arte** is in a dated 1960s cylindrical building, west of the Plaza de las Américas Mall in the ProNaf Zone and just east of the curve of Av. Lincoln at Coyoacán. The museum contains a small collection of art by contemporary artists influenced by classic Spanish and Mexican modernism. (☎616 7414. Open Tu-Su 11am-7pm. Free.) To escape the clamor of downtown Ciudad Juárez, head to **Parque Chamizal,** south of the Chamizal Bridge, 1km north of ProNaf, and 2km east of the *centro*. The park sits on what used to be a natural islet carved by the meandering Rio Grande. The area has often changed hands, and is now considered Mexican territory. Its large shade trees, picnic tables, fountains, grass, and recreational fields provide welcome respite from the sprawling, concrete-laden city. Every October, the park hosts **Las Chupacabras,** a 100km bike race that is considered one of the most extreme sporting events in Mexico. The **Museo Arqueológico,** in Parque Chamizal, houses plastic facsimiles of Pre-Hispanic sculptures as well as prehistoric fossils, rocks, and bones. Heading east on Av. Presidencia alongside the park, take the first (unnamed) major street to the left into the park. Another block down, past the curve in the road, the museum is on the right. Heading south from the Chamizal bridge, take the second right once in the park. (☎611 1048. Open Tu-Sa 9am-5pm, Su 11am-5pm. Free.)

Bullfighting was once a fixture of life in Juárez but in recent years animal rights activism has dampened enthusiasm for the sport. With fewer Americans buying

NORTHWEST MEXICO

SOTOL ME ALL ABOUT IT

Although tequila has gained a worldwide reputation, few people have heard of its cousin, *sotol*.

Along with tequila and *mezcal*, *sotol* is made from a plant of the agave family. Unlike tequila, which is made from blue agave, *sotol* is distilled from the *Agavacea dasylirion*, a smaller plant that grows in the mountains and deserts of Chihuahua. *Agavacea* hearts are cooked, shredded, fermented, distilled, and finally aged from six months *(reposado sotol)* to over a year *(añejo sotol)*.

Local *indígenas* first discovered *sotol*'s intoxicating properties over 800 years ago; it didn't take the Spanish long to catch on and, with the aid of European distillation techniques, enhance the purification process. Despite having been enjoyed for centuries in Chihuahuan *haciendas*—indeed, many families brew their own version of the drink—*sotol* has only recently begun to achieve international recognition. Take caution with a homemade version of *sotol*, called *bacanora*, as it has a high alcohol content and is equivalent to moonshine. *Bacanora* can also cause blindness if poorly distilled.

Sotol admirers claim that it has a smoother taste than its better-known relative. But perhaps *sotol*'s strongest selling point is its price—a bottle of top-notch *sotol* costs only a fraction of the price of similar-quality tequila.

tickets, weekly fights are less sustainable. However, it is still possible to catch occasional shows at the **Plaza Monumental de Toros,** Paseo Triunfo de la República, 500m east of López Mateos. Fights are held sporadically in the summer only on Sundays at 10am and/or 6pm. (Shady side 250/140 pesos. Sunny side 150/70 pesos. Children 15 pesos.) **Lienzo Charro,** on Av. del Charro, 500m north of República, hosts the *charreada* (rodeo) on weekend afternoons during the summer. Call ahead for times. (☎611 0465. Prices typically 25-50 pesos, children free.)

♫ NIGHTLIFE

The nightclubs lining the first few blocks of Av. Juárez south of the border cater primarily to Americans, particularly those under 21, who only need to walk a few hundred yards from the US to drink legally. These clubs play Top 40 hits and usually have a US$7-10 cover charge. For less tourist-oriented nightlife, head to the corner of Mejía and Av. Lincoln in the ProNaf Zone (taxi US$7).

Dalí, Mejía 3118 (☎611 4898). Intellectuals, pseudo-intellectuals, and sophisticates-in-training mingle and sip java (with and without alcohol; 25-30 pesos) in this decidedly un-Juárez relaxed atmosphere. Hookah bar. Wi-Fi available. Open M-Th and Su 5pm-1am, F-Sa 5pm-2am. MC/V.

La Mulata, Lincoln 1055 (613 0020). The city's best dressed swing the corner here to the newest Latin pop beats. Don't be surprised if you see some Versace. Mixed drinks from 30 pesos. Cover 50 pesos most nights. Open F-Sa 8pm-2am. MC/V.

Palacio Coin, Av. Juárez across from Gonzales. The friendly female bartenders in this local hole-in-the-wall away from the bigger clubs of Av. Juárez will keep you well refreshed. F-Sa 9pm live *cantina* band music. Beer 15 pesos. Margaritas 25 pesos. Open daily noon-midnight. Cash only.

Chamuco's, Mejía and Franklin 2nd fl. (616 8937). Catering to a slightly older crowd, this large sports bar, popular with Americans, has a congenial atmosphere and cheap drinks. Billiards 40 pesos per hr. Th all-you-can-drink beer US$10. Yard of beer 80 pesos. Open M-Th 11am-1am, F-Sa 11am-2am. MC/V.

La Serata, Lincoln 1045 (611 5785). A popular electro-bar in the ProNaf area. Lasers and lamplights dance to various trance and house beats. Th 2-for-1 beer. Mixed drinks from 30 pesos. Yard of beer 80 pesos. Billiards 40 pesos per hr. Cover 50 pesos. Open Th-Sa 8pm-2am. MC/V.

NUEVO CASAS GRANDES (NCG)   ☎ 636

Nuevo Casas Grandes (pop. 80,000) is an aging, dreadfully quiet town in the blistering Chihuahuan desert where *vaqueros* (Mexican cowboys) still run the streets. NCG arose at the beginning of the 20th century after a group of pioneer families from Casas Grandes moved their kids—children *and* goats—to the newly constructed railroad station. Nuevo Casas Grandes is still an agricultural center, but the city itself is of little interest to the budget traveler, other than as a base for exploring surrounding archaeological sites. Of these, the most popular are the ruins of **Paquimé**, Casas Grandes's Zuñi namesake and **Gran Chichimeca**, northern Mexico's pre-Hispanic capital.

◧ TRANSPORTATION. Nuevo Casas Grandes is most easily reached by bus, and the ride into town through the Sierra Madre is breathtaking, albeit painfully hot. To get from the **bus station** on Obregón and 16 de Septiembre to the *centro*, walk one block on 16 de Septiembre to Constitución, which runs past the railroad tracks that form the backbone of the city. **Chihuahuenses** and **Ómnibus de México** (☎ 694 0780) run buses to: **Chihuahua** (4hr., every hr., 206 pesos); **Ciudad Juárez** (3½hr., every hr., 161 pesos); **Cuauhtémoc** (6½hr., 3 per day, 175 pesos); **Monterrey** (16hr., 6 per day, 737 pesos); and **Nogales** (8½hr., 1 per day, 330 pesos.) **Taxis** loiter near the corner of 16 de Septiembre and Constitución but most places in Nuevo Casas Grandes are only a short walk from the city center.

◪ PRACTICAL INFORMATION. Constitución, Calle Juárez, 5 de Mayo, and **16 de Septiembre** form the grid that is the city center. The **tourist office** is located on Benito Juárez and Ignacio Zaragoza, near the car dealerships. (Open daily from 9am to 5pm), **Casa de Cambio California,** Constitución 207 offers **currency exchange.** (☎ 694 3232 or 4545. Open M-Sa 9am-6pm.); several **banks** line 5 de Mayo; most have **24hr. ATMs.** Laundry services are available at **Lavasolas la Chiquita,** Minerva 423, right before Madero. (Wash, dry, and detergent 30 pesos per kg. Open daily.). Other services include: **emergency:** ☎ 060; **police** (☎ 694 0973), on Blanco and Obregón; **IMSS hospital** at 1961 Benito Juárez Ave; **Farmacia Benavides,** on the corner of 5 de Mayo and Obregón. (☎ 694 3545. Open daily 7am-11pm.); **LADATELs** at most street corners; phone cards can be purchased at **Celcom** (☎ 694 6876) on 419 Constitución Ave; **Copias y Fax,** at Obregón and 5 de Mayo, offers **Internet access** (☎ 694 6876; 20 pesos per hr.; copies 0.60 pesos; open daily 8am-9pm.); and the **Post Office** at 16 de Septiembre and Madero. (☎ 694 2016. Open M-F 9am-3:30pm.) **Postal Code:** 31700.

⌂◖ ACCOMMODATIONS AND FOOD. The rooms at **Hotel Paquimé ❺**, Benito Juárez 401, come with white tile floors, spotless bathrooms, hot tub, kitchenette, full bar, and valet parking. (☎ 694 1320; hotel paquime@paquinet.com.mx. Singles 270 pesos; doubles 340 pesos.) At **Hotel California ❺**, 211 Av. Constitución, there are no mirrors on the ceiling; there is no pink champagne on ice. Nonetheless, large, spotless rooms with A/C and satellite TV offer a comfortable stay. (☎ 694 1110 or 2214; fax 694 0834. Singles 325 pesos; doubles 350 pesos. Cash only.)

Most of NCG's restaurants cluster on Constitución and Juárez between 5 de Mayo and Urueta. NCG's more expensive restaurants combine American diner decor with *norteño* cuisine. **Tortas Chuchy ❷**, on Constitución and 5 de Mayo, offers an extensive selection of excellent *tortas* (sandwiches), grilled hot dogs and convenience store junk food, with a sputtering fan and a television tuned to *fútbol* in the corner. (*Torta*, drink, and fries combo 25 pesos. Cash only.) A family business for over 50 years, **Restaurante Constantino ❹**, on Juárez at Minerva, serves up hot *comida* on red-and-white checkered tables. Chicken tacos 45 pesos. Steaks 80-110 pesos. (☎694 1005. Open daily 7am-midnight. MC/V.) **Supermercado el Triunfo,** on Constitución and 2 de Abril, is a brand-new, air-conditioned and well-stocked supermarket. (Open M-Sa 7am-8pm, Su 7am-4pm).

▶ DAYTRIPS FROM NUEVOS CASAS GRANDES

LAS RUINAS DE PAQUIMÉ

Best visited as a daytrip from Nuevo Casas Grandes, Paquimé is an easy 15min. walk from the town of Casas Grandes. From NCG, catch a yellow bus labeled "Pueblo" from the intersection of Constitución and 16 de Septiembre (10min., every hr., 5.50 pesos). Get off at the main plaza of Casas Grandes and walk back in the direction the bus just came on Constitución. A few bends in the road lead to Paquimé. Be sure to note the return bus to NCG does not depart until 4pm

Up until colonization, the entire valley surrounding Nuevo Casas Grandes was filled with loosely allied indigenous villages. At the center of this cultural network was the city of Paquimé, the ancient hegemon of all Gran Chichimeca (see below). Today, many archaeological sites of the Chichimecan system can be easily explored from NCG.

The huge network of crumbling adobe walls rising out of the desert plain just beyond the old town of Casas Grandes comprises what used to be the commercial center of Gran Chichimeca, a pre-Hispanic indigenous civilization. The inhabitants of Paquimé, a people culturally related to the Anasazi of the American Southwest, once built cisterns and aqueducts to trap rainwater in order to irrigate the bean and corn fields. Paquimians used minerals and shells mined from the Sierra Madres as currency, and revered the Guacamaya Verde (Military Macaw), a green-plumaged bird used in many religious ceremonies. Decadence in the 15th century caused the city to fall into ruin about 100 years before the arrival of the Spanish and the torching of the city that followed. The attached museum contains an amazing collection of artifacts found on-site, including religious items and exquisite pottery, with explanations in English and Spanish. The museum also features a miniature model of the city to help explain the partially eroded site. On Allende, one of the roads leading up to Paquimé, about a half-dozen stores sell cheap "Paquimean" pottery. (Ruins and Museo de las Culturas del Norte ☎692 4140. Open Tu-Su 10am-5pm. 45 pesos, children and students free.

OTHER SIGHTS IN GRAN CHICHIMECA. A bus leaves daily around 4pm from the corner of Constitución and 16 de Septiembre for **Mata Ortiz** (40km south of NCG), a town famous for its revival of Paquimé-style pottery. Be sure to ask around for the most accurate departure time, as bus schedules vary, and *camiones* only make one or two stops a day. When boarding, make sure to check when the last bus departs. On the way to Mata Ortiz, the dirt road passes Colonia Juárez (23km southwest of NCG), a Mormon colony founded by Latter-day Saints escaping the 19th-century prosecution of polygamy in the US. Although Colonia Juárez can be reached by staying on the "Pueblo" bus past Paquimé, most sites are inaccessible without a car; it is best to hire a guide who has a truck. Keep in mind that guides and hotel staff are a great source of information about the archeological sites.

Equally fascinating archaeological sites are at **Arroyo de los Monos** (35km southeast of NCG), which has ancient cave paintings, and **Cueva de la Olla** (55km southwest of NCG), a series of adobe structures built into a cave. About 254km southeast of NCG is **Madera,** from which the **Cuarenta Casas** site can be reached (54km north).

CHIHUAHUA

☎ 614

Founded in 1709, the city of Chihuahua (pop. 775,000) is considered the heart of the Northwest, thanks mostly to three centuries of havoc and gunfire. It was here that Conservative forces executed Mexican Independence martyr Manuel Hidalgo in 1811. It was here that Benito Juárez established his government-in-exile after the invasion of the D.F. by French Imperial forces under Maximilian. It was here that Pancho Villa marshaled his Revolutionary forces during the Porfiriato, and also where the General's not-so-intact remains rest in peace. Though locked in memory, the city nonetheless remains aware of its current importance. Many characters saunter the wide streets of modern Chihuahua, from cowboy-clad *vaqueros*, Tarahumara weavers, Mennonite milkmaids, to the historically enlightened and culturally conscious *Let's Go* budget traveler.

⊏ TRANSPORTATION

Flights: Gen. Fierro Villalobos Airport (CUU; ☎ 420 5104), 14km from town. The "Aeropuerto" bus stops near Niños Héroes and Independencia; look for the sign. Airlines include **AeroCalifornia** (☎ 437 1022), **Aeroméxico** (☎ 415 6303 or 416 1171), and **Continental** (☎ 411 8787).

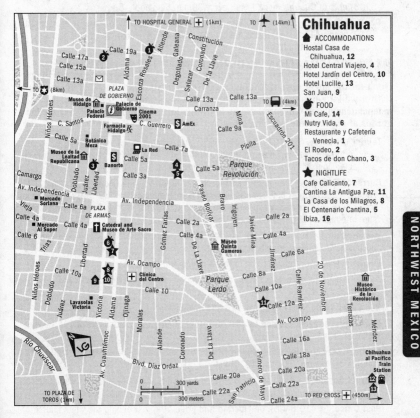

Chihuahua

⌂ ACCOMMODATIONS
Hostal Casa de
  Chihuahua, **12**
Hotel Central Viajero, **4**
Hotel Jardín del Centro, **10**
Hotel Lucille, **13**
San Juan, **9**

◆ FOOD
Mi Cafe, **14**
Nutry Vida, **6**
Restaurante y Cafetería
  Venecia, **1**
El Rodeo, **2**
Tacos de don Chano, **3**

★ NIGHTLIFE
Cafe Calicanto, **7**
Cantina La Antigua Paz, **11**
La Casa de los Milagros, **8**
El Centenario Cantina, **5**
Ibiza, **16**

NORTHWEST MEXICO

Trains: The **Chihuahua al Pacífico (CHEPE)** station, Méndez at Calle 24, south of the center off Ocampo and 2 blocks from 20 de Noviembre. To shorten the 20min. walk, hop on one of the public buses (4 pesos) that run up and down Ocampo to Libertad. The station is popular with backpackers for its daily CHEPE train that runs between **Chihuahua** and **Los Mochis**, cutting through the breathtaking Barrancas del Cobre (Copper Canyon; p. 264) (16hr.; 7am; 1st-class 1451 pesos; 2nd-class 660 pesos) via main stop **Creel** (1st-class 726 pesos, 2nd-class 330 pesos), **San Juan, El Divisadero, Posada Barrancas, Bahuichivo,** and **El Fuerte**. A second station, **Estación Central de los FFNN,** features the nighttime División del Norte train, with service between **Ciudad Juárez** and **Mexico City.**

Buses: From the **bus station,** a municipal bus (3 pesos) will take you to the cathedral. Taxis cost 70 pesos. **Ómnibus de México** (☎420 1580 or 0132) sends buses to: **Aguascalientes** (14hr., 7 per day, 688 pesos); **Ciudad Juárez** (every hr., 264 pesos) **Cuauhtémoc** (1½hr., 7 per day, 69 pesos); **Durango** (8hr., 9 per day, 421 pesos); **Guadalajara** (4 per day, 856 pesos); **Hidalgo del Parral** (3hr., every hr., 108 pesos); **Mexico City** (2 per day, 1052 pesos); **Monterrey** (4 per day, 546 pesos); **Nuevas Casas Grandes** (4hr., 4 per day, 206 pesos); **Torreón** (6hr., 315 pesos); **Zacatecas** (596 pesos). **Estrella Blanca** (☎429 0218) has a slightly older fleet that chugs to nearly all the same locations for about the same price. **Rápidos Cuauhtémoc** (☎410 5208) runs to **Cuauhtémoc** (1½hr., every 30min. 5am-noon, 64 pesos).

Car Rental: Alamo, Borunda 2500 (☎410 9707), before Revolución. **Avis** (airport ☎420 1919, *centro* 414 1919). **Hertz,** Revolución 514 (☎415 7818), at Santos.

■★🛈 ORIENTATION AND PRACTICAL INFORMATION

Don't let the sheer size of Chihuahua intimidate you—all sights of interest are within walking distance of the *centro*. With the exception of **Victoria, Aldama, Independencia,** and **Carranza,** streets in Chihuahua are poorly lit and may be dangerous at night. Avoid walking alone.

Tourist Office: (☎410 1077; fax 416 0032), on Aldama between Carranza and Guerrero, in the Palacio del Gobierno. Helpful staff and tourist guides. Tourist trolley service available. Open M-W 9am-7pm, Th-F 9am-5pm, Sa-Su 10am-5pm.

Currency Exchange: Casas de cambio cluster along Victoria. **Banorte,** Victoria 104 (☎410 1593). Open M-F 9am-3pm. **Hotel San Francisco** (☎439 9000), down the street, has 24hr. **currency exchange. ATMs** crowd the streets near the cathedral. Make sure late-night ATM transactions are done in well-lit areas.

Laundromat: Lavasolas Victoria, Victoria 1009, south of the San Juan hotel. Laundry 50 pesos. Open M-Sa 9am-8:30pm.

Emergency: ☎060. Quickest way to reach police and Red Cross.

Police: Homero 500 (☎442 7300), across from the Ford plant. **Tourist Security** Hotline ☎800 201 5589.

Red Cross: (☎411 9500), at Calle 24 and Revolución.

Pharmacy: Farmacia Hidalgo (☎410 6508), at Guerrero and Aldama. Open M-Sa 9am-9pm, Su 10am-2pm.

Medical Services: Hospital General (☎415 6305), at Av. Rosales and Calle 33a. **Clínica del Centro,** Ojinaga 816 (☎416 0022).

Internet Access: La Red, Ojinaga 508-1 (☎415 5615). 15 pesos per hr. Copy and fax 5 pesos per page. Open M-F 9am-8pm, Sa 10am-8pm.

Post Office: (☎410 6408), on Libertad and Calle 19a, just behind the white church of San Francisco. Open M-Sa 9am-5pm. **Postal Code:** 31000.

ACCOMMODATIONS

While the numerous hotels on Niños Héroes near the marketplace may be cheap, their cleanliness and safety can be suspect. A better bet would be paying the extra 20 pesos per night to stay in a hostel next to the CHEPE train.

Hostal Casa de Chihuahua, Méndez 2203 (☎410 0843), directly across from the CHEPE station. The hostel is brand-new and run by an international family. 5-peso coffee and 30-peso breakfasts as early as 5:30am are perfect for early morning train-hopping. Wi-Fi available. Dorms 140 pesos per person; 2-person groups 250 pesos. Cash only. ❷

Hotel Central Viajero (410 2683), on the corner of Calle 5a and Coronado. The best budget deal in the *centro* sports posters and photos of Revolutionary heroes and matadors on the walls. Rooms are a little dusty with low beds, but have A/C and TV. Singles 135 pesos; doubles 165 pesos. Cash only. ❷

Hotel Lucille, directly across from the CHEPE station. Rooms are clean and suitable for backpackers. Few amenities other than the attached restaurant. Reception 24hr. Check-out noon. Singles 140 pesos; doubles 200 pesos. Cash only. ❷

San Juan, Victoria 823 (☎410 0036). A 1930s relic with a tile courtyard, in a convenient location. All rooms with cable TV, some with A/C. Boasts a popular *cantina* and a small restaurant. Towel deposit 10 pesos. Internet access 10 pesos per hr. Singles 135 pesos; doubles 145 pesos. Cash only. ❶

FOOD

Chihuahua's eateries favor function over form. The city's many 1960s-style diners serve hearty meals for around 50 pesos a head. The small *cantinas*, where bands serenade drunken, rowdy men, guarantee cowboys late-night *antojitos*.

El Rodeo, Libertad 1705 (☎416 3080), at Calle 19a. Steaks, well worth the price, are the specialty (starting from 130 pesos). The *arrachera chihuahua especial* (flank steak; 95 pesos) is delightful, but don't tease: the *filete cabrería* (Porterhouse tenderloin; 140 pesos) is why you came. Open daily noon-8pm. MC/V. ❺

Nutry Vida, Victoria 420. An air-conditioned refuge for vegetarians. Also offers herbal supplements, yogurt dishes, and baked goods. Vegetarian *comida corrida* 30-40 pesos. Whole-wheat donut 4 pesos. Open daily 8am-8pm. Cash only. ❸

Tacos de Don Chano, Libertad 319 (☎437 0399), also accessible from Juárez. Located right in the middle of Mercado Libertad. A great, clean cafe for a quick lunch. Offers an array of tacos (4 for 40 pesos), burritos (20 pesos), and *antojitos* (30-40 pesos) served with delicious, homemade red and green salsas. Open daily 11am-8pm. Cash only. ❸

Restaurante y Cafetería Venecia, Rosales 1901 (☎416 5934). Turn right on Calle 19a going up Aldama. The Venecia serves a full range of *antojitos* and *carne,* and business always seems brisk. Combos 25-40 pesos. Open daily 7:30am-10pm. Cash only. ❸

SHOPPING AND SIGHTS

After you buy your cowboy hat and boots at the **Mercado Libertad** (Libertad between Independencia and Carranza), an even more eye-opening shopping experience awaits at **Botánica Meza,** Juárez 523, which sells a wide selection of herbs, talismans, *milagros,* magic powders, and charms to a serious clientele of *curanderas* (traditional healers) and the occasional witch. Even if you think it's moonshine, don't say so—*botánica* is not a good place to make enemies. (Open M-Sa 9am-2pm and 3-8pm; hours less predictable Su.) For produce and cheap clothing, **Mercado Al Super, Mercado Soriano,** and the surrounding shops on Niños Héroes are a more practical choice. A note for Chihuahua's museums: more times than not, simply asking for assistance will get you a free private tour. Most museums are overstaffed and have English-speaking guides ready to help.

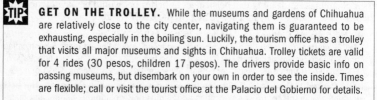

GET ON THE TROLLEY. While the museums and gardens of Chihuahua are relatively close to the city center, navigating them is guaranteed to be exhausting, especially in the boiling sun. Luckily, the tourism office has a trolley that visits all major museums and sights in Chihuahua. Trolley tickets are valid for 4 rides (30 pesos, children 17 pesos). The drivers provide basic info on passing museums, but disembark on your own in order to see the inside. Times are flexible; call or visit the tourist office at the Palacio del Gobierno for details.

■ **MUSEO HISTÓRICO DE LA REVOLUCIÓN.** Also known as **Quinta Luz,** this 50-room mansion was the home of Pancho Villa's (legal) widow Luz Corral, who maintained the museum and led tours until her death in 1981—60 years after her husband's. It is by far the most frequented museum in Chihuahua and paints a vivid portrait of the life and times of Villa and the fascinating events surrounding the Mexican Revolution of 1910. Items on display include Villa's personal effects, photographs, and heavy weapon collection. The star of the show is the bullet-ridden Dodge in which the unsuspecting Villa was assassinated in 1921. *(Calle 10a 3010. Walk 1.5km south on Ocampo, turn left on 20 de Noviembre, go 2 blocks to Calle 10, and turn right. The museum is in the large off-pink building to the left. ☎416 2958. Open Tu-Sa 9am-1pm and 3-7pm, Su 10am-4pm. 10 pesos.)*

■ **MUSEO REGIONAL DE CHIHUAHUA.** Commonly known as **Quinta Gameros,** this building is one of the more stunning mansions in Mexico, and a prime example of the French art nouveau style. Mining engineer Manuel Gameros, the aristocrat who contracted the building (1907-11), never had a chance to live here before the Revolution drove him to Texas. The house, itself a magnificent work of art, was seized by Revolutionaries, and at one point served as Pancho Villa's barracks and Venustiano Carranza's home. Owned and operated by the Universidad Autónoma de Chihuahua, Quinta Gameros is dedicated to providing recognition to Chihuahua's artists. The ground floor contains rotating exhibits from current local artists whose work is often for sale, while the upstairs houses an impressive collection of *chihuahuense* art from the past two centuries. *(On the corner of Calle 4 and Paseo Bolívar, a 10min. walk from the cathedral. ☎416 6680. Open Tu-Su 11am-2pm and 4-7pm. 20 pesos, students and children 10 pesos; W half-price.)*

PALACIO DE GOBIERNO. A 19th-century testament to *chihuahuense* history, the palace holds imposingly large Aarón Piña Mora murals, with flames marking the spots of Hidalgo's and Allende's executions, as well as a nude statue of Emiliano Zapata, whose modesty is maintained by a well-placed rifle brandished upright by a fallen comrade. It also houses the ever-helpful tourist office and two brand new museums. ■ **El Museo Galería de Armas** displays a collection of weapons used during Mexico's many wars, including a 3m long rifle used by the Spanish. ■ **El Museo de Hidalgo** depicts the life and times of Miguel Hidalgo with audio-visual commentary (English language assistance available). Although free at the moment, museum prices are subject to change. Contact the tourist office for details. *(At the center of Chihuahua on Aldama and Victoria. Palacio open daily 8am-7pm. Museums open Tu-Su 9am-5pm.)*

GRUTAS DE NOMBRE DE DIOS. Located 15min. from downtown in the *cerros* to the east of the city, this series of caverns contains fossils of fauna from the state's prehistoric age, when the land was an inner sea. Time has carved a series of passages wide enough for a walking tour, but not quite deep enough for spelunking. Among the impressive formations are the locally dubbed "Quixote," "La Torre de Pisa," and "El Aguila." Trained guides offer tours of the 17-room system. *(At Av. Colegio Militar. ☎400 7059. Open Tu-F 9am-4pm. Contact the tourist office prior to visit for directions and tour prices.)*

MUSEO DE LA LEALTAD REPUBLICANA CASA DE JUÁREZ. This museum chronicles the years the Mexican government spent in exile during the Maximilian-Hapsburg reign. Spanish writings by Benito Juárez and timelines elaborate the renovated rooms of Juárez's Chihuahuan home, where he lived from 1864 until 1866, when the Republican government was restored. The museum is an interesting glimpse of the influential minds and activists of Chihuahua's past. *(On Juárez between Independencia and Carranza in a rose building marked "Museo de Casa Juárez." ☎410 4258. Captions in Spanish. Open Tu-Su 9am-7pm. 10 pesos, students and children 5 pesos.)*

PALACIO FEDERAL. Constructed on the foundation of a much older Jesuit college that was the center of Spanish colonial Chihuahua, this Neoclassical building was finished in 1910. Walk down the stairs and to the back of the building to find the Calabozo de Miguel Hidalgo, the dungeon where Hidalgo was held by the Spanish government prior to his execution in 1811. The small entrance is visible several steps below street level. The museum displays his writings, crucifix, and the wall of his jail cell, on which he scrawled a few parting words to his captors with a piece of charcoal. *(The entrance to the Calabozo is on Juárez. ☎429 3300, ext. 1056. Open Tu-Su 9am-6pm. 10 pesos, students and children 5 pesos.)*

CATHEDRAL. Due to Apache raids and the unpredictable nature of mining money, it took 100 years to construct Chihuahua's Nuestra Señora de Regla y San Francisco de Asís. Finally finished in 1826, the beautiful Churrigueresque facade features the apostles and a large pipe organ. A great place to escape from the heat, the cathedral also attracts many visitors each day. In the southeastern corner is the small **Museo de Arte Sacro,** housing pastoral 18th-century religious paintings and a chair on which the late Pope John Paul II sat during his 1990 visit. *(In the centro. Entrance is on Victoria. Open M-F 10am-2pm and 4-6pm. 20 pesos, students 12 pesos.)*

🎵 📷 ENTERTAINMENT AND NIGHTLIFE

For those interested in grabbing the bull by its horns, the **Expogan,** Chihuahua's regional cattle show featuring rodeo, *palenque*, horse races, and fascinating agro-industrial exhibits, is held the first week of October. Chihuahua also sports its very own **Plaza de Toros,** at Reforma 2001. *Corridas* occur during the summer, but only intermittently—inquire at the tourist office for more details. Tickets run around 200 pesos in the shade and 150 pesos in the sun and can be purchased at the Plaza.

> **THE LOCAL STYLE.** Shopping in the dusty streets for a headpiece may be intimidating—the signature cowboy hat claims unrivaled importance in western North American culture. In the past, one could tell the origin of a farmhand by the shape and shade of his top. Although form is not so important as fashion in today's market, the shape is still key. The hippest and baddest *duranguenses* and *chihuahuenses* usually wear the hats with the sides turned up tight to the crown. This has led to some stereotyping—as one popular saying goes, *"Sombrero tejano, anteojos oscuros, traficante seguro."* (Texan hat, dark glasses, definitely a drug-trafficker.)

While Chihuahua has a disco scene in the Zona Dorada (north of the *centro*), visitors may prefer a more typical *norteño* evening at one of the many *cantinas* in the city. *Cantinas* are El Norte's version of the traditional cowboy saloon, with dark wood interiors, endless rivers of tequila, and rowdy *vaqueros*. Lounging at a bar's outdoor courtyard, and listening to live guitar music can be a more relaxed way to take advantage of Chihuahua's beautiful nights.

Cafe Calicanto, Aldama 411 (☎410 4452), across from the Casa de Cultura. Chihuahua's sophisticates come to enjoy mixed drinks and snacks at this idyllic cafe, where local singers and songwriters serenade the beautiful open-air, umbrella-blessed patio. After 9pm on weekends, *tortas* are 25 pesos. Beer 20 pesos. Tequila from 30 pesos. Open Tu-Sa 6pm-2am. Cash only.

La Casa de los Milagros (☎437 0693), 1½ blocks south of the cathedral on Victoria. Beautiful people wind down to the sounds of live guitar music among statues of angels and saints. Serves Bohemia and Tecate, the Northwest's favorite beers (25 pesos), and an impressive selection of wine. Cigars 25 pesos. Open M-Th and Su 5pm-midnight, F-Sa 5pm-1am. Cash only.

El Centenario Cantina, Coronado 503 (☎410 2019). A safe bar patronized by *fútbol*-fanatic locals on weeknight and raucous cowboys on the weekends. Beer 20 pesos. Open M-Th and Su 6pm-midnight, F-Sa 6pm-2am. MC/V.

Cantina La Antigua Paz, Calle 12a 2201 (☎410 1466). A traditional *cantina* (they're rare) offering the usual *machismo* in a 90-year-old setting, complete with inspiring reliefs and old newspaper clippings. A great place to rest after visiting the Museo Histórico de la Revolución. Beer 20 pesos. Open daily 10am-midnight. Cash only.

▶ DAYTRIP FROM CHIHUAHUA

CUAUHTÉMOC

Cuauhtémoc lies halfway between Creel and Chihuahua, a 1½hr. bus ride from each. From Chihuahua, both Ómnibus de México (☎582 1201) and Estrella Blanca (☎429 0240) run 4 buses per day to Cuauhtémoc for about 69 pesos. Rapiditos Cuauhtémoc runs back and forth every 45 min for 64 pesos. Take the Aeropuerto or Circunvalación-1 buses from the corner of Niños Héroes and Independencia (4 pesos) to the Terminal Central del Autobuses. Cuauhtémoc's Módolo de Información Turística, an information kiosk in the Plaza Principal on Morelos between Melgar and Suárez, offers general advice and will organize outings to local restaurants for groups of 5 or more. (☎581 3488. Generally open M-F 9am-1pm and 3-5pm, Sa 9am-noon.)

Cuauhtémoc is both a modern center for agricultural production and a supply station for the extremely conservative societies of the Germanic Mennonites and the indigenous Tarahumara. Buses to Cuauhtémoc travel through spectacular desert landscapes, which alone make the trip worthwhile.

For visitors passing through Cuauhtémoc on their way to or from **Las Barrancas del Cobre** (Copper Canyon; p. 264), the Mennonites and their tidy *campos* in the surrounding valley are the city's main attraction. Founded in the 15th century, this German pacifist religious group moved from Europe to Russia to Canada trying to escape persecution and forced military service. After the British government forced Mennonites into military service during WWI, many migrated to Mexico with the stipulation that they would not fight any wars. Since the 1920s, they have become the most important agricultural producers in the state and enjoy traditional agrarian lifestyles in numbered *campos*.

To see the famous Mennonite cheese in production, your best bet is to head to **La Quesería América,** Campo 2b, a modern factory that uses traditional techniques. (☎587 7249 or 7300. Cheese about 50 pesos per kg. Open M-F 8am-6pm, Sa 8am-5pm.) The **Museo de los Mennonitas,** near the entrance to Campo 21, features displays on all aspects of Mennonite life, from agriculture to the home, and has a series of English-language videos on the history of the Mennonites. (20 pesos, ages 12-18 10 pesos. Open M-Sa 9am-5pm.)

Since many *campos* don't allow visitors, the best way to see these sights is with a Mennonite guide. ▣**Jacob Harms Loepke,** a member of the Mennonite church who used to live in the communities near Cuauhtémoc, conducts half-day tours of the above mentioned sites, traditional churches and schools, and even to a Mennonite household where you can buy fantastic homemade cookies (3 pesos each) and experience a traditional Mennonite buffet (50 pesos per person). Tours in English, German, and Spanish can be booked at the plaza tourist kiosks, or directly through Jacob Loepke by calling his cell phone (☎283 6971. 4-person groups 350 pesos. Tour bus for larger groups 150 pesos per person.)

HIDALGO DEL PARRAL ☎627

In 1640, when silver from local mines began pouring into Spain, King Philip IV himself christened Parral the "Silver Capital of the World." The title remained until the mines became unprofitable in the 1950s. Locals—unphased by this turn of fate—simply dropped the silver bit, renaming Hidalgo "Capital of the World." The *pueblo* was notably the site of Pancho Villa's breakfast-time assassination. Buses also connect Parral to Guachochi on the eastern end of the Sierra Madre Occidental, making Parral the backdoor to surreal, unparalleled Copper Canyons (p. 264).

▐ **TRANSPORTATION.** To go downtown from the **bus station,** exit left out of the front door and walk two blocks down Pedro de Sille. Turn left onto Independencia and follow it downhill to the *centro*. A 25-peso taxi ride can replace the 15min. walk and is often a better alternative to navigating the confusing streets. **Estrella Blanca** (☎523 0075) runs buses to: **Chihuahua** (4hr., 7 per day, 108 pesos); **Ciudad Juárez** (7hr., 8 per day, 372 pesos); **Guadalajara** (1 per day, 713 pesos); **Mexico City** (20hr., 3:30pm, 856 pesos); **Guachochi** (2hr., 66 pesos). To get to **Torreón,** change buses at Jiménez (1hr., 8 per day, 48 pesos). **Taxis** can be hailed at Plaza Principal, along Mercaderes or Jesús García.

▐ **PRACTICAL INFORMATION.** The 9am to 5pm routine is unheard of in Parral; this city takes its *siesta* seriously. Except for a few *cantinas* and restaurants, everything closes from 1-3:30pm. Expect no help during *siesta* hours, even if you beg. Parral has **no official tourist office,** but hotel and museum staff—especially the history buffs at the **Museo de Pancho Villa**—will be happy to point out sights. Parral has many competing *casas de cambio*, and the most centrally located **ATM** is at **Banamex,** on Mercaderes just before Ojinaga. Other services include: **police,** at Independencia and Lozoya (☎523 0575); **Red Cross,** at Balderas and Chapultepec (☎523 4700); **Farmacia Independiente de Parral,** Independencia 43, in the *centro* (☎523 2584; open daily 8am-midnight); **Hospital de Jesús,** at Cintrón and Zaragoza (☎522 0027 or 0064); **Internet** access, copy and fax service at **AMPM Ciber Cafe,** on Jesús García across from Hotel Chihuahua on the second floor, (Internet access 10 pesos per hr.; open M-Sa 9am-9pm); and the **post office,** at Rago and Libertad, a few blocks from the cathedral (open M-F 8am-3pm). **Postal Code:** 33800.

LOCAL LEGEND

HIDALGO HEARSAY

Years before his assassination, Pancho Villa claimed: *"Parral me gusta para morirme"* (I like Parral enough to die here). On July 23, 1923, the famous general left his home for breakfast, accompanied in his black 1919 Dodge Roadster by a few bodyguards. Driving past the corner of the plaza, the Dodge and the *dorados* were shot over 150 times in under a minute. Villa himself took 10 bullets to the body and 4 to the head, and died instantly.

From there the story gets shady. It is generally accepted that Villa was buried in a grave within the Parral cemetary. His assassins surrendered, receiving a partial pardon from the government. As the assassins were imprisoned rather than executed, suspicions grew about former President Plutarco Elías Calles's role in the massacre.

When Pancho's corpse was exhumed three years after burial, it was discovered that he had been decapitated. Rumors say one of Villa's German mercenaries, Captain Holmdahl, cut off and sold the head to a skull-collecting Chicago millionaire. Others say it was taken by his lieutenants, marched in funeral procession to Villa's birthplace in the Durango mountains.

Many years later, the government called for Villa's body to be taken to the Tomb of Illustrious Men in the capital. According to Parral's citizens, the anthropologists did not recover Villa's portly body from the grave, but instead the corpse of a peasant woman. Whispers still insinuate Mayor Don Pedro Alvarado secretly switched the bodies, hiding Villa's remains somewhere below Parral's streets.

ACCOMMODATIONS AND FOOD. The most central budget option is **Hotel Chihuahua ❸,** Colón 1. From Plaza Baca, walk on Mercaderes toward the *centro* and turn left on García. Keep left on García until Colón. The hotel is across from Club Viet-Nam. The friendly, helpful staff keeps clean rooms with good ventilation and hot showers. (☎522 1513. Singles 150 pesos, with cable TV 180 pesos; doubles 200/250 pesos. Cash only.) **Hotel San Miguel ❷,** Jesús García 41, across from the Chihuahua, has cheap green-brick rooms with TV. (☎522 6066. Singles 150 pesos; doubles 200 pesos).

Watch as your food is cooked over a wood fire at **Restaurante el Aseradero ❸,** Independencia 345, after Primavera toward the *centro*. Chow down on chicken, beef, and *cabrito* (goat) for 40-50 pesos. (☎523 0271. Open daily 10am-10pm. Cash only.) Closer to the *centro*, **Cafe Chihuahua ❷,** attached to the hotel, serves excellent egg-based *desayunos* for under 30 pesos. (Open daily 8am-10pm. Cash only). Buy groceries at **El Camino** (☎523 0663), on Independencia just outside downtown.

SIGHTS AND ENTERTAINMENT. Parral's mining days may be over, but the city has just begun to capitalize on the history left behind. A good place to get a sense of Parral's former wealth is the **Palacio Alvarado,** at Calle Riva Palacio and Licenciado Verdad. Constructed from 1899 to 1903 by French architect Amérigo Rouvier for Don Pedro Alvarado—a mine owner so wealthy he once offered to pay off Mexico's entire national debt—the building has just been extensively restored and decked out with all its original furniture. (☎522 0290. Photography prohibited. Open daily 10am-6pm. 10 pesos, children 7 pesos.) Pancho Villa spent the last years of his life in Mercaderes across the river until assassins riddled him and his car with 150 bullets. Right next to the scene is the **Museo de Francisco Villa,** Gabino Barrera 13, which indulges his cult-like followers with a downstairs shrine and an upstairs exhibit focusing on Villa's martyrdom, complete with pictures of his gory end. A starred plaque next to a small tree outside the museum marks the spot of Villa's assassination. (☎525 3292. Open Tu-Su 9am-1pm and 3-7pm. 10 pesos, children 5 pesos.) Many artifacts of Parral's former glory are still kept at **Museo Regional en La Mina La Prieta** outside of town. (☎525 4400. Call for hours and directions; generally open daily 10am-5pm). A visit to the **Templo de la Virgen de Fátima,** Barrio de Fátima 19, gives a sense of the local devotion to the patron saint of miners. The walls are constructed from thousands of glittering chunks of local ore, and the square pews copy those in the mine's shrines. Many of the city's other churches are also elaborately decorated. The oldest is the **Templo de San José** at Morenos and 20 de Noviembre, which was finished in 1684 and is an excellent example of the Spanish Baroque influence in Mexican architecture.

For big-screen fun, visit **Mega Cinema** (☎ 523 3060), at Independencia and Constitución. Outside of the usual male-dominated *cantinas* found in the *centro*, good times roll at **J. Quísseme,** a lounge and dance club on Independencia near the bus station. Things start hopping after 10pm. (Beer 25 pesos. Cover 30 pesos. Open Th-F 8pm-1am, Sa 9pm-2am.) The club **Lone Star,** by the stadium, is another local favorite, especially among Parral's youth. (Beer 25 pesos. Cover 30 pesos. Open W-Sa 9pm-3am.) Every July 14-21, **Las Jornadas Villistas** take hold of Parral. This festival, commemorating the assassination of Pancho Villa, draws thousands of cult enthusiasts and bikers to Parral, where they participate in days of cultural activities and nights of debauchery. The streets fill with cockfights, concerts, bike rallies, and theater shows, culminating on July 21 with a dramatic reenactment of Villa's assassination.

CREEL ☎ 635

Creel's railway—the CHEPE train—now hauls loads of tourists rather than gold, but the high altitude and dramatic, rocky surroundings of the western boom town help it stay cool and collected in the midst of this backpacker bombardment. The town (pop. 5000) has frigid temperatures in the winter, making it a great place to escape the summer heat and humidity of lowland Mexico. While the steady flow of foreigners has turned the main street into a row of hotels, restaurants, and gift shops, it hasn't diluted Creel's rugged ambience. The town still hosts local lumber industries as well as a hospital and school for indigenous Tarahumara children. Creel is the most popular base for excursions into Las Barrancas del Cobre and the Sierra Tarahumara, and the wilderness surrounding Creel is picturesque and easily accessible. Creel's incongruous mix of budget travelers, *indígenas*, and small-business entrepreneurs make it a worthy stop in its own right.

▨ TRANSPORTATION

Creel is one of the few towns in the Sierra Tarahumara accessible both by bus and train and is the best starting point for trips into the canyons. The only transportation between Creel and the coast is the train. Buses only go north and east, since the Sierra is very difficult to traverse by road.

Trains: CHEPE trains (☎ 456 0015; www.CHEPE.mx.com) leave Las Barrancas daily for **Chihuahua** (1st-class 6hr., 3:30pm, 660 pesos; 2nd-class 6hr., 7pm, 330 pesos) and **Los Mochis** (1st-class 10hr., 11:15am, 793 pesos; 2nd-class 11hr., 1:20pm, 397 pesos). Rates are lower for a trip to an in-between stop such as **Divisadero** or **El Fuerte.** 2nd-class tickets are not sold in advance from the Creel station, so scramble on quickly when the train pulls up and elbow for a seat. Cash only.

Buses: The **Estrella Blanca** station (☎ 456 0073) is a small white-and-green building uphill across the tracks from town. Buses to **Chihuahua** (5hr., 7per day 7am-5:30pm, 195 pesos) pass through **Cuauhtémoc** (4hr., 121 pesos). To travel to **Hidalgo de Parral,** take a bus to **Guachochi** (noon, 5:30pm; 82pesos) and transfer to **Parral** (185 pesos). Buses also go to Ciudad Juárez (8:30am, 476 pesos). Buses to **Batopilas** (6hr.; M, W, F 9:30am and Tu, Th, Sa 7:30am; 160 pesos) leave from Hotel los Piños on Mateos. Tickets are available from Hotel los Piños, as well as on the bus. Service is highly contingent upon weather and road conditions. **Noroeste,**

next to the Estrella Blanca station, offers service to **Chihuahua** and **Cuauhtémoc** (3 per day) and **San Rafael/Divisadero** (2 per day) for similar prices.

Bike Rental: Margarita's Casa de Huéspedes (p. 266) rents cheap bikes (80 pesos per day). **Los 3 Amigos** rents newer bikes. (90 pesos for 5hr. or 150 pesos per 24hr.) Free Internet access included with the price of bike rental.

✦ 🛈 ORIENTATION AND PRACTICAL INFORMATION

The railroad tracks function as a rough compass: toward **Chihuahua** is north and toward **Los Mochis** is south. The *zócalo* is the best place in which to get your bearings. The main street, **Mateos,** runs parallel to the tracks on the opposite side of the *zócalo* and is the only street near the *zócalo* that extends any distance. Most listings are south of the train station on Mateos, or on **Batista** or **Flores,** which branch off Mateos to the east. **Villa** parallels the tracks on the opposite side of Mateos. The areas beyond Mateos are very underdeveloped and mainly residential. Most activity takes place on Mateos.

■ **Tourist Information:** In Creel and Las Barrancas del Cobre, it's extremely important to get reliable, honest information before setting out anywhere. There is no Chihuahuense Tourism Information office, but it is not necessary: ■ **Los 3 Amigos,** Mateos 46 (☎ 456 0179; www.amigos3.com), prides itself on providing tourists with thorough information in English, Italian, Spanish, and Thai. Ivan, Yolanda and Salvador have an amazing knowledge of the area, its history, and its accessibility, and arrange tours and guides as well. Norberto, owner of **El Aventurero,** Mateos 68, next to Casa de Huéspedes Margarita, is another great source of information and runs tours on horseback throughout the valleys surrounding Creel.

Bank: Banco Santander, next to Casa de Huéspedes Margarita, (☎ 456 0250), has a **24hr. ATM.** Exchanges US$ and traveler's checks M-F 9am-3pm.

Police: (☎ 456 0450), in the Presidencia Seccional, on the south side of the *zócalo.*

Pharmacy: Farmacia Rodríguez, Mateos 43 (☎ 456 0052). Open M-Sa 9am-1pm and 3-8pm, Su 10am-1pm.

Medical Services: Clínica Santa Teresita (☎ 456 0105), on Parroquia, at the end of the street behind Margarita's Casa de Huéspedes, 2 blocks from Mateos. Open M-F 10am-1pm and 3-5pm, Su 10am-1pm.

Fax Office: Papelería de Todo, Mateos 30 (☎/fax 456 0122). Open M-Sa 9am-8:30pm, Su 9am-1pm.

Internet Access: Compu Center, Mateos 33 (☎ 456 0345). 20 pesos per hr. The 6 computers fill up quickly during high backpacker season. Open 9:30am-10pm.

Post Office: (☎ 456 0258), in the Presidencia Seccional, on the south side of the *zócalo.* Open M-F 9am-3pm. **Postal Code:** 33200.

🛏 ACCOMMODATIONS AND CAMPING

Due to Creel's popularity with Canyon-bound tourists, a large number of establishments compete for tourist pesos. The result is straight out of an economics textbook: plentiful budget rooms and negotiable prices during low season. Many accommodations are within a couple of blocks of the *zócalo.* The **Villa Mexicana** campground offers relatively safe and affordable camping. Free camping is available near **Lake Arareco** or around the bike trail, but may be unsafe—use caution.

Margarita's Casa de Huéspedes, Mateos 11 (☎ 456 0045). Always full of travelers, this is the best deal around by a long shot: 1 night in a dorm room, 1 dinner, 1 breakfast, and loads of information for only 80 pesos. Younger staff members often wait at the train station to guide backpackers to the hostel, and provide English-language tours of the area. Breakfast and dinner included. Laundry 50 pesos. Bike rental 80 pesos per day. Dorm bed 80 pesos. Private singles with hot shower 250 pesos; doubles 300 pesos. Cash only. ❶

Casa de Huéspedes Perez, Flores 257 (☎456 0391). From the train station, head to the main plaza and turn right on Mateos. Make a left at Video BJ, walk down the street, cross the green bridge, and walk directly uphill to the first house. Comfortably rustic accommodations with clean bath, heater, and the tremendous hospitality of Luli and her family. Kitchen and laundry facilities available. English-language tours offered by **M&M Tours,** run by Luli's sons. Singles 160 pesos; doubles 200 pesos; triples 300 pesos. Cash only. ❷

Hotel Los Valles (456 0092), on Batista just off Mateos. Relatively new, spotless, centrally located, and in great shape. Room price includes private bath, heater, and satellite TV. Singles 220 pesos; doubles 300 pesos. ❸

Hotel la Posada de Creel (☎456 0142), across from the train tracks from the *zócalo* and to the left. A cheap option for private rooms. Tidy rooms with wood paneling have gas heating and 24hr. hot water. Bunk-bed singles 100 pesos; private single with bath 150 pesos; doubles with bath 180 pesos. Cash only. ❶

Hotel la Villa Mexicana (☎/fax 456 0665 or 0666; www.vmcoppercanyon.com), on Mateos. From the train station, cross the *zócalo* and turn right on Mateos; the campground is on the left after about 1.5km. A good place to answer the call of the wild or look for longer-term group lodgings. Log cabins, RV hookups, and camping spots cluster around a main clubhouse. 4-bed cabins US$65 per night. Campsites US$10 per night. AmEx/D/MC/V. ❶

🍴 FOOD

Cheap, tasty food is easy to find in Creel and comes with a smile. There is a supermarket, **Comercial de Creel,** on Mateos 55. (Open M-Sa 9am-8pm.) After-hours hot dog stands dot Mateos. (Jumbo hot dogs 20 pesos.)

▨ **El Tungar** (☎456 0130), on the train tracks south of the station. A sign outside proclaims El Tungar is "the hospital for hangovers." Appropriately, all the food is on the spicy side. You'll find *menudo, pozole,* and *mariscos* from 30-50 pesos. Burritos 14 pesos. ▨**Arí,** a local drink made from ant excretions, is also available. Open M-Sa 8pm-5pm, Su 8am-1pm. ❸

▨ **Tío Molcas,** Mateos 35 (☎456 0033). The local hang-out. Cheerful waitresses banter with customers during commercial breaks. The attached **bar** is the only bar in Creel. Burritos 15 pesos. Fried chicken 40 pesos. Filling beef dishes 40-50 pesos. Open daily 8am-11pm. Cash only. ❸

Cafetería Gaby, Mateos 50. Look for the "Cafe Combate" illustration. Offers a full range of Mexican treats (burritos and *tortas* 12 pesos) and combo meals for 35 pesos. If confused by the door, pull the string. Open daily 7am-10pm. Cash only. ❷

Veronica's, Mateos 34. Creel's flag-ship restaurant, and one of the best places to escape the heat with a hearty meal. *Ráramuri filete* (Ráramuri steak) 110 pesos. Open daily 7:30am-10:30pm. AmEx/MC/V. ❺

El Manzano, next door to El Tungar. Serves delicious beef, chicken, and pork dishes for 30-50 pesos. Open M-Sa 9am-7pm. Cash only. ❸

👁 🎵 SIGHTS AND ENTERTAINMENT

Tourists come to Creel to visit the breathtaking **Barrancas del Cobre,** which surround the entire town. To explore the canyons, you'll need a car, a tour guide, or a strong legs and a brave streak. Still, the town has some sights closer to home. **Museo Creel Tarahumara,** on Ferrocarril 17 in the old railroad station across from the *zócalo*, has exhibits on the town's eponymous founder, former Chihuahua governor Enrique Creel (1854-1931), as well as the Chihuahua-Pacific Railroad and Tarahumara history and mythology. (☎ 456 0080. Open Tu-F 9am-1pm and 3-6pm, Sa 9am-6pm, Su 9am-1pm. 10 pesos, students 7 pesos, children 5 pesos.) Dinosaur fossils and relics from the region's mining past can be found at **El Museo de Paleontogía,** near the beginning of Mateos. Look for the building with dinos on it. (Open Th-Tu 9am-1pm and 3-6pm. 10 pesos.)

While most of the establishments in Creel close before 9pm, there are a few late-night options. Tourists roam the streets and people strum guitars until midnight. **Tío Molcas,** Mateos 35 at Caro, is the only bar in the *centro*. Filled with tourists, locals, and Mexican sports fanatics, its relaxed atmosphere breaks *cantina* stereotypes. You'll find no trouble unless you bring it along. (Beer 15 pesos, free shot of tequila available upon request. Open daily 3pm-1am. Kitchen closes at 11pm.)

OUTDOOR ACTIVITIES

Creel has some of the best **mountain biking** terrain in the entire world, rivaling the legendary trails of Moab, Utah. Every July, **La Onza Copper Canyon Race** attracts hundreds of young cycling aficionados from all over the Western Hemisphere. Bikers will find single-track trails winding through tall pines, volcanic formations, and Tarahumara villages on the eastern mesas. It is recommended that beginners rent a sturdy bike from a travel agency before starting out on the **San Ignacio Loop,** a roughly 3hr. circuit around Creel's nearest daytrip sites. Longer excursions to the canyon towns are popular, but travelers should hire a guide familiar with the riding surface (slick rock and quick switchbacks). **Los 3 Amigos** rents new bikes (90 pesos for 5hr., 150 pesos for 24hr.), and has a permanent mechanic on staff. Free Internet access at the office is included in the package. **Umarike Tours** rents mountain bikes with front suspension in excellent shape, and also provides expert information. (120 pesos for 4hr., 180 pesos per day.)

The many cliffs and gorges in the area are perfect for **rock climbing, bouldering,** and **rappelling.** Most of the beautiful crag and face, however, is not for amateurs—climbing requires not only grit but also professional familiarity. The area inside **Chapultepec Park,** near the Plaza Mexicana, is the best site for beginner lessons or a few veteran hours with some overhang. Arturo Gutierrez at **Umarike Tours** is an expert spider-man and rents out gear and info. Visit www.umarike.com.mx to contact Arturo in advance.

Creel is also the starting point of several **ultra-marathons.** This is more than appropriate as the Tarahumara—whose tribal name means "runners on foot" in the Rárarmuri tongue—are considered to be some of the greatest long-distance runners in the world. A Tarahumara may run in his *huarachis* for up to four days, covering 50-80 miles per day. Although it's unlikely that you'll be doing any such marathoning, you'll likely see one or two running Tarahumara. Several locations along Mateos rent ATVs and dirt bikes, and the area behind the Hotel Villa Mexicana has excellent moguls for the more adventurous.

> **TIP**
> **WATCH THE PRICE.** Many tourists don't know that the municipality has a set price chart for tours that all companies and guides are expected to follow. The chart delineates how much guides are allowed to charge for a set number of people for certain locations. Ask to see the chart (it's on the wall at Los 3 Amigos; p. 266) to make sure you're not getting fleeced.

DAYTRIPS FROM CREEL

The valleys surrounding Creel are home to impressive rock formations, former cave dwellings, and breathtaking scenery. Above the canyon floors, there are many additional sights just a few hours from Creel, but none are accessible via the

CHEPE train. While many hotels and companies offer tours to Creel's vicinity, exploring on your own for free is probably your best option.

LAGUNA ARARECO AND ENVIRONS. Most sights are en route to **Laguna Arareco,** a semi-clean freshwater lake, and the best way to see all of them is to follow the loop around the water. Free maps of this route are available at Casa de Margarita (p. 266) and Los 3 Amigos (p. 266). Just past the park entrance, on the left, is **Cueva Sebastian** and **Misión de San Ignacio.** The caves have been home to one Tarahumara tribe for hundreds of years, and travelers are invited to pass through their homes. The mission, built in 1744, celebrates a Jesuit-style mass in Rára-muri, the native Uto-Aztecan language of the Tarahumara people.

Continuing straight past the mission, you will come to a sign for the **Valle de los Hongos** (Valley of the Mushrooms), named for the mushroom-like appear-ance of the rock formation at the bottom of the hill. Turn right, and you will come to the valley, beyond which are the **Valle de las Ranas** (Valley of the Frogs) and the **Valle de las Chichis** (Valley of the Boobies). Going back along the path and following the main gravel road, you will find signs pointing to the (appro-priately far away) **Valle de los Monjes** (Valley of the Monks), whose spectacular vertical, spiral rock formations are the most impressive of the area. Before reaching Valle de los Monjes, you will see a sign on the right pointing down a path to **Laguna Arareco.** After gawking at the Valle de los Monjes, head back to this sign and follow the 3km path to reach Laguna, which is cold and not ideal for swimming. Boating used to be popular on the lake, but has recently been banned. From the water, follow the path to the highway. Turn right on the high-way to head back to Creel (8km). The entire trip is 22km long and takes 6-7hr. on foot. Mountain biking through the area is popular and takes about half the time (see **Outdoor Activities,** p. 262). Los 3 Amigos rents two-seat scooters for US$10 per hr. No matter how you choose to cruise, pack plenty of water and a snack. *(To reach the park entrance, take Mateos south all the way past the centro, continuing onward as it becomes a gravel road. When the road forks, go left, up a hill past a cemetery, until you reach the park gates. Park admission 15 pesos, students and children 10 pesos.) Alterna-tively, start the loop from the highway to Batopilas. Small houses along the path are supposed to charge a 10-peso toll, but the booths are usually unmanned in low season.)*

REKOWATA HOT SPRINGS. The Rekowata Hot Springs bubble about 20km out-side of Creel. The pools are about as clean as the lake, and the temperature usually hovers around 98°F. The hot springs are difficult to reach by foot or bike, and the roads there are not conducive to travel by scooter or pickup truck. *(The best option to see the hot springs is to book a tour with one of the hotels in Creel.)*

CUSÁRARE. There are three exits for Cusárare. The first and third lead to the **Cusárare waterfall,** and branch off to the right. The first path (3km) is fairly hilly, while the other (1.9km) is considerably more gentle. Although the waterfall is only 98 ft. high, it can reach a width of 85 ft. during the rainy season (July-Sept.). The rest of the year it is little more than a trickle, but that doesn't stop schoolchildren and tourists from walking the poorly maintained path to the base and playing in the pools. The second exit, which branches off to the left, leads to the town of **Cusárare** itself, with the **Misión** and its museum. The mission is over 270 years old and features strong Tarahumara elements in its design and decoration. Several restored paintings are now being housed in the custom-built **Museo de Loyola** located next door. Turning right instead of left at the second exit takes you to the Sierra Lodge, the only hotel in Cusárare. Park your car near the lodge and follow the green arrow pointing to the "Cascada"; the hike to the falls (3km) is breathtak-ing. Watch out for falling rocks. *(Cusárare waterfall is situated 25km southeast of Creel, and most guides offer 1- or 2-day trips. Alternatively, Estrella Blanca runs buses to Hidalgo del Par-ral via Cusárare. 20min., 2 per day, 22 pesos. Museo open Tu-Su 9am-6pm. The last bus leaves Cusárare at 6pm. Joint mission/waterfall ticket can be purchased at either site, 15 pesos.)*

LAS BARRANCAS DEL COBRE (COPPER CANYON)

The Sierra Tarahumara—home to the indigenous Tarahumara—is an achingly beautiful mountain range. A view of the 11 interlocking canyons known as Las Barrancas del Cobre from the highest peaks shows earth at mind-boggling scale: the chasms reach depths of almost 2km and the entire system spans an area over four times the size of the US's Grand Canyon. Commonly referred to simply as Copper Canyon, the area is quickly becoming one of North America's most popular ecotourism destinations. The countless gorges, ravines, and rugged adventure trails are home to arid deserts, snow-capped peaks, pine forests, river valleys, and sub-tropical rainforests.

A ride on the **Chihuahua al Pacífico (CHEPE) train**, a modern engineering marvel spanning more than 700km, is the quickest, safest way to see the best canyon spots. Hiking, riding, biking, and driving through the canyon is very difficult, but infinitely more rewarding. The area lacks trails, transportation, adequate topographical maps, administrative infrastructure, and even decent roads, making advanced outdoors skills—or the aid of a knowledgeable guide—a requirement for any excursion. Infrastructure problems are exacerbated by the fact that most people visit during the rainy monsoon season (July-Aug.), when storms routinely wash out the roads and the train tracks, stranding visitors for days on end. Because of this, most travelers resort to being shuttled to the sights by a Creel-based tour company.

AT A GLANCE	
AREA: 1500 sq. km	**SUGGESTED ITINERARY (2 WEEKS):** Take the CHEPE Train from Los Mochis (1 day) to **Creel** (2 Days) before exploring **Candameña Canyon** (2 Days), **Urique Canyon** (2 days), **Batopilas Canyon** (3 Days), **Divisadero** (1 day), and **Sinforosa Canyon** (2 days). Depart via CHEPE to **Chihuahua** (1 day).
CLIMATE: Arid and dry, except during the rainy months of July-Sept., when daily monsoons inundate the region. Extreme temperatures abate during the peak travel months of Apr.-May and Oct.-Nov.	
HIGHEST ALTITUDE: 2000m	

The CHEPE train, although painfully slow, is one of the best ways to take in the stunning scenery of Las Barrancas del Cobre and is a perennial favorite with visitors. Mexicans boast that the trip is "the greatest train ride in the world," and the rail voyage is the only way to see the virtually inaccessible Copper Canyon, the particular chasm that is the area's namesake. Two types of trains make the daily journey between Los Mochis and Chihuahua. The **second-class train** has spacious reclining seats and clean bathrooms and is well air-conditioned. The **first-class train** is twice as expensive, but for your extra money all you get is tilt-o-matic seats, a nicer dining car, and, occasionally, an open-air viewing car.

HOT SEAT. In order to see the most spectacular scenery, which lies between Temoris and Creel, grab a seat on the right side of the Chihuahua-bound train or the left side of the Los Mochis train.

Trains go from Los Mochis to Chihuahua (1st-class 13hr., 6am, 1451 pesos; 2nd-class 14hr., 7am, 726 pesos) and from Chihuahua to Los Mochis (1st-class 6am, 1451 pesos; 2nd-class 7am, 726 pesos). Trains, especially those heading towards Chihuahua, usually run late (up to 2hr.). Stops, listed for second-class trains from Los Mochis, are: **Sufragio, El Fuerte, Loreto, Temoris, Bahuachivo, Cuiteco, San Rafael, Divisadero, Creel, San Juanito, La Junta, Cuauhtémoc,** and **Chihuahua.** You don't want to get stranded at any of these tiny destinations, as most lack even electricity and

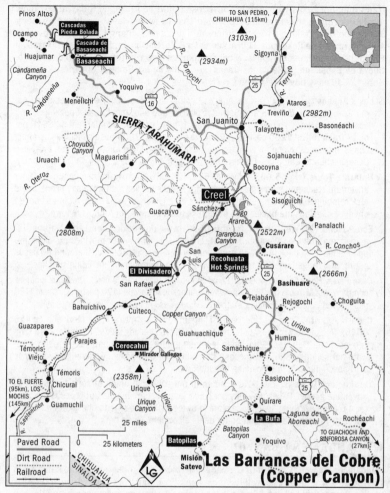

Las Barrancas del Cobre (Copper Canyon)

plumbing. At Divisadero, the trains stop for 15min., allowing passengers to take in the spectacular view and be bombarded by *gorditas*, tropical fruits, and arts and crafts vendors. Though often overlooked, El Fuerte is just as decent a place to get on or off as Los Mochis. The city is not particularly attractive in the high summer, but any time of year it is more appealing, cheaper, and safer than Los Mochis. Furthermore, whichever way you're going, it allows for an extra 2hr. in bed.

🏔 TOURS

One of the safest and surest ways to explore Las Barrancas is with a tour, which costs only slightly more than doing it solo. Band together with as many other interested travelers as possible to keep costs down. Booking a tour is the best course of action when planning an overnight trek or going somewhere inaccessible; daytrip tours may not be as worthwhile. Daytrips should be arranged a day in advance, while overnight treks must be planned two to three days in advance. Check around before booking a tour, as prices and deals may change. Most tours head to **Aguas Termales de Rekowata, El Divisadero, La Bufa, Basihuare, Río Urique, Basaseachi Falls,** and sometimes **Batopilas.** Most companies also run tours to **Lago de Arareko, Cueva de Sabastián, Valle de las Ranas,** and **Valle de los Hongos,** but these destinations are all easy day hikes from Creel.

■ **Los 3 Amigos** (☎456 0179; www.amigos3.com), on Mateos. Only travel agency in Copper Canyon. Yolanda, Ivan and Salvador provide free info, maps, travel packages, and assistance in hiring guides on foot, horseback, bike, or truck. Scooter rental US$10 per hr. ■ **Truck rental** 1200 pesos per 24hr., in low season 1000 pesos; includes camping chairs, insurance, lunch for 5, maps, and full gas tank. Ideal for sights farther away like Basaseachi and Batopilas. Cheaper than a tour if split 4 ways. Open daily 9am-8pm.

■ **Umarike Tours** (☎456 0632, mobile 614 406 5464; www.umarike.com.mx), is for adventure studs and stud-esses. Arturo, who speaks English with a Welsh accent, offers rock climbing and leads mountain bike tours for a variety of skill levels. All tours booked online. Excursions are pricier than other bike tours because of Arturo's renown.

Eco-Paseos "El Aventurero" (☎456 0558; www.ridemexico.com), on Mateos 68, across from the Best Western. Friendly, English-speaking owner provides excellent info and guides horseback rides with exceptionally tame horses. Tours cost around 60 pesos per hr. and range from 2hr. to 10 days. 800 pesos per day, not including supplies.

Casa Pérez, Flores 257 (☎456 0391), off Mateos, in their family's hotel. The Pérez brothers' company, **M&M Tours** (p. 261), runs group outings to Rekowata (120 pesos), Cusárare (180 pesos), and Batopilas (350 pesos). The M&M and Casa Margarita tours are very similar.

Casa Margarita, Casa de Huéspedes Margarita or Margarita's Plaza Mexicana (☎456 0045). Reasonably priced van tours led by English-speaking guides to all standard Canyon locations. Bag lunches included for larger groups. The most popular trip visits Rekowata hot springs. (8hr., 120 pesos). Batopilas tour 350 pesos. General guide services 100 pesos per day, not including transportation.

Tarahumara Tours (☎456 0184), booth in the *zócalo*. A union of sorts for numerous adventure guides. Prices may vary per guide, but most excursions 2500 pesos per night for 4-6 people. While these leaders are knowledgeable, be sure to check around before booking; you may be able find better deals elsewhere. Open daily 9am-4pm.

⚠ CANDAMEÑA CANYON

Candameña Canyon (Canyon of Cascades) is one of the most accessible canyons in the Sierra Tarahumara, as well the most sparsely populated. The two most popular sights, **Basaseachi Falls** and **Piedra Volada Falls**, are best seen as a combined daytrip from Creel. The CHEPE train stops a few hours away at **San Juanito**—Bocoyna municipality's largest town—but the only lodging available is an extremely expensive hotel. The canyon is cut in half by the very calm **Río Candameña,** which is easily navigated with prior advice from a knowledgeable guide. Backpackers often make the 3-day trek from the river's source to its drop at the falls.

BASASEACHI. The town of **Basaseachi** ("Place of the Cascade in Ráramuri) lies west of Creel on Mex. 16, which runs between Hermosillo and Chihuahua. To reach Basaseachi from Creel, take Mex. 127 north 45km, and then Mex. 16 110km west. Otherwise, take a tour or a bus. Estrella Blanca sends **buses** to Hermosillo from Chihuahua (5hr., 2 per day, 212 pesos) and Cuauhtémoc (3½hr., 2 per day, 178 pesos). From Creel, take a bus toward Chihuahua and get off at San Pedro, where Mex. 16 meets Mex. 127. The 7am and noon buses (1hr.,

75 pesos) will get you to San Pedro in time to catch the Basaseachi-bound buses at 9am and 2:30pm (3hr., 100 pesos), but you'll have to wait at least an hour. The last bus leaves Basaseachi at 5pm.

CASCADAS BASASEACHI. Water cascades from a height of 311m at **Basaseachi Waterfall.** During the rainy season (July-Sept.), it becomes Mexico's second largest waterfall. Tucked into a corner of Canyon Candameña, the falls don't get many visitors, but those who do make the trip are rewarded with scenery from a postcard photographer's wildest dreams. Unfortunately, the falls area can run dry during the months of September through June. The route to the falls (45min., each way) is clearly marked with signs reading "C. Basaseachi" and leads to a natural window that affords a breathtaking view of the falls and surrounding canyon. The walk along the slippery path is comparable to standing in a hurricane; the spray and spume from the falls literally jumps off the face of the cliff. Adventurous souls can trek to the base of the falls by following the path. The hike is difficult and takes another hour from the window, but the reward is a subtropical paradise. *(The falls can be reached either from the town of Basaseachi or from the military checkpoint. From the military checkpoint the trip is only 6km, instead of the 12km from the Las Estrellas junction in town where the bus stops. Either way, the road is paved, and the entrance fee is only 10 pesos.)*

CASCADAS PIEDRA VOLADA. About 4km from the Basaseachi falls, **Piedra Volada** (453m) is considered the highest waterfall in Mexico and the 12th highest in the world. Piedra Volada carries less water than Basaseachi, however, and is similarly only impressive during the rainy season (July-Sept.). The way to the falls is poorly marked; the best way to get there is to hire a guide in either Creel or Basaseachi. About 800m before you reach the window, you'll pass the Rancho San Lorenzo, which runs **Lobo Turismo de Aventura,** offering a wide variety of activities, including tours to Piedra Volada on foot or on horseback. They also offer camping facilities, cabins, and a restaurant, all within the park. *(☎614 414 6046; lobo-waterfalls@yahoo.com.mx. Piedra Volada tours 5hr., 6 person min., 250 pesos Camping 100 pesos; 4-bed cabin 526 pesos, with kitchen 650 pesos; 10-bed cabin 1111 pesos.)*

◪ BATOPILAS CANYON

The views from Batopilas Canyon are second only to those at Urique. If you choose to drive yourself, it's best to stay under 60km per hr. on the paved road and under 30km per hr. (first and second gear) on the dirt roads. The last gas station is after the town of **Napuchi,** 1km before the turn-off to Batopilas (p. 268), 74km south of Creel on Mex. 23. From here, the road turns to dirt and is wide enough for only one car, with canyon pressing close on both sides. Be careful driving, especially during July to Sept., when rain often washes out sections of the switchback dirt route. Check weather conditions and drive slowly, allowing up to 9hr. if you want to stop at the sights along the way. Manual transmission is recommended, and it is always best to let fast-moving trucks pass.

ENVIRONS. Canyon attractions include **Misión Satevo,** a former 18th-century Jesuit mission known as the "Lost Cathedral," featuring unusual brick architecture. (8km south of Batopilas., 20min. ride following the main street past Batopilas's end.) To see abandoned mines, such as **Penasquito** and **La Bufa,** it's highly advised to hire a guide in Creel—the structures are old and can be dangerous for those unfamiliar with the area—or to take the bus, which is relatively safe. **Buses** from Creel leave across the street from Los Pinos hotel (5-6 hr.; M, W, F 9:30am, Tu, Th, Sa 7am; 160 pesos). Travelers will arrive in Creel before any of the CHEPE trains pass through. Tickets available at Hotel Los Pinos, Cafe Creel, and onboard.

GRAND EXHAUST

Nine-hundred ninety one dollars. It cost one grand to fix the truck's manifold and exhaust pipe after my misadventurous descent into Urique Canyon. A price only half-worthy of the 2000m deep near-death experience I managed to climb back up with.

Logistical nightmares are gospel in Northwest Mexico. Admittedly, my *pesadilla* was extreme—only insane travelers are reckless enough to drive solo down North America's deepest canyon in a monsoon—but episodes of busted equipment, fickle weather, and dangerous roads are extremely common in Las Barrancas del Cobre, and bound to frustrate even the most seasoned veteran.

Don't panic—just be prepared. If you consult a guide, keep to day travel, and bring snacks—your canyon experience will be sublime. At no point should you kick your rental vehicle, shout multi-lingual obscenities, or take it out on the town mule. You will at best draw awkward glances from trekkers and at worst wind up with a horseshoe-shaped tattoo on your forehead.

Travel in any of the accessible canyons is not for the faint of heart, nor the stubborn. No matter how far you are below the crest, remember that you've got friends in high places—guide businesses in Creel depend on word of mouth, and they won't lead you astray.

– Raúl Carrillo

BATOPILAS. The town of **Batopilas** (pop. 1150) was founded in 1708 by Pedro de la Cruz, and quickly gained prominence as the canyon's center for mining operations. It is considered by many to be the "most remote town in North America." The real attraction is the drive to Batopilas from Creel: you can stop to see the falls at Cusárare (km 112), the caves at Basihuare (km 133), the canyon bottom at Humira (km 150), and the Batopilas canyon rim (km 27 on the dirt road), reaching Batopilas just in time for dinner.

If you don't bring your own tent and tour guide Batopilas has a few places to stay, including **Hotel Juanita ❸,** across the main plaza where the bus stops (☎456 9043; doubles 250 pesos; cash only) and **Casa Monse ❷,** next-door (☎456 9027; singles and doubles 200 pesos) From the main plaza, walk past the church and turn left, right, and left again up the rock steps. Knock on the door of the nearby house to ask to be let in.

🏔 SINFOROSA CANYON

Sinforosa Canyon, often called the "Queen of the Canyons," is farthest away from Creel (4hr.), but very close to **Hidalgo del Parral** (p. 257). The largest town in the canyon, 160km from Creel southeast on Chihuahua Highway 25, **Guachochi** (pop. 10000), the Tarahumara cultural center, is almost twice the size of Creel. There are a number of Tarahumara **caves** to visit, and many **waterfalls** with 5-80m drops, the tallest being the **Rosalinda.** These falls and caves are accessible via walking trails. Hot springs are located at **Agua Caliente** and **Esmeralda,** on the Nonoava river.

🏔 URIQUE CANYON

Urique Canyon is the deepest chasm in Las Barrancas del Cobre. The altitude drop from Creel to the river bottom is approximately 2000m. The least treacherous way to make the tremendous descent is to take a 4WD vehicle from Creel down the switchbacks. **Los 3 Amigos** (p. 266) rents Nissan double-cabs (1200 pesos per 24hr., in low season 1000 pesos; includes camping chairs, insurance, satellite radio, lunch for 5, excellent maps, and one full gas tank). The agency is more than happy to send a guide along—it is highly recommended that travelers take advantage of this service, as driving in the canyon can be extremely perilous.

RÍO URIQUE. To reach Río Urique by vehicle, travel south from Creel on the highway into San Rafael. At San Rafael, follow the signs directing you to Cerocahui. Here the paved road turns to dirt and can be dangerous during the summer, as monsoon rains often pool into creeks in the middle of the road and sometimes wash it out completely. Eventually, you'll come to a fork in the road. Take the right-hand path. You should pass the tiny towns of Cuiteco and Bahuichevo before arriving in **Cerocahui.** The road from Cerocahui goes uphill, followed by a terrific plunge into the canyon—all on dirt and gravel. The drive from Cerocahui village over the hill and down to Río Urique is perilous under certain conditions, but without a doubt the most beautiful in all the canyon system. The two most astounding viewpoints are the **Mesa de Arturo** and, farther down, the **Mirador Gallegos.**

CEROCAHUI. It takes about 5hr. to reach the bottom of Urique Canyon and 5hr. to climb back out. It's best to make it a long daytrip with a picnic at the river, but if you can't head out of Creel at dawn, Cerocahui (pop. 900) is a nice place to set up camp. **Hotel Plaza** 3 (☎456 5256), across from the old mission, is the cheapest hotel in town and has very hospitable owners. (Doubles with TV, showers, and excellent view of the surrounding ranches 350 pesos. Cash only.) Local caballeros (cowboys) offer horse tours to nearby **Huichochi Waterfall** for flexible prices. The Muñoz brothers, owners of the **San Isidro Lodge** and *amigos* of **Los 3 Amigos,** offer custom bike and horse tours of the canyon. (☎456 5257; www.coppercanyonamigos.com.)

▚ DIVISADERO

This spot, 35km away at the rim of the Urique Canyon, is an excursion that many tourists miss. Three canyons (Cobre, Tararecua, and Urique) can be seen merging into each other from the **Mirador** (7316 ft. above sea level). This view extends over 100 mi., and is especially magnificent at sunrise, when the light appears to rise out of the ravines themselves.

At Divisadero there are plenty of trails leading down from the canyon rim where the hotels are. Using the expensive hotels as a reference point, you can venture to the bottom of the canyon and return without a guide with plenty of time to catch the **CHEPE train** to Creel. (6pm, 50 pesos. 1st-class 4pm, 129 pesos; 2nd-class 6pm, 65 pesos.) To get there without the train, follow Mex. 23 towards San Rafael or take a Noroeste bus from the stations across the railway tracks (1st bus leaves 10:30am, 40 pesos). It is best to go early because tickets sell out.

La Piedra Volada (p. 267), is worthy of the moderate 2hr. hike from Divisadero. From the wobbly giant boulder you can see **Las Escaleras,** a natural staircase cut into the mountainside. Tourists are invited to jump up and down on the precariously perched boulder. Trust us: the boulder won't fall. If you want to spend more than a day here, it's best to hire a guide in Creel who knows the area.

SINALOA

EL FUERTE ☎698

Founded in 1564 by Don Francisco de Ibarra, El Fuerte (pop. 30,000) takes its name from a seemingly impenetrable fort—the last of three—that once stood on this site, guarding the Spanish from the native Zuaque and Tehueco warriors. The former stronghold's cannons, however, have failed to keep pesky budget travelers at bay, and rumor has it that the city's wardens will betray their isolationist roots and open El Fuerte as a southern exploration base for Las Barrancas del Cobre.

▐▜ TRANSPORTATION AND PRACTICAL INFORMATION. From the station, **trains** leave daily for **Chihuahua** (1st-class, 8:30am, 1271 pesos; 2nd-class, 10:15am,

636 pesos) and **Los Mochis** (1st-class 1½hr., 6:15pm, 267 pesos; 2nd-class 2hr., 10:30pm, 133 pesos). From the train station, take a taxi into the El Fuerte *zócalo* (7km, 45 pesos). Visit www.chepe.com.mx for more information. **Buses** to **Los Mochis** (50 pesos) leave from Juárez and 16 de Septiembre. Taxis gather on Juárez, the main street. To get to the *zócalo* from Juárez, walk west from Juárez and turn left onto 5 de Mayo, which puts you in front of the Palacio Municipal.

Services include: the **tourist office,** on the second floor inside the Palacio Municipal (☎893 0290); **Bancomer,** Constitución 101 at Juárez (☎893 1145; **24hr. ATM;** open M-F 8:30am-4pm); **Red Cross,** Hidalgo 530 (☎893 0707); **Farmacia del Fuerte,** Juárez 112 (open daily 8am-10pm); **Clínica el Buen Samaritano** (☎893 0688), on the corner of Ocampo and Cecena; **Internet** access at **Cibercafe Urias,** Juárez 103 toward the *zócalo*, above the Librería Urias (☎893 0615; 10 pesos per hr; open M-Sa 8am-8pm, Su 8am-3pm); and the **post office,** in the Palacio Gobierno on the first floor (open M-F 9am-4pm). **Postal Code:** 81820.

⌂⌂ ACCOMMODATIONS AND FOOD. El Fuerte's budget accommodations lie along and downhill of Juárez. An air-conditioned escape from El Fuerte's humidity is **Villa de Villa ❷,** Juárez 407. (☎893 1032. Singles 200 pesos; doubles 250 pesos.) **Hotel San Jose ❶,** Juárez 108, has large, musty, rooms with high ceilings. (☎893 0845. Cots 30 pesos; bare-bones singles 100 pesos; doubles with fan and bath 200 pesos.) **Hotel Guerrero ❷,** Juárez 210, has dim rooms with baths, high ceilings, and comfy beds. (☎893 1350. Singles 200 pesos; doubles 250 pesos.)

Cheap food in El Fuerte can be found in the numerous *comida corrida* stands on Juárez, with delicious taco plates and *pozole* for under 30 pesos. **Chinaloa ❸** dishes up Chinese food on the corner of Juárez and 16 de Septiembre. To sample the fish from the river and surrounding dams, however, you'll have to pay more. Toward the *zócalo* lies **Restaurante El Mesón General ❺,** Juárez 202. Food is served around an open courtyard, and there is occasionally live music on weekends. (☎893 0206. *Tacos machaca* 53 pesos. Octopus 82 pesos. Open daily 8am-10:30pm.) Better *mariscos* and better views are along the river at **El Paseo de Los Aves ❺,** Camino la Galera. Follow 5 de Mayo past Fuerte Museo Mirador as it curves to the right and then to the left (15-20min. by foot). Sit on the patio and enjoy a variety of fish filets for 70-90 pesos. (☎893 0986. Open daily 8am-10pm.)

◙ SIGHTS. The imposing *fuerte* on the hill dates back to 1610. To reach it, take 5 de Mayo past the Palacio de Gobierno and turn right at the sign that reads "Fuerte Museo Mirador." On the lower level, there are rooms filled with colonial and indigenous artifacts (including giant artillery pieces), along with galleries featuring the work of current Sinaloan artists. The real attraction, however, is the view of the sub-tropical valley from the upper level. (☎823 1501. Open daily 9am-9pm. 5 pesos, students and children 3 pesos.) Continuing on 5 de Mayo will lead you along the **Río Fuerte.** Keep your eyes peeled for native birds such as the **Crested Caracara,** the **Mexican Blue-Rumped Parrotlet,** and the **Plain-Capped Starthroat.** Also keep your eyes on the path ahead of you as it's a frequently used cow passage.

LOS MOCHIS ☎668

Unfortunately, the grimy, densely populated city of Los Mochis (pop. 275,000) is a necessary stopover for adventurers on their way to Las Barrancas del Cobre (Copper Canyon). As the westernmost stop for the CHEPE train—the railroad snaking through Copper Canyon—the city was first founded and developed by expats as a Robert Owens-esque utopian socialist colony, and later became part of a sugar-growing money-making scheme. While both its socialist and sugar days are over, Los Mochis continues to be an important link between the coast and the interior, funneling goods and backpackers into the mountains.

■ **TRANSPORTATION.** The **CHEPE** (Chihuahua al Pacífico) train (☎824 1151) runs between Los Mochis and Chihuahua, with stops throughout the Copper Canyon. The posh first-class train leaves daily at 6am for **Creel** and **Chihuahua** (1453 pesos). Equally comfortable, but with smaller seats and dining cars, the second-class train leaves daily at 7am for **Creel** (397 pesos) and **Chihuahua** (727 pesos). Tickets are available in the station or on board. During peak backpacker season (July-Aug.), you may wish purchase tickets in advance. **Viajes Flamingos,** Hidalgo Pte. 419 (☎812 1613), in the Hotel Santa Anita, also sells tickets.

RAIL JABBER. You'll hear a lot of talk from ticket-sellers, TI agents, and even taxi drivers about how sweet it is to travel CHEPE first-class. Don't be fooled! Both trains roll on the same set of mountain tracks, both serve food, and both stop in the same places so passengers can ogle scenic Copper Canyon vistas. The 6am train has larger seats and a less crowded coach, but you won't get a chance to meet other backpackers. Sleep in and pay half-price.

Though many **bus** carriers serve the city, finding the individual stations can be a challenge. Most obvious is the modern **Elite** station (☎812 1757), at Juàrez and Degollado. **Transportes Norte de Sonora** also leaves from Elite to **Guaymas** (5hr., every hr., 205 pesos). **Tufesa** (☎800-737-8883) on Morelos and Zapata, is a good deal for the long trips, and sends buses to: **Hermosillo** (7hr., 313 pesos); **Culiacán** (2½ hr., 162 pesos); **Mazatlán** (5½ hr., 310 pesos); **Nogales** (10hr., 486 pesos), and **Guadalajara** (14hr., 572 pesos). **Transportes del Pacífico** (☎812 0347), on Morelos between Leyva and Zaragoza, sends *de paso* buses to similar destinations.

Buses to **El Fuerte** and nearby destinations leave from Zaragoza, between Ordoñez and Cuauhtémoc. Buses to **Topolobampo** and **Mavari** (every 20 min., 14 pesos), leave from a stop on Cuahtémoc between Prieta and Zaragoza, one block north of Obregón. Los Mochis also has **Pacífico** (for coastal destinations to the south) and **Azteca de Oro** stations on Zaragoza, just north of Independencia.

Ferries to **La Paz** leave from Topolobampo daily at 11pm. (2nd-class 710 pesos, 4-bed cabin 760 pesos in addition to fare). **Baja Ferries** sells tickets until 2pm the day of departure. (☎817 3752. Open daily 8am-10pm.) **Viajes Ahome,** Prieto 105-1 at Morelos, also brokers tickets. (☎812 3752. Open M-Sa 9am-2pm and 3-7pm, Su 9am-2pm.) **Municipal buses** (4 pesos) run throughout the city. The main stop is on Zaragoza at Obregón; ask the driver if he goes to your destination. **Taxis** (☎812 0283) wait on the corner of every major intersection. Negotiate prices beforehand.

∎ **PRACTICAL INFORMATION.** The city is laid out in a grid. Downtown, the principal north-south avenues are (from east to west) Degollado, Zaragoza, Leyva, Guerrero, and Rosales. Perpendicular to these (from north to south) are Juan de Dios Bátiz, Cárdenas, Morelos, Independencia, Obregón, Castro, and Ordóñez. Information on Los Mochis, Sinaloa, and the Copper Canyon can be found at the **tourist office** at Ordoñez and Allende, inside the Palacio del Gobierno. (☎815 1090. Open M-F 9am-4pm.) Other services include: **Bancomer** (☎812 2323) on Leyva and Juárez has **24hr. ATMs** (open M-F 8:30am-4pm.); **American Express** (☎612 0590) between Flores and Morelos (open M-F 9am-2pm and 4-6pm, Sa 9am-1pm); **emergency** ☎060; **police** (☎812 0333), on the corner of Cuauhtémoc and Degollado; **Red Cross** (☎815 0808) on Tenochtitlán and Pueblo, one block off of Castro; **Centro Médico** (☎812 0198) at Castro 130 Pte.; **Internet** access at **WebSurf,** outside the mall at Obregón and Rosales. (10 pesos per hr.; open M-Sa 9am-9pm, Su 9am-7pm); and the **post office** on Ordoñez 226, between Prieto and Zaragoza. (☎812 0823. Open M-F 9am-3pm). **Postal Code:** 81200.

∎∎ **ACCOMMODATIONS AND FOOD. Hotel Hidalgo** ❷, Hidalgo Pte. 260, between Prieta and Zaragoza, offers basic rooms. (☎818 3453. Singles 140 pesos,

NORTHWEST MEXICO

with A/C 175 pesos; doubles 240 pesos; triples 270 pesos. Cash only.) Across the street, **Hotel Beltran ❺,** has pale orange rooms with soft mattresses, A/C, and TV. (☎812 0688. Singles 275 pesos; doubles 320 pesos. Cash only.) The rooms at **Hotel Lorena ❺,** Obregón 186, come furnished with everything but a butler, including A/C, clean baths, TV, purified water, and Wi-Fi. (☎812 6847; fax 812 0239. Singles 300 pesos; doubles 360 pesos; each additional person 40 pesos. MC/V.) **Hotel América ❺,** 655 Allende, offers a more elegant, cleaner stay for a few more pesos. Rooms have A/C and TV. (☎812 1355. Singles 390 pesos; doubles 455 pesos. MC/V.)

Tacos la Cabaña de Doña Chayo ❶, Obregón 99 at the corner of Allende, is a great place for late-night grub. The size of the tacos justifies their relatively high price. (Tacos 18 pesos. Quesadillas 18 pesos. Open daily 8am-1am. Cash only.) **El Taquito ❸,** on Leyva between Hidalgo and Independencia. serves super early, pre-travel breakfasts. Try eggs with bread, tortillas, beans, coffee, a full plate of fruit, and fresh orange juice—all for just 45 pesos. (Open 6am-10pm. Cash only.) **eSalads ❸,** on the corner of Hidalgo and Allende serves chicken, vegetables, and salad dishes for 30-42 pesos. (☎818 0016. Open M-Sa 9am-6pm. MC/V.) For groceries, head to **VH Supermercado,** on Obregón and Zaragoza. (☎815 7285. Open daily 7am-10pm.)

◧ ⬛ SIGHTS AND NIGHTLIFE. An extensive collection of exotic flora grows in the **Parque Sinaloa y Jardín Botánico,** located half a block down Rosales from the end of Castro. The gardens are the former property of North American sugarcane tycoon Benjamin Johnston, and contain plants from Africa, India, Australia, Java, and the West. (Free). The city's locals often enjoy hot dogs, cold *raspados,* and other cheap snacks in **Plaza Solidaridad** on Obregón and Rosales, diagonally opposite to the mall. Adjoining the plaza is **Sanctuario del Sagrado Corazón de Jesús,** Mochi's oldest church, built after the founder's Protestant wife donated the land to the people. Nightlife in Los Mochis tends to be surly and male-dominated, with belligerent men in cowboy hats at every watering hole. Bars and shady strip clubs cluster on Obregón near Allende, and most fill with rowdy patrons by midnight. **La Marea,** (☎817 0570) is the hottest under-30 spot. The DJ plays *banda, norteño,* and reggaeton. (Beer 20 pesos. Tequila 40 pesos. Open daily 9pm-2am. Cash only.)

About 12 miles south of Los Mochis, the port of **Topolobampo** offers a little more in the way of sight seeing. Topolobampo, the original site of Owen's farmers's collective, occupies a distinct geographical position. From here, 11 rivers feed into the bay—the world's third deepest, after Sydney and San Francisco. Boat trips to the **mangrove estuaries**—home to a wealth of bird life—can be easily booked at the harbor for negotiable prices. Ask if you can see **◧Pechocho,** the friendly neighborhood dolphin. The port's most popular beach is **Maravari.** The area is not very developed, but does offer sweet jet-skiing, banana-boating, and wind-surfing. Buses to Topolobampo (20min.) and Maravari (30min.) leave from Cuauhtémoc and Prieto (every 30min., 15 pesos).

CULIACÁN ☎667

Due to the large amount of budget traffic to seaside destinations, Culiacán (pop. 600,000) has become an important tourist transportation hub in Sinaloa and is the state's largest city. Unfortunately, this isn't the only traffic that passes through Culiacán; the capital, nicknamed "little Medellín" after the notorious Colombian city, is one of Mexico's primary drug centers and is home to several drug-running *bandidas,* constantly at war. Extra effort has kept the *centro* beautiful, and what little artistic wealth falls to Sinaloa is gathered here.

▣ TRANSPORTATION. The **airport** (☎760 0676) is 10km southeast of downtown. Major carriers include **AeroCalifornia** (☎716 0250), **Aerolineas Internacionales** (☎712

5443) and **Aeroméxico** (☎714 0181 or 800 021 4000). Culiacán's modern **bus station** (☎712 4875) is 12km from downtown. Local buses to the station leave from stops throughout the *centro* and from the **old bus station** on Solano (3 pesos). **Taxis** cost 50 pesos and are often the only option after dark. **Élite** sends buses to: **Guadalajara** (11hr., 463 pesos); **Hermosillo** (366 pesos); **Monterrey** (17hr.; 5, 7:30pm; 800 pesos); **Tepic** (8hr., 339 pesos). **Pacífico** (☎761 4730) goes to **Ciudad Obregón** (every hr., 140 pesos), **Guaymas** (8hr., every hour., 170 pesos), and **Mazatlán** (2½ hr., every hr., 147 pesos). **Norte de Sinaloa** heads to **Los Mochis** (every hr. 7am-9pm, 120 pesos).

▚ PRACTICAL INFORMATION.

The city concentrates on the south side of **Río Tamazula** but is very spread out. Luckily, buses (4 pesos) run all over and save time and energy. The downtown area is roughly delineated by **Madero, Granados,** the edge of the river along which **Niños Héroes** runs, and Bravo. In 2003, President Fox sent extra federal police to Culiacán as a signal to the city's drug barons. A large contingent ends up standing on the street corners in the *centro*, toting rifles—they don't see much action, but look imposing nonetheless. While the area between Bravo and Obregón is relatively safe, other parts of Culiacán can be dangerous, especially at night.

Services include: **Tourist office,** in the Palacio de Gobierno, at Insurgentes and Barraza (open M-F 8am-3pm and 5-7pm.); **Banamex,** Rosales 103 (☎715 0700), with **currency exchange** and a **24hr. ATM** (open M-F 8:30am-4:30pm); another **24hr. ATM** on the corner of Hidalgo and Obregón; **emergency** ☎060; **police** at Federalismo 2500 (☎761 0152); **Red Cross** (☎752 0707) at Solano; **24hr. Farmacia Red Cross,** Solano and Paleza; **Hospital Civil de Culiacán** (☎716 4650), at Obregón and Romero; **Internet** access at **MegaClub** (☎712 4312), on Obregón in the *zócalo* (10 pesos per hr; open daily 10am-10pm); and the **post office,** Domingo Rubi 560 (☎712 2170; open M-F 8am-3pm). **Postal Code:** 80000.

▙▟ ACCOMMODATIONS AND FOOD.

The safest accommodations and cheapest eateries can be found close to the cathedral. Although farther away from the *centro* than the other budget hotels, **Hotel Louisiana ❷,** at 478 Villa Ote., is a bargain. (☎713 9152. Singles 150 pesos; doubles 160 pesos. Cash only.) **Hotel Nevada ❷** on Juárez, two blocks below Obregón, also has cheap stays right in the middle of town. (Singles 150 pesos, with A/C 180 pesos; doubles 160/200 pesos.) **Hotel Salvador ❹,** Solano Ote. 297, offers large, clean rooms with A/C, bath, and a pretty decent view. (☎713 7462. Singles 200 pesos; doubles 250 pesos. MC/V.) Of Culiacán's upper-tier hotels, **Hotel Francis ❺,** at 135 Escobedo Pte., has the most amenities (A/C, bar, cable, Wi-Fi) for the lowest price. (☎712 1808. Singles 320 pesos; doubles 390 pesos. MC/V.)

A variety of cut-rate chow can be found in the area surrounding Obregón and Hidalgo. **Tacos Ranas ❶,** at the corner of Morelos and Flores offers cheap food, including three *tacos al pastor* for 15 pesos. (Open M-Sa 9am-9pm.) Culiacán's flagship restaurant, **Los Antiguos Portales de Culiacán ❺,** Paliza Nte. 574 (☎752 1978), has a great view of Plaza Obregón and affordable breakfasts (30-60 pesos) with *huevos al gusto*. (Open daily noon-10pm. AmEx/D/MC/V.) **Tentu Sushi ❸,** 30 Hidalgo Pte. (☎715 7738), serves seafood and greens. (Open daily 10am-8pm.) **Wings Yogurt ❷,** on the corner of Obregón and Juárez, has a variety of chicken, fruit, and yogurt dishes for 25-35 pesos.

⬛ SIGHTS.

The city's shrine to **Jesús Malverde,** a 19th-century bandit whose Robin Hood-esque practices led to his execution in 1909, is a landmark on Independencia. Malverde is also called the "narco-saint," as he has become the spiritual figure of Culiacán drug trafficking. To reach the shrine from the *centro*, head west toward Bravo until you reach Madero as it runs along the train tracks. Follow this away from the *centro* until it turns into Independencia. Just off the Plaza

Obregón, the **Museo de Arte Sinaloa**, on Rafael Buelna and Paliza, houses the works of artists such as Diego Rivera, López Saenz, and Frida Kahlo in its wonderfully air-conditioned chambers. (☎716 1750. Open Tu-Sa 10am-3pm and 5-7pm, Su 11am-5pm. 5 pesos, students and children 3 pesos; Su free.) **Casa de la Cultura** and the attached **Galería Frida Kahlo,** on Noris and Flores, are beautiful, air-conditioned houses with fantastic Mexican artwork. (☎715 2111. 10 pesos.) Culiacán's majestic yellow **Catedral,** on Obregón and Juárez in the *centro*, is one of *el norte's* most impressive. **La Lomita,** a large building at the top of a hill, offers a *mirador* with a view of the whole city. Follow Obregón all the way past Solano up hill.

MAZATLÁN   ☎ 639

The locals say that some nights, lying quietly on the well-trodden sands, you can still hear the sounds of the 1980s dying in the waves. Mazatlán (pop. 400,000) is certainly past its heyday—when the resorts opened in the Zona Dorada during the 80s—but the 500-year-old port continues to be an attractive travel destination. *Mazatlecas* are very proud of their beach-side haven, and keep the *malecón* (boardwalk) spotless both in and out of *Carnaval* time. The beaches stretch for kilometers and the clubs are all-night affairs.

MAZATLÁN FOR POCKET CHANGE. To get the most out of your budget, stay in the *centro* and play in the Zona Dorada. After getting a room at **Hotel del Rio,** grab a quick bite to eat in the **Mercado Municipal** and take advantage of the sweet, fresh roadside **manguitos** and seafood **taquitos.** When you're ready to head to the beach, hop on the 8-peso **Sábalo-Centro bus** and relax with a packed meal for dinner. Buy your drinks from a liquor store and enjoy them on the beach before sand-crawlin' to **Joe's Oyster Bar.** Dance until dawn, and share the cost of a *pulmonía* to the *centro* with your new friends.

◼ TRANSPORTATION

An efficient bus and taxi system makes navigating the city a breeze. At some point, all municipal buses pass the public market on Juárez, three blocks north of the *zócalo* at Ocampo. The air-conditioned Mercedes **"Sábalo-Centro"** bus runs from the downtown market, with stops a few blocks from the *malecón* in Ola Altas and at Playa Sábalo in the Zona Dorada (10 pesos). The **"Cerritos-Juárez"** bus continues up to Playa Bruja at Puerta Cerritos. The **"Insurgentes"** route services bus and train stations, and **"Playa Sur"** goes to the southern ferry dock and lighthouse (every 15min. 5am-10pm, 4 pesos). For late-night disco-hopping, take a **taxi** or **pulmonía** (like a large golf cart). Standard fare between Old Mazatlán and the Zona Dorada is 40-50 pesos, and about 10-20 more pesos in a *pulmonía*, depending on the time of night (later is more expensive). The walk is more than an hour, giving drivers bargaining leverage, but don't be afraid to haggle with *pulmonía* drivers—there are plenty to choose from.

Flights: Rafael Buelna International Airport (**MZT;** ☎982 2399), 18km south of the city. "Central Camionera" bus goes to the *centro,* but you must return by taxi (200 pesos). Served by: **AeroCalifornia,** in El Cid Resort (☎913 2042); **Aeroméxico**, Sábalo 310A (☎914 1111 or 800 021 4000); **Alaska Airlines** (☎800 252 7522); **Mexicana,** Pasco Claussen 101-B (☎982 7722 or 800 502 2000).

Buses: The bus station is 3 blocks from the *malecón* and about 2km north of Old Mazatlán, between downtown and the Zona Dorada. To get downtown, catch any of the red "Centro" or "Mercado" buses, 1 block west of the station and about 1 block south, to your right along Benemerito de las Americas. (3 pesos, after 9pm 3.50 pesos; buses stop running at 10pm). Avoid the "Sábalo-Coco" bus, as it goes downtown only after an

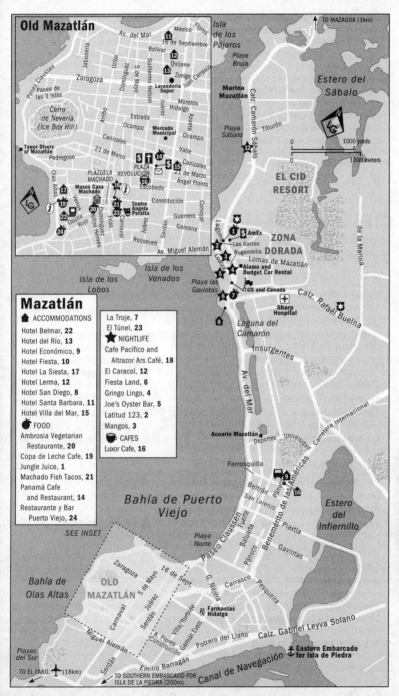

Old Mazatlán

Isla de los Pájaros

Cerro de Nevería (Ice Box Hill)

Tower Divers of Mazatlán

PLAZUELA MACHADO

Museo Casa Machado

Teatro Angela Peralta

PLAZA REVOLUCIÓN

Mercado Municipal

Lavandería Super

Estero del Sábalo

Marina Mazatlán

Playa Bruja

Playa Sábalo

EL CID RESORT

ZONA DORADA

AmEx

Las Garzas

Bugambilia

Lomas de Mazatlán

Alamo and Budget Car Rental

US and Canada

Sharp Hospital

Laguna del Camarón

Insurgentes

0   1000 yards
0   1000 meters

Isla de los Venados

Playa las Gaviotas

Isla de los Lobos

Mazatlán

⌂ ACCOMMODATIONS

Hotel Belmar, **22**
Hotel del Río, **13**
Hotel Económico, **9**
Hotel Fiesta, **10**
Hotel La Siesta, **17**
Hotel Lerma, **12**
Hotel San Diego, **8**
Hotel Santa Barbara, **11**
Hotel Villa del Mar, **15**

🍎 FOOD

Ambrosia Vegetarian
  Restaurante, **20**
Copa de Leche Cafe, **19**
Jungle Juice, **1**
Machado Fish Tacos, **21**
Panamá Cafe
  and Restaurant, **14**
Restaurante y Bar
  Puerto Viejo, **24**

La Troje, **7**
El Túnel, **23**

★ NIGHTLIFE

Cafe Pacífico and
  Altrazor Ars Café, **18**
El Caracol, **12**
Fiesta Land, **6**
Gringo Lingo, **4**
Joe's Oyster Bar, **5**
Latitud 123, **2**
Mangos, **3**

☕ CAFES

Luxor Cafe, **16**

Acuario Mazatlán

Deportes

Universidad

Carretera Internacional

Ferrosquilla

Bahía de Puerto Viejo

Beltrán

San Lorenzo

Estero del Infiernillo

SEE INSET

Bahía de Olas Altas

OLD MAZATLÁN

Playa Norte

Paseo Clausen

Farmacias Hidalgo

Playas del Sur

TO EL FARO, ✈ (18km)

TO SOUTHERN EMBARCADO FOR
ISLA DE LA PIEDRA (200m)

Canal de Navegación

Eastern Embarcado
for Isla de Piedra

Calz. Gabriel Leyva Solano

NORTHWEST MEXICO

enormous loop around the city. *Pulmonías* and cabs also make the trip for around 40 pesos. **Transportes de Pacífico** (☎981 5156) travels to: **Culiacán** (every hr., 127 pesos); **Durango** (8hr.; 4 per day, 259 pesos); **Guadalajara** (8hr., 310 pesos); **Guaymas** (10hr., 441 pesos); **Los Mochis** (6hr., every hr., 240 pesos); **Mexico City** (18hr., every hr., 703 pesos); **Monterrey** (17hr., 3 per day, 584 pesos); **Nogales** (15hr., 643 pesos); **Puerto Vallarta** (7½hr., 305 pesos); **Tepic** (4½hr., every hr., 145 pesos). **Estrella Blanca, Tufesa,** and **TuriStar** offer similar services.

Ferries: Baja Ferries (☎981 0470), at the end of Carnaval, south of Flores. A 20min. walk from the *centro* or a quick ride on the blue "Playa Sur" bus (4 pesos). Taxis 30-35 pesos. Tickets sold only on the day of departure. Arrive at least 2hr. early to get a seat. Ticket office open M-F and Su 8am-3pm, Sa 9am-1pm. Make reservations at least 2 weeks ahead in high season (Dec. and July-Aug.). Daily ferry to **La Paz** (17½ hr., 2:30pm, call for fares).

Car Rental: Alamo, Sábalo 410 (☎913 1010). **Budget,** Sábalo 402 (☎913 2000). **National,** Sábalo 7000 (☎913 6000).

✦ ❷ ORIENTATION AND PRACTICAL INFORMATION

Mazatlán is strictly divided into **Old Mazatlán,** home to the *zócalo* and budget hotels and restaurants, and the **Zona Dorada,** home to high-rise hotels and big-money entertainment. The *malecón* (boardwalk) follows the beach and connects the two sides of town. Mazatlán is spread out; the easiest way to traverse the city is by bus.

Tourist Office: State office (☎981 8883), at Escobero and Carnaval. Open M-F 9am-5pm. Small municipal office, Olas Altas 11-7 (☎981 8435), past Hotel Belmar, in the *centro.* Open M-Sa 8am-7pm.

Consulates: Both at Playa Gaviotas 202, across from Hotel Playa Mazatlán in Zona Dorada. **Canada** (☎913 7320). Open daily 9am-1pm. **US** (☎916 5889). Open daily 10am-2pm.

Currency Exchange: *Casas de cambio* are open all day in the northern downtown area, but have poor rates. Stick to banks in the *centro* and the *zócalo.* **Banca Serfín** (☎982 6666), 21 de Marzo and Nelson, across from the *zócalo.* Open M-F 8:30am-5pm, Sa 10am-2pm. **Bancomer,** on the other side of the cathedral. Both have **24hr. ATMs.**

American Express: (☎913 0600; fax 916 5908), in Centro Commercial Plaza Balboa on Sábalo. Open daily 9am-5pm.

Laundry: Lavandería Super, Azuelta 1817, in the *centro.* 12 pesos per kg. Open M-Sa 8:30am-7pm, Su 8:30am-1pm.

Emergency: ☎066.

Police: (☎983 4510), on Buelna in Colonia Juárez.

Tourist police: (☎914 8444), on Ruiz and Santa Monica in the Zona Dorada.

Red Cross: (☎981 3690), on Zaragoza and Corona.

24hr. Pharmacy: Farmacias Hidalgo (24hr. emergency hotline ☎985 4545), at Evey and Hidalgo. Other locations in Old Mazatlán and the Zona Dorada.

Medical Services: Sharp Hospital (☎986 5678 or 983 1717), on Kumate and Buelna, near Zaragoza park, know as the tourist's hospital.

Internet Access: Ciber el Punto, Flores 810 (☎981 8730), in the *centro.* 15 pesos per hr. Also offers **fax** service. Open daily 8:30am-9:30pm.

Post Office: (☎981 2121), on Flores at Juárez, across from the *zócalo.* Open M-F 8am-6pm, Sa 9am-1pm. **Postal Code:** 82000.

▟ ACCOMMODATIONS

It's expensive to stay in the Zona Dorada or in the mid-range waterfront hotels of Olas Altas, but budget hotels line Juárez and Serdán in Old Mazatlán. The truly self-denying can find even cheaper lodgings in the area around the bus station. Rates may rise substantially during the high season (July-Aug. and Dec.-Apr.), but you can usually bargain.

OLAS ALTAS

Back in the 1950s, Olas Altas was the focal point of Mazatlán's fledgling resort scene. Although newer establishments have sprung up, the area remains mostly unchanged since its glory days. Copper plaques on every edifice list the big stars who have passed through its doors. A 10min. walk from the *centro*, and easily accessible, Olas Altas connects to the rest of Mazatlán by the "Sábalo-Centro" and other bus lines.

Hotel Belmar, Olas Altas 166 (☎985 1112), at Osuna. Spacious rooms with bath, and 2 queen beds. Internet access in the lobby. Free phone calls within North America. Pool and library. Rooms with A/C and TV 279 pesos, with ocean view 350 pesos; each additional person 30 pesos. AmEx/MC/V. ❺

Hotel la Siesta, Olas Altas Sur 11 (☎981 2640 or 800 711 5229), at Escobedo. Tiered wooden walkways connect small, clean rooms set around a lush courtyard with an ocean view. Rooms with A/C, phone, and TV. Singles in low season 300 pesos, with ocean view 315 pesos; in high season 351/468 pesos. Doubles 530 pesos. MC/V. ❺

OLD MAZATLÁN

Downtown, though congested, offers easy access to most points in the city.

Hotel del Río, Juárez Nte. 2410 (☎982 4430). Clean white halls and small rooms await at a family-run hotel a few blocks north of the *mercado*. A bit out of the way, the hotel has pleasant furniture and management, and sufficiently tacky business cards. Reserve 2-3 days in advance. Singles 150 pesos, with A/C 200 pesos; doubles 300/350 pesos. Cash only. ❷

Hotel Milan, Canizales 717 (☎985 3499), across from the Telmex building in the business district. A/C and TV make up for the brown color scheme. Singles 163 pesos; doubles 187 pesos. Prices rise 30-40% July-Aug. Cash only. ❷

Hotel Lerma, Bolívar 622 (☎981 2436), at Serdán. 10min. from the *centro*. Light blue rooms and ceiling fans make the heat bearable. Singles 90 pesos, with bath 110 pesos; doubles 120 pesos. Prices rise 10 pesos July-Aug. and Dec.-Apr. Cash only. ❶

Hotel Santa Barbara, Juárez 2612 (☎982 2120), on the corner of 16 de Septiembre. Up the hill from the *centro*. Doubles 180 pesos, with A/C 230 pesos. Cash only. ❶

Hotel Villa Del Mar, Serdán 1506 (☎981 3426). Jigsaw puzzles decorate the walls of these tiny cathedral-side doubles, with 2 single beds, TV, and a ceiling fan. Doubles 300 pesos, each additional person 100 pesos. Cash only. ❸

NEAR THE BUS STATION

These hotels are a long walk from both the *centro* and the Zona Dorada but are close to the "Sábalo-Centro" bus lines.

Hotel Fiesta, Ferrosquila 306 (☎981 7888), near the bus station. Clean rooms with hot water. Enjoy "hot kakes" (20 pesos) or a "homlet" (18 pesos) at the hotel's cafe. Singles and doubles 160 pesos, with A/C and TV 200 pesos. Cash only. ❷

Hotel Económico, Río Panuco 4 (☎118 4076), right across from the bus station. Perfect if you're just looking for a few hours of shut-eye before the morning bus. No amenities. Singles 120 pesos; doubles 150 pesos; triples 180 pesos. Cash only. ❶

LA ZONA DORADA

Hotel San Diego (☎983 5703; www.hotelsandiego.tripod.com), on Av. Del Mar and Buelna right by Fiesta Land. The best hotel rates in the Gold Zone. Clean rooms feature

A/C, large baths, and TV. Singles low season 250 pesos, doubles 350 pesos; high season 350 pesos/550 pesos. Cash and traveler's checks only. ❺

La Posta (☎983 5310), on Buelna. Trailer park. Hookup 85 pesos. ❶

█ FOOD

Restaurant prices soar as you get closer to the glam of the Zona Dorada. You may have to pay a little extra to sample the catch of the day, but it's guaranteed to be fresh. The busy **mercado municipal,** between Juárez and Serdán, three blocks north of the *zócalo,* serves the best and cheapest food in the area. If you need a headless pig (or a pig's head), look no further. For something more formal, with a view, head to an establishment along the *malecón* in Olas Altas. Enjoy your meal with the local █**Pacífico** beer, the pride of Mazatlán.

ZONA DORADA

The only restaurants close to budget in the Zona Dorada are on **Las Garzas,** but they serve basically the same food and are constantly competing for *gringo* dollars. Prices may be negotiable in low season.

La Troje, on Buelna across from Hotel San Diego. Cheap and filling breakfasts. *Burritos de huevo, frijól,* or *jamón* 10 pesos. Open daily 8am-11pm. Cash only. ❶

Jungle Juice, Av. Las Garzas 101 (☎930 3315). Daily specials in this seafood restaurant. Fish 50-60 pesos. Open daily 7am-10pm. Bar open daily 6pm-2am. MC/V. ❹

OLAS ALTAS

Copa de Leche Cafe, 1220A Sur (☎982 5753), on the *malecón* next to Hotel Belmar. Various gigantic egg dishes (50-75 pesos) and classic *café con leche* (15 pesos) served well into the afternoon. Open daily 7:30am-11pm. MC/V. ❺

Restaurante y Bar Puerto Viejo, Olas Altas and Osuna. Friendly staff serves fresh seafood right on the boardwalk with a great view of Olas Altas and the surrounding cliffs. 5 beers 55 pesos. Filling orders of ceviche 45 pesos. *Marlin ahumado* 55 pesos. Occasional live music on weekends. Open daily 10am-10pm. Cash only. ❹

NEAR PLAZUELA MACHADO

El Túnel, in the tunnel that starts at Carnaval 1207, across from the theater. Great ambience upstaged only by the amazing food. Dedicated to serving classic *sinaloense* cuisine, this place has dished out delicious *gorditas* since 1945. Try the *Tonicol* (13 pesos), a vanilla soda made exclusively in Sinaloa. *Gorditas* or *agua de horchata* 13 pesos. *Pozole sinaloense* 40 pesos. Open daily noon-midnight. Cash only. ❸

Machado Fish Tacos, Osuna 34 (☎981 1375), on the Plazuela Machado. Specializes in a variety of seafood tacos (fish, shrimp, clam, octopus, oyster) for 15 pesos each. Egg breakfasts 35 pesos. Open daily 8am-midnight. Cash only. ❸

Ambrosia Vegetarian Restaurant, Dominguez 1406 (☎985 0333). Excellent salads, such as the *ensalada rusa con ostiones y hongos* (russian salad with oysters and mushrooms; 55 pesos). AmEx/MC/V. ❹

Cafe Luxor, 828 Flores across from the cathedral. Free Internet with purchase of drink, baked good, or giant chicken salad (29-45 pesos). *Té Hindú* 29 pesos. Cash only. ❸

Panamá Cafe and Restaurant, Juárez and Canizales, and at Serdán and Morelos. Gusty A/C accompanies quick service. Local patrons devour amazing pastries or *antojitos sinaloenses* (45-55 pesos). Salads 25-35 pesos. Breakfasts 40-50 pesos. Open daily 7am-10pm. MC/V. ❹

👁 🕭 SIGHTS AND BEACHES

BEACHES. Mazatlán's famous beach stretches 16km from Olas Altas, well past the Zona Dorada. North of Old Mazatlán, along del Mar, is **Playa Norte.** Its small waves and general lack of activity make it a decent stretch of sand on which to find some solitude and maybe do a little bait-and-tackle, though loud traffic may spoil the mood. As you approach the Zona Dorada, the beach gets cleaner, the waves larger, and Playa Norte eases into **Playa las Gaviotas,** a popular spot among local surfers. Past Punto Sábalo and Hotel Los Sábalos, in the lee of the islands, is **Playa Sábalo,** the reason why Mazatlán is Mazatlán. Beware the vendors hawking cheap souvenirs. As Playa Sábalo recedes to the north, crowds thin rapidly. "Sábalo-Centro" buses pass all these beaches. In most places, boogie boards (40 pesos) and sailboats (500 pesos per hr.) are available. Renting snorkels is not worth it, as the water is very sandy near shore. Take the "Cerritos-Juárez" bus (5 pesos) to the last stop and walk left (walking straight ahead brings you to a rocky outcropping with restaurants but little sand) to nearly deserted **Playa Bruja,** with beautiful sand and 1-2m waves. **Camping** is permitted, but exercise caution after dark and camp in groups whenever possible.

> 🌴 **BEACHED.** The Mexican government owns all coastal land 20m from the high tide mark, meaning that there is no such thing as a private beach in Mexico. This means that you can spend as much time as you want, whenever you want, on any of Mazatlán's beaches, even if there is a hotel right behind it. So if you find the perfect secluded beach, don't worry—you're not trespassing. Even so, don't be surprised if you are denied access by overzealous property owners.

EL FARO. For a 360° view of Mazatlán and the sea, climb to the top of El Faro, the second tallest lighthouse in the world. The 30min. hike is almost unbearable in the summer; ascend in the early morning or late evening to avoid the heat. *(At the end of the "Playa Sur" bus route south of the centro.)*

TOWER DIVERS. Mazatlán's tower divers perform acrobatic and dangerous plunges into rocky surf from an 18m high ledge. Dives take place during the day, but be warned that divers will not perform unless they pull in a sufficient amount of money beforehand. The best times to watch are 10-11am and 4:30-6:30pm during high season, when tour buses arrive and tourists fork over their pesos, allowing you—the savvy (and unscrupulous) budget traveler—to see dives for free. Grab a spot just south of the high-dive towers. *(On Claussen, south of Zaragoza and north of La Siesta Hotel.)*

ISLA DE LOS VENADOS. Deer Island is a relatively deserted strip with fine diving, snorkeling, and beautiful beaches; catamaran boats leave from the Aqua Sports Center at El Cid Resort in the Zona Dorada. Bring your own food and water if you plan to spend some time here. *(☎913 3333, ext. 341. Boats depart daily 10am, noon, 2pm. Round-trip 100 pesos.)*

MAZAGUA. Water park mania hit Mazatlán with Mazagua, a large, clean park north of the Zona Dorada near Puerto Cerritos, in the area dubbed "New Mazatlán." Go bonkers in the wave pool and shoot down slides or the mammoth pipe flume. Be sure to pack a lunch. *(Take a "Cerritos-Juárez" bus, 4 pesos. ☎988 0041. Open Mar.-Oct. daily 10am-6pm. Snack bar. Inner tubes, lifevests 30 pesos. Storage lockers 20 pesos.)*

ACUARIO MAZATLÁN. One of the largest aquariums in Latin America, the Acuario Mazatlán keeps sharks and other feisty fish (250 breeds in all) in a slew of cloudy, small tanks, and hosts performing sea lions and birds. *(Av. De los Deportes 111. Off Av. del Mar, 1 block back from the beach, halfway between Zona Dorada and the centro; the turn-off is marked with a blue sign. ☎981 7815. Open daily 9am-6pm. 50 pesos, ages 5-10 25 pesos.)*

OTHER SIGHTS. The newly restored and luxurious **Teatro Ángela Peralta**, at Carnaval and Libertad near Plazuela Machado, hosts an impressive variety of cultural programs. *(☎982 4447; www.teatroangelaperalta.com. Prices vary by show.)* **Museo Casa Machado,** housed in a 19th-century mansion, is filled with relics from Mazatlán's glory days as the state capital. The museum houses a collection of spectacularly gaudy old *Carnaval* costumes. *(Constitución 79, just off Plazuela Machado. ☎982 1440. Open daily 10am-6pm. 20 pesos, children and students 10 pesos.)* The small but interesting **Museo Arqueológico** displays clay figurines, rocks, and dioramas. *(Osuna 72, between the centro and Olas Altas. Open M-F 10am-6pm, Su 10am-3pm. Free.)*

🔲 NIGHTLIFE

From March through October, Mexican youth swarm to the dozen *discotecas* surrounding Playa Norte. The ones that aren't solely electronica blast a mix of salsa, hip hop, and reggaeton. Prices for transportation and cover are steep, and most nightclubs cut deals with package-tour companies—the unpackaged tourist often pays more. Mellower amusements entertain older crowds around the *centro*.

THE CENTRO AND OLAS ALTAS

The bars lining the Plazuela Machado offer 15-peso beers and attract both locals and tourists hoping to enjoy the warm night air while listening to live music.

  Cafe Pacífico, Constitución 501 (☎981 3972), across from Plazuela Machado. A pub with an odd assortment of animal skins, rifles, and stained-glass windows. Cool interior—dedicated to the namesake Mazatlán brew—attracts a fun crowd of amiable locals seeking respite from the sun. Tourists lounge on their patio with nightly live music. Beer 15 pesos. *Jalapeños* stuffed with marlin 45 pesos. Open daily 10am-2am. MC/V.

  Altrazor Ars Cafe, Constitución 517, at Plazuela Machado. Enjoys local fame for serving Corona across from the birthplace of Pacífico beer. Local hipsters come for the beer (15 pesos), snacks, and live music nightly at 8:30pm under the umbrellas. Their *salciadas* (17 pesos) are hard to beat. Sandwiches 20-40 pesos. Large quesadillas 30 pesos. Open M-Sa 9am-2am, Su 4pm-1am. MC/V.

ZONA DORADA

Nightlife in the Zona Dorada is all about excess. Two-for-one beer deals abound.

  🔲**Joe's Oyster Bar,** Playa Goviatas 100 (☎983 5353), next to Los Sábalos Hotel. The best. Beachfront location and relaxed atmosphere make Joe's extremely popular for drinks (2 beers for 30 pesos) and dancing under the *palapas* on the beach. Cover Th-Su 50 pesos; includes 2 beers or 1 *bebida nacional* (any locally produced alcohol). Open daily 11am-5am. AmEx/D/MC/V.

  Mangos, Playa Gaviotas 403 (☎916 0044), set off from the street toward the beach. Young and trendy beach crowd. Mango margaritas are the house specialty (40 pesos, 2 for 60 pesos). Dress code prohibits tennis shoes, flip-flops, and shorts; it is enforced at the management's discretion. Cover 50 pesos when crowded. Draws more locals than foreigners. Open M-Th and Su noon-12:30am, F-Sa noon-4am.

  Fiesta Land, (☎989 1600, ext. 176 and 177), on Sábalo toward the southern end of the Zona Dorada, atop a white castle. A grouping of several nightspots that, despite all being in the same complex, operate as relatively separate entities. **Valentino's** is a disco with an incredible clifftop view and pulsing electronica music. Dress code: no shorts or sneakers. **Cantabar,** part of Valentino's, features karaoke and live *música norteña* on Su. **Bora-Bora** has an urban feel, and the club pumps salsa and hip hop. **Bali Hai** is a sports bar, while **Maui** is a snack bar. 2-for-1 beers 30 pesos. Mixed drinks from 35 pesos. Cover for the complex is 50 pesos, but individual clubs will charge their own on packed nights; Su women free at Bora Bora and Cantabar. After 12:30am, a hand stamp lets you into all clubs; before then you are restricted to 1. Cantabar open until 6am on weekends, others open until 3am. Crowds don't arrive until midnight, and beforehand it's usually filled with young high schoolers.

Latitud 123, on the corner of Las Garzas and Loaiza (☎913 1413). New club plays a lot of US hits, yet strangely attracts many older Mexican couples. Dress code: no shorts, no sandals. Beer 20 pesos. Cash only.

Gringo Lingo, Playa Gaviotas 313 (☎913 7737; www.gringolingo.com.mx), across from Hotel Sábalo. A young foreign crowd comes to hear music that speaks their language and enjoy some of the least-gouged prices the Zona Dorada has to offer. The live rock music. 2-for-1 beers 30 pesos. Hamburgers 45-60 pesos. Open daily noon-1am. MC/V.

El Caracol (☎913 3333, ext. 3245), in the El Cid Hotel on Sábalo. A premier 4-level dance club, with insane laser beams and endless *música electronica*. Drinks 30-45 pesos. Cover 50 pesos; discounts for El Cid guests. Open daily 9pm-2am. AmEx/MC/V.

✺ FESTIVALS

As if the nightly scene weren't rowdy enough, the city comes out in full force each year to celebrate a notoriously debaucherous ✦**Carnaval,** where clothes are optional and pick-up trucks pump salsa through the streets. More than just a money-making scheme hatched by local hoteliers, Mazatlán's *Carnaval* during the week before Lent has a history dating back to the 17th century. Hotel reservations should be made several weeks in advance for this party.

▶ DAYTRIP FROM MAZATLÁN

◗ ISLA DE LA PIEDRA

Take a green "Independencia" bus (4 pesos) from the market at Serdán to the Embarcadero de la Isla de la Piedra, the small jetty about 250m east of the Baja Ferries station. Another jetty lies east of the centro, but is only accessible by pulmonía or taxi (40 pesos from the centro). From there, take a boat to the island (5min., every 10min., round-trip 15 pesos; boat prices double after 7pm.) Life jackets are mandatory. Pulmonías and taxis (20 pesos) take passengers to the beach from the ferry landing. By foot, go straight from the boat landing and follow the concrete path left, taking the first dirt road that branches to the right across the island (10-15min.) At the larger disembarking points, tractors drag wagons of passengers all the way to the beach for free.

A short boat ride from the mainland, Isla de la Piedra boasts 18km of glistening sand, crashing waves, and rustling palm trees. Coconuts are king here, with thousands harvested every weekend in the summer. Less crowded and not as developed as the mainland, the island is a haven of sunshine and ocean popular with both Mexican families and Americans escaping the tourists. Take a trip on a banana boat (80 pesos), and rent snorkeling equipment (150 pesos per hr.) or a body board (30 pesos per hr.). Horses can be hired (85 pesos per hr.) up the beach; ask for Martín.

AGUASCALIENTES

AGUASCALIENTES   ☎449

Named for the hot springs near the city center, Aguascalientes (pop. 800,000) is famous throughout Mexico for its no-holds-barred Feria de San Marcos, when the whole city goes wild for three weeks from mid-April to mid-May. For the rest of the year, residents—referred to as *los hidrálicos* (thermal water people)—settle down to work, play with their kids in the many plazas, and attend the city's myriad of cultural events. Modern concrete buildings are interrupted by unusual churches, the mural-covered Palacio del Gobierno, and unexpected green spaces. Aguascalientes stood on the old silver trail between Zacatecas and Mexico City, but other than a few museums and a lovely plaza, it does not offer as much for tourists as the nearby colonial cities of Guanajuato and Zacatecas.

▣ TRANSPORTATION

Aguascaliente's **bus station** is on Convención Sur and Av. 5, a few blocks west of José Mari Chavez. Green-and-white city buses numbered in the 20s and 30s (4 pesos) run from outside the bus station to the Mercado Morelos, two blocks north of the Plaza de la Patria, in the center of town. To get back to the station, take a "Central Camionera" bus or a taxi (under 40 pesos). **Ómnibus de México** (☎978 2770) goes to: **Ciudad Juárez** (15hr., 6 per day, 951 pesos); **Durango** (7hr., 7 per day, 292 pesos); **Torreón** (6hr., 5 per day, 370 pesos); **Zacatecas** (2½ hr., 8 per day, 91 pesos). **Futura** (☎978 2758) goes to: **Durango** (6hr., 10 per day, 292 pesos); **Guadalajara** (3hr., every hr. 5am-9pm, 172 pesos); **Mexico City** (6hr., 10 per day, 423 pesos); **Monterrey** (9hr., 8 per day, 376 pesos); **San Luis Potosí** (3hr., 15 per day, 132 pesos). **Primera Plus** (☎978 2671) and **ETN** (☎978 2429) also go to major cities.

◪ ▣ ORIENTATION AND PRACTICAL INFORMATION

Aguascalientes is 168km west of San Luis Potosí, 128km south of Zacatecas, and 252km northeast of Guadalajara. **Circunvalación** encircles the city, while **López Mateos** cuts through town from east to west. From **Plaza de la Patria,** most sights are within walking distance. The city takes its *siestas* quite seriously; many sights and businesses close from 2 to 4pm.

Tourist Office: (☎915 9504 or 0051), on the south side of the Plaza de la Patria, in the Palacio de Gobierno. Note: there are two adjacent palaces, the other is the Palacio Municipal. The door opens right onto the plaza. Decent maps and several brochures, some in English. 3 different trolley tours of the city cost 25 pesos per person. Inquire at the office for times. Open M-F 8am-7:30pm, Sa-Su 9am-6pm.

Currency Exchange and Bank: Bancomer, 5 de Mayo 120 (☎915 5115), 1 block from Plaza de la Patria. Offers good rates. Open M-F 8:30am-4pm, Sa 10am-1pm.

Emergency: ☎066 or 080.

Police: (☎910 2881 or 2883), at the corner of Héroe de Nacozari and López Mateos. **LOCATEL** (☎910 2020) assists with missing persons.

Red Cross: (☎916 4200 or 4714; emergency ☎065) at Dr. Medina and El Dorado. Has ambulance service.

24hr. Pharmacy: Farmacia Sánchez, Madero 213 (☎915 3550), 1 block from Plaza de la Patria.

Hospital: Hidalgo, Galeana 465 (☎918 4448 or 918 5054).

Fax Office: Telecomm (☎916 1427), on Galeana at Nieto. Open M-F 8am-7pm, Sa 9am-1pm, Su 9am-noon. Another in the bus station. Open M-F 8am-7:30pm, Sa 9am-noon.

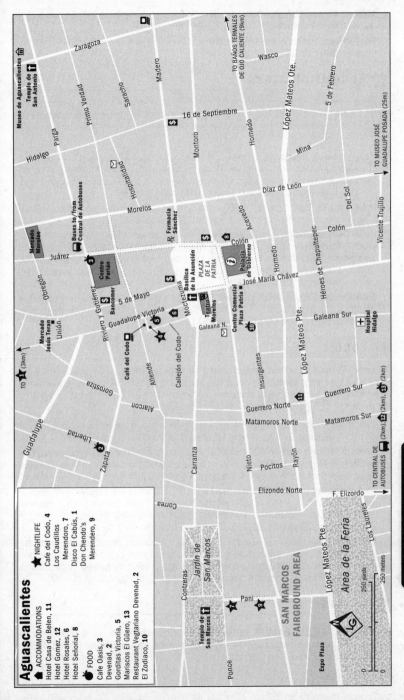

NORTHWEST MEXICO

Aguascalientes

ACCOMMODATIONS
Hotel Casa de Belen, **11**
Hotel Gomez, **12**
Hotel Rosales, **6**
Hotel Señorial, **8**

FOOD
Cafe Oasis, **3**
Devenad, **2**
Gorditas Victoria, **5**
Mariscos El Güero, **13**
Restaurant Vegetariano Devenad, **2**
El Zodiaco, **10**

NIGHTLIFE
Cafe del Codo, **4**
Los Caudillos
Merendero, **7**
Disco El Cabús, **1**
Don Chendo's
Merendero, **9**

Museo de Aguascalientes 🏛
Templo de San Antonio 🕇

TO BAÑOS TERMALES DE OJO CALIENTE (9km)

TO MUSEO JOSÉ GUADALUPE POSADA (25m)

Zaragoza
Wasco
Madero
Saracho
Primo Verdad
Parga
Hidalgo
16 de Septiembre
Montoro
Hornedo
Mina
López Mateos Ote.
5 de Febrero

Díaz de León
Hospitalidad
Del Sol
Vicente Trujillo
Colón

Morelos
Buses to/from Central de Autobuses
Mercado Morelos
Juárez
Farmacia Sánchez ℞

Obregón
Centro Parián
Bancomer
5 de Mayo
Basílica de la Asunción
PLAZA DE LA PATRIA
Palacio de Gobierno
Colón
Hornedo
Héroes de Chapultepec

Mercado Jesús Terán
Unión
Riviero y Gutiérrez
Guadalupe Victoria
Montezuma
Teatro Morelos
José María Chávez
Galeana Sur
Hospital Hidalgo

Café del Codo
Allende
Callejón del Codo
Centro Comercial Plaza Patria
Galeana N.
López Mateos Pte.

Gorostiza
Alarcon
Insurgentes
TO (3km)

Guadalupe
Liberad
Zapata
Carranza
Guerrero Norte
Matamoros Norte
Nieto
Pocitos
Rayón
Guerrero Sur
Matamoros Sur
(2km)
(2km)

Elizondo Norte
F. Elizondo
TO CENTRAL DE AUTOBUSES
(2km)

Correa
Contreras
Jardín de San Marcos
Pani
SAN MARCOS FAIRGROUND AREA
López Mateos Pte.
Area de la Feria

Templo de San Marcos
Ponce
Expo Plaza
250 yards
250 meters

Internet Access: Cafe del Codo, Callejón del Codo 15 (☎994 1587), on a small alley off Victoria. 10 pesos per hr. Open M-Sa 8am-midnight.

Post Office: Hospitalidad 108 (☎915 2118). Open M-F 8am-6pm, Sa 9am-1pm. **Postal Code:** 20000.

▲ ACCOMMODATIONS

Budget hotels in Aguascalientes are located on side streets extending from Plaza de la Patria. As a general rule, hotels in the *centro* are of higher quality than those by the bus station and charge similar rates. During the Feria de San Marcos (mid-Apr. to mid-May), reservations are a must.

Hotel Rosales, Guadalupe Victoria 104 (☎915 2165), off Madero, across from the Basilica and Plaza de la Patria. The shady courtyard invites midday lounging. Excellent location, especially for the price. Clean, antique rooms come with cable TV and fans. Singles 180 pesos; doubles 200 pesos; triples 220 pesos. ❸

Hotel Casa de Belen, (☎915 8497) on the corner of Galeana Sur and López Mateos. This 5-story sliver offers singles with fans for 130 pesos. Cash only. ❷

Hotel Señorial, Colón 104 (☎915 1630), at the corner of Montoro, on Plaza de la Patria. Fantastic location. Ask for a room with a balcony overlooking the plaza and cathedral; the view is worth the higher price tag. Nice rooms with phone, cable TV, and purified water. Singles 220 pesos; doubles 330 pesos; triples 405 pesos; 6-bed rooms 750 pesos. Cash only. ❹

Hotel Gomez, Circunvalación 602 (☎978 2120), to the left of the *camionera central* as you exit. The best bargain around the bus station. Rooms come with TV. Restaurant attached. Singles 200 pesos; doubles 250 pesos. ❸

◖ FOOD

Countless numbers of **food vendors** selling juice, popcorn, *tamales*, and fruit fill the *centro*, especially on weekends at the Plaza de la Patria. Aguascalientes has a **Tepoznieves,** in Centro Parian at Juárez and Primo Verdad, which is proudly hailed as the home of Mexico's best ice cream and offers over 131 flavors.

Cafe Oasis, Juárez 222 (☎915 9409). Popular fast food in the *centro* on the corner of Riviero y Gutiérrez. 2 slices of pizza and a soda for 25 pesos. Cash only. ❷

Gorditas Victoria, Victoria 108 (☎918 1792), next to the Hotel Rosales. Local families enjoy a wide range of filling *gorditas* (15 pesos) throughout the day. Grab your food *para llevar* (to go) and enjoy it in the plaza. Open daily 8am-8pm. ❶

Restaurant Vegetariano Devenad (☎918 2721), at Zapata and Libertad, just north of Jardín San Marcos. A decent walk from the Plaza de la Patria, but worth it if you're tired of meat dishes. Quesadillas 15 pesos. Veggies and rice 40-50 pesos. Open M-Sa 11am-7:30pm. Cash only. ❸

El Zodiaco, Galeana Sur 113 (☎915 3181). The eye-opening decor includes live canaries, orange chairs, an open kitchen, a painted shrine to the Virgen de Guadalupe, and formica tables. Specialties include generous egg breakfasts (30-40 pesos). Sandwiches and hamburgers 15-20 pesos. Open daily 8:30am-10pm. Cash only. ❸

◉ SIGHTS

▨**MUSEO JOSÉ GUADALUPE POSADA.** The museum displays a selection of grimly delightful engravings by locally born artist José Guadalupe Posada (1852-1913). Cavorting skeletons, nightmarish devils, drunks, and lovers populate his images, which tend to portray the darker, unromanticized side of rural Mexican life. Posada, an ardent critic of the dictator Porfirio Díaz (1830-1915), set the stage for the scathing social commentary of later Mexican muralists, such as Diego Rivera (1886-1957) and José Clemente Orozco (1883-1949). The collection includes 220 of his original works and images, the most famous of which, *Calavera de la Catrina*, depicts the *calavera* (skull) of a high-society female wearing an outlandish hat. Rivera recreated Posada's *La Catrina* as a part of his *Sueño de Una Tarde Dominical en la Alameda*, now on display in Mexico City. *(On León, next to the Templo del Encino, 4 blocks south of López Mateos. ☎ 915 4556. Open Tu-Su 11am-6pm. 10 pesos, students 5 pesos, children free; Su free.)*

PLAZA DE LA PATRIA. Bountiful shade, benches, and bubbling fountains invite the weary to take a break. To the south, it is bordered by the Palacio de Gobierno and the Palacio Municipal. Fascinating and bitter historical murals cover the Palacio de Gobierno's interior. Next to the Palacio on the eastern end is a large golden tower with the national emblem of an eagle on a cactus eating a serpent. Also south of the plaza is the Teatro Morelos, the site of the 1914 Convention of Aguascalientes, in which rival factions led by Zapata, Carranza, and Villa clashed over the selection of the new president, prolonging the Revolution. Posters outside the theater list event information.

ESTADIO VICTORIA. The home of Aguascalientes' 1st division soccer team, Club Necaxa. **"Los Rayos"** draw large crowds, especially when they play the more popular teams from Guadalajara and Mexico City. *(☎ 976 1830; www.clubnecaxa.com.)*

BASÍLICA DE LA ASUNCIÓN DE LAS AGUASCALIENTES. The soft gray-and-rose-colored Solomonic Baroque facade of the 18th-century basilica make it the city's most remarkable structure. The cathedral's interior, restored in the 18th and 19th centuries, is graced with high ceilings, ornate icons, and gold trimmings along with 17th- and 18th-century paintings by Jose de Alcibar, Andres López, and Miguel Cabrera. *(In the center of Plaza de la Patria. Open daily 7am-2pm and 4-9pm.)*

TEMPLO DE SAN ANTONIO. A 10min. walk from the Plaza de la Patria down Zaragoza, a unique onion-domed church rises up at the end of the street. Construction of the church began in 1895 and was completed in 1908 under self-taught architect José Refugio Reyes (1862-1945). The patterns on the interior murals, frescoes, oil paintings, and delicate stained-glass windows matches the eclectic exterior, which blends Baroque, Classical, and Oriental styles. *(On Pedro Parga at Zaragoza. From the plaza, walk 3 blocks down Madero, go left on Zaragoza, and continue for 3 blocks. ☎ 915 2898. Open M-Sa 6:30-10am, 11:30-12:30pm, and 6-9pm; Su 6:30am-noon and 5:30-9pm.)*

MUSEO DE AGUASCALIENTES. This small, interesting art museum in a building designed by José Refugio Reyes exhibits the works of Aguascalientes native Saturnino Herran (1887-1918). Though Herran died at 31, he left behind a masterful collection. His 1917 design for a mural, *Nuestros Dioses*, blends indigenous with Catholic worship in a visually stunning sketch. Rotating exhibits feature Mexican painters, sculptors, and photographers. *(Across from Templo de San Antonio. Open Tu-Su 11am-6pm. 10 pesos, students and seniors 5 pesos; Su free.)*

JARDÍN DE SAN MARCOS. Around 1600, *indígenas* erected the Templo Evangelista San Marcos on this site, originally an indigenous settlement. The small church still has services, and is the center of a crowded pedestrian thoroughfare filled with Mexican families in the evenings. The adjacent arcade is lined with bars and vendors and is active late into the night. *(The Jardín is a 5-10min. walk on Carranza from Plaza de la Patria. Church open daily 7am-2pm and 4-9pm.)*

HOT SPRINGS. Aguascalientes does, after all, mean "hot waters," and sure enough, there are several thermal *balnearios* (hot springs) at the edge of town. Most are overrated—waters tend to be lukewarm at best. The most accessible springs are at **Baños Termales de Ojocaliente.** The turn-of-the-20th-century building consists of many private thermal showers and an outdoor swimming pool. The waters are reputed to have cured cases of rheumatism, which helps explain the elderly clientele. *(Balneario located across the Parque Urbano la Pona at the fork of Revolución and San Luis Potosí. To get there from the city center take a Ruta 14 or 19 bus eastbound from Madero and ask the driver if it is bound for the Balneario. Open daily 7am-7pm. 70-180 pesos per hr.)*

OTHER SIGHTS. Around the *centro* are other museums worth a look. The **Museo de Arte Contemporaneo** displays rotating exhibits of contemporary Latin American artists and houses a small library. *(At Morelos and Verdad. ☎918 6901. Open Tu-Su 11am-6pm. 10 pesos, students and teachers 5 pesos.)* The **Museo Regional de Historia** occupies another building designed by Refugio Reyes. The collection explores the area's past, from prehistoric to Revolutionary times. *(Carranza 118. ☎916 5228. Open Tu-Su 9am-7pm. 30 pesos, students and children free; Su free.)*

🎵 🎭 ENTERTAINMENT AND NIGHTLIFE

Unless you catch the Feria de San Marcos, Aguascalientes doesn't have much of a nightlife. By city ordinance, *discotecas* are prohibited in the *centro histórico*, and even on the outskirts they can only open their doors Thursday through Saturday. Bars or *merenderos* (open-air cafes), on the other hand, are open every night of the week. They are concentrated on **Pani,** between Ponce and Nieto, in the area of the San Marcos Fairgrounds just south of the Jardín. Buses stop running around 10pm, when taxis become the best way to get around.

Don Chendo's Merendero, Arturo Pani 144. This bar and grill is one of the most happening places in town. Drinks and live, heartfelt *mariachi* music are served to a mix of tourists and locals. Beer 20 pesos. Tequila 30 pesos. Open daily 1pm-2am. Cash only.

Los Caudillos Merendero, Arturo Pani 127. A cheaper, more relaxed alternative. *Ranchero*-themed interior. Very popular among young *hidrálicos*. Beer 15 pesos. Tequila from 30 pesos. Cash only.

Cafe del Codo, 225 Codo (☎994 1587). Perfect for winding down without having to leave the *centro*. Aside from being an Internet cafe, it's also a hangout for the young, artsy crowd. Beer 20 pesos. Common 2-for-1 specials. Live jazz Th-F. The waiters play on the weeknights. Open M-Sa 8am-midnight. AmEx/MC/V.

Disco El Cabús (☎913 0432), on Zacatecas at Colosia, in the Hotel Las Trojes. Shake your caboose at the most popular disco in Aguascalientes, with the usual flashing lights and bass-heavy dance beats. Don't wear shorts—you may be apprehended by the fashion police. Cover 50 pesos. Open Th-Sa 9pm-3am. MC/V.

✿ FESTIVALS

During the **Feria de San Marcos** (mid-April to mid-May) everything from cockfights to milking contests takes place in the Jardín de San Marcos. The Feria de San Marcos is commonly referred to as the "largest *cantina* in Mexico," and cheap outdoor bars pop up on every street corner. To reach the Expo Plaza, walk two blocks to the left as you face the Templo in Jardín. The festival of the patron saint of Aguascalientes, **La Romeria de la Asunción** (August 1-15), is celebrated with dances, processions, and fireworks. The **Festival de las Calaveras** (late Oct.-early Nov.) is another occasion for the city to cut loose and celebrate.

ZACATECAS

ZACATECAS ☎492

Almost 400 years ago, the founding Spanish silver barons swore an oath to pave the streets of Zacatecas (pop. 125,000) with the precious metal. Using indigenous labor, they extracted more than 6000 tons from the mountains before abandoning their plans. The city's high altitude (2500m) wards off high temperatures, making Zacatecas a pleasant place to while away the time. The *centro*—recently dubbed a ◪UNESCO World Heritage site—boasts leftover mansions, glorious temples, cable cars, and a dozen museums with impressive modern art collections. During the summer, students and professors from across the world come to study at the university, learn Spanish at the Instituto del Fénix, or decipher Náhuatl at the Ethnography Center. Zacatecas is a college town that knows how to have fun, with Corona—brewed on the outskirts of town in the world's second largest *cervecería*—fueling the most of the city's nightlife.

▣ TRANSPORTATION

Flights: Aeropuerto La Calera (**ZCL**; ☎928 0338), accessible by *combis* (☎922 5946) from the Mexicana office (20min., departs 2hr. before flight, 50 pesos). Serviced by: **AeroCalifornia**, Juan de Montoro 203 (☎925 2400); **Mexicana**, Hidalgo 406 (☎922 7470; open M-F 9am-7pm); **Taesa**, Hidalgo 306 (☎922 0050 or 0212; open M-F 9am-7pm, Sa 10am-6pm).

Buses: Central de Autobuses (☎922 1112), on Lomas de la Isabélica, at Tránsito Pesado on the outskirts of town. "Ruta 8" city buses (5 pesos) and taxis (30 pesos) to the *centro* wait outside. After dark, a taxi is the only option. To get to the station from the *centro*, take a "Ruta 8" bus along Genaro Codino, Hierro, Hidalgo, or González Ortega (all on the same bus route). **Ómnibus de Mexico** (☎922 5495) has the broadest range of destinations, including service to: **Aguascalientes** (3hr., every hr., 91 pesos); **Ciudad Juárez** (26hr., every hr., 862 pesos); **Durango** (5hr., 15 per day, 202 pesos); **Guadalajara** (5hr., every 45min., 261 pesos); **Matamoros** (11hr., 7 per day, 498 pesos); and **Mexico City** (8hr., 10 per day, 459 pesos). **Futura** (☎922 0042) and **Estrella Blanca** (☎922 0684) provide similar services.

Car Rental: Autos Último Modelo, Alcatraces 147 (☎/fax 924 5509). From 450 pesos per day. First 200km free. **Avis**, López Mateos 615 (☎922 3003, airport office 985 1100). Open M-Sa 8:30am-3pm and 5-7:30pm. **Budget**, López Mateos 104 (☎922 9458; www.budget.com.mx). From 500 pesos per day.

✴◪ ORIENTATION AND PRACTICAL INFORMATION

Zacatecas is 610 km from the D.F. on the silver trail and 190km from San Luis Potosí. The city's narrow cobblestone streets are not only mercilessly snarled, but their names change frequently, they're sprawled over hills, and many are *callejones* (alleys often ending in stairways). **Hidalgo** is the main street, and the **cathedral** is a useful landmark visible from all over town.

Tourist Office: Hidalgo 403 (☎922 3426), on the 2nd fl. Helpful staff answers questions in both Spanish and English, and provides a variety of maps and pamphlets. Open M-F 8am-8pm, Sa-Su 10am-6pm. Office operates an equally helpful **booth** a block south on Hidalgo, just across from the Teatro. Open Tu-Su 10am-6pm.

Currency Exchange and Banks: Banca Promex, González Ortega 122 (☎922 9369), has good rates and a **24hr. ATM**. Open M-F 8:30am-5:30pm, Sa 10am-2pm. More banks on the 1st blocks of González Ortega and Hidalgo away from Juárez.

NORTHWEST MEXICO

Zacatecas

ACCOMMODATIONS
Hostal Villa Colonial, **10**
Hotel Colón, **15**
Hotel del Parque, **14**
Hotel María Conchinita, **16**
Hotel Zamora, **13**

FOOD
Acrópolis, **4**
Los Dorados de
Villa, **2**
Gorditas Doña Julia, **8**
El Pueblito, **6**
La Única Cabaña, **12**

NIGHTLIFE & CAFES
Café Dalí, **5**
Gaudí, **7**
Las Quince Letras, **11**

El Malacate, **1**
Subterráneo Cafe, **3**
Todos Santos, **9**

Luggage Storage: At the bus station. 5 pesos per hr. Open 24hr.

Laundromat: Lavamatic Plus, Rosadela 18 (☎923 4706), at México. Open M-Sa 9am-5:30pm. 40 pesos per 3kg.

Emergency: ☎066

Police: Héroes de Chapultepec 1000 (☎922 0507). 24hr. **tourist police** hotline (☎927 2654 or 0180).

Red Cross: Calzada de la Cruz Roja 100 (☎922 3005 or 3323), off Héroes de Chapultepec, near the exit to Fresnillo.

24hr. Pharmacy: Farmacia Guadalajara, López Mateos 305 (☎922 3862), across the street from the Howard Johnson. Many other pharmacies line Tacuba and Hidalgo.

Hospital: General, García Salinas 707 (☎923 3004 or 3005), in Guadalupe.

Fax Office: Telecomm (☎922 0060; fax 922 1796), on Hidalgo at Juárez. Open M-F 8am-7pm, Sa-Su 9am-noon.

Internet Access: Optimus Prime, Tacuba 118 (☎922 0423), across from the fountain. Has good service and assistance. 15 pesos per hr. Open M-Sa 9am-9pm.

Post Office: Allende 111 (☎922 0196), off Hidalgo. Open M-F 9am-4pm, Sa 9am-1pm. **Mexpost** next door. Open M-F 9am-6pm, Sa 9am-1pm. **Postal Code:** 98000.

ACCOMMODATIONS

Most budget accommodations have been priced out of the *centro* and linger at its fringe, on López Mateos—the main thoroughfare bordering the historic core. Reservations are a good idea at the cheapest hotels.

Hostal Villa Colonial (HI), 1 de Mayo (☎922 1980; hostalvillacolonial@hotmail.com), up Callejón Mono Prieto, behind the cathedral. The Lozano clan runs one of the city's most popular hostels. Internationals and backpackers revel in the amenities: book exchange, dining room, kitchen, terrace, TV, and storage. Sells the cheapest beer in town: 9 pesos per bottle. Frequent outings to La Quemada and the Corona brewery. Su outings to Real de Catorce. Laundry 25 pesos per 10kg. Internet access 15 pesos per hr. Free Wi-Fi. Free pickup from the bus station if arranged in advance. Reservations recommended. 4-bed dorms 90 pesos, with ISIC or HI card 80 pesos; private rooms 200 pesos; studio apartments 1000 pesos per week. Prices may vary by season. MC/V. ❶

Hotel del Parque, González Ortega 302 (☎922 0479), near the aqueduct. Has a pretty view of the greenery and fountain in Parque Enrique Estrada. A 10min. walk uphill to most museums and sights, but worth it for the price. Clean bathrooms and TV. Singles 175 pesos; doubles 200 pesos; triples 225 pesos; quads 250 pesos. Cash only. ❸

Hotel Colón, López Mateos 508 (☎922 0264). White marble rooms with cable TV are an excellent bargain. Noise from the highway might be bothersome. Singles 190 pesos; doubles 290 pesos; triples 330 pesos. MC/V. ❸

Hotel María Conchita, López Mateos 401 (☎922 1494), across Mateos from the *zona centro*. Well-maintained rooms equipped with phone and cable TV. 4th- and 5th-floor rooms are slightly newer, but don't merit the higher price (or stair) hike. Light sleepers should ask for a room away from the noisy highway. The late-night restaurant next door offers cheap breakfasts (33 pesos) and other Mexican standards. Singles 180 pesos; doubles 230 pesos; triples 260 pesos. Cash only. ❷

Hotel Zamora, Plazuela de Zamora 303 (☎922 1200), on the continuation of Independencia downhill from the Jardín de Independencia. With a lobby that lingers in the eternal twilight of *telenovelas*, Hotel Zamora has a good location but a high price tag for its off-green, shabby rooms. Singles 170 pesos; doubles 210 pesos. Cash only. ❸

FOOD

Zacatecas is famous for its rich sweets and heavy enchiladas. Get that sugar rush with *dulce de leche* (caramelized milk), *camote* (yams), *coco* (coconut), or *batata* (sweet potato)—they all cost around 5 pesos, and are peddled by vendors in the *centro*. Zacatecas also hosts a thriving cafe culture.

La Única Cabaña (☎922 5775), on Independencia at Juárez. The most popular restaurant in town, this *taquería* knows how to satisfy. Fast, delicious food served with excellent salsas. Tacos 6 pesos, with cheese 8 pesos. Quesadillas 7 pesos. Roasted half-chicken 60 pesos. Open daily 7am-midnight. Cash only. ❶

Los Dorados de Villa, Plazuela de Garcia 314 (☎922 5722), across the street from Taquería Wendy. Serves 10 varieties of enchiladas. *Enchiladas duranguenses* for 60 pesos. Open daily 8am-9pm. MC/V. ❹

El Pueblito, Hidalgo 403 (☎924 3818), downstairs from the tourist office. Cozy, colorful interior with an upscale feel. Classy enough to impress a date. Try the Zacatecan enchiladas (54 pesos) or the regional sampler (60 pesos). Open daily 1-11pm. MC/V. ❹

Acrópolis (☎922 1284), on Hidalgo and Plazuela Calendario Huízar next to the cathedral. Brightly decorated. Serves Zacatecas's professional set. Coffee 25 pesos.

Chicken *chimichangas* 57 pesos. Wide range of cheesecakes 30 pesos each. Open daily 8am-10pm. MC/V. ❹

Gorditas Doña Julia, Hidalgo 409 (☎923 7955). Additional locations on Tacuba (across from the fountain) on Obregón, on the freeway out of town. Despite floods of locals and tourists, they're still able to ensure fast service and 11 varieties of filling *gorditas*, including *huevos con nopal* (8 pesos). Open daily 8am-11pm. Cash only. ❶

👁 SIGHTS

Because of its extraordinary beauty, Zacatecas's entire *centro* is a ◪**UNESCO World Heritage site.** Strict building codes and prohibitions against gaudy advertisements make it hard to tell where the city ends and the museums begin, but it hardly matters, as both are spectacular. Not to be missed are the two Coronel museums and the vista of the city from **La Bufa.** If you've got a few more days, leave time for the neighboring town of **Guadalupe** (p. 293) and the ruins of **La Quemada** (p. 293).

◪**CATEDRAL BASÍLICA.** This pink sandstone cathedral was begun in 1729, completed in 1752, and consecrated in 1862. The intricate three-story facade is perhaps the best example of Mexican Baroque and depicts Christ blessing the Apostles and images of the Eucharist. The northern facade bears a representation of Christ on the cross, and the European Baroque southern facade pays homage to Nuestra Señora de las Zacatecas. The interior of the cathedral is surprisingly plain, though legend has it that prior to the War of Reform (1858-1861) it was as splendid as the outside. *(On Hidalgo, 4 blocks northeast of Juárez. Open daily 7am-1pm and 3-9pm. Free.)*

◪**MUSEO RAFAEL CORONEL.** Bristle-faced tigers, swarthy Moors, caimans, devils, and gods stare out from the walls of this superb museum that stresses the power of *máscaras*. Masks are housed in the dramatic Ex-Convento de San Francisco, built in the 17th century by Franciscans and then occupied by the Jesuits until the late 18th century. The exhibits showcase an enormous collection of figurines, pottery, and puppets donated by Rafael Coronel. Don't miss the rooms with Coronel's recent photographs and paintings. *(To reach the museum from the cathedral, follow Hidalgo, bearing left at the fountain at the 1st fork, and right at the 2nd. Open M-Tu and Th-Su 10am-5pm. 20 pesos, students and seniors 10 pesos, children free.)*

◪**MUSEO DE PEDRO CORONEL.** Housed in the former Colegio de San Luis Gonzaga, a Jesuit college established in 1616 that later became a jail, the museum is now home to the unparalleled paintings, sculptures, and tomb of Zacatecan artist Pedro Coronel. It also has one of the best modern art collections in Latin America, with works by Braque, Chagall, Dalí, Hogarth, Goya, Miró, and Picasso. Check out the view of the Plazuela Santo Domingo from the second-floor windows. The Historical Library of Zacatecas attached to the museum is home to thousands of volumes, some dating back to 1560. *(On Villapando at Serdán. Facing away from the cathedral entrance, cross Hidalgo going right. Turn left into the first alleyway, left as it ends on Dondina, and right at your first opportunity, following Villapando to the museum. ☎922 1821. Open M-W and F-Su 10am-5pm. 20 pesos, students and seniors 10 pesos, children free.)*

CERROS AND TELEFÉRICO. Most people walk up **Cerro El Grillo** to catch the ◪**teleférico** (cable car) to the much higher Cerro de la Bufa. El Grillo also has a splendid view over Zacatecas, and the Mina el Edén east entrance neighbors the *teleférico* stop here. Named in Basque for its resemblance to a Spanish wineskin, the **Cerro de la Bufa** peers down on the city from its highest crag. Museums, a church, and tons of clambering kids stand at the top, but the real attraction is the view. The **Museo de la Toma de Zacatecas,** adjacent to the Cerro de la Bufa, was built to commemorate Pancho Villa's decisive victory over federal troops in the summer of 1914, and displays an array of revolutionary memorabilia, including photographs, a cannon, and small weapons. *(☎922 8066. Open daily 10am-4:30pm. 20 pesos, students and children 10 pesos.)* On one side of the museum lies the 18th-century **Capilla del Patrocinio,** with a graceful facade and cloistered courtyards carved from the pink stone that graces many of Zacatecas's monuments. A short but steep walk up the hill leads to the Moorish **Mausoleo de los Hombres Ilustres de Zacatecas** (Mausoleum of the Illustrious Men of Zacatecas), worth the hike if only for the view of the city. There's yet another view behind the museum, from the castle where the **Meteorological Observatory** is housed. Climbing around is half the fun. *(To get to La Bufa, either take a taxi from the centro (35 pesos), or the teleférico from Cerro del Grill. Teleférico open daily 10am-6pm. 23 pesos. Teleféricos also leave from La Bufa below the Capilla, but depending on the time of day, you may have to wait in line for 1hr.)*

MUSEO DE ARTE ABSTRACTO MANUEL FELGUÉREZ. This converted prison houses a wide range of Mexican abstract art from the past 40 years. On prison-guard catwalks, you can survey the Manuel Felguérez collection, which takes the former prisoners' position. The museum also boasts superb giant canvases from the Osaka 70 exhibit and temporary displays on Mexican and international figures. *(Colón 1. ☎924 3705. Open M and W-Su 10am-5pm. 20 pesos, students 10 pesos.)*

PARQUE ENRIQUE ESTRADA. Southeast of the downtown area, 39 pink stone arches mark the end of Zacatecas's famous colonial aqueduct, **El Cubo.** Beside the aqueduct is the beautifully manicured **Parque Enrique Estrada.** On the western side of the park is the former governor's mansion, now the **Museo de Francisco Goitia,** Enrique Estrada 101. The museum displays contemporary art from the last half-century, examining the influence of modern Mexican artists on the international scene. *(☎922 0211. Open Tu-Su 10am-5pm. 10 pesos.)*

PALACIO DEL GOBIERNO. Built in 1727 as the count Joseph de Rivera Bernández's residence, the building distinguishes itself with a mural that surrounds its interior stairwell. Painted in 1970 by Antonio Rodríguez, the work traces the history of Zacatecas from antiquity to the present. *(Next to the cathedral. Open M-F 9am-8pm. Free.)*

TEMPLO DE SANTO DOMINGO. Built by the Jesuits in 1746, the temple contains nine Baroque altarpieces covered with enough gold to make the whole church gleam. There's also a rare 18th-century German pipe organ. *(At the end of Villapando. Open daily 7am-1pm and 5-8pm. Mass held frequently on weekends. Free.)*

MUSEO ZACATECANO. This museum has a permanent exhibit on the art of the region's native Huichol people as well as a collection of 19th-century *retablos* (icons) that provide something of a crash course in Mexican Catholicism. *(On Dr. Ignacio Hierro, 2 blocks down from Santo Domingo. ☎922 6580. Open M and W-Su 9:30am-5pm. 20 pesos, students and seniors 10 pesos.)*

MINA EL EDÉN. Discovered in 1583, the Mina el Edén was one of Mexico's most productive silver mines until the 1960s, when continual flooding made mineral extraction futile. Now reopened as a tourist attraction, the interior lacks the beauty of natural caves. Its cramped depths make it easy to see why it was sarcastically called "The Mine of Eden," in reference to the miserable conditions suffered by its workers—five to seven workers died each day during the mine's peak. The 45min. tour includes some fairly tame treks across rope bridges and auto-pilot descriptions by Spanish-speaking guides. *(The mine has 2 entrances; enter at the east entrance, close to the Grillo teleférico stop. An old mine train will take you to the tour starting point. Open daily 10am-6pm. 60 pesos, children 30 pesos.)*

🎵 🎭 ENTERTAINMENT AND NIGHTLIFE

Folkloric dance, all kinds of music, and parades constantly enliven the **cathedral square.** Every Thursday, the Zacatecas **state band** stages a free classical concert at 7pm, and clowns entertain children on the steps surrounding the cathedral almost nightly. The yearly cultural highlight is **Zacatecas en la Cultura,** a festival during *Semana Santa,* in which concerts, operas, and plays are held in the elegant **Teatro Calderón,** on Hidalgo near the cathedral, and throughout the city. Zacatecas is also reputed to have Mexico's best **Morismo** (reenactment of the battle between the Moors and the Spanish) held in mid-August. Call the tourist office for specific details. From September 8 to 22, the city celebrates the **Feria Nacional de Zacatecas** with bullfights, agricultural and crafts shows, music, and sporting events.

Nights in Zacatecas can be expensive, but the combination of fun crowds, *mezcal,* and nonstop party music is worth it. There are plenty of cheap, colorful *cantinas* and pool halls, and there's even an occasional rodeo. The nightlife listed is in the *centro,* where well-lit, relatively safe streets eliminate the need for taxis. By far, the best parties are *callejoneadas*: Zacatecans are prohibited from possessing alcohol in public, so they hang buckets of *mezcal* from a donkey's neck and follow it around the city.

> **TIP**
> **MIXED UP.** That stuff you're downing during the *callejoneadas* is the black sheep of the tequila family. Unregulated by the government, the maguey juice served in the street festivals may be unsettling for foreign stomachs and also contains about 25% water—hence the propensity for weak drinkers to turn into super-*hombres*. Zacatecan restaurants serve higher grade *mezcal,* and glasses with high proof may hold a little surprise: a pickled *gusano,* the local agave worm and sign of good quality.

🏛 **El Malacate** (☎922 3002), 600m in from the side entrance of the Mina del Edén. Also called **La Mina,** this recently renovated club is the hottest spot in Zacatecas, and claims to be the world's only disco buried within a mineshaft. An abandoned cart takes clubbers into the inner chamber, where Latin techno reverberates from the rock walls as laser beams pulse, justifying the 100-peso cover. Beer 20 pesos. Mixed drinks from 30 pesos. Open Th-Sa 10pm-3am. MC/V.

Cafe Subterráneo (☎923 0413), up the hill from Cafe Dalí. The Cafe Sub has a jazz-club lay-out, with tables hanging over the boulevard and kitschy lighting. Patrons often borrow the chill management's guitar and perform karaoke. Occasionally the staff joins in. Cappuccino 25 pesos. Beer 20 pesos. Open from 5pm-late. Cash only.

Cafe Dalí, Ignacio Hierro 504 (contacto@cafedalizacatecas.com). This coffee shop/bar fills with students drinking *micheladas* (25 pesos) and playing pool (40 pesos per table). Melting clocks adorn the walls. Bathrooms are marked by portraits of Dalí (men) and his wife, Gaia (women). Beer 15 pesos. Open daily 5pm-midnight. Cash only.

Todos Santos, Aguascalientes 235, near the Hostal Villa Colonial. Authentic enough to hold *quinceañeras* in the basement, this local bar/restaurant gets packed with zapped Zacatecans late at night. 1 free round of tequila may be included for large parties. Beer 15-20 pesos. Complimentary nuts. Cash only.

Gaudí (☎922 1433), on Tacuba and Aguascalientes in the *centro.* A favorite among university students for its relatively large dance floor and nonstop international hip hop and reggaeton. Beer 20 pesos. Th 10 pesos. Open Th-Sa 10pm-3am. Cash only.

Las Quince Letras, Mártires de Chicago 309 (☎922 0178). It may be best to stop and ask for directions. This classic *cantina* witnessed vicious brawls between miners and *vaqueros* for almost a century. Dimly lit and smoky atmosphere. F-Su live *conjuntos.* Beer 15 pesos. Zacatecan *mezcal* 15 pesos. Open daily 5pm-1am. Cash only.

⚡ DAYTRIPS FROM ZACATECAS

▓ LA QUEMADA

Take a Villanueva bus from the small bus station in Zacatecas on López Mateos to La Quemada (45min., every 30min., 20 pesos). Specify that you want to get off at the ruins (Las Ruinas de la Quemada). The road to the ruins is on the left of the main route, right after the restaurant with the Corona sign. As there are no buses, walk about 3km to reach the entrance. Site open daily 10am-5pm. 37 pesos, with museum 8 pesos. You'll have to get off in Malpaso and change buses to get to Jérez. Hostal Villa Colonial offers recorridos between the hostel and the ruins for 90 pesos. (4-person min., van leaves at 10:30am and returns at 3:30 pm).

About 50km south of Zacatecas lie the well-preserved ruins of **La Quemada** (AD 500-800). The ruins have not yet yielded any spectacular artifacts, nor is it attributed to any major Mesoamerican civilization, so the ruins are more or less untouristed. Hikers will love scrambling around this adobe pyramid city, as the trails can sometimes be unnervingly steep. The ball court, dwellings, fortresses, and temples of La Quemada were built into a mountain with a stunning 360° view of the surrounding countryside. A 170km network of dirt and clay roads runs between the citadel and what used to be ranching villages in the fertile lake-area below. Some theorize that La Quemada was the site of the legendary Aztec city Chicomostoc, Tenochtitlán's precursor Tlascan, and capital of the region north of the Río San Antonio. It is only that known the city-dwellers traded with almost all of the cultures of Ancient Mexica at one time or another. The oldest representation of the eagle-serpent-cactus symbol was also found here.

The scaled museum model of the ruins is a helpful guide to the more remote sections. Few parts of the expansive ruins are off-limits, so it is a good idea to take a few hours and a lot of water when exploring. Beware: the tall grass surrounding the hillsides is a favorite hiding spot for rattlesnakes, among other venomous predators.

LA CERVECERÍA CORONA. The world's second largest brewery does not accept walk-in tourists, and reservations for alcoholic excursions must be made through someone who can pull strings. Guillermo and Ernesto, the boys at the **Villa Colonial** (p. 289), are good friends of the management and offer transport to and from the brewery Monday through Saturday. (*Tours 100 pesos per person, 4-person min. Tours depart Zacatecas at 2pm and return around 7pm.*) The trip includes a tour of the factory and all the 🍺beer you can drink. A small souvenir shop is also located outside the *cervecería.* (*The "Cía. Cervecera de Zacatecas, S.A. de C.V.," is on Antonino Fernandez Rodriguez 100, Calera de Victor Rosales. Call ☎478 985 4040, ext. 1194, 2200 or 1123 for directions, and to schedule an official tour.*)

GUADALUPE. The village, named after the town church, was founded in 1707 as a training site for Franciscan missionaries. The **Ex-Convento de Guadalupe,** located on the main plaza, is known not only for having produced over 3000 missionaries, but for its famous statue of the **Virgen de Guadalupe,** above the altar. Next to the cathedral is the **Museo de Guadalupe,** which contains paintings depicting scenes from the life of St. Francis and of nearly every known incident in the life of Jesus Christ. (*From Zacatecas, catch a Transportes Guadalupe bus from the* *bus station or the smaller station on López Mateos 30min., 5 pesos. Tell the bus driver you want to get off in Guadalupe's centro. From the bus station in Guadalupe, walk a short distance to your left along Mateos and turn right on Constitución at the monument in the center of the street. The cathedral is a couple of blocks ahead. Catch a return bus to Zacatecas from the same bus station. Cathedral open daily 10am-4:30pm. 20 pesos.)*

DURANGO

DURANGO   ☎ 618

Far from both the D.F. and the border, Durango (pop. 500,000) is *norteño* to the core, from its unique culture to summertime triple-digit temperatures. Declared a national monument by the government, Durango has diverse architecture ranging from colonial mansions in the *centro* to makeshift saloons leftover from American Western movie sets towards the outskirts. Despite ample, inexpensive food, museums, and a beautiful countryside, few tourists besides film buffs alight here—possibly because of the menacing scorpion mascot.

▐ TRANSPORTATION

The Central de Autobuses is on the eastern outskirts of town. **Ómnibus de Mexico** (☎818 3361) send **buses** to: **Aguascalientes** (7hr., 9 per day, 292 pesos); **Chihuahua** (8hr., 4 per day, 388 pesos); **Ciudad Juárez** (18hr., 7 per day, 689 pesos); **Guadalajara** (10hr., 6 per day, 702 pesos); **Mexico City** (11hr., 8 per day, 652 pesos); **Zacatecas** (5hr., every hr., 202 pesos). **Estrella Blanca** (☎818 3061) goes to: **Aguascalientes** (7hr., 3 per day, 274 pesos); **Parral** (6hr., 4 per day, 257 pesos); **Torreón** (3hr., 7 per day, 182 pesos); **Zacatecas** (5hr., 4 per day, 202 pesos). **Transportes de Durango** serves smaller cities in the state. To reach the *centro*, exit the station and take the Ruta 2 *camioneta* (4 pesos), which runs from the front of the station, down 5 de Febrero to the Plaza de Armas. City buses don't run at night; take a **taxi** (28 pesos).

✸ ⁊ ORIENTATION AND PRACTICAL INFORMATION

Most establishments cluster near the **Plaza de Armas** and the **Catedral.** The main streets are **5 de Febrero,** which runs east-west past the plaza, and **20 de Noviembre,** parallel to and one block north of 5 de Febrero. **Independencia** is the main north-south street. The surrounding countryside is where most of the marijuana in Mexico is grown. If you choose to go exploring on your own, do so during daylight and stay close to major roads, as the hazy off-roads are dangerous.

Tourist Office: Dirección de Turismo y Cinematografía, Florida 1106 (☎811 1107; www.durango.gob.mx), next to the Museo de Cine. Staff provides useful information, brochures and maps. Open M-F 9am-6pm.

Currency Exchange: Scotiabank Inverlat, Constitución 310 Sur (☎812 8270). Exchanges money and has a **24hr. ATM.** Open M-F 9am-5pm; exchange M-F 9am-3pm. More **24hr. ATMs** dot the Catedral area.

Luggage Storage: In the bus station. 5 pesos per hr. Open 24hr.

Laundromat: Lavamatic Plus, on Zarco Sur, between 20 de Noviembre and 5 de Febrero Negrete. 30 pesos per 3kg. Open M-Sa 9am-7:30pm.

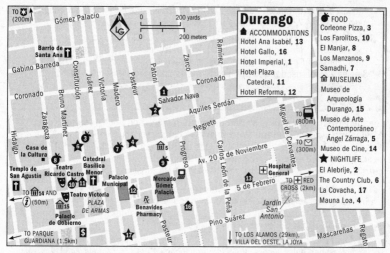

Emergency: ☎066.

Police: (☎817 5406), at Felipe Pescador and Independencia. **Tourist Police** ☎800 903 9200.

Red Cross: (☎817 3444 or 3535, emergency 065), at 5 de Febrero and Reforma. Open 24hr.

Hospital: General (☎811 9115), at 5 de Febrero and Norman Fuentes.

Pharmacy: Farmacia Benavides, at Pasteur and 5 de Febrero. Open daily 9am-9pm.

Internet Access: Internet, at 20 de Noviembre 119, up the narrow staircase. 10 pesos per hr. Open daily 10am-11pm.

Post Office: 20 de Noviembre 500 (☎811 4105), at Roncal. **Fax** and **Mexpost** inside. Open M-F 8am-6pm, Sa 9am-1pm. **Postal Code:** 34000.

ACCOMMODATIONS

Durango's relatively inexpensive hotels are right in the *centro*. Scorpions can be a reality in some rooms without A/C—shake your shoes before putting them on to avoid the painful sting.

Hotel Gallo, 5 de Febrero 117 (☎811 5290). Lobby is punctuated by ceaseless chatter from 2 canaries in the corner. Spacious rooms with private baths and hot water; those with TV tend to be cleaner and larger. Singles and doubles from 120 pesos, with TV 160 pesos. Cash only. ❶

Hotel Imperial, Salvador Nava 164 (☎813 3795), on an offshoot of Patoni before Coronado. Dirt cheap rooms come with a toilet, desk, fan, and tiger-themed blankets. Singles 93 pesos; doubles 165 pesos. Cash only. ❶

Hotel Ana Isabel, 5 de Febrero 219 Ote. (☎813 4500). Sparkling white walls line a sunny atrium decked out with hanging plants. Airy rooms in good condition with clean, tiled bath and dark carpet. Management speaks excellent English and dispenses useful advice. Singles 180 pesos; doubles 250 pesos. Cash only. ❸

Hotel Reforma, Madero 303 Sur (☎813 1622 or 1623). Buried inside the *centro*, Reforma is a well-maintained hotel offering spacious, comfortable rooms with cable TV.

Friendly staff gives info on Durango's sights. Adjacent cafe open 8am-8pm. Singles 225 pesos; doubles 275 pesos; triples 375 pesos. MC/V. ❹

Hotel Plaza Catedral, Constitución 216 Sur (☎813 2660), off 20 de Noviembre, next to the cathedral. Beautiful, historic building with a romantic open interior. Rates are a steal, considering antique quality. Well-maintained rooms have phones and cable TV. Singles 225 pesos; doubles 250 pesos; triples 300 pesos. Cash only. ❹

📇 FOOD

Inexpensive meals are easy to find in Durango. Taco and hot dog stands line 20 de Noviembre at night, and the *tuna* (prickly-pear cactus fruit) rules during the day. Vendors remove the spines and sell bags of the green, kiwi-shaped fruit (about 5 pesos) off 5 de Febrero. Durango also prides itself on its milk-based sweets and *caldillo duranguense*, a thick beef stew eaten at most meals.

Los Farolitos (☎812 7987), on Martínez, 1 block from the *teatro*. Delicious meals, including quesadillas, are great to go. Try a couple of the big tacos with *rajas de queso* or *carne deshebrada con chile verde* (7.50 pesos). Drinks 10 pesos. Open M-F 8:30am-10pm, Sa-Su 9am-8:30pm. Cash only. ❶

Los Manzanos, 20 de Noviembre Pte. 128, at Patoni. Diner-style 70s furniture, with tasty food and quick service. *Caldillo duranguense* 45 pesos. Dinners with soup, salad, dessert, and drink 50-78 pesos. Open daily 8am-11pm. MC/V. ❸

Samadhi, Negrete 403 Pte. Healthy and 100% veggie fare pleases a crowd of foreigners, students, and the rare vegetarian *duranguense*. Gargantuan goblets of fruit, nuts, yogurt, and granola 30 pesos. Lunch 35-55 pesos. Open daily 9am-7pm. Cash only. ❸

Corleone's Pizza, Constitución 114 Nte. (☎813 3138). 45-peso personal pan pizzas are the offer you can't refuse at this dimly lit bistro behind the cathedral. MC/V. ❸

El Manjar, at Negrete and Zaragoza, west of the cathedral. Giant feline masks, a blow-up tarot magician, a ceramic clown, a wooden Don Quixote, and countless plants all cram into this small space. Breakfast with freshly squeezed orange juice 17-25 pesos. Open M-Sa 8am-8pm. Cash only. ❷

👁 SIGHTS

By far the most hyped-up attraction in Durango is its **cinematic history.** Over 200 films, including *The Wild Bunch* (1968), *Blueberry* (2002), and several John Wayne classics, have been filmed in the dusty desert outskirts of Durango. The city recently opened 📷**Museo del Cine,** Florida 1106 at Independencia and 20 de Noviembre, commemorating the city's golden age of Westerns. The old sound-recording equipment, camera, and Victoria 8 projector give insight into how cumbersome earlier productions must have been. Most of the museum seems to be dedicated to John Wayne, although Clint Eastwood makes a few appearances. (Open Tu-Su 9am-6pm. 10 pesos, children 5 pesos.) Some of the original **movie sets** have been left standing and are now popular tourist attractions. **Villa del Oeste,** at km 12 on the Carretera Parral, is the only set that allows visitors. It has been converted into a Wild Wild West theme park of sorts, with simulated gunfights and real can-can dancers. Corny fill-in costume photographs are available upon request. (Tourist buses from Plaza de Armas Th-Sa 1, 3pm; Su 1, 2:30, 4:30pm. ☎827 3001. Open Th-Su 10am-6pm. 25 pesos.)

The Spanish colonial architecture and silver barons' mansions occupy the *centro* along with pink sandstone buildings and grassy, tree-lined parks. The most resplendent of these is the **Catedral Basílica Menor,** on the northern edge of the **Plaza de Armas.** Built between 1691 and 1770, the glowing pink cathedral has frescoes, gilding, and massive pillars. Its bishop once presided over the largest diocese in the world—most of modern Mexico and a large swath of the American southwest. Be sure to check out the haunted confessional at the back of the cathedral, in the east nave to the right of the altar. In 1738, a dying Spanish *don* tried to gain salvation; according to legend, a beam of light struck him down. Locals have stayed away from the accursed confessional ever since. Durango's **Palacio de Gobierno** was once the home of Spanish mining tycoon Juan José Zambrano. After Mexico gained its independence, the government seized the mansion for state use. The inside walls and stairwell are decorated with Benito Juárez's golden death-mask, and murals depicting the state's history. (On 5 de Febrero between Martínez and Zaragoza. Open daily 8am-8pm.) Just west of the cathedral stands the pink **Teatro Ricardo Castro,** on 20 de Noviembre, which hosts theatrical productions and screenings, and is considered to be one of the best theaters in northern Mexico. Inquire at the tourist office or theater box office for shows, prices, and schedules.

The **Museo de Arte Contemporaneo Ángel Zárraga** displays Mexican paintings and sculptures from the past 10 years. Highlights include startling abstract paintings from Dulce María Nuñez Rodríguez and sculptures by Juan Soriano. (Negrete 301. Open Tu-Su 10am-6pm. Free.) The **Museo de Arqueología Durango** dramatizes Durango's desert cultures with cinematic tricks and fairly impressive archaeological exhibits. (At Zaragoza 315 Sur. ☎813 1047. Open Tu-F 10am-6:30pm, Sa-Su 11am-6pm. 10 pesos, children 5 pesos.)

♫ 🅟 ENTERTAINMENT AND NIGHTLIFE

Though most farmers are kept busy raising cattle, a select few have chosen scorpion ranches instead. **Mercado Gómez Palacio,** on 20 Noviembre, three blocks east of the cathedral, is full of the poisonous creatures. Thankfully, most are entombed in transparent plastic bubbles adorning belt buckles, keychains, and fabulously kitschy Durango souvenir clocks. Vendors keep aquariums full of the state arachnid on-site, lending the market a certain edge. Be careful—you never know what you'll find in your new cowboy boots. (Open daily around 10am-9pm.)

Starting the second week of July, Durango commemorates the city's founding with the 10-day **Feria Nacional.** Parades, fireworks, auctions, and carnival rides liven things up. Most of the festivities take place at the **Parque Guardiana,** quite a distance from the *centro*—you may have to take a taxi (30 pesos). Buses to the Feria leave from 5 de Febrero and Independencia (4 pesos). Admission to the festival is 15 pesos.

Unfortunately, nightlife in Durango is restricted to weekends, leaving the *centro* eerily empty on weeknights. The best clubs are located on the outskirts of town; it's best to ask locals which ones are hottest in season. A variety of courtyard bars featuring live music have sprouted off Negrete behind the cathedral. The patio at **Mauna Loa,** on the corner of Negrete and Madero, is perfect for relaxing. Live *mariachi* music and local *rocanrol* sounds better with 15-peso beer and 22-peso tequila. (Open F-Su 4pm-midnight.) Though slightly more touristy, **Country Club,** 112 Constitución, is a quiet place to watch a football game with your brew of choice. (☎811 0066. Open 8am-2am. Cash only). Come sundown, get your groove on at **La Covacha,** Pino Suárez Pte. 500, at Madero, where locals dance to international and Latin hits. (☎812 3969. Cover 30 pesos. Open Th-Su 9pm-4am.) Slightly more upscale is **El Alebrije,** Serdán 309 Pte. Live romantic music (Th-Sa 9pm-midnight) echoes through the brightly painted courtyard. Learn how the *pasito duranguense*, a traditional dance step. (Beer 15 pesos. Tequila 30 pesos.)

NORTHEAST MEXICO

At first glance, Northeast Mexico seems like nothing but desert country: hot, dry, and dotted with cacti. *Norteño* music pumps from every speaker, and residents devour *cabrito* (roasted goat) with their famous beers—Bohemia, Corona, Carta Blanca, and Sol. But beneath the dusty surface of cowboy culture, the Northeast holds gems undiscovered by most tourists. Silver veins once made the country rich, leaving fabulous colonial architecture, and forest and coastal lagoons hold diverse natural riches. The towns and cities of the Northeast, home to parched white missions and wide streets, exude a sense of calm fostered by small-town hospitality and an authentic rural lifestyle.

Vaquero culture still lives on in **Tamaulipas, Nuevo León,** and **Coahuila.** These border states have plenty of American-owned factories and big cities, especially along the Texas border, but the drunken daytrippers detract only slightly from the rich history of music, food, and agriculture of the borderlands. The capital of *el norte* is Monterrey, Mexico's third largest city. The view from Monterrey's central plaza, packed with skyscrapers, colonial churches, and mountains, is a synthesis of modernity and tradition that embodies today's *noreste*. Natural beauty hides just outside city limits, with spectacular, cliff-faced peaks drawing climbers to the central region; farther east, cloud forests and mangroves hold some of Mexico's greatest biodiversity.

The coast of Tamaulipas offers a taste of the Gulf, with beaches ranging from busy Tampico, where you can munch on fresh seafood, to tiny La Pesca, where the waves and the fishes will be your only company. Several native endangered species make their home in La Reserva Biosfera El Cielo, a majestic cloud forest.

Many of the riches in *el norte* lie in the state of **San Luis Potosí,** with strong indigenous traditions and natural beauty of desert-to-jungle extremes. The town of Real de Catorce, a favorite stop for peyote-hungry backpackers, is largely untouched by modernity. *Burros* track through the town, and visitors enjoy mountaintop panoramas. Xilitla offers caves, waterfalls, rivers, wild parrots, semi-tropical rainforests, and surrealist ruins. The capital city of San Luis Potosí is a jewel—a playground of regional culture, Baroque architecture, and colonial appeal.

HIGHLIGHTS OF NORTHEAST MEXICO

DELIGHT in the glorious architecture and raging nightlife of **Monterrey** (p. 312).

BATHE in the waterfalls of a kooky Englishman's tropical homage to surrealism at **Las Pozas** (p. 341); spend the day in nearby of **Xilitla**, the *noreste*'s very own Eden.

HONEYMOON in tiny **Real de Catorce** (p. 337), an ex-mining town high in the Sierra Madres that now specializes in peyote and gorgeous mountain views.

DAYDREAM in lovely **San Luis Potosí** (p. 330), dubbed "the city of plazas," and enjoy *música en vivo* while soaking up the brilliant northeast sun.

HIKE through of the bird- and butterfly-filled **Reserva de la Biosfera El Cielo** (p. 308).

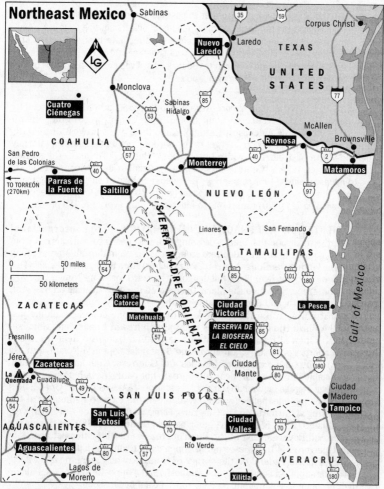

Northeast Mexico

0   50 miles
0   50 kilometers

TAMAULIPAS

NUEVO LAREDO   ☎ 867

Nuevo Laredo (pop. 500,000) pulses with commerce. From small souvenir shops to enormous trucks bulging with NAFTA-spurred trade, pesos and dollars pour in and out of Nuevo Laredo at a dizzying pace. The city manages to maintain a Mexican soul, separating itself from the "other Laredo" across the border in Texas. Afternoon tourists pass through looking for cheap crafts, and after a hard day of buying *sombreros*, pass the time with locals in the town's green plazas before gulping *cerveza* at border bars. Due to safety concerns, Nuevo Laredo is frequently subject to tourist travel advisories; monitor the situation prior to arrival.

GOOD COP, BAD COP. If at all possible, avoid contact with police officers in Nuevo Laredo. There are many reports of officers abusing their power to rob tourists. Additionally, police officers themselves have been the victims of drug-related violence, and passersby have gotten caught in the crossfire. That said, many officers are only trying to do their jobs; if you are approached by one, be as polite and cooperative as possible.

⌨ TRANSPORTATION. The **airport**, Aeropuerto Quetzalcóatl (NLD), serviced by **Mexicana** (☎718 1264 or 1492; www.mexicana.com), is southwest of the city, off Mex. 2. The **Central de Autobuses**, Refugio Romo 3800, is southwest of the city, quite a far trek from the *centro*. To get to the border from the **bus station**, take any blue-and-white or green-and-white bus marked "Puente." To get to the station from the border, take a "Central" bus (5 pesos). **Ómnibus de México** (☎714 0617) goes to **Aguascalientes** (10hr., 8 per day, 520 pesos), **Saltillo** (4½hr., 230 pesos), and **Zacatecas** (9hr., 8 per day, 490 pesos). **Sendor** (☎714 2100) provides similar service. **Estrella Blanca** (☎714 0670) runs a bus to **Monterrey** (3hr., every hr., 185 pesos).

⌨ 🛈 ORIENTATION AND PRACTICAL INFORMATION. From **International Bridge #1**, the most popular tourist crossing point, (5 pesos to walk across from the US side, 6 pesos to return), **Guerrero** emerges as the main thoroughfare running south. Three landmarks along Guerrero, **Plaza Juárez, Plaza Hidalgo,** and **Palacio Federal,** define the downtown. **Plaza Hidalgo** and Guerrero make up Nuevo Laredo's center. Four streets surround the plaza: **Guerrero** on the east, **Ocampo** on the west, **Dr. Mier** on the north, and **González** on the south.

The **tourist office,** in the Palacio Federal (a giant stone colonial building just south of the Plaza Hidalgo), provides many brochures in English and Spanish. (☎712 7397. Open M-F 8am-3pm.) Major banks line Guerrero near the Plaza Hidalgo. **Banorte** (open M-F 9am-4pm) and **Santander** (open M-F 9am-4pm, Sa 10am-2pm), both on the corner of Canales and Guerrero, each have **24hr. ATMs. Casas de cambio** line Guerrero near the border, but banks have better exchange rates. **Luggage storage** is available at the bus station. (5 pesos per hr. Open 24hr.) Other services include: **police** (☎060), available at the Palacio Federal or at the border crossing at the north end of Guerrero; **Farmacia Calderón,** on Guerrero, west of Plaza Hidalgo (☎712 5563; open 24hr.); **medical services** at **ISSSTE,** at the corner of Victoria and Reynosa, east of the Plaza Juárez (☎712 3491); **Internet** access at **Net Time,** Guerrero 2448. (15 pesos per hr.; open daily 10am-9pm); **post office,** in the back of the Palacio Federal on the corner of González and Camargo (☎712 2090; open M-F 9am-3pm, Sa 9am-1pm); and **Mexpost,** on the opposite side of the Palacio (☎713 4717; open M-F 9am-4pm, Sa 9am-1pm). **Postal Code:** 88000.

🛏 🍴 ACCOMMODATIONS AND FOOD. Hotels of all prices are found within a few blocks of the main plazas. There are good bargains if you're willing to look around. **Hotel Alameda ❸,** González 2715, offers clean, comfortable rooms with A/C, phone, and TV. (☎712 5050. 24hr. bell. Singles 230 pesos; doubles 275 pesos. Cash only.) **Hotel La Finca ❷,** Reynosa 811, just off González in the southeast corner of the Plaza Hidalgo, sits on a quiet street just a few steps from the *centro*. Spacious rooms rise above a red-tile patio and have A/C, and cable TV. (☎712 8883. Budget singles 130 pesos, singles 290 pesos; doubles 370 pesos. Cash only.)

Pricey tourist border joints aside, most eateries are similar in quality and price, with plenty of tacos, enchiladas, and *carne asada* (grilled meat). Local favorite **Lonchería El Popo ❶,** on Dr. Mier across from the Palacio Federal, specializes in *lonchos,* simple sandwiches with either *ternera* (brisket) or hamburger. Locals fill the folding-chair patio at all hours; you may want to get your meal to go. (*Lonchos* 12-14 pesos. Open daily 11am-10pm.) On the corner of Perú and Reynosa, **El Quinto Sol ❷** sells all-natural cookies and soy hamburgers (35 pesos). For dessert, *nieve* (shaved ice; 15-32 pesos) with granola cereal or sweet sauce is a must. (☎ 715 5275. Open daily 7am-10:45pm.) **Los Super Frutería Primes,** five blocks south of the Plaza Hidalgo on Ocampo and Arteaga, is the closest supermarket to the center of town. (Open M-Sa 7am-9pm, Su 7am-7pm.)

REYNOSA ☎ 899

Reynosa (pop. 1 million) specializes in two symbiotic businesses: wrecking tourists with drinking and dancing each night, then piecing them back together each day with dirt-cheap medical care. The city teems with open-air *taquerías*, carts selling *licuados*, and leather shops. As the heat eases, locals chat in the Plaza Principal, where clowns and musicians compete for their attention. At night, underage Texans mix with Mexicans in the clubs of the Zona Rosa.

⌐ TRANSPORTATION. Reynosa lies across the border from McAllen, Texas, and can be reached by taking 23rd St. 12km south to the town of Hidalgo, Texas, and crossing the **International Bridge.** Routes 2 and 40, from Matamoros and Monterrey, respectively, lead straight into town. The **Central de Autobuses** is on Colón to the southeast of the *centro.* The easiest way to get to the *centro* is by walking: take a left out of the station, turn left on Colón, walk seven short blocks, and take a right onto Hidalgo; the plaza is six blocks down. A **taxi** will cost about 30 pesos, but probably isn't worth the hassle. **ADO** (☎ 922 8713) runs **buses** to **Tampico** (7hr., 6 per day 4:30-11pm, 301 pesos), **Veracruz** (16hr.; 4:30, 8:30pm; 687 pesos), and **Villahermosa** (24hr.; 4:30, 7, and 9pm; 912 pesos). **Futura** (☎ 922 1452) offers *ejecutivo* service to **Guadalajara** (15hr.; 6, 8pm; 908 pesos) and **Mexico City** (15hr.; 5:20, 7:30pm; 928 pesos). **Ómnibus de México** (☎ 922 3307) runs to **Chihuahua** (15hr.; 9am, 10:30pm; 750 pesos) and **Saltillo** (5hr.; 6:30am, every hr. 9am-1pm, 221 pesos). **Grupo Sendor** (☎ 922 0206) goes to: **Matamoros** (2hr., every 45min., 64 pesos); **Monterrey** (3hr., every hr., 168 pesos); **Nuevo Laredo** (4hr., every 2hr. 5:15am-9:40pm, 176 pesos); **San Luis Potosí** (11½hr., 8 per day 7am-10:45pm, 381 pesos).

▰▱ ORIENTATION AND PRACTICAL INFORMATION. Reynosa is 97km from Matamoros and Brownsville, Texas, and 220km from Monterrey. Central Reynosa is square, with the International Bridge border crossing at the northeast corner. The central **Plaza Principal** is bound by Zaragoza on the north, Hidalgo on the west, Morelos on the south, and Juárez on the east. A few blocks east of the Plaza lies the **Zona Rosa,** dotted by bars and the city's budget accommodations. A pedestrian market runs south down Hidalgo, from Plaza Principal to Colón.

Tourist information can be found in the Presidencia Municipal, on Morelos facing the Plaza Principal. A friendly staff has free maps with listings of restaurants, bars, and hotels. (☎ 922 0005. Open M-F 9am-5pm.)**Banorte,** on Morelos at Hidalgo (☎ 938 2212; open M-F 9am-4pm) and **Bancomer,** opposite Banorte on Zaragoza (☎ 922 7004; open M-F 8:30am-4pm, Sa 10am-3pm), offer competitive rates, exchange traveler's checks, and have **24hr. ATMs.** Other services include: **emergency** (☎ 066); **police,** at the border crossing at Aldama and Virreyes in the northeast corner of town (☎ 922 0008); **Red Cross** (☎ 922 1314); **Farmacia Benavides** at the corner of Hidalgo and Guerrero, also has groceries and film-processing (open daily 7am-10pm); **Internet** access at **Internet Paseo Reynosa,** inside the Paseo Reynosa mall on the corner of Hidalgo and Mendez, 2nd fl. (☎ 946 2289; 10 pesos per hr.; open daily 9am-9pm); **Lavandería Genova,** next to Hotel

Genova on Matamoros and Canales (wash and dry 36 pesos; open M-Sa 8am-8pm, Su 8am-2pm); and the **post office,** on the corner of Díaz and Colón (☎922 0110; open M-F 9am-3pm). **Postal Code:** 88500.

▐▐ ACCOMMODATIONS AND FOOD. Reynosa's hotels are pricey, with the cheapest located in the Zona Rosa near the border. **Hotel Capri ❹,** at the corner of Allende and Canales, has rooms with A/C and cable TV, and a reasonably priced 24hr. restaurant attached. (☎922 6584. 24hr. bell. Singles 280 pesos; doubles 330 pesos; triples 410 pesos. AmEx/MC/V.) For a cheaper stay, try the clean, blue rooms at **Hotel Genova ❸,** on Matamoros near Canales. (☎922 1342. 24hr. bell. Singles and doubles 160 pesos, with A/C 220 pesos. Cash only.)

Reynosa overflows with delicious, super-cheap Mexican fare, served at outdoor stands and open-air cafeterias near the plaza and at the south end of the Hidalgo market. A shining example is **Tacos El Pingüino ❷,** on Morelos facing the Plaza Principal. *Tacos de barbacoa* (barbecued beef; 28 pesos) or 15-peso *tortas* are made right in front of you. Pingüino also has a full-service restaurant serving Mexican entrees around the corner on Juárez. (Open daily 10am-11pm. Cash only.) For a splurge, try the specialty—roasted *cabrito* (goat)—at **Restaurante El Jardín ❺,** Juárez 835, half a block from the plaza. Goats roast behind a glass window as attentive, well-dressed waiters deliver goat tacos to cafeteria-like tables in front of brick walls. (☎922 1824. Tacos 45-130 pesos. Open M-Sa 7am-11pm, Su 8am-10pm.) Pick up fresh groceries at **Frutería Matehuala,** at Colón and Hidalgo. (☎922 1188. Open daily 7am-7pm. Cash only.)

◙◪ SIGHTS AND ENTERTAINMENT. In the evening, locals of all ages crowd the main plaza to enjoy street performers and cool off after the day's heat. The pedestrian street **Hidalgo,** lined with stores, is a good spot for people-watching; duck into the **Antiguo Mercado Hidalgo** for all your souvenir needs. For an abridged history lesson, check out the beautiful storefront **mural** on the corner of Zaragoza and Ocampo. The mural depicts scenes of Mexican life, pre-Hispanic glory, conquest, revolution and, finally, tourists buying crafts in a market place. The **Museo Histórico de Reynosa,** at Ortega and Allende, houses a collection of masks, dolls, antique guns, old coins, and other historical artifacts. (☎922 1512. Open Tu-F 9am-2pm and 4-8pm, Sa 10am-2pm and 4-8pm, Su 10am-2pm. Free.)

To catch the latest Hollywood flicks, go to **Multicinemas,** right on the main plaza. (44 pesos; 27 pesos before 3pm; 34 pesos before 6pm.) Check out Reynosa's community theater for free at **La Casa de la Cultura,** next door to the Cámara de Comercio on Chapa and Allende, a block from the main plaza. The Casa regularly hosts plays, exhibits, concerts, and dances; drop in to see the schedule of upcoming events. (☎922 9989. Open M-F 9am-1pm and 3-7pm. Most performances at 7pm.)

OFF THE STREETS AND OUT OF TROUBLE. Mexico's drinking age (18) may be lower than that of the US, but they still have laws concerning alcohol. In Reynosa, you cannot consume alcohol in the streets; keep this in mind before you leave a bar with a drink in hand.

Underage visitors to Reynosa beware: clubs have recently started to enforce the Mexican drinking age of 18. Be sure to bring your ID. Clustered along Ocampo near the border, most nightspots in Reynosa have high and low seasons. During US spring break (Mar.-Apr.), the town turns into a miniature Cancún—all the booze, but (alas!) none of the beaches. During the low season, these bars are deserted a good chunk of the week, coming alive only on weekends, with *mariachis* and enthusiastic Texans. Young people head to the **Alaskan Bar and Disco,** on

Ocampo between Allende and Zaragoza, a *discoteca* with two levels and an enormous dance floor. (Beer US$1. Mixed drinks US$1.50. Open high-season daily, low season F-Sa 9pm-4am. Cash only.) The new **Bar 1040**, at Ocampo and Allende close to the border, offers clubbers a cavernous dance floor; the enormous orange building is hard to miss. (Beer US$1. Cover some nights US$10. Open high season daily 8pm-2am, low season W-Sa 8pm-2am.)

MATAMOROS   ☎ 868

Like Brownsville, Texas, its counterpart across the river, Matamoros (pop. 365,000) sprawls out into the dusty heat of the desert, exuding a transience typical of many border towns. Nonetheless, the center of Matamoros is a vibrant capsule of Mexican culture. Music blasts from every storefront as crowds gather daily to stroll and shop. A business boom in the 1970s saw much of Matamoros's historic *centro* torn down, but in recent years new cafes, a theater, and museums have revitalized the areas surrounding the plaza and old markets.

CROSSING THE BORDER. To reach Matamoros from Brownsville, Texas, walk or drive across the **International Bridge.** To cross from the US to Mexico, pedestrians pay US$0.50 (5 pesos) and cars pay US$2.50 (28 pesos). To cross from Mexico to the US, pedestrians pay 3 pesos (US$0.30) and cars pay US$2.50 (28 pesos). Much of the **Río Grande** has been diverted for irrigation, so it's only a 2min. walk over the bridge. If you're traveling farther south than the 22km border zone, pick up your tourist card (US$20) and vehicle permit (US$28). If you are leaving Matamoros by bus, you can buy your tourist card at the Central de Autobuses along with your bus ticket. See p. 32 for more info on border crossings.

▐ TRANSPORTATION. From the border crossing, the city extends out in a V-shape following the bend in the Río Grande. To reach the *centro* from the border area, take one of the yellow **minibuses** labeled "Centro" (5 pesos). If you don't mind being instantly branded a tourist, the tourist office (see below) also runs a free trolley into town. To return to the border, catch a minibus marked "Puente." These converted school buses (called *peseros*) make continuous stops and congregate on Calle 7 between Matamoros and Abasolo. Wave your hand at them and they'll stop almost anywhere—just yell "¡Baja!" (Local transit department ☎817 8881).

Bus traffic to out-of-town destinations flows through the **Central de Autobuses,** on Canales at Guatemala, off Calle 1. (Open 24hr.) To get there, catch a bus labeled "Central" on Calle 8. **ADO** (☎812 0181) goes to **Tampico** (7hr., 7 per day, 280 pesos), **Tuxpan** (11hr., 5 per day, 440 pesos), and **Veracruz** (16hr., 4 per day, 636 pesos), with numerous stops in between. **Noreste/Sendor** (☎813 2768) services **Monterrey** (6hr., 18 per day, 238 pesos), **Reynosa** (2hr., 18 per day, 70 pesos), and **San Luis Potosí** (10 hr., 11 per day, 462 pesos). **Transportes del Norte** (☎812 0262) runs to **Mexico City** (14hr.; *ejecutivo* at 7pm, 876 pesos; 1st-class 6 per day, 682 pesos) and **Saltillo** (7hr., 6 per day, 262 pesos). **Ómnibus de México** (☎813 7693) offers similar services. Travelers to the northeast may find it more convenient to depart from the **Noreste station** downtown (☎813 4050), at the corner of Calle 12 and Abasolo, where you can catch buses coming from Central de Autobuses en route to their destinations.

▐ PRACTICAL INFORMATION. The center of town is dominated by **Abasolo,** which hosts a pedestrian shopping area, and **Plazas Hidalgo** and **Allende.** At the border, the **tourist office,** Av. Alvaro Obregón No. 23 (☎868 812 0212, www.matamoros.com), on the right just past the immigration office, offers pamphlets and advice in English and Spanish. (M-F 9am-6pm, Sa 9am-3pm.) Better maps of Matamoros are available at the **Brownsville Chamber of Commerce** on the Texan side of the border. **Casas de cambio** dot the *centro* along Calles 5 and 6. The best exchange rates are available in the immigration office at the Mexican border checkpoint, in the bus station, or at banks. Most major banks will exchange traveler's checks (M-F only) and have **24hr. ATMs. Police** (☎817 0135) are stationed around the International Bridge and the border. **Internet** access is widely available for about 10 pesos per hr.; try **C@fe Ciber**, at Calle 5 and González (☎812 4691. Open daily 9am-10pm). Other services include: **emergency** ☎066; **Red Cross** (☎812 0044); **Cruz Verde** (☎817 0287); **Farmacia Regis**, on Calle 10 between Matamoros and Abasolo (☎830 8579; open M-Su 8:30am-8:30pm); **Hospital Guadalupe**, 72 Calle 6, between Victoria and Rayon. (☎812 1655); and the **post office**, at Calle 11 and Río Bravo, with **Mexpost** inside (open M-F 9am-3pm, Sa 9am-1pm). **Postal Code:** 87330.

> **WARNING:** It is not recommended to walk around the market area—where most of Matamoros's budget accommodations are located—after the shops close (around 10pm).

⚷◻ ACCOMMODATIONS AND FOOD. Although prices in Matamoros are reasonable, expect little more than the basics. The rose-filled tile courtyard at ▨**Casa de Huéspedes Las Margaritas ❷**, on Calle 4 between Abasolo and Matamoros, makes up for the occasional leak or spider. Away from the *centro's* bustle, it's the quietest place in town. All rooms come with private bath, fan, and TV. (☎813 4024. 24hr. bell. Singles 150 pesos; doubles 150-200 pesos. Cash only.) Closer to Matamoros's markets and shops, **Hotel Majestic ❷** and **Hotel Mexico ❷**, both on Abasolo between Calles 8 and 9, provide spartan, sterile rooms with private bath and fan. (Hotel Majestic: ☎813 3680. 24hr. bell. Singles 160 pesos; doubles 180-220 pesos; each additional person 40 pesos. Cash only. Hotel Mexico: ☎812 0856. 24hr. bell. Singles and doubles 140 pesos, with TV 200 pesos; each additional person 50 pesos. Cash only.) **Casa de Huéspedes "Rosey" ❷**, Plaza Allende, on Calle 10 between Morelos and Guerrero, offers smaller rooms and similar amenities, with a pronounced smell of cigarettes. (☎813 1826. Singles and doubles 120 pesos, with TV 150 pesos. Cash only.)

Ice cream stores, fruit stands, and *taquerías* crowd Abasolo and the streets near Plaza Hidalgo, hawking snacks to hungry shoppers. For the cheapest tacos, walk over to Plaza Allende, and pick the stand with the longest line: it means the food is good and the high turnover ensures freshness. For a quick bite near Plaza Hidalgo, sit counter-side at **Doña Tota Gorditas ❶** and scarf down mini-tortillas stuffed with *nopales* (cactus) or *carne con mole*. (☎813 3959. Gorditas 8-12 pesos. Open daily 9am-3:30pm. Cash only.) Nearby, **Mayo's Cafe ❸**, at Morelos and Calle 7, serves hearty portions of classic dishes like *huevos rancheros* (40 pesos), *carne asada* (50 pesos) and a variety of *antojitos* (35-50 pesos.) Breakfast, such as *pan dulce* (12 pesos) and hotcakes (30 pesos) is served all day. (☎816 5210. Open M-Sa 7am-10pm, Su 7am-3pm. Cash only.) **Las Dos Repúblicas ❹**, on Calle 9 between Abasolo and Matamoros, lures tourists with faux-*hacienda* decor and famous 18-ounce margaritas. Texan families and underage teenagers chow down on nachos (US$3.75) and browse the adjoining gift shop. (☎812 2766. Beer US$1.50. Margaritas US$2. Entrees US$3-6. Open 10am-7pm, MC/V.) Several supermarkets line Calles 11 and 12. The largest is **Waldo's Mart**, on the corner of Calle 11 and Morales (open daily 7am-10pm). **La Estrella** is an open market on Abasolo between Calles 11 and 12. (Open M-Sa 8am-8pm, Su 8am-5pm.)

◉♫ SIGHTS AND ENTERTAINMENT. Abasolo, a pedestrian street between Calles 6 and 13, is lined with shops and vendors from Calles 6 to 9, where it becomes a cacophonous market. Known for its shoes, Abasolo is peppered with *zapaterías* (shoe stores); if you've always wanted cowboy

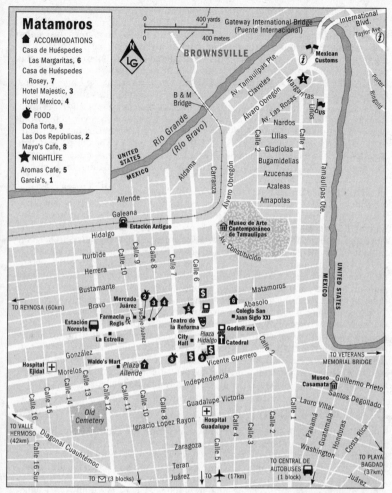

Matamoros

🏠 ACCOMMODATIONS
Casa de Huéspedes
  Las Margaritas, **6**
Casa de Huéspedes
  Rosey, **7**
Hotel Majestic, **3**
Hotel Mexico, **4**

🍴 FOOD
Doña Torta, **9**
Las Dos Repúblicas, **2**
Mayo's Cafe, **8**

⭐ NIGHTLIFE
Aromas Cafe, **5**
García's, **1**

boots, now's the time. Stock up on *sombreros* and souvenir shotglasses on **Pasaje Juárez**, on Calle 9 between Matamoros and González. Peek into *dulcerías* (candy stores) and watch artisans craft huge *piñatas* on Calle 10 and Bravo, or inhale the scent of spices among the *hierberías* (herb stores) on Calle 11 between Abasolo and Morelos.

Beat the heat in Matamoros's stellar ⭐**Museo de Arte Contemporaneo de Tamaulipas,** on Constitución at Calle 5. The building is a fantastic example of 1960s experimental architecture. Its blinding white towers loom over a shady, sculpture-laden garden. Nonetheless, the building never upstages the exhibits—knowledgeable guides lead tours of polygonally-shaped galleries displaying a variety of Mexican media. Two galleries house monthly visiting exhibits.(☎ 813 1499. www.mact.tamaulipas.gob.mx. Open Tu-Sa 10am-2pm and 3-6pm. 15 pesos, students 10 pesos, children 12 and under free, W free.)

Discover the history of Matamoros in **Museo Casamata** at the corner of Guatemala and Santos Degollado. The museum houses artifacts, such as cannons, collected during Matamoros's rise from a minor Spanish port to 1860s boomtown. Inside the courtyard sits the restored Fort Casamata, constructed in 1830. One of 13 forts forming a ring around the city, the old fort features interactive time lines chronicling the defense of Matamoros since the 1700s. (☎813 5929; mcasamata@hotmail.com. Tu-F 8:30am-4:30pm, Sa-Su 9am-2pm. Free.) Matamoros's **cathedral**, on Calle 5 across from Plaza Hidalgo, is home to a full-size replica of Christ in a glass coffin.

For an evening of high culture, visit the **Teatro de la Reforma** on Calle 6 between González and Abasolo. The colonial brick building is home to everything from classical drama to ballet folklórico—look for event posters throughout town. (☎812 5120. Tickets range from free to 150 pesos or more.) The **Colegio San Juan Siglo XXI,** a conservatory at the corner of González and Calle 4, holds an annual classical music festival in late May and periodic concerts throughout the year.

🎵 **NIGHTLIFE.** Bars and nightclubs line Av. Alvaro Obregón from the border crossing onwards, baiting daytrippers with drink specials and entertainment. Anywhere drunk tourists go, thieves will follow. Use due caution. By far the most popular with border-hopping tourists is **García's** (☎812 3929), on the left side of Obregón, straight ahead after you cross the International Bridge. Garcia's is a three-in-one stop: listen to live music and grab a beer at the Fiesta Bar (open M-Th and Su 10am-midnight, F-Sa 11am-3am. MC/V.), feast on filet mignon in the restaurant (lunch and dinner specials US$10; open daily 11am-11pm), or search for bargains in the gift shop and pharmacy. The gift shop sells liquor, but beware: you must be over 21 to bring it across the border. While US-bound travelers may want to take advantage of this last-stop souvenir mecca, cheaper, more authentic goods can be found in town on Abasolo (p. 304) In town, try **Las Dos Repúblicas** (p. 304), or for a swankier outing, sip from a variety of specialty drinks (30-50 pesos) at **Aromas Cafe,** Calle 6 and Abasolo. Listen to live music in the bar upstairs or enjoy coffee on the patio. (☎812 6232; www.aromascafe.com.mx. Soups, *cremas*, and salads 30-45 pesos. Pasta and meat entrees 60-150 pesos. Full breakfast menu available. Wi-Fi access 6 pesos per hr. Open daily 7am-midnight. MC/V.)

CIUDAD VICTORIA   ☎834

Ciudad Victoria (pop. 300,000) may be the sleepiest state capital in Mexico. Nestled at the foot of the Sierra Madre, the laid-back town is worth a trip in itself for the surrounding natural beauty. Ecotourism adventures abound, including diving, cavern exploring, mountain biking, kayaking, and birdwatching. Just a few kilometers away, sights include Las Altas Cumbres, a protected forest home to jaguars, endangered bird species, and archeological sites, and Jaumave, a sanctuary for the Guacamaya Verde (Military Macaw), an endangered parrot. Cañón del Novillo has great camping, hiking and spelunking; during the canyon's rainy season, Boca de San Juan Capitán morphs into a beautiful stream with several waterfalls. Approximately 100km from the city lies Reserva de la Biosfera el Cielo (p. 308), Ciudad Victoria's true natural gem.

🚌 **TRANSPORTATION.** From the Central de Autobuses, a "Boulevard" minibus runs to the *centro* (4 pesos). Make sure the driver knows you want to exit near Plaza Hidalgo. From there, walk two blocks up Calle 8 or 9 to the plaza, home to most of Ciudad Victoria's attractions. A taxi costs 30 pesos. From the station, **Transpaís** (☎218 4619) runs buses to: **Ciudad Valles** (4hr., every hr., 146 pesos); **Matamoros** (4½hr., every hr., 197 pesos); **Reynosa** (4½hr., every hr., 192 pesos); **Tampico** (3½hr., every hr., 150 pesos); **San Luis Potosí** (5-6hr., every hr.,

204 pesos). **Senda** (☎890 9090; www.gruposenda.com.mx) has service to **Mexico City** (11hr., every hr., 556 pesos), **Monterrey** (4hr., every hr., 194 pesos), and **San Luis Potosí** (5-6hr., every hr., 205 pesos).

🛈 PRACTICAL INFORMATION. Main streets in Ciudad Victoria running north-south have both a name and a number (e.g., Calle 8 is also Calle Juan B. Tijerina). To get to the **tourist office**, Calle 9 136 at Lomas del Santuario, walk south along Calle 9, cross Río San Marcos, and continue until you see a yellow building labeled "El Peñón." The bilingual staff will be happy to tell you everything you need to know about Victoria and the state of Tamaulipas. (☎315 6249, toll-free 800 710 6539; www.ciudadvictoria.gob.com.mx. Open M-F 9am-5pm, Sa-Su 9am-5pm.) **Exchange currency** or traveler's checks at **Slotiabank Inverlat**, on the corner of Calle 9 and Hidalgo in the plaza, which also has a **24hr. ATM.** (Open M-F 9am-5pm, Sa 10am-3pm.) Other services include: **Lavandería Vic Deme**, on Calle 8 between Matamoros and Guerrero (wash 13-20 pesos, dry 50 centavos per min. Open M-Sa 8am-8:30pm); **emergency** (☎066); **police** (☎312 0195); **Red Cross**, on Col. López Mateos (☎065 or 316 2077); **Hospital General**, Libramiento Fidel Velázquez Ote. 1845 (☎316 2197); **Pharmacy Benavides**, on the corner of Hidalgo and Calle 9 (Open daily 7am-midnight); **Internet** access at **Copy-Ciber Express**, just off Plaza Hidalgo on Calle 8 between Morelos and Matamoros (7 pesos per hr.; open M-F 9am-8:30pm) or **Ultranet**, Calle 16 and Morelos (☎134 0874; 5 pesos per hr.; open daily 10am-10pm); and the **post office**, on Calle 8 between Morelos and Matamoros, in the Palacio Federal (open M-F 8am-3pm). **Postal Code:** 87000.

🛏🍴 ACCOMMODATIONS AND FOOD. While expensive luxury hotels surround Plaza Hidalgo, quality budget lodging can be found hiding in nearby streets. **Hostal de Escandón ❷**, Calle 8 143 just off the plaza, provides cool, comfortable rooms and classic boarding-house ambience. Interior rooms face a roofed courtyard. (☎312 9004. 24hr. bell. Singles 171 pesos, with A/C, bath, and TV 220 pesos; doubles 220/270 pesos; each additional person 50 pesos. Cash only.) If you have several travelers in your group, **Hotel Posada "Don Diego" ❸** will house four of you for only 300 pesos in large, airy rooms encircling a pleasant, palm-filled courtyard. (☎312 1279. 24hr. bell. Singles with bath 225 pesos; 4-bed rooms 300 pesos; each additional person 25 pesos. Cash only.) In the middle of the market area, **Hotel del Centro ❸**, on Calle 6 between Hidalgo and Juárez, offers clean but noisy rooms. (☎312 3968. 24hr. bell. Singles with bath and TV 180 pesos, with A/C 200 pesos; doubles 200/230 pesos. Cash only.)

Street-side vendors line the shopping area on Calle 7 until about 6pm. If you get the urge to dine more luxuriously, try the fancier restaurants in hotels around the *centro*. At **Restaurante Los Monteros ❸**, on Hidalgo facing the plaza, elegant waiters serve unusually light Mexican dishes such as papaya lime salad for 12 pesos and delicious fruit salads for 15 pesos. (Breakfast 20-30 pesos. Entrees 35-40 pesos. Open M-Sa 8am-4pm. Cash only.) Despite Chinese-inspired decor, **Cafe Canton ❸**, at Calle 8 114 just south of Plaza Hidalgo, serves traditional Mexican food sure to beat the empty-wallet blues. (Meals 25-60 pesos. Open daily 6am-10pm. Cash only.)For groceries, head to **Supertiendas Modelo,** on the corner of Morelos and Calle 7. (Open M-Sa 8am-9pm, Su 10am-8pm. MC/V.)

🎭🎵 SIGHTS AND ENTERTAINMENT. To the east of the busy Plaza Hidalgo, **mercados** line Calles 6 and 7, offering everything from cartoonish *piñatas* and crafts to goat liver. The plaza itself is filled from dawn to dusk with shoppers and families. Those interested in the history of the Tamaulipas should head to the **🏛Museo Regional de Historia de Tamaulipas,** located in a yellow building at the corner of Allende and Calle 22. Walk five blocks north from Plaza Hidalgo to Allende, then take a left and walk to Calle 22. The museum combines videos, artifacts, models, fossils, and a guided tour (in Spanish) which winds through 12 rooms and a tree-filled courtyard while detailing the history of Tamaulipas, from pre-colonial natural history to indigenous cultures. (☎315 1456. Open M-F 10am-6pm, Sa-Su 10am-4pm. Free.) To get to the more tranquil **Plaza Constituciónal,** walk west from the plaza on Hidalgo to Calle 16, where a verdant square dotted with fountains stands in the shadow of the pink-and-white **Catedral de Sagrado Corazón** and the **Palacio de Gobierno,** a grandiose building with impressive murals depicting the nation's history. Also along the plaza, the **Centro Cultural Tamaulipas** hands out cultural calendars and schedules of upcoming concerts and festivals. Escape the heat with a stroll down **La Alameda 17** (Calle 17), a stretch lined with flowering trees, ice cream stores, and parks. Victoria also boasts the **Parque Zoológico Tamatán,** which features both Mexican and other exotic wildlife, on the outskirts of the city. If you come to Ciudad Victoria in the second week of October, don't miss the **Ciudad Victoria Expo,** featuring music, dancing, and *artesanías* from the area

RESERVA DE LA BIOSFERA EL CIELO

Victoria provides relatively easy access to Reserva de la Biosfera El Cielo, the state's most impressive nature reserve. Often referred to as simply "La Reserva," it encompasses more than 300,000 acres of lush vegetation, mountains, and wildlife. The mountains and valleys within the reserve support several different ecosystems, from semi-tropical rainforest to pine forest, and contain over 400 species of birds, 60 different reptiles, and 92 mammals, including bears, armadillos, pumas, and jaguars. Rare orchids bloom among the trees during certain parts of the year, lining miles of trails ascending into the cloud forest. Ardent birders or hikers will enjoy the pleasant hikes; the more adventurous should look out for guided kayaking, mountain biking, horseback rides, and rappelling excursions.

TRANSPORTATION AND PRACTICAL INFORMATION. To reach the reserve by bus, go to the **Transpaís** booth at the bus station in Victoria and ask for a ticket to **Gómez Farías.** The bus heads toward **Cuidad Mante** but makes numerous stops along the way; be sure to have the driver let you off at Gómez Farías, about 2hr. (112km) from Victoria. The bus stops along the highway; from there, a blue minibus (every hr., 5 pesos.) takes you downtown, although it often runs a few hours late. Local mini-van taxis will also offer their services (15-60 pesos, depending how many passengers the driver picks up along the way.) From Gómez Farías, you can hike into the reserve or hire a *camioneta*, a 4WD truck that can bring you all the way up to **San Jose.** In Gómez Farías, you can pick up information on the sights at the **tourist office.** (Open Sa-Su 9am-5pm.) For more information on ecotourism, visit www.tamaulipas.gob.mx. Also in Gómez Farías, ask around about kayaking, mountain-biking and rappelling adventures. Many of the *camioneta* businesses also provide guides for these activities. Plan ahead: there are no **banks** or **ATMs** in Gómez Farías, and credit cards are not accepted at most places.

UPHILL BATTLE. If you decide to hike, bring water and sturdy shoes: from Gómez Farías, it is 10km to Alta Cima, 18km to San Jose, 24km to La Gloria, and 36km to Joya de Mantiales—virtually all uphill. You may also want to bring extra water and snacks into the reserve. Food is available, but *tiendas* often run out of certain supplies and restaurants need advance notice for groups.

ACCOMMODATIONS AND FOOD. Lodgings are available in Gómez Farías but are relatively expensive. Further down the road from the tourist office,

Posada Campestre ❺ offers bungalow-style rooms with individual porches. (☎832 236 2200. Singles and doubles 300 pesos. Cash only.) Within the reserve, accommodations are a bit more reasonable. In Alta Cima, **◪Hotel El Pino ❸** provides charming pine cabins, comfortable wooden beds and gorgeous views of the surrounding mountains (Guided tours available; www.elcielotours.com. Guests can arrange for food to be prepared at **Restaurante La Fe,** just down the hill. Singles and doubles 250 pesos; triples and quads 300 pesos. Camping with firepit and bath 25 pesos per person.) In San Jose, **Cabañas Dona Marina ❷,** offers dozens of decorative doilies and cabins with comfortable bunks. (☎834 304 7621. Guide services available. Will provide food 25-30 pesos per person. Singles, doubles 150 pesos; quads 300 pesos. Camping 20 pesos per person.) **Comedor Buganbilia ❷,** right next to the tourist office in Gómez Farías, serves up freshly-made fare under a hut in a garden (*Gorditas* and *tostadas* 6 pesos. Open 9am-6pm.)

◪ OUTDOOR ACTIVITIES. The four inhabited hamlets of **Alta Cima, San Jose, La Gloria,** and **Joya de Manantiales** make excellent bases from which to explore the reserve. Villagers make their living cutting palm and cactuses. Nearby sights include **La Cueva Del Agua,** a three-level cave home to a species of glowing fish. **Valle de Los Viveros,** a sunny, picnic-perfect glade bordered by small waterfalls, and the massive, unusual rock formations at **La Piedra del Elefante** and **El Cerro de La Campana.** Each campsite and bungalow rental offers awe-inspiring vistas of mist-shrouded mountains, providing a serene escape well worth the trouble of getting there. The reserve gets the most visitors on weekends; come during the week and you will ll most likely have it to yourself. As much of the reserve is a cloud forest, expect rain, especially in the afternoons and chilly nights.

LA PESCA   ☎835

Cool breezes off Río Soto La Marina, the Laguna Morales, and the Gulf of Mexico provide relief from the brutal sun and make La Pesca (pop. 1600) a dream getaway for beachgoers, boaters, and of course, fishermen. Visitors pour into town during school holidays (Jul.-Aug.), but during off-season, it's practically empty. In the evenings, villagers gather in the storefronts on the main road to talk and watch impromptu ball games.

◨◪ TRANSPORTATION AND PRACTICAL INFORMATION. Transportes Taumalipecos de la Costa (☎834 312 1496) runs **buses** to **La Pesca** from Ciudad Victoria (3hr., 11 per day, 110 pesos.) To return to Victoria, catch the bus at the Transportes Taumalipecos office in La Pesca, just off the town square. Plan ahead: **there are no banks and no ATMs in La Pesca.** Other services in La Pesca include: **Lavandería La Pesca,** on your left as you head towards the beach, one block before Hotel Titanic (wash 13 pesos per kg.; open daily 8am-8pm; cash only); **emergency** (☎066); **police** (☎327 1141); **Red Cross** (☎327 1086); **Centro de Salud,** one block past the school heading towards the beach (open M-F 9am-3pm); **Farmacia Linda,** (☎327 0623; open daily 8am-10:30pm; cash only); **Internet** access at **Chat@Maryal,** 3 blocks from the bridge on the left as you come into town (☎327 1291; 10 pesos per hr.; open daily 9am-10:30pm); and the **Telegram Office,** next to the bus office, off the town square, which also wires money (☎327 0723; open M-F 9am-3pm, Sa 9am-1pm). **Postal Code:** 87670.

◨◪ ACCOMMODATIONS AND FOOD. Scenic camping is free anywhere along **Playa La Pesca,** which is roughly 4km down the road from the center of town. You can easily walk, or wait for the bus from Ciudad Victoria out to the peninsula's tip (11 per day). On the road leading into La Pesca, several hotels offer riverside camping. Before you reach town, **Hotel Marina del Río ❷**, at Km 44, has shaded grounds with a dock, camping and grills. (☎327 0699. Camping 70 pesos per person. Bungalows for 4-12 people 600-1200 pesos. Cash only.) On the other side of town, **Hotel Tropicana ❷**, about 1km towards the beach, rents candy-colored thatched roof huts furnished with beds, sofas, kitchenettes and BBQ pits. (☎327 8302. Camping with bath 75 pesos per person. Bungalows for 4-10 people 600-1200 pesos. Cash only.)

No license is required to use the beach's fishing pier, and you are free to keep whatever you catch. Most hotels have docks with grills for cooking your catch, and many restaurants will cook your fish for you if you bring it to them. Near the lighthouse on the beach, **Magui's ❷** serves seafood *a la veracruzano* under a thatched roof. (Spicy shrimp and fish dishes 30 pesos. Open M-Th 10am-5pm, F-Su 10am-8pm, Cash only.) For the freshest oysters visit **Cocina Economica ❶**, a nearby blue shack that lives up to its name with cheap, tasty snacks. (Tacos 5 pesos. Shrimp cocktail 25 pesos. Open M-Th 10am-5pm, F-Su 10am-sundown. Cash only.)

🏖🎭 BEACHES AND ENTERTAINMENT. La Pesca's gorgeous white sand *playa* (beach) is one of the few nesting places of the endangered *tortuga lora* (Kemp's Ridley Sea Turtle). Nesting season is from March until June. Every June and July, governmental environmental agencies celebrate the release of baby sea turtles into the ocean in an effort to preserve the species. The **turtle center** is located a 500m away from the lighthouse on Playa La Pesca. (☎834 318 9483; www.tamaulipas.gob.mx. Opening hours vary.) Throughout the year, clubs in nearby cities organize **fishing tournaments**; the largest public one is at the end of November. Hotels can arrange boat rentals (½-day 300-400 pesos; full day 800 pesos).

TAMPICO   ☎833

While the tropical heat and crowded chaos can be overwhelming, Tampico (pop. 295,000) is the northeast's seaside getaway and a refreshing break for landlocked travelers. Though Tampico may not be ideal for a week-long stay, there is plenty here to reward the intrepid tourist. The seafood is wonderfully fresh, the main plazas are filled with greenery and colonial architecture, the nightlife is swinging, and the pleasant beach, often deserted on weekdays, is an oasis in this desert region.

📧 TRANSPORTATION. The **Central de Autobuses Tampico (CAT)** is on Zapotal. Directly in front of the station, taxis (25 pesos), minibuses (4.50 pesos), and *colectivos* (4 pesos) can take you to the *centro*. To get back to the bus station, take any "Perimetral" *colectivo* (4 pesos). **Ómnibus de México** (☎213 4339) runs **buses** to: **Ciudad Valles** (2½hr., 6 per day, 114 pesos); **Guadalajara** (12hr., 4 per day, 478 pesos); **Mexico City** (8½hr., 8 per day, 368 pesos); **Saltillo** (9hr., 3 per day, 390 pesos); **Tuxpan** (3½hr., 4 per day, 156 pesos). **Transpaís** (☎213 0047) heads to Matamoros (7hr., 15 per day, 290 pesos), **Monterrey** (7hr., 23 per day, 358 pesos), and **Reynosa** (7½hr., 17 per day, 296 pesos). **ADO** (☎213 5512) goes to **Puebla** (9hr., 2 per day, 362 pesos) and **Xalapa** (9hr., 2 per day, 358 pesos).

CHEAP AND QUICK. *Colectivos* are communal taxis that run to select destinations throughout town and can be a money- and time-saving trick for tourists. Since most visitors only want to go to 2 destinations—the *centro* and the beach—*colectivos* are as cheap as a bus and much faster. Look for ordinary cars with placards in the windshields reading "Centro" or "Playa."

◪ PRACTICAL INFORMATION. The **tourist office,** Colón 102, on the third floor of the Palacio Municipal, has maps, brochures, and a friendly staff. (☎229 2765. Open M-F 9am-7pm.) **Banks** with **24hr. ATMs** are on and around both plazas. Other services include: **emergency** (☎066); **police** (☎212 1157), on Tamaulipas at Sor Juana de la Cruz; **Red Cross,** with ambulance service (☎212 1333; open 24hr.); **Hospital Beneficencia Española,** on Hidalgo and Francita Ejército Nacional (☎241 2363); **La Parroquia Lavandería,** 301 Lopéz de Lara (☎214 9790; wash/dry 8 pesos per kg.; open M-Sa 8am-10pm); **Farmacia Fénix,** on the corner of Aduana and Altamira (☎212 3922; open daily 8am-11pm); **Internet** access at **Cyber Cafe Combo Aduana,** upstairs at Aduana 319 Nte. (☎144 0458; 10 pesos per hr; open daily 9am-9pm); and the **post office,** Madero 309 Ote., on Plaza de la Libertad (☎212 1927; Mexpost ☎212 3481; open M-F 9am-5pm, Sa 9am-1pm). **Postal Code:** 89000.

◪◪ ACCOMMODATIONS AND FOOD. Four hundred pesos or more buy an excellent room in one of the larger hotels on Madero and Díaz Mirón near the plazas, but cheaper options do exist. During the summer, keep an eye out for special promotions, when hotels slash rates to drum up business. Situated in an antique colonial building overlooking Plaza de la Libertad, the ◪**Hotel Posada del Rey ❹,** Madero Ote. 218, offers sizeable, plush rooms; some have splurge-worthy balconies. (☎214 1024. Singles and doubles 270-500 pesos. MC/V.) The hotel's restaurant **La Troya ❺** specializes in Spanish cuisine. (☎214 1155. Breakfast 25-40 pesos. Entrees 50-120 pesos. Open daily 8am-10pm. MC/V.) Climb the narrow staircase at **Hotel Capri ❸,** Juárez Nte. 202, to reach surprisingly sunny, high-ceilinged rooms. All rooms have bath, fan and TV, and beer and snacks are available in the lobby. (☎212 2680. Singles and doubles 235 pesos; each additional person 50 pesos. Cash only.) **Hotel Plaza Inn ❸,** Madero Ote. 204, offers a great location and comfortable rooms with A/C. (☎214 3757. Singles and doubles 270 pesos. MC/V.)

Seafood is standard fare in Tampico, where specialties include *jaiba* (blue crab), but the city's best known dish is *carne asada a la tampiqueña* (seasoned grilled steak served with guacamole, refried beans, and enchiladas with red sauce). ◪**Refresquería el Globito de Tampico ❷,** two buildings in middle of the Plaza de Armas, treats crowds to an array of delicious *tortas* (20-34 pesos), hamburgers (30 pesos), and *licuados* (29 pesos). Top it all off with a fantastic banana split for 35 pesos. (☎212 8627. Open 24hr. Cash only.) Chow down at a seaside stand or in the covered food court, the **Centro Gastronómico de Tampico,** on the Cañonero side of Plaza de la Libertad. Upstairs, you will be accosted by small "restaurant" (countertop) owners pushing their fresh food at low prices. The most crowded counters generally serve the tastiest and cleanest food. **Naturaleza ❷,** Aduana 107 Nte., one of Tampico's only vegetarian restaurants, prepares a wide variety of soups, *licuados*, and massive salads, as well as Mexican entrees—from *bistec* to *chorizo*—made entirely of soy. The *comida del día* (daily special) is a steal: 45 pesos includes bread, soup, entree, salad, and juice. (☎212 4979. Entrees 20-35 pesos. Open M-Sa 9am-9pm, Su 10am-6pm. MC/V.) Find groceries at **Arteli,** a supermarket at 601 Díaz Mirón Ote. (Open daily 8am-10pm. MC/V.)

◪◪ SIGHTS AND ENTERTAINMENT. with its gentle waves and stretches of white sand, **Playa Miramar** is by far the best beach in the northeast. It is accessible by the "Tampico Playa" bus (30min., 4 pesos), a shared "Tampico Playa" taxi (15min., 4 pesos), or a private taxi (35 pesos), all of which can be caught near the plazas. Stake out a spot under a rented palm-frond umbrella (50-60 pesos) on the beach's 10km of sand and expect a stream of vendors to disrupt your relaxation.

Tampico is known for its nightlife. While the scene changes constantly, the general rule is that it gets trendier the farther you go from the *centro*. If you really want to party, take a taxi (35-40 pesos) to ▨**Byblos,** at Calle Byblos 1, a large black pyramid adorned with Versace images, three fountains, and a black marble bar. Recently named one of the top 10 clubs in Mexico, Byblos plays everything from pop to reggae to electronic amid pulsating lasers and video screens. Note that there are two different entrances: one for the under-18 crowd and another for those of age. The last Saturday of every month morphs into a blowout birthday bash; those born during the month enjoy drink specials and no cover. (☎217 3050; www.byblos.com.mx. Cover 70 pesos, includes open bar. Open W-Sa 10pm-4am. MC/V.) Many of the hotels on the central plazas have swanky bars, or try **Azul Disco,** on the corner of Juárez and Carranza, featuring beer (10 pesos), fog, lasers, and predictably blue decor. (Cover 50 pesos. Open W-Sa 9pm-4am.) In October, actors, artisans, folk dancers, and singers from around the world gather for the annual **Festival Internacional Tamaulipas.** Check the tourist office for schedules.

NUEVO LEÓN

MONTERREY   ☎81

A neon cross crowns the centuries-old cathedral in Monterrey's central plaza—just one example of how *regios* (Monterrey residents) have seized their city's past and refashioned it to serve the present. The city has marvelous museums, but it lives vibrantly in the moment, bursting with hip clubs, restaurants, and art-filled public parks. Monterrey is the third largest city in Mexico, with a population of three million people and growing. Founded in 1596 by Diego de Montemayor at the foot of Cerro de la Silla (Saddle Mountain), the small trading outpost's location between Mexico and the US made it an important center of business and commerce. Today, the city is home to many of the country's wealthiest businesspeople, and one of Mexico's most prestigious universities, the Universidad Tecnológica de Mexico. The youthful, cosmopolitan flair of a university town pervades even the most industrial sections of the city: *norteño* music, theater, and dance abound.

▐▌ TRANSPORTATION

Flights: Gen. Mariano Escobedo Intl. Airport (MTY), in the far northeastern corner of town, off Mex. 54. **Taxis** 200 pesos for 20km trip to the *centro* (20-30min.). Serves **Aeroméxico** (☎800 021 4010; www.aeromexico.com) and **Mexicana** (☎800 509 8960; www.mexicana.com).

Buses: All buses pass through Monterrey's huge **Central de Autobuses** on Colón between Villagrán and Pino Suárez. To reach the *centro* from the bus station, walk 2 blocks east to the gray Metro station at Cuauhtémoc and Colón and take the Metrorrey (Line 2, 4.50 pesos) to Padre Mier or Zaragoza.

Intercity Buses: Ómnibus de México (☎8375 7063) runs to: **Aguascalientes** (8hr., 4 per day, 376 pesos); **Chihuahua** (12hr., 3 per day, 546 pesos); **Guadalajara** (12hr., 3 per day, 538 pesos); **Mexico City** (12hr., 3 per day, 637 pesos); **Saltillo** (1½hr., 55 pesos); **Zacatecas** (6hr., 5 per day, 292 pesos). **Noreste** (☎8375 5488) heads to **Matehuala** (4hr., every hr., 213 pesos). **Frontera** (☎8318 3751) goes to **León** (10 hr., 5 per day, 475 pesos) and **Saltillo** (1½hr., every 20min., 55 pesos). Similar service is provided by **Estrella Blanca** (☎8318 3737), **Transporte del Norte** (☎8151 5253), **Líneas Americanas,** and luxurious **Futura** and **Turistar. Sendor** and the many lines it runs, such as **Tamaulipas,** share offices (☎8375 7577) near Sala 5.

Local Buses: *Urbano* buses (5-8 pesos) usually move in only 1 direction on any given street, except on Constitución and Juárez. Popular routes include stops at the **Gran Plaza** (#18 or 42), points along **Padre Mier** and **Hidalgo** (#15), and along the perimeter of the **downtown** area (#69). To get from the budget hotel area to the *centro*, take the #1 Central or #17 Pío X bus, both of which run the lengths of Pino Suárez and Cuauhtémoc. Buses run daily 6am-midnight. For more detailed route information, ask locals waiting at the bus stops or the staff at the tourist office.

Car Rental: Hertz, located at the airport (☎8369 0696 or 0822; open daily 10am-6pm), and downtown, in the Hotel Crown Plaza, on Hidalgo and Zaragoza (☎8342 5156; open daily 10am-6pm). Rentals from 500 pesos per day.

Metro: Monterrey's amazing Metro system, the ■**Metrorrey,** is the best way to get around—it's clean, cheap, efficient, and the ride from the bus station to the Gran Plaza takes only 6min. The Metrorrey runs on 2 lines: **Line 1** (yellow) extends from the western station of **San Barnabe** to **Exposición** in the east; **Line 2** (green) runs from the north, at **Anaya** station, to the Gran Plaza at the **Zaragoza** stop. Line 2 stops at **Padre Mier,** in the Zona Rosa, and ends close to the Barrio Antiguo. The lines intersect at **Cuauhté-moc,** which is next to the bus station and close to many budget hotels. Consult the maps posted in each station to figure out which train you should take, and check the walls for the extremely accurate *horario* (schedule). Machines sell electronic ride passes in quantities of 1 (4.50 pesos), 2 (8.50 pesos), and 4 (16 pesos), as well as passes for the **Metrobús** (6 pesos). At the larger stations, such as Cuauhtémoc, you can buy multi-ride passes of up to 100 pesos. There are vending machine-style **book dispensers** at major stations (50-200 passes). Metro runs daily 4:30am-12:30am.

◀ ▎ ORIENTATION AND PRACTICAL INFORMATION

Aside from the budget hotel district, near the Cuauhtémoc stop of the Metrorrey, visitors will spend most of their time in Monterrey's *centro*. The Gran Plaza, usually referred to as the Macroplaza, lays a green swath of grass through the downtown area. The *centro* forms a cross shape, with the Zona Rosa on one side, the Barrio Antiguo on the other, and the Macroplaza down the center.

TIP   **HELLO, OPERATOR.** Due to population growth, Monterrey has a unique two-digit area code (81) to accommodate more telephone number combinations. Always make sure you get an 8-digit number to avoid dialing confusion.

Tourist Office: Washington 638, in the Antiguo Palacio Federal, 1st fl. (☎8155 3333; www.nl.gob.mx), between Escobedo and Zaragoza at the north edge of the Macroplaza. Very helpful staff. Has bilingual brochures, coupons, and very useful maps of the city, *centro*, and Metrorrey. Open daily 8:30am-6:30pm. The magazines **What's On, Común,** and **La Rocka,** all free and available at the tourist office and many hotels, have listings on cultural events, music, and nightlife.

Consulates: Canada, Zaragoza 1300 Sur, Edif. Kalos (☎8344 3200 or 2961, emergency ☎800 706 2900). Open M-F 9am-1:30pm and 2:30-5:30pm. **UK,** Av. Ricardo Margain Zozaya 240, 2nd fl., Valle de Campestre (☎8356 5359). Open M-F 8am-5pm. **US,** Constitución Pte. 411. (☎8345 2120, emergency ☎8362 9126), downtown. Open M-F 8am-1pm for passports and citizens' concerns, 9am-5pm for telephone information. 24hr. guard and emergency service. The Monterrey tourist office also has consulate information for other countries.

Currency Exchange and Banks: Banks dot Madero near the budget hotels and flood the Zona Rosa, especially along Padre Mier. Many refuse to cash traveler's checks and charge high service fees (10%). All have **24hr. ATMs.** Most open M-F 9am-4pm. Most Metrorrey stations also have ATMs. **Mexdollar Internacional,** 1136 Suárez (☎8374 4311), right by the bus station and Cuauhtémoc Metro stop, offers 24hr. currency and traveler's check exchange. **Western Union** (☎8354 2254), Ómnibus de México office at the Central de Autobuses, and several are in stores along Morelos in the Zona Rosa.

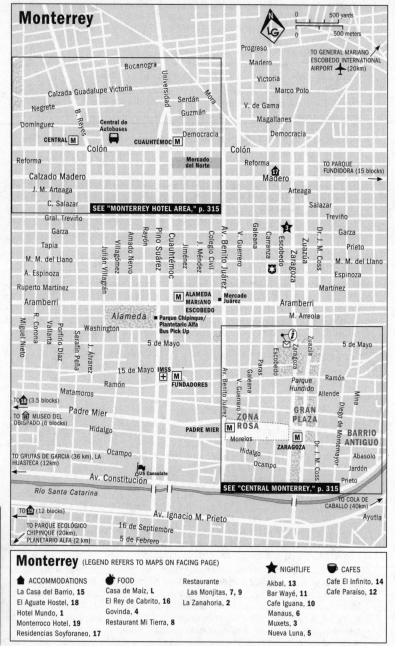

Monterrey

0 ——— 500 yards
0 ——— 500 meters

TO GENERAL MARIANO
ESCOBEDO INTERNATIONAL
AIRPORT ✈ (20km)

Bocanegra

Progreso
Madero
Victoria
Marco Polo
V. de Gama
Magallanes
Democracia

Calzada Guadalupe Victoria
Universidad
Serdán
Mora
Guzmán
Negrete
B. Reyes
Central de
Autobuses
Democracia
Domínguez
CENTRAL Ⓜ
Colón
CUAUHTÉMOC

Colón

Reforma
Calzado Madero
J. M. Arteaga
C. Salazar

SEE "MONTERREY HOTEL AREA," p. 315

Mercado
del Norte

Reforma
Madero
TO PARQUE
FUNDIDORA (15 blocks)
Arteaga
Salazar

Gral. Treviño
Garza
Tapia
M. M. del Llano
A. Espinoza
Ruperto Martínez
Aramberri

Villagómez
Julián Villagrán
Amado Nervo
Rayón
Pino Suárez
Cuauhtémoc
Jiménez
J. Méndez
Colegio Civil
Av. Benito Juárez
V. Guerrero
Galeana
Carranza
Escobedo
Zuazúa
Zaragoza

Treviño
Garza
Prieto
M. M. del Llano
Espinoza
Martínez
Dr. J. M. Coss

Ⓜ **ALAMEDA
MARIANO
ESCOBEDO**
Mercado
Juárez
Aramberri
M. Arreola

Alameda
Parque Chipinque/
Planetario Alfa
Bus Pick Up

Miguel Nieto
R. Corona
Vallarta
Porfirio Díaz
Serafín Peña
J. Álvarez
Washington

5 de Mayo
15 de Mayo **IMSS** ✚ Ⓜ
FUNDADORES
Ramón
Matamoros

TO ⑱ (3.5 blocks)

TO 🏛 MUSEO DEL
OBISPADO (6 blocks)

Padre Mier
Hidalgo
Ocampo

TO GRUTAS DE GARCIA (36 km), LA
HUASTECA (12km)

Av. Constitución
🇺🇸 US Consulate

Río Santa Catarina

TO ⑲ (12 blocks)

TO PARQUE ECOLÓGICO
CHIPINQUE (20km),
PLANETARIO ALFA (2 km)

16 de Septiembre
5 de Febrero

Av. Ignacio M. Prieto

Paras
Escobedo
Zuazúa
5 de Mayo
Ramón
Allende
Mina

Av. Benito Juárez
V. Guerrero
Galeana
ℹ
Parque
Hundido

**ZONA
ROSA** Ⓜ

**GRAN
PLAZA**

Diego de Montemayor

Morelos
Hidalgo
Ocampo

PADRE MIER

Ⓜ **ZARAGOZA**

Dr. J. M. Coss

**BARRIO
ANTIGUO**
Abasolo
Jardón
Prieto

SEE "CENTRAL MONTERREY," p. 315

TO COLA DE
CABALLO (40km)
Ayutla

Monterrey (LEGEND REFERS TO MAPS ON FACING PAGE)

🏠 ACCOMMODATIONS
La Casa del Barrio, **15**
El Aguate Hostel, **18**
Hotel Mundo, **1**
Monterroco Hotel, **19**
Residencias Soyforaneo, **17**

🍴 FOOD
Casa de Maíz, **L**
El Rey de Cabrito, **16**
Govinda, **4**
Restaurant Mi Tierra, **8**

Restaurante
Las Monjitas, **7, 9**
La Zanahoria, **2**

⭐ NIGHTLIFE
Akbal, **13**
Bar Wayé, **11**
Cafe Iguana, **10**
Manaus, **6**
Muxets, **3**
Nueva Luna, **5**

☕ CAFES
Cafe El Infinito, **14**
Cafe Paraíso, **12**

NORTHEAST MEXICO

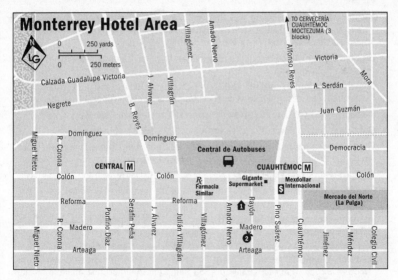

Monterrey Hotel Area

N LG

0 — 250 yards
0 — 250 meters

TO CERVECERÍA
CUAUHTÉMOC
MOCTEZUMA (3 blocks)

Calzada Guadalupe Victoria

Victoria

A. Serdán

Negrete

Juan Guzmán

Domínguez

Domínguez

Central de Autobuses

Democracia

CENTRAL M

CUAUHTÉMOC M

Colón

Colón

Colón

R Farmacia Similar

Gigante Supermarket

Mexdollar Internacional

Reforma

Reforma

Mercado del Norte (La Pulga)

Madero

Madero

Arteaga

Arteaga

Miguel Nieto · R. Corona · Miguel Nieto · R. Corona · Porfirio Díaz · Serafín Peña · J. Álvarez · Julián Villagrán · Villagómez · Amado Nervo · Rayón · Pino Suárez · Cuauhtémoc · Jiménez · J. Méndez · Colegio Civil

B. Reyes · J. Álvarez · Villagrán · Amado Nervo · Alfonso Reyes · Mora

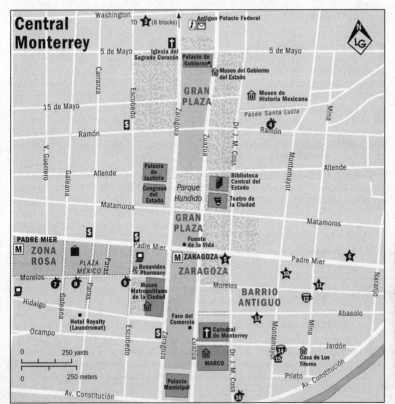

Central Monterrey

N LG

Washington

TO (8 blocks)

Antiguo Palacio Federal

Iglesia del Sagrado Corazón

Palacio de Gobierno

5 de Mayo

5 de Mayo

Museo del Gobierno del Estado

GRAN PLAZA

Museo de Historia Mexicana

Paseo Santa Lucía

15 de Mayo

Ramón

Ramón

Palacio de Justicia

Congreso del Estado

Biblioteca Central del Estado

Allende

Allende

Parque Hundido

Teatro de la Ciudad

Matamoros

GRAN PLAZA

Matamoros

Fuente de la Vida

PADRE MIER

M ZONA ROSA

PLAZA MÉXICO

Padre Mier

M ZARAGOZA

Padre Mier

Morelos

Benavides Pharmacy

ZARAGOZA

Museo Metropolitano de la Ciudad

Morelos

BARRIO ANTIGUO

Hidalgo

Hotel Royalty (Laundromat)

Faro del Comercio

Abasolo

Ocampo

Catedral de Monterrey

Jardón

0 — 250 yards
0 — 250 meters

MARCO

Casa de Los Títeres

Palacio Municipal

Prieto

Av. Constitución

Av. Constitución

Carranza · Escobedo · Zaragoza · Zuazua · Dr. J. M. Coss · Montemayor · Mina · Naranjo

V. Guerrero · Galeana · Paras · Paras · Escobedo · Zaragoza · Zuazua · Dr. J. M. Coss · Montemayor · Mina

American Express: San Pedro 215 Nte. (☎8318 3304). Catch bus #214 headed for "San Pedro" on Pino Suárez at the stop just past Ocampo. Get off before Calzada del Valle and cross the street. Open M-F 9am-5pm, Sa 9am-1pm.

Luggage Storage: At the bus station. 5 pesos per hr., up to 30 days. Available at Sala 2 and Sala 5. Open 24hr.

Laundry: Hotel Royalty (☎8340 2800), on the corner of Hidalgo and Carranza. Open M-Sa. Laundry services available at most *centro* hotels for about 40 pesos per load.

Police: (☎8343 0173 or 2576), on the corner of Carranza and Espinosa.

Red Cross: Alfonso Reyes 2503 Nte. (☎065 or 8372 5832), at Calle Henry.

Pharmacy: Farmacia Vida, in the bus station. Open daily 9am-11pm. **Benavides** (☎8345 0257), on the corner of Morelos and Escobedo. Open daily 7:30am-10:30pm.

Medical Services: Cruz Verde (☎8371 5311 or 5050), at Ciudad Madero and Ciudad Victoria.

Fax Office: Telecomm, in the bus station, next to the post office. Open M-F 8am-7pm, Sa-Su 9am-4pm.

Internet Access: Internet Hidalgo, Hidalgo 147. 10 pesos per hr. Open daily 10am-10pm. **E-connection,** Escobedo 831. 20 pesos per hr. Open daily 9:30am-10pm.

Post Office: (☎8344 9364) on Zaragoza at Washington, inside the Antiguo Palacio Federal, ground fl. Open M-F 8am-7pm, Sa 9am-1pm. **Mexpost** is next door (☎8344 9255). Open M-F 9am-5pm, Sa 9am-1pm. Another post office is on the 2nd fl. of the bus station (stairs near Sala 5). Open M-F 8am-4pm, Sa 9am-1pm. **Postal Code:** 64000.

ACCOMMODATIONS

Monterrey can be expensive, but budget hotels do exist. Cheaper accommodations dot the less glamorous area near the bus station, and most accept only cash. A smattering of hostels in various neighborhoods throughout the city offer far more comfortable lodging and amenities than similarly priced hotels. Hotels located near the Zona Rosa tend to be of four- or five-star quality, and even three-star accommodations inflate their rates to gouge tourists and business travelers. If you feel like spending 600 pesos, a hotel downtown will reward you with luxury: restaurants, room service, and elegantly decorated rooms.

La Casa del Barrio, Diego Montemayor 1221 (☎8344 1800; www.casadelbarrio.com.mx), at the corner of Jardón. A bit pricey for a hostel, but the dorms are gorgeous, large, and airy with rustic wooden furniture. The location, right in the middle of the Barrio Antiguo, can't be beat. Kitchen access and complimentary coffee. Free Internet access and Wi-Fi. Dorms 182 pesos per person; private rooms with shared bath 350 pesos, with private bath 370 pesos. Discounts on longer stays. MC/V. ❸

El Aguacate Hostel, Priv. Manuel Gutiérrez 505 (www.elaguacatehostal.com). From the Central, catch bus #126 "Huasteca/Fama2." Get off at the intersection of Carranza and 15 de Mayo, walk right on 15 de Mayo and take a left on Gutiérrez. A laid-back hostel with an earthy vibe, in a friendly residential area a short hike or bus ride from the *center*. Clean dorms, lovely painted patios, and friendly owner make you feel right at home. Kitchen available. Free Internet access. Dorms 75 pesos, campsites with access to hostel facilities 55 pesos. Private rooms available with reservation. Cash only. ❶

Residencias Soyforaneo, Madero Ote. 431, top floor (☎8374 2164; www.soyforaneo.com), 7 blocks east of the bus station. Clean, simple dorms concrete balconies. Kitchen facilities and a helpful, English-speaking staff make this the best value near the station. Dorms 130 pesos per person; private rooms 320 pesos. Cash only. ❷

Monterroco Hostel, Av. Lomas de San Francisco 205 (☎1365 4690. www.monter-roco.com). From the bus station, take bus #17, which will cross the river and make a right onto 16 de Septiembre/Loma Redonda. Get off at the HSBC and Monterroco is uphill on your left. Not exactly central, but a swimming pool, exercise equipment, free Internet, cable TV, and kitchen make it worth the trip. Dorms 130 pesos. Discounts on longer stays. Cash only. ❷

Hotel Virreynes, Amado Nervo 902 (☎8374 6610), at the corner of Arteaga. Simple, clean rooms with A/C will do for a cheap stayover, but don't expect many frills. Singles 100 pesos; doubles 200; triples 300. Cash only. ❶

Hotel Mundo, Reforma 736 (☎8374 6850), off Amado Nervo. Slightly more luxurious than other bus station hotels. All rooms include A/C and TV. Uniform rooms—reminiscent of chain hotels—with brightly shining floors. Singles 280 pesos; doubles 320 pesos; triples 360 pesos; quads 380. MC/V. ❺

Hotel Nuevo León, Amado Nervo 1007 (☎8374 1900 or 0713), 1½ blocks from the bus station. A statue of Buddha welcomes you to a maze of rooms, some with dresser and table. Singles with TV and A/C 300 pesos; doubles 500 pesos. Cash only. ❺

🍴 FOOD

Roasted meat is king in Monterrey. Make sure to indulge your carnivorous tooth by eating plenty of *bistecs* (steaks), a regional speciality. Other popular dishes include *frijoles a la charra* (beans cooked with pork skin, coriander, tomato, peppers, and onions) and *machaca con huevos* (scrambled eggs mixed with salsa and dried, shredded beef). For dessert, you'll love *piloncillo con nuez* (a hardened brown sugar candy with pecans) and the heavenly *glorias* (candies made of nuts and goat's milk). The Zona Rosa caters to hungry businesspeople and shoppers with dozens of mid-range restaurants. The neighboring Barrio Antiguo boasts delicious, upscale international cuisine. For the cheapest food downtown, visit the taco stands that line Coss between 5 de Mayo and Allende, or on Matamoros west of the Macroplaza. Cheap eats also abound on Colón near the bus station. **Gigante supermarket,** on Colón across from the bus station, has an adjoining pharmacy. (☎8255 2925. Open daily 7am-10pm.)

Restaurante Las Monjitas (☎8342 8537), on Escobedo at Galeana; another on Morelos at Galeana in the Zona Rosa. Escobedo branch is an imitation cathedral where the waitresses dress as nuns. Heavenly specialty tacos (45-75 pesos) have names like *La Monjita* (The Nun; beef with bacon, onions, and soft cheese) and *Tres Misioneros* (3 Missionaries; chicken, beef, pork, and bacon). Open daily 8am-11pm. Cash only. ❸

La Zanahoria, Rayón 932 (☎8372 3258), between Madero and Arteaga. A vegetarian oasis in a meat-lover's capital. Mexican entrees such as mushrooms, *chiles rellenos,* enchiladas, and veggie burgers come with a drink, salad, soup, and whole wheat bread for 52 pesos. Just the entree 35 pesos. Open daily noon-6pm. Cash only. ❸

Cafe Paraíso (☎8344 6616 or 6617), on Morelos on the corner of Mina. A great place to take a break from sightseeing in the heart of the Barrio Antiguo. This hip spot also serves alcoholic drinks and good French and Mexican cuisine. Delicious flavored cappuccinos 30 pesos. Entrees 25-60 pesos. Sweet crepes 50 pesos. Open M-Th 5pm-1am, F-Sa 5pm-2am, Su 5pm-midnight. Cash only. ❷

El Rey de Cabrito, Coss 817 (☎8345 3352), on the corner of Constitución, behind the Museo de Arte Contemporáneo. Famous throughout Monterrey, El Rey reigns supreme for roasted meat, especially their *cabrito* (150-300 pesos.) This regional specialty, comes smoking straight off the flames. Traditional Mexican entrees 50-120 pesos. Open daily 11:30am-midnight. Cash only. ❺

NORTHEAST MEXICO

Casa del Maíz, Abasolo 870 (☎8340 4332), between Mina and Naranjo. Dim lights, flowers, and low tables invite romantic whispers. Enjoy inventive Mexican cuisine such as *memelas, tamales,* and *tostadas* with your choice of fillings and toppings, from mushrooms to *bistec* (35-70 pesos). Portions are small, but tasty. Drinks 15-50 pesos. Open M 6-11:30pm, Tu-Th 6pm-1am, F-Sa 2pm-1am, Su noon-10:30pm. Cash only. ❹

Govinda, 841 Ramón, off Coss in the Barrio Antiguo. This Indian-inspired restaurant serves a massive vegetarian *comida corrida* (60 pesos), which includes access to a salad bar. Come also for the *licuados,* fruit cocktails, and fresh-squeezed juices (15-30 pesos.) Open M-Sa noon-6pm. Cash only. ❸

Restaurant Mi Tierra (☎8340 5611), on Morelos across from the Plaza México in the Zona Rosa. Some of the city's best tacos in an open-air setting. If you can't find a seat, get it to go. Try their specialty *milanesa* (38 pesos). Open daily 9:30am-9:30pm. Tacos, *enchiladas, tostadas,* and more 28-46 pesos. Cash only. ❸

🜨 SIGHTS

Monterrey's architects were kind to tourists. Not only is the city beautiful and easy to navigate, but most sights are packed into the 40-acre **Macroplaza** and adjacent **Barrio Antiguo.** A visitor could easily spend the day strolling through the Macroplaza and admiring the statues, architecture, and greenery, all surrounded by the stunning gray mountains that ring the city. Monterrey's state-of-the-art museums and parks will keep you busy all day, while at night, the Barrio Antiguo is the place to be for drinking and dancing.

■ MUSEO DE ARTE CONTEMPORÁNEO (MARCO). MARCO's colorful building is a work of art in itself—enormous windows showcase Monterrey's mountains, while a giant geometric fountain inside spouts like a broken water main. The art is just as spectacular as the building. MARCO exhibits the best of Mexico's innovative artists, including Juan Soriano (1920-2006) and Enrique Canales (1936-2007). Rotating special exhibits feature international artists and 20th-century movements. *(Zuazúa and Padre Raymundo Jardón. Across from the cathedral. ☎8262 4500. www.marco.org.mx. Open Tu and Th-Su 10am-6pm, W 10am-8pm. 50 pesos, students and children 30 pesos; under 5 free, W free. Cash only.)*

MACROPLAZA. Bounded by Washington to the north, Constitución to the south, Zaragoza to the west, and Coss to the east, the Macroplaza (also called the Gran Plaza) displays all elements of Monterrey—art, commerce, government, religion, and romance. It hosts three government palaces: the **Antiguo Palacio Federal,** the **Palacio de Gobierno,** and the **Palacio Municipal.** The Palacio del Gobierno houses a free museum, **Museo del Gobierno,** showcasing the old congress of the state and Mexico's movement from a colonial government to representative democracy. (☎2033 9900; www.museodelpalaciodelgobierno.org.mx. Open Tu-Su 10am-7pm.) Beyond these immense structures lies the resplendent **Catedral de Monterrey.** Built between 1603 and 1753, the cathedral features a multicolored dome with a neon cross atop it. Towering above the cathedral is the bright orange **Faro del Comercio** (Commerce Lighthouse). Built in 1983 it represents Monterrey's lifeblood—business. The lighthouse begins to pulse with laser light after 10pm on weekend nights, when thousands pack the adjoining Barrio Antiguo. Across Zaragoza from the Faro, the **Museo Metropolitano de Monterrey** has relics, photos, and doctrines from Monterrey's founding to its modern-day life. (☎8344 2503. Open Tu-Su 10am-7pm. Free.) Beneath these towers and spires, the cool garden of the **Parque Hundido** (Sunken Park) draws lovers of all ages as well as families with boisterous kids. The nearby **Fuente de La Vida** (Fountain of Life), built in 1984 by the government of Nuevo León, contains a gaggle of naked, cavorting demigods surrounding an imposing statue of Neptune.

MUSEO DE HISTORIA MEXICANA. In this state-of-the-art museum, you can witness thousands of years of Mexican history (in Spanish) through an interweaving of historical artifacts, movies, interactive computer displays, replicas, art, and models. The ground floor houses fascinating bilingual exhibits utilizing the same blending of presentation methods as found upstairs. (*Dr. Coss 445 Sur. At the far end of the Plaza 400 Años. ☎8345 9898; www.museohistoriamexicana.org.mx. Open Tu-F 10am-7pm, Sa-Su 10am-8pm. 12 pesos, children under 12 free; Tu free. Cash only.*)

MUSEO DEL OBISPADO AND MIRADOR. A beautifully restored colonial palace holds a well-presented history of Nuevo Leon, detailing its rise from a remote frontier outpost of the Spanish empire to the economic capital of northern Mexico. The real reason to come, however, is the location: the museum sits atop the highest hill in Monterrey and offers spectacular views of the city and surrounding mountains, including Monterrey's icon **Cerro de la Silla.** (*Located on Rafael Jose Vergel, in the Colonia Obispado, west of the center. To get there from the center, catch a west-bound bus on Padre Mier until Padre Mier reaches a dead end into a garden. Walk up through the garden, take a left on Benitez, then a right on Verger and the museum is at the top of the hill. If you want to spare yourself the hike, a taxi will cost about 30 pesos. ☎8346 0404. Museum open Tu-Su 10am-7pm; mirador open daily 6am-11pm. 37 pesos.*)

LA CASA DE LOS TÍTERES. The tiny Casa is one of the only museums in Latin America devoted to the art of puppet-making and puppetry. Rooms are filled with puppets of all epochs and cultures. The museum also features regular shows by local and international performers: some traditional puppet shows aimed at children, but also more avant-garde work that will surprise any theatre enthusiast. (*910 Jardón, on the corner of Mina. ☎8343 0604; www.baulteatro.com. Open M-F and Su 2-6pm. 15 pesos, children 10 pesos.*)

CERVECERÍA CUAUHTÉMOC MOCTEZUMA. Beer and sports go hand in hand. With this in mind, Monterrey's leading beer manufacturer attached a brewery to the Mexican Baseball Hall of Fame and Museum. Brewery tours take you through the production of Carta Blanca, Dos Equis, and Tecate beers, and conclude in the Beer Garden, where adults can sample a glass or two under the shade of trees and fermentation tanks. Afterward, head to the **Salón de la Fama,** a museum that chronicles the birth of baseball in the mid-1800s and its arrival in Mexico shortly thereafter. Interactive exhibits allow kids of all ages to try their luck at batting, pitching, and catching. (*On Alfonso Reyes, 1½ blocks south of the Anaya Metrorrey station on Line 2. ☎8328 5355; www.salondelafama.com. Brewery and museum open M-F 9:30am-6pm, Sa-Su 10:30am-6pm. Tours given throughout the day in both Spanish and English. Free.*)

PARQUE FUNDIDORA. This massive park blends relaxing expanses of greenery, manmade lakes and rivers with countless entertainment options, from ice-skating to theatre. One end of the park is dominated by the **Arena Monterrey,** a massive venue that draws big-name international performers. Check newspapers and the tourist office for schedules. At the other end theme park **Plaza Sesamo** (the Mexican name for Sesame Street) stays packed with children from dawn to dusk. (*☎8354 5400; www.parqueplazasesamo.com. Open M-F 3-8pm, Sa-Su 11am-8pm. 159 pesos, after 6pm 109 pesos, children under 6 free.*) In between, make sure to visit the **Cineteca-Fototeca,** a gallery and movie theater showcasing cutting-edge photography exhibits and alternative films. (*☎8479 0015; www.conarte.org.mx. Open daily 10am-9pm. Most exhibits and screenings free.*) To explore the park, rent a bike next to Lago Aceración. (*20 pesos per hr. Open daily 1-9pm.*) As of 2007, the construction is underway to extend the manmade Canal Santa Lucia that runs by the Museo De La Historia Mexicana into the Parque Fundidora, creating a pleasant riverwalk from downtown to the Parque. (*To get to the park, take Line 2 of the Metrorrey to the Fundidora stop. ☎8340 7150; www.parquefundidora.org. Park open daily 6am-11pm. Free.*)

PLANETARIO ALFA. Located on the southern outskirts of the city, this massive oval sphere houses a museum of science and technology with rotating hands-on exhibits, a planetarium, observatory, and IMAX theatre. *(Av. Roberto Garza Sada 1000, in the Colonia San Pedro. Free shuttles leave from the Alameda Mariano Escobedo Tu-F every hr. from 1:30pm-7:30pm, Sa-Su every 30min. from 11:30am-7:30pm. ☎8303 0001; www.planetarioalfa.org.mx. Open Tu-Su noon-9pm. Museum 45 pesos, with IMAX 80 pesos.)*

TEATRO DE LA CIUDAD. For a calmer evening, stop by Macroplaza's enormous theater. The Teatro regularly hosts plays, operas, and dance performances. Amateur actors occasionally perform outside. *(On the plaza across from the Fuente de la Vida. ☎8343 8975. Opens 1hr. before evening performances. Information and tickets available at the office facing the Macroplaza, down the steps near the theater entrance. Office open M-F 9am-7pm. Prices vary by show; some available through ticketmaster.com. Cash only at box office.)*

📷 🎵 SHOPPING AND ENTERTAINMENT

Most of Monterrey's dozens of malls lie outside the center, especially the ones with the most upscale shopping. Ask at the tourist office for directories and directions. The **Zona Rosa,** particularly along Morelos, is the city's commercial center, a cacophony of clothing and shoe stores, boutiques, and street vendors. Bargainhunters may prefer the **Mercado del Norte** (also known as **La Pulga**), a seemingly endless maze of vendor stalls covering Reforma, just south of Colón. The clothing vendors, *taquerías*, and music stores stretch from Cuauhtémoc all the way to Juárez. Enter on Cuauhtémoc, directly across from the Metrorrey station. (Open daily 9am-7pm.) Every Sunday, from about 10am-6pm, stalls line **Mina** in the Barrio Antiguo, selling paintings, jewelry, crafts, and antiques.

Monterrey celebrates **Mexican Independence Day** in style, with partying and parades September 15-16. Expect hotel prices to rise. In late November, the **Festival del Barrio Antiguo** closes streets around the Barrio Antiguo for a week of cultural events, including open-air theater, music festivals, dance, and art exhibitions.

🏔 OUTDOOR ACTIVITIES

There is ample opportunity to leave Monterrey for the nearby hills, with an astounding number of sights just outside the city limits. Many of them are easily explored solo, but the Monterrey tourist office also has information on reasonably priced tours, which may be less of a hassle and offer more exotic opportunities such as bungee-jumping, rappelling, and rafting.

PARQUE ECOLÓGICO CHIPINQUE. Just a few kilometers south of Monterrey, on the Carretera a Chipinque, this park has over 4000 acres of pristine mountain paths for hiking, mountain biking, rock-climbing and birdwatching. Camping is also available. *(☎8303 2190; www.chipinque.org.mx. Free buses leave from the Alameda Mariano Escobedo W-F 9 and 11am, Sa-Su at 8, 10am, and noon; schedule subject to change—check the park website for the best info. Open daily 6am-8pm. 20 pesos, with car or bike 30 pesos, children under 12 free.)*

GRUTAS DE GARCIA. West of the city on Route 40, these deep caves are high up on the side of breathtaking stone mountains. You can hike up to the entrance, or take the *teleférico*, a spectacular, if short, gondola ride. The guided tour through the cavern (in Spanish) takes about 45min., walking past natural structures such as the "Mano de La Muerte," a sinister, hand-shaped stalagtite, and "El Divino Rostro," a patch on the ceiling bearing a striking resemblance to Jesus Christ. Grupo Senda sends buses to the cave (45min., 20 pesos) on weekends, while on weekdays, buses go only to the village of Garcia (40min., 15 pesos). Taxis can bring you to the caves (10min., 50 pesos). (☎8347 1533. Open daily 9am-5pm. Entrance to the caves via teleférico 60 pesos adults, children under 10 45 pesos; if you choose to walk 45/35 pesos.)

PARQUE LA HUASTECA. For a more rough-and-tumble experience of Monterrey's gorgeous mountains, head to this park, 20min. outside the city on Route 40. Tour companies offer mountain climbing and rappelling, but the striking, arid mountain landscape also invites solo travelers looking to hike and camp. (☎2020 7400. To get there, catch a bus marked "Huasteca" on Reforma near the Central de Autobuses, or anywhere along Av. Vestuviano Carranza; 8 pesos. Buses pick up and drop off at the entrance to the park. Free. Open daily 7am-7pm).

⬛ NIGHTLIFE

Head over to **Barrio Antiguo** for fun after 10pm. Monterrey is transformed when cafes begin to serve liquor and become more like bars, while bars crank the music and turn into clubs. The bar and cafe scene is relatively static, but the club scene changes radically; ask locals at the cafes what clubs are currently hot. After its first-ever Pride March in the summer of 1997, Monterrey has quickly become one of the most gay- and lesbian-friendly cities in Mexico. Although most GLBT nightspots cater primarily to men, women are also welcome. For more listings, ask for a copy of the free gay and lesbian monthly magazine, *Rola Gay*, at **Muxets** (see below), or check the website gaymonterrey.net.

> **HAPPY HOUR.** Going out in Monterrey can be pricey, but not if you do some coupon scavenging first. Steep competition in the Barrio Antiguo means many bars put out promotional cards offering drink specials and no-cover passes. Look for them in restaurants around the center, the tourist office, and the hostel Casa del Barrio.

▨ **Cafe Iguana,** Diego de Montemayor 927 (☎8343 0822; www.cafeiguana.com.mx.). A standing-room-only bar of paint-splattered rooms and patios playing rock videos or occasionally a live group give way to a cavernous, laser-filled dance floor where local and celebrity DJs keep the crowd going till dawn. Don't miss their pizza window outside, a local favorite for a late-night snack (20 pesos). Beer 20 pesos. Mixed drinks 40 pesos. Cover only for special events. Open W-Sa from 9pm. Cash only.

▨ **Akbal,** Abasolo 870 (☎1257 2986), above **Casa del Maíz** (p. 318). This swanky lounge mixes new and old with electronica and videos pulsing above cabaret-style lush red velvet couches and lamps adorned with feathers. Su is the official gay night. Beer 30 pesos. Mixed drinks 50 pesos. Open Tu-Su 8:30pm-2am. Cash only.

Cafe El Infinito, Jardón 904 Ote. (☎8989 5252; www.cafeinfinito.com). This cafe/bar/used-bookstore/arthouse/movie theater promises politically charged, challenging conversation. Sip international wine (35-52 pesos) or exchange a book (free). Free Wi-Fi. Coffee 20 pesos. Beer 30 pesos. Open Tu-Su 5pm-1am. Cash only.

Bar Wayé, on the corner of Mina and Morelos. A thatched roof over the bar and African masks create a beach atmosphere perfect for the phenomenal live reggae played daily in this laid-back bar. Su nights are especially popular. Beer 15 pesos. No cover. Open Tu-Su 5pm-2am. Cash only.

Manaus, Padre Mier 1045 (☎8989 1920; www.manaus.com.mx), inside the complex called El Zócalo. This sleek, minimalist club gets going late with reggaeton and hip hop, and frequent live groups. No formal dress code, but shorts and flip-flops are frowned upon. Th 50% discount off bill. Cover 60-100 pesos. Open W-Sa 9:30pm-late. MC/V.

Muxets (☎8252 9773), Zaragoza 345 on the corner of Garza. Dark, lounge-style bar primarily geared towards gay men. Drinks 15-50 pesos. Drag shows *(show transvesti)* F-Sa 12:30 and 3:30am. Cover Sa 20 pesos; includes 2 beers. Open W-Sa 9pm-late. Cash only.

COAHUILA

SALTILLO ☎844

Saltillo (pop. 900,000) is an often overlooked retreat from Monterrey. Cosmopolitan yet friendly, Saltillo is home to cafes, bustling markets, rows of book stores, and sunny, pink-paved plazas. Founded in 1577, the city was named for the small *salto de agua* (spring) that sprung miraculously from the desert. Today, Saltillo is famous for its hand-woven *sarapes* (shawls), *pan de pulque*, abundant silver, and calming *centro*, an oasis of relaxing plazas and a gorgeous cathedral.

■ TRANSPORTATION. The **Central de Autobuses** is 3km southwest of the *centro* on Echeverría Sur. To get to the *centro*, exit the terminal and catch minibus #9 (20min., 6:30am-11pm, 5 pesos). To return to the station, catch minibus #9 at the corner of Aldama and Hidalgo, a block down the street from the cathedral, in front of the furniture store's entrance. A taxi from the bus station to the *centro* costs 35 pesos. From the bus station, **Frontera** (☎417 0076) runs to **Matehuala** (3hr., 7 per day 6:15am-11pm, 178 pesos) and **Monterrey** (1½hr., every hr., 55 pesos). **Ómnibus de México** (☎417 0315) serves: **Aguascalientes** (7hr., 10 per day 4am-11pm, 321 pesos); **Guadalajara** (10hr., 5 per day, 479 pesos); **Reynosa** (5hr., every hr. noon-9pm, 207 pesos); **San Luis Potosí** (6hr., 278 pesos); and **Zacatecas** (5hr., 6 per day, 240 pesos). **Transportes del Norte** (☎417 0902) goes to many of the same destinations for similar prices. **Autobuses Saltillo-Parras** (☎417 0063) goes to **Parras de la Fuente** (2½hr., 9 per day 6:30am-7:15pm, 85 pesos).

■ PRACTICAL INFORMATION. The **tourist information** on Saltillo and the state of Coahuila can be found in the hut on the corner of Acuña and Coss. (☎432 3690 or 3692; www.saltillomexico.org. Open M-Sa 9am-2pm and 4-7pm.) Pick up a copy of the bilingual magazine *"Saltillo, una ciudad de altura,"* in hotels or in the kiosk in Plaza de Armas. Other services include: **Banamex,** Allende at Ocampo, behind the Palacio de Gobierno and right off the Plaza de Armas, with a **24hr. ATM.** (open M-F 9am-4pm); **luggage** available at the bus station (5 pesos per hr.; open 24hr.); the **police** (☎434 0450) at Treviño and Echeverría Ote., with another branch in the same building as the tourist module on Acuña and Coss; **emergency** ☎066; **Red Cross** (☎414 3333) at the corner of Cárdenas and Cepeda; **Madero pharmacy** across from Mercado Juárez at the corner of Aldama and Allende (☎412 2559; open daily 8am-11pm) and **Internet** access at **CyberBase,** upstairs at 159 Padre Flores (8 pesos per hr.; open M-Sa 8am-10pm, Su noon-10pm). The local government also provides ▧**free Wi-Fi,** accessible in the areas surrounding Plaza de Armas. The **post office** is on Victoria 303, and has **Mexpost** inside. (☎412 0242. Open M-F 9am-5pm, Sa 9am-1pm.) **Postal Code:** 25000.

■◻ ACCOMMODATIONS AND FOOD. Echeverría, which runs past the bus station at the town's periphery, has several cheap, low-quality places to rest your head. There are few lodgings in the *centro*, except for some luxury options. Don't be put off by having to walk into a shopping center to reach **Hotel Bristol ❷,** Aldama 405. The simple, clean rooms are arranged around an indoor *sala* totally insulated from the noise of the street below. Rooms come with a TV and there is free coffee in the lobby. (☎154 0134. 24hr. bell. Singles and 1-bed doubles 150 pesos; 2-bed 200 pesos. Cash only.) **Hotel Jardín ❷,** on Pedro Flores across from the Mercado Juárez, has plastic-covered chairs, turquoise walls and dim lights straight out of the 1960s. The rooms, while large, are less than sparkling. (☎412

Saltillo

⌂ ACCOMMODATIONS

Hotel Bristol, **4**
Hotel Jardín, **3**
Hotel Saade, **5**
Hotel Urdiñola, **9**

🍎 FOOD

El Vegetariano Feliz, **11**
Mena Pan de Pulque, **8**
Restaurant Principal, **2**
Tacos el Pastor, **6**

★ NIGHTLIFE

Cerdo de Babel, **7**
Frug's, **1**
Los Gitanos, **10**

5916. Reception 24hr. Singles with TV 150 pesos; each additional person 50 pesos. Cash only.) **Hotel Urdiñola ❺**, Victoria 211 (☎414 0940), behind the Palacio de Gobierno, is exquisite but expensive. This retreat comes equipped with fans, cable TV, phones, and room service. (☎414 0940. Singles 300 pesos; doubles 328 pesos; triples 355 pesos; quads 395 pesos.) **Hotel Saade ❺**, Aldama Pte. 397, just before Hotel Bristol, has quiet, well-furnished rooms; top-floor digs offer a panorama of Saltillo. There are three types of rooms: *económico* (singles only), standard, and *ejecutivo*. (☎412 9120. Singles 265/300/320 pesos; doubles 355/375 pesos; triples 410/430; each additional person 55 pesos.)

The area in and around Mercado Juárez holds a huge number of cheap *taquerías*, selling tacos, *tortas* and *licuados*. The most popular is **Tacos El Pastor ❷**, on Plaza Acuña at the corner of Aldama and Padre Flores. Four types of salsa adorn each table, waiting for your order of *bistec* for 30 pesos or *verduras* for 28 pesos. (Open daily 8am-10pm. Cash only). More upscale cafes surround the Plaza de Armas and its neighboring streets. Be sure to sample Saltillo's *pan de pulque* (bread made with an unrefined cactus juice). Sweet and full of pecans and brown sugar, it's available at ☒**Mena Pan de Pulque ❶**, Madero 1350, three long blocks west from Carranza. (☎412 1671. 4 buns for 18 pesos. Open daily 7am-8pm. MC/V.) **Restaurante Principal ❺**, Allende Nte. 702, seven blocks north of Palacio de Gobierno, will satisfy your inner caveman with their *cabecita* (steamed goat's head; 70

THE LOCAL STORY

NEVER TOO MUCH ACCORDION

Whether it's blaring out of a rusty pickup truck, floating out of a bar, or crackling through the speakers of a rickety city bus, *norteño* music is inescapable in the state of Chihuahua. Mournful accordions accompanied by rhythmic guitar riffs are characteristic of this incredibly popular musical style, whose diverse roots mirror those of Mexico itself.

Norteño music, like the name suggests, flourishes in northern Mexico and southern Texas, where Spanish, Creole, and *mestizo* soldiers had a significant presence in the 18th and 19th centuries. Their musical influences, like the guitar and Afro-Caribbean beats, were mixed with folk rhythms of German and Czech immigrants, mainly polkas and waltzes, creating incredibly unique and complex hybrid styles: the storytelling, ballad-oriented *corrido* and the more lively *norteño*.

Santiago Jiménez and Narciso Martínez popularized *norteño* music in the 1930s, and by the 1950s their recordings had spread throughout the Americas to dance halls and bars. *Norteño* is still evolving, with modern groups like **Costumbre** combining western music with traditional *norteño* melodies. Turn on Mexican music channels and you'll find that *norteño* has even made it into the currently exploding reggaeton genre, a fusion between Latin and hip-hop music.

pesos) or a goat leg or kidney (130 pesos). Squeamish diners can try the *enchiladas* (60-65 pesos) and delicious cheese and chicken *chilaquiles* (corn tortilla casserole) for 54 pesos. (☎414 3384. Open daily 8am-midnight. Cash only.) On the other end of the dietary spectrum, **El Vegetariano Feliz ❸**, Hidalgo 423, serves soy-filled *burritos* (35 pesos), vegetable *tamales* (35 pesos), yogurts, and fresh-squeezed juices. *Comida corrida* 45 pesos. (☎410 0875. Adjoining Internet cafe; Internet access 10 pesos per hr. Open daily 9am-9pm. Cash only.)

🟦 **SIGHTS.** Saltillo's pride and joy is the recently opened 🟦**Museo del Desierto,** Pérez Treviño 3745, in Parque Las Maravillas. An incredible variety of prickly cacti grow in the museum's garden, mingling with tortoises and prairie dogs. Inside, exhibits range from dinosaur skeletons unearthed in the Coahuilan desert to a massive ant farm. Getting here is complicated: Friday through Sunday, take the *tranvía* trolley from the cathedral (4 per day 10:25am-5:25pm, 20 pesos). Otherwise, take a taxi for about 35 pesos. (☎410 6633. Open Tu-Su 10am-6pm. 34 pesos, children 24 pesos.) Back in town lies **Museo de las Aves de México,** Hidalgo 600, at Bolívar. The museum is home to more than 2350 species of birds, stuffed and displayed in natural settings. Over 75% are species native to Mexico. A rear garden holds live raptors and other birds currently being rehabilitated for release into the wild. (☎414 0168; www.museodelasaves.org. Open Tu-Su 10am-6pm, Su 11am-6pm. 10 pesos, students and children 5 pesos.)

Saltillo's most stunning sights are its cathedral and open plazas. The **Catedral de Santiago** was built from 1745 to 1800 and towers above the city. Pilgrims visit the Catedral's Santo Cristo chapel to venerate its 1608 image of Christ. (Open daily 9am-1pm and 4-8pm.) A few blocks east of the center lies **Alameda Zaragoza,** a pleasant park which features statues of heroes of Mexico's independence and a small lake in the shape of Mexico. To explore Saltillo's history and panoramic view, hike up Miguel Hidalgo and turn left on Gómez three blocks after the Museo de las Aves. The **Iglesia del Ojo de Agua** was built in 1905 on the spot where the *saltillo* was first discovered in 1577. Continue past the church up to the small pink-painted plaza. Known as **Plaza Mexico** or **El Mirador,** this is where US President Zachary Taylor's army camped before their battle with Santa Anna's troops in the Mexican-American War in 1846-48. The site offers a breathtaking view of Saltillo.

🟦🟦 **SHOPPING AND ENTERTAINMENT.** Since the 1600s, Saltillo has been known for its tradition of weaving. Famed throughout Mexico for its colorful wool *sarapes* (shawls), the city has invented its own style, called the "saltillo." The best place to buy *sarapes* is **El Sarape de Saltillo**, Hidalgo 305, before Museo de las Aves. (☎414 9634 or 4889. Open M-Sa 9am-1pm and 3-7pm.) For less expensive *sarapes*, crafts, and silver, visit **Mercado Juárez** behind Plaza Acuña.

The downtown **Centro Cultural (Teatro García Carrillo)**, on Aldama in Plaza Acuña, presents regular sculpture and art exhibitions, films, and concerts free of charge. Drop by to check the list of weekly events. (Open Tu-Su 10am-2pm and 4-7pm. Free.) The **Instituto Coahuilense de Cultura (ICOCULT)**, on the Plaza de Armas at Juárez and Hidalgo, has an artsy cafe, bookstore, and gallery featuring local and international artists, as well as information on cultural events throughout Saltillo and the state. (☎410 2033; www.icocult.gob.mx. Open Tu-Su 10am-9pm.) In mid-summer, catch the two-week **Feria de Saltillo,** featuring agricultural and art exhibitions, performances, and *sarapes*, a celebration that dates back to the 16th century. Most of the action takes place outside the city, on Mex. 57. On the weekends, trams leave from Plaza de Armas; alternatively take a taxi (25-30 pesos). Pick up a schedule of performances at hotels or the tourist office.

⬛ NIGHTLIFE. Most of Saltillo's nightlife is concentrated around the *centro*, with bars featuring live music on the streets Padre Flores, Ocampo, and Juárez. Heavy wooden tables, alternative rock, and cubist paintings lend an artsy air to **⬛Cerdo de Babel Taverna,** Ocampo 324, popular with young locals. (☎103 3934. Beer 17-20 pesos. Mixed drinks 30 pesos. Open Tu-Sa 7pm-3am. Cash only.) **Los Gitanos,** upstairs at Juárez 259, behind Palacio del Gobierno, offers live rock or *trova* nightly, free chips, and a 2-for-1 Happy hour daily 7-9pm. (Beer 20 pesos. Mixed drinks 30 pesos. Open Tu-Sa 7pm-late. Cash only.) True clubbers will want to hit **Frug's,** at Acuña and Aguirre. This big club with an open pavilion plays *norteño* and Spanish pop music. (Beer 15 pesos. Open Th-Sa 9:30pm-4am.)

TORREÓN ☎871

Torreón (pop. 550,000) began its days as a railroad hub, and for most tourists it remains a waystation seen only in transit., a northern center of light industry. If you must stay in scorching Torreón, see Cristo de Las Noas—the 31m tall statue of Christ is the world's third largest—and make the daytrip to the heavenly vineyards of Parras de La Fuente.

▐ TRANSPORTATION. The Central de Autobuses de Torreón, Juárez 4700 (720 3124), is about 7km east of the *centro*. **Estrella Blanca** (☎720 0808) sends **buses** to: **Durango** (3hr., 9 per day, 173 pesos); **Guadalajara** (10hr., 4 per day, 431 pesos); **Matamoros** (10hr., 4 per day, 430 pesos); **Mexico City** (13hr., 1 per day, 731 pesos); **Zacatecas** (6hr., every hr., 280 pesos). From the bus station, catch a very slow *pesero* to the *centro* (40min., 3.60 pesos). **Ómnibus de México** provides service to **Chihuahua** (7hr., 6 per day, 315 pesos) and **Hidalgo del Parral** (4hr., 3 per day, 212 pesos). **Autotransportes Parras-Torreón** services **Parras de la Fuente** (3hr., 7 per day, 105 pesos) and smaller towns on the way. **Transportes Coahuilenses** serves smaller towns within the state, including **Cuatro Ciénegas** (3½hr., 137 pesos). **Taxis** to the *centro* cost 40 pesos. **Budget,** Paseo de la Rosita 910, or at the Hotel Fiesta Inn in the *centro*, offers **car rentals.** (☎721 9091; torreon@budgetansa.com. Cars from 800 pesos per day.) A special **street car** shuttles tourists from the Fiesta Inn Hotel to all major sites in Torreón, including the museums, Cristo de las Noas, and the many plazas. (Fiesta Inn Hotel, Paseo de la Rosita 910. ☎732 2244 or 720 1861. Daily 9am-6pm, frequency depends on demand. Prices vary.)

⬛▐ ORIENTATION AND PRACTICAL INFORMATION. Hotels, restaurants, and most services listed are located in the area immediately surrounding the **Plaza de**

Armas, which is bordered by **Morelos** to the north and **Juárez** to the south. **Cepeda** is at the eastern edge of the plaza, **Carrillo** at the western. The **Bosque Venustiano Carranza** is 2km east of the plaza. One can catch buses and *carritos* (collective taxis) going to almost any part of Torreón.

The **tourist office,** Pasco de la Rosita 308, is a hike from the *centro.* It posts informative maps in front of the Palacio de Gobierno and the Plaza de Armas. (☎732 2244, toll-free English line 800 718 4220. Open M-F 9am-6pm.) **Banks** with **24hr. ATMs** cluster near the Plaza de Armas. **Banco Santander,** at the corner of Carrillo and Morelos on the Plaza de Armas, **exchanges currency.** (Open M-F 9am-4pm.) **American Express** is on García 95 Sur at Matamoros. (☎718 3620. Open M-F 9am-2pm.) **Luggage storage** is available at the bus station. (4 pesos per hr. Open 24hr.) To get to **Lavandería los Ángeles,** Independencia 37 Ote., at Colón, walk to Independencia and then catch a bus (3.30 pesos) to Colón. (☎713 4459. 50 pesos. Open M-F 10am-2pm and 4-8pm, Sa 10am-5pm.) Other services include: **emergency** ☎060; **police,** at Colón and Revolución (☎733 6759); **Red Cross,** Cuauhtémoc 462 (☎713 0088 or 0192); **Farmacia Santander,** at Morelos and Carillo (☎712 8738; open 24hr.); **Hospital los Ángeles,** Paseo del Tecnológico 909 (☎729 0400 or 0415); **Telecomm,** Morelos 775, east of the Plaza de Armas, which has **fax** and **Western Union** (☎/fax 716 6848; open M-F 8am-7pm); **Internet** access at **Copias e Internet,** Morelos 1175 Pte. (open daily 9am-9pm; 15 pesos per hr.); and the **post office,** at Juárez and Galeana, nine blocks east of Plaza de Armas, on the first floor of Palacio Federal (☎712 0264; **Mexpost** next door; open M-F 9am-5pm, Sa 9am-1pm). **Postal Code:** 27000.

⌖⌂ ACCOMMODATIONS AND FOOD. Torreón's budget accommodations cluster around the Plaza de Armas and tend to be large hotels from the 1930s and 1940s. Plenty of functional options can be found along Morelos, east of the Plaza de Armas. **Hotel Galicia ❶,** Cepeda 273 Sur, between Juárez and Morelos, has funky rooms with individual balconies. Fans are available upon request. (☎716 1111. Singles 125 pesos; doubles 160 pesos; triples 210 pesos. Cash only.) **Hotel Paseo ❺,** Morelos 547 Pte., is relatively pricey but without a doubt the best deal in Torreón. Amenities include pristine individual bath and cable TV. Wi-Fi in the lobby. (☎716 0303. Check-out 2pm. Singles 280 pesos; doubles 360 pesos. MC/V.)

The *centro*'s curbs and sidewalks teem with *torta* and *gordita* vendors. Locals crowd **Lonches Roz y Morelos ❶,** one such cart with a small TV at Rodríguez and Morelos. (Sandwiches 12-16 pesos. Open daily 11am-6pm. Cash only.) **De Granero ❷,** on Morelos 444 Pte., is a vegetarian restaurant popular with Torreón's health-conscious residents. They serve fruit salads with granola and yogurt (35 pesos), soy *chorizo* burritos (10 pesos), and a wide selection of *licuados* (10-20 pesos). There is also an attached health-food store and bakery. (☎712 7144. Open daily 8am-9pm. MC/V.) Other locations are at Estadio and Carranza (☎717 8441) and Constitución 712 (☎718 7661)

◪ SIGHTS. Parks and museums dot the downtown area, including the 30-block **Bosque Venustiano Carranza,** on Cuauhtémoc between Juárez and Bravo, a favorite among Torreón's families. The optimistically named Bosque (forest) is home to the **Museo Regional de la Laguna,** Juárez 1300 Ote. The museum holds Licio Lago's collection of pre-Hispanic art and artifacts, complete with several well-executed fakes, which managed to fool Lago and still confound some archaeologists, in addition to a display on the Laguna area's nomadic desert cultures. (☎713 9545. Open Tu-Su 10am-6:30pm. 27 pesos, children free.) Not far from the museum, a crew of **break dancers** monopolizes the Bosque's open-air stage with elaborate footwork and headspins. (To get to the Bosque, catch a 4-peso *colectivo* labeled "Ruta Centro" on Juárez at the Plaza de Armas. It drops off and picks up 2 blocks from the entrance. Taxis 20 pesos.) Torreón is also home to the third largest statue of Christ in the world, ▧**Cristo de las Noas,** which spreads its imposing arms over the city and surrounding walls, towers, and rotundas. Follow the stairs to the summit for an amazing view of the town with gospel accompaniment courtesy of the large speakers nearby. A recreated Holy Land—with a calvary and caves of Gethsemane in the works—flanks the statue. The year 2007 marked the statue's centennial anniversary. To get there, take a taxi from the *centro* (round-trip 70 pesos).

▧▧ **ENTERTAINMENT AND NIGHTLIFE.** Lounging in the **Plaza de Armas** is by far the most popular type of entertainment in Torreón. On weekends, the whole city comes out to polka, salsa, and tango under the trees as the speakers blare *música norteña. Caballeros* (gentlemen) sport cowboy hats, tight jeans, and boots, while *damas* (ladies) wear shimmering dresses. Torreón's bars often feature live musicians. Across from the plaza, inside Hotel Palacio Real, is **El Greco,** Morelos 1280 Pte., which often hosts live bands on weekends. Check the schedule posted outside for a listing of events. (☎716 0000. Corona 20 pesos. Happy hour 7-9pm, 2-for-1 drinks. Open Tu-Sa 6pm-2am. MC/V.) **El Tecolote Bar Bohemio,** on Morelos 657 Pte., is a popular hangout in the *centro.* (Beer 15 pesos. Open daily 8pm-2am. AmEx/MC/V.) The giant, zinc-plated **Teatro Nazas,** Cepeda Sur 150, is considered one of Mexico's most modern theatres and can hold up to 2000 audience members. The auditorium hosts plays, musical concerts, and even operas. (For information on shows and times, call ☎712 4797.) Torreón has two main festivals, the **Feria del Algodón** (cotton fair; mid-Aug. to mid-Sept.) and the **Feria Laguna** (regional fair; early Oct.). The **Gran Reguta del Río Nazas** is a boat race on the city's river in early July.

▧ **DAYTRIP FROM TORREÓN**

PARRAS DE LA FUENTE

Parras de La Fuente (pop. 27,000) lies between Torreón and Saltillo, about a 2½ hour bus ride from each city. From Torreón, Autotransportes Parras-Torreón (☎422 1139) services Parras (7 per day, 105 pesos) and returns to Torreón (5 per day, 6:30am-7pm). The local camioneta #12 runs to the vineyards and the tourist office via the Central (8 pesos). The easiest way to get around Parras is by car; taxis are available at the Central or by phone (☎422 1111). The bus stops at the tourist office, 3km outside of town on the highway that runs north to Mex. 40. (☎422 0259. Open daily 10am-1pm and 3:30-7pm.)

True to its nickname, the "Oasis of Coahuila," Parras de la Fuente blooms in the desert. Fields of *parras* (grapevines) and walnut trees surround the little colonial town. Parras's attractions are few but tranquil: visiting a historic winery, swimming in freshwater *estanques* (ponds), and relaxing on patios and in plazas.

The oldest **vineyard** in the New World—established in 1597—still produces wine at ▧**Casa Madero,** 4km outside town. The dark cellars, period mosaics, 20 ft. fermentation tanks, ancient wine presses, and vine-shaded paths are worth seeing, even if you can't understand the tour. Dark and white grapes are in season from July-September (A taxi from the *centro* to the vineyard costs 40 pesos, or you can take the local Paila-bound bus from the bus station for 8 pesos. ☎422 0055; www.madero.com.mx. Guided tours in Spanish begin whenever a group arrives. Open daily 9am-5pm. Free.) Wines and brandies made at the Casa Madero estate are for sale near the winery's entrance. Most are of lower quality—the good stuff is quickly bought by local restaurants and resorts—but are still worth a taste. (45-650 pesos per bottle, depending on size). For true Bacchic excess, visit Parras from August 3 to 19, during the **Feria de la Uva** (Festival of the Grape). New wines are uncorked, processions snake through town, and everyone takes part in the grape-stomping celebration. The rowdiest days are August 9 and 10. Non-booze-related sights also grace Parras. **Estanque Hacienda** and **Estanque de la Luz** are two popular ponds great for swimming and waterside relaxation. (Taxis from the *centro* around 30 pesos. 10 pesos. Open daily 10am-6pm.)

CUATRO CIÉNEGAS   ☎869

Although the town of Cuatro Ciénegas (pop. 8000) is not well-equipped for tourism, the 843km wildlife preserve surrounding the community makes for a not-to-be-missed eco-adventure. Located in the valley between two mountain ranges, the Cuatro Ciénegas marsh area offers a unique biosphere of mixed desert and swampland flora and fauna unavailable anywhere else in the Chihuahua Desert. Indeed, there is no other place like Cuatro Ciénegas in the entire world.

🖪🛈 TRANSPORTATION AND PRACTICAL INFORMATION. The **Camionera Central** (☎696 0711) is right in the *centro* on Hidalgo, and offers second-class bus service. **Autotransportes Coahuilenses** runs to: **Monterrey** (180 pesos); **Monclova** (2hr., every hour, 45 pesos.); **Torreón** (3½hr., 8 daily, 137 pesos) via **San Pedro** (2hr., 119 pesos); **Saltillo** (5½hr., 167 pesos). There are no taxis in town.

The **tourist information office** located on the corner of Juárez and Venustiano Carranza can give helpful advice about the area, but is likely to hold sporadic hours (☎696 0574. Open M-Sa 10:30am-5pm). Accurate and free information about the reserve can also be obtained at **Herpetarium.** Other services include: **Banco Santander** on 201 Zaragoza cornered with Escobedo (**24hr. ATM;** open M-Sa 9am to 4pm, Su 10am-2pm); **emergency** ☎066; **police** (☎696 0810); **Clínica de Salud,** Juárez Ote. (☎696 0210); **Farmacia Similar,** 202 Juárez Ote. (open daily 10am-2pm and 4pm-8pm); **Cyber Cafe** 200 Juárez Pte. (Internet access 10 pesos per hr.; open daily 8am-10pm); and the **post office,** Hidalgo 216 Pte. (☎696 0196). **Postal Code:** 27640.

🖍🛏 ACCOMMODATIONS AND FOOD. Hotel Ibarra ❸, Zaragoza 200, offers basic amenities including TV and hot showers. (☎696 0129. Singles 200 pesos; doubles 300 pesos. Cash only.) **Hotel Cuatro Ciénegas ❶,** Hidalgo 206 across from the Hotel Plaza, has even cheaper rooms and TV, but no private baths. (☎796 0693. Singles 150 pesos; doubles 200 pesos. Cash only.) **Camping** is readily available at **Río Los Mezquites, Poza la Becerra,** and **Las Playitas** as long as you bring your own tent. Costs are subject to the whim of the particular landowner, but are rarely more than 50 pesos per person.

La Casona ❹, Zaragoza 109, serves excellent steaks any style (90-110 pesos) in front of a big screen TV. (☎696 0073. Beer 20 pesos. Traditional *antojitos* 40-60 pesos per plate. Open daily 8am-10pm. Hours likely to change during soccer games. AmEx/MC/V.) For cheaper fare and hearty breakfasts, head to El Padrino ❸, at 204 Juárez. Enjoy chicken *flautitas* (8-for-25 pesos) or *huevos al gusto* for 20-35 pesos. (Open daily 8am-6pm. Cash only.)

🔲 SIGHTS. In town, check out the 🖾**Acuario y Herpetario Minckley,** Morelos Sur 112, run by the extremely knowledgeable *biologista* Arturo Contreras, who claims to have once been the world's youngest ecotourism guide. Among the main attractions are venomous *cascabeles* (rattlesnakes), giant vinagroons (whip scorpions), and extremely aggressive red-eared turtles. Photos can be taken with the non-poisonous vipers for 30 pesos. The Acuario is staffed entirely by enthusiastic volunteer adolescents. (☎696 1102. Admission 20 pesos. Open M-Sa 10am-1pm and 4-8pm.) Also open to visitors is the **Museo Casa de Carranza,** V. Carranza 105, where Mexico's first constitutionalist president passed his childhood years. Many of the revolutionary leader's documents and personal effects are still kept intact within. Permission must be granted by Venustiano's fifth-generation granddaughter in order to take photos. (Open Tu-Su 9am-1pm. Free.) Wineries such as **Bodegas Ferriño,** share part of Cuatro Ciénegas's 150-year old vintner tradition. (☎ 696 0033. Call ahead for directions and tour arrangements. Open M-Sa 8am-8pm. Free tours and tastings.)

◢ DAYTRIP FROM CUATRO CIÉNEGAS

AREA DE PROTECCIÓN DE FLORA Y FAUNA CUATRO CIÉNEGAS

The Reserve is about 20min by car, southwest of the town along Hwy. 30. If you've brought your own vehicle, you shouldn't have any problems moving around, although a few sites are restricted to guided tours. ◣Arturo Contreras and the Minckley Acuario team (p. 328) offer car tours and excellent biological info on the various critters and vegetation. (500 pesos to take a guide along with you in your own vehicle. 1000 pesos for a bilingual tour of every inch with Arturo himself. It is advisable to arrive at the visitor's center, Morelos 112, Su early on the weekends.)

There are few indications that an oasis exists in the arid and unforgiving desert, within the 4000 hectares surrounding the strip off Hwy. 30. Yet, the misplaced marshlands known simply as **La Reserva** are home to almost 300 native species of flora and fauna—about three dozen of which are endemic and isolated, meaning they are native to the area and never migrate out of the biosphere. Even more surprising is the fact that there are only a handful of each species, meriting La Reserva's nickname: the Galapagos of Mexico. Among the pocket endemics are foxes, scorpions, snails, and poisonous frogs. The system of underground rivers flowing under the clay-baked soil, along with over 550 lagoons, bogs, lakes, and ponds—collectively known as *pozas*—provide specimens with vital nutrients.

For those interested in a quick, pre-ecoadventure picnic, the turnoff for **Río Los Mezquites** is 6km down the road on the left. Follow the road to a refreshing stream, complete with barbecues, *palapas*, and public toilets. Swimming is allowed in most parts of the river. Camping is also available with landowner's permission and the payment of a small fee.

> **🆃🅸🅿 ALL NATURAL.** Although swimming is allowed in many of the *pozas* on the reserve, suntan lotions, hair gels, hand salves, and oily lubricants are entirely prohibited. The many fish and microflora inhabiting the water will perish if introduced to certain chemicals.

Begin your explorations at **Poza las Tortugas.** One of the largest and clearest *pozas*, Las Tortugas is also the only artificial watering hole in the park. Almost 50 species of fish live under the water's surface, the majority of which are named after founding biologist Dr. Minckley. Turtle Pond is also the host of the reserve's informative **Visitor's Center.** (Open Tu-Su 10am-7pm. 25 pesos.) A short walk away is the clean, cerulean **Poza Azul,** maintained entirely by local funding. Buses from town (25min., 25 pesos) run twice daily to the popular **Poza la Becerra,** which offers the marshland's only chance to soak in hot, pristine waters right in the middle of the desert. Schools of *coahuilense* children stock the *pozas* in this area with schools of *coahuilense* fish. (☎ 696 0574. Open daily 9am-9pm. 40 pesos, children 20 pesos.) Don't miss the stretch of gleaming, white gypsum sand known as **Las Arenales**, the second largest sand deposit in the world after New Mexico's White Sands. Guided tours are mandatory for this section; inquire at the tourist office. The dunes are also home to the rare camel-hoof *alacrán* (scorpion).

SAN LUIS POTOSÍ

SAN LUIS POTOSÍ ☎ 444

In 1592, prospectors dreaming of gold and missionaries seeking to convert the indigenous Guachichil and Tlaxcaltec tribes to Catholicism founded San Luis Potosí (pop. 900,000). Their legacy lives on in "The City of Plazas," where mining financed the construction of gorgeous cobblestone squares, gardens, palaces, and churches. Having twice served as the capital of Mexico, San Luis Potosí also housed the jailed Francisco Madero, whose 1910 Plan de San Luis Potosí sparked the Mexican Revolution. *Potosinos* are immensely proud of the historical importance of their city, as well as its modern-day beauty, occupying their music- and art-filled plazas from dawn to dusk.

▟ TRANSPORTATION

Flights: Aeropuerto Internacional Ponciano Arriaga (**SLP;** ☎822 2119), 25min. north of the city. Buy tickets at **2001 Viajes**, Obregón 604 (☎812 2953). Open M-F 9am-2pm and 4-8pm, Sa 9:30am-2pm. Served by: **AeroCalifornia** (☎811 8050), **AeroMar** (☎817 5062), **Aerolitoral** (☎818 7371), **American Airlines** (☎822 1860), **Continental** (☎817 8445), and **Mexicana de Aviación** (☎813 3399).

Buses: To get downtown from the **Transportes Terrestres Potosina** (**TTP;** ☎822 3180) catch an "Alameda" or "Centro" bus (5:30am-10:30pm, 5 pesos) to the end of Plaza Alameda at Constitución. Continue down Othón, past Plaza del Carmen, until the *centro*, Plaza de Armas (also called Jardín Hidalgo). A **taxi** costs 28 pesos; get your fixed-price taxi ticket at the bus station counter.

Estrella Blanca (☎816 5477) has regular and *de lujo* service. Prices listed below are for *economico* (regular). Buses run to: **Aguascalientes** (3hr., every hr. 5am-9pm, 101 pesos); **Guadalajara** (6hr., 22 per day, 221 pesos); **Monterrey** (7hr., 5 per day, 336 pesos); **Zacatecas** (3hr., 19 per day, 105 pesos). **Ómnibus de México** (☎816 8161) runs to: **Mexico City** (6hr., every hr., 298 pesos); **Reynosa** (9hr.; 8:30pm, 1:30am; 380 pesos); **Saltillo** (5hr., 7 per day, 278 pesos); **Tampico** (7hr., 3 per day, 315 pesos). **Transportes Tamaulipas** (☎816 6964) serves **Matehuala** (2hr., every hr. 7am-1am, 121 pesos) and **Matamoros** (10hr., 3 per day, 467 pesos).

Car Rental: Hertz, Obregón 670 (☎812 9500). Rates start at 250 pesos per day plus insurance and mileage. 25+. Open M-F 9am-2pm and 4-8pm, Sa 9am-2pm.

✳ ❷ ORIENTATION AND PRACTICAL INFORMATION

San Luis Potosí is at the center of a triangle formed by Mexico's three largest cities—Guadalajara, Mexico City, and Monterrey. Five main routes, **Rutas 57, 85, 70, 49,** and **80,** make their way here. Once in the city, streets have a habit of changing names as they pass through the main plazas—keep that in mind and a map in hand. The city centers on the neighboring squares, **Plaza de Armas, Plaza de Los Fundadores,** and **Plaza del Carmen.** South of the center, other neighborhoods of interest include **Jardín de San Francisco** and **Barrio del San Miguelito,** south on Zaragoza. To the east lies **Parque Alameda** and **Barrio de San Sebastian.** To the west **Zona Carranza,** along Carranza, hosts more upscale and modern shopping, restaurants, and bars.

Tourist Office: Turismo Municipal, Jardín Jidalgo 5 (☎812 2770; www.san-luis.gob.mx/turismo) on the 1st fl. of the Palacio Municipal, in the northeastern corner of Plaza de Armas. Great English-speaking staff and information. Open M-F 8am-

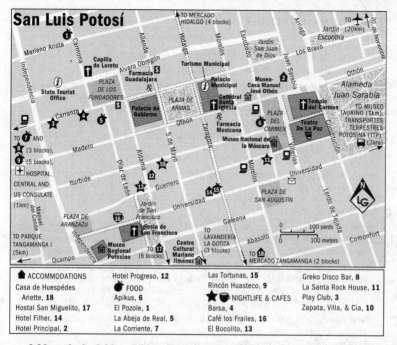

San Luis Potosí

ACCOMMODATIONS	Hotel Progreso, 12	Las Tortunas, 15	Greko Disco Bar, 8
Casa de Huespédes	● FOOD	Rincón Huasteco, 9	La Santa Rock House, 11
Ariette, 18	Apikus, 6	★ ● NIGHTLIFE & CAFES	Play Club, 3
Hostal San Miguelito, 17	El Pozole, 1	Barsa, 4	Zapata, Villa, & Cia, 10
Hotel Filher, 14	La Abeja de Real, 5	Café los Frailes, 16	
Hotel Principal, 2	La Corriente, 7	El Bocolito, 13	

8:30pm, Sa-Su 9:30am-7:30pm. **State tourist office,** Obregón 520 (☎812 9939), 1 block west of Plaza de los Fundadores. Information on attractions throughout the state. Open M-F 8am-9pm, Sa-Su 8am-2pm.

Consulate: US, Carranza 2076, 4th fl. (☎811 7802 or 7803). Open M-F 8:30am-1:30pm. In case of emergency, police and tourist office have consulate employees' home numbers.

Currency Exchange and Banks: Casas de cambio lie along Morelos, north of Plaza de Armas. Many banks lie near Plaza de Armas and are open M-F 9am-4pm, Sa 10am-2pm. **Banamex,** at Allende and Obregón, 1 block east of Plaza de Armas, has a **24hr. ATM** and exchanges traveler's checks with no commission.

Luggage Storage: At the bus station. 5 pesos per hr. Open 24hr.

Laundromat: Lavandería La Gotita, 5 de Mayo 870A (☎814 2783), at Hernandez. 30 pesos per load. Open M-F 10am-8pm, Sa 10am-3pm.

Emergency: ☎066.

Police: (☎072 or 812 2244), at the corner of Hidalgo and Reforma.

Red Cross: (☎815 3635 or 820 3902), on Juárez at Gutiérrez.

Pharmacy: Farmacia Mexicana, Othón 180 (☎812 3880). Open daily 8am-2am.

Hospital: Central, Carranza 2395 (☎817 9600), 20 blocks west of the *centro*.

Fax Office: Ahorratel (☎822 1912), outside at the bus station between the 1st- and 2nd-class terminals. Open daily 8am-9pm.

Internet Access: Cafe Plaza, Escobedo 315, on Plaza del Carmen. 12 pesos per hr. Open daily 9am-9pm.

Post Office: Universidad 526A, 2 blocks south of Plaza del Carmen. **Mexpost** inside. Open M-F 8am-5pm, Sa 9am-1pm. **Postal Code:** 78000.

🏠 ACCOMMODATIONS

Cheap hotels can be found off Alemeda Juan Sarabia, at Los Bravos and 20 de Noviembre, but better options are available. Meanwhile, in the *centro*, old hotels relive their glory days with large rooms and plaza views.

🏅 **Hostal San Miguelito,** Fernando Rosas 530 (☎814 8382; http://mx.geocities.com/hostalsanmiguelito/). Walk south on Aldama as it becomes Vallejo. Bear right around the Plaza San Miguelito, walk 2 blocks, and take a right on Fernando Rosas. About 15min. from the center, the cobblestoned neighborhood is charming and cheap—this homey hostel is worth the walk. Large cheery dorms, TV room, kitchen, and painted rooftop patio. Free coffee and tea. Internet access 10 pesos per hr. Laundry 25 pesos. 24hr. bell. Dorms 100 pesos per person. Cash only. ❶

Casa de Huéspedes Arlette, Zaragoza 855 (☎812 7441). Just south of the center. Slightly dark, but large and clean, the rooms here ring a lovely blue-and-yellow tiled courtyard with parakeets and tables. Kitchen facilities available. 24hr. bell. Singles and doubles with shared bath 110 pesos, with private bath 170 pesos. Cash only. ❶

Hotel Principal, Juan Sarabía 145 (☎812 0704), near the Templo del Carmen. Bright yellow walls light up this otherwise unremarkable hotel, but it is a good deal for the location. Rooms have cable TV. Singles 153 pesos; doubles 204 pesos; triples 255 pesos. Cash only. ❷

Hotel Progreso, Aldama 415, off Guerrero, near Plaza de San Francisco. No longer the luxury hotel it once was, but the high ceilings and grand lobby maintain an antique allure. Tall, dark hallways lead to clean, dark rooms. Fans in all rooms. Singles and doubles from 275 pesos; triples 345 pesos; quads 395 pesos. Cash only. ❸

Hotel Filher, Universidad 375 (☎812 1562), at Zaragoza, 3 blocks south of Plaza de Armas. Gorgeous rooms, with bright paintings, beautiful wool bedspreads, and wooden furniture. Amenities include fan, phone, cable TV, and free bottled water. Singles 415 pesos; doubles 465 pesos. MC/V. ❺

🍴 FOOD

The sheer number and range of restaurants near the *centro* will satisfy everyone, including vegetarians and those looking for international cuisine. *Enchiladas potosinas*, a regional favorite, are stuffed with cheese and then fried. Cactus is used to make such diverse dishes as *melcocha* (molasses candy) and *nopalitos* (cactus slices cooked in a salty mixture of garlic, onion, and tomato sauce). The cheapest Mexican food can be found at the countertop restaurants in **Mercado Tangamanga,** south of the center on Zaragoza, off the Jardín Colón, and **Mercado Hidalgo,** north of the center on Hidalgo. **Farmacia Guadalupe**, on the Plaza de Armas, also has a full grocery section. (Open daily 7am-2am. MC/V.)

🏅 **La Corriente,** Carranza 700 (☎812 9304 or 1965). A cross between a ranch house and the garden of Eden: red tile floors and stuccoed walls meet a skylight and hanging vines. The traditional Mexican food manages to surpass the relaxing ambience. Try the divine *enchiladas potosinas* (40 pesos) or a juicy steak with guacamole and black beans (90 pesos). *Comida corrida* 60 pesos. Open M-Sa 8am-midnight, Su 8am-6pm. AmEx/MC/V. ❺

La Abeja de Real, 104 Díaz de Leon (☎814 1365). Just off the Plaza de los Fundadores, this restaurant serves health food, with cafeteria-like seating and speedy service. Mushroom quesadillas and veggie burgers 10-20 pesos. Yogurt parfaits 16 pesos. Fresh juices 15 pesos. Open M-Sa 9am-6pm, Su 9:30am-5pm. Cash only. ❶

Rincón Huasteco, Cuauhtémoc 232 (☎814 6003). Walk west on Carranza for 5 blocks after Independencia, take a left on Tres Guerras, and walk 4 more blocks.

Named after the pre-Hispanic culture native to San Luis Potosí, this restaurant specializes in traditional regional dishes, such as *bocoles* (8 pesos), *tamales* in banana leaves (15 pesos) and *huastecán* bread (3.50 pesos). *Antojitos* 7.50-38 pesos. Entrees 30-90 pesos. Open daily 8am-11pm. MC/V. ❸

Las Tortunas, Zaragoza 396 (☎812 8263) at Universidad. A bright cafe popular with local students for cheap *tortas*, with fillings such as avocado and egg (14 pesos) and *chorizo* (16 pesos). Breakfast and *antojitos* from 17 pesos. Open daily 8am-10pm. ❶

El Pozole, Carmona 205 (☎814 9900), at Artista. Bright eating area when the sun is shining and a friendly staff add to the enjoyment. Serves a limited menu of regional specialties, such as *pozole* (45 pesos) and tacos (30 pesos). Open Tu-Su noon-11:30pm. Cash only. ❸

🔘 SIGHTS

As the former center of the state's booming silver and gold trade, prosperous San Luis Potosí had the money and the stature to build some of the country's finest museums, cathedrals, and plazas. The sheer number of beautiful sights can be almost intimidating; fortunately, the majority have historical markers in English and Spanish and are within easy walking distance of one another.

PLAZA DE ARMAS. Called the "City of Plazas," San Luis Potosí has four main town squares. The most central of these is Plaza de Armas, filled with trees and lounging *potosinos*. At the start of the 17th century, residents watched bullfights from the balconies of the surrounding buildings. Since 1848, a red sandstone gazebo bearing the names of famous Mexican musicians has graced the plaza, which hosts local bands. Today, loudspeakers hooked up to the gazebo blare popular music, political announcements, and soccer games. Check the Turismo Municipal for events. *(Concerts Th and Su evenings.)* The **Santa Iglesia Cathedral** is the city's main landmark, with two bell towers that play different melodies every hour. It began as a simple church completed in 1710, and "upgraded" to a cathedral when San Luis Potosí became a diocese in 1855. Miners donated gold and silver to glorify the interior, and marble statues of the apostles stand between the Solomonic columns of the Baroque facade. *(Open daily 7:30am-2pm and 4:30-8:30pm. Free.)* Located on the east side of the Plaza sits the **Palacio Municipal,** constructed in 1838 where the old Royal Houses were located. It served as the City Hall until being converted into a center of fine arts. The rest of the building houses the tourist office and provides the local artist community with gallery space and other services. The west side of the plaza is marked by the Neoclassical facade of the **Palacio de Gobierno,** constructed in 1798. Briefly serving as Mexico's capital in 1863, the structure was renovated in 1950 and is now San Luis Potosí's administrative center. Displays on the second floor feature murals, statues, and plaques. In 1867, President Benito Juárez signed former emperor Maximilian's death sentence here.

PLAZA DEL CARMEN. This bright, lively plaza hosts street performers, vendors, and crowds of teenagers and college students milling around at night. Towering over the northeastern corner is the **Templo del Carmen,** a serene church constructed from 1749 to 1764 and regarded by many *potosinos* to be the city's most beautiful religious building. Worshippers pray here all day. It features hanging chandeliers, golden altars, and a huge mural of the Crucifixion. During the Mexican Revolution, the government used the convent to jail local rebels. Once released, the prisoners went on to lead the revolt of San Luis Potosí. *(Open daily 7am-1:30pm and 4-9pm. Free.)* South of the Templo sits the **Teatro de La Paz,** a theater so acoustically well constructed that most performers don't even need microphones. The *salón* holds a collection of modern art, the foyer is filled with sculptures and murals, and the theater hosts everything from international dance festivals to children's theater. *(Teatro behind Templo del Carmen. ☎812 5209. Pick up a schedule at the tourist office or look for posters outside the theater. Tickets from 50 pesos.)*

JARDÍN DE SAN FRANCISCO. San Luis Potosí has at least one garden for each of its seven districts. This one, on Plaza de San Francisco, is distinguished by its bronze fountain, cobblestone streets, and pink sandstone buildings. Recently, the west side of the garden on Universidad has become a nightlife hot spot. Many bars, cafes, and art vendors crowd the street. It's the perfect spot for an evening stroll.

PARQUE TANGAMANGA. With lakes for boating and fishing, a baseball field, electric cars, and bike paths, this *parque* is an ideal place to picnic and spend the day. The park is filled with trees and expansive lawns; rent a bike to explore it all. *(Catch a Route #10 "Perimetral" bus on Constitución across from the Alameda; 15min., 4 pesos. Get off at Monumento a la Revolución, in the middle of a rotary. Facing the soldiers' backs, take a left and go 3 blocks. Park open Tu-Su 7am-6pm. Bike rental 25 pesos per hr.)*

BARRIO SAN MIGUELITO. The closest and prettiest of the city's five barrios, San Miguelito lies south of Plaza de Armas following Zaragoza. This historic, cobblestone neighborhood is home to beautiful churches, markets, and tree-filled parks. **Jardín Colón** offers shade and fountains, and just south of it rises the **Caja de Agua,** a massive Neoclassical font that has fed the city water since the 18th century.

MUSEO REGIONAL POTOSINO. The museum occupies the grounds of the former Franciscan convent at Iglesia de San Francisco, built in 1590. The first floor contains artifacts from all over Mexico, focusing on the pre-Hispanic Huastecan civilization. On the second floor, the marvelous Baroque **Capilla a la Virgen de Aranzazu** sparkles with gilding and pink paint. According to legend, a local 18th-century shepherd found the altar's wooden image of the Virgin Mary in a prickly thicket. The name *aranzazu* means "from within the thorns." *(On Independencia near the corner of Galeana. ☎814 3572. Open Tu-Sa 10am-7pm, Su 10am-5pm. 34 pesos; Su free.)*

OTHER SIGHTS. The **Museo-Casa Manuel José Othón** was once the house of one of Mexico's greatest poets, Manuel José Othón (1858-1906). The museum displays some of his manuscripts and photographs and has preserved the appearance of the house as it was at Othón's death. *(Othón 225, between Escobedo and Morelos. ☎812 7412. Open Tu-F 10am-2pm and 4-6pm, Sa-Su 10am-2pm. 5 pesos.)* The Centro Cultural Mariano Jiménez is the birthplace of the 1910 Revolutionary Mariano Jiménez, and features richly painted murals and a rotating gallery that shows some of San Luis Potosí's best artwork. *(5 de Mayo 610, between Abasolo and Comonfort. ☎814 7393. Open M-F 8am-2:30pm. 5 pesos.)* By 1895, San Luis Potosí had an active bullring that housed up to 7500 spectators. Today, the abandoned **Plaza de Toros** contains statues of bullfighters. Across the street, the **Museo Taurino** shows off an impressive collection of posters and suits of famous bullfighters, paying homage to the romance and the violence of the bullfighting culture. *(On Universidad and Triana, east of Alameda. Walk up the stairs and over the highway. Open Tu-Sa noon-2:30pm and 5-8pm. Free.)* The **Museo Nacional De La Máscara,** located in the Plaza del Carmen houses a collection of over 2500 masks from every region and epoch. The museum is closed for remodeling, and is scheduled to reopen by the end of 2007.

🎵 ENTERTAINMENT

Shops line Morelos north of Plaza de Armas, and vendors sell silver and crafts on Universidad, east of Plaza de San Francisco. The best shopping is along Hidalgo, called Zaragoza south of the plaza. This street has blocks of stores, coffee shops, and *heladerías*. **Puros Habanos,** Carranza 325, is a gorgeous shop that sells Cuban, Dominican, Jamaican, and Mexican cigars. (☎810 4300. Open daily 10am-9pm.)

The **Feria Nacional Potosina (FeNaPo)** takes place during the last three weeks of August on the fairgrounds at the southeast edge of town. During FeNaPo, *potosinos* come from all over town to see live animals, concerts, bullfights, cockfights, fireworks, a car race, and a parade. The Feria reaches its apex on August 25, the celebration of the **Festival Patronal de la Ciudad,** commemorating King Louis of France, after whom the city was named. However, the festival pales in comparison with the city's celebration of *Semana Santa*. The culmination of *Semana Santa* is the **Procesión del Silencio** on Good Friday. This silent procession involves 25 *cofradías* (local groups), who carry lifelike statues portraying the events leading to Christ's death. The **Festival Internacional de Danza Contemporánea** invades San Luis Potosí in October as dance groups from around the world come to participate in Mexico's most important dance festival. The **Muestra Internacional de Folklore** highlights dance, music, and arts and crafts from all over the world during the end of September. The **Festival Internacional de San Luis,** held during the month of April, has artists from all over the world present high-quality works.

▌ NIGHTLIFE

Much of San Luis Potosí's nightlife revolves around upscale bars and live music. The area around Plaza de San Francisco has become very popular with the large student population. You're sure to find students from the university mingling at **Cafe los Frailes,** Universidad 165. (☎812 5826. Beer 22 pesos. Mixed drinks 30-45 pesos. Live music F-Sa after 10pm. Cover for upstairs only F-Sa 10 pesos. Open Tu-Th 4-11pm, F-Sa 4pm-midnight, Su 4pm-11pm. Cash only.) Futuristic decor and blacklights welcome you into **La Santa Rock House,** Escobedo 125, a suave bar which features live rock bands every weekend, starting at 10pm. (☎812 4533; www.lasantarockhouse.com. Beer 18 pesos. Mixed drinks 30-40 pesos. Cover 15 pesos F-Sa. Open Th-Sa 9pm-4am. Cash only.) **Barsa,** upstairs at Carranza 250, just off Plaza de los Fundadores, is a sleek, popular sports bar which features beer specials during soccer games and life-size statues of basketball and soccer players. (☎812 5239. Beer 15-20 pesos. AmEx/MC/V.) Mural portraits of Revolutionaries cover the walls of the patio at **Zapata, Villa, & Cia,** at Iturbide 635 between Aldama and 5 de Mayo. (Beer 12 pesos. Mixed drinks 35 pesos. F-Sa live music. Open Th-Sa 6pm-2am. Cash only.)

At night, some restaurants turn into bars. One is **El Bocolito,** Guerrero 2, in the north corner of the plaza. A rowdy crowd of all ages congregates here for live music. (☎812 7694. Beer 20 pesos. Mixed drinks 35 pesos. Cover varies depending on the band. Open F-Sa 9pm-5am. Cash only.) For some dancing, head over to **Play Club,** Carranza 333, which features live bands playing commercial covers. (☎812 5692. Beer 20 pesos. Mixed drinks 30 pesos. Cover varies. Open Th-Sa 10pm-2:30am. Cash only.) The municipal tourist office will also gladly tell you where the latest disco spots are. The gay and lesbian crowd should check out the popular Cafe Greko, Carranza 763, a lounge and coffeehouse that transforms into a club, **Greko Disco Bar,** Th-Sa after 9:30pm. (☎812 3200. Beer 15 pesos. Mixed drinks 30 pesos. Cover Sa 30 pesos. Open M-W and Su 5pm-1am, Th-Sa 5pm-3am. Cash only.)

MATEHUALA ☎488

Although Matehuala (pop. 65,000) derives its name from a Náhuatl phrase meaning "don't come," this former mining town is actually quite friendly, and makes an easy stopover for the few backpackers who pass through en route to Real de Catorce.

⌐TRANSPORTATION. Matehuala has two bus stations. The large **Central de Autobuses** is on 5 de Mayo, just south of the city and near the Arco de Bienvenido. The Central sends **buses** to more destinations than the **Terminal de Autobuses a Real de Catorce** but is more of a hike. To get downtown from the Central, take a *pesero* labeled "Centro" (10min., 6:30am-10pm, 4.50 pesos); get off at the intersection of Madero and Hidalgo, next to the market, then make a left to get to the central plazas. **Taxis** make the trip for 25 pesos.

The Central de Autobuses provides the services of **Transportes del Norte, Frontera,** and **Estrella Blanca** (☎882 2650) to: **Mexico City** (7hr., 8 per day, 415 pesos); **Monterrey** (4hr., 6 per day, 213 pesos); **Nuevo Laredo** (7hr., 5 per day, 396 pesos); **Querétaro** (6hr., 6:05am, 255 pesos); **Saltillo** (3hr., 5 per day, 178 pesos); **San Luis Potosí** (2hr., 6 per day, 121 pesos). **Noreste** (☎882 0997) serves **Monterrey** (4hr., every hr., 203 pesos) and **Reynosa** (7hr., 6 per day, 314 pesos). **Autobuses Tamaulipas** (sometimes ticketed through the parent company, Grupo Senda; ☎882 2777) goes to **Real de Catorce** (1½hr.; 8, 10am, noon, 2, 6pm; 47 pesos) and **San Luis Potosí** (2hr., every hr. 6am-midnight, 121 pesos). Buses to Real de Catorce also stop at the **smaller bus station** (☎822 0840), at Guerrero and Mendez, and then continue on to the Central de Autobuses and other destinations.

🛂 PRACTICAL INFORMATION. Limited **tourist information** can be found at the **Cámara de Comercio,** Morelos 427, a block east of Hidalgo. (☎882 0110, tourist helpline ☎882 5005. Open M-F 9am-2pm and 4-7pm.). **Maps** are sold at many *papelerías* around the *centro*. Other services include: **Banamex,** Constitución 105 next to the cathedral, which **exchanges currency** and traveler's checks and has a **24hr. ATM** (☎882 5151; open M-F 9am-3pm, Sa 9:30am-2pm); **Lavandería Acuario,** Madero 131A, at Betancourt (☎882 7088; 12 pesos per kg; open M-F 8am-8pm, Sa 8am-7pm); **police,** next to the bus station (☎882 0647); **Red Cross,** on Ramírez north of the cathedral (☎882 0726 or 0911); **Farmacia Guadalajara,** Morelos 611, with groceries and **Western Union** inside (open 24hr.); **Hospital General,** on Hidalgo a few blocks north of the *centro* (☎882 0445); **Internet** access at **Libertad,** Colón 102, one block south of the cathedral on Hidalgo (☎102 0905; 6 pesos per hr.; open daily 8am-10pm); and the **post office,** Bocanegra 102 Interior 25, off Hidalgo inside Mercado Bocanegra (☎882 0071; **Mexpost** inside; open M-F 8am-4pm). **Postal Code:** 78700.

▐▐ ACCOMMODATIONS AND FOOD. Budget accommodations populate the *centro*. For a cheap stopover, *casas de huéspedes* of varying degrees of cleanliness line Bocanegra, near the intersection with Hidalgo. **Casa de Huéspedes "El Jacalito"** ❶, Bocanegra 111, has tiny, clean rooms with shared bathrooms around a cheery orange courtyard. (☎882 1407. 24hr. bell. Singles 80 pesos; doubles 100. Cash only.) The colorful rooms at **Hotel Blanca Estela** ❸, Morelos 406, have beautiful wooden furnishings, fan, cable TV and powerful showers. Check in early; this may well be the most crowded place in town. (☎882 2300. 24hr. bell. Singles 180 pesos; doubles 220 pesos; triples 300 pesos. Cash only.)

The few restaurants in Matehuala are family-owned cafeterias, and cafes, clustered around Plaza de Armas, with good food at low prices. Visit **Las Tortonas** ❷, next to the PEMEX sign on Hidalgo, north of the cathedral for *tortas* (16-26 pesos) with egg, cheese, and avocado. (☎882 6666. Open M-Sa 8am-10pm, Su 10am-6pm. Cash only.) **Gorditas Panchita** ❶, Morelos 509 between Cuauhtémoc and Julián de los Reyes, a block from the cathedral, is a local favorite for breakfast and lunch. A circle of women continually pats out fresh *gorditas*, which their male coworker stuffs with *nopales, frijoles, rajas de queso,* and various meats. (*Gorditas* 5 pesos each. Open daily 9am-4pm. Cash only.) An indoor **market** is next to the Catedral de la Immaculada Concepción. (Open daily 9am-6pm.)

Otel.com

Are you aiming for a budget vacation❓

DO NOT
DISTURB

Clockwise from top left: Caño Negro Wildlife Refuge; Tortuguero Park Canal Cruise; Toucan; Rainforest; Manuel Antonio Park

Costa Rica Natural Paradise 10 Days $995
Call Now for Choice Dates

Caravan makes it so easy - and so affordable - for you to explore the magnificent rainforests, beaches and volcanoes of Costa Rica. Your Caravan Costa Rica tour includes all meals, all activities, all hotels, a great itinerary, all airport transfers, all transportation and excursions within Costa Rica.

A professional tour director accompanies you for the entire tour. With naturalist guides, see exotic birds and wildlife, hike in jungle rainforests, view volcanoes, soak in hot springs and cruise through biological reserves.

Join the smart shoppers and experienced travelers who rely on Caravan to handle all the details while you and your family enjoy a well-earned, worry-free vacation in Costa Rica. Or, choose from one of our other tours, priced at just $995. Call today.

Choose Your Tour—Only $995

8 days	Canadian Rockies
8 days	Nova Scotia, Prince Edward Isl.
8 days	Grand Canyon, Zion, Bryce
8 days	Mount Rushmore, Yellowstone
8 days	California Coast and Yosemite
8 days	New England Fall Colors
8 days	Mexico's Copper Canyon Train
8 days	Mexico's Ancient Civilizations
11 days	Guatemala
10 days	Costa Rica Natural Paradise

"Caravan is very reasonably priced"
— *New York Times*

"The distinguished Caravan Tours has virtually daily departures throughout January, February and March for its escorted 10-day tour. And what a tour it is: Usually, travelers have to choose from among Costa Rica's beaches, volcanoes and rain forests. This tour goes to all those places and includes every major sight, as well as three meals a day on all but two days, and excellent hotels and lodges.**"**
— *Arthur Frommer's Budget Travel*

◐◧ SIGHTS AND ENTERTAINMENT. Matehuala was founded in 1550, but the city's buildings are mostly modern and its main attractions are its placid parks and 20th-century cathedral. Standing solemnly at the center of Matehuala between Juárez and Hidalgo is the recently completed **Catedral de la Inmaculada Concepción,** a copy of Saint Joseph's Cathedral in Lyon, France. Construction began in 1905 but lack of funding slowed progress. In front of the main cathedral is **Plaza Juárez,** now permanently occupied by vendor stalls and makeshift cafes. Sprawling onto adjoining streets, the bazaar is collectively known as **Mercado Arista,** selling leather and ceramic goods and a slew of cheap plastic trinkets. Trees shade the pleasant **Plaza de Armas,** a few blocks south of the Catedral on Hidalgo and neighboring the stuccoed walls of the **Templo San Salvador.** Relax amid the limited greenery and street vendors in **Parque Vicente Guerrero.** For a larger expanse of grass or a pickup game of basketball, head to **Parque Álvaro Obregón,** just south of Insurgentes. During the first week of September, Matehuala celebrates the **Festival del Desierto** (Festival of the Desert) with food, music, and art.

REAL DE CATORCE ☎ 488

Once a thriving mining town with 30,000 inhabitants, Real de Catorce (pop. 1500) now looms mysteriously on the side of a mountain—a virtual ghost town. At one time, Real de Catorce was one of the country's largest silver producers, but its glory crumbled as its mines ran dry. The 20th century brought on flooding, destruction, and desertion, leaving behind the empty mine shafts and carts that give Real de Catorce its eerie feel. Today, backpackers and pilgrims trek to see this town's *burro*-trodden paths and brick ruins, and to pay respect to the town's patron saint, St. Francis.

▟ TRANSPORTATION. To get to Real de Catorce, you must go through Matehuala. With your back to Matehuala's cathedral, take a right on Hidalgo, following it as it passes the Hotel Matehuala; take a left on Guerrero and walk two blocks to Mendez. **Buses** leave Matehuala from the small station at the corner of Guerrero and Mendez, also stopping at the **Matehuala Central de Autobuses. Autobuses Tamaulipas** (☎ 882 0840) will bring you to **Real de Catorce** (1½hr., 5 per day 8am-6pm, 47 pesos). Confirm schedules with the bus driver and arrive early. The ride is guaranteed to whiten the knuckles of the timid traveler near the end, as the bus rambles along a winding path chiseled into the mountain. Riders change to a smaller bus for a 2.5km ride through a long and narrow table. Buses drop off and pick up at the tunnel on the Real de Catorce side. Get there early, as there tends to be a mad rush once the bus comes through the tunnel. Return buses to Matehuala depart from the same spot (5 per day 8am-5:45pm.)

▟ PRACTICAL INFORMATION. The town's main road is **Lanzagorta,** which runs from the bus stop and is lined with stalls selling *gorditas*, T-shirts, and *artesanías*. **Constitución** lies uphill from Lanzagorta and parallel to it; both streets run through **Plaza Principal** and the famed cathedral, as well as **Jardín Hidalgo,** two blocks west. There are **no financial services** in Real de Catorce. The **tourist office** is in the Presidencia Municipal, Constitución 27, right on the Plaza Principal, but it is not always staffed even during opening hours. (☎ 887 5071. Open daily 10am-4pm.) A **town map** is posted outside the office; all the hotels also have free maps and are often better sources of information. Services include: **emergency** (☎ 887 5112; open 24hr.); **police** (☎ 888 8751), at the Presidencia Municipal; **Centro de Salud,** near the tunnel to Matehuala; **LADATEL** at the Presidencia Municipal and around town; **Farmacia Juan Pablo II,** Calle Ramón Corona and Zaragoza, one block below Lanzargota (open daily 9am-2pm and 3pm-7pm); **Internet** access at **El Cafe Quemado,** Calle Libertad 5 (20

THE LOCAL STORY

HALLOWED HALLUCINOGENS

The region surrounding Real de Catorce is the spiritual center of the indigenous Huichol culture. Every year, thousands of Huichol pilgrims come to pay homage to *hikuri*, the deer deity. The *indígenas* commune with their deer-god through the ritual consumption of peyote. A key ingredient in mescaline production, peyote is a small, button-shaped cactus with hallucinogenic properties.

In the 1960s and 1970s, the Mexican-American writer Carlos Castaneda made this ritual famous in his book *The Teachings of Don Juan,* which claimed to be a firsthand account of the peyote ceremonies. Real de Catorce became flooded with hippies and travelers seeking spiritual guidance and mind-altering experiences. This has continued until today, to the point where many environmentalists and indigenous activists worry that peyote may be in danger of extinction due to over-harvesting. It can take up to a decade for a peyote button to grow to harvestable size, and if improperly cut, the entire plant will die.

The state of San Luis Potosí has designated much of the region surrounding Real de Catorce as a nature preserve, but still allows indigenous Huichol access and permission to harvest and use peyote for religious purpose. Be aware that in North America, it is illegal for non-indigenous people to possess peyote.

pesos per hr.; open M-Tu and Th-F 10am-2pm and 4pm-8pm, Sa-Su 2pm-8pm); and the **post office,** on Constitución to the right of the Presidencia Municipal as you are facing it, on the right side of the street (open M-F 9am-3pm). **Postal Code:** 78550.

ACCOMMODATIONS AND FOOD. Real de Catorce has two classes of accommodations: very cheap *casas de huéspedes,* usually marked with a sign saying "Se Rentan Cuartos," and exquisitely decorated, full-service luxury hotels. Hotel prices vary drastically according to season and day of the week (weekends and festivals are the most expensive). Those traveling to Real de Catorce during *Semana Santa,* December, or July through August should book in advance and be prepared for steeper prices. The clean, homey rooms at **Hospedaje Familiar "Real de los Alamos" ❶**, Constitución 21 just past the Plaza Principal, also have access to a lovely roof terrace—it's the best deal in town. (☎887 5009. Reception 24hr. Rooms 100 pesos per person. Cash only.) **Hostal Alcazaba ❶**, Calle Zaragoza 33, on the way to the Panteon, offers campsites and bungalows with access to a kitchen and firepits. (☎887 5075; alcazaba@realde-catorce.net. Camping 50 pesos per person; bungalows up to 4600 pesos. Cash only.) On Zaragoza just above Jardín Hidalgo, **Hotel San Juan ❶** offers clean, if not very spacious, rooms for very negotiable prices. (☎887 5099. 24hr. bell. Singles 90-100 pesos; double 150 pesos. Cash only.) For a splurge, go all out at **El Mesón de la Abundancia ❺**, Langazorta 11, which lies in the former town treasury. It's the oldest building in town, with large rooms adorned with private terraces and sitting rooms. (☎887 5044; www.mesonabundancia.com. Doubles 850 pesos; triples and quads 950 pesos. MC/V.)

Mysteriously, most of Real de Catorce's restaurants serve Italian food. Hotel El Real's **Restaurant El Real ❺**, with its dim lights and intimate atmosphere, proves that Mexico really can do Italian. (Pizza and pasta dishes 50-120 pesos. Open daily 8am-10pm. MC/V.) **La Esquina Chata ❸**, at the corner of Lanzagorta and Hidalgo on Plaza Hidalgo, serves excellent pizza and famous foccaccia sandwiches (35-65 pesos), as well as hearty crepes (35 pesos) in a relaxed atmosphere with wooden furnishings and soothing music. Everything—from the bread to the mayonnaise—is fresh. (☎887 5060. Open daily 9am-10pm.) Uphill from Jardín Hidalgo, **El Toletino ❸**, Callejón Teran 7, serves Mexican and international dishes downstairs (20-50 pesos), and features live music most weekends in the upstairs bar. (Beer 15 pesos. Open Tu-Th noon-10pm, F-Su noon-1am.)

◙ ⬛ SIGHTS AND ENTERTAINMENT. Real de Catorce is home to the most beautiful church in northeast Mexico, the ⬛**Parroquia de la Purísima Concepción,** in the Plaza Principal. The altar retains its original stucco and painting of the Virgen de Guadalupe and houses a life-size statue of St. Francis. The squares of wooden flooring are actually doors to subterranean tombs. Decades of painted tin sheets cover the walls in the back, testifying thanks to St. Francis's miraculous cures and visa waivers. Across Juárez from the cathedral, the **Casa de Moneda,** formerly a mint, houses a photography exhibit of the town. (Open daily noon-2pm. Free.)

Norteño and *mariachi* bands occasionally play at the gazebo at **Jardín Hidalgo,** beyond the cathedral between Lanzagorta and Constitución. On Xicotencatl off Zaragoza, the terraced steps of the **Palenque de Gallos** (cock-fight ring) replicate the layout of a classic Athenian theater. At the top of Zaragoza stands the white **Capilla de Guadalupe** (also called the **Panteón**). At the high end of Constitución lies **El Mirador,** an area full of ruined miners' homes that grants a vista of the city. The surrounding cliff, known as **El Voladero,** grants breathtaking views of mountains and valleys, dry riverbeds, and herds of cows on distant hilltops.

Cowboys offer **horseback tours** of the region on every street corner, especially on the west side of Plaza Hidalgo along Zaragoza between Lanzagorta and Constitución, and at the end of Lazargota near the bus stop (from 40 pesos per hr.). Try a 2hr. trip to ⬛**Ciudad de las Fantasmas** (Ghost City), an abandoned mining town nearby, where you can explore ruined churches, mine shafts, and tunnels. You can also **hike** up to Ciudad de las Fantasmas—just follow the track from the end of Lazargota (near the bus stop) uphill toward the ruins, following the ancient stone wall (6km round-trip).

Semana Santa is the most celebrated festival in Real de Catorce. Nightly parades and glittering candles light up the usually peaceful mountain evenings. October 4, known as the **Feria de San Francisco,** is the feast day of St. Francis of Assisi, Real de Catorce's beloved patron saint. From the end of September through October, the normally quiet town explodes with activity as visitors come from all over Mexico to pray at the cathedral. This festival packs the streets with daily and nightly *fiestas* outside the cathedral. Note that local hotels often double their rates; book rooms far in advance.

CIUDAD VALLES
☎ **481**

Ciudad Valles (pop. 110,000) is a crossroads between northeast and central Mexico. The city itself doesn't offer much in the way of sights, but the lush mountains surrounding it are rife with gorgeous fruit trees, coffee farms, indigenous villages, caves, and waterfalls of the Huastecan region. For travelers on the way to Xilitla, Valles is a convenient stopover. The rainy season lasts from July to September—so if you visit during those months, expect to get wet.

If you've got enough time in the city, you might want to check out **Museo Regional Huasteco "Joaquín Meade,"** which provides an introduction to the pre-Hispanic Huasteco civilization. The one-room museum houses a collection of artifacts as well as a series of photographs, old and new, of the surrounding area. All information is in Spanish. To get to Joaquín Meade, take the "Mercado" bus up Laredo past the rotary and get off at the museum sign, pointing to the left, before the curve in the road. Take a left onto Juan Sabaría for three blocks and turn left onto Rotarios; the museum is at the end of the block on the left on the corner of Artes. (☎381 1448. Open Tu-Su 10am-5pm. Free.)

While pricier hotels populate the *centro* of Valles, a traveler just passing through will be equally comfortable at one of the many mid-range hotels surrounding the bus station. **Hotel San Carlos ❸,** on Venegas 140, across from the station, provides aqua-colored rooms with cable TV, firm beds, and A/C. (24hr. bell. Singles 234 pesos; doubles 351 pesos. Cash only.) For an easy meal, **Restaurant "Don Felix"** ❷, also across from the station, serves *comida corrida* for 30 pesos and *antojitos* for 15-30 pesos. (Open daily 7:30am-11:30pm. Cash only.There is a massive supermarket, **Mercado Soriano,** within a few blocks of the station. Take a left out of the station, then an immediate right, and the store is straight ahead.

The **Central de Autobuses** is on Luis Venegas near the outskirts. To get to the center of town, take a "Mercado" bus (4 pesos). To take a **taxi,** purchase a ticket from the ServiBus stand inside of the station (25 pesos to the *centro*). From the station, **Oriente** (☎382 3912) serves: **Ciudad Victoria** (4hr., 15 per day, 148 pesos); **Guadalajara** (10hr., 4 per day, 425 pesos); **Matamoros** (8hr., 4 per day, 343 pesos); **Monterrey** (7½hr., 11 per day, 322 pesos). **Vencedor** (☎382 9309) goes to **San Luis Potosí** (5hr., every hr. 4am-11pm, 221 pesos), **Tampico** (2½hr., every hr. 5am-8pm, 114 pesos), and **Xilitla** (2hr., every hr. 4am-7pm, 52 pesos). **Banorte,** at Hidalgo and Carranza, has a **24hr. ATM.** Other services include: **emergency** (☎060); **Red Cross** (☎382 0056); **police** (☎382 0074); **Internet** at **Cyber Boss,** Galeana 29B (take the "Mercado" bus, get off at Laredo after the sign for the museum, continue up a block, go left onto Juárez for a block, and turn right onto Galeana; 4 pesos per hr.; open M-Sa 9am-9pm, Su 9am-5pm); and the **post office,** Juárez 520 (☎382 0104; open M-F 8am-3pm, Sa 9am-1pm). **Postal Code:** 79000.

XILITLA ☎489

Xilitla (hee-LEET-la; pop. 8000), the pot of gold at the end of a long, winding road, welcomes visitors with friendly locals, fruit fresh from the tree, and low prices. Houses sit perched on green mountains, where the mainly indigenous population works the fields of coffee plantations. The stunning landscape surrounding Xilitla is peppered with over 150 caves (including the 6-acre, 450m deep El Sótano de las Golondrinas), dozens of waterfalls, wild orchid sanctuaries, exotic animals, horseback trails, and rivers ready for rafting. The most notable attraction is the beautiful and bizarre architectural feat of *Las Pozas* (the pools). Built by English millionaire Edward James, this tribute to surrealism channels three waterfalls into a fantasy landscape of multicolor concrete and live flowers.

■ TRANSPORTATION. The **bus station** sits on the hillside at the lower edge of town. All buses to Xilitla pass through Ciudad Valles, 2hr. to the north. From Valles, buses frequently head to Xilitla. **Vencedor** runs to **Ciudad Valles** (2hr., 16 per day, 52 pesos), **San Luis Potosí** (6½hr.; 9am, 1pm; 228 pesos), and **Tampico** (4½hr., 3 per day, 170 pesos). To get to Plaza Central, officially Jardín Hidalgo, by foot, go up the stairs to the right of the bus station and turn right on Zaragoza. The plaza is a few blocks up the hill. **Taxis** to Las Pozas wait up the stairs to the left of the station (60 pesos).

■ PRACTICAL INFORMATION. Xilitla is a small town with only a few, seldom-labeled streets. **Zaragoza** runs east from just above the bus station and borders the southern edge of **Jardín Hidalgo,** the main square. The Jardín is bordered by **Hidalgo** to the north, **Ocampo** to the west, and **Bravo** to the east. Two blocks north of the Jardín, **Morelos** runs west to **Las Pozas** 4km away. **Tourist information** for Xilitla can be found at the website of El Castillo (www.junglegossip.com), a lovely guest house down the hill from Xilitla's main plaza. **Exchange currency** or traveler's checks at **Centro de Cambio,** on the right-hand side of Zaragoza as you walk toward the plaza. (☎365 0281. Open daily 8am-4pm.) **Banorte,** on the Zaragoza side of the plaza, also exchanges currency and checks and has a **24hr. ATM.** (☎365 0029. Open M-F 9am-3pm.) Other services include: **emergency** (☎066); **police,** in the Palacio Municipal (☎365 0680); **Red Cross** (☎365 0318); **Farmacia San Agustín,** on Hidalgo, at the northwest corner of Plaza Principal (☎365 0125; open daily 8am-8:30pm); **Lavandería Dona Tere,** Arriaga 112 (15 pesos per kilo; open 9am-7pm; cash only); **LADATELS,** on Hidalgo, at the north edge of Jardín Hidalgo; and the **post office,** in the back of the Palacio on Zaragoza (2nd fl.; open M-F 9am-4pm). **Postal Code:** 79902.

▐▌ **ACCOMMODATIONS AND FOOD.** In mid-summer and during *Semana Santa*, Xilitla's star hotels—El Castillo and the cabins at Las Pozas—fill up fast and require reservations. **Campsites** with toilets are also available next to Las Pozas, just across the road from the garden. Reception 9am-8pm. Register at the Las Pozas entrance. (☎365 0367. 30 pesos per person. Cash only.) The cheapest rooms in town can be found in the market area behind the church; however, expect a minimum of amenities and services. **Hotel Casa Maria ❶,** behind the church on Hidalgo, is dirt cheap and dirty, with peeling walls and hard beds. All rooms have private bath. 24hr. bell. (☎365 0049. Singles 100 pesos; doubles 130 pesos. Cash only.) **Hotel San Ignacio ❷,** on the corner of Arriaga and Zaragoza, is a cheery yellow building with several floors of clean, simple rooms, all with private bath and TV. (☎365 0621. Reception 6am-midnight. Singles 170 pesos; doubles 270 pesos; triples 330 pesos. Cash only.) Down the hill from Jardín Hidalgo is gorgeous **Posada el Castillo ❺,** Ocampo 105. El Castillo was the former home of Plutarco Gastelum, close friend of Edward James and foreman of the Las Pozas project, and is a surrealist tribute itself. James used to stay here when in Xilitla. Each of the nine rooms has huge windows and a balcony or veranda. All meals can be arranged upon request. (☎365 0038; www.junglegossip.com. Check-in between 9am-11am and 5pm-7pm. Rooms 550-1210 pesos. Cash only.) Solitude-seekers can stay in one of the six cabins at **Las Pozas ❺.** The experience of sleeping surrounded by surreal sculpture and rushing waterfalls promises to be unforgettable. (☎365 0367. Reception 9am-8pm in the small stores at the entrance of Las Pozas. Rooms for 1-15 people 300-1500 pesos. Cash only.)

Xilitla's streetside vendors sell freshly picked **fruit**—don't miss the mangos, oranges, and lychees. Locally grown **coffee,** sold in bulk or brewed, is flavorful and fierce. Little lunchtime *comedores* line the market area just east of Jardín Hidalgo and the church. ▌**La Flor de Cafe ❷,** Hidalgo 215, alongside the church, fills locals with *mole poblano*, fresh *aguas de frutas* (fruit juice; 25 pesos), and marvelous *café con leche* (5 pesos). Women from surrounding communities rotate chef duties. (☎365 0376. *Tamales* 2 pesos. Enchiladas 3 pesos. Meat entrees with rice, beans, and a drink 27 pesos. Open daily 9am-9pm. Cash only.) Those looking for a change from *bistec* and enchiladas will love ▌**Ambar ❹,** also known as "El Lugar de Doña," on the corner of Hidalgo and Ocampo. Feast on rich pizzas (small 65 pesos, large 120 pesos), or one of the many vegetarian options, such as mushroom lasagna (50 pesos). The menu features entirely local food, and the family also runs a store selling local handicrafts. (☎365 0405. Open high season daily, low season W-Su 3pm-11pm.) For a classier meal, **Cayo's ❹,** Alvarado 117, serves steak and seafood entrees (70 pesos) and specialty drinks (20-30 pesos) in giant goblets from its full bar on a patio overlooking the mountains. (Beer 12 pesos. Breakfast 20-40 pesos. Open daily 7am-midnight. MC/V.) The **tienda** at Las Pozas sells overpriced soda, ice-cream, beer, and snacks. (Open daily 9am-8pm.)

◩ **SIGHTS.** ▌**Las Pozas** (The Pools), formally called the **Enchanted Garden of Edward James,** is Xilitla's main attraction. The swimmable pools and overgrown greenery do seem to have an enchanted aura, enhanced by the experimental concrete sculpture that appears to be growing from the landscape. Edward James himself was an old-fashioned English eccentric. An aspiring artist and member of the surrealist group, James dabbled in poetry and the high life. In the late 1940s,

James visited Xilitla and, caught up in its natural beauty, decided to build his home as a living surrealist monument. The result is a universe of concrete, steel, and stone, in wild colors and shapes, overflowing with flowers, butterflies, and jungle vines. Doors open into nothing, winding staircases lead nowhere, and the library has no books. To walk to Las Pozas, head downhill on Ocampo, the street parallel to and farthest from the church at Jardín Hidalgo, for two blocks, and make a left onto Morelos. At the fork in the road take a left up the hill followed by an immediate right at the top of the hill onto a stone road and follow this road as it turns into a gravel path. Las Pozas will be on your left after a longish walk (4km, 40min.). From the top of the stairs near the bus station, a taxi can take you right to the gate for 60 pesos. (☎365 0367. Open daily 9am-8pm. 30 pesos.)

Before you leave Xilitla, **Museo de Edward James,** on Ocampo just off the plaza, is certainly worth a visit. Beneath vaulted concrete arches, the museum, which opened in 2005 in the other half of Plutarco Gastelum's home (now Posada El Castillo), explains the process by which Las Pozas was created, showing James's sketches for the building as well as the wooden molds used to build the concrete structures. The museum also devotes a room to James's life and artistic vision; most interesting is the collection of James' correspondence with Gastelum, as well as his other surrealist friends, including Salvador Dalí. (Open high season daily 10am-6pm, low season M and Th-Su 10am-6pm. 30 pesos, children under 12 and students with ID 15 pesos.)

In town, Xilitla's historical draw is the quietly graying **Templo de San Agustín,** on the east side of the plaza. Built between 1550 and 1557, this ex-convent is the oldest colonial building in the state. The crumbling stucco exterior exposes the stone walls beneath, but the interior is beautifully preserved, with life-size plaster figures of saints surrounding the chapel and courtyard. Every August 28, the plaza comes alive with fireworks and regional dances for the **Feria de San Agustín.**

⚑ OUTDOOR ACTIVITIES. Xilitla is famous among **spelunkers** for its deep and varied **caves.** Many tour guides lead informal explorations: ask at the Las Pozas ticket office about 3hr. tours. (English and French spoken. 200 pesos per hr. for 1-2 people.) For a tour with more equipment and experience, contact Benito Guzmán Ibargüen at **SierrAventura** at least a week in advance. He offers guided tours and provides all the necessary equipment. (guzmanbenito@hotmail.com. Prices vary.) For more options, ask hotels for locals who run hiking and mountain bike tours. The **Cueva del Salitre** (Parrot Cave) makes a good early-evening excursion. Each night at dusk, hundreds of green-and-yellow parakeets gather outside the cave. To reach the cave, head down Ocampo, take a right at Morelos, and follow the road to the end. Take a left and walk down the curved hill past the PEMEX station. A few hundred meters later, you will come to a mechanic's shop. The cave is a 5min. walk downhill, and the mechanics will take you for 20 pesos.

CENTRAL MEXICO

Central Mexico is the nation's heartland, home to alluring colonial cities and stunning Aztec ruins. For centuries, fertile hills, access to Mexico City, and a silver-rich underground made this heavily populated area the key to controlling the nation, leading to invasions by the Aztecs, Spanish, and French and many bloody battles during the War of Independence and the Mexican Revolution. Today, the area's tumultuous history and beautiful setting in the mild Mexican altiplano draws history buffs and nature lovers alike.

After docking in Veracruz in 1519, Cortés worked his way inland, convincing local tribes from **Puebla** and **Tlaxcala** to join his entourage—and massacring those who didn't. Despite his best efforts, images from *indígena* mythology still mingle with Catholic icons in the area's many churches, pointing to a vibrant indigenous culture. Pre-Hispanic heritage is also preserved in nearby archaeological sites, including the impressive structures in Cholula and Cacaxtla.

To the northwest, the states of **Guanajuato** and **Querétaro** occupy a vast, bowl-shaped plateau sheltering some of the nation's richest colonial heritage. Mining began in the area soon after the Spanish arrival, and by the 18th century the state of Guanajuato supplied the majority of Mexico's silver, which transformed its capital city into the region's commercial and banking center. Now a bona fide University town, its well-preserved colonial buildings make it one of the most beautiful stops in the state. San Miguel de Allende, located just east on the silver trail, lures expats with Siren songs of hot springs, perfect weather, and a lively artistic life. Mountainous **Hidalgo** attracts tourists to the stunning archaeological site of Tula and numerous hiking opportunities in the Sierra Madre Oriental. Impressive ruins, solemn convents, and picture-perfect towns speckle the **Estado de Mexico** before giving way to green plains and snowy mountains.

South of Mexico City, the state of **Morelos** is a prime vacation destination for Mexicans and foreigners alike, who come to take a dip in Cuernavaca's "eternal spring," explore Xochicalco's beautifully desolate ruins, and bask in Tepoztlán's striking landscape.

HIGHLIGHTS OF CENTRAL MEXICO

MUM'S THE WORD at the **Museo de las Momias** in Guanajuato (p. 351).

TUNNEL into the great **pyramid of Cholula** (p. 416), one of the largest in the world.

BUILD UP your knowledge at archaeological site of **Tula** (p. 370), once the capital of the Toltec Empire.

BRAVE the waters at Lake Avándaro in picturesque **Valle de Bravo** (p. 376).

SALSA through the nightclubs in sophisticated **Cuernavaca** (p. 383).

INDULGE in delicious *mole* dishes and the million and one types of sweets conjured up by centuries of cloistered **Puebla** cooks (p. 403).

CENTRAL MEXICO

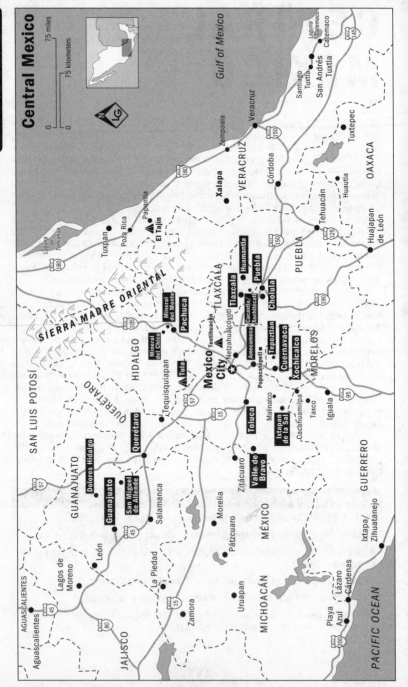

Central Mexico

75 miles
75 kilometers

Gulf of Mexico

SIERRA MADRE ORIENTAL

SAN LUIS POTOSÍ

HIDALGO

QUERÉTARO

GUANAJUATO

Mexico City

VERACRUZ

PUEBLA

TLAXCALA

MORELOS

MÉXICO

MICHOACÁN

GUERRERO

JALISCO

OAXACA

PACIFIC OCEAN

Laguna de Tamiahua
Tuxpan
Poza Rica
Papantla
El Tajín
Veracruz
Zempoala
Xalapa
Córdoba
Tuxtepec
Huautla
Tehuacán
Huajapan de León
Santiago Tuxtla
San Andrés Tuxtla
Catemaco
Laguna Catemaco
Pachuca
Mineral del Monte
Mineral del Chico
Tula
Teotihuacán
Netzahualcóyotl
Cacaxtla/Xochitécatl
Huamantla
Puebla
Cholula
Amecameca
Tepoztlán
Cuernavaca
Xochicalco
Popocatépetl
Tequisquiapan
Querétaro
Dolores Hidalgo
San Miguel de Allende
Guanajuato
Salamanca
Morelia
Pátzcuaro
Zitácuaro
Valle de Bravo
Toluca
Ixtapan de la Sal
Malinalco
Cacahuamilpa
Taxco
Iguala
Ixtapa/Zihuatanejo
Lázaro Cárdenas
Playa Azul
Uruapan
Zamora
La Piedad
León
Lagos de Moreno
Aguascalientes

180
105
57
15
150
150
125
190
145
95
45
80
200

GUANAJUATO

GUANAJUATO   ☎473

Once one of the three greatest mining centers in the Americas, Guanajuato enriched the Spanish crown for more than 200 years after massive veins of silver were discovered in the area in 1558. Wealth without liberty, however, did not satisfy the *guanajuatenses*; it was here, during Hidalgo's stop in 1810, that the Spanish were defeated at Alhóndiga de Granaditas. Today, Guanajuato (pop. 71,000) is a bona fide college town and livelier than ever, offering visitors affordable prices and plenty to do both day and night. A superstitious city still haunted by its colonial-era legends and stories of hidden treasures, Guanajuato attracts Don Quixote fans for the Cervantes festival in October, and Diego Rivera (the world-famous muralist was born here) enthusiasts year-round. The city's tangle of serpentine streets overflows with monuments to silver barons and revolutionary luminaries. A small-town feel and colonial charm earned the city its **✪UNESCO World Heritage** status in 1988 and the carved wooden doors, Spanish archways and courtyards, and rusting mine carts now serving as planters around the historic district recall the Old World's influence.

▐ TRANSPORTATION

Flights: The **Bajío airport** (☎472 748 2021), located between Guanajuato and León, is just 30min. away from Guanajuato by taxi (275 pesos).

Buses: Guanajuato's **bus station**, Guanajuato a Sila km 7 (☎733 1329 or 1340), is located about 8km west of town. To get to the *centro*, take a "Pozuelos" bus from the station; "Mercado" buses go to the market. **Local buses** criss-cross the entire city, running westward above ground and eastward under ground (every 10min. 6am-10:30pm, 4 pesos). **Taxis** into town run about 30 pesos. To get to the bus station, take a "Central de Autobuses" bus from Plaza de la Paz. **Primera Plus/Flecha Amarilla** (☎733 1333) sends first-class **buses** to: **Celaya** (2¼hr., every 40min. 9am-7pm, 63-82 pesos); **Guadalajara** (4hr., 10 per day 8:40am-11:30pm, 246 pesos); **León** (1hr., 10 per day 8:40am-11:30pm, 36 pesos); **Mexico City** (4½hr., 11 per day 5:30am-11:59pm, 287 pesos); **Salamanca** (1½hr., 5 per day 5:30am-4:45pm, 51 pesos); **San Miguel de Allende** (1½hr., 7 per day 9:30am-7:30pm, 81 pesos). Second-class service reaches **Dolores Hidalgo** (1½hr., every 20min. 5:20am-10:20pm, 41 pesos); **San Luis Potosí** (5hr.; 7:20am, 1pm; 142 pesos). **Ómnibus de México** (☎733 2607) travels to more distant locations such as **Monterrey** (11hr., 8:40pm, 503 pesos); **Tampico** (10hr., 6:45pm, 328 pesos); and **Torreón** (11hr., 9pm, 481 pesos). The **Estrella Blanca** group (☎733 1344) goes to **Mexico City** (5hr.; 10:20am, 1pm, midnight; 265 pesos) and **Tijuana** (38hr., 6pm, 950 pesos). **Transportes del Norte** (☎733 4928) goes to **Nuevo Laredo** (14hr., 8:15pm, 683 pesos).

◢▐ ORIENTATION AND PRACTICAL INFORMATION

Guanajuato, 380km northwest of Mexico City, is a tangled maze of streets and *callejones* (colonial alleyways) that will leave you dizzy. **Plaza de la Paz,** the **Basílica,** and **Jardín Unión** mark the *centro*, with the university's Moorish architecture looming in the background. **Juárez,** the main pedestrian street, climbs eastward past the *mercado* and Plaza de la Paz, becoming **Obregón** just past the Basilica, then **Sopeña** after Teatro Juárez.

Tourist Office: Secretaria de Desarrollo Turístico, Plaza de la Paz 14 (☎732 1574 or 1982; www.guanajuato-travel.com). Free maps and cultural pamphlets. Open M-F 9:30am-7:30pm, Sa 10am-5pm, Su 10am-2pm.

Tours: Transportes Turísticos de Guanajuato, Bajos de la Basílica 2 (☎732 2134), across from the tourist office, offers comprehensive city tours. Go 1hr. ahead to arrange for an English guide. (4hr.; 10:30am, 1:30, 4pm; 100 pesos, excluding museum entrance fees.) Open daily 8:30am-9pm. The tiny **Travelling** office, Plazuela de la Compañía 12-A (☎732 0637; travelling_gto@hotmail.com), specializes in student airfare and adventure activities. Open M-F 10am-2pm and 4-9pm, Sa 9am-3pm.

Currency Exchange: Banks line Juárez and Plaza de la Paz. **Banorte,** Obregón 1 (☎732 2568), is open M-F 9am-6pm and has a **24hr. ATM. Casa de Cambio "Divisas Dimas,"** Juárez 33 (☎732 1058), next to Hotel Mesón del Rosario, has good rates. Open M-Sa 10am-4pm and 5-8pm.

Beyond Tourism: For a language school try the **Academia Falcón,** Paseo de la Presa 80 (☎731 1084 or 2114; www.academiafalcon.com) or the Escuela de Idiomas at the Universidad de Guanajuato. (☎732 0006, ext. 8003; www.ugto.mx/idiomas).

Laundromat: Tintorería y Lavandería del Centro, Sopeña 26 (☎732 0680). 50 pesos per 3-5kg. Open M-F 9am-8:30pm, Sa 9am-4pm.

Police: Alhóndiga 10 (☎732 0266 or 2717).

Red Cross: Juárez 131 (☎732 0487 or 5750), 2 blocks east of the *mercado.*

Pharmacy: San Francisco de Asís, Aguilar 15 (☎732 8916), just off Plaza de la Paz. Open daily 7am-11pm. **Farmacia ISSEG,** Estacionamiento San Pedro (☎734 2353), in front of the Plaza Allende, is open 24hr.

Medical Services: Médica Integral Guanajuatense, Plaza de la Paz 20 (☎732 2305 or 1338, ext. 1). Open 24hr. **Centro Médico la Presa,** Paseo de la Presa 85 (☎731 1135 or 1074). Open 24hr.

Fax Office: Telecomm, Sopeña 1 (☎732 2747), to your left facing Teatro Juárez. Open M-F 8am-7:30pm, Sa-Su 9am-12:30pm.

Internet Access: Abounds in the *centro.* **Y2K Internet,** Cabecita 3 (☎732 3878), off Plaza del Baratillo. 4 pesos per 20min. Open daily 10am-midnight. Internet cafe **El Mexiquito,** Libertad 6 (☎733 9039), also has good rates for domestic and international calls. Open daily 10am-10pm.

Post Office: Ayuntamiento 25 (☎732 0385), across from the Templo de la Compañía. Open M-F 9am-5pm, Sa 9am-1pm. **Postal Code:** 36000.

ACCOMMODATIONS

Inexpensive and charming hotels populate the area around the Basílica. Don't be tempted to settle for the cheap but unpleasant lodgings surrounding the *mercado.* On weekends or during *Festival Cervantino* in October, make reservations well in advance and expect higher prices. All of the hostels listed are within a few minutes walk of the *centro.*

■ **Hostalito Guanajuato,** Sangre de Cristo 9 (☎732 5483; www.hostalitoguanajuato.com), just off Plaza Allende. This homey hostel with *guanajuatense* decor and a bathtub garden in the dining area attracts a loyal crowd. Extremely helpful management provides breakfast and unlimited coffee as well as a welcome drink and walking tour. Free Internet. Check-out noon. Dorms 135 pesos, 100 pesos for longer stays; private room 160 pesos per person, with bath 190. 10% discount with HI card. MC/V. ❷

■ **Casa Mexicana,** Sóstenes Rocha 28 (☎732 7393; www.casamexicanaweb.com), near Teatro Cervantes. Colorful hostel with an inviting courtyard and kitchen, and an attached language school. Laundry 35 pesos per 3kg. Internet 10 pesos per hr. Check-out noon. Dorms 65 pesos; private rooms 105 pesos per person, with bath 145 pesos. Cash only. ❶

Casa Bertha, Tamboras 9 (☎732 1316; www.paginasprodigy.com/casabertha), a short walk up a *callejón* from Plaza Mexiamora. Labyrinthine stairways lead to cozy rooms, most with cable TVs and sparkling baths, some with kitchens. View from the

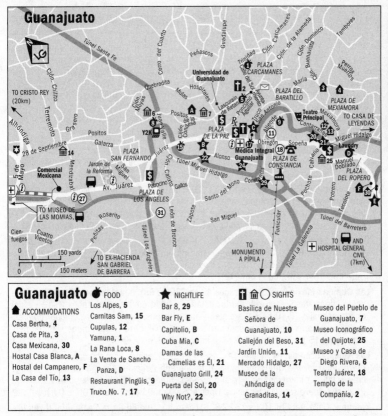

Guanajuato

FOOD
Los Alpes, **5**
Carnitas Sam, **15**
Cupulas, **12**
Yamuna, **1**
La Rana Loca, **8**
La Venta de Sancho
   Panza, **D**
Restaurant Pingüis, **9**
Truco No. 7, **17**

ACCOMMODATIONS
Casa Bertha, **4**
Casa de Pita, **3**
Casa Mexicana, **30**
Hostal Casa Blanca, **A**
Hostal del Campanero, **E**
La Casa del Tío, **13**

NIGHTLIFE
Bar 8, **29**
Bar Fly, **E**
Capitolio, **B**
Cuba Mia, **C**
Damas de las
   Camelias es Él, **21**
Guanajuato Grill, **24**
Puerta del Sol, **20**
Why Not?, **22**

SIGHTS
Basílica de Nuestra
   Señora de
   Guanajuato, **10**
Callejón del Beso, **31**
Jardín Unión, **11**
Mercado Hidalgo, **27**
Museo de la
   Alhóndiga de
   Granaditas, **14**
Museo del Pueblo de
   Guanajuato, **7**
Museo Iconográfico
   del Quijote, **25**
Museo y Casa de
   Diego Rivera, **6**
Teatro Juárez, **18**
Templo de la
   Compañía, **2**

huge terrace looks the Monumento al Pípila right in the eye. Check-out noon. Rooms 130-180 pesos per person. Cash only. ❷

La Casa del Tío, Cantarranas 47 (☎ 733 9728; www.travelbymexico.com/guan/casadeltio), across the street from the Plazuela Cantarranas. Bright hostel popular among international clientele for its clean dorms with big windows, kitchen, and TV room. View of the city from the colorful rooftop terrace. Breakfast and Wi-Fi included. Laundry 35 pesos per load. Check-out 1pm. Dorms 100 pesos; private rooms 150 pesos per person. Cash only. ❶

Casa de Pita, Cabecita 26 (☎ 732 1532; www.casadepita.com), near Plaza Mexiamora. The motherly owner welcomes you into her antique home, traditionally decorated with *azulejo* ceramics and miraculously equipped with Wi-Fi and cable TV. Breakfast 9-10am daily. Check-out noon. Reservations required. Rooms 250-600 pesos; 3-bed dorms 360 pesos. Cash only. ❸

Hostal del Campanero, Campanero 19 (☎734 5665), near Teatro Cervantes. Newly renovated rooms face a cheery, enclosed courtyard. Rooftop terrace overlooks the Don Quixote statues. Breakfast 20 pesos. 30min. of Internet 20 pesos. Check-out noon. Dorms 80 pesos; private room with shared bath 150 pesos per person. Cash only. ❶

Hostal Casa Blanca, Positos 17 (☎733 4118; bcolmene@hotmail.com). Attentive management. High ceilings and tiled floors keep even the interior rooms refreshingly cool. The balcony rooms have an intimate view into the offices of the Legislative Palace. Single-sex communal baths. Check-out noon. Dorms 100 pesos; private rooms 120 pesos per person. Cash only. ❶

CENTRAL MEXICO

🍴 FOOD

Guanajuato's plazas host an abundance of inexpensive restaurants. Near **Jardín Unión**, prices rise in direct proportion to the number of *gringos* per block. You can catch several open-air bargains at **Mercado Gavira**, by Mercado Hidalgo. Vegetarian and organic options are available at **El Unicornio Azul** market, Plaza del Baratillo 2 (☎732 0700. *Menú del día* 30 pesos. Open M-F 9:30am-9pm, Sa 9:30am-2:30pm.) Supermarkets in town include **Comercial Mexicana**, Juárez 131, two blocks east from the market on Juárez (☎732 9628; open daily 8am-10pm) and **Super Ahorremas**, Cantarranas 50, which is smaller but closer to many hostels (☎732 3930; open daily 9am-9pm).

🍽 **Truco No. 7,** Truco 7 (☎732 8374), the 1st left west of the Basilica. Artsy, spacious, dark, and popular. Cappuccino 18 pesos. Fruit salad 22 pesos. Try the cheese-smothered *enchiladas mineras*, a Guanajuato specialty (30-50 pesos). Open daily 8:30am-11:30pm. Cash only. ❸

Restaurant Pingüis, Allende 3 (☎732 1414), at the back of the Jardín Unión. Casera cooking and budget-friendly prices attract both locals and travelers. Enjoy the curious decor while feasting on egg platters (23 pesos) or tacos (30 pesos). Their spicy *sopa azteca* (20 pesos) is a filling vegetarian starter. *Comida corrida* 40 pesos. Open daily 8am-9:30pm. Cash only. ❷

Carnitas Sam, Juárez 6 (☎732 0355). If Sam could make even the tortillas out of meat, he just might. Savory *carnitas* (marinated pork) and other treats draw locals late for post-party feasting. Tacos 12 pesos. Quesadillas 6-8 pesos. Open daily 8am-6pm and 7pm-5am. Cash only. ❶

Las Cupulas Mexicanas, Cantarranas 43 (☎732 6763), near the Teatro Principal. Grab some cheap, tasty eats with the locals after a night on the town. Tacos (6-12 pesos) and quesadillas (6-10 pesos) are meaty and delicious. Known for their *chicharron prensado* (crispy pork stew; 20 pesos) and the veggie *pambazo* (suffed bread with red pepper sauce; 15 pesos). Open daily 10am-5am. Cash only. ❶

Los Alpes, Lascurain de Retana 14-2 (☎732 6299), across from the university. This *cafetería* and *nevería* offers inexpensive meals and delicious ice cream to the college crowd. Interior courtyard seating and jukebox. Breakfast 15-22 pesos. *Comida corrida* 28 pesos. *Nieve sencilla* 10 pesos. Open M-Sa 9am-9:30pm, Su 5-10pm. Cash only. ❷

Yamuna, Calle del Sol 10 (☎732 1873), near the Templo de la Compañía. If you like your enchiladas curried, you'll love this tiny Indian-influenced vegetarian restaurant with a pleasant vibe and delicious food. Salads 25 pesos. *Comida del día* 45 pesos. Open M-Sa 9am-7pm. Cash only. ❷

La Venta de Sancho Panza, Manuel Doblado 12 (☎732 1020), facing the Plaza del Ropero. In keeping with the town's Quixote obsession, dishes bear the names of Cervantes' characters. Ask for their fresh, flakey *empanadas* to go (18 pesos). Breakfast 50 pesos. Salads 45-60 pesos. Open daily 7:30am-11pm. Cash only. ❸

La Rana Loca, Juan Valle 22 (☎733 4245), across from Diego Rivera's house. Buffet-style. Good food, big servings, and delicious *agua de jamaica* (flower drink with cranberry-like taste). Open M-Sa noon-7pm. Cash only. ❷

👁 SIGHTS

Guanajuato's attractions range from the historically fascinating to the morbidly grotesque. Most are near the *centro*; they are ordered below from east to west.

SIGHTS NEAR THE CENTRO

MUSEO ICONOGRÁFICO DEL QUIJOTE. This gorgeous example of 18th-century Spanish architecture contains 18 large galleries with over 800 works of art inspired by Cervantes's anti-hero Don Quixote. Sculptures, stained-glass windows, clocks, and chess pieces illustrate the story's penetration of popular culture. Paintings include pieces by Dalí, Daumier, Ocampo, and Coronel. Ask about evening concerts. *(Manuel Doblado 1, by Sopeña. ☎ 732 3376 or 6721; www.museoiconografico.guanajuato.gob.mx. Open Tu-Sa 10am-6:30pm, Su 10am-2:30pm. 20 pesos; students, teachers, and children free.)*

JARDÍN UNIÓN. One block east of the Basilica, the 200-year-old triangular *jardín* is the town's social center. Adjacent shops and cafes are visible through the trees, and musicians add a pleasant voice to the vibrant park. In the afternoons and evenings, crowds gather on shady benches. Mexico's 1000-peso note pictures the fountain in the Plaza Baratillo, just across the street.

TEATRO JUÁREZ. Inaugurated in 1903 by dictator Porfirio Díaz for a performance of *Aida*, the theater has an ornate Roman facade—columns, statues, bronze lions, and eight staring muses. Its posh interior has the feel of an old European opera house. Note the depiction of the Santa Sofía on the house curtain. Besides housing government offices, the *teatro* hosts plays, operas, ballets, classical music concerts, and the main events of *Festival Cervantino*. *(Calle Sopeña. Faces the corner of Jardín Unión. ☎ 732 0183. Check schedule in front of theater for weekly performances. Open Tu-Su 9am-1:45pm and 5-7:45pm, except performance days. Admission 35 pesos; students 15 pesos. Performances 3 times per month; tickets 50-100 pesos. Cash only.)*

MONUMENTO AL PÍPILA. The 28m-high monument, built in 1939, commemorates the miner who torched the Alhóndiga's front door, opening the way for a riotous massacre of the Spanish during Mexico's War of Independence. The Pípila looks best at night when illuminated by spotlights. For a magnificent panoramic view of the city, descend the hill following the steeper path down the western side, which ends near the Túnel de los Ángeles. If you're walking up at night, you may want to take a friend. *(Hop on a "Pípila" bus from Plaza de la Paz; 4 pesos. Alternatively, take the 12-peso funicular to the Mirador. Open M-F 8am–9:45pm, Sa 9am–9:45pm, Su 10am-8:45pm.)*

MUSEO VIVIENTE DE LAS LEYENDAS. Brings to life nine Guanajuatense legends with eerily life-like animated replicas of the city's tragic and humorous myths, set to recorded narration. Cringe as the story of the Tuzos Cucos unfolds before your eyes and see the famous father of the Callejón del Beso (p. 350) violently stab his daughter. *(At the upper funicular station at Pípila. ☎ 756 5991. Spanish only. Open M-F 9am-6:30pm, Sa 10am-7pm, Su noon-7pm. 30 pesos, children and seniors 15 pesos; combo ticket with funicular 35 pesos, children and seniors 25 pesos.)*

BASÍLICA DE NUESTRA SEÑORA DE GUANAJUATO. This elegant Baroque structure was finished in 1696 but did not become a basilica until 1957. Dozens of candelabra illuminate the interior, decorated with fine ornamental frescoes. A wooden image of the city's protectress, Nuestra Señora de Guanajuato, rests on a pure silver base and is believed to be the oldest piece of Christian art in Mexico. Rumor has it that it was hidden in a grotto in Grenada for eight centuries before being sent to Guanajuato as a gift from King Carlos I of Spain. *(On Plaza de la Paz. Open daily 8am-9pm.)*

TEMPLO DE LA COMPAÑÍA. Completed in 1765, this Jesuit temple and college, much larger than the Basilica, was shut down in 1785. Just two years later, the Jesuits were expelled from Spanish America altogether. In 1828, the building hosted the Colegio del Estado, which spawned the city's modern university. The ornate stone exterior is striking, with four Churrigueresque facades still intact and a contrasting Neoclassical dome from 1808. The entrance to a small art museum lies to the left of the altar and includes a 17th-century painting of San Ignacio de Loyola and an 18th-century representation of San Francisco de Asís. Ending the exhibit is a spooky *relicario*, a wooden shelf enveloped in gold leaf and holding human bones. *(Calle del Sol 16, next to the university. ☎732 1827. Templo open daily 7:30am-9:30pm. Museum open Tu-Sa 10am-5pm, Su 10am-2pm. 10 pesos, students and children 5 pesos. Guided tours: in Spanish Tu-Su 1pm, in English Sa 2pm.)*

MUSEO DEL PUEBLO DE GUANAJUATO. This 18th-century colonial mansion, home to one of the signatories of the Declaration of Independence, houses a permanent collection of 18th- and 19th-century Mexican art. It also includes many intricately detailed crafts and over 1000 pieces of miniature art-work, along with rotating contemporary art exhibits. An impressive reconstruction of a Baroque church facade on the second floor houses José Chávez Morado's *Estipite Fracturado*, a mural recounting the horrors of colonial exploitation. *(Positos 7. ☎732 2990. Spanish only. Open Tu-Sa 10am-6:30pm, Su 10am-2:30pm. 15 pesos; students 5 pesos.)*

▨ **MUSEO Y CASA DE DIEGO RIVERA.** This museum chronicles the life of Guanajuato's most famous native son, born in 1886 in this house. Visitors can see old furniture from his childhood home before moving upstairs to chronologically arranged works representing his different artistic periods. Don't miss the watercolor illustrations of the *Popol Vuh* (the sacred book of the Maya), or his preliminary sketch for a section of the mural commissioned in 1933 for New York City's Rockefeller Center. Rotating exhibits occupy the top floor. *(Positos 47. ☎732 1197. Open Tu-Sa 10am-7pm, Su 10am-3pm. 15 pesos, students 5 pesos; ticket sales stop 30min. before closing.)*

CALLEJÓN DEL BESO. This is the legendary narrow alleyway across which a Spanish aristocrat's daughter flirted with her impoverished—and forbidden—lover. According to local lore, her father flew into a rage and stabbed his daughter to death upon discovering their "Kissing Alley" tryst. Today, local superstition dictates that passing lovers should kiss on the third step or face bad luck. Local capitalism dictates that they climb up to the balcony for a 60-peso photo. *(From Juárez, walk south along Plaza de los Ángeles and turn left into the alley.)*

MUSEO DE LA ALHÓNDIGA DE GRANADITAS. Originally built in 1809 to guard the city's grain supply, this Neoclassical building witnessed the victory of Mexican hero "El Pípila," who massacred over 300 Spaniards here on September 28, 1810. After squelching Hidalgo's rebellion later that year, angry Spaniards displayed the severed heads of the executed leaders—Hidalgo, Allende, Aldama, and Jiménez—from the corners of the building. Today,

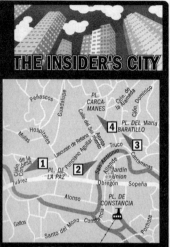

THE INSIDER'S CITY

STORIED STREETS

Chances are locals will tell you the tale of Callejón de los Besos, where a man killed his daughter after catching her kissing her forbidden lover. Little known to tourists, almost every street in Guanajuato has a sordid legend behind it:

1 West of the Palacio Legislativo is **Callejón de la Condesa,** which the Condesa de Valenciana used as an escape route to avoid public embarrassment after discovering that her husband, Conde Don Diego de Rul, had cheated on her.

2 Today, the **Calle del Truco** is a very frequented street, but did you know that this *calle* was once home to the gambling house where Don Ernesto gambled away his wife to the devil? When he delivered the alarming news to his lovely wife, she died from shock and was promptly handed over to the devil. Residents of this street will assure you that when the silence and darkness of the late night settle, the ghost of Don Ernesto paces nervously up and down the street.

the Alhóndiga is an ethnographic, archaeological, and historical museum. Captivating murals covering the ceiling and sides of the stairwells, painted in 1955 and 1966 by José Chávez Morado, resemble those of José Clemente Orozco or Diego Rivera. One of his most striking murals is an interpretation of the display of Hidalgo's severed head—lit by unearthly fire and stuck in a bird cage. *(Mendizabal 6, at the western end of Positos. Entry at the side, not the front facing Plaza 28 de Sept. ☎ 732 1180. Open Tu-Sa 10am-6pm, Su 10am-3pm. 33 pesos; students with Mexican credentials, seniors, and children under 13 free; Su free for Mexicans. Free guided tours in English W 10am-4pm.)*

MERCADO HIDALGO. Established in 1910 in honor of the 100th anniversary of the struggle for independence, the *mercado* sells everything from meat to hand-crafted dolls. Most of the fun is haggling over prices. The first floor houses some of the best and cheapest food and candy in town. *(On Juárez, by Jardín de la Reforma. Most stalls open daily 9am-9pm; top-floor stalls selling crafts tend to open later and close earlier.)*

> **TIP**
> **FROGGY BOTTOM.** Wondering about the frog souvenirs in the Mercado de Hidalgo? The name Guanajuato comes from Quanax-Huato, meaning 'hilly place of frogs' in Purépecha, spoken by the land's original Tarascan inhabitants. You'll also see playful cement frogs if you join local families for a weekend picnic in the Los Pastitos park.

MUSEO DE LAS MOMIAS. The high mineral content of Guanajuato's soil naturally mummified the 111 corpses and four heads now on display at the museum, though now only 58 currently being exhibited. Gag at the purplish, inflated body of a drowning victim; at a woman buried alive, frozen in her attempt to scratch her way out of the coffin; and at two fashionable Frenchmen, one hanged and one stabbed. The museum's oldest mummy has been here for around 140 years, while the most recent acquisition has been around since 1985. Tread cautiously through catacombs in the attached **Museo de Culto de la Muerte** and view morbid holograms and torture weapons of the colonial era, including a coffin of spikes. Pose for a photo with replica mummies outside. *(Esplanada del Panteón, next to the city cemetery east of town. Take a "Las Momias" bus from in front of the Basilica or the market; 4 pesos. Buses drop off and pick up in front of museum. ☎ 732 0639. Open daily 9am-6pm. 50 pesos, students 35 pesos, children 30 pesos, seniors with Mexican credentials 15 pesos. Museo del Culto de la Muerte 10 pesos.)*

3 At the time of the 1910 Revolution, a house in the **Plaza del Baratillo** was home to the greediest man in town, known as the *"usurero del Baratillo"* (Baratillo's loan shark). He hoarded his treasure and then made money by lending a sum and asking for great interest in return. One day, a client ran off without returning a large amount, driving the *usurero* crazy. Supposedly, he spent days locked in his house counting gold and tormenting his neighbors with the clinking of his precious coins.

4 The most sordid story of all is attached to the **Plaza Carcamanes,** a short hike from the Plaza del Baratillo. Two brothers with the last name Karkaman immigrated from Europe and took up residence in a house on this plaza more than 150 years ago, but their lives in Guanajuato were far from peaceful. It is said that both brothers were betrayed by the same young lady, who lived around the corner. When Arturo, one of the brothers, found out, he used the same sword to kill his own brother, the unfaithful girl, and eventually himself. The next morning, neighbors discovered all three bodies; the girl suffered from a bloody wound directly to her heart.

SIGHTS AWAY FROM THE CENTRO

EX-HACIENDA DE SAN GABRIEL DE BARRERA. The 17 glorious gardens, covering about three acres, are perhaps the most beautiful of Guanajuato's many natural attractions. Cobbled paths, well-groomed flora, and whistling birds create the perfect atmosphere for a stroll. The ex-*hacienda* itself, which is just as impressive, borders the gardens. Its rooms contain 16th- and 17th-century furniture, silverware, and paintings, but lack detailed labels. *(Catch a 4-peso "Noria Alta/Marfil" bus across from the mercado and tell the driver you're headed to San Gabriel de la Barrera. Get off at Hotel Misión and follow the road next to the hotel across the street from the bus stop down into the hacienda. ☎ 732 0619. Open daily 9am-6pm; closed from Christmas to New Year's Day. 22 pesos; children and students 15 pesos.)*

MONUMENTO A CRISTO REY. The Cerro del Cubilete, 2660m above sea level and 20km from Guanajuato, is considered the geographical heart of Mexico. The monument, a dark bronze statue of Jesus, at the summit is 20m tall and weighs more than 250 tons. The views from the summit are just as striking. On the way back to Guanajuato, ask the driver if the *Bocamina* mine is currently open to tourists; if so, get off at La Valenciana to see the mine and a lovely church, and take a 10min. taxi back to town. *(From the stop in front of the Alhóndiga, take a "Cristo Rey" bus. ☎ 734 5165 or 732 2635; www.santuariocristorey.org. Round-trip bus 4hr.; 10 per day 6:45am-4:45pm; 15 pesos each way.)*

🎵 ENTERTAINMENT

Theater, dance, and musical performances abound. Ask at the tourist office or consult posters around town. *Callejonadas* (sing-alongs) depart from Templo de San Diego. (Daily, starting around 9pm.) Costumed musicians invite you to join them for 80 pesos (including drink), but you can take in their slurred jokes and boisterous chants from the Jardín, or walk their route during the day by following the "Ruta Callejonada" signs starting near the Túnel de los Ángeles.

Check out **Teatro Principal,** Hidalgo 18 (☎732 0006, ext. 2717; 25 pesos, students and seniors 20 pesos, other events 40 pesos), or **Teatro Cervantes,** on Plaza Allende (☎732 1169). Check www.extension.ugto.com for an events listing.

Guanajuato explodes for the first three weeks in October during the **Festival Internacional Cervantino.** The city invites repertory groups from all over the world to make merry with the *estudiantinas* (strolling student minstrels), at local theaters, museums and churches. Tickets are sold by Ticketmaster a month in advance and sell out rapidly; an event at Teatro Juárez will set you back up to 600 pesos. The **Office of the Festival Internacional Cervantino** (☎731 1150; www.festivalcervantino.gob.mx) can provide more information.

Guanajuato also celebrates the **Feria de San Juan** (June 24), at **Presa de la Olla** park, with an entire week of dancing, cultural events, fireworks, and sports, and **Día de la Cueva** (July 31), when residents gather for a picnic on the **Cerro de la Bufa,** overlooking the city; those who are up for a nighttime hike can walk to a cave's entrance to honor San Ignacio de Loyola, the patron saint of Guanajuato and founder of the Compañía de Jesús. The **Día de la Toma de la Alhóndiga de Granaditas** (Sept. 28) is celebrated with a parade in honor of the day the Spanish were defeated. The **Día de las Flores** coincides with *Semana Santa* and reflects upon Guanajuato's mining days. On the third Wednesday of every May, the city morphs into a madhouse in honor of the **Día del Estudiante** (Day of the Students).

🎭 NIGHTLIFE

Guanajuato is a college town and its nightlife hops even during exam period. Most places listed below are in walking distance from the *centro*.

Bar 8 (☎732 7179), at Constancia and Santo del Mono. With a laid-back atmosphere and cheap drinks, Bar 8 fills its 3 floors with a student crowd. Play pool upstairs or toast your friends with the house drinks, the flaming *canelazo* shot (35 pesos) and Wikiwaki-woo (65 pesos), a tequila-based concoction. Beer from 15 pesos. M-Tu 2 beers for 25 pesos. Open daily 1pm-3am. Cash only.

Damas de las Camelias es Él, Sopeña 32. A sophisticated crowd of professionals and 30-something tourists groove to traditional latin (flamenco, jazz, and Portuguese) rhythms in this elegantly decorated bar. *Cerveza* 20 pesos. Mixed drinks 40-45 pesos. Open M-W 8pm-4am, Th-Sa 8pm-5am. Cash only.

Why Not?, Alonso 34 (☎732 9759). Che posters line the walls, and Mexicans mingle with internationals to the strains of ska, *sur,* reggae, and hip-hop. Is Tiste (40 pesos) is the bar's special creation of rum, vodka, tequila, and coke. Beer 15 pesos. Mixed drinks from 30 pesos. Open M-Sa 9pm-3am. Cash only.

Cuba Mia, Truco 1 (☎733 5762), next to the Basilica. Head upstairs and you'll forget you're in Mexico: dim lights, Cuban flags and sweaty salsa (as well as *merengue, cumbia,* and *bachata*) transport you to Havana. There may be a guest list on the weekend, when a live band takes the stage. Salsa lessons M-Th 6-10pm (50 pesos). Beer 20-25 pesos. Shots and mixed drinks 50 pesos. Open M-Sa 10pm-5am. Cash only.

Guanajuato Grill, Alonso 4 (☎732 0287). Fake stars in the covered courtyard, gilt-framed pictures on maroon walls, and pounding electronic and pop music set the mood for hip *guanajuatenses.* Flag down a waiter to avoid long lines at the bar. Beer (25 pesos). Mixed drinks (40 pesos). Cover Sa, 60 pesos after 11pm. Tu and Th-F beer specials. Open Tu and Th-Sa 10pm–4am. AmEx/MC/V.

Capitolio, Plaza de la Paz 62 (☎732 0810). Descend underground to this sleek club, with pulsing techno and reggaeton music, throbbing lights, and leather booths. Dress to impress the university crowd; come later for dancing. Cover Th-Sa 50 pesos. Tu beer special 5 pesos, Th-Sa 25 pesos. Open Tu and Th-Sa 9pm-4am. Cash only.

Bar Fly, Sóstenes Rocha 30 (☎141 5092), next to Casa Mexicana. A chill bar on the 2nd fl. plays world music like reggae and French hip hop. House special is the rastafa drink (from 35 pesos) with red, green, and yellow layers. Also offers flavored *shisha* (35 pesos). Open daily 8pm-midnight. Cash only.

Puerta del Sol, Sopeña 14 (☎732 6903). Heart-break ballads and warm candlelight provide a relaxed, romantic setting. Their specialty drink is La Momia, a kahlúa and *rompope* (Mexican eggnog spiked with rum) mix (45 pesos.) Beer 15-25 pesos, accompanied by popcorn. Live music nightly. Open W-Sa 6pm-3am. Cash only.

SAN MIGUEL DE ALLENDE ☎415

You're as likely to see greying hippies as *mariachis* in this diverse town known for its influx of artists, who say the sunshine is particularly inspirational here. In the 18th and 19th centuries, San Miguel de Allende (pop. 138,000) was a bustling commercial center and played a pivotal role in the struggle for independence. On September 16, 1810, Hidalgo, the priest of nearby Dolores, led his rebel army into the city. Under the leadership of Ignacio Allende—the town, originally named San Miguel—rallied in opposition to Spanish rule. In 1826, the infant republic recognized Allende's role in the drive for independence by joining his name to San Miguel's. Today, expats account for up to 12% of the population. Despite a surfeit of English-speakers, the city's lively *mercado,* shady plazas, colonial churches, and quiet gardens retain a calm appeal.

▣ TRANSPORTATION

Buses: To get from the bus station to the *centro,* take a "Centro" bus (every 15min. 7am-10pm, 4 pesos) to the corner of Colegio and Mesones, near the statue of Allende on horseback. Walk 2 blocks west on Mesones, then 1 block left on Relox to Plaza Principal. Alternatively, take a taxi (20 pesos). **Flecha Amarilla** (☎ 152 0084) goes to: **Aguascalientes** (4½hr.; 12:30, 2:30pm; 154 pesos); **Dolores Hidalgo** (45min., every 15min. 4:30am-9:15pm and 11:45pm, 26 pesos); **Guadalajara** (5½hr., 5 per day 7:15am-8pm, 336 pesos); **Guanajuato** (1¼hr., 7 per day 7:15am-8pm, 81 pesos); **León** (2¼hr., 7 per day 7:15am-8pm, 119 pesos); **Mexico City** (3½hr.; M-Sa 9:40am and 4pm, Su 9:40am, 4, 5pm; 212 pesos); **Querétaro** (1½hr.; 5:30, 6:30, 7:20am, and every 40min. 8am-8pm; 42 pesos); **San Luis Potosí** (4hr., 7 per day 7:30am-6:45pm, 126 pesos). **Herradura de Plata/Pegasso Plus** (☎ 152 0725) and **ETN** (☎ 152 6407) provide similar service to fewer locations. The **Estrella Blanca** group (☎ 152 2237) travels to more distant locations such as **Nuevo Laredo** (12hr., 426 pesos) via **Monterrey** (10hr., 7pm, 346 pesos); and **Ciudad Acuña** (17hr., 749 pesos) via **San Luis Potosí** (3hr., 6pm, 133 pesos), **Saltillo** (9hr., 409 pesos), **Moncloa** (10hr., 510 pesos), and **Piedras Negras** (16hr., 734 pesos).

Car Rental: HOLA, Plaza Principal 8 (☎ 152 0198 or 154 8621; www.holarentacar.com). Rates start at 402 pesos per day, plus insurance and mileage.

■■ ❼ ORIENTATION AND PRACTICAL INFORMATION

San Miguel is 97km southeast of Guanajuato and 274km northwest of Mexico City. Most attractions are within walking distance of the *centro*, **Jardín Principal** (in the **Plaza Principal**). **Calles San Francisco, Relox, Correo,** and **Hidalgo** border the Jardín. The names of east-west streets change every few blocks. The towering *parroquia* in front of the Jardín Allende is always visible.

Tourist Office: Consejo Turístico (☎ 152 0900; www.turismosanmiguel.com.mx), Plaza Principal 8, opposite the Parroquia. Open M-F 8:30am-8pm, Sa 10am-8pm, Su 10am-5:30pm.

Tours: Tranvía Turístico "El Mayorazgo", Plaza Principal 18 (☎ 154 5408; www.transturimperial.com), offers comprehensive 1½hr. trolley tours (6 per day, M-Tu and Th-Su 10am-8pm; English-language tour 4pm; 60 pesos, children 40 pesos). The library runs a colonial **House & Garden** tour, departing from the library (Su noon, 150 pesos), to benefit an educational charity. Private tours offered in high season by private guides like **Ricardo Salgado González** (☎ 154 5965, cell 111 3817; ricardo_salgado60@yahoo.com.mx).

Consulate: US, Macías 72 Interior 111-112 (☎ 152 2357, after-hours emergencies 0068 or 0653), between San Francisco and Mesones. Open M-F 9am-1pm or by appointment. For other countries, or to extend visas or visitors' permits, contact the **Delegación Regional de Servicios Migratorios,** Calzada de la Estación (☎ 152 2542), at Calle Lupita, near the bus station. Open M-F 9am-1pm.

Currency Exchange: Intercam, Correo 15 (☎ 154 6660 or 6707). Additional locations at San Francisco 4, another at Juárez 27. Offers great rates. Open M-F 9am-6pm, Sa 9am-2pm. **Banamex,** Canal 4 (☎ 152 1040 or 1004; fax 152 3732), on the west side of the Jardín. Open M-F 9am-4pm, Sa 10am-2pm. Has **24hr. ATMs.**

American Express: Hidalgo 1 (☎ 152 1856; fax 152 0499), between San Francisco and Mesones. Open M-F 9am-2pm and 4-6:30pm, Sa 10am-2pm.

English-Language Bookstore: Libros El Tecolote, Jesús 11 (☎ 152 7395), between Umarán and Cuadrante. Open Tu-Sa 10am-6pm, Su 9am-4pm.

Library: Insurgentes 25 (☎ 152 0293), between Relox and Hidalgo. Expats and students gather in the courtyard. Wide selection of books in English and Spanish. Sells old paperbacks Th 10am-1pm. Library, gift shop, and cafe open M-F 10am-7pm, Sa 10am-2pm.

Laundromat: Lavandería el Reloj, Relox 34 (☎ 152 3843), between Mesones and Insurgentes. Full-service wash and dry 45 pesos per 4kg. Open M-F 8am-8pm, Sa 8am-5pm.

CENTRAL MEXICO

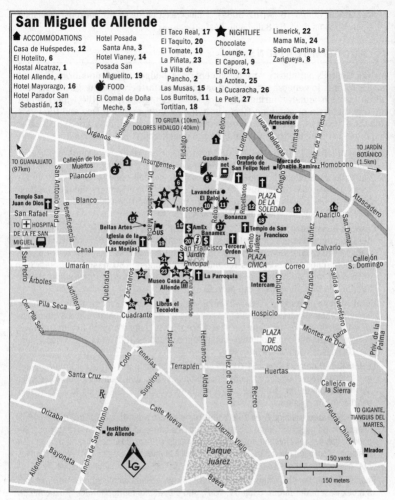

San Miguel de Allende

⌂ ACCOMMODATIONS
Casa de Huéspedes, **12**
El Hotelito, **6**
Hostal Alcatraz, **1**
Hotel Allende, **4**
Hotel Mayorazgo, **16**
Hotel Parador San
Sebastián, **13**

Hotel Posada
Santa Ana, **3**
Hotel Vianey, **14**
Posada San
Miguelito, **19**

♣ FOOD
El Comal de Doña
Meche, **5**

El Taco Real, **17**
El Taquito, **20**
El Tomate, **10**
La Piñata, **23**
La Villa de
Pancho, **2**
Las Musas, **15**
Los Burritos, **11**
Tortitlan, **18**

★ NIGHTLIFE
Chocolate
Lounge, **7**
El Caporal, **9**
El Grito, **21**
La Azotea, **25**
La Cucaracha, **26**
Le Petit, **27**

Limerick, **22**
Mama Mía, **24**
Salon Cantina La
Zarigueya, **8**

Emergency: (☎ 152 0911). Direct contact with **police and fire department.**

Red Cross: (☎ 152 1616), 1km outside of town on Carretera Celaya.

24hr. Pharmacy: Farmacia Guadalajara, Ancha de San Antonio 13 (☎ 154 9047; fax 154 9048). Next to Domino's Pizza, near Instituto Allende. Store with full-service pharmacy in the back. MC/V.

Hospital: Hospital de la Fe San Miguel, Libramiento José Manuel Zavala 12 (☎ 152 2233 or 2320, emergency 2545), near the bus station. In emergencies, you may also call **Hospital Civil** (☎ 152 6015).

Fax Office: Telecomm, Correo 16-B (☎ 152 3334; fax 152 0081), 2 doors west of the post office. Open M-F 9am-7pm, Sa-Su 9am-12:30pm.

Internet Access: Guadiananet, Insurgentes 48 (☎ 154 7042), between Relox and Loreto. Through main entrance, on left. 5 pesos per 20min. Open daily 10am-9pm.

Post Office: Correo 16 (☎152 0089), 1 block east of the Jardín. **Mexpost** available. Open M-F 8am-4pm, Sa 8am-noon. **Postal Code:** 37700.

ACCOMMODATIONS

As San Miguel's popularity with foreigners rises, budget accommodations become harder to find. In general, prices drop as you move farther from the Jardín. Rooms fill up fast, particularly during *Semana Santa*, September, and the winter, when the city throws a month-long *fiesta* in honor of Independence Day and the city's founding. Reservations are recommended for these times. Many hotels will offer discounts for longer stays. All require noon check-out.

Hostal Alcatraz, Relox 54 (☎152 8543; www.geocities.com/alcatrazhostel). Popular, homey hostel with single-sex dorms. Everyone mingles in the kitchen, TV room, and central patio. Free Internet. 20-peso key deposit. Reception open M-Sa 9am-10pm, Su 10am-9pm. 4- to 6-bed dorms 102 pesos. Cash only. Also manages the modern **Hostel Inn,** a few blocks north, popular with large groups. Dorms 120 pesos; doubles with bath 270 pesos. Cash only. Alcatraz ❶, Inn ❷

Casa de Huéspedes, Mesones 27 (☎152 1378), around the corner from the Templo del Oratorio. Tastefully decorated, spacious rooms branch off the courtyard; some with balconies and *talavera* baths. Top-floor terrace has spectacular views of the city's churches. Reservations recommended. Singles 180 pesos; doubles 300 pesos; up to 2 additional people, 100 pesos each. Monthly rates available for apartments with kitchens. Cash only. ❸

Hotel Allende, Hidalgo 22 (☎152 7929; hotelallendesma@yahoo.com.mx). Simple, carpeted rooms all have cable TV and Wi-Fi. Room #15 has a bathtub and a grandiose view through a floor-to-ceiling window. Receptionist Leobardo gives Spanish classes (1½hr., 80 pesos). Reservations recommended. Doubles 350; up to 2 additional people 100 pesos each. Cash only. ❸

El Hotelito, Hidalgo 18 (☎152 0121), located 2 blocks north of the Jardín. Courtyard and rooms are full of contemporary sculptures, vases, and paintings, some for sale. Ask for a room on the 3rd fl. for bigger windows. Doubles 300-400; up to 2 additional people, 100 pesos each. MC/V. ❸

Hotel Mayorazgo, Hidalgo 8 (☎152 1309; posadamayorazgo@hotmail.com), between San Francisco and Mesones. Huge rooms with spacious bath and TV surround a grassy outdoor patio in this centrally located hotel. Cozy apartments with small kitchen and living area also available. Reception open 8am-midnight; ring bell if unattended. Singles 250 pesos; doubles 300 pesos; apartments 350 pesos for 2 people, 100 pesos per additional person. ❸

Posada San Miguelito, Canal 9 (☎154 8393; www.posadasanmiguelito.com), just half a block west of the Jardín. Cable TV, Wi-Fi, and a beautiful rooftop terrace. Rustic decor. Rooms on the second fl. have balconies. Reservations requested. Doubles 450-600 pesos; up to 2 additional people 100 pesos each. MC/V. ❹

Hotel Parador San Sebastián, Mesones 7, (☎152 7084) between Colegio and Nuñez. Pleasant yellow rooms have tiled baths. Books and TV in the large sitting room. 5min. walk to the *centro* makes this a find only for big groups. No reservations. Singles and doubles 300 pesos; triples 400 pesos; quads 520 pesos; quints 560 pesos; 6-bed rooms 660 pesos. Cash only. ❹

Hotel Vianey, Aparicio 18 (☎152 4559). Comfortable, quiet rooms with bath open onto a pleasant courtyard. Good prices for groups, but a bit of a walk from the *centro*. Doubles and triples (optional kitchenette) 350 pesos; quads sleep up to 6 people 450 pesos. Cash only. ❷

Hotel Posada Santa Ana, Insurgentes 138 (☎152 0534), between Macías and Quebrada. Along with its regular hotel rooms, this *posada* runs a small 1-room hostel with cheap bunk beds. Same-sex baths and co-ed showers inside dorm. 12-bed dorm 100 pesos. Cash only. ❶

☕ FOOD

Restaurants and cafes occupy almost every corner of San Miguel, and the sweet aroma of international cuisine wafts through the cobbled streets. Unfortunately, prices can be high. For the best values, visit the streets around the **mercado** on Colegio. You can get delicious and cheap *tortas* (13-40 pesos) at **Tortitlán ❶**, Juárez 17, between San Francisco and Mesones. (☎152 3376 or 154 6688. Tacos 9-19 pesos. Open M-Sa 9am-7pm, Su 10am-5pm. Cash only.) **Bonanza**, Mesones 43A, is a local supermarket. (☎152 1260. Open M-Sa 8am-8pm, Su 8am-5pm. Cash only.) The covered **Mercado Ignacio Ramírez**, where Colegio meets Animas, is where most locals do their daily food shopping. The **Mercado de San Juan de Dios** and *el parian* pedestrian area between Insurgentes and San Rafael also offer cheap eats.

🍴 **El Comal de Doña Meche,** Insurgentes 62 (☎152 0012), facing the library. Under colorful paper streamers, Doña Meche herself serves up fat *gorditas* and tortillas stuffed with anything from *migaja* (breadcrumbs; 11 pesos) to the smokey *mole con pollo* (chicken; 13 pesos). Put out the fire from a greasy, spicy, and delicious *chile relleno* (stuffed peppers; 25 pesos) with *horchata* (7 pesos). Open daily 9:30am-8:30pm. Cash only. ❷

🍴 **Los Burritos,** Mesones 69-A (☎152 3222). Tasty and economical *comida rápida*. Family-run local staple offers huge selection of burritos (4-6 pesos). Carnivorous travelers will like the *burrito maxi* (10 pesos) and the hot and cheesy *burriqueso maxi* (15 pesos). Fresh fruit juice (6 pesos) puts a sweet end to the meal. Open M-Sa 10:30am-6pm. Cash only. ❶

La Villa de Pancho, Quebrada 12 (☎152 1247), near the corner of Pilancón. Welcome to the home of the friendly father-daughter duo, Carlos and Cristina. *Cerveza* 12-16 pesos. Breakfast all day 25-35 pesos. *Comida corrida* from 40 pesos. Open daily 11am-9pm. Attached Casa de Huéspedes and lavandería. Wash and dry 10 pesos per kg. ❸

La Piñata, Jesús 1 (☎544 001), on Umarán, a block west of the Jardín. Enjoy a seemingly bottomless *licuado* (18 pesos) with the mellow mix of locals, students, and backpackers feasting on veggie *tostadas* (10 pesos) and sandwiches (20-25 pesos) in this small but animated spot. Breakfast 40 pesos. *Comida corrida* 50 pesos. Open daily 8:30am-10pm. Cash only. ❷

El Taco Real, Relox 15 (☎152 6677). Serves up an affordable and stylish Mexican feast. Daily vegetarian-friendly buffet (65 pesos) includes creamy mushroom *rajas* and *pozole* (chicken and corn soup). All the *agua fresca* you can drink 10 pesos. Breakfast 45 pesos. Open daily 9am-8pm. Cash only. ❹

El Taquito, Hidalgo 1-A (☎152 4850), on the northwest corner of the Jardín. Locals scoop up these tasty tacos (5 pesos) and burritos (5 pesos) at the 4-stool counter, or order takeout or delivery. Come after the late-morning rush. Open M-Sa 9am-4:30pm. Cash only. ❶

El Tomato, Mesones 62 (☎151 6057), between Relox and Hidalgo. Mostly frequented by foreigners, this cheery nook is adorned with images of its edible namesake. *Menú del día* (80 pesos) features creative dishes like tofu croquettes. Salads 60 pesos. Homemade wheat bread accompanies orders. Open M-Sa 9am-9pm. Cash only. ❸

Dulces Típicas, Ancha de San Antonio 3 (☎152 2882). This *dulcería* dishes out savory tacos (3 for 12 pesos) from 9am until noon. While there, ogle the marzipan and cinnamon cactus in its glass box (298 pesos), or snap up the more reasonably priced champagne- or tequila-flavored *cajeta* sweets (28 pesos per box). Coffee 6 pesos. Open M and W-Su 9am-8pm. Cash only. ❶

Las Musas, Macías 75 (☎152 4946), inside Bellas Artes. Italian and Mexican cuisine among the cultural center's murals. Feast on sweet pastries created under the supervision of the Italian-born owner. Salads 59-65 pesos. Lasagna 70 pesos. Pizzas 79-95 pesos. Open M-Sa 9am-6pm, Su 10am-2pm. Cash only. ❺

CENTRAL MEXICO

🛇 SIGHTS

The best way to experience San Miguel is by foot—nearly all sites of interest lie within walking distance of the Jardín. They are listed in order of prominence.

LA PARROQUIA. San Miguel's most impressive sight was built in the 17th century by indigenous forced labor as punishment for killing Spanish herds. The neo-Gothic facade and tower were added to the church in 1890 by *indígena* mason Zeferino Gutiérrez, who is rumored to have learned the style from postcards of French cathedrals. Pointed arches and flute-like towers enclose chandeliers and gold trim that glitter in the sunlight. At the front is a tremendous gold-leaf altar. The basement holds the tomb of Anastasio Bustamante, three-time president between 1830 and 1841, although his heart resides in a chapel in Mexico City. Spotlights illuminate the church at night. *(Calle Plaza Principal Sur, in front of the Jardín. ☎ 152 4197. Open daily 6am-9pm. Mass daily 6, 7, 9am, noon, 8:15pm, Su also 8am, 1pm.)*

> **SAN MIGUEL FOR POCKET CHANGE.** To see the sights without spending a dime, check out the murals in the 18th century Bellas Artes center (always free). On Sundays the **Casa de Allende** is free also. For the biggest selection of ceramics and silverwork, descend the stairs at the corner of Relox and Palmar to the **Mercado de Artesanías.** Nearby, the covered **Mercado Ignacio Ramírez,** where Colegio meets Animas, is where most locals do their daily food shopping. The **Mercado de San Juan de Dios** and the pedestrian area between Insurgentes and San Rafael also offer cheap eats. After dark, take advantage of 2-for-1 drinks at **La Azotea,** then continue on to **El Caporal** for live Mexican music.

CENTRO CULTURAL IGNACIO RAMÍREZ "EL NIGROMANTE" (BELLAS ARTES). Housed in a former 18th-century convent, this cultural center and art school has become one of the most important spaces in San Miguel. The building previously functioned as a primary school for girls and a fortress before taking shape as an art school in the 1930s. Today, the cultural center presents magnificent temporary exhibits and is a common venue for the town's varied festivals, including the Chamber Music Festival. The stunning murals around the peaceful, manicured courtyard are by Pedro Martínez, David Alfaro Siqueiros, and Eleanor Cohen. The center also offers various classes, including ceramics, dance, art, and guitar, some in English. There are also occasional European and US film showings. *(Macías 75, next to Iglesia de la Concepción. ☎ 152 0289; cceninba@prodigy.net.mx. Galleries open Tu-Sa 10am-5:30pm.)*

MUSEO CASA DE ALLENDE. The birthplace of the town's namesake, Ignacio Allende, now houses a respectable collection of ancient ceramics, pre-Classical artifacts, historical exhibits, and, of course, a tribute to the man himself. Even if you don't know Spanish, you'll enjoy the collection of regional art, which includes an armadillo guitar. *(Cuna de Allende 1, to the east of La Parroquia. ☎ 152 2499. Open Tu-Su 9am-5pm. 34 pesos, children and students free; Su free. Audio guide 8 pesos.)*

TEMPLO DEL ORATORIO DE SAN FELIPE NERI. Founded in 1712 and rebuilt many times, the church is an amalgamation of styles: beyond its Baroque and *indígena* fusion, the floors and lower wall are covered with glazed tiles from China, Spain, and Puebla, Mexico. On the west side, the towers and dome are connected to **Santa Casa de Loreto,** a reproduction of the building of the same name in Italy. Enter through the doorway west of San Felipe Neri. *(Insurgentes 12, at Loreto. ☎ 152 0521. Templo open daily 6:30am-1pm and 5:30-8:30pm. Santa Casa open daily 7-9am and 6-8pm.)*

IGLESIA DE LA INMACULADA CONCEPCIÓN (LAS MONJAS). The enormous Las Monjas church, built between 1755 and 1891, still functions as a convent. A representation of the Immaculate Conception graces the two-story dome, a replica of the cupola at Les Invalides in Paris. The ornate gold altar features a likeness of the Virgin. *(At the corner of Canal and Macías; entrance on Zacateros. ☎ 152 0148. Open daily 7:30am-8pm. Mass M-F 7:30am, 7pm; Su 9:30, 11:30am, 7pm.)*

OTHER SIGHTS NEAR THE CENTRO. The **Instituto de Allende,** a downhill hike south on Zacateros from Las Monjas, houses a gallery with exhibits by student artists and offers Spanish and art classes, some in English. *(Ancha de San Antonio 20. ☎ 152 0190; www.instituto-allende.edu.mx. Office is open M-F 8:30am-2pm and 4-6:30pm, Sa 9am-2pm.)* Every Tuesday, vendors converge upon the **Tianguis del Martes** (Tuesday market) near the municipal stadium to sell their wares. Assorted odds and ends like clothing, groceries, and old doorknobs await the adventurous shopper. *(Take a "Gigante" bus from Juárez for 4 pesos or a taxi for 20 pesos. Open daily 9am-4pm.)* Reverberating with the calls of tropical birds, **Parque Juárez** is a large, lush garden just south of the *centro*. *(South of the Jardín on Hermanos Aldama.)*

OTHER SIGHTS AWAY FROM THE CENTRO. The **Jardín Botánico el Charco del Ingenio** is home to colonial ruins and a dazzling array of cacti and succulents. About 1300 species grow along 8km of walking paths in the park (1 sq. km). *(Taxi from Jardín Principal, 30 pesos. You can also take a 4-peso "Gigante" bus from Colegio and Mesones; get off at the Gigante stop and walk 15min. north along the highway. Signs will guide the way. ☎ 154 4715; www.laneta.apc.org/charco. Camping available. Open daily 9am-4pm. 30 pesos, students and children 15 pesos.)* Enjoy the breathtaking view of San Miguel and the surrounding mountains from the **mirador** above the city. *(From the Jardín, go east 3 blocks on Correo to Salida Real a Querétero; take a right and walk south for 15min. The mirador will be on your left. Or, take a 4-peso "Gigante" bus from Colegio and Mesones or Juárez, but tell the driver you're going to the mirador.)* Hot springs fans will find paradise at **La Gruta,** just outside of town. Set amidst verdant gardens, their four pools, one of which is in a man-made grotto, are very popular with locals on weekend afternoons. *(Carretera San Miguel a Hidalgo km 10. From the station, take a "Dolores Hidalgo" bus and get off at El Cortijo; 10min., 6 pesos. Alternatively, take a "Santuario" bus from Calzada de la Luz and Relox and tell the driver you're going to La Gruta; 20min., 7 pesos. Turn left on the dirt road directly ahead and follow the signs down the path. When returning to San Miguel, flag down a bus along the road. Or, continue to Dolores Hidalgo by walking right to El Cortijo, crossing the highway and flagging down a bus that says "Dolores"; 40min., 20 pesos. ☎ 185 2099. La Gruta open daily 8am-5pm. 80 pesos. Cash only.)*

🎵 🎧 ENTERTAINMENT AND NIGHTLIFE

There are as many clubs as churches in San Miguel, and music flows the through the city streets night and day. The magazine **Atención,** available every Monday in the tourist office and local newsstands, is the best source of information on upcoming concerts, theatrical productions, and lectures. **Bellas Artes** and the **Instituto Allende** post advertisements for art exhibits and other events. Expect cover charges at clubs to skyrocket during festivals, especially *Semana Santa*.

🎸 **Mama Mía,** Umarán 8 (☎ 152 2063; www.mamamia.com.mx), just off the Jardín, is a favorite of foreigners and *gringo*-friendly locals. This enormous building offers a restaurant and 4 bars. **Mama's Bar,** to your right as you enter, attracts a 20-something crowd and features live salsa, rock, and funk. Cover sometimes F-Sa 50 pesos. Open Th-Sa 9pm-3am. **Leonardo's,** across the entryway, scores points for its big-screen TV and comfy sofas. Open daily 7pm-3am. Straight in is **El Patio** bar, which shares a kitchen with the pricey **restaurant.** The restaurant has live music daily (M-W *folklórica*, Th-Sa salsa, Su jazz). Both places offer M-Th and Su 5pm-8pm 2-for-1 martinis. Open M-Th and Su 7am-1am, F-Sa 7am-3am. Upstairs, a young crowd enjoys the view of the city and DJ beats at **La Terraza.** Beers 25 pesos. Mixed drinks 40 pesos. Rooftop taco stand open F-Sa (40 pesos for 4 tacos). Open Th-Sa 6pm-3am. MC/V.

Chocolate Lounge, Mesones 99 (☎ 152 1958), between Hidalgo and Macías. Gay-friendly bar and lounge is the after-hours locale for those craving a pounding beat and a big drink. DJs spinning loud house music thrill a large, local crowd in the Chocolate Bar. Head upstairs to recline on leopard-print benches in the trendy **Liquid Zoo Lounge.** Beer 25 pesos. Cover Sa 30 pesos. Open W-Sa 9pm-5am. MC/V.

Salon Cantina La Zarigueya, Mesones 97 (☎ 150 7676; www.saloncantina-lazarigueya.com), next to Chocolate Lounge but a world apart. Locals kick it up to live music (F rock or salsa; Sa *norteño, sinaloense, and duranguense*) in a rustic atmosphere. Beer 20 pesos, bucket 90 pesos. Mixed drinks 30 pesos. Cover Sa 60 pesos. Open F-Sa 10pm-4:30am. Cash only.

Limerick, Umarán 24 (☎ 154 8642). Past the red phone booth you'll find a classic Irish pub. Throw darts or shoot pool with a mixed crowd, and compare national beers (20 pesos) to the 20 imported varieties (35-60 pesos). Irish car bombs (90 pesos). Open Tu-W and Su 5pm-1am, Th-Sa 5pm-3am. Cash only.

Le Petit, Macías 95 (☎ 152 3229), between Cuadrante and Umarán, attached to El Market Bistro restaurant. Wine racks, watercolor paintings, and colonial architecture pull in a relaxed, sophisticated crowd. Bar menu features swank items like breaded calamari (45 pesos). Beer 20 pesos. Margaritas and martinis from 40 pesos. Bar open daily 5pm-1am. AmEx/MC/V.

La Azotea, Umarán 6 (☎ 152 4977 or 8265), above Pueblo Viejo restaurant. San Miguel's chic young professionals take in a spectacular view and the daily 2-for-1 drink special (50 pesos). Unique tapas like shrimp tacos (75 pesos). Try the cactus martinis (90 pesos). Open daily noon-3am. AmEx/MC/V.

El Grito, Umarán 15 (☎ 152 0048; elgrito@cybermatsa.com). Wealthy students from around the area converge at this upscale *discoteca*, where you'll find several rooms of pounding dance music, artificial smoke, and antique statues. Upstairs tables for VIP. Come early to avoid a long line. Cover Sa 150 pesos for open bar. Open F-Sa 8pm-5am.

El Caporal, Mesones 97-A (☎ 152 5937), next to Salon Cantina La Zarigueya and run by the same family. Live Mexican *ranchera* music in a relaxed atmosphere. Beer 25 pesos. Mixed drinks from 45 pesos. Open daily 8pm-late. Cash only.

La Cucaracha, Zacateros 22A (☎ 152 0196). Popular Mexican *cantina* with lots of history and an eclectic array of art. A slow-paced place to nurse beers (15 pesos) as jukebox tunes play in the background. Mostly male clientele. Th free bar snacks. Open M-W and Su 9pm-3am, Th 5pm-3am, F-Sa 9pm-5am. Cash only.

🌿 FESTIVALS

San Miguel boasts more *fiestas* than any other Mexican town—a celebration of some sort takes place nearly every weekend. In September, the city commemorates its independence and founding on the Friday after **Día de San Miguel** (Sept. 29), with traditional dances, fireworks, and a running of the bulls in the Jardín. San Miguel celebrates the birthday of **Ignacio Allende** (Jan. 21) with parades and fireworks. Tourists pour in for the raucous **Festival de Locos** the Sunday after **Día de San Antonio** (June 13). Bellas Artes hosts the world-renown **International Chamber Music Festival** during the first two weeks in August. (Ticket packages from 1000 pesos. Program and tickets available through the Chamber Music office at Bellas Artes, or www.chambermusicfestival.com.) Recent additions include the **Festival Internacional de Cine Expresión en Corto** in late July, featuring a competition and showing of short films, and the **Jazz Festival** in November.

DOLORES HIDALGO ☎ 418

Though it receives few foreign visitors, the sleepy town of Dolores Hidalgo is a site of pilgrimage for patriotic Mexicans following the *"Ruta de Hidalgo."* Its recent population boom (growing from 40,000 to 60,000 in 10 years) has hardly affected Mexico's dusty "Cradle of Independence," whose quiet streets still echo the rousing words of the town's heroic priest, Miguel Hidalgo y Costilla: "Mexicanos, viva Mexico!" Calling his flock to arms in 1810 with the famously electrifying *Grito de Dolores*, Hidalgo rallied an indigenous army to march towards Mexico City. With this brazen move, Hidalgo not only signed his own death warrant—he was executed for treason a year later—but also single-handedly began the movement that led to Mexican independence. In addition to its historical significance, Dolores has also built up a reputation for its *talavera* ceramics (colorful, glazed earthenware). Its other main attraction is the tasty *nieve* (ice cream) sold around the *jardín* in a variety of unusual flavors, including avocado, shrimp, tequila, and chili. The town can be visited as a daytrip from San Miguel de Allende or Guanajuato.

⊏ TRANSPORTATION. To get downtown from the **Flecha Amarilla bus station,** Hidalgo 26-A (☎ 182 0639), walk straight out the door and left on Hidalgo. **Flecha Amarilla** (☎ 182 0639) goes to: **Aguascalientes** (3½hr., 1:30 and 3:30pm, 137 pesos); **Guadalajara** (8hr., 9:40am and 12:40pm, 249 pesos); **León** (3hr., 71 pesos) via **Guanajuato** (1½hr., every 20min. 5:20am-9pm, 41 pesos); **Mexico City** (5hr., every 40min. 5:30am-7pm, 200 pesos) via **Querétaro** (2½hr., 66 pesos); **San Luis Potosí** (3hr., every 2hr. 5:30am-8:10pm, 96 pesos); **San Miguel de Allende** (1hr., every 30min. 5:10am-9:25pm, 26 pesos). **Herradura de Plata** (☎ 182 2937) goes to some of the same destinations, as well as to **Monterrey** (9hr., 7:30pm, 336 pesos) and **Nuevo Laredo** (12hr., 7:30pm, 516 pesos).

⚄ PRACTICAL INFORMATION. Three blocks down the street from the **bus station** are the *jardín*, the tourist office, Plaza Principal, and the Parroquia. To get to Plaza Principal from the **Herradura de Plata bus station,** on the corner of Chiapas and Yucatán, go out the door on your left as you face Yucatán. Walk down Chiapas, which turns into Tabasco, take a left on Hidalgo, and follow it to the plaza. Streets change names as they cross the plaza, and the town's points of interest all lie within blocks of the *centro*. Services include: **tourist info** at **Delegación de Turismo,** Plaza Principal 1 (☎ 182 1164; www.dolores.gob.mx; open M-F 10am-4pm, Sa-Su 10am-3pm); **currency exchange** at **Centro Cambiar Paisano,** Plaza Principal 22 (☎ 182 4535; good rates; open M-Sa 9am-6pm, Su 10am-3pm) and **Bancomer,** Hidalgo 29 (☎ 182 0590; **24hr. ATMs;** open M-F 8:30am-4pm); **emergency** (☎ 182 0911); **police,** México 2, (☎ 192 0021) 11 blocks north of the plaza; the **pharmacy Botica de San Vicente,** Zacatecas 2, at Potosí (☎ 182 2417; open daily 9am-10pm); **Red Cross** (☎ 182 0000); **Hospital General,** Hidalgo 12 (☎ 182 0013); **Internet** access at **Sports Cafe Internet,** Zacatecas 3 (☎ 182 0747; 7 pesos per hr.; open M-F 9am-10pm, Sa-Su 10am-9pm); and the **post office,** Puebla 22, (☎ 182 0807; open M-F 9am-4pm) between Jalisco and Veracruz, a block from Plaza Principal. **Postal Code:** 37800.

⚃⚄ ACCOMMODATIONS AND FOOD. Quality budget rooms are scarce in Dolores Hidalgo. Prices rise and vacancies fall dramatically during *Semana Santa* and from September 9 to 17, when Independence Day celebrants overrun the town; reservations are recommended. **Posada Dolores ❶,** Yucatán 8, a block east of the plaza, has simple rooms. Though some feel like windowless concrete cubes, they're very clean, and the family atmosphere is welcoming. More expensive rooms are much nicer and come with bath and TV. The communal baths have hot water but lack toilet seats. Grab cheap *comida corrida* (25 pesos) in the **adjoining restaurant ❷**. (☎182 0642. Singles 60 pesos, with bath 160 pesos; doubles 120/220 pesos. Cash only.) **Hospedaje La Posada ❸**, Chihuahua 4, between Zacatecas and Oaxaca, offers small rooms with tiled baths and TV. (☎182 4266 or 5226. Doubles 250 pesos; quads 380 pesos; 5- to 8-bed rooms 720 pesos. Cash only.)

Around the *jardín*, many restaurants are reasonably priced. **Torticlán ❶**, Plaza Principal 28, next to the Casa de Visitas, serves *tortas* (13 pesos) with juice (8.50 pesos) or beer (10 pesos) to local families. (☎182 2676. Open daily 9am-5:30pm. Cash only.) **D'Jardín ❷**, Plaza Principal 30, has substantial portions of Mexican favorites such as *chilaquiles* for 30 pesos. (☎182 0252. Open daily 9am-7pm. Cash only.) **Las Tortugas ❷**, Querétaro 8, one block north of the plaza, provides *tortas* (15-26 pesos) and pizza (one slice plus beverage 20 pesos) to hordes of hungry schoolchildren. (☎182 2239. Open daily 9am-midnight. Cash only.) A number of hopping bars and *discotecas* can be found along Calzada de los Héroes and Colonia Mariano Balleza, near the Salida a San Miguel on the northeast side of town.

◐ ✿ SIGHTS AND FESTIVALS. Most of Dolores's sights lie within four blocks of the bus station and revolve around the huge bronze statue of Hidalgo, in the center of the plaza. On the north side of the plaza is the beautiful **Parroquia de Nuestra Señora de los Dolores**, from which Hidalgo delivered the *Grito de Dolores*. Constructed between 1712 and 1778, the church's lavish interior features a main altar surrounded by intricately ornamented gold leaf columns and two lateral altars, one Churrigueresque and the other baroque. Dress appropriately—no shorts or tight dresses are allowed. (Open daily 5:30am-9pm.) Next to the church is the **Recepción de la Presidencia Municipal**, whose courtyard contains a replica of the parish bell that Hidalgo rang at 5am on September 16, 1810 to rouse the town to action (the original is now positioned atop Mexico City's Palacio Nacional), and a stained-glass skylight representing the Mexican effort to cast off the chains of Spanish servitude. (☎182 0193. Open M-F 9am-4pm.) On the west side of the plaza is the **Casa de Visitas**, Plaza Principal 25, built in 1786 to house Spanish officials and used today to accommodate the person who gives the *grito* in the September festival. (☎182 0645. Only patio open to tourists. Open M-Sa 10am-6pm, Su 11am-3pm.) **Museo de la Independencia**, Zacatecas 6, lies less than a block northwest of the Parroquia in the former colonial prison. Gory paintings detail the physical and spiritual costs of Spanish rule and the fight for independence. Relive the *grito* in an eerie life-size diorama with wax statues of an inspired Hidalgo and anxious Mexicans. The museum also includes an exhibit on the history of the Mexican flag and national anthem. (☎182 0908. Open M-Sa 9am-4:45pm, Su 9am-3pm. 15 pesos; students and seniors 7.50; children free; Su free.) The **Museo Casa Hidalgo**, Morelos 1, at Hidalgo, a block from Plaza Principal, was Hidalgo's home from 1804-1810. The museum displays personal items owned by Hidalgo, from his priestly robes to his eyeglasses, and other artifacts. (☎182 0171. Open Tu-Sa 9am-5:45pm, Su 9am-4:45pm. 27 pesos; students, seniors, and children free; Su free.)

Dolores Hidalgo's biggest shindig is the **Fiestas de Septiembre** (Sept. 9-17), the highlight of which is the reenactment of the *Grito de Dolores* on September 16th. Until Zedillo broke the tradition in 1996, the president himself made an appearance at the Casa de Visitas to re-issue the speech. A week later, the town celebrates their patron saint with **Día de la Virgen de los Dolores** (Sept. 23). The **Purísima Concepción** celebration (Nov. 28-Dec. 8), when many pilgrimages take place, includes massive *artesanía* sales and pyrotechnic displays.

QUERÉTARO

QUERÉTARO ☎ 442

Declared a ■UNESCO **World Heritage Site** in 1995, Querétaro (pop. 870,000) has witnessed some of the most decisive moments in Mexican history. This patriotic city, which has served as the nation's capital three times, is located on a busy stretch of road between Mexico City and Guadalajara, and in recent years the Mexican government has taken measures to polish Querétaro's image. Visitors enjoy live music in shady plazas, stroll through narrow *andadores* (walkways), and admire the beautifully preserved Baroque churches. Many of the city's museums recreate, among other important events, Emperor Maximilian's last days. A hike up the Cerro de las Campanas (Hill of the Bells) will bring you to the site where the ill-fated ruler spoke his famous last words: "Mexicans, I am going to die for a just cause: the liberty and independence of Mexico." He was sentenced to death in the city's Teatro, where, 50 years later, Venustiano Carranza drafted the 1917 Constitution, establishing modern Mexico. Today, a prosperous agricultural and industrial center that also boasts an active student population, Querétaro and its colonial charm have grown increasingly attractive to vacationers both foreign and domestic.

▆ TRANSPORTATION

Querétaro lies between Mexico City and Guadalajara on **Mex. 57.** The modern **bus station** (☎229 0181 or 0182) is on the southeast side of town, but it is not within walking distance of the *centro*. To catch a bus to the *centro*, walk toward the highway and to the right, past an eclectic market, toward the sign that says "Paradero de Micros." Take the "Ruta 25" bus on Allende and Zaragoza, "Ruta 8" at Ocampo and Constituyentes, "Ruta 19" on Madero at Guerrero, or "Ruta 72" on Universidad—all are labeled "Central." (Every 5-10min. 6am-10:30pm, 5 pesos.) **Taxis** to most destinations are 30 pesos—tickets are sold inside the station and handed to the driver. Querétaro's bus station is divided into two terminals: Terminal A offers first-class service, and Terminal B offers second-class service.

Flights: Querétaro's new **Aeropuerto Intercontinental (QRO;** ☎192 5500; www.aiq.com.mx.), about 30km east of the city, offers limited domestic flights and only one international destination, Houston, TX.

Buses:

Terminal A: Élite (☎229 0022) drives to: **Acapulco** (9hr.; 11am, 7:45, 10pm; 483 pesos); **Cuernavaca** (5hr.; 11am, 7:45pm; 210 pesos); **Mexico City** (3hr., every hr. 7:30am-8pm, 160 pesos); **Monterrey** (10hr., 8 per day 9am-11pm, 482 pesos). **Primera Plus/Servicios Coordinados** (☎211 4001) travels to: **Aguascalientes** (4½hr., 9 per day 6:45am-7:45pm, 234 pesos); **Guadalajara** (5hr., 20 per day, 284 pesos); **Guanajuato** (2½hr.; 8:20am, noon, 5:30pm; 116 pesos); **León** (2½hr., 20 per day, 137 pesos); **San Luis Potosí** (2½hr., 22 per day, 154 pesos). **Ómnibus de México** (☎229 0029) has similar service. **Autobuses Americanos** (☎229 0003) goes to the US.

Terminal B: Flecha Amarilla (☎211 4001) sends buses to: **Morelia** (4hr., 22 per day, 131 pesos); **San Miguel de Allende** (1½hr., every 40min. 6:20am-10:20pm, 42 pesos); **Tula** (2½hr., 8 per day, 91 pesos); **Uruapan** (7hr.; 8:30am, 11:40pm; 236 pesos). **Flecha Roja/Herradura de Plata** (☎224 0245) provides similar service. The **Estrella Blanca** group (☎229 0067) travels farther north.

Car rental: A number of car rental agencies have counters in the bus station and in town. **Thrifty Car Rental** (☎245 1500 or 1429), located downtown in the Centro Comercial at Plaza Alamos, rents from 600 pesos including tax and unlimited miles. Open M-F 9am-7pm, Sa-Su 9am-4pm.

PRACTICAL INFORMATION

Tourist Office: Pasteur Nte. 4 (☎238 5067 or 800-715-1742; www.queretaro.travel). Helpful staff provides maps, festival info, and event schedules. Rents audio tours in English, French, German, and Spanish. Max 8hr. rental, 50 pesos. Open daily 9am-8pm. AmEx/MC/V only.

Tour Operator: Sierra Aventura (☎182 4876; www.sierraventuramex.com) offers ecotourism and adventure trips, including spelunking and cycling, in the surrounding area from 600 pesos per person.

Currency Exchange: Banks line the *centro*. **Banamex,** Juárez and 16 de Septiembre (☎225 3000). Has **24hr. ATM** and exchanges currency and traveler's checks. Open M-F 9am-5pm, exchange window closes by 3pm, Sa 10am-2pm. **Casa de Cambio,** Juárez 3 (☎212 0220). Open M-F 9am-4pm, Sa 10am-2pm.

Luggage Storage: At the bus station. 5 pesos per hr. Open daily 6:30am-midnight.

Laundromat: Speed Wash, Montes Nte. 42. Wash and dry: 10 pesos per kg., 2 kg min. Dry cleaning available. Open M-F 9:30am-8pm, Sa 9:30am-3pm.

Police: Pie de la Cuesta 107 (☎220 9191 or 8363), in Colonia Desarrollo San Pablo, at the corner of Río Tuxqpan. The **Ángeles Verdes** (☎213 8424) assist stranded motorists. **LOCATEL** (☎229 1111) helps with missing persons. **Emergency:** ☎060.

Red Cross: (☎229 0505, ambulance 229 0669), at Balustradas and Circuito Estadio, near the bus station.

Pharmacy: Farmacias del Ahorro, Juárez 2 (☎216 1760). Open 7am-11pm.

Hospital: Sanatorio Alcocer Poza, Reforma 23 (☎212 0149), near Corregidora.

Internet Access: Internet cafes abound in the *centro*. **Ciber@Net,** Madero 49 (☎214 2557), at Allende. Centrally located, but pricey. 5 pesos for 1-10min.; 15 pesos per hr. Open M-F 9am-9pm, Sa 10am-6pm. Cash only.

Post Office: Arteaga Pte. 5 (☎212 3119), between Juárez and Allende, 2 blocks south of the Jardín. Open M-F 8am-6pm, Sa 9am-1pm. **Postal Code:** 76000.

ACCOMMODATIONS

Querétaro has few budget options (most of which require adjusting to a new standard of cleanliness) and only two true hostels. There are several colorful places near the main *jardín*, **Jardín Zenea**; the cheapest require a bit of a hike from the *centro*. Call ahead for summer weekends, *Semana Santa*, and the end of December—Querétaro is a favorite for Mexico City's weekend travelers.

Hostal K'angi, Altamirano Nte. 8 (☎212 2324; www.kangihostal.com.mx). Join international backpackers lounging at cafe tables on the patio or in the shared kitchen. Breakfast included. Towels 15 pesos. Reception daily 9am-11pm; late arrivals ring bell. Check-out 11am. Dorms 140 pesos; private room 180 pesos. Discounts for ISIC, HI, and longer stays. MC/V. ❶

La Mansión del Burro Azul, Altamirano Sur 35 (☎224 2410 or 148 7157; www.depaseo.com/Burroazul/MansionBurroAzul.htm). Despite the proximity to the bustle on Zaragoza, cast iron chandeliers, fountain, and *talavera* details make this colonial hotel tranquil. Cable TV and bath. Breakfast 45 pesos, or cook your own in the shared kitchen. Reservations required; 50% advance deposit in high season. 1Doubles 350 pesos; quads 550 pesos, with microwave and fridge 750 pesos. 0% discount for stays longer than 1 week. AmEx/D/MC/V. ❹

La Jirafa Roja Hostel, 20 de Noviembre 72 (☎212 5133 or 213 7785; jirafarojahostel@yahoo.com.mx), a few blocks from the *centro*. Run by siblings Atu and Ivan, who provide info about the area in English, Japanese, or Spanish. Kitchen, TV lounge, patio,

Querétaro

ACCOMMODATIONS
Hotel del Marqués, **1**
Hotel Hidalgo, **25**
Hostal K'angi, **13**
La Jirafa Roja Hostel, **30**
La Mansión del Burro Azul, **28**
Posada Colonial, **18**
Posada la Academia, **24**
Villa Juvenil Youth Hostel, **29**

FOOD
La Antojería, **15**
Cafe del Fondo, **23**
Los Compadres, **11**
Ibis Natura Vegetariana, **5**
La Mariposa, **10**
Pettra Bar, **14**
Realizzato, **27**
Restaurante de la Rosa, **3**
Restarant Don Jorge, **2**
Taquería El Jardín, **4**
Tortas Willy's, **9**

SIGHTS
Convento de la Santa Cruz, **26**
Museo de Arte de Querétaro, **22**
Museo de la Ciudad, **8**
Museo de la Matemática, **9**
Museo Regional, **19**
Palacio de Gobierno, **16**
Santuario de Nuestra Señora de Guadalupe, **12**
El Teatrito la Carcajada, **21**
Teatro de la República, **7**

NIGHTLIFE
Alkimia, **17**
Backstage Bar, **20**
La Cantina de los Remedios, **31**

and terrace. Email for reservations and info. Towels 10 pesos. Dorms 110 pesos. 10-peso discount for stays longer than 2 nights. Cash only. ●

Posada la Academia, Pino Suárez 3 (☎224 2739), close to the Jardín del Arte. Great location for the price. Rooms and courtyard are slightly worn, but compensate with private baths and ceiling fans. Singles with bath 150 pesos; doubles from 200 pesos; up to 5 people 300 pesos. Cable TV 40 pesos extra. Cash only. ❷

Villa Juvenil Youth Hostel, on Ejército Republicano within the sports and recreation complex. While a bit remote, it's a bargain and, despite the numerous athletes, space is usually available. Communal baths. Reception open daily 7am-10pm; to check-in late, leave a message at the desk. Single-sex dorms 30 pesos. Cash only. ●

Hotel Hidalgo, Madero Pte. 11 (☎212 8102; reservaciones@hotelhidalgo.com.mx), just off the Jardín Zenea. The city's oldest hotel. A huge courtyard with fountain leads to comfy rooms with small baths and cable TV. Attached restaurant serves moderately priced food. Reservation required. Singles 340 pesos; doubles 390-460 pesos; each additional person 50 pesos, 4-person max. Accepts US$. D/MC/V. ❹

Posada Colonial, Juárez 19 (☎212 0239). Rooms sport naked light bulbs and lack windows. Some room partitions don't reach the rafters. Reception 24hr. No reservations. Pay in advance. Singles from 120 pesos, with bath and TV 190 pesos; doubles from 150/250 pesos; triples 200/330; quads 240/350. Cash only. ●

CENTRAL MEXICO

Hotel del Marqués, Juárez Nte. 104 (☎212 0414 or 212 0554), about a 10min. walk from the Plaza de Armas. Stained-glass depiction of Querétaro welcomes guests to a sizable reception area. Musty rooms have small, clean baths; most with cable TV, phone, and purified water. Parking available. Singles 210 pesos; doubles 260 pesos; triples 290 pesos; quads 320 pesos. Cash only. ❸

🍴 FOOD

Excellent, moderately priced restaurants line the *andadores* in Querétaro, and pricier places dot the Plaza de Armas. **Comercial Mexicana,** Zaragoza Pte. 150, is a supermarket about eight blocks west of Corregidora. (Take any westbound "Zaragoza" *micro* or walk 20min. ☎216 3357. Open M-Sa 8am-10pm, Su 8am-9pm.) You can also visit **Mercado Hidalgo,** on Montes between Hidalgo and Morelos, a small market full of fresh produce, meat, and taco stands. (Tacos 10-15 pesos. Open daily 7am-6pm.)

🏛 **La Antojería,** Andador 5 de Mayo 39 (☎224 2760, ext. 113; www.lacasona5.com). The whimsical jumble of *artesanía* from all over Mexico is as much a draw as the food. A tourist favorite is the spicy *torta ahogada* (25 pesos). Vegetarians will like the mushroom *taco con huitlacoche* (14 pesos). Open Tu-Su noon-midnight. Cash only. ❷

Taquería El Jardín, Corregidora 40 (☎144 1031). Soak in the ambience of the Jardín de la Corregidora from this unassuming *cocina* with the best *queso fundido* (melted cheese; 21 pesos) in town. All dishes served with guacamole, *pico de gallo, chile del arbol,* and chipotle salsas. Quesadillas 10 pesos. Open daily 9am-1am. Cash only. ❶

La Mariposa, Peralta 7 (☎212 1166), by the Jardín Zenea. A local favorite for almost 70 years. The cafeteria and *pastelería* prides itself on serving less-spicy, traditional *comida queretana. Enchiladas queretanas* (55 pesos) are popular, but the homemade ice cream (30 pesos) is the real attraction. Open daily 8am-9:30pm. Cash only. ❸

Los Compadres, 16 de Septiembre 22 (☎212 9886), west of the Santuario de Nuestra Señora Guadalupe. Wooden benches, old photos of the city, and meaty dishes take you back to an earlier Querétaro. Offers a variety of *tortas* (15-20 pesos) and fantastic *pozole* (30 pesos), served very quickly. Open Tu-Su 9am-10:30pm. Cash only. ❷

Tortas Willy's, 16 de Septiembre and Juárez (☎212 7354). A great place to stop for a quick meal and watch the world go by from your diner stool. Offers any and all things *torta* (15-20 pesos), and fast. Coffee 6 pesos. Delivery available. Open daily 8am-10pm. Cash only. ❶

Restaurante de la Rosa, Juárez Nte. 24 (☎224 3445). Traditional Mexican cuisine accompanied by *hacienda*-style decor. *Enchiladas queretanas* (42 pesos) are a local treat, or splurge on the sweet, nutty *chile en nogada* (86 pesos). 4-course *menú del día* 38 pesos. Open daily 9:30am-6pm. Cash only. ❸

Cafe del Fondo, Pino Suárez 9 (☎212 0905). This local hangout boasts an enormous coffee grinder and strong, exotic coffee (12-40 pesos). Chess games run all day. *Tortas* 12 pesos. Quesadillas 24 pesos. Daily specials 30 pesos. Mostly male clientele. Open daily 8am-10pm. ❶

Ibis Natura Vegetariana, Juárez Nte. 47 (☎214 2212), at the Jardín Zenea. Tasty veggie cheeseburgers (18 pesos), hearty *menú del día* (44 pesos), salads (25-39 pesos), and 20 different flavors of yogurt (16 pesos). The shop also sells faux-*chicharrón* (23 pesos), as well as vitamins, books, and other nutritional products. Open M-F 8am-9:30pm, Su 9am-9pm. Cash only. ❷

Realizzato, Arteaga 30 (☎212 9703). Local professionals come here for a working lunch in a refined setting. Choose from 3 daily 3-course *paquetes*, with unlimited beverages (30 pesos). Cappuccino 15 pesos. Open daily 9am-10pm. Cash only. ❷

Pettra Bar, Madero 66 (☎ 214 3245), between Guerrero and Ocampo. Restaurant by day, bar by night. The patriotic *huaraches,* covered with red and green salsas and white cheese, are topped with any kind of meat (20 pesos). Beer 15 pesos, or 2 for 25 pesos before 6pm. Open M-Sa 8am-3am, Su 8am-7pm. Cash only. ❷

Restaurant Don Jorge, Corregidora 147 (☎ 212 3421), north of the main plaza. Friendly staff serve up breakfasts for 32-54 pesos, including juice, coffee, and fresh bread. Vegetarian *enchiladas querétanas* 48 pesos. Open daily 8am-10pm. Cash only. ❸

👁 SIGHTS

In addition to museums and churches, Querétaro's picturesque *centro histórico* has beautiful plazas and parks, and the *andadores* are perfect for evening strolls.

▨ MUSEO REGIONAL. The **Ex-Convento Franciscano de Santiago,** begun in 1693, now houses a modern museum. The first floor highlights Mexican history with *indígena* artifacts, including a reproduction of a Nanho (a modern indigenous group) chapel and fascinating rotating exhibits. The second floor is divided between the Constitutional Congress of 1917 and the ex-Convent's history; it features old church music, audiovisuals that translate Spanish into a native tongue, and an impressive collection of religious paintings. Beware of the mummy. *(At Corregidora and Madero, on the eastern side of the Jardín. ☎ 212 2031; museoregional.qro@inah.com.mx. Open Tu-Su 10am-7pm. 37 pesos; under 13, students, seniors free; Su free for nationals.)*

TEATRO DE LA REPÚBLICA. Over 150 years old, the Teatro has witnessed many decisive events in Mexico's history: the 1867 judgment of Emperor Maximilian, the drafting of the constitution in 1917 in the **Sala de Constituyentes,** and the 1929 founding of the Partido Nacional de la Revolución (PNR)—the precursor to today's Partido Revolucionario Institucional (PRI; see p. 59). The theater resembles a European opera house, with four levels of red velvet seating. *(Peralta 2, 1 block from the Jardín. ☎ 212 0339. Open Tu-Su 10am-3pm and 5-8pm. Free. Performance prices vary; check www.culturaqueretaro.gob.mx for schedules and prices. Tickets for performances at the theater, including those by the Philharmonic Orchestra of Querétaro, are sold at Carranza 4, M-F 9am-3pm.)*

CONVENTO DE LA SANTA CRUZ. Built where the Spaniards defeated the Chichimeca Indians in 1531, this convent proudly touts its role in the evangelist movement in Mexico and Baja California. It was the first place in the Americas to train priests and still displays the stone cross that presided over the brutal conversions of 1531. Nearly everything inside Santa Cruz (built in 1640) is original: the clay pipes and rain-catching system date from the city's aqueduct days, and monks still live in the convent. The cell where Maximilian spent his last moments, on the second floor, has been left with all of its Victorian furniture intact, exactly as it was on the day of his execution in 1867. In one courtyard, there are mimosa bushes with thorns in the shape of crucifixes, known as the **Árbol de la Cruz** (Tree of the Cross). Legend has it that it spontaneously grew where a Spanish-born priest tapped his walking stick. Ask about access to the terrace, which has a fantastic view of Querétaro and the surrounding hills. *(East of Juárez on Independencia. ☎ 212 0235. Open Tu-Sa 9am-2pm and 4-6pm, Su and festival days 9am-4pm. Free; small donation requested. Courtyard accessible only during 20min. tours in English, French, Italian, and Spanish.)*

SANTUARIO DE NUESTRA SEÑORA DE GUADALUPE. The church's white towers and central dome date from 1680 and pay homage to the Virgen de Guadalupe, Mexico's patron saint. The red-and-green-stained facade is intended to represent the colors of the Mexican flag. Imposing pillars contrast with the delicate chandeliers hanging against a backdrop of dimly lit stained-glass windows in this intricately designed church. The image of "La Guadalupana" is by Miguel Cabrera. *(At Pasteur and 16 de Septiembre. ☎ 212 0732. Open Tu-Su 9am-2pm and 5-8pm. Mass Tu-Sa 10am, 8pm; Su 10am, 1, 2, 7, 8pm.)*

LA ALAMEDA DE HIDALGO. Built in 1790, the Alameda is a huge park that manages to block out the press of the city, making it an ideal spot for a morning jog or afternoon stroll. The markets along Zaragoza, near the entrance, sell cheap clothes and music. Be careful at night, as this area can be unsafe. *(3 blocks south on Corregidora from the Jardín. Entrance on Zaragoza. Open M-Tu and Th-Su 8am-7pm.)*

MUSEO DE ARTE DE QUERÉTARO. Formerly an Augustinian monastery, the building's beautiful stone courtyard features columns topped with grimacing heads. European paintings, modern Mexican art, and Cristóbal de Villa Pando's 19th-century depictions of the apostles round out the formidable collection. *(Allende Sur 14, between Madero and Pino Suárez. 2 blocks from the Jardín. ☎ 212 2357. Open Tu-Su 10am-6pm. 20 pesos; nationals under 12, students, and seniors free; Tu free.)*

MUSEO DE LA MATEMÁTICA. A genealogy at the entrance traces the origin of mathematics to the pre-Aztec indigenous peoples. Explore more about that "magical language to speak with nature" in one big hall with over 110 science-fair-quality exhibits. Popular with school groups. *(16 de Septiembre Ote. 61. ☎ 192 1200, ext. 3770; www.uaq.mx/museo. Open M-F 10am-6pm. 25 pesos; under 7, students, and seniors 15 pesos.)*

CERRO DE LAS CAMPANAS (HILL OF THE BELLS). The Hill of the Bells is a beautiful garden with a bloody past. Named for the peculiar sound its rocks make as they collide, this is where Maximilian surrendered his sword in 1867 before his execution. Directly ahead of the park entrance is the small neo-Gothic **chapel,** built in 1900 by Porfirio Díaz to placate Maximilian's family and reestablish economic ties with Austria. It marks the spot where the emperor and two of his generals were shot. Some monarchists still leave flowers, a reminder of the divisive period in Mexican history. Flowering trees and quiet paths lead the way to an impressive, tree-lined view of Querétaro and a large stone statue of Benito Juárez, who stands triumphant over the memorial to his imperialist predecessor. Behind the statue is the **Museo La Magia Del Pasado,** with interactive exhibits spanning Querétaro's history; the fourth room explains the republican *sitio* (siege) of 1867 heralding Maximilian's downfall. *(Walk north of the Jardín on Corregidora and turn left onto Escobedo. Walk 30min. until Escobedo ends at Tecnológico, take a right, and then take the 1st left at the park entrance. Or, catch a 5-peso "Ruta R" bus on Allende anywhere south of Morelos or a "Tecnológico" bus going west on Zaragoza, and get off at "Ciudad Universitaria"; enter in front of the statue of Escobedo. Alternatively, take a 30-peso taxi. Park open daily 6am-6pm. Chapel open Sa-Su. Museum open Tu-Su 9am-5pm. Buy the museum ticket at park entrance. Park entrance 1 peso; museum ticket 15 pesos; under 15 and seniors free.)*

OTHER SIGHTS. Querétaro's **Acueducto** stretches along los Arcos, west of the *centro*. Constructed in 1735 as a gift to perpetually parched Querétaro from the Marqués de Villas del Águila, this distinctive structure, with 74 original arches of pink sandstone and gardens at its base, still brings water to the city. The largest archway divides Los Arcos and Zaragoza. A *mirador* overlooks all 1280m of the aqueduct from Ejército Republicano, about three blocks past the Convento de la Santa Cruz. The **Museo de la Restauración de la República** and the **Museo de la Ciudad,** housed in a former convent on Guerrero between Balvanera and Hidalgo, are host to the history of Maximilian's reign in Mexico and revolving exhibits of contemporary art, respectively. *(Guerrero 27, near Hidalgo. ☎ 212 4702 or 224 3756. Open Tu-Su 11am-7pm. 5 pesos, students and children free, Su free.)* Up 5 de Mayo to the east of the

Jardín is the **Plaza de la Independencia (Plaza de Armas),** a monument to the Marqués. Faithful stone dogs surround his statue, drooling respectfully into a fountain. The plaza is bordered by trees, cafes, shaded benches, and beautiful colonial buildings, including the **Casa de la Corregidora (Palacio de Gobierno),** which housed government officials during colonial times. Today, the Casa is the seat of the state government. **Andador Libertad,** two blocks from the Jardín, connects Plaza de la Independencia and Corregidora. It is host to a slew of mellow vendors and *artesanía* shops. *(Shops usually open M-Tu and Th-Su 10am-9pm.)*

🎵 🎭 ENTERTAINMENT AND NIGHTLIFE

Outdoor activities abound in the *centro*'s **Jardín Zenea.** Jugglers, *mariachis*, and magicians perform sporadically, and brass bands play concerts in the gazebo on Sunday evenings from 6-8pm. Outdoor theaters are also popular, especially in the Jardín del Arte. Pick up a copy of *Asomarte*, a comprehensive monthly bulletin on art, dance, theatre, literature, music, and workshops, from the tourist office, bus station, or area hotels. On Wednesday nights movies are half price. The jester hats hanging on the back wall at **El Teatrito La Carcajada,** 5 de Mayo 48, reveal the true role of this cafe as a comedy club. (☎200 1100; www.lacarcajadadeljugalar.com. Frappuccinos and sweet crepes each 25 pesos. Shows in Spanish F-Sa reception 8:30pm, show 9pm. 120 pesos.)

Querétaro has a number of weekend nightclubs popular with locals, students, and 20-somethings visiting from Mexico City. The *centro* has a few bars lining the *andadores*, but they tend to be mellow. The area around Constituyentes and Bernardo Quintana has plenty of options for late-night parties—dress to impress. Taxis from the *centro* usually cost 25 pesos, but prices increase later at night.

La Cantina de los Remedios, Constituyentes Pte. 125a (☎248 2350). Western-style saloon doors welcome customers to this decked-out *cantina*. Posters of celebrities and witty Spanish graffiti cover the walls, and *sombreros* and paper lanterns hang from the ceiling. The huge bar packs enough liquor to give pause to even the most hardened *charro* (cowboy). Beer 34 pesos. Mixed drinks from 39 pesos. Live *mariachi* music from 8pm. Open M-Sa 1:30pm-3am. Doors close at 1:30am.

Backstage Bar, 5 de Mayo 70 (☎182 0768). Start your night off shooting pool at this tourist-friendly bar. Plays mostly 70s, 80s, and 90s American rock. Fruity beers like apple, mango, or coconut (35 pesos). W 2-for-1 imported beers (40 pesos). Open W-Sa 7pm-3am. MC/V.

Alkimia, 5 de Mayo 71 (☎212 1791), one block from the Plaza de Armas. A wood-panelled bar projects funk, electronica, and rock music videos. Sip on a lychee martini (70 pesos) or a pink mojito (60 pesos) on leather lounges in the second room with a clean-cut 20-something crowd. Beer 25 pesos. Tu 7-11pm 2-for-1 mixed drinks (60 pesos). Open Tu-Sa 7pm-2:30am. D/MC/V.

🎆 FESTIVALS

The annual **Feria de Querétaro** usually takes place during the second week of December on the outskirts of the city. The **Festival de Santiago de Querétaro** commemorates the city's founding on July 25, with free concerts and street fairs. The **Feria de Santa Ana,** complete with a running of the bulls through the congested streets, happens the next day. The whole town dances during the **Celebración de la Santa Cruz de los Milagros** and the **Fiestas Patrias,** which take place September 13-16. Other festivals include the **Día del Albanil** (May 3), with fireworks and dancers, and, of course, *Semana Santa*, the week before Easter. Be sure to make reservations if visiting Querétaro during a festival. For information about cultural events, stop by the library and performance space **Casa de la Cultura Gómez Morín,** on Pasteur south of Constituyentes past the Alameda (open Tu-Su 10am-6pm).

Two traditional towns east of Querétaro host important festivals and can be reached in a day trip. From Querétaro's Central de Autobuses Terminal B, take a bus (1hr.) to **Peña de Bernal,** the site of a 350m monolith (dwarfed only by Spain's Gibraltar and Brazil's Pan de Azucar), and a massive celebration of the spring equinox (March 19-21), when traditional dancers hike to the *peña's* summit. Continue on to **Tequisquiapan** (3hr.), a small town noted for its **Feria Internacional del Queso y del Vino** during the first two weekends in June.

HIDALGO

TULA   ☎ 773

Tula (pop. 27,500) is a little town with one main attraction: one of the most important archaeological sites in Mesoamerica. With little else to offer, except a few refreshingly quiet, untouristed streets, travelers usually come for the day. Mexico City is an 80km jaunt, and Pachuca is only 75km away.

▐ TRANSPORTATION. From Mexico City to Tula, take an **AVM bus** (☎ 737 9691) from Central de Autobuses del Norte, Sala 8 (1¾hr., 7am and every 30min. 8am-8pm, 52 pesos). Once in Tula, to reach the *zócalo* from the **bus station,** Xicotencatl 14 (☎ 732 9600), make a right when you exit the station, turn left at M. Rojo del Río, and walk to Hidalgo, where you'll make a right and see the cathedral on your left. AVM (☎ 732 0118) runs to **Mexico City** (1¾hr., 21 per day 5:30am-8pm, 52 pesos) and **Pachuca** (2hr., every hr. 5:30am-6:30pm, 47 pesos). **Flecha Amarilla** (☎ 732 0225) goes to **Guanajuato** (5hr., 10:30am, 191 pesos) and **Querétaro** (2½hr., 8 per day 5:15am-7pm, 91 pesos) via **San Juan del Río** (2hr., 68 pesos).

▐ PRACTICAL INFORMATION. An understaffed **tourist office** can be found within the Presidencia Municipal, several blocks southeast of the Zona Arqueológica. (☎ 733 6210 or 100 2181; turismo@tulahidalgo.com.) You can also pick up information from the **Sala Histórica Quetzalcóatl,** on Zaragoza next to Hotel Catedral. (☎ 732 7749. Open Tu-Su 9am-5pm. Free.) **Santander Serfín,** Hidalgo 201, **exchanges currency** and **traveler's checks,** and has **24hr. ATMs.** (☎ 732 0154. Open M-F 9am-4pm, Sa 10am-2pm.) The Omnibus Mensajería y Paquetería office, 16 de Septiembre 50, will hold your **luggage** until 6pm. (☎ 732 6068. 15 pesos.) Other services include: **Lavandería Diana,** on Ferrocarril (18 pesos per kg.; open M-F 8am-8pm, Sa 8am-5pm); **police,** 5 de Mayo 408 (☎ 733 2049); **Red Cross** (☎ 732 1250); **Farmacia del Ahorro,** on M. Rojo del Río (open daily 7am-11pm); **LADATELs,** near the bus station and on Zaragoza and Hidalgo; and the **post office,** on Ferrocarril (☎ 732 0068; open M-F 9am-4pm). **Postal Code:** 42800.

▐▐ ACCOMMODATIONS AND FOOD. Because most tourists visit Tula as a daytrip, the town lacks quality budget accommodations. The business-oriented hotels, however, are in great shape. **Hotel Catedral ❸,** Zaragoza 106, next to the cathedral, has comfortable rooms with cable TV. (☎ 732 0813; fax 732 3632; www.tulaonline.com/hotelcatedral. Breakfast included. Parking available. Check-out 2pm. Singles and doubles 411 pesos; each additional person 100 pesos. AmEx/D/MC/V.) **Hotel Casablanca ❸,** Pasaje Hidalgo 11, has recently been remodeled and all rooms have TV. (☎ 732 1186 or 3223; www.casablancatula.com. Check-out 1pm. Singles 280 pesos; doubles 300 pesos; triples 350 pesos;

6-bed suite 750 pesos. MC/V.) **Auto Hotel Cuéllar ❸**, 5 de Mayo 23, offers rooms of two varieties: regular and more comfortable. The regular rooms come with private bath but are older and lack TVs. (☎732 0170 or 0442; www.hotelcuellar.com. Regular singles 265 pesos, upgraded 315 pesos; doubles 315/415 pesos; triples 385/475 pesos; quads 465/555 pesos; quints 565 pesos. D/MC/V.)

Good, cheap food is cooked right in front of you in the **Mercado Tianguis** and the **Plaza del Taco ❷**, on 5 de Mayo, behind the cathedral. (*Comida corrida* 25 pesos. Open daily 6am-8pm. Cash only.) **Cafetería y Nevería Campanario ❷**, Zaragoza 110, offers cheap fare with colorful paintings and *piñatas*. (☎732 3825. Sandwiches 14 pesos. Ice cream 18 pesos. Open daily 8am-9pm. Cash only.) **Super Comercial,** 5 de Mayo 13, has all your supermarket needs. (☎732 1228. Open daily 8am-9pm.)

◉ THE ARCHAEOLOGICAL SITE OF TULA

The best way to get to the archaeological site is to take a combi (5 pesos) with the destination Tlahelipan, Actupan, or Iturbe from the terminal on 5 de Mayo, across the street from Plaza del Taco. Tell the driver to stop at the site. Taxis will take you from the sitio stand at the bus station or on Zaragoza and Hidalgo in town (☎732 0039; 25 pesos). Site ☎732 0705. Open daily 9am-5pm. 37 pesos; students, teachers, and under 13 free; Su free for nationals. The site includes the archaeological ruins and 2 musuems, both in Spanish; 5-peso English brochures sold near the entrance. Ask at the entrance about private tours (150 pesos).

Tula's importance in pre-Hispanic Mexico cannot be overstated. The first town in northern Mesoamerica with historical records, it was settled and occupied by various small nomadic tribes during the pre-Classic and Classic Periods, and it is believed to have come under the sway of powerful Teotihuacán (p. 141). In the late Classic Period, however, the area was abandoned and then resettled by a different group—the Tolteca-Chichimeca (more commonly known as the Toltec). By the early post-Classic Period (AD 900-1200), the Toltec capital entered a period known as the Tollán phase, marked by construction and expansion. New pyramids arose, the city was carefully realigned, and the population peaked at around 80,000. A close resemblance in architecture between Tula and the post-Classic Mayan center at Chichén Itzá (p. 646) has led archaeologists to speculate that the two had a relationship, perhaps through trade or conquest. The Toltecs, whose name means "builders" in Náhuatl, relied heavily on irrigation and modeled their architecture after Teotihuacán. When crop failure and drought weakened the capital in 1165, neighboring Chichimecs sacked the city, burning temples and destroying much of what the Toltecs had built. The devastated city went through another ravaging when the Aztecs, who viewed themselves as rightful heirs to the Toltecs' cultural inheritance, later occupied and looted the city in 1168. Today remnants of the Aztec occupation can be found among the Toltec remains in bits of scattered ceramics and pottery. The ruins at Tula, first excavated in 1872, are not the best-preserved in central Mexico; nonetheless, they are still impressive, and the giant Atlantes statues alone make the trip worthwhile.

JUEGO DE PELOTA I (BALL COURT I). From the entrance area, an 800m dirt path zigzags past cacti through two sets of vendor stalls before arriving at the main plaza. The first structure to the right as you reach the main plaza is Ball Court 1, just north of the large Edificio de los Atlantes. At 12.5m wide and 67m long, the I-shaped court is the smallest of Mesoamerican ball courts. Part of a statue depicting a ball player was found here, but now only the feet are visible, on display in the museum. The public sat atop the platform to watch the game.

EDIFICIO DE LOS ATLANTES (PYRAMID B). To the left lies the monumental Edificio de los Atlantes, Tula's most impressive and best-preserved building. Three rows of 14 columns stand in the Great Hall in front of the pyramid. Archaeologists suspect they comprised a covered walkway leading to the pyramid. On top of the pyramid are the 4.8m basalt Atlantes statues—Toltec warriors in the shape of columns—which originally supported a temple and altar dedicated to the priest-king Quetzalcóatl. Close inspection of the statues reveals traces of the original red pigment. From the platform, there is a great view of the site and the surrounding countryside. The sides of the pyramid were decorated with reliefs of jaguars, coyotes, eagles, and feathered serpents—each symbolizing a different class of warrior—some of which are still visible on the north and east sides.

EL COATEPANTLI (THE WALL OF SNAKES). On the east side of Pyramid B, closest to the Palacio Quemado, lies El Coatepantli—the wall of snakes. Reliefs of giant rattlesnakes devouring humans relate to the practice of human sacrifice, and the conch shells represent Quetzalcóatl as the planet Venus. For the Toltec, walls marked the limits of sacred space; these walls are the prototypes of the ceremonial enclosures later built by the Aztecs.

PALACIO QUEMADO (BURNT PALACE). The name of this building (to the left facing the front of Atlantes) is only half true. While its large rooms with numerous columns were indeed deliberately destroyed by fire, it was not a *palacio*, but rather an administrative center for government advisors. A perfectly preserved *chac mool* (a Mayan statue often used as an altar for offerings) was found in the central room; it is exhibited in the museum when not traveling with other expositions. In other areas of the building, offerings of conch shells and turquoise, and what appears to be a storeroom for ceramics and other materials have been found.

TEMPLO PRINCIPAL (PYRAMID C). The Toltecs built their largest building, Templo (or Edificio) Principal, on the eastern boundary of the plaza to face the sunrise. Deliberately destroyed by the Chichimecas and others following Tula's abandonment at the end of the 12th century, Templo Principal now pales in comparison to Edificio de los Atlantes. Because it is not fully excavated, Templo Principal cannot be scaled from the front—you must scramble up a steep path on the side closest to Atlantes. Tula's main religious building likely was adorned with the massive sculptural slab located nearby; its imagery of Quetzalcóatl in his manifestation as Tlahuizcaltec Uhtli, "the morning star," symbolizes the triumph of light over darkness.

EL ADORATORIO (THE SHRINE). In front of Pyramid C lies the small Adoratorio, with two distinct stages of construction. The original platform of the shrine measured 8.5m on each side. Unfortunately, the shrine has been looted extensively since the pre-Hispanic era.

EL JUEGO DE PELOTA II (BALL COURT II). This ball court was discovered in an extreme state of disrepair. Originally, the walls were covered with carved panels and stone rings embedded in each side wall. Only a small fragment of this adornment, which rests on a small altar in the northeastern corner of the exterior facade, is preserved. The altar, called the **Tzompantli,** held the skulls of sacrificial victims associated with the game. The Aztecs made a series of modifications to the original plan, making the court smaller and constructing it inside the old Toltec ruins. Later, a steam bath was built on top.

PACHUCA ☎ 771

Despite its proximity to Mexico City, Hidalgo's capital (pop. 300,000) has limited attractions for sightseers. The gorgeous *zócalo*, with its Reloj Monumental, presents a stark contrast to the rest of the unimpressive city streets. The heritage of

Spanish settlers and English miners has left a unique mark on the region, which is most palpable in the outlying towns of Mineral del Chico (p. 375) and Mineral del Monte (p. 375). One day is plenty of time to see both the towns of Mineral del Chico and Mineral del Monte, though you'll need a few more days if you plan on exploring the surrounding wilderness.

TRANSPORTATION. Pachuca is approximately 90km northeast of Mexico City on Mex. 85. The **bus station**, on Camino Cuesco (☎713 3447), is a fair distance from downtown. Frequent *combis* run from the station to Plaza de la Constitución and the *zócalo* (6am-9:30pm, 3.50 pesos). From the bus station, **ADO** (☎713 2910) goes to **Mexico City's** Cien Metros (1½ hr.; every 15min. M-F 4:30am-10:15pm, Sa-Su 5:45am-10:15pm; 56 pesos), **Poza Rica** (4½hr., 4 per day 8:30am-8:45pm, 118 pesos), and **Tuxpan** (6hr.; 3, 8:45pm; 162 pesos). **Flecha Roja** (☎713 2494) goes to **Mexico City** (1¼hr., every 10min. 4am-10:30pm, 51 pesos). **Futura/Estrella Blanca** (☎713 2747) goes to **Mexico City** (2hr., every 15min. 5:30am-10pm, 56 pesos) and **Querétaro** (5hr., every hr. 5am-9:40pm, 135 pesos). The bus station has **luggage storage.** (4-8 pesos, depending on size. Open daily 8am-9pm.)

TIP

BLOWN AWAY. One of Mexico's coldest and highest cities, Pachuca is known as La Bella Airosa, Mexico's "Windy City." Even a hot summer day can get blustery, so bring a jacket.

ORIENTATION AND PRACTICAL INFORMATION. Finding your way in Pachuca can be difficult, as many streets curve and change names and maps are not readily available. Be prepared to ask for directions. Facing the Reloj Monumental in Pachuca's *zócalo*, the **Plaza de la Independencia, Matamoros** is on the right and **Allende** on the left. **Guerrero** is parallel to Allende, one block to the left. Matamoros and Allende converge a few blocks away from the Reloj at **Plaza Juárez,** which has two parts: an open cement space with a statue of the man himself, and a small park. **Avenida Juárez** juts out from the statue's base, while **Revolución** extends from the park.

Services include: **tourist office,** at the bottom of the clock tower, facing Matamoros (☎715 1411; open M-F 9am-6pm, Sa-Su 10am-6pm); **currency exchange** and **ATMs** surround the Reloj; **emergency** (☎066); **police,** in Plaza Juárez (☎711 1880); **Red Cross** (☎065); the **24hr. Farmacia Guadalajara,** Matamoros 207 (☎715 6871); **Sociedad de Beneficiencia Española** hospital, Av. Juárez 908, far from downtown (☎718 6900; www.benepachuca.com); **Internet** access at **@ADI,** Hidalgo 401 (☎715 6299; 12 pesos per hr.; MC/V); **Tintorería y Lavandería Modelo,** Doria 205 (☎715 2971; 16 pesos per kg., 4 kg. min.; open M-Sa 8am-9pm); and the **post office,** Juárez at Iglesias, two blocks south of Plaza Juárez (☎713 2592; open M-F 9am-5pm, Sa 9am-1pm). **Postal Code:** 42070.

ACCOMMODATIONS AND FOOD. Equidistant from both the Reloj and Plaza Juárez, **Hotel América ❶,** 3 de Victoria 203, is simple and cheap. (☎715 0055. No reservations. Singles and doubles 120 pesos, with bath 150 pesos, with bath and TV 180 pesos, with king bed 200 pesos; quad with 2 beds 250 pesos; each additional person 50 pesos. Cash only.) Across the street, **Hotel Cuauhtémoc ❶,** Allende 311, offers similarly bare rooms. (☎715 5349. Singles and doubles 100 pesos, with bath and TV 150 pesos, with king bed 200 pesos. Cash only.) **Hotel de los Baños ❹,** Matamoros 205, right on the *zócalo*, has worn but comfortable rooms with clean baths, phone, TV, and purified water. (☎713 0700; fax 715 1411. Singles 235 pesos; doubles 295 pesos; triples 330 pesos; quads 365 pesos; quints 400 pesos. AmEx/D/MC/V.) A block south of the *zócalo* is **Hotel Noriega ❸,** Matamoros 305. Rooms show their age, but they have large private baths, and the hotel interior has a pleasant colonial touch. (☎715 1555; fax 715 1844. Singles 200 pesos, with TV 220 pesos; doubles 240/265 pesos; triples 280/300 pesos; quads 300/330 pesos. D/MC/V.)

Mercado Juárez, Carranza 105, lies north of Plaza de la Constitución. Although most of the hotels contain restaurants, little *pastes* stores are a better, cheaper option. Locals agree that the place to go is mini-chain **Pastes Kikos ❶,** with locations on the *zócalo* and in Plaza Juárez. (*Pastes* 6 pesos. Open daily 8am-9pm. Cash only.) **La Luz Roja ❷,** Plaza Juárez 108, at the corner of Guerrero in the *portal* facing the statue's left shoulder, is a bit cramped due to immense popularity. Try the delicious *pozole* or *morelianas*, each 27 pesos. (☎714 2321. Open daily 10am-8pm. Cash only.)

 PACHUCA MUSEUM PECULIARITIES. Since the small city of Pachuca is not used to a large tourist crowd, most museums will run on their own schedule. Your best bet is to plan to get to a museum 30min. after the supposed opening time and one hour before closing. The tourist office tends to follow similar rules and is most likely to open for service on weekends rather than weekdays.

◙ **SIGHTS.** Pachuca's Neoclassical **Reloj Monumental,** 40m high, dominates the *zócalo*. Construction began in 1904 by the same manufacturers who built London's Big Ben, but was stopped a year later due to a shortage of funds. When it was finally completed in 1910, it cost a total of 300,000 pesos, paid in gold. Four female statues on the third level represent the Independence of 1810, the Liberty of 1821, the Constitution of 1857, and the Reform of 1859. (Open M-F 9am-6pm, Sa-Su 10am-6pm. 20 pesos to climb to the top for a view of the city's office buildings.) To reach **Archivo Histórico y Museo de Minería** from the Reloj, walk one block south on Matamoros, turn left onto Mina, and follow it for 1½ blocks. A former mining company office, the museum holds a notable collection of rocks, minerals, mining tools, and heavy machinery. (Mina 110. ☎715 0976. Open W-Su 10am-2pm and 3-6pm. 15 pesos; children, students, teachers, and seniors 10 pesos; miners and ex-miners free. English brochures 5 pesos.)

The **Ex-Convento de San Francisco,** on Hidalgo between Arista and Casasola, now houses several museums, a gallery, and an outdoor theater. To get there from the Reloj, take Matamoros south for one block, turn left on Mina, take it for two blocks, turn right on Hidalgo (not to be confused with Viaducto Hidalgo), and continue for three blocks. Pass the **Church of San Francisco** on the corner of Arista and Hidalgo, and turn left to enter the Plazuela Ortega. To the left is the **Museo Nacional de la Fotografía,** which surveys the technological history of photography and displays historical Mexican photographs from the end of the 18th century on, including photos by the famous Casasola brothers and Nacho López. (☎714 3653, ext. 104; museodelafotografia@inah.gob.mx. Open Tu-Su 10am-6pm. Free.) Across from the museum is the **Cuartel del Arte,** a small gallery of temporary art exhibits. (☎715 4186; galerias_cecultah@hotmail.com. Open Tu-Sa 10am-6pm. Free.) Exit the other end of Plazuela Ortega and turn left on Casasola. The first entrance on the left is the **Museo Archivo Histórico del Exposición Fotografía,** also known as the Fototeca, which holds temporary exhibits from its collection of 900,000 photos spanning 160 years of Mexican history. (☎715 1977; fototecanacional@inah.gob.mx. Open M-F 10am-3pm. Free.) The next entrance, opposite Plaza Bartolomé de Medina, is the **Centro INAH Hidalgo,** which houses a permanent exhibition on the history of the convent in the Sala de los Arcos. The Sala Nacho López, which holds the photography museum's temporary exhibitions, can be found opposite the Sala de los Arcos. (☎714

3520. Open M-F 10am-6pm. Free.) Returning down Casasola to Hidalgo, one block to the left brings you to **Parque Hidalgo,** a favorite hangout for local teens and the playground of the neighboring primary school.

▶ DAYTRIPS FROM PACHUCA

MINERAL DEL CHICO

Mineral del Chico can be easily visited as a daytrip from Pachuca. Combis (☎683 4757) run to Mineral del Chico from the stop on Carranza in Pachuca, right after Mercado Juárez (40min., every 35min. 6am-8:30pm, 10 pesos; last combi returns from Mineral del Chico 7:30pm).

Forty minutes of winding mountain roads separate Pachuca from the tiny town of Mineral del Chico (pop. 580). Nestled within **Parque Nacional el Chico,** numerous hikes and striking views of nearby rock formations make Mineral del Chico a great escape from urban congestion. Follow the Carretera a Carboneras, the road that runs uphill to the right from the *combi* stop, to reach the spectacular vista point, **Peña del Cuervo** (6km). Hire a guide to accompany you past the church and follow the winding road up to the rock formation, dubbed **Las Monjas** (a 5hr., 17km hike) due to its resemblance to nuns bowed in prayer. On the way there, turn right at the dirt road alongside the **Río del Milagro,** which meanders past old entrances to mines and the ruins of the once-glorious **Hacienda de Plan Grande.** From there, you can either go right to the **Unión de Dos Ríos,** or left to the **Trucha Poderosa,** which houses the **Mina del Poder de Dios,** dating to 1790. The trail goes on for miles, and it is easy to just keep walking—remember that you will eventually have to turn around and go back. Abandoned mines frequently collapse, so be careful exploring on your own.

The town has a few convenience stores, a handful of small restaurants selling tacos, *pastes* (local, meat-filled pastry), and more expensive plates, a church with a small *zócalo*, and some houses. For more information, head to the **tourist office** in the Presidencia Municipal, across from the church. (☎715 0994, ext. 114; premineral38@hotmail.com. Open M-F 9am-4pm, Sa 9am-2pm, Su 10am-2pm.) Several companies organize outdoor activities: **Adven-Tours** (☎715 2941; www.adven-tours.com), based out of the family-run Las Güeras restaurant behind the church, offers single- and multi-day trips like rappelling (400 pesos for 5hrs.), while **Mountain Gate** (☎713 5599; www.mountaingate.com.mx), organizes ATV tours from 400 pesos. Options for horseback riding and fishing abound as well.

MINERAL DEL MONTE

Catch a "Mineral del Monte" combi (20min., 6.50 pesos) in front of the Iglesia de la Asunción in Pachuca, on Villigran at the corner of Carranza. Last return combi from Mineral del Monte 10pm. Tour trolleys, such as Rafabus, depart from the bottom of Hidalgo and Héroes for a quick visit to 5 mines and 2 miradores. (☎797 0195. Spanish only. 50min., 25 pesos.)

Mineral del Monte (pop. 10,600), 9km north of Pachuca, is a quiet town with brightly painted houses and an exceptional number of small silver shops. Stroll north of the Plaza Principal to visit **Mina Acosta,** on Guerrero (a 20min. walk), to see a relic of Mineral del Monte's mining history. An active mine for over 250 years, Mina Acosta passed through the hands of Spanish, English, Mexican, and American owners before finally coming under government control in 1947. The building to the left of the entrance once housed mine managers. Silver robbers were kept out of the mine by the obsidian shards that line the tops of the surrounding walls. If the tunnels in Mina Acosta alone were laid end-to-end, they would reach from Pachuca to Tijuana. (Guided tours in Spanish include a 450m walk through a mine tunnel. Open W-Su 10am-5pm. 25 pesos, students and teachers 15 pesos, miners and ex-miners free.)

Mineral del Monte offers good hiking and climbing opportunities. *Combis* depart from La Madre in front of Deportivo de la Ciudad, also known as the Escuela Primaria, across from the Instituto de Artes, for **Peñas Cargadas** (every hr. 6am-5pm, 5 pesos), a massive rock formation up in the hills. At the site, **Cargada Mayor,** on your left, is 100m tall. To its right is **Cargada Menor,** a mere 80m tall. Next to Menor stands **El Pilón** (70m), and on the far right, **Cerrote** (30m). Many hiking paths weave through the area, which, due to its isolation, can be dangerous. **You should not attempt to go alone. Only very experienced rock climbers should attempt to scale the rocks.** Crosses at the bottom mark spots where several climbers have met their deaths. Interested climbers should contact **Lucio Ramírez** (Club Alpino, Lerdo de Tejada 4 in Mineral del Monte) or stop by **Club Alpino's** headquarters in Deportivo de la Ciudad. (Climbing excursions Su 7am. Open Su 7am-7:30pm.)

The town gets wild during its two week-long festivals, celebrating the patron saint of miners in **La Feria del Dulce Nombre** (2nd week of January), and the product of their labor in **El Festival de la Plata** (2nd week of July). For more information, visit the **tourist office** in the Presidencia Municipal. (www.el-real.com. Open M-F 10am-3pm, Sa-Su 10am-5pm.)

ESTADO DE MEXICO

VALLE DE BRAVO   ☎726

From the mountain views at the end of every cobblestone street to the luscious fruit sold in the market by *indígenas*, this 16th-century town is a picturesque dream. Despite the influx of new businesses and wealthy Mexico City residents who keep vacation homes here, Valle de Bravo (pop. 60,000) still retains a cozy, traditional feel. This is no accident: in 1972, Valle de Bravo was declared a "typical town," and construction on new buildings is strictly regulated. The architecture maintains a uniform colonial touch—all the buildings have a red base and white walls with tile roofing. Mountain biking, hang gliding, boating, and horseback riding beckon tourists and Mexican urbanites, who marvel at the beauty of Lake Avándaro and its surrounding pine forests.

🖪🚻 **TRANSPORTATION AND PRACTICAL INFORMATION.** To get to the *centro* from Valle's **bus station,** Calle 16 de Septiembre, turn right as you exit, walk downhill one block, and make a right on Zaragoza. Continue for two blocks until you see Centro Comercial Isseymym and turn left. You will see the large church of San Francisco de Asís at the end of the street. **Autobuses Mexico-Toluca Zinacantepec** (☎262 0213) sends 2nd-class buses to **Mexico City** (3hr., every hr. 6am-8pm, 85 pesos) via **Toluca** (2hr., 48 pesos). Tickets are sold inside the station.

Several blocks uphill from the lake, **Plaza Independencia** is to the right of San Francisco de Asís, **5 de Mayo** runs in front of the church, and **Toluca** is on the opposite side of the plaza, becoming **Bocanegra** as it continues uphill. **Pagaza** intersects Toluca and 5 de Mayo. The **tourist office** is on Blvr. Juan Herrera y Piña, inside the fire department (☎262 6200; d_turismo_valle@hotmail.com; open M-F 9am-5pm), but **booths** by the lake (☎262 0458; open M-F 8am-11pm, Sa-Su 7am-1am) and in the

Mercado de Artesanías (open in high season daily 9am-4pm) are closer to the *centro*. **Bancomer**, at Independencia and 5 de Febrero, across from the church, changes checks and currency and has a **24hr. ATM**. (☎262 1328. Open M-F 8:30am-4pm.) **Librería Arawi Valle**, Coliseo 101, facing the plaza, has a small selection of English-language books and periodicals. (☎262 2557. Open daily 9:30am-3pm and 5-9pm. D/MC/V). Other services include: **Laundry** at **Lavandaría Lavanet,** Monte Alegre 201, at Bravo (☎262 6716; full-service wash and dry 12 pesos per kg; self-service 60 pesos; open daily 9am-8pm); **emergency** ☎060; **police,** at Díaz and 5 de Febrero (☎262 4498); **Farmacia Farmapronto,** Arcadio Pagaz 100, in front of the plaza facing the church (☎262 1441; open daily 8am-10pm); **Red Cross,** at Herrera y Piña and Jiménez de la Cuenca (☎262 0391); **IMSS,** at Zaragoza and Díaz (☎262 0559); **Computel,** Plaza de la Independencia 6, which offers **fax** and long-distance **phone** service (☎262 6481; open daily 7am-8:45pm); **Internet access** at **Cafe Internet/ Videoclub,** Plaza de la Independencia 3, several doors down from Computel (☎262 5126; 12 pesos per hr.; open daily 9:30am-10pm); and the **post office,** Pagaza 200 (☎262 0373; open M-F 8am-3pm). **Postal Code:** 51200.

⌨⛶ ACCOMMODATIONS AND FOOD. Lakeside lodging means parting with a lot of pesos, as does staying uphill from town, where rustic, no-frills *posadas* take advantage of the breathtaking view to charge exorbitant rates. Most budget options are in the *centro*. **Casa Abierta ❺,** Coliseo 107, is a small cultural center with four charming rooms and one apartment for rent. A cafeteria, classes, movie screenings (W 7:30pm, Sa 7pm), and live Cuban *trova* music (Sa 10pm) are also offered on the premises. Rooms go quickly, so reserve ahead. (☎262 5190; casabiertavalle@hotmail.com. Check-out 1pm. Rooms 400-500 pesos. Prices rise on weekends. D/MC/V.) **Posada Mary ❹,** Plaza Independencia 1, has a prime location across from the *jardín*, relatively affordable prices, and clean, comfortable rooms with sturdy wood furniture. The one single with a balcony facing the plaza is the catch of the lot. (Check-out noon. Singles 250 pesos; doubles 250-360 pesos; triples 360-460 pesos; quad 460 pesos. Cash only.) **Hotel Las Bugambilias ❸,** Bocanegra 101, behind the church, has basic rooms with cable TV, fan, and clean, tiled bath, though noise from the upstairs pool hall detracts. (☎262 3889. Another location 2 blocks from the bus station, at 16 de Septiembre 406. Check-out noon. Singles 150 pesos; doubles 300 pesos; triples and quads 500 pesos. Cash only.)

Restaurants in this town vary widely by cuisine and price. The nicer places surround the *jardín*, in the shade of the *portales* (the imposing arches). The spaciousness and traditional decor at **El Portal Restaurante-Bar ❸,** Plaza de la Independencia 101, create a pleasant atmosphere. Try the delicious local specialty, *trucha empapelado* (steamed trout; 70 pesos), on the upstairs terrace overlooking the plaza. (☎262 1343. Beer 20 pesos. *Antojitos* 40 pesos. Pastas 40 pesos. Meat entrees 44-85 pesos. Open daily 8am-11pm. AmEx/D/MC/V.) Across the plaza, **El Tortón ❷,** Plaza Independencia 2, is a cheaper, faster option popular with locals. (Coffee 12 pesos. Beer 15-17 pesos. Hamburgers 24 pesos. *Tortas* 18-31 pesos. Open daily 10am-11pm. Cash only.) By the lake, visit **Trucha La Estrella ❹,** Rinconada San Vicente at Fray Gregorio, for a cup of trout ceviche (40 pesos) or fresh trout prepared any way you like (65 pesos). (Shrimp cocktail 50 pesos. Beer 10-12 pesos. Open daily 10am-7pm. Cash only.) A short walk from the plaza can save a few pesos: stop at one of the small family-run restaurants on **16 de Septiembre** between the bus station and the *centro*, or track down food vendors at the **Mercado Municipal,** three blocks from the church on Independencia, serving *comida corrida* for 30-50 pesos. Stock up on vitals at supermarket **Centro Comercial isseymyn,** Independencia 404, is also available. (☎262 2273. Open daily 9am-8pm.)

◙ **SIGHTS.** The huge **San Francisco de Asís** church, which marks the center of town, dwarfs everything around it. Inside there is baptismal font from the 17th century. (On Plaza de la Independencia. Open daily 8am-2pm and 5-8pm.) One block from the lake, the **Templo de Santa Maria** houses the venerated 17th-century Cristo Negro, which—according to legend—miraculously survived a fire set in a surprise attack. In awe, the rival indigenous groups ceased fighting, bringing peace to the region. (On Calle Ameyal. Open M-F 8am-2pm and 4-8pm, Sa-Su 8am-8pm.)

A good place to lose yourself for a few hours is the **Mercado de Artesanías**, at Juárez and Peñuelas, five blocks down Bocanegra from the *jardín*, left on Durango for two blocks, then right on Juárez. Begun in 1985 as a way to preserve native Orcondo artistic traditions, the Mercado has been a successful attraction ever since; artisans competing to sell clay pottery, embroidered fabrics, and *ocoxal* baskets allow for plenty of comparison shopping and bargaining. (Open daily 10:30am-7pm.) The lake-front **Centro Regional de Cultura**, at Archundio and Salitre, hosts diverse art expositions as well as a youth-oriented *cineclub* (F 6:30pm) and a number of dance, theater, and musical events; check the weekly calendar of events at the front door. (☎ 262 1948; casaculturavallede-bravo@yahoo.com.mx. Open M-Sa 9am-6pm. Free.)

◪ **OUTDOOR ACTIVITIES.** The huge, manmade **lake** is a popular attraction for all visitors, whether they sit back to enjoy the view or take part in some watersports. Walk away from the plaza on Pagaza, make a right on Salitre and walk down to the Embarcadero Municipal. Hour-long boat tours depart from the *muelle municipal*. (Private excursions 300 pesos, *colectivos* 40 pesos per person. M-Sa 11:30am, 12:30pm, 2pm, 3pm. Twilight cruise with live music Sa 9pm.)

There are also other adventures to be had outdoors, including a hike up to **La Peña** (2km), a nearby overlook that was also the site of many ancient sacrifices. From the Embarcadero Municipal, go north on Jiménez de La Cuenca, or La Costera, for about 1km and turn left after you pass 16 de Septiembre. Continue straight up for about 30min. until you reach the top. A bit farther away lies the natural wonder of the **Velo de Novia**, a 35m high waterfall. (Taxi from the *centro* will get you there the fastest. 15min., 20 pesos.) Those seeking an adrenaline boost should contact **Fly Mexico**. (☎ 262 0048; flymexico@prodigy.net.mx. 5 de Mayo 111, in the Hotel Mesón del Viento. Instructor-accompanied hang gliding and paragliding 1300-1500 pesos per person; group discounts available. Open daily 7am-10pm. D/MC/V.)

IXTAPAN DE LA SAL ☎ 721

Ixtapan de la Sal (pop. 35,000), nestled in a valley and protected by the mountains, has long been identified with its namesake mineral; in fact, records indicate that its ancient *matlatzinca* inhabitants paid a 2000-sack salt tribute to the Aztec empire. It seems as if the town is always blessed with good weather, escaping rainy days even when it is storming in nearby cities. The refreshing weather has already been capitalized upon: a snazzy water park has become the main attraction in town. However, just past the touristy water park, fancy resorts, and a myriad of small hotels, the town is peaceful and charming. In the evening, people of every age hang out in the beautiful central plaza; on weekends, they party it up at themed discos.

▣ **TRANSPORTATION.** The **bus station** (☎ 141 1006), on Carretera Ixtapan-Tonatico, lies between Ixtapan and a small town just south of it, Tonatico. Buses usually stop in front of Ixtapan's water park before proceeding to the station. Only a short walk from the center of town, the park is a much more convenient place to disembark, provided you haven't stowed anything under the bus. To get there from the bus station, take an "Ixtapan" *combi* (3 pesos). To get to the bus terminal, catch a bus either at the resorts or on Juárez, or take a taxi for 20 pesos. **Tres Estrellas de Centro** (☎ 141 1005) sends buses to **Mexico City** (3hr., every 15min. 3:30am-7:45pm, 72 pesos; express 2hr.; M-F every hr. 6am-6pm, Sa every 30min. 5:30am-7pm, Su every 30min. 4:30am-7pm; 83 pesos); **Taxco** (1¼hr., every 40min. 6:10am-8pm, 40 pesos); **Toluca** (1hr., every 20min. 5:20am-8pm, 36 pesos); and other locations. **Flecha Roja** (☎ 141 1805) sends second-class buses to **Acapulco** (6hr., 5 per day 10am-5:20pm, 180 pesos), **Cuernavaca** (2½hr., 6 per day 8am-6pm, 64 pesos), **Taxco** (1¼hr., 37 pesos), and other destinations.

▦ ⁊ ORIENTATION AND PRACTICAL INFORMATION. Ixtapan's main street is **Juárez**, which ends after 500m at the spa, water park, and resorts. **Allende** runs parallel to Juárez, to the right while looking toward the resorts. Some of the main streets perpendicular to Juárez, listed starting from the resorts, are: **Constitución, Aldama, 16 de Septiembre, Independencia,** and **20 de Noviembre.**

The **tourist office** is located inside the **Balneario Municipal.** (Allende at 20 de Noviembre. ☎ 145 5387. Open daily 10am-5pm.) **Banamex,** on the corner of Allende and Zaragoza, **exchanges currency** and traveler's checks, and has a **Western Union.** (☎ 143 2995. Open M-F 9am-4pm.) Other services include: **luggage storage,** at the bus station (5 pesos per day; open daily 7am-8pm); **police,** Plaza de los Mártires 1, in the Presidencia Municipal (☎ 143 0297; open 24hr.); **Red Cross,** on Carr. Ixtapan-Tonatico, between the water park and the bus station (☎ 143 1939; open 24hr.); **Farmacia Madrid,** Allende 8, at 16 de Septiembre (☎ 143 0273; open daily 8am-9:30pm); **fax** at **Telecomm,** next to the post office (☎ 143 5616; open M-F 9am-3pm, Sa 9am-1pm); **Internet** access at **Cyberplanet,** 16 de Septiembre 208 (10 pesos per hr.; open daily 9am-10pm, though hours vary); and the **post office,** 16 de Septiembre 403, two blocks from the church (☎ 143 0223; open M-F 9am-4pm). **Postal Code:** 51900.

⌐⊡ ACCOMMODATIONS AND FOOD. If you avoid obscenely priced resorts and spas, you can find some great deals in Ixtapan. **⬧Hotel María Isabel ❶,** Kiss 11, is the best bargain. To get there from Juárez, facing the resorts, turn right on 20 de Noviembre, take the first right onto Matamoros, and then the first left. The hotel is in the middle of the block on the right. It has impeccable rooms with bath and cable TV, as well as a top-floor sun deck. (☎ 143 0102. Check-out 12:30pm. 125 pesos per person, with 3 meals per day 210 pesos. Cash only.) **Casa de Huéspedes Sofía ❸,** 20 de Noviembre 4, one block off Juárez, boasts large baths with purple fixtures, fluffy bedspreads, cable TV, and pink walls. (☎ 143 1851. Check-out noon. Singles 175 pesos; doubles 300 pesos; triples 425 pesos. Cash only.) Pleasant **Hotel Casa Sarita ❶,** Obregón 512, near the church, has large doubles that are a little worn, but clean and comfortable. (☎ 143 2745. Check-out 1pm. 150 pesos per person. Cash only.)

Taquerías are easy to find and good for a quick bite, and the **snack bar** in the bandstand in the *centro* is a great place to grab a *torta* (14-18 pesos). **Chimbombo ❷,** on the corner of Juárez and 16 de Septiembre, has a great atmosphere, tasty food, and agreeable prices. (☎ 143 1467. Tacos 10 pesos. *Tortas* 16-20 pesos. Enchiladas 40 pesos. Open Tu-Su 6pm-2am. Cash only.) **Pepe's Pizza and Pasta ❷,** at Juárez and Aldama, is a pizzeria with a Mexican flair. (☎ 143 1115. Pasta from 17 pesos. Pizzas from 28 pesos. Beer 15 pesos. Open daily noon-10pm. D/MC/V.) **Panificadora "Salgado" ❶,** Obregón 101B, near Allende, sells freshly baked bread for 2 pesos and various *panes dulces* for 4 pesos. (☎ 143 0654. Open daily 7am-10pm. Cash only.) The supermarket, **Servicio Comercial Gari's,** 20 de Noviembre 100, is located at Allende. (☎ 143 3100. Open M-Sa 9am-8pm, Su 8am-7pm.)

◙ SIGHTS. Most people visit Ixtapan to enjoy the massive water park, **Ixtapan,** at the end of Juárez. With 16 pools (including four thermal springs and a wave pool), a water roller coaster, and a 150m long slide, the park provides hours of family entertainment. (☎143 0331 or 0878; www.ixtapan.com. Open daily 9am-6pm. 150 pesos, children 0.9-1.3m 70 pesos, under 0.9m free. Lockers 5 pesos. AmEx/D/MC/V.) For a relaxing splurge, the park **spa,** directly next door, offers facials for 250-600 pesos, massages for 150-670 pesos, and body treatments for 300-500 pesos. (Open daily 8am-7pm.) For a less expensive dip in soothing thermal waters, go to the **Balneario Municipal,** in town at Allende and 20 de Noviembre, which has thermal and hydro-massage pools inside, and a slide and regular pool outside. Indulge in free mud baths, which you can apply yourself. (☎145 5387. Massage 130 pesos per 25min. Thermal pools open daily 7am-6pm. Hydromassage pools open daily 7am-4pm. Outdoor slide pool open daily 7am-5pm. 60 pesos.) The 50m **Tzompantitlán** waterfall, accessible via a short trip from Tonatico in taxi (25 pesos), is a great spot for rappelling.

To reach **Plaza de los Mártires,** facing the water park turn right off Juárez onto Independencia and continue straight for three or four blocks. The plaza is a bright, beautiful combination of old and new architecture, with an obelisk-like monument dedicated to the martyrs of the Revolution. At the side of the plaza, up the steps to the left when facing the school, is the **Santuario de la Asunción de María,** a striking white church with mauve and rust trim in the plateresque style. Mosaic benches surround the atrium, while gold ornamentation, stained-glass windows, and murals adorn the interior. A glass case holds a life-size sugar-cane Christ in the adjoining 16th-century **Capilla del Santísimo y del Señor del Perdón.** (Main entrance at 16 de Septiembre and Obregón. Open daily 6am-8pm. Office open M-F 10am-2pm and 6-8pm, Sa-Su 10am-2pm.)

TOLUCA   ☎722

Residents of Toluca (pop. 475,000) the capital of Mexico State since 1830, are more likely to think of themselves as *mexiquenses* (residents of Mexico State) first, and *mexicanos* second. Today, old-timers wistfully recall the old Toluca, before industry expanded rapidly, and traffic congestion and pollution became serious problems. A small-town atmosphere and some worthwhile cultural attractions charm visitors that find themselves here for a day or two.

▐ TRANSPORTATION. The **bus terminal,** Berriozabal 101, near Paseo Tollocan, is southeast of the *centro.* To reach the station from the *centro,* board a "Terminal" bus (5 pesos) on Juárez north of Independencia or on Morelos at Bravo. Taxis also make the trip (40-50 pesos). Of the many companies that serve Mexico City, check their final destination to make sure you end up at a convenient stop. **Flecha Roja** (☎217 0285) has direct and indirect service to **Mexico City** (1hr., every 5min. 5am-10:30pm, 34 pesos) and **Querétaro** (3hr., every hr. 4:50am-7:40pm, 110 pesos). **Naucalpan** (☎212 2400) goes to **Mexico City** (1½hr., every 7min. 5am-9:30pm, 38 pesos). **Herradura de Plata** (☎217 0024) heads for **Morelia** (4hr., every hr. 5:30am-7:30pm, 200 pesos) and other destinations. **Tres Estrellas,** (☎217 3396), under the "Aguila" sign serves: **Cuernavaca** (2½hr., every 30min. 5am-7:45pm, 54 pesos); **Ixtapan** (1hr., every 20min. 6am-8:15pm, 36 pesos); **Taxco** (2½hr., every 40min. 6:20am-6:40pm, 76 pesos); and other destinations.

◆▐ ORIENTATION AND PRACTICAL INFORMATION. Paseo Tollocan connects Toluca to Mexico City. The Plaza Cívica (Plaza de los Mártires), cathedral, and *portales* make up Toluca's *centro,* which is bounded by **Lerdo de Tejada** to the north, **Juárez** to the east, **Hidalgo** to the south, and **Bravo** to the west.

A word of warning: address numbers on Hidalgo increase in either direction from the center of the *portales*, dividing them into Oriente (Ote.) and Poniente (Pte.) addresses. Most of Toluca's attractions are a short walk from the *portales;* blue signs marked "M" for "museum" point the way.

The municipal **tourist office,** Building C, 2nd fl., in Plaza Fray Andrés de Castro, operates an information booth and *artesanía* shop within the *portales.* (☎214 5346 or 2494. Open M-F 9am-6pm. **Banamex,** on Hidalgo 223 at Galeana has **24hr. ATMs** and **Western Union.** (☎279 9900. Open M-Sa 9am-4pm.) There is **luggage storage** at the bus terminal (5 pesos per bag per day; open Th-M 6am-9pm, Tu-W 10am-6pm) and **laundry** at **Lavandería Carolina,** Av. Villada 217 (☎215 0110), at Morelos. (Wash and dry 8 pesos per kg. Open M-F 9am-7pm, Sa 9am-3pm.) Emergency services include: **emergency:** ☎066; **police,** Av. Baja Velocidad 1008 (☎216 1812), and Morelos 1300 (☎214 9352. Both open 24hr. **Avanzatel** (☎01 800 696 9696) helps with missing persons. Medical services include: **Red Cross,** at Jesús Carranza and Cirilo T. Cancelada, southwest of the *centro* (☎217 2540 or 3333; open 24hr.); **Farmacia Guadalajara,** Av. Villada 400, at Gómez Fariz (☎214 9008; open daily 7am-11pm); **IMSS,** Paseo Tollocan 620 (☎217 0733), 5 blocks from the bus station. Other services include: **Internet** access at **Magic Network,** Hidalgo 401, just west of the *portales.* (5 pesos per hr; open M-F 7:30am-9pm, Sa 9am-9pm, Su 10am-9pm); **Fax** at **Telecomm,** Berriozabol 101-2, in the bus station(☎217 0774; open M-F 9am-3pm, Sa-Su 9am-1pm); and a **post office,** Hidalgo Ote. 300, at Sor Juana Inés de la Cruz (☎214 9068; open M-F 8am-4pm, Sa 8am-1pm). **Postal Code:** 50090.

⌂ ACCOMMODATIONS. Toluca's budget accommodations offer little besides location. The city has a less-than-buzzing nightlife, so you may spend more time than you might like in a hotel. Beware: A number of hotels in the *centro* are *de paso,* rented by the hour to couples looking for a good time. The well-located **Hotel San Nicolás ❷,** Bravo 105, one block off Hidalgo, boasts spacious, clean rooms. (☎214 7196 or 213 8468. Check-out 1pm. Singles 180 pesos, with TV 210 pesos; doubles 180/210-230 pesos; triples with TV 270 pesos; quads with TV 300 pesos. Cash only.) Pink-and-blue rooms at **Hotel San Carlos ❺,** Portal Madero 210, in the *portales* on Hidalgo, come with two full-size beds, telephone, and cable TV, but the extra comfort comes at a higher price. (☎214 9419; hotelsancarlos@prodigy.net.mx. Check-out 1pm. Singles 300 pesos; doubles 400 pesos; triples 500 pesos; quads 600 pesos. AmEx/D/MC/V.) A few blocks west of the *centro,* the **Hotel Maya ❶,** Hidalgo 413, is small and quirky. Singles have metal walls through which you can hear your neighbors; doubles are more private. (☎214 4800. Check-out 11am. Singles 100 pesos; doubles 150 pesos, with bath 200 pesos. Cash only.)

☖ FOOD. Restaurants and cheap food stands clutter the storefronts of the *portales.* Red or green *chorizo* (spicy sausage), a local specialty, is served with everything—from *queso fundido* (melted cheese) to *tortas.* Traditional candies include *palanquetas* (peanut brittle), candied fruits and *mosquitos* (fruit liqueurs), and *dulces de leche* (milk sweets). Toluca has two markets, **Mercado 16 de Septiembre,** on Manuel Gómez Pedraza, two blocks uphill from the Cosmovitral (open daily 8am-7:30pm), and **Mercado Juárez,** behind the bus station on Fabela (open daily 8am-6:30pm). There is also a supermarket, **Gigante,** Juárez 231, at Instituto Literario. (☎215 9400. Open M-F 8am-10pm, Su 9am-10pm.)

Great breakfasts (50-70 pesos) and filling *comida corrida* (55 pesos) make **Cafe Hidalgo ❹,** Hidalgo 231, popular with locals. (☎215 2793. Open daily 8am-10pm. D/MC/V.) At the well-established **Rancheros del Sur ❸,** Aquiles Serdán 109, even the smallest serving will satisfy two people. (Walk toward Independencia on 5 de Febrero and turn right on Serdán. 3 other locations outside of the *centro.* ☎215 9950. Open daily 12:30pm-midnight. Cash only.) Faux-Burberry upholstered

LOCAL LEGEND

LA MALINCHE

Cortés's native interpreter during the conquest, La Malintzin, remains an iconic figure in Mexico. She is revered as the savior of a race, reviled as a treacherous conspirator, and regarded as a victim of the conquest.

Though the origins of her nickname, *La Malinche*, are as controversial as her significance to Mexican history—the name may refer to Náhuatl words for "noble captive" or "bad luck"—it's known that she was baptized Doña Marina after she was given to Cortés by the Chontal Maya in 1519.

The young woman spoke Maya and Náhuatl, the language spoken by Moctezuma's people. Because of this, she was able to translate between Cortés's interpreter and the Aztecs. Cortés and Doña Marina became lovers, and she soon gave birth to his son.

During the time of the conquest, Cortés is rarely pictured in drawings and paintings without Doña Marina by his side, leaning conspiratorially towards his ear. Her prominence in the events of the conquest led Cortés to write once in a letter, "After God we owe this conquest of New Spain to Doña Marina." Because Cortés had a wife back home, Doña Marina was married off to a wealthy conquistador and effectively fell off the radar in historical accounts.

Though many now believe that her translations saved thousands of lives, La Malinche is still generally regarded as a traitor, and the word *malinchista* is today used in Mexico to identify people who betray their race and culture.

benches set the tone at **Cafe con Leche ❸**, 5 de Febrero 111, across from the *portales* facing Bravo. (☎213 7179. Specialty *cafe con leche* 16 pesos. Breakfast 37-60 pesos. Entrees 40-80 pesos. *Comida corrida* 45 pesos. Open daily 8am-10pm. D/MC/V.) **El Arte Cafe and Cocktail's ❶**, Portal 20 de Nov. 111, may not be ideal for a full meal, but it's the place to be at all hours of the day. (Inside the *portal* between Independencia and Hidalgo. ☎215 8535. Coffee 14 pesos. Beer 16 pesos. Desserts 22-30 pesos. F-Sa live rock music 7-10pm. Open M-Th and Su 11am-10pm, F 11am-1am, Sa 11am-midnight. Cash only.

◪ **SIGHTS.** Built in 1909 for Porfirio Díaz's *centenario*, ▨**Cosmovitral**, a steel art nouveau structure housed a market from 1910 to 1975. In 1980, the building was reinaugurated as the world's largest stained-glass complex. Half a million tiny pieces of colored glass convey the struggle with the forces of the universe, including the masterpiece at the entrance, *El Hombre Sol*. The spring equinox sends sunlight through his heart, creating an explosion of translucent colors. The left wall represents death and night, while the right represents life and day; look up to see the Milky Way depicted on the ceiling. The building also holds a **botanical garden,** housing 400 types of plants from all over the world. (*Av. Juárez, at Lerdo de Tejada. ☎214 6785. Open Tu-Su 9am-5pm. 10 pesos, children 5 pesos.*)

Outside of town, the **Centro Cultural Mexiquense** houses the **Museo de Culturas Populares,** a beautifully restored *hacienda* with a large collection of Mexican folk art, the **Museo de Antropología e Historia** with all manner of Mexican artifacts, and the **Museo de Arte Moderno,** which features paintings by Leopoldo Flores and Rufino Tamayo. (*Blvr. Jesús Reyes Heroles 302. 8km out of town. Accessible by "C. Cultural" buses running along Lerdo de Tejada; 30min., 5 pesos. ☎274 1277. All museums open Tu-Sa 10am-6pm, Su 10am-3pm. 1 ticket gains entrance to all 3 museums. 10 pesos, students and children 5 pesos; W free.*)

The Instituto Mexiquense de la Cultura, known simply as the **Casa de Cultura,** Ascencio Nte. 103 off Hidalgo, has art exhibits and movie viewings. Check the cultural agenda for upcoming events. (*☎215 1075; www.edomex.gob.mx/imc. Open M-F 9am-8pm, Sa 10am-2pm. Free.*) Landscapes, still lifes, and abstract pieces by Japanese-Mexican artist Luis Nishizawa (b. 1918) are on display at the **Museo Taller Nishizawa,** Bravo Nte. 305, next to the Museo Felipe Gutiérrez. The artist himself drops by on some Saturday afternoons to meet with art students. (*☎215 7468. Open Tu-Sa 10am-6pm, Su 10am-3pm. 10 pesos; students, teachers, children, and seniors 5 pesos; W and Su free.*) Striking watercolors by masters like Vicente Mendiola and Ignacio Barrios fill the **Museo de la Acuarela,** Melchor Ocampo 105, conveniently located on the Alameda. *(☎214 7304. Open Tu-Sa 10am-6pm, Su 10am-3pm. 10 pesos, students and children 5 pesos; W and Su free.)* Originally a Carmelite convent, the **Museo de Bellas Artes de Toluca,** Santos Degollado 102, near Cosmovitral, houses temporary exhibits of modern art in addition to its collection of 18th-century religious art, the highlight of which is the 16th-century *Virgen del Apocalípsis* made entirely of hummingbird feathers, mother-of-pearl, and silver thread. *(☎215 5329. Open Tu-Sa 10am-6pm, Su 10am-3pm. 10 pesos, students and children 5 pesos; W and Su free.)*

FESTIVALS. Toluca fetes its patron saint during the **Fiesta de San José** on March 19, but two other festivals overshadow this religious celebration. An agro-industrial affair, the **Feria de Toluca,** during the last two weeks of September, features cockfights, rodeos, *lucha libre,* and plenty of dance and theater performances. (Check www.expoferiadelvalledetoluca.com.mx for event schedule.) Soon afterward, the whole town starts to prepare for *Día de los Muertos* with the **Feria del Alfeñique** (Oct. 15-Nov. 2), when vendors craft *calaveras de azúcar* (sugar skulls) to compete for your tastebuds' attention and a municipal prize.

MORELOS

CUERNAVACA   ☎777

Cuernavaca (pop. 370,000) is—and always has been—full of visitors. First were the Tlahuicans, who founded the city of Cuauhna'huac. In 1520, Cortés arrived with an army of Tlaxcaltecans and conquered the city as a stepping stone to Tenochtitlán. Later, generations of *criollos* corrupted the indigenous name to "Cuernavaca." Today, students flood innumerable Spanish-language schools, "living the language" in the company of thousands of other international travelers. Locals aid the learning process by shouting in English at anyone who looks vaguely foreign. Cuernavaca has attracted the famous and infamous, from Gabriel García Márquez to the Shah of Iran, and draws droves of Mexico City residents seeking comparatively clean air on weekends. Visitors have generated a wealth of restaurants, museums, nightlife, and a stylish international scene. Even as Cuernavaca becomes more expensive, the city's rich history, from its Tlahuican pyramid to its grand 20th-century mansions, continues to entice.

▐ TRANSPORTATION

Buses: The Estrella Blanca **bus station,** Morelos 329 (☎312 2626), is several blocks from Jardín Borda, between Arista and Victoria. **Estrella Blanca** goes to: **Acapulco** (4hr., 6 per day 8am-6pm, 265 pesos); Guadalajara (9hr.; 10am, 10pm; 581 pesos), **Mexico City** (1¼hr., 5 per day 6am-6pm, 76 pesos), and **Taxco** (1¾hr., every hr. 7am-9pm, 52 pesos). **Tres Estrellas** (☎310 1114), in the back left corner of the station, serves **Toluca** (2½hr., every 30min. 5am-7:45pm, 54 pesos). **Turistar** offers 1st-class service to **Mexico City** (1¼hr.; 7am, 12:30, 3:30pm; 63 pesos). Those arriving via Estrella de Oro should cross the street and flag down a northbound *minibús* (4.50 pesos) on Morelos—they run past the *centro.* **Estrella Roja** (☎318 5934), at Galeana and Cuauhtemotzín, runs to **Puebla** (2¾hr., 11 per day 5:30am-7pm, 140 pesos). **Pull-man de Morelos** (☎312 6063 or 318 9205), at Abasolo and Netzahualcóyotl, goes to **Mexico City** (1¼hr., every 15min. 4:30am-11pm, 63 pesos).

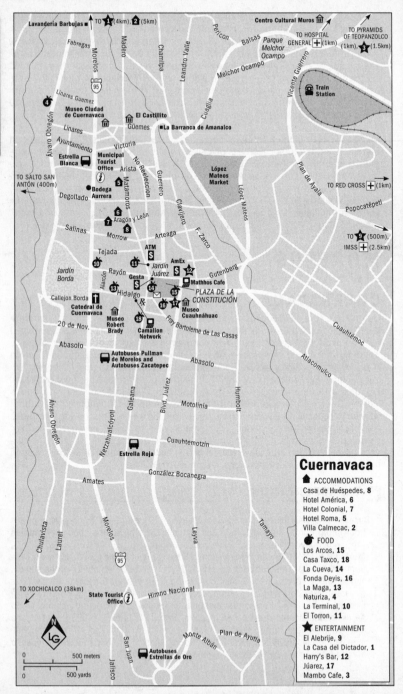

Lavandería Barbujas ■ TO ⭐(4km), 🚌(5km)   Centro Cultural Muros 🏛

Fabregas   TO HOSPITAL GENERAL ➕(1km)   TO PYRAMIDS OF TEOPANZOLCO (1km), ⭐(1.5km)

Morelos   Madero   Champa   Leandro Valle   Peñcon   Balsas   Parque Melchor Ocampo

Melchor Ocampo   Vicente Guerrero

🚉 Train Station

Linares Guemez

95

Museo Ciudad de Cuernavaca 🏛   El Castillito 🏛

Álvaro Obregón   4 🍎   Guemes   ■ La Barranca de Amanalco

Linares   Victoria

Ayuntamiento   López Mateos Market

Estrella Blanca 🚌   Municipal Tourist Office   Arista   No Reeleccion   Guerrero   Clavijero   F. Zarco   Plan de Ayala

TO SÁLTO SAN ANTÓN (400m)   ℹ️   5 ⬆   Matamoros   TO RED CROSS ➕(1km)

Degollado   ● Bodega Aurrera   Popocatépetl

Salinas   6 ⬆   Aragón y León   7 ⬆   8 ⬆   Morrow   Arteaga   TO ⭐(500m), IMSS ➕(2.5km)

Tejada   ATM 💲   AmEx 💲

Jardín Borda   10 ⬆   11 ⬆   ● Jardín Juárez   Gutenberg

Rayón   Gesta 💲   Mathhos Cafe ☕

Callejon Borda   13 ⬆   14 ⬆   Hidalgo   15 ⬆   PLAZA DE LA CONSTITUCIÓN   Cuauhtémoc

Catedral de Cuernavaca 🏛   ℞   16 ⬆   Museo Cuauhnáhuac 🏛

20 de Nov.   Museo Robert Brady 🏛   18 ⬆   Camalión Network   Fray Bartoleme de Las Casas

Abasolo   Autobuses Pullman de Morelos and Autobuses Zacatepec 🚌   Abasolo   Atlacomulco

Galeana   Blvd. Juárez   Motolinía   Humbolt

Netzahualcóyotl   Cuauhtemotzín

Estrella Roja 🚌

González Bocanegra   Tamayo

Álvaro Obregón   Amates

Chulavista   Laurel   Morelos   Leyva

95

TO XOCHICALCO (38km)   State Tourist Office ℹ️   Himno Nacional

N   LG

0   500 meters
0   500 yards

San Juan   Monte Albán   Plan de Ayutla

Autobuses Estrellas de Oro 🚌   Jalisco

Cuernavaca

🏠 **ACCOMMODATIONS**
Casa de Huéspedes, **8**
Hotel América, **6**
Hotel Colonial, **7**
Hotel Roma, **5**
Villa Calmecac, **2**

🍴 **FOOD**
Los Arcos, **15**
Casa Taxco, **18**
La Cueva, **14**
Fonda Deyis, **16**
La Maga, **13**
Naturiza, **4**
La Terminal, **10**
El Torron, **11**

⭐ **ENTERTAINMENT**
El Alebrije, **9**
La Casa del Dictador, **1**
Harry's Bar, **12**
Júarez, **17**
Mambo Cafe, **3**

Public Transportation: Frequent **local buses** (4.50 pesos) run along Morelos and Álvaro Obregón and congregate at the *mercado;* the sign indicates the bus's final stop, and the route numbers are either on the hood or over the windshield.

Taxis: Citlalli (☎311 5325 or 317 3766). Almost anywhere in the *centro* can be reached for under 30 pesos.

ORIENTATION AND PRACTICAL INFORMATION

Carretera 95 from Mexico City intersects Cuernavaca's main avenues. To reach the *centro*, exit onto **Domingo Diez** or **Emiliano Zapata,** which splits into **José María Morelos** and **Obregón** to the south. Cuernavaca is not easily navigable—expect random turns and abrupt name changes, especially near the plaza. Even and odd numbers usually stay on different sides of the street but, because of two different numbering systems, buildings opposite each other may have addresses several hundred numbers apart. The official address system changed a while ago, and on some streets it's not uncommon to see two addresses on each building: "400/antes 17" means the official address is 400 and the previous one was 17.

Tourist Offices: Municipal Office, Morelos 278 (☎329 4404; www.cuernavaca.gob.mx). A 10min. walk north of Hidalgo, below the Museo de la Ciudad. Open M-F 9am-5:30pm, Sa-Su 10am-5pm. 2 info booths in the *zócalo* and 1 in front of Museo de la Ciudad. **State Office,** Morelos Sur 187 (☎314 3920), a 15min. walk south of Hidalgo. Look for a yellow wall on the right side of the street. Open daily 9am-6pm.

Currency Exchange and Banks: Some establishments accept US$. **Gesta,** Galeana y Lerdo de Tejada 2-A (☎314 0195), near Jardín Juárez. Exchanges currency and traveler's checks. Open M-F 9am-6pm, Sa 9am-2pm. **Bancomer,** Matamoros 1 (☎312 5740), at Lerdo de Tejada, has **24hr. ATMs.**

American Express: Marín Agencia de Viajes, Gutenberg 3-13 (☎314 2266), in Las Plazas shopping mall on the *zócalo.* Open M-F 9am-7pm, Sa 10am-2pm.

Luggage Storage: At the Estrella Blanca bus terminal. 3 pesos per hr. Open 24hr.

Laundromat: Lavandaría Burbujas, Morelos 397, past Fabregas. Wash and dry 24 pesos for up to 3kg; each additional kg 8 pesos. Open M-F 8am-7pm, Sa 9am-3pm.

Emergency: ☎066 or 080.

Police: Policía Metropolitana (☎313 2436 or 101 1027), on Av. Colegio Militar. Open 24hr. Oversees **Agrupamento Turístico,** Morelos 278 (☎318 9739). Open daily 8am-8pm. **Tourist security hotline:** ☎800 903 9200.

Red Cross: (☎315 3505 or 3555), on Ixtaccíhuatl at Río Amatzmac. Open 24hr.

24hr. Pharmacy: Farmacia del Ahorro, Hidalgo 7 (☎322 2277), at Galeana.

Hospital: Hospital General C.P.R. (☎311 2210 or 2237), at Díaz and Gómez Ascarrate.

Fax Office: Telecomm, Plaza de la Constitución 3 (☎314 3181), next to post office. Offers **Western Union.** Open M-F 8am-7:30pm, Sa 9am-4:30pm, Su 9am-12:30pm.

Internet Access: Mathhoscafe, Gutenberg 2L-3 (☎318 3936), at Juárez. 6 pesos per hr. Free Wi-Fi with beverage purchase. Coffees 12-14 pesos. House special, *mathhoschino,* 18 pesos. Open M-F 9am-11pm, Sa-Su 11am-9pm.

Post Office: Plaza de la Constitución 3 (☎312 4379), on the side of the *zócalo* closest to Hidalgo. **Mexpost** inside. Open M-F 8am-6pm, Sa 10:30am-1:30pm. **Postal Code:** 62001.

ACCOMMODATIONS

Hotel rooms don't come cheap in Cuernavaca, though some affordable options can be found in the *centro* and in outlying *colonias.* On weekends, you're competing with half of Mexico City's middle class—make reservations.

Hotel Roma, Matamoros 17 (☎318 8778), between Degollado and Arista. Rooms with cable TV and small baths off a maze of white-washed corridors. Heated pool with waterfall (open 9am-8pm). Free Wi-Fi. Parking available. Check-out 1pm. Singles 300 pesos; doubles 340-450 pesos, each additional person 50 pesos. MC/V. ❺

Hotel América, Aragón y León 14 (☎318 6127), between Morelos and Matamoros. Modest hotel with great location and well-kept rooms with private bath and TV. Ring bell after midnight. Check-out 1pm. Singles 240 pesos, with TV 270 pesos; doubles 370 pesos. Prices drop 50 pesos in low season. Cash only. ❹

Hotel Colonial, Aragón y León 19 (☎318 6414; www.tourbymexico.com/hotelcolonial), uphill between Matamoros and Morelos, right by the *zócalo*. Spacious peach-colored rooms with hard mattresses surround a small grassy patio. Check-out 1pm. Front door locked after 11pm; ring to be let in. Singles 250 pesos; doubles 300 pesos; triples 400 pesos; quads 450 pesos. ❹

Villa Calmecac, Zacatecas 114 (☎313 2918; www.villacalmecac.com), at Tanque in Col. Buenavista. From the *centro*, take a Ruta 12 bus north on Morelos. Get off past the Zapata statue, walk 1 block and turn left onto Zacatecas. Gorgeous surroundings, including a functioning steam bath in the garden. Cozy rooms with clean, communal baths. Breakfast buffet (8am-1pm). Check-out 1pm. 4-bed dorms 280 pesos; doubles with private bath 760 pesos. 10% discount with HI or ISIC. Cash only. ❺

Casa de Huéspedes San Juan, Aragón y León 11 (☎312 7357), between Matamoros and Morelos. The most appealing of several slummy options in the Aragón y León backpacker ghetto. Less-than-glamorous rooms with bare bulbs and sagging mattresses face an overgrown garden, but the price just can't be beat. Communal bath. Hot water upon request. Singles 80 pesos; doubles 100 pesos. Cash only. ❶

🄵 FOOD

If you have any money left over after paying your hotel bill, there's no better place to spend it than in Cuernavaca's restaurants, which offer some of the tastiest meals in the region. There are plenty of decent, cheap places to eat in the *centro*, especially around **Galeana and Juárez.** For fresh food, visit the **Mercado López Mateos.** Head east on Degollado, up the pedestrian bridge, and past the vendor stands until you exit onto Clavijero. The market is below the stairs on Clavijero. Food items are all the way in the back. (Open daily 7am-8pm.) The supermarket **Bodega Aurrera,** Morelos 249, is half a block toward the *zócalo* from the Estrella Blanca bus station. (☎312 8120. Open daily 8am-10pm. AmEx/D/MC/V.)

🍴 **La Maga,** Morrow 9, 2nd. fl. (☎310 0432), between Morelos and Matamoros. A restaurant, cafe, book club, cultural forum, and bar in one. Excellent veggie-friendly buffet with fresh fruit, salad, soups, and traditional entrees (1-5pm; 66 pesos). *Comida corrida* (35 pesos) takeout only. Salads (22-30 pesos) and sandwiches (27 pesos) served after 5pm. F-Sa live world music 9pm. Open M-W 1-9pm, Th-Sa 1-11pm. ❹

🍴 **El Torton,** Matamoros 20 (☎314 4136), at the corner of the Jardín. Another around the corner on No Reelección. Clean, quick, cheap, and centrally located, with *tortas gigantes* (20-30 pesos) that are truly gigantic. Natural flavored *aguas* 12 pesos. Open daily 8:30am-9:30pm. Cash only. ❷

Los Arcos, Jardín de los Héroes 4 (☎312 4486 or 1510). Sit on this restaurant-bar's outdoor patio for good music and huge portions. Savor the red *enchiladas cuernavaca* (57 pesos). Don't worry—the *oreja de elefante* (110 pesos) is a type of local fish, not a pachyderm. Breakfasts before 1pm, 47-80 pesos. *Menú del día* after 1pm, 70 pesos. *Tortas* 22-40 pesos; 15 pesos takeout. Happy hour daily 2-4pm and 8-10pm. Live *ranchero* or salsa music daily 9-11:30pm. Open daily 8am-midnight. AmEx/D/MC/V. ❹

La Cueva, Galeana 2 (☎312 4002), facing the Gobierno del Estado building, west of the *zócalo*. Friendly service and the well-stocked bar attract local youth, who pour in around

9pm. Floor has a steep slope; hold on to your coffee! Breakfast 25-65 pesos. *Comida corrida* 35 pesos. All-you-can-eat *pozole* 45 pesos. *Tortas* and sandwiches from 17 pesos. Open M-Th and Su 8am-11pm, F-Sa 8am-midnight. Cash only. ❸

Casa Taxco, Galeana 12 (☎318 2242), between Hidalgo and Abasolo, near the Plazuela del Zacate. Delicious and inexpensive. *Comida corrida* 40-55 pesos. Salmon or *conejo* (rabbit) in garlic chili sauce 90 pesos. Open M-Sa 8am-8pm, Su 9am-8pm. Cash only. ❹

Naturiza, Álvaro Obregón 327-1 (☎312 4626), 1 block past Morelos, behind Hotel Canarios. Tasty vegetarian food far from the crowded *centro*. *Comida corrida* 55 pesos. A la carte specialities like eggplant parmesan or soy *chile en nogada* 55-75 pesos. Open M-Sa 9am-5pm. Cash only. ❹

Fonda Deyis, Hidalgo 10 (☎312 2310), half a block from the Palacio de Cortés. The most affordable option for a sit-down, home-style meal in the centro. Squeeze into a tiny booth for the 28-peso comida corrida. Open Sa-F 10am-6pm. Cash only. ❷

La Terminal, Rayón 28 (☎318 7186), on the corner with Morelos. This corner staple has served thick and tasty tortillas and filling meals with a traditional touch since 1925. *Comida corrida* 35 pesos. Regional dishes 40-67 pesos. Th-Sa live *trova* music from 8pm. Open M-F 1-10pm, Sa-Su 9am-10pm. Cash only. ❸

◎ SIGHTS

For a city that's mostly visited for its "eternal springtime," Cuernavaca has an array of museums to keep you indoors—if only for a little while. Once you step back outside, you can take in the fresh air in some of the city's natural havens.

SIGHTS IN THE CENTRO

PLAZA DE LA CONSTITUCIÓN AND JARDÍN JUÁREZ. The Plaza de la Constitución is the heart and soul of the city. Food and balloon vendors, *mariachis*, and shoe shiners seek to capitalize on the locals and tourists that always pack the park. Gustave Eiffel (of Eiffel Tower fame) designed the bandstand, or *kiosko*, in Jardín Juárez, at the northwestern corner of the plaza. A graying band belts out polka, classical music, and Mexican folk music (Th and Su 6pm). *(Across from the Palacio de Cortés.)*

MUSEO CUAUHNÁHUAC (PALACIO DE CORTÉS). The fortress-like Palacio de Cortés stands as a reminder of the city's grim history. Cortés conquered Cuernavaca in 1521 and built this two-story fortress atop the remains of the ruined Cuauhnáhuac pyramid. He lived here on and off until his return to Spain in 1540, and his Spanish widow remained here until her death—her skeleton can be seen outside the entrance. The building served as a prison in the 18th century and became the city's Palacio de Gobierno during the Porfiriato. Thanks to restoration work done in the 1970s by the Instituto Nacional de Antropología e Historia, the Palacio was transformed into the Museo Cuauhnáhuac, displaying artifacts from pre-Hispanic times to the Revolution, including indigenous depictions of the conquest such as the 1493 *Codice Moctezuma*. Its most famous attraction is on the second floor: a 1929 Diego Rivera mural illustrating the state's history (*De la conquista a la revolución;* "From conquest to revolution"), commissioned by then-US ambassador Dwight Morrow, father-in-law of transatlantic flyer Charles Lindbergh. *(Leyva 100, at Hidalgo and Blvr. Juárez. ☎312 8171; mrcinah@prodigy.net.mx. Signs in English and Spanish; call ahead for free guided tours Tu-Sa 10am-2pm. Camera use 35 pesos. Open Tu-Su 9am-6pm; tickets sold until 5:30pm. 37 pesos; discounts for Mexicans; Su Mexicans free.)*

CATEDRAL DE CUERNAVACA. Built with volcanic rock mainly by indigenous craftsmen, the construction of this cathedral was begun in 1529 and completed in 1552. The former Franciscan convent is the 5th-oldest church in the Americas. That age hides secrets: about 20 years ago, restoration of the modernized *templo* revealed **Japanese frescoes** depicting the persecution and martyrdom of Christian missionaries in Sokori, Japan. These frescoes may have been painted in the early 17th century by a converted Japanese artist, but how they ended up in Mexico remains a mystery. To the right is the 17th-century **Capilla de la Tercera Orden,** with a beautiful golden Churrigueresque altar; to the left is the late 19th-century **Capilla de El Carmen,** which has a mass in English on Sunday at 10:30am. *(Hidalgo 17, 3 blocks from the zócalo, at Morelos. ☎ 318 4590. Open daily 8am-2pm and 4-7pm.)*

MUSEO ROBERT BRADY. The "Casa de la Torre," the former friary converted into a private home by a rich American expat, houses an eclectic, beautiful collection of art, with pieces by Max Beckman, Paul Klee, Frida Kahlo, Diego Rivera, and Rufino Tamayo. The museum also features colonial Mexican furniture, pre-Hispanic figurines, and indigenous art from many parts of the world. Visitors might feel a little voyeuristic peeking into Brady's brightly tiled kitchen and closets full of Mexican caftans, and admiring snapshots of his celebrity friends. *(Netzahualcóyotl 4, 1 block off Morelos behind the cathedral. ☎ 314 3529 or 318 8554; www.bradymuseum.org. Open Tu-Su 10am-6pm. 30 pesos, students with ISIC 15 pesos.)*

JARDÍN BORDA. In 1783, Friar Manuel de la Borda built this garden of magnificent pools and fountains as an annex to the home of his father, wealthy silver tycoon José de la Borda. In 1865, Emperor Maximilian and his wife Carlota established a summer residence here. Don't miss the small door in the wall by the southwest *mirador* through which the emperor's lovers entered unannounced. Today, the garden's splendor has faded. Modern additions include four temporary exhibit rooms near the entrance comprising the **Instituto de Cultura de Morelos**, a small theater, a cafe, and a *museo del sitio* near the emperor's summer home. **Rowboats** are available for rent on the small duck pond. The Jardín also hosts a weekly crafts fair, **Jardín del Arte.** *(Morelos 271. Enter through a stone building on Morelos, across from the Cathedral. ☎ 318 1050; www.arte-cultura-morelos.com. Open Tu-Su 10am-5:30pm. 30 pesos; students, teachers, and children 15 pesos; Su free. Rowboats 15 pesos per 30min., 20 pesos per hr. Jardín del Arte fair Su 11am-5pm.)*

SIGHTS AWAY FROM THE CENTRO

CENTRO CULTURAL MUROS. This new museum holds the impressive **Gelman Collection of Mexican Art.** The first floor features current Mexican artists pushing the limit with curious mixed-media work, while the second floor houses modernist pieces by greats such as Frida Kahlo, José Clemente Orozco, Diego Rivera, and Rufino Tamayo, as well as renowned contemporary artists. Restored murals by Joseph Renau and Jose Reyes Meza, taken from the Hotel Casino de la Selva, can also be found near the entrance. *(Vicente Guerrero 205, to the right within the Costco/Mega shopping complex. Take a Ruta 5 bus from the centro to the shopping complex. ☎ 310 3848; www.muros.org.mx. Open Tu-Su 10am-6pm. 30 pesos, students and teachers 15 pesos, seniors and children under 6 free; Tu and Su free.)*

PYRAMIDS OF TEOPANZOLCO. This small site in the middle of a residential neighborhood contains 15 different constructions, including the ruins of a pyramid and two temples built by the Tlahuicans, who were conquered by the Aztecs in 1427. Little remains of the temples, located atop the pyramid and dedicated to the god of war, Huitzilopochtli, and the god of rain, Tlaloc. Another temple honors the wind god, Ehe'catl, an incarnation of the feathered serpent Quetzalcóatl, with its round base showing Aztec influence. *(Calle Río Balsas at Ixcateopan, in Col. Vista Hermosa* *beyond the train station on Balsas. From the marketplace or Morelos, take a taxi for 25 pesos. Alternatively, take bus #10 "Río Mayo" for 4.50 pesos from Degollado and No Reelección—ask to be let off at Ixcateopan, where you will make a right and walk 3 blocks to the site. ☎ 314 1284. Spanish brochure 5 pesos. Call ahead for free guided tours in Spanish. Open daily 9am-5:30pm. 34 pesos; children under 13 free; Discounts for Mexicans; Su free.)*

> **TIP** **STEPPING UP.** If you find yourself descending your umpteenth pyramid on all fours, take a lesson from how the Aztecs handled these steep steps. To avoid turning their back on the temple's deity, Aztecs ascended and descended in a serpentine fashion. You, too, can scale the pyramid more easily by adopting this zigzag approach.

OTHER SIGHTS. The scenic little building holding **El Castillito (Museo Fotográfico de la Ciudad de Cuernavaca)** was built in 1903 as a residence for the caretaker of the gardens across the street. Today it houses a small, free collection of old photographs and city plans of Cuernavaca. *(Güemes 1, past the church. ☎ 329 4405. Open Tu-Su 10am-5pm. Free.)* Next to the tourist office on Güemes is **La Barranca de Amanalco**, where you can take a peaceful stroll through nature (and some garbage) right in the middle of the city. *(Open daily 9am-6pm. Free.)* Another natural sight that has sadly become a magnet for trash is the 41m tall waterfall, **Salto de San Antón.** Despite its unappreciated state, the waterfall is still impressive; convenient benches at San Antón have great views. *(To get to Salto de San Antón, follow Degollado toward Obregón, cross the bridge and continue down Callejón del Salto, slightly to the left. Turn left when the road ends, and walk down the steps and the dirt road to another main road. Walk left to a small parking area; the entrance to the salto is on the right. Alternatively, take a "Carolina" combi from Morelos at Hidalgo and get off at La Virgen; turn to the left and walk 3 short blocks. Open daily 8am-6pm. Free.)*

NIGHTLIFE

Cuernavaca's popularity as a vacation spot fuels a glitzy nightlife. Discos are typically open from 9 or 10pm to 6am on Friday and Saturdays; a few spots are also open during the week. The more popular discos lie beyond walking distance from the *zócalo* in the *colonias*, best reached by taxi (*rutas* end at about 10pm). Only Harry's and Juárez are within walking distance of the *zócalo*. All the spots listed are familiar to taxi drivers. An alternative to clubs is the busy **Plazuela del Zacate** on the corner of Hidalgo and Galeana, where bars with outdoor seating and live music attract plenty of people.

La Casa del Dictador, Jacarandas 4 (☎ 317 3186), a few blocks south of the Zapata statue, at Zapata in Col. Buenavista. Raging music and gay (mostly male) clientele. Cover F 50 pesos with 2 beers; Sa 50 pesos with 5 beers. Open F-Sa 10:30pm-4am. Cash only.

Mambo Cafe (☎ 313 5813), on Guerrero at Nueva Italia. The spot to salsa, merengue, and cumbia. Tropical decor, live band, and round tables create a 1950s Cuban club scene. DJ plays reggaeton between live salsa and *norteño* acts every hour midnight-3am. Beer 35 pesos. Mixed drinks from 50 pesos. Th 3 free drinks for women. F 49% off bottles. Cover F-Sa 80 pesos. Doors open W-Sa 10pm. AmEx/D/MC/V.

Juárez, Blvr. Juárez 4 (☎ 312 7984), facing the Palacio de Cortés. Billowing sheets set a cool atmosphere for dancing and drinks. Balcony on 2nd fl. overlooks the dance floor and the zócalo. Beer 30 pesos; 10 for 100 pesos. Mixed drinks 60-80 pesos. 100-peso drink min. for men. Doors open F-Sa 10pm. AmEx/D/MC/V.

El Alebrije, Av. Plan de Ayala 405 (☎ 322 4282; www.elalebrijecuernavaca.com). Light and smoke effects energize you as you bump and grind to pop hits on the raised oval dance floor. A young and stylish crowd fights to get into this exclusive club—VIP areas separate the somebodies from the nobodies. Beer 40 pesos. Mixed drinks 65-80 pesos. Cover men 150 pesos. Doors open F-Sa 10pm. AmEx/D/MC/V.

Harry's Bar, Gutenberg 5 (☎312 7679; harrys@netcall.com.mx), at Guerrero on the south-eastern corner of Jardín Juárez. Downstairs bar with sassy American decor fills up after midnight. Tu foreigners drink free. Beer 30 pesos. Mixed drinks 40-60 pesos. F-Sa *bebidas nacionales* 10 pesos 9-11:30pm. Open Tu and F-Sa 10pm-6am. AmEx/D/MC/V.

Enygma, Alazar 34 (☎183 9343), off Juárez in the *centro.* Head upstairs to this relaxed gay bar. Alex, the songbird in drag, peppers hilariously raunchy (Spanish) jokes while serenading a lively crowd (Th-Sa 11:30pm). Beer 2 for 39 pesos. Mixed drinks 45-55 pesos. Open W-Sa 8pm-1am. Cash only.

🔳 DAYTRIP FROM CUERNAVACA

🔲 XOCHICALCO

From Cuernavaca, Pullman de Morelos buses go to the Crucero de Xochicalco (30min., every 30min. 6am-9:45pm, 25 pesos). Ask the driver to announce the stop. From there, take a taxi to the site (20 pesos) and ask the driver to meet you at the exit to the site for the return trip. Alternatively, take a "Cuentepec" bus (12 pesos) from the southern side of Cuernavaca's mercado, which leaves you at the entrance to the site; last bus back departs at 6pm. To return, take a taxi back down to the buses. Expect to wait for some time for the bus or pay a little more for the taxi to the Crucero de Alpuyeca (50 pesos), where buses run more frequently back to Cuernavaca. Site and museum on Carr. Xochicalco. ☎374 3092. Museum open daily 9am-5pm. Site open 9am-6pm; last entrance at 4:45pm. 45 pesos. There are few signs in the museum, but extremely helpful guided tours in English and Spanish 250 pesos; larger groups 300-350 pesos.

Atop a steep plateau amid beautiful rolling hills, Xochicalco (zoh-chee-CAL-co; "house of flowers" in Náhuatl) is one of Mexico's most fascinating—and myste-rious—archaeological sites. More of a religious and trading center than a city, it was first settled during the early Classic Period, around the time neighboring Teotihuacán was reaching its 7th-century zenith. It was not until Teotihuacán's demise (700-900) that Xochicalco truly flourished. The city became an important trading and cultural center with diplomatic and trading relations with the Maya, Zapotecs, and Toltecs, as evidenced by the architecture. Among the many con-struction projects initiated in 700 was a ball court almost identical to those of the Classic Maya. Accordingly, some archaeologists speculate that Xochicalco may have been a Mayan outpost; others believe that Xochicalco was the mythi-cal **Tamoanchan,** the city where Mayan, Zapotec, and Toltec sages met every 52 years to synchronize calendars and renew the cult of Quetzalcóatl. Xochicalco fell around AD 1200, likely due to internal conflict.

> **⚡TIP** **XOCHICALCO OBSERVATORY.** Try to plan your trip to Xochicalco between April 28 and August 14. During this time, the light from the sun is best observed during the 1:15pm viewing; make plans to get to the site by 11:30am so you can make it to the observatory by 1pm. The absolute best days to enter the cave are May 14-15 and June 28-29, when the light from the sun fills the opening at full force.

Before entering the ruins, visit the solar-powered **Museo del Sitio de Xochicalco,** to the right of the entrance. Comprehensive exhibits and the ticket office make the museum a necessary stop. You can purchase a Spanish mini-guide (8 pesos) in the bookstore at the entrance to the site, or shell out 35 pesos for a comprehensive English booklet. From there, a rocky path leads to the ruins, which are best explored along a 3hr. circular route. After you enter, walk past the first entrance until the road curves and leaves you in front of steps that will take you to the **Plaza de la Estela de los Glifos** (Plaza of the Stela with Glyphs), explored in 1960 and named for the altar at the center whose stela bears two glyphs related to the god Quetzalcóatl. It is believed that priests plotted the sun's trajectory over the pyramids by tracing the stela's shadow. Behind the altar is the **Gran Pirámide (Structure E),** the biggest structure at the site, topped by a temple. Twin pyramids on the east and west of the plaza, **Structure C** and **Structure D,** were used for sun worshipping: one is oriented toward sunrise, the other toward sunset.

To the left of the Gran Pirámide is a good view of the southern **Juego de Pelota** (ball court) below. Many archaeologists believe that this ball court was one of the earliest in Mesoamerica; ball courts as far south as Honduras show signs of a heavy Xochicalco influence. Also left of the Gran Pirámide is the stairway/portico section, used to protect the city from invasion. Past the portico and up two sets of impressive steps is the **Plaza Principal,** rebuilt in 1910, which held homes of dignitaries, as well as government offices. The top of the Pirámide de la Estela de los Glifos is accessible from here, enclosing a huge central pit that was the burial site for high priests and a place for ritual offerings. In the center of the plaza is the renowned **Pirámide de la Serpiente Emplumada** (Pyramid of the Plumed Serpent). Reconstructed in 1909, it bears eight enormous serpent reliefs, referring to serpent-god Quetzalcóatl; the northern side is the most complete.

At the rear of the plaza is the tremendous **Acrópolis,** first explored in 1994, the highest area of the site and supposedly the area where the rulers of Xochicalco lived. The east side was for daily activities, while the west was exclusively ceremonial. Descend from the Acrópolis down the same slope used to go up, and to your left there will be a path down to the **Hall of the Polichrome Altar,** a colored altar protected by a reconstruction of Toltec roofing. To the right is a well-preserved *temezcal,* where ballplayers ritually purified themselves pre-game. Down the steps in the direction of the blue arrow is the **Teotlachtli,** the northern ball court. Two massive rock rings were originally attached in the middle of its unusually high walls—most Mesoamerican ball courts have only one ring. Teams competed for the privilege of being sacrificed atop the Pyramid of Quetzalcóatl, a true honor and a sign of good sportsmanship. Walking through the ball court and turning left will bring you to the entrance to the **observatorio,** which is in a manmade cave. (Open daily 10am-5pm.) On the summer solstice, Aztec sages and stargazers adjusted their calendar by peering through an aperture in the ceiling to trace the path of the sun. Tourists may enter every 15min.; wait outside and a guide will meet you. If you are in a small group, he might even let you stand beneath the hexagonal shaft of light.

TEPOZTLÁN   ☎ 739

Tepoztlán (pop. 25,000) is a village of cobblestone streets, hidden among sheer cliffs and crowned by a mysterious, ancient pyramid. Many villagers still speak Náhuatl and protect their heritage by prohibiting commercial development. The town has remained friendly to small-scale settlement, attracting throngs of expats and tourists while causing prices to soar. So, pack a picnic lunch, spend the night in a cheap hotel, and buy your crafts elsewhere.

◪◪ TRANSPORTATION AND PRACTICAL INFORMATION. Tepoztlán's **bus terminal** (☎395 0852), on Prolongación 5 de Mayo, sends **Ometochtli** (☎310 1877) buses to **Cuernavaca** (45min.; every 15min. 6am-8:20pm; 15 pesos, students 13 pesos) from the east side of Mercado López Mateos, in the "andenes del Mercado" from the last *andén* (platform). To get to **Mexico City,** take a **Pullman de Morelos** or **Cristóbal Colón,** 5 de Mayo 35 (☎395 0520) bus (1¼hr.; 22 per day 5:15am-7:50pm; 64 pesos).

The *centro,* consisting of the *zócalo,* several government buildings, and the church, is bound by **5 de Mayo** to the west, **La Conchita** to the east, **Revolución** to the south, and **Zaragoza** to the north. South of the *zócalo,* 5 de Mayo becomes **Tepozteco,** which leads straight to the pyramid. The **tourist office,** at Envila and 5 de Mayo, is in the Palacio Municipal and offers informative brochures with simple maps. (☎395 0009. Open M-F 8am-4pm, Sa 8am-1pm.) It also manages two information **booths** during high season, one in the *zócalo* (open daily 10:30am-4:30pm) and one in the gas station, near where buses drop off (open daily 10am-4pm). **Bancomer,** on 5 de Mayo facing the *zócalo,* has **24hr. ATMs.** (☎397 3939. Open M-F 8:30am-4pm. Across the street, **Divisas Tepoztlán,** 5 de Mayo 3B, **exchanges currency** and traveler's checks (☎395 2676; open M-F 9am-4:30pm, Sa 9am-4pm). Other services include: **police** (☎395 2113); **Farmacia Villamar,** at 5 de Mayo 20, on the *zócalo* (☎395 0424; open daily 8am-9pm); **Internet** access at **Internet Tepoztlán,** Zaragoza 9 (☎395 1033; 10 pesos per hr.; open daily 10:30am-9pm); and the **post office,** Revolución 52 (☎395 0122; open M-F 9am-2pm). **Postal Code:** 62520.

◨◧ **ACCOMMODATIONS AND FOOD.** Most of the hotels in town are pricey, but do not despair—many **casas de huéspedes** are willing to strike a deal. Most hotels have lower prices during the week, and some negotiate deals on weekends. **Hospedajes Karlita ❷,** Campesinos 4, down the street on your left as you come out of the Museo de Arte Prehispánico, has clean rooms with communal baths. There are only four rooms, so act quickly. (☎395 0190. Check-out noon. Singles and doubles 150 pesos; triples and quads 400 pesos. Cash only.) **Hospedaje Mely ❸,** 5 de Mayo 25, near the entrance to the *centro* from the bus station, offers immaculate, rooms with ceiling fans and a sparkling communal bath. (☎395 3719. Check-out 1pm. Singles and doubles 220 pesos; triples and quads 320 pesos. Cash only.)

Dozens of restaurants serving both trendy and traditional Mexican food line **5 de Mayo** and **Revolución.** Prices hover around 40-90 pesos for entrees. There are some small *taquerías* and *torterías* behind the *zócalo,* but they are few and far between. On the town's market days, vendors open stalls right in the *zócalo,* with *comida corrida* for 20-30 pesos (W and Sa-Su 7am-6pm).**Tepozteca Bonita ❸,** Isabel la Católica 1, is a family-run restaurant where delicious *menú del día* (50 pesos) and handmade tortillas come at a reasonable price. (Open Sa-Su 11am-9pm. Cash only.) Right in front of the *zócalo,* **Cafe Amor ❷,** Zaragoza 2, serves *tortas gigantes* (13-28 pesos), crepes (30 pesos), and pizza (40-90 pesos) in a cafe with a balcony. (at 5 de Mayo. ☎395 4584. Open M-F 12:30-11pm, Sa-Su 2:30pm-2am. Cash only.) The nationwide *nevería* chain **Tepoznieves ❶** got its start here in Tepoztlán, with decor as Mexican as its flavors: tequila, *tejocote,* rose petals, and fig with *mezcal, canto de sirenas* (siren song) and *beso del angel* (angel's kiss), among other poetic concoctions. Visit its newest, biggest branch at 5 de Mayo 21 (☎395 2148. Cup or cone 10-20 pesos. 45 pesos per liter. Open daily 10am-9pm. Cash only.) Tepoztlán has a supermarket, **Super Tepoz,** at 5 de Mayo 6. (☎395 2266. Open daily 8am-midnight.) The town's only bar is the laid-back **Los Balcones,** where locals sip beer (20 pesos) and survey the *zócalo* from the bar's balconies. (5 de Mayo 14. Open F 7pm-1am, Sa 11am-1am, Su 11am-11pm. Cash only.)

◧▧ **SIGHTS AND FESTIVALS.** Tepoztlán's crowning attraction is the ▨**Pirámide del Tepozteco.** Although only 10m high, the clifftop pyramid is still imposing. The area was originally occupied in AD 1200, but was conquered by the

Aztecs in 1438. The pyramid itself is a shrine to Tepoztécatl, the patron god of the people; he is related to the *pulque* (a *maguey* plant) and the moon. The shrine originally held a statue of Ometochtli, but a Dominican friar destroyed it in the 16th century. From the bus station, follow 5 de Mayo into town (past the *zócalo* on your right) until the road ends. The 2km hike is a brisk hour-long walk, and the scenery is beautiful, though the trail is steep (and treacherous when wet—frequently the case in summer). Besides appropriate footwear and water, you may want to bring insect repellent. Some people have died by falling from the pyramid; exercise caution. (Open daily 9am-5:30pm. 34 pesos; students 20 pesos, children under 12 and seniors free; Su free.) The tiny **Museo de Arte Prehispánico** (commonly known as Museo Carlos Pellicer), Pablo González 2, is at the rear of Capilla Asunción, behind the *zócalo*. The collection consists of beautifully displayed pieces of Aztec, Mayan, Olmec, Tlahuican, and *teotihuacano* applied and religious art. (☎395 1098. Open Tu-Su 10am-6pm. 10 pesos.)

Celebrations every **September 8** honor Tepoztécatl, the town's ancient patron god, who was thought to have been born here over 1200 years ago. The night before, participants ascend the mountain to the pyramid where they dance *concheros* (local, pre-Hispanic dance) by candlelight through the night. The next day, they parade down to the Plaza Cívica, where they've built a representation of the pyramid. In March during **Carnaval**, *chinelos*—colorfully attired folk dancers—invite visitors to join in their traditional dance, *el salto*, while musicians play age-old tunes during a three-day celebration.

TLAXCALA

TLAXCALA   ☎246

The colonial city of Tlaxcala (pop. 90,000) surprises visitors with well-preserved, colorful buildings, a breathtaking *zócalo*, and an abundance of cultural and social activities. Despite a growing population and steady modernization, the capital of the nation's smallest state retains its provincial feel. Tlaxcalans were not always so peaceful; unable to withstand the Spanish onslaught during the 16th century, they made a pact with Cortés and sent 6000 warriors to raid and plunder the city of Cholula, ultimately helping Cortés to take Tenochtitlán in 1521. In return, Tlaxcala was granted Spanish protection and recognized as *"muy noble y muy leal"* (very noble and very loyal). Today, few traces of Tlaxcala's mercenary history remain, and its tranquil beauty draws weekend guests from Mexico City and Puebla. Tlaxcala serves as a great base from which to explore the state's now deserted convents and *haciendas*, relatively untouched *indígena* communities, and well-preserved ruins. As well, the city's museums, art galleries, and cultural center provide a satisfying taste of the heartland.

▐▀ TRANSPORTATION

Buses: To get to the *centro* from the **bus station** (☎462 1347) on Carretera Tepeihtec, exit through the glass doors to a swarm of idling *colectivos*. Those facing right go to the downtown area, the market, and the hotel district along Revolución (4 pesos). To return to the bus station, take any *combi* marked "Central" from the *mercado*, or flag one down behind San José at 20 de Noviembre and 1 de Mayo. **Autotransportes Tlaxcala** (☎466 0087; www.atahejecutivo.com.mx) runs **buses** to **Mexico City** (2hr., every 20min. 5am-9pm, 90 pesos) and **Veracruz** (6hr., 4 per day 6am-midnight, 147 pesos). **Autotransportes Mexico-Texcoco** (☎462 0362) also has service to **Mexico City** (2hr.,

9 per day 6:20-9pm, 90 pesos). **Flecha Azul** (☎462 3392) serves **Puebla** (1hr., every 10min. 5:30am-9:30pm, 15 pesos).

Car Rental:Kar, Topógrafos Pte 7, Col. Loma Bonita (☎462 4500), just outside of town, rents from 500 pesos per day. Open M-Sa 9am-8pm.

✴ 🔋 ORIENTATION AND PRACTICAL INFORMATION

Tlaxcala is approximately 85km east of Mexico City and is most easily reached by **Mex. 150.** Don't be fooled by the large number of *colectivos* leaving from the market—Tlaxcala is a very walkable city. Distances are manageable, and it's 4 pesos cheaper and often more direct to chug up the hills yourself than to ride in the VW vans whose 1600cc engines can't handle the steep grades, forcing drivers to take longer routes. 20 de Noviembre shoots north-south, connecting the Mercado Municipal (a hub of *colectivo* stops) and the main plazas, **Plaza Juárez, Plaza de la Constitución** (the *zócalo*), and the diagonally adjacent **Plaza Xicoténcatl.** A parallel landmark street, **Juárez,** becomes **Independencia** south of the *zócalo.*

Tourist Office: Juárez s/n (☎465 0960 or 0961; www.tlaxcala.gob.mx/turismo), at Lardizábal. Attentive and friendly staff provide a wealth of information, pamphlets, and touch-screen computer presentation (also available online). Open M-F 9am-7pm, Sa-Su 10am-6pm. The city's 3 tourist information kiosks keep the same hours. Office sponsors cheap, comprehensive **trolley tours** that leave from in front of the Correos building. (F-Sa 11am, 1:30, 4, 5pm, Su 11am, 1, 2, 3pm; 20 pesos.)

Budget Travel: Viamex, Camargo 5-B (☎462 9284; www.viamex.com.mx), has student rates and packages. Open M-F 9am-8pm, Sa 9am-2pm.

Currency Exchange and Banks: Centro de Cambio Puebla, Juárez 33 (☎462 5050), at Guridi y Alcocer. Exchanges cash and traveler's checks. Open M-F 9am-6pm, Sa 9am-1:30pm. **Banamex,** Plaza Xicoténcatl 8 (☎462 2055). Open M-F 9am-4pm. **Banorte,** Portal Hidalgo 10 (☎462 6743). Has **24hr. ATMs** under the *portales,* as do several banks on Juárez, past the tourist office. Open M-F 9am-6pm, Sa 9am-2pm.

Laundromat: Lavandería de Autoservicio Acuario, Alonso de Escalona 13A (☎462 6292 or 3717). Full-service 42 pesos. 3kg min., 14 pesos per extra kg; 2hr. service available. Self-service wash 14 pesos per 4kg, dry 10 pesos per 10min. Open M-Sa 8:30am-7pm, Su 8am-2pm.

Police: Xicoténcatl 13 (☎462 0735 or 1079), at Lardizábal. Open 24hr. **Tourist police** also available at the same number.

Red Cross: Allende Nte. 48 (☎462 0920), at the corner where Allende ends on Guerrero. 24hr. walk-in emergency service.

24hr. Pharmacy: Farmacia Cristo Rey 2, Lardizábal 15 (☎462 2913), between Xicoténcatl and Independencia.

Hospital: Hospital General, Jardín de la Corregidora 1 (☎462 0030 or 3555), 5 blocks from the *zócalo* at the corner of Camargo and Josefa Castelar.

Fax Office: Telecomm, Díaz 6 (☎462 4998). Offers **Western Union** services. Open M-F 8am-7:30pm, Sa-Su 9am-noon.

Internet Access: Cafes abound near the *zócalo.* **Sistemas Teycom,** on Independencia across from the Plaza Xicoténcatl (☎466 7109). Fast connection. 10 pesos per hr. Open M-F 9am-8:30pm, Sa 11am-4pm. **Cafe Internet,** 20 de Noviembre 14 (☎462 0716), just north of Lardizábal. 8 pesos per hr. Open daily 9am-9pm.

Post Office: Plaza de la Constitución 20 (☎462 0004), on the corner of Camargo. Open M-F 8am-6pm, Sa 9am-1pm. **Postal Code:** 90000.

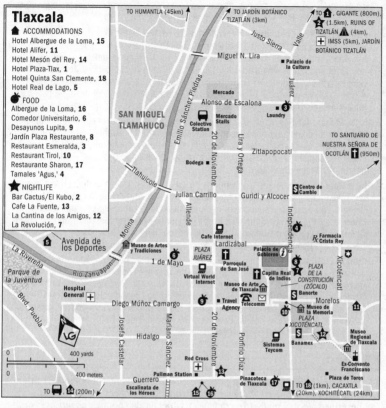

Tlaxcala

🏠 ACCOMMODATIONS
Hotel Albergue de la Loma, **15**
Hotel Alifer, **11**
Hotel Mesón del Rey, **14**
Hotel Plaza-Tlax, **1**
Hotel Quinta San Clemente, **18**
Hotel Real de Lago, **5**

🍴 FOOD
Albergue de la Loma, **16**
Comedor Universitario, **6**
Desayunos Lupita, **9**
Jardín Plaza Restaurante, **8**
Restaurant Esmeralda, **3**
Restaurant Tirol, **10**
Restaurante Sharon, **17**
Tamales 'Agus,' **4**

⭐ NIGHTLIFE
Bar Cactus/El Kubo, **2**
Cafe La Fuente, **13**
La Cantina de los Amigos, **12**
La Revolución, **7**

ACCOMMODATIONS

Though you won't find dirt-cheap accommodations in Tlaxcala, 200-250 pesos pays for some very comfortable rooms. Most hotels charge a standard price for rooms with one bed (for 1-2 people), so sharing is the best way to save. Be sure to make reservations on weekends and holidays, as lower-cost hotels, especially those near the *zócalo*, tend to fill up quickly.

Hotel Alifer, Morelos 11 (☎462 5678 or 3062; www.hotelalifer.com), a short hike east of Plaza Xicoténcatl, just before Morelos starts to curve. Airy rooms with stucco walls and blindingly bright bedspreads include cable TV, phone, and marble baths. Remarkably close to the *centro*. Rooms on 2nd fl. command a view of the surrounding hillside. Complimentary bottled water, parking, and Wi-Fi. Check-out 1pm. 1-bed double 350 pesos; triple 450 pesos; quad 550 pesos. MC/V. ❺

Hotel Albergue de la Loma, Guerrero 58 (☎462 0424), equidistant from the bus station and the *centro*. The 61 steps leading to Albergue's hilltop perch may be daunting, but clean rooms with bath, cable TV, and large windows with inspiring views await. Elevator accessible from the parking lot. Spacious rooms with 2-3 beds and sofas are perfect for family stays. Downstairs **restaurant** serves reasonably priced food daily 8am-

10pm. Check-out 1pm. Singles 350 pesos, with breakfast 400 pesos; doubles 450/ 530 pesos; triples 550/670 pesos; quads 650 pesos. MC/V. ❺

Hotel Quinta San Clemente, Independencia 58 (☎462 1989; hotelsanclemente@prodigy.net.mx), about 10min. south of Plaza Xicoténcatl. The yellow-colored hotel is on the left 4min. after Independencia starts to curve to the right. A tinkling fountain in the courtyard and rooms with tiled bath, phone, and cable TV compensate for the distance from the *zócalo*. Parking, Wi-Fi, and coffee included. 10% discount for stays longer than 4 nights. Check-out 1pm. 1-bed doubles 249 pesos, king-size 349 pesos; with 2 beds for 2-4 people 449 pesos. Cash only. ❹

Hotel Mesón del Rey, Calle 3 1009 (☎462 9055; hotelmesondelrey@hotmail.com), with a regal-looking entrance immediately to the left after exiting the bus station. The modern rooms—spacious but gloomy with small bath, phone, and cable TV—are the cheapest singles in town. Singles 180 pesos; doubles 230 pesos, each additional person 50 pesos. Cash only. ❸

Hotel Real de Lago, Av. de los Deportes 15 (☎462 0399), next to the convention center. Take Primero de Mayo from Plaza Juárez, cross the foot bridge, and follow Molina to the left. When the road splits, veer right on Col. Aldolfo López Mateos until it turns; the hotel is on the corner. Spacious, carpeted rooms with spotless bath and cable TV. Check-out 12:30pm. 1-bed doubles 295 pesos, king-size 490 pesos; rooms with 2 beds for 2-4 people 450 pesos; for 5 people 650 pesos. Cash only. ❹

Hotel Plaza-Tlax, Revolución 6 (☎462 7852). From the *zócalo*, head north on Juárez, which changes into Valle; the hotel will be on your left soon after Valle becomes Revolución. Alternatively, take a "Santa Ana" or "Gigante" *colectivo* from behind San José, and get off near the large Hotel Jeroc complex. Location close to the small Valle club scene, but far from the *zócalo*. Clean rooms with small bath and TV. Check-out 12:45pm. Singles 200 pesos; doubles 230 pesos, 2-bed 270 pesos; 2-bed triples 300 pesos, 3-beds 500 pesos. Cash only. ❸

◖ FOOD

Tlaxcalteca specialties include *pollo en xoma* (chicken stuffed with fruit and other meat), *barbacoa en mixiote* (meat cooked in maguey leaves), and *pulque* (an unrefined alcohol made from maguey), which is also popular as *pulque verde*, (mixed with honey water, spearmint, and lemon juice). For delicious midday meals, duck into one of the small family-run restaurants on Juárez between Zitlalpopocatl and Alonso de Escalona, where *comida corrida* is usually 35 pesos or less. Around the *zócalo*, meal prices rise to 60-90 pesos. For *antojitos* and rarer regional specialties, try the vendors around the **mercado,** on the corner of Alonso de Escalona and Lira y Ortega, along 20 de Noviembre from Zitlapopocatl. (Open M-Sa 8am-8pm, Su 8am-5pm.) There is also a supermarket, **Gigante,** Valle 66 (☎462 5846), in the *centro* on the corner of Vera, and accessible by any *colectivo* of the same name. (Open daily 8am-10pm. AmEx/D/MC/V.)

▨ Restaurante Sharon, Guerrero 14 (☎462 2018), between Independencia and Díaz. Big glass windows slide away to reveal an enormous and unassuming dining room. Tlaxcalans melt for their 9 varieties of *quesos fundidos* (melted cheese; 41-48 pesos). Make a meal out of 3 stuffed-to-the-brim tacos (36-39 pesos). Meat dishes (50 pesos) come with salad and beans. Open M-F and Su 2-9pm. Cash only. ❸

Jardín Plaza Restaurante, Portal Hidalgo #5 (☎462 4891). The ideal location makes the Jardín a popular spot for lunch. Savor a *molcajete jardín* (120 pesos) or the far more affordable and filling *menú del día* (50 pesos). Regional dishes 45-90 pesos. Seafood 75-90 pesos. F-Sa 9pm-midnight live music. Open M-Th and Su 7:30am-11pm, F-Sa 7:30am-12:30am. 100-peso min. for D/MC/V. ❹

Tamales 'Agus,' Juárez 23-A (☎462 1107), between Lardizábal and Guridi y Alcocer. Doesn't seem like much from the outside, but you can feast on inexpensive *tamales* (5 pesos), *taquitos* (5 pesos) and *tostadas* (7 pesos). Wash them down with *atole,* a warm, milk-based, blue-corn beverage (5 pesos). Open M-Sa 7:30am-12:45pm and 6-9pm. Cash only. ❶

Restaurant Tirol, Independencia 7A (☎462 3754), along Plaza Xicoténcatl. Catering to weekday business lunchers and a hip evening crowd, Tirol offers *zócalo*-quality service and food at more reasonable prices. *Sopa tlaxcalteca* 25 pesos. Regional specialties 50-85 pesos. 4-course *comida corrida* 65-90 pesos. Open M-Sa 7am-midnight, Su 7am-7pm. D/MC/V. ❹

Comedor Universitario, Primero de Mayo 11 (☎460 3239), at Sánchez. Line up with fellow scholars for cheap Mexican cafeteria chow. 3-course lunch with unlimited juice refills 16 pesos with student ID. Open early Aug. to late March and mid-Apr. to late June M-F noon-5pm. Cash only. ❶

Restaurant Esmeralda, Alonso de Escalona 7, between Lira y Ortega and Juárez. Small, family-run restaurant packed with locals on their lunch breaks. Cheap and tasty *menú del día* 25 pesos. Breakfasts 28 pesos. Entrees 30-35 pesos. Open daily 9am-7pm. Cash only. ❷

Desayunos Lupita, Camargo 14 (☎462 6453), at Allende. This egg-yolk-yellow breakfast joint at the end of Tlaxcala's *mariachi* row makes scrumptious *huaraches* (cornmeal pizza dish; 55 pesos). Enjoy the full breakfast (39-52 pesos) before 1pm, or the *menú del día* (30 pesos) after. Open M-F 8:30am-4pm, Sa-Su 8:30am-1:30pm. Cash only. ❸

👁 SIGHTS

Most of Tlaxcala's attractions center around the streets off **Plaza de la Constitución,** but *colectivos* make the trek to farther sights manageable. Visit the vendors in **Plaza Xicoténcatl** on weekends for all your *artesanía* needs. Make sure to see **Cacaxtla** and **Xochitécatl,** two well-preserved archaeological sites nearby.

SIGHTS NEAR THE CENTRO

▨ PLAZA DE LA CONSTITUCIÓN (EL ZÓCALO). The serene Plaza de la Constitución is the heart of Tlaxcala. Look for the octagonal fountain of Santa Cruz in the center by the bandstand. Built in Europe during the 14th century, it was given to the city by King Phillip IV in 1646—no small token considering the distance those stones were hauled—to symbolize Spanish gratitude toward *La Ciudad Leal* (The Loyal City) and its instrumental role in Mexico's colonization. Four other fountains, a charming 19th-century gazebo, and the surrounding landscape contribute to the attraction of this plaza.

PLAZA XICOTÉNCATL. Southeast of the *zócalo* is Plaza Xicoténcatl, dedicated to the young Tlaxcalan warrior **Xicoténcatl Axayacatzin** (1484-1521) who defied his chieftan father's support of the Spanish and fought for Tlaxcala's independence. Today, his statue commands a center spot in the plaza. Normally a tranquil area, the plaza livens up on weekends, when a small artisan market occupies the grounds. *(F-Su 9am-8pm.)*

PALACIO DE GOBIERNO. The former palace of the viceroys, where Cortés stayed when he was in Tlaxcala, now commemorates the history of the region's people. Covering the interior walls of the 16th-century palace are immense, brilliantly colored **▨murals by Desiderio Hernández Xochitiotzin** (b.1922), depicting everything from early inhabitants of the Valley of Mexico to the Wars of Independence, accompanied by reproductions of the 16th-century codices that inspired the work. At the time of its construction in 1545, the palace was divided into three parts. The west end of the building housed the granary, the center contained the home of the four indigenous lords, and Spanish viceroys had quarters in the west. Don't miss the representation of Tlaxacala ("corn tortilla" in Náhuatl) at the top of the far right arch. *(Plaza de la Constitución 3. On the north side of the zócalo. Open daily 9am-6pm. Free. Guides loiter inside, offering to explain the murals. Spanish 100 pesos, English 150 pesos.)*

MUSEO DE ARTE DE TLAXCALA. This new museum holds temporary modern and contemporary art exhibits as well as a small permanent collection of seven early works by Frida Kahlo. The building, built in 1898, was a home, a court-house, a prison, and a hospital before its inauguration as the Museo de Arte in 2004. The **Pinacoteca,** a bit farther away on Guerrero, is affiliated with the museum and holds smaller but still impressive, exhibits by local artists. Eight large sculptures by artist Juan Soriano (1920-2006) spill out into the plaza from in front of the Museo de Arte, including an obstinate-looking bronze bull. *(Plaza de la Constitución 21. Pinacoteca at Guerrero 15. ☎ 462 1510 or 466 0352; www.mat.org.mx. Both open Tu-Th and Sa-Su 10am-6pm, F 10am-10pm. 20 pesos, students 10 pesos, under 14 and seniors free, Su free for Mexican nationals.)*

MUSEO DE LA MEMORIA. A great first stop for history buffs, El Museo de la Memoria guides visitors through Tlaxcalan history from 1521 through the end of the 18th century. The museum occupies a 16th-century building that once housed the sisterhood of Santa Cruz of Jerusalem. Today, interactive computer programs and videos throughout help explain the various exhibits. The first room on the right holds temporary exhibits. *(Independencia 3, across from Plaza Xicoténcatl. ☎ 466 0792; museodelamemoria@hotmail.com. Open Tu-Su 10am-5pm. 10 pesos, students 5 pesos, under 10 and seniors free; Tu free. Guided tours upon request W-Su 30 pesos, in English US$5.)*

EX-CONVENTO FRANCISCANO DE LA ASUNCIÓN. Built between 1537 and 1542, this was one of the first convents in the Americas. The thick, wooden door of the cathedral opens into a beautiful Romanesque nave and a ceiling of intricate Moorish-influenced *mudéjar* (woodwork) crafted in the Philippines. The main altar contains, among other artifacts, *La Conquistadora*, the canvas of the Vir-gin that Cortés is said to have kept between his armor and his breast. In the first of four chapels is a corn-paste sculpture of Christ, *El Cristo de Centi*, which dates back to the 16th century. The side chapel to the right, closest to the altar, **La Capilla de la Tercer Orden,** holds the basin used to baptize the four Tlaxcalteca lords at the time of the alliance in 1520. *(Calzada San Francisco, on the southeast side of Plaza Xicoténcatl. A 400-year-old cobblestone way leads about 200m up to the ex-convent. Open M-F 6:30am-2pm and 3:30-8pm, Sa-Su 6am-7:30pm.)*

MUSEO REGIONAL DE TLAXCALA. Meandering through the cloisters of the once imposing ex-convent, the museum presents a fascinating permanent exhibit, including artifacts from nearby archaeological zones, colonial religious-inspired art upstairs, and a library with works on Tlaxcalan history. Take a peek through the fence across the cobblestone road at one of Tlaxcala's prized sites, the **Plaza de Toros.** Named for famed bullfighter Jorge "El Ranchero" Aguilar, the plaza has been used since 1788 and comes to life in the last week of October and first week of November, when Tlaxcala celebrates its annual fair. *(Calzada San Francisco, next door to the ex-convent, on the side closest to the entrance. ☎ 462 0262. Open daily 10am-6pm. 37 pesos; children, teachers, students, and seniors free; Su free for Mexican nationals.)*

PARROQUIA DE SAN JOSÉ. Originally built atop a hermitage dating from 1526, the old parish church, once known as the Catedral de Tlaxcala, became an impor-tant center of Church administration in the 1640s. Today, the immense yellow structure remains an important religious place. At its entrance stand two stone founts of holy water, where weary pedestrians often pause to relax. The interior contains a stone image of Camaxtli, the ancient Tlaxcalteca god of war. The *tala-vera* tiles and bricks now covering the exterior of the church were laid over the original mortar facade in the 17th and 18th centuries. *(Northwest of the zócalo. Open daily 6am-8pm. Mass M-F 7:30am, 7:30pm; Su 7 per day 7:30am-7:30pm.)*

MUSEO DE ARTES Y TRADICIONES POPULARES DE TLAXCALA. The museum features six exhibition halls in which local artisans demonstrate their crafts. Presentations include a tour of a traditional Otomi *temezcal* (steam bath), an explanation of textile production, and an exhibit about the making of *pulque*. *(Mariano Sánchez 1, on the corner of Lardizábal. A short walk west on Lardizábal from the Parroquia. ☎462 2337; artesanias_tlax@yahoo.com.mx. Open Tu-Su 10am-6pm. 6 pesos, students 4 pesos, artisans free.)*

SIGHTS AWAY FROM THE CENTRO

SANTUARIO DE NUESTRA SEÑORA DE OCOTLÁN. Though the Parroquia de San José is Tlaxcala's main place of worship, Ocotlán boasts greater religious, symbolic, and historical significance and is a prime example of the Churrigueresque style, with lavish use of gold throughout the interior and on the altar. According to legend in 1541, Tlaxcala's own Virgin, Nuestra Señora de Ocotlán, appeared to a sick *indígena* named Juan Diego Bernardino. She provided him with a miraculous substance to cure those suffering from the mysterious epidemic and ordered him to build the church. The modern-day *santuario* holds a 16th-century wooden image of the Virgin—supposedly the same one that appeared inside a burning tree to Juan Diego—which is carried through the city streets every year on the third Monday of May. The star of the show is the *camarín*, a small octagonal room located behind the altar where the Virgin is "dressed" for important festivals. *(Hidalgo 1. Head 2 blocks past the tourist office on Juárez until you reach Zitlalpopocatl. Then turn right and follow the steep road uphill for about 1km. Alternatively, take a 4-peso "Ocotlán" colectivo from 20 de Noviembre and Lardizábal and tell the driver to let you off at the Santuario. ☎462 1073. Open daily 9am-7pm.)*

THE RUINS OF TIZATLÁN. These tiny ruins, discovered in 1924 4km northeast of Tlaxcala, were the site of the fateful Tlaxcalteca-Spanish alliance and are all that remains of one of the four *señoríos* (warrior city-states) in the Chichimeca valley. The unusual use of brick—only two other ruins in Mexico use the material in construction—along with the remains of some murals can be seen in the **Basamento de los Altares.** The ruins themselves are underwhelming, but the view from the site is magnificent. A one-room *museo del sitio* provides a short historical account and displays Tlaloc (rain god) figurines. In front of the site is the golden-domed **Templo de San Estéban,** built on top of the Xicoténcatl *señorío* by indigenous workers in 1527. Access to the original, humidity-stricken 16th-century *capilla* of the church is included in admission. *(To reach the ruins, take a 4-peso "Tizatlán" colectivo from the corner of Sánchez and 1 de Mayo or Guerrero. Tell your driver you want to go to the Iglesia, and he or she will drop you off in front of a bright green building on the Calzada Xicoténcatl. Walk left on this street, then up several flights of stairs and cross the bridge until you reach the ruins on your left behind the yellow Templo de San Estéban. Open daily 9am-6pm. 27 pesos.)*

JARDÍN BOTÁNICO TIZATLÁN. A showcase of the state's natural beauty, this garden, encompassing about eight hectares, displays native plants in an otherworldly setting. Rocky paths meander across a creek to reveal a hidden greenhouse. No bikes, balls, radios, or alcoholic beverages are allowed in the pastoral paradise. A movie theater, **Sala Miguel N. Lira,** is located within the gardens. *(Take a "Camino Real"* colectivo *from the market and tell the driver you want to go to the Jardín, in front of the Casa de Gobierno. By foot, follow Juárez past the tourist office until it turns into Valle and then Revolución. From the hotel district on Revolución, turn left at Camino Real before the brick bridge passes over the road. ☎465 0900, ext. 1702 or 1711; ecologia@tlaxcala.gob.mx. Office open M-F 9am-1pm and 4-6pm. Gardens open daily 6am-7pm. Free.)*

♪ 🎬 ENTERTAINMENT AND NIGHTLIFE

On weeknights in Tlaxcala, lights go out early and most of the raucous nightlife can be found outside the city in **Santa Ana** or **Puebla**. However, more options pop up on weekends when the few discos in the *centro* and on Valle and Revolución open their doors to a young, eager crowd. Many of the restaurants and bars under the *portales* feature live music and outdoor seating that attract swarms of hip, coffee-sipping sophisticates. In Tlaxcala, many of the bars also function as discos on weekends. Early in the evening, patrons sit calmly at their tables. Later on, around 11:30pm, a sort of universal twitch sinks in, and the crowd surges to its feet, grinding and gyrating in sweaty, drunken bliss. Check www.mundotlax.com for a listing of what's hot at the moment.

La Revolución, Portal Hidalgo 9 (☎466 1637), under the *portales*. One of the most popular spots in town, this restaurant by day/bar by night boasts rare tequila bottles—including one bathed in gold and worth over 6000 pesos and another shaped like a rifle. Pop, reggae, and salsa. F-Sa live rock midnight-1am. Beer 16-20 pesos. Mixed drinks from 45 pesos. Cover F-Sa 40 pesos. Open Tu-Th and Su noon-11pm, F-Sa noon-6am. D/MC/V.

Bar Cactus, Valle 63A (☎462 6864). 20-somethings gather in packs at all times of day to enjoy the beer (20-30 pesos) and desert-themed decor. In **El Kubo**, the disco next door, the same crowd gets down on the large dance floor to all music spun by one of Tlaxcala's best DJs. 4 VIP zones guarantee that you'll feel special. Drinks from 35 pesos. Bar open M-Sa noon-10pm. El Kubo open F-Sa 8pm-late. Cash only.

La Cantina de los Amigos, Plaza Xicoténcatl 6 (☎458 7397). This centrally located, old-school cantina draws a mature crowd for 2-for-1 beer and *copeo* Happy hour (6:30-8pm). *Botanas* served 1-6pm. Beer 24 pesos. Live *trova* and *mariachi* music F after 10pm and Su 2-6pm. Open T-Su 1pm-midnight. D/MC/V.

Cafe-Bar La Fuente, Av. 20 de Nov. 56 (☎462 9722), at Guerrero. An alternative to the bar scene along the *zócalo*. Couples sip drinks and share semi-private balconies as Latin ballads play and dim lights throw the *artesanía*-clad ceiling into shadows. Beer 18 pesos. Live music Th-Sa 8:30pm. Open M-Th and Su 11am-11:30pm, F-Sa 11am-2am. Cash only.

🌸 FESTIVALS

For information on cultural events in Tlaxcala, check out www.culturatlaxcala.com.mx or head to the **Palacio de la Cultura** (☎462 6069), Juárez 62, four blocks from the *zócalo* at the corner of Justo Sierra. To the right as you enter are monthly schedules and announcements of theater and dance productions, as well as art expositions. The Palacio also stages concerts, exhibits, and performances in its courtyard and all over town. **Teatro Xicoténcatl,** Juárez 21, hosts Theater Tuesdays and most of the Palacio's weekend events. The theater's bookstore offers some books in English on Tlaxcalan culture. (☎462 4073. Hours vary, depending on event schedule.)

Tlaxcala's state fair, the **Feria de Tlaxcala,** is held from mid-October to mid-November. During the month-long *feria*, exhibitions of crafts and livestock dot the town, while Tlaxcalans from across the state participate in cultural and sporting events. If you have a taste for religious events, stop by Tlaxcala on the third Monday in May to see the sacred pine image of the **Virgen de Ocotlán** paraded through the streets or during **La Fiesta de San José,** March 19, when the national celebration centers on the Parroquia. The city livens up with street parades and folkloric dance during **Carnaval,** the first week of February, when *tlaxcaltecas* sport wooden masks and traditional costumes to mock colonial-era European *hacienda* owners. The **Feria San Pablo del Monte,** inaugurated in 2005, is celebrated from late June to early July. This festival features an impressive crafts fair and exposition. For more information on festivals, contact the tourist office.

⚡ DAYTRIPS FROM TLAXCALA

▨ CACAXTLA

In Tlaxcala, take a bus marked "Nativitas" or "San Miguel de Milagros" from 20 de Noviembre next to the market or behind San José. Tell the driver you want to go to Cacaxtla, and he or she will drop you off at the main entrance (50min., 8 pesos). If you happen to be dropped in San Miguel de Milagros, walk up the windy road, following the signs. To return, catch another colectivo in the same direction, get off at Nativitas (2.50 pesos) and take a "Tlaxcala" colectivo (7 pesos) back to town. By car, take Mex. 119 towards Tepetitla. ☎ 416 0000. Open daily 9am-5:30pm. 43 pesos, students and teachers with Mexican credentials and children free; Su free. Spanish mini-guides 5 pesos. Private Museo tour guides 100 pesos.

One of the best-preserved and best-presented archaeological sites in the country is the hilltop ruin of Cacaxtla (kah-KASH-tla), 18km southwest of Tlaxcala. The Olmec-Xicalancas, who once dominated the southwest corner of Tlaxcala state and most of the Puebla Valley, built and expanded the city during the Classic Period (AD 650-900). By AD 1000, Cacaxtla was abandoned, its inhabitants driven from the area by Toltec-Chichimec invaders. Excavation began here in 1975; since then 4000 sq. m of ruins have been unearthed.

The small museum on the right by the entrance contains artifacts and bones collected from the site, including a mutilated corpse and reproductions of the the site's most important murals. From the museum, a paved road leads toward the ruins which, to prevent erosion, are covered by the world's second largest archaeological roof.

Once upstairs, visitors move clockwise around 18 different points of interest including ceremonial courtyards, temples, tombs, and palatial remains. Location markers provide historical information in Spanish, English, and Náhuatl. Near the entrance to the ruins, visitors pass the **Palacio** complex, principally priests' quarters, where archeologists found the remains of over 200 sacrificed children. Opposite the entrance, marvel at the free-standing latticework window, **La Celosía.** Made by surrounding interwoven twigs and branches with mud, lime, and sand, it is one-of-a-kind in Mesoamerica.

Another attraction is the series of murals throughout the site, considered to be among the best-preserved pre-Hispanic paintings in Mesoamerica. The largest of these murals, the **Mural de la Batalla,** stretches along a 26m wall and depicts a historical-mythological battle of two armies, one dressed in jaguar skins, defeating another dressed in eagle feathers. The still-visible original mineral-based colors show a distinct Mayan influence, which may indicate the existence of a trading network linking the Maya and the Olmec-Xicalancas. The walkway ends on one of the pyramid's edges, providing a final touch to the tour: a breathtaking view of the surrounding countryside.

XOCHITÉCATL

There is no direct transportation to Xochitécatl; the best way to reach the site is from Cacaxtla. After visiting Cacaxtla, take the 2.5km dirt path to the right of the steps leading to the pyramid and walk for 35min. Ask for directions at Cacaxtla to make sure you take the right path and bring bottled water with you from Tlaxcala, as you won't see a vendor for hours. To return to Tlaxcala, walk down the mountain road to the town of San Miguel Xochitecatitla and take a "Tlaxcala" colectivo (8 pesos), or walk back to Cacaxtla and take the colectivo from there. Open daily 9am-5:30pm. 43 pesos, students and teachers with Mexican credentials and children free; Su free. Spanish mini-guides 5 pesos. Free with Cacaxtla ticket.

The Nahua ceremonial center at Xochitécatl (so-chee-TE-cahtl, "place of flowers" in Náhuatl) predates Cacaxtla by several hundred years, and its ruins are located on a hill just opposite Cacaxtla. Before the Olmec-Xicalancas conquered the city in AD 300, the inhabitants of Xochitécatl constructed the temple to honor Xochiqueteali, the goddess of fertility. For this reason, archaeologists hypothesize that many of the artifacts at the site are remains of women or babies, who were sacrificed with some regularity at the site. There are four pyramids, the largest of which, the **Pirámide de las Flores**, is actually a pyramid on top of a pyramid. During the spring equinox, the sun passes through the columns on top, which are thought to have been constructed to bring fertility to all women who passed through them. Visitors are not guaranteed the same, but will surely appreciate the spectacular view of nearby volcanoes **Popocatépetl, Ixtaccihuatl,** and **La Malinche (Malintzin).** To the left of the floral pyramid is the **Edificio de la Serpiente.** The basin on top of this pyramid caught water and served as a mirror in which to observe the stars. Perpendicular to these two pyramids is a smaller, flatter structure, the **Basamento de los Volcanes.** At the western side of the site is the **Spiral Pyramid,** built in the late pre-Classic period. Dedicated to the wind god Ehecatl, it is the only such spiral pyramid known to exist. As no steps were found that lead up the structure, it is believed that priests actually walked the spiral walkway all the way to the top. The pyramid of Ehecatl now has a white cross dating from 1632 at its peak, which serves as a ceremonial center for the inhabitants of the area. On your way to the site, peek into the small museum near the entrance and see some of the many ceramic and basalt artifacts found atop the various pyramids.

HUAMANTLA

*From Tlaxcala, take an "ATAH" bus from the station to Huamantla (1hr., every 8min., 16 pesos). Ask to be let off near Parque Juárez. To return, continue past Museo Taurino to Abasolo and make a right. Buses marked "Tlaxcala" return to the city from the corner of Abasalo and Bravo Nte. By car, take Mex. 119 to Mex. 126. Or, continue on to Puebla via Autobuses a Puebla (45min., every hr. 5am-7pm, 20 pesos), which departs from the terminal on Matamoros, between Juárez and Allende. Huamantla makes a great base for exploring the **La Malinche** volcano, just 20min. away. Arrange excursions at Ecoturismo Tlaxcala Extremo. (Guerrero Nte 103. ☎473 0501 or 220 4927; contactotlaxcalaextremo@hotmail.com.)*

Most tourists visit Huamantla (pop. 32,000), located 45km east of Tlaxcala, for its its famous bull-runnings. Sights are centered around the *zócalo,* **Parque Juárez,** which has a 100-year-old gazebo in the center. Northeast of the *zócalo,* the **Museo Taurino,** Allende Nte. 205, commemorates Huamantla's famous bullfighting history and holds models of Mexico's main bullfighting rings. Displays feature posters, bullfighting attire, and photographs dating from the early 1900s, including some of famous female bullfighter Sono Díaz. After leaving the museum, walk down the alley on its left and ring the bell to see **La Taurina,** Huamantla's famous bull ring.

(Museum open M-F 8:30am-6:20pm, Sa-Su 10am-1:30pm. Free.) The spectacular **Feria de Huamantla** fills the town with visitors, carpets of flowers, and sawdust, and newly freed bulls, beginning on August 14, ◼**La Noche que Nadie Duerme,** with a parade of the Virgin down the carpeted path from the Basílica de la Caridad. On the following Saturday, the streets close for the traditional *huamantlada*, the running of the bulls (Consult www.huamantlalaferia.org for event information.)

In 1835, Huamantla also gained renown for its *títeres* (puppets), when the Rosete Aranda troupe began to perform shows with more than 5000 hand-made puppets. The **Museo Nacional del Títere,** Parque Juárez 15, on the west side of the *zócalo* along Reforma, contains the third largest collection of original Rosete Aranda puppets in Mexico, as well as early pre-Hispanic figurines made of clay. (☎472 1033. Open Tu-Sa 10am-2pm and 4-6pm, Su 10am-3pm. 10 pesos, students 5 pesos.) The city also hosts the annual **Festival Internacional de Títeres** during the third week of July.

PUEBLA

PUEBLA   ☎222

Puebla (pop. 1.3 million) was a great social experiment, in which Renaissance met ruffian, and Enlightenment met real world. Conceived in 1531 by a group of humanist Spaniards, the "City of Angels" was to be a crossroads of faith and education, with libraries, schools, and administrative buildings designed to civilize and Christianize. Surprisingly enough, Puebla was completed as planned and to this day is a mix of 17th- and 18th-century European ideals and colorful Mexican art. Built on solid, empty ground, Puebla's streets are said to have been laid by angels who streaked ribbons across the land, forming the grid that makes the city so simple to navigate. Angels notwithstanding, the city has been shaped by pious visitors. Franciscans and Dominicans built orphanages for illegitimate children, hospitals, and libraries, while nuns from a variety of orders set up cloisters and kitchens, where they invented some of Mexico's most famous dishes and the sugar-candy sweets for which the city is known.

▐ TRANSPORTATION

Most sights and accommodations are within walking distance of the *zócalo*. When traveling by **taxi,** set a price before getting in and don't be shy about haggling. Municipal **buses** and **micros** *(combis)*—white VW vans that operate like buses— cost 4 pesos. Anything labeled "Centro" will take you close to the *zócalo*.

Flights: Aeropuerto Hermanos Serdán (☎774 2408), in Huejotzingo, 22km northwest of Puebla on Mex. 150. Regional airline **Aeromar** (☎232 9633) flies to **Monterrey** and **Guadalajara. AeroCalifornia** (☎230 4896) goes to **Tijuana** and Guadalajara.

Buses: Central de Autobuses Puebla (CAPU; ☎249 7211; www.capu.com.mx), at Norte and Tlaxcala. One of the largest bus stations in the country. Services include: **Luggage storage** at GuardaPlus (5-12 pesos per hr; open 24hr.); **24hr. ATMs** and free **Wi-Fi** around the food court; **tourist information** booths in the Arrivals terminal (open daily 9am-8pm). To get to the *zócalo*, exit to the street, take one of the walking bridges over the nearby highway, and flag down a "Centro" bus. To get back to the bus station, take a northbound bus labeled "CAPU" on Blvr. Héroes de 5 de Mayo. Official yellow taxis, labeled **taxis controlados,** will make the trip for 40 pesos. **ADO**

CENTRAL MEXICO

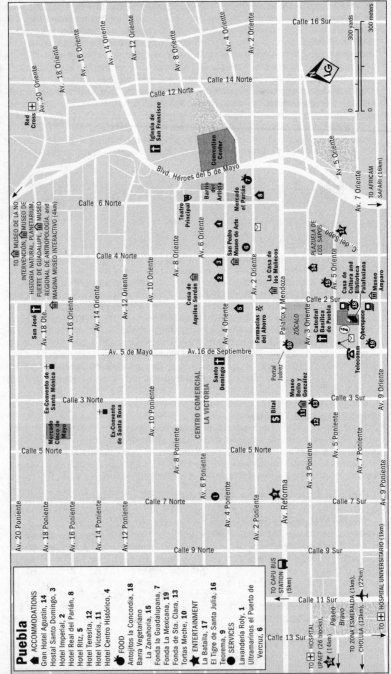

Puebla

♠ ACCOMMODATIONS
Gran Hotel Agustín, **14**
Hostal Santo Domingo, **3**
Hotel Imperial, **2**
Hotel Real del Parián, **8**
Hotel Ritz, **5**
Hotel Teresita, **12**
Hotel Victoria, **11**
Hotel Centro Histórico, **4**

● FOOD
Antojitos la Concordia, **18**
Barra Vegetariano
La Zanahoria, **15**
Fonda la Guadalupana, **7**
Fonda La Mexicana, **19**
Fonda de Sta. Clara, **13**
Tortas Meche, **10**

★ ENTERTAINMENT
La Batalla, **17**
El Tigre de Santa Julia, **16**
Teorema, **9**

SERVICES
Lavandería Roly, **1**
Ultramarinos el Puerto de
Vercruz, **6**

TO MUSEO DE LA NO
INTERVENCIÓN, MUSEO DE
HISTORIA NATURAL, PLANETARIUM,
FUERTE DE GUADALUPE, MUSEO
REGIONAL DE ANTROPOLOGIA, and
IMAGINA MUSEO INTERACTIVO (4km)

(☎225 9000; www.adogl.com.mx) goes to: **Cancún** (20hr., 11:45am, 1092 pesos); **Mexico City** (2½hr., every hour 5:15am-10:10pm, 96 pesos); **Oaxaca** (4½hr., 7 per day, 270 pesos); **Veracruz** (3½hr., 8 per day, 218 pesos). **Estrella Roja** (☎273 8300; www.estrellaroja.com.mx) offers service to **Mexico City** (20hr., every 20min. 5am-11:30pm, 82 pesos). **Cristóbal Colón** (OCC; ☎225 9007) goes to **Puerto Escondido** (14hr.; 7:30am, 10pm; 638 pesos) and other resort cities. **Estrella Blanca** (☎249 7433), under the "Futura" sign, goes to **Acapulco** (7hr., 7 per day, 450 pesos), **Cuernavaca** (3½hr., every hr. 5am-7pm, 140 pesos), and **Taxco** (5hr.; 8am, 8pm; 210 pesos). **Autotransportes Tlaxcala,** under the "Verdes" sign, services **Tlaxcala** (1hr., every 10min. 4:45am-10:10pm, 15 pesos). Smaller buses also serve the CAPU station. If you are **Cholula**-bound, exit to the right of the Futura ticket window and look for the rows of red-and-white buses.

Car Rental: The many agencies in town include **Avis** (☎249 6199) and **Security** (☎268 2210; puebla@securitycarrental.com). 21+. Valid driver's license from country of residence required.

ORIENTATION AND PRACTICAL INFORMATION

Puebla, capital of the state of the same name, is connected through an extensive network of routes to **Mexico City** (120km northwest along Mex. 150), **Oaxaca** (Mex. 190, 125, 131), **Tlaxcala** (Mex. 119), **Veracruz** (Mex. 150), and countless other cities. Street names change as they pass the *zócalo*. Note that there are two major streets in Puebla celebrating the date of Mexico's victory over the French: **Avenida 5 de Mayo** (which becomes Av. 16 de Septiembre in the *centro*) and **Bulevar Héroes del 5 de Mayo.** The main east-west drag, **Avenida Reforma,** becomes **Palafox y Mendoza** east of the *zócalo*.

> **TIP**
>
> **AT A CROSSROADS.** Numerical addresses follow a rigid pattern: they correspond to the number of the lowest cross street. For example, Av. 4 Ote. 237 would be bounded by Calle 2 Nte. and Calle 4 Nte. One block farther down, between Calles 4 Nte. and 6 Nte., addresses are in the 400s.

Tourist Office: Av. 5 Ote. 3 (☎777 1519 or 1520; www.sectur.pue.gob.mx), next to the Casa de la Cultura. Efficient staff offers free maps and pamphlets. Open M-F 8am-8pm, Sa 9am-8pm, Su 9am-2pm.

Currency Exchange and Banks: Banks line Reforma and 16 de Septiembre around the *centro*. Most have **24hr. ATMs. Casas de cambio** offer slightly better rates and cluster in the Zona Esmeralda along Juárez, far from the *zócalo*. Try **Casa de Cambio Puebla,** Juárez 1706 (☎248 0199). Open M-F 9am-6pm, Sa 9am-1:30pm.

American Express: Blvr. Héroes del 5 de Mayo 312 (☎229 1500). Cashes and replaces AmEx checks. Open M-F 9am-5pm.

Laundromat: Lavandería Roly, Calle 7 Nte. 404 (☎232 8772). Full-service 51 pesos per 3kg. Self-service 40 pesos per 3kg. Open M-Sa 8am-8pm, Su 9am-3pm.

Emergency: ☎066.

Police: Seguridad Pública (☎243 1022).

Red Cross: Av. 20 Ote. 1002 (☎234 0000), at Calle 10 Nte. 24hr. ambulance service.

Pharmacy: Farmacias del Ahorro, Av. 2 Ote. 15A (☎231 3383). Open daily 7am-11pm.

Hospitals: Hospital UPAEP, Av. 5 Pte. 715 (☎229 8100), between Calles 7 and 9 Sur. 24hr. service. **Hospital Universitario** (☎229 5500, ext. 6000), on Calle 13 Sur at Av. 25 Pte. 24hr. emergency service.

Fax Office: Telecomm, 16 de Septiembre 504 (☎246 4188), just south of the post office. **Western Union** and telegrams. Open M-F 8am-6pm, Sa-Su 9am-noon.

Internet Access: Internet cafes line Calle 2 Sur; shop around for the best price. **Internet Cyber-Byte,** Calle 2 Sur 505B (☎246 4469). Plenty of computers with fast connections. 15 pesos per hr. Open M-Sa 10am-midnight, Su noon-midnight. **Cafe Internet**

Cyber Space, Calle 2 Sur 701 (☎242 7236). 8 pesos per hr. Open M-F 8:30am-9:30pm, Sa-Su 10:30am-9:30pm.

Post Office: (☎232 6448), on 16 de Septiembre at Av. 5 Ote., 1 block south of the *zócalo*, around the corner from the state tourist office. **MexPost** inside. Open M-F 8am-7pm, Sa 9am-1pm. **Administración 1,** Av. 2 Ote. 411 (☎242 1136). Open M-F 8am-6pm, Sa 9am-1pm. Each has separate **Listas de Correos** for mail pickup. **Postal Code:** 72000 or 72001.

■ ACCOMMODATIONS

Puebla is well stocked with hotels, most of which are within a five or six block radius of the *zócalo*, though real budget options are hard to find. Those willing to make the trek might want to stay 30min. away in Cholula, where you'll hit the cheap hotel jackpot.

■ **Hotel Imperial,** Av. 4 Ote. 212 (☎/fax 242 4980; www.hotelimperialpuebla.com). On the expensive side, but perfect for splurging. Rooms come with beautiful bath, phone, and cable TV, while the hotel offers miniature golf, gym, ping-pong tables, pool, purified water, elevator, and parking. Includes breakfast in the downstairs cafe (7:30-10:30am) and *cena del patrón* (snacks and drinks; 8-9:30pm). Free self-service laundry and Internet access. Fills up on weekends. Singles 380 pesos; doubles 480 pesos; triples 580 pesos; quads 660 pesos. 30% discount with *Let's Go.* AmEx/MC/V. ❺

Hotel Centro Histórico, Av. 4 Pte. 506 (☎246 8942 or 6796). A colonial courtyard and elegant staircase leads to small but modern rooms. Complimentary bottled water. Singles 280 pesos; doubles 340 pesos. Cash only. ❹

Hostal Santo Domingo, Av.4 Pte. 312 (☎232 1671; hostalstodomingo@yahoo.com.mx). Basic rooms feature high wood-beamed ceilings and shared baths. Breakfast included (8-10:30am). Internet 8 pesos per hr. during the day, 10 pesos per hr. at night; free Wi-Fi. The dorms are the cheapest option in town, so book ahead for weekends or high season. Check-out noon. 12-bed dorms 125 pesos; singles 280 pesos; doubles 340 pesos; triples 410 pesos; quads 505 pesos. Cash only. ❷

Gran Hotel Agustín, Av. 3 Pte. 531 (☎232 5089). With an antique stained glass entryway depicting Puebla's landmarks, this hotel oozes faded glory. Small but servicable rooms, most with phone and cable TV, named after Puebla's municipalities. Plan your showers around the hot water schedule (6-11am and 6-11pm). Includes breakfast (8-11am) at attached **restaurant.** Parking available. Check-out 1pm. Singles 170 pesos, with TV 210 pesos; doubles 295 pesos; triples 335 pesos; quads 380 pesos. MC/V. ❷

Hotel Teresita, Av. 3 Pte. 309 (☎232 7072). The small rooms are models of modernity, with clean and attractively tiled baths, coordinated bedspreads, soft lighting, cable TV, and stuccoed walls. Check-out 2pm. Singles 240-270 pesos; doubles 380 pesos, each additional person 30 pesos. Cash only. ❷

Hotel Victoria, Av. 3 Pte. 306 (☎232 8992, toll-free 800 849 2793). Convenient location, accommodating staff, and affordable prices compensate for dingy rooms with unappealing baths. Check-out 2pm. Singles 150 pesos; doubles 190 pesos; triples 270 pesos; quad 360 pesos. Cash only. ❷

Hotel Real del Parián, Av. 2 Ote. 601 (☎246 1968), across the street from the *mercado* and upstairs from some of Puebla's best bargain restaurants. The Parián offers comfortable beds in clean, brightly painted rooms, some with balconies. Check-out 1pm. Singles 180 pesos; doubles 250 pesos; triples 320 pesos. Cash only. ❸

Hotel Ritz, Calle 2 Nte. 207 (☎232 4457; hotelritz@terra.es). The Ritz offers many of the same amenities as Hotel Teresita (tiled private baths, TV), but has not been as thoroughly renovated. Still, the location is good, and the free coffee is drinkable. Complimentary bottled water. Free Wi-Fi. Check-out 2pm. Singles 200 pesos; doubles 250 pesos; triples 400 pesos; quads 500 pesos. Cash only. ❸

🍴 FOOD

Puebla is the birthplace of the *mole poblano* (dark chocolate chile sauce), which can be found slathered on chicken, rice, or just about anything, and has been incorporated into other regional specialities, such as *mole pipián* (pumpkin seed and chile sauce) and *mole adobo* (a spicier blend with cumin powder). The patriotic green, white, and red *chiles en nogada* (green peppers stuffed with beef and fruit, smothered in white walnut sauce and adorned with pomegranate seeds) was devised by the nuns of Santa Mónica as a birthday present for Mexican Emperor Agustín de Iturbide when he visited the city in 1821. Sample the other centuries-old recipes of Puebla's cooking nuns in the *dulcerías* along **Avenida 6 Ote.,** just east of 5 de Mayo.

A multitude of *taquerías*, can be found on Calle 5 Nte. between Av. 10 and 12 Pte., on Av. 5 de Mayo at Av. 14 Ote., and at the **Mercado El Alto,** on the far side of La Iglesia de San Francisco. In addition to the staples, these joints sell *cemitas*, sandwiches made with special long-lasting bread. Other markets include **Mercado 5 de Mayo,** on Av. 18 Ote. between Calles 3 and 5 Nte., which sells everything from fresh veggies to raw meat (open daily 8am-7pm) and **Ultramarinos el Puerto de Veracruz,** Av. 2 Ote. 402. (☎232 9052; open M-Sa 8am-9:30pm, Su 9am-3pm. Cash only.)

🌿 Barra Vegetariano la Zanahoria, Av. 5 Ote. 206 (☎232 4813; rest_-lazanahoria@yahoo.com.mx). Another at Av. Juárez 2104 (☎246 2990). A high ceiling, bubbling fountain, and winding cast-iron stairs give this vegetarian hangout the most agreeable ambience around. Huge burgers served on whole-wheat buns (from 16 pesos) satisfy even the most ravenous diner. 5-course *menú del día* includes fruit beverage (49 pesos). Sa-Su buffet 79 pesos. Open daily 7am-9pm. MC/V. ❸

Antojitos la Concordia, Calle 2 Sur 509 (☎232 1373). A local favorite for the past 45 years, Concordia offers good food at good prices. Surrounded by religious fixtures and Mexican couples, you'll be charmed by the speedy service and friendly staff. The *plato del día* satisfies at 35 pesos; leave room for the ice cream float or banana split (35 pesos). *Antojitos* 17-38 pesos. Open daily 8:30am-9pm. Cash only. ❷

Fonda de Sta. Clara, Av. 3 Pte. 307 (☎242 2659), next to Hotel Teresita. A classy, touristy dining experience awaits at the Fonda de Sta. Clara. Waitresses in "traditional" costumes serve seasonal *chapulines* (grasshoppers), *escamoles* (ant larvae), or *gusanos de maguey* (agave worms) to the brave (85-140 pesos). *Antojitos* 36-55 pesos. Traditional *poblano* dishes 80-115 pesos. Open daily 10am-10pm. AmEx/D/MC/V. ❺

Fonda la Guadalupana, Av. 2 Ote. 806 (☎242 7691), between Blvr. Héroes del 5 de Mayo and Mercado el Parián. Worth the short walk past the strip of similar family-run *fondas*. Clay pots adorn the walls of this homey restaurant, where backpackers feast on the 4-course *comida corrida* (35 pesos) or share a 2-for-1 *cemita* special (35 pesos). *Tortas* 15 pesos. *Tostadas* 10 pesos each. Open M-Sa 10am-7pm. Cash only. ❷

Tortas Meche, Portal Juárez 111B (☎232 8628). The most affordable fare on the *zócalo*, with all the usual varieties of *tortas* and *cemitas* (18-45 pesos), as well as local hits like *mole poblano* or *pierna endiablada* (pork, bacon and ham, in a chipotle-prune sauce). Breakfasts 25-50 pesos. Open daily 7:30am-11pm. Cash only. ❸

Fonda la Mexicana, 16 de Septiembre 706 (☎232 6747), 3 blocks south of the *zócalo*. Another around the corner at Av. 9 Ote. 6B. Strings of *papel picado* line the ceiling and *folklórico* items adorn the walls of this patriotic restaurant. Fonda serves good but expensive *mole* and *pipián*. Speedy, no-frills service. *Menú económico* M-F 52 pesos, Sa-Su 57 pesos comes with soup, entree, and dessert or coffee. Entrees 55-90 pesos. Open daily 10am-9pm. MC/V. ❹

SIGHTS

Historic Puebla is a sightseer's paradise. Mexican students and North Americans from nearby language schools file into the *zócalo* every weekend. Most sights are clustered around the *zócalo*, but some are located a few minutes away in the **Centro Cívico 5 de Mayo.** The 1999 Puebla earthquake damaged several major sights near the *zócalo*, though extensive restoration has helped return most of Puebla's sights to their former glory.

■ **CATEDRAL BASÍLICA DE PUEBLA.** Visible from all directions, this massive cathedral is the obvious starting point for any tour of the city. Built between 1575 and 1649 by indigenous labor working under Spanish direction, the cathedral's dark Baroque facade is enlivened by bright *talavera* domes. No less impressive is the interior, with ornate, inlaid choir stalls and a statue of the Virgin, known as *La Conquistadora* because of her arrival with the first Spaniards. The freestanding **Altar Mayor** was designed by Manuel Tolsá in 1797, using marble from all over Mexico, and a model of it sits in the Museo Amparo. Circle around the altar to the left to face the **Capilla de la Virgen de Guadalupe,** which houses the tomb of Puebla's first archbishop, as well as one of three 18th-century Virgin paintings by the Zapotec master artist Miguel Cabrera (1695-1768). Guides loiter outside offering tours but the helpful explanatory signs in English and Spanish inside should suffice. *(Open M-Sa 10:30am-12:30pm and 4-6pm.)*

> **TIP**
>
> **DOTTING YOUR TILES.** Wondering which *talavera* tiles are antique and which are modern replacements? Check for the three raised dots left by the colonial kilns which fired Puebla's original ceramics.

■ **MUSEO AMPARO.** Three blocks south of the *zócalo*, the Museo Amparo traces the social history of Mesoamerica through art and architecture. Enter past the celestial mural by Pedro Diego Alvarado, Diego Rivera's grandson, depicting Puebla's mythical origin. Upstairs in the Conquest room, another Alvarado painting shows the horrifying Cholula Massacre. An impressive timeline shows artistic and architectural advancement on five continents, and the extensive pre-Hispanic art collection begins with small artifacts. The rooms also show stunningly restored religious art. You can probably skip the 10-peso audio presentations, as much more information is available in the written guides (in English, French, and Spanish) available for free in each room. *(Calle 2 Sur 708. ☎ 229 3850; www.museoamparo.com. Camera use 50 pesos. Su noon guided tour in English 180 pesos, in Spanish 120 pesos. Headphones 10 pesos plus 10-peso deposit. Open M and W-Su 10am-6pm. 35 pesos, students 25 pesos; M free.)*

CASA DE LOS MUÑECOS. Closed for seven years after suffering extensive damage in the 1999 earthquake, the Casa is worth a visit as one of Puebla's most entertaining buildings. This "House of the Dolls" is decorated on the outside with *talavera* renditions of the labors of Hercules. Some say the sculptures on the outside are the architect's rivals, while others say they are meant to be the city aldermen who protested when the Casa was built higher than the municipal palace. Inside, the **University Museum** displays exhibits on regional history and portraits of over 200 martyrs. *(Calle 2 Nte. 4, at the zócalo's northeastern corner. ☎ 229 5500. Free guided tours in Spanish by appointment. Open Tu-Th 10am-5pm, F-Su 10am-7:30pm. 30 pesos, students 10 pesos, children under 12 and seniors 5 pesos; W free.)*

IGLESIA DE SANTO DOMINGO. This extravagant, gilded church was Puebla's first great religious structure and is now a stunning example of Spanish and international Baroque. The building was constructed between 1571 and 1611 by rural Dominican converts. Statues of saints and angels adorn the unrestored wooden altar, but the church's real attraction is the resplendent ☒Capilla del Rosario, a chapel to the left of the altar, laden with enough 22-karat gold to make the King of Spain jealous. Masks depicting an *indígena*, a conquistador in armor, and a *mestizo* hang above the three dazzling doors on the side of the chapel. On the ceiling, three statues represent Faith, Hope, and Charity. The altar's 12 pillars correspond to the 12 apostles. The six on the upper level were each made from a single onyx stone. Because there was no room for a real choir, the designers painted a chorus of angels with guitars and woodwinds on the wall over the door. *(On 16 de Septiembre, between Av. 4 and 6 Pte. ☎ 242 3643. Open daily 8am-2pm and 4-8:30pm. No visitors allowed during mass: 8:30am, 6:30, 8pm. Free.)*

MUSEO BELLO Y GONZÁLEZ. The Museo Bello, like the Casa de los Muñecos, was badly damaged in the 1999 earthquake, and only the first floor is currently open to the public. The museum displays the private art collection of late textile magnate José Luis Bello, including a diverse selection of earthenware, iron, ivory, and porcelain artifacts. Bello amassed an impressive array of *talavera poblana* from several centuries. Blue and white dominate the 16th- and 17th-century pieces, while the 18th-century pieces are more colorful. Blue made a comeback in the 19th century with *azul punche* ware, named for the candy of the same color eaten in Puebla for Día de los Muertos. Call ahead to arrange guided tours in English or Spanish. *(Av. 3 Pte. 302 at Calle 3 Sur, 1 block west of the southwestern corner of the zócalo. ☎ 232 9475. Open Tu-Su 10am-5pm. 15 pesos, students 10 pesos; Tu free.)*

CASA DE AQUILES SERDÁN. Originally the home of Aquiles Serdán (1876-1910), printer, patriot, and martyr of the 1910 Revolution, the house is now the **Museo Regional de la Revolución Mexicana.** Hundreds of bullet holes, both inside and out, bear witness to Serdán's assassination. The museum also includes photos of Serdán and other Revolutionaries, newspaper clippings, and correspondences that narrate the development of the Revolution. One room is dedicated entirely to his Serdán's sister Carmen and other female Revolutionaries. Since the museum lacks thorough explanatory signs, ask at the entrance for a free guided tour in English, Spanish, or German. *(Av. 6 Ote. 206. ☎ 242 1076. Open Tu-Su 10am-4:30pm. 15 pesos, children and students 10 pesos; Tu free.)*

SAN PEDRO MUSEO DE ARTE. At the time of its inauguration in 1544, this weighty stone building served as the male-only Real Hospital de San Pedro. It began to treat the public only in 1832 after converting into Puebla's Academia Médico-Quirúrgica and later, the Hospital General del Estado (1867). It subsequently functioned as a sports complex, theater school, and public library, before being restored and re-opened as an art museum in 2001. The second-floor galleries display a permanent collection documenting the building's hospital history, with interesting dioramas depicting colonial medicine, as well as several temporary exhibitions of modern art in diverse media. *(Calle 4 Nte. 203. ☎ 246 6618 and 5858. Open Tu-Su 10am-5pm. 15 pesos; children, students, teachers, and seniors 10 pesos; Tu free.)*

EX-CONVENTO DE SANTA MÓNICA. When Benito Juárez's Reform Laws went into effect in 1857, they not only weakened the Church's power, but forced the nuns at the convent into hiding. The convent operated in secrecy for 77 years before it was rediscovered. Today, it serves as the **Museo de Arte Religiosa Santa Mónica** with curious and sporadically labeled religious art, much of which was produced by the nuns themselves. Particularly eerie is a life-size recreation of the Last Supper, in which plaster apostles in real robes sit around a colonial dinner table. Even more unnerving is the nuns' crypt, where those who died during the period of hiding were plastered into the walls and honored with scrawls that spoke of their lives. The beautiful kitchen (doubling as a laboratory) where the nuns first made *chiles en nogada* is also open to visitors. *(Av. 18 Pte. 103. ☎232 0178. Open Tu-Su 9am-6pm. 27 pesos, under 13 free; Su free.)*

EX-CONVENTO DE SANTA ROSA. This building—the birthplace of the original recipe for *mole*—housed the nuns of the order of Santa Rosa from 1683 to 1861. Today, the *ex-convento* is a museum of *artesanía poblana*, offering examples of arts and crafts from different areas of the state. The kitchen and a nun's cell have been preserved in their original condition and provide a glimpse into the combination of piety and joyous cooking that was cloistered life. On Sunday afternoons, the courtyard doubles as a theater for free concerts. *(Entrance on Calle 3 Nte, at Av. 14 Pte. ☎232 9240. Open Tu-Su 10am-4pm. 10 pesos, includes a guided tour.)*

IGLESIA DE SAN FRANCISCO. Across Blvr. Héroes de 5 de Mayo from El Parián, Puebla's oldest neighborhood contains the city's oldest church. Built by the Franciscans between 1535 and 1585, it features an incredible *talavera* and an orange-red tile facade that contrasts sharply with the ominous bell tower. Experience the legacy of the city's nuns with the delectable *dulces típicos* (from 5 pesos), being sold in the surrounding plaza. *(At Av. 14 Ote. and Blvr. Héroes del 5 de Mayo. Open 24hr. Mass: M-Sa 6:30, 7:30, 8:30am, 6, 7pm; Su every hour 6:30am-1:30pm, 6, 7pm.)*

CASA DE LA CULTURA. A base for exploring cultural events in the city, the Casa houses the **Biblioteca Palafoxiana,** an impressive 43,000-volume library that began with Juan de Palafox's 6000-book collection, donated to the city in 1646. His original library includes an illuminated copy of the Nuremberg Chronicle from 1493. Although it sustained extensive damage in the 1999 earthquake, the library has been beautifully restored, with a display showing the damage. Ask for a monthly calendar of cultural events at the information desk in the front of the courtyard. *(Av. 5 Ote. 5. Casa de la Cultura ☎246 6922. Open daily 10am-6pm. Library ☎242 8073. Open Tu-F 10am-5pm, Sa-Su 10am-4pm. 10 pesos, students 5 pesos; Tu free.)*

CENTRO CÍVICO. A short trip from the *centro*, the Centro Cívico was the location of the May 5, 1862 **Battle of Puebla,** when general Ignacio Zaragoza defeated the French in their advance toward Mexico City. The former battleground is now a large, unkempt park, which contains several sights and austere patriotic signs that curiously omit the fact that, one year later, fortified French forces overpowered Zaragoza's troops and occupied Puebla for five years. *(Catch a #72 bus or #8 colectivo, each 4 pesos, on Blvr. Héroes de 5 de Mayo, 3 blocks east of the zócalo. Get off when you see a large, multi-armed cement fountain, a monument to Zaragoza, that sits on an empty square. Facing away from the monument, cross the street and walk uphill toward the park.)* Located inside the **Fuerte de Loreto,** the oddly named **Museo de la No Intervención** (Museum of No Intervention) documents the Battle of Puebla and General Zaragoza, with artifacts and a panoramic recreation of the battlefield as it might have looked in 1862 and exhibits on the French rule in Mexico. *(From the Zaragoza monument, follow the road as it curves past a defunct information center. A large concrete Mexican flag marks a fork in the road. The museum is on the right. ☎235 2661. Open Tu-Su 10am-5pm. 34 pesos, children under 13 free.)* The one-room **Museo Regional de Antropología** narrates the social history of Puebla state. The museum's highlight is the display of traditional folk costumes near the exit. *(Retrace your steps from the Fuerte Loreto up the road. The yellow museum is on the right before the intersection. ☎235 9720, ext. 27. Call ahead for Spanish tours. Open Tu-Su 10am-5pm. 37 pesos.)* The giant silver pyramid nearby is the park **planetarium,** now active after renovations following the 1999 earthquake. The planetarium's **Omnimax** theater has showings every hr. 10am-6pm. *(Next to the Museo Regional de Antropología. ☎235 2099 or 236 6998. Open daily 10am-6pm. IMAX 40 pesos, children and students 30 pesos.)* The **Recinto Ferial,** an exposition center and fairground, is across from the planetarium, and next door is the state-of-the-art **Imagina Museo Interactivo,** with over 150 hands-on exhibits targeted to youngsters. The best is the 15-peso Venture Simulator, a virtual roller coaster. *(Next to the Planetarium.* ☎ *236 7580 or 213 0289; www.imagina.pue.gob.mx. Open M-F 9am-1pm and 2-6pm, Sa-Su 10am-2pm and 3-7pm. 40 pesos, children 35 pesos.)* The semi-ruined **Fuerte de Guadalupe** honoring the Cinco de Mayo victory would offer stunning views of Puebla and the surrounding mountains, if it weren't for the many trees that block the view. The steep entrance fee makes the long walk to the ruins even less attractive. *(Follow the road to the left of the Museo de la No Intervención and take a right at the 2nd intersection. The fort is all the way at the end of the road. Open Tu-Su 9am-5:30pm. 34 pesos; under 13 free; Su free.)*

AFRICAM SAFARI. A longer trip takes you to this zoo, which holds over 3000 free-roaming animals, representing approximately 250 species and the Americas, Antarctica, and Asia. Visitors can drive through the park, stopping at designated locations to take photos and mingle with the animals. *(16km southeast of Puebla, the Safari is best reached by bus. Estrella Roja offers packages that include round-trip fare from CAPU or the zócalo and park admission. From CAPU: M-F 11am, Sa-Su 10am. From the zócalo: daily 11am, 2pm. 190 pesos, children 160 pesos. By car, head to the south of the city and then east, following the signs to Valsequillo on Blvr. Cap. Carlos Camacho.* ☎ *281 7000; www.africamsafari.com.mx. Open daily 10am-5pm. 125 pesos, children 120 pesos. Tip Tours organizes tours that depart from the zócalo.* ☎ *248 5580; www.tiptours.com.mx. Daily 11am, 2pm.)*

🎵 ENTERTAINMENT

The **Casa de la Cultura,** Av. 5 Ote. 5, is the place to go for information about Puebla's cultural events. Pick up a monthly calendar and check the board at the rear of the courtyard for the latest schedules. (☎ 246 6922. Films Th-Su. Folk dances Sa and Su. Open daily 8am-8pm.) Also be sure to check the schedule posted inside the **Teatro Principal,** which lists weekly performances. (Av. 4 Nte. 203. ☎ 232 6085. Open daily 10am-5pm for visits.) A new program at the **Centro Cultural Santa Rosa** (☎ 232 9240), in the **Ex-Convento de Santa Rosa,** includes performances of popular and traditional music and experimental theater. On Sunday afternoons, the courtyard hosts free concerts and dance performances.

🍸 NIGHTLIFE

Bars and theaters pile up in the *zócalo,* while a younger local crowd heads for the bars in the **Plazuela de los Sapos,** creating a loud and social weekend scene. Farther from the *zócalo,* on Juárez between Calles 21 and 29 Sur, is the **Zona Esmeralda,** lined with even more bars and discos. If you're prepared to spring for a taxi, you may as well continue on to the clubs and bars on the **Recta Cholula,** the highway connecting Puebla and Cholula. The true center of the area's thriving nightlife, the Recta is jam-packed with college and language-school students on weekends. Buses stop running around midnight, so take a taxi (60 pesos). Ask to be let off by the clubs near UDLA (Universidad de las Américas).

■ **Rumba Cafe,** Av. Juárez 2313 (☎ 225 6375 or 226 6692), in the Zona Esmeralda. This 1000-person club recreates the atmosphere found at seaside cities by showering tourists and locals with confetti, balloons, and inflatable hats. Come early to avoid a long line. Dress code: no sneakers or sportswear. Live salsa midnight-1am and 2-3am. Cheesy choreographed variety show 1-2am. Beer 32 pesos. Mixed drinks from 55 pesos. Cover 50 pesos. Open Th-Sa 10pm-4am. AmEx/MC/V.

Teorema, Reforma 540 (☎ 298 0028), 3 blocks west of the *zócalo.* A bookstore/cafe by day, Teorema is a trendy alternative to the bar scene by night. After 9pm, the intellectual clientele crowds in to hear music, chat with friends, and drink *café con licor* (35 pesos) in this literary lair. Live music daily 9:30pm: M-Th *trova*, F-Sa classic rock. Cover M-W 10 pesos, Th 20 pesos, F-Sa 30 pesos. Open M-Sa 10am-2:30pm and 4:30pm-2:30am. D/MC/V.

Boveda Bar, Calle 6 Sur 503C (☎246 2555), in Plazuela de los Sapos. Hordes of hard-drinkers pack into this dark and smoky den. Live music daily from 9pm: M and Th-Su rock, Tu-W *norteño* and *cumbia.* Beer 30 pesos, 10 beers 180 pesos. *Cemitas* 15-20 pesos. *Antojitos* 25-50 pesos. Open daily 5pm-3am. MC/V.

Bar 2, Blvr. del Niño Poblano 403 (☎225 2888), in Centro Comercial Las Palmas. One of several bars inside this shopping mall, the retro ambience at Bar 2 is complete with disco balls and neon bubble lights illuminating the split-level dance floor. Beer 18 pesos. Mixed drinks from 30 pesos. Open Tu-Sa 1pm-3am. AmEx/D/MC/V.

La Kiwa, Av. 5 Pte. (☎242 7247), between 16 de Septiembre and Calle 3 Nte. Squeeze past the carved metal entrance to join a diverse rock-loving crowd at the *centro*'s liveliest bar. Live rock F-Sa from 5pm. Beer 10 pesos. Mixed drinks 40 pesos. Open M-Sa noon-3am. Cash only.

█ SHOPPING

Home to embroidered textiles, clay ornaments, woven palms, and a 450-year tradition of *talavera*, Puebla offers diverse shopping opportunities. At the **Mercado el Parián,** with entrances on both Av. 2 Ote. and 4 Ote. at Calle 6 Nte., tourists gather to buy hand-painted *talavera* ceramics and tiles, as well as leather purses, beads, and other trinkets. (Open daily 10am-8pm.) For less expensive *talavera* purchases, head to **Avenida 18 Pte.,** west of Av. 5 de Mayo. North of El Parián, at Calle 8 Nte. 410, is the **Barrio del Artista,** where *poblano* artists paint and hawk their works on the street. Sundays 10am-6pm, the **Plazuela de los Sapos,** south of the *zócalo* on Calle del Sapo, fills with antique bazaars selling bronze figures, old coins, and *talavera*.

▒ FESTIVALS

In addition to June's *mole* cook-off and August's *Festival de Chiles en Nogada*, the city of Puebla celebrates several secular events throughout the year. The end of April kicks off the month-long **Feria de Puebla** (Apr. 27-May 27), which includes the city's **Cinco de Mayo** celebration. Each day, the streets fill with various types of artisan expositions. Special events include *corridas de toros* (runnings of the bulls) and cock fights. Juan de Palafox (1600-1659), who served as bishop of Puebla from 1640-1655, is remembered in the **Festival Palafoxiana** for his religious influence and the generous donation of his namesake library to the city. The celebration runs from the last Friday in September until November 19 and features dances, concerts, theatre performances, and art. Additionally, Puebla's various municipalities each host exuberant *ferias* in the *centro* to honor their patron saints, including **San Jose** (March 19), **San Francisco** (October 4), and **Guadalupe** (December 12).

CHOLULA   ☎222

The exuberance of the students at the Universidad de las Américas (UDLA) unite with small-town hospitality to make Cholula (pop. 95,000) a welcome alternative to the big-city anonymity of nearby Puebla. The Olmecs, Zapotecs, and Toltecs each had their moment of glory here, in the oldest continually inhabited city in the Americas, and each added another tier or temple to the city's Great Pyramid. Upon his arrival in 1520, Hernán Cortés named Cholula "the most beautiful city outside of Spain"; shortly thereafter, he and his troops slaughtered 6000 *cholutecos* in the Cholula Massacre—punishment for a sup-

Cholula

⌂ ACCOMMODATIONS
Corintios, **2**
Hostal Cholollan, **1**
Hotel Las Américas, **16**
Hotel Noche Buena, **15**

🍴 FOOD
Cemitas La Roca, **5**
Güeros, **13**
La Lunita, **8**
El Pecas Parilla, **14**
Soloburguer, **3**
Los Tulipanes, **6**
Tortas Alex, **12**

★ ENTERTAINMENT
Bar Reforma, **11**
Bar-Restaurant
  Enamorada, **9**
Burbula, **17**
Café Tal, **7**
La Casa del
  Mojito, **4**
Jazzatlán, **10**
El Tigre, **19**
Unit, **18**

posed alliance between the *choluteca indígenas* and the Aztecs. To further punish the city, Cortés vowed to erect 365 churches—one for every day of the year—on top of the city's native temples. While he never completed his goal, Cholula's 37 churches today have ensured the city's place on the route for pilgrims. An easy trip from Puebla or Mexico City, Cholula draws urban escapists with its churches, balmy weather, and lively *portales*. Just don't expect to get much sleep—bells from the 37 churches start ringing early Sunday morning.

▐ TRANSPORTATION

To get to the *zócalo* from the Estrella Roja **bus station,** Av. 12 Pte. 108 (☎247 1920), between 5 de Mayo and Calle 3 Nte., walk east to the intersection of Av. 12 Pte. and 5 de Mayo and turn right on 5 de Mayo. Walk 4 blocks downhill toward the large yellow church of San Pedro. **Estrella Roja** runs buses to **Mexico City** (2½hr., every hour 5am-7pm, 61 pesos). **Super Rápidos,** which stops directly across the street from the station, goes to **Puebla** (30min., every 10-15min. 5am-11pm, 5 pesos). For more destinations, try Puebla's CAPU (p. 403).

    Colectivos to Puebla and locations within Cholula can be flagged down at many locations in the *centro*, including Av. 8 Pte. and Calle 3 Nte. and Morelos and Calle 2 Sur (30min. to Puebla's CAPU, 5 pesos). *Colectivos* stop running at 10pm; after hours, negotiate a price with a local **taxi** (from 75 pesos). **Sitio taxis,** available throughout the city, can be found at the southeast corner of the *zócalo*.

✦ ▐ ORIENTATION AND PRACTICAL INFORMATION

Cholula is on Blvr. Forjadores, 122km east of Mexico City and 8km west of Puebla. As in Puebla, the street grid simplifies navigation. *Calles* run north-south with odd-numbered ones to the west (Pte.) and evens to the east (Ote.). *Avenidas* travel east-west, with odd-numbered ones to the south (Sur) and evens to the north (Nte.). **Bulevar Forjadores** runs north-south and becomes **Calle 4.** The main east-west axis, Av. Hidalgo, becomes Av. Morelos at the *zócalo* and Av. 14 Ote. east of the Great Pyramid. The town encompasses two small municipalities, **San Pedro Cholula** and **San Andrés Cholula.** The verdant *zócalo*, tourist office, and most restaurants are located in San Pedro. San Andrés contains everything east of the Great Pyramid, and is mostly residential. The walk between San Pedro and San Andrés can be lonely on weeknights when bars and clubs are closed, and taxis will make the trip for 35 pesos.

Tourist Office: Portal Guerrero 3 (☎261 2393), on the *zócalo*. Offers basic info and a photocopied map. Open M-F 9am-7pm, Sa-Su 9am-2pm.

Budget Travel: Find student deals at **TIPS Viajes,** Morelos 202 (☎130 9577; www.tip-tours.com.mx), on the southeastern corner of the *zócalo*. Also offers Internet, 10 pesos per hr. Open daily 10am-10pm.

Currency Exchange and Banks: Casa de Cambio Azteca, Calle 2 Sur 104 (☎247 2190). Open M-F 9am-5:30pm, Sa 9am-1:30pm. Banks on Morelos at the *zócalo* have more limited hours but offer comparable rates and have **ATMs. HSBC,** Morelos 14 (☎247 6591), at 2 Sur, exchanges traveler's checks. Open M-Sa 8am-7pm.

Laundromat: Clean Experts, Av. 3 Pte. 101, local 4 (☎261 4421), near Alemán. Wash, dry, and fold 12 pesos per kg. Open M-F 8am-8pm, Sa 8am-4pm. Cash only.

Police: (☎247 0562), on Calzada Guadalupe at Av. 12 Ote.

Red Cross: Calle 7 Sur 301 (☎247 8501), at Av. 3 Pte., a bit of a hike from the *centro*. Walk-in service. Open 24hr.

24hr. Pharmacy: Droguería Medina, Hidalgo 502 (☎247 1644), at Calle 5 Nte.

Medical Services: Centro de Médicos San Gabriel, Av. 4 Pte. 503 (☎247 0014), between Calles 5 Nte. and 7 Nte. Open 24hr.

Fax Office: Telecomm, Portal Guerrero 9 (☎247 0130). Telegrams and **Western Union.** Open M-F 8am-7pm, Sa-Su 9am-noon. **Papelería Toño,** Morelos 8 (☎/fax 247 1149), between Alemán and Calle 2 Sur. Open daily 8am-8pm.

Telephones: LADATELs line Morelos and Hidalgo on the south side of the *zócalo*.

Internet Access: Tierra Virtual Internet Cafe, Calle 2 Sur 310 (☎247 8834), at Av. 5 Ote. 10 pesos per 1¼hr. Open M-Sa 9am-10pm, Su 10am-8pm.

Post Office: Calle 7 Sur 505 (☎247 5917), just past Av. 5 Pte. Open M-F 8am-4pm. **Postal Code:** 72760.

ACCOMMODATIONS

Near the *zócalo* and the pyramid, budget hotels are scarce. Several moderately priced hotels are located north of Cholula on **Carretera Federal Mexico-Puebla,** but Cholula's lodgings are high quality, so your pesos stretch farther here than in the big city of Puebla. The city is overrun with visitors during its festivals; be sure to make reservations in advance.

Corintios, Calle 5 Nte. 801 (☎247 0495 or 9440), 4 blocks from the *zócalo*. Spacious, blue-and-white rooms with balcony, private bath, cable TV, and a central location. Sunny roof-top terrace puts plenty of church steeples and a volcano in focus. Check-out 1pm. After 8pm, ring the bell to enter. Singles 140 pesos; doubles 220 pesos; triples 330 pesos. Discounts for 3-day and week-long stays. Cash only. ❷

Hotel Las Américas, Av. 14 Ote. 6 (☎247 0991). From the *zócalo*, follow Morelos (which becomes Av. 14 Ote) 2 blocks past the pyramid—hotel is on the right after 5 de Mayo. The clubs are right next door. Bright flowers, trimmed grass, and pet ducks surround a peaceful pool. Rooms are comfortable though slightly worn, with TV and phone; baths are 1 giant shower with no curtain. Shell out an extra 20 pesos to upgrade to a king-size bed and nicer showers. Check-out 1pm. Singles 180-250 pesos; doubles 210-340 pesos; triples 330-370 pesos; quads 360-400 pesos. Cash only. ❸

Hostal Cholollan, Calle 2 "C" Nte. 2003 (☎247 7038 or 371 9139; hostalcholol-lan@hotmail.com), on the "Privada de Choyollan" between Av. 20 Ote. and 22 Ote. A 15min. walk from the *zócalo*. Meet young travelers in this cozy, colorful hostel. Commu-nal kitchen, TV room, patio with hammocks, and a small rock-climbing wall. Organizes mountain climbing excursions (150 pesos per person, 4-person min.). Check-out 1pm. 4-bed dorms 70 pesos; private double 220 pesos. Cash only. ❶

Hotel Noche Buena, Av. 7 Ote. 7 (☎247 0564 or 247 495), between Alemán and Calle 2 Sur. Drafty but affordable rooms with firm beds just 3 blocks south of the *zócalo*. Room quality varies significantly. Singles 110 pesos; doubles 200 pesos. Cash only. ❷

▶ FOOD

Influenced in part by Puebla's culinary traditions, most of Cholula's restaurants feature variations of *mole poblano*. For good, cheap local food, wander through the **Cosme del Razo** market (entrances on Calles 3 and 5 Nte.; open daily 8am-8pm) and the food stands in the *zócalo* and along the western side of the pyra-mid. Cholula's most affordable establishments are on **Hidalgo,** perpendicular to the *portales*. Toward the bus station, family-owned *torta* shops and market stands offer even better prices, but eating in the *zócalo* buys you a pyramid-view and strolling musicians. For pre-packaged food and toiletries, try **Tienda Sindical de Consumo Crom,** Alemán 116, a supermarket near the corner of Av. 3 Ote. (☎247 0355. Open daily 7:30am-10pm. D/MC/V.)

Güeros, Hidalgo 101 (☎247 2188; www.restaurantegueros.com). Select your favorite tunes from the jukebox as you sample *antojitos* (16-32 pesos) or regional specialties (26-98 pesos) in the modern, spacious eating area. Try one of their inventive pizzas (46-92 pesos) for a Cholulan twist on a familiar dish. Tacos from 9 pesos. Sand-wiches, *tortas,* and *cemitas* (sub-like sandwiches) 15-24 pesos. Accepts $US. Open daily 9am-midnight. 100-peso min. MC/V. ❸

El Pecas Parrilla, Alemán 512A (☎247 1618; www.elpecasparrilla.com), at Av. 7 Pte. Offers the quality and ambience of tourist joints at lower prices. Wi-Fi. *Cemitas* and *tor-tas* 12-25 pesos. Tasty *molletes con chorizo* (rolls with sausage) 20 pesos. Tacos 21-60 pesos. Open daily 10am-midnight. Cash only. ❸

La Lunita, Av. Morelos 419 (☎247 0011; www.lalunita.com), at Calle 6 Nte. This bar-restaurant dating from 1939 has become a colorful local staple with its quirky decor and storied history. It gets packed during sports games and in the evening, when patrons enjoy their famous sangria (from 55 pesos). *Tortas* and *cemitas* 25-35 pesos. Regional specialties 40-90 pesos, but their breakfasts and *menú del día* are a better deal (75 pesos). Open daily 9am-midnight. D/MC/V. ❹

Tortas Alex, Hidalgo 101-B (☎247 2249), on the *zócalo* next to Güeros. This popu-lar *torta* shop lures the hungry with its cheap, satisfying fare. Enjoy *tostadas* (12 pesos), *tortas* (17-30 pesos), and *platos típicos* (22-35 pesos) while watching *telenovelas*. The Guerrero-style *pozole* is a must-try (27 pesos). Open Tu-Su 9am-11pm. Cash only. ❷

Soloburguer, Av. 6 Pte. 105 (☎500 4144), at 5 de Mayo. True to its name, this cheery little place serves only burgers (from 15 pesos), all with a Mexican twist—*chile poblano* garnish. Cheesy vegetarian burgers 20 pesos. Open daily 11am-11pm. Cash only. ❶

Los Tulipanes, Portal Guerrero 13 (☎247 1707), on the west side of the *zócalo*. Stands out from a row of pricey restaurants competing for scenic views of the *zócalo*. Delicious 4-course *menú del día* (45 pesos), 1:30-6:30pm. Breakfast from 35 pesos. Entrees 15-50 pesos. Specialties 42-70 pesos. Open Tu-Su 8am-9pm. MC/V. ❸

Cemitas La Roca, Alemán 502 (☎893 4679), at Av. 5 Pte. Another on Morelos 409. Bring a friend or a big appetite to gobble up the meaty *cemitas* at this simple but popular locale. *Cemitas* 1 for 18 pesos or 2 for 30 pesos. Frozen yogurt 5 pesos. Open daily 9:30am-9pm. Cash only. ❷

⊙ SIGHTS

Cholula's chief attractions are the brightly colored towers of its 37 **churches** jutting above the rest of the city, and its spectacular ruins, the **Teneapa Pyramid complex.** The archeological site consists of the **Great Pyramid** and the **Courtyard of the Altars,** with the **Santuario de Nuestra Señora de los Remedios** built atop the pyramid at the time of conquest. It has limited explanatory markers and is best explored with a tour (guides can be found at the entrance to the site; Spanish 90 pesos, English 120 pesos). The June 1999 earthquake that devastated so many of Puebla's sights also impacted Cholula, and many churches sustained extensive damage. The combined efforts of the government, churches, and community enabled the reconstruction of many of them. Most are within easy walking distance of Cholula's *zócalo*, the second largest plaza in Mexico. With its 46 covered arches, it also boasts Latin America's longest *portales*.

THE GREAT PYRAMID AND ENVIRONS

TENEAPA PYRAMID. When Cortés destroyed the Toltec temple atop the misshapen hill that dominates Cholula, he was unaware that the lump was actually a pyramid. When explorations of the "hill" first began in 1934, archaeologists discovered three other pyramids built one on top of the other, with onion-like layers indicating the successive constructions by the different cultures that occupied the area. Archaeologists believe the original pyramid was built around AD 200 by the Olmecs or a related group. When a Toltec-Chichimec group settled in Cholula in the 12th century, fleeing from a rival faction in Tula (giving Cholula its Náhuatl name "place of escape"), they built the fourth and final pyramid, named Tlachi-aualtepetl ("man-made hill"), and may have conducted human sacrifice atop it. Sophisticated drainage systems kept the structure—the largest pyramid in the world by volume, nearly 400m at its base and 66m in height—intact. The last excavations took place in the early 70s; today, certain tunnels and some excavations on the southern and western sides of the pyramid are the only areas open to visitors. *(Entrance on Morelos, across from the small yellow building. ☎247 9081. Ruins and tunnels open daily 9am-6pm. 37 pesos; under 12, students, and teachers free; Su free.)*

MUSEO DE SITIO. Before entering the tunnels, visit the museum across the street from the ticket booth. Centered around a helpful diorama of the pyramid (designed to persuade skeptics that it is not, in fact, a hill), the museum features local artifacts tracing Cholula's rise as a ceremonial center and a reproduction of the **Codice of Cholula,** a 17th-century account of the Cholula massacre from the *indígena* perspective. A reproduction of the 56m *Los Bebedores*, one of the site's two famous frescoes and one of the largest murals in pre-Hispanic Mesoamerica, graces the back room, which is connected to the main exhibit by a tunnel. *(Calle 8 Nte. 2, down the ramp or stairs just east of the entrance to the tunnels. ☎247 9081. Info in both English and Spanish. Open daily 9am-6pm. Free with tickets to the pyramid.)*

TUNNELS AND PATIOS. To reach the excavations on the side of the pyramid opposite the entrance, most visitors walk through the labyrinthine tunnels that riddle the pyramid's base. Though there are a total of 8km of tunnels burrowed out by archeologists, visitors can only explore 300m of the mostly well-lit, arched passages. A particularly stunning section affords a glimpse of the main staircases of one of the interior pyramids whose 9 floors have been excavated from bottom to top—visitors stand on the second. The underground adventure ends at the south side of the pyramid in the outdoor **Patio de los Altares** (Courtyard of the Altars), which shows six stages of construction. English-language pamphlets (5 pesos) can be purchased at the bookstore near the end of the outdoor excavations, though the bare essentials can be gleaned from the explanatory English and Spanish markers. Guides are also a great help.

SANTUARIO DE NUESTRA SEÑORA DE LOS REMEDIOS. Built atop the pyramid in 1594, the Santuario looms over the city of Cholula. The trek to the Santuario, though taxing, is well worth it. The Spanish dedicated the sanctuary to La Virgen de los Remedios to safeguard against the Aztec gods from whose ruined temple the walls were constructed. After collapsing in an 1864 earthquake, the structure was rebuilt using much of the original material. Cholulans again had to repair the flower-filled sanctuary after the 1999 earthquake. Fortunately, the Virgin, set in her Fabergé jewelry box, remained unharmed, and celebrations in her honor take place each June and September. Her name is now spelled out in blue neon lights. On a clear day, the majestic view from the top of church courtyard extends as far as the snow-capped volcanoes at **Popocatépetl** and **Iztaccíhuatl,** as well as the rest of Cholula and its sea of churches. *(Santuario accessible from the uphill path off Calle 6 Sur, between Morelos and the exit from the Courtyard of the Altars. ☎ 271 0122. Open daily 6:30am-8pm. Free.)*

CHURCHES AND THE ZÓCALO

TEMPLO DE SAN GABRIEL. Hoping to use the church for a mass conversion, the Franciscans used indigenous labor to construct San Gabriel on top of the Templo de Quetzalcóatl in 1549. Despite San Gabriel's imposing size, the Franciscans found it too small for their epic conversion campaign, and in 1575 they began work on the Capilla Real, two doors down. The current altar was built in 1897, utilizing a Neoclassical style designed to emphasize the mass of the already weighty church. The **Convento de San Gabriel,** behind the church, is still in use but is not open to the public. Next door is the **Biblioteca Franciscana,** a UDLA library that holds more than 25,000 volumes published between the 16th and 19th centuries. *(Calle 2 Nte. 201, at the southeastern corner of the zócalo. Templo: ☎ 247 0028 or 0122. Open daily 6am-7pm. Library: ☎ 261 2395; http://ciria.udlap.mx/franciscana. Open M-F 8am-7pm.)*

CAPILLA REAL. The Capilla Real is the most visually striking of the city's churches. This 49-domed structure was finished in the early 17th century, fulfilling its role as the long-awaited auditorium for thousands of *indígenas* to hear mass. The wall behind the splendid altar features three paintings depicting the story of the Virgen de Guadalupe. The Capilla Real lacks the ornate gold filigree of the surrounding churches; its simplicity is defined by the ever-changing panorama of whitewashed arches, soaring cupolas, and uniquely decorated side chapels. *(On Calle 2 Nte. at Av. 6 Pte., the northernmost church on the eastern side of the zócalo. ☎ 247 6088. Open daily 9am-1pm and 4:30-6pm.)*

CAPILLA DE LA TERCERA ORDEN. Gold ornamentation and seven large 18th- and 19th-century paintings decorate the interior, while the church's small dome balances Capilla Real's vastness. A recent renovation introduced two huge windows on either side of the altar that light up the church. *(Between San Gabriel and Capilla Real. Open Tu and Th-F 5-7pm; Sa 10am-1pm and 5-7pm.)*

PARROQUIA DE SAN PEDRO. As a 17th-century construction, San Pedro boasts an architectural style unique to its age: Baroque meets Renaissance in ornate fashion. The interior has been spectacularly restored and features a Churrigueresque

TAKING A BITE OUT OF CORRUPTION

Mexico is commonly stereotyped as a country where a few extra dollars can get anything done a lot faster. The tradition of *La Mordida* (the bite: common slang for asking for a bribe) has deep roots in Mexican history. Spaniards commonly bestowed government positions in colonial Mexico on the highest bidder. The Catholic Church was also infamous for dispensing power in exchange for money. After independence, the cash-strapped government couldn't afford to pay bureaucrats, so they supplemented incomes with bribes. State officials enjoyed legal immunity, as did anyone who paid them enough. As a result, Mexicans became highly cynical about politics and law.

This continued well into the 20th century, until President Carlos Salinas entered into self-imposed exile after a corruption scandal. Though he has since returned to Mexico, in 2000, the former president has found it difficult to re-enter the country's political scene. The following administrations, driven by voter demand, have cracked down on *La Mordida*. The public believes successful drug traffickers get by with cooperative, well-paid police officers and bureaucrats, so corruption was the hot-button issue in the 2000 and 2006 elections.

In 2007, the Mexican government subjected over 200 top police officers to "loyalty testing," in order to prove they were not connected to drug traffickers. Ordinary Mexicans remain skeptical but are hopeful that *La Mordida* will be a thing of the past.

cupola. Eighteenth-century paintings adorn the walls, including one of Diego de Borgraf's powerful depictions of Christ. *(On 5 de Mayo at Av. 4 Pte., at the northwestern corner of the zócalo. ☎ 247 0030. Open M-Tu and Th-Su 6:30am-1pm and 4:30-6pm.)*

THE ZÓCALO AND OUTSKIRTS OF CHOLULA

MUSEO DE LA CIUDAD DE CHOLULA. The **Casa del Caballero Aguilar,** which today houses the Museo de la Ciudad, is considered to be one of the oldest residential structures in the Cholula area. This small museum traces the habitation of Cholula from about 1000 BC. The first three rooms showcase pre-Hispanic pots and artifacts, while the next two contain colonial arts. The second-to-last room features a John O'Leary exhibit presenting photographs of the city's religious festivals. The last stop is a visit to the ▨**restoration laboratories** of the museum, where visitors watch UDLA technicians apply a mix of high- and low-tech restoration methods to recently excavated objects. *(Av. 4 Ote. 1. ☎ 261 9053. Open M-Tu and Th-Su 9am-3pm. 20 pesos; students, teachers, and seniors 10 pesos; Th and Su free.)*

SANTA MARÍA TONANTZINTLA. Almost as famous as Cholula itself, several churches reside in surrounding villages, including **Santa María Tonantzintla,** an impressive example of the popular Baroque style. Built atop a pre-Hispanic temple, the church's saffron, *azulejo*-decorated facade hides a startling ▨**interior**—an explosion of iconography, the handiwork of the same indigenous artisan who executed the plans of European artists in Puebla's Capilla del Rosario (p. 408). Guides outside will pick out references to Quetzal-cóatl and other pre-Hispanic elements from over 450 stucco faces staring from the walls and ceilings for 100 pesos. *(Plaza Principal Tonantzintla. Take a colectivo marked "Chipilo" at Morelos and Calle 6 Nte.; 4 pesos. Get off when you see a beige-and-red church on your left (approx. 20min.); Tonantzintla is a short walk down the pedestrian street to the right. Open daily 9am-6pm.)*

SAN FRANCISCO ACATAPEC. A 15min. walk (or a 3-peso bus ride) away from Tonantzintla lie the town and church of San Francisco Acatapec. Built in 1588, the facade of the church is almost as ornate as Tonantzintla's walls: the church's dome and front wall are entirely covered in brilliant custom-made *talavera* tiles set into an overgrown graveyard in one of the most exquisite applications of the famous tiles. A 1940 fire destroyed much of the gilt wood interior, though visitors can admire the original mirrored panels flanking the altar. A golden sun, thought to be the pre-Hispanic god Tonatiuh, smiles down from the ceiling of the nave. *(On Av. Puebla. To go directly from Cholula to Acatapec, simply ride a few km farther on the same "Chipilo" bus to Tonantzintla. To return, wait for the same 5-peso bus to loop around on its "Cholula" route. Open daily 10am-3pm and 4-6pm.)*

UNIVERSIDAD DE LAS AMÉRICAS. The elite, private university UDLA (OOHD-lah), established in Cholula in 1967, is as well-groomed as its students, and its verdant, bench-filled campus can serve as a respite from the city's mayhem. Students, locals, and visitors find cheap diversion watching UDLA's *béisbol* and *fútbol* teams face neighboring colleges at the **Estadio Templo de Dolor.** *(Tickets 50 pesos; 2-for-1 on game day with any student ID. ☎ 229 2000, ext. 6502.)* Most cultural events take place in the **auditorio,** behind the library. The auditorio is also home to the **Cine Club Las Américas,** where students present independent films. *(Open when school is in session. For events schedule, check www.udlap.mx/temporadacultural. Screenings Tu 6 and 8pm; for more info, call recreación estudiantil ☎ 229 2076.)* The university's two galleries, the **Sala José Cuevas** and **Sala Bertha Cuevas,** both in the Rectoría, often hold temporary exhibits. *(Open M-Sa 8am-5pm, Su 8am-3pm.)* **Cafetería Santa Catarina,** the only one of the campus's five cafeterias open year-round, serves institutionalized Mexican food. *(31-48 pesos. Open daily 8am-9pm.)* Souvenirs are available in the nearby social center kiosk. *(Ex-hacienda Santa Catarina Mártir. Leave an ID with the guards for admission to the grounds. Take an eastbound "UDLA" or "Intermedio" bus from the stop on Av. 12 Ote. at Calle 2 Nte. General info ☎ 229 2000; www.udlap.mx. Guided tours available upon request from the Departamento de Incorporación Estudiantil. ☎ 229 2025. Open M-F 9am-5pm.)*

🎵 🎭 ENTERTAINMENT AND NIGHTLIFE

Vibrant by day, Cholula is even better by night. For more high-powered, high-cost activity, try closer to the university in **San Andrés Cholula** (where a strip of bars lines Av. 14 Ote. between 5 de Mayo and Calle 2 Nte.) or 20min. away to the Zona Esmeralda in Puebla (p. 411). The bars in San Andrés attract university students, while those in the *centro* cater to a more diverse crowd.

Unit, Av. 14 Ote. (☎ 403 2502; unitdepuebla@hotmail.com), at Calle 4 Nte, in San Andrés. Smartly dressed, upbeat 20-somethings mingle and move to pop, reggaeton, and 80s hits in this mod hot spot. Cool off on the 2nd-fl. balconies. Beer 15 pesos. Mixed drinks from 20 pesos. Open T-Sa noon-3am. MC/V.

Bar-Restaurant Enamorada, Portal Guerrero 1 (☎ 247 0292 or 247 7022), under the *portales.* Named for the classic 1942 Mexican chick-flick filmed in this spot, this stained-glass bar feeds and inebriates a social set. Young crowd flocks to its outdoor tables for live *trova* music (7:30-10:30pm), followed by *rancheros* and more dance tunes indoors (10:30am-2:30am). Beer 20 pesos. Mixed drinks from 40 pesos. Open Tu-Su 8am-2am. MC/V.

La Casa del Mojito, Av. 6 Ote. 205 (☎ 247 0667; www.casadelmojito.com), closer to the *centro.* A local favorite, this Cuban-owned bar packs its small dance floor every night with sweaty *salseros.* Beer 25 pesos. Mixed drinks from 40 pesos. Live salsa music 11pm-2am. Cover 40 pesos; 2-for-1 8-9pm. Open Th-Sa 8pm-2am. MC/V.

Jazzatlán Cafe-Bar, Morelos 419 (☎ 304 3643; www.jazzencholula.com), at Calle 6 Nte, in Cholula *centro.* Rotating local art expositions grace the walls of this intimate, candlelit jazz lounge. Beer 20 pesos. Mixed drinks 45-50 pesos. *Antojitos* 30-90 pesos. Live music 10pm; W blues, Th-Sa jazz. Open W-Sa 6pm-2am. D/MC/V.

Burbula, Av. 14 Ote. 422, in San Andrés. A hip and artsy crowd starts off the evening dining and imbibing in this relaxed atmosphere. Cross the 2nd-fl. footbridge to a more intimate seating area. Beer 15 pesos. Liqueur coffees 20 pesos. Open M-Sa 2pm-11pm. Cash only.

Bar Reforma, Calle 4 Sur 101, connected to Hotel Reforma. The oldest cantina in Cholula has quirky decor—Marilyn Monroe make eyes at a mosaic of all the Catholic temples in Cholula. Beer 20 pesos. Mixed drinks from 30 pesos. Sangria 45 pesos. Open M-Sa 6pm-1am. Cash only.

El Tigre, Av. 14 Ote. 611 (☎261 7759), in San Andrés. A popular spot for university students. DJ spins electronic music until midnight, when the crowds pile in for the latest dance hits. 2-for-1 beer 30 pesos. Sangria-like *Jarra Sangre del Tigre* 155 pesos for 2 liters. Open T-Sa 10pm-3am. MC/V.

Cafe Tal, Porral Guerrero 7 (☎404 9947), under the *portales* in the *centro*. Fuschia sofas and chill music provide coffee lovers with a moderately priced place to relax. Beer 14-16 pesos. Liqueur coffees from 20 pesos. Open daily 8am-11:30pm. Cash only.

✿ FESTIVALS

Cholula celebrates its religious festivals with flair. Since 1640, Cholula has hosted the **Bajada de la Virgen** for two weeks in May or June, when the Virgen de Remedios descends from her celestial sanctuary to visit the city and surrounding towns. Cholulans carry the figurine through the streets by motorcycle every morning at 7am during the festival week. In the evenings, locals revel under the elaborate gateways of flowers, seeds, and glitter decorating the Virgin's route. She descends again on August 11, all the way to the town of San Luis Tehuiloyocan. An even bigger festival, the secular **Feria Milenaria de San Pedro Cholula,** takes up the first two weeks in September, centering around the Virgen de Remedios's **Día Santo** (September 8). Around November 28, **Concierto de las Campanas** features 130 bell ringers and the continuous playing of 33 church bells from 8-9pm. The **Ritual a Quetzalcóatl,** on the spring equinox (March 21), involves traditional dancing in the Courtyard of the Altars in honor of the indigenous god. Celebrations for *Carnaval, Semana Santa,* and Christmas are also big events, when Cholula fills with visitors from Puebla, Mexico City, and surrounding villages.

CENTRAL PACIFIC COAST

Stretching from the quiet fishing hamlets near San Blas to the busy port of Manzanillo, the central Pacific coast claims a stunning diversity, enclosing dense jungle estuaries in the north and craggy, snow-topped volcanoes in the south, all with a common fringe of flat sand and a sweltering heat just palliated by a sea breeze.

In the north lies **Nayarit,** a quiet state of thick vegetation inhabited by the republic's oldest indigenous group, the Huichol, who infuse the streets of Tepic with a distinctly indigenous flavor. The area grows the lion's share of the nation's marijuana and serves as the setting for *Journey to Ixtlán*, Carlos Castañeda's renowned book describing experiences with hallucinogens in a small town between Tepic and Guadalajara. Hallucinogen use has long been part of Cora and Huichol *indígena* traditions and is still common practice among shamans in their incantations.

South of Nayarit lies **Jalisco,** the most touristed state along the central Pacific coast. *"Jalisco es Mexico,"* the message emblazoned on signs around the state, rings true. *Mariachi* music, *charrería* (cowboy culture), and tequila all originated in this state. For much of its history, however, the semi-arid hills of the province remained isolated from the rest of the republic, possessing neither silver nor gold, jewels nor water, fertile land nor an agricultural climate. It wasn't until the 1920s—when railroad tracks extended to Guadalajara—that this Sierran town (elevation 1552m) grew into a metropolis, and today it is Mexico's second largest city. Away from the sweaty streets of the capital lies Puerto Vallarta, a glittering international city of discos, resorts, and vacationing Americans. Had Hollywood not found Vallarta in *Night of the Iguana* (1964), it might have gone the same way as tiny Pérula, not two hours away, home to one paved road and almost uninhabited beaches.

The tiny state of **Colima** is home to spectacular black sand beaches and pleasant mountain towns where tourists can escape the resort scene and breathe in cool, crisp air. The benevolent coast is subject to the whims of seismic uncertainty, with occasional earthquakes and rumblings from the state's imposing volcano, *Volcán de Fuego*—the most active in Mexico. The state is also home to the city of Colima, a sparkling, untouristed gem full of gardens, and Manzanillo, the workhorse of Mexico's Pacific coast. This port has not paused once in 700 years of commerce to wipe its sweaty brow, and only recently has it begun to lure travelers with its golden beaches.

HIGHLIGHTS OF THE CENTRAL PACIFIC COAST

REVEL in **Guadalajara** (p. 428), Mexico's second largest city: home to *jarabe tapatío, la avenida de zapatos,* and many *mariachis.*

FLAUNT IT in **Puerto Vallarta** (p. 447), which is no longer the quiet, secluded paradise of the 1960s. The thriving tourist industry has transformed the city with glitzy nightlife, luxury hotels, shop-lined streets, and a happening gay scene (p. 453). The **best beaches** lie south of the city (p. 454).

DRINK in **Tequila** (p. 445), the kitschy and fun birthplace of your favorite liquor.

SNEAK AWAY from it all in **Bahía de Navidad** (p. 456), where you can swim, surf, and sunbathe on your choice of beautiful beaches. Both **Bahía de Navidad** and **Melaque** (p. 457) offer budget accommodations and gorgeous beaches on the bay.

CONQUER El Nevado (p. 470), Colima's own snow-capped volcanic peak.

NAYARIT

SAN BLAS ☎323

The corner of the Nayarit Coast occupied by San Blas (pop. 9000) is a benevolent Bermuda Triangle. Travelers who run aground here first glance at the scruffy *zócalo* and start to wonder why they came, but are soon mesmerized by the sounds of crashing surf and humming jungle. The easy lifestyle, where bikes outnumber cars and everyone stops to talk on their way to the beach or the bar, makes it hard to get on the bus to leave. Some get stranded permanently, drawn by the mythical mile-long wave, the surrounding jungle estuaries, the banana trees, and the Nayarit mountains, full of waterfalls and coffee plantations.

TRANSPORTATION. To get to San Blas, you have to travel to Tepic first and change buses. **Transportes Norte de Sonora buses** leave from Tepic for San Blas every hour (42 pesos) from both the old and new bus stations. The **bus station** is in the *zócalo*, on the corner of Canalizo and Sinaloa. **Estrella Blanca** (☎285 0043) goes to **Guadalajara** (5hr., 7am, 170 pesos), **Puerto Vallarta** (3hr.; 7:30, 10am, 1:30, 4:30pm; 180 pesos), and **Tepic** (1¾hr., every hr. 6am-8pm, 44 pesos). **Transporte Noreste y Nayarit** goes to: **Culiacán** (8hr., 296 pesos); **Mazatlán** (5hr., 180 pesos); **Santiago** (noon, 5pm; 40 pesos); and other local destinations.

> TIP **JEJÉN TODAY, GONE TOMORROW.** San Blas is notorious for its *jejenes*—nasty biting sand flies that plague tourists and locals alike. A common misconception is that *jejenes* are unavoidable, but the reality is that they only infest San Blas during the days around the new moon and the full moon, and are worse in the early morning and after dusk. Plan your visit accordingly, and if you happen to be on the beach at these times, put on bug repellent or wear long pants and a long-sleeved shirt.

ORIENTATION AND PRACTICAL INFORMATION. San Blas is 69km northeast of Tepic by Mex. 15 and 54. **Juárez,** the town's main street, runs parallel to the bus station on the south side of the *zócalo*. **Batallón** runs perpendicular to Juárez from the *zócalo*'s center and leads to the closest beach, **Playa Borrego.**

The **tourist office** is upstairs in the Palacio Municipal, on the *zócalo*. (☎285 0005. Open daily 9am-4pm.) Another branch is located on Playa Borrego, on the left across from Restaurant Alicia. (Open daily 9am-3pm.) **Banamex,** on Juárez east of the *zócalo*, exchanges currency and has a **24hr. ATM.** (☎285 0030. Bank open M-F 8am-3pm.) Other services include: **police** (☎285 0021 or 0028), on Sinaloa opposite the bus station, through the last door in the Palacio Municipal as you walk away from the *zócalo;* **Farmacia Económica,** Batallón 49 (☎/fax 285 0111; open daily 8:30am-2pm and 4:30-9pm); **Centro de Salud,** on Batallón and Campeche, five blocks south of the *zócalo*, at the turnoff for Hotel Garza Canela (☎281 1207; open 8am-8pm); **IMSS,** at Batallón and Guerrero (☎285 0227; open daily 7am-6pm; after-hours entrance on Canalizo); **Caseta,** Juárez 64, with long-distance **phone** and **fax** service (open daily 7am-10pm); **Internet** access at **Cafe-Net San Blas**, Batallón 6, off the *zócalo* (☎285 1082; 10 pesos per hr.; open daily 9am-10pm); **laundry** at **Lavandería Express,** on Sinaloa half a block from the *zócalo* (10 pesos per kg.; open daily 7am-9pm.); and the **post office,** at Sonora and Echeverría, one block northeast from the northeastern corner of the *zócalo* (☎285 0295; open M-F 8am-3pm, Sa 8am-noon). **Postal Code:** 63740.

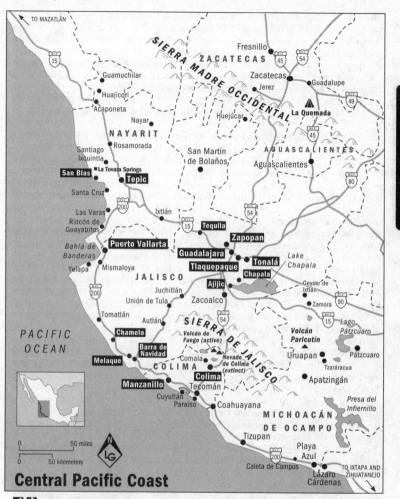

CENTRAL PACIFIC COAST

Central Pacific Coast

◼◻ ACCOMMODATIONS AND FOOD. All accommodations in San Blas are within walking distance of Playa Borrego. **Hotel Morelos ❸**, Batallón 108, three blocks south of the plaza, has a flowery courtyard full of dusty used books and a kitchen, leading to clean rooms with fan and bath. (☎285 0892. Reception 3pm-midnight. Singles 200 pesos; each additional person 50 pesos. Cash only.) **Estancia las Flores ❹**, Juárez 49, offers rooms with white tile, wicker furniture, big bronze beds, and TV, all centered around a courtyard brimming with beautiful vines and flowers. (☎285 0120. Singles and doubles 240 pesos. Cash only.) For the more frugal traveler, there's **Posada Irene ❶**, Batallón 122, which has rooms with fan and bath near the beach. (☎285 0399. Singles and doubles 120 pesos. Cash only.)

Serving reasonably priced seafood in the *centro*, ◼**La Familia ❸**, Batallón 18, is half-arboretum, half-depository for bizarre sundries: shark jaws, percussion instruments, and a young Mike Tyson's boxing tape. Large portions and friendly all-in-the-family staff transform the fisherman's impressive daily catch into a savory *pescado frito* (55 pesos), making this place a must. (☎285 0258. Open daily 8am-10pm.) For *antojitos* on homemade tortillas among sepia prints of the pantheon of Mexican heroes, head to **La Parrillada ❶**, on Canalizo facing the *zócalo*. Fill up with the enormous *torta vampizo* for 20 pesos. (Open daily 9am-midnight. Cash only.) For simple seafood right off the dock, try **El Jejenero ❺**, on the right on Juárez near the bridge. Exquisite garnish accompanies the *ceviche de camarones* for 80 pesos. (☎285 0345. Open daily 5pm-9pm. Cash only.) If you get hungry on the beach, check out any of the straw-roofed restaurants doling out fish and beer.

⬛ SIGHTS. While San Blas's beaches are the town's obvious natural beauty, locals will all point you in the direction of the **springs** at the source of the estuary nearby as the area's most worthwhile spot. Traveling upstream in small *lanchas* (skiffs) through the choke of mangroves and other aquatic plants—with the help of a knowledgeable guide—is a great way to see the incredible biological diversity of the region. Colonies of tropical birds and spindly herons, termite mounds and streams of tall white butterflies amid the macagua flowers, furtive turtles and lizards sunning themselves on rocks, and the open jaws of crocodiles on branches greet the visitor along the route inland. At a fork in the river, there's the option to see the **crocodile farm**, where monstrously large reptiles are held and bred as they're slowly reintroduced to the local waters. At the end of the route is a spring, a swimming hole with lucidly clear water and a swing to make the perfect entrance. While people from the restaurant overlooking the spring are generally around to keep watch, swim at your own risk. Tours are best in the early morning during the week. **La Tovara,** located in Matanchén, is the only company that runs tours, which should be booked at their office. To get there, take the same bus that goes to Playa Las Islitas from the corner of Sinaloa and Paredes (6 pesos) and look for a huge "La Tobara" sign on the left, right by the tiny town of Matanchén. (Tours 360 pesos for up to 4 people for the springs, 470 for the group to the springs and the crocodile farm.)

A small shrine to the town's connection with surfing exists in the **Museo de Surfing,** located on Borrego along the beach. Displays provide information about San Blas's waves and its surfers. (Open Sa-Su 10am-2pm and 4-7pm.) To survey the sweep of the beaches, the impenetrable jungle, and the local mountains in one glance, head up to **La Contaduría** overlooking the town. Wild grapes grow against the sheer walls guarding the remains of a 17th century fort. A short walk away are the ruins of the church which once housed the bells immortalized by Longfellow in "The Bells of San Blas." There are no bells, no white doves, and Longfellow never actually made it to San Blas, but the quiet walk, crumbling stone, and view from the top make it worth the walk. To get there, walk east on Juárez towards the bridge and turn right past the seafood places. Follow the signs. (Open 9am-6pm. 7 pesos.) Other hikes in the region include trips to waterfalls, coffee plantations, and the Aztec Island of Mexcalitlán. Getting to most trailheads requires a taxi or car. For information, ask at the tourist office, which will put you in touch with a guide, or inquire at Stoner's Surf Camp (see below), which offers some of the cheapest tours to the waterfalls, Mexcalitlán, and the fort for negotiable prices.

⬛ BEACHES. Known for its long, symmetrical waves and safe, sandy bottom, San Blas's coast has long been a haven for surfers. The currents and topography of the surrounding beaches make it the best place in Mexico to learn how to surf. Although Stoner's Cafe—the heart and soul of San Blas surf culture—was destroyed in October 2002 by Hurricane Kenna, its spirit and services live on at **⬛Stoner's Surf Camp,** Ramada 7, located at Restaurante Playa Azul. Their motto for surf lessons is *"si no te paras, no pagas"* (if you don't stand up, you don't pay), and with instructors like Pompis, the Mexican longboard champion, the confidence is understandable. Besides surfing and food there are showers, *palapas*, and a professional ✪**massage therapist.** All equipment, including tents, sleeping bags, and mosquito nets, is provided. (www.stonerssurfcamp.com. Longboard rental 50 pesos per hr., 100 pesos per day; shortboard 30 pesos per hr., 100 pesos per day; 1hr. with instructor and board 150 pesos. Bike rental 30 pesos per day. Open daily 7am-10pm. Camping 30 pesos; *palapas* in back with electricity and mosquito nets 100 pesos. Beachfront *palapas* 300 pesos per night.)

The jewel of San Blas's beaches is **Playa Las Islitas,** actually located in nearby Matanchén. A long, deserted cove on one end looks across to towering nearby mountains partly lost in the clouds. The beach stretches indefinitely toward the south, perfect for both the idle walker and the avid surfer. Intrepid wave-riders flock to the area during the stormy months of September and October, looking to catch the famous annual wave with its mile-long tunnel that spans the entire **Bahía Matanchén.** To reach Las Islitas, take a bus from the station (every hr. 6am-5pm, 8 pesos; returns 7:30am-4pm) or from the corner of Sinaloa and Paredes in front of the green-trimmed building (15min., 4 per day 8:30am-2:30pm, 6 pesos) The latter continues on to other beaches, passing Las Islitas on its return to town one hour later. A taxi to Las Islitas costs 40-60 pesos; a taxi back can cost as few as five. The first few stretches of sand that greet you are lovely, but more seclusion and prettier coves await farther along. At the southern end of Batallón, **Playa Borrego** is the closest beach to the center of San Blas, sitting at the end of Batallón. Soft sand and good currents make it fun for swimmers and surfers, but Borrego's mosquitoes feast on those who dare venture out at sunrise or sunset. **Playa del Rey,** an extension of Barrego, has stronger currents. A *lancha* will take you there from the pier at the western end of Juárez (round-trip 30 pesos) or you can walk down Playa Barrego (1km) towards the lighthouse. In the other direction lies **La Puntilla,** a rocky point where the ocean meets one of the rivers surrounding San Blas. Add your name next to thousands of others on the sand wall along the 2km walk east.

▎ **NIGHTLIFE.** The hum of bar talk and the occasional rumble of motorbikes speeding by are the background to San Blas's quiet nights. **Mike's CantaBar,** Juárez 75, is a throwback to the 70s—when the owner isn't performing in the "Mike and Mike" show, oldies and funky hits play in the intimate space of the bar. (☎285 0432. Beer 15 pesos. Mixed drinks 36 pesos. Live music Th-Su 10pm. Open daily 6pm-2am.) **Torino's,** Juárez 63, fills with older locals and their *gritos* (cries) to the *mariachi* music from the jukebox. (☎285 1395. Beer 8-12 pesos. Open daily noon-midnight. Cash only.) For a quieter bar and the chance for conversation without straining to hear, try **Viejano's,** on Batallon near the *zócalo*. (☎285 0090. Beer 15 pesos. Mixed drinks 30 pesos. Open daily 10pm-2am. Cash only.)

TEPIC
☎311

Tepic (pop. 300,000), nestled among the mountains of Nayarit, has served as a center of commerce since its founding by the Spanish in 1531. While a regional capital and a city in its own right, with numerous museums showcasing the culture of both the indigenous peoples and its own greats like poet Amado Nervo (1870-1919), it is largely a transportation hub to the beaches and jungles of Nayarit.

▐ **TRANSPORTATION. Buses** leave from the **Central Camionera,** the newer station east of the *centro*. To reach the *centro*, cross the street and catch a yellow bus

(6am-10pm, 3 pesos), or a taxi (30 pesos). To return, take a "Central" or "Mololoa Llanitos" bus from the corner of México Sur and Hidalgo. **Transportes del Pacífico** (☎213 2320) travels to: **Culiacán** (6hr., every hr., 221 pesos); **Guadalajara** (3hr., every 30 min., 169 pesos); **Mexico City** (10hr., every hr., 525 pesos); **Puerto Vallarta** (3½hr.; every hr. 6am-7pm; 115 pesos); **San Blas** (2hr., every 30min. 5am-7pm, 42 pesos). Various other small carriers also provide service to these destinations. Buses to San Blas also leave from the old bus station, southeast of the *centro*.

7 PRACTICAL INFORMATION. Situated 170km north of Puerto Vallarta and 280km south of Mazatlán, Tepic links Guadalajara (230km to the southeast) with the Nayarit beaches. **Dirección de Turismo Municipal,** in the green building on Puebla at Nervo, one block from the local bus station, hands out maps and organizes free tours of the city. (☎212 8037 or 6465. Tour of historic downtown daily 11am, 1, 4, 6pm. Office open daily 8am-8pm.) There is also a tourist office located in the new bus station (☎210 3111; open daily 8am-8pm), and the Secretary of Tourism of the state of Nayarit is located outside the *centro* at the corner of México and Ejército. (☎214 8071. Open daily 8am-8pm.) **Casas de cambio** are scattered along México Nte. (most open M-Sa 9am-2pm and 4-7pm), while **Bancomer,** on México Nte. 123, south of the plaza, has **24hr. ATMs.** Other services include: **luggage storage,** in the new bus station (3 pesos per hr., open 7am-6pm); **emergency** (☎066); **police,** Tecnológica Ote. 3200, only accessible by taxi (☎211 6900 or 216 5766); **Farmacia Guadalajara,** Zapata 79A (☎216 7110; open 7am-11pm. MC/V.); **Red Cross** (☎213 1160), on Insurgentes well east of the city; **Hospital General,** on Paseo de la Loma and the corner of Calzada de la Cruz next to La Loma Park (☎214 2315); **Internet** access at **Neonet,** Lerdo 256C (☎217 9935; 8 pesos per hr.; open M-F 9:30am-10pm, Sa-Su 10am-10pm); **laundry** at **Lavandería del Centro,** Querétaro 282A, 4 blocks east of México (☎212 1332; wash/dry 10 pesos per kg.; open 8am-2pm and 4-8pm.); and the **post office,** Durango Nte. 33, between Allende and Morelos (☎212 0130; open M-F 8am-6:30pm, Sa 8am-noon). **Postal Code:** 63000.

⌂ ACCOMMODATIONS AND FOOD. ◪**Hotel Morelia ❶,** Morelia 215, has a lush courtyard and big, clean, white rooms with shining floors. (☎216 6085. Reception 24hr. Singles 100 pesos, with bath 120 pesos; doubles 120/140 pesos. Cash only.) The curved white railings of **Hotel Mérida ❸,** Mérida 135, lead to large rooms with bath and fan. (☎212 6163. Reception 24hr. Singles 180 pesos; doubles 210 pesos. Cash only.) Next door to Hotel Morelia, **Hotel Posada Pasadena ❶,** Morelia 215A, is the cheapest option in town, with big, simple rooms. Rooms without bath compensate with massive couches. (☎212 9140. Reception 24hr. Singles 70 pesos, with bath 100 pesos; doubles 80/120 pesos. Cash only.) For those with an itch to camp, try **La Noria ❺,** located 12km from Tepic along the Carretera Miramar (#66). Furnished cabins with hot water are surrounded by green hills, where visitors can ride horses, mountain bike, or go on various hiking excursions. (☎213 1423. Open year-round. 2-bed cabins 480 pesos per night; 4-bed cabin 4600 pesos per night. To arrive, either drive or take a taxi.)

The best of Nayarit's bounty—most notably seafood and fruit—gets served in Tepic. **La Placita ❷,** Zapata 77 near the cathedral, serves great *comida corrida* for 25 pesos, including soup and dessert. (☎217 2753. Open daily 8am-4pm.) **Fonda de Mamá Tolla ❷,** Veracruz 254, one block off the plaza, serves gargantuan meals with refills of *agua fresca*, tortillas, and *frijoles* for 35 pesos. (☎212 4119. Open daily 8am-5pm. Cash only.) **Restaurant Vegetariano Quetzalcóatl ❹,** on León Nte. at Lerdo, four blocks west of Plaza Principal, hosts a popular breakfast and lunch buffet for 70 pesos (Tu-Sa 1pm) in its leafy courtyard. (☎212 9966. Open Tu-Sa 8:30am-9pm.)

◎ SIGHTS. Tepic—the Nayarit capital—is also the cultural center of the state, reflected by a wealth of museums densely clustered in the *centro*. Two of these museums are dedicated to Tepic's most famous artists. The **Museo Amado Nervo,** Zacatecas 284 Nte., celebrates the life and works of the famous poet in the house where he was born. (☎212 2916. Open M-F 9am-2pm and Sa ·10am-2pm. Free.) The **Museo Emilia Ortiz,** Lerdo 192 Pte., houses award-winning art by locals in addition to some of the photography and art of Emilia Ortiz, inspired by the indigenous peoples of Nayarit. (☎212 2652. Open daily 9am-7pm. Free.) The **Casa Museo de Juan Escutía,** Hidalgo 71 Ote., is the birthplace of the "Niño Héroe de Chapultepec," a military cadet who died at 17 fighting off American troops in 1847. The museum holds flags and a monument to his death, which is graced by the eulogy of his fellow-resident Nervo. (☎212 3690. Open M-F 9am-2pm and 4-7pm, Sa 10am-2pm. Free.) The **Museo Regional de Antropología e Historia de Nayarit,** México Nte. 91, south of the plaza at Zapata, offers an extensive exhibit on Huichol embroidery, indigenous ceramic work, and the impressive carcass of a San Blas crocodile, which are being reintroduced to the area. (☎212 1900. Open M-F 9am-6pm, Sa 9am-3pm. 34 pesos.) The **Museo de los Cuatro Pueblos,** Hidalgo Ote. 60, details the art of Huichols, Náhuatls, Coras, Tepehuanos, and Mexicaneras, including dress, pottery, and mock-up *palapas.* (☎212 1705. Open M-F 9am-2pm and 4-7pm, Sa 10am-2pm. Free.) For those seeking respite from museums, take a stroll in **Parque Loma** (north of Insurgentes along Puebla) or **Alameda Central** (7 blocks east of Mexico on Allende).

◪ NIGHTLIFE. Despite its status as regional capital, Tepic is a sleepy city, and its nightlife consists of bars and *cantinas* scattered around the city, with no central street or location. **etc.,** México 55, emits a casual, alternative vibe with back rooms, warm-toned plush seats, and Escher-esque cubed floor patterning. (☎217 0988. Beer 12 pesos. Mixed drinks 40 pesos. Open M-W and Su 6pm-1am, Th-Sa 6pm-3am. Cash only.) The locals head over to **El Submarino,** Zaragoza 175, a simple joint with plastic deck chairs, a working jukebox, and plenty of spiced nuts to go along with the 10-peso beer. (Open daily 9pm-midnight. Cash only.) **Sanangel Bar,** México 39, joins red and blue lighting with music to set the mood. Sip a beer (12 pesos) or tequila (35 pesos) from atop a barstool. (Open M-Tu noon-midnight, W-Su noon-3am. Cash only.)

◪ DAYTRIP FROM TEPIC

IXTLÁN DEL RÍO

The archaeological site of Ixtlán del Río lies between Tepic and Guadalajara on Mex. 15. The 88km journey takes about 1½hr. Most bus services from Tepic to Guadalajara will stop here (40-50 pesos). The town stretches along Av. Hidalgo, down which the bus service runs. The tourist office, Hidalgo Pte. 672, offers a series of brochures on the archaeological site and the town. (☎243 5639. Open M-F 9am-6pm, Sa-Su 10am-2pm.)

Although there is evidence of human habitation in Nayarit as far back as the 3rd millennium BC, early residents did not reach the highlands until the 4th century BC. **Ixtlán,** or "place of obsidian," was one of their earliest and perhaps most significant settlements. The early Ixtlán period (300BC-AD300) is characterized by a form of subterranean funerary known as **Las Tumbas de Tiro.** One of these sites has been excavated to reveal evidence of the familial burial practices and the ceramics that characterize this period. The culture developed significantly during roughly the next half-millennium, peaking in the Middle Ixtlán period (750-

1110AD). During that time, this group, known as the Aztatlán, built a network of stone structures, earning the site the name of **Los Toriles.** The Aztatlán culture worshipped the four elements, and it is believed that each of the series of central altars delineated by stone colonnades was dedicated to gods representing each element. The stepped circular pyramid has a different shape than the others and is the only one with a recognizable dedication. A close examination of the walls reveals a series of spirals, representing moving air and hence the wind god Ehecatl, who is closely identified with Quetzalcóatl. Although the architecture bears strong Toltec influences, some features appear to be unique, such as the cruciform windows. There are no guided tours of the archaeological site, but it is attached to a **museum,** which explains the excavations. The museum, to the left as you enter, sets out other aspects of the culture, as well as the significance of this site in the context of the region's archaeological record. (Open daily 8am-5pm. 25 pesos; students, teachers, and over 60 free; Su free.)

JALISCO

GUADALAJARA ☎ 33

Skirting the line between the semi-arid deserts to the north and the tropics to the south, Guadalajara (pop. 4 million) has produced many of the country's most recognizable cultural treasures: bittersweet *mariachi* music, the *jarabe tapatío* (Mexican hat dance), and tequila. Soon after Guadalajara's founding in 1532 by conquistador Nuño de Guzmán, most of the region's *indígenas* were slaughtered and few pre-Hispanic traditions survived. In the years following, the city served as the capital of Mexico and a key battleground in the War for Independence, producing such local heroes as Father Miguel Hidalgo. Guadalajara's markets, clubs, and modern buildings mix smoothly with plazas, promenades, and churches, showcasing local *artesanía*. Painters, thespians, dancers (including the renowned Ballet Folklórico), and street performers continue the city's artistic traditions. Meanwhile, the Universidad de Guadalajara, the second oldest in Mexico, keeps the city young and adds a measure of intellectual sophistication. Though not specifically geared toward tourists, Guadalajara's natural charm and friendly *tapatíos* (as the city's residents call themselves) nevertheless draw a steady stream of visitors.

◼ INTERCITY TRANSPORTATION

Flights: Aeropuerto Internacional Miguel Hidalgo (GDL; ☎3688 6399 or 5127), 17km south of town on the road to Chapala. Served by: **AeroCalifornia** (☎3616 2525); **Aeroméxico** (☎01 800 021 4000), office on Corona at Madero (open M-Sa 9am-6pm); **American** (☎3616 4402 or 4408); **Continental** (☎3647 6675); **Delta** (☎3616 3748); **United** (☎3813 4002 or 4008). A yellow-and-white "Aeropuerto" bus passes through the *centro* on Independencia at Los Ángeles (every hr. 5:45am-8:45pm, 10 pesos) and makes the return trip from outside "Sala Nacional." Get off at 16 de Septiembre and Constituyentes. Metered taxis to the airport run 120 pesos, but you can often bargain the price down to 80 pesos. To get to the center of the city from the airport, go to the taxi stand at the end of building and buy a ticket for a taxi (190 pesos) or take the "Centro" bus outside (30min., every 30min., 10 pesos).

Buses: Central Vieja (☎3650 0479 or 0480), Los Ángeles 218, at Dr. Michel across from Parque Agua Azul. This convenient old **bus station** services many nearby destinations (up to 2-3hr. away). **Nueva Central Camionera** is in nearby Tlaquepaque. An old shopping mall now makes up the new **bus station** with 7 terminals. Fixed-fare buses and taxis (40-70 pesos, depending on time of day) head downtown frequently, as do

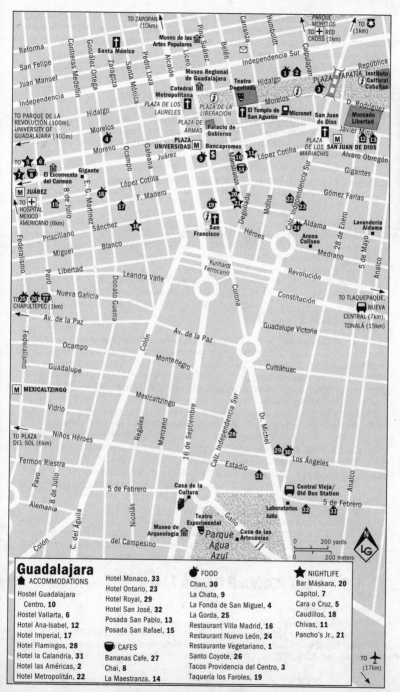

Guadalajara

ACCOMMODATIONS

Hostel Guadalajara
  Centro, **10**
Hostel Vallarta, **6**
Hotel Ana-Isabel, **12**
Hotel Imperial, **17**
Hotel Flamingos, **28**
Hotel la Calandria, **31**
Hotel las Américas, **2**
Hotel Metropolitán, **22**
Hotel Monaco, **33**
Hotel Ontario, **23**
Hotel Royal, **29**
Hotel San José, **32**
Posada San Pablo, **13**
Posada San Rafael, **15**

CAFES

Bananas Cafe, **27**
Chai, **8**
La Maestranza, **14**

FOOD

Chan, **30**
La Chata, **9**
La Fonda de San Miguel, **4**
La Gorda, **25**
Restaurant Villa Madrid, **16**
Restaurant Nuevo León, **24**
Restaurante Vegetariano, **1**
Santo Coyote, **26**
Tacos Providencia del Centro, **3**
Taquería los Faroles, **19**

NIGHTLIFE

Bar Máskara, **20**
Capitol, **7**
Cara o Cruz, **5**
Caudillos, **18**
Chivas, **11**
Pancho's Jr., **21**

"Centro" buses (4.5 pesos). From downtown, catch a #275, #275A, or TUR-706 bus on Revolución or 16 de Septiembre, across from the Cathedral. In a taxi, be sure to specify the station or it might take you to the old bus station, **Central Vieja.** Only partial listings provided; call for more info:

Terminal 1: Primera Plus (☎3600 0354) and **Flecha Amarilla** (☎3600 0398 or 0270) go to all major destinations.

Terminal 2: Overflow from **Ómnibus de México** (Terminal 6) and local carriers.

Terminal 3: Élite (☎3679 0404).

Terminal 4: Transportes del Pacífico (☎3679 0405 or 0495) sends 1st- and 2nd-class buses to many coastal destinations. Also home to **Transportes Norte de Sonora** (☎3679 0463 or 3600 0298), which has cheap 2nd-class service to distant northern destinations like **Guaymas** (19hr., 522 pesos).

Terminal 5: Línea Azul (☎3600 0112) goes to many destinations in northeastern Mexico.

Terminal 6: Ómnibus de México (☎3600 0590 or 3600 0468) provides comprehensive service to: **Aguascalientes** (24 per day 6:30am-midnight, 172 pesos); **Ciudad Juárez** (22hr., 10 per day, 1120 pesos) via **Chihuahua** (856 pesos); **Durango** (9 per day, 476 pesos); **La Piedad** (3 per day, 115 pesos); **Matamoros** (6 per day, 717 pesos); **Mexico City** (7hr., 12 per day, 410 pesos); **Monterrey** (16hr., 11 per day, 538 pesos); **Querétaro** (5hr., 3 per day, 271 pesos); **Reynosa** (13hr., 7 per day, 698 pesos); **Tampico** (12hr., 4 per day, 478 pesos); **Tepic** (3hr., every 30min. 4am-11:45pm, 194 pesos); **Torreón** (10hr., daily 8pm, 539 pesos); **Tuxpan** (7 per day, 116 pesos); **Zacatecas** (every hr. 4:30am-12:30am, 261 pesos).

Terminal 7: Estrella Blanca (☎3679 0405) is the parent company of numerous smaller lines, including **Rojo de los Altos** and **Transportes del Norte.** This is the biggest terminal, and buses from here will take you to almost every major city in the Republic for competitive prices.

▓ ORIENTATION

The heart of the city is the *centro histórico* around **Plaza Tapatía** and **Plaza de la Liberación.** Two major streets—**Calzada Independencia** (known as "Calzada Independencia Norte" north of Hidalgo, and "Calzada Independencia Sur" south of Morelos) and **Morelos** (running west from Calzada, where it begins)—divide Guadalajara into quadrants. Note that in addition to Calzada Independencia, Guadalajara has **Calle Independencia,** crossing the city east-west just north of the *centro,* and **Juárez,** which runs east west just south of the plazas and becomes **Vallarta** west of the university. The surrounding cities of **Tlaquepaque** to the east, **Zapopan** to the west, and **Tonalá** east of Tlaquepaque are all joined seamlessly to the outskirts of Guadalajara. When taking a bus to Guadalajara's *centro histórico,* verify with the driver that you're going to the correct *centro,* and not one of a neighboring city. The poorer *colonias* (neighborhoods) of Guadalajara can be dangerous at any time of day; check with the tourist office before blazing new trails. Throughout Guadalajara, travelers should keep to well-lit streets and take taxis after 10pm. Women traveling alone may wish to avoid Calzada Independencia after dark, as the neighborhoods southeast of the Mina-Calzada Independencia intersection are poorly lit and primarily frequented by raucous drunken men and prostitutes. The *barrio* area, even as close to the *centro histórico* as the Plaza de los Mariachis, is dangerous despite large crowds of *mariachis* and bar patrons.

▐ LOCAL TRANSPORTATION

Public Transportation:

Buses: Though usually crowded, bumpy, and always noisy, **minibuses, regular buses** (4.50 pesos), and big blue **TUR buses** (9 pesos) are a convenient way to get to sites farther away from the *centro histórico,* such as the Zoológico Guadalajara, Tlaquepaque, and Nueva Central. Buses run 6:30am-10pm; TUR buses run slightly later. Be sure to check the line (A, B, C, or D) of your bus. Generally, A and B run almost the same route along the main drags (with the same numbers), and C and D buses have different routes into the residential neighborhoods. Always check with the driver to confirm the bus's destination. **Buses #60** and **#62** run the length of Calzada Independencia, from the train station in the south all the way past Plaza de Toros. The wired **"Par Vial" bus** runs west on Calzada Independencia, then Hidalgo, before turning onto Vallarta, just short of Mateos. Returning eastward, it cruises Hidalgo 3 blocks north of Juárez. **Bus #258** from San Felipe, 3 blocks north of Hidalgo, runs from near Plaza Tapatía down Mateos to Plaza del Sol, the nightlife hot spot. **Bus #275** runs from Zapopán down to 16 de Septiembre and Revolución, and continues on to Tlaquepaque and Tonalá. Schedule and route information available at the tourist office. Comprehensive schedules on sale at most newsstands for 40 pesos.

Metro: (☎3827 0000). The two Metro lines run smoothly (every 5-10min. 6am-10:30pm, 4.50 pesos) and offer a great alternative to the bus system for anyone tired of breathing exhaust. An excellent map is posted in the stations. **Line 1** runs from the northern boundary of the city, Periférico Nte., more or less along Federalismo to Periférico Sur, with a central stop at Federalismo and Juárez. **Line 2** runs from Juárez and Alcalde/16 de Septiembre, conveniently passing Mina, to Patria in the east. The Metro is convenient both for locals and tourists, since it passes through the city center and downtown areas on its way out to the suburban residential areas.

Car Rental: Dollar Rent-a-Car, Federalismo Sur 380 (☎3825 5080), at La Paz. Open M-F 9am-7pm and Sa 9am-2pm.

⑦ PRACTICAL INFORMATION

TOURIST AND FINANCIAL SERVICES

Tourist Office: State Office, Morelos 102 (☎3668 1600). Friendly staff with useful maps of Guadalajara's *centro histórico*. Pick up the free, English-language tourist papers **Punto de Interés** and **Guadalajara Weekly** (free, English-language tourist papers). Open M-F 9am-8pm, Sa-Su 10am-2pm. Another branch in the Palacio de Gobierno. Open daily 9am-2pm. Guadalajara, Tlaquepaque, and Zapopan each maintain separate offices. Guadalajara also has 2 **tourist information booths** in Plaza Tapatía, 1 in Plaza de la Liberación, 1 in Plaza Guadalajara, 1 next to the Hospicia Cabañas, and 1 in the Jardín de San Francisco. All are open M-F 8:30am-2pm and 4-7:40pm, Sa 9:30am-3:30pm, Su 9:30am-2:30pm.

Consulates: Australia, Cotilla 2030 (☎3615 7418; fax 3818 3390), between Vega and Bara. Open M-F 8am-1:30pm and 3-6pm. **Canada,** Local 31 (☎3615 6270 or 3616 5642, emergencies 800 706 2900; fax 3615 8665), at Hotel Fiesta Americana, on the Minerva traffic circle. Catch a "Par Vial" bus. Open M-F 8:30am-5pm. **UK,** Jesús de Rojas #20 (☎3343 2296), near the Gran Plaza. Open M-F 9am-2pm and 5-8pm. **US,** Progreso 175 (☎3825 2700; fax 3826 6549). Open M-F 8am-4:30pm. The **Oficina de la Asociación Consular,** at the UK consulate, can provide listings for other consulates.

Currency Exchange: The streets off of Cotilla and Maestranza offer little else besides *casas de cambio:* a mecca for the cash-strapped. For banking services and a **24hr. ATM,** head to **Bancapromex,** 237 Juárez. Open M-F 9am-4pm, Sa 10am-2pm.

LOCAL SERVICES

English-Language Bookstore: Sandi Bookstore, Tepeyac 718 (☎3121 0863), near the corner of Rosas in Colonia Chapalita. Take bus #50 or 51B from Garibaldi or the green "Plus" bus from Juárez. New books and newspapers. Open M-F 9:30am-7pm, Sa 9:30am-2pm. Larger Mexican bookstores often carry English bestsellers.

Laundromat: Lavandería Aldama, Aldama 129 (☎3617 6427), 2½ blocks off Calzada Independencia. Full-service up to 7kg (35 pesos). Self-service: wash and dry 14 pesos. Open M-Sa 9am-7pm. Laundry service also available at **Chan** (p. 435).

EMERGENCY AND COMMUNICATIONS

Emergency: ☎080.

Police: (☎3668 0800 or 3684 2919), at the corner of Calzada Independencia Nte. 840 and Hospital.

Red Cross: (☎3613 1550 or 3614 5600, emergencies ☎085), at Manuel and San Felipe behind Parque Morelos.

24hr. Pharmacy: Farmacia Guadalajara, Mina 221 (☎3617 8555), at Cabañas.

Medical Services: Hospital Mexico Americano, Colomos 2110 (☎3642 7152 or 3641 3323). **Green Cross Hospital** (☎3614 5252), at Barcenas and Veracruz.

Fax Office: Laboratorios Julio, 5 de Febrero 110, at Dr. Michel, sends and receives faxes. Prices vary based on destination. Open M-Sa 8am-7pm.

Internet Access: Juárez has a large offering of Internet cafes around 8 de Julio. Among them is **Micronet,** 60 Juárez, a no-frills Internet cafe offering a fast connection and a variety of candy. 12 pesos per hr. Open daily 8pm-2am. **Compucan,** Martínez 46 (☎3614 0797), provides Internet access for 12 pesos per hr. Open daily 9am-8pm. Cafes offering Wi-Fi line the strip of Chapultepec just south of Vallarta.

Post Office: (☎3613 6425 or 3614 6697), on Carranza between Manuel and Calle Independencia. Open M-F 8am-6:30pm, Sa 9am-1pm. **Postal Code:** 44100.

♥ ACCOMMODATIONS

Guadalajara is chock full of low-cost hotels and hostels, most located within easy walking distance of the *centro histórico*. Most hostels are located west near Federalismo, while cheap hotels abound along Mina and Calzada Independencia. The latter areas occasionally suffer typical big city problems—24hr. traffic, poor room quality, and prostitution. Some of the best values are around the old bus station, a 20min. walk from Plaza Tapatía. This area's advantages include proximity to Agua Azul and easy access to buses going to Guadalajara's appealing surroundings, including Lake Chapala, Tequila, Tlaquepaque, and Tonalá. Accommodations run on the small side, so arrive early or call ahead to ensure a room. Hotels advertising that they cater to families are declaring themselves to be prostitution-free.

AROUND THE CENTRAL VIEJA BUS STATION

Away from the action, this area offers a slew of quality, low-priced hotels. Beware of the traffic; to ensure a relatively quiet night, request a room that doesn't face the large streets.

▨ Hotel San José, 5 de Febrero 116 (☎3619 2811; hotelsanjose@hotelsanjose.com.mx). An unremarkable exterior hides a lush, beautiful lobby and immaculate, elegant rooms. All rooms with TV, fan, and private bath. More expensive rooms have been recently remodeled. Singles 160-230 pesos; doubles 190-270 pesos. Cash only. ❷

Hotel la Calandria, Estadio 100 (☎3619 6579). Wood paneling and brass decor greet visitors to this well-kept hotel. Rooms are clean and come with fan and private bath. Singles 115-180 pesos, with TV 135 pesos; doubles 150-200 pesos. Cash only. ❶

Hotel Royal, Los Ángeles 115 (☎3619 8473 or 3650 0914). Shocking pink walls and a plethora of tropical plants give this place a kitschy vibe wholly distinct from its urban setting. Clean rooms come with TV, fan, bath, and a little street noise. Singles 135 pesos; doubles 155 pesos. Cash only. ❷

Hotel Monaco, 5 de Febrero 152 (☎3619 0018 or 3619 0019). A gleaming white lobby leads to tiled, slightly worn rooms with bath, TV, and fan. Hotel restaurant serves cheap Mexican fare. Singles 110 pesos; doubles 130 pesos. Cash only. ❶

ALONG CALZADA INDEPENDENCIA

While hotels in this area are generally safe, it is not recommended to walk on the Calzada alone after dark. The 24hr. diners, bus routes, and cheap *cantinas* with *mariachi* bands make Calzada a noisy place at night.

Hotel Metropolitán, Calz. Independencia Sur 278 (☎3614 9382). Rooms with clean, comfortable beds and tiled bathrooms open to a pleasant, sky-lit lobby adorned with old maps. Avoid rooms with windows facing the street. Reception 24hr. Singles 140 pesos; doubles 200 pesos; triples 230 pesos; quads 260 pesos. Cash only. ❷

Hotel Flamingos, Calz. Independencia Sur 725 (☎3619 8764), near Los Ángeles. Enamelled wooden desks and dressers make the simple rooms a bit more classy. All rooms with TV. Reception 24hr. Singles 170 pesos; doubles 210 pesos. Cash only. ❷

Hotel Ontario, Calz. Independencia Sur 137 (☎3617 8099). Across from Hotel Metropolitán, Ontario offers unbeatable prices (if not rooms) and good access to the *centro*. Simple, slightly run-down rooms with private baths. Reception 24hr. Singles 100 pesos; doubles 120 pesos; triples 150 pesos. ❶

WEST OF CORONA

Upscale restaurants and shops replace the *taquerías* and markets downtown as you travel west on Juárez, but the hostels nearby still offer solid lodgings for moderate prices.

Posada San Pablo, Madero 429 (☎3614 2811). Basic but large rooms come with private or communal bathrooms. Travelers chat in the kitchen and courtyard. Laundry 50 pesos. Checkout 1pm. Curfew 11pm on Sunday. Singles 190 pesos, with bath 270 pesos; doubles 280/330 pesos; triples 299/399 pesos; quads 550 pesos. MC/V. ❸

Posada San Rafael, López Cotilla 619 (☎3614 9146). This former monastery-turned-*posada* had its 19th-century roots in mind when renovating. The original stone walls still guard the colorful courtyard. Rooms with phone, remodeled bathroom, and TV. Internet 12 pesos per hr. Singles 270 pesos; doubles 330 pesos. AmEx/MC/V. ❹

Hostel Vallarta, Rayon 135 (☎3825 7278; www.hostelworld.com), off Juárez. This secluded hostel lies west of Federalismo, a short walk from the Parque Revolucionario and the Ex-Convento del Carmen. Lounge with talkative, amiable staff in the breezy courtyard. Kitchen, TV, lockers, and Internet available. Breakfast and linens included. Reception 24hr. Singles 135 pesos; doubles 300 pesos. Cash only. ❷

AROUND PLAZA TAPATÍA

The hotels clustered around Tapatía charge more than others in Guadalajara, but the easy access to the plazas and downtown sights more than make up for the extra pesos. Word of caution: the cheapest hotels may be frequented by prostitutes; the tourist office advises visitors to avoid lodgings southeast of Mina and Calzada Independencia.

🖼 **Hostel Guadalajara Centro (HI),** Maestranza 147 (☎3562 7520; www.hostelguadalajara.com). Funky art and plush couches set the tone for this hostel in the heart of the downtown area. Communal bathrooms and dorms with balconies overlooking the streets. Breakfast and linens included. Private rooms for 1-3 people have fan and TV. Laundry 50 pesos. Kitchen and storage available. Free Wi-Fi and Internet. Reception

24hr. Check-out 10am. Dorms 145 pesos; private rooms 250 pesos. 10 peso discount for ISIC members, 30 peso discount for HI members. Cash only. ❶

Hotel las Américas, Hidalgo 76 (☎3613 9622 or 3614 1604), at Humboldt. Paintings and well-groomed native plants complement clean and simple rooms. Carpeted rooms have fan, phone, private bath, purified water, and TV. Ask for a room away from the noisy street. Reservations recommended during the summer. Reception 24hr. Singles 200 pesos; doubles 255 pesos; triples 285 pesos; quads 315 pesos. Cash only. ❸

Hotel Imperial, Mina 180 (☎3686 5718; fax 3586 5719). Good upkeep, friendly staff, and the cool, protected lobby/courtyard make the Imperial worthwhile. Spacious rooms come with fan and private bath; some with cable TV. Wi-Fi access. Reception 24hr. Singles 150 pesos; doubles 200 pesos. Cash only. ❶

🍴 FOOD

Guadalajara is a city that revels in its culinary identity. Hundreds of *taquerías*, scattered in long lines around the city, serve tacos of all sorts for a mere handful of pesos. Almost as common are local specialties like *tortas ahogadas* (pork rinds stuffed in a soft shell and topped with onions and salsa) and *birria* (stewed meat, usually pork, in tomato broth thickened with cornmeal and spiced with garlic, onions, and chiles). Estrella beer, brewed *clara dorada* (golden clear) right in Guadalajara, is perfect for cooling off after all the *comida picante*. The city caters to everyone; food from faraway places is available, too, at slightly higher prices. **Mercado Libertador,** at Mina and Calzada Independencia, sells every kind of food imaginable at cheap market prices. A 24hr. supermarket, **Gigante,** Juárez 573 (☎3613 8638), is located on Juárez and Martinez, near the "Super G" sign.

THE CENTRO

Tacos and ice cream dominate the menus of most joints in the *centro,* but with a little energy you can find sit-down spots with broader offerings. **Mercado Libertad,** on Calz. Independencia Nte., next to the plaza, is a sensory overload—find anything in this market from *birria* and fried chicken to live animals. (Huge meals around 26 pesos. Open daily 6am-8pm. Cash only.)

▨ **La Chata,** 126 Corona (☎3613 0588), off Juárez. The yellow walls decorated with pictures and pottery from Jalisco have complemented La Chata's exquisite food since 1942, creating the perfect *tapatío* ambience. The *platillo jalisciense* (70 pesos) comes with a little bit of everything. Beer and wine 25-45 pesos. Entrees 40-85 pesos. Open daily 8am-midnight. AmEx/MC/V. ❹

La Fonda de San Miguel Arcángel, Guerra 25 (☎3613 0809 or 0793). Standing in a building first completed 1694, la Fonda—once called Santa Teresa de Jesús—is the oldest convent in the city. Golden colonnades, exotic birds, and a fountain make for a relaxed mood. Breakfast specials 50-80 pesos. Mixed drinks 40-70 pesos. Entrees 90-140 pesos. Open M and Su 8:30am-6pm, Tu-Sa 8:30am-midnight. AmEx/D/MC/V. ❺

Tacos Providencia del Centro, Morelos 86 (☎3613 9914), next to the state tourist office. This white-tiled *taquería* on the corner offers quick service, good food, and even better people-watching. Tacos 5 pesos. Quesadillas 7 pesos. Drinks 8 pesos. Open Tu-Su 10am-7pm. Cash only. ❶

Restaurant Nuevo Leon, Calz. Independencia Sur 233 (☎3617 2740), between Aldama and Medrano. Wood floors and plush orange chairs are a comfortable setting for watching Chivas games. The specialty is Monterrey-style *cabrito al pastor* (goat; 135 pesos). Drinks 40-70 pesos. Entrees 100-140 pesos. Open daily 11am-10:30pm. ❺

Restaurant Villa Madrid, Cotilla 553 (☎3613 4250). Watch as staff convert a wall of fruits into great smoothies and huge *licuados* (15-25 pesos). *Tostadas* (40 pesos), burritos (44 pesos), and other hearty dishes are served with plenty of sides. Open daily noon-9pm. Cash only. ❸

Restaurante Vegetariano, Hidalgo 112 (☎3658 1354), at Humboldt. Creative salads (15-20 pesos) make up for what the ambience lacks. Veggie burgers 19 pesos. *Licuados* 10 pesos. Open M-Sa 8am-7pm, Su 10am-6pm. Cash only. ❶

Chan, Los Ángeles 131 (☎3619 9446). Metal chairs with green tops and a jukebox give Chan the feel of a 50s diner. Seafood is their specialty. *Sopa de mariscos* 60 pesos. Entrees 40-60 pesos. Laundry service 50 pesos. Open daily 7am-11pm. Cash only. ❸

ZONA ROSA

The places listed below are around the Vallarta and Chapultepec intersection or just west of it (on the "Par Vial" and #321 buses), where a few extra pesos buy excellent food and a bit more elegance. Past Chapultepec, Vallarta both a 24hr. **Sanborn's** and **VIPs** (offering drugstore, coffee shop, and newsstand items) for those seeking a late-night refuge from their hotels.

Santo Coyote, Lerdo de Tejada 2379 (☎3343 2265 or 2266). A Hawaiian luau with all the stars of the Mexican culinary canon. Waiters serve tropical dishes like cactus-and-cilantro-infused *filete "el patrón"* (147 pesos) or *crema hacienda de cortez* (pumpkin flower, grilled chile, and maize soup; 55 pesos). Open daily 1pm-1am. AmEx. ❺

La Gorda, Niños Héroes 2810 (☎3121 2126), by Los Arcos. Though slightly geared toward tourists, La Gorda cooks up large portions for the right price. Another location at Juan Álvarez 1336 (☎3825 2239). Full meals under 50 pesos. Open M-Sa 1:30pm-midnight, Su 1-11pm. MC/V. ❸

◉ SIGHTS

Guadalajara preserves its deep cultural and historical heritage while embracing the bustle and flow of modern city life in its plazas and markets. The city's many shopping malls spill over into wide public spaces, packed with *mariachis*, tourists, vendors, and street performers. That said, many of the city's finer sights are in its scattered parks and suburbs: Zapopan's cathedral (p. 440), Tonalá's market (p. 441), Tequila's blue agave (p. 445), and the picturesque towns around Lake Chapala. The tourist office offers a free comprehensive pamphlet called *Puntos de Interés*, complete with maps, sites, and suggested walks.

THE CENTRO

PLAZA DE LA LIBERACIÓN. Guadalajara's cultural wealth is concentrated amid *tapatía* activity in this central plaza. Horse-drawn *calandrias* line up near the Museo Regional, waiting to cart you around the city (50-60min., 200 pesos). Surrounded by the cathedral, Museo Regional, Palacio de Gobierno, and Teatro Degollado, this spacious plaza at the corner of Corona and Hidalgo has a bubbling fountain and a large Mexican flag. Military personnel ceremonially retire the colors daily at 7pm. An enormous sculpture on the northern side of the plaza depicts Hidalgo breaking the chains of servitude above a plaque with his 1810 decree abolishing the slave trade.

PALACIO DE GOBIERNO. The palace, built in 1774, served as the headquarters of renegade governments under Hidalgo from 1810 to 1811 and under Juárez in 1858. A stairwell features one of José Clemente Orozco's most brilliant and shocking frescos, depicting Father Hidalgo brandishing a fiery sword against the forces of the military parties and a corrupted Church. Nearby is the room where Hidalgo signed his famous decree. *(Corona 31. Palacio's General Director ☎3668 1808. Open daily 9am-8pm. Tours available in English.)*

CATEDRAL METROPOLITANA. Facing Teatro Degollado across Plaza de la Liberación, this Neoclassical church—the most visible symbol of the city—was begun in 1568 and completed 57 years later. After an 1818 earthquake destroyed its original towers, ambitious architects replaced them with much taller ones. Fernando

VII of Spain donated the cathedral's 11 richly ornamented altars in appreciation of Guadalajara's aid during the Napoleonic Wars. Beautiful white stone interior arches support soaring naves, and the largest organ in Mexico, imported from France, stands at the back. Take the steps on the right-hand side to descend beneath the altar, where the tombs of three cardinals and two bishops lie. *(Between Hidalgo and Morelos. Open daily 8am-8pm. Masses still take place—plan accordingly.)*

INSTITUTO CULTURAL CABAÑAS. Just past the spiraling fountains of the Plaza Tapatía lies the flat stone edifice and its gorgeous chapel rotunda. Also known as the Hospicio Cabañas, this building was constructed in 1801 to house an orphanage. It served as an art school and a military barracks before its present status as an exhibition, performance, and office space; the last orphans were transferred elsewhere in 1980. Orozco murals decorate the building's chapel, and the Institute houses the world's foremost collection of Orozco art. The striking *El Hombre de Fuego* (The Man of Fire)—a dramatic reversal of heaven and hell that tops off Orozco's disturbing portrait of Mexican history—peers down from the dome. *(Calle Hospicio #8, Hospicio and Cabañas, 3 blocks east of Independencia. Open Tu-Sa 10am-6pm, Su 10am-3pm. 10 pesos, students 5 pesos, children 6-12 2.50 pesos; Su free. 10 pesos for camera use—no flash.)*

MUSEO DE LAS ARTES POPULARES. North of the centro, this contemporary museum houses offbeat "popular art" (not to be confused with pop art) artifacts. The permanent exhibits upstairs showcase chess sets, daggers, guitars, and photography, while mixed media pieces with tequila bottles, figurines, and a papier-mâché dragon are displayed downstairs. The cultural relics are well kept, and the warehouse is often empty, ensuring a crowd-free experience. *(San Felipe 211. ☎3614 3891. Open Tu-Sa, 10am-6pm and Su 10am-4pm. Free.)*

MUSEO REGIONAL DE GUADALAJARA. The old San José seminary chronicles the history of western Mexico starting with the Big Bang and also displays works of art. Skip the paintings in favor of the enormous, complete skeleton of a prehistoric elephant and indigenous handicrafts. *(Liceo 60 at Hidalgo, on the northern side of Plaza de la Liberación. ☎3614 9957. Open Tu-Sa 9am-6pm, Su 9am-4:30pm. 37 pesos, children under 12 and seniors free; Su free.)*

TEATRO DEGOLLADO. Attend the Guadalajara Philharmonic for a good look at the breathtaking Teatro Degollado, named for former governor Santos Degollado. Built in 1856, the Neoclassical structure can seat hundreds beneath its gilded arches, sculpted allegories of the seven muses, and Gerardo Suárez's interpretation of Dante's *Divine Comedy* on the ceiling. In addition to the Philharmonic, the theater seasonally hosts amateur acts. Every Sunday the Universidad de Guadalajara performs *ballet folklórico*. *(On the eastern end of Plaza de la Liberación. Office ☎3613 1115. Open to visitors daily noon-2pm. Guadalajara Philharmonic performs F at 8:30pm and Su at 12:30pm. Tickets available at the theater box office. ☎3614 4773. Open daily 10am-8pm. Tickets from 50 pesos.)*

TEMPLO DE SAN AGUSTIN. This unassuming church, built in 1573, stands off a corner of the Plaza de la Liberación. Built with a combination of Baroque and Neoclassical styles, it has no nave or dome, just a few altars and two sculptures of Saint Augustine and his mother. The church was once a convent, and its abutting cloister now houses the University of Guadalajara's music school. Pass quietly through the arch to enjoy the peaceful courtyard and music. *(Located at the corner of Morelos and Degollado. ☎3614 5365. Regularly scheduled mass. Open daily 6am-9pm.)*

PLAZA DE LOS MARIACHIS. Immediately after you sit down in this crowded plaza full of jewelry stands, roving *mariachis* will pounce. Most will expect a donation after their song, even if you didn't ask for the performance. Full during the day, the plaza overflows at night as hundreds of *mariachis* spill over nearby streets. Beware: in early evening the plaza fills with roving unsavories, who have been known to mug unsuspecting passersby. *(On the southern side of San Juan de Dios, the church with the blue neon cross on Independencia at Mina. Songs 20-35 pesos.)*

OUTSIDE THE CENTRO

PARQUE AGUA AZUL. Hidden to the south of the old bus station, this 168,000 sq. m park features tropical aviaries, an orchid greenhouse, and a butterfly garden. Couples relax in the grass as children play soccer on the park's scattered greens. *(South of the centro on Calz. Independencia. Take bus #60 or 62 south. Open Tu-Su 10am-6pm. 4 pesos, children 2 pesos.)*

EL EX-CONVENTO DE CARMEN. A venue for exhibits and film showings, the ex-convent holds an immense collection of contemporary pieces by local artists. The galleries are full of lurid, gorgeous paintings and other modern installations by talented Jalisco artists. The building is also home to the Center for Audiovisual Studies and screens international film classics. *(Juárez 630, one block east of Federalismo. ☎3587 7825. Open Tu-Sa, 10am-8:30pm and Su 10am-8pm. Movies run every day at 4, 6, and 8pm. Donations accepted.)*

NORTH OF THE CENTRO

To reach the following sights, take Ruta #60 or 62 north on Calz. Independencia.

ZOOLÓGICO GUADALAJARA. A nice break from the grime and bustle of the *centro*, the zoo holds over 300 species from around the world. Other highlights include a kangaroo farm and an aquarium. The far end of the zoo affords a grand view of the 200 mi long Barranca de Huentitán ravine. *(Continue north on Calzada Independencia past Plaza de Toros and walk 1.5km from the bus stop on Independencia to the entrance of the zoo. ☎3674 1034. Open in summer daily 10am-6pm; in low season W-Su 10am-6pm. 45 pesos, children 25 pesos. Call ahead 3-5 days to schedule swimming with dolphins. ☎3674 0138. Prices vary.)*

CENTRO DE CIENCIA Y TECNOLOGÍA. The center houses a planetarium, as well as exhibits on stars, rocks, and the history of communication. Check out the topiary garden. *(A 20min. walk south from the zoo. Open daily 9am-6pm. ☎3674 4106. Museum and planetarium 12 pesos, children 6 pesos.)*

🎵 ENTERTAINMENT

LIVE PERFORMANCES

Guadalajara ardently keeps in touch with its cultural side, and the government actively promotes artistic and musical endeavors. To keep abreast of all the happenings, from avant-garde film festivals to bullfights, check the listings in *The Guadalajara Weekly* and *La Gaceta*, the University's weekly newspaper. Information is also available in the kiosks and bulletin boards in places like **Instituto Cultural Cabañas.** Be prepared to take a taxi—buses stop running at 10pm.

The **Ballet Folklórico** performs stunning intricate dances from regions throughout Mexico. The University of Guadalajara troupe, reputedly the best, performs in **Teatro Degollado.** Tickets are available on the day of performance and one day in advance. *(☎3614 4773. Performances Su noon. Box office open daily 10am-8pm. Tickets 80-300 pesos.)* **Ballet Folklórico de Cabañas,** the Jalisco state troupe, performs in the **Instituto Cultural Cabañas,** three blocks east of Calzada Independencia. *(Performances W 8:30pm. Tickets 60 pesos.)*

> **GUADALAJARA FOR POCKET CHANGE.** Much of Guadalajara's culture and history is available on the cheap. Spend the night in **Hotel Vallarta** and enjoy the breakfast (included) before walking downtown to the free **Museo de Artes Populares.** Visit the **Catedral Metropolitana,** a fantastic piece of architecture and the city's quintessential symbol. To fuel up, the **Mercado Libertador's** restaurants and food stands provide good fare for a good value. In the late afternoon, stroll over to the **Ex-Convento del Carmen** and catch a classic flick before retiring to the **Parque de la Revolución,** just west of Federalismo, where couples, friends, and youth while away the evening.

For a dose of theater, there's the **Teatro Experimental,** which despite its name performs major mainstream works as well. The theater, recognizable by the large obelisk in front of it, is nestled in a corner of the Parque Agua Azul along Calzada Independencia Sur. Shows run for several days. Check La Gaceta and other papers for what's showing. (Tickets available at ☎3818 3800 or 1-2hr. before the show at the box office. Tickets 80-120 pesos, students ½-price.)

Finding a bench in the Plaza de Armas, across from the Palacio de Gobierno, can be a tricky task, as the Jalisco State Band's public performances draw large crowds. (Performances Th and Su 6:30pm; seat-seekers should arrive before 6pm. Free.) **Plaza de los Fundadores,** behind Teatro Degollado, serves as a stage every afternoon and evening for clown mimes. Watch and give tips, but unless you like being the butt of jokes, keep out of the mime's view. Every October, Guadalajara explodes with the **Fiestas de Octubre,** a surreal, month-long bacchanalia of parades, dancing, bullfights, fireworks, food, and fun. Each day of the month is dedicated to a different state or territory in Mexico. Information and a schedule of events can be found at the tourist office at Morelos 102 (☎3668 1600).

University facilities, scattered throughout the city, provide high culture for low budgets. The **Departamento de Bellas Artes,** García 720, coordinates activities at many venues throughout the city. A blackboard in the lobby lists each day's attractions. (Open M-Sa 9am-5pm. Price depends on event.)

CINEMA

Cinepolis at the Centro Magno, shows current Hollywood films dubbed in Spanish. (☎3630 3940. Tickets 50 pesos, matinees 40 pesos, W 32 pesos. AmEx/MC/V). International films and classics show daily at the **Ex-Convento del Carmen** (p. 437). (☎3587 7825. Movies run every day at 4, 6, and 8pm. Donations accepted.) Guadalajara has dozens of cinemas (about 30 pesos); check newspapers for listings.

SPORTS

Bullfights take place most Sundays (Oct.-Mar.) at either 4 or 5:30pm at **Plaza de Toros,** on Nuevo Progreso at the northern end of Independencia. (Take Ruta #60 or 62 buses north. ☎3651 8506. Tickets 70-520 pesos. Open M-Sa 10am-2pm and 4-6pm.) **Lucha libre,** or wrestling, is a crowd favorite. Local wrestlers take on opponents who are subjected to the audience's filthiest possible abuse and return it in kind. Acrobatics and drama are fundamental, and fights sometimes make it out ring into the seats—be prepared to clear out. (Arena Coliseo, Medrano 67 off Calz. Independencia. ☎3617 3401. Matches Su 5:45pm and Tu 8:15pm. Prices 70-110 pesos per match, about 5-6 fights.) **Fútbol** is enormous in Guadalajara, and the **Chivas,** the local professional team, are perennial contenders for the national championship. Matches take place September through May in **Jalisco Stadium** on Calzada Independencia Nte. in front of Plaza de Toros. (☎3637 0563. Open daily 8am-4pm. Tickets 5-200 pesos.)

◨ SHOPPING

Mercado Libertad, at the intersection of Independencia and Mina East, is a labyrinth of alleys and stalls stretching some seven blocks. The range of items sold is broad and eclectic—pirated films, *sombreros*, Chivas jerseys, herbal remedies, and equestrian equipment are all on offer. Plenty of prepared food is available in the restaurant section (open daily 6am-8pm), or head over to the food stalls and pick out some produce or poultry as vendors hawk their wares. The Sunday market **El Baratillo,** is on Mina approximately 15 blocks east of Mercado Libertad. From Mercado Libertad, walk two blocks north to Hidalgo and catch bus #40 heading east or a "Par Vial" bus on Morelos. El Baratillo sometimes sprawls over 30 blocks—that's more market area than in all of Mexico City! Vendors sell everything imaginable, from *tamales* to houses. (Open all day every Su.)

> ✴**TIP** **IT'S JUST A NUMBER.** In most parts of Mexico, bargaining is completely acceptable—and even expected. Taxi drivers and artisan stands alike will automatically name a higher price than is fair. Most taxis don't run on meters, so their original price is arbitrary and very easy to bargain down. Browsing the wares of competitors will often cause sellers to drop their prices.

For boutique stores, brand names, and a food court, head over to the newly opened shopping mall **Centro Magno** at Vallarta 2455 (☎3630 1113 or 1772). The Centro has a **Hard Rock Cafe** (☎3616 4560), its own **Chili's** franchise (☎3616 5216), and upscale shops where you can expect to shell out pesos. The mall is busy with window-shoppers late into the night, offering a surreal vision of the commercialized Mexican "Plaza of the Future"—a far cry from the traditional *mercados*.

◪ NIGHTLIFE

Clubs and cafes, bars and burlesque, Guadalajara lays claim to all varieties of nightlife. The cafes and quieter spots generally close in the early evening, but the nightlife crowd dances well into early morning hours. Plaza del Sol and Vallarta host the city's club scene, while bars are further east. Guadalajara's downtown area supports a thriving gay culture. Since public transportation ends at 10pm, taxis are the best way to get around the city's scattered nightspots.

BARS AND CAFES

Cheaper, calmer, and closer to the *centro*, Guadalajara's bars and cafes are much more intimate than its pulsating clubs. Loud saloons and bars line Calzada Independencia, while a cafe culture predominates along Vallarta heading west.

La Maestranza, Maestranza 179 (☎3613 5878), near Cotilla. Bullfighting memorabilia lines the walls, a backdrop to the loud dance hits blaring over the intimate wicker tables. Open daily noon-3am. AmEx/MC/V.

Bananas Cafe, Chapultepec 330 (☎3615 4191), at Tejada. Pop art and pop stars surround raised tables and colorful light fixtures. Outdoor seating has a tropical feel. Drinks named after rock stars 17-20 pesos. Open M-Th and Su 9am-1am and F-Sa 9am-3am. Cash only.

Chai, Vallarta 1509 (☎3615 9426 or 3616 1299). Hip locals lounge on white sofas while resting their mugs on coffee tables cluttered with magazines and the occasional laptop. Iced lattes 19 pesos. Gourmet sandwiches 37-64 pesos. Wi-Fi access. Open M-Th and Su 8am-midnight and F-Sa 8am-1am. AmEx/MC/V.

CLUBS

The upscale clubs lining Vallarta come to life around midnight. Taxis (50-60 pesos) are the best mode of transport, since partiers clad in dress shoes and heels won't appreciate the 30min. walk from the *centro*. More traditional discos with complex track lighting, pulsing music, and elevated dance floors surround Plaza del Sol (near Mateos Sur and Otero), accessible by taxi for about 70 pesos.

Capitol, Vallarta 2648 (☎3615 8999), at Los Arcos. A flashy neon palm tree at the door sets the tone for fancy art, flatscreen TVs, and pretension galore. Pulse to electropop dance music with trendy clientele in this converted 2-story 19th-century mansion. Dress to impress. Cover women 60 pesos; men Tu-Th 60 pesos, F-Sa 80 pesos. Open Tu-Sa 11:30pm-5am.

Cara o Cruz, Vallarta 2503 (☎3615 7621). This lively saloon is packed on weekends. Patrons dance in a friendly environment. Cover 30-50 pesos. Beer 15 pesos, tequila 40 pesos. Open W-Sa 8:30pm-3am, Su 5pm-3am.

GLBT NIGHTLIFE

Locals in Guadalajara's gay scene claim it's the most vibrant in Mexico. GLBT clubs and bars cluster around the downtown area, where there's generally no cover or dress code. For event listings, check *Amadeus News*, which covers events in both Guadalajara and Puerto Vallarta (available at Chivas, below).

Caudillos, Sánchez 407 (☎3613 5445), near Hotel Cervantes, 3 blocks from the *centro*. Bumping music and strobe lights fill the small dance floor and the smoky corners of Caudillos. The black-and-white pictures on the wall contrast with the ambience. 2 beers for 25 pesos. Tequila 30 pesos. Open W and F-Sa 5pm-6am.

Chivas, Cotilla 150 (☎3613 1617), near the corner of Degollado. After 35 years in the business, Chivas is home base for the Guadalajara scene. Animated regulars converse around small tables. Beer 25 pesos for 3, 80 pesos for 12. Open daily 6pm-3am.

Pancho's Jr., Maestranza 264 (☎3613 9938), at Sánchez. A wide dance floor surrounded by cheap deck chairs is perfect for karaoke and transvestite shows on the weekends. Beer 2 for 25 pesos. *Micheladas* 2 for 40 pesos. Open daily 6pm-3am.

Bar Màskara's, Maestranza 238 (☎3614 8103), at Madero. A popular jungle-themed gay bar with a mixed male and female crowd. Don your favorite mask and step into the fun. Packed on weekends. 2-for-1 beers (25 pesos) and 2-for-1 tequila shots (60 pesos). Open daily 9pm-3am.

▶ DAYTRIPS FROM GUADALAJARA

ZAPOPAN

Catch a local #275 bus northbound on 16 de Septiembre (40min., 4.50 pesos). Ask the driver when to get off, or get off when you see the massive arch. Last bus back 10pm.

A soaring 20m arch next to the bus route is the first indication that Zapopan is an unusual suburb. The arch and its sculptures stand over the entrance of the beautiful **Paseo Teopitzintli,** a shady walk that leads to the stunning **Basílica de la Virgen de Zapopan,** at Hidalgo and Matamoros Nicolás Bravo, erected around the turn of the 18th century after a local peasant's vision of the Virgin. The altar holds Our Lady of Zapopan, a small cornstalk figure made by *indígenas* in the 16th century and still venerated by locals. Her healing powers are commemorated by decades worth of *ex votos*, small paintings on sheet metal offering a visual testimony of the cured. During the early fall, the figure of Our Lady of Zapopan frequently moves from church to church throughout Jalisco—each move is occasion for a festive parade in honor of the saint. One of the most hallowed transfers occurs on Día de la Raza (Oct. 12; p. 72), when the figure makes her way from Guadalajara's Cathedral back to Zapopan's church in a large procession. The late Pope John Paul II visited the basilica in 1979, and a statue of the pontiff holding hands with a beaming village boy now stands in the courtyard in front of the church. The **Sala de Arte Huichol**, on one side of the cathedral, offers a comprehensive display of indigenous culture, including a replica of a Huichol home. (Open M-Sa 9am-1:30pm and 3-6pm, Su 10am-2pm. 5 pesos.) The basilica faces the **Plaza de las Américas**, which stands at the end of the Paseo. Along the Paseo is the **Museo de Arte de Zapopan**, local art in a sleek, modern building. (☎3818 2515. Open Tu-Su 10am-6pm. 24 pesos.) Surrounding it are plenty of small shops and places to grab roasted chicken or a cheap taco.

TLAQUEPAQUE

Take a local #275 or 275A bus or the "Tlaquepaque" TUR bus (30min., 10 pesos) from 16 de Septiembre on the southbound side. For the main markets, get off at Independencia by the Pollo-Chicken on the left; if the driver turns left off Niños Héroes, you've gone too far. To get back to Guadalajara, take a #275 or TUR bus on Reforma or Niños Héroes.

Tlaquepaque has both preserved and profited from its colonial past. The streets off the plaza, farther from the *centro*, are lined with brightly painted 17th- and 18th-century homes; most have been converted into *artesanía* shops. Products tend to be of higher quality and price than similar goods piled high in the market shops aimed at unsuspecting tourists. Independencia, the main pedestrian route, is a shady walk lined by expensive galleries of ceramics and other fine handcrafted items. **Museo Regional de las Cerámicas y los Artes Populares de Jalisco,** Independencia 237, at Alfareros, sells an interesting collection of regional crafts. (☎3635 5404. Open Tu-Su 10am-6pm.) There are daily outdoor performances of *jarabe tapatío* in the square, and on Sunday *mariachis* perform in the **Parian,** at the corner of Independencia and Madero. A small **tourist information booth** (☎3562 7050) is on Calle Morelos, between Verde and Medellín. There are few dining options for the budget traveler apart from taco and fruit stands. More affordable meals can be found near the *mercado*, just off Tlaquepaque's main square.

TONALÁ

Catch bus #275 (4.50 pesos) or TUR-707 (9 pesos), both on Revolución. From the 275, get off at the corner of Av. Tonalá and Tonaltecas to greet rows of pottery stores. From TUR-707, get off at Juárez and Tonaltecas. Pass 3 blocks of market stalls to reach the Plaza Principal, at Juárez and Madero.

The dusty town of Tonalá is renowned for its finely wrought, earth-toned pottery. Due to its high quality and manufacturing costs, the town's *cerámica* often bypasses the local market of bargain hunters and goes straight to upscale department stores and boutiques. For a closer look, start at the **tourist office,** Zapata 244 (☎1200 3913; open M-F 9am-8pm), two blocks off the plaza on the right, and ask for information on local pottery factories such as **Concotzín, Erandi,** and **Kent Edwards.** Most factories offer tours, which often include the opportunity to buy slightly imperfect merchandise at discount prices. If you're not looking to buy, visit the **Museo Nacional de Ceramica,** Constitución 104, which displays award-winning work by native talents. The huge number of shops surrounding the *plaza principal* multiplies on ◪**market days** (Th and Su) into an endless expanse of stands sprawling down Juárez for blocks. Vendors sell local products (glassware, silver jewelry, basketry, miniature pottery sets), as well as *artesanía* from throughout Mexico. Taco stands punctuate the stalls for those in search of a cheap, quick bite.

NORTH SHORE OF LAKE CHAPALA

Guadalajara straddles the line between Mexico's arid North-Central plain and the lush overgrown hillsides of the Central Pacific Coast. For a taste of the latter, head south from the city to the fresh air and pretty villages on the north shore of Lake Chapala, Mexico's largest lake. The cooling effect of its waters and the mountain barrier conspire to keep the air 22°C (72°F) year-round, giving the coastal towns what National Geographic once called "the perfect climate." Such temperate weather has attracted everyone from D. H. Lawrence to Porfirio Díaz to thousands of US and Canadian retirees. Unfortunately, swimming is not recommended due to pollution and fluctuating water levels, which change substantially from year to year due to changes in rainfall and Guadalajara's sizeable water consumption. That aside, the temperate climate, relaxed atmosphere, and natural beauty make the north shore a worthwhile trip.

CHAPALA   ☎376

Chapala (pop. 20,000), founded by Tecuexe Indian Chief Capalac in 1510, is the first stop along the road from Guadalajara. It was here that D. H. Lawrence began writing *The Plumed Serpent* during the 1920s. The town now doubles as both a busy gateway to the lake's *pueblitos* and larger cities and as a quiet town, with the occasional burro clacking down the unpaved streets. Although the North Shore tends to be expensive, Chapala hosts the area's most affordable accommodations and is a great place to experience the lake and the mountains without too much of a tourist veneer.

⊟ TRANSPORTATION. To get to Chapala from Guadalajara, take a "Guadalajara-Chapala" **bus** (45min., every 30min. 5:30am-9:30pm, 35 pesos) from the old station. The new bus station also serves **Chapala** (1¼hr., every hr. 7:45am-5:45pm, 24 pesos). From Ajijic, take any bus (20min., every 20min., 7 pesos). In Chapala, the entrance of the **bus station** is on Madero at Martínez. Turn left on Madero as you exit the station to reach the lake. "Guadalajara-Chapala" buses back to Guadalajara leave the station on roughly the same schedule as they arrive.

⚠ PRACTICAL INFORMATION. The lake forms the town's southern and eastern boundaries. **Hidalgo** (called **Morelos** east of Madero) runs west to Ajijic from two blocks north of the lake. **Corona** runs along the southern waterfront. **Madero** is the main road, and runs north-south. The **tourist office,** Madero 407, is opposite the Palacio Municipal. (☎765 3141. Open M-F 9am-7pm, Sa-Su 9am-1pm.) **Banamex,** Madero 222, has an **ATM** (☎765 2271 or 2272; open M-F 9am-4pm), as does **Bancomer,** Madero 212. The **mercado de artesanías,** on the waterfront, extends four blocks east of Madero's end, on Corona. Other services include: **police,** Madero 413 (☎765 4444); **Red Cross,** on Av. Gallo adjacent to Cristania park on the *malecón* (☎765 2308, emergencies 065); **Farmacia Morelos,** Madero 435A (☎765 4002); and the **post office,** Degollado 323, near Guerrero (☎765 6809; open M-F 8am-3pm). **Postal Code:** 45900.

⊓⊡ ACCOMMODATIONS AND FOOD. An outstanding lodging choice three blocks from the shores of Lake Chapala is ⊠**Hotel Cardilejas ❸,** Cotilla 363, a rambling, colorful building on a hill with all the ambience of an Italian villa. Small, well-kept rooms with lace bedspreads have been known to lure the accidental tourist into month-long stays. Conveniently located one block off Madero near the bus station (look for the red-and-white sign), the hotel furnishes a great view of the lake and Chapala's charming rooftops. (☎765 2279. Singles 200 pesos; doubles 250 pesos; triples 290 pesos.) **Las Palmitas ❹**, Juárez 531, is across the street and two blocks away from the food market. A long, open white-tile courtyard leads to rooms with large beds. (☎765 3070. Singles 220 pesos; doubles 310 pesos; triples 415 pesos.) **Hotel Villa Samary ❹**, Juárez Morelos 199, offers massive rooms just a block away from the *malecón*. (☎765 3960. Singles 215 pesos; doubles 300 pesos.)

For a town its size, Chapala boasts plenty of dining options. The many coffee and pastry shops have relaxed outdoor seating, giving the town a summery, European feel. There are also plenty of taco stands along Madero that offer tasty and filling food on the go. **La Leña ❺**, Madero 236C, serves a range of seafood and *carne* amid old vinyl and paper snowflakes hanging from the ceiling. Try the *tostadas de marlin* (20 pesos) or one of the meat dishes (50-80 pesos). (☎765 2654. Open daily noon-midnight. Cash only.) For something lighter, try **Coffee Break ❷**, Madero 415. Order a coffee (15 pesos) or an Italian soda (22 pesos) and take advantage of the Wi-Fi access. (☎765 5931. Open M-Sa 8am-10:30pm. MC/V.) For a quick bite, try **Piccirilos Pizzeria ❷**, near the statue of Los Ausentes at the back of the plaza. In between slices (16 pesos), check out the arcade in back. (☎765 7777. Open daily 10am-10pm. Cash only.)

⬛🎵 **SIGHTS AND ENTERTAINMENT.** While brave weekenders may occasionally rev up their jetskis and tear through the calm waters of the lake, pollution and a receding shoreline prevent most watersports. Most prefer to satisfy their lakeside craving by leisurely drifting through the water on small boats. Many local boat owners can be found on the pier at the end of Madero offering to take tourists out to the two islands, Isla de los Alacranes and Riberas, where there are a couple of restaurants. (Piloted boats to Isla de los Alacranes 280 pesos per 30min., 350 pesos per hr.) Despite the grime, the lake remains picturesque. For the best view of Chapala, the lake, and the surrounding hills, walk up López Cotilla and turn left down the small alley. Climb up the stone stairway and continue up the roughly hewn stairs in the hillside for 15-20min., until you get to the cross.

⬛ **NIGHTLIFE.** After sunset, people head to Corona and Madero near the *malecón* for nighttime frolics. One popular place is **Ever's,** Corona 6, where a young crowd sits out on the patio with drink of choice in hand. (Beer 10-15 pesos. Open M-Th 4pm-midnight, F-Sa 4pm-2am. Cash only.) Just down the street is **Jony's Place,** Corona 2, with a jukebox and pool table in the back. (☎765 3182. Beer 15 pesos. Sangria 35 pesos. Margaritas 40 pesos. Open Su-Th 9am-midnight, F-Sa 9am-2am. Cash only.) **El Gavilan,** at the corner of Cotilla and 5 de Mayo, is full of locals singing loud *mariachi* songs. (☎765 2352. Beer 15 pesos. Tequila 30 pesos. Open daily 9pm-1am. Cash only.)

AJIJIC ☎376

Ajijic's (pop. 18,000) perfect weather and idyllic setting could not stay secret forever, and today the town supports a thriving expatriate community and tourism industry. Nevertheless, the city's cobblestone streets and well-tended gardens of Ajijic retain the charm of old Mexico. The town's renowned beauty has always drawn crowds of artists and writers; their efforts fill the cobblestone streets and lakeside galleries. The town's modern amenities and natural *pueblito* ambience merit the hype and a visit from even the most tourist-wary traveler.

📞 TRANSPORTATION AND PRACTICAL INFORMATION. From the old bus station in Guadalajara, take a "Guadalajara-Chapala" bus (1hr., every 30min. 5:30am-9:30pm, 35 pesos), which, after stopping in Chapala, will continue along the lake to Ajijic and destinations beyond. From Chapala, take a bus to Ajijic via San Antonio from the bus station on Madero and Martínez (20min., every 15min. 6am-8pm, 7 pesos), or catch it at various bus stops along Madero. Buses back to Chapala or Guadalajara can be caught along Chapala, the same route by which the bus arrived (1hr., every 30min. 6am-8pm, 35 pesos).

If you're lost, locals are often willing to point you in the right direction. The only paved street in Ajijic is Carretera Chapala, which divides the town into north and south. West of Colón it is called Poniente, and to the east Oriente. To reach the plaza, turn left at the traffic light onto Colón. **Tourist information** can be found at the Lake Chapala Society's outpost in a former silkworm nursery at 16 de Septiembre 16. (☎766 1140. Open M-Sa 10am-2pm.) **Bancomer,** Parroquia 2 on the plaza, has a **24hr. ATM.** Other services include: **Lavandería,** just off the plaza at Colón 24A (wash and dry 40 pesos; open M-F 9am-6pm, Sa 9am-3:30pm); **police,** Colón 23 on the plaza (☎766 1760) and **Red Cross** (☎765 2308 or 2553) in Chapala, both reachable in an emergency by dialing ☎080; **Hospital Ajijic,** Carretera Chapala 33 (☎766 0662); **Farmacia Jessica,** Parroquia 18 on the plaza (☎766 1191; open daily 9am-2pm, 5-9pm); **Copy-Top,** Guadalupe Victoria 2, on the Plaza (☎766 4464; **Internet** 20 pesos per hr.; open daily 10am-9pm) or **CiberTec** PC, Chapala Pte. 9B (10 pesos per hr.; open M-F 10am-6pm); and the **post office,** Chapala Pte. 7A (☎766 1888; open M-F 8am-3pm, Sa 9am-1pm). **Postal Code:** 45920.

📍 ACCOMMODATIONS AND FOOD. Ajijic has no budget hotels, but the extra pesos bring appropriate luxuries. Keep in mind that Chapala, where rooms are cheaper, is a short bus ride away. **Las Casitas ❺,** Carretera Pte. 20, is one of the best hotel options, with red tile floors, fans, cable TV, private baths, a kitchen, and a cozy living room with chimney. (☎766 1145. 2-bed bungalows 395 pesos. Cash only.) Rooms at **Hotel Italo ❺,** Guadalupe Victoria 8, two blocks east of the plaza, are white-tiled with refrigerator, TV, and capacious beds. The hotel provides a laundry service, sauna, and hot tub. (☎766 2221. Singles 300 pesos; doubles 400 pesos; triples 490 pesos. MC/V.) **Posada las Calandrías ❺,** Carretera Chapala 8, has a flower-filled garden, barbecue space, and a great view of the laguna from the terraces. (☎766 1052. Small bungalows with 2 beds, a kitchenette, and refrigerator start at 400 pesos; larger rooms 500 pesos. MC/V.) All establishments have pools.

Although expensive restaurants dominate the scene, Ajijic will not disappoint the budget traveler. For breakfast, coffee, and *antojitos* in a lush garden replete with exotic birds, try **🐦Cafe In Acálli ❶,** 16 de Septiembre 6A. (☎766 4859. Coffee 9 pesos. Regular and veggie burgers 15 pesos. Sandwiches 11 pesos. Open M-Sa 9am-5pm. Cash only.) Another cheap local favorite is **Tepalo Restaurant ❷,** on Parroquia 10B at the plaza. Try the deep-fried shrimp sandwiches (40 pesos), fish filets (50 pesos) or enchilada plates (28 pesos). (☎766 0727. Open M-F 8am-5pm, Sa-Su 8am-6pm. Cash only.) The walls of **Saint Peter's ❺,** Hidalgo 17 off Colón, are studded with paintings, giving this upscale restaurant an art gallery vibe. Tapas (30 pesos) are served at the bar, and entrees run 90-115 pesos. (☎766 1919. Open M-Sa 1pm-midnight, Su 1-7:30pm. MC/V.) For organic, fair-trade coffee in a stylish setting, there's **Cafe Grano Cafe ❶,** Marcos Castellanos 15C, across from the church. (☎766 5684. Coffee 12 pesos, latte 19 pesos. Open M-Th 9am-2pm and 6-9pm, F-Su 9am-2pm and 5:30-9:30pm. Cash only.) At night, people of all ages head to the bar at **Posada Ajijic,** Morelos 1 on the laguna at Colón, which features live music Tu-F

7-11pm and Sa 9pm-1am. (☎766 0744. Beer 15 pesos. Tequila 40 pesos. Cover F-Sa 40 pesos. Open M-F noon-11pm, Sa noon-1am. MC/V.) **Taberna de Garrik,** at 16 de Septiembre #4, inside Hacienda Los Alcatraces, has live music on Saturdays from 8:30pm-1am. (☎766 5238. Cover 25 pesos. Open Th-Sa 5:30pm-1am. Cash only.)

TEQUILA
☎374

The smell of its namesake liquor—made here for over four centuries—suffuses the streets of Tequila (pop. 20,000). Surrounded by gentle mountains covered with the prickly, blue-green agave cactus plants as far as the eye can see, this small town is home to 16 tequila distilleries, including those of tequila giants Sauza and José Cuervo. Nearly every business in town is linked to alcohol in some way, and tourism sustains a slew of T-shirt, souvenir, and liquor shops, selling every variety of tequila and *mezcal*. A great daytrip from Guadalajara, Tequila makes for good times and even better nights.

◼◪ TRANSPORTATION AND PRACTICAL INFORMATION. Transportes Teo-cuitatlan buses (☎3619 3989) leave for Tequila from Guadalajara's old bus station (2hr., every 15min. 5:30am-9:30pm, 50 pesos). In Tequila, walk to the left from the bus stop and head down Sixto Gorjón into town. Turn right at Juárez, and then left at the cathedral to get to **Plaza Principal.**

All the distilleries are close to Plaza Principal. The giant José Cuervo and Sauza plants are right next to each other two blocks north of the plaza on a street that starts off as **Corona;** to the left, as you walk towards the Sauza plant, it becomes **Sauza Mora.** Turn off Corona to the left on Cuervo to reach the factory gates. Though it's hard to get lost in a town so small, you may want to pick up a map at the **Gobierno Municipal,** at the corner of Cuervo y Corona. The **tourist office's** module is located in a corner of the plaza across from the Palacio Municipal. (Open daily 10am-4pm.) **Bancomer,** on Gorjón at Juárez, has a **24hr. ATM.** (Open M-F 9am-4pm, Sa 9am-1pm.) **Farmacia Gema,** Gorjón 206 (☎742 4733), is open 24 hours. **Sergio Cyber** (☎742 4817), upstairs at Gorjón 88, has **Internet** access (12 pesos per hr). The **police** (☎742 0056) are right next door at Cuervo 33. In a **medical emergency,** call ☎080 or 116 for an ambulance. The **post office** is located at the corner of Juárez and Madero. (Open daily 9am-3pm.) **Postal code:** 46400.

◪◖ ACCOMMODATIONS AND FOOD. Tequila has a range of hotels close to the main plaza. **Hotel Colonial ❷,** Morelos 52, one block to the right before the plaza, has clean rooms with fan, bathroom, and TV overlooking a tranquil lobby. (☎742 4540. Singles start at 135 pesos. Cash only.) **Hotel San Francisco ❸,** 10 Vallarta, next to the cathedral, is a clean, comfortable sanctuary with large rooms. All rooms have private bath, fan, and TV. (☎742 1757. Singles 200 pesos; doubles 250 pesos. Cash only.) For a few more pesos, **Hotel Posada del Agave ❹** offers tequila-themed digs. Clean rooms decorated in tiles painted with agave plants have private baths, fans, and cable TV. (☎742 0774. Reception 24hr. Singles 210 pesos; doubles 299 pesos. Cash only.) **Casa Dulce Maria Hotel ❺,** Abasolo 20, off Gorjón, catches the eye with stunning columns surrounding the fountain in the courtyard. Spotless rooms come with large, comfortable beds and equally immaculate baths. (☎742 3200. Reception 24hr. Singles 300 pesos; doubles 480 pesos. MC/V.) **Hotel Abasolo ❸,** Abasolo 80A, provides spacious rooms with bath and TV, some with balconies overlooking the street. (☎742 8518. Reception 24hr. Singles 180 pesos; doubles 250 pesos; triples 380 pesos. Cash only.)

FORGET THE TEQUILA— PASS THE PULQUE!

Chances are you may be intimately acquainted with the *maguey* cactus (a.k.a. agave)—or, more likely, the tequila and *mezcal* it produces. What Mr. José Cuervo never told you is that when its sap (called *agua miel*, or honey water) is fermented instead of distilled, *maguey* yields the wondrous drink of the Aztecs: **pulque.**

Pulque is thought to have originated over 2000 years ago. Legend has it that it was discovered by the goddess Mayahuel. Associated with virility and fertility, *pulque* was used as an aphrodisiac and was given to the sick as medicine.

The supreme god of *pulque* is Ometotchitli, also known as Two Rabbit, who was said to have 400 sons. There are other *pulque* gods, who together are known as Centzon Totochtin, or 400 Rabbit, representing the 400 stages of inebriation.

Pulque is made by harvesting *agua miel* from 12-year-old *maguey*. The *agua* is transported by hand to a fermenting house, or *tinacol*, a sacred area where men must remove their hats and women are forbidden. (Long ago, *pulque* producers weren't allowed to even have contact with women.)

Today, *pulque* drinkers pay homage to the gods by pouring some on the ground before taking some for themselves.

A diverse cross-section of restaurants surrounds the plaza and the nearby streets. **El Mesón de Mezcal ❹,** Gorjón 152, flavors most of its food with its very own brand of tequila. (☎742 0476. *Torta ahogada* 20 pesos. Shrimp 72 pesos. Open daily 9am-10pm. Cash only.) For a nice evening view of the plaza, try **Cafe de Rossy ❸,** Vallarta 4. (☎742 2030. Espresso 10 pesos. Cappuccino 18 pesos. Club sandwiches 20 pesos. Coffee with tequila 20-30 pesos. Open daily 8am-2pm, 6:30-11pm. Cash only.) Right across from the Cuervo factory is the elegant, breezy **La Fonda Cholula ❹,** Corona 55. The enchiladas (50 pesos) go well with a little tequila, which starts at 30 pesos. (☎742 1079. Open daily 11am-6pm. AmEx/MC/V.) Taco stands also cluster on the right-hand side of the church as you face the entrance.

🎵 **ENTERTAINMENT.** Entertainment in Tequila is limited to drinking, taking a **tequila factory tour,** and visiting tequila museums. The tourist office runs tours (85 pesos) every hour from 11am-3pm from their module on the plaza. A better option may be to head straight to the **Sauza** factory tour. Join in at the factory or trek to the tour's official start: 50m down the highway past the entrance to Tequila at Rancho Indio, where a demonstration of blue agave cultivation precedes a visit to the factory. At the factory, a detailed demonstration of the production process, from agave to bottle, culminates predictably with shots. (☎742 0013. Tours M-F 11am, 12:30, 3, 4pm; Sa 11am, 12:30pm. 35 pesos.) Two blocks back toward the plaza is the less impressive **José Cuervo** factory, with a significantly more expensive, less detailed tour. For the price of a few shots, you'll learn more than you ever wanted to know about agave, the distillation and aging processes, and the history of the famous liquor. The guides will ply you with tequila and margaritas throughout the tour. Those under 18 get virgin margaritas. (Tours every hr. M-F, 10am-4pm, Sa 10am-5pm. The 3pm tour is in English. 100 pesos.) The **Museo Nacional de Tequila,** Corona 34, teaches tequila history, and has an impressive bottle collection and a gift shop. (☎742 2410. Open Tu-Su 10am-4pm. 15 pesos, students and children 7 pesos.) The **Museo Familia Sauza** in the old Sauza family mansion at Rojas 22 can be visited via guided tour. (Open M-F 10am-1:30pm, Sa-Su 10am-4:30pm. Tours approx. every 30min. Donations suggested.)

For the first 12 days of December, Tequila celebrates its *Feria Nacional de Tequila.* Each of the town's factories claims one day, on which it holds rodeos, concerts, cockfights, fireworks, and other festivities. Obviously, there are plenty of drinks to go around.

▚ NIGHTLIFE. Despite Tequila's diminutive size, throngs of well-dressed people pack the town's streets on weekends. Most cafes close before midnight, but the occasional bar is there for those who want a longer night. Tequila flows with its namesake drink at night, but many locals actually prefer beer. **Carajo's,** Corona 109, a few blocks from the plaza to the right, is a lively bar with a disco ball and cramped tables. On the weekends, people and loud club music overflow onto the street. (☎742 2885. Beer 15 pesos. Tequila 35 pesos. Open daily noon-1am. Cover F-Sa 30 pesos. Cash only.) For a quieter time, hit up **La Revolución Cafe y Bar,** upstairs at Corona 3A. Friendly regulars and nonstop *banda* music set the intimate tone. (Beer 15 pesos. *Michelada* 18 pesos. Tequila 35 pesos. Open daily 8pm-1am. Cash only.)

PUERTO VALLARTA ☎322

Half a century ago, Puerto Vallarta (pop. 350,000) was just another sleepy fishing village lost in the jungle between the mountains and a massive bay on the Pacific. Richard Burton, Liz Taylor, and droves of reporters following the lovers invaded the tiny village in 1963 to film *Night of the Iguana*, uncovering the beauty of the area for the world to see. The film thrust Vallarta into the public eye, jumpstarting the development of the city of 200,000 that is now famed as a tourist destination. While *Night of the Iguana* is long forgotten, Vallarta's massive resorts, epic nightlife, and timeless allure ensure it will remain a popular destination far into the future.

▐ TRANSPORTATION

Flights: Ordaz International Airport (PVR), 8km north of town. To get downtown from the airport, take a blue "Centro" or "Olas Altas" bus or a taxi. To get back from town, catch a "Novia Alta," "Marfil," or "Aeropuerto" bus on Cárdenas, Insurgentes, or Juárez. Served by **Aeroméxico** (☎224 2777, toll-free ☎800-021-4000); **Alaska** (☎221 1350); **American** (☎221 1799, toll-free ☎800-904-6000); **Continental** (☎221 2213); and **Mexicana** (☎221 1266, toll-free ☎800-501-9900).

Buses: The bus station is north of the *centro*, just beyond the airport. To get downtown, take a "Centro" or "Olas Altas" bus or taxi. To get to the bus station from downtown, take an "Ixtapa" bus (4.50 pesos) northbound at the plaza. **Primera Plus/Flecha Amarilla** (☎290 0715) offers service to: **Mexico City** (12hr., 7pm, 823 pesos); **Aguascalientes** (8hr., 2:45pm, 551 pesos); **Guadalajara** (5hr., every hr. 8am-1am, 336 pesos); **León** (8hr.; 11:45am, 1:45, 10:30pm; 578 pesos); **Manzanillo** (5hr.; 7, 10:30am, 1:30, 4:30, 10pm; 184 pesos) via **Barra de Navidad** (4½hr., 173 pesos); **Melaque** (4hr., 168 pesos); **Querétaro** (12hr., 9pm, 620 pesos). **Futura** (☎290 1001), **ETN** (☎290 0996 or 290 0997), and **Pacífico** (☎280 1008) offer similar services.

Taxis: Leave from the *centro* for the airport, bus station, or Marina Vallarta (60 pesos). Rides into town are much cheaper.

Buses: Local buses enter the city on México, which becomes Díaz Ordaz. All *combis* and any municipal bus operating south of the Sheraton or labeled "Centro" pass the main plaza, while those labeled "Hoteles" service the hotel strip. Buses stop at the clearly marked *parada* signs and at the covered benches, but you can flag one down almost anywhere. Buses going to points south go along Badillo, while those heading north travel along Juárez. (Buses and *combis* operate daily 6am-10pm. 4.50 pesos.)

Car Rental: National, Ascencio km 1.5 (☎01 800 003 9500), at the airport. **Thrifty,** Ascencio 7926 (☎221 2984).

CENTRAL PACIFIC COAST

▓ 🛈 ORIENTATION AND PRACTICAL INFORMATION

Running roughly east-west, **Río Cuale** bisects Puerto Vallarta before hitting the ocean. **Mex. 200** from Manzanillo runs into town south of the river, becoming **Insurgentes.** The ritzy waterfront between **Plaza Mayor** and **31 de Octubre,** called the **malecón,** is home to pricey restaurants, hotels, clubs, and the quintessential souvenir shops. North of the *malecón,* **Morelos** becomes **Perú** before joining the coastal route. Farther north lie the **airport, marina,** and **bus station.** The Zona Romántica, southwest of the river, is a mixture of bars, cafes, businesses, shops, and restaurants of all sorts. The southern end has almost all the cheap hotels, best beaches, and budget restaurants.

Tourist Offices: (☎226 8080 or 223 2500, ext. 230 or 231), on Juárez in the Presidencia Municipal. The **Secretaria de Turismo del Estado de Jalisco (SETUJAL;** ☎221 2676 or 2677), on the 2nd fl. of Plaza Marina. Free maps, brochures, and local English-language newspapers. Distributes *Bay,* a free publication that lists entertainment options in the city. Open M-F 8am-9pm, Sa 9am-noon. Another branch located inside the Parque Hidalgo (☎226 8080 ext. 230.) Open daily 11am-6pm.

Consulates: Canada, Blvr. Ascencio 1951 (☎293 0099, emergencies 800 706 2900; fax 293 0098), in the hotel zone. Open M-F 9am-3pm. **US** (☎222 0069, emergencies 013 332 682 145 in Guadalajara; fax 223 0074), in Nuevo Vallarta north of the city. Open M-F 8:30am-12:30pm.

Currency Exchange and Banks: Banamex (☎226 6110), at Juárez and Zaragoza, in front of the Presidencia Municipal. Open M-F 9am-4pm, Sa 10am-2pm. **Banorte,** Olas Altas 246 (☎223 0481), between V. Carranza and Badillo. Open M-F 9am-5pm, Sa 10am-2pm. Both have **24hr. ATMs. Casas de cambio** are everywhere, especially near the *malecón.* Rates vary, but are lower than at banks. Most open daily 9am-7pm.

American Express: Morelos 660 (☎223 2955; fax 223 2926), at Abasolo. Open M-F 9am-6pm, Sa 9am-1pm.

Luggage storage: At the bus station. 3 pesos per hr. Open 24hr.

Bookstore: Una Página en el Sol, Olas Altas 339 (☎222 3608), at Diéguez. Additional location at Aldama 180 (☎223 0115). Book exchanges welcome. Most English-language books 20-40 pesos. Huge sandwiches 30-40 pesos, small desserts 16-25 pesos. Open daily 7:30am-midnight.

Laundromat: Laundry Aguamátic, Constitución 279 (☎222 5978), between Cárdenas and Carranza. 12 pesos per kg. Open M-Sa 9am-8pm.

Emergency: ☎060.

Police: Revolución 350 (☎290 0507 or 0512), by the airport. Take a "Las Juntas" bus.

Red Cross: (☎222 1533) on Río de la Plata at Río Balsas. Take the "Cruz Roja" bus from Cárdenas and Insurgentes.

Hospitals: CMQ Hospital, Badillo 365 (☎223 1919), at Insurgentes. Also has a **24hr. pharmacy** (☎222 1330). **Hospital Medasist,** Diéguez 360 (☎223 0444 or 0656), at Insurgentes.

Internet Access: PV Cafe.com, Olas Altas 250 (☎/fax 222 0092), at Rodríguez. Cafe, small bar, fax, and copy service. Internet 35 pesos per hr. Wi-Fi available. Significant discounts for members; temporary memberships available. Open daily 8am-1am. A 24hr. Internet cafe is located inside the **Hotel Río,** Morelos 170. (☎222 0366. 15 pesos per hr. Cash only.)

Post Office: Colombia 1014 (☎223 1360 or 222 6308) , about 12 blocks north of the plaza on Juárez. Open M-F 8am-6pm, Sa 9am-1pm. **Postal Code:** 48300.

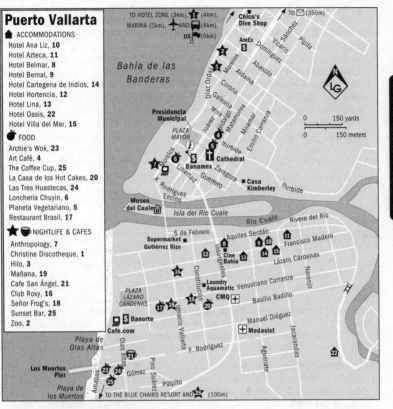

Puerto Vallarta

⌂ ACCOMMODATIONS

Hotel Ana Liz, **10**
Hotel Azteca, **11**
Hotel Belmar, **8**
Hotel Bernal, **9**
Hotel Cartegena de Indios, **14**
Hotel Hortencia, **12**
Hotel Lina, **13**
Hotel Oasis, **22**
Hotel Villa del Mar, **15**

🍅 FOOD

Archie's Wok, **23**
Art Café, **4**
The Coffee Cup, **25**
La Casa de los Hot Cakes, **20**
Las Tres Huastecas, **24**
Lonchería Chuyin, **6**
Planeta Vegetariano, **5**
Restaurant Brasil, **17**

★ ☕ NIGHTLIFE & CAFES

Anthropology, **7**
Christine Discotheque, **1**
Hilo, **3**
Mañana, **19**
Cafe San Ángel, **21**
Club Roxy, **16**
Señor Frog's, **18**
Sunset Bar, **25**
Zoo, **2**

ACCOMMODATIONS

A city of ritzy resorts and condos, the only budget hotel options in Puerto Vallarta are south of the river, clustered on a small strip of Madero. Reservations are recommended during *Semana Santa* and December, when vacationers from the interior and the north swoop in. Camping on the beach is prohibited in Puerto Vallarta, but once you pass into Nayarit it is permissible. Look for stretches of beach not adjoining hotels, and exercise caution overnight.

Hotel Azteca, Madero 473 (☎222 2750), between Jacarandas and Naranjo. Beautiful, potted plants extend through the courtyard to the 2nd fl., where clean rooms with bath and fan await. Towel deposit 50 pesos. Reception 24hr. Singles 200 pesos, with TV 250; doubles 300/350 pesos. Up to 50 pesos extra in high season. Cash only. ❹

Hotel Villa del Mar, Madero 440 (☎222 2885 or 0785), 2 blocks east of Insurgentes. A high-ceilinged lobby winds around a sweeping staircase surrounded with eclectic posters from faraway lands. Large, clean rooms with bath and fan; some with access to the pretty green side courtyard. Rooftop terrace with a view of the *centro*. Towel deposit 50 pesos. Singles 230 pesos, with balcony 300 pesos; doubles 260/350 pesos. All rooms at balcony prices during high season. 6% fee for MC/V. ❹

Hostel Oasis, Libramiento 222 (☎222 2636; www.oasishostel.com). Take a "Tunel" bus and get off at the first traffic light. Located a short walk from the *centro*, the only youth hostel in town offers simple dorms, communal bathrooms, laundry service, Internet access, luggage storage and lockers, and a communal kitchen. Breakfast included. Check-in 6am-midnight. 140 pesos per night. Cash only. ❷

Hotel Belmar, Insurgentes 161 (☎223 1872), at the corner of Serdán. A gleaming staircase leads past the lobby to gorgeous white rooms with large beds, luxurious bathrooms, outdoor sinks, and balconies overlooking most of Vieja Vallarta to the river. Reception 24hr. Singles 290 pesos; doubles 370 pesos; A/C 60 pesos extra. AmEx/MC/V. ❺

Hotel Lina, Madero 376 (☎222 1661). Lina's vivid color scheme lends a tropical ambience that carries over into comfortable rooms with TV, bath, and fan. Reception 24hr. Singles 200 pesos; doubles 250 pesos. 30 pesos more in high season. Cash only. ❹

Hotel Ana Liz, Madero 429 (☎222 1757). Small rooms with funky curtains hold wood-framed beds, bath, fan, and lots of furniture. Reception 24hr. Singles 190 pesos; doubles low season 220 pesos, high season 250 pesos; triples 300 pesos. Cash only. ❸

Hotel Bernal, Madero 423 (☎222 3605). An inviting courtyard leads to clean, spare rooms. Private bath and fans. Free purified water. Towel deposit 30 pesos. Reception 24hr. Singles 220 pesos; doubles 280 pesos; triples 340 pesos. 30-40 pesos more in high season. Cash only. ❹

🍴 FOOD

Puerto Vallarta, living up to its international billing, serves cuisine from around the globe. It comes with a hefty cost, though, and finding cheap food can be a challenge. The best place to look is south of the river, where a slew of restaurants serve traditional tacos and *antojitos* for decent prices. Innumerable street vendors along Madero and Cárdenas hawk decent tacos at all hours of the day and night for the lowest prices in the city. Olas Altas and the surrounding streets are home to a variety of cafes and delis with lighter options. There is also a supermarket, **Gutiérrez Rizo,** at Constitución and Serdán. (☎222 0222. Open daily 6:30am-11pm. AmEx.)

▨ Planeta Vegetariano, Iturbide 270 (☎222 3073; www.planetavegetariano.com), at Hidalgo, a few blocks inland from Plaza Mayor. This intimate, muraled vegetarian restaurant deserves its glittering reputation, with new dishes and themes every day. The all-you-can-eat buffet (65 pesos) includes 5 gourmet dishes (non-dairy options available), soup, salad bar, *agua fresca,* coffee, tea, and dessert. Breakfast buffet M-Sa 8am-11:30am. Dinner buffet daily 11:30am-10pm. Open daily 8am-10pm. Cash only. ❸

Restaurant Brasil, Carranza 210 (☎222 2909), off Vallarta. This Brazilian grill is for the ambitious, serving up course after course of exquisitely prepared meats complemented by mountains of garnish and fried plantains—tell the waiter when you can't lift the fork anymore and he'll stop bringing meat. Mens dinner 190 pesos, for women 160 pesos. Open daily 2-9pm. MC/V. ❺

La Casa de los Hot Cakes, Badillo 289 (☎222 6272), at Constitución. A piece of genuine Americana in Vieja Vallarta, with the full run of breakfast foods on the menu. Waffle and pancake specials 31-40 pesos. American coffee 13 pesos. Pressed orange juice 12 pesos. Open daily 8am-2pm. Cash only; US dollars accepted. ❸

The Coffee Cup, Gómez 146-A (☎222 8584; www.thecoffeecuppv.com), near Olas Altas. A blend of Mexican beans from around the Republic flavors the air in this cafe/deli. The fruit smoothies (37 pesos) go well with the large deli wraps (55 pesos). Coffee beans 95 pesos per ½kg. Free Wi-Fi. Open daily 8am-10pm. Cash only. ❸

Las Tres Huastecas, Olas Altas 444 (☎222 3017), on the corner of Rodriguez. The poetry of "El Querreque," as the *oaxaqueño* owner refers to himself, is immortalized on the walls of his simple breakfast spot. Quick scrambled eggs with tortillas and fried potatoes 30 pesos. Open daily 7am-8pm. Cash only. ❷

Archie's Wok, Francisca Rodríguez 130 (☎222 0411), just before the beach. Archie made his name as John Huston's personal chef, known for his Asian fusion dishes. Now his widow Cyndi maintains the tradition, turning out some of Vallarta's finest food in a candlelit setting. Th-Sa evenings graced with soft harp music. *Pancit de puerco* 89 pesos. Chicken stir fry 79 pesos. Open M-Sa 2-11pm. MC/V. ❺

Lonchería Chuyin, Libertad 187 (☎222 6411), between Juárez and Morelos. Take the food to go and sit in Plaza Mayor or on the *malecón*. Serves an abundance of options for a quick bite: 2 burritos or 3 *sincronizadas* (toasted tortillas) for 25 pesos. Sandwiches 23-30 pesos. Fruity *licuados* 17-22 pesos. Open daily 8am-10pm. Cash only. ❷

Art Cafe, Hidalgo 390 (☎222 4812), on the corner of Iturbide. Choose from healthful options: tea, coffee, sandwiches, salads, and desserts. A Mediterranean smorgasbord at its finest in an artsy downtown setting. Espresso 15 pesos. Pastrami and other sandwiches 55-65 pesos. Open 9am-9pm. Cash only. ❸

👁🅒 SIGHTS AND BEACHES

Vallarta's most popular attractions are its natural gifts: the striking green mountains and the miles of coastline and warm water. Watersports enthusiasts have a lot to choose from in Vallarta—activities like parasailing (8-10min. ride US$30) are extremely popular, especially in the morning. Jet skis (doubles 550 pesos per 30min.), banana boats (350 pesos per person for 1hr.), and kayaks (150 pesos per hr.), are also available—ask around at the pier and on the *malecón*. **Chico's Dive Shop,** 772 Díaz Ordaz, offers scuba diving courses, certification classes, and trips. (☎222 1895 or 1875 at Mismaloya; www.chicos-diveshop.com. 1hr. course US$25. Certification classes US$370. 4hr. of snorkeling 400 pesos per person. English-speaking staff lowers rates for returning customers and groups. Open daily 8am-10pm.) **Equestrian** fanatics can take to the hills on horseback; sign up at the stand in the plaza on Olas Altas at Carranza. (☎222 0386. 150 pesos per hr.)

Some of the least crowded and most gorgeous beaches stretch south of town on the road to Mismaloya (p. 454) and north into Nayarit (p. 422). The beaches near the *centro* are used most often for chatting and people-watching along the *malecón*, or for the watersports centered around *Muelle de los Muertos* (Pier of the Dead), which separates **Playa de los Muertos** (Beach of the Dead) from **Playa de Olas Altas** (Tall Waves Beach). The former has clearer water and is a better swimming area. The muddy river empties into

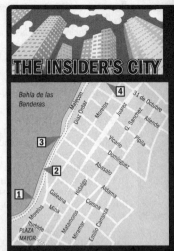

THE INSIDER'S CITY

SCULPTURES OF THE MALECÓN

The sculptures lining Puerto Vallarta's *malecón*, unknown to many except as convenient landmarks, are a testament to the flourishing artistic spirit within the city.

1 Seahorse (Rafael Zamarripa; 1976). The bronze figure of the boy riding a seahorse is the most recognizable and iconic of Vallarta's statues.

2 In Search of Reason (Sergio Bustamante; 1999). This piece celebrates the new millennium. The ladder is a photo-op favorite, as people clamber several rungs up to match the poses of the children.

3 Rockeater (Jonas Gutierrez; 2006). The most recent addition to the *malecón*, features the mystifying image of a rotund, 8 ft. tall man eating rocks.

4 The Millennium (Mathis Lidice; 2001). This gorgeous sculpture at the northern end of the *malecón* beautifully symbolizes man's constant evolution through time.

the ocean at Olas Altas, which is a more popular spot for watersports. To get to either, walk west along Cárdenas or Badillo. Near the southern end of Playa de los Muertos is **The Blue Chairs** resort, the world's largest gay and lesbian beachfront resort.

Isla del Río Cuale is accessible by short stairways from both bridges spanning the Río Cuale, as well as by a bridge on the seaward side that connects the island with Playa de Olas Altas. A tree-shaded pathway runs the length of the diminutive island, past restaurants, boutiques, a club, and merchants' stands with handicrafts and souvenirs. The **Museo del Cuale,** at the seaward end of the island, houses interesting displays on Mesoamerican culture and regional history. (Open M-F 9am-2pm and 3-6pm. Free.) Steep stairs beginning behind the Church of Guadalupe lead up the mini-mountain into the wealthy **Zaragoza** neighborhood, known locally as "Gringo Gulch," where the first Americans and Canadians relocated. The rose-colored bridge spanning the rooftops connects **Casa Kimberley,** Zaragoza 445, the former love nest of Richard Burton and Elizabeth Taylor, to its rooftop pool in the building across the street.

While best known for its beaches and clubs, Puerto Vallarta has a startlingly large art community demonstrated by the numerous art galleries all over town, which feature all types of media. Each week from October to May, a program called **ArtWalk** showcases different galleries around the city. Each Wednesday from 6-10pm, some of the galleries have free cocktail exhibitions of their work. Pick up a program from the tourist office or look for ArtWalk flags around town. Most ArtWalk galleries have regular summer hours. Call specific galleries for more information. For a thrill, head to **La Paloma** bullring, located on Av. Las Palmas across from the Marina. Four bullfighters are showcased each week on Wednesday night at 5pm. (☎221 0414. Tickets 350 pesos. Take a 60-peso taxi or a 5-peso bus to **SAM'S/Wal-Mart** and walk down Las Palmas.) A quieter night waits at **Cine Bahía,** Insurgentes 63, showing American and international films, often dubbed into Spanish. (☎222 1717. 30 pesos, senior citizens and children 25 pesos; Tu 25 pesos)

◪ NIGHTLIFE

Like any resort destination, Puerto Vallarta boils over every night with thousands of well-dressed locals and foreigners streaming onto the *malecón* and nearby streets. The boardwalk sees the most action at night, while the lively gay scene centers south of the river on **Olas Altas.** The **Zona Romántica** offers smaller, more intimate bars, while the Plaza Marina far north of the city (reachable by taxi, 60-80 pesos, or a 15min. hike from the last bus route) has a series of clubs catering to college student staying in nearby hotels. The party doesn't really start until 11pm-midnight, but go a little early to beat the lines outside the bigger clubs, which generally charge a hefty cover of 100-150 pesos. US dollars are accepted at most clubs.

Zoo, Díaz Ordaz 630 (☎222 4945). Pumping music keeps the beat for the revelers on the cramped dance floor, drinks in hand. The bravest move into the iron cages. An elephant statue adds to the animal motif. Cover Sa-Su 150 pesos; includes 2 drinks. Open daily noon-6am. MC/V.

Hilo, Díaz Ordaz 622 (☎223 5361), on the waterfront. Most of the club is a dance floor, with a young crowd packing into the standing room and groups of girls dancing atop the bar. Private seating upstairs offers some relief from the sweaty crowds and loud rap below. Beer 30 pesos. Mixed drinks 50 pesos. Cover F-Sa 100 pesos. Open daily 4pm-6am. Cash only.

Cafe San Ángel (☎223 1273), Olas Altas 449, on the corner of F. Rodríguez. Modern art, chill music, and the occasional acoustic performance give this bistro/bar an alternative, intellectual vibe. Relax in the wicker chairs and enjoy the tapas (45-65 pesos). Breakfast served all day. Coffee 25 pesos, hard drinks 35-40 pesos. Open daily 8am-2am. Cash only.

Señor Frog's (☎222 5171), Carranza 218. Bands of dressed-up Mexican youth line up outside the door in anticipation for the special events, which include foam parties (Tu) and beach parties with wet T-shirt and thong contests (F). Cover Sa-Su 100 pesos; Tu-F 350 pesos includes open bar. Beer 35 pesos. Hard drinks 50 pesos. Open daily 11am-2am. AmEx/MC/V.

Christine Discotheque (☎224 0202 or 2990) on Av. Las Garzas, located in the NH Krystal hotel just before the marina. The proximity to resorts north of the city draws crowds of college kids who pack the dance floor and the seating area. Massive video screen. Occasional concerts and special events; drop by for a schedule. Dress code F-Sa, no shorts or t-shirts. Cover W and F-Sa 200 pesos for men, 100 pesos for women; Th and Su 440 pesos with open bar. Open W-Su 10pm-6am. AmEx/D/MC/V.

Club Roxy, Ignacio Vallarta 217, between Madero and Carranza. A mix of ages frequents Roxy to hear the live reggae-rock and 70s dance music. Live music starts at 10:30pm. Beer 25 pesos. *Bebidas nacionales* 2-for-1 8-11pm. Open M-Sa 8am-4pm.

GLBT NIGHTLIFE

Vallarta supports a large gay community, with nightlife clustering around the southern end of Olas Altas. Two **gay cruises** are available, both booked through the Blue Chairs Resort. The **Blue Ocean** cruise leaves from Los Muertos pier and travels to the southern beaches. (☎222 5040. Includes breakfast, lunch, open bar, and afterparty at the Sunset Bar. Th 10am-5:30pm. 750 pesos.) **Pegaso Charters** hosts their cruise the next day. (☎290 0705. F 10am-3pm. 700 pesos.) Two magazines, *Zona Romántica* and *Gay Guide Vallarta*, available in most gay establishments, offer a comprehensive listing of gay and gay-friendly establishments.

Mañana, Carranza 290 (☎222 7772; clubmanana.com). A new, dimly-lit club whose ambience and shows attract droves of people. Indoor and outdoor seating, strippers every night at 11:30pm, with dance and cross-dressing diva shows on the schedule as well. Lesbians welcome. Cover M-Th and Su 50 pesos includes 1 drink; F-Sa 100 pesos. Open daily 10pm-6am. Cash only.

Sunset Bar, Malecón 4 (☎222 5040), on the rooftop of The Blue Chairs resort on Playa de los Muertos. A laid-back bar filled with hotel patrons, featuring an unusual variety of weekly activities: M karaoke, Tu 7pm gay bingo with Ida Slapter, occasional pool parties and performances by local band The Dirty Bitches. 2-drink min. on nights with shows or bingo. Happy hour 10am-5pm with 2-for-1 margaritas. Open daily 11am-11pm. MC/V.

Anthropology, Morelos 101, on Plaza Río next to the Vallarta Bridge. Look for the rainbow flag and follow the steps down; then follow the snake decor upstairs. Racy fun for all. Men clad only in the slimmest of thongs gyrate all night on top of the faux-stone bar and then make rounds among the customers for tips. Beer 25 pesos. "National drinks" 40 pesos. Disco holds strip shows at 11:30pm and 12:30am. 2-for-1 drinks all night. Rooftop Happy hour 9-10:30pm. Open daily 9pm-4am. Cash only.

◪ DAYTRIPS FROM PUERTO VALLARTA

The 26mi. **Bahía de Banderas** (Bay of Flags) that shelters Puerto Vallarta owes its name to a blunder: when the conquistador Nuño Beltrán de Guzmán landed here in 1532, he mistook the colorful headdresses of the thousands of natives awaiting him for flags. With a little effort, the quieter beaches and the untouched splendor that originally drew the crowds to Vallarta can still be found at the outer edges of the bay, all reachable within an hour's travel from the downtown area.

SOUTHERN COAST

Buses go to Mismaloya and Boca de Tomatlán from Constitución and Badillo in Vallarta (every 10min. 5:30am-11pm, 5.50 pesos). Taxis 80 pesos. "Tuito" buses run to Chico's Paradise from Carranza and Aguacate (every 30min. 5am-9pm, 10 pesos). Taxis acuáticos (water taxis) are the cheapest way to get to the boats-only beaches. They leave from Muelle de los Muertos (Pier of the Dead) and stop at Las Ánimas, Quimixto, and Yelapa. (45min., 11am, 90 pesos round-trip, return at 4pm.) Taxis acuáticos also travel between Boca de Tomatlán and the farther beaches for lower prices. (Boca to Yelapa, 50-60 pesos.) Cruises to points south of Vallarta leave from the marina. (9am, from US$25, return at 4pm.) Information is available in the tourist office, at large hotels, in smaller tourist offices strewn along the malecón, or at the marina.

The most secluded of Vallarta's beaches lie down the coast to the south amid thick tropical growth and sheer rock faces. The first few are monopolized by resorts, and hotels do their best to restrict public access. Past Boca de Tomatlán, the beaches are accessible only by boat.

LOS ARCOS. Down the coast lies Los Arcos, a group of towering rock islands shaped by pounding waves. Boats drop anchor next to the islands for a scenic afternoon lunch. The rocky coast is the starting point for the 200m trek out to the islands past the coral. Bring a mask or goggles, or risk missing the tropical fish that flutter through the underwater reefscape. **Mind your step—the coral is sharp enough to draw blood. Use caution and swim with a friend.** *(Take the bus to Mismaloya and ask the driver to stop at Hotel de los Arcos.)*

MISMALOYA. Best known as the site of *Night of the Iguana*, the movie that put Vallarta on the map, Mismaloya is a smoothly curving sandy beach just south of the city. The turquoise water affords a much clearer view than the rest of the turbid Pacific, but the beach is a little more crowded than those that surround it. Keep an eye out for part of the crashed helicopter from the set of Arnold Schwarzenegger's action movie, *Predator*, filmed here in 1987.

BOCA DE TOMATLÁN. The final beach on the southern road is nestled in a tiny, sheltered cove. Enjoy your large plot of sand or catch a *taxi aquático* to the distant beaches, which leave on the half-hour. The last spot to visit on the southern road is **Chico's Paradise**, 5km inland from Boca de Tomatlán. Wash down the view of nearby Tomatlán Falls and its brave cliff divers with a beer (20 pesos) at Chico's huge *palapas*, or splash in the river and admire the lush, green hills that surround it. *(To get to Chico's from Boca de Tomatlán, take a 5-peso "Tuito" bus from the main highway. 5 pesos. ☎ 223 6005. Open daily 10am-6pm.)*

LAS ÁNIMAS QUIMIXTO AND MAJAHUITA. About as deserted as they come, these beaches (accessible only by *taxi aquático*) play host to a few scattered straw-roofed shacks serving mixed drinks along empty stretches of sand. Some surrounding rocky areas are good for scuba diving—arrange times and prices with a *taxi aquático* service.

YELAPA. The southernmost beach along the bay is surprisingly developed, with timeshares and *palapa*-themed bungalows with modern amenities available for seasonal rental. This aside, the soft white beach spans the cove, making for idyllic swimming among bobbing boats. Kayakers, snorkelers, and vendors hawking the occasional souvenir also share the beach. For the truly dedicated traveler who finds the rumored seclusion of Yelapa's beaches not up to their billing, there are freshwater pools up the steep hillside. To get there, begin walking up the path that follows the riverbed and ask someone how to get to the pools. They will point you to a path that leads over some pipes to the right of the trail. If (when) you lose this narrow, meandering path, start following the riverbed upstream—it's hard to miss with the large boulders lining it. After 10-15min. of hiking, complete solitude awaits you in the refreshingly cool pools.

NORTHERN COAST

Step on a "SAM'S/WalMart bus" (25min., 5 pesos) in Puerto Vallarta. From the Wal-Mart, get on to a gray "ATM" bus heading for Punta de Mita and ask to be let off at Piedra Blanca (45min., 18 pesos), Destiladeras (50min., 20 pesos), or ride it all the way to Punta de Mita (1hr., 20 pesos). Last return bus 9pm.

The northern part of the bay, actually in Nayarit, offers uncrowded beaches with a bay view largely untarnished by massive resort development. Nuevo Vallarta, the largest and southernmost of nine small towns on the north bay, is 150km south of Tepic and 20km north of Puerto Vallarta. Protected by a sandy cove, **Playa Piedra Blanca** (White Rock Beach) has wonderfully calm waters that invite people of all ages into the ocean. Just past Piedra Blanca is **Destiladeras**, a beach bordered by a sharp precipice through which the water passes. Not entirely a sand beach, its smooth stones still make it a prime spot for swimming and body-surfing. The northernmost point of the bay separating it from the ocean is **Punta de Mita.** Smooth stones mingled with mostly empty stretches of sand make it a worthwhile destination far from the bustle of the city's beaches. Bordered by rocky islets, it has a live coral reef out past the first few breaks. Bring bottled water and a bag lunch to avoid inflated prices at the beachside *palapas*.

BAHÍA DE CHAMELA   ☎ 315

Many a fisherman's bay with glorious miles of golden sand have gone the way of Puerto Vallarta, but Bahía de Chamela, 60km northwest of Melaque, lies forgotten by the outside world. The largest *pueblo*, Pérula (pop. 700), has few services and just one paved road, but its desolate dirt roads lined with shockingly bright flowers, empty expanses of sand punctuated by fishing *lanchas*, and village hospitality have an irresistible pull. Though Chamela receives its share of tourism, especially in December and April, Pérula remains uncommercialized—the Midas touch has yet to spoil the natural beauty and seclusion of the bay. Crime is virtually nonexistent in Pérula, but lone travelers should exercise caution on the deserted beaches and dark roads leading to town.

▐ TRANSPORTATION. Second-class **buses** from **Puerto Vallarta** to **Manzanillo** (5hr., 184 pesos) pass through **Pérula** (4hr., 90 pesos), and buses going from **Melaque** or **Barra de Navidad** to **Puerto Vallarta** (5hr., 140-145 pesos) also stop in Pérula. Always tell the bus driver where you're going in advance and sit in the front so you don't miss the stop. To get to Playa Pérula, descend at the big, white "Playa Dorada" sign and walk 30min. down a winding dirt road. *Let's Go* does not recommend hitchhiking, but friendly locals will most likely offer a ride. To get to Playa Chamela, get off farther south at "El Súper," where a sign points to the beach 1km away. Pérula is a 40min. walk along the shore. Hotels in Pérula may pick you up from the station; otherwise, since Pérula lacks a formal taxi system, contact Felipe Santana (☎1004 5756), who will take you to points around the area; Playa Chamela costs 80 pesos both ways. To return to Pérula, catch a **Primera Plus** bus from the stop on the main highway. They also head to: **Guadalajara** (3hr.; 8, 10:30am, 4pm; 67 pesos); **Manzanillo** (2½-5hr., every hr. 7:30am-10:30pm, 75 pesos) via **Melaque** (1½hr., 47 pesos); and **Puerto Vallarta**

(3hr., every hr. 7:30am-10:30pm, 88 pesos). To get out of town without having to walk back to the highway, catch a **Transportes Cihuatlan** bus from the corner of Tiburón and Independencia at 8am or midnight to **Aútlan** (2hr., 158 pesos), **Guadalajara** (3hr., 315 pesos), or **Melaque** (1½hr., 70 pesos).

✷ PRACTICAL INFORMATION. The **Centro de Salud** is at the corner of Juárez and Pargo, three blocks west of the plaza. (☎333 9804. Regular hours M-F 9am-4pm, weekends and 24hr. emergency service available: knock loudly.) **Farmacia Villa del Mar**, on the east side of the plaza, has 24hr. service. (☎333 9800.) There is a **LADATEL** phone outside the Primera Plus Station, one outside Hotel Punta Pérula, and a couple scattered on the paved road through town. **Internet** is available in the orange house at the corner of Pargo and Independencia. (☎100 2381. Open M-F 10am-9pm. 20 pesos per hr.)

⌂⌂ ACCOMMODATIONS AND FOOD. Pérula offers few lodgings, so you won't have to spend too much time looking. **Hotel Punta Pérula ❹**, on the corner of Juárez and Tiburón 98 two blocks from the beach, is the best deal in this *pueblito*. Spacious rooms with antique-looking wooden shutters, bath, and TV open onto a large courtyard with hammocks drooping over flowers. (☎333 9782. Call ahead. High season singles 250 pesos; doubles 350 pesos. Low season 200/300 pesos. Cash only.) A more luxurious option is **Estancia Dolphins ❺**, on Juárez and Paiva two blocks east of the plaza, featuring a gated courtyard with lush lawn and pool adorned with a life-size cayman statuette. The enormous rooms come with fittingly large beds, fan, TV, glass dolphin-themed side tables, and lovely tile bathrooms. (☎333 9850. Call ahead. Rooms 350 pesos, for up to 4 people. Cash only.)

The diner in Pérula faces the toughest of choices: seafood or tacos. If you opt for the former, head over to **La Prieta ❹**, on the beach near the rock jetty. *Mariscos* (seafood) here are served up fried, filleted, in salads—however you like. The staple *camarones* (shrimp; 70 pesos) go well with a 10-peso bottle of Pacífico. (Open daily low season 7-11pm, longer hours in high season. Cash only.) The long row of seafood restaurants stretching along the beach are open intermittently, mostly during the late summer months, but a couple are usually open at any time—ask the fishermen on the beach. **Taquería Michel ❶**, just southeast of the plaza on Independencia, is good for a cheap taco fix. The usual *antojitos* and *agua fresca* are on tap. (Tacos 7 pesos. Quesadillas 10 pesos. Open daily 6-11pm. Cash only.)

⊿ BEACHES. Fishing boats far outnumber people on the sleepy local beaches. The bay's northernmost point, Punta de Pérula, shelters **Playa Pérula,** perfect for swimming. A 40min. walk down the virgin beach will bring you to the Villa Polinesia Motel and Campsite, marking **Playa Chamela.** Kilometers of empty sand invite absent-minded, tranquil walks south to Playa Rosada, where rougher waters cater to bodysurfing more so than casual swimming. Occasional *palapas* refresh the parched and weary bodysurfer, and *lanchas* from Playa Pérula transport wanna-be Robinson Crusoes to the nearby islands or on fishing trips (600 pesos each way; ask around for deals). Inquire from the fishermen at the northern end of Playa Pérula, about 1km north of town.

BAHÍA DE NAVIDAD

Down the coast from the glittering lights of Vallarta lies the unspoiled hideaway of Bahía de Navidad. While the two towns on the bay, **Melaque** and **Barra de Navidad,** do feel a jolt of tourism during Mexican vacation periods, December and *Semana Santa,* for the most part they remain quiet fishing towns with nowhere to go except the beach. It's a wonder more vacationers year-round don't visit the *bahía* and its sheltered cove of powdery sand, shimmering water, and scenic, embracing cliffs. The empty beach bungalows and clubs scattered about the towns come alive again in December, but their presence during the low season is unobtrusive to the point they can be forgotten, as can the days and hours on the breezy streets and beaches of the bay. Melaque and Barra de Navidad lie 55km northwest of Manzanillo on Mex. 200, and 240km southwest of Guadalajara on Mex. 54. Melaque is the northernmost of the two. The two towns are well connected by municipal buses that shuttle between them. (20min., every 15min. 6am-8:30pm, 4 pesos). Taxis cost 50 pesos. If you are really pinching pesos, the walk along the beach takes 40min., but may be dangerous after dark as robberies have been reported.

MELAQUE ☎315

While vacationers flow into the beachfront hotels during December and the early spring, Melaque (pop. 12,000) sleeps for the rest of the year. A cool sea breeze over the golden beaches staves off what would otherwise be stifling heat, allowing for leisurely walks around the town and *zócalo*, quiet outdoor meals, and peaceful days on the beach.

▊ TRANSPORTATION. Melaque's **bus stations** are side by side on Farías, the main drag parallel to the beach. From the bus station, turn left on Farías and walk two blocks to reach Mateos. Another left takes you to the plaza, a few blocks inland. Mateos and Hidalgo are the main cross-streets running toward the ocean. **Autocamiones Cihuatlán** (☎355 5003) offers second-class service. **Primera Plus/ Flecha Amarilla** (☎355 6110) offers first- and executive-class service. The two are side by side at Farías 34. First-class service goes to: **Guadalajara** (5hr., 9 per day 9:15am-1:15pm, 242 pesos); **Manzanillo** (1½hr., 8 per day 3am-8pm, 50 pesos); direct to **Mexico City** (5:15pm, 780 pesos); **Tomatlán** (2hr.; 5, 9pm; 103 pesos). Second-class service heads to: **Guadalajara** (6½hr., every hr. 6:30am-10:30pm, 205 pesos); **Manzanillo** (1¾hr., every 30min. 5am-midnight, 41 pesos); **Puerto Vallarta** (5hr., 12 per day, 140 pesos); **Tomatlán** (3 hr., 3 per day, 90 pesos).

▊ PRACTICAL INFORMATION. Banamex, on Farías across from the bus station, has a **24hr. ATM.** (☎355 5277 or 5342. Open M-F 9am-4pm, Sa 10am-2pm.) Exchange money or traveler's checks at **Casa de Cambio,** Farías 27A, inside the commercial center across from the bus station. (☎355 5343. Open M-Sa 9am-6pm, Su 9am-3pm.) Other services include: **police,** upstairs at Mateos 52, north of the plaza (☎355 5080 or 6090); **Red Cross** (☎355 2300), 15km away in Cihuatlán, accessible by the "Cruz Roja" bus (every 15min. 6am-8pm, 6 pesos) from the plaza, or by taxi (100 pesos); **Superfarmacia Plaza,** Mateos 48, on the southern side of the plaza (☎355 5167; open daily 8:30am-3pm and 6-11pm); **Centro de Salud,** Guzmán 11, left out of bus station on Farías for three blocks, then half a block to the left (☎355 5880); **LADATEL phones** on both Farías and Mateos; **casetas,** next to the bus station (☎355 6310; fax 355 5452; open M-Sa 8:30am-8:30pm, Su 8:30am-1pm); **Internet access** at **Mundo Cibernetico,** Guzmán 20, two blocks from the plaza (☎355 5061; 20 pesos per hr.; open daily 9am-2pm and 5-10pm); and the **post office,** Orozco 13, between Farías and Corona (☎355 5230; open M-F 8am-noon). **Postal Code:** 48980.

▊▊ ACCOMMODATIONS AND FOOD. Expensive beachfront hotels dominate the center of Melaque, but more affordable—though still pricey—options exist, clustering at the end of Farías. Rates rise during high season. Camping is feasible in Melaque if you arrange to stay next to one of the beachside restaurants. Expect to pay a small fee to the restaurant owner. **Hotel Los Caracoles ❺**, Farías 26, offers a little luxury for a few more pesos. White stucco walls in the courtyard greet the visitor to gorgeous, immaculate rooms with fan, cable, bath, and large, soft beds. (☎355 7308; www.loscaracoles.com.mx. Reception 24hr. Singles 250 pesos; doubles 350 pesos; triples 450 pesos; quads 500 pesos; 8-bed bungalow with kitchenette 650 pesos. Call ahead in high season. MC/V.) The straw-thatched overhang of **Casa Paula ❹**, Vallarta 6, leads to a courtyard alive with children, leafy greens, and a menagerie of random clutter. An odd paint scheme graces the medium-sized rooms, which come with refrigerator, fan, TV, and beautiful blue-tiled bathrooms. (☎355 5093. Reception 24hr. Rooms for 1-2 people 200 pesos; triples 250 pesos; quads 350 pesos. Cash only.) **Bungalows los Arcos ❹**, Farías 2, charges similar prices. Take a right at the bus station and walk to the end of the street, and it's on the left. Massive, spotless rooms come with fan, TV, A/C, and a cramped, private bath. Those tired of the saltwater should take advantage of the pool in the back courtyard. (☎355 5184. High season 1-3 people 400 pesos; quads 500 pesos. Low season singles 200 pesos; triples 350 pesos; quads 380 pesos; each additional person 50 pesos. Cash only.)

More traditional restaurants with *antojitos* and tacos are scattered around the plaza, while the ubiquitous straw-roofed seafood restaurants with cheap deck chairs cover the beach. **Lonchería María Luisa ❷**, on Hidalgo, serves an incredible number of fruit concoctions of all flavors and consistencies. Sit on the high stool watching the blender while eating burritos (6 pesos) and other cheap staples. (☎355 6279. *Jugos batidos* 25 pesos. Hamburgers 25 pesos. Open daily 7am-11pm. Cash only.) Locals idle the time away at **Restaurant Ayala ❷**. Turn left on Carrillo Puerto, the street before Mateos, and walk a block. Tasty fish (38 pesos) and burgers with fries (23 pesos) are hearty dinner options, while the eggs (23 pesos) and the *comida corrida* (25 pesos) are lighter options for earlier in the day. (☎355 6680. Open daily 8am-5pm.) **Las Palmas ❺**, on the waterfront a few blocks towards the rock jetty, seats its patrons a stone's throw away from the wake. Along with the view, it serves up shrimp and octopus (70 pesos) and enchiladas (40 pesos) as well as *antojitos*. (Beer 15 pesos. Open daily 9am-6pm. Cash only.)

◪ ⅃ BEACHES AND ENTERTAINMENT. There is not much to do in Melaque except go to the beach. Toward the western end waves shrink and the beach becomes more crowded. Rent jet skis at **Restaurant Moyo,** the last restaurant on the far western end of the beach. (☎355 6104. 2- and 3-person jet skis 450 pesos per 30min. Small launches available 400 pesos per hr. Available daily 10am-5pm.) By night, people gather in the *zócalo* and drink beer or stroll casually along the shore. For a casual ambience with a young crowd, hit up **Surfo's Bar,** Juárez 43 off the *zócalo*. Surfboards deck the walls and catchy Mexican rhythms set the mood. Pool available when the table's open. (Beer 15 pesos. Mixed drinks 35 pesos. Open M and W-Su 8pm-2am. Cash only.) **Caxcan,** Mateos 48, overlooking the *zócalo* from above the pharmacy, offers cheap drinks along with a quiet view over the hum of conversation below. (2-for-1 drinks 30 pesos. Open daily 4pm-midnight. Cash only.) In general, don't get your partying hopes up unless you come during December or *Semana Santa*, when the town fills with tourists—even then there are only a couple bars to satisfy the nightlife craving.

BARRA DE NAVIDAD   ☎315

Barra de Navidad (pop. 7000) is smaller than its sister Melaque, but it attracts more tourists and expats to its shaded streets, numerous sidewalk eateries, and popular seaside bars, giving it a concentrated energy conspicuously absent in

Melaque. The quiet downtown area between the *laguna* and the sea offers little of anything except small restaurants, and once again the beaches and the fishing boats are the destinations of choice for locals and tourists alike.

E TRANSPORTATION. Veracruz, the main street, runs northwest-southeast, angling off its end to meet Legazpi, which runs north-south along the beach. The **bus stop** is at Veracruz 226, on the corner of Nayarit. Turn left on Veracruz from the bus station to get to the *centro.* **Primera Plus/Costa Alegre,** Veracruz 269 (☎355 6111), at Filipinas, has first-class service to: **Guadalajara** (5hr.; 6 per day 8am-6pm; 246 pesos); **León** (10hr., 8pm, 485 pesos); **Manzanillo** (1½hr.; 11:30, 11:45am, 2:30, 7:45pm; 49 pesos); **Mexico City** (13hr., 5pm, 718 pesos). Second-class buses go to **Guadalajara** (6hr.; 8:30, 11:30am, 2:30pm; 205 pesos); **Manzanillo** (1½hr.; 7 per day 7:15am-7:30pm; 41 pesos); and **Puerto Vallarta** (5hr., 7 per day, 145 pesos).

🛈 PRACTICAL INFORMATION. The **tourist office,** at Jalisco 67, offers brochures and photocopied, hand-drawn maps. (☎355 5100 or 8383. Open M-F 9am-5pm.) Barra has no bank, but there is a **24hr. ATM** at Banamex, next to the police station. **Cyber@Money,** Veracruz 212C, **exchanges money** and traveler's checks at high rates without commission. **Internet** access is 25 pesos per hr. (☎355 6177. Open M-F 9am-2pm and 4-7:30pm, Sa 9am-6:30pm.) Other services include: **police,** Veracruz 179 at the corner of Guanajuato (☎355 5398 or 5399); **Centro de Salud,** on Puerto de la Navidad down Veracruz, just out of town (take a right where a traffic island divides Veracruz; ☎355 6220; 24hr. emergency service); there are no *casetas,* but **LADATEL** phones line the main streets; and the **post office,** on Veracruz at the plaza (open M-F 8am-noon). **Postal Code:** 48987.

🛏🍴 ACCOMMODATIONS AND FOOD. Lodgings in Barra are nicer, cheaper and cleaner than they are in Melaque. All prices are subject to high-season hikes. **Posada Pacífico ❸,** Mazatlán 136, has a walkway overlooking the garden, which gives it the feel of a villa. Big rooms come with fan and clean bath. (☎355 5359; fax 355 5349. Boogie board rentals 30 pesos. Reception 24hr. Singles 180 pesos; doubles 280 pesos; triples 320 pesos. Cash only.) The best bargain in town is **Casa de Huéspedes Mamá Loya ❶,** Veracruz 69. Blue tile saturating the lobby gives it a smooth Mediterranean ambience. Simple, spotless rooms come with fan a soft bed, and clean white bath. (Reception 24hr. Singles 100 pesos; doubles 150 pesos. Cash only.) **Hotel Caribe ❷,** Sonora 15, has simple rooms with big blue bath and fan. The fountain in the courtyard is surrounded by massive hanging potted plants. (☎355 5952. Singles 150 pesos, with TV 200 pesos; doubles 200/250 pesos. Cash only.) **Hotel Jalisco ❸,** Jalisco 81, offers bike rentals in addition to its rooms with TV, fan, and slightly battered wooden furniture. Balconies offer a view overlooking the quiet streets. (☎355 8505. Bike rental 20 pesos per hr., 100 pesos per day. Reception 24hr. Singles 150 pesos; doubles 200 pesos; triples 250 pesos. Cash only.) **It's illegal to camp in Barra de Navidad: if you brought a tent, try Melaque.**

Barra doesn't offer too much culinary variety. **Restaurant Bar Ramon ❺,** Legazpi 260, is a classy, brick-bordered joint with a semi-formal evening ambience. Consider the fisherman's box lunch (50 pesos) if you're going out to sea the next day. (☎355 6435. Beer 15 pesos. Seafood entrees 75-95 pesos. Open daily 7am-11pm. Cash only.) For tasty, inexpensive Mexican food in a pleasant atmosphere, **Restaurant Paty ❷,** Jalisco 52 at Veracruz, is the place to be. The breakfast special is just 35 pesos, and there are vegetarian options. (Beer 15 pesos. *Antojitos* 35-45 pesos. Quesadillas 40 pesos. Meat dishes 40-45 pesos. Open daily 8am-11pm.) **Felix' Bar ❹,** Jalisco 48, attracts talkative old American expats to its relaxed outdoor seating. Sandwiches and *chimichangas* (40 pesos) are plentiful and tasty. (Beer 15 pesos. Open daily 8am-11pm. Cash only.)

CENTRAL PACIFIC COAST

🏖🏊 **BEACHES AND OUTDOOR ACTIVITIES.** Fishermen are available to ferry you to nearby destinations. They'll wait as you eat in the rustic farming atmosphere of Colimilla, across the lagoon. (200 pesos for an indefinite restaurant stay for up to 10 people; 150 pesos otherwise.) Deserted **Playa de los Cocos,** 1km away, has larger breakers than those in Barra. Continue on to **Playa Viejo,** further past Cocos. If you don't want to swim back, remember to set a time to be picked up. 600 pesos round-trip for up to 10 people. Other trips include snorkeling off Tenacatita (2500 pesos for 10 people); Isla de Navidad (150 pesos, 10 people); Tamarindo bay (1500 pesos, 10 people); or a 7hr. fishing/snorkeling trip (2500 pesos, 10 people). To arrange any of these, head down during the day to the **Sociedad Cooperativa de Servicios Turísticos,** on Legazpi on the lagoon. Ask about discounts—individual fishermen are likely to give them, especially for groups. You can also charter your own fishing boat at **Mary Chuy Fishing Charters.** Six hour trips for groups ranging from 4-14 persons cost 3000, 5500, and 6500 pesos, respectively, for the three boat sizes. (☎355 5416. Open daily 7am-7pm.) If you want to skip the expensive tours, ask around town at hotels and bait shops for fishing equipment and boogie board rentals.

🎭 **ENTERTAINMENT.** While Barra de Navidad positively pulses during December and the Mexican vacation months, it has a small but quality selection of bars and nightspots during the low season. Trendy **Sea Master,** Legazpi 146, plays host to an equally trendy clientele that populate its funky plush chairs. Orange lighting, modern art, and music set the mood, as does the gorgeous ocean overlook. (☎355 8216. Beer 10 pesos. Mixed drinks 40-50 pesos. Happy hour with 2-for-1 drinks 3-9pm. Open daily 6pm-1am. MC/V.) For an earthier atmosphere, try **Jarro Video Bar,** on Legazpi next to the fishing co-op, featuring pumping dance music, big screen TV, pool table, plush chairs, and vulgar witticisms painted on the walls. (☎355 5540. Beer 15 pesos. Mixed drinks 40 pesos. Open M-Th and Su 9pm-1am, F-Sa 9am-4pm. Cash only.) Various establishments along Legazpi offer 2-for-1 Happy hours that make the giddy trip toward inebriation that much cheaper. At **Terrace Capri,** on Legazpi across from the church, hit the dance floor or relax with a drink while watching the waves. Perhaps you'll be lucky enough to see a stunning sunset. (☎355 5217. Beer 20 pesos. Mixed drinks 40 pesos. 2-for-1 drinks during Happy hour 6-9pm. Open daily 5pm-2am.)

COLIMA

MANZANILLO   ☎314

Manzanillo (pop. 130,000), long the grimy capital of Mexican shipping on the Pacific and a paradise for sailfish hunters, has slowly awakened to the golden beaches between its two bays and the tourist appeal they generate. Today, the city has a dual identity, with its bustling historic center totally divorced from the beaches housing its newer resorts, separated by miles of industrial shipyards, containers, and cranes. The burgeoning resort industry has brought a slew of upscale restaurants and clubs with it, and this is where the action centers after the sun sets. Those seeking only sand and surf would do better to retreat to a secluded village such as Barra de Navidad, but for those excited by lively, crowded beaches—and the nightlife of a real city—Manzanillo delivers.

Manzanillo

▐ TRANSPORTATION

Flights: Aeropuerto Internacional de Manzanillo (ZLO; ☎333 2525) on Playa de Oro between Barra de Navidad and Manzanillo. Taxis (☎333 1999) to the *zócalo* 250 pesos. Airlines include **AeroCalifornia** (☎334 1250; open M-F 8am-8pm, Sa-Su 9am-5pm) and **Mexicana** (☎333 2323; open M-F 9am-6:45pm, Sa 9am-6pm). Both have offices in the Comercial Mexicana shopping center, along the "Miramar" bus route.

Buses: Station on Oceano Pacífico in Colonia Valle de las Garzas, next to the Laguna las Garzas. Take a taxi (35 pesos) or bus (5 pesos) to the *centro*, also called Jardín Obregón. From the station, take a "Centro" bus until you reach the Jardín Obregón; ask the driver when to get off. **Estrella Blanca** (☎336 7617) goes to: **Acapulco** (12hr.; 6:30am, 6:30, 9:30pm; 460 pesos); **Lázaro Cárdenas** (6½hr.; 6:30am, 6:30, 9:30pm; 224 pesos); **Mazatlán** (12hr.; 2:30, 8pm; 563 pesos); **Mexico City** (14hr.; 7:30am, 9pm; 623 pesos); **Puerto Vallarta** (6hr., 5am, 1, 8:05pm, 204 pesos); **Tepic** (7hr.; 1, 8:05pm; 396 pesos); **Zihuatanejo** (9hr.; 6:30am, 6:30, 9:30pm; 316 pesos). **Autobuses del Sur** (☎322 1003), **La Línea/Autobuses de Occidente** (☎322 0123), **Transportes Cihuatlán** (☎322 0515 or 336 8315), and **Primera Plus** (☎336 4802) offer similar services. **Autobuses Nuevo Horizonte** (☎322 3900) runs to **Colima** (2½hr., every 30min. 5am-7pm, 46 pesos).

Public Transportation: White-and-blue "Miramar" and "Centro" **buses** run between the *centro* and the resort strip (30min., every 15min. 5am-11pm, 5 pesos).

Car Rental: Hertz (☎333 3141, airport office ☎333 3191), on Costera de la Madrid 1246-B. 750 pesos per day. Open M-Sa 9am-1pm and 3-7pm, Su 9am-5pm. MC/V.

▐ PRACTICAL INFORMATION

Tourist Office: Costera Miguel de la Madrid 875A (☎333 2277; www.visita-colima.com.mx), next to Suites Caradoles. Catch a "Miramar" bus (5 pesos) on México or near the Jardín Obregón and tell the driver where you're headed. Get off and cross the highway. Provides great maps. Open M-F 9am-3pm and 5-7pm, Sa 10am-2pm. Information booths in front of the Palacio, around town, and along the beaches offer many of the same maps. Open daily 8am-10pm. Helpful **tourist police** (☎332 1002) in the Presidencia Municipal in the *zócalo* distribute maps and brochures. Another branch located in the bus station (☎334 5154. Open Tu-Su 9am-5pm.)

Currency Exchange: HSBC, México 99 (☎332 0950), at 10 de Mayo. Changes traveler's checks. **24hr. ATM.** Open M-Sa 8am-7pm.

Laundromat: Lavandería Savi, Bocanegra 44. Laundry 15 pesos per kg., 30-peso min. Open M-Sa 9am-8pm.

Emergency: ☎066.

Police: (☎332 1004), in the Palacio Municipal.

Red Cross: (☎336 5770), on Barotes west of the *centro*.

24hr. Pharmacy: Farmacia Guadalajara, México 301 (☎332 2922), at Cuauhtémoc, 4 blocks from the *zócalo*. Also sells snacks and has a small deli.

Medical Services: Centro Médico Quirúrgico, Costera 1215 (☎334 0444 or 1666).

Fax Office: Caseta de Teléfonos Computel, México 302 (☎322 3926). National calls 3.50 pesos per min. Calls to the US 6 pesos per min. Open daily 7:30am-10pm.

Internet Access: Internet, Madero 324 (☎332 8237). Internet 10 pesos per hr. Open M-Sa 9am-9:30pm, Su 9:30am-8:30pm.

Post Office: Galindo 30 (☎332 0022). Open M-F 9am-4pm, Sa 9am-1pm. **Postal Code:** 28200/28201.

ACCOMMODATIONS

The city's budget hotels, mostly decent digs for standard price, cluster around a few streets in the *centro*. Camping is permitted on Playa Miramar, but is only recommended during *Semana Santa* and in December, when bathroom facilities are available and security is heightened.

Hotel Flamingos, Madero 72 (☎332 1037), by the Jardín Obregón. Antique wooden chairs and tables furnishing the lobby and rooms lend Flamingos a measure of class. Rooms with big, low beds and clean, small baths. Singles 200 pesos; doubles 250 pesos. Cash only. ❹

Hotel Azteca Central, Madero 265 (☎332 7343; www.hotelaztecacentro.com), off Cuauhtémoc. In what feels like a converted office building, rooms have simple white walls inlaid with elegant tile. All come with TV, bath, fan, and patterned curtains. Reception 24hr. Singles 200 pesos; doubles 320 pesos. Cash only. ❹

Hotel Costa Manzanillo, Madero 333 (☎332 2740). Sunflowers filling the courtyard and peeking out from stairwells make for a bright, colorful ambience. Standard rooms come with bath, fan, and TV. Reception 24hr. Singles 180 pesos; doubles 230 pesos. A/C 100 pesos extra. Cash only. ❸

Hotel Emperador, Dávalos 69 (☎332 2374), near the Jardín Obregón. The monastic feel of the simple rooms is alleviated by the balcony in the 2nd fl. hallway overlooking a beautiful garden. Small, spare rooms have fan and cramped but clean bath. Singles 200 pesos; doubles 250 pesos. Cash only. ❹

Hotel San Jose, Cuauhtémoc 138 (☎332 5105). The absence of a lobby gives Hotel San Jose a sort of non-ambience you won't find anywhere else. Basic rooms with clean bed and small bath with hot water. Reception until 11pm. Singles 200 pesos; doubles 300 pesos. Cash only. ❹

🔲 FOOD

Food is plentiful and cheap in the *centro*, far away from the big restaurants in the hotel zone. The local specialty, unsurprisingly, is fresh seafood. Whether you prefer them in a spicy *diabla* sauce, sizzled up with lots of garlic, or in soup, fresh shrimp and fish dishes are easy to come by and inexpensive on any corner near the Jardín. Manzanillo also has a **market,** Mercado 5 de Mayo, on 5 de Mayo at Guerrero. (Open daily 5am-5pm.) A **supermarket,** Comercial Mexicana, is at Costera de la Madrid km 11.5. Take a "Miramar" bus (5 pesos) from the *zócalo.* (☎333 1375. Open daily 8am-10pm.)

■ **Mercado de Comida,** on the corner of Cuauhtémoc and Madero. A breeze runs through the small eateries here, where customers sit on bar stools and enjoy their cheap *antojitos* and *mariscos* served within a minute or two of ordering. Most dishes 25-40 pesos. Open daily 7am-10pm; however, most dishes are not ready until 9am and most stands close shop around 8pm. Cash only. ❷

Yacatecuhtli, Allende 24 (☎332 5670), off Madero behind the nutrition store. Garish red and lime green walls and a tall ceiling lend an odd arthouse vibe to this cafe-restaurant, which serves a variety of *antojitos,* like *gordotas* 15 pesos and sandwiches (50 pesos). Open daily 8am-9pm. Cash only. ❸

Restaurante Chantilly, Madero 60 (☎332 0194), by the massive swordfish statue. Professionals and tourists feast on good staples in the *malecón* as busy waitresses bustle around serving tasty enchiladas (35-40 pesos), tuna or chicken salad (40 pesos), and meat dishes (40-85 pesos). Open M-F and Su 7:30am-10:30pm. Cash only. ❸

Jugo Lunch, Madero 164 (☎332 7100), in the portales. Fruit drinks and meat dishes are the specialty here. *Agua fresca* (18 pesos) goes well with *carne con chile* (50 pesos) in the laid-back atmosphere with chatty, jocular waiters. Open daily 8am-10:30pm. Cash only. ❹

Restaurant del Río, México 330 (☎332 2525). A cheap hole-in-the-wall joint right in the heart of the *centro* that will fill you up in no time with *comida corrida* (45 pesos) or Mexican specialties (20-40 pesos). Wash down your meal with a cold beer (10 pesos) or *licuado* (12 pesos). Tacos 4 pesos. Open M-Sa 8:30am-6pm. Cash only. ❷

🔲 BEACHES

Manzanillo's beaches stretch along two bays formed by the Santiago and Julupan peninsulas: **Bahía de Manzanillo** and **Bahía de Santiago.** Bahía de Manzanillo is extensively developed and not ideally suited for swimming because its beach slopes steeply, creating a strong and sometimes dangerous undertow. Bahía Santiago has quieter beaches and gentler slopes, allowing for more secluded sunbathing and easier swimming.

PLAYA LAS BRISAS. Golden sand covers Las Brisas, but so do massive resort hotels and expensive restaurant plots. During low season, the beach is fairly quiet but during high season it is packed with vacationers. The main advantage of Las Brisas is its proximity to the *centro. (Take a taxi for 35 pesos, the "Las Brisas" bus for 5 pesos, or a "Miramar" bus and ask to be let off at the crossroads. Go left for more populated beaches or stake out a private spot near the junction.)*

PLAYA SANTIAGO. Smooth, well-worn beach glass adorns the sands of Playa Santiago. Less developed than its fellow beaches on the other side of the peninsula, Santiago gets moderately busy during the high season but its soft sand and the tiny motes that glitter gold and green in its shallow waves make it worth the trip. *(Take a "Miramar" bus for 5 pesos to any point just past the peninsula. Walk down towards the beach along any of the streets perpendicular to the main road for 5-10min.)*

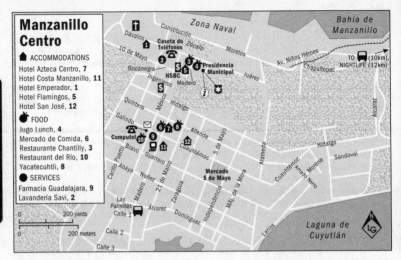

Manzanillo Centro

▲ **ACCOMMODATIONS**
Hotel Azteca Centro, **7**
Hotel Costa Manzanillo, **11**
Hotel Emperador, **1**
Hotel Flamingos, **5**
Hotel San José, **12**

🍴 **FOOD**
Jugo Lunch, **4**
Mercado de Comida, **6**
Restaurante Chantilly, **3**
Restaurant del Río, **10**
Yacatecuhtli, **8**

● **SERVICES**
Farmacía Guadalajara, **9**
Lavandería Savi, **2**

PLAYA LA BOQUITA. Private and sheltered by the Juluapan Peninsula, with small waves and a shallow bottom, La Boquita is a popular destination for families and children. The surrounding restaurants offer chartered tours for fishing, snorkeling, and sea tours, mostly during high season. Launches are also available, but the primary attraction of this beach is its relatively undeveloped setting and tranquil waves. *(Take a "Miramar" bus to Club Santiago. 40min., 4 pesos. The beach is a 25min. walk through the white gate and along a cobblestone street, which becomes a dirt road. Don't be intimidated by the gate security guards; just ask for Playa Boquita and they will wave you through. Taxis 30 pesos.)*

PLAYA LA AUDIENCIA. Swimmers, divers, and watersports enthusiasts alike enjoy this small, protected cove on the peninsula. La Audiencia offers a gorgeous view across the bay, the flattest sand, and row upon row of beach umbrellas to take refuge under from the hot midday sun. *(Take a "Las Hadas" bus for 5 pesos from Niños Héroes or anywhere on Miramar Rte. to the Sierra Radison, and follow the path to the beach to avoid having to navigate the rough hillsides.)*

GRUTA LA FLOREÑA. This impressive complex of grottoes is a mere 30min. away from Manzanillo. Visitors can explore every nook and cranny in the maze of caves surrounded by lush green vegetation. Contact a local tour guide for the best (and safest) experience. *(Guides can be found through the tourist office. ☎ 333 2277.)*

🎵 NIGHTLIFE

Manzanillo won't disappoint those in search of nocturnal amusement. Clubs and bars with dance floors and pricey drinks line the resort strip. "Miramar" buses run until 10pm. Taxis back to the *centro* cost 50 pesos.

Colima Bay Cafe, Costera de la Madrid km 6.5 (☎ 333 1150), on the beach side. Frogs in jerseys and other strange decor outfit the walls around the busy dance floor, where music at a comfortable volume invites a mixed crowd. Two bars and a stunning view over the ocean provide a break from dancing. Beer 30 pesos. National drinks from 45 pesos. Cover in high season F-Sa 100 pesos. Open M-Sa 2pm-2am. Cash only.

Sunset Lounge, Costera de la Madrid km 7 (☎333 6400), across from 5 de Mayo Sports Complex. Loud alt-rock and plush white lounge seating draw crowds of well-dressed 20-somethings. People pour out onto the patio, which overlooks the ocean. Beer 30 pesos. Mixed drinks 50-60 pesos. Bottle of Moët Brut Imperial 140 pesos. Sa nights live rock music. Open M-W 6pm-1am, Th-Su 6pm-5am. Cash only.

Senor Jalapeños, Costera de la Madrid 1165 (☎333 9286), near Nautilus. Half restaurant, half sports bar, the laid-back atmosphere and 70s music attracts both old husbands taking their wives out and a younger crowd shooting pool. Beer 25 pesos. Mixed drinks 50-60 pesos. Open daily 10:30am-2am. MC/V.

Nautilus, Costera de la Madrid 1161 km 9 (☎334 3331). The huge lighthouse and a merman on the side of the building beckon you to the 2-story, nautical-themed disco. Ramps lead to a deck where young crowds party hard to electronica, pop, and hip hop. Beer 25 pesos. Mixed drinks 50-60 pesos. Cover in high season 100-150 pesos. Open in high season daily 10:30pm-5am; in low season Th-Sa only. MC/V.

K'melia, Costera de la Madrid km 9.5 (☎333 7487), opposite the beach side. Strange hanging objects, tin statues, and a cow on the wall ornament the seating area of this bar, filled with the sound of 70s American motown and dance hits. An older crowd sits under the massive straw roof and eats their *antojitos*. F-Sa live rock music. Beer 23 pesos. Mixed drinks 45-50 pesos. Open daily 1pm-midnight. Cash only.

COLIMA ☎312

Nestled in a ring of mountains and the smoky *calderas* of El Volcán de Fuego and El Nevado, Colima (pop. 130,000) is a leafy, quiet city ripe with history. Despite its size, a dense *centro* and inviting population make Colima a small, intimate place for even the briefest of visits. The twin gods on the horizon have given the area its share of seismic trouble—El Volcán de Fuego recently awoke from its slumber, and in 2003 a massive earthquake in Colima registered 7.6 on the Richter scale—from which the city has only recently finished rebuilding. A constant breeze, beautiful green plazas, a thriving student population, and a history and culture preserved in museums combine to lure even the most ardent beachgoer away from the sands of the coast toward this untouristed inland gem.

▌▀ TRANSPORTATION

Flights: Aeropuerto Colima (CLQ; ☎314 4160), 2hr. from town. Served by **AeroCalifornia** (☎314 4850 or US 800-080-9090), **Aeromar** (☎313 1344), and **Aeroméxico** (☎313 8057). **Taxis** (☎313 0524) from the airport to the *centro* cost 120 pesos.

Buses: Colima's **Central de Autobuses** is on the northeastern side of town, about 5km from the *centro*. To get there from the *centro*, take a "Ruta 4" *combi* on Zaragoza (every 10min. 6am-9pm, 4 pesos) or a taxi (25 pesos). From the station, **Primera Plus** (☎314 8067) sends 1st-class buses to: **Aguascalientes** (6hr., 4pm, 370 pesos); **Guadalajara** (3hr., every hr., 160 pesos); **León** (6hr.; 4am, 12:30, 5:30pm; 332-350 pesos); **Manzanillo** (1½hr., every hr., 61 pesos); **Mexico City** (10hr.; 9, 11:30pm; 580 pesos); **Puerto Vallarta** (6½hr., 10:40pm, 230 pesos); **Tecomán** (40min.; 6:40, 9pm; 35 pesos). **Autobuses de Occidente/La Línea** (☎314 8781), **Estrella Blanca** (☎312 8499), **Ómnibus de México** (☎312 1630), and **Autotransportes Galeana** (☎313 4785) have similar service.

Taxis: One of the most convenient and popular ways to get around Colima. Service is fairly cheap (15 pesos gets you to most places listed).

Car Rental: SuperAutos, Av. Rey Coliman 381 (☎312 0752). Economy cars with insurance and taxes from 500 pesos per day. Open daily 9am-8pm. MC/V.

⚡ PRACTICAL INFORMATION

Tourist Office: (☎312 4360), Madero 203 in the Presidencia Municipal. Friendly staff offers helpful brochures and information on Colima state. Open M-F 8:30am-8pm, Sa 10am-1:30pm.

Banks: Several throughout the city. **Banamex,** Hidalgo 90, in the *centro.* Major banks like Madero east of the centro.

Emergency: ☎066.

Police: Libramento Ejército Mexicano 200 (☎312 0967 or 2566).

Red Cross: (☎313 8787), at Aldama and Obregón. Open 24hr.

24hr. Pharmacy: Farmacia Guadalajara, Obregón 16 (☎314 7474) at Madero.

Internet: Internet Cafe, Juárez 92 at Morelos. 10 pesos per hr. Open M-F 9am-11pm, Sa 10:30am-3pm and 5-11pm. Free Wi-Fi located in the Presidencia Municipal and throughout the *plaza principal.*

Post Office: (☎312 0033), on Gen. Núñez at Madero, in Col. Centro. Open M-F 8am-6pm, Sa 8am-noon. **Postal Code:** 28000.

♠ ACCOMMODATIONS

Cheap lodging may be found near **Jardín Núñez,** but you get what you pay for—rooms are generally sparse and a little crumbly.

Hotel La Merced, Juárez 82 (☎312 6969). Try to get a room off the driveway in the quiet courtyard, which is filled with flowers and plush leather furniture. High-ceilinged rooms have big beds, cable TV, fan, and clean bath. Parking available. Reception 24hr. Singles 260 pesos; doubles 330 pesos; triples 330-460 pesos. Cash only. ❺

Hotel Colonial, Medellín 142F (☎313 0877), 1½ blocks from the cathedral. Colonial has 2 sections, an older one and a remodeled one. Rooms vary in style and price—all have comfortable beds and hot water, older rooms have TV, newer rooms have cable TV. Reception 24hr. Singles 120-200 pesos; doubles 170-250 pesos. Cash only. ❷

Hospedaje San Antonio, Medellín 179 (☎330 0789), south of Bravo. A quiet lodging with only 5 rooms. A simple hallway leads to small, clean rooms with comfortable beds, bath, fan. Reception 24hr. Singles 150 pesos, with cable TV 180 pesos; doubles 230/250 pesos. Cash only. ❸

Gran Hotel Flamingos, Av. Rey Coliman 18 (☎312 2525), 3 blocks from the *centro.* A pleasant breeze runs through hallways of flamingos and volcano pictures, past the wood-paneled lobby. Rooms have bath, fan, and cable TV, some with balcony. Reception 24hr. Singles 230 pesos; doubles 270 pesos; triples 300 pesos. Cash only. ❸

Hotel San Cristóbal, Reforma 98 (☎312 0575), at Morelos. The budget option—barren walls in the lobby foreshadow similarly lifeless tiled rooms. Long, narrow beds give the feel of an after-hours clinic. Rooms have fan. Reception 24hr. Singles 115 pesos, with bath 160 pesos, with TV 180 pesos; doubles with TV 140 pesos, with bath 200 pesos. Cash only. ❶

🍴 FOOD

Inexpensive meals with traditional favorites like *pozole blanco* (chicken or pork stew with homily in white broth) and Colima-style *sopitos* (small, thin tortillas topped with beans, meat, and shredded lettuce), are easy to come by. A jaunt down the side streets of **Plaza Principal** leads to taco stands, and *churros* aplenty.

Los Naranjos, Barreda 34 (☎312 0029), in the *centro.* Fairly fine dining at small tables to the tune of soft piano music. Serves up various *carnes* (including filet mignon), an

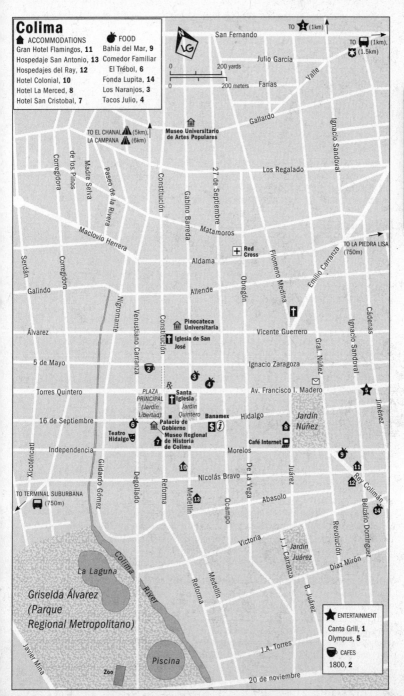

CENTRAL PACIFIC COAST

Colima

ACCOMMODATIONS
Gran Hotel Flamingos, 11
Hospedaje San Antonio, 13
Hospedajes del Ray, 12
Hotel Colonial, 10
Hotel La Merced, 8
Hotel San Cristobal, 7

FOOD
Bahía del Mar, 9
Comedor Familiar
El Trébol, 6
Fonda Lupita, 14
Los Naranjos, 3
Tacos Julio, 4

ENTERTAINMENT
Canta Grill, 1
Olympus, 5

CAFES
1800, 2

extensive breakfast selection (30-55 pesos). *Comida corrida* 63 pesos. F seafood specials. Open daily 8am-11pm. AmEx/D/MC/V. ❺

Fonda Lupita, Coliman 230 (☎139 3058) at the corner of Victoria. This corner stone does a brisk business during midday with its generous helpings of *comida corrida* (35 pesos). Su a la carte only. Open M-F 8am-10pm, Sa-Su 8am-4pm. Cash only. ❸

Comedor Familiar el Trébol, Degollado *59* (☎312 2900), at 16 de Septiembre, in Plaza Principal. A casual place. Regulars order *antojitos* and *comida típica*. *Tortas* and tacos 20-25 pesos. *Comida corrida* 30 pesos. Open daily 8am-11pm. Cash only. ❷

Bahía del Mar, Morelos 264 at Coliman. Open-air seating and deck chairs hint at the sea, while the *mariscos* seal the deal. *Camarones* (shrimp; 80 pesos). Fish any style 75 pesos. Beer 15-20 pesos. Open M-Sa 7am-11pm. Cash only. ❺

Tacos Julio, Madero 87A (☎314 7022), just west of Ocampo. Nothing more than a taco stand with a seating area. No atmosphere, but definitely the cheapest tacos you'll find in the city, ready in less than a minute, with every kind of meat you could want. Tacos 5 pesos. Soft drinks 8-10 pesos. Open daily 9am-11pm. Cash only. ❶

🔍 SIGHTS

Colima is famous for the natural splendor that surrounds it on all sides. Within the city itself, there's a wealth of archaeological, historical, and cultural sites to enjoy as well. Before you leave town, make sure you head over to the **Piedra Lisa,** at the corner of Aldama and Galván, to slide down the smooth surface and, as the legend goes, ensure your eventual return to Colima.

PLAZA PRINCIPAL. The gazebo and fountains of the plaza (officially Jardín Libertad) are bordered on the north by the **Palacio de Gobierno,** which contains historical murals. The double arcade around the plaza holds the **Museo Regional de Historia de Colima,** which houses an extensive collection of pre-Hispanic artifacts that detail Aztec culture, and showcases temporary exhibits of local art in its airy courtyard. *(Portal Morelos 1 at 16 de Septiembre and Reforma. Museum ☎312 9228. Open Tu-Sa 9am-6pm, Su 5-8pm. 37 pesos, students with Mexican credentials free; Su free.)*

SANTA IGLESIA CATHEDRAL. Originally built in 1527. the church was destroyed multiple by times by Colima's regular earthquakes, fires, and other natural disasters. It acquired its present look, with an elegant Neoclassical facade and cupola, between 1820 and 1894, when it was consecrated to the Virgin Mary of Guadalupe. The damage from a recent earthquake has since been repaired, and the church is open to the public in all its splendor. *(Adjoining the Palacio de Gobierno. ☎312 0200. Office open M-Sa 10am-2pm and 4-7pm. Mass M-Sa 7:30, 11:30am, 7:30pm; Su 7, 8, 11am, noon, 6, 7, 8pm.)*

PINACOTECA UNIVERSITARIA. The quiet galleries adjacent to the university hold an enormous amount of art by students and locals in various media, including a prominent room full of its most recent artistic acquisitions. The auditorium doubles as a lecture hall and poetry performance venue. Call for a listing of events. *(Guerrero 35 between Barreda and Constitución. ☎312 2228. Open Tu-Sa 10am-2pm and 5-8pm, Su 10am-1pm. 10 pesos, children and students 5 pesos.)*

MUSEO UNIVERSITARIO DE ARTES POPULARES. Traditional costumes, meticulously preserved musical instruments, extensive displays about regional festivals, and an amazing exhibit on puppetry fill the rooms of the museum. Twelve-foot puppets called *mojigangos* decorate the courtyard. *(At Barreda and Gallardo. Catch the 4-peso "Ruta 7" bus on Barreda between Zaragoza and Guerrero, or walk 7 blocks 15min. northeast of the centro. ☎312 6869; www.ucol.mx/arte/museos/populares.php. Open Tu-Sa 10am-2pm and 5-8pm, Su 10am-1pm. 10 pesos, children and students 5 pesos; Su free.)*

PARQUE GRISELDA ÁLVAREZ. A nice break from museums, these orchards were converted into a sprawling public park in 1985. A small zoo, picnic areas, and an artificial lake with rowboats for rent are hidden among the well-kept greenery and gorgeous flowers. *(At Degollado and 20 de Septiembre southeast of the* centro. *Take a 15-peso taxi or walk down Degollado for 15-20min. Open W-Su 10:30am-5pm.)*

EL CHANAL AND LA CAMPANA. Tucked away north of the city lie El Chanal and La Campana, two excavated archaeological sites revealing massive pre-Hispanic ruins. The former, discovered in 1945, has ball courts, altars, and small pyramids built in honor of indigenous deities. La Campana, thought to be among the historically most heavily populated sites in Western Mexico, is home to monuments, small altars, roads, and rudimentary plumbing. *(El Chanal is at the northern end of Carranza. Take a 25-peso taxi and walk several km up the cobblestone road. Open Tu-Su 10am-6pm. To get to La Campana, take a taxi to the western end of Tecnológico in the Villa de Álvarez. Open Tu-Su 9am-5pm. Both free.)*

CENTRAL PACIFIC COAST

ENTERTAINMENT

Volcanoes aren't the only things erupting in Colima. A large student population ensures a vibrant club and bar scene, fueled by small covers and cheap booze. For something more relaxing, try a movie at **Cine Soriana**, Gómez 371. (☎311 3213. Open in high season M-Tu and Th-F 3pm-midnight, W and Sa-Su 1pm-midnight. 42 pesos, children 35 pesos.)

Olympus, Madero 372 (☎313 4281) between Cárdenas and Dominguez. Jam-packed with stylish youth, this place gets going at midnight when the music goes up and the fog comes down over a laser-lit dance floor. Navigating your way to the bar is difficult, as is finding a seat, but the liveliness more than makes up for the confusion. Beer 25 pesos. Mixed drinks 45-55 pesos. Cover 50 pesos. Open F-Sa 10:30pm-3am. Cash only.

1800, 5 de Mayo #15 (☎312 9300) between Carranza and Constitución. Patrons nibble at *antojitos* with their drinks or relax on couches in small, intimate groups of friends under the strange orange lighting and overhanging drapes. Hip international music plays quietly enough to allow for conversation. Meals 45-65 pesos. Beer 20 pesos. Mixed drinks 25-50 pesos. Open Tu-Su 7pm-2am. Cash only.

Canta Grill, Felipe Sevilla 211 (☎330 1390) 10 blocks north of the *centro*—it's best to take a taxi. Young professionals in small packs descend on this karaoke joint to massacre popular Mexican hits while enjoying the dense, lively atmosphere. Beer 25 pesos. Mixed drinks 40-55 pesos. Cover 50 pesos. Open Th-Su 9pm-2am. Cash only.

DAYTRIPS FROM COLIMA

VOLCÁN DE FUEGO AND LAGUNA MARÍA. In Náhuatl, Colima means "place where the old god is dominant"—the "old god" being **El Volcán de Fuego** (3960m), located 25km from the city of Colima. Puffs of white smoke continuously billow from the volcano and lava flowed in 1994, when El Fuego reasserted its status as an active volcano. Since then there have been fairly regular ash eruptions, including one in 2005 which measured over 5km high and led to the evacuation of nearby villages. Lava bombs shot from the volcano and ash covered nearby settlements. The volatility of the volcano in past years has led to the closing of the summit. To see the Fire Volcano, tourists may approach as close as Laguna María, which lies along the path up to the volcano. The still, green water of the lagoon acts as a mirror, perfectly reflecting the natural beauty of Colima and attracting a bevy of creatures. The park also offers hiking trails (some of which lead up to spectacular views of the nearby volcano) and horseback riding. *(Take a "Zapotitlán" bus from the Terminal Suburbana and tell the driver where you're going. 30min.; 7:10am, 2:40, 5pm; 50 pesos. From the bus drop-off, it's a 10min. walk up a steep cobblestone road. Service is infrequent. Let's Go does not recommend hitchhiking, but locals may offer you rides to Comala or Colima if they see you waiting at the intersection. Laguna María administration has schedules for return buses to Colima.)*

EL NEVADO DE COLIMA. Near Volcán del Fuego in the same volcanic system is the slightly taller **El Nevado de Colima** (4335m), which earned its name from the blanket of snow that drapes over it during winter. The vegetation near the summit changes from the native temperate arbor to taiga, with rare pines and conifers foreign to this part of Mexico. The entire volcano system, made into a national park by Lázaro Cárdenas in 1936, offers great opportunities for challenging mountain hiking, but the park is open sporadically. If you're planning a trip to the top, get in contact with the **Seguridad Pública**, reachable through Colima's tourist office, and they will check current conditions of the Nevado for you. The ascent should not be attempted solo or by those without sufficient hiking experience, especially during the rainy season. The tourist office can locate a tour guide to take you up to the summit and back down again. *(El Nevado is accessible by car or bus, but the last leg of the trip is suitable only for offroad vehicles. "Suburbanos" buses run to Ciudad Guzmán across the border in Jalisco state from the new bus station at the base of the volcano. From there, 2nd-class buses at the far right end of the bus station limp up to El Fresnito, a village at the base of the mountain and home to several guides. Guides with vans will transport you to La Joya, at 4000m, the highest point on the mountain accessible by automobile and the starting point for your epic mountain assault. From there, it's a steep 1km hike to the summit.)*

LAGUNA CARRIZALILLO. Families and couples dominate the land surrounding the small lagoon, enfolded in the rocky hills 27km north of the city center of Colima. The land around affords a beautiful view of the valley down to Colima and the volcano standing imperially in the distance. Children play in the shallows of the small lagoon, home to appropriately small fish and amphibians. Otherwise, the water is fairly dirty and unsuitable for swimming. Paddleboats (30 pesos), however, are a common form of recreation on the laguna. Most of the people here come for picnics, renting a grilling space (20 pesos) and bringing meat to cook for all-day affairs as children run around and adults drink beer. Camping is also available (40 pesos per night), but the park only provides the plot of land—you have to furnish everything else. While the park technically closes at 6pm, many drive in after hours to catch the sunset. When the sun hits the lagoon at a certain angle, the whole park lights up gold. *(Take an "El Naranjal" bus from the Terminal Suburbana and tell the driver you want to visit the lagoon. Admission 10 pesos. Open daily 10am-6pm.)*

SOUTHERN PACIFIC COAST

The Southern Pacific Coast is a melange of natural beauty, indigenous culture, and colonial splendor, from coastal beaches and swamps to serrated inland hills, wooing backpackers, and families alike. On the water's edge, the glitzy resorts of the north give way to surfers and hippies roughing it further south. Inland, indigenous villages dot the cities and hills, next to the Baroque stone of Mexico's colonial past. Because the region's Purépecha peoples survived by fishing, the Aztecs named the lands surrounding Lake Pátzcuaro **Michoacán** (Country of Fishermen). Michoacán's fertile soil, abundant rain, and mild weather make for bountiful crops—potatoes, avocados, and strawberries are just a handful of the goods that make their way to markets across Mexico. The gentle hills inland give way to violent, tortuous cliffs on Michoacán's wild coast. Hundreds of miles of remote beaches are inaccessible, except for the occasional secluded surf spots.

The state of **Guerrero** is home to Taxco, the first silver mining town in North America—a tangle of narrow cobblestone streets nestled into a quiet mountainside. During the colonial period, silver kept the state and most of New Spain swimming in the precious metal. Nowadays the state's riches come primarily from tourist dollars flooding the coastal resorts. Former international vacation hot spot, Acapulco now attracts hordes of Mexican tourists ready to party hard come sundown. Sister cities Ixtapa and Zihuatanejo have now eclipsed their neighbor's reputation, attracting droves of sun-worshipping foreigners.

Fractured into an assorted quilt of terrains by the rugged heights of the Sierra Madre del Sur, **Oaxaca** has inspired a violent possessiveness in its many different peoples. Zapotecs, Mixtecs, Aztecs, and Spaniards have all fought and died for the region. More than 200 indigenous tribes have occupied the valley over the past two millennia, and more than one million *oaxaqueños* still speak indigenous languages. Stunning indigenous ruins, exquisite colonial architecture, and savory local culinary dishes characterize inland Oaxaca state, while miles of unpolished coast and record-breaking pipelines attract surfers and hippies alike.

HIGHLIGHTS OF THE SOUTHERN PACIFIC COAST

RETREAT to the gorgeous beaches of the stormy **Michoacán Coast** (p. 490), which boast powerful waves, privacy, and rugged terrain.

FIGHT your way through the crowded market places of **Pátzcuaro** (p. 481), where the Purépecha sell every conceivable type of handicraft.

TREAD the stone streets of **Morelia** (p. 475), where glorious cathedrals, obsolete aqueducts, and colonial houses preserve the long history of the republic.

ADORN yourself with silver jewelry in **Taxco** (p. 493), and enjoy magnificent mountain views from the narrow hillside streets.

BASK in the competing aromas of chocolate, *mezcal*, and *tlayudas* in **Oaxaca** (p. 530), the culinary mecca of southern Mexico.

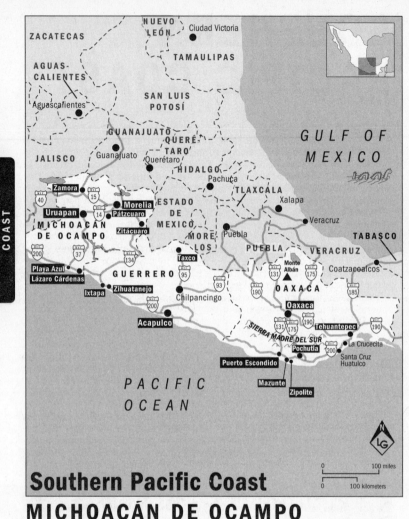

Southern Pacific Coast

MICHOACÁN DE OCAMPO

ZITÁCUARO   ☎ 715

Zitácuaro (pop. 200,000) would have been a much larger city had it not been destroyed three times during the 19th century—once during the War of Independence (1812), again by Santa Anna's troops (1855), and finally during the French Intervention (1865). The city's long tradition of defiance and survival led Benito Juárez to name it the *Ciudad de la Independencia* (City of Independence). The city is tucked into the eastern edge of the Sierra Madre Occidental, and mountains seem to loom at the end of every street. Outdoors enthusiasts will find plenty of opportunities for hiking, camping, birdwatching, kayaking, and horseback riding nearby, but there is little for the cosmopolitan traveler. The city also makes a good base for exploring during butterfly season (Nov.-Mar.) Despite its growing population and increasing urbanization, Zitácuaro's cultural traditions have remained as steadfast as the mountains.

⌷ TRANSPORTATION. The **bus station,** Pueblita Nte. 17 (☎ 153 7265), is at the end of Cuauhtémoc Nte., two blocks north of Hidalgo and six blocks east of Revolución Nte. Tickets for taxis to the *centro* are sold at a booth inside (20 pesos). "Centro" *combis* (5am-7pm, 4.50 pesos) are outside the station. **Flecha Amarilla** (☎ 153 1488) provides 2nd-class service to **Mexico City** (2¾hr., 4am, 97 pesos) via **Toluca** (1¾hr., 58 pesos), and 1st-class service to **Morelia** (3hr., 7 per day 4am-4:30pm, 89 pesos) via **Ciudad Hidalgo** (50min., 23 pesos). **Autobuses de Occidente/La Línea** (☎ 153 0866) goes to **Mexico City** (3hr., every 20min. 3am-10:40pm, 97-110 pesos) and **Zamora** (6hr.; 11:30am, 12:50pm; 180 pesos). **Estrella Blanca** (☎ 153 7173) drives to northern destinations and sends buses to **Querétaro** (6hr., 1:30pm, 115 pesos). **Autobuses Mexico-Toluca Zinacantepec** (☎ 153 7163) has limited local service.

⌷▪ ORIENTATION AND PRACTICAL INFORMATION. Zitácuaro sits on **Mex. 15,** 165km west of Mexico City. **Plaza Principal,** the city center, consists of Plaza Cívica de Benito Juárez, Plaza Municipal, and Mercado Juárez. **Plaza Municipal** is bordered by **Lerdo de Tejada** to the south, **García** to the west, **5 de Mayo** to the east, and **Ocampo** to the north. **Hidalgo** runs parallel to Ocampo on the northern side of the market. The main avenue, **Revolución,** is one block east of 5 de Mayo. Streets end in "Nte." (North) or "Sur" (South), indicating their relation to Hidalgo.

The **tourist office,** Carretera Zitácuaro-Toluca km 4, is far from the *centro* but provides helpful regional maps and brochures. Take an orange *combi* (4 pesos) south on Revolución and tell the driver where you would like to disembark. (☎ 153 0675; delregdeturzitacuaro@prodigy.net.mx. Open Apr.-Oct. M-F 9am-4:30pm, Sa-Su 9am-2pm; Nov.-Mar. M-F 9am-7pm, Sa-Su 9am-2pm.) **Banamex,** Tejada 30, **exchanges currency** and has a **24hr. ATM.** (☎ 153 1920. Open M-F 9am-4pm, Sa 10am-2pm.) The bus station has **luggage storage.** (10 pesos per 4hr. Open 24hr.) Other services include: **emergency** (☎ 066); **police,** Ocampo 13, in the Palacio Municipal (☎ 153 1137); **Red Cross,** Prieto 11 (☎ 153 1105, from cell phones 114); **Farmacia Guadalajara,** 5 de Mayo Sur 12A (☎ 153 8633; open 24hr.); **Clínica Sanitorio Memorial,** Valle Nte. 10, (☎ 153 6539); **Telecomm,** Ocampo Ote. 7, with **fax, Western Union,** and telegraph (☎ 153 1281; open M-F 8am-7:30pm, Sa 9am-1pm); **Internet** access at **Evolución Internet,** Hidalgo Ote. 17B, near Salazar (☎ 153 7314; 10 pesos per hr., 3 peso min.; open daily 9am-9pm); and the **post office,** Revolución Sur 133 (☎ 153 1283; open M-F 8am-3pm). **Postal Code:** 61516.

▟▙ ACCOMMODATIONS AND FOOD. Reservations are a good idea for the start of the butterfly season (Nov.-Dec.). Most inexpensive hotels offer surprisingly attractive rooms at great prices. Put your pesos to good use at the **Hotel América ❸,** Revolución Sur 8, which has parking spaces and clean rooms with spotless baths, tiled floors, and cable TV. The balcony rooms look out onto busy Av. Revolución. (☎ 153 1116. Check-out 1pm. Singles 190 pesos; doubles 250 pesos; triples 310 pesos; quads 370 pesos. Cash only.) Another good option is the recently remodeled **Hotel Lorenz ❸,** Hidalgo Ote. 14. The spacious rooms have cable TV and charming white, wood furniture; some overlook the courtyard and its fountain seating. (153 8458. Check-out noon. Singles 180 pesos; doubles 250 pesos; triples and quads 350 pesos. Cash only.)

Try the friendly **Cafetería Chipps ❸,** Hidalgo Ote. 22, east of Revolución, where the whole family takes part in the restaurant business. The daily *comida corrida* (45 pesos) always includes vegetarian options. (☎ 153 1195. Milkshakes 15 pesos. Open M-Sa 11am-6pm. Cash only.) Sit on pink wooden

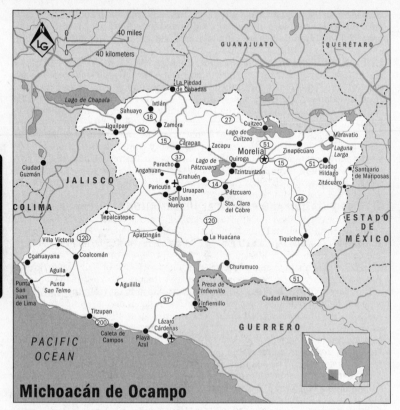

Michoacán de Ocampo

benches overlooking the plaza at **Bambino's ❷,** on Lerdo de Tejada Pte. at 5 de Mayo, which fills with locals in the evenings. (☎153 7753. Breakfasts 38-55 pesos. *Tortas* and burgers 16-18 pesos. Pizza 10 pesos per slice. Ice cream sundae 16 pesos. Open daily 8:30am-10pm. Cash only.) Stands with fresh fruits and vegetables, tacos, quesadillas, and ice cream line **5 de Mayo**—sarcastically nicknamed the Calle del Hambre (Hunger Road)—between Hidalgo and Ocampo, outside the **mercado municipal.** (Market open daily 8:30am-6pm. Most outdoor stands open until 10pm.) **Super ISSTE** is a supermarket at Revolución Nte. 2. (☎153 0291. Open daily 9am-9pm. D/MC/V.)

TIP **A MOVEABLE FEAST.** Wondering why that scrumptious carbohydrate treat you enjoyed yesterday evening is nowhere to be found this morning? Zitácuaro's gastronomic gurus follow a strict selling schedule: white breads are sold in the morning, sweet buns and pastries in the afternoons. Zitacuarenses are so proud of their bread, they coined a rhyming jingle: "Para mujeres y pan, Zitácuaro Michoacán" (For women and bread, Zitácuaro Michoacán).

🔲 **SIGHTS.** Afternoons in Zitácuaro slip by quietly beneath the sun in the **Plaza Cívica de Benito Juárez,** where vendors gather, uniformed school children play *fútbol,* and the elderly relax on shaded benches. The **Palacio Municipal,**

Ocampo 13, at the north end of the plaza, has a mural by Abel Medina bringing to life Zitácuaro's history, from Mazahua settlement to the present. (☎153 0021. Open daily 8am-9pm.) The small **Jardín de la Constitución,** on Ojeda Sur three blocks west of the plaza, is filled with flowers, grassy areas, and shady seats for starry-eyed lovebirds and budding artists. Zitácuaro's **Cerrito de la Independencia,** where the monument to Don Ignacio López Rayón stands, looks out over not only the city itself, but also miles of lush valleys, forested hills, and spectacular distant blue peaks. (Follow Tejada as it crosses Revolución Sur until it reaches Altamirano. Turn right and follow the paved path. Alternatively, take an orange 4.50-peso *combi* south on Revolución to Cañonaso and walk the 4 blocks uphill. Open 24hr.) The **Mora del Cañonazo Garden,** on Moctezuma, still preserves the site where a cannon ball landed during the War of Independence and has a small, pleasant garden perfect for an afternoon stroll. (From the *centro,* take a *combi,* 4.50 pesos, going north on Revolución, get off at Moctezuma, and walk 6 blocks to the right. Open 24hr.)

One of Zitácuaro's most impressive sights is the monarch butterflies that can be seen in nearby **El Capulín** (11km) from November to March. If you happen to be in town during this season, head to the ecotourist center at El Capulín, Carr. Zitácuaro-Aputzio km 11, where you hike (1½hr.) to the site by foot—on your own or with a guide—or on horseback. (☎140 6171. Guides 100 pesos. Horse rides 100 pesos. Open daily 9am-4pm. 25 pesos, children 15 pesos.) The migrating monarchs are celebrated in the last weekend of February and the first two weekends in March during the **Festival Cultural de la Mariposa Monarca.**

For a change of pace, visit the traditional Otomí town of **San Felipe de Los Alzati,** which surrounds an impressive though not fully excavated stepped pyramid. The four groupings of pre-Classic constructions at the site, including three *temezcal* (steam) baths, are believed to have marked the eastern frontier of the Purepechan empire (AD1200-1500) To get to the ruins, take a "Soriana" *combi* from the corner of Revolución Nte. and Moctezuma (15min.; 4.50 pesos) to San Felipe and ask for the stop at the turn-off to Ziráhuato; from there, take a taxi or walk 2km to the archeological site. (Open daily 10am-5pm. 24 pesos.)

10km south of town on the Huetamo Rte., **Presa del Bosque** also provides spectacular views of the countryside. The dirt road to the right of the main road leads to a lake where adventurous souls swim, hike, fish, and camp. (Take a *taxi colectivo* on the corner of Zaragoza and Benedicto López; 25-30 pesos.) For more organized outdoor excursions, contact **Papalotzín,** Prieto 26, one of the more established companies in town. They offer everything from camping and hiking (500 pesos per day), to birdwatching tours and guided visits to see the monarch butterflies (500-1000 pesos per group, 6-person min.). They also organize mountain biking (bikes 500 pesos; guide 500 pesos) and climbing excursions (500 pesos) in the nearby waterfalls. (☎109 2530; papalotzintour@yahoo.com.mx. Open M-F 9am-2pm and 4-7pm.)

MORELIA ☎443

State capital Morelia (pop. 575,000) anchors the proud traditions of Michoacán culture and history. Art exhibits, concerts, museums, dance productions, and theater create a vibrant cultural scene fueled by the city's sizable student population. Once Valladolid, it was renamed in 1828 to honor its native son and hero of the War of Independence, Jose María Morelos (1765-1815). Its history, however, extends well into the 21st century, evident in the museums and churches alongside the banks and fast-food chains now occupying antique houses, relics of Morelia's colonial magnificence. The capital's youthful pulse and stunning stone architecture are testaments of its vitality in the colonial era and the present day.

▐ TRANSPORTATION

Morelia lies 230km west of Mexico City on Mex. 15. Buses and *combis* traverse the city (6am-10pm, 4.50 pesos), and taxis wait at the bus station.

Flights: Aeropuerto Francisco J. Múgica (MLM), Carr. Morelia-Zinapécuaro km 27 (☎313 6780). No buses serve the airport; taxis cost 150 pesos. Airlines include: **Aeromar** (☎313 6886), **Aeroméxico** (☎313 0140), and **Mexicana** (☎312 4725).

Buses: The new **TAM** station is on the outskirts of town, in front of the stadium housing the popular Monarcas del Morelia. To get downtown, take a brown *combi*, which will drop you off in front of La Casa de la Cultura. Taxis to the *centro* cost 30 pesos. **Primera Plus/ Flecha Amarilla** (☎338 1081) provides 1st-class service to: **Aguascalientes** (5½hr., 7 per day 12:15am-5:30pm, 265 pesos); **Guadalajara** (3½hr., 14 per day 6:15am-midnight, 242 pesos); **León** (3hr.; every 30min. 6:30am-7:30pm, 9:30, 11pm; 150 pesos); **Mexico City** (5hr.; every hr. 7:15am-6:15pm, 8, 11pm, midnight; 240 pesos); **Pátzcuaro** (1hr.; 5:45, 7:45am, 3pm; 35 pesos); **Puerto Vallarta** (9hr., 8:10pm, 588 pesos); **Querétaro** (3hr., 23 per day 1:45am-midnight, 131 pesos); **San Luis Potosí** (6hr., 18 per day 1:45am-midnight, 279 pesos); **Uruapan** (2hr., 8 per day 1am-9:30pm, 99 pesos); **Zamora** (2½hr., 5 per day 9am-5:30pm, 112 pesos). 2nd-class service covers the same destinations. **ETN** (☎334 1059) provides similar, but more expensive, services. **Élite** (☎334 1051) goes farther north, with intermittent service to US destinations.

▐ PRACTICAL INFORMATION

Tourist Office: Secretaria de Turismo, Tata Vasco 80 (☎317 8052 or 8054) across from Plaza Morelos 1km east of the *centro*. Maps, event guides, and information about Michoacán's sites. Open M-Sa 9am-6pm, Su 10am-2pm. **Information booths** in front of Palacio Clavijero and the cathedral have maps and more info. Open M-Sa 9am-8pm.

Banks: Banks cluster on Madero near the cathedral. **Bancomer,** Madero Ote. 21 (☎312 2990). Has a **24hr. ATM.** Open M-F 9am-4pm, Sa 10am-2pm.

Banamex, Madero Ote. 63 (☎322 0338). Open M-F 9am-5pm, Sa 9am-2pm.

Luggage Storage: Most bus lines have luggage storage. 5 pesos per hr.

Laundromat: Lavandería Burbuja, Alzate 650 at the corner of Guzman. 10 pesos per kg. Open M-F 9am-2pm and 4:30-8pm, Sa 10am-2pm.

Emergency: ☎070.

Police: Periférico 5000 (☎316 3100), on the outskirts of town. Open 24hr. The **Módulo de Policía,** in the *zócalo*'s northwest corner, is more accessible. Open daily 7am-11pm.

Red Cross: Ventura 27 (☎314 5073; emergency 314 5151), by Parque Cuauhtémoc.

24hr. Pharmacy: Farmacia Guadalajara, Morelos Sur 117 (☎312 1360), near the cathedral. Also a mini-market.

Hospital: Civil (☎312 0102), at Ramos and Huarte. Open 24hr.

Fax Office: Computel, Ruiz 553 (☎313 5537), also has phones. Open daily 7am-9pm. **Telecomm,** Madero Ote. 369 (☎312 2693), in the Palacio Federal. Open M-F 8am-7:30pm, Sa-Su 9am-12:30pm.

Internet Access: Internet y Más, Allende 332 (☎324 2407). 8 pesos per hr. Open M-Sa 9am-8:30pm, Su 9am-3pm.

Post Office: Madero Ote. 369 (☎312 0517), in the Palacio Federal, 5 blocks east of the cathedral. Open M-F 9am-6pm, Sa 9am-1pm. **Postal Code:** 58000.

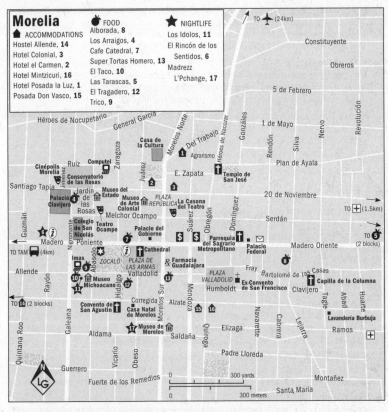

Morelia

▲ ACCOMMODATIONS
Hostel Allende, **14**
Hotel Colonial, **3**
Hotel el Carmen, **2**
Hotel Mintzicuri, **16**
Hotel Posada la Luz, **1**
Posada Don Vasco, **15**

🍴 FOOD
Alborada, **8**
Los Arraigos, **4**
Cafe Catedral, **7**
Super Tortas Homero, **13**
El Taco, **10**
Las Tarascas, **5**
El Tragadero, **12**
Trico, **9**

★ NIGHTLIFE
Los Idolos, **11**
El Rincón de los
  Sentidos, **6**
Madrezz
L'Pchange, **17**

SOUTHERN PACIFIC COAST

ACCOMMODATIONS

Weekend vacancies are hard to come by in Morelia, and hotels in general are not as common as one might expect in a state capital. But among the scattered hotels, budget accommodations are available if you know where to look.

Hostel Allende, Allende 843 (☎312 2246), 2 blocks west of Quintana Roo. Low prices and a cozy courtyard full of palms and parasols. Private rooms and 4-bed dorms with clean baths. Offers communal kitchen, Wi-Fi, and cable TV. Dorms 110 pesos, with HI or ISIC 100 pesos; singles 180 pesos, with TV 250 pesos; doubles 360 pesos; triples 400 pesos. Cash only. ❶

Hotel Mintzicuri, Vasco de Quiroga 227 (☎312 0664). Antique wooden furniture accentuates the lobby and the cozy, wood-paneled rooms individually named for *michoacáno* towns. Rooms come with phone and cable TV. Popular with tourists; come early or call ahead. Singles 220 pesos; doubles 250 pesos; triples 280 pesos. Cash only. ❹

Hotel Colonial, 20 de Noviembre 15 (☎312 1897). Simple white walls, high ceilings, and a soft bed come with enormous hot-water bath. Most of the rooms are different; ask for one with a balcony. Singles 250 pesos, with TV 350 pesos; doubles 300/400 pesos; triples 450 pesos. MC/V. ❺

Hotel Posada La Luz, del Trabajo 32 (☎317 4878), across Morelos from Casa de la Cultura. Strong rays of ambient light give the rooms and lobby an airy, expansive feel. Rooms come with big firm beds and clean, cramped (and aging) private baths. Reception 24hr. Singles 200 pesos; doubles 300 pesos. Cash only. ❹

Hotel el Carmen, Ruiz 63 (☎312 1725), across the garden from Casa de la Cultura. Wooden beds take up space, but the sparkling bath, cable TV, and high ceilings make up for it, and the couches in the bustling courtyard are plenty comfortable. Singles 250 pesos; doubles 350 pesos; triples 490 pesos. Cash only. ❺

Posada Don Vasco, Vasco de Quiroga 232 (☎312 1484), 2 blocks south of Madero. Stone stairs and interior arches typical of *moreliano* architecture lead to small, secure rooms. Clean, narrow beds, small cable TV, carpet, and bath round out the rooms. Singles 220 pesos; doubles 250 pesos; triples 280 pesos. Cash only. ❹

█ FOOD

Morelia is a haven for cheap, quick food—taco stands and small restaurants serving up *comida corrida* dot all of Morelia, and *torterías* are found on nearly every block in the *centro*. Restaurants on the *zócalo* and in the *portales* are pricier but tend to stay open later. For local specialties, try *sopa tarasca* (a creamy soup made with beans, cheese, and bits of crispy tortilla, flavored by a bitter, black chile) or *sopa tlalpeño* (a chicken-based soup with vegetables and *chipotle*), legacies of the Purépecha and Tarasco indigenous groups that once controlled this region.

▨ **Trico,** Valladolid 8, 2nd fl. (☎313 4232). Restrained elegance, excellent service, and a glorious view of the cathedral make the prices a pleasant shock. Serves regional specialties and its very own, like the chicken Trico (49 pesos). Baguettes from 25 pesos. Breakfast 40-50 pesos. Open daily 7am-9pm. AmEx/MC/V. ❸

El Taco, Allende 329A, east of Galeana. The name says it all—don't come here for the variety. Large helpings in a jiffy. Wash it down with *agua fresca* (7 pesos). Tacos 5 pesos. *Tortas* and quesadillas 13 pesos. Open daily 10am-10pm. Cash only. ❶

Cafe Catedral, Portal Hidalgo 197A (☎312 3289), across from the cathedral. Packed tables perfect for people-watching under dazzling cathedral lights. The salads (40-50 pesos) and *tortas* (35 pesos) are a better deal for the peso than the meat dishes (80-100 pesos). Open daily 9am-midnight. MC/V. ❹

Super Tortas Homero (delivery ☎333 0673), on Abasolo at Allende. Great *tortas* (24-30 pesos) in a casual setting draw the crowds—getting a seat is difficult. "El Super" (37 pesos) is a prime choice. Open daily 9am-11:30pm. Cash only. ❷

Los Arraigos, Nigromante 32B (☎312 9222), north of Ocampo. Simple tablecloths, aged wood, and a strange iron wagon wheel complement exquisite *comida michoacána*. Try the *sopa tarasca* (35 pesos), the *mole* dish (80 pesos) or the *paella* (85 pesos). Open daily 9am-10pm. Cash only. ❺

Alborada, Lejarza 36 (☎313 0171), right off Madero. Push past the bakery to the quiet restaurant in back, which offers *comida corrida* (60 pesos) and a generous salad bar. *Energéticos* (yogurt, fruit, and honey) 25 pesos. Breakfasts 22-42 pesos. Open M-Sa 8am-6pm. Bakery open M-Sa 8am-9pm. Cash only. ❹

El Tragadero, Hidalgo 63 (☎313 0092). Tiny cacti and sepia photos dot the dining area. *Comida corrida* (45 pesos) and large helpings of local specialties, like *tlalpeño* or *tarasco* soup (30 pesos). Open M-Sa 7:30am-11pm, Su 7:30am-8pm. Cash only. ❸

👁 SIGHTS

Many of Morelia's famous buildings are ornamented in a style peculiar to the city—imitation Baroque, frequently identifiable by a flat decorative motif on pilasters and columns. The cathedral is an impressive example.

🏛 CATHEDRAL. Overlooking the *zócalo*, the imposing cathedral is a masterpiece of elegant restraint, with simple patterns covering the walls and nave. A gorgeous, 4600-pipe organ commands the back, while the front is dominated by the cathedral's oldest treasure, the 16th-century **Señor de la Sacristía,** an image of Christ sculpted by *indígenas* out of corn cobs and orchid nectar. It is capped by gold crown donated by Phillip II of Spain, covered by its own rotunda. *(Open daily 5:30am-8:30pm. Mass Su every hr. 6am-noon and 6-8pm.)*

MUSEO MICHOACÁNO. This museum hosts exhibits on the anthropology, archaeology, art, ecology, and history of Michoacán. The real treasure here is the odd assortment of artifacts on display, like the monolithic carved crucifix depicting a face, polyglot bibles, suits of armor and old weapons, and an exhaustive exhibit on Tarasco culture. *(Allende 305, at the zócalo. ☎ 312 0407. Open Tu-Sa 9am-4:30pm, Su 9am-3:30pm; 34 pesos, students, seniors, and under 14 free; Su free.)*

CASA DE LA CULTURA. Artists, musicians, and backpackers gather in the sprawling connected courtyards, decked with machine-part statuary. The Casa houses a bookstore, art gallery, theater, and lovely cafe, in addition to hosting art festivals, book signings, and literature workshops. Dance, guitar, piano, sculpture, theater, and voice classes are available. Ask for the weekly schedule of events. *(Morelos Nte. 485, northeast of the zócalo. ☎ 313 1215 or 313 1320. Open daily 8am-6pm.)*

CALZADA FRAY ANTONIO DE SAN MIGUEL. Cutting through the heart of Old Morelia, this pedestrian walk stretches 1km under shady poplars bordered by well-preserved, gorgeous 18th-century stone houses. The eastern end spills onto Plaza Morelos, where there is a bronze statue of the city's namesake hero on horseback. *(Starts just east of Fuente de las Tarascas, under the Acueducto.)*

MUSEO DE MORELOS. Originally a house purchased by José María Morelos, local parish priest and War of Independence hero, the converted museum inside follows his birth, education, and martyrdom, and houses a vast collection of mundane objects that belonged to the family, including agricultural tools, fine china, and sewing scissors. *(Morelos Sur 323, southeast of the cathedral. ☎ 313 2651. Open daily 9am-7pm. 27 pesos; students, seniors, and under 13 free; Su free. Video use 30 pesos.)*

MUSEO DEL ESTADO. A mishmash of exhibits and artifacts from Michoacán, the museum houses a loom, several suits of armor, and an entire reconstructed pharmacy from 1868. The ethnology exhibits explain in fastidious detail the history of the Purépecha and Tarasco peoples, and the modern history of the state is covered as well. *(At Tapia and Guzman, across from Conservatorio de las Rosas. Open M-Sa 9am-2pm and 4-8pm, Su 9am-2pm. Free.)*

CONSERVATORIO DE LAS ROSAS. Built in the 18th century to protect and educate widows and poor or orphaned Spanish girls, the building and its rose-filled courtyard now house Morelia's premiere music school—the oldest in the Americas. Check with the conservatory's public relations office or with the Casa de Cultura for performance schedules. *(Tapia 334, north of the tourist office. ☎ 312 1469. Open M-F 7am-9pm, Sa 8am-2pm. public relations office open M-F 9am-4pm. Some performances free, others 20 pesos. Check schedule for prices.)*

CASA NATAL DE MORELOS. More of a civic building than a museum, the rooms guide you through Morelos's life, with his letters, wartime maps, and baptismal font all on display. Like most other official buildings in the city, it features large murals by Michoacán artist Alfredo Zalce (1908-2003). The house also holds conferences and a bookstore. *(Corregidora 113. ☎312 2793. Open daily 9am-7pm. Free.)*

PALACIO DEL GOBIERNO. Across from the cathedral, the Palacio de Gobierno, Madero 63, has more historical murals by Zalce, including one on the staircase ceiling, imitative of José Orozco's in Guadalajara. *(Palacio de Gobierno open M-F 8am-10pm, Sa-Su 8am-9pm.)*

CASA DE LAS ARTESANÍAS. The **Ex-Convento de San Francisco** houses this massive indoors bazaar, which sells every conceivable handicraft from the towns surrounding Morelia. Downstairs, marvel at prize-winning clay jars, clay figurines, copper ornaments, and hand-carved and -painted wooden furniture. Along the upstairs hallway, crafts are displayed in rooms labeled with their town of origin; Paracho carries guitars, Tocuaro contains devil masks, Huetano sells gold and silver jewelry, and Santa Clara has copper. For better bargains, visit the towns themselves, or nearby Pátzcuaro (p. 481). *(Humboldt, east of the zócalo. ☎312 1248. Open M-Sa 10am-8pm, Su 10am-3:30pm. Free.)*

TIP

CRAFTY SHOPPING. *Artesanías* overflow in the marketplaces of inland Michoacán, from concert guitars to devil masks. The vendors in cities are well aware of their novelty value to tourists, and in cities charge more than the handicrafts are worth. Find out what village the craft is produced in, and head out to buy straight from the producer, where you'll get the lowest price.

BOSQUE CUAUHTÉMOC. The tranquility of the trees and lawns attracts dog-walkers, families, and lovers. Find a patch of grass or head over to the mini-amusement park, with bumper cars (10 pesos) and a train (3 pesos). The **Museo de Historia Natural,** on the east side of the Bosque, features exhibits on the reptiles and plants of the state and a homily to recycling. On the northern side of the Bosque is the **Museo de Arte Contemporaneo Alfredo Zalce,** which displays works in all media by Zalce—one of Michoacán's most celebrated artists—as well as temporary exhibits of contemporary art. *(To get to the Bosque, take a "Ruta Rojo" combi from behind the cathedral on Allende; 4.50 pesos. Amusement park open daily 11:30am-7:30pm. Museo de Historia ☎312 0044. Open daily 10am-6pm. Donations suggested. Museo de Arte ☎312 5404. Open M-F 10am-8pm, Sa-Su 10am-6pm. Free.)*

PARQUE ZOOLÓGICO BENITO JUÁREZ. Housing over 440 species, the zoo has all the exotic safari animals you could want; the herpetarium is excellent and always busy—line up early. The Friday 8pm tour (100 pesos) includes dinner. *(Take a maroon combi south on Nigromante or a pink "Santa María" combi from the tourist office; 4.50 pesos. Or, walk south 3km on Nigromante until it becomes Juárez. Entrance on the west side of zoo. ☎314 0488. Open M-F 10am-5pm, Sa-Su 10am-6pm. 20 pesos, children 10 pesos.)*

OTHER SIGHTS. At the eastern end of Madero is the city's most recognizable landmark, the statue of **Las Tarascas,** three bare-breasted indigenous women offering of *michoacáno* fruit to the heavens. Nearby is **El Acueducto,** built in the 18th century to meet the city's growing water needs. The 253 arches are all that remain of what was once a 7km Baroque marvel. Though no longer functional, it is a magnificent sight at night. Av. Acueducto runs along the aqueduct to the university.

🎵 📷 ENTERTAINMENT AND NIGHTLIFE

The Casa de Cultura and tourist office carry event listings. Lights, music, and theater draw crowds to **Teatro Morelos** (☎314 6202), on Camelina at Ventura Pte., and to **Teatro Ocampo**, Ocampo 256, at Prieto. (☎312 3734. Tickets 50-120 pesos.) **La Casona del Teatro**, Serdán 35, at Morelos one block north of Madero, hosts comedic dramas in Spanish. (☎317 4920. Stop by for a schedule of shows. 75 pesos.) The **Casa Natal de Morelos** (p. 480) shows family movies and holds cultural events. (Films Tu-W 5 and 7pm, 5 pesos.) **Cinepolis Morelia**, on Tapia at Jiménez, next to the conservatory, screens Hollywood's latest. (☎312 1288. Open daily 1:30-10:30pm. Before 6pm 35 pesos, after 6pm 41 pesos.) There is also a **Planetario**, on Ventura Pte. at Ticateme, in the Centro de Convenciones. Take the "Ruta Rojo #3" *combi* from Allende/Valladolid, and watch for the convention center on the right. (☎314 2465. IMAX movies F-Sa 7pm, Su 6:30pm. 25 pesos.)

Classy bars lie at the heart of Morelia's nightlife. Casual establishments pepper the *centro*, while along Camelinas, best reached by taxi (25-30 pesos), upscale clubs and bars draw young, well-dressed clientele.

🃏 Skina Bar, Camelinas 524, down the street from Emporio. Well-dressed, blasé youth smoke at high tables, stealing glances at those entering the space-age tunnel. American and Mexican hip hop fill the massive, high-ceilinged bar. Beer 20 pesos. Mixed drinks 50-70 pesos. Open W-Sa 9pm-4am. Cash only.

El Rincón de los Sentidos, Madero Pte. 485 (☎312 2903). Bright lighting and funky light fixtures complement mellow acoustic music, quiet enough to enjoy your conversation. Beer 20-22 pesos. Liqueur coffee 40-44 pesos. Salads and *antojitos* 40-50 pesos. Th-Sa live music. Open daily 9am-1am. Cash only.

Los Idolos, Allende 355, just east of Galeana. Loud electronica competes with the roar of conversation from the tables and booths packed into an antique stone courtyard. People of all ages drink cheap beer (10 pesos). Mixed drinks 35-45 pesos. Open daily 10pm-3am. Cash only.

Madrezz L'Pchange, Aldama 116 (☎317 5380), at Obeso. A casual gay and lesbian establishment. A loud lounge-bar where patrons nurse their drinks in oversized chairs, talking over the music. Cover 30 pesos. Beers 20 pesos. Mixed drinks 40-55 pesos. Open F-Sa 9pm-3am. Cash only.

Emporio, Camelinas 1194. Split-level chaos as thumping music draws dancers to the central floor, rendering conversation impossible on the raised level above, where young and beautiful clientele sip drinks. Cover men 100 pesos, women 50 pesos. Beer 20 pesos. Mixed drinks 55-75 pesos. Open Th-Sa 11pm-3:30am. Cash only.

PÁTZCUARO
☎434

Out-of-the-way Pátzcuaro (pop. 75,000) is a small frenzy, with market stalls and traffic competing for the dirty street space in front of the town's monotonous red-and-white colonial buildings. To spur economic development in the 1530s, Spanish Bishop Vasco de Quiroga encouraged residents of each Purépecha village around picturesque (but polluted) Lake Pátzcuaro to specialize in different crafts; today an overwhelming array of *artesanías* draws tourists from all over Michoacán. Pátzcuaro's major sights may be best suited as a daytrip from Morelia.

📧 TRANSPORTATION. Pátzcuaro lies 56km southwest of Morelia and 62km northeast of Uruapan. To reach the *centro* from the bus station off Circunvalación, 8 blocks south of the *centro*, catch a combi (7am-9:30pm, 4 pesos) or city bus (6:30am-10pm, 4 pesos) from the lot to the right of the station. Taxis cost 20 pesos. **Primera Plus/Flecha Amarilla** (☎342 0960) sends first-class buses to: **Guadalajara** (4½hr., 11:30pm, 231 pesos); **Mexico City** (6hr.; 12:15am, 11:20am, 3pm; 270 pesos); **Morelia** (1hr.; 6am, 8:20pm, midnight; 30 pesos); **Puerto Vallarta** (8hr., 8:10pm, 588 pesos). **Autotransportes Galeana/Ruta Paraíso** (☎342 0808) heads to **Uruapan** (1hr., every 30min. 5:30am-9:30pm, 37 pesos).

⌐ PRACTICAL INFORMATION. For **tourist information,** maps, and lots of helpful info about Pátzcuaro and the state, head to the **Delegación Regional,** Ahumada 9B, just north of Plaza Grande. (☎342 1214. Open M-F 9am-2pm and 5-7pm, Sa-Su 9am-2pm.) **Banamex,** Portal Juárez 32, on the west side of Plaza Chica, has a **24hr. ATM** and **currency exchange.** (☎342 1550. Open M-F 9am-4pm, Sa 10am-2pm.) **Luggage storage** available at the bus station. (5 pesos per hr. Open daily 7am-10pm.) Other services include: **emergency: Protección Civil** (☎342 5656); **police** on Ibarra, between Espejo and Tangara, inside the Agencia del Ministero Público (☎342 2016); **Farmacia Popular,** on Ibarra at Codallos. (☎342 3242. Open daily 9am-10pm); **Hospital Civil,** Romero 10, next to San Juan de Dios (☎342 0285. Open 24hr.); **Internet access** at **Meg@Net,** Mendoza 8, between Plaza Chica and Plaza Grande (10 pesos per hr. Open M-Sa 9am-9pm, Su 10am-9pm.); and the **post office:** at Obregón 13, half a block north of Plaza Chica. (☎342 0128. Open M-F 8am-4pm, Sa 9am-1pm). **Postal Code:** 61600.

⌐ ACCOMMODATIONS AND FOOD. Hotel Valmen ❸, Lloreda 34, 1 block east of Plaza Chica. is a gorgeously painted retreat from the *centro*. Beautiful tile and big, airy rooms come with equally big and clean baths. Valmen is popular with travelers; make reservations for weekends. (☎342 1161. Singles 180 pesos; doubles 240 pesos; triples 300 pesos. Cash only.) For couples or groups, **Mandala ❺,** Lerín 14, near Casa de los Once Patios, is unbeatable. A cozy lobby with elegant art leads to spacious rooms with candles and hand-crafted wood furniture. Baths are immaculate. (☎342 4176. Singles and doubles 300 pesos; triples 400 pesos. Upstairs rooms with private bathrooms are 200 pesos more. Prices vary for *Semana Santa* and *Noche de los Muertos*. Cash only.)

Cheap restaurants surround Plaza Chica and the accompanying market, while fancier joints crowd the hotels on Plaza Grande. *Pescado blanco* (whitefish), *charales* (small fried fish, eaten whole), and *caldo de pescado* (fish soup) are regional specialties—most restaurants can whip them up. Massive dishes come with plenty of sides at **Cha Cha Cha ❹,** Buena Vista 7 at the top of the hill. *Artesanía* plates and tablecloths lend a local charm to the tables packed with families. (☎342 1626. Meat dishes 65-75 pesos. Vegetarian pastas 55-70 pesos. Open daily noon-9:30pm. Cash only.) For cheap and fast Mexican staples, hit **El Asadero ❶,** Ibarra 16, west of Plaza Grande. Huge, cheap *tortas* (15-20 pesos) and *antojitos* (10-25 pesos) satisfy your hunger in a pleasant, tiled courtyard. (Traditional Mexican dishes 45-50 pesos. Open daily 9am-9pm. Cash only.) There is a supermarket, **Merzapack,** at Mendoza 24 (☎342 5255; open daily 7am-10pm). For late-night eats, head to the food stands that pop up in Plaza Chica after dusk.

◙ SIGHTS. Conceived of and ordered by the bishop who towers in the region's history, the simple yet elegant **Basílica de Nuestra Señora de la Salud** has an unusual, asymmetrical set of five chapels off the nave. Conflicting tales explain their significance: they may represent five major body parts (the head, two arms, and two legs), Christ's five wounds, or Quiroga's ideals for Christian society—honesty, justice, love, wisdom, and work. Locals pray to la Virgen de la Salud, a figure made of Tarascan *tatzingue* (corn cob paste and honey), housed in a domed, gilded booth in back. (At Lerín and Serrato. Open daily 7am-8pm. Mass Su every hr. 7am-1pm, 7, and 8pm. Office open M-F 10am-1:30pm and 5-7pm.)

CROSSING OVER. By far the most spectacular of Pátzcuaro's religious festivals is **Noche de los Muertos** (Oct. 31-Nov. 2). Mexicans and tourists crowd on to candle lit *lanchas,* which travel to the island of Janitzio all day and night. The first night commemorates lost children; the second honors deceased adults.

Built in 1540 to house the Colegio de San Nicolás de Obispo, the fort-like walls of the **Museo Regional de Artes Populares** enclose a flower-filled courtyard with *artesanías* from the villages around the lake. In the back are Purépecha ruins. (Enseñanza 20, at Alcanterilla, 1 block south of the Basílica. ☎342 1029. Open Tu-Sa 9am-7pm, Su 9am-3pm. Admission and tour 34 pesos.) The back wall of **Biblioteca Gertrudis Bocanegra**—a church dating from 1576, now converted into a library—displays an incredible 1941 mural by Juan O'Gorman. La Historia de Michoacán begins with the Purépecha creation story and ends with the Revolution. Painted into it are O'Gorman and his wife, Vasco de Quiroga (1470-1565; Michoacán's 1st bishop), Morelos, and, harder to spot, Hitler. (Next to the Teatro Caltzontzín. ☎342 5441. Open M-F 9am-7pm, Sa 10am-2pm.)

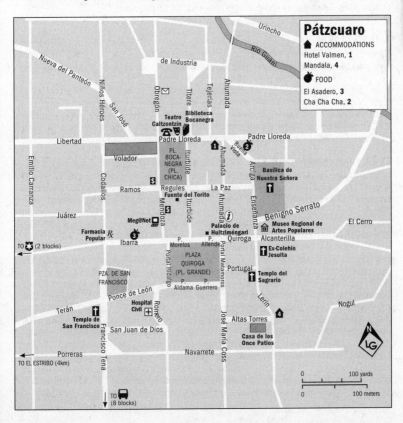

On **Isla de Janitzio**, a 20min. boat ride away in the middle of the lake, *indígena* inhabitants have largely preserved their dress and customs, including the beautiful spectacle of *Noche de Muertos*. Masks, pottery, and other *artesanías* are much cheaper here than on the mainland. On part of the island stands a 40m monument to Morelos, hero of the War for Independence. (☎342 0681. Round-trip *lanchas colectivas* available daily 8am-5pm, 30 pesos.) Outside of town, **El Estribo** is a lookout point near the top of a hill. The view of the Lago de Pátzcuaro and the surrounding hills is magnificent. The trip is best made in the morning, when other people make the climb; it's inadvisable to walk the dark road there after dusk. (Approx. 4km from town west on Navarrete; about a 1hr. walk.)

🗋 **SHOPPING.** Markets and storefront on **Plaza Chica** and the western side of **Plaza Grande** hawk Pátzcuaro's unique crafts—hairy Tócuaro masks, elegant Sierra dinnerware, and thick wool textiles. Bargaining is easier in the market or when you buy more than one item, but Pátzcuaro's special wool sweaters, *sarapes* (blankets), *rebozos* (shawls), and *ruanas* (capes) are often non-negotiable. *Artesanías* from farther afield are for sale, too. (Most shops open daily 8am-8pm.) Higher-quality and more expensive items are at **La Casa de los Once Patios,** on Lerín near Navarrete. Prices may be fixed to discourage haggling. Dance performances are held in the main courtyard, usually on weekends. (Open daily 10am-8pm; some shops close in the afternoon.)

ZAMORA ☎351

Zamora (pop. 156,000), affectionately known as *"la cuna de hombres ilustres"* (the cradle of illustrious men), has nurtured such greats as poet Manuel Martínez de Navarrete (1768-1809) and Alfonso García Robles (1911-1991), whose nuclear disarmament efforts earned a Nobel Peace Prize. A city with a small-town feel, it thrives on its potatoes, sweet strawberries, and even sweeter *dulces* (candies). Zamora doesn't have much in the way of attractions—the gorgeous Gothic cathedral in progress is worth a visit, but other than that, it's best suited as a pit stop between Guadalajara and Morelia for exploring Michoacán's natural beauty.

📧 🛂 **TRANSPORTATION AND PRACTICAL INFORMATION.** To get to the *centro* from the **bus station,** on Juárez at the edge of town, take a "Central" bus (5 pesos) from Colón and Hidalgo or a **taxi** (20 pesos). **Autobuses de Occidente/La Línea** (☎515 1119) goes to: **Guadalajara** (3hr., 7 per day 5:15am-5:30pm, 128 pesos); **Colima** (5hr.; 2:45am, 2:15, 11:30pm; 161 pesos); **Mexico City** (9hr., 11pm, 273 pesos) via **Toluca** (7hr., 208 pesos); **Uruapan** (2½hr., 5 per day 5:15am-4:45pm, 65 pesos). **ETN** (☎515 6400), **Estrella Blanca** (☎515 1133), and **Primera Plus** (☎515 1316) provide similar services. **Transportes del Pacífico** (☎515 1125) motors to the north.

Most activity is centered in or around the *centro*, bordered by **Nervo** to the north, **Guerrero** to the south, **Morelos** to the west, and **Allende** to the east. **Hidalgo** curves north behind the cathedral, intersected by **Ocampo,** which runs east-west a block north of the *centro*. The **tourist office,** Morelos Sur 76, two and a half blocks north of Nervo, provides maps and other info. (☎512 4015 or 7781. Open M-F 9am-2pm and 4-7pm, Sa-Su 10am-2pm.) **Bancomer,** Morelos 250 at Nervo, has a **24hr. ATM.** (☎512 2600. Open M-F 8:30am-4pm, Sa 10am-2pm. **Currency exchange** M-F 8:30am-3:30pm.) Other services include: **emergency** ☎060; **police,** Ejercito Nacional 243B at Ocampo, 5 blocks east of the *centro*. (☎512 0022 or 0133); **Red Cross,** on Calle Mendoza, 1km south of the *centro* (☎512 0534); **Farmacia Guadalajara,** Nervo 21, in the plaza (☎515 7055; open 24hr.); **Hospital Municipal,** Serdán 256 (☎512 1202 or 532

0746); **Internet** access at **Oficom,** Hidalgo 99, at Colón (☎ 512 1713; 8 pesos per hr.; open M-Sa 9am-9pm); and the **post office,** Hidalgo 112, at Colón, in the Palacio Federal (☎ 512 0205; open M-F 8:30am-4pm, Sa 9am-noon). **Postal Code:** 59600.

▐▀▐▘ ACCOMMODATIONS AND FOOD. Lodgings are not plentiful in Zamora, but what exists is affordable and clean. For your money's worth, head over to **Hotel Alameda ❸,** Corregidora 88, off the *centro*. Thoroughly furnished rooms are clean and open, with enormous bed, cable TV, and fan. (☎ 512 0722. Singles 170 pesos; doubles 210 pesos; triples 250 pesos; quads 300 pesos. Cash only.) Family-oriented **Hotel Nacional ❸,** Corregidora 106, just off the *centro*, has small yet comfy rooms, tidy baths, and a fourth-floor terrace. (☎ 512 4224. Singles 170 pesos; doubles 290 pesos. Cash only.)

Zamora's small selection of restaurants often close by 7pm, but candy shops are open until 9pm or so. For pizza, try **Buona Pizza ❶,** on Madero at Corregidora, southwest of the *centro*. Excellent fare makes up for the lack of decor. (☎ 512 2525. Hamburgers 40 pesos. Pasta 55 pesos. Pizzas from 80 pesos. Open daily 10am-9pm. Cash only.) **La Pantera Rosa ❸** (The Pink Panther), Hidalgo Sur 234, has pink-clad waiters serving up the exquisite house special, *carnes asadas en su jugo* (grilled beef with beans in broth; 46-52 pesos) and 25-peso quesadillas. (☎ 512 1866. Open daily 10am-10pm. Cash only.) For local sweets, hamburgers, and tacos try the **Mercado Morelos,** by the *centro* across from the cathedral. (Entrees 25-35 pesos. Open daily 8am-8pm. Cash only.)

◪ SIGHTS. The **Catedral Inconclusa,** formally known as Santuario Guadalupe, is a shocking and glorious departure from standard Mexican Baroque architecture. Building began in 1898 but was halted in 1914. Renovations started in 1988, and are estimated to continue for the next few years. The Gothic spires, though not yet at their completed height of 90m, are nonetheless awe-inspiring. The austere stone interior supports soaring naves with tiny cupolas on top. The swirling blue-and-red stained glass behind the altar is startlingly beautiful. Wander around—it's largely empty besides a few onlookers and the occasional hammering workman. (Office outside to the left of the church. Open M-F 9:30am-2pm and 5-8pm, Sa 9:30am-2pm.) Nearby, marvel at the **Géiser de Ixtlán's** occasional bursts and soak in the surrounding hot springs. (Served by a "Ixtlán" bus, every hr. from 5 de Mayo and Juárez, 15 pesos.)

URUAPAN ☎ 452

Green hills capped with clouds and grove upon grove of avocado trees hide Michoacán's second largest city, Uruapan (pop. 300,000). The city's temperate climate is sullied by dust, diesel, and crumbling, graffitied buildings that surround the *zócalo*, a surprising oasis in the midst of unremarkable semi-squalor. However, it serves as a prime base for exploring the natural beauty and diverse climates of Michoacán. Tourists come in droves to explore the nearby waterfalls and Parque Nacional Tzarácua, as well as to make the pilgrimage to the 16th-century crucifix in nearby San Juan Nuevo.

▐▘ TRANSPORTATION. To reach the *centro* from the **bus station,** on Juárez in the northeastern corner of town, hail a taxi (20 pesos) or hop on a "Centro" bus. Later in the day, you may have to board at the alternate bus stop on the street in front of the station (5 pesos). From the station, **La Línea/Autobuses de Occidente** (☎ 523 1871) sends first-class buses to: **Colima** (6hr., 9:45pm, 210 pesos); **Guadalajara** (4½hr., 6 per day 3am-midnight, 189 pesos); **Manzanillo** (9hr., 9:45pm, 278 pesos); **Mexico City** (7hr., 13 per day 12:15am-midnight, 335 pesos); **Zamora** (2hr.; 6:30, 11:30am, 12:30, 4:30pm,

65 pesos); **Zihuatanejo** (8 hr., 7pm, 230 pesos). Second-class buses serve the same destinations at slightly lower prices. **Primera Plus/Flecha Amarilla** (☎524 3982) and **ETN** (☎523 8608) have similar service at higher prices. **Autotransportes Galeana/Ruta Paraíso** (☎524 4154) and **Parhikuni** (☎523 8754) go to regional destinations.

⚡ PRACTICAL INFORMATION. Uruapan lies 120km west of Morelia and 320km southeast of Guadalajara. Most services are clumped near the *zócalo*, where two streets—**Vicente Carranza** (running north-south) and **Emilio Carranza** (the principal east-west road)—honor the Carranza clan. Find **tourist information** at **Casa Regional del Turista**, E. Carranza 20, a short walk from the *zócalo*. (☎524 0677. Open daily 9am-3pm and 5:30-7:30pm.) The **Delegación Regional de Turismo,** Ayala 16, offers information on the city as well as destinations throughout the state. (☎524 7199. Open daily 9am-2pm and 4-7pm.) On weekends, you can get the same maps from the **info booth** in the bus station. (Open Sa-Su 9:30am-6pm.) **Bancomer,** E. Carranza 7, **exchanges currency** at good rates and has a **24hr. ATM.** (☎524 1460. Open M-F 8:30am-4pm, Sa 10am-2pm.) **Luggage storage** is available at the bus station. (5 pesos per bag per hr. Open daily 7am-11pm.) Other services include: **laundry** at **Autoservicio de Lavandería,** E. Carranza 47 at García (☎523 2669; full service 30 pesos per 3kg; open M-Sa 9am-2pm and 4-8pm.); **emergency** ☎060; **police,** at Eucaliptos and Naranjo (☎523 5515 or 2733); **Red Cross,** Del Lago 1, a block from the hospital (☎524 0300); **24hr. Farmacia Guadalajara,** E. Carranza 3 (☎524 2711; open 24hr.; AmEx/MC/V); **Hospital Civil de Uruapan,** San Miguel 6, seven blocks west of the northern edge of the *zócalo* (☎524 2550); **Internet** access at **Cyber@home,** Independencia 10A (10 pesos per hr.; open daily 9am-8:30pm.); and the **post office,** on Jalisco just east of Villa, 1km east of the *centro* along 16 de Septiembre. (☎523 5630. Open M-F 9am-3pm, Sa 9am-1pm). **Postal Code:** 60000.

⧈⧇ ACCOMMODATIONS AND FOOD. Budget options are plentiful on the east side just south of the market. Creeping vines and the ambient heat at **Hotel Moderno ❶,** Portal Degollado 4, on the east side of the *zócalo*, make the courtyard an antique greenhouse. Rooms have firm beds, charming dark green furniture, and cavernous baths. (☎524 0212. Singles and doubles 100 pesos; triples 150 pesos. Cash only.) West of the *zócalo* and half a block from the Parque Nacional, **Hotel del Parque ❸,** Independencia 124, is a peaceful retreat from the dirt and noise of the *centro*. Small, quaint rooms with big beds open onto a tranquil patio. All rooms have gorgeous new bath and cable TV. Reservations are recommended in high season. (☎524 3845. Singles 195 pesos, with TV 225 pesos; doubles 275 pesos; triples 295 pesos. Cash only.) **Nuevo Hotel Alameda de Uruapan ❺,** 5 de Febrero 11, half a block from the *zócalo*, is a better deal for groups. The hefty price pays for a bit of luxury, with marble floors, bellhops, and spotless bath. Rooms also come with A/C, cable, and picture windows. (☎523 4100. Reception 24hr. Singles 370 pesos; doubles 440 pesos; triples 520 pesos. MC/V.)

Cheap joints and slightly classier cafes vie for space in the *zócalo*. Coffee and avocados are the local specialties, available on every corner. For the cheapest meals in town, try the food stands and small restaurants inside the *mercado*. **Mercado de Antojitos,** between Constitución and V. Carranza, on the north side of the *zócalo*, is a zoo of noise, sizzling meat, and rambunctious children. Aggressive owners call out the litany of menu items, offering up an amazing variety of Mexican staples. Try the fabulous *atole de leche* (a hot, thick, cornstarch-based sweet drink) for 6 pesos. (Open daily 8am-midnight. Cash only.) At **Cafe La Pergola ❹,** Portal Carrillo 4, on the south side of the *zócalo*, suited waitstaff and stiff black chairs lend class to the half-lit, brick-and-vine eatery. Admire the lurid, menacing

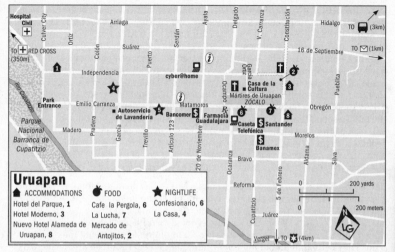

Uruapan

▲ ACCOMMODATIONS
Hotel del Parque, 1
Hotel Moderno, 3
Nuevo Hotel Alameda de
    Uruapan, 8

🍎 FOOD
Cafe la Pergola, 6
La Lucha, 7
Mercado de
    Antojitos, 2

★ NIGHTLIFE
Confesionario, 6
La Casa, 4

SOUTHERN PACIFIC COAST

mural while sampling *enchiladas uruapan* for 55 pesos, avocado drinks for 30 pesos, or soup for 40 pesos. (☎523 5087. Open daily 8am-11:30 pm. Cash only.) Locals pack **La Lucha ❷**, Portal Matamoros 15, on the plaza. The overpowering aroma as you sip a chocolate or coffee (10 pesos) or eat some *pastel* (sweet bread; 15 pesos) will make you feel alive. (☎524 0375. Open daily 9am-9pm. Cash only.)

🎫 🎵 **SIGHTS AND ENTERTAINMENT.** During *Semana Santa*, regional artisans flood the city, parading in alphabetical order according to their home community. The craftsmen (and women) compete for the title of best artisan, proffering clay figurines, dresses, and more. Otherwise, most of Uruapan's dazzling sights are located just outside the city. **Parque Nacional Barranca del Cupatitzio,** on San Miguel at the western end of Independencia, is a stunning bit of jungle on the edge of town. The park brims with waterfalls, dense vegetation, shaded cobblestone walkways, and a fishing pond. Local lore maintains the spring formed where the devil tripped while running from a priest's blessing. (☎524 0197. Open daily 8am-6pm. 15 pesos, under 10 and over 70 12 pesos.)

For nighttime entertainment, **Confesionario,** E. Carranza 25A, is a classy cantina-bar with live acoustic music on weekends and karaoke contests on other nights. (☎526 0489. Beers 23-25 pesos. Mixed drinks 40-60 pesos. Open daily 7pm-3am. Cash only.) **La Casa,** Revolución 3, four blocks west of the *centro*, offers a more laid-back vibe. Couples and friends come here to relax and chat in the leafy courtyard with fountain. (Beer 20-22 pesos. Happy hour M-F 7-8pm. Mixed drinks 40-45 pesos. Open M-W and Su 10am-midnight, Th-Sa 10am-2am. MC/V.)

📌 **DAYTRIPS FROM URUAPAN**

Uruapan's saving grace is its location in the heart of the beautiful interior of Michoacán. Mountains, old cinder cones, and national parks with massive cascades are all a short bus ride away. If you are saturated with natural beauty, check out the revered image of Christ in San Juan Nuevo that was rescued by the village after a volcano eruption.

TZARÁRACUA AND TZARARECUITA. Just 15km from Uruapan is **Parque Nacional Tzaráracua,** a lush jungle area housing two roaring 20m **waterfalls.** The first, Tzaráracua (sah-RA-ra-kwa), is only 2km from the parking lot. Walk down the steps to the right or ride a horse (round-trip from the parking lot 70 pesos), down the rocky path to the left. At the main waterfall look but don't swim—there's a dangerous undercurrent. Gaze from the bridge, or for an epic view above, take the cable car over the river (50 pesos). Tzararecuita (sah-ra-reh-KWEE-ta), 2km farther, is a totally secluded waterfall with two smaller pools perfect for swimming. To get there, cross the bridge and head to the right. A small path leads to the top of the hill. Descend the other side of the hill, the pools are at the bottom. For a guide, ask one of the horse handlers or many boys hanging around the bridge; most request a fee of 50 pesos. *(Park open daily 8am-6pm. 10 pesos, children 5 pesos. Parking 5 pesos. "Zapata-Tzaráracua" or #4 buses leave the south side of the zócalo (25min., every hr. 7am-5pm, 4 pesos.) Return bus departs parking lot every hr. until 6pm. Taxis 70-80 pesos.)*

NUEVO SAN JUAN. 17km west of Uruapan, Nuevo San Juan was founded after the destruction of the old village by the Paricutín Volcano in May of 1944. Many penitents visit the village to see the **Lord of Miracles,** an image of Christ dating back to the late 16th century. When the volcano erupted, San Juan's 2000 inhabitants abandoned the village and began a three-day 33km pilgrimage carrying their beloved icon. They settled in an old *hacienda,* and built a beautiful rose-brick sanctuary with pastel tiles to house the image. Gold leaf, stained-glass windows, and intricate designs adorn the two domed towers; on the walls, murals visually retell the story. (Open daily 6am-8pm; mass Su approx. every hr. 6:30am-1:30pm and 5-7pm.) **Museo de Volcán Paricutín,** on Av. 20 de Noviembre, a block past the cathedral to the right once you exit the church, has photos of the eruption. (Open daily 9am-7:30pm. Free.) A **mercado** in front of the cathedral sells *artesanías* and much more at good prices. Toward the back of the cathedral, you'll stumble upon the cheapest and tastiest food in town. *(From the Uruapan bus station, take a Purhépechas bus to San Juan Nuevo.* ☎524 4154. *40min., every 10min. 5am-8pm, 7-10 pesos. Alternatively, catch the bus as it passes the "San Juan Nuevo" bus stop on Juárez between 5 de Febrero and Cupatitzio. To return, catch the bus on the corner of Obregón and Iturbide, 2 blocks from the cathedral.)*

LÁZARO CÁRDENAS   ☎753

Named after the famed *Michoacáno* president who nationalized oil in 1938 and instituted radical land reform, the hot, noisy city of Lázaro Cárdenas (pop. 163,000) is one of Mexico's most important Pacific ports. The services you won't find in many other places on the Michoacán coast are the city's main draw, since there is little or nothing to do here, and the lack of an off-shore breeze makes the city noticeably more sweaty and uncomfortable than the tranquil towns that line the coast nearby. This and the lack of beaches or natural beauty make Lázaro Cárdenas good for little more than an overnight stay or a pit stop.

▐ TRANSPORTATION. Lázaro Cárdenas Airport (**LZC;** ☎532 1920), on the town's outskirts, hosts **Aerolínea Cuahonte** (☎532 3635 or 4900) and **Transporte Aeromar** (☎537 1084). **Buses** depart from independent stations around the main drag. **Autotransportes Cuauhtémoc** and **Estrella Blanca,** Villa 65 (☎532 0426), two blocks west of Cárdenas, goes to: **Acapulco** (5½hr., 8 per day 6am-midnight, 196 pesos); **Morelia** (6hr.; 2:30, 10pm; 253 pesos); **Puerto Escondido** (5:30pm, 400 pesos); **Zihuatanejo** (2hr., every 2hr. 4:45am-midnight, 72 pesos). **Estrella Blanca** provides second-class service to: **Acapulco** (6½hr., every hr. 6:30am-4:30pm, 151 pesos); **Mexico City** (10hr.; 8am, 5, 10, 10:05pm; 455 pesos); **Zihuatanejo** (2½hr., every hr. 2:30am-9pm, 66 pesos). **Autotransportes Galeana,** Cárdenas 1810 (☎532 0262),

Estrella de Oro, Corregidora 318 (☎532 0275), and **La Línea,** Cárdenas 171 (☎537 1850), offer similar service. **Parhikuni** (☎532 3006), at the Galeana station, sends buses to **Morelia** (310 pesos) and **Uruapan** (210 pesos).

⚑ PRACTICAL INFORMATION. Get the maps and info you need to conquer the coast from the **Delegación Regional de Turismo,** Rector Hidalgo 120E, three blocks west of the Palacio Municipal (☎/fax 532 1547. Open M-F 9am-2pm and 4-7pm, Sa 9am-2pm.) **Banamex,** Cárdenas 1646, **exchanges currency** and has an **ATM.** (☎532 2020. Open M-F 9am-4pm, Sa 10am-2pm.) **HBSC,** Cárdenas 1940, also has one. (☎537 2376. Open M-Sa 8am-7pm.) **Luggage storage** is in the Estrella Blanca bus station. (5 pesos per bag per hr.) Other services include: **police** (☎532 2030), in the Palacio Municipal on Cárdenas at H. Escuela Naval; **Red Cross,** Aldama 327 (☎532 0575); **Farmacia París,** Cárdenas 2002 (☎532 1435; open 24hr.); **Hospital General,** Av. 20 de Noviembre 314 (☎532 2842); **Centro de Salud** (☎535 0004), on Cárdenas; **Caseta Goretti,** Corregidora 79, with long-distance **phone** and **fax** service (☎537 3155; open daily 8am-midnight); **Internet** at **Discotienda e Internet,** Cárdenas 1738, at Mina (10 pesos per hr.; open daily 8am-10pm); and the **post office,** Bravo 1307 (☎532 0547; open M-F 8am-4pm, Sa 9am-1pm). **Postal Code:** 60950.

⛏♨ ACCOMMODATIONS AND FOOD. Lázaro Cárdenas unfortunately matches its lack of attractions with a lack of budget accommodations. Expensive hotels with aquatic names are interspersed with a few cheaper options. **Hotel Costa Azul ❸,** 5 de Mayo 276, is a quiet option off the main drag, with clean tile grounding medium-size rooms, some with caged balconies. All rooms have big beds, TV, fan, and bright. (☎532 1816. Reception 24hr. Singles 160 pesos; doubles 195 pesos; triples 230 pesos; quads 260 pesos. Cash only.) A little more luxury comes with **Hotel Delfín ❹,** Cárdenas 1633, whose beautiful pool offsets the green stucco of the lobby. Rooms lack ornament but clean and well-kept, with fan, bath, and phone. (☎532 0373. Reception 24hr. Singles 250 pesos, with A/C 400 pesos; doubles 350/450 pesos. MC/V.) **Hotel Veronica ❸,** Mina 47, is the cheapest option in town. Small, stark rooms come with fan and bath. (☎532 3409. Reception 24hr. Singles 160 pesos; doubles 190 pesos; triples 220 pesos; quads 250 pesos. Cash only.)

For cheap eats, the street beside the Galeana bus station is full of *torta* and taco stands that are always crowded with people. **Alen's Burger ❸,** Plaza Zirahuen L-42, upstairs on Morelos, brings in a young crowd with soft alt-rock and patterned metal light fixtures. Alen's offers hamburgers (25 pesos) and veggie burgers (30 pesos), as well as traditional Mexican *botanas* (appetizers). (☎532 0687. *Antojitos* 30-35 pesos. Beer 15 pesos. Open daily 3-11pm. Cash only.) **El Tejado ❺,** Cárdenas 1670, is a classy sit-down eatery with families occupying the big wicker chairs. Vines creep out from under the ceiling, contrasting with the sepia pictures of the city in past years. The chipotle beef (100 pesos) is the house special. (☎532 0140. Entrees 75-100 pesos. Beer 20 pesos. Indulgent flutes of Courvoisier 80 pesos. Open daily noon-midnight. Cash only.) **El Paraíso ❷,** Cárdenas 1862, by the Galeana bus station, offers traditional fare but little illumination in a central location. The *sopa de tortilla* (20 pesos) and chicken (35 pesos) are both worth a try. The pool tables and bar, busy at night, suit the dark, smoky atmosphere. (☎532 3233. Beer 16-20 pesos. *Comida corrida* 25 pesos. Cash only.)

▧ NIGHTLIFE. Most of Lázaro Cárdenas shuts down after dark, but trendy video-bars, full of young people and occasional live music, dot the city. Adolescents and college-age kids line the couches of **7 Pecados,** Matamoros 508, one block off Cárdenas. An intimate lounge with low tables sits under flickering strobe lights. The occasional live acoustic music distracts from the videoscreen playing Madonna videos in the back. (☎532 0913. Beer 20-25 pesos. Mixed drinks

45-60 pesos. Open daily 6pm-3am. Cash only.) **Video Bar NH,** Circuito de las Univ. 60, outside the *centro*, is a similar but more distant option. Wednesday through Saturday, this small bar area features live acoustic music starting at 10pm and a big screen for current hits and eclectic ones from past decades. (☎533 2900. Beer 25 pesos. Mixed drinks 50-60 pesos. Open Tu-Sa 6pm-1am. Cash only.)

MICHOACÁN COAST

Michoacán's coast is wild land, with sheer cliffs hundreds of meters tall guarding totally inaccessible beaches, broken occasionally by a stretch of flat, uninhabitable land. Tropical vegetation lends a touch of green to the state's 260km of virgin beach. Mex. 200, the solitary coastal route, twists up, down, and around the angry terrain, making for beautiful vistas, though possibly nauseating rides. The surf is rough and the tide dangerous: good for surfing but dangerous for swimming.

> ❗ **ALONE IN THE DARK.** Use extreme caution when exploring the Michoacán coast—there are **no lifeguards.** As always, it is not a good idea to walk on the beach at night. Mex. 200 tends to be deserted at night: *Let's Go* does not recommend traveling after dark.

PLAYA AZUL   ☎753

Playa Azul (pop. 5000), a small Pacific town 26km west of Lázaro Cárdenas, is renowned for its soft, golden sands and majestic, rose-colored sunsets. Despite the wide, well-paved roads, Playa Azul is a small *pueblito* at heart—residents all make sure to greet visitors warmly. The tempting waves attract surfers and boogie boarders, but the strong undercurrent makes swimming treacherous. Though crowded with Mexican tourists during December and *Semana Santa*, the beach is otherwise very quiet. All the usual accoutrements of a *pueblo* are present: unmarked dirt roads, thatched-roof houses, and open-air markets criss-cross the town, while chickens and tanned locals in bathing suits walk the streets. The village is so small that street names are seldom used (or known) by residents.

■■ **TRANSPORTATION AND PRACTICAL INFORMATION.** The *malecón* runs along the beach; it is called **Serdán** to the west of the plaza and **Zapata** to the east. The other streets bordering the plaza are **Montes de Oca** to the west and **Filomena Mata** to the east. **Lázaro Cárdenas** runs from **Mex. 200** into Playa Azul, perpendicular to the beach, intersecting Carranza, Madero, and Independencia, which parallel the beach. From Lázaro Cárdenas, in front of Coppel by Corregidora, catch a "Playa Azul" *combi* straight to the beach (45min., every 20min. 5am-9pm, 12 pesos). To get to **Caleta de Campos** from Playa Azul, catch a *combi* across from the PEMEX station (5min., every 10min., 5 pesos) and ask the driver to let you off at Acalpican, a marked intersection near a bridge just to the north. From there, hail a bus labeled "Caleta" (1hr., every 30min. 5:45am-8:30pm, 40 pesos).

Playa Azul has **no bank or casa de cambio,** but does offer most other services: **surf board** and **boogie board rental** from several beachfront shops, including Coco's Pizza; **police,** across from the PEMEX station on Cárdenas and Independencia (☎532 1855 or 0370; staffed 8am-8pm); **Farmacia Cristo Rey,** on Magón in front of Martita (open daily 9am-9pm); **Centro de Salud,** next door to the post office, (open 8am-6pm); **LADATEL phones,** on the *malecón* or along Independencia; and the **post office,** on Venustiano Carranza at Montes de Oca, just behind Hotel María Teresa (☎536 0113; open M-F 9am-3pm). **Postal Code:** 60982.

ACCOMMODATIONS. The lodgings in Playa Azul range from hammocks to luxuriously spacious rooms. The disparity is reflected in the price. Call ahead in August, December, and during *Semana Santa*. **Hotel del Pacífico ❶**, on Zapata (the *malecón*), six blocks from Lázaro Cárdenas, is the best value for your money in Playa Azul. The simple, comfortable beds and fan offset the slightly worn bathrooms. (☎536 0106. Reception 9am-midnight, but open for guests 24hr. Singles 100 pesos; doubles 150 pesos. Cash only.) The upstairs rooms at **Hotel Andrea ❺**, Zapata 879, command a sweeping view of the rough breakers. Sparkling rooms and fan give a bright, airy feel, complemented by clean, white-tile bathrooms. At 600 pesos, the large six-bed room with bath is ideal for groups. (☎536 0251. Reception 24hr. Singles 200 pesos, rooms for 2-3 300 pesos; for 4-6 450 pesos. Cash only.) **Hotel Costa de Oro ❷**, on Madero, three blocks from Lázaro Cárdenas, is an inviting option overlooking a dirt courtyard and a small pool. Small, simple rooms come with linens and clean spacious bathrooms. (☎536 0086. Singles 150 pesos; doubles 200 pesos, with TV. Cash only. Ring bell for reception after 11:30pm.)

FOOD. *Palapa* seafood joints outline the town's beaches, while inland you can find more traditional Mexican fare. At **⊠Nuestro Bar ❺**, upstairs at Zapata and Lázaro Cárdenas, you can sip coconut milk straight out of the husk (20 pesos) as you watch the waves roll over the shore from the second-floor deck. The view makes the splurge on the food worth it, though the seafood entrees (125-145 pesos) are excellent on their own. (☎536 0098. Hamburgers 30 pesos. Cheap *antojitos* 35-50 pesos. Open M-Th and Su 5-11pm, F-Sa 5pm-2am. AmEx/MC/V.) **Restaurante Familiar Martita ❷**, on Magón at Madero, two blocks inland, is a cozy, family-run restaurant with reasonably-priced breakfast plates that leave you full all day long. (☎536 0111. Breakfast 30 pesos. *Comida corrida* 35 pesos. Open daily 7am-11pm. Cash only.) The beachfront pizza-*antojitos* fusion joint **Coco's Pizza ❸**, Malecón 100, affords prime space for watching surfers catch the breaks. Their *camarones a la diabla* (shrimp with chile; 85 pesos) are a spicy taste of heaven. The fried fish (50 pesos) comes with plenty of sides. (☎536 0222. Open daily 8am-9pm. Cash only.) Playa Azul also has a market, **Flores Magón**, two blocks east of the plaza on Magón. (Open daily 8am-5pm.)

NIGHTLIFE. After dark the stray dogs of Playa Azul outnumber people on the streets. A couple *cantinas* and lounges around town offer relaxed atmo-

GIVING BACK

PARTY FOR THE TURTLES' SAKE

Every year, thousands of endangered sea turtles emerge from the ocean to lay eggs in the sands of Mexico's Pacific coast. Between July 15 and December 23, volunteers in Mexico's national turtle conservation program, **La Tortuga Marina para Protección**, scour the beaches for turtle eggs, collect them, and take them to safe houses to protect them from being eaten by predators such as birds, dogs, and even humans.

After 45 days, the eggs hatch and the volunteers have one day to make sure the baby turtles are in good health before releasing them into the ocean. On average, 25,000 *tortuguitas* are hatched and released in the five-month span.

In the small beachside town of **Playa Azul**, the *Tortuga Marina* is cause for celebration. For three days every year, during the third weekend of Oct., exhibits in the plaza house sea turtles of all sizes taken from the ocean for the day by federal permit. The huge block party is aimed at raising awareness of the endangered species and teaching kids to protect and respect the docile creatures. Films are shown in *palapas* and groups are taken to watch the turtles lay eggs in the sand and occasionally assist with their release to the sea.

Festivities begin Sa 10am, in Playa Azul's zócalo. Turtle release Su 11am, weather permitting.

spheres and moderately priced alcohol. **La Hacienda,** on Carranza one block east of Cárdenas, is a *vaquero*-themed *cantina* with sandy walls adorned by guns and cowboy hats. Locals play cards and watch soccer as they down their drinks. (Beer 15 pesos. Mixed drinks 35-40 pesos. Open daily 8pm-2am.) If you want some fresh air, head to **Nuestro Bar.** Couples sit on the sectionals on the deck, casually drinking and soaking in the ocean breeze. (Beer 10 pesos. *Michelada* 20 pesos. Mixed drinks 40-55 pesos. Open M-Th and Su 5-11pm, F-Sa 5pm-2am. AmEx/MC/V.)

◪ **BEACHES.** The 53km of coastline between Playa Azul and Caleta de Campos alternate between abrupt, jagged rocks and beautiful white sand. The waves are rough and make for stellar surfing, but swimming is not the best idea. In springtime, around *Semana Santa,* the waters are calmest and most crowded. At **Las Peñas,** 13km west of Playa Azul, the waves are turbulent enough to discourage swimmers, but great for surfing. **El Bejuco,** only 2km west, has a sandy cove with tamer waves and fewer rocks, and perhaps the best option for swimming and laying out on the beach. Go west another 12km and you'll find **Chuquiapan,** a longer beach surrounded by tall green palms but littered with stones and driftwood, and an ideal site for surfing, swimming, and camping on the beach. **La Soledad,** enclosed by cliffs 4km farther west, is cozier and more populated. The patchwork of rocks produces a layered tide of different colors that crash against the rocks, one of which resembles an enormous elephant. **Mexcalhuacán,** 2km west, is little more than a thin strip of sand next to a rock, which affords a sweeping view. **Caleta de Campos** begins 7km later. **Nexpa,** a sandy beach with a steep slope and powerful waves, is a surfer haven 5km west of Caleta, attracting boarders from all around the world.

CALETA DE CAMPOS

Caleta de Campos is a tiny fishing village 53km west of Playa Azul and one of the few places along **Mex. 200** with services. The hills in town offer sweeping views of the ocean, while the sleepy beach allows you to enjoy the moderate surf up close. Caleta has two hotels; both are nice, affordable, and fill up during *Semana Santa* and Christmas. From the hotels, walk to the end of Principal, pass the church on the right, and follow the dirt road to the beach (10min.).

The **Hotel los Arcos ❸,** Colegio Militar 5, next to the church as Principal veers left, is a cathedral of white tile and light. Gorgeous rooms come with fan, TV, and sparkling bath, and balconies overlook the steep coast below. (☎531 5038. Singles 200 pesos, with TV pesos; doubles 250/300 pesos, with A/C 350/400 pesos.)

The entire town lies along one main street, **Melchor Ocampo** (known locally as Principal); blink and you'll miss it. The **police station** is by the radio tower on the left as you turn onto Principal from the main highway. (☎532 2030.) There is also a phone next to the station. **Farmacia Nena,** located on Ocampo half a block off the highway, is open 8am-8pm. To reach the **Centro de Salud,** turn right before Principal goes left and walk three blocks up **Vasco de Quiroga.** (Open daily 8am-2pm and 4-8pm. 24hr. emergency service.) **Phones** are located on Ocampo.

Buses (labeled "Michoacános") running from Lázaro Cárdenas to Caleta de Campos on Mex. 200 leave from Galeana bus station and pass each of the beaches listed above (1½hr., every 20min. 6am-8pm, 55 pesos). From the highway, you can see signs labeling each beach, usually at a bridge—keep an eye out for them, as bus drivers won't always accurately drop you off. The beaches are a short walk from the highway (5-10min.), usually down a dirt road. To return to Playa Azul or Lázaro Cárdenas, wave down a bus going in the opposite direction (last return at 7:40pm). To get to Nexpa, take a white *combi* from the bus depot at the beginning of Principal in Caleta de Campos (10min., every 40min. 7am-7pm, 10 pesos). Be advised that bus service is intermittent on the road back to Playa Azul, and the road's narrow shoulder makes walking dangerous. While *Let's Go* does not recommend hitchhiking, drivers are often willing to give rides to passersby.

GUERRERO

ZIHUATANEJO AND IXTAPA ☎ 755

At one time, Zihuatanejo (see-wah-tah-NEH-ho) relied on the sea's bounty for sustenance and Ixtapa's landscape was a tangle of coconut palms, rocky cliffs, and mangrove swamps. It wasn't until the 1970s that Ixtapa and its counterpart found themselves on the tourist circuit. Today, the towns (combined pop. 80,000) thrive almost exclusively on tourism, as the siren song of the Pacific and the flat golden beaches of the area draw tourists from all over the continent. Zihuatanejo's quiet pedestrian alleys and window shops sharply contrast Ixtapa's chic restaurants, wide boulevards, and soaring beachfront highrises that lie one small valley away. The differences between the two will make your trip feel like two vacations in one; stay in Zihuatanejo and play in both for the best budget experience.

▐ TRANSPORTATION

Ixtapa's main road, **Bulevar Ixtapa,** lies between a bundle of waterfront luxury hotels on one side and overpriced stores on the other. **Buses** shuttling between the two cities leave Zihuatanejo from Juárez and Morelos, across from the yellow Elektra store, and Ixtapa from various points on Blvr. Ixtapa (15-25min., daily 6am-10pm, 7 pesos). **Taxis** also make the trip between the towns (50 pesos during the day, 75 pesos at night). In Zihuatanejo, they can be found on Juárez, in front of the market, and in Ixtapa from Señor Frog's.

Flights: Aeropuerto Internacional de Ixtapa/Zihuatanejo (ZIH; ☎554 5408 or 0223), 15km outside of town. Taxis leave to Zihuatanejo (150 pesos) and Ixtapa (190 pesos). *Combis* depart from the left side of the airport parking lot to the intersection of Morelos and Juárez in Zihuatanejo (6am-11pm, 7 pesos). You can catch a *combi* marked with a plane from the intersection of González and Juárez in Zihuatanejo (6:30am-10:30pm, 7 pesos). Served by: **America West** (☎554 8636; open M-Sa 9am-5pm, Su noon-4pm); **Continental** (☎554 4219; open daily 9am-5pm); and **Mexicana,** in Ixtapa (☎554 2227; open daily 8am-8pm) and **Zihuatanejo** (☎554 2208 or 4767; open M-Sa 9am-7pm), with offices on the corner of Guerrero and Bravo.

Buses: In Zihuatanejo, buses arrive at the **Estrella de Oro** station, Paseo de Zihuatanejo 34, and next door at the **Estrella Blanca** station, on the *centro*'s outskirts. *Combis* (5 pesos), across the street as you leave the station, or taxis (25 pesos) bring you to the *centro*. To reach the bus station from the *centro*, hop on a "Coacoyul" *combi* (7am-8:30pm, 4 pesos) across from the market on Juárez. **Estrella de Oro** (☎554 2175) sends buses to: **Acapulco** (5hr., every hr. 6am-8pm, 99 pesos); **Cuernavaca** (7hr., 8, 9:15am, 10pm, 362 pesos); **Mexico City** (9hr.; 6:40am, 8, 10pm; 425 pesos); **Papanoa** (1½hr., every hr. 7am-2pm, 32 pesos). **Estrella Blanca** (☎554 3477) offers 1st-class service to: **Acapulco** (4hr., 15 per day 1am-9:35pm, 129 pesos); **Lázaro Cárdenas** (2½hr., 7 per day, 66 pesos); **Morelia** (7½ hr., 8pm, 293 pesos); **Puerto Escondido** (11hr., 7:30pm, 373 pesos). 2nd-class service to local destinations.

Car Rental: Hertz, Bravo 29 (☎554 2255; fax 554 3050), in Zihuatanejo. Cars available from 300 pesos per day without insurance. Open daily 9am-2pm and 4-7pm. Also has an office in the airport (☎554 2952). AmEx. **Alamo** (☎553 0206), Local 28 in the Centro Comercial de los Patios in Ixtapa and at the airport. Cars 400-900 pesos per day with insurance. Open daily 9am-9pm. AmEx.

🛈 PRACTICAL INFORMATION

Tourist Office: SEFOTUR (☎544 8350 or 544 8361), Galo 1, just off Paseo del Palmar in Zihuatanejo. Open M-F 8am-3:30pm and 5-7pm, Sa 8am-1pm. For complaints or emergencies, call the **Agencia de Ministerio Público en Atención al Turista** (☎554 6103), or **Profeco** (☎554 5236), both in Zihuatanejo.

Currency Exchange: Bancomer (☎554 7492), Juárez 9 at Bravo, in Zihuatanejo. **24hr. ATM.** Open M-F 8:30am-4pm, Sa 10am-2pm. Banks scattered throughout Plaza de los Patios in Ixtapa.

Laundromat: Lavandería Express, González 35 (☎554 4393), just west of Cuauhtémoc, in Zihuatanejo. 15 pesos per kg. Open daily 10am-6pm.

Luggage Storage: Estrella Blanca station in Zihuatanejo. 5 pesos per hr. per bag.

Emergency: ☎060.

Tourist Police: Álvarez 19 (☎554 2040 or 5846) in Zihuatanejo.

Red Cross: Huertas 116 (☎554 2009), as you leave Zihuatanejo. 24hr. service.

Pharmacy: Farmacia Principal, Ejido 34 (☎554 4217), at the corner of Cuauhtémoc in Zihuatanejo. Open M-Sa 9am-9pm.

Medical Services: IMSS, Olinala 1 (☎554 4822), across from the Estrella Blanca station. **ISSSTE,** on Paseo de la Boquita just east of the canal. 24hr. emergency service.

Internet Access: Barnet Zihuatanejo, Ramírez 2. A/C, very fast connections, and plenty of computers. 10 pesos for 1st 30min.; 20 pesos per hr., students 15 pesos per hr. Open daily 9am-11pm. **Xtapa Conexión** (☎553 2253), Ixtapa Plaza Local 15 on the walkway to the left of Señor Frog's. High-speed connection 35 pesos for 15min., 80 pesos per hr. Open daily 8am-11pm.

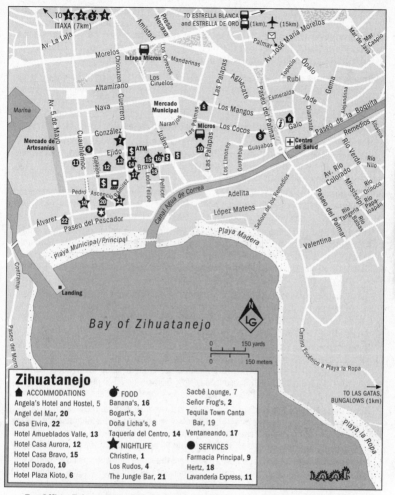

Zihuatanejo

🏠 ACCOMMODATIONS
Angela's Hotel and Hostel, 5
Angel del Mar, **20**
Casa Elvira, **22**
Hotel Amueblados Valle, **13**
Hotel Casa Aurora, **12**
Hotel Casa Bravo, **15**
Hotel Dorado, **10**
Hotel Plaza Kioto, **6**

🍎 FOOD
Banana's, **16**
Bogart's, **3**
Doña Licha's, **8**
Taquería del Centro, **14**

★ NIGHTLIFE
Christine, **1**
Los Rudos, **4**
The Jungle Bar, **21**

Sacbē Lounge, 7
Señor Frog's, **2**
Tequila Town Canta
Bar, **19**
Ventaneando, **17**

● SERVICES
Farmacia Principal, **9**
Hertz, **18**
Lavandería Express, **11**

Fax Office: Telecomm (☎553 0680; fax 554 3381), next to Zihuatanejo's post office in Edificio SCT. **Western Union** service. Open M-F 9am-7pm, Sa-Su 9am-noon.

Post Office: (☎554 2192), Edificio SCT between Telegrafistas and Palmar in Zihua-tanejo. Walking southwest towards the beaches on Morelos, turn right on Telegrafis-tas and walk 1 block. Open M-F 8am-6pm, Sa 9am-1pm. **Postal Codes:** 40880 (Zihuatanejo); 40884 (Ixtapa).

🏠 ACCOMMODATIONS

For a small town, Zihuatanejo has an awe-inspiring number of accommodations, many of them reasonably priced. Prices rise substantially during high season (Dec.-Apr.). In the low season, you will have excellent leverage for negotiating discounts if you come with a large group or plan to stay several days. Hot water is unreliable in most budget hotels. Camping is prohibited in Zihuatanejo and on Playa Palmar in Ixtapa, but is popular on **Playa Quieta**, near Club Med in Ixtapa, and on **Playa Linda**, just around the pier. All of the following are in Zihuatanejo, as no budget accommodations exist in Ixtapa.

Angela's Hotel and Hostel, Mangos 25 (☎554 4748). The sign in front says it all: "Canadian spoken here, *un poco español*, eh." Owners Gregg and Amanda welcome guests with open arms. Scruffy, young travelers hang out in the flower-filled hallways. Communal hot shower and well-appointed kitchen. Luggage storage available. Dorms 90 pesos; singles and doubles 50 pesos; triples 330 pesos. Cash only. ❶

Hotel Plaza Kioto, Galo 5 (☎554 0494). Fresh-smelling, spacious rooms are hidden behind the wicker-chaired lobby of Plaza Kioto. Rooms have low, colorful bed, cable TV, fan, and immaculate bath. Reception 24hr. Singles 200 pesos; doubles 300 pesos; triples 400 pesos. Cash only. ❸

Hotel Dorado, Las Palapas 5 (☎544 7556). The small, bright courtyard is compressed by rooms on all sides, with standard bed and bath, fan, and TV. Tiny, tucked-away pool. Singles 200 pesos, with A/C 250; doubles 300/350 pesos. Cash only. ❸

Angel del Mar, Ascencio 10 (☎554 5084). Wins points for its location in the heart of the *centro*, a stone's throw away from Playa Principal. Private rooms come with cold-water bath. Dorms come with fan and linen. Communal kitchen. Hot water available. Reception 24hr. Dorms 100 pesos; private rooms 250 pesos. Cash only. ❶

Casa Elvira, Álvarez 29 (☎554 2061), 1 block from Playa Municipal. Zihuatanejo's 1st guest house, opened in 1956. The best deal for a private room. Creeping plants over-take the courtyard, while iron staircases are festooned with Christmas lights. Tiny but clean rooms come with fan. No hot water. Rooms 100-200 pesos. 1 room with hall-way bath 80 pesos. Prices often negotiable. Cash only. ❶

Hotel Amueblados Valle, Guerrero 33 (☎554 2084; fax 554 3220), between Ejido and Bravo. 8 huge, comfortable apartments with balcony, ceiling fan, couch, stocked kitchen, and daily towel service. A good deal for groups. Make reservations up to 5 months in advance for high season. May-Nov. 500 pesos., 1-3 people Dec.-Apr. 600 pesos. 2-bedroom apt. 750 pesos. Discounts for longer stays. Cash only. ❺

Hotel Casa Aurora, Bravo 42 (☎554 3046), between Guerrero and Galeana. Long, airy hallways lined with couches and potted plants give Aurora a peaceful ambience. Classy armoires and bedspread distract from the sallow walls. Rooms come with TV, fan, and large bath. Singles and doubles 300 pesos; triples and quads 350 pesos. Cash only. ❸

Hotel Casa Bravo, Bravo 20 (☎554 2548). Past the small lobby lie spacious rooms with white bedspread and sparkling bath. All rooms with TV, some with cable. Singles 300 pesos, with A/C 350; doubles 350/400 pesos. Cash only. ❸

🍴 FOOD

Dining, like most other activities in Ixtapa, comes at a hefty price. Try eating early in the day or hitting up cheaper eateries on the back side of the main plaza. You can also go to Zihuatanejo, where fish is fresh and *antojitos* are relatively inexpensive. Zihuatanejo also has a **market** with fresh produce and small eateries (open daily 6am-7pm), and a supermarket, **Comercial Mexicana,** behind the Estrella Blanca bus station (☎483 2184; open daily 8am-10pm).

■ **Dona Licha's,** Cocos 8 (☎554 3933), 1 block west of Paseo del Palmar in Zihuatanejo. This family restaurant offers great food and a convivial atmosphere. Arched wooden roof has fans to keep you cool until your delicious *carne* plate (50 pesos) arrives. Seafood 60-70 pesos. Omelettes 35 pesos. Cash only. Open daily 8am-6pm. ❹

Taquería del Centro, Bravo 36, on the corner of Guerrero in Zihuatanejo. An amiable owner and cheap tacos available late into the night make this place a winner. 3 tacos for 20 pesos, served with heaps of toppings. Open daily 6:30pm-2am. Cash only. ❷

Banana's, Bravo 4 (☎556 1080 or 559 3294), in Zihuatanejo. A great breakfast place for a quick bite, with a bustling diner vibe. The *comida corrida* (30 pesos) has a variety of main courses and sides. Eggs with fruit juice or coffee 20 pesos. Chicken and beef *fajitas* 60 pesos. Seafood 45-70 pesos. Open daily 8am-4pm. Cash only. ❸

Nueva Zelanda, Local 1 on the plaza in the middle of Ixtapa's *centro comercial*. White paper serving hats and metal diner tables lend a vintage 50s touch. Serves *antojitos* at reasonable prices. *Chilaquiles* (tortilla casserole) 50 pesos. Soup 38 pesos. *Molletes* (Mexican pizza) 48 pesos. Open daily 8am-10pm. Cash only. ❸

Bogart's (☎553 0333) on Blvr. Ixtapa next to Krystal Hotel, in Ixtapa. If you have a hankering to splurge on dinner, there is no better place to do so than here. Step into Bogie's most famous movie, Casablanca: Moorish arches, a fountain, reflecting pool, and a white piano give it old-world class. Make sure to pause for a picture with your fez-topped waiter. Entrees average 180 pesos. Open daily 6pm-midnight. AmEx/MC/V. ❺

◤ BEACHES

Neither Zihuatanejo's self-conscious charm nor Ixtapa's resorts can eclipse the area's natural beauty. Zihuatanejo's four beaches, clockwise from the municipal pier, are **Playa Principal, Playa Madera, Playa la Ropa,** and **Playa las Gatas.** The latter two are easily the best. Ixtapa overlooks the unbroken stretch of **Playa del Palmar** on Bahía del Palmar, but less touristed beaches lie beyond Laguna de Ixtapa: **Playa Quieta, Playa Linda,** and, at the west edge of the bay, **Isla Ixtapa.**

ZIHUATANEJO

PLAYA PRINCIPAL. Not the most stunning, pristine, or private of the beaches in town, but it's only a few minutes walk from downtown and its mildly choppy waves are suitable for a swim. Start up a game of volleyball or beach soccer, or show off on the adjacent basketball court. *(Downtown Zihuatanejo, in front of the Paseo del Pescador.)*

PLAYA MADERA. Only 200m long, Playa Madera (Wood Beach) was once a loading site for the local hardwood export. The fine sand and moderate waves show no trace of the beach's lumberyard past, but offer a great place to play in the waves. Restaurants and bungalows cramp the shore, and posh hotels lie off to one side. *(Follow the cement path at the end of Playa Principal.)*

PLAYA LA ROPA. Protected from the rough Pacific by the bay, Playa la Ropa is the largest of the four beaches. Uncrowded and gently curving, it's the ideal beach for carousing in the surf, walking idly along the shore, or parasailing over the waves. If you tire of the surf, try to catch a glimpse of the crocodile in the estuary behind. *(Take a "Ropa" bus from along Juárez; 6am-7pm, 5 pesos. You can also make the 4km trip by foot: follow Paseo de la Boquita along the canal over the bridge and turn left, passing Playa Madera. The road curves to the right, past Hotel Casa que Canta; follow the stone road to the left down to the beach. If you're planning to leave late, you may want to arrange a taxi pickup beforehand; 25 pesos. Waveriders 400 pesos per 30min. Parasailing 200 pesos per 10min.)*

PLAYA LAS GATAS. According to local legend, the Purépecha king Calzontzín ordered the construction of the stone wall in Playa las Gatas to keep out whiskered sharks while he bathed. Since then, coral (most of which has died by now), and marine life have overtaken the stone barricade that divides the crystalline waters. Lawn chairs and umbrellas (free) from local restaurants have invaded the beach. The calm, clear waters welcome snorkelers (equipment rental 50 pesos per day) and kayakers (1-person kayaks 150 pesos per hr.). Escape the shops and restaurants by walking the 2km path behind the last restaurant to the **Garrobo Lighthouse** for a panoramic view. Ask any of the waiters for specific directions to the well-hidden path. *(To reach Playa Las Gatas, take a lancha from the pier in downtown Zihuatanejo; 10min., every 15min. 9am-4pm, round-trip 35 pesos; last return 5pm. It is possible, but not easy, to walk over the rocks to Las Gatas from La Ropa. Alternatively, you can walk on the road that brought you to La Ropa for another 45min., keeping to the left as it splits.)*

IXTAPA

PLAYA DE PALMAR. Well guarded from Blvr. Ixtapa by a line of posh hotels, Playa de Palmar is the pin-up model of beaches, long and sandy, populated but not crowded with beautiful people swimming, playing volleyball, and sipping classy drinks on beach chairs. *(The beach can be reached by public access paths at either end, to the left of Barcelo's resort or to the right of the Krystal Hotel. Otherwise, clutch your Let's Go confidently, wear your swimsuit proudly, and cut through the fancy hotel lobbies—this may work best when you're leaving the beach.)*

PLAYA QUIETA AND PLAYA LINDA. About 6km northwest of downtown lie Playas Quieta and Linda, separated by a large pier. Playa Quieta, a little busier than its neighbor, is backed by restaurants. Playa Linda has a small boardwalk with *mariscos* shacks, a few beach chairs, and a long expanse of open beach, yours for the taking if you're willing to walk a few hundred meters. *(From Ixtapa, follow Blvr. Ixtapa northwest beyond most of the hotels and turn right at the "Playa Linda" sign. From Zihuatanejo, it is better to use the access road from Mex. 200: take the left, marked "Playa Linda," beyond the exit for Ixtapa as you head toward Puerto Vallarta. The road skirts Laguna de Ixtapa and hits the beach farther northwest. Taxis from Ixtapa 40 pesos, from Zihuatanejo 70 pesos. A "Playa Linda" bus from either town visits the 2 beaches; 6 pesos. Buses return to Ixtapa and Zihuatanejo every 15min. until 7pm; 6 pesos. You can also bike the 4km roadside path.)*

ISLA IXTAPA. Some of the most picturesque beaches lie on Isla Ixtapa, 2km offshore from Playa Quieta—a must-visit for snorkeling enthusiasts. Facing the mainland, many restaurants take advantage of the captive audience. The main beach is **Playa Cuachalalate,** frequented by fishermen and waterskiers. **Playa Varadero** is a small beach with calm waters and *palapa* restaurants. On the ocean side of the island, **Playa Coral** is a haven for snorkeling. Rent a mask and flippers (60 pesos) to see the gaudy tropical fish, but be careful not to wash up on the reef in the strong, irregular tide. *(Catch a microbús from Zihuatanejo or Ixtapa to get to the pier at Playa Linda; 6 pesos. From there, catch a lancha; every 15min. 9am-5pm, round-trip 35 pesos. Alternatively, board a lancha from Playa Principal's pier in Zihuatanejo; round-trip 120 pesos, 8-person min.)*

⚡ NIGHTLIFE

Although beaches in both towns promise spectacular sun, sand, and waves, the only place to go for crazy nightlife is Ixtapa. **Bulevar Ixtapa,** like most resort strips, is studded with fancy clubs and relaxed bars that rock to the beat of a crowd of young people. Zihuatanejo's sports bars and karaoke joints come to life at night, and a small but vibrant club scene is on the rise.

IXTAPA

Christine (☎553 0456), Blvr. Ixtapa in front of Hotel Krystal. Massive crowds of well-dressed youth form outside as opening time approaches. Inside, the party explodes with an open bar, energetic lighting, and approving cheers from the partiers inside. Cover 300 pesos with open bar. Open daily 10pm-late. AmEx/MC/V.

Señor Frog's (☎553 2282), in the Ixtapa Commercial Center, across from the Hotel Presidente. A restaurant by day, but when the clock strikes midnight, tipsy Americans and Mexicans climb on tables and stadium seats and start breaking it down. Beer 35 pesos. *Bebidas nacionales* 50-70 pesos. Yard-long drinks 100 pesos. Cover 100 pesos, includes one drink. Open daily 6pm-3am. MC/V.

Los Rudos, (☎755 113 1984), on Blvr. Ixtapa across from the Park Royal. A calm change from the pulsing clubs around it. Couples share drinks on the patio overlooking the street. *Lucha libre* (wrestling) paraphernalia and a mounted VW Beetle add personality. Beer 35 pesos. Mixed drinks 55-75 pesos. Open daily 7pm-3am. Cash only.

ZIHUATANEJO

The Jungle Bar, Ramírez 3 (lajunglazihua.com), at Ascencio. An intimate group of tables in the bar area, a lot of conversation, and a friendly crowd make for a good vibe. The cheapest beer (10 pesos) and liquor (double shot 40-50 pesos) around are popular with everyone. Mixed drinks 35 pesos. Live music on weekends. Open daily high season noon-3am, low season 7pm-2am. Cash only.

Sacbê Lounge, Ejido 22 at Guerrero. Zihuatanejo's only full-fledged club is a gleaming metal palace covering 3 floors, where the town's young and sexy come to dance or lounge on the sides, drink in hand. The bravest climb to the cage on the 3rd fl. and show off what they're working with. Beer 30 pesos. Mixed drinks 45-65 pesos. Open daily 8pm-4am. Cash only.

Tequila Town Canta Bar, Cuauhtémoc 3. Dark, absolutely crammed disco bar. Strobe lights and loud Latin beats inspire people to hit the dance floor. Beer 30 pesos. Mixed drinks 60-70 pesos. 50-peso drink min. Open daily 10pm-3am. Cash only.

Ventaneando, Guerrero 108A, 3rd fl. (☎554 5390), across from D'Latino at Bravo. Seizure-inducing green lighting and loud, pulsing club hits mixed with *banda* orchestrate the sweaty dancing on the small, crowded floor. Snowboarding videos seem entirely out of place. Beer 25 pesos, 5 beers 100 pesos. Mixed drinks 50-60 pesos. Open daily 8pm-4am. Cash only.

COSTA GRANDE

The Guerrero coast north of Acapulco is often called Costa Grande, pairing it with a smaller counterpart, Costa Chica, to the south. Though the stretch from Acapulco to Zihuatanejo and Ixtapa has few inviting beaches, ■**Barra de Potosí,** 20km southeast of Zihuatanejo, is a hidden treasure ideal for wasting a day in the waves.

BARRA DE POTOSÍ   ☎755

For the traveler sick of tourists, cheap T-shirts, and general kitsch, no better tonic exists than a spell on the seemingly infinite stretch of sand of Barra de Potosí. This small town consists of a shallow lagoon, a forest of palm trees, and waterfront huts; overlooked by developers, it seems caught in perpetual siesta. Be warned—there's nothing here but the beach, so bring a towel and some sunscreen. The waves are rough nearer the rocks, good for novice surfers, and milder back towards the town, drawing a weekend crowd of swimmers from as far as Michoacán. Accommodations are surprisingly expensive here; Barra de Potosí may be best suited as a daytrip from Zihuatanejo.

⊟ TRANSPORTATION. From Zihuatanejo, "Petatlán" or "Peta" **buses** leave for Potosí from a station on Las Palmas, by Ejido and Juárez (30min., every 15min.

6am-9pm, 14 pesos) or catch it along Los Cocos. Ask to be let off at **Achotes,** a *pueblito* announced by a single black-and-white sign. A **pickup truck** (30min., 10 pesos) with wooden benches nailed in the bed will be waiting (or arriving soon) on the side road to collect passengers for the trip to the *enramadas* (open-air seaside restaurants) by the coast. Trucks return to the intersection from the same spot (daily 7am-6pm). The bus to Zihuatanejo leaves from the other side of the route.

⬛⬛ ACCOMMODATIONS AND FOOD. In this town lacking A/C and most basic services, the only lodgings available cost a pretty penny. On the road into town **Casa Puesta del Sol ❺**, offers beautiful, well-painted rooms with airy windows, fully equipped kitchens, and large *azulejo*-tiled baths—a villa ambience. (☎114 5078. Good for groups. Suites from 600 pesos, larger suite with deck and ocean view 800 pesos. Cash only.) **Hotel Barra de Potosí ❺**, a resort-style hotel on the road into town, offers a large beachside pool and restaurant. The large rooms have a little dirt in the corners and the occasional bug along with TV, fan, and unexceptional bath. (☎544 8290. Not all rooms have the same amenities. 1-bed interior rooms for 1-2 people 300 pesos, with parking lot view 400 pesos, ocean view 500 pesos; suite for 3-4 600 pesos, 800 pesos with ocean view. Cash only.)

There are 10 or so *enramadas*, practically identical, which serve simple seafood dishes. Enjoy homecooked food while relaxing in one of the hammocks swinging in the shaded restaurants. In keeping with the casual spirit, some do not have set menus, instead asking you what type of seafood you'd like to eat (expect to spend 80-120 pesos per person). The usual staples—shrimp, fish, and octopus—are cooked as you'd like. (Open daily 9am-8pm.)

◩◪ SIGHTS AND BEACHES. Off the beach, a daunting hike up **Cerro Guamilule** (200m) offers a spectacular view of the beaches, the lagoon, and the vast expanse of the ocean. The hill lacks a well-worn trail, and the trek is not an easy or quick one by any means, but the rewarding view is equal to the exertion. The southernmost beach on the bay is **Playa Potosí,** running alongside the town from the lighthouse for several kilometers. Farther north is the aptly named **Playa Blanca** (White Beach; 3km), completely empty except for a few *palapas*. Follow the dirt road where the main road veers to the right to reach the beach. **Playa Coacoyul** (8km), is accessible through the town of the same name just before Achotes. Farther north and more accessible from other towns are **Playa Riscaliyo** (19km), and pebbly **Playa Manzanillo** (24km), before a lighthouse (26km) overlooking the northern edge of the bay. All beaches are free of tourists in the summer months but fill with hundreds of domestic vacationers during Christmas. Around the southern point from Playa Potosí is **Playa Larga,** a beach with absolutely nothing on it: no *palapas*, people, or fishing boats. Getting there is difficult: walk around the lagoon or take a *lancha* across, and walk through 600-700m of forest and pine grove. Sit back and revel in total solitude.

ACAPULCO   ☎ 744

Once upon a time, Acapulco (pop. 2 million) was a stunningly beautiful playground for the rich and famous. Along with cities like Havana, it served as a tropical getaway: a place for dancing and romancing and walking through the shallows of blue-green beaches. Since then, international tourism has more or less settled down, giving way to flocks of middle-class vacationers. Now a swelteringly hot modern city, with incredible traffic and the constant cacophony of horns, Acapulco is learning to cope without its former allure. While the city is now filled by ordinary faces and buildings, the rich still come and 20-story high-rises still dominate the beachfront strip. Despite occasional periods of intense drug violence, tourism continues unabated, partly because Acapulco still merits its reputation as a party city, boasting infinite ways to paint the town red and make the nights memorable—or forgettable. After the sun sets the grime and heat of the city disappears, and the beautiful twinkling lights on the hillsides flare up like a candlelight vigil watching over those heading out into the night.

▢ TRANSPORTATION

Flights: Aeropuerto Internacional Álvarez de Acapulco (ACA), on Mex. 200, 26km south of the city. Taxis to the airport 200 pesos; shared cabs (☎462 1095) 100 pesos. Served by **Aerolíneas Internacionales** (☎486 5630), **Aeroméxico** (☎466 9109), **American** (☎466 9227), **America West** (☎466 9257 or 800 235 9292), **Continental** (☎466 9063), and **Mexicana** (☎486 7585).

Buses: Acapulco has 3 bus stations.

Estrella de Oro Cuauhtémoc 1490 (☎485 8705), at Massiu. To reach the *zócalo,* cross the street and catch any "Zócalo" bus (30min., 4.50 pesos). Taxis 50 pesos. Goes to: **Cuernavaca** (4hr., 5 per day 10:30am-5:30pm, 265 pesos); **Mexico City** (5hr., every hr. 6am-midnight, 288 pesos); **Taxco** (4hr.; 2:10, 4:10, 6:10pm; 158 pesos); **Zihuatanejo** (4hr.; 6, 7:50am, 1:50, 4:20pm; 119 pesos); **Lázaro Cárdenas** (6hr., every 30min. 5:30am-6:30pm, 151 pesos).

Centro Papagayo (☎469 2081), on Cuauhtémoc behind Parque Papagayo. One of Estrella Blanca's 2 stations in Acapulco. *Ejecutivo* buses travel to: **Cuernavaca** (4hr., 4 per day 2:20am-6:30pm, 265 pesos); **Mexico City** (5hr., every hr., 315 pesos); **Puebla** (7hr.; 7 per day, 6am-midnight; 450 pesos); **Guadalajara** (10hr.; 5:15, 6:30, 7, 8:15pm; 646 pesos). To get to Centro Papagayo from the *zócalo,* take a "CICI" bus (4.50 pesos) to Parque Papagayo. Cross the park; the bus station is on Cuauhtémoc behind it.To get to the *zócalo,* take a "Zócalo" bus.

Centro Ejido (☎469 2028), on Ejido north of the *zócalo.* All other Estrella Blanca buses leave from this 2nd station, including those to **Morelia** (7hr., 9pm, 488 pesos) and **Puerto Escondido** (8hr.; 7:45, 11:45am, 1:45, 4:45, 11pm; 248 pesos). Take an *"Ejido"* bus from the *zócalo* (4 pesos). To get to the *zócalo,* take a "Zócalo" bus.

Car Rental: Hertz, Costera 137 (☎485 6889), across from Universidad Americana. Small VWs with insurance 575 pesos per day. Open daily 8am-8pm. Airport location open daily 6am-10pm. Other rental places on Costera.

◼▢ ORIENTATION AND PRACTICAL INFORMATION

Acapulco Bay lies 400km south of Mexico City and 239km southeast of Ixtapa and Zihuatanejo. **Mex. 200** becomes **La Costera** (Costera Miguel Alemán), the main drag that skirts the waterfront for the length of the city. Acapulco Dorado, or **Zona Dorada,** is full of restaurants, malls, and hotels; it stretches from **Parque Papagayo** to the naval base. The ultra-chic resorts are on **Acapulco Diamante,** farther east. Budget accommodations and restaurants lie between the *zócalo* and **La Quebrada,** the famous cliff-diving spot. You will lose precious beach time trying to walk the main drag, so get familiar with the basics of public transportation. Buses run along Costera from Playa Hornos or Playa Caleta in the west to **CICI water park** or **Base** in the east and back (4.50 pesos, yellow bus with A/C 5 pesos). Along Cuauhtémoc, buses run between "Cine Río" in the west and "La Base" in the east (3.50 pesos).

Tourist Offices: SEFOTUR, Costera 4455 (☎484 4583 or 4416), in the Centro Cultural de Acapulco, diagonally across from the CICI water park. Helpful staff will gladly answer any questions. Open daily 8am-11pm. In an emergency, contact the **Procuraduría del Turista** in the same office.

Consulates: Canada (☎484 1305 or 1349), Centro Comercial Plaza Marbella, on Local 23 at Diana. Open M-F 9am-2pm. **US,** Costera 121, #14 (☎481 0100), in the Emporio Acapulco. Open M-F 10am-2pm.

Currency Exchange: Banks on Costera have good rates. Most with **24hr. ATMs** and open M-F 9am-4pm. **BBVA Bancomer** (☎482 2097), in the *zócalo*. Open M-F 8:30am-4pm, Sa 10am-2pm. **Banamex**, Costera 364 (☎469 4104). Open M-Sa 9am-4pm. **Casas de cambio** line Costera. Most open until 8pm.

American Express: Costera 121. (☎485 2200). Open M-F 9am-6pm, Sa 9am-1pm.

Luggage Storage, in both **Estrella Blanca** stations, 4 pesos per piece per hr.

Emergency: ☎066.

Police: LOCATEL (☎481 1100) offers aid in missing-person cases.

Red Cross: Ruiz Cortines 126 (☎065), north of the *zócalo*. Take a "Hospital" bus.

Pharmacy: Botica de Acapulco, Carranza 3 (☎783 8429), 1 block from the *zócalo*. Open daily 6am-10pm. **Farmacia de Ahorros** (☎442 6789), on the corner of Farallón and Costera. Open 24hr. MC/V.

Medical Services: ISSSTE, Ruíz Cortines 128 (☎445 5370), north of the *zócalo* along Madero next to the Red Cross. Take a "Hospital" bus.

Telephones: LADATELs line the Costera. **Caseta Carranza,** Carranza 9, 1 block from the *zócalo*, also offers **fax** service. Open M-F 9am-7pm, Sa 9am-3pm.

Internet Access: Vig@net, just west of the *zócalo* at Hidalgo 8. A/C and 8 pesos per hr. make for a good deal. Open daily 8am-midnight.

Post Office: Costera 215 (☎483 2405), 2 blocks east of the *zócalo,* in the Palacio Federal. Open M-F 8am-6pm, Sa 9am-12:30pm. **Postal Code:** 39301.

▛ ACCOMMODATIONS

West of the white, 20-story hotels dominating the skyline, the area around the *zócalo* has plenty of budget options. Rates increase dramatically during *Semana Santa* and late December; it's a good idea to make reservations ahead. Camping is only permitted during December on **Playa Hornos** and **Playa Tamarindo**.

▨ **Hotel Asturias,** Quebrada 45 (☎483 6548), up the hill to the left behind the *zócalo*. Comfy beds, powerful fans, and reliable hot-water baths well off the street provide an oasis in the frenzied city. A shady pool offers much-needed relief from the inexorable heat. Free parking for guests. Ring the bell after 11pm to return. Singles 150 pesos, renovated rooms with A/C and TV 250 pesos; doubles 220/320 pesos; triples 300/400 pesos. Cash only. ❷

Hotel Misión, Felipe Valle 12 (☎482 3643), at La Paz, 2 blocks left of the *zócalo* as you face the church. The old mission retains the feel of a sanctuary, with quiet vegetation and traditional brickwork lining the walls and stairs making for a nice remove from the city. Rooms with tiled baths (but no toilet seats) and fans; some with desks and sofas. Reception 24hr. Singles 200 pesos; doubles 400 pesos. Cash only. ❹

Hotel Queen Merry, Carranza 4 (☎482 0821), between Valle and Azueta. Through the white patterned gate and up the stairs, rooms with indulgently large, soft beds and balconies overlooking the street greet guests. Rooms come with clean, light-filled bath, TV and fan. Reception 24hr. Singles 140 pesos; doubles 220 pesos. Cash only. ❸

Hotel Angelita, Quebrada 37 (☎483 5734), behind the cathedral, 2 doors from Hotel Asturias. The hallway facing the rooms is a small arboretum offering a bizarre mix of real and fake plants with small ceramic birds. Bright blue walls, purified water, top sheets, and a comfy lobby with cable TV make life easier. All this and a big, tiled bath give the place a homey, optimistic feel. Singles 100 pesos; doubles 200 pesos. Cash only. ❶

K3 Youth Hostel, Costera 116 (☎481 3111 and 3133; www.k3acapulco.com), across from hip Condesa beach. Small dorms, reminiscent of crowded closets, come with A/C.

SOUTHERN PACIFIC COAST

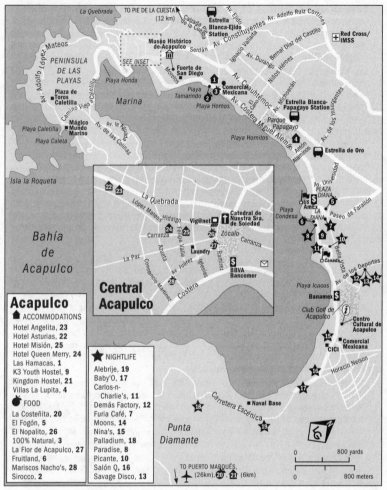

Acapulco

🏠 **ACCOMMODATIONS**
Hotel Angelita, **23**
Hotel Asturias, **22**
Hotel Misión, **25**
Hotel Queen Merry, **24**
Las Hamacas, **1**
K3 Youth Hostel, **9**
Kingdom Hostel, **21**
Villas La Lupita, **4**

🍎 **FOOD**
La Costeñita, **20**
El Fogón, **5**
El Nopalito, **26**
100% Natural, **3**
La Flor de Acapulco, **27**
Fruitland, **6**
Mariscos Nacho's, **28**
Sirocco, **2**

⭐ **NIGHTLIFE**
Alebrije, **19**
Baby'O, **17**
Carlos-n-
    Charlie's, **11**
Demás Factory, **12**
Furia Café, **7**
Moons, **14**
Nina's, **15**
Palladium, **18**
Paradise, **8**
Picante, **10**
Salón Q, **16**
Savage Disco, **13**

Communal bathrooms are spotless. Expensive for a hostel—you pay for close proximity to the beach and discos. Breakfast included. Has a bar (beer 12 pesos, *bebidas nacionales* 25 pesos), a kitchen, and a terrace over vibrant Costera. Internet access 20 pesos per hr. Reception 24hr. Lockout 11am-3:30 pm. 4-bed dorms 160 pesos, with ISIC or HI membership 145 pesos; private rooms 400/365 pesos. MC/V. ❸

Villas La Lupita, Anton de Alaminos 232 (☎486 3917; villaslalupita.com), 1 block north of Costera. If you're seeking a little quiet luxury closer to the heart of the city, La Lupita is a good place to drop some cash. A gorgeous pool stands next to a breezy *palapa* lounge in the courtyard. Spacious rooms have soft comforters and beds, fan, A/C, cable, safety deposit boxes, keycard entry, and shining baths. Wi-Fi in the courtyard. Reception 24hr. Doubles 800 pesos; each extra person 160 pesos. AmEx/MC/V. ❺

Kingdom Hostel, Carretera Escénica (☎466 3736), on the way to Puerto Marques. A converted athletic facility, Kingdom Hostel offers an unusual mix of amenities, reflected in the price. A large courtyard pales next to the amazing pool, the tennis court, and the soccer field. Linens and breakfast included. Kitchen, parking, and Internet available. Reception 24hr. Co-ed dorms 200 pesos; private rooms 300 pesos. Cash only. ❹

Las Hamacas, Costera 239 (☎483 7006; www.hamacas.com.mx). A pricier option brings that bring more amenities and more proximity to the nightlife. Rooms with A/C, phone, cable TV, refrigerator, and a small terrace overlook the restaurant and oddly shaped pool. Singles 500 pesos; doubles 600 pesos; triples 700 pesos. Cash only. ❺

◖ FOOD

Acapulco's international restaurants cater to tourists' palates, and the chic restaurants between Playa Condesa and the naval base are meant for travelers who don't fret about money. Many local eateries ready to satisfy any craving without the high prices, are interspersed along Costera. For the cheapest eats, grab a barstool in one of the many *torta* shops or taco stands on the streets surrounding the *zócalo*. A supermarket, **Comercial Mexicana,** has two locations on Costera, one east of the tourist office and the other four blocks east of the *zócalo*. (☎484 3373. Open daily 7am-midnight.)

▨ **La Flor de Acapulco,** Juárez 1 (☎482 0286). Enjoy the homey ambience, the view over the *zócalo,* and the terrific food in an Acapulco mainstay, open since 1939. The *bistec encebollado* (65 pesos) will leave you sated. Filling *platillos mexicanos* from 35 pesos. Meat and seafood entrees from 60 pesos. Open daily 8am-midnight. Cash only. ❶

Mariscos Nacho's, Azueta 7 (☎482 2891), at Juárez, 1 block west of the *zócalo.* A staggering amount of seafood is on offer here—this open-air *marisquería* serves everything from octopus (75 pesos) to baby shark quesadillas (25 pesos), and bustles with sunburned families straggling in from the beach and party people dolled up for a night on the town. Various cool fish parts adorn the walls. Fish filet 60 pesos. Open daily 9am-9:30pm. AmEx/MC/V. ❸

La Costeñita, Puerto Marqués Local 46 (☎466 3816), on the main drag in Puerto Marqués. Around since 1952, this casual seafood restaurant's food has distinguished it from the hundreds of similar restaurants that line the beach around it. For breakfast try the *huevos al gusto* (30 pesos), and for larger meals the seafood tacos (85 pesos) or octopus (75 pesos) will do just fine. Open daily 8am-9pm. Cash only. ❸

El Nopalito, La Paz 230 (☎482 1876), a block off the *zócalo.* This popular place has nothing in the way of decoration, but does have a friendly, bustling atmosphere. Brings in locals with its *menú del día* (soup of the day, entree, and jello dessert; 38 pesos). *Pozole* (Th) and paella (Su) specials 42 pesos. Open daily 8am-7pm. Cash only. ❷

Frutiland, Costera 116, in the Plaza Condesa. Specializes in concoctions made from all manner of exotic and familiar fruits, with sweet mixed juices (23 pesos) and breakfast fruit plates (20 pesos). Open daily 8am-10pm. Cash only. ❷

100% Natural, Costera 248 (☎486 2033), at the corner of Vizcaíno. Other branches line the Costera, though the beachside location has the greatest allure, with the option of eating in the chilly interior or out on the pier. Serves up tasty organic health food. A good variety—traditional *antojitos* (55-65 pesos) complement pizza (51 pesos) and pasta (55 pesos). Open daily 7am-11pm. MC/V. ❸

Sirocco, (☎485 9490) on Costera next to Playa Hornos. An upscale joint serving Spanish-Mexican fusion dishes by day and tapas by night. A cool, red interior makes a casual, elegant mood. Expensive paella dishes (185-300 pesos per person) require

1hr. preparation. For something lighter on the stomach and the wallet try the quesadillas (65-75 pesos). Drinks 65 pesos. W 2-for-1 paella. MC/V. Open daily noon-1am. ❺

El Fogón (☎484 3607), Costera and Yañez, across from the Continental Plaza Hotel. Convenient hours make up for the slightly overpriced food, nevertheless filling. Eat tacos (53 pesos) or filling breakfast combos (21-41 pesos) beneath arches and clay pots hanging from the wooden-beamed ceiling. *Chilaquiles* 50 pesos. *Carnes* 95-115 pesos. Mexican specialties 51-185 pesos. Open 24hr. AmEx/MC/V. ❹

🗺 SIGHTS AND BEACHES

If you're in Acapulco, chances are you seek two things: beaches and booze. Have no fear, intrepid traveler—Acapulco delivers. There are a few chances to get away from sunburn and hangovers: the main museum is the **Museo Histórico de Acapulco**, in the Fuerte de San Diego, built in 1616 to protect the bay from pirates. The 12 exhibits describe life in the old city and the city's maritime importance, with emphasis on the cross-cultural exchange between China, Spain, and the Phillipines. Interesting artifacts and chinoiserie on display. A better reason to come to the fort, however, is the **view of the bay** from the ramparts. Enjoy the sweeping vantage over the city and the bay without having to pay the admission fee. (☎482 3828. Open Tu-Su 9:30am-6:30pm. 37 pesos, students free; Su and festival days free. Camera use, no flash, 35 pesos.) Just outside the fort's gate on Morelos is the **Casa de la Mascara**, an extensive collection of masks from around Guerrero with captions explaining their significance. (Open Tu-Su 10am-4pm. Donation suggested.)

PENÍNSULA DE LAS PLAYAS. At the westernmost tip of Acapulco Bay, on the seaward side of the peninsula, lie **Playas Caleta** and **Caletilla**. Bobbing boats share the soft, crystalline water, ideal for swimming. Droves of families pack the beach, making peaceful towel space difficult to find. A narrow road separating the two beaches leads to **Mágico Mundo Marino,** a water park with slides, pools, and a small zoo. You can also study the marine fauna on a glass-bottomed boat ride across the bay to the forested island **La Roqueta,** which has its own zoo. *(Boats from Mágico Mundo daily 9am-6pm. 50 pesos. Mágico Mundo ☎483 1215. Open daily 9am-6pm. 40 pesos, children 20 pesos. Zoo open M and W-Su 10am-5pm. 5 pesos.)*

FROM HOTEL LAS HAMACAS TO PARQUE PAPAGAYO. This stretch of sand along the Costera, away from Old Acapulco, is blessed with fewer high-rises and smaller crowds than other beaches. **Playas Tamarindo, Hornos,** and **Hornitos,** between Las Hamacas Hotel and the Radisson, are called the "afternoon beaches" because fishermen haul in their midday catches here, and indeed Tamarindo smells like seafood for much of the day. The waves are moderate and the sand is ideal for beach sports, and the beaches present a long view directly out of the bay to the horizon of the open Pacific. Those needing a break from the relentless sun should head to **Parque Papagayo,** which sprawls from Costera to Cuauhtémoc. Bike and walking paths, an aviary, a skate park, a roller rink, and an island in the middle of the lake inhabited by a monkey are a sampling of what the park offers. Children will enjoy the wading pool, exotic birds, and million spots for hide-and-seek. Cool off in the pool amid shrieking children. *(☎485 2490. Park open daily 7am-8pm; rink open daily 4-10:30pm. 15 pesos, with skate rental 25 pesos. Pool open 7am-8pm. 15 pesos.)*

FROM LA DIANA TO THE NAVAL BASE. A trip to **Playa Condesa,** at the center of the bay, brings you to the sandy center of Acapulco. Strong waves and a rapidly dropping sea floor discourage swimmers but open the waters to windsurfers and jet skiers. Ashore, throngs of sun worshippers lounge under their blue umbrellas (20-30 pesos), while hordes of vendors offer everything from mangos-on-a-stick to bathing suits. As the day wears on and the sun sets, friends meet on the beach to hang out, eat, drink, and play the occasional beach soccer game. Farther down, between the golf course and naval base, is **Playa Icacos,** the longest of the bay. The eastern edge of the beach is popular with families, with fine sand and calm waves. The **CICI,** a water park, is the perfect chance to plunge down winding water slides or watch trained dolphins perform. For big-spending dolphin-lovers, the CICI lets you frolic with them in the tank for short intervals. Above water you can experience the thrill of the sky coaster. *(Costera at Colón. Follow Costera until the orange walls painted with large blue waves; otherwise take a "CICI" or "Base" bus. ☎484 1970. Open daily 10am-6pm. 100 pesos. Dolphin shows M-F 2pm, Sa-Su 2 and 4pm, 15 pesos. Swim with dolphins: ☎481 0294. 30min. 900 pesos, 1hr. 1300 pesos. Make reservations 1 day in advance.)*

PUERTO MARQUÉS. Just west of Acapulco Diamante and in sharp contrast is the dusty, crumbling town of Puerto Marqués. The protection of the cove makes for gentle waters, backed by a narrow beach and a line of *marisco* restaurants stretching at least 1km. The bus ride is the real attraction; the hilltop view of Acapulco and the bay are unbeatable. As the bus rambles along, the **Bahía de Puerto Marqués** and the pounding surf of **Playa Revolcadero** come into view. Both offer a variety of watersports, including surfing and scuba diving. Catch a *colectivo* from Puerto Marqués (6 pesos) to get to the quieter and less crowded **Playa Bonville** farther east. *(From the bus station across from Comercial Mexicana at Playa Hornitos, on the beach side of the street, take a "Glorieta" bus to La Glorieta. From there, catch a "Puerto Marqués" bus. For snorkel, scuba, and jet ski rental, ask around at the beachfront restaurants.)*

PIE DE LA CUESTA. Northwest of the city and around the other side of the sheltered bay is **Pie de la Cuesta,** a small village bordering a long beach exposed to the open Pacific. The beach, impossible to miss behind the palm grove, is a beautiful untouristed gem of golden sand. Enjoy it to its fullest, because swimming here is ill-advised, with monster waves crashing close to the shore even during low tide. *(To get to Pie de la Cuesta, take a "Pie de la Cuesta" bus near the zócalo on Costera.)* The area's other natural attraction, the **Laguna de Coyuca,** is full of tropical birds, fish, and reptiles. Tours take you around the perimeter of the laguna, with time to swim and take pictures of the wildlife, and if you should want to, a partial set from the classic Rambo II. *(☎460 0229. 4½hr. tours 11am, noon, 1:30pm from Restaurant "Pacífico" near the lagoon. Call for prices. Cash only.)*

🎵 ENTERTAINMENT

Those too tired for another day on the beach or night at a club will find milder entertainment at **Plaza Bahía,** a large shopping mall on Costera, four blocks east of La Gran Plaza, on the beach side. Bowl away at **Bol Bahía** on the fourth floor. (☎485 0970. 30 pesos per person per game or 200 pesos per hr. for a group; shoes 11 pesos. Open M-Sa noon-1am, Su noon-midnight.) East of Plaza Bahía is **Galerías Diana**, where you can window shop or catch a first-run Hollywood film at **Cinépolis,** on the third floor. (Movies daily 3-11pm. Tickets 40 pesos, W 32 pesos.)

Corridas take place at **Plaza de Toros Caletilla,** 200m west of Playa Caleta near the abandoned yellow jai alai courts. (☎483 9561. Tickets sold at 4:30pm at the plaza on fight days. Dec.-Apr. Su and occasional Th 5pm.) **Cliff diving** may be Acapulco's most famous form of entertainment. Head out to the cliffs at **La Quebrada,** at the western end of the street of the same name, and watch the *clavadistas* first scale the nearly vertical cliffs, pray, and then plummet into the churning waters below. (☎483 1400. Take a bus to the *zócalo* and walk 15min. west on La Quebrada. Dives at 12:45, 7:30, 8:30, 9:30, 10:30pm. Tickets 35 pesos.) The Acapulco tourist office organizes a variety of festivals to lighten tourists' wallets. **Festival**

Acapulco, a celebration of music, occurs in May, and the **Black Film Festival** takes place during the first week of June. On December 9, men and women from around the globe journey to Acapulco to test their cliff-diving skills (or watch others) during the **Torneo Internacional de Clavados en La Quebrada.**

NIGHTLIFE

Acapulco has a reputation for partying, and it is well deserved. Discos, bars, and more vintage dancing clubs, all along the Costera, get going at midnight and don't stop until sunrise. Almost all include open bar, which warrants a hefty cover. The city has a small but active gay nightlife scene, centered on a few small blocks. It is always easier and cheaper for women to get in, and many clubs offer deals to women on weeknights. For further discounts (albeit small ones), grab the cards from the cabbies and solicitors as you walk down Costera—they get a commission and you get 20 pesos off the cover price.

CLUBS AND BARS

Palladium (☎446 5486), on the Carretera Escénica las Brisas. A massive glass front commands the best view of the entire bay. The latest trance and techno pulse as trendy youth dance under the frenzied lights. You'll have to shell out for Acapulco's best. Open bar. Cover men 400 pesos, women 300 pesos; Tu and Th women 150 pesos until 12:30am. Open Tu and Th-Su 11pm-5am. MC/V.

Salón Q, Costera 3117 (☎481 0114). Traditional Latin rhythms fill "La Catedral de la Salsa" and draw a mixed crowd to dance or nurse their drinks with friends. Relives Acapulco's glory days, when places like this were the norm, not the exception. Dance show and live music 12:45am. Beer 40 pesos. Mixed drinks 45 pesos. Cover with open bar 240 pesos. Open Tu-Su 10pm-4am. Cash only.

Furia Cafe, Farallón 1 (☎484 2179), on the 10th fl. above the parking garage. A seemingly bizarre location for a club, the classy lounge empties at midnight when the live music starts and couples crowd the floor to *banda* and *norteño* favorites. Rest and enjoy the beautiful view of the surrounding hills. Pants and suitable dancing shoes required. Open bar for *bebidas nacionales*. Cover Th men 120 pesos, women 60 pesos; F-Sa 140/80 pesos. Open Th-Sa 11pm-4am. Cash only.

Paradise, Costera 107 (☎484 5988), on Condesa beach. A fun *terraza* bar over the ocean, where tourists and locals move unself-consciously to reggaeton and club hits or relax at high tables watching the bungee jumping next door. 60-peso drink min., which includes 2 *bebidas nacionales*. Beer 30 pesos. Mixed drinks 45-55 pesos. Open daily 10pm-4am. Cash only.

Alebrije, Costera 3308 (☎484 5902). Stadium seating and rectangular lounge couches lend a sports arena vibe, only dispelled by the darkness and the groups of girls getting low on the bartop. Open bar. Cover men 400 pesos, women 300 pesos; W-Th women 100 pesos before midnight. Open daily 10:30pm-5am. Cash only.

Nina's, Costera 2909 (☎484 2400), on the beach side near CICI. The gaudy tropical exterior matches the bright motion inside, with an older crowd grooving to live cumbia, salsa, and merengue with impersonations of famous Latin dancers and singers. Elaborate costume show 1am. Open bar. Cover Th-Sa 250 pesos. Open Th-Su 10pm-4am. Cash only.

Carlos'n Charlie's, Costera 112 (☎484 1285). Take the freight elevator up to bar the 2nd-fl. overlooking the Costera. Young groups of friends and infatuated couples come to have a peaceful night out or enjoy mixed drinks at the encouragement of the friendly waitstaff. International pop hits play on a big screen TV in the background.

Beer 40 pesos. Mixed drinks 75 pesos; yard-long drinks 140 pesos. No cover. AmEx/MC/V. Open daily noon-3am. Cash only.

Baby'O (☎ 484 7474; www.babyo.com.mx), on Costera. Extremely posh and exclusive—a night here could easily run you as much as night in a resort, and there's not even a pool. Cave-and-jungle interior houses a slightly less frenetic and more sophisticated atmosphere than its rambunctious neighbors. Beer 50 pesos; *bebidas nacionales* 110 pesos. High season cover men 600 pesos, women 200 pesos. Low season cover men 400 pesos, women 100 pesos. Open high season daily 10:30pm-7am, low season W-Su 10:30pm-7am. AmEx/MC/V.

GLBT NIGHTLIFE

Demás Factory, Av. de los Deportes 10A (☎ 484 1800), next to Savage. An odd assortment of tin foil streamers, balloons, and a large disco ball decorate the dark club. Loud techno pounds in the background as a naked stripper makes the rounds on the bartop. Beer 30 pesos. *Bebidas nacionales* 40-45 pesos. Chippendale shows daily at midnight. Cover 70 pesos, includes 1 drink. Open daily 10pm-5am.

Moons, Av. de los Deportes 10C (☎ 484 1800), next to Demás Factory. Scantily clad men traipsing across the white-tiled disco floor, replete with stripper's pole, is the main draw of Moons. Customers sit at small, high tables and enjoy the show. Beer 30 pesos. *Bebidas nacionales* 45-50 pesos. Cover 70 pesos, includes 1 drink. Open Th-Su 10:30pm-5am.

Picante, Privada Piedra Picuda 16 (☎ 484 2342), behind Carlos'n Charlie's. Flashing green lights and blacklights illuminate the graphic, racy entertainment on tap while the young, lithe male clientele looks on. Dress code prohibits cross-dressing to avoid possible harassment. Beer 30 pesos. *Bebidas nacionales* 45 pesos. Strip show begins at midnight. Cover 50 pesos, includes 1 drink. Open daily 10pm-4am. MC/V.

Savage Disco, Av. de los Deportes 10B (☎ 484 1800). Stand-out features include leopard-print chairs, zebra-striped bar, strobe lights, and booming music. Beer 30 pesos. Transvestite shows 1 and 3am; mixed crowd for shows. Cover 70 pesos, includes 1 drink; good for Demás and Moons as well. Open F-Sa and holidays from 10pm.

TAXCO ☎ 762

White buildings topped with red roofs, winding streets, and sparkling *platerías* (silver shops) make the old mining town of Taxco (pop. 100,000) an antique gem set in the mountains. Clouds pass at arm's reach, cobblestone alleys coil around colonial churches, and the streets are so narrow that pedestrians must hug the walls to let cars pass. The steep hills wind even the most athletic traveler, and getting lost in the maze of streets and markets alternately frustrates and surprises visitors with glorious views of the valley below. Beneath the old-fashioned beauty run the veins of silver that shaped Taxco's history. When silver was discovered in 1524, Taxco became the continent's first mining town, luring craftsmen and treasure-seekers from all over the world. It was not until the 1930s, when the tourist industry took hold, that Taxco exploded with *platerías*. Today, the streets are aflutter with tourists drawn to the exquisite jewelry. Even the most budget-conscious travelers are inclined to take home a little bit of treasure.

▐ TRANSPORTATION

There are two main **bus stations** in Taxco. **Estrella de Oro,** Kennedy 126 (☎ 622 0648), has first-class service to: **Acapulco** (4hr., 13 per day 5:10am-7:10pm, 145 pesos); **Cuernavaca** (1½hr., 6 per day 10:20am-7:40pm, 50 pesos); **Mexico City** (2½hr., 7 per day 7am-7pm, 100 pesos); **Iguala** (1¾hr., 11 per day 5:10am-6:10pm,

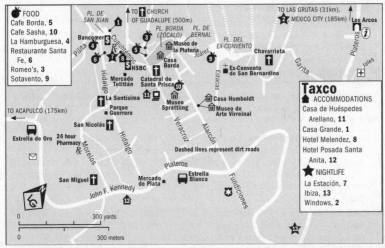

FOOD
Cafe Borda, **5**
Cafe Sasha, **10**
La Hamburguesa, **4**
Restaurante Santa
Fe, **6**
Romeo's, **3**
Sotavento, **9**

TO LAS GRUTAS (31km),
MEXICO CITY (185km) Los Arcos

PL. DE
SAN JUAN
TO CHURCH
OF GUADALUPE (500m)
PL. BORDA   PL. DE
(ZÓCALO)   BERNAL
Bancomer
Cuauhtémoc
Pilita
Museo
de la Platería
PL. DEL
EX-CONVENTO
Chavarrieta
Casa
Borda
Juárez
HSBC
Ex-Convento
de San Bernardino
Estacas
Garita
Jales
Mercado
Tetitlán
Catedral de
Santa Prisca
TO ACAPULCO (175km)
La Santísima
Museo
Spratlling
Casa Humboldt
Parque
Guerrero
Museo de
Arte Virreinal
San Nicolás
Veracruz
Alarcón
Estrella de Oro   24 hour
Pharmacy
Morelos
Hidalgo
Dashed lines represent dirt roads
San Miguel
Plat..os
Estrella
Blanca
Mercado
de Plata
John F. Kennedy
Fundiciones

Taxco
ACCOMMODATIONS
Casa de Huéspedes
Arellano, **11**
Casa Grande, **1**
Hotel Melendez, **8**
Hotel Posada Santa
Anita, **12**
★ NIGHTLIFE
La Estación, **7**
Ibiza, **13**
Windows, **2**

0 ___ 300 yards
0 ___ 300 meters

28 pesos). To get to the *zócalo*, the lightly laden or heavily ambitious can cross the street and walk up the steep hill known as Pilita. When you reach Plazuela de San Juan, which has a small fountain, veer left and you will emerge facing Santa Prisca in the *zócalo*. Otherwise, a "Zócalo" *combi* will make the trip (3.50 pesos), as will a taxi (12 pesos almost anywhere in the city). **Estrella Blanca,** Plateros 104 (☎622 0131), goes to: **Acapulco** (4½hr., 6 per day 4am-6:40pm, 168 pesos); **Cuernavaca** (1½hr., 12 per day 6am-8pm, 58 pesos); **Toluca** (3hr.; 2:40, 11:30am, 1:40pm; 79 pesos); **Mexico City** (2½hr., 10 per day 6am-8pm, 105 pesos.) To reach the *zócalo* from the bus station, turn right onto Plateros, left on Alarcón, and then left on Agostín de Tolsa.

⚙ 🛈 ORIENTATION AND PRACTICAL INFORMATION

Taxco lies 185km southwest of Mexico City. The town, built into a hillside, is a labyrinth of crisscrossing cobblestone streets and dead-end alleys—a map is essential. The *zócalo*, **Plaza Borda**, is marked by **Catedral de Santa Prisca**, which is visible from most places in town. **Avenida de los Plateros,** the main traffic thoroughfare and home to most official services and the bus stations, skirts the land downhill from the *zócalo*.

Tourist Office: Subsecretaría de Fomento Turístico, Plateros 1 (☎622 2274), at the entrance to town. "Los Arcos" *combis* (3.50 pesos) end in front of the office. Open M-Sa 10am-8pm. Tourist info also at Estrella Blanca station. Most hotels have maps.

Banks: Bancomer, Cuauhtémoc 14 (☎622 4966). Open M-F 8:30am-4pm. **HSBC,** Plaza Borda 3-A (☎622 7300). Open M-Sa 8am-7pm.

Emergency: Procuraduría del Turista, Plateros 1 (☎622 2274 or 6616). Open M-F 9am-6pm, Sa 9am-2pm.

Police: Fundiciones 27 (☎622 8462 or 0007), at the hill's base across from Alarcón.

Red Cross: (☎622 3232 or ☎065 in emergencies), on Jales, next to the tourist information caseta. 24hr. emergency service.

24hr. Pharmacy: Farmacia Genericos y Similares, Morelos 31 (☎627 3889), up the hill from Plateros. Also, **Farmacias del Ahorro,** Cuauhtémoc 4 (☎627 3444). Open daily 7am-11pm.

Medical Services: IMSS, Plateros 330 (☎622 3510 or 0336). Open 24hr.

Internet Access and Fax Office: Torril 4 (☎622 0789), upstairs on the way to Casa de Huéspedes Arellano. 8 pesos per hr. Open M-F 9am-8:30pm, Sa-Su 10am-8pm.

Post Office: Plateros 382 (☎622 0501), near the Estrella de Oro station. Open M-F 8am-2:30pm. **Postal Code:** 40200.

ACCOMMODATIONS

A good night's sleep does not come cheap in Taxco, but the few budget accommodations are sleaze-free and situated in beautiful, old-fashioned buildings with generally clean rooms, many with gorgeous views over the city. Reservations are recommended.

Casa de Huéspedes Arellano, Pajaritos 23 (☎622 0215). From the *zócalo*, walk down the street to the right of the cathedral and descend the 1st set of stairs to the right. Continue 3 levels down through the vendor stands; on the left is Taxco's best deal. Spotless, simple rooms with soft beds complement clean communal bath. 3 charming terraces with couches and a sweeping view over the city. Dorms 140 pesos; singles 160 pesos, with private bath 320 pesos; 3- to 4-bed rooms 400/480 pesos. Cash only. ❷

Casa Grande, Plazuela de San Juan 7 (☎622 0969), on the *zócalo*. You won't fall asleep before 1am, when the adjacent bar turns out its lights. Small, slightly unmaintained rooms with gargantuan beds, dressers, clean bath, and balcony view for dirt cheap. Like rooms, communal baths are small and dark. Singles 155 pesos, with bath and TV 230 pesos; doubles 230/355 pesos; triples 270/412 pesos. MC/V. ❸

Hotel Posada Santa Anita, Plateros 320 (☎622 3975). A little more street noise and the lack of a view make for a cheap stay, but rooms are clean, and pleasantly bright with spotless hot baths. Reception 24hr. Singles 200 pesos; 1-bed doubles 320 pesos, 2-bed 370 pesos; triples 420 pesos; quads 550 pesos. Cash only. ❹

Hotel Melendez, Cuauhtémoc 6 (☎622 0006), just off the *zócalo*. The center courtyard affords a healthy measure of repose, if you don't mind the occasional zealous Bible quote painted on the wall. The rooms are large, with pretty wooden furniture. Hot water in morning and evening. Singles 250 pesos; doubles 350 pesos. Cash only. ❺

FOOD

The *taquerías* and *torterías* peppering the streets of other cities are conspicuously lacking in Taxco, making quick and cheap food hard to find. Menus here are fairly uniform and reflect the tourist presence, with egg specials and hamburgers as the mainstays. Most restaurants are a little pricier than in other regions, but afford great terrace views. There is also a market, **Mercado Tetitlán,** on the street to the right of Santa Prisca or off Hidalgo, which sells everything from jewelry to meat. (Open daily 8:30am-8pm.)

Cafe Sasha, Alarcón 3 (☎627 6464; cafesasha@hotmail.com). An incredible menu selection caters to every palate. Vegetarians can try the thai curry special or falafel with tabouli (75 pesos), while jumbo burgers (55 pesos) and nachos (48 pesos) are heavier yet cheaper options. Funky art, exotic curios, and some useless *Lonely Planets* complete the coffeehouse ambience. Wi-Fi. Open daily 8am-12am. Cash only. ❹

Restaurante Santa Fe, Hidalgo 2 (☎622 1170), downhill from Plazuela de San Juan. A welcoming clutter of gaudy tablecloths, signed posters, earthenware dishes, and family photos have added to Santa Fe's charm since 1954. The bold should try the rabbit in garlic sauce (65 pesos), while the cheap *tortas* (14 pesos) are excellent. Open daily 8am-9pm. Cash only. ❷

La Hamburguesa, Plazuela de San Juan 5 (☎622 0941), across from Casa Grande. Hearty food comes at the drop of a hat, including the namesake burgers (23 pesos) with fries. Terrace seating overlooking the Plazuela is marred by mosquitoes. Entrees 25-50 pesos. Open daily 9am-midnight. Cash only. ❷

Romeo's, Plazuela de los Gallos 2 Altos (☎622 6922), uphill on Crayem off the *zócalo*. March up the numerous staircases straight past the indoor seating to the roof, where a gorgeous panorama of the city accompanies the pricey food. *Comida corrida* 76 pesos. Chicken dishes more reasonable at 60 pesos. Breakfast specials from 35 pesos. Open daily 10am-6pm. Cash only. ❺

Casa Borda, Plaza Borda 3A, on the *zócalo*. Coming here is a gamble, since there are only 3 tables, but it's worth the effort for the lovely breakfast. Posters of Marilyn Monroe and other profligate stars of the 50s hang on the wall. Eggs 30 pesos. Excellent breakfast combos 40-50 pesos. *Antojitos* 45-55 pesos. Open daily 8am-9pm. Cash only. ❹

🌀 SIGHTS

MUSEO GUILLERMO SPRATLING. William Spratling, the genius artist who transformed Taxco in the 1930s, donated his massive collection of pre-Hispanic artifacts, which are housed here. Stunning examples of his virtuoso silverwork are on display downstairs. *(Delgado 1. Follow the road to the left of the cathedral downhill. ☎622 1660. Open Tu-Sa 9am-6pm, Su 9am-3pm. 27 pesos.)*

CATEDRAL DE SANTA PRISCA. "God gives to Borda, Borda gives to God," said José de la Borda, devout silver tycoon, whose financing of the gorgeous church left him broke. The glittering dome and towers, which top the rosy Baroque facade, are visible from throughout the city. Inside are paintings by indigenous artist Miguel Cabrera (1695-1768), whose racy subjects include a pregnant Virgin Mary and the circumcision of baby Jesus. Admire the gorgeous organ, and 12 ornamented gold altars for the apostles. *(Open daily 8am-8pm. Su Mass every hr. 6am-2pm.)*

CASA HUMBOLDT. Bas-reliefs in Moorish *mudéjar* style, beautiful patios, and a petite garden hidden within decorate this 18th-century colonial home, which continues to get mileage out of being a rest stop for explorer Alexander von Humboldt one night in 1803. The house now holds the collection of the Museo de Arte Virreinal, including exhibits on 17th- and 18th-century Catholic rituals and dress. *(Alarcón 12, past Hotel los Arcos. ☎622 5501. Open Tu-Sa 10am-5:45pm, Su 10am-3:45pm. 20 pesos, students 15 pesos, children 10 pesos.)*

CASA BORDA. Once the 18th-century home of silver tycoon José de la Borda, the Casa now serves as the Instituto Guerrerense de Cultura. Poke around and enjoy the architecture, including the precipitous multi-story drop to the street in back. In addition to hosting a library, a dance studio, and several galleries, the center hosts book readings and concerts. Ask for a schedule. *(Enter on the zócalo. ☎622 6617. Open daily 9am-8:30pm.)*

MUSEO DE LA PLATERÍA. This museum traces the history of silver artisans in Taxco from when silver was discovered in the viceregal period, featuring beautiful work by local artists and testaments to Taxco silver throughout the centuries. *(Buried in the Patio de las Artesanías. Enter on the zócalo, walk to the left and head downstairs. Open Tu-Su 10am-6pm. 10 pesos.)*

EX-CONVENTO DE SAN BERNARDINO. Buried and half-forgotten off the center of town, the Ex-Convento was built in 1592 as a Franciscan monastery and destroyed in a fire, then reconstructed in Neoclassical style in 1823. The struggle for independence officially ended when the Plan de Iguala was signed here in 1821. Today, the temple houses two popular devotional images, including *El*

Cristo de los Plateros (Christ of the Silversmiths). *(In Plaza del Convento. Follow Juárez past city offices. Open daily 8am-1pm and 2-6:30pm. Free.)*

VIEWS OF TAXCO. The vistas of the city and surrounding hills are best from the Church of Guadalupe. From the *zócalo*, take Crayem, to the right of Cuauhtémoc, to Guadalupe, and veer right until you reach the plaza before the church. The walk is steep even for Taxco, so taking a "Guadalupe" *combi* or a taxi is probably a good idea. For a more sweeping view, take a cable car to Hotel Monte Taxco. To get a gorgeous postcard view of the city and the cathedral from the front, climb the hill called **Bermeja**. To get there, head down Morelos, cross the street, and begin climbing. *(Take a "Los Arcos" combi to the white arches at the city's entrance; 3.50 pesos. Before passing through the arches, turn left up a hill and bear left into the parking lot.* ☎622 1468. *Cable car runs daily 7:40am-6:50pm. Round-trip 35 pesos, children 22 pesos, Hotel Monte Taxco guests free.)*

♫ 🎭 ENTERTAINMENT AND NIGHTLIFE

Taxco's crowded streets somehow manage to accommodate the hordes of tourists that descend on the town during its two major festivals: **Feria Nacional de la Plata,** a national contest during the last week of November that celebrates silver artisanship, and the more popular **Semana Santa** festivities. Biblical reenactments fill the streets and on Good Friday, hooded *penitentes* process through the streets carrying logs made out of cactus trunks on their shoulders, and subject themselves to flagellation to cleanse their sins. During the annual **Día del Jumil,** on the first Monday of November, Taxco residents make a pilgrimage to the Huizteco hill, where they collect and eat insects known as *jumil*. The brown bugs contain more protein per gram than beef and only appear during this time of year. In December, the Church of Guadalupe, from which you can see all of Taxco, comes alive with celebrations of the Virgin. On **Día del Santa Antonio Abad,** on January 17, townspeople bring their animals to be blessed in the atrium of the Cathedral in an age-old ritual. The next day, during the **Feast of Saint Sebastian and Saint Prisca,** the streets are filled with food, music, and fireworks.

As shops close and vendors pack their wares, people head to Plaza Borda, in front of the illuminated cathedral. Those with enough energy to dance after hiking Taxco's hills will get their chance at **Windows,** in Hotel Monte Taxco. Accessible only by taxi after 7pm, this bar/dance club offers a party atmosphere with an unparalleled view. *(*☎622 1300. *Cover 60 pesos. Open F-Su 10:30pm-late. MC/V.)* Well-dressed groups head to **Ibiza,** Plateros 137, to laugh over drinks and break it down on the dance floor to loud techno and house music. *(*☎627 1664. *Cover 70 pesos. Open Th-Su 10pm-4am. MC/V.)* **La Estación** is a more laid-back option closer to the *centro*. Couples and groups young and old drink beer and watch soccer or play pool (30 pesos per hr.) in this vaguely western-themed bar. *(Beer 20 pesos. Mixed drinks 45-55 pesos. Open daily noon-1am. Cash only.)*

📷 SHOPPING

More than 300 *platerías* cater to a steady stream of tourists drawn to Taxco by its silver sheen. If you're dipping uncomfortably deep into your pockets, browse the shops that sell *artesanías* as well as silver. Stop by **Mercado Tetitlán,** southwest of the *zócalo*. (Open daily 8:30am-8pm.) **Mercado de Plata,** just behind the Estrella Blanca station, is where locals buy the work of silversmiths from the countryside, who often sell fine goods at cheaper prices. (Open Sa 10am-6pm.) Shopping outside the *centro* will usually garner cheaper prices, if less interesting designs.

🔁 DAYTRIP FROM TAXCO

🏛 **GRUTAS DE CACAHUAMILPA.** A stunning, deep set of natural caves lie just 30km away from Taxco, chiseled out millions of years ago by the subterranean Río

San Jeronimo. Bats perch in the 75m heights, and stalactites, stalagmites, and other sinuous mineral formations cover the surfaces. Legend has it the cave has played host to runaway *indígenas*, General Porfirio Díaz, Santa Anna, and Alexander von Humboldt, among others. Guides lead a 2km tour into the caves. Aside from the caves, there's a recently-opened botanical garden and nature reserve, housing 39 endemic species and other spectacular animals like the royal eagle. (*"Grutas" combis leave every hr. from Taxco's Estrella Blanca station, stopping at the parking lot; 20 pesos. Taxis cost 120 pesos. Buses make the trip as well but will drop you farther away; 50min., every 40min., 6:30am-3:30am, 21 pesos. To get to the parking lot, take a right off the highway, then another right after the curve. ☎ 734 346 1716. Open daily 10am-5pm. 60 pesos, ages 5-12 40 pesos. Private guides 200 pesos. 2hr. tours leave visitors center every hr. You can only enter the caves with a guided tour. Wear loose clothing and shoes with traction.*)

OAXACA

PUERTO ESCONDIDO ☎954

The narrow highway that runs into Puerto Escondido winds through the mountains and parallels the coast. Lined on both sides by jungle, it doesn't reveal the blue Pacific Ocean to the south until the forest parts for the city. In this surfer's—and wannabe-surfer's—paradise, Playa Zicatela is considered one of

Oaxaca State

the world's best surfing beaches, while others nearby have waves perfect for beginners. Puerto Escondido (pop. 60,000) transformed itself from a fishing and surfing town into a hip tourist locale, drawing droves of young people from around the world, some of whom take up permanent residence. Although Puerto Escondido constantly sees new faces—bringing a young, international flavor—it nevertheless holds on to a tight-knit community feeling.

▛ TRANSPORTATION

Flights: Puerto Escondido Airport (PXM; ☎ 582 0492). Best reached by taxi (35 pesos). **AeroCaribe** (☎ 582 2023) flies to **Bahías de Huatulco, Mexico City,** and **Oaxaca. Aerovega** (☎ 582 0151), Gasga 113, flies to **Oaxaca** daily.

Buses: Estrella Blanca station (☎ 582 0086) is the farthest from the tourist corridor at Oaxaca and 10 Nte. Buses go to **Acapulco** (semi-direct 8hr., 4, 10, 11am; direct 9½hr. 8am, 2, 5pm; each 216 pesos), **Bahías de Huatulco** via **Pochutla** (2½hr., 5 per day 4pm-12:30am, 38-62 pesos), and **Mexico City** (12hr.; 6:30, 7:30, 8:30pm; 430 pesos). **Cristóbal Colón,** (☎ 582 1073) just west of the *crucero* on the carretera, sends buses to: **Bahías de Huatulco** (2hr., 9 per day 7am-9:30pm, 68 pesos); **San Cristóbal de las Casas** (14hr.; 6:30, 9:30pm; 372 pesos); **Oaxaca** (7hr., 7am, 6:30, 8:45pm, 228 pesos) and **Tuxtla Gutiérrez** (12hr.; 6:30, 9:30pm; 324 pesos). Semi-direct service runs to **Bahías de Huatulco** via **Pochutla** (2½hr., 21 per day, 35 pesos). *Micros* to **Pochutla** leave from the *crucero* (1hr., every 30-60min., 20 pesos).

✦ ▟ ORIENTATION AND PRACTICAL INFORMATION

Built on a hillside 294km south of Oaxaca on **Mex. 175,** Puerto Escondido is bisected by **Mex. 200,** also known as **Carretera Costera,** which divides uphill from downhill. The main tourist corridor is **Perez Gasga,** which loops down from the *crucero* and skirts the beach before rejoining Mex. 200 near Playa Marinera. The flat area of Gasga nearest the beach, full of shops and restaurants, is known as the **Adoquín.** It closes to traffic at 5pm and fills with pedestrians. Going east from the *crucero* will take you to **Zicatela.** Since the town is so small, most businesses do not have exact addresses, often making it difficult to find establishments. Locals may insist that Puerto Escondido is safe, but recent assaults on tourists have prompted the tourist office to recommend that travelers stay in groups and avoid isolated beaches, even during daylight hours. **Taxis** can be found by the tourist information booth and along **Carretera Costera** and **Calle del Morro** on **Zicatela;** they are the safest way of getting around after nightfall (25-30 pesos).

Tourist Office: Módulo de Información Turística, the booth at the beginning of the pedestrian walkway, down Gasga from the *crucero.* Open M-F 9am-2pm and 4-6pm, Sa 10am-1pm.

Currency Exchange: Money Exchange (☎ 582 2800), on the Adoquín halfway up the hill. Open M-F 8am-8pm, Sa-Su 8am-5pm. **Banorte,** on Hidalgo between Oaxaca and 1 Pte. (open M-F 9am-4pm, Sa 10am-2pm) and **HSBC** (☎ 582 1824), 1 Nte. at 3 Pte. (open M-F 8am-7pm) both have **ATMs.**

Luggage Storage: At the **Estrella Blanca** station. 3 pesos per piece per hr. The **Hotel Mayflower** (p. 516) also offers storage for 10 pesos per day.

Library: IFOPE Library, Juárez 10 (IFOPE2002@yahoo.com), on Rinconada on the way to Playa Carrizalillo. 900 books in English, French, German, and Spanish; membership required. Used books for sale 20-30 pesos. Open M, W, Sa 10am-noon.

Laundromat: Lava Max, Gasga 405, uphill from the walkway on the right, next to Banamex. Wash 13 pesos per kg. Dry 14 pesos. Open M-Sa 8am-7pm, Su 8am-4pm.

Emergency: International Friends of Puerto Escondido (IFOPE) (☎ 540 3816). A neighborhood watch group of area expats will get you in contact with your embassy, the

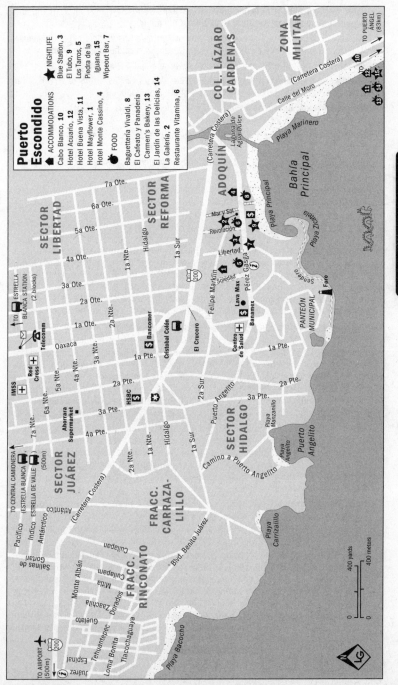

SOUTHERN PACIFIC COAST

Puerto Escondido

♣ ACCOMMODATIONS
Cabo Blanco, **10**
Hotel Acuario, **12**
Hotel Buena Vista, **11**
Hotel Mayflower, **1**
Hotel Monte Cassino, **4**

✦ FOOD
Baguettería Vivaldi, **8**
El Cafeato y Panadería
  Carmen's Bakery, **13**
El Jardín de las Delicias, **14**
La Galería, **2**
Restaurante Vitamina, **6**

★ NIGHTLIFE
Blue Station, **3**
El Tubo, **9**
Los Tarros, **5**
Piedra de la
  Iguana, **15**
Wipeout Bar, **7**

police, or medical help. If no one answers, go to the **Hotel Mayflower** (p. 516) and find owner **Minne Dahlberg** (☎582 0367), one of the founders.

Police: (☎582 0498), on 3 Pte. at the corner of Carretera Costera, ground fl. of Agencia Municipal. **Tourist Police** (☎582 3439), on Gasga, west of the tourist corridor.

Red Cross: (☎582 0550), on 7 Nte. between Oaxaca and 1 Pte. 24hr. service.

24hr. Pharmacy: Farmacia La Moderna 1, Gasga 203 (☎582 0698 or 2780), as it curves down from the *crucero*. Many others along the Adoquín.

Medical Services: Centro de Salud, Gasga 409 (☎582 2360). Small, minimal-expense medical clinic. Open 24hr. for emergencies.

Fax Office: Telecomm (☎582 0232), next to the post office. Open M-F 8am-7:30pm, Sa 9am-noon.

Internet Access: Internet Copa Cabaña, on the Adoquín just east of Libertad. 15 pesos per hr. Open daily 9am-10:30pm.

Post Office: 7 Nte. 701 (☎582 0959), at Oaxaca, a 15min. walk uphill from the *crucero*. Open M-F 8am-3pm. **Postal Code:** 71981.

🏠 ACCOMMODATIONS

While plenty of budget options are available in Puerto Escondido, those looking to surf and lounge on the beach should take advantage of comparably priced lodgings on Playa Zicatela. The cheapest *cabañas* (around 50 pesos) might not be secure; lock your valuables if possible. Prices vary in Puerto Escondido, rising during the high-season months of March-April, July-August, and December, and reservations are recommended. Rates listed below are for the low season.

▨ **Hotel Mayflower** (☎582 0367), on Libertad. From the bus station, cross the *crucero* and go left downhill, stairs descend on the right to the entrance. A Puerto mainstay, Mayflower offers clean beds and spotless, communal baths. Common areas, a rooftop bar and pool table, and a bevy of backpackers provide the tight-knit ambience. Wi-Fi, computer, purified water, lockers, book exchange, communal kitchen, and all the wisdom and knowledge of the owner. Rooms fill up every day—call ahead or arrive early. Reception 24hr. Dorms 90 pesos, 5% HI discount. Rooms 220 pesos. Cash only. ❶

▨ **Hotel Buena Vista** (☎582 1474; buenavista101@hotmail.com), on Playa Zicatela. Perched on a hill above Calle del Morros, Buena Vista rewards the seemingly endless climb with its spectacular, unequaled view of the beach. Tiled bath, fan, and refrigerator furnish the room. Splurge a little for the rooms with the gorgeous, sweeping balcony view. Be sure to call weeks in advance. Singles and doubles 200 pesos, with kitchen or A/C 300 pesos; each additional person 50 pesos. Prices double in high season. Monthly rates available. Cash only. ❸

Hotel Monte Cassino (www.hostalpuerto.com), on the eastern end of the Adoquín. Blessed solitude is the strength of Monte Cassino, with a simple, flowery courtyard located off the quiet end of the street. Rooms are simple but bright, with plain white beds and clean bath. Singles and doubles 150 pesos. Cash only. ❷

Hostel Shalom, in Puerto Escondido. A 7min. walk west on Calle Hidalgo above Carrizalillo, between Playas Manzanillo and Angelito and Playa Carrizalillo. A colorful mishmash of bungalows, tents, bathrooms, and mismatched paint. Dorm sheets are natty; bring your own or stick to the hammock. Communal kitchen and 24hr. bar, with a laidback vibe. Espresso 10 pesos. Hookahs for sale 80 pesos. Bikes 180 pesos per day. Surfboards 60 pesos per day.) Baths are sparse and cramped, but serviceable. Hammock 40 pesos; tent 50 pesos; dorm bed with mosquito net 60 pesos; 6-bed bungalows and private rooms 60 pesos per person. Cash only. ❶

Cabo Blanco (☎582 0337), on Playa Zicatela. Some of the cheapest *cabañas* on the strip. Clean, pleasant rooms range from tiny to spacious, all with fan and mosquito net. Has a popular adjacent restaurant with packed fish-fry parties with 2-for-1 mixed drinks on M nights. Singles and doubles 100 pesos, slightly larger 150 pesos, with bath 300 pesos. Cash only. ❶

🗋 FOOD

Puerto Escondido features the typical Mexican Pacific fare, seafood and *antojitos*, overlaid with a large helping of international cuisine imported by the sizeable expat community. Vegetarian fare is also abundant, especially along Zicatela. Local markets include: **Mercado Benito Juárez**, 8 Nte. at 3 Pte., which has typical goods in an organized setting (very busy on W and Sa when fresh produce arrives; open daily 5am-8pm); and **Ahorrara** (☎582 1128), at 3 Pte. and 4 Nte. (open M-Sa 8am-9pm, Su 8am-4pm).

El Jardín de las Delicias (☎582 0094), near the western end of Calle del Morro. A mixed bag of surfers, families, and couples chat with the amiable polyglot owner and chow down on hearty Italian food under the gigantic straw roof. Enormous salads (40-45 pesos) and low-fat brick-oven pizzas (75-90 pesos; after 5pm) are menu highlights. Open daily 9am-midnight. Cash only. ❹

Baguettería Vivaldi (☎582 0800), at the east end of the Adoquín. Tasty food for the homesick or anyone tired of the abundant Mexican and Italian fare. Vivaldi offers a number of enormous baguette sandwiches (from 35 pesos) and crepes (from 30 pesos) in a European cafe setting. Open daily 7am-midnight; in high season open longer. Cash only. ❷

La Galería, on Gasga just west of Andador Libertad. The brick floor and pastel paintings covering the walls give this Italian place its own artsy vibe. Pizza (55 pesos) goes well with fantastic ice cream desserts (42 pesos). Open daily 8am-11pm. Cash only. ❸

El Cafecito y Panadería Carmen's Bakery (☎582 0516), on Calle del Morro. A favorite of backpackers and tanned surfers, they whip up large breakfasts (32-43 pesos) before you head out into the waves. For later meals the veggie burgers (42 pesos) or garlic shrimp (89 pesos) might be a better option. 2nd location on Benito Juárez up from Carrizalillo. Open daily 7:30am-10pm. Cash only. ❸

Restaurante Vitamina T (☎582 3045), on the east end of the Adoquín. A good place to grab a quick breakfast. Eggs, any style (35 pesos) are perfect. For dinner and lunch, go elsewhere. Open daily 8am-midnight. MC/V after 2pm. ❸

🗋 BEACHES

Snorkelers may rent equipment from **Puerto Angelito** (40 pesos per hr.) or **Aventura Submarina,** on the Adoquín across from the tourist booth (☎582 2353; 150 pesos per day). Aventura Submarina also leads diving trips (inquire for prices). At most beaches, restaurants rent out umbrellas (35-50 pesos per day); but if you buy a drink you can use them for free. The following beaches are relatively safe. Still, you should stay in a group and not visit at night unless heading to a restaurant. Adventurers exploring secluded beaches must exercise caution.

PLAYA ZICATELA. Walking on the path behind the rocks on the east end of Marinero will take you to Zicatela, Mexico's pipeline and one of the best surfing beaches anywhere. Mesmerizing waves with 5-6m faces regularly break, so unless you've got the know-how and experience, stay on shore and enjoy the show. The best times for surf-watching are around 7:30am and 6:30pm, though times vary with the tide.

PLAYA CARRIZALILLO. The 167 stairs down the steep hill keep Carrizalillo secluded in its petite cove, allowing for good swimming and a little tranquility away from the town. The beach is fairly small but should afford you a small place to lay out or leisurely soak in the waves and sun. To get here, take a taxi (20 pesos). To walk, go west on Gasga to Banamex, until you come to the Rotary Club basketball courts. Follow the sign to Playa Carrizalillo, make a left, and keep walking downhill. Stairs lead down from Benito Juárez. Past Carrizalillo, the waves again turn dangerous—do not attempt to swim there.

PLAYA PRINCIPAL. The main beach of Puerto Escondido, Playa Principal lies just beyond the stores and restaurants that line Adoquín. *Lanchas* crowd the waters, which are gentle enough for swimming, while the sand is covered with soccer games, sunbathers, and beachcombers.

PLAYA MARINERO. Continuing east along the shore, you'll pass a small contaminated lagoon on your left. Immediately after is Marinero, less crowded than Principal and good for swimming and sunbathing. Waves get rougher near the point, inviting hordes of boogie boarders and rookie surfers.

PLAYAS MANZANILLO AND ANGELITO. On the other side of Playa Principal, Manzanillo and Angelito are crammed with vacationing Mexican families and their screaming children with inflatable tubes. Manzanillo is the better bet for swimming. Taxis (20 pesos) will bring you here, but if you prefer to walk (20min.), go west on Gasga to Banamex and take a left (10min.); continue left toward the ocean at the sign for Playa Angelito. You will come to a fork in the road; the left path leads to Manzanillo, the right leads to Angelito. The two beaches are separated by an easily crossed rock barrier.

PLAYA BACOCHO. Less scenic (and slightly dirtier) than other beaches, Playa Bacocho is noteworthy because it provides the best sunset view around and features two beach clubs, **Coco's** and **Club de Playa Villasol,** which allow use of their bars and pools for 40 pesos per day. Beware of the powerful current on the east side of the beach. Bacocho is best reached by taxi (45 pesos).

🏔 OUTDOOR ACTIVITIES

If you get tired of the beach, there are plenty of ecotourism opportunities in the area and experienced companies to guide you—as with most guided tours, you have to be willing to shell out. **Lalo Ecotours** offers seasonal tours of the lagoon of San Jose Manialtepec, 30min. outside of Puerto Escondido. Kayaking trips through the mangrove swamps, hikes through the bird-rich forests, and night trips to see the bioluminescent plankton are just a few of the tours on offer. (☎582 2853; www.lalo-ecotours.com. Call to arrange tours and pickup from your hotel. Available in English. Most are 350 pesos per person.) **Rutas de Aventura** allows you to personalize longer eco-vacations through Guerrero's interior, where you can mountain bike, hike through jungles and coffee plantations, kayak lagoons and rivers, and enjoy the extensive bird, reptile, and crocodile population of the state. (☎582 0170; www.rutasdeaventura.com.mx. Prices based on tour length and itinerary.)

🎵 NIGHTLIFE

The Adoquín is the center of Puerto Escondido's nightlife, with lively bars blasting music into the street well into the morning. All the best places are right on the strip, eliminating the need for a taxi, or making for an easy ride from Playa Zicatela (20 pesos). In the early evening, every restaurant and bar has a Happy hour, which usually lasts 3-4hr. and features cheap beers and two-for-one mixed drinks. Some bars let women drink free for an hour in the evening. Head to the tourist corridor for the ideal bar-hopping setting. After a day of surfing and sun, most are too tired to dance, leaving the disco scene pretty small. Most clubs close during low season.

Wipeout Bar, in the middle of the strip. A relaxed bar overlooking the bustle and breeze of the street. Loud reggaeton and hip hop fails to deter conversation as the young and beautiful play pool or sip drinks in cool blue lighting. Beers 20 pesos, 2-for-1 mixed drinks 50 pesos. Sa 11pm-midnight women drink free. Open W-Sa 7:30pm-2am. Cash only.

Piedra de la Iguana, at the eastern end of Zicatela. A yard with a bar in the corner. The unsuspecting nightspot hosts raging afterparties for surfers, the Zicatela crowd, and those who aren't finished when the Adoquín shuts down. Beer 20 pesos. Mixed drinks 40 pesos. Open weekends and occasional weekdays 2am-late. Cash only.

Blue Station (☎582 3842), across from Wipeout Bar. A psychedelic mix of neon paint and blacklights along with pounding club music makes the air a little heavy in here. Beer 20 pesos. Mixed drinks 45-55 pesos. Open high season daily 9pm-2am; low season closed M. Cash only.

Los Tarros, on the Adoquín—hard to miss. The occasional table is lost amid the crush of dancing bodies. Fight your way to the bar, get a drink, and then find a space and camp on it or you'll lose it to one of the sweaty bodies writhing and singing to the loud Latin dance hits. Cover 30 pesos. Beer 30 pesos. Mixed drinks 35-50 pesos. Open daily 10:30pm-4am. Cash only.

El Tubo, behind Wipeout Bar on Playa Principal. Beachgoers don't bother to change much before heading out to El Tubo, where the reggaeton and hip hop keeps the casual dance floor moving well into the morning, when people spill out onto the beach. Beer 20 pesos. Mixed drinks 40-50 pesos. Open daily in high season 10pm-4am. Cash only.

MAZUNTE   ☎958

International backpackers in Mexico inevitably make the pilgrimage to Mazunte (pop. 700), the new hot spot to waste away the day. One of the most beautiful beaches on the southern Pacific coast, Mazunte is much more relaxed and less surfer-oriented than nearby Puerto Escondido. At night, the hostel bars come alive as guests spill out onto the beach and commune under the starry sky.

TRANSPORTATION AND PRACTICAL INFORMATION. Mazunte can be reached by taking a "Mazunte" **camioneta** from Zipolite (every 20min. 6am-7pm, 5 pesos). *Camionetas* also run to and from Pochutla (approx. 10 pesos). From Puerto Escondido, catch a **micro** at the *crucero* and get dropped off at the intersection named San Antonio (approx. 1hr., 15 pesos). From there, catch a *camioneta* to Mazunte (every 30min., 8 pesos) or take a taxi (25 pesos).

Mazunte is a 1km stretch of beach with a secluded cove on the far west end. Parallel to the beach is the main road, **Avenida. Paseo del Mazunte** (also known as **Principal**), which runs between Mazunte and nearby towns. Two dirt roads, **Calle La Barrita** and **Calle Rinconcito,** run between Mazunte and the beach and are lined with signs for rooms to rent. A small **tourist information** stand on the east end of the main road is open sporadically. Outside of the stand is a large town map; the **Centro de Salud** lies along a dirt road called Maguey at the western edge of town. Go straight as it breaks off from Principal, which veers right. (Open M-F and Su 8am-2pm and 4-8pm, 24hr. emergency service). The **police station** is headquartered in the Agencia Municipal behind the basketball courts in the middle of town. The station is unstaffed during the day—your best bet is early evening. There are no amenities in

GIVING BACK

LA VENTANILLA

At the mouth of the Tonameca River, just west of Mazunte, 25 families have formed a commune on an ecological reserve, dedicated to protecting the biodiversity of the area. They finance their wetland conservation efforts by leading tours through the surrounding mangrove swamps, paddling small boats through the dense foliage.

Along the way, keep your eyes peeled for lurking crocodiles, white heron mating colonies, camouflaged toucans, and the magical *majagua* flower, which changes color over the course of the day. The tour culminates with a visit to an island in the middle of the lagoon, where rare, native crocodiles and deer are bred in captivity. Nearby, the colony's female residents serve up fresh coconut refreshments and sell small handicrafts.

Many of the guides grew up around the colony. Their knowledge of the area is comprehensive and intimate—no question goes unanswered. With most similar tours of lower quality going for ten times as much, this one can't be missed.

To get La Ventanilla, take a camioneta from Mazunte bound for the crucero at San Antonio (5 pesos) and get off at the sign that says "La Ventanilla," then walk 1.5km down the road. Alternatively, take a taxi (25 pesos). Open daily 8am-5pm. Tours 40 pesos per person, children 20 pesos.

town other than a few convenience stores and houses with **laundry** signs. There is **Internet** access at **Marcos Net,** on Principal on the eastern edge of town. (12 pesos per hr. Open daily 10am-10pm.)

⚏ ACCOMMODATIONS AND FOOD. In addition to the hotels, many houses between the main road and the beach rent rooms for cheap and may be worth checking out. The *palapa* restaurants, *posadas* and hostels rent out hammocks and camping space on their grounds. (40-50 pesos for a hammock, roughly the same per person for campsites.) **La Luna Nueva ❶,** off Calle La Barrita midway down the main road, offers one of the best deals in town. The B&B has four rooms with fan, hammock, and mosquito net, and a clean common bath. The charming owners also run a popular bar in the front of the *cabañas*. (Singles 80 pesos; doubles 100 pesos. Cash only.) A cheap option with a range of rooms is **Posada Agujon ❶,** on the right side of Rinconcito a block from the beach. Despite the gaudy exterior stripes, all rooms are clean and basic, some with simple baths. The courtyard below doubles as a restaurant-bar, full of sand and bric-a-brac. (Singles and doubles 100-150 pesos, with bath 250 pesos. Cash only.) **Posada del Arquitecto ❶,** on the left side of Calle Rinconcita, is a rambling collection of *palapa* bungalows and dorms separated by cacti and palm trees. *Palapas* come with clean beds and mosquito nets. Dorm mattresses are thin foam pads. Bring your own lock for the lockers. (Hammocks 50 pesos; dorms 50 pesos; *cabañas* 200-300 pesos. Cash only.) If you're tired of roughing it and want to splurge, **La Alta Mira ❺,** down Calle Rinconcita and up a hill on the right, has 10 elegant bungalows with gorgeous tiled baths overlooking the cove, and stairs leading to the beach. (☎584 3104; www.altamira-hotel.com. Bungalows 450-600 pesos. Prices fall in low season. Cash only.)

Most of the restaurants at the beach are open late and double as bars until even later. Away from the beach there's **Armadillo ❹,** up a hill on Callejón del Armadillo off Rinconcito. Doubling as a gallery for bronze statuary, it serves up Mexican and Italian food at low prices. The *pasta a la mexicana* (45 pesos) is superb. Fresh bread available; ask for prices. (armadillomaxunte@yahoo.com.mx. Quesadillas 35-45 pesos. Seafood 70-85 pesos. Open daily 8am-11pm. Cash only.) For sumptuously fresh food, there's **Maíz Azul ❹,** on Playa Ventanilla near the tourist office. Let them know if you're in a hurry—they lavish care and time on the meals here, and it's easy to forget about the time watching the powerful waves crash on the beach. The *pescado* (70 pesos) is well worth the wait. (Octopus any style 60 pesos.

Shrimp 80 pesos. Open daily 8am-6pm. Cash only.) On the west end of the main road, popular **Palapa Tania ❷** has huge platters of food at lower prices. (Vegetarian dishes 35 pesos. *Pollo a la mexicana* 45 pesos. Open daily 2-11pm. Cash only.)

🖼 🖼 **SIGHTS AND NIGHTLIFE.** Besides the excellent and popular beach, the town's main attraction is the **Centro Mexicano de la Tortuga,** the first thing you see coming into town. Though the number of people looking out for the health of the Oaxacan coast is still dangerously small, interest is growing, thanks in part to the education provided by the center. The specialized aquarium contains six sea turtle species, five river species, and three land species. (☎/fax 584 4476. Open W-Sa 10am-4:30pm, Su 10am-2:30pm. Entrance with guided tour approx. every 10min.; tours in English available. 20 pesos.)

A short 1.5km camioneta ride west of Mazunte is **Playa Ventanilla,** which has vicious, swimmer-hostile waves and dirty sand. The reason to make the trip is the **Cooperativa Ventanilla,** a 1km walk down the road marked by the "La Ventanilla" sign, the site of a communal colony of 25 families who have dedicated themselves to protecting the wetlands at the mouth of the Tonameca River. The group runs amazing 🖼**lancha tours** that pass through the mangrove swamps (1¼hr.; 40 pesos, children 6-12 20 pesos). Guides paddle the lagoon in small boats, pointing out enormous crocodiles, iguanas, and members of the vast bird population. Through the choke of mangroves the guides paddle to an island in the middle, where they protect small native deer, mammals, and baby mangroves. Adjacent to the pens the women of the island sell coconuts, tacos, and small handicrafts. (Open daily 9am-5pm.) The Cooperative also collects sea turtle eggs from the beach to protect them from predators, and, after they hatch, releases them into the ocean. **La Luna Nueva** bar, on Calle la Barrita, is a laid-back joint with rope swings at the bar and reasonably priced mixed drinks (40 pesos). (Open daily 10pm-1am. Cash only.)

ZIPOLITE
☎**958**

Zipolite's (pop. 1500) distinction of having the only nude beach in Mexico fails to arouse the town from its sleepy languor, and sunbathers baring it all are far outnumbered by children playing in the surf. The action centers on the western end of the beach, lined by cheap hotels that double as restaurants and bars. There's little to do but sit on the beach or swim, but the latter activity is risky due to the hidden seaward currents. If you're not the gambling type, head to Mazunte's more benevolent waves.

> ⚠ **RIPTIDES.** Zipolite's beaches have brutal waves coming in from 2 directions, creating a series of channels that suck unsuspecting swimmers out to sea. Although ferocious, these channels are not very wide. If you find yourself being pulled from shore, do not panic and do not attempt to swim directly toward the beach; rather, swim parallel to the beach until clear of the seaward current. Many people have drowned at Zipolite, and warnings should be taken seriously—watch for red and yellow warning flags on the beach that mark especially dangerous areas. If you do swim, keep close to the shore.

📧 **TRANSPORTATION.** Just 4km west of Puerto Ángel, Zipolite is easily accessible by any vehicle rumbling down the poorly paved coastal road. **Camionetas** (5 pesos), **taxis colectivos** (10 pesos), and **taxis especiales** (30 pesos) pass frequently. To reach Pochutla, *taxis colectivos* are 15 pesos during the day. At night, take a private taxi. (25min., 100 pesos.)

■ 🛈 ORIENTATION AND PRACTICAL INFORMATION. Zipolite consists of one 2km stretch of beach and the roads that run behind it. The western end of the beach, where most of the hotels and restaurants are located, is called **Roca Blanca**. It's lined by a paved road called **Paisan** that runs parallel to the larger east-west road; the two are connected by a dirt road on the west end and a paved road on the other end.

While there is **no currency exchange** in Zipolite, most hotels and *cabañas* accept US$, and some of the bigger ones accept traveler's checks. The **police** station is largely unmanned; the branch in Puerto Ángel (☎584 3207) is a much safer bet. The nearest hospital, **General Hospital,** is between Puerto Ángel and Pochutla. (☎584 0219.) **Internet** access at **Danydoquin,** on the eastern edge of Paisan where it intersects the other paved road. (☎584 3363. 15 pesos per hr. Open daily 10am-9pm.) **Posada Lavandería Navidad,** on the western edge of Paisan across from Posada Esmeralda, offers next-day service. (Wash and dry 12 pesos per kg. Open daily 8am-6pm.)

> **⚡TIP** **PACK YOUR HAMMOCK.** In the beach towns along the south of Oaxaca, many hotel and restaurant owners will let you tie up your hammock between 2 trees or near their own hammocks for a nominal fee, which saves the cost of a room and affords more protection and ambience than two trees in a dark forest.

🏠 🍴 ACCOMMODATIONS AND FOOD. Almost every *palapa* on the beach has huts out back, most with relatively clean shared baths. Whichever you choose, be sure to put valuables in a safe box. Nicer, more secure *cabañas* and rooms are on the west side of the beach. Ask around for prices for hammocks and camping space. At the far western end of the beach where Paisan meets the dirt road, **🔾Posada Esmeralda ❸** stands as a sanctuary of cleanliness. Simple rooms with fan and sparkling bath add to the quiet order—a delightful change form the hit-or-miss grime and dirt of nearby hotels. (No hot water. Singles and doubles 150 pesos; triples and quads 250 pesos. Cash only.) Alongside the beach is **Hotel Brisa Marina ❶,** a multi-story hotel with rooms from the simple to near-luxurious. Beds are soft and clean, while bathroom tile shows its age. (☎584 3193; brisamarinaca@yahoo.com. Singles 80 pesos; singles and doubles with bath 150 pesos, with bath and balcony 250 pesos. Prices often negotiable.) **La Choza ❶,** in the middle of Paisan, offers dirt cheap prices. Hammocks, palms, and courtyard walls have all been visited by psychedelic paint. (☎584 3190. Hammocks 40 pesos. Rooms 100 pesos, with bath 120 pesos. Cash only.) Almost to the west end of the beach is **Posada San Cristóbal ❸.** Soaring tropical plants blot out the sun in the courtyard, making the hammocks below perfect midday relief from the heat. Communal bathrooms are clean, and each bed comes with a mosquito net. (☎584 3191. Singles and doubles 150 pesos, with bath 250 pesos. Discounts for longer stays. Cash only.)

Seafood and pasta restaurants abound, and the hordes of health-conscious environmentalists ensure that vegetarian dishes are easy to find. Most of the best restaurants are at the west end of the beach. For good Mexican try **Los Almendros ❹,** near the eastern end of Paisan, where you can get cheap *antojitos* (25-35 pesos) or larger dinner dishes. (*Tlayudas* 30 pesos. Chicken dishes 60-70 pesos. Open daily 10am-10pm. Cash only.) At **3 de Diciembre ❸,** a block north of the Paisan on the other paved road, indulge with a piece of *pay* (pie) from the gorgeous selection lining the counter, ranging from fruit pies to the rich *pay de chocolate*. (Pie 25 pesos. Open W-Sa 7pm-2am. Cash only.) **El Terrible ❺,** at the eastern end of Paisan, serves up pizzas and crepes, a nod to the French owner's homeland. Hot pizza is fresh and cheesy. (Pizzas 80-90 pesos. Open Tu-Sa 6pm-midnight. Cash only.)

☒ NIGHTLIFE. Nightlife in Zipolite is subdued. Many of the beachfront hotels have their own small bars, but if you want to head out, try **Buonvento,** on the paved street off the east end of Paisan. Under the open sky people drink and watch music or sports on the big-screen TV. (Beer 20 pesos. Mixed drinks 40-50 pesos. Open daily 6:30pm-12:30am. Cash only.) For a little dancing there's **Disco-Bar La Puesta,** where Paisan meets the paved road. A mixed crowd, mostly women, alternate drinks at the bar with grooving to dance hits. (Beer 20 pesos, Mixed drinks 40-55 pesos. W salsa night. Open W-Sa 10pm-2am. Cash only.)

☒ DAYTRIP FROM ZIPOLITE: SAN AGUSTINILLO

Four kilometers from Zipolite, the small town of San Agustinillo lies on a beach of the same name, which offers less crowded beaches than Zipolite but little beyond that, with only a few restaurants, convenience stores, and bungalows rounding out the town. The two coves that form the harbor have fairly manageable surf (stay away from the rocks), which can be harnessed with body boards, fins, or surfboards rented from **Mexico Lindo y Que Rico** (50 pesos per hr., boogie boards 30 pesos), on the western edge of town. Many beginners start here before braving the bigger waves at Zipolite. Mexico Lindo also rents some of the best rooms on the beach: new and clean with fans, private baths, and double beds. (Singles and doubles 250 pesos, with ocean view 350 pesos.) For a cheaper stay across the street from the beach, go to **Casa de Huéspedes Kaly ❹,** which has extraordinarily well-kept, quiet rooms with big fans, comfortable beds with mosquito nets, and spotless bath. (No hot water. Singles and doubles 200 pesos. Cash only.) The adjacent restaurant serves *mariscos* (starting at 70 pesos) and hearty meat dishes. (Open daily 9am-8pm.) (*San Agustinillo is accessible via a "Mazunte" camioneta from Zipolite (every 20min. 6am-7pm, 3 pesos), or any Zipolite-bound camioneta from Pochutla.*)

POCHUTLA ☎958

Pochutla's (pop. 66,000) thick, hot air hints to its proximity of the ocean, but do not be misled into disembarking. You will find yourself not in a beachside paradise but rather in a transportation hub filled with buses, taxis, and dust. Come here only to stock up on money and other necessities.

Taxis colectivos heading to **Puerto Escondido** (50 pesos), **Puerto Ángel** (10 pesos), **Zipolite** (20 pesos), and beyond leave from the downhill part of town, across from the Estrella del Valle bus station. The most efficient way to travel between coastal towns is by *camioneta* (every 20min. 6am-8pm; 7 pesos to Puerto Ángel, 10 pesos to Zipolite or Mazunte). The second-class **bus station,** on the right side of Cárdenas as you enter the city, sends buses to **Oaxaca** (7hr., 11 per day 5am-10:30pm, 70 pesos) and **Mexico City** (12hr.; 6, 7pm; 355 pesos). **Tránsitos Rápidos de Pochutla,** just past the second-class station, goes to **Bahías de Huatulco** (1hr., daily every 15min. 5:30am-8:50pm, 16 pesos). **Eclipse 70,** next door, goes to **Oaxaca** (7hr., every 1½ hr. 4am-11pm, 120 pesos).

Hotel Santa Cruz ❷, just up the street from the Cristóbal Colón station, has clean, medium-sized rooms good for crashing in the event of a long layover. (☎584 0016. Singles 100 pesos, with bath 120 pesos; doubles 150 pesos. Cash only.) **Hotel Izalo ❷,** on Cárdenas just past Juárez, offers a little more luxury, with large rooms and big, clean baths. (Singles 150 pesos, with A/C 250 pesos; doubles 350/500 pesos.) For a quick bite, try **Restaurant Lichita ❸,** Cárdenas 79, where large portions come quickly. (*Comida corrida* 35 pesos. Open daily 9am-8pm. Cash only.)

To reach the *zócalo*, church, and main outdoor market, follow Cárdenas uphill and turn right on Juárez a block after the area where the *colectivos* drop-off. **24hr. ATMs** available at **Banamex,** on the *zócalo*, opposite the Agencia Municipal offers financial services (open M-F 9am-4pm); **Scotiabank,** uphill on Cárdenas, just after the intersection with Juárez; **HSBC** on the left just past Scotiabank. Other services include: **police,** in the Palacio Municipal to the left of the church (☎584 0159); **Farmacias de Más Ahorro** (☎584 1213), just before Juárez on Cárdenas, open 24hr.; **Hospital General,** also known as **SSA,** between Pochutla and Puerto Ángel (☎584 0219); **Internet** access at **Ciberespacio,** in front of the church in the *zócalo* (10 pesos per hr.; open M-Sa 9am-9pm); and the **post office,** right on Juárez toward the *zócalo* and to the left of the church, behind the Palacio Municipal. (Open M-F 8am-3pm.) **Postal code:** 70900.

BAHÍAS DE HUATULCO   ☎958

Just over an hour away from the rougher, undeveloped beaches of Mazunte and Zipolite, Huatulco (pop. 50,000) offers ritzy hotels, expensive food, and wide boulevards that gleam with the government's money. The area unabashedly sells itself to vacationing Mexican families, but is clean and manageable enough to distract from the kitsch. Transportation is expensive, and even the most budget-friendly hotels in La Crucecita are still pricey. The high costs mean that the clientele is almost exclusively middle- and upper-class families, with few backpackers.

◰ TRANSPORTATION

Flights: The **Bahía de Huatulco International (IATA)** airport (☎581 9007), 19km from the town of Santa Cruz, is served by **Aerocaribe** (☎587 1220) and **Mexicana** (☎587 0243). To get to the airport, take a taxi (25min., 100 pesos) or a "Sta. Maria" *micro* from the corner of Guamuchil and Carrizal in Santa Cruz (10 pesos). Ask to be let off at the airport, and walk approximately 500m to the right of where the driver drops you.

Buses: The **Cristóbal Colón station** (☎587 0261) is on Blvr. Chahué across from Gardenia in La Crucecita. To get to the *zócalo,* cross Chahué and walk 8 blocks down Gardenia. Cristóbal Colón goes to: **Mexico City** (15hr.; 4:30, 5:55, 8:20pm; 564 pesos); **Oaxaca** (8hr.; 9:20am, 4:50, 11pm; 216 pesos); **Puerto Escondido** (2hr., every 40min. 5:40am-7pm, 35 pesos); **San Cristóbal** (11hr.; 8:30, 11:50pm; 306 pesos); **Tuxtla Gutiérrez** (8hr.; 8:30, 11:50pm; 260 pesos). **Estrella Blanca** (☎587 0103), down Gardenia at Palma Real, travels to: **Acapulco** (10hr.; 11:30am, 10pm; 307 pesos); **Mexico City** (14hr., 6pm, 525 pesos); **Salina Cruz** (3hr.; 2, 8pm; 85 pesos). The best way to get to **Pochutla**—gateway to Mazunte, Puerto Ángel, Puerto Escondido, and Zipolite—is a **Transportes Rápidos de Pochutla** *micro;* they leave from Carrizal after it curves into an east-west road at the north end of town (1hr., every 15min. 5:30am-9pm, 15 pesos).

✦ ⍰ ORIENTATION AND PRACTICAL INFORMATION

Huatulco and its *bahías* (bays) consist of 35km of beach and cove on the southern Oaxacan coast between the Coyula and Copalita rivers, about 295km south of Oaxaca de Juárez. The most practical place to stay is **La Crucecita,** in the middle of a string of nine bays, called, from east to west: Conejos, Tangolunda, Chahué, Santa Cruz, El Órgano, Maguey, Cacaluta, Chachacual, and San Agustín. La Crucecita houses the bus stations and the few existing budget accommodations. **Santa Cruz,** the bay closest to La Crucecita, offers the best access to the airport.

Tourist Office: FONATUR (☎587 0285), on Blvr. Chahué south of the *zócalo* in La Crucecita. Practical tourist information is more accessible at the **Módulo de Información,** in the *zócalo* in La Crucecita toward the east side and in the main plaza in Santa Cruz. Helpful maps and advice. Be sure to check the **official taxi tariffs,** posted near the Módulo; many tourists pay more than they should. Open M-F 9am-2pm and 4-7pm during high season.

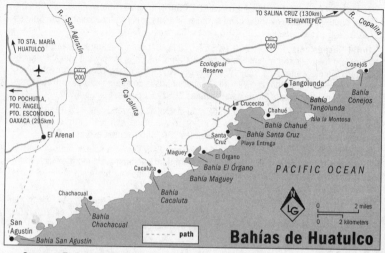

Bahías de Huatulco

TO SALINA CRUZ (130km), TEHUANTEPEC

R. San Agustín

TO STA. MARÍA HUATULCO

TO POCHUTLA, PTO. ÁNGEL, PTO. ESCONDIDO, OAXACA (295km)

R. Cacaluta

Ecological Reserve

El Arenal

Cacaluta

Maguey

Chachacual

San Agustín

Bahía San Agustín

Bahía Chachacual

Bahía Cacaluta

Bahía Maguey

Bahía El Órgano

El Órgano

Santa Cruz

La Crucecita

Chahué

Bahía Chahué

Bahía Santa Cruz

Playa Entrega

Tangolunda

Bahía Tangolunda

Isla la Montosa

Bahía Conejos

Conejos

Copalita

PACIFIC OCEAN

N

path

0   2 miles
0   2 kilometers

SOUTHERN PACIFIC COAST

Currency Exchange: HSBC, Bugambilias 1504 at Sabali, has a **24hr. ATM.** Open M-Sa 8am-7pm. There's a **Bancomer** ATM on the *zócalo* as well. Major banks line the main street in Santa Cruz. Large hotels exchange money at slightly less favorable rates.

Car Rental: Budget, at the airport (☎581 9000). Open daily 8am-8pm.

Police: Blvr. Chahué 100 (☎587 0675), in back of the peach-colored government building, 200m south of the intersection of Guamuchil and Chahué.

Emergency: ☎068.

Red Cross: Blvr. Chahué 110 (☎587 1188), next door to the post office and police. 24hr. service.

Pharmacy: Farmacia La Clínica, Sabali 1602 (☎587 0591), at Gardenia, 8 blocks northeast from the *zócalo*. Open 24hr.

Hospital: Centro de Salud, Carrizal 202 (☎587 1421) at the corner of Guamuchil. Also **Centro Médico Santa Cruz,** Flamboyan 204 (☎587 0448 or 1030), on the *zócalo*.

Fax: Telecomm (☎587 0894; fax 0885), next to the post office. Open M-F 8am-7:30pm, Sa-Su 9am-12:30pm.

Internet Access: El Telefonito, Bugambilias 501 (☎587 1794). 15 pesos per hr. Open daily 8am-10:30pm.

Post Office: Blvr. Chahué 100 (☎587 0551), in the peach-colored government building. Open M-F 8am-3pm, Sa 9am-1pm. **Postal Code:** 70989.

ACCOMMODATIONS

Camping is a way to escape Huatulco's high-priced hotel scene, but it is allowed only on Chahué, Cacaluta, and Conejos bays. Even in these locations, camping is a risky affair; there is little security, no services, and very few—if any—other campers. **Under no circumstances should you attempt to camp on Santa Cruz or Tangolunda;** hotel security will not be kind. If you want a normal night's stay, be prepared to shell out. All affordable hotels are in La Crucecita, and even those tend be overpriced. Some families rent out rooms, and those willing to search around and negotiate will be rewarded for the effort. Rates rise 20-50% during high season (July-Aug.); listings below are low/high season ranges.

Posada del Carmen, Palo Verde 307 (☎587 0593), in between Bugambilias and Gardenia. White tile covers all the ground surfaces. Rooms come with cable and fan. Singles 200/250 pesos; doubles 300/350 pesos. Cash only. ❹

Hotel Posada Jois, Chacah 209 (☎587 0781), between Bugambilias and Carrizal. Ambient light fills the atrium-like downstairs area, which is simply but elegantly decorated. Simple white beds, fan, TV, and excessive closet space come with each room. The communal bath that comes with cheaper rooms is comparable to the private baths in terms of cleanliness. Singles and doubles 200/250 pesos. Cash only. ❺

Hotel Posada San Agustín (☎587 0368), on Macuil at Carrizal. Spotlessly clean, bright, and run by a young family. Small, sparkling rooms come with fan, bath, balcony and street view. Singles 140/200 pesos; doubles 220/350 pesos. Cash only. ❷

Hotel Sol Posada (☎583 4947), on Gardenia at Palo Verde. A splash of luxury in the form of A/C and cable offset the otherwise standard, medium-sized rooms, which come with soft bed, redundant fan, bath, and balcony overlooking the quiet street. Singles 250/300 pesos; doubles 400/450 pesos. Cash only. ❺

Hotel Benimar, Bugambilias 1404 (☎587 0447), at Pochote. Narrow, plain beds are crammed into the tiny rooms—no calisthenics here. Singles and doubles 200/250 pesos; triples 250/300 pesos; quads 350/400 pesos. Cash only. ❹

◧ FOOD

Tourist restaurants offer both international cuisine and Mexican staples with dressed-up names at inflated prices. *Antojitos* generally come at reasonable prices, but for the cheapest full meals try heading out of the *zócalo* to the tacos on **Bugambilias** and **Carrizal. 3 de Mayo,** on Guamuchil off the *zócalo*, sells trinkets, produce, and meat. (Open daily 7am-8pm.)

La Crucecita (☎587 0906), 1 block past the *zócalo* at Bugambilias and Chacah. Upgrade from the plastic tables of taco shops to the wicker chairs and flowers of La Crucecita, where you can linger and enjoy the ambience at a reasonable price. *Tlayudas* 40 pesos, *salads* 35-45 pesos. Enormous *oaxaqueño* specials 100 pesos. Open M and W-Su 7am-10pm. Cash only. ❷

Taquería Los Parados, on Carrizal at Macuhite. This taco joint provides a little class and a lot of relief from expensive fare. Patrons waiting for taco orders (15-20 pesos) pack the wooden chairs and tables. Combo platters (70 pesos). Open daily 9am-11:30pm. Cash only. ❶

Oasis Cafe (☎587 0045), at Bugambilias and Flamboyan. The strange Mexican-Japanese fusion draws an evening crowd of young hipsters. Try the sumashi (45 pesos) or stick to Mexican standbys, like the *tlayudas* (90 pesos). Open daily 7am-midnight. Cash only. ❸

Restaurant-Bar La Tropicana (☎587 0661), Guanacastle at Gardenia, across from Hotel Flamboyant. What it lacks in ambience and quality is more than made up for by the hours and location. *Antojitos* (35-40 pesos) or the wild variety of *tortas* (30 pesos) are the best bet. Open 24hr. Cash only. ❸

La Tropicana (☎587 0170), on Carrizal at Chacah. Families come and linger over large meals at the breezy, tranquil tables of La Tropicana. The *comida corrida* (35 pesos) is always a midday winner, while salads (40-45 pesos) and *carnes* (60 pesos) are larger portions. Open daily 7am-midnight. Cash only. ❹

◪ BEACHES

Huatulco's nine bays and 36 beaches, spread over 35km, pose a sizeable transportation challenge. It's hard to get off the beaten track without handing over pesos for a taxi or *lancha*. Fortunately, three of the bays are accessible by *colectivos* that leave from the intersection of Guamuchil and Carrizal (5 pesos to Tangolunda, 5 pesos to Santa Cruz, 3 to Chahué). If you plan to take a tour, the tourist bureau recommends going through an official agency in town rather than one of the "guides" vending their services in the street; many tourists have been ripped off in the past. Storefronts such as the **Módulo de Información** next to the Cristóbal Colón station are not official; only the *módulo* in the *zócalo* (p. 524) offers solid advice. If you plan on indulging in watersports, consider going through the company itself or renting directly off the beach to save pesos, rather than dealing with a travel agency. **Piraguas** (☎587 1333), in La Crucecita, guides white-water rafting trips down nearby Río Capolita.

> **EARLY TO RISE.** Getting to the various bays of Huatulco can be a frustrating and costly enterprise, but if you head out early enough, you can catch a *taxi colectivo* and split the fare. These taxis stop running shortly after midday, so plan ahead and leave early or you'll be paying for your own taxi.

BAHÍA SANTA CRUZ. Bahía Santa Cruz, with its accessibility and gentle waves, is often a riot of families filling the shallows and the deck chairs of the numerous *palapa* restaurants onshore. **Playa Santa Cruz,** just behind the main plaza in Santa Cruz, is small and packed but a good launching point for tours of the bay, which leave from the pier on the left side. **Playa Entrega,** a 36-peso ride through the hills, offers a little more space to swim and snorkel. Fins and masks are available at the left side of the beach facing the water. **Restaurant Ve el Mar,** on the side of the beach nearest the *lanchas*, is known to have the best seafood in the area. *(36-peso taxis or lanchas (150 pesos per 10 people) will take you from Santa Cruz to Playa Entrega. Snorkeling equipment 50 pesos per day. Tours of the bay start at 150 pesos per person; tickets available at the booth on the pier in Santa Cruz. To get to Santa Cruz, continue down the right branch of Blvr. Chahué, a 15min. walk or 5min. ride past Bahía Chahué. Restaurant ☎587 0364. Dishes start at 80 pesos. Open daily 8am-10pm.)*

BAHÍAS MAGUEY Y ÓRGANO. Two kilometers from Playa Santa Cruz and much less crowded, the twin bays offer more solitude. The white sand and open water is excellent for swimming and sunbathing. *(Taxis 50 pesos. 10-person lanchas 500 pesos.)*

BAHÍA TANGOLUNDA. Massive luxury hotels dominate the beachfront and own the sand here, which is just as well because the steep banks and rough tide make swimming here an uncertain affair. Pricey restaurants and malls cluster the rest of the town. *(Take a 5-peso colectivo.)*

OTHER BAHÍAS. The only other beaches accessible by land are **La Bocana, Bahía Cacaluta** (4WD only), and **Bahía San Agustín;** taxis charge hefty rates to travel this far. Another option is renting a bike or car for the day (see **Practical Information,** p. 524). *Lanchas* from the **Cooperativa Tangolunda** in Santa Cruz travel to other beaches (prices vary by beach and size of boat, but are guaranteed to be high— over 400 pesos). If you don't mind splurging on transportation, **La India,** San Agustín, and **Cacaluta** are best for snorkeling and diving, with extensive reef systems in the western bays. San Agustín is the most crowded, while Cacaluta, La India, and **Conejos,** are the best shots at solitude. **Playa Chachacual,** in between Cacaluta and San Agustín, is only available by boat, but is little more than an ecological reserve with a mangrove swamp. If you go in the morning you may find people to share the ride, and during the low season you can bargain for lower rates. The *cooperativa* offers the most economical all-day tour of the bays, stopping at **Maguey** and San Agustín, where you can eat lunch and snorkel with an English-speaking guide. *(☎587 0081. Open daily 8am-6pm. Tours 10 and 11am in high season; 11am in low season. 250 pesos. Call 1 day in advance.)*

◧ NIGHTLIFE

The family vacation factor means that nightlife in Huatulco is a pretty laid-back affair, centering on bars on the *zócalo*, most of which don't stay open too late.

Casa Mayor, Bugambilias 601 (☎587 1881), upstairs on the *zócalo*. Remixed American classics and the aroma of organic coffee suffuse the air in this hip terrace bar. A young clientele sip their coffee liqueurs (45 pesos) and mixed drinks (40-50 pesos) and laugh over the music. Open daily 9am-1am. Cash only.

La Perla, Bugambilias 701, at the corner of Guamuchil. A jazz club with all the trappings, dim lights, and slightly smoky atmosphere to boot. When the live music isn't playing, the older crowd helps belt out jazzy favorites. Happy hour 6-8pm. Live music every night from 9pm. Beer 20 pesos. Mixed drinks 45-55 pesos. Open daily 7pm-1am. Cash only.

Iguana Bar, at the northwest corner of the *zócalo*. Grab a beer and watch some sports at this quiet, no-frills bar. Tacos 44 pesos. Beer 18 pesos. Specialty drinks from 35 pesos. Open daily 8pm-2am. Cash only.

Huatul Tropic, in Santa Cruz, on Mitla near the corner of Otitlan del Valle. The only option for dancing in Huatulco plays cumbia, salsa, and merengue at penetrating levels, energizing the couples on the dance floor. Grab a mixed drink (50 pesos) or a cheap *cucaracha* (vodka, kahlua, tequila and soda water; 25 pesos) in between dances. Cover 80 pesos. Open daily 11pm-late. Cash only.

ISTHMUS OF TEHUANTEPEC

East of Oaxaca, the North American continent narrows to a slender strip of land 215km wide, known as the Isthmus of Tehuantepec, or El Istmo. The isthmus is the shortest division between the Gulf of Mexico and the Pacific Oceans, and is home to the indigenous Zapotec culture of Oaxaca state. Many of El Istmo's residents speak only *Chatino*, their native dialect, or Zapotecan—Spanish is rarely heard. Traditionally an agricultural civilization, modern Zapotecs are famed for their weaving, jewelry and political achievements—Benito Juárez himself was of Zapotec origin.

TEHUANTEPEC   ☎971

Tehuantepec (pop. 60,000), derives its name from the Náhuatl word *Tecuantepec*, meaning "maneater hill." Founded by Zapotec emperor Cosijoeza in the early 1500s, the oldest and most historically significant of El Istmo's three principal cities contains some of the first churches built by *indígenas*. In the 19th century, the city served as Porfirio Díaz's base during initial skirmishes with the French. Tehuantepec is famous for preserving Zapotec flavor in all aspects of modern life.

Tehuantepec's most notable sight is also the best place to find **tourist information.** Library staff at the **Casa de la Cultura,** on Calle Guerrero, will be happy to fill you in. (☎715 0114. Open M-F 9am-2pm and 5-8pm, Sa 9am-2pm.) The Casa is housed in the **Ex-Convento Rey Cosijopi,** a 16th-century Dominican building named after the Zapotec leader who ordered its construction. A 15min. walk south of the *zócalo* will bring you to **San Blas,** a traditional **mercado.** Between May and September, each of Tehuantepec's 18 communities holds its own week-long ◧**festival,** beginning with a *baile velorio* at night and followed the next morning by a special mass and several days of parades, live music, dancing, and extensive consumption of *cerveza*. The whole town turns out, with women in traditional Zapotec dress and men and boys on horseback. Tourists are welcome, though a local chaperone is usually needed to get into some social events. During the **Vela Sandunga** (the last week of May), each *barrio* picks a representative to compete for

the title of "Reina de la Vela" (Queen of the Candle).
Native *tehunos* from all over Mexico return to celebrate the annual **Vela Tehuantepec** (Dec. 26), a party held in the main square. Both require traditional dress for women and *guayaberas* for men.

Travelers to Tehuantepec should head to **Hotel Oasis ❷**, Ocampo 8, a block south of the *zócalo* at the corner of Romero. Sparse, floral-themed rooms are clean with fan, bath, and lots of empty space. (☎715 0008. Singles 150 pesos; doubles 190 pesos. Cash only.) **Restaurant El Almendro ❷**, inside Hotel Oasis, is one of the nicer establishments. Its wood-furnished bar, cheap beer, and satellite TV draw a crowd come evening-time. (☎715 0835. Breakfast 35 pesos. Pizza from 40 pesos. Open daily 8am-11pm. Cash only.) For budget meals, try the **Mercado de Jesús Carranza ❶**, on the plaza's west side (open daily 8am-8pm; cash only), or the numerous taco stands that pop up in the *zócalo* or behind the Palacio Municipal after dark.

To get to town from the Cristóbal Colón/ADO **bus station**, 1.5km north of the *centro*, make an immediate left as you exit the station. This street becomes Héroes, veers to the right, and eventually leads to a dead end. Turn right and walk a few more blocks; make a left on Hidalgo and follow it to the *zócalo*. From the station to town **taxis** cost 15 pesos and **mototaxis** 5 pesos. **Cristóbal Colón** (☎715 0108) **buses** travel to: **Huatulco** (3hr.; 12:10, 2:30, 7:30pm; 100 pesos); **Mexico City** (12hr.; 7:45, 8, 9:55pm; 572 pesos); **Oaxaca** (5hr., 12 per day, 142 pesos); **Tuxtla Gutiérrez** (6hr.; 2:45, 8:20am, 11:45pm; 178 pesos). Buses also go to neighboring **Juchitán** (30min., 5 per day 10:40am-9:40pm, 16 pesos) and **Salina Cruz** (30min., 12 per day 5:30am-midnight, 10 pesos), though the fastest, cheapest way to travel to either is to walk two blocks on 5 de Mayo to the *carretera*. Southbound buses to **Salina Cruz** (8 pesos) and northbound buses to Juchitán (10 pesos) stop frequently.

Services include: **tourist office** at the **Casa de la Cultura**, on Guerrero, two blocks north of the *zócalo;* **Banorte** and **Bancomer** on 5 de Mayo just west of the *zócalo*, have **24hr. ATMs; police** (☎715 0001), at the back of the Palacio Municipal; Farmacia San Jorge, on Juárez south of the *zócalo* (open daily 8am-8:30pm); **Centro de Salud**, Guerrero 16, two blocks north of the *zócalo* (☎715 0180; 24hr. service); **Telecomm**, next to the post office (open M-F 8am-7:30pm, Sa 9am-noon); **LADATELs**, in the *zócalo;* **Internet** access, on 5 de Mayo at the *zócalo* (10 pesos per hr.; open daily 8am-10:30pm); and the **post office**, at the corner of 22 de Marzo and Hidalgo, on the north side of the *zócalo* (open M-F 8am-3pm). **Postal Code:** 70760.

FROM THE ROAD

BIG QUESTIONS

It's not everyday that public transportation makes you think about "Big Questions," but as I sat in a sweltering bus in Tehuantepec, I began to wonder "Why are we here?" Ten minutes later the question assumed even greater philosophical proportions: "Why the *hell* are we still here?"

Welcome to Mexico's intercity bus transportation service, where buses frequently wait in the choking heat for more passengers. There's no A/C to temper the suffocating heat, and windows are useless like the idling buses.

When they do start rolling, the seats are crammed so full that the press of passengers negates any relief a breeze might bring. The "routes" lack formal stops; buses frequently pull over roadside to pick up passengers—from old men toting guitars to snake oil salesmen—all of whom make the ride more pleasant.

No one complains though. It's simply how life is here. Getting around by cheap public transportation requires factoring it into your schedule, or grinning and bearing it like the locals.

If you come from a country where public transportation runs on a precise schedule, the Mexican bus system can be difficult at first. Travelers who spend enough time here, however, will get used to it, and maybe even start relying on it. I do—I arrived late to my second bus, but with no worries. It left twenty minutes late.

— Russell Rennie

OAXACA

☎951

High amid the cool mountain air, Oaxaca (pop. 500,000) woos visitors with a combination of art, activism, food, and festivals all its own. A fusion of *indígena* color still present in the markets and the festivals and colonial Mexican charm flush in the cathedrals and manors figure prominently in the history of the city that produced both *indígena* hero Benito Juárez and dictator Porfirio Díaz. Diesel fumes duel the perfume of *mezcal* and chocolate, permeating dusty market stalls hawking Zapotec crafts and trinkets. Glorious golden churches buttress the past, while modern cafes, posters, and museums fill by day the younger generations that graffiti their anger by night. This is the peculiar mix that gives Oaxaca its pulse.

▐ TRANSPORTATION

Oaxaca, between the Sierra Madre del Sur and the Puebla-Oaxaca mountain ranges, sits in the Oaxaca Valley 523km southeast of Mexico City. Principal access to Oaxaca from the north and east is via **Mex. 190** as well as the "súper-carretera" **Mex. 135** from Puebla. Most parts of the city are easily accessible by foot. **Local buses,** called *urbanos,* cost 3.50 pesos; most run west on Mina, cutting east to the north of the *centro* before heading south again on Juárez; ask around for the correct line. **Taxis** run anywhere in the city for 30-40 pesos. Walk along a major street or find a *sitio* sign for an unoccupied taxi.

Flights: Aeropuerto Internacional de Oaxaca Xoxocotlan (OAX; tourist info booth ☎511 5040), on Mex. 175, 8km south of the city. To get to the *centro,* take a taxi (100 pesos) or share a van (25 pesos) with other travelers through **Transportes Aeropuerto,** with an office on Plaza Alameda, near the post office. (☎514 4350. Tickets available at airport exit. Vans will also take you from your hotel to the airport; prices vary by hotel. Arrangements should be made a day in advance by phone or in person. Open M-Sa 9am-2pm and 5-8pm. Airport serves: **AeroCalifornia,** Morelos 1207 (☎241 8570); **AeroCaribe,** Fiallo 102 (☎516 0229); **Aeroméxico,** Hidalgo 513 (☎516 3229 or 3765); **Aviacsa** (☎518 4555, airport office ☎511 5039); **Mexicana,** Independencia 102 (☎516 8414 or 7352), at Fiallo.

Buses: 2 bus stations serve Oaxaca.

1st-class bus station: Niños Héroes de Chapultepec 1036 (☎513 3350), 11 blocks north of the *centro.* To get to the *centro,* cross the street and take a westbound "Centro" *urbano* (3.50 pesos) or a taxi (30-40 pesos). **ADO** (☎515 1703) heads to: **Mexico City** (6½hr., 20 per day, 362 pesos); **Puebla** (4½hr., 11 per day, 270 pesos); **Tuxtepec** (6½hr.; 9:30, 11:30pm; 266 pesos); **Veracruz** (7hr.; 8:30am, 10:15pm, midnight; 356 pesos). **Cristóbal Colón** goes to: **Bahías de Huatulco** (8hr.; 9:30am, 9:30, 11pm; 228 pesos); **San Cristóbal de las Casas** (12hr.; 7, 9pm; 362 pesos); **Tehuantepec** (4½hr., 18 per day, 142 pesos); **Tuxtla Gutiérrez** (10hr.; 7, 9, 10:30pm; 322 pesos); **Puerto Escondido** (10hr.; 9:30am, 9:30, 11pm; 240 pesos). Tickets for ADO and Cristóbal Colón available at 20 de Noviembre 204, or at the *zócalo*'s travel agencies.

2nd-class bus station: 7 blocks west of the *zócalo,* just north of the Central de Abastos market. To get to the *centro,* take a taxi (25 pesos) or a "Centro" *urbano* in front of the main terminal. By foot, exit left out the terminal, cross busy Periférico, and follow the street as it turns into Trujano. After 7 blocks, Trujano reaches the *zócalo.* Bus station services regional bus lines. On market days, buses to surrounding towns leave every 10min. It's a good idea to buy tickets early.

Car Rental: Budget, 5 de Mayo 315 (☎516 4445). Also at the airport (☎511 5252). Open daily 9am-3pm and 4-7pm. **Alamo,** 5 de Mayo 205 (☎514 8534). VWs 600 pesos per day. Open M-Sa 8am-8pm, Su 9am-7pm.

✦ 🛈 ORIENTATION AND PRACTICAL INFORMATION

Oaxaca is a delightfully walkable city. The city's *zócalo* is comprised of the square and the block-long **Plaza Alameda de León** just north of the square. **Alcalá's** five-block stretch

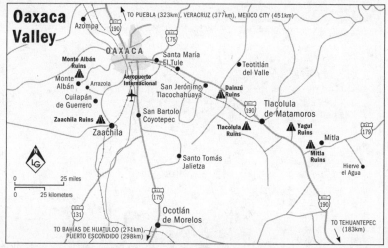

Oaxaca Valley

TO PUEBLA (323km), VERACRUZ (377km), MEXICO CITY (451km)

Azompa

OAXACA

Santa María El Tule

Monte Albán Ruins

Monte Albán
Arrazola
Aeropuerto Internacional

Teotitlán del Valle

San Jerónimo Tlacochahuaya

Dainzú Ruins

Cuilapán de Guerrero

San Bartolo Coyotepec

Tlacolula de Matamoros

Zaachila Ruins
Zaachila

Tlacolula Ruins

Yagul Ruins
Mitla

Mitla Ruins

Santo Tomás Jalietza

Hierve el Agua

0   25 miles
0   25 kilometers

Ocotlán de Morelos

TO BAHÍAS DE HUATULCO (271km),
PUERTO ESCONDIDO (298km)

TO TEHUANTEPEC (183km)

between the *zócalo* and the Iglesia de Santo Domingo to the north features a high concentration of museums, restaurants, craft shops, and tourists. South of the *zócalo* is a hive of open-air markets, *mezcal* stores, cheap eateries, and chocolate cafes. Many street names change as they pass the *zócalo*, and sometimes even when they don't.

Tourist Offices: SEDETUR, Murguía 206 (☎516 0123; http://oaxaca.gob.mx/sedetur or www.aoaxaca.com). Provides maps, brochures, and the free English newspaper *Oaxaca Times* (www.oaxacatimes.com) and free monthly *Guía Cultura*. Open daily 8am-8pm.

Consulates: Canada, Suárez 700 #11B (☎513 3777). Open M-F 10am-2pm. **US,** Alcalá 407 #20 (☎514 3054 or 516 2853; fax 516 2701), in Plaza Santo Domingo. Open M-F 10am-3pm.

Currency Exchange: Banamex, Hidalgo 821, east of the cathedral. Open M-Sa 9am-4pm. Buys and sells dollars at good rates. **HSBC,** Guerrero 117, at the corner of Armenta y López. Open M-Sa 8am-7pm. Both have **24hr. ATMs.** Numerous smaller **casas de cambio** surround the *zócalo*.

Bookstores: Librería Universitaria, on Guerrero between Armenta y López and Valdivieso. Buys and sells a small number of English paperbacks. Open M-Sa 10am-3pm and 4:30-8:30pm. **Amate Books,** Alcalá 307 #2 (☎516 6960), in Plaza Alcalá. Sells North American magazines and books about Mexico in several languages. Open M-Sa 10am-8:30pm, Su 2-7pm.

Libraries: Oaxaca Lending Library, Suárez 519 (☎518 7077; www.oaxlibrary.com). Everything from the *New Yorker* to *Sports Illustrated* for 1 peso. Also sells used books. Open M-F 10am-2pm and 4-7pm, Sa 10am-1pm. **Instituto de Artes Gráficos de Oaxaca,** Alcalá 507 (☎516 6980), across from Santo Domingo. Has a library with works in various languages and a museum with rotating art exhibits. Library open M-Sa 10am-8pm. Museum open M and W-Su 10am-8pm. Donations suggested.

Laundromat: Azteca Lavandería, Hidalgo 404 (☎514 7951), just east of Díaz Ordaz. Open M-Sa 8am-8pm, Su 10am-2pm. 65 pesos per 3.5kg. MC/V.

Emergency: ☎066.

Police: Morelos 108 (☎516 0455), west of the *zócalo*. Open 24hr. From 8am-8pm, go first to **CEPROTUR,** Murguía 206 (☎514 2192; fax 516 0984), which handles all tourist safety matters. The **Agencia Ministerio Público** (☎514 2192) handles **tourist**

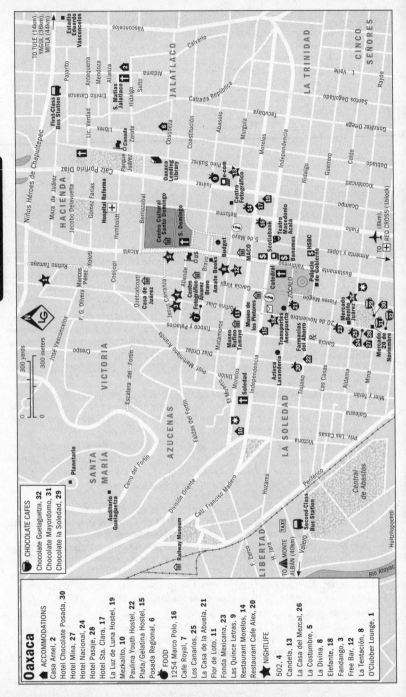

Oaxaca

↑ ACCOMMODATIONS
Casa Arnel, 2
Hotel Chocolate Posada, 30
Hotel Mina, 27
Hotel Nacional, 24
Hotel Pasaje, 28
Hotel Sta. Clara, 17
La Luz de Luna Hostel, 19
Mezkalito, 10
Paulina Youth Hostel, 22
Plata/Gelatina Hostel, 15
Posada Regional, 6

♦ FOOD
1254 Marco Polo, 16
Cafe Royal, 7
Los Canarios, 25
La Casa de la Abuela, 21
Flor de Loto, 11
Fonda Mexicana, 23
Las Quince Letras, 9
Restaurant Morelos, 14
Restaurant Cafe Alex, 20

★ NIGHTLIFE
502, 4
Candela, 13
La Casa del Mezcal, 26
La Costumbre, 5
La Divina, 8
Elefante, 18
Fandango, 3
Free Bar, 12
La Tentación, 8
O'Clubber Lounge, 1

♦ CHOCOLATE CAFES
Chocolate Guelaguetza, 32
Chocolate Mayordomo, 31
Chocolate la Soledad, 29

SOUTHERN PACIFIC COAST

police issues. Open daily 8am-8pm. **Info Booth** (☎511 0740), at the airport and in Museo de los Pintores, Independencia 607.

Red Cross: Armenta y López 700 (☎516 4803 or 4805), between Pardo and Burgoa. 24hr. ambulance service.

24hr. Pharmacy: Farmacias Similares, 20 de Noviembre 304 (☎514 9098), between las Casas and Aldama. MC/V.

Hospitals: Hospital Civil, Díaz 400 (☎515 1300 or 3709), 1.5km north of town. **Hospital Reforma,** Reforma 613 (☎516 6100), at Humboldt.

Fax Office: Telecomm (☎516 4902), on Independencia at 20 de Noviembre, around the corner from the post office. Open M-F 8am-6pm, Sa 9am-4pm.

Telephones: LADATELs are everywhere; many in the *zócalo*. *Casetas* clustered on Independencia. Open daily 7am-10pm.

Internet Access: Everywhere in Oaxaca, usually for 10 pesos per hr. or less. **e-com,** Juárez 302 (☎516 9925). Speedy connection 5 pesos per hr. Open M-Sa 9am-8:30pm. MC/V.

Post Office: (☎516 2661), on the west side of Plaza Alameda de León. Open M-F 8am-7pm, Sa 9am-1pm. **Postal Code:** 68000.

ACCOMMODATIONS

Cheap beds abound in Oaxaca. Amid the loud, busy streets and markets south of the *zócalo*, rooms go for around 200 pesos, more for private bath. North of the *centro* are rooms of similar quality but often with bath and a little more tranquility. Nowhere in the city will you reliably find baths with toilet seats. Reservations are advised on *fiesta* weekends, especially during *Semana Santa*, the *Guelaguetza* (the two Mondays after July 16), and *Día de los Muertos* (Nov. 1-2). For longer stays, rooms are available for rent. Check the tourist office and the *Oaxaca Times* for listings.

NORTH OF THE ZÓCALO: THE CENTRO

This area is the best location for those looking to stay close to Oaxaca's artifacts and galleries, and its hotels provide a little peace from the chaos of the *zócalo* and the markets south. Casa Arnel and Posada Regional, lie northeast of the *centro* in Jalatlaco, about 10 blocks from the *zócalo*.

Casa Arnel, Aldama 404 (☎515 2856; casa.arnel@spersaoaxaca.com.mx), at Hidalgo, across from the Iglesia San Matías Jalatlaco. Gates enclose the secluded, vibrant courtyard, whose leafy plants, jars, and moisture give Arnel its flavor. Boasts a stunning view of the Oaxaca skyline and cozy, simple rooms. Communal baths are spotless. Offers bar, currency exchange, travel agency, library, and laundry service. Breakfast 7:30-9:45am. Internet access 15 pesos per hr. Singles 150 pesos, with bath 400 pesos; doubles 250/500 pesos. Prices rise in high season. Cash only. ❸

Posada Regional, Libres 600 (☎518 4626), at Cosijoeza. Another option away from the *centro* offering peace and privacy. A leafy staircase leads to a little luxury—rooms have giant, rosy bed, *azulejo* sink, and gorgeous, patterned bath with skylight. Also come with fan and TV. Singles 300 pesos; doubles 400 pesos. Cash only. ❺

Hotel Sta. Clara, Morelos 1004 (☎516 1138). The bright lobby's leather couches provide respite for weary travelers. Carpeted rooms come with clean, wide beds, classy armoires, and well-scrubbed baths. Singles 200 pesos; doubles 300 pesos; triples 400 pesos. Cash only. ❸

La Luz de Luna Hostel, Juárez 101 (☎516 9576). The small courtyard ensures intimacy, as guests lie in hammocks and chat, surrounded by plants and a pack of cute dogs. Linens included. Baths a little small and rusty. Beds 70 pesos. 1- to 2-person *cabañas* 180 pesos. Slightly bigger private rooms 200 pesos. Cash only. ❶

SOUTH AND WEST OF THE ZÓCALO

Filled with cheap hotels—four or five on the same block, particularly along Díaz Ordaz and Mina—this area can oblige discriminating tastes on a budget. Many hotels face noisy streets; ask for a room in the back or on an upper floor.

Mezkalito Hostel, Independencia 101 (☎512 3464; www.hostelmezkalito.com), 6 blocks west of the *zócalo*. A clean, comfortable night's stay with a mountain of amenities makes for the best deal in town. An idler's coastal paradise moved inland, the colorful courtyard's hammocks and the upstairs pool overshadow the plain rooms. Communal baths are clean. Luggage storage, lockers, kitchen, and 24hr. Internet available. Breakfast and linens included. Reception 24hr. Dorms 90-110 pesos. MC/V. ❶

Paulina Youth Hostel, Trujano 321 (☎516 2005 or 514 4210). A well-groomed hedge separate Paulina from the drab city around it. Though a bit pricey for a hostel, amenities include sparkling communal baths, a very hefty breakfast, private lockers, Internet, terrace, and small lounge space. Lockout 3:30am. Dorms 155 pesos; singles 280 pesos; doubles 330 pesos. 5-peso discount with HI or ISIC. 10% price increase with MC/V. ❷

Hotel Chocolate Posada, Mina 212 (☎516 5760). A treat for die-hard dessert fans, the courtyard houses the elegant cafe of adjacent chocolate shop **Chocolate la Soledad** (p. 536). Cozy rooms have antique bedframes and quilted covers, TV, and fan. Small, clean communal baths. Singles and doubles 200 pesos; triples 300 pesos. MC/V. ❷

Hotel Nacional, 20 de Noviembre 512 (☎516 2780), north of Mina. Lacks charm and any sort of ornament, but a solid, cheap option. Small, clean bed, and private bath, as well as TV. Reception 24hr. Singles 180 pesos; doubles 200 pesos. Cash only. ❷

Hotel Pasaje, Mina 302 (☎510 4213), 3 blocks south of the *zócalo*. A leafy courtyard leads to large, tiled rooms with short beds, cable TV, fan, and dresser. Baths are top-notch—large and clean. Not-so picturesque location provides convenient access to markets, restaurants, and chocolate shops, but also to car horns and diesel exhaust. Singles 200 pesos; doubles 250 pesos; triples 350 pesos. Cash only. ❹

Plata/Gelatina Youth Hostel, Independencia 504 (☎514 9391), 1 block west of the *zócalo*. Flowers growing out of a toilet, cacti, old-fashioned milk cans, and eclectic art decorate the interior of this funky, social hostel. Cafe, communal kitchen, and ping-pong available. Dorm beds are comfy, and communal baths large and clean. Singles 200 pesos; doubles 250 pesos. Cash only. ❶

Hotel Mina, Mina 304 (☎516 4966), near 20 de Noviembre. One of the cheapest options for private rooms. Small rooms are clean but quite dim, with big comfy beds. Communal baths are clean, but lack toilet seats, and showers are really just elevated faucets. Singles 120 pesos; doubles 150 pesos; triples 250 pesos. Cash only. ❶

◪ FOOD

Considered by many the culinary capital of Mexico, Oaxaca offers up menus laden with international food, typical Mexican dishes, and a vast array of local specialties. Oaxacan cooking features seven kinds of *mole*, a heavy chile-and-chocolate sauce. Other staples include *tlayudas* (tortillas jammed with toppings), *quesillo* (boiled string cheese), *chorizo* (spicy sausage), *tasajo* (thinly cut steak), and *chapulines* (tiny cooked grasshoppers doused in oil and chile). Another local specialty now found in all parts of the republic, *tamales* are made of ground corn stuffed with beans, chicken, or beef and wrapped in banana or corn leaves before being steamed. Oaxaca's trademark drink, sold everywhere, is the fiery, cactus-based tequila cousin *mezcal*.

The *zócalo* itself is besieged by middle-priced, middle-quality bar-restaurants, while the edges of the Alameda have upscale places with fancy versions of standard Mexican fare for tourists. Alcalá has pricey food, and García Vigil is home to

> **IT'S ON THE HOUSE.** There's no better way to take home a little piece of Oaxaca then to buy a bottle of *mezcal*. Big chains have outlets all over the southern half of the city, but to save a few pesos, try the individual retailers with only one store location; you can often get quality *mezcal* at lower prices. When in bars, ask if there's a house *mezcal*, which is usually just as good but much cheaper than the name brands.

a bevy of hip French cafes. Cheaper and more authentic *fondas* and *comedores* can be found southwest of the *centro*. The fastest and cheapest regional meals are at the markets and taco stands on Trujano and Las Casas, southeast of the *zócalo*.

Restaurant Cafe Alex, Díaz Ordaz 218 (☎514 0715). Classy, quiet establishment with an enormous menu selection including all the *oaxaqueño* favorites. Gorgeous tropical parrots and shady fronds come with garden seating. *Tlayudas* 40 pesos. *Comida corrida* 48 pesos. Open M-Sa 7am-10pm, Su 7am-1pm. Cash only. ❸

Fonda Mexicana, 20 de Noviembre 408 (☎514 3121). One of the most popular spots south of the *zócalo*. The friendly, family-run restaurant is packed with locals on lunch break. *Comida corrida* (40 pesos) includes dessert. Beer 8 pesos. Open M-Sa 8am-5pm. Cash only. ❸

Cafe Royal, García Vigil 403 (☎514 5235), just north of Bravo. An eatery "with a French touch," where hip Mexicans and Europeans sip lattes. The baguettes (45-50 pesos) are the best bet. Crepes from 40 pesos. Open M-Sa 8am-11pm. Cash only. ❹

1254 Marco Polo, 5 de Mayo 103 (☎514 4360), north of Independencia. A charming seafood joint away from the sea, filled with the hum of old couples and young tourists alike. The *comida corrida* (42 pesos) serves either seafood or *comida tipica*, while the ceviche (50-60 pesos) is a cheap, filling option. Shrimp 110 pesos. Open daily 8am-9pm. Cash only. ❺

Las Quince Letras, Abasolo 300 (☎514 3769). An upscale eatery full of families and enamored couples, with leafy outdoor seating available. For the bold, *chapulines* (grasshoppers; 50 pesos) are the perfect appetizer. Salads 45-55 pesos. Entrees 75-95 pesos. Open daily 9am-9pm. MC/V. ❺

Restaurant Morelos, Morelos 1003 (☎516 0558). Try this homey, orange-walled eatery, where you can sit down and have a quick bite. *Comida corrida* (40 pesos) comes with sweet flan dessert. Breakfast 30 pesos. Open M-Sa 7am-7pm. Cash only. ❷

Flor de Loto, Morelos 509 (☎514 3944). A haven for vegetarians with requisite tie-dyed tables. Regional (i.e., meaty) food also served. Try the soy meatballs with spinach (38 pesos) or the *menú del día* (48 pesos). Open daily 8:30am-10pm. Cash only. ❸

Los Canarios, 20 de noviembre 502 (☎514 1937), just south of Aldama. Bland music and a lack of personality and decor are more than made up for by convenient hours and reasonable prices. Try the barbecue chicken special (58 pesos) or the eggs, any style (30 pesos). Mexican plates 58 pesos. Open 24hr. Cash only. ❸

CHOCOLATE CAFES AND SHOPS

Many chocolate shops near the corner of Mina and 20 de Noviembre produce Oaxaca's favorite confection. The smell is overpowering—follow your nose to see the chocolate-making process and grab plenty of ■**free samples.** If you don't make it to the area, don't worry—nearly every restaurant in the city serves *chocolate caliente* (hot chocolate). You can order it *oaxaqueño*-style *con agua* (with water), or *con leche* (with milk). Also keep an eye out for *café de olla*, a sweet, spicy coffee. Many cafes line Alcalá and Abasolo between 5 de Mayo and Reforma.

■ **Chocolate Mayordomo,** Mina 219 (☎516 1619), at 20 de Noviembre. Additional locations across the street as well as a third down the street. King of Oaxaca's sweets market with 10 stores in the city. World-renowned confectioners lure the uncertain with free samples. Buy some solid chocolate for the road (25-30 pesos per 500g) or sit with a cup of the city's cheapest hot chocolate (small 10 pesos). Open daily 7am-9pm. ❶

Chocolate la Soledad, Mina 221 (☎526 3807), across the street from Mayordomo. This chocolate and spice shop fronts the **Hotel Chocolate Posada** (p. 534) and sells the sweet stuff in all shapes, sizes, and flavors. Indulge yourself with a double hot chocolate (15 pesos) in the vine-covered courtyard cafe or grab a simple cup (10 pesos). As a bonus, they have plenty of free samples and sell *mezcal* in every form imaginable. Open M-Sa 7am-9pm, Su 7am-8pm. D/MC/V. ❶

Chocolate Guelaguetza, 20 de Noviembre 605, south of Mina. Less hectic than the others on the block. A large selection of *moles*, chocolate figurines, chocolate picture frames, and other candied bric-a-brac are on offer here, along with a good ol' cup of hot chocolate (12 pesos). Open daily 8am-8pm. Cash only. ❶

◎ SIGHTS

Oaxaca's long history permeates its streets, museums, colonial mansions, and Baroque churches. Many sites of interest are between the *zócalo* and Santo Domingo, including the numerous studios and galleries that give Oaxaca its reputation as an art mecca. Oaxaca also boasts several markets, including the enormous **Central de Abastos,** on Trujano, eight blocks west of the *zócalo*. (Open daily 8am-8pm.) **Mercado Benito Juárez,** at the corner of 20 de Noviembre and Aldama, two blocks from the *zócalo*, sells crafts, produce, flowers, and clothing. Its annex, **Mercado 20 de Noviembre,** on the next block, has an array of cheap food stalls. (Both open daily 6am-9pm.) **Mercado de Artesanías,** at the corner of García and Zaragoza, offers artisan wares. Prices and quality are often better in nearby villages where the crafts originate. (Open daily 8am-8pm.)

■ **CENTRO CULTURAL SANTO DOMINGO.** The ex-convent next to the Iglesia de Santo Domingo was converted into the prestigious **Museo de las Culturas de Oaxaca** in the *centro*. The stellar museum houses room upon room of Mixtec, Zapotec, colonial, and more recent Mexican artifacts, but the prime attraction is the treasure extracted from Tomb 7 in Monte Albán: the largest single collection of Mixtec treasure ever found. The burial site features jewelry and art made with gold, silver, copper, amber, jade, opal, turquoise, obsidian, coral, and alabaster. The Center also houses the new **Jardín Etnobotánico,** a fairyland of giant cacti and flowering trees, and the 17th-century Fray Francisco de Burgoa **library** collection, with 23,000 antique volumes and a large set of Old World maps. (☎516 2991. *Open Tu-Su 10am-7pm. The only way to view the garden is through a free guided tour; English tours Tu, Th, Sa 11am. 45 pesos. Video rights 35 pesos. Audiotour 40 pesos.)*

■ **MUSEO DE LOS PINTORES.** The unremarkable building houses an extensive permanent exhibit by *oaxaqueño* painter Rafael Morales, among other locals, but the real attractions are the rotating special exhibits, which display incredible works from the oeuvre of masters like Rembrandt and Picasso. *(Independencia 607, at the corner of García Vigil ☎516 5645. Open Tu-Sa 10am-8pm, Su 10am-6pm. Admission 20 pesos, students 10 pesos.)*

IGLESIA DE SANTO DOMINGO. Higher, mightier, and in better shape than the cathedral, Santo Domingo is the city's tallest building. The priory was begun in 1555, but not completed for another 111 years, when the trademark Mexican Baroque stylizations inside were completed. During the Reform Wars, the governor ordered the destruction of all 14 altars, which were restored by local artists in

1959, with gold matching the gorgeous gilt inlays on the walls and nave. It is one of the most elaborate—and expensive—of its kind, and a treat for even the most jaded tourist. The Capilla de la Virgen del Rosario, to the right as you walk in, is from 1731. Though much older, it, too, holds relatively new altar works, some of them inaugurated as late as 1969. *(3 blocks past MACO, on the Andador Turístico. Open daily 7am-1pm and 4-8pm. Capilla open daily 9:30am-1pm and 4-7pm.)*

BASÍLICA LA SOLEDAD. A minor but absorbing attraction is the **Museo Religioso de la Soledad,** housing art and religious relics from first archbishop's time and an odd assortment of gifts sent to the Virgin, who is said to have appeared here in 1620, including black coral, a giant seahorse, a stuffed cat, architectural figurines, and money from around the world. *(Independencia 107, 4 blocks west of the post office. ☎516 5076. Open daily 8am-2pm and 4-7pm. Donations suggested.)*

 OAXACA FOR POCKET CHANGE. After a stroll through the huge **Central de Abastos** or the more manageable **Mercado Benito Juárez** (p. 536), check out **Mercado 20 de Noviembre** (p. 536), where everything from barbecued meat to *quesillo* is available for your dining pleasure. Spend the evening at the **Pochote Theater** (p. 538), which has free nightly screenings of international movies. Wind down the night at **La Tentación** (p. 539) with a Sól beer while enjoying live salsa.

CASA DE BENITO JUÁREZ. Mexico's most beloved president lived here for 10 years as a child (1818-28), after being adopted by a nun who owned a bookbinding shop. Scenes of everyday 19th-century life are juxtaposed with far more interesting placards on the socioeconomic and political conditions in Mexico in Juárez's time. *(García Vigil 609, 1 block west of Alcalá. ☎516 1860. Open Tu-Su 10am-7pm. 34 pesos; Su and holidays free. Video rights 35 pesos.)*

CATEDRAL DE OAXACA. Originally constructed in 1553 and reconstructed after earthquake damage between 1702 and 1733, the cathedral dates from a time when the Mexican Church and State were unified. The interior is dim and stark, with equally austere paintings adorning the walls. The altar is small—the main focus of the room is the bishop's seat in the middle. The King of Spain donated the English clock in the back. *(On the northeastern corner of the zócalo. Open daily 7:30am-8pm.)*

CENTRO FOTOGRÁFICO ALVAREZ BRAVO-FONOTECA EDUARDO MATA. The small courtyard full of young, artsy types hosts a few small exhibits of contemporary photography by *oaxaqueños* and other Mexican nationals, as well as a library on the art. In an adjacent room is a music library amassed by local Eduardo Mata. *(Bravo 116, east of Vigil. ☎514 1933. Open M and W-Su 8am-9:30pm. Donations suggested.)*

MUSEO DE ARTE PREHISPÁNICO DE MEXICO RUFINO TAMAYO. This museum features the artist's immense, well-preserved personal collection of pre-Hispanic objects from all over Mexico. The figurines, ceramics, and masks that Tamayo (1899-1991) collected were meant to be appreciated as works of art rather than artifacts, resulting in a hybrid of an art gallery and an archaeological museum. *(Morelos 503, between Díaz and Tinoco y Palacios. ☎516 4750. Open M and W-Sa 10am-2pm and 4-7pm, Su 10am-3pm. 30 pesos, students 15 pesos.)*

MUSEO DE ARTE CONTEMPORÁNEO DE OAXACA (MACO). This colonial building is known as the Casa de Cortés, although he never lived here, and it was built after his death. Today, the 18th-century home hosts rotating exhibits of modern art from around the world. In the past it has showcased work by *oaxaqueños* Rodolfo

Morales, Rufino Tamayo, and Francisco Toledo. *(Alcalá 202, 1 block down Andador Turístico on the right. ☎514 2228. Open M and W-Su 10:30am-8pm. 10 pesos; Su free.)*

OTHER SIGHTS. If you're looking for a beautiful view of the city and surrounding hills, head to the **Cerro de Fortín** (Hill of the Fortress), which once housed a fort to protect the city. The Escalera de Fortín begins on Crespo, leading past the Guelaguetza amphitheater to the Planetarium Nundehui. The climb is grueling, and should only be undertaken during daylight hours, as the area has been known to harbor a few thieves after dark. *(☎514 7500. Open Th-Su 10am-1pm and 5-8pm. 25 pesos.)* Porfirio Díaz left a mark on his native city, one of the most beautiful Porfiriato additions being the **Teatro Macedonio Alcala,** with its gorgeous dome and stonework. *(5 de Mayo at Independencia, 2 blocks behind the cathedral. ☎516 3387. Weekly shows 6, 8pm. 25 pesos.)* The off-beat **Museo de la Filatelia (MUFI)** houses a stamp collection that will put others to shame, with a mish-mash of stamps from around the Republic dating back to the early days of *correo* service. *(On Juárez just south of Berriozabal. Open Tu-Su 10am-6pm. 20 pesos.)*

♫ ENTERTAINMENT

Pochote Theater, García Vigil 817, hosts international movies, short films, and documentaries. *(☎514 1194. Shows daily 8pm. Free.)* The **Guerreros,** Oaxaca's professional baseball team, play at the Estadio Eduardo Vasconcelos, on the corner of Vasconcelos and Niños Héroes de Chapultepec. (Tickets 5-60 pesos.) Oaxaca's cultural centers provide various other types of entertainment. **Casa de la Cultura,** Ortega 403, at Colón, hosts theater productions, concerts, summer music and art classes, and art exhibits. *(☎516 2483. Open M-F 9am-6pm, Sa 9am-3pm and 4-6:30pm, Su 9am-2pm.)* **Instituto Oaxaqueño de las Culturas** *(☎516 3434),* at Madera and Tecnológica, has a similar program. To get there, take a westbound "Sta. Rosa" *urbano* for 2.50 pesos from Independencia and Tinoco y Palacios.

Those debilitated by the previous night's activity can catch a flick in English with Spanish subtitles at the **Mulitmax** cinema, Av. Universidad 139 *(☎514 7929;* tickets 40 pesos), in the Plaza del Valle mall, or at **Cinépolis,** Av. Castillejos 502 *(☎506 0885;* tickets 40 pesos), at Plaza Oaxaca. Both plazas can be reached by taking a "Plaza del Valle" bus on Juárez. SEDETUR (p. 531) has movie listings.

◈ NIGHTLIFE

Oaxaca boasts a thriving bar scene, sustained by droves of hip youth and criminally cheap *mezcal*. The *zócalo* empties around 10 or 11pm, and gangs of mixed groups whistle and laugh along the Alcalá. Dancing here requires a little skill, as most clubs play salsa and merengue. Some bars are closed on Sunday, but Monday is the quietest day by far. Most nightlife can be reached by foot or taxis (35 pesos).

BARS

Bars cluster the street along Matamoros and Porfirio Díaz, which are well lit and close to the *zócalo*.

■ **Elefante,** 20 de Noviembre 110 *(☎514 5916),* just south of Independencia. The Mughal India theme surrounds young couples drinking on lounge couches under interior arches with elaborate red drapes. Persian carpets and elephant posters mix strangely with the alt, reggae, and Spanish rap. Cover 30 pesos. Beer 20 pesos. Mixed drinks 45-60 pesos. Open daily 10pm-3am. MC/V.

FreeBar, Matamoros 100C, across from La Tentación. Groups of friends pack the dark corners of this small bar, getting tipsy off the dirt cheap alcohol. A DJ mixes loud Spanish hip hop while a few people dance in the back. *Mezcal* 10 pesos. Beer 20 pesos. Mixed drinks 35 pesos. Open Tu-Su 10pm-3am. MC/V.

La Divina, Gurion 104, across from the south side of Santo Domingo. Popular among the city's hipster crowd. Trippy ceramic artwork, slightly disturbing masks and skeletons, and nooks for close conversation. Movies screened M-Tu, Th and Su. F-Sa live music. Beer 20 pesos. Mixed drinks 50 pesos. Open daily 8pm-1am. Cash only.

Fandango, Díaz 503 (☎514 9584), at Allende. Walls are a collage of magazine clippings, tarot cards, and flyers in this funky cafe-bar. The front is bright with candlelight, and hums with conversation. The back is darker, with louder music. Wi-Fi. Live music F-Sa 10pm-1am. Beer 15-20 pesos. Mixed drinks 40-50 pesos. *Mate* 40 pesos. *Lassi* 20 pesos. Open Tu-Sa 7pm-2am. Cash only.

La Casa del Mezcal, Flores Magón 209. This classy-but-casual establishment is the premier place to try Oaxaca's favorite beverage. Fight locals for a seat in the back, or make a spectacle of yourself at the bar with a flaming *mezcal* shot. Plain *mezcal* 20 pesos; specially aged/flavored types 40 pesos. Open daily noon-2am. Cash only.

La Costumbre, Alcalá 501, opposite the entrance to Santo Domingo. Soft music and bright lighting make for a super-casual, conversational sort of bar good for a quiet night out. Beer 20 pesos. Mixed drinks 40-55 pesos. Open M-Sa 9pm-3am. Cash only.

CLUBS

Most clubs cater to salsa and merengue dancers here, so put on some nice shoes. Walk or save your heels and grab a taxi (35 pesos).

⧫ Candela, Murguía 413 (☎514 2010), at Pino Suárez. Situated in an elegant, well-lit courtyard, surrounded by candlelit tables, and rocked by a great salsa band. Dance floor draws a diverse crowd. Live music Tu-Sa from 10:30pm. Cover Tu-W 30 pesos; Th-Sa 50 pesos. Mixed drinks 50 pesos. Bottle of Courvoisier 1700 pesos. Restaurant open M-F 1-7pm. Dancing Tu-Sa 9pm-2am. Cash only.

La Tentación, Matamoros 101 (☎514 9521). The dance floor is on fire with couples dancing to casual salsa and cumbia rhythms, impatiently downing their drinks between songs. Grab a cheap cocktail (35 pesos) and let the *oaxaqueños* teach you how it's done. Salsa Th-Sa nights. Cover F-Sa 35 pesos. Open daily 9pm-2am. MC/V.

502, Díaz 502 (☎516 6020), across from La Resistencia. As the city's only gay and lesbian nightclub, 502 can afford to be selective. The club is private; ring the bell outside the door and wait for the bouncer to unlock it. Lesbian-friendly. Patrons sip drinks at the edges and occasionally foray onto the dance fl. No drugs, heavy drinking, or transvestism allowed. Cover F-Sa 50 pesos, includes 1 drink. Open high season Tu-Su 10:30pm-6am; low season Th-Sa only.

O'Clubber Lounge, Díaz 102B (☎515 0477), 1 block from Héroes de Chapultepec. Electronica, trance, and house music move the young crowd on the metal bridge spanning the room and on the crazy floor below. Beer 25 pesos. *Bebidas nacionales* 40-60 pesos. Cover Sa 50 pesos. Open W-Th 10pm-3am, F-Sa 9pm-4am.

✷ FESTIVALS

Oaxaca explodes with festivals in late July, celebrating its abundant culinary and cultural wealth. On the two Mondays following July 16, known as **Los Lunes del Cerro** (Hill Mondays), representatives from all seven regions of Oaxaca state converge on the **Cerro del Fortín** for the festival of ⧫**Guelaguetza,** held at the Auditorio

Guelaguetza. Guelaguetza recalls the Zapotec custom of reciprocal gift-giving. At the end of the day's traditional dances, performers throw goods typical of their regions into the outstretched arms of the crowd gathered in the 12,000-seat stadium. In between the gatherings are festive food and handicraft exhibits, art shows, and concerts. (Call Ticketmaster in Mexico City for reservations, as tickets sell out. Ticketmaster ☎ 55 5325 9000. Front-section seats 400 pesos; back-section seats free, but you must come very early to get a seat.)

As the *mezcal* capital of the world, Oaxaca is justifiably proud of itself. During the **Fiesta Nacional del Mezcal,** held in late July, Oaxacans and foreigners alike gather to drink themselves numb. Vendors crowd the park, and everyone stumbles from booth to booth, giddy from the unlimited free shots of the earthy drink. If you've exceeded your taste-test tolerance, take a seat and enjoy the festival's live music, traditional dances, and fireworks. (Locations and exact date changes from year to year. Check the tourist office for current info. Entrance fee 15-20 pesos.)

Around the same time, *mole*—Oaxaca's local delight—commands its own week-long **Festival de los Siete Moles,** held in hotels and restaurants around the city. Each night the featured venues crowd up as they serve and celebrate one variety of the *oaxaqueño* sauce. (Check the tourist office for a complete listing of locations.)

Oaxaca's exquisitely beautiful **Día de los Muertos** celebrations (Nov. 1-2) have become a huge tourist attraction in recent years. Most travel agencies offer expeditions to the candlelit, marigold-filled village graveyards. Shops fill with molded sugar *calaveras* (skulls), while altars are erected throughout the city to memorialize the dead. Because these celebrations can be very personal, locals might not appreciate being photographed as they remember the deceased.

On December 23, Oaxacans celebrate **Noche de los Rábanos** (Night of the Radishes). The small tuber is honored for its frequent use in Oaxacan cuisine and its easily carved form. Masterpieces of historic or biblical themes made entirely in radish fill the *zócalo*, where they are judged. Hundreds of people admire the creations and eat sweet *buñuelos* (fried tortillas with honey). Upon finishing the treat, make a wish and throw the ceramic plate on the ground; if the plate smashes into pieces, your wish will come true.

◼ DAYTRIP FROM OAXACA

◾ MONTE ALBÁN

Autobuses Turísticos buses to Monte Albán leave the Hotel Rivera del Ángel, Mina 518 (☎ 516 5327), between Mier y Terán and Díaz Ordaz, several blocks southwest of the zócalo (30min., every 30min. 8:30am-3pm). Tickets must be purchased exactly 10min. before departure; round-trips with fixed return are 38 pesos, but don't allow much time at the site. Tickets to return later (20 pesos) are sold in the Monte Albán parking lot. Site open daily 8am-5pm. 45 pesos. Videocamera use 35 pesos. Though many travel agencies can set you up with hassle-free transportation and excellent guides, it is usually cheaper to transport yourself and, if you want, find a guide once you reach the mountain. English-language guides charge 200-300 pesos for a 1hr. tour, depending on the size and negotiating skills of your group.

Commanding the valley high above Oaxaca is Monte Albán, the one-time capital of the Zapotec empire. Visitors to Oaxaca should not leave without seeing the ruins, which are some of the most important and spectacular in Mexico, and an enduring legacy of both Zapotec and Mixtec culture. Built atop the mountain to be nearer their gods, the city was abandoned in all its advanced splendor over a millennium ago, largely untouched until the 20th century. Unless you're an expert on pre-Hispanic civilizations, a good guide (or the 80-peso guidebook from the museum store) to Monte Albán can really illuminate your visit.

> **TIP**
> **GO GO GROUP.** Private guides have the most intimate knowledge of Monte Albán's many mysterious ruins, but they often charge steep prices. Get a price quote from a guide and then collect your group or wait near the entrance and try to get some compatriots to join you—you can save big by splitting the original price with others.

HISTORY. The history of Monte Albán can be divided into five parts, spanning the years from 500 BC until the Spanish conquest in the 16th century. During periods I and II, Monte Albán rose as the Mayan and Zapotec cultures intermingled. The Zapotecs adopted the Olmec's *juego de pelota* (ball game) and steep pyramid structure, while the Maya inherited the Zapotec calendar and writing system. These developments, along with the observatories and drainage systems and varied forms of art like the stelae, are evidence of the city-state's advanced infrastructure. Almost all of the extant buildings and tombs, as well as several urns and murals of nobles and leaders, come from Period III (AD 350-700). Around AD 800, the city began to decline for reasons which remain unknown, perhaps involving political instability or over-exploitation of resources. By 850 the settlement was practically uninhabited, and in its stead rose smaller Mixtec cities like Yagul and Zaachila. The Mixtecs assumed control of Monte Albán, but did not settle it, using it instead as burial site, depositing some of their finest art and treasure inside. In 1931, Dr. Alfonso Caso began the first comprehensive excavation of the city, systematically detailing it in its entirety in a project spanning more than two decades. In 1932, he and Juan Valenzuela discovered Tomb 7, which held the largest single collection of Mixtec treasure ever found. The treasures from Tomb 7 are now on display at the Museo de las Culturas de Oaxaca (p. 536).

The monolithic, geometric stone structures are all that remain of the Zapotec capital, which once sprawled 20km over three mountaintops. First constructed circa 550 BC, Monte Albán was the massive undertaking of a confederation of local communities, ruled by the religious elite. The city flourished during the Classic Period (AD 200-700), when it shared the spotlight with Teotihuacán (p. 141) and Tikal as the major cultural and ceremonial centers of Mesoamerica. Here, people cultivated maize, built complex water drainage systems, and engaged in extensive trade networks, especially with Teotihuacán. Daily life was carefully constructed to harmonize with supernatural elements: architecture adhered to the four cardinal directions and the 260-day sacred calendar. To emphasize the congruence between household and cosmos, families buried ancestors beneath their houses to symbolize their journey to the underworld. Excavations of burials in Monte Albán have yielded not only dazzling artifacts, but also valuable information about social stratification; pottery, figurines, burial sites, and engravings indicate a highly rigid social order, as ordained by the gods. The educated priests ruled, with the holiest living on the mountaintop, while the laboring lower classes lived and worked farther down in the valley in a physical and symbolic hierarchy.

BALL COURT. After passing through the ticketing station just beyond the museum, walk left up the inclined path leading diagonally toward the ruins. Before reaching the Main Plaza, you will see the remains of several small buildings on your left and the ball court (constructed c. 100 BC) in front of you. The sides of the court, which now look like bleachers, were once covered in stucco and plaster and served as bouncing boards for the ball toward the goal, which stood in the middle of the grassy area. The motion of the ball symbolized the movement of the heavenly spheres, and the game was used in rituals as well as to resolve land disputes.

MAIN PLAZA. Passing the ball court on your left, you will enter the huge Main Plaza, with the mountain-like North Platform on the right, smaller structures lined up on the left, and the enormous South Platform bounding it on the other side. The Main Plaza is flat, and was covered entirely in stucco—remarkable when one considers that the mountain from which it was cut originally had a high peak. On your left, look for **Building P,** with its massive staircase leading up the platform. The structure was scientific as well as religious, with a shaft that filled a chamber below only on the two days of the year when the sun was at its zenith. Just past that is the **Palace,** containing a complex set of passageways and rooms that served as the residence of a high priest.

SOUTH PLATFORM. Angled with the Palace and forming the Plaza's south end is the South Platform, one of the site's highest structures. The top affords a commanding view of the ruins, valley, and mountains beyond, accessible by half-meter stairs. On both sides of the staircase on the plaza level are replicas of the original stelae carved with priests and tigers and a defense wall running along the front of the platform. One stela is believed to depict a former king of Monte Albán.

BUILDING OF DANCERS (BUILDING L). Walking left of the platform to the plaza's west side, you will first come across System M and then the Building of Dancers. Once thought to be performing ritual dances, the "dancers" in the reliefs on the center building more likely depict chieftains conquered by Monte Albán, almost all with mutilated genitals. Over 400 figures date from the 5th century BC and are nearly identical to contemporary Olmec sculptures on the Gulf Coast.

BUILDING K (SYSTEM IV). Just north of the Buildings of the Dancers is Building K, a dual complex with a central courtyard. The staircase in the middle leads to the temple platform on top. Just north of the system is a massive monolith with early calendar markings on it.

BUILDINGS G, H, I, AND J. Crossing back to the center of the platform, the first structure you'll find is Building J, in the shape of an arrowhead. Unlike any other building here, it is asymmetrical and built at a 45° angle to nearby structures. The Zapotecs often used astronomy to detect seasonal changes, and Building J was positioned to line up with Orion's Belt when the rainy season was coming. Its broad, carved slabs suggest that the building is one of the oldest on the site, dating from 100 BC to AD 200, but it was rebuilt multiple times. The so-called **Conquest Stones,** incongruous with the others on the backside of Building J, feature strange glyphs with upside-down heads. These represent the chieftains of groups conquered by the Zapotecs. The next group of buildings moving north, dominating the center of the plaza, includes buildings G, H, and I—likely comprising the principal altar of Monte Albán. From here, the religious leader addressed citizens from ground level and the Zapotec leader addressed them from the North Platform.

NORTH PLATFORM. Finish off the Main Plaza by visiting the North Platform near the entrance, a structure almost as large as the plaza itself. It consists of a platform overlaid with a collection of pyramids and smaller stone platforms connected by small staircases. The platform contains the Sunken Plaza as well as the site's highest altar, the best place to view the entire site and lose yourself in passing clouds. Between the Sunken Plaza and the Main Plaza are 12 restored columns from a colonnade called the **Royal Portico,** where the Zapotec leader once addressed those in the Main Plaza and lesser nobles in the sunken plaza. The sight has amazing acoustics, and snatches of conversation echo throughout the Main Plaza. Around the east side of the platform is the **Bejeweled Building,** so called for the streaks of red painted on its stuccoed discs, showing some of the influence of Teotihuacán.

TOMBS AND MUSEUM. Continue straight on the path, exiting the site to **Tomb 104.** Although none of the 260 tombs in Monte Albán are open to the public, you can still get an idea of the tomb from its exterior structure and the information placard with a map. On your way out of the site, be sure to stop by the **museum,** which gives a chronological survey of Monte Albán's history and displays the originals of the stelae (the ones outside are replicas). The most interesting exhibit is a case of human skulls, some deformed by disease, and others by the deliberate manipulation of infants' skulls, presumably for ritual beautification or to show social status. Although the collection is still impressive, some of the more spectacular artifacts have been hauled off to museums in Oaxaca and Mexico City. Near the parking lot is the entrance to Tomb 7, where the spectacular cache of Mixtec ornaments mentioned above was found.

GULF COAST AND CHIAPAS

Gorgeous beaches, natural reserves, and pleasant small towns welcome travelers to the states of the southern Gulf Coast, which are united by tropical beauty, indigenous traditions, Caribbean music, and sweeping poverty.

Stretching 300km along the Gulf of Mexico, steamy **Veracruz** is ripe with breathtaking beaches, burgeoning cities, and vast spaces filled only with roaming cattle and lush vegetation. The ancestral home of the Huastec, Totonac, and Olmec civilizations, Veracruz witnessed Cortés's first steps on American soil and has since endured foreign intervention and invasion by Spain (1825), France (1839), and the US (1847 and 1914). Today, many residents continue to live off the land, cultivating tobacco and coffee and running small-scale cattle ranches. Veracruz's main income, however, comes from oil and fishing. *Veracruzanos*, also known as *jarochos*, are renowned for their delightful sense of humor, tasty seafood and coffee, and Afro-Caribbean-inspired music. *Marimba* rhythms and Caribbean colors flow through the steamy port city of Veracruz day and night.

Undertouristed **Tabasco** lies southeast of Veracruz along the Gulf of Mexico, dotted with lakes and swamps, crisscrossed by rivers, and swathed in dense jungle. Empty beaches line the northern coast, and the southeastern border overflows banana and cacao plantations. Once the center of Olmec territory, Tabasco offers a glimpse into Mexico's mother culture with the ruins at La Venta. Villahermosa, the capital, rises from the center of the jungle, its colonial identity in constant conflict with modernization.

Chiapas sits south of Tabasco and for centuries has been known for environmental diversity—its cloud-enveloped heights contrast with dense, lowland rainforests. One of Mexico's most beautiful cities, San Cristóbal de las Casas, renowned for its cobblestone streets and surrounding *indígena* villages, sits high among these peaks. Chiapas encompasses part of the Mayan heartland, and the Lacandón Rainforest shields the remote ruins of Bonampak and Yaxchilán as well as fiercely traditional groups of Lacandón Maya. Chiapas's *indígenas* remain true to their roots—in many communities, schools teach in the local dialect as well as Spanish. The Ejército Zapatista de Liberación Nacional (EZLN) rebellion of 1994 drew the world's attention to Chiapas and the highland region's constant land conflicts, which pit small-scale Mayan farmers against wealthy ranchers and the national government.

HIGHLIGHTS OF THE GULF COAST

INHALE the rich vanilla aromas of **Papantla** (p. 548), "the city that perfumes the world," and carry the scent with you to the awesome ruins at **El Tajín** (p. 551).

STRIKE a pose at the stunning **Cascada de Texolo** (p. 558), where movie stars galore have filmed countless scenes under the glistening falls.

GULP the thin air of **San Cristóbal de las Casas** (p. 590), set atop lush green mountains in the Chiapan cloud forest.

GAWK in amazement at the Olmec artifacts situated in a spectacular outdoor jungle-setting in Villahermosa's **Parque-Museo La Venta** (p. 580).

VERACRUZ

TUXPAN (TUXPAM) ☎ 783

With its beautiful river, welcoming atmosphere, and palm trees, Tuxpan (pop. 75,000) draws tourists from all over Mexico. Perhaps due to the heat and humidity, many foreigners have yet to join in the fun, though tranquil Tuxpan offers vacationers leisurely strolls and great bar-hopping along the Río Tuxpan, as well as nearby escapes to coral reefs and mangrove forests.

⊡ TRANSPORTATION. Tuxpan, 347km northwest of Veracruz, spreads along the northern bank of Río Tuxpan. Each bus line has its own station; to get to the *centro* from any one, walk to the river and turn right. **ADO**, Rodríguez 1 (☎834 0102), close to the bridge and three blocks east of Parque Cano down Reyes Heróles, sends **buses** to: **Matamoros** (11hr., 3 per day, 482 pesos); **Papantla** (1½hr., 9 per day, 50 pesos); **Tampico** (3½hr., 29 per day, 156 pesos); **Veracruz** (5½hr., 19 per day, 210 pesos). **Ómnibus de México**, Independencia 30 (☎834 1147), under the bridge, runs first class to: **Guadalajara** (10hr., 3 per day, 570 pesos); **Mexico City** (6hr., 9 per day,

Veracruz State

190 pesos); **Monterrey** (10hr., 5 per day, 481 pesos); **Querétaro** (10hr., 3 per day, 292 pesos). Second-class buses run to most nearby destinations.

⚐ PRACTICAL INFORMATION. The **tourist office,** Juárez 20, at the back of the Palacio Municipal in Parque Rodríguez Cano, has maps and brochures as well as information on boat rentals for the reefs and mangrove forests. (☎834 2155, ext. 125; www.tuxpan.com.mx. Open M-F 9am-7pm, Sa 10am-4pm.) **Exchange currency** and traveler's checks at **Bancomer,** on Juárez and Zapata between the 2 parks, which has a **24hr. ATM.** (Open M-F 8:30am-4pm.) Other services include: **emergency** (☎060); **police,** Libramiento López Mateos 520 (☎834 0252); **Red Cross,** next to the police (☎834 0158); **Hospital Civil** (☎834 0199); **Súper Farmacia,** on Morelos and Mina, between the 2 parks (☎835 3395; open 24hr.); **LADATELS,** scattered around the two plazas; **Lavandería Plus,** Mina 9, two blocks from Juárez (☎840 2710; 11-13 pesos per kg; open M-Sa 8am-8pm); and **Internet** access at **Intermix Internet Cafe,** Ortega 22, 2 blocks off Morelos (5 pesos per hr. 7am-noon, 7 pesos per hr. noon-midnight; open daily 7am-midnight). To reach the **post office,** Mina 16, from Parque Reforma, follow Morelos toward the bridge, take the first left onto Mina and walk three blocks. (☎834 0088. **Mexpost** inside. Open M-F 9am-4pm.) **Postal Code:** 92801.

⚐ ACCOMMODATIONS. Hotels in Tuxpan are concentrated around the plazas, and they are all quite expensive. While Tuxpan is hot, some rooms have A/C—you can expect to shell out considerably more for it. **Hotel España ❷,** Clavijero 11, near the bus station, is a bit of a walk from the *centro,* but it is clean and comfortable and probably the best value in town. (☎834 8527. Singles and doubles 140 pesos, with A/C 220 pesos. Cash only.) Right off the Parque Reforma, **Posada San Ignacio ❸** welcomes guests with bright murals and flowery rooms, and the courtyard is filled with parakeets. Cheerful and adorable during the day, these birds will likely wake you around 8am. Rooms have private bath, fan, and TV. (☎834 2905. 24hr. bell. Singles and doubles 200 pesos, each additional person 50 pesos. Cash only.) Not quite as homey, but perfectly located, is **Hotel El Parque ❸,** offering plain rooms with fan and TV right on the Parque Reforma. (24hr. bell. Singles and doubles 200 pesos; triples and quads 250 pesos. Cash only.) **Hotel Tuxpan ❹,** Mina 2, is a pleasant, family-run hotel with sunny rooms and friendly staff. Rooms have private bath and fan. (☎834 4110. 24hr. bell. Singles 230 pesos, with A/C 270 pesos; doubles 270/300 pesos. Cash only.)

◖ FOOD. Along *el bulevar,* especially near the bridge, **food vendors** grill seafood tacos and *gorditas,* while the downtown area is rife with small restaurants and *taquerías.* On a hot, humid evening, nothing is more refreshing than a *licuado* (8-16 pesos) made from fresh, seasonal fruits, from **Refresqueria Estudiante ❶,** the teenage hang-out in the middle of Parque Reforma. **El Mejicano ❸,** on Morelos 49 opposite Parque Reforma, seats you amid bright colors and imitation Diego Rivera paintings. The regional menu includes *enfrijoladas* (warm tortillas rolled in a black bean sauce and stuffed with cheese or chicken; 32 pesos) and seafood dishes. (☎834 8904. Entrees 30-90 pesos. Buffet 50 pesos. Open daily 6am-midnight. Cash only.) Set back from the bustle of the plazas, **Los Pilares ❷,** Mina 27, serves cheap, tasty *comida corrida* (28 pesos) in a lovely white building shaded by bougainvillea-covered pillars. (*Antojitos* 20-35 pesos. Desserts 8 pesos. Open daily 7am-9pm. Cash only.) Indulge your sweet tooth at **El Tulipan ❷,** at Juárez 34 off Parque Reforma and at Reyes Heróles next to Los Girasoles, which offers combination plates (18-20 pesos) of luscious cakes and pies served with cappuccino and *refrescos* in a chintzy cafeteria atmosphere. (Sandwiches 20-30 pesos. Open daily 9am-10pm. Cash only.) **Super Alan,** on Juárez and Mina, is a supermarket between the two parks. (☎834 9008. Open daily 8am-9pm.)

◙ **SIGHTS.** Mexico has a storied and intimate relationship with Cuba, beautifully illustrated at the ◙**Museo de la Amistad Mexico-Cuba,** across the river via any of the ferries along Reyes Heróles (2.50 pesos). From the ferry, walk two blocks away from the river, then turn right on Obregón and follow it to its end; the museum is on your left. Exhibits include photos of Castro and Che taken during Castro's exile in Tuxpan in the late 1950s and sculptures celebrating Cuban accomplishments in art, music, and sports. (Tours in Spanish and English; ask for details. Open M-Sa 9am-7pm, Su 9am-3pm. Free.) **El Museo de Arqueología,** in the Parque Reforma, has artifacts from the pre-colonial settlements of the Olmec, Huastec, and Toltec. The museum closed for renovation in 2007, but plans to reopen by early 2008.

◪ **BEACHES.** *Tuxpeños* are justifiably proud of their beautiful river and scenic shores. Palm trees line the boardwalk and piles of well-priced pineapples, bananas, shrimp, and fish await visitors to the market under the bridge. Take the "Playa" bus on Reyes Heróles (8 pesos) to **Playa Azul,** 12km from the *centro*. Though it may be slightly dirty and crowded with families, the fine sand stretches far enough for you to stake a claim somewhere under the wild coconut palms. For a pricier but worthwhile adventure, rent a launch to explore the nearby *manglares* (mangrove forests), the **Laguna de Tampamachoco,** one of Tuxpan's three *arrecifes* (coral reefs), and the **Isla de Los Lobos,** a fisherman's paradise. From the riverside at Reyes Heróles and Rodriguez, by the ADO bus station, the **ferry boats** will take you on cruises of the Laguna and *manglares*. Get a group together and split the cost. (☎ 835 4564. 1-18 people. 1hr. 215 pesos, 2hr. 440 pesos.) Snorkeling, fishing, and scuba-diving expeditions to the reefs and to Isla de Los Lobos can be arranged at restaurants by Puente Tampamachoco, just before Playa Azul. Costs vary greatly depending on the length and nature of the trip, and again, it helps to go in groups. The tourist office in town can also provide you with contacts for adventure guides.

▣▨ **ENTERTAINMENT AND NIGHTLIFE.** Tuxpan's waterfront stays alive long after dark, and the most popular places are all within walking distance of the *centro*. Friday nights, head over to **Vida en los Museos** at the Museo de la Amistad Mexico-Cuba at 7pm for entertainment ranging from intimate intellectual conversations to large rock concerts. On Sunday nights, locals crowd the parks for *Domingos Culturales/Familiares* (Cultural/Family Sundays). In Parque Rodríguez Cano, children jump on trampolines and drive bumper cars while parents chat. In Parque Reforma, older couples dance to Latin classics. All the while, adolescents march in single-sex packs, eyeing each other from afar. August 6 marks the beginning of **Feria Exposición,** a week-long display of town spirit, complete with traditional song and dance, cockfights, and an open-air theatre. On December 7, Tuxpan celebrates **El Día del Niño Perdido**.

Countless bars line the streets around Parque Reforma, but the best place to be on the weekends is down the river, where bars and nightclubs cluster on Juárez and Reyes Heróles between Perez and Hernandez. By far the most popular is the restaurant ◙**Los Girasoles** (☎ 834 0392), on Reyes Heróles, which transforms into a dancer's paradise on weekends. (Mixed drinks 30-40 pesos. Happy hour daily 7pm-10pm.) Right next door on Hernandez, **Bulldog Dance Hall** thumps out techno and electronica and offers drink specials for women (open Th-Sa 9pm-5am), while one block over on Perez, **Bar London** plays reggaeton, salsa, and pop. (Sa 2-for-1 entry. Cover 30-50 pesos. Open Th-Sa 9pm-5am.) For a mellower drink, **Safari,** on Reyes Heróles and Perez, offers a large riverfront patio and free Wi-Fi. Skip the pricey food and have a beer (15 pesos) or mixed drink (20-50 pesos). (2-for-1 Happy hour daily 8pm-9pm. Open daily noon-last customer.)

GULF COAST AND CHIAPAS

POZA RICA   ☎ 782

Known more for its industry than its history or culture, Poza Rica (pop.
148,000) is one of the busiest oil centers in the country. The lush, green city is a
transportation hub for northern Veracruz, with easy access to nearby Papantla
and the ruins of El Tajín. If you find yourself on a long layover between buses,
check out the **MMCinema** on the Soriana Plaza, which shows the latest American
movies for low prices (matinees 45 pesos).

Several mid- to high-priced hotels are located in the *centro*, along Cortines.
Check in at the tourist office in the ADO bus station for promotional coupons. Otherwise, **Hotel Farolito ❶**, to the left as you exit either station, is dirt cheap, but the
rooms have peeling paint and a musty smell. All rooms have fans. (☎824 3466. Singles and doubles 115 pesos, with A/C 170 pesos. Cash only.) The restaurant and bar
Palma Sola ❸, next door to Los Arcos, is an excellent place to relax and grab some
antojitos (20 pesos) and drinks. (☎823 5373. Entrees 30-80 pesos. Beer 10 pesos.
Open daily 7am-11pm. Cash only.) For a quick meal, a number of countertop restaurants dot **Plaza Soriana ❶**, just a few steps away from the station. (*Gorditas* and
enchiladas 7-30 pesos. Most open daily 8am-10pm. Cash only.) The supermarket
Soriana is to the right as you exit the bus stations. (Open daily 8am-10pm. MC/V.)

From the two adjoining **bus stations** in the northwest corner of town, the *centro*
is accessible by "Centro" or "Juárez" minibuses. (10-15min., 4.50 pesos.) The station
on the left is served exclusively by **ADO** (☎824 8881), which services: **Matamoros**
(12hr., 4 per day, 504 pesos); **Mexico City** (5hr., every hr., 178 pesos); **Papantla**
(30min., every hr., 16 pesos); **Tampico** (5hr., every 30min., 192 pesos); **Tuxpan**
(45min., every 30min., 30 pesos); **Veracruz** (4½hr., every hr., 180 pesos); **Villahermosa**
(12hr., 12 per day, 506 pesos); and **Xalapa** (5hr., 15 per day, 180 pesos). From the
other station, **Ómnibus de México** (☎822 5866) goes to **Guadalajara** (10hr., 5 per day,
540 pesos), and **Transportes Papantla** (☎822 5666) heads to smaller regional destinations. **Tourist Information** is inside the ADO bus station, to the right of the ticket
counter. They offer brochures for El Tajín and coupons for hotels. (Open M-F 9am-
4pm). Services include: **Bital,** in Plaza Soriana, next to the bus stations, which
exchanges currency and traveler's checks and has a **24hr. ATM** (☎822 1877; open M-Sa
8am-7pm); **24hr. ATMs** in either bus station; **luggage storage,** in the ADO bus station
(5 pesos per hr.; open 24hr.); **emergency** ☎060; **police** (☎822 0407); **Red Cross** (☎822
0101); **Farmacia La Vida** in the non-ADO station (open 24hr.); **Telecomm,** next to the
post office (open M-F 8am-7:30pm, Sa 9am-5pm, Su 9am-noon); and the **post office,**
Calle 16 Ote., facing Parque Juárez, accessible by minibus from the *centro* (☎823
0102; **Mexpost** inside; open M-F 9am-4pm, Sa 9am-1pm). **Postal Code:** 93261.

PAPANTLA   ☎ 784

Papantla (pop. 49,000) has all the ingredients for a perfect, out-of-the-way stop.
Nestled in the green foothills of the Sierra Madre Oriental, Papantla is one of the
few remaining centers of Totonac culture. The city sits 12km north of the El Tajín
ruins, an important Totonac city during the Classic Period. Conquered by the
Aztecs in 1450, the Totonacs soon took revenge by joining Cortés in his march to
Tenochtitlán. After the conquest, the Spanish discovered the city's delicious, traditionally cultivated vanilla and introduced it to the rest of the globe, titling Papantla
"the city that perfumes the world." Papantla now combines traditional Catholicism
and *indígena* pride with its hallowed cathedral, showcasing a Totonac mural and
Totonac dances every weekend. The surrounding landscape of fertile orchards
and vanilla plantations is both beautiful and impressive, and its proximity to the
ruins of El Tajín makes a stopover in Papantla almost a requirement.

TRANSPORTATION

Papantla lies 250km northwest of Veracruz and 21km southeast of Poza Rica on Mex. 180. To get from the **ADO bus station**, Juárez 207 (☎842 0218), to the *centro*, turn left on Juárez and veer left at the fork; the walk is steep but short. ADO buses go to: **Mexico City** (5hr., 7 per day, 198 pesos); **Poza Rica** (45min., 20 per day, 16 pesos); **Tuxpan** (1½hr., 4 per day, 50 pesos); **Veracruz** (4hr., 13 per day, 150 pesos); **Xalapa** (4hr., 10 per day, 162 pesos). A **taxi** along Juárez from the ADO station to the *centro* is about 16 pesos. If you're arriving at the second-class bus station, **Transportes Papantla** (☎842 0015) 20 de Noviembre 200, turn left outside the station and ascend 20 de Noviembre three blocks to the northwest corner of the plaza.

ORIENTATION AND PRACTICAL INFORMATION

The central plaza, **Parque Téllez,** is bordered to the south by a whitewashed **cathedral** on Nuñez y Domínguez, and to the north by **Enríquez. Zamora** lies to the east, and **Reforma** to the west.

Tourist Office: (☎842 3837), near the northwestern corner of the plaza at the intersection of Azueta and Artes. Enter at the TelCel store on Azueta and walk to the 2nd fl. A helpful staff doles out information packets and recommendations. Open M-F 9am-3pm and 5-8pm. During festivals and weekends in summer, Totonac "Ambassadors" roam the plaza offering practical information and cultural context.

Bank: Santander Serfín (☎842 4300), along the northern side of the plaza. **Currency exchange** and **24hr. ATM.** Open M-F 8am-4pm, Sa 10am-2pm.

Emergency: ☎060.

Police: (☎842 0075), in the Palacio Municipal.

Red Cross: (☎842 0126), on Escobedo off Juárez.

Pharmacy: El Fénix, Enríquez 103E (☎842 0636), on the northern side of the plaza. Open M-Sa 8am-11pm, Su 8am-10pm.

Medical Services: IMSS (☎842 0194), on 20 de Noviembre at Lázaro Cárdenas. **Clínica del Centro Médico** (☎842 0082), on 16 de Septiembre.

Laundromat: Lavandería Chagcanan, on the corner of Juárez and Madero, down the hill from the plaza. 10 pesos per kilo. Open M-Sa 8am-8pm.

Fax Office: Telecomm, on Olivo, off 20 de Noviembre near Hotel Totanacapán. Open M-F 8am-7pm, Sa 9am-5pm, Su 9am-noon.

Telephones: LADATELs are along Enríquez in the main plaza.

Internet Access: Terry-Net (☎842 2707), at 16 de Septiembre 123, behind the cathedral. 8 pesos per hr. Open daily 10am-10pm.

Post Office: 5 de Mayo 625. **MexPost** inside. Walk west on 16 de Septiembre (the street behind the cathedral), then take a left on 5 de Mayo. The post office is on your left. Open M-F 9am-4pm. **Postal Code:** 93400.

ACCOMMODATIONS

Hotel Totonacapán, 20 de Noviembre at Olivo (☎842 1220). 4 blocks downhill from the plaza. Hallway murals lead to spacious rooms with large windows, free bottled water, A/C, and TV. 24hr. bell. Singles 350 pesos; doubles 400 pesos. Cash only. ❺

Hotel Familiar Arenas, 307 Enriquez (☎842 0283). About 5 blocks from the plaza. Few niceties, but large, airy, teal-colored rooms are pay-by-the-bed, meaning that if two people bunk

THE BIG SPLURGE

A SWEET DEAL

Vainilla has flavored sweets and treats all over the world for millennia. Cultivated by indigenous farmers on Mexico's rainy coast, the plant itself is an orchid—a vine-like species that bears greenish-yellow flowers and thin bean pods. According to legend, the vine grew out of the blood of a pair of ill-fated lovers—hence the sweet aroma of the shriveled fruit. The spice's heady flavor and rich scent so captivated the Spaniards that they believed it was an aphrodisiac, and consumed it only in moderation. Mexico remained the sole cultivator of vanilla until the late 18th century, when plantations in Asia and Madagascar began out-producing small-scale, Mexican farms.

Papantla remains the epicenter of Mexican vanilla production, and a visit to the plantations surrounding the city makes for an exquisite outing. Vanilla is an extremely labor-intensive crop: it must be hand-pollinated, hand-picked, and hand-cured. The gorgeous ◪ **Casa Larios,** one of Papantla's largest plantations, offers tours of the manufacturing process—from seed to bottle—and free samples of fresh vanilla.

Casa Larios will arrange pickup from Papantla. ☎842 0160; luzo68@yahoo.com. Spanish- and occasional English-language tours 100-200 pesos per person, depending on the size of the group and type of refreshments provided.

up, it's the same price as one. 24hr. bell. 100 pesos per bed with shared bath; 150 with private bath. Cash only. ❶

Hotel Kátlen, Juárez 311 (☎842 3990). Located immediately after the fork as you come from the bus station. Somewhat plain rooms on a noisy street, but perks like free bottled water and a lovely lobby equipped with computers with cheap Internet access (5 pesos per hr.) make this a great stop for budget travelers. 24hr. bell. Singles 150 pesos; doubles 200. Cash only. ❷

Hotel Pulido, Enríquez 205 (☎842 0036). 2 blocks off the main plaza facing the cathedral. Set back off the street around a tiled courtyard, with lots of space and powerful fans. 24hr. bell. Singles and doubles 180 pesos, with A/C 350 pesos. Cash only. ❷

Hotel Tajín, Núñez y Domínguez 104 (☎842 0121; www.hoteltajin.com). Half a block left of the plaza as you face the cathedral. A step up in class, Tajín has a miniature replica of one of its namesake's pyramids in the lobby. The rooms feature shared balconies with panoramic views, A/C, phones, cable TV, and bottled water. Reception 24hr. Singles 350 pesos; doubles 400 pesos, each additional person 100 pesos. MC/V. ❺

Hotel Mexico, Núñez y Domínguez 110 (☎842 0086). If you can get past the hole-in-the-wall lobby, the rooms are quite decent and the price is nice. 24hr. bell. Singles and doubles with private bath 150 pesos. Cash only. ❷

◖ FOOD

Papantla's best and most popular restaurants are around the *zócalo*. These touristed spots serve regional goodies, usually beef and pork. Specialties include *molotes*, Mexican dumplings of spiced meat wrapped in a boiled corn shell, and *bocoles*, stout fried tortillas filled with egg, cheese, sausage, or chicken. Countertop restaurants inside **Mercado Juárez** and **Mercado Hidalgo** have cheap tacos, *comida corrida*, and the like. For groceries, **Super Alan** is on the corner of 5 de Mayo and Serdan. From the plaza, walk down Azueta and take a left on 5 de Mayo. (☎842 6201. Open M-Sa 8am-10pm, Su 9am-8pm. MC/V.)

La Hacienda, Reforma 100 (☎842 0633), on the western end of the central square. Treats diners to excellent service, a terrace-top view of the plaza, and delicious food. *Bocoles* 25 pesos. Entrees 20-45 pesos. Open daily 7:30am-11pm. Cash only. ❸

Taquería el Vaquero, just steps away from the plaza on 20 de Noviembre. This tiny stand has only one thing on the menu: tacos (2.50 pesos) with your choice of meat filling and the spiciest salsa in town. Open daily 8am-6pm. Cash only. ❶

Restaurante Por Si Acaso Me Recuerdas, Juan Enríquez 102 (☎842 1112), to the left of the main plaza when facing the cathedral. Enjoy the quiet of this small local hideaway. The food comes fast, hot, and cheap. 4 *bocoles* 15 pesos. Chicken *mole* with rice 32 pesos. Open daily 7am-2am. Cash only. ❷

Restaurante Sorrento, Enríquez 105 (☎842 0067). Caters to locals with a full bar, a view of the plaza, and many regional specialties, such as *molotes de picadillo*. Entrees 15-80 pesos. Open daily 7am-midnight. Cash only. ❸

🔵 SIGHTS

Papantla's biggest attractions are relics of its Totonac heritage. Even the Catholic **Catedral Señora de la Asunción,** overlooking the *parque*, has a remarkable 50m long, 5m high stone relief, called *Homenaje a la Cultura Totonaca*, on its outer wall. The relief—based on a relief from El Tajín—depicts Totonac ballplayers jumping amid spiraling, naturalistic patterns. On Sunday afternoons in the cathedral's spacious courtyard, **Plaza de los Voladores,** *voladores* (fliers; p.333) acrobatically entreat the rain god Tlaloc to water local crops. The show can be seen from the *parque* below, but if you watch from the cathedral, the dancers pass around a basket after the performance; a peso or two is expected as a donation. High above the center of town, **Monumento al Volador** is a gigantic statue of a flute-wielding *indígena* erected atop a hill in 1988 and visible from all around. To reach the monument, which offers a sweeping view of Papantla and of the local make-out spot below, take a steep walk up Reforma (5-10min.), the road that passes the entrance to the cathedral. **Museo de la Ciudad,** at Pino Suárez and Madero, displays artifacts from ancient Totonac history. The museum displays an impressive photographic timeline of the city's history, as well as traditional costumes and exhibits on local, modern indigenous culture. There is also a small store with an interesting selection of literature on indigenous culture, all in Spanish. (☎842 0221. Open Tu-Su 10am-2pm and 4-8pm. 10 pesos.)

📋 🎋 SHOPPING AND FESTIVALS

Activities besides Totonac-related sightseeing are few and far between. The town's two **markets** are situated next to the *zócalo*. **Mercado Juárez,** at Reforma and 16 de Septiembre, in the pink building off the southwest corner of the *zócalo*, specializes in fruits, vegetables, and freshly butchered meat. **Mercado Hidalgo,** on 20 de Noviembre off the northwest corner, is packed with *artesanías*, clothing, meat, and souvenirs. This is the best place to buy Papantla's world-renowned **vanilla**—a few stands sell high-quality extract (from 6 pesos) and wonderfully sweet liqueur (from 70 pesos per bottle). Others sell figurines made with vanilla sticks. If you're counting pesos, shopkeepers are usually happy to give out small free samples.

In early June the town celebrates the 10-day **Corpus Christi festival,** a merging of Papantla's indigenous and Catholic religious traditions. Most of the action occurs at a fair just outside town, with artistic expositions, fireworks, concerts, cockfights, and even a running of the bulls. To get to the *feria* (festival) from the *centro*, take a taxi (16 pesos) or *pesero* (4.50 pesos) from 16 de Septiembre behind the cathedral. In town, *voladores* perform throughout the day, and the plazas fill with traditional dancers and musicians. Once every 52 years—the traditional Totonac epoch—the festival takes on larger proportions.

🔺 DAYTRIP FROM PAPANTLA

EL TAJÍN

El Tajín is accessible from Papantla via peseros that stop on the corner of Francisco I Madero and 20 de Noviembre, on the other side of the road from the centro. *(30min., every 10min. 5:30am-9pm, 8 pesos.) Hop on a "Poza Rica" bus (it may say*

"Chote" or "Tajín"), but first check with the driver to make sure it stops at El Tajín. The bus goes through El Chote and stops at the rotary at the entrance to El Tajín. To return, catch a "Papantla" bus (7 pesos, last bus 10pm) from the rotary. Ruins open daily 9am-5pm. 45 pesos, under 13, over 60, and students with Mexican or ISIC identification free; Su free.)

The ruins at El Tajín give a grand impression of the thriving Totonac civilization that spread across modern-day northern Veracruz. The name Totonac is a Spanish derivative of the Náhuatl *Tutu Nacu*, which means "three hearts" and refers to the three major city centers of Totonac culture, one of which was El Tajín. In Totonac, "Tajín" means "thunder," "lightning," or "hurricane"; it is believed that the Totonacs dedicated this city to the god of rain. The area was probably settled around AD 100 by Huastec peoples before the Totonacs razed their structures and developed the area early in the Classic Period (AD 300-400). Located between two rivers, El Tajín exploited its position as a link between the Gulf Coast and Central Mexico. The city reached its hey-day in the mid-Classic Period (AD 600-900), when it grew from a minor rural center with primarily religious significance to the economic and religious capital of the Totonac empire, second in prominence only to Teotihuacán in the Valley of Mexico. The area's importance declined in the post-Classic Period, around AD 1200; it is unclear whether the inhabitants died or fled. Most archaeologists believe the city was conquered and burned by invading nomadic tribes, such as the Chichimeca (p. 250). The Totonacs who remained in the area were brought under the control of the Aztecs in the late 15th century. Though the ruins were "discovered" by the Spanish in 1785, restoration did not begin until 1939. El Tajín now sits as a maze of stone-carved temples and pyramids, perfect for a day's exploration.

MUSEUM AND ENTRANCE AREA. In front of the entrance stands the *voladores'* large pole. *(Performances daily every hr., requested donation 20 pesos.)* Books *(50 pesos)* on El Tajín are sold at the store adjacent to the **information desk.** A restaurant at the entrance, **Cafetería "El Tajín" ❸,** serves seafood and *comida corrida. (Entrees 20-52 pesos. Open daily 10am-5:30pm.)* Before you reach the museum, a sea of *comedors* and stalls selling souvenirs, jewelry, and embroidered clothing hawk their wares. Entering the ruins, you pass **Museo de Sitio,** a museum featuring original mural fragments, sculptures, models of the site, and a morbidly fascinating display of ancient skeletons. The relics are labeled in English and Spanish. From the museum, a straight path leads to the ruins, dotted occasionally with information placards, in Spanish, English, and Náhuatl. The best sources of information are the Spanish *miniguías* (guidebooks; 8 pesos) or a guided tour. *(Tour groups limited to 5 persons. English 200 pesos, Spanish 150 pesos.)*

PLAZA DE ARROYO. The plaza, a central rectangle formed by four tiered pyramids, lies just to the left of the gravel road. Each pyramid points toward the northeast at a 20° angle, a common feature among the site's early buildings.

JUEGO DE PELOTA SUR (SOUTH BALL COURT). Past the pyramids, two low-lying, slanted constructions to the left of the main path frame a central grass ball court, where the Totonac's famous one-on-one ball game was played as part of a rain ceremony. Every 52 years, the most valiant ballplayers held a contest that ended with the ritual decapitation of one or more of the winners. Seventeen such courts grace the ruins of Tajín; this one is famous for its carved stone walls depicting the ball games, and the fact that it has a space for spectators.

THE CENTRAL ZONE. Across from the plaza stands a central altar surrounded by two temples. Left of the altar is a split-level temple with a statue of Tajín. This area is the Central Zone, notable for the diverse styles and functions of its buildings.

LA PIRÁMIDE DE LOS NICHOS. To the northwest stands the Pyramid of Niches, El Tajín's most recognizable structure, with seven levels and a total of 365 niches corresponding to the days of the year. Each niche was once painted crimson and blue. The Totonacs kept time in 52-year epochs, during which a single flame was kept continuously burning. At the end of each epoch, the carefully nurtured flame was used to ritually torch many of the settlement's buildings; each new epoch of rebuilding and regeneration was inaugurated by the lighting of a new flame. Ritual ceremonies are now held annually at the pyramid. During the vernal equinox, farmers place seeds in the pyramid's niches and later retrieve them for planting. Like many of the site's most elaborate buildings, the pyramid was built during the decline of El Tajín, in the late-classic period, in what many archeologists view as a desperate attempt by the ruling elite to maintain their diminishing prestige.

TAJÍN CHICO. Atop a hill to the north, a series of large stepping stones and a staircase lead to Tajín Chico. While Tajín was a public religious and social center, Tajín Chico contained the living quarters of the ruling class and wealthy elite. This area also underwent bursts of great construction in the late-Classic period, a reflection of the isolation of the elite and their anxiety about their waning influence.

XALAPA (JALAPA) ☎ 228

The first thing you notice upon entering Xalapa (pop. 390,000) is the weather—the cool, temperate climate of Veracruz's capital city provides a welcome oasis in the muggy state. A self-proclaimed cultural center, Xalapa boasts an upstanding university, an excellent orchestra, and one of the top archaeological museums in the Americas. Conquered by the Aztecs in 1460, this Totonac city was part of the empire until Cortés claimed the land for Spain. Xalapa is the birthplace of the *xalapeño* (jalapeño) pepper, and the city's fertile soil nourishes Mexico's rich, mellow coffee. Visitors today will find artistic performances, vibrant nightlife, and a number of beautiful parks. Though the *centro* bursts with commerce and boisterous students, Xalapa can be what you make of it: a whirlwind tour of art, archaeology, and culture, or just a place to take in the glorious breeze and relax.

TRANSPORTATION

The **train station** is at the northeastern edge of the city, a 40min. walk or 22-peso taxi ride from the *centro*. There are two **bus stations,** so make sure to specify which one if taking a taxi. **CAXA,** 20 de Noviembre 571, east of the *centro*, services distant cities and has long-distance phones, telegraph and luggage service, restaurants, and shopping. You can catch buses to neighboring towns at **Terminal Excelsior,** west of the *centro* on Allende. From the bus stations to the *centro*, catch a bus marked "Centro" or "Terminal" (4.50 pesos); taxis cost 23 pesos.

From CAXA, **ADO** (☎842 2500) sends first-class **buses** to: **Catemaco** (5hr., 7 per day, 176 pesos); **Mexico City** (5hr., 20 per day, 206 pesos); **Papantla** (4hr., 10 per day, 162 pesos); **Puebla** (3hr., 11 per day, 120 pesos); **San Andrés Tuxtla** (3hr., 9 per day, 164 pesos); **Santiago Tuxtla** (3hr., 5 per day, 156 pesos); **Tuxtepec** (5hr.; 6am, 3:20pm; 174 pesos); and **Veracruz** (every 20-30min. 5am-11pm, 74 pesos). **Autobuses Unidos** (AU; ☎842 2500) runs first class to **Puebla** (3hr., 12 per day, 98 pesos), **Mexico City** (5hr., 16 per day, 170 pesos), and other regional destinations.

ORIENTATION AND PRACTICAL INFORMATION

Located in the center of the state, Xalapa is 106km northwest of Veracruz on **Mex. 140** and 315km east of Mexico City. Downtown centers around the **cathedral** and the **Palacio de Gobierno,** separated by **Enríquez.** Streets that branch from Enríquez toward **Parque Juárez** and the Palacio de Gobierno run downhill, while those on the cathedral side travel uphill to the markets.

Tourist Office: Edificio Nachita Desp. 214 (☎842 1214; www.turistenadoxalapa.com), on Enríquez. 1st entrance to the Palacio Municipal after the cathedral, 2nd fl., to your right at the end of the hallway. Helpful, English-speaking staff. Open M-F 9am-3pm and 5:30-8:30pm. Also a small **kiosk** in front of Palacio del Gobierno with info on whitewater rafting and other ecotourism opportunities. Open M-F 10am-8pm.

Currency Exchange: Banks with **24hr. ATMs** line Enríquez and the surrounding streets. Most will exchange currency and traveler's checks.

Luggage Storage: At the bus stations. Supervised. 5 pesos per hr., 30 pesos per day. Open 24hr.

Bookstores: Several at Xalapeños Ilustres and Mata, past the Centro Recreativo, and the surrounding streets.

Laundromat: Ciclos Lavandería, Landero y Coss 16 (☎818 6254). Laundry 10 pesos per kg. Open M-F 9am-7pm, Sa 9am-4pm.

Emergency: ☎066.

Police: (☎818 7199; tourist security unit ☎800 903 9200), on Alcalde y García at Cuartel San José, north of Iglesia San José.

Red Cross: Clavijero 13 (☎817 3431), 1 block from Parque Juárez.

24hr. Pharmacy: Farmacia Rex Centro, Enríquez 41 (☎817 2220).

Hospital: Civil, (☎818 4400), on the corner of Guido and Bravo.

Fax Office: Telecomm, Zamora 70 (☎816 2167), just before the Palacio Federal. Open M-F 8am-7:30pm, Sa 9am-5pm, Su 9am-noon.

Internet Access: Internet @lex, Callejón del Diamante 17. 8 pesos per hr. Open daily 9am-11pm.

Post Office: (☎817 2021), at Zamora and Diego Leño in the Palacio Federal. **Mexpost** inside. Open M-F 8am-4pm, Sa 9am-noon. **Postal Code:** 91001.

🏠 ACCOMMODATIONS

Without the need to splurge on A/C, it's possible to find comfortable, convenient, and cheap lodging on **Revolución,** especially past Mercado Jaureguí, which is close to the *centro*, market, and parks.

Hostal de la Niebla, Zamora 24 (☎817 2174; www.delaniebla.com.) Located right in the *centro*, sparkling 6-bed dorms, lovely terrace, and common areas suit students seeking cheap rooms and a true hostel experience. Breakfast included. 15min. of free Internet. Reception 24hr. Single-sex dorms 145 pesos, with ISIC 130, with HI 110. Singles 200 pesos; doubles 300 pesos. Cash only. ❷

Hotel Dulcelandia, Revolución 61 (☎817 3917). Purple and pink, with clean (if a bit cramped) rooms surrounding a 3-story courtyard. Rooms have TV and private bath. 24hr. bell. Singles 100 pesos; doubles 150; triples 175. Cash only. ❶

Hotel Limón, Revolución 8 (☎817 2204; fax 817 9316), just past the cathedral. Brightly colored tiles lend a cheerful glow. Clean rooms with TV. Free bottled water. 24hr. bell. Singles 140 pesos; doubles 185 pesos; triples 200 pesos. Cash only. ❷

Hotel California, Gonzáles Ortega 1, on the north side of a small park, where Juárez intersects with Carrillo Puerto. Not exactly lovely, but it compensates with simple rooms for low prices. 24hr. bell. Singles 60 pesos, with private toilet 85 pesos, with full bath 100 pesos; doubles 100/110/170 pesos; triples 120/225 pesos. Cash only. ❶

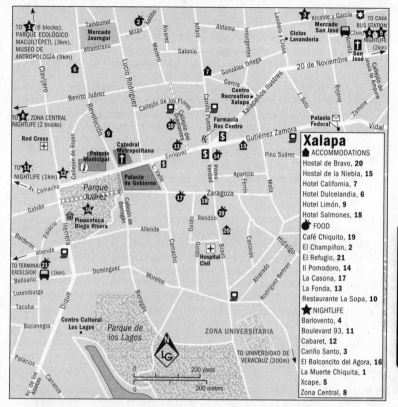

Xalapa

▲ ACCOMMODATIONS
Hostal de Bravo, **20**
Hostal de la Niebla, **15**
Hotel California, **7**
Hotel Dulcelandia, **6**
Hotel Limón, **9**
Hotel Salmones, **18**

🍴 FOOD
Café Chiquito, **19**
El Champiñon, **2**
El Refugio, **21**
Il Pomodoro, **14**
La Casona, **17**
La Fonda, **13**
Restaurante La Sopa, **10**

★ NIGHTLIFE
Barlovento, **4**
Boulevard 93, **11**
Cabaret, **12**
Cariño Santo, **3**
El Balconcito del Agora, **16**
La Muerte Chiquita, **1**
Xcape, **5**
Zona Central, **8**

Hostal de Bravo, Bravo 11 (☎818 9038), below Zaragoza. Tidy rooms in a sunny court-yard with large windows, fans, and TV. Free bottled water. 24hr. bell. Singles 280 pesos; doubles 310 pesos; each additional person 30 pesos. Cash only. ❸

Hotel Salmones, Zaragoza 24 (☎817 5431). For a few extra pesos, enjoy large rooms with fan, phone, and TV; some with balcony. Reasonably priced adjoining restaurant and bar. Singles 350 pesos; doubles 400 pesos; triples 420 pesos. AmEx/MC/V. ❺

🍴 FOOD

Xalapeño food is cheap and plentiful. Coffee—especially *lechero*, or *café con leche*—is the city's official drink; cafes line the streets in the *centro*, and even vendors make a delicious brew. Visitors should also be sure to sample the regional delicacies: pickled chiles, jalapeño peppers, *picaditas* (flat corn cakes with mashed beans and cheese), and *garnachas* (bean-filled, fried corn cakes). Don't miss the *pambaza*, served on round bread and stuffed with beans, tomato, lettuce, and other goodies. Tortillas are handmade in almost every restaurant. For fresh groceries and cheap *taquerías*, head to the open-air **Mercado Jaureguí**, two blocks behind the cathedral, which sells meat, fresh produce, and other goods (open M-Sa 7am-9pm, Su 7am-5pm), or **Mercado San José**, northwest of La Iglesia de San José, which sells bushels of fruits and vegetables (open daily 7am-8pm).

La Fonda, Callejón del Diamante 1 (☎818 7282). Quite simply the best food around. Eat upstairs for better ambience. Delicious *pambazas* 18 pesos. Steak prepared *al gusto* 55 pesos. Open M-Sa 8am-6pm. Cash only. ❸

El Refugio, Palacio 27. Inventive food and drinks in a lounge atmosphere, with low tables and floor cushions. Be sure to try the extraordinary, homemade herb-and-chili sauces and dips. Some of the many vegetarian options include the Technicolor salad, with mint, oranges, lettuce, and cheese (35 pesos). Pasta 35 pesos. Unbelievable sangria 17 pesos. Beer 12 pesos. Open Tu-Sa 6pm-1am, Su 6-11pm. ❷

Cafe Chiquito, Bravo 3 (☎812 1122), 2 blocks south of Enríquez. Sit inside amid local paintings or in the back garden with a gurgling fountain. Enjoy yogurt, honey and granola for breakfast (24-28 pesos). Lunch buffet 35 pesos. Chicken and steak entrees 30-50 pesos. Open daily 8am-11pm. Live music M-Sa after 9pm. AmEx/D/MC/V. ❸

El Champiñon, 20 Xallitic (☎818 3291). Past Mercado Jaureguí down the stairs from Revolución. A *comedor*-style restaurant serving classic Mexican, minus the meat. Very little soy on the menu, just lots of veggies. Fresh *tamales* 15 pesos. *Comida del día* (fruit, soup, entree, juice, and dessert) 35 pesos. Open daily 10am-7pm. Cash only. ❷

Il Pomodoro, Primo 11 (☎841 2000). Excellent pizzas (40-100 pesos), pastas (36-40), and tiramisu (21 pesos) amid giant wooden wine racks and Roman murals. Open M-Th 9am-midnight, F-Sa 9am-1am, Su 9am-10:30pm. Cash only. ❹

La Casona, Zaragoza 20 (☎818 2119). Relaxed, comfortable atmosphere and walls filled with photos of old Xalapa. Courtyard tables, a fountain, and attentive waiters add class. Quality menu packed with standard Mexican fare alongside more creative dishes. Entrees 35-115 pesos. Th-Sa 9pm-midnight live *folklórico* music. Open daily 8am-midnight. AmEx/MC/V. ❺

Restaurante La Sopa, Callejón de Diamantes 3A (☎817 8069). Lunch changes daily and includes drink, soup, entree, and dessert (35 pesos). More extensive dinner menu available. Entrees 10-50 pesos. Open M-Sa 1-5:30pm and 7:30-11:30pm. ❷

👁 SIGHTS

MUSEO DE ANTROPOLOGÍA (MAX). The finest in the country after Mexico City's Museo Nacional de Antropología (p. 118), Xalapa's museum focuses on the state of Veracruz. The museum is organized chronologically, showcasing the area's pre-Hispanic civilizations as each came to power. Highlights include huge Olmec heads, each weighing more than two metric tons, murals from the Higuera civilization, codices documenting the arrival of the Spaniards, and countless artifacts, fossils, and skeletal remains. *(Catch a 5-peso yellow "Tesorería" bus on Enríquez; or take a 20-peso taxi. Otherwise, take the 45min. walk, starting on Enríquez/Camacho away from the cathedral; make a left on Av. Xalapa, and continue for several blocks until you see the museum on your left. ☎815 0920. Open Tu-Su 9am-5pm. 45 pesos, students with ID 25 pesos, under 12 free. Video camera use 100 pesos. English, French, and Spanish audiotours 20 pesos.)*

PARQUE ECOLÓGICO MACUILTÉPETL. Xalapa's biggest and most beautiful park, where, with a little trekking, you can enjoy the native flora and fauna. A brick path meanders past lip-locked lovers to the summit of an extinct volcano 186m above Xalapa, where a spiral tower looks out over the city and mountains. If you don't feel like walking the 4km path to the top, you can cheat and take the stairs. *(Take a 5-peso "Mercado-Corona" colectivo from Revolución and Altamirano, or hail a 20-peso taxi. Open daily 7am-6pm.)*

UNIVERSITY DE VERACRUZ. The large manmade "lakes" of **Paseo de los Lagos** lap against the university's hillsides below Enríquez. Not exactly architectural masterpieces, UV's institutional box-style buildings are painted in pleasing shades of blue and green. Still, pine trees and a lakeside path make it worth a visit. Pop into one of the art galleries for information on workshops and exhibitions.

PARQUE JUÁREZ. This park serves as Xalapa's surrogate *zócalo*. Relax, catch the breeze, and take in the superb vista of the surrounding buildings and vegetation. Two staircases in the park's platform lead to **Agora de la Ciudad.** The center harbors a small cafe, several galleries, and a theater screening alternative films on weekends, with occasional film festivals. *(Open M 9am-6pm, Tu-Su 8am-10pm.)*

PINACOTECA DIEGO RIVERA. This small museum is Xalapa's artistic gem, housing many of Rivera's more experimental canvases, ranging from Impressionism, collage, Cubism, and travel sketches to a charming dose of horse-human bestiality. The museum also features rotating exhibits by contemporary Mexican artists. *(Herrera 5, just below Parque Juárez. ☎818 1819. Open Tu-Su 10am-8pm. Free.)*

CALLEJONES. Xalapa takes pride in its old cobblestone alleys, many of which are associated with gory legends. **Callejón del Diamante,** off Enríquez, honors a diamond that detected infidelity. Legend has it that a Spaniard gave the diamond to his Mexican wife, who then played hanky-panky with a local while he was away. The darkened diamond alerted the Spaniard who, enraged, slaughtered his wife. Cafes and vendors now line the *callejón.***Callejón de la Calavera,** in the southwest corner of the city, is named for a woman who decapitated her cheating, drunkard husband. The lovers of **Callejón de Jesús te Ampare** were killed by a widower who went mad with jealousy upon seeing the happy couple. *"Jesús te ampare"* ("Jesus protect you") was the last thing the girl managed to say to her lover.

🎵 🍸 ENTERTAINMENT AND NIGHTLIFE

For information on cultural events, visitors should check listings in the local newspapers or head to the **Centro Recreativo Xalapa,** on Dique near Bocanegra. In addition to offering brief classes and lectures on almost anything you would want to know about the city and local culture, the Centro posts information on upcoming concerts and ballets. (☎817 3110. Open daily 10am-8pm.) **Agora de la Ciudad** (☎818 5730), in Parque Juárez, offers similar services, keeping Xalapa's students up-to-date. Events include weekly performances by the **Orquesta Sinfónica de Xalapa,** university expositions, recitals, and art exhibits. Staff at both the Centro and Agora can tell you where to find what you're looking for.

During the **Festival de Junio Musical** in June, the symphony hosts concerts, and performers stage theater productions and recitals throughout the city. Xalapa also celebrates the **Feria Internacional de Xalapa,** which features a variety of cultural, artisan, and sporting events during the month of April.

Nightlife in Xalapa centers around the cultural (theatre, classical music, *ballet folklórico*) and the bawdy (drinking, dancing, and what follows). After attending a high-class performance, lounge in one of the city's cafes—most of which are full until about 11:30pm—before dancing the night away at one of the clubs on **Camacho** or **20 de Noviembre.** Bars and cafes in Xalapa are very student-oriented, and patrons enjoy live music nearly every night. Late-night jaunts, especially when returning from near the bus station, will probably require a taxi (20 pesos).

BARS AND CLUBS

La Muerte Chiquita, Azueta 125 (www.muertechiquita.com.mx.) Despite the lengthy walk from the *centro*, students, artists, and musicians flock to this grotto-like bar, decorated with graffiti of everything from elephants to Andy Warhol prints. Live music almost every night, from jazz to classic rock to hip hop. Beer 18 pesos. Mixed drinks 30-40 pesos. Open Tu-Su 7pm-3am. Cash only.

Zona Centro, Benito Juárez 123 (☎841 1961; zonacentro13@yahoo.com.) A relaxed bar with electronic music, pop art on the walls, and fantastically delicious fruit cocktails—try the Guanabana (25 pesos). Sit upstairs if you want to eat—the tables get better service than the low cushions downstairs. Falafel 25 pesos. Beer 17 pesos. Mixed drinks 20-30 pesos. Open M-Sa 6pm-3am. Cash only.

Cariño Santo, Aldama 75 (☎817 3288). Lounge on plush couches or sit under the stars in the romantic courtyard at this opulent tapas bar. Mellow alternative rock adds some edge to the scene. Mojitos and other mixed drinks 35 pesos. Beer 20 pesos. Tapas 20-40 pesos. Open M-Sa 7pm-last customer. MC/V.

Barlovento, 20 de Noviembre 641 (☎817 8334), next to XCAPE (see below; p. 558). Shake it to salsa and Caribbean music on a large dance floor under mobile lights. Professional male salsa dancers roam the floor; women receive 2 tickets at the entrance to exchange for a spin around the dance floor and pointers from the pros. Beer 22 pesos. Mixed drinks 30-40 pesos. Cover 30 pesos; more during special events. Open Th-Sa 10pm-3am. Cash only.

Boulevard 93, Camacho 87 (☎817 6820). This bright bar/club fills up early with well-dressed students. At midnight the lights go down and the music switches to remixes of Spanish and American hits. Look out for flyers with drink specials. W free martinis for women. Beer 20 pesos. Mixed drinks 30-50 pesos. W-Sa 9:30pm-4am. MC/V.

XCAPE, 20 de Noviembre 635 (☎812 5075), 4 blocks down 20 de Noviembre to the right of the bus station. Dance the night away under a disco ball to hip hop, rock, and techno. Su nights are especially popular. Th nights live *norteño* band. Beer 23 pesos. Mixed drinks 32-40 pesos. Cover 40 pesos. Open Th-Su 10pm-4am. Cash only.

Cabaret, Clavijero 4 (cabaretxalapa@gmail.com). Cabaret is the place to be for Xalapa's gay and lesbian community. Slightly below street level, this bar features electropop music under a dark, red glow. Not much room to dance, but plenty of standing room. Beer 25 pesos. Mixed drinks 30-40 pesos. No cover. Open W-Sa 9pm-4am.

El Balconcito del Agora, Bajos del Parque Juárez s/n, 2nd fl., inside Parque Juárez. Outdoor tables on the balmy balcony offer a magnificent view of the city, and the location can't be beat. Loud music and soccer games blast inside. Beer 20 pesos. Mixed drinks 50 pesos. Open Tu-Su 6pm-2am. Cash only.

⬛ DAYTRIP FROM XALAPA

⬛ **XICO'S CASCADA DE TEXOLO.** In the town of Xico, 19km outside of Xalapa, mules and horses share the road with automobiles. Besides pastoral bliss, Xico has one huge selling point—the dramatic waterfall of **Texolo,** just 3km from town. If it looks like it's out of a movie, that's because it is. Several US movies were filmed here, including *Romancing the Stone* (1984) and *Clear and Present Danger* (1994). Somewhat less glamorous car and deodorant commercials have also been shot at the falls. In any case, Hollywood has left no trace of its presence, and few tourists frequent the site. The rocks are often slippery and deserted, so exercise extreme caution and wear appropriate footwear. The walk to the falls is long and lonely: try not to go by yourself and don't hike to the falls at night. The insects are silent but ferocious—bring bug repellent. *(To get to Xico from Xalapa, walk west on Allende until you reach Galeana and a large park. You will see a roundabout: this is Terminal Excelsior. From there, take any "Xico" bus; 30min., 11 pesos. You will drive through a few towns on the way. When you see signs saying "Xico" and "Entrada de la Ciudad," alert the driver and exit the bus, which will drop you on Calle Hidalgo. From there, turn left and walk a block uphill to Calle Zaragoza. Turn left onto Zaragoza, which eventually becomes the path to the falls. The road forks at 2 points along the way; take the right fork both times.)*

VERACRUZ ☎229

The oldest port city in the Americas, Veracruz (pop. 412,000) is an assault on the senses. Intense humidity and often unbearable heat envelop the city, while the powerful odor of saltwater and fish pervades the air. A curse by day, the city's tropical climate makes for gorgeous nighttime strolls along the beach and through the *zócalo*. Small *marimba* bands and lone guitarists provide a constant soundtrack for the bars and restaurants, while nighttime vendors holler sales pitches over the music. The city has a storied military past; it survived occupations by Spain, France, and the US. Though the fortresses have long since been knocked down, Veracruz is immensely proud of *veracruzano* culture, a rich synthesis of traditions as a result of its seafaring history.

▐ TRANSPORTATION

Flights: Aeropuerto General Heriberto Jara (VER; ☎934 7000), 8km south of downtown Veracruz on Mex. 150. Taxis to the airport cost 120 pesos. Served by **Aeroméxico** (☎938 3711) and **Mexicana** (☎938 9192).

Buses: Central de Autobuses Veracruz (CAVE), Mirón 1698. To get to the *centro,* take a "Díaz Mirón" bus north to Parque Zamora (5 pesos). Some buses run to the *zócalo;* others stop at the park. To return to the station, take a southbound "Díaz Mirón" bus from anywhere along 5 de Mayo. **ADO** (☎937 5788) goes to: **Cancún** (21hr.; 4:45, 8:45pm; 789 pesos); **Catemaco** (3hr., 10 per day, 99 pesos); **Córdoba** (1½hr., 29 per day, 86 pesos); **Fortín de las Flores** (2hr.; 1, 6pm; 89 pesos); **Mexico City** (5½hr., 18 per day, 280 pesos); **Oaxaca** (6½hr., 3 per day, 279 pesos); **Orizaba** (2½hr., 29 per day, 92 pesos); **Tuxtepec** (3hr., 6 per day, 100 pesos); **Puebla** (4½hr., 8 per day, 202 pesos); **Xalapa** (1¾hr., every 20-30min. 6am-11:30pm, 70 pesos). **AU** (☎937 5732), 1 block behind the ADO station, has cheaper 2nd-class service to similar destinations.

Bike Rental: On Camacho at Bolívar, along Villa del Mar beach. 25-30 pesos per hr.

✸ ▐ ORIENTATION AND PRACTICAL INFORMATION

Veracruz sprawls along the coast in the southwestern corner of the Gulf of Mexico, 104km south of Xalapa and 424km east of Mexico City. Along the southern coast, Veracruz merges with the suburb **Boca del Río.** Home to luxury hotels, shopping malls, and sparkling shorelines, it is easily reached by the "Boca del Río" buses which leave from **Zaragoza,** one block toward the bay from the *zócalo* (5 pesos). Buses are less frequent at night; taxis are a safer choice.

Tourist Office: (☎989 8817), inside the Palacio Municipal, facing the *zócalo*. Tons of brochures and friendly staff. Open daily 10am-6pm.

Currency Exchange and Banks: Banks and **casas de cambio** pack the corner of Juárez and Independencia, 1 block north of the *zócalo*. **Banamex** (open M-F 9am-4pm) and **HSBC** (open M-F 8am-7pm, Sa 8am-3pm) have **24hr. ATMs.**

American Express: Serdán 704 (☎931 0838). English-language travel advice and services. Open M-F 9am-7:30pm, Sa 9am-1:30pm.

Luggage Storage: In the 2nd-class bus station. 19 pesos per day. Open 24hr.

Laundromat: Lavandería Mar del Sol, 610 Madero (☎101 7088). 22 pesos per load; 3kg max. Open M-Sa 8am-9pm.

Emergency: ☎066.

Police: (☎938 0664), at Colonial Palieno.

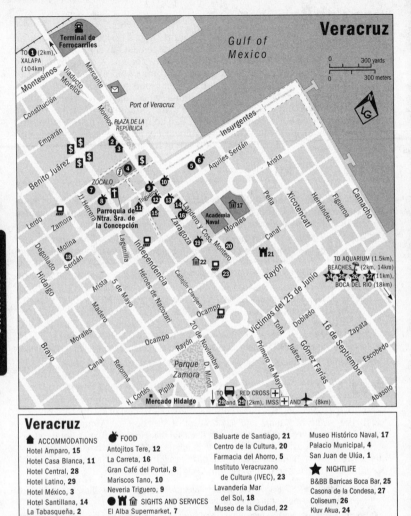

Veracruz

♠ ACCOMMODATIONS
Hotel Amparo, **15**
Hotel Casa Blanca, **11**
Hotel Central, **28**
Hotel Latino, **29**
Hotel México, **3**
Hotel Santillana, **14**
La Tabasqueña, **2**

🍎 FOOD
Antojitos Tere, **12**
La Carreta, **16**
Gran Café del Portal, **8**
Mariscos Tano, **10**
Neveria Triguero, **9**

● 🏠 🏛 SIGHTS AND SERVICES
El Alba Supermarket, **7**

Baluarte de Santiago, **21**
Centro de la Cultura, **20**
Farmacia del Ahorro, **5**
Instituto Veracruzano
  de Cultura (IVEC), **23**
Lavandería Mar
  del Sol, **18**
Museo de la Ciudad, **22**

Museo Histórico Naval, **17**
Palacio Municipal, **4**
San Juan de Ulúa, **1**

★ NIGHTLIFE
B&BB Barricas Boca Bar, **25**
Casona de la Condesa, **27**
Coliseum, **26**
Kluv Akua, **24**

Red Cross: (☎937 5411), 1698 Díaz Mirón, between Orizaba and Abascal, 1 block south of the Central de Autobuses. Ambulance service.

24hr. Pharmacy: Farmacia del Ahorro, Gómez Farías 2 (☎937 3525).

Medical Services: Hospital Español, 16 de Septiembre 955 (☎932 0559).

Fax Office: Telecomm (☎932 2508), on Plaza de la República next to the post office. Open M-F 8am-7pm, Sa 9am-5pm, Su 9am-noon.

Internet Access: Cibernet Reds (☎939 6999) on the corner of Lerdo and Zamora. 10 pesos per hr. Open M-Sa 10am-11pm. **Internet Satelital,** 719 Arista. 12 pesos per hr. Open daily 10am-10pm.

Post Office: Marina Mercante 210 (☎932 2038), at Plaza de la República. **Mexpost** inside. Open M-F 8am-4pm, Sa 9am-1pm. **Postal Code:** 91700.

ACCOMMODATIONS

Accommodations in Veracruz fall into two categories: expensive, luxurious beachside hotels and cheaper, less glamorous abodes closer to the *centro*. Veracruz has three high seasons: *Carnaval* (the week before Lent), *Semana Santa*, and midsummer. Many of the hotels fill up well in advance during these times; be prepared to pay extra, too. The added necessity of A/C in this steamy city ups the price even more. Most rooms near the bus stations offer A/C for a good price.

Hotel Amparo, Serdán 482 (☎932 2738). If there are backpackers in Veracruz, they're probably here. Very comfortable, neat rooms with fans and hot water. Reception 24hr. Singles 150 pesos, with cable TV 180 pesos; doubles 180/220 pesos. Cash only. ❷

Hotel Casa Blanca, Callejón Trigueros 49 (☎200 3974 or 3975). A slightly higher price tag represents a major step up in class and service. Newly renovated rooms have TV, fan, and large bathrooms. Room service available from the Spanish restaurant downstairs (open daily 8am-10pm). Singles 200 pesos; doubles 200-300 pesos; each additional person 50 pesos. ❸

Hotel Santillana, Landero y Coss 209 (☎932 3116). A few steps away from the waterfront, Santillana offers reasonably sized rooms with fan and TV. The purple-and-green courtyard, interesting wallpaper schemes, and caged parrots emanate garish charm. 24hr. bell. Singles 200 pesos; doubles 300 pesos. Cash only. ❸

Casa de Huéspedes La Tabasqueña, Morelos 325, just around the corner from the *zócalo*. Dark but comfortable rooms with fan and TV. 24hr. bell. Singles 150 pesos; doubles 250 pesos. Cash only. ❷

Hotel Mexico, Morelos 343 (☎931 5744). Don't be put off by the garage-like lobby: big rooms with charming wood paneling, fan, and TV await. 24hr. bell. Singles 200 pesos; doubles 250 pesos; each additional person 50 pesos. Cash only. ❸

Hotel Latino, La Fragua 1180 (☎937 6599), 1½ blocks from the ADO station. The best bet for a stay near the station, with soft beds, bright colors, and large bathrooms. Singles 200 pesos, with A/C 250 pesos; doubles 300/380 pesos. Cash only. ❸

Hotel Central, Díaz Mirón 1612 (☎937 2350), to the right of the ADO station. Modern-looking hotel with a faux-marble lobby. Big rooms with bath, phone, and TV. Inquire about budget singles (150 pesos) on the roof, which, despite the unusual setting, aren't much worse than the standard rooms. Singles 250 pesos, with A/C 300 pesos; doubles 300/380 pesos. Cash only. ❷

FOOD

Small restaurants surround the fish markets on **Landero y Coss.** Eccentrically decorated, these are the places to dig into the mountains of crab, fish, shrimp, and octopus hauled out of the gulf on a daily basis. For a cheaper, slightly more frantic experience, try **Mercado Hidalgo,** on Cortés at Madero, one block from Parque Zamora, where seafood stands sell fish and shrimp entrees for around 15-30 pesos. (Open daily 8am-8pm.) Pricier restaurants under the *portales* in the *zócalo* offer yummy dishes and a *marimba* beat. Wherever you choose to dine, don't miss out on distinctive *veracruzano* fare—just steer clear of raw fish. Regional specialties include *huachinango* (red snapper), *filete relleno* (fish fillet stuffed with *mariscos*), *arroz a la tumbada* (rice in a sauce that includes—of course—shellfish), and *jaiva* (large local crab). Seafood is becoming increasingly expensive, so if you find yourself blanching at the prices, look beyond the *mariscos*—even the restaurants in the *zócalo* have decently priced *antojitos* and meat dishes. For groceries, head to **El Alba,** on Lerdo 270, between Independencia and 5 de Mayo. (☎932 2424. Open M-Sa 9am-9pm.)

Gran Cafe de la Parroquia, Gómez Farías 34 (☎932 2584), on the *malecón*. A Veracruz tradition—the enormous space seems filled with the entire town drinking tall glasses of the famous coffee (*lechero*; 15 pesos). Entrees 100 pesos. Sandwiches 20-45 pesos. Open daily 6am-1am. D/MC/V. ❹

El Cochinito de Oro, Zaragoza 190 (☎932 3677), at Serdán. Relatively cheap, quality seafood and friendly service explain El Cochinito's 50-year popularity with locals. Mixed drinks 30 pesos. Breakfast 30 pesos. Entrees 70-75 pesos. Ever-changing *menú del día* 50 pesos. Open daily 7am-7pm. Cash only. ❸

Gran Cafe del Portal, Independencia 1187 (☎931 2759), at the southwest corner of the *zócalo*. Sit on the patio at another of Veracruz's favorite hangouts, with delicious food and elegant waiters. *Antojitos* 29-75 pesos. Entrees 85-132 pesos. Open daily 7am-midnight. Cash only. ❺

El Torbellino, Zaragoza 384 (☎932 1357), near the naval museum. Locals crowd around plastic tables drinking beer (15 pesos) and consuming mountains of *mariscos*. Apart from a small selection of meat dishes, everything on the menu, from salads to entrees, is seafood. Mixed drinks 15 pesos. Entrees 60-70 pesos. Open daily 11am-7pm. Cash only. ❸

Antojitos Tere, Zaragoza 155. Cheap tasty *antojitos* are few and far between in the *centro*. Satisfy late night cravings at this bright *comedor,* just a block from the *zócalo*. *Empanadas* stuffed with everything from meat to squash blossoms 15 pesos. *Comida corrida* 35 pesos. Tu-Su 10am-midnight. Cash only. ❷

Nevería Triguero, Plaza Trigueros 1, just off Zaragoza, 1 block from the *zócalo*. While it claims to be an ice cream shop, Triguero also serves hearty breakfasts (20-30 pesos) and *antojitos* (20-40 pesos). Don't miss the "Mondongo," a humongous pile of fresh, exotic fruit topped with the ice cream or yogurt of your choice (45 pesos). Open daily 8am-1am. Cash only. ❷

La Carreta, Arista 574, near the naval museum. Not much for ambience, but this simple cafeteria serves cheap, filling Mexican dishes quickly. *Menú del día* 25 pesos. Breakfasts 22-28 pesos, including coffee and juice. Entrees 22-28 pesos including drink. Open daily 7am-7pm. Cash only. ❶

Mariscos Tano, Molina 20 (☎931 5050), 1 block south of the *zócalo*. Veracruz's seafaring pride is on full display here, with a model ship at the counter and stuffed sea creatures filling the rafters. The owner proudly displays pictures of his reign as king of *Carnaval. Mariscos* and popular regional entrees 30-100 pesos. English menu available. Open daily 9am-10pm. Cash only. ❺

La Gaviota, Callejón de Trigueros 21 (☎932 3950), half a block from Zaragoza and Serdán. Simple ambience and regional specialties at more affordable prices than *antojitos* 15-45 pesos. *Filete a la veracruzano* 70 pesos. Open 24hr. Cash only. ❸

◉ SIGHTS

Veracruz's importance to Mexico was clear to past foreign invaders, who often targeted the port as their first point of attack. This history has left its mark on the sights, imbuing remnants of the military past with deep, nationalist meaning. Students from the Naval Academy amble about the streets even today, testimony to Veracruz's perpetual military readiness.

▧ **MUSEO HISTÓRICO NAVAL.** The museum, located on the grounds of Veracruz's Naval School, is a sailor's air-conditioned dream, highlighting Mexico's rich maritime history from pre-Hispanic to modern times. All the history is in Spanish, but gallery after gallery of model ships, entertaining dioramas of battles and forts, and dozens of antique and modern weapons will pique even a casual interest in military history. *(The Naval Museum occupies the entire block bordered by 16 de Septiembre, Arista, Montero, and Morales; the entrance is on Artista. ☎ 931 4078. Open Tu-Su 9am-5pm. Free.)*

CASTILLO DE SAN JUAN DE ULÚA. The fortress, Veracruz's most important historic site, rests on a fingertip of land jutting into the harbor. Using coral chunks as bricks, construction began sometime after Cortés's arrival by order of Charles V. It was intended as part of the system of fortifications built to protect Spanish treasure from Caribbean pirates. After 1825, it became a high-security jail for the likes of presidents Benito Juárez and Porfirio Díaz, as well as folk hero **Chucho el Roto,** San Juan's best-known prisoner, who supposedly escaped three times. *(Take a 4.50-peso "San Juan de Ulúa" bus in front of the Aduana building in Plaza de la República. ☎ 938 5151. Open Tu-Su 9am-5:30pm. 20 pesos. Guided tours in Spanish 10 pesos.)*

BALUARTE DE SANTIAGO. Built in 1635, the Baluarte is the last remnant of the stone wall that once encircled a good part of the city, protecting the inhabitants from pirates. The wall, along with the eight other *baluartes* (small forts), was torn down in the late 19th century. The museum inside displays a collection of pre-Hispanic gold ornaments called *Las Joyas del Pescador,* named for their rescue from the ocean by a lucky octopus fisherman. Around the back of the fort, a spiral staircase leads up to a pleasant view. *(On Canal, between 16 de Septiembre and Farías, 1 block from the Naval School. ☎ 931 1059. Open Tu-Su 10am-4:30pm. 37 pesos. Under 13 free.)*

MUSEO DE LA CIUDAD. The lower level of this museum features paintings and dioramas that depict the history of the city from pre-Hispanic times to the present. Indigenous artifacts, colonial accounts, and fantastic photos of musicians, clubs, and the beaches of Veracruz's past will bring you up to speed on everything you ever wanted to know about the city. Check for special exhibits on art and history upstairs. *(Zaragoza 397. Head down Canal away from the water, turn right on Zaragoza. ☎ 932 6385. Open M-Sa 10am-6pm, Su 10am-3pm. Downstairs free; special exhibits upstairs 25 pesos, students 15 pesos.)*

ACUARIO DE VERACRUZ. A popular family beachside attraction, the aquarium features fish, sharks, and turtles native to the gulf. *(In the Centro Comercial Plaza Acuario, on the left facing the ocean. Catch a 5-peso "Villa del Mar" bus on Zaragoza. ☎ 931 1020. Open M-Th 10am-7pm, F-Su 10am-7:30pm. 60 pesos, children 30 pesos.)*

🌊 BEACHES

The general rule for beaches in Veracruz is that the farther from the city, the nicer the beach. Still, it's practically impossible to escape the distant oil barges and tugboats. **Playa Villa del Mar** is a pleasant hour-long walk from the *zócalo* along the waterfront. It is also accessible via one of the frequent "Villa del Mar" or "Boca del Río" buses (4.50 pesos) that stop on Zaragoza and along Camacho. Few people swim at Villa del Mar; dirty, thatch-roofed restaurants have set up camp along the boardwalk, making frolicking in the sand almost impossible. Still, the restaurant huts and bars create a lively atmosphere at night.

For a more deserted beach, head over to **Playa Mocambo,** in the neighboring city of **Boca del Río.** Take a "Boca del Río" bus (30min, 5 pesos) and get off at the mall, Plaza de las Américas. The beach is on the other side of the Holiday Inn. Those who define their beach experiences by attitude rather than turquoise water will enjoy laid-back lounging in the residential area further down the coast.

PARA BAILAR LA BAMBA

The iconic Mexican song "La Bamba" is perhaps Veracruz's most famous export. The rhythms of *veracruzano* musical tradition are a fusion of Afro-Caribbean and Latin beats. After the conquest of Mexico, the Spaniards brought slaves from West Africa to the Mexican coast. Over time the blend of indigenous, Spanish, and African cultures created Veracruz's unique *jarocho* music—airy, danceable string and percussion rhythms embodying the relaxed *veracruzano* lifestyle.

Many musicologists believe that "La Bamba" gets its name from Mbamba, the ancestral home of many African slaves who settled in Veracruz. Versions of "La Bamba" existed as early as the late 1600s, and it has evolved ever since. Since the song's first recording in 1908, the tune has spread to dance halls across the country and is often featured in Mexican films.

The song's popularity peaked in 1946, when conservative Miguel Aleman (a Veracruz native) used it as his campaign song in his successful run for presidency. "La Bamba" became an international sensation after it was covered by Richie Valens, an American rock-and-roll artist, and in the 1970s, even the US Chicano movement tweaked the original lyrics to reflect their cause. Today, you cannot pass an evening in Veracruz's *zócalo* without hearing a few catchy bars.

ENTERTAINMENT AND NIGHTLIFE

In the evening, the hymns of the cathedral spilling out into the *zócalo* yield to the rhythms of salsa, *jorocho*, and *marimba*. Vendors spread their wares on the paths, and bars and restaurants fill with drinkers and dancers. *Veracruzanos* love to dance, and do so beautifully. Salsa rules the bars at night, as well as *la bamba* and *danzón*, a distinctly Veracruz style similar to salsa. On weekend nights, free live music in the *zócalo* woos dancers of all ages.

For some culture in the *centro*, the **Instituto Veracruzano de la Cultura (IVEC)** on the corner of Canal and Zaragoza, and **Centro Cultural Altarazanas,** next to the Naval Museum on Montero, hand out brochures and schedules, keeping tourists and college students posted on the latest concerts, art exhibitions, and performances in the city. Both centers also feature dance lessons every week in *danzón* and salsa—ask inside for times and prices. (IVEC ☎931 4396. Open Tu-Su 9am-9pm. Centro ☎922 8921. Open M-F 9am-7pm, Sa-Su 10am-6pm.) Every December 31, from midnight until dawn, *veracruzano* families dress in their Sunday best and fill Camacho, looking east to the Gulf of Mexico to witness the first sunrise of the year. With that auspicious start, a year of celebrations begins. Veracruz's most famous activity comes early, in the days before Ash Wednesday, when Carnaval invades the *zócalo* with nine days of festivities. The Festival Internacional Afrocaribeño spans ten wild days in mid-July.

Apart from merrymaking in the *zócalo*, most action takes place along **Camacho,** the seaside road connecting Veracruz and Boca del Río, and **Ruiz Cortines,** which runs more or less parallel to Camacho. Just before the purple high-rise Hotel Lois, where Ruiz Cortines branches off Camacho, is a good place to get off the "Boca del Río" bus. The club scene shifts rapidly, and the titanic discos along Camacho and Cortines change hands constantly. Nevertheless, the nightlife is fairly concentrated and it's easy to see where people are headed.

Casona de la Condesa, Camacho 2015 (☎933 5451; www.casonadelacondesa.com), plays live music: *norteño*, pop, rock, and salsa. Beer 25 pesos. Mixed drinks 50 pesos. Cover F-Sa 50 pesos, Sa women free. Open Tu-Su 10pm-5am. MC/V.

B&BB Barricas Boca Bar, Camacho 4 (☎121 4266), next to the Hotel St. Louis, has a massive stage featuring live music from Mexican rock to salsa. While the lack of space between tables isn't conducive to dancing, that doesn't stop the crowd. Beer 18 pesos. Mixed drinks 30 pesos. Cover varies 20-70 pesos. Open W-Sa 10pm-4:30am. MC/V.

Klub Akua, Camacho 621 (☎130 2421). If it's a crowded dance floor, wild lights, and excess-inducing drink specials you crave, Klub Akua—often called Klub—delivers. Beer 25 pesos. Mixed drinks 30-50 pesos. Cover 30 pesos. W-Sa 10pm-4am. Cash only.

Coliseum, Cortines 1006. On nights with live acts, this club fills its arched facade to the ramparts with a hip crowd dancing to electronica or rock. Call ahead to find out who's playing; when it's just a DJ, the club can be dead. Cover for live acts only 20-70 pesos. Open Th-Sa 10pm-4am. Cash only.

◢ DAYTRIPS FROM VERACRUZ

THE RUINS AT ZEMPOALA

From the 2nd-class bus station on La Fragua behind the ADO station, Autobuses TRV sends buses to Cardel (55min., every 10 min., 23 pesos). Exit the right side of the station onto Azueta, and walk 2 blocks to the right; the Zempoala bus pickup is on the cross street at the T-intersection. From there, take a bus to Zempoala (15min., 9 pesos). Ask the driver to let you out at the ruins, at the intersection of Ruiz and Troncoso Nte. Veracruz buses return from Cardel (every 10min. 5am-11:30pm). Site open daily 9am-6pm. 34 pesos. Students with ID, children under 13, seniors over 60 free.

The impressive ruins at **Zempoala (Cempoala)** lie 40km north of Veracruz off Mex. 180. Zempoala was one of the largest southern Totonac cities and part of a federation that covered much of Veracruz. During its peak in the 14th and 15th centuries, the city may have had as many as 120,000 inhabitants, and many believe it was the Totonac post-Classic successor to El Tajín (p. 551). In 1458, however, the Aztecs conquered Zempoala and forced the Totonac to join the Aztec Empire. When Cortés arrived in 1519, the humbled city had only about 30,000 residents and was eager to assist an enemy of the Aztecs, lending Cortés soldiers and supplies.

To the left as you enter, a small **museum** holds examples of pottery, stone statues, and artifacts from the ball game, as well as a model of the site and explanations (in Spanish) of the various buildings' functions. The site itself consists of stone structures surrounding a grassy field next to present-day Zempoala. The palm trees and peaceful setting of the ruins seem incongruous with their bloody history. The structure closest to the entrance is the **Temple of Death.** To the left of the main path are three **pyramids.** The pyramid on the left is dedicated to Tlaloc (the rain god), the one on the right to the moon, and the one in the center to the sun, decorated with circular stone receptacles for the hearts of people sacrificed in religious offerings. To the right of the main path is the **Templo Mayor,** the largest building on the site. When Cortés arrived, the Spaniards erected an altar to the Virgin on top of the temple, imposing Catholicism on the Totonacs. In front of the Templo Mayor is the **throne** where the king observed sacrifices. The throne faces the temple known as **Las Chimeneas.** This area played a central role in the Totonac "New Five Ceremony," a five-day fast that took place every 52 years, when a cycle of the ritual calendar ended. Every spring equinox, people still come to the circle to expel negative energy.

LA ANTIGUA

Take a 2nd-class TRV bus from the Central, behind the ADO station (40min., 15 pesos). Tell the driver you want to get off at La Antigua—on the way to Cardel and Zempoala—and watch for the stop, marked by the tollbooth and a "La Antigua" sign pointing left. Cross the street and follow the main road for 15min. until the main drag. To return, go back down the road; buses to Veracruz from Cardel pass every 10min. 5:15am-11:45pm.

When Cortés landed on the coast of Mexico in 1519, he and his army moved north, settling here and founding the first Spanish town in Mexico. Cortés named the town Villa Rica de la Vera Cruz, but when the city was reestablished in 1599 in its present location 28km away, the old town came to be known as just that—La Antigua. The modern-day reality is an interesting juxtaposition of 16th- and 21st-century architecture.

Many unlabeled streets and the jungle's tendency to interrupt all things orderly make finding the town's older buildings a bit of a scavenger hunt. On the left coming into town you'll see the **Parroquia de Cristo del Buen Viaje,** an orange-and-blue cathedral dating to the mid-17th century; the interior contains two 16th-century baptismal fonts carved by early indigenous converts. After the cathedral, take a left onto Cortínez and you'll find the **Edificio del Cabildo** on the right. Built in 1523, this was the first Spanish government office in Mexico. Continuing along Cortínez past the *zócalo*, take a left onto Independencia after one block to find the famous **Casa de Cortés,** another administrative building where the conquistador supposedly lived for a time. Farther down the street, the tree that divides the road holds legendary status as the site where Cortés first armed himself for the fateful 1519 expedition. Four long blocks back on Independencia towards the *zócalo* is the most beautiful of the buildings: the **Emerito del Rosario.** Finished in 1524, it features the stations of the cross rendered in *talavera* tile.

CÓRDOBA ☎ 271

Friendly Córdoba (pop. 134,000) greets visitors with a lively green *zócalo* surrounded by colonial architecture: a busy modern city still very much connected to its history. The Spanish founded Córdoba in 1618, intending for it to serve as a defensive post against anticipated slave rebellions at nearby sugarcane plantations. Later, the city would establish itself as a place of freedom and compromise—the Treaty of Córdoba (p. 56) was signed here on August 21, 1821, bringing Mexico independence from Spain.

▐ TRANSPORTATION. All buses arrive at Cordinados Córdoba (☎ 727 0468), 3km from the *zócalo* along Av. 4. To get to the *zócalo*, also called the Plaza de Armas, from the bus station, exit to the right and take a "Centro" bus (4.50 pesos). **ADO** sends first-class buses to: **Mexico City** (5hr., 21 per day, 224 pesos); **Oaxaca** (6hr., 4 per day, 258 pesos); **Orizaba** (40min., 18 per day, 16 pesos); **Puebla** (3hr., 14 per day, 136 pesos); **Tulum** (6hr., 5:40pm, 846 pesos); **Tuxtepec** (3hr., 3 per day, 94 pesos); **Tuxtla Gutiérrez** (8hr., 3 per day, 476 pesos); **Veracruz** (1½hr., 24 per day, 82 pesos); **Villahermosa** (5½hr., 11 per day, 358 pesos); **Xalapa** (3hr., 17 per day, 120 pesos). Other lines offer second-class service to some destinations. Hop on a northwest-bound bus on Av. 11 to reach Orizaba (13 pesos) or **Fortín de las Flores** (7 pesos) from Córdoba.

▐ PRACTICAL INFORMATION. The **tourist office** is under the *portales*, to the right of the Palacio Municipal, on the northwestern side of the *zócalo* at Av. 1 and Calle 1. (☎ 717 1700, ext. 1778. Open M-F 8:30am-8pm.) You can **exchange currency** at **Casa de Cambio Puebla,** 117 Calle 2, between Av. 1 and 3. **Scotiabank,** on the *zócalo* at Av. 1 and Calle 3, has a **24hr. ATM.** (Open M-F 9am-5pm, Sa 10am-3pm.) Other services include: **Emergency:** ☎ 060; **police:** (☎ 712 6720) in the Palacio Municipal; **Red Cross,** Calle 11 between Av. 7 and 9 (☎ 712 0300); **Farmacias de Dios,** Av. 1 510 (☎ 712 2873); **Hospital Covadonga,** Av. 7 1610 (☎ 714 5520); **Luggage Storage,** at the bus station (4-11 pesos per hr.; open 24hr.); **Internet** access at **Liz Internet Cafe,** at Calle 3 and Av. 2 (10 pesos per hr.; open daily 9am-9pm); and the **post office,** Av. 3 303, 1 block southwest of the *zócalo* (☎ 712 0069; open M-F 8am-6pm, Sa 9am-1pm). **Postal Code:** 94500.

ⅢⒸ ACCOMMODATIONS AND FOOD. Córdoba's affordable establishments, concentrated on Av. 2 between Calles 9 and 11, make it ideal for a budget traveler. ⓈHotel Iberia ❷, Av. 2 919, is the best bargain. Luxurious rooms feature fans, dark wood furnishings, free bottled water, phone, TV, and extremely powerful showers. Free coffee and 15min. of free Internet are available in the lobby. (☎712 1301. Budget singles 150 pesos, with cable TV 165 pesos; budget doubles 150 pesos, with cable TV 180-265 pesos; triples 280-330 pesos; each additional person 50 pesos. Cash only.) **Hotel Tress Cado ❶**, on Av. 2 between Calles 9 and 1, is good for a cheap, no-frills stay. (☎712 2374. 24hr. bell. Singles 70 pesos, with TV 90 pesos; doubles 140/200 pesos. Cash only.) The location of **Hotel Los Reyes ❷**, Calle 3 No. 10, is unbeatable; with sunny, well-priced rooms. (☎712 2538. 24hr. bell. Singles and doubles with cable TV and fan 160 pesos; triples 220 pesos. Cash only.) Indulge yourself at **Hotel Virreynal ❺**, Av. 1 309, across from the church in the *zócalo*. The spacious rooms include A/C, phone, and TV, and the adjoining restaurant offers room service. (☎712 2377. Singles 330 pesos; doubles 360 pesos; each additional person 20 pesos. MC/V.)

El Patio de la Abuela ❷, on Calle 1 between Av. 2 and 4, has served up quality, affordable meals for two generations. The photos on the wall enhance the family feel. (☎712 0606. *Antojitos* 5-30 pesos. Traditional entrees 15-40 pesos. *Tortas* 12-30 pesos. Open daily 8am-midnight. MC/V.) **Taquitos La Fogata ❶**, Av. 2 between Calles 5 and 7, has tacos and quesadillas with dozens of fillings. (M and W 6pm-midnight 2-for-1 tacos. Tacos 5-10 pesos. Open daily 9am-midnight. Cash only.) Restaurants and cafes fill the porticos of the *zócalo* on Av. 1, but the most popular is **El Tabachin ❸**, Av. 1 101, which has classy steak entrees (80-90 pesos) and more affordable, generous portions of traditional Mexican fare, like *panuchos* and *enchiladas* for 30 pesos.) (☎712 1989. Open daily 8am-11pm. Cash only.) **Las Delicias ❷**, on Av. 3 between Calles 7 and 9, offers *antojitos* (15-25 pesos), meat entrees (40-45 pesos), and *comida corrida* (27 pesos) in an open-air environment. (☎712 3185. Second location on Av. 2 and Calle 3. Open daily 7:30am-9:30pm. Cash only.) **Restaurante Virreynal ❹**, adjacent to **Hotel Virreyal** (p. 567), serves quality *antojitos* (17-41 pesos), fish, and meat. (☎712 2377. Entrees 15-75 pesos. Open daily 9am-10:30pm. MC/V.) The grocery store, **Mercado Revolución,** is bounded by Calles 7 and 9 and Av. 8 and 10. (Open daily 7am-9pm.)

ⒼⒿ SIGHTS AND ENTERTAINMENT. Dominating the *zócalo*'s southeastern side is the **Parroquia de la Inmaculada Concepción.** Constructed in 1621, the church combines both Baroque and Neoclassical styles. Now the city's primary place of worship, the *parroquia* is distinctive not only for its size and age, but also for its famous bells, which can be heard for miles. Under the *portales* on the *zócalo*'s northeastern side is **Casa Zevallos.** Formerly a hotel, Zevallos has a plaque outside commemorating the site where Juan O'Donojú (acting Spanish viceroy) and Agustín de Iturbide (conservative rebel leader) agreed on the terms of Mexico's independence on August 24, 1821. Across the *zócalo*, half a block away, is the **Museo de la Ciudad de Córdoba,** Calle 3 No. 303, home to murals, archaeological finds, and a small art gallery. (Open daily 9am-2pm and 4-8pm. Free.) At night, the *zócalo* comes alive with music, but nightlife is mostly limited to restaurant-bars around the *centro*. Fantastic balcony seating overlooking the *zócalo* and live music draw a hip young crowd to **La Divina Comedia,** Calle 3 No. 1, upstairs. (☎405 2106. Open daily from 5:30pm. Live rock or acoustic bands F-Sa. Beer 20 pesos. Mixed drinks 30 pesos. Cash only.) **Utopia,** on Av. 7 between Calles 4 and 6, has a blacklit bar and live *trova* bands. (Beer 15 pesos. Mixed drinks 20 pesos. Cover F 10 pesos. Open W-Sa 10:30pm-3am.)

Calm and tranquil, neighboring **Fortín de las Flores** comes alive during the last week of April through the first two weeks of May, when the **Expo Feria de la Flor Fortín** takes center stage. Florists, merchants, and horticulturists descend

GULF COAST AND CHIAPAS

upon the city to enjoy the best that the area has to offer. If you're itching to see plantlife the rest of the year, you can head 7.5km north to **Tropical World** (☎702 0024), in nearby Santa Elena, which specializes in orchids and tropical flowers from Hawaii to Brazil. To get there, take a bus from Cordinados Córdoba to Huatusco and get off in Monte Blanco.

ORIZABA
☎272

Near the base of Mexico's highest peak sits Orizaba (pop. 115,000). Formerly a center for sugarcane distillation, modern Orizaba has turned to production, churning out barrels of beer and cement. Dozens of parks and gorgeous churches, mountain views, and excellent climate make Orizaba a peaceful stopover between central Mexico and the warm, humid regions in the south of Veracruz.

▐ TRANSPORTATION. Orizaba's two main **bus** lines maintain separate stations. To get to the *zócalo* from the ADO station (☎724 2723), at Av. 6 Ote. 577, between Calles 11 and 13 Sur, exit left and walk to Calle 3 Sur; cross the road and continue 3 blocks to the *zócalo*. **ADO** has first-class service to: **Cancún** (19hr.; 2:05, 8:35pm; 932 pesos); **Córdoba** (40min., 30 per day, 16 pesos); **Mexico City** (4hr., 14 per day, 210 pesos); **Oaxaca** (6hr., 3 per day, 244 pesos); **Veracruz** (2hr., 24 per day, 96 pesos); **Villahermosa** (7hr., 11 per day, 392 pesos). To get to the *centro* from the second-class AU station, Calle 8 Pte. 425 (☎725 1979) between Calles 5 and 7 Nte., exit left and cross the bridge; take the first right toward the church towers.

▐ PRACTICAL INFORMATION. Orizaba lies 18km west of Córdoba and 25km northwest of Mexico's tallest mountain, **Pico de Orizaba.** Most points of interest are near **Parque Castillo,** bounded by Madero to the west, Colón to the south, Calle 3 Sur to the east, and Av. 3 Ote. to the north. **Av. 6 Ote.,** three blocks south of the *zócalo,* is the main thoroughfare. The **tourist office,** in the Palacio de Hierro at Madero and Av. 2, displays photos of Orizaba, hands out maps, and arranges adventure tours. (☎728 9136; www.orizaba.gob.mx. Open M-F 8am-3pm and 4-8pm, Sa-Su 10am-2pm and 4-8pm.) Several **banks** south of the *zócalo* **exchange currency** and have **24hr. ATMs,** including **Santander,** on Av. 2 Ote and Madero. (Open M-F 9am-4pm, Sa 10am-2pm.) Other services include: **luggage storage,** at the ADO station (4-11 pesos per hr.; open daily 10am-6pm); laundry at **Súper Lavandería Orizaba,** Calle 11 Sur and Av. 4 Ote. (12 pesos per kg; open M-Sa 9am-8pm); **emergency** ☎060; **police** (☎724 6400), at the corner of Circunvalación Nte. and Av. 5 Ote.; **Red Cross,** Colón Ote. 253 (☎725 4767), between Calles 4 and 6 Nte.; **24hr. Farmacia Guadalajara,** Colón 50, between Calles 2 and 3; **Hospital Civil,** at the exit to the highway to Puebla (☎725 2774); **LADATEL phones,** on the northwest side of the *zócalo,* past the *parroquia;* **Ritchi Internet Infinitum,** Av. 4 Pte. 61 (☎726 5322; 6 pesos per hr.; open daily 10am-9pm); and the **post office,** Av. 2 Ote. 282, at Calle 7 Sur (☎725 0330; **Mexpost** inside; open M-F 8am-6pm, Sa 9am-1pm). **Postal Code:** 94300.

▐▐ ACCOMMODATIONS AND FOOD. The rooms at **Hotel Arenas ❷,** Calle 2 Nte. 169, between Av. 3 and 5 Ote., are clean and come with fans, cable TV, and access to a jungle-like courtyard. (☎725 2361. 24hr. bell. Singles 120-130 pesos; doubles 170 pesos. Cash only.) **Hotel Plaza ❷,** Calle 4 Nte. 253, offers dark but very comfortable rooms with fans, bottled water and cable TV. Check-out (strictly enforced) is 24hr. after check-in—great if you're coming in late, not so great if you arrive in Orizaba at 8am. (☎724 8808. 24hr. bell. Singles 160 pesos, doubles 200. Cash only.) For a cushier stay, **Hotel Plaza Palacio ❹,** Poniente 2 No. 2, offers large, airy rooms (some overlooking the park and church), a spacious lobby, and reasonable restaurant. (☎725 9933. 24hr. bell. Singles 230; doubles 290; triples 350. Cash only.) The more luxurious **Grand Hotel de France ❺,** Av. 6 Ote. 186, has a giant courtyard and large, plush rooms with phone and cable TV. (☎725 2311. Singles 320 pesos; doubles 360 pesos. MC/V.)

Orizaba has fantastic street food; you'll find *tamales*, salads, and *gorditas* in every park, and concentrated around Av. 5, towards the market, **Mercado Melchor Ocampo,** bounded by Av. 5 and 7 Ote. **Candilejas Restaurant** ❹, Colón Ote. 35B, offers a menu of *antojitos* (10-40 pesos) and entrees (40-90 pesos) served on a patio overlooking Parque Castillo. (☎725 0863. Live music after 7pm. Open daily 8:30am-1am. Cash only.) **Tamales Gourmet** ❶, Calle 7 Sur 182, on the corner of Av. 4, boasts 15 varieties of *tamales*, over half of them vegetarian. (☎726 3119. *Tamales* 6-10 pesos. Open M-Sa 9am-1pm and 6-10:30pm. Cash only.) Visit **Antojitos Mexicanos McDaniel's** ❶, Calle 2 Nte. 174, for some quick 8-peso *tortas* or four *taquitos* for 18 pesos. (☎723 4724. Open daily 8am-11pm. Cash only.)

🄶 🎵 **SIGHTS AND ENTERTAINMENT.** The ◪**Museo de Arte del Estado,** on Av. 4 Ote. between Calles 23 and 25, is a bit of a trek, but you won't regret it. You can walk or take an eastbound bus from Av. 6 Ote. The museum hosts fabulous rotating exhibits featuring some of Mexico's best modern art, a collection of Diego Rivera works, and 19th-century etchings and paintings of Veracruz cities. (☎724 3200. Open Tu-Su 9am-6pm. 10 pesos, students and seniors 5 pesos; Su free.)

Part waterfall, part hiking trail, the **Parque Nacional 500 Escalones** awaits just outside the city limits, attracting *orizabeños* who want to jog or picnic. Most of the water in the **Cascada de la Trompa del Elefante** has been diverted for hydroelectric power, but the walk to the river is fun. Just make sure you're willing to pay the price of climbing back up the stairs. To get there, catch a red-and-yellow Estrella Roja bus (4 pesos) on the corner of Av. 3 Ote. and Calle 2 Nte. Descend at Calle Isabel la Católica and walk down as it curves left around a small blue church and over a bridge. Buses return to the *centro* on Calle Isabel, picking up from a block beyond the drop-off point.

At night, much of Orizaba gathers in **Parque Alameda,** where you can run, watch kids play on the giant trampolines, take in the breeze, and snack on fried plantains and *papas fritas.* To get there, simply follow Colón Pte. away from the *zócalo* and over the bridge. Nightlife in Orizaba is limited, but there are a few bars scattered throughout the *centro.* The outdoor patio at **Monte Casino,** Av. 4 on the corner of Calle 19 Sur, is a great place to have a few beers and watch soccer. From 6pm-9pm nightly, enjoy the 2-for-25 peso beer special. (Beer 18-20 pesos. Open daily 11am-midnight. Cash only.) For dancing, **Genesis Club,** Av 6 Ote. 796, plays pop and electronica. (Cover 30 pesos. Mixed drinks 30-40 pesos. Open Th-Sa 10pm-4am. Cash only.)

THE HIDDEN DEAL

PEAK CONQUEST

The highest mountain in Mexico, 18,696 ft. Pico de Orizaba looms tall over Orizaba. The massive peak is noteworthy for more than its natural beauty: just north of it winds the trail Hernan Cortés followed from Veracruz to Tenochtitlán to conquer the Aztecs. A formidable Aztec garrison guarded the traditional passage to Central Mexico—the stronghold of Aztec power—so Cortés opted for the more dangerous mountain route. Legend has it that Cortés's mistress, Doña Marina or La Malinche, knew the route was foolishly difficult, and on her return to the coast chose an alternate route descending through modern-day Orizaba.

You don't have to be intent on conquest and pillaging to scale the Sierra Madre Occidental's sky-high altitudes today. The Pico de Orizaba is a challenging hike, and best done with guides who customize the experience to your skill level. Less experienced trekkers can hike to a base camp about three-quarters of the way up, but mounting the actual summit requires rock and ice-climbing equipment, as well as professional training.

Several Orizaba-based outfitters offer trips, including the respected Rodolfo Hernandez, of Desafio Tours, located at Poniente 3, No. 536. ☎725 0696; informacion@desafio.cjb.net. Treks including equipment 400-3000 pesos.

LOS TUXTLAS

Nestled in the foothills of southern Veracruz, Los Tuxtlas are a relaxing trio. The three towns—San Andrés Tuxtla, Santiago Tuxtla, and Catemaco—have distinct personalities. With cheap, quality accommodations and transportation options, the relatively large town of **San Andrés Tuxtla** makes a good base for exploring the foothills. Only 30min. from the Olmec site of Tres Zapotes, the small **Santiago Tuxtla** is primarily an archaeological stop. More touristed **Catemaco** is known for its *brujería* (witchcraft) and beautiful lagoon.

SAN ANDRÉS TUXTLA   ☎294

Lodged between the lush lakeside resorts of Catemaco and the Olmec artifacts of Santiago, San Andrés (pop. 55,000) binds Los Tuxtlas together. The tobacco and cattle-raising town offers an entertaining *zócalo* and nearby natural attractions.

⧉ TRANSPORTATION. Both the first- and second-class **bus stations** are on **Juárez,** which branches off of **Mex. 180.** To get to the *centro* from either station, exit left and follow Juárez for 15min. down a steep hill, across a small stream, and up to the cathedral in the northern corner of the *zócalo.* You can also catch second class buses to **Catemaco** and **Santiago** just a block from the *zócalo,* in front of Felix supermarket on the corner or Ignacio de la Llave and Constitución. **Taxis** travel the same route (3min., 13 pesos). **ADO** (☎942 0871), at the first-class station, sends **buses** to: **Mexico City** (7½hr.; 10:05, 11:30pm; 296 pesos); **Puebla** (6hr.; 10:05, 11:30pm; 276 pesos); **Veracruz** (2½hr., 12 per day, 94 pesos); **Villahermosa** (5hr., 4 per day, 198 pesos). **AU** (☎942 0984) goes to **Xalapa** (4hr., 3 per day, 115 pesos). **Autotransportes los Tuxtlas** (☎942 1462), based in the second-class station, serves **Catemaco** (20min., every 10min. 4:30am-6pm, 6.50 pesos), **Santiago Tuxtla** (20min., every 10min. 4:30am-6pm, 6.50 pesos), and **Veracruz** (3½hr., every 10min. 4:30am-6pm, 71 pesos). *Colectivos* also drive to Catemaco and Santiago Tuxtla (13 pesos).

YOU'VE GOT A TICKET TO RIDE. When traveling by any bus, it's always a good idea to hang on to your ticket stub. This is especially important on rural second-class buses, which are subject to constant inspections. Keep that stub the driver handed you, or you may get charged twice!

⧉ PRACTICAL INFORMATION. San Andrés is located midway between Catemaco and Santiago. Before the cathedral, **Juárez** intersects **Constitución** to the left and **Madero** to the right, in front of the Palacio Municipal. Both **Banamex** and **Santander** have **24hr.** ATMs under the portico of the Palacio Municipal, on the *zócalo.* **Bancomer,** half a block south on Madero, **exchanges currency** and traveler's cheques. (Open M-F 8:30am-4pm). **Farmacia Garysa,** Madero 3, is open 24hr. (☎942 1506). **Hospital Civil** is located on Barerra at the edge of town. (☎942 0447.) Other services include: **police,** in the Palacio Municipal (☎942 0235); **Red Cross,** Boca Negra 25, north of the *zócalo* (☎942 4995); **Lavendería "Chapala,"** in the Plaza Comercial "Mi Favorita" (☎942 1043); **Internet** access at Bynn@r Internet, Constitución 6 (☎942 7494; 8 pesos per hr.; open M-Sa 10am-midnight, Su 2pm-midnight); and the **post office,** Fragua 23, at 20 de Noviembre 1 block from the *zócalo.* (**Mexpost** inside. Open M-F 8am-3pm). **Postal code:** 95701.

⧉⧉ ACCOMMODATIONS AND FOOD. San Andrés has great budget accommodations. Three of the best bargains are within a stone's throw of each other on Suárez. To get to them, walk left from the cathedral and turn right onto

Suárez, continuing uphill past the movie theater. **Hotel Colonial ❶**, Suárez 7, has small clean rooms, ceiling fans, and a grand, tiled lobby that radiates dilapidated chic. (☎942 0552. 24hr. bell. Singles 80 pesos; doubles 140 pesos. Cash only.) On the corner of Bocanegra and Suárez, one block down, **Hotel Catedral ❶** offers sizeable rooms with fans. (☎942 0237. 24hr. bell. Singles 90 pesos; doubles 120 pesos. Cash only.) Across the street from Hotel Colonial, **Hotel Figueroa ❷,** Suárez 10, has balconies draped in flowers and free bottled water, but the rooms aren't much fancier than its budget counterparts. (☎942 0257. 24hr. bell. Singles and doubles 150 pesos, with cable TV 180 pesos. Cash only.) Tuxtla nights can be sweltering, so if you want A/C your best bet is **Hotel Isabel ❹**, Madero 13 (☎942 5123), to the left of Hotel Parque. (☎942 5123. 24hr. bell. Singles 230 pesos, with A/C 300; doubles 310/380 pesos. Cash only.)

Sidewalk cafes on the *zócalo* serve breakfast and coffee, accompanied by a pleasant view of small-town life. From lunchtime until around 7pm, taco and *torta* stands line the park as well. Right on the *zócalo*, on the corner of Lerdo de Tejada and 20 de Noviembre, **Winni's Restaurant ❷** draws chatting locals to its outdoor tables (or air-conditioned dining room) with tasty *licuados*, sandwiches, and pastries. (☎942 0110. Tacos and *tortas* 20-30 pesos. Entrees 40-60 pesos. Open daily 7am-2am. Cash only.) On Madero, across from Hotel Isabel, **La Surianita ❷** prepares filling, traditional meals. (☎942 2389. *Antojitos* 10-30 pesos. Entrees 25-48 pesos. Open M-Sa 8am-10:30pm, Su 8am-2pm. Cash only.) For a classier meal, join the old men of the town drinking coffee and smoking cigars at the **Restaurante del Parque ❸**, on the ground floor of Hotel Parque in the *zócalo*. (☎942 0198. *Antojitos* 21-40 pesos. Entrees 50-90 pesos. Open daily 7:30am-11:30pm. MC/V.) The **Mercado 5 de Febrero** lies near the *zócalo*. To get there, walk on Madero, turn right on Carranza, and continue to the market. (Open daily 8am-8pm.)

◨ **SIGHTS.** Even non-smokers will be impressed by the **Fábrica Tabacos San Andrés,** the birthplace of Santa Clara cigars. The management welcomes visitors, and a staff member walks you through the entire process. The store at the entrance sells the final product. Bottom-of-the-line cigars are affordable (from 76 pesos), but a box of 25 of the finest *puros* goes for much more (up to 2000 pesos). Look out for the Magnum (109 pesos); measuring more than 45cm, it holds the Guinness record as the world's longest marketed cigar. Note that customs regulations may limit the number of cigars you can take back into your country. (☎947 9900. From the *zócalo*, walk up Juárez to the ADO terminal. Take a right and continue about 200m past the bus parking lot. Open M-F 8am-5pm.) To cool down in the steamy Las Tuxtlas weather, visit nearby **Cascada del Salto de Eyipantla** at 50m high, it's worth the 245 requisite steps and 6-peso fee. Take an "El Salto" microbus from the second-class bus station in San Andres. It makes dropoffs and pickups at the entrance to the falls. (30min., 5 pesos, last return bus 8pm).

◪ **DAYTRIP FROM SAN ANDRÉS TUXTLA**

SANTIAGO TUXTLA AND TRES ZAPOTES

To get to Santiago, take a bus (20min., 6 pesos) from in front of the Super Felix in San Andrés. To get to Tres Zapotes from Santiago, walk uphill on Morelos from the bus station and turn left onto Ayuntamiento to the zócalo. Turn left onto Zaragoza, and walk three blocks downhill to a T intersection. Turn right on Hidalgo and make a quick left over the footbridge, which will carry you to Morelos, from which a taxi colectivo will whisk you to Tres Zapotes (30min., 15 pesos). From the taxi stop in Tres Zapotes, take a left on Obregón and walk to the end of the street; the museum will be on the left. Buses marked "Tres Zapotes" also pass through this stop, which are cheaper (10 pesos) and slower (40min.)

Of Tuxtla's three cities, the smallest, Santiago (pop. 15,000), has the least to offer visitors. The most impressive sight is the massive **Olmec head** at the far end of the *zócalo*. The **Museo Tuxteco** on the *zócalo* on Ayuntamiento, holds another such head, along with other Olmec artifacts from Tres Zapotes and some colonial era suits of armor and tapestries. (Open M-Sa 9am-6pm, Su 9am-5pm. 34 pesos.)

Small-town charm aside, Santiago's main draw is the nearby archaeological site of **Tres Zapotes,** more remarkable for its age than its appearance. Tres Zapotes was a chief Olmec ceremonial center between 300 BC and AD 300, though evidence indicates the area may have been occupied as early as 1200 BC. The site remains largely un-excavated, but the small **museum** has a few well-preserved artifacts on display. The casual observer may be disappointed—Tres Zapotes is better suited to those with an academic interest. The centerpiece of the site is a large Olmec stone head. At a heavy 45 tons, it's the largest such head ever discovered. The first of the dozen or so Olmec heads excavated, it was discovered in 1862 by a *campesino* who at first thought it was an overturned cooking pot.

To the left of the head is **Estela C,** which, together with its more famous upper half, bears the oldest written date in the Americas—31 BC—inscribed in late Olmec, or Spi-Olmec, glyphs similar to those later used by the Maya. The date is depicted as a bar (representing the number 5) and two dots, totaling seven on the Olmec calendar. **Estela A** lies in the transept to the left. Decorations on the stela include an Olmec face, a man holding an axe, and a serpent coiling in upon itself. **Estela D,** to the right of the head, depicts four people whose relative heights symbolize their power and importance.

CATEMACO ☎294

The most touristed town in Las Tuxtlas, Catemaco (pop. 24,000), is surrounded by a gorgeous lagoon. The small town, famed for its *brujería*, has plenty of natural magic to offer as well. Head out on the lake next to local fishermen and seek out secluded swimming holes, hiking, fishing, posh spas, rare wildlife, and miles of Gulf Coast beaches. Fairly quiet in the low season, Catemaco picks up during *Semana Santa* and during the summer celebration of the town's patron saint, Santa Carmen.

▐ TRANSPORTATION. Catemaco lies on **Mex. 180.** From the Autotransportes los Tuxtlas second-class **bus stop,** turn right and follow the curved road past the "Bienvenidos a Catemaco" arches. Take a straight path for 10-15min. to the spires of the *basílica*. **Autotransportes los Tuxtlas** travels to **San Andrés** (20min., every 20min. 3am-8pm, 9 pesos) and other regional destinations. The ADO station is along the waterfront on the *malecón*. To get there from the church, walk to the *malecón* and take a left. The station is several blocks down the street. **ADO** (☎943 0842) heads to: **Mexico City** (9hr., 4 per day, 390 pesos); **Puebla** (6hr., 3 per day, 304 pesos); **Veracruz** (3hr., 7 per day, 100 pesos); **Xalapa** (3hr., 4 per day, 176 pesos). **AU** (☎943 0842) goes to **Mexico City** (9hr.; 11:30am, 9pm; 309 pesos).

▐ PRACTICAL INFORMATION. Streets are poorly marked, but the *basílica* in the *zócalo* is almost always visible. Standing with your back to the front door of the *basílica*, **Carranza** is the street to the right that runs past the Palacio Municipal. To the left is **Aldama,** and one block downhill from that is **Playa,** followed by the **malecón.** Perpendicular to these streets is **Boettinger,** across the *zócalo*. **Ocampo** is the street behind the church. The **tourist office,** in the Palacio Municipal on the *zócalo*, offers maps of *pirata* (public transportation pickups) routes, brochures, and helpful, though limited, advice. (☎943 0016. Open M-F 9am-3pm.) **Bancomer,** on Boettinger directly across from the *basílica*, has **24hr. ATMs.** Other services include: **police,** in the Palacio Municipal (☎943 0055); **Farmacia Unión,** on the corner of Madeo and Boettinger, (open daily 7am-11pm; AmEx/MC/V); **Centro de Salud,** on Carranza, in a white building with a blue roof, three blocks from the *zócalo* on the left (☎943 0247); **Internet,** Adama 25, behind the *basílica* (8 pesos per hr., open daily 8am-11pm); **Lavandería Sofi,** on Boettinger, four blocks from the *zócalo* (8 pesos per kg., open M-F 9am-8pm, Sa 9am-5pm); and the **post office,** on Cuauhtémoc, which branches off Carranza some blocks from the *zócalo*, away from the *basílica* (open M-F 9am-3pm). **Postal Code:** 95870.

▐▌ ACCOMMODATIONS AND FOOD. Most hotels lie around the *zócalo* and the waterfront. During *Semana Santa,* most of July, and Christmas, hotels fill up quickly. For A/C, soft beds, and TV, skip the waterfront and head to **Hotel del Centro ❷,** Zaragoza 33, a block from the *zócalo*. (☎943 0189. Singles 170 pesos; doubles 220 pesos. Cash only.) Right next door, **Hotel Loud-Pasc,** Zaragoza 52, has slightly more cramped rooms with TV, fan, and A/C for lower prices. (☎943 1381. Singles 150; doubles 200. Cash only.) If A/C isn't an issue try **Hotel Julita ❷,** Playa 10, a block downhill from the *zócalo*. It has an unbeatable location, downstairs restaurant and very large, clean rooms. (☎943 0008. Singles and doubles 150 pesos. Cash only.) The only place to camp in town is at **La Ceiba RV Park ❶,** on the *malecón,* which—despite the name—is more geared toward tent camping. (Showers and bathrooms. Tent sites and parking on the small waterfront lawn 50 pesos per person.) Infinitely nicer camping facilities can be found on the lake or at the beaches en route to Montepío. **La Jungla ❶** is a secluded retreat where—as the owners will proudly tell you—parts of Mel Gibson's film "Apocolypto" were shot. The facilities include camping, docks, kayaks and ecotours. (Accessible by *pirata* from Catemaco for about 15 pesos—ask the driver to let you off at the entrance, or at Nanciyaga, the resort next door. Campsites 50 pesos.)

Lake views differ more than menu choices in Catemaco's waterfront restaurants. Mojarra and *topote* fish are endemic to the lagoon, as are *tegogolos,* the famous Catemaco sea snails. Mojarra is prepared in a variety of ways, while bite-sized *topote* is fried whole and often heaped on *tamales.* Massive restaurant-bars line the *malecón,* often empty during the low season, but if you can fight the temptation to eat on the waterfront, the best food is at **La Casona ❸,** on the *zócalo* on Aldama. Your view will be of a peaceful wooden garden rather than the lake, but the seafood and steak entrees (30-90 pesos) are delicious. (☎943 2002. Open daily 7am-10pm. Cash only.) If it's lakeside ambience you want, **Gorel's ❹**

THE LOCAL STORY

MAGIC MEDICINE

Faith in Catemaco's *brujería* (witchcraft) varies from complete devotion to total skepticism. The practice can be traced to deep within the surrounding jungle, where hundreds of species of medicinal plants have been used by *indígenas* for centuries. Catemaco's natural mineral springs are touted as healing water—and bottled as Cayame brand sodas, on sale throughout the area.

Traditionally, the gathering and application of medicinal plants and minerals was performed by *curanderos* (shamans). These healers performed *limpias* (cleansings involving herbs and amulets) to rid the body of illness and bad spirits, while *culebreros* specialized in snake bites and *hueseros* tended to broken bones and joint problems. Under Spanish rule, the practice blended with Catholic tradition, incorporating rosaries and saints into the *brujería.*

Curanderos summon "white magic," used purely for healing. *Brujos,* however, claim to practice "black magic" (the devil's work) which can cause misfortune. In the 1950s, Gonzalo Aguirre Bech, the *Brujo Mayor,* set up shop in Catemaco, organizing annual witchcraft festivals. Bech's fame—and that of Catemaco—spread worldwide, and today *brujos* rule the market in Catemaco, performing *limpias* for about 100 pesos, while complicated "operations" can cost upwards of 2000 pesos.

serves regional seafood specialties (45-70 pesos) and beer (17 pesos) under a thatched roof and twinkling lights. When things get crowded, the management sets up tables right on the beach. (Open daily 8am-11pm. Cash only.) Cheaper eats abound in the *comedors* in the market area between Madero and Playa to the right of the *basílica*. **Fonda La Campesina ❷,** Playa 29, serves filling breakfasts for 15-25 pesos, and *antojitos* for 20-40 pesos. (Open daily 7am-7pm. Cash only.) You can find classic mojarra at **Los Sauces ❹,** on the *malecón* at Rayón, to the left coming downhill from the *basílica*. (☎943 0548. Entrees 25-150 pesos. Open daily 9am-10pm. Cash only.) There is also a supermarket, **Súper de Todo,** right next to the *basílica*. (Open M-Sa 8:30am-9pm, Su 8am-3pm.)

◪ SIGHTS. The rocky beaches of **Laguna Catemaco** are a refreshing break from the hot *Veracruzano* sun. The water immediately in front of town is not safe for swimming, but a hiking path runs along the edge of the lake (walk down from the *zócalo* to the waterfront and turn left). The trail will guide you 1.5km to **Playa Expagoya** and then another 500m to the more secluded and sandier **Playa Hermosa,** the first swimmable beach. The path can be extremely dark at night; employ all due caution. It's also possible to swim off a *lancha* in the deeper and sometimes clearer waters in the middle of the lake.

The best way to see Catemaco is on a **◪lancha tour** that departs from the shore of the lagoon. The tour lasts 1¼hr. and takes you past several small islands and various attractions. (*Lancha colectiva* 50 pesos. 1- to 6-person private boat 350 pesos.) Exotic birds, crocodiles, and water lilies aside, the most popular sight is **La Isla de los Changos.** A group of wild, red-cheeked *changos* (mandrills, a type of baboon) was brought from Thailand for a scientific experiment at the University of Veracruz in 1979—scientists wanted to see if the animals could survive in a new environment. Lo and behold, 25 years later the *changos* are alive, well fed, and posing for snapshots. En route to the island, you'll pass a cave-shrine that stands on the spot where the town's namesake, local fisherman Juan Catemaco, had a vision of the Virgin Mary over a century ago; his statue overlooks the calm waters today. Negotiate with *lanchistas* for longer trips, including explorations of the rivers that feed the lake or trips past the nearby tropical forests. On the *malecón* about three blocks from the ADO bus station, **Catemaco Turs** offers paddleboats (50 pesos per hr.) and kayaks (singles 40 pesos per hr., doubles 45 pesos per hr., 180/ 185 pesos per day) for self-guided exploration.

◪ ◪ NIGHTLIFE AND ENTERTAINMENT. Catemaco's nightlife heats up only in high season. Many bars and clubs shut down or operate irregularly in low season. Most of the best bars are right on the beachfront, so your best bet is likely to walk along the street until you find a place that strikes your fancy. Street lamps and blacklights aside, the *malecón* can get very dark at night, and all travelers are advised to be cautious. To experience the witching hour, head to **El Bule,** Malecón 33, near Playa and Hotel Julitais, one of most popular spots in the city. Depending on the night, people here get moving to cumbia, hip hop, merengue, rock, and salsa. (Beer 15 pesos. Mixed drinks 30 pesos. Some F nights live music. Cover Sa 30 pesos. Open Th-Su 8pm-4am.) To get away from the city, take a taxi (30 pesos) to **Chanequa's,** a chic video bar in Hotel Playa Azul. (☎943 0042. Open only when bands are playing; call ahead to inquire.)

Catemaco's major secular celebration, **Día de los Pescadores** (Day of the Fishermen) occurs on May 30, when a procession of manually powered *lanchas* parades across the lagoon, and locals compete in a fishing tournament. The town also celebrates the day of its patron saint, **Santa Carmen,** on July 16. The first week in March, Catemaco fills with the occult for the **Festival de las Brujas** (Witches).

🔲 DAYTRIP FROM CATEMACO

🔳 MONTEPÍO AND THE GULF COAST

Public transportation is limited to Transportes Rurales pickup trucks, called piratas *by locals, which depart from the eastern edge of town. To get there from the zócalo, walk east on Adama or Playa until you reach the ADO bus station. Take a left and walk about 4 blocks, and you'll see a lot full of pickups. Just outside town, the road forks into 2 main routes. One heads north to Montepío on the Gulf Coast and the other east to Coyame on the opposite side of Lake Catemaco. When enough passengers have boarded,* piratas *depart for both; every 30min. 6am-7pm.*

The road from Catemaco to **Montepío,** a small fishing village on the coast, offers a tour of jungle landscapes, rural villages, and gorgeous beaches. First off is **Sontecomapán** (18km from Catemaco), a small town beside a saltwater lake that empties into the gulf. *Lanchas* are available for excursions on the lake and down the coast (*lancha colectiva* 50 pesos; private boat 250 pesos). If you want to go to **Playa Jicacal** and **Playa Escondida,** ask the *pirata* driver in advance to let you off, then walk 30min. to stony, empty Playa Jicacal. Visitors who want a secluded beach without a walk through the jungle can have the *pirata* drop them off at the second-to-last stop, **Balzapote.** Most people get off at the beach at **Montepío** (34km from Catemaco), but the *pirata* route continues on 5-10min. to **Playa Hermosa,** a small but swimmable beach which lives up to its name. Between there and Montepío you can find **waterfalls** up from the beach—the best way to reach them is with a guide. You can find one at the driveway to Posada San José. Most people go by horse, taking the guided trip inland and midway down the beach to **Cascadas de Revolución** (80 pesos). You can arrange excursions to other *cascadas* or rent a horse and try to find them on your own (25 pesos per hr., 40 pesos with guide). From Montepío, you can also find a *lancha* to take you to impressive **caves** along the coast (50 pesos per person).

ACAYUCAN ☎924

At the junction of Mex. 180, which runs between Veracruz and Villahermosa, and Mex. 185, which crosses the Isthmus of Tehuantepec, lies Acayucan (pop. 48,000), a transportation hub for southern Veracruz that lacks any major sites.

Hotels and restaurants surround the *zócalo.* **Hotel Joalicia ❷,** Zaragoza 4, immediately off the *zócalo,* has well-furnished rooms for excellent prices, and purified water in the hallways. (☎245 0877. 24hr. bell. Singles with fan 130 pesos, with A/C and TV 140; doubles 190/200. Cash only.) **Soyamar ❶,** Guerrero 601, serves vegetarian and meat entrees, and every fruit and vegetable juice imaginable. (☎245 1744. Entrees 7-25 pesos. Open M-F 7:30am-8pm, Sa 8:30-8pm. Cash only.) Hordes of taco stands and *torta* shops crowd the **market,** which occupies the block below the *zócalo,* bordered by Victoria, Hidalgo, Enrique Luz, and Montezuma. Most are open from around 7am-7pm.

Acayucan's **bus station** (☎245 1142), on Acuña in Barrio Tamarindo, is on the eastern edge of the city. Many buses are *de paso* and tickets go fast, so get to the station early. To get to the *zócalo,* exit right and walk straight to Hidalgo. Turn left and walk straight for 10min. to reach the *centro,* then catch a westbound "Centro" *colectivo* or bus (5 pesos), otherwise take a **taxi** (15 pesos). **ADO** sends **buses** to: **Mexico City** (7hr., 3 per day, 446 pesos); **Oaxaca** (8hr., 3 per day, 288 pesos); **San Andrés Tuxtla** (2hr., 3 per day, 54 pesos); **Veracruz** (3½hr., 9 per day, 166 pesos); **Villahermosa** (4hr., 17 per day, 144 pesos); **Xalapa** (6hr., 5 per day, 236 pesos). *Urbanos* line the street outside and go to nearby destinations.

Santander Serfín, at Victoria and Zaragoza, **exchanges currency** and has **24hr. ATMs.** (Open M-F 9am-5pm.) Next door, **Farmacia Union** is a **24hr. pharmacy.** Other services include: **emergency** ☎066; **police,** in the *palacio municipal* on the *zócalo* (☎245 1078); **Red Cross,** at Ocampo Sur 4, between Victoria and Negrete (☎245 0028); **Cybernet-ICO,** Victoria 22, opposite the plaza (☎245 8085; 10 pesos per hr.; open daily 9am-11pm); and the **post office,** a block north on Moctezuma and left on Guerrero (☎245 0088; open M-Sa 8am-4pm). **Postal Code:** 96001.

TABASCO

VILLAHERMOSA   ☎993

Villahermosa (pop. 1.6 million) is neither a *villa* (small village), nor is it *hermosa* (beautiful). The capital of Tabasco state is as flat and hot as a frying pan, and sprinkled liberally with satellite dishes, luxury hotels, and fast-food joints. What holds this lovely concoction together? Crude oil, of course. The city has capitalized on oil discoveries and its strategic location along the Río Grijalva, one of the few navigable rivers in the Republic. Nevertheless, the city is far from crude. Studded with lagoons, parks, and pedestrian walkways, Villahermosa is actually quite conducive to daytime rambling. If your aim is to explore a large Mexican city while escaping the typical tourist circuit, Villahermosa is the place; while it's often frequented by those connected to the oil industry, *gringos* remain few and far between.

▌ TRANSPORTATION

Flights: Aeropuerto Capitán Carlos Pérez (VSA; ☎356 0156), on the Villahermosa-Macupana Hwy., 13km from downtown. Taxis shuttle between the airport and the *centro* (*especial* 150 pesos, *colectivo* 100 pesos). Major airlines have offices in Tabasco 2000, including: **Aerocaribe,** Via 3 120 Locale 9 (☎316 5047); **Aeroméxico,** Cámara 511 Locale 2 (☎800-021-4000); **Aviacsa,** Via 3 120 Locale 10 (☎316 5733); **Mexicana,** Via 3 120 Locale 5-6D (☎316 3132).

Buses: There are 2 main bus terminals in Villahermosa.

1st-class terminal: on Mina at Merino. To reach downtown from the station, walk 2½ blocks to your right on Mina to Méndez Magaña. From there, take a *combi* to Parque Juárez (5 pesos). Or, take a left at Méndez Magaña and walk 5 blocks until Madero. 3 blocks to the right will bring you to the Parque (15-20min.). **ADO** (☎312 7692 or 314 5818) runs to: **Cancún** (11hr., 16 per day, 572 pesos); **Campeche** (5hr., every 30min. 9am-noon, 278 pesos); **Mexico City** (11hr., every hr., 618 pesos); **Oaxaca** (11hr., 4 per day 4:18am-9:25pm, 476 pesos); **Palenque** (2hr., 11 per day 7:15am-9:15pm, 94 pesos); **Puebla** (8hr., 9 per day, 528 pesos); **San Andrés Tuxtla** (4hr., 9 per day, 208 pesos); **San Cristóbal de Las Casas** (6hr.; 9:30am, 12:30pm; 220 pesos); **Tuxtla Gutiérrez** (7hr., 4 per day 7:15am-10:25pm, 216 pesos). **OCC, ATS,** and **TRT** also serve the station.

2nd-class terminal: on Ruiz Cortines, 2 blocks left of Mina. To reach downtown from the terminal, cross the highway on the pedestrian bridge left of the station and hop on an "Indeco Centro" bus (5 pesos) to Parque Juárez on Madero. Get off the bus, cross the bridge, and walk toward the Best Western for 2 blocks. Go left on Mina and continue south for 3 blocks until you reach the ADO station. Taxi to the *centro* 15 pesos. 2nd-class service reaches many regional destinations such as **Paraíso, Tacotalpa,** and **Teapa.**

Taxis: Radio Taxi (in the *centro* ☎314 3456, in Tabasco 2000 316 6421), is slightly more expensive than the *taxis colectivos* (20 pesos within the *centro*). On call 24hr. Min. charge for roaming **yellow taxis** 15 pesos. Between neighborhoods 20 pesos.

Car Rental: Dollar, Tabasco 1203 (☎315 4830). 598 pesos per day for economic 2-door car includes 300km and insurance. Open daily 8am-8pm. MC/V. **Autos del Grijalva** (☎312 9184 or 314 2986), on Melchor Ocampo at the *malecón* and Paseo

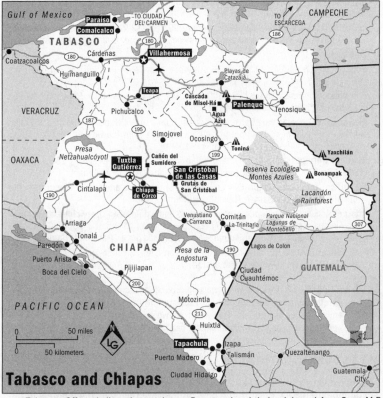

Tabasco and Chiapas

Tabasco. Offers similar prices and cars. Reserve ahead during July and Aug. Open M-F 8:30am-8pm, Sa 8:30am-4pm. MC/V.

ORIENTATION AND PRACTICAL INFORMATION

Landlocked Villahermosa is 20km from the Chiapas border and 71km from the Gulf of Mexico. The city spreads out in all directions. **Paseo Tabasco** links the *centro* to **Tabasco 2000,** a complex of newer buildings with a shopping mall and government offices. **Tabasco, Bulevar Cortines,** and the **Río Grijalva** enclose the main downtown tourist area. At the heart of it all is the **Zona Luz,** a small grid of perpetually buzzing pedestrian streets next to Parque Juárez. *Saetas* (public buses) and *combis* (5 pesos) run 6am-10pm.

Tourist Office: De los Ríos 113 (☎310 9700, ext. 5238), in Tabasco 2000. From the Paseo, take a left and walk until you reach another traffic circle; office is ahead on the left. Open M-F 8am-4pm. **Booth** at the Parque Museo la Venta. Open daily 8am-4pm.

Banks: Banks abound in Zona Luz and on Paseo Tabasco. **Banamex** (☎312 0011), on Madero at Reforma, and **Santander,** on Madero between Zaragoza and Lerdo de Tejada, have **24hr. ATMs.** Both open M-F 9am-4pm.

American Express: 1404 Tabasco 2000 (☎315 3999), in the office of Turismo Creativo. Exchanges traveler's checks. Open M-F 9am-7pm, Sa 9am-2pm.

Luggage Storage: Guarda Plus, at the ADO bus station. 5-12 pesos per hr. Open daily 6am-10pm.

Laundromat: Lavandería Top Klean, Madero 303 (☎312 2856), next to Hotel Madero. 16.50 pesos per kg. 25 pesos per kg for same-day service. Open M-Sa 8am-8pm.

Emergency: ☎066.

Police: (☎315 2517), at 16 de Septiembre and Periférico, and at Aldama 101 (☎315 2633 or 2630), in Zona Luz.

Red Cross: Sandino 716 (☎315 5600 or 5555), in Col. 1 de Mayo. Reachable by taxi (15 pesos). 24hr. ambulance service.

Pharmacy: Farmacias del Ahorro, Méndez 1405 (☎314 0603, delivery 315 6606). Also in the Zona Luz, near Reforma and Aldama, across from the Howard Johnson. Both branches open M-Sa 6am-10pm, Su 7am-10pm.

Medical Services: IMSS, Carretera Villahermosa km 205 (☎315 2015 or 2691). **ISSSTE** (☎315 1986 or 6295), on Ciudad de Ceiba s/n, Colonial Atasta.

Fax Office: Telecomm, Lerdo 601 (☎314 2525), at Sáenz around the corner from the post office. Open M-F 8am-7:30pm, Sa-Su 9am-12:30pm.

Internet Access: Several options near Zaragoza and Aldama. **Multiservicios Computacional,** Aldama 621 (☎312 8334). 10 pesos per hr. Open daily 8:30am-9pm. **G&G,** Zaragoza 405-A (☎131 0915), in Parque Juárez. 10 pesos per hr. Open daily 8am-1am.

Post Office: Sáenz 131, at Lerdo. Open M-F 9am-3pm, Sa 9am-1pm. **Mexpost** inside. Open M-F 9am-4pm. **Postal Code:** 86000.

> **!** **HEADS UP.** Be alert when walking around the **Zona Luz,** the areas around **Parque Canabal,** the **market,** and **Tabasco 2000** after lights go out. Robberies and assaults on tourists have been known to occur. Don't wear jewelry or watches, carry only a small amount of cash, and walk in groups.

ACCOMMODATIONS

Villahermosa firmly refuses to cave into backpacker demands for budget accommodations. As a result, the best options are the overpriced hotels in the Zona Luz. Call ahead for reservations July-August.

Hotel Oriente, Madero 425 (☎312 0121), between Tejada and Reforma. The best of the bunch. Clean rooms and spotless baths in various shades of pale green, all with TV. The staff is friendly and fairly knowledgeable about the Zona Luz. Free purified water. Singles with fan and TV 210 pesos, with A/C 300 pesos; doubles 280/360 pesos; triples 330/420 pesos, each additional person 30 pesos. Cash only. ❸

Hotel del Centro, Suárez 209 (☎312 5961), between Sánchez and Mármol. Another branch at Madero 411. Large, fairly clean rooms with fan and TV, though the mattresses have seen better days. Singles 200 pesos, with A/C 350 pesos; doubles 250/350 pesos; triples 300/450 pesos. Cash only. ❸

Hotel San Francisco, Madero 604 (☎312 3198), between Sánchez and Mármol. Rooms are homey, and baths are brand-new and clean. The institutional hallways and lobby with fluorescent lighting do not promote socializing. All rooms with A/C and TV; some with good views of the city. Singles 220 pesos; doubles 270 pesos, with king-size beds 285 pesos; triples 350 pesos; quads 390 pesos. Cash only. ❸

Hotel Madero, Madero 301 (☎312 0516), near 27 de Febrero. Friendly, family-run hotel with a central location. Light sleepers should ask for a room away from the street. All of the large, clean rooms have A/C, phone, and TV. Singles 300 pesos; doubles 400 pesos; triples 500 pesos. Cash only. ❺

Villahermosa

ACCOMMODATIONS
Hotel del Centro, **3**
Hotel Madero, **11**
Hotel Oriente, **6**
Hotel Palma de
  Mallorca, **5**
Hotel San Francisco, **2**

FOOD
Cafe La Cabaña, **10**
Cocktelería Rock
  and Roll, **9**
Restaurant Bar
  Impala, **7**
Restaurant Madan, **8**
Restaurant Los
  Tulipanes, **14**
Soy Aquarius, **1**
Tacolandia, **4**

NIGHTLIFE
Bfore, **12**
La Bohemia, **13**

GULF COAST AND CHIAPAS

Hotel Palma de Mallorca, Madero 510 (☎312 0144 or 0145), near Zaragoza and Madero. A dark hotel with tacky interior and worn-out mattresses. Singles with fan 160 pesos; doubles with A/C 250 pesos. Cash only. ❷

FOOD

Villahermosa, like the rest of Tabasco, specializes in *mariscos* (seafood). A typical *tabasqueño* dish—not for the faint of heart—is tortoise sauteed in green sauce and blood and mixed with pickled armadillo. Crab is often served in *chirmol* sauce, made from ground squash seeds and burnt tortillas. To wash down your meal, try traditional *pozol*, made from ground cornmeal, cocoa, and water. Although *taquerías* litter the downtown area, most restaurants specializing in seafood are either in far-off suburbs or very expensive. The best places for regional seafood are roadside restaurants and *palapas* along tourist routes, like the **Teapa Comalcalco route.** In the Zona Luz, coffee shops line **Benito Juárez.** Stock up on grocery goods at **Mercado Pino Suárez,** at Pino Suárez and Hermanos Zozaya next to the highway, in the northeastern corner of town (open daily 5am-8pm), and a supermarket, **Maz,** on Madero at Zaragoza next to Parque Juárez (open daily 8am-10pm).

Soy Aquarius, Mina 309 (☎312 8968), between Méndez and Magallanes. Popular with vegetarians and health-conscious carnivores. *Menú del día* includes salad, 2 main

GOOD WILL HUNTING. *Venado*, or venison, is a popular dish throughout the Yucatán peninsula. But those with a flair for conservation may want to think twice before digging into *venado* and radish tacos. The wetland deer are a rare species and the hunting process is often destructive to the animals as well as the marshes they live in.

dishes, a starch, bread, dessert, and *agua de fruta* (55-65 pesos). Soyburgers 20 pesos. Fish and poultry 49 pesos. Open M-F 8am-5:30pm, Sa 8am-2pm. Cash only. ❹

Restaurant Madan, inside the Best Western Madan. The most reliable breakfast spot in town, Madan has Mexican favorites such as *huevos rancheros* (40 pesos) and huge stacks of hotcakes (28 pesos). Open daily 7am-11pm. MC/V. ❹

Restaurant Los Tulipanes (☎312 9217 or 312 9209), in the CICOM complex. Specializes in *comida tabasqueña*. Enjoy fresh seafood on the banks of the Río Grijalva in this local favorite, where high cost means high quality, not tourist-inspired extortion. Breakfast buffet 8am-10am, 108 pesos. Seafood entrees 85-140 pesos. Open M-Sa 8am-9pm, Su 8am-6pm. AmEx/MC/V. ❺

Tacolandia, on Aldama in the Zona Luz. Casual and extremely popular, Tacolandia wins the prize for most tacos turned out daily in the Zona Luz. The roasting pork on the spit is a sight to behold. Tacos from 6 pesos. Open M-Sa 9am-9pm. Cash only. ❶

Cafe la Cabaña, Juárez 303, near 27 de Febrero. Part of a popular chain of cafes in town, the Zona Luz location draws out all of Villahermosa's gossiping old men. Cappuccinos 21 pesos. Iced coffees 27-30 pesos. Chocolate malts 34 pesos. Coffee beans 110 pesos per kg. Open M-Sa 7am-10pm, Su 8:30am-9pm. MC/V. ❷

Restaurant Bar Impala, Madero 421 (☎312 0493). One of the many restaurant-bars along Madero, Impala has a cluttered atmosphere and a menu of Mexican standards. Tasty *tamalitos de chipilín* (10 pesos), *panuchos* (fried tortilla shells stuffed with meat and beans; 20 pesos), and tacos (20 pesos). Open M-Sa 10am-9pm. Cash only. ❷

Coctelería Rock and Roll, Reforma 307 (☎314 7465), across from Hotel Miraflores. Specializes in large seafood cocktails (70-95 pesos) and old men guzzling Corona. The party really kicks into high gear when the Mexican national soccer team plays. Beer 12 pesos. Open daily 10am-midnight. Cash only. ❹

👁 SIGHTS

For a city unconcerned with tourism, Villahermosa has a surprising number of worthwhile museums and tourist activities. Downtown is home to cafes, ice cream shops, hair salons, and shoe shops as far as the eye can see.

PARQUE-MUSEO LA VENTA. Located south of Tabasco 2000, La Venta features 33 Olmec sculptures lifted from their original locations in La Venta, Tabasco, and replanted in Villahermosa by poet and tireless anthropologist Carlos Pellicer Cámara. Immediately beyond the entrance, a small museum details the recovery of the Olmec artifacts by Pellicer Cámara and the creation of the park as well as the history of the ancient Olmec peoples. From the museum, a well-marked 1km **jungle walk** reveals mammoth Olmec altars and sculptures, leading eventually to a **zoo,** with all manner of local flora and wild animals. Past the museum, the sprawling **Parque Tomás Garrido Canabal** has a large lagoon, landscaped alcoves, and hidden benches and fountains—which lure plenty of hormonal teenagers. Beware: the *mirador* claims to offer a panoramic view of the city, but the 40m climb yields only an aerial view of blooming trees and the lagoon. *(Take a "Tabasco 2000," "Carrisal," or "Palacio" bus, 5 pesos, to the Tabasco and Ruiz Cortines* *intersection and walk 1km through Parque Canabal to the entrance. Taxis 15 pesos. ☎314 1652. Ticket office, archaeological area, wildlife area, and museum open daily 8am-5pm. 40 pesos. Light-and-sound show Tu-Su 8, 9, 10pm. 100 pesos.)*

MUSEO DE HISTORIA DE TABASCO. The small museum displays a series of poorly labeled artifacts and pictures on state history, but the building itself is the most interesting exhibit. A wealthy merchant had the famous blue edifice, known as the **Casa de los Azulejos** (House of the Tiles), built between 1889 and 1915 and decorated with Italian and Spanish Baroque tiles, a different style in every room. Also check out the Egyptian tiles along the ledge of the outside walls. Eleven classical sculptures decorate the roof, and the seated female figures are said to be the merchant's family members. The museum is also home to an excellent bookstore. *(At Juárez and 27 de Febrero in Zona Luz. ☎314 2172. Exhibits in English and Spanish. Open July-Aug. M-Sa 9am-7pm, Su 10am-6pm; Sept.-June closed M. 15 pesos.)*

CENTRO PARA LA INVESTIGACIÓN DE LAS CULTURAS OLMEC Y MAYA (CIMCOM). The main draw in CIMCOM, the **Museo Regional de Antropología Carlos Pellicer Cámara** is a testament to 1970s design. The museum displays Olmec and Mayan artifacts from nearby archaeological sites La Venta and Comalcalco. The center also houses a public library, art school, and theater. *(From Zona Luz, the museum is a 15min. walk south along Río Grijalva. #1 and "CICOM" buses, 5 pesos, pass frequently. ☎312 6344. Open Tu-Su 9am-5pm. 25 pesos.)*

YUMKÁ. A far cry from an African safari, Yumká is nonetheless a good way to escape the stifling heat of downtown. Just 16km from the bustle of Villahermosa, animals run freely throughout the 101-hectare park, which reproduces the four *tabasqueño* ecosystems: jungle, savannah, wetlands, and gift shop. Visitors travel about in boats, by foot, and on trolleys, seeing animals in their natural habitats. *(On Las Barrancas, next to the airport. Buses leave from Parque La Venta Sa-Su and vacation days at 9, 10:30am, noon, 1:30pm; 15 pesos. ☎356 0115, 0119, or 0107; www.yumka.org. Open daily 9am-4pm. 50 pesos, children 25 pesos.)*

▣ SHOPPING

Northwest on Paseo Tabasco, away from the *centro* and Río Grijalva, lies **Tabasco 2000,** a futuristically bland complex of buildings and pedestrian-unfriendly streets light years away from the car-free walkways of Zona Luz. The long strip of stucco and concrete buildings includes the city's Palacio Municipal, a convention center, several fountains, an upscale shopping mall, most of the larger discos, and a planetarium with beautiful murals and Omni-Max flicks dubbed in Spanish. To get to Tabasco 2000, take a 5-peso "Tabasco 2000" or "Palacio" bus from Parque Juárez. (☎316 3641. Mall shops open daily 10:30am-8:30pm; planetarium shows most days 4, 5, 6pm. 25 pesos.)

♫ ▣ ENTERTAINMENT AND NIGHTLIFE

Villahermosa attracts artists and academics with a well established network of lectures and workshops. Travelers should check out the **Centro Cultural Villahermosa,** on Madero at Zaragoza, across from Parque Juárez, for a weekly program of events around the city and at the Centro, including recitals and screenings. (Open 10am-8pm.) The cafe in the back of **Galería el Jaguar Despertado,** Sáenz 117, near Reforma in the Zona Luz, features live classical and jazz performances. A weekly program of cultural events is often outside the door; performances are usually at 8pm. There is a small gallery upstairs featuring local artists with works for sale. (☎314 1244. Open M-F 9am-9pm, Sa 10am-8pm, Su 10am-3pm.)

GULF COAST AND CHIAPAS

Across the street, **Colegio de Arte Tabasco**, Sáenz 122, features contemporary *tabasqueño* art; much of it is for sale. (☎312 8170. Open M-F 9am-9pm.)

The Zona Hotelera in and around Tabasco 2000 is home to a number of discos and clubs. Here, Villahermosa's young and wealthy dress up and get down to a mix of salsa and electronica music. Taxis are the only safe means of night transportation.

Bfore, Paseo Tabasco (☎352 1191; www.bforelounge.com), at Obrero Mundial, 1 block past the intersection of the Paseo and Magaña. This hip, 2-story club attracts partiers of all ages with its sleek leather couches, artsy black-and-white photos, and DJs. Beer 60 pesos per liter. Mixed drinks 40 pesos. Su karaoke. Cover Th 30 pesos. Open Th-Su 8pm-3am. MC/V.

La Bohemia de Manrique, Calle Vía 2 (☎316 9224), on Paseo Tabasco. A more tranquil scene with tasty regional food. Beer 18 pesos. Mixed drinks 32-43 pesos. *Antojitos* 24-60 pesos. Entrees 60-110 pesos. Live *trova* music nightly. Cover Tu-W women 40 pesos; Tu-Th men 40 pesos; F-Sa 60 pesos. Open Tu-Th 8pm-3am, F-Sa 8pm-4am.

▶ DAYTRIPS FROM VILLAHERMOSA

As the largest city in the mostly rural state of Tabasco, Villahermosa serves as a base for dozens of daytrips into the state's northern coast and wetlands, southwestern jungle, and southeastern mountains.

▨ TAPIJULAPA AND PARQUE NATURAL DE LA VILLA LUZ

Two buses serve the town, leaving every hr. from Tacotalpa. To get to Tacotalpa, catch a taxi colectivo (1hr., 37 pesos) from the lot behind and to the right of Villahermosa's Chedraui supermarket as you face it. 2nd-class buses leave for Tacotalpa (1½hr., every hr. from 5:25am, 26 pesos). Colectivos stop on Tacotalpa's main drag. ½ block farther down, in front of the market, red-and-white buses leave for Tapijulapa (40min., every hr. 5am-6pm, 8 pesos); buses also leave from Teapa. The bus will stop at an archway. To reach the plaza, walk downhill through the arch, keeping right. To reach the Tapijulapa lancha *dock, from which you can access the Parque, walk 2 blocks parallel to the river; at the end of the street, turn right and head 1 block downhill. Arrange a pick-up time before disembarking. Return buses to Tacotalpa leave from the same archway, 2 blocks north of the plaza (every hr., last bus 7pm). Buses and colectivos returning to Villahermosa from Tacotalpa stop running around 8pm. Wear shoes appropriate for walking in mud and bring bug repellent for the evening. Returning to the* lancha *dock will take about 25min.; the entire trek takes approximately 2hr. If you get a guide in Tapijulapa, they will expect a tip of at least 20-25 pesos.*

In Tapijulapa, 90km south of Villahermosa, the air smells as fresh as the white-washed houses look. High in the mountains by the Amatán and Oxolotán rivers, this small and relatively untouristed town is a nice change from Villahermosa. The **Parque Natural de la Villa Luz** features pearly-blue sulfuric waters that seem to glow from within. Getting to the Parque, 3km from Tapijulapa, requires a *lancha* (round-trip 20 pesos). Small boys will likely chase you on your way to the *lancha* dock and offer to be your guide; hiring one of them is not really necessary, as the paths are well marked. Climb the stairs and go through the orange gates on the other side of a field, passing a shack on your right. A bit farther, you'll come to the home of former governor Tomás Garrido Canabal (1891-1943), whose name you might recognize from Villahermosa. The house has been outfitted with some token artifacts (including an old sewing machine) and declared a museum. There are signs pointing to the **cascadas** (waterfalls with pools popular for bathing; 600m to the left), the **albercas** (mineral pools; 900m to the right), and the **Cueva de las Sardinas Ciegas** (Cave of the Blind Sardines; 900m to the right). The cave's odd name comes from the native sardines that, having adapted to their dark environment, are all blind. Every year on Palm Sunday, residents of Tapijulapa gather at the cave for the **Pesca de la Sardina.** While dancing to the music of the *tamborileros*, celebrants toss *barbasco* (powdered narcotic plants) into the water, which stun the fish and cause them to float to the top of the water for easy harvesting.

THE RUINS OF COMALCALCO

The ruins are 3km outside the city of Comalcalco, 56km northwest of Villahermosa. Combis to Comalcalco marked "Comalli" leave from a station on Gil y Sáenz between Reyes and Cortines; walk past the ADO station on Mina and turn left on Reyes, then right on Sáenz. (Every 20 min., 25 pesos.) Ask to be let off on Comalcalco's main drag at the hub near Súper Max, the ADO station, and the clock tower, and from there snag a northbound Paraíso bus and ask to be let off at "las ruinas" (5 pesos). From the access road, walk 1km, or wait for an infrequent minibus (3 pesos). To get back, reverse the directions. In Comalcalco, the Comalli station is at Reforma and Calle N. Bravo. The last combi back to Villahermosa leaves at 9pm. Site open daily 8am-5pm; last entrance 4pm. 37 pesos.

Unpublicized and generally ignored by backpackers, the Mayan ruins of Comalcalco are surprisingly extensive, though the mosquitoes are enough to discourage many. Named after the *comal*—a griddle (originally made of clay) for cooking tortillas—the city was built and rose to its height during the Classic Period (100 BC-AD 800) at the western frontier of Mayan territory. Because the Tabasco Maya, known as Chontals, lacked stone for their temples, they used baked clay, making Comalcalco the oldest brick city in all the Americas. In the museum, you will see dozens of these bricks, the surfaces of which are carved with animals, temples, humans, and hieroglyphics.

The main road, left from the museum entrance, will take you into the main plaza. The 10-level, 20m **pyramid** left of the site entrance is Comalcalco's landmark. Under an awning on the building's north face, the relics of a carving of a giant, winged toad and several humans are all that remain of decorations that once covered the structure's surface. Past Temples II and III, a path leads to the **Gran Acrópolis,** a 175m long complex of temples and private residences. Look closely at the dilapidated walls and you can see the insides of Comalcalco's brickwork and oyster-shell mortar. Among the ruins is the precarious-looking **Palacio,** stretching for 80m, with half a vault somehow still intact, and what is thought to have been a bathtub and cooling system. From the top of the acropolis, it's possible to imagine how the jungle might have appeared before deforestation and radio towers. On the way down, watch for sculptural remnants preserved in protected corners. Especially interesting reliefs are on the eastern side in the **Tumba de los Nueve Señores;** the figures are believed to represent the nine night gods of the Mayan pantheon.

RESERVA DE LA BIOSFERA PATANOS DE CENTLA

For information on visiting, contact the on-site Centro de Interpretación Uyotut-Ja, on Carr. Frontera-Jonuta km 12.5. It's also the site of an observation tower, restaurant, and lancha pier. (☎ 310 1422 or 313 9290; pantanos@intrasur.net.mx. Open Tu-Su 9am-5pm.)

Though Tabasco's ecotourism industry has been slow to take flight, the state's predominant feature (after its oil reserves) is its natural beauty. One of the best places to explore Tabasco's vast wilderness is the Reserva de la Biosfera Patanos de Centla, a preserve encompassing 302,000 hectares of wetlands. Sediments left behind by the converging Usumacinta and Grijalva rivers create an ideal habitat for mangrove and jungle ecosystems, home to over 434 plant species and 365 species of vertebrates, including numerous birds, crocodiles, jaguars, manatees, otters, and turtles. Set aside by the government in 1992, the land is also home to 50,000 people, most of whom live in small fishing villages along the river systems deep inside the preserve. Unfortunately, the Reserve's ecological goals sometimes pit it against the broader economic interests of the indigenous peoples who live here. Small turtles sell for 100 pesos in the open market, and venison goes for more, giving residents incentive to hunt protected animals. This hunting is a major concern of workers at reserve's station at Tres Brazos.

The best way to see the reserve is through one of the many guided tours organized by travel agencies in Villahermosa. Going it alone is possible, but much more expensive and it is often difficult to gain access to the more protected areas of the reserve. **Turismo Nieves,** Sarlat 202, offers full-day tours to the area which include guides, the *lancha* trip, and lunch. (☎314 1888; www.turismonieves.com.mx. Tours start at 1035 pesos for 6-8 people.)

PARAÍSO ☎933

Only 71km from Villahermosa, Paraíso and its beaches are the only real spot in the state of Tabasco to enjoy the warm Gulf Coast waters. Public **beaches** lie east and west of the city. **Varadero, El Paraíso, Pal Mar,** and **Paraíso y Mar** are reachable by the "Playa" *combi* (20min., every 30min., 5 pesos) that leaves from the second-class bus station. All about 500m from the road, they have *palapas* where you can hang a hammock for free. Varadero and El Paraíso are by far the nicest but are often closed during the week; both have restaurants and the latter has hotels and a pool. Alternatively, an eastbound bus to Chiltepec leaves every 30min. from the second-class bus station. The first stop is **Puerto Ceiba** (15min., every 20min., 5 pesos), a small fishing village on the edge of **Laguna Mecoacán,** a 51,000-hectare oyster breeding ground. Local fishermen give *lancha* tours of the lagoon (300 pesos; 14-person max.). Ask at any of the docks along the way. Across the bridge from Puerto Ceiba is **El Bellote** (every 20min., 6 pesos), another small fishing town located between the lagoon and the Río Seco, with several affordable restaurants. Near the end of the bus route, 27km east of El Paraíso, is the town of **Playa Bruja;** just east is the beach itself, with *palapas* and a restaurant.

The city of Paraíso has several hotel options, though the best bargain is to sleep in a hammock at one of the several *palapa* beach *balnearios.* Make sure to check in with management about beach safety before hanging your hammock. For those interested in a bed, **Hotel Solimar ❺,** Ocampo 114, half a block north of the plaza, is the best option. The rooms are blissfully breezy and air-conditioned and the attached restaurant has a reasonable menu. (☎333 2872. Rooms from 350 pesos. Cash only.)

Combis run from Villahermosa to Paraíso (1¼hr., every 30min., 50 pesos) from the blue tarp on Av. Arboledas (Castellanos), next to the **Chedraui supermarket.** Get off at the first stop, before the traffic circle. From there catch any passing bus to the station (5 pesos). To reach the 2nd-class bus station from the *zócalo,* walk two and a half blocks away from Juárez to Buenos Aires and continue for nine blocks.

TEAPA ☎932

Surrounded by banana and cacao farms and cattle ranches 52km south of Villahermosa, Teapa is a pleasant base for exploring the mountainous southern region of Tabasco. The town itself has several 18th-century churches, including the Franciscan **Temple of Santiago Apostol,** two blocks from the fountain next to the central plaza (mass Su 7am and 1pm) and the Jesuit **Temple of Tecomájica.** The real gems, however, are ◪**Las Grutas Coco.ná,** 2km outside of the city. Discovered in the late 1800s by two adventurous brothers hunting in the woods, a visit to the caves is like a trip to another planet. A concrete path winds 500m into the hillside as eerie, piped-in flute music and dramatic lighting enhance the enormous caverns, underground lagoons, and bizarre geological formations. Guides offer their services, pointing out formations that resemble the Virgin Mary, a moose head, and other objects. The explanations are interesting but, as the caves are lit, your time may be better spent exploring on your own. (Any taxi in town can take you to the caves, 10min., 30 pesos. Open daily 9am-5pm. 25 pesos, children 15 pesos. Guides 40-60 pesos; 10-person max. Rock and rappel tour 100 pesos. Small on-site museum open daily 10am-5pm; free.)

Teapa also draws tourists with its many riverside *balnearios* and sulfurous thermal spas. The popular mud bath is said to cleanse the spirit and the pores. **Hacienda Los Azufres ❺,** at km 5.5 along the Teapa-Pichucalco Carretera, offers day services (thermal pools 30 pesos, children 15 pesos) as well as a few rooms. (☎327 5806. Singles 300 pesos; suites with small kitchen 450 pesos. Cash only.)

Other sleeping options in Teapa include the tidy but impersonal **Hotel Los Candiles ❺,** Carlos Ramos 101 (☎932 322 0431). All rooms have A/C and TV as well as cheery orange decor. Free purified water. (Singles 300 pesos; doubles 350 pesos. Cash only.)

Teapa has several banks along the main drag. **Banamex,** at the corner of Gregorio Mendez and Bastar, has a **24hr. ATM.** (☎322 0284. Open M-F 9am-4pm.) To get to Teapa from Villahermosa, look for an infrequent red *taxi colectivo* in front of Maz supermarket on Parque Juárez, or take a 2nd-class bus (1¼hr., every 30min., 32 pesos).

CHIAPAS

TUXTLA GUTIÉRREZ ☎961

A plain of smooth white marble, the vast central plaza of Tuxtla Gutiérrez (pop. 568,000) is the hub of Chiapan political and social life. This capital city is a dizzying amalgam of markets, flashing signs, and the omnipresent Mexican shoe store. It's a crowded and noisy city, and it has a radical streak. A case in point is Miguel Gutiérrez, a progressive *chiapaneco* governor who in 1838, rather than succumb to imperialist forces, wrapped himself dramatically in the Mexican flag and jumped to his death from a church spire. As in much of the highlands, rain showers are common in the afternoon, so unless you want a liberating natural bath, keep your poncho handy.

▐ TRANSPORTATION

Flights: Aeropuerto Llano San Juan (TGZ), 15km west of town. Taxis to town 60 pesos. **Aerocaribe,** Av. Central Pte. 206 (☎602 5649 or 800 623 4518, at the airport 671 5218 or 5220). **Aviacsa,** Av. Central Pte. 160 or 1144 (☎612 8081 or 800 006 2200, at the airport 671 5246).

Buses:

ADO/Cristóbal Colón Station: 3km from the city center on 5 Nte. Pte. next to the Gigante Bodega supermarket. **Cristóbal Colón** (☎612 5122) goes to: **Cancún** (18hr.; 10:15am, 12:30pm; 688 pesos); **Mexico City** (15hr., 6 per day from 6pm, 738-770 pesos); **Oaxaca** (10hr.; 11:30am, 7:15pm, midnight; 322 pesos); **Palenque** (6hr., 4 per day 5am-midnight, 158 pesos); **Puebla** (13hr., 4 per day 6pm-midnight, 633 pesos); **Puerto Escondido** (11hr.; 8:15, 11pm; 342 pesos); **San Cristóbal de las Casas** (2hr., 17 per day 5am-midnight, 32 pesos); **Tapachula** (6hr., 10 per day 6am-midnight, 230 pesos); **Veracruz** (12hr.; 9:45, 11:45pm; 500 pesos); **Villahermosa** (7hr., 7 per day 6am-11:45pm, 216 pesos).

Autotransportes Tuxtla Gutiérrez (ATG) Station: Av. 3 Sur 712 (☎611 2310), next to Mercado San Roque. **ATG** serves similar destinations, including **Cancún** (371 pesos), **Palenque** (87 pesos), and **San Cristóbal de las Casas** (12 pesos).

Transportes Chiapa-Tuxtla Station: (☎611 2656 or 615 5301), at Calle 2 Ote. and Av. 2 Sur. To reach **Chiapa de Corzo,** hop on a Transportes Chiapa-Tuxtla *microbús* at the station (25min., every 2min., 9 pesos) or grab one leaving town on Blvr. Corzo.

Tuxtla Gutiérrez

🏠 ACCOMMODATIONS
Hotel Casablanca, **2**
Hotel del Pasaje, **9**
Hotel Plaza Chiapas, **3**
Villas Deportivas Juvenil, **7**

🍴 FOOD
Las Canteras, **1**
Naturalissmo, **5, 6**
Las Pichanchas, **8**
Restaurante Imperial, **4**

Parque Madero/Botanical Gardens

City Center

Public Transportation: VW van **colectivos** run frequently throughout the city. (R1 6am-10pm, other routes 6am-9pm; 4 pesos.) **Combis,** including **Transportes de Pasaje,** go to San Cristóbal from the area around Mercado Andador San Roque. Services and costs are similar. (1¼hr., every 10min., 35 pesos.)

Taxis: Within the city 20-30 pesos. To the bus station 30 pesos.

Car Rental: Hertz, Blvr. Domínguez 1195 (☎617 7777). Child seats available. Open M-Sa 8am-10pm, Su 9am-5pm. Airport location (☎153 6074) open daily 7am-6pm.

🚩 🛈 ORIENTATION AND PRACTICAL INFORMATION

Tuxtla lies 85km west of San Cristóbal and 293km south of Villahermosa. *Avenidas* run east-west and *calles* north-south. The city's central axis, intersecting the *zócalo*, is formed by **Avenida Central** (which becomes Blvr. Ángel Albino Corzo to the east and Blvr. Belisario Domínguez to the west) and **Calle Central.** Streets are numbered according to their distance from the central axis. For example, Calle 2 Sur Ote. lies south of Av. Central and two blocks east of Calle Central. Addresses on Av. Central are numbered according to how many blocks from the *centro* they lie (Av. Central Pte. No. 554 is about 5 blocks west of center). **Bulevar Domínguez** is dotted with American megastores, chains, shopping malls (Plaza Crystal and Plaza Galería), and many of the city's more expensive restaurants.

Tourist Office: The most central location is in front of the Palacio Municipal in the **Sec. de Desarollo Económico** booth. Open M-Sa 9am-4pm. **Dirección Municipal de Turismo,** Av. Central Pte. 554 (☎613 2099 or 7904, ext. 111, 112). Open M-F 8am-8pm, Sa 8am-1pm. **State Tourism Office,** Blvr. Domínguez 950, about 15 blocks west of the *zócalo.* The booth on the *zócalo* has maps and brochures. Open M-Sa 9am-2pm.

Banks: The area around the *zócalo* and Av. Central has plenty of banks and **ATMs. Bancomer,** on Av. Central at the corner with Ca. 2a Pte. **exchanges currency** and has **24hr. ATM.** Open M-F 8:30am-4pm. **Scotiabank,** on Av. Central at the corner with Calle 4a Ote. Open M-F 9am-5pm.

Emergency: ☎060.

Police: Protección Civil, Ca. 3a Ote N. 414 (☎615 3646). Another office on Av. 3a Sur. **Policía de Seguridad Pública** (☎604 1130 or 614 0435). **Tourist police:** tourist assistance (☎800 903 9200).

Red Cross: Av. 5a Nte. Pte. 1480 (☎612 0096 or 0492).

24hr. Pharmacy: Farmacia del Ahorro, at Av. Central and Calle Central (☎602 6677).

Medical Services: Sanatorio Rojas, 2 Av. Sur Pte. 1487 (☎602 5138 or 5004). **IMSS** (☎612 3143 or 3155), on Calzada Emilio Rabasa.

Laundry: Lavandería Automatica, at the corner of Av. 5 Nte and Ca. 2 Ote., offers same-day service at reasonable rates. 12 pesos per kg. Open M-F 8am-8pm, Sa 8am-5pm.

Fax Office: Telecomm (☎613 6547; fax 612 4296), on Av. 1 Nte. at Ca. 2 Ote., next to the post office. Open M-F 8am-7:30pm, Sa 9am-3pm.

Internet Access: Internet cafes cluster on Calle Central past Av. 4 Nte. and on Av. Central east of the *zócalo.* **ProbiNet,** Av. Central Ote. 551 (☎714 7745). Fast connection and A/C. 10 pesos per hr. Open daily 8:30am-11pm.

Post Office: (☎612 0416), on Av. 1 Nte. at 2 Ote., on the northeast corner of the *zócalo,* in the corridor to the right of the Palacio Municipal. **Mexpost** inside. Open M-F 8:30am-4pm, Sa 9am-1pm. **Postal Code:** 29000.

ACCOMMODATIONS

There are not enough backpackers in Tuxtla to support the hostel industry, but there are plenty of reasonable, uninspired hotels, especially near the *mercado* around **Av. 5 Sur** and just northeast of the *zócalo.* However, bathing in these places may be a lukewarm experience at best, as the hot water is less than reliable.

Hotel Casablanca, Av. 2a Nte. Ote. 251 (☎611 0142 or 0305), a block from the Palacio Municipal. The best of the bunch in Tuxtla. Clean rooms, gardens, and sitting areas. Rooms have no working outlets and guests may have to request hot water at reception. Free purified water. Reception 24hr. Check-out 1pm. Singles from 154 pesos; doubles from 214 pesos, with A/C and TV 409 pesos; triples 291/467 pesos. Cash only. ❷

Hotel del Pasaje, Av. 5 Sur Pte. 140 (☎612 1550), half a block west of Calle Central. Though a little out of the way, this large hotel has quiet rooms that include private bath, fan, and purified water. Singles 120 pesos, with A/C 165 pesos; doubles with A/C and TV 190 pesos; triples 220 pesos. V. ❶

Hotel Plaza Chiapas, Av. 2a Nte. Ote. 299 (☎613 8365), 1 block east of Palacio Municipal. Basic rooms are dark but clean. Purified water and morning coffee included. Singles 180 pesos; doubles with fan 210 pesos; triples 300 pesos. Cash only. ❷

Villas Deportivas Juvenil, Blvr. Corzo 1800 (☎612 1201), 3km east of the *zócalo*. From any stop on Av. Central, catch an eastbound *combi* and get off at "Índejech" (EEN-deh-hetch). Huge community sports center with dorm-style rooms. Institutional and deserted, but clean and cheap. Bring your own sheets or sleeping bag. Cafeteria open M-F 7am-9pm, Sa 7am-3pm. Breakfast 17 pesos. Lunch and dinner 25 pesos each. Dorms 50 pesos. Cash only. ❶

⬛ FOOD

Uncorrupted by foreign travelers, Tuxtla Gutiérrez is a good place to get to know the region's earthy and delicious cuisine. *Carnes* come prepared in *pepitas de calabaza* (squash seeds) or *hierba santa* (holy herbs). *Tamales* in Tuxtla come with every filling imaginable for only 5-8 pesos. For the adventurous, *nucús* (ants) are plentiful at the start of the rainy season. Tuxtla's bustling **Mercado Díaz Orden,** on Calle Central between Av. 3 and 4 Sur, has food and trinket stands. (Open daily 6am-6pm.) **Mercado Andador San Roque,** Calle 4 Ote. between Av. 3 and 4 Sur, has the best straw hats in town, oodles of wicker, and several cheap eateries. (Open daily 7am-4pm.) There is also a supermarket, **Chedraui's,** on Blvr. Corzo, on the left just past the military base. Take an eastbound "Ruta 1" *combi* from a block west of the *zócalo* on Av. Central.

⬛ Las Pichanchas, Av. Central Ote. 837 (☎612 5351), between Calles 8 and 9 Ote. One of the best for Chiapan food. Waiters ring bells for orders of *pumpo,* the house drink. *Marimba* music and *ballet folklórico* (9, 10pm) complement the decor. Scrumptious *tamales* (2 for 26 pesos), *carne salada con pepita de calabaza* (salted meat with pumpkin seeds; 65 pesos), and *tascalate* (traditional chocolate drink; 12 pesos). 70-peso min. after 8pm. Open daily noon-midnight. AmEx/MC/V. ❸

Restaurante Imperial, Calle Central Nte. 263 (☎612 0648), 1 block from the *zócalo*. A popular local favorite. Excellent breakfasts (24 pesos), *antojitos* (24-28 pesos), and *comida corrida* (36 pesos). Open daily 8am-6pm. Cash only. ❷

Naturalissimo, Calle 6 Pte. 124 (☎614 5343), half a block north of Av. Central. Another location on Av. Central between Calle 4a and 5a Ote. The famous health-food chain has the only vegetarian options in town with meatless tacos (15-28 pesos), delicious *licuados* (32 pesos), and vegetarian *comida corrida* (68 pesos). Delivery available. Open M-Sa 7am-10:30pm, Su 8am-10:30pm. Cash only. ❸

Las Canteras, Av. 2a Nte. Pte. 148-A (☎611 4310). Well-known for authentic Chiapan food without all the flash. Breakfasts 29-35 pesos. *Comida corrida* 48 pesos. Entrees 25-65 pesos. Open M-Sa 7am-9pm, Su 8am-6pm. Cash only. ❸

⬛ SIGHTS

More than 1200 animals live at the **Miguel Álvarez del Toro Zoo (ZOOMAT).** Animals, children, and refreshment stands roam freely. From Calle 1 Ote., between Av. 6 and 7 Sur, take the R60 bus; 20min., every 30min., 4 pesos. (Open Tu-Su 8:30-4:30pm. Non-nationals 20 pesos, students 10 pesos. Guided tours in Spanish 20 pesos, in English 40 pesos.)

Many of Tuxtla's attractions are located in **Parque Madero,** in the northeast part of town at Ca. 6a Ote. and Av. 5 Nte. In the middle of the park is **Teatro de la**

Ciudad Emilio Rabasa. To the north of the theater is a children's amusement park, **Conviviencia Infantil,** with games, playgrounds, and a mini-train. (Open Tu-Su 8am-8pm.) Down the paved walkway lined with fountains and busts of famous Mexicans is **Museo Regional de Chiapas,** which displays regional archaeological finds along with Olmec and Mayan artifacts and history. (Open Tu-Su 9am-4pm. 37 pesos.) To the left is the new **Museo de Paleontología,** which has a small collection of regional fossils and a display of unique Chiapan amber. (Open Tu-F 10am-5pm, Sa-Su 11am-5pm. 15 pesos.) Down the concourse on the left you'll find the **Jardín Botánico Dr. Faustino Miranda,** a miniature Chiapan jungle. (Open Tu-Su 9am-6pm. Free.) The **Museo Botánico** is right across from the garden. To reach Parque Madero, walk or take a R3 or R26 *combi* from Av. 5a Nte; 4 pesos.

CHIAPA DE CORZO   ☎ 961

Originally settled by the Zoques in 1000 BC because of its location at the crossing of two rivers, Chiapa de Corzo (pop. 59,000) is a booming tourist stopover, largely for the same reason. The town's main attraction is its proximity to the towering El Cañón del Sumidero, an impressive natural wonder and nationwide landmark. It has been said that the Zoques pitched themselves from the limestone cliffs rather than be conquered by the Spaniards.

 TRANSPORTATION. **Buses** and **minibuses** from Tuxtla Gutiérrez are the only direct means of transportation to Chiapa de Corzo and stop on the north side of the *parque central.* Return buses leave from the same drop-off point (every 5min., 30min., 9 pesos). To get to **San Cristóbal,** take one of the "Tuxtla-bound" buses from the park to Highway 190, the main road (5 pesos), and wait for a San Cristóbal bus at the gas station (32-35 pesos).

 ORIENTATION AND PRACTICAL INFORMATION. Located 15km east of Tuxtla Gutiérrez and 68km west of San Cristóbal on the bank of the **Río Grijalva,** Chiapa del Corzo is small and easily navigable, especially given that most services are located around the *parque central,* with its distinctive Moorish fountain.

The **tourist office** is at No. 1 Av. Ruiz, just off the *parque central* (☎ 616 1013. Open M-F 8am-4pm.) **Bancomer,** on the east side of the park, **exchanges currency** and has a **24hr. ATM** (open M-F 8:30am-4pm), as does **Banamex** on the west side (open M-F 9am-4pm). Other services include: **emergency** ☎ 060; **police** (☎ 616 0076, ext. 2) in the municipal building on the northeastern corner of the *parque;* **Red Cross,** on the main highway (☎ 616 1900); **Súper Farmacias Esquivar,** Av. Grajales 2 at Chiapaneca (☎ 611 2525; open daily 7am-11pm); **fax** office at **Los Portales,** on the east side of the park (☎ 600 6421); **Internet** access at **White,** Calle 5 de Febrero 117, on the west side of the park (☎ 616 1551; 6 pesos per hr.; open daily 10am-1am); and the **post office,** on the north side of the park (open M-F 8am-3pm). **Postal Code:** 29000.

 ACCOMMODATIONS AND FOOD. Chiapa's accommodations are, on the whole, not budget-friendly. The upscale **Los Ángeles ❹,** Av. Grajales 2 on the southeastern corner of the park, is popular with family groups and has very clean rooms with cable TV and a good **restaurant** downstairs. The hotel also offers parking and purified water. Book ahead July-Aug. (☎ 616 0048. Reception 24hr. Doubles 250 pesos, with A/C 300 pesos; triples 280/320 pesos; quads 300/340 pesos; quints 310/360 pesos. Cash only.) Just up the block is the sparkling **Posada Real ❺,** Av. Grajales 192, where spotless rooms come with A/C, stationery, cable TV, washcloths, and bottled water. Book two weeks ahead July-Aug. (☎616 1015. Singles 200 pesos, with A/C 300 pesos; doubles 300/400 pesos. Cash only.)

Restaurante Charita ❷, on the east side of the *parque central*, serves typical Mexican fare for 30-35 pesos, as well as some interesting *licuados* (15 pesos), including alfalfa and cactus. (☎616 0417. Open daily 7am-10pm. Cash only.) **Jardínes de Chiapa ❸**, Av. Madero 395, serves authentic Chiapan food for around 45 pesos, as well as standard Mexican food for 25-89 pesos. (☎616 0198. Open daily 9am-7:30pm. AmEx/MC/V.) Cheap *comedores* are located in the **mercado municipal,** at Calle Mexicanidad and Av. López, across from the Templo de Santo Domingo. A **Mini Súper Chiapas** is on the north side of the park. (☎616 0041. Open M-Sa 8am-8:30pm, Su 8am-3pm.)

◐ **SIGHTS.** Far and away, the main tourist draw of the town is **Parque Nacional Cañón del Sumidero.** A *lancha* journey through the canyon begins with views of cornfields, but shortly after the Belisario Domínguez bridge, the hills leap to form near-vertical cliffs, rising over 1.2km above the water. Protected as a natural park, the steep walls are home to troops of monkeys, hummingbirds, and falcons, while the murky waters harbor crocodiles and turtles. Along the river lie several caves and waterfalls. The park's most famous waterfall is **Árbol de Navidad,** which dashes over a series of moss-covered rock formations in the shape of a pine tree before disintegrating into a fine mist that envelops passing boats. Past the waterfall is the pricey **Parque Ecoturístico Cañón del Sumidero,** which lures tourists with a pool, zoo, walking path, and restaurant. The 200m hydroelectric dam **Netzahualcóyotl** marks El Sumidero's northernmost extremity; along with three other dams on Río Grijalva, it provides 25% of Mexico's electricity. When the *indígenas* of Chiapas were defeated by Cortés in 1528, they threw themselves from these cliffs rather than be captured. These days, people who are finished with sodas and snacks heroically throw their detritus in the water—in the rainy season, the thick layers of trash in the river make it practically unnavigable. (The **embarcadero,** where you can hire a *lancha* to reach El Cañón del Sumidero, is two blocks south of the park on 5 de Febrero. From the bus stop, walk across the park toward the arched walkways and take the street downhill on your right. *Lancha* tours leave as they fill from the *embarcadero;* 2hr., 7am-4pm, 12-person min., 120 pesos. Round-trip boats plus Parque Ecoturístico entrance 290 pesos, children 210 pesos.)

SAN CRISTÓBAL DE LAS CASAS ☎967

Most Mexican cities pack their charm into a pedestrian walkway lined with museums and cafes, surrounded by diesel-burning trucks with loud horns threatening the cobblestoned peace. San Cristóbal (pop. 142,000), on the other hand, is wonderful through and through, filled with friendly locals and top-notch dining, and surrounded by a ring of lush green mountains. Founded in 1528, the city was named for its mythical patron saint, San Cristóbal, and Bartolomé de las Casas (1484-1566), a crusader for indigenous rights. It sits in the midst of several indigenous villages on the edge of the politically unstable Lacandón Rainforest. On January 1, 1994, the Zapatistas took over parts of the city and surrounding territory. Since 1998, they have become a symbol of rebellion for young travelers to Chiapas, though they have lost much of their local support. Despite the tensions, San Cristóbal's lovely buildings, Mayan markets, diverse eateries, and happening nightlife make for an inviting city.

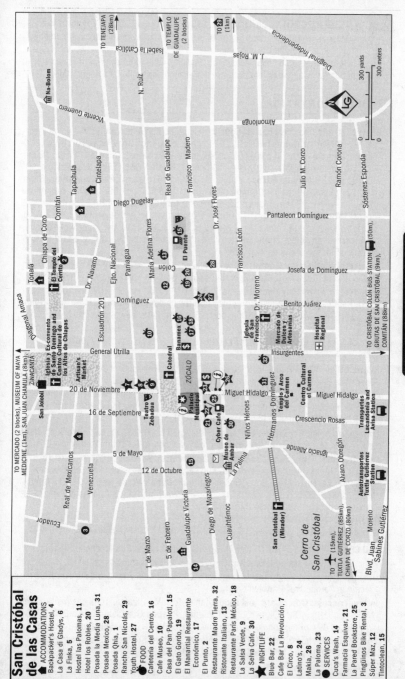

San Cristóbal de las Casas

▲ ACCOMMODATIONS
Backpacker's Hostel, 4
La Casa di Gladys, 6
La Finka, 5
Hostel las Palomas, 11
Hotel los Robles, 20
Posada la Media Luna, 31
Posada Mexico, 28
Posada Qhia, 1
Rancho San Nicolás, 29
Youth Hostel, 27

● FOOD
Cafeteria del Centro, 16
Cafe Museo, 10
Casa del Pan Papalotl, 15
El Gato Gordo, 19
El Manantial Restaurante
  Económico, 17
El Punto, 2
Restaurante Madre Tierra, 32
Ristorante Italiano, 13
Restaurante Paris México, 18
La Salsa Verde, 9
La Selva Cafe, 30

★ NIGHTLIFE
Blue Bar, 22
Cafe Bar La Revolución, 7
El Circo, 8
Latino's, 26
Makia, 23
La Paloma, 23

● SERVICES
Cuca's Wash, 14
Farmacia Esquívar, 21
La Pared Bookstore, 25
Pingüinos Bike Rental, 3
Súper Maz, 12
Tintoclean, 15

❗ INSURRECTION. On January 1, 1994, over 9000 *indígena* Zapatista insurgents took over parts of San Cristóbal in a 12-day siege. The situation is currently stable; tourists to the city and neighboring villages should not encounter problems as long as they carry their visas and passports. Those who come with political or human rights agendas, however, are unwelcome and could face deportation.

TRANSPORTATION

Buses: 1st- and 2nd-class **bus stations** are along the Pan-American Highway near Insurgentes. **Cristóbal Colón** (☎678 0291) sends buses to: **Campeche** (6:20pm, 330 pesos); **Cancún** (17hr., 4 per day 12:15-6:30pm, 630 pesos); **Comitán** (1½hr., 12 per day, 32 pesos); **Mérida** (6:20pm, 448 pesos); **Mexico City** (16hr., 6 per day 4:10-11:30pm, 788 pesos); **Oaxaca** (12hr.; 6, 10pm; 362 pesos); **Palenque** (5hr., 8 per day, 122 pesos); **Playa del Carmen** (4 per day 12:15-6:30pm, 608 pesos); **Tapachula** (7hr., 7 per day 7:30am-midnight, 206 pesos); **Tuxtla Gutiérrez** (2hr., 15 per day, 32 pesos); **Villahermosa** (11am, 11:05pm; 204 pesos). To get downtown, take a right (north) on Insurgentes and walk 7 blocks to the *zócalo*. From the other bus stations, walk east on any cross street and turn left onto Insurgentes. Or, call for a **taxi** (☎678 9340). 15 pesos to the *centro*.

Car Rental: Optima Car Rental, Diego de Mazariegos 39 (☎674 5409), 2 blocks south of the *zócalo*. Open M-Sa 9am-2pm and 4-7pm, Su 9am-1pm.

Bike Rental: 🐧 **Los Pingüinos,** Ecuador 4-B (☎678 0202; www.bikemexico.com/pinguinos). Rentals from 100 pesos per 4hr., 150 pesos per day. Also offers excellent tours (p. 596). Open M-Sa 10am-2:30pm and 3:30-7pm. Cash only.

PRACTICAL INFORMATION

Tourist Office: SECTUR (☎678 6570 or 1467), half a block south of the *zócalo* on Hidalgo. Open M-Sa 8am-9pm, Su 9am-2pm. **City office** (☎678 0665), at the northwestern end of the Palacio Municipal. Open daily 8am-9pm. Both have maps and helpful tour information.

Bank: Bancomer, Plaza 31 de Marzo 10 (☎678 1351), on the south side of the *zócalo*, has a **24hr. ATM.** Open M-F 8:30am-4pm, Sa 10am-3pm.

English-Language Bookstore: La Pared, Hidalgo 2 (☎678 6367), half a block south of the *zócalo*. Buys and sells new and used books. Open Tu-Su 10am-2pm and 4-8pm.

Laundromats: Tintoclean Tintorena y Lavandería, Guadalupe Victoria 20 (☎678 7231), 2 blocks west of the *zócalo*. Full-service: 12 pesos per kg. Self-service: 10 pesos per kg. Open M-Sa 9am-1pm and 4-8pm. **Cuca's Wash** (☎678 3139), Guadalupe Victoria 76, 6 blocks west of the *zócalo*. Wash and dry 30 pesos per 3kg. Fast same-day service. Open M-Sa 8am-8pm.

Emergency: ☎066.

Police: (☎678 0554), in the Palacio Municipal.

Red Cross: Allende 57 (☎678 0772), 3 blocks south of the Pan-American Highway.

24hr. Pharmacy: Farmacia Esquivar (☎678 6669), on Mazariegos at Rosas.

Hospital: Hospital Regional, Insurgentes 24 (☎678 0770), 4 blocks south of the *zócalo* in Parque Fray Bartolomé.

Internet Access: Cyber Cafe, just south of the *zócalo* on Hidalgo. 10 pesos per hr. Open M-Sa 9am-10pm, Su 10am-10pm. **El Puente,** Real de Guadalupe 55 (☎678 3723), 2½ blocks east of the *zócalo*. 6 pesos per hr. Free Wi-Fi. Open daily 8am-10:30pm.

Post Office: Allende 3 (☎678 0765), 2 blocks southwest of the *zócalo*. **Mexpost** inside. Open M-F 9am-7pm, Sa 9am-1pm. **Postal Code: 29200.**

ACCOMMODATIONS

An influx of backpackers has created a demand for cheap hotels and hostels, and San Cristóbal has responded with a plentiful supply near the *centro*. Camping is available outside town, but temperatures often drop below 10°C (50°F), making heavy blankets or a sleeping bag indispensable.

Posada Mexico (HI), Josefa Ortiz de Domínguez 12 (☎678 0014). A backpacker resort disguised as a hostel. Spacious gardens with views of the hills, well-appointed common areas with pool table and TV, a huge kitchen, and nightly activities ranging from karaoke to bonfires. Unlimited purified water. Friendly management can arrange any kind of tour. Breakfast included. Free Internet access. Laundry 16 pesos per kg. Check-out 11am. Hammock 40 pesos; high-season single-sex dorms 100 pesos; singles 140 pesos, with private bath 200 pesos; doubles 240/300 pesos. Cash only. ❶

Backpacker's Hostel, Real de Mexicanos 16 (☎674 0525; www.backpackershostel.com.mx). This lively hostel has "fire time" daily 8-11pm, in addition to camping space, communal kitchen, and daily tours to some of the area's attractions. Dorms 75-90 pesos; all-female dorm available. 10% discount with HI and ISIC. Cash only. ❶

Posada la Media Luna, Hermanos Domínguez 5 (☎631 5590 or 3355; www.hotel-lamedialuna.com.mx), between Hidalgo and Insurgentes. A clean, beautiful *posada* with courtyard and original artwork in every colorful room. Quieter than other hostels in the area, Media Luna attracts a slightly older crowd. All rooms have Wi-Fi and cable TV. Laundry 15 pesos per kg. Singles 250 pesos; doubles 350 pesos; triples 450 pesos; quads 550 pesos. Cash only. ❸

Posada Qhia, Tonala 5 (☎678 0594). Near the market in quiet Barrio del Cerrillo, Qhia offers unparalleled views of the nearby mountains as well as comfortable dorm beds around a well-tended garden. Lounge in the rooftop sitting area. Continental breakfast included. Dorms 60 pesos; singles 120 pesos; doubles 130 pesos. Cash only. ❶

La Finka, Av. Diego Dugelay 42, on the corner of Tapachula. Perhaps the cheapest spot in town, La Finka has dorm beds in cramped, messy, intimate rooms. The friendly staff serves homecooked, all-organic lunches (23 pesos) which draw outsiders as well as Finka regulars. Foosball table. Lockers available. Beds 30 pesos. Cash only. ❶

La Casa di Gladys, Cintelapa 6 at Dugelay (☎678 5775; casagladys@hotmail.com). This hostel has a communal kitchen, small TV area, and halls lined with plants, artwork, and cozy alcoves. Rooms have shared baths. Free taxi from bus station. Verify reservations. Dorms 80 pesos; singles 150 pesos; doubles 150-180 pesos; triples 220 pesos; quads 260 pesos. Cash only. ❶

Youth Hostel, Juárez 2 (☎678 7655; youthhostel2004@yahoo.com), between Madero and Flores. The name says it all. Cheap, clean, slightly dark rooms with spotless communal baths, kitchen, and common area with TV. Dorms 50-75 pesos; doubles 120 pesos. Cash only. ❶

Hostel las Palomas, Guadalupe Victoria 47 (☎674 7034; hostel_laspalomas@yahoo.com.mx). Travelers congregate at all hours in the central courtyard and cozy kitchen, and the new staff is anxious to display local knowledge. Big common room with cable TV. Free Internet and purified water. Dorms 75-80 pesos; private rooms 100 pesos, with bath 350 pesos. Cash only. ❶

Hotel los Robles, Madero 30 (☎678 0054), 2 blocks from the *zócalo*. Rooms come with private bath and TV. Singles 200 pesos; doubles 250 pesos; triples 300 pesos; quads 350 pesos. Discounts may be available for larger groups. Cash only. ❸

Rancho San Nicolás, Calz. Ranulfo Tovilla 47 (☎674 5887 or 678 0057), 1km east of town. Take a taxi (15 pesos) or follow León out of town, bear right at the split, and continue until the road reaches a dead end. The ranch is through the gate on your right. Beautiful, quiet spot on the edge of town, thick with pines. Kitchen, common room with fireplace, electricity, and hot water. If no one is around, ring the bell at the *hacienda* across the road. Camping 40 pesos; rooms with shared bath 50 pesos per person. ❶

◖ FOOD

San Cristóbal gets top marks for its international cuisine. Funky restaurants with a youthful feel keep their prices low and quality high to attract scores of backpackers. San Cristóbal has one of the largest **markets** in Mexico, at Utrilla and Domínguez, seven blocks north of the *zócalo* (open daily 6am-4pm), and a supermarket, **Súper Maz,** Real de Guadalupe 22, two blocks east of the *zócalo* (☎678 0256; open daily 8am-9:30pm).

▨ **Restaurante Madre Tierra,** Insurgentes 19 (☎678 4297), opposite Iglesia de San Francisco, 2½ blocks south of the *zócalo*. All-natural homemade food served in a courtyard or candlelit dining room. Exceptional bakery and bar upstairs. Breakfast 33-45 pesos. *Menú del día* 65 pesos. Open daily 8am-10pm. Bar open daily 8pm-3am. Cash only. ❸

▨ **El Punto,** Comitan 13 (☎678 7979), on El Cerrillo Plaza. Authentic thin-crust Italian pizza with elaborate toppings like curry, artichoke, and mushroom (90 pesos). With only 4 tables, it fills up after 8:30pm. Takeout available. Open daily 2-11pm. Cash only. ❸

El Gato Gordo, Madero 28 (☎678 0499), between Domínguez and Colón. Fresh, delicious food ideal for budget-style face-stuffing. Vegetarian *menú del día* 23 pesos. Sandwiches on homemade bread 25 pesos. Open M and W-Su 1-10:30pm. Cash only. ❷

Ristorante Italiano, Real de Guadalupe 40C (☎678 4946). The tortellini with mushrooms and sauce (81 pesos) may seem pricey, but it's worth it. Super-delicious pastas 50-65 pesos. Great brick-oven pizza 65-100 pesos. Open Tu-Su 2-11pm. MC/V. ❸

Casa del Pan Papalotl, Real de Guadalupe 55 (☎678 3723; www.casadelpan.com), inside El Puente language school, 2½ blocks from the *zócalo*. This cheerful restaurant overflows with fresh flowers and gets organic produce direct from local farmers. Breakfast 39 pesos. Lunch buffet (2-5pm, 60 pesos) is often serenaded by roving troubadors. Wi-Fi. Kitchen open 8am-10pm. 10% student discount with ID. Cash only. ❸

La Salsa Verde, 20 de Noviembre 7 (☎678 7280), 1 block north of the *zócalo*. Large taco diner stays busy into the night. *Tacos al pastor* 5 for 28 pesos. Open daily 8am-midnight. Cash only. ❶

Restaurante París Mexico, Madero 20, 1 block east of the *zócalo*. French or Mexican *menú del día* 55 pesos. Unholy "Francomex" *menú del día* 60 pesos. Terrace on 2nd fl. has great views of the surrounding mountains. Open daily 8am-1am. Cash only. ❸

Cafetería del Centro, Real de Guadalupe 7 and 15B (☎678 3922), near the *zócalo*. Simple food with great service in a no-frills atmosphere. Breakfast 28-47 pesos. *Comida corrida* 45-51 pesos. Open daily 7am-10pm. Cash only. ❸

El Manantial Restaurante Económico, Francisco Madero 14, half a block from the *zócalo*. Popular hole-in-the-wall restaurant with large portions. Classic *menú del día* (23 pesos) includes soup, starch, and main dish. Open daily 8am-6pm. Cash only. ❶

Cafe Museo, María Flores 10 (☎678 7876), between Utrilla and Domínguez. Coffee museum/garden/pastry shop all in one. Organic coffee 8-15 pesos. Live music every night 8pm. Open daily 9am-9:30pm. Cash only. ❶

La Selva Cafe, Rosas 9 (☎678 7243; www.laselvacafe.com.mx), at Cuauhtémoc. Coffee and pastry enthusiasts enjoy the jungle patio. Organic coffee and tea 12-28 pesos. Coffee beans 27 pesos per .25kg. Free Wi-Fi. Open daily 9am-11pm. Cash only. ❷

👁 SIGHTS

🏛 NA-BOLOM. San Cristóbal's most famous attraction is the "House of the Jaguar," a private home that turns into a live-action museum during the day. Guided tours explore the estate of Frans and Trudy Blum, whose name was misinterpreted as *bolom* (jaguar). The Blums worked among the dwindling *indígena* communities of the Lacandón Rainforest on the Guatemalan border from 1943 until Trudy's death in 1993. Today, international volunteers continue the Blums' work by conducting tours of their Neoclassical *hacienda* and library. The library's manuscripts focus on Mayan culture, rainforest ecology, and the plight of indigenous refugees. The small chapel (originally intended to be a Catholic seminary) serves as a gallery of religious art. Other rooms are devoted to archaeological finds from the nearby site of **Moxviquil** (mosh-VEE-queel), religious artifacts from the **Lacandón Rainforest,** and a selection of the 50,000 pictures Trudy took of the jungle and its inhabitants. Na-Bolom also rents rooms furnished by Frans and decorated by Trudy, complete with fireplace, mini-library, antique bath, and original black-and-white photos. *(Guerrero 33, in the northeastern section of the city at the end of Chiapa de Corzo. ☎678 1418; www.nabolom.org. Guided tours in Spanish 11:30am, in English and Spanish 4:30pm, followed by a 15min. film. Shop open daily 9am-2pm and 3-7pm. Library open M-F 10am-4pm. Dinners in the old dining room daily 7pm, 110 pesos. Make reservations 3hr. ahead. Rooms from 500 pesos for 2 people. Museum 35 pesos.)*

MUSEUM OF MAYA MEDICINE. Also called the **Centro de Desarrollo de la Medicina Maya (CEDEMM),** this museum features life-size models recreating Mayan healing methods, including strong-smelling herbs, hypnotic shaman prayers, and a display that explains the use of black spiders' teeth to treat inflammation of the testicles. The graphic video on Mayan midwifery is only for those with strong stomachs. *Ilol,* or medicine men, are on hand to dispense advice. *(Blanco 10, 1km north of the market. ☎/fax 678 5438. Open M-F 9am-6pm, Sa-Su 10am-4pm. 25 pesos.)*

ZÓCALO. Since its construction by Spanish settlers in the 16th century, San Cristóbal's *zócalo,* **Plaza 31 de Marzo,** has been the geographical and spiritual center of town. The **Palacio Municipal** stands on the west side of the plaza while the yellow **Catedral de San Cristóbal** dominates the northern side. Inside, the cathedral features a splendid wooden pulpit and chirping birds in the rafters. *(Cathedral open daily 7am-7pm.)*

MUSEO DEL AMBAR. This old monastery houses an exquisite collection of Chiapan amber, from pre-Hispanic jewelry to modern sculptures. An exhibit downstairs shows you how to identify genuine amber, an important skill in the markets of San Cristóbal. *(Plaza de la Merced, in the Ex-Convento de la Merced, at Cuauhtémoc and 12 de Octubre. ☎678 9716; www.museodelambar.com.mx. Open M-Sa 9am-2pm and 4-7pm, Su 9am-2pm. 20 pesos.)*

IGLESIA Y EX-CONVENTO DE SANTO DOMINGO. The most beautiful church in San Cristóbal, Santo Domingo was built by the Dominicans from 1547 to 1560 and enlarged to its present size in the 17th century. The elaborate if poorly maintained stone facade houses an inner sanctuary covered in gold leaf and dozens of portraits, most of which were painted anonymously in the 18th century. *(Open M-Sa 7am-7pm. Mass Su 7:30, 11am, 1, 7:30pm.)* Inside, the **Centro Cultural de los Altos de Chiapas** features an excellent multimedia exhibit in Spanish on the history of San Cristóbal and Chiapas, with colonial artifacts, photos, and *chiapaneo* textiles. *(Open Tu-Su 9am-6pm. 37 pesos.)* The *Ex-Convento*'s grounds make up the **artisan market.** *(On Utrilla beyond the Iglesia de la Caridad.)*

VISTA. Two hilltop churches overlook San Cristóbal. **El Templo del Cerrito San Cristóbal,** on the west side of town, is accessible by a set of stairs at the intersection of Allende and Domínguez. **El Templo de Guadalupe,** to the east, can be reached by walking west on Real de Guadalupe. Both areas can become deserted at night and El Templo de Guadalupe is closed at night.

TOURS. One of San Cristóbal's most prized recreational activities is **horseback riding.** Guided rides to San Juan Chamula leave from Cafetería del Centro *(Real de Guadalupe 7; ☎967 100 9611; 4hr.; daily 9am, 1pm; 100 pesos)*, and La Casa di Gladys *(Cintelapa 6; ☎678 5775; daily 9am, 2pm; 100 pesos)*. **Rancho San Nicolás** rents horses (p. 593). For a chance to see the villages in the surrounding hills, take a two-wheeled tour with **Los Pinguinos** (p. 592). Tours pass through the remarkable landscape, including natural limestone bridges and villages with no road access. The basic tours leave daily 8:15am, returning around 1pm, and cover 20-40km on rough dirt paths. *(From 300 pesos, 12-person max. Multi-day tours also available. Book 24hr. in advance.)* Walking tours to indigenous villages are also a great way to delve a little deeper into traditional practices and beliefs. **Alex y Raul** *(☎678 3741 or 9141; alexyraultours@yahoo.com.mx)* offer a popular half-day tour. *(4½hr. Departs from the San Cristóbal Cathedral daily 9:30am. 125 pesos.)*

♪ 🌺 ENTERTAINMENT AND FESTIVALS

Both party animals and mellower folks will enjoy a night out on this town. For those with aching feet or technophobia, **Cinema el Puente,** Real de Guadalupe 55 (☎678 3723), three blocks from the *zócalo* inside Centro Cultural el Puente, screens American and Mexican films and documentaries (25 pesos; 6 and 8pm daily). During high season, the park hosts dances and live *marimba* music (Th 6pm-midnight).

A schedule of events is posted at the Centro Cultural el Carmen, three blocks south of the *zócalo* on Hidalgo, on the left side of the Arco del Carmen. An annual film festival is held in the **Sala de Bellas Artes Alberto Domínguez** (July 28-Aug. 9; 20 pesos). On Easter Sunday, *Semana Santa* gives way to the week-long **Feria de la Primavera y de la Paz.** Before riotous revelry begins, a local beauty queen is selected to preside over the festivities, which include concerts, dances, bullfights, cockfights, and baseball games. During the **Fiesta de San Cristóbal** (July 16-25), the city's saint is vigorously celebrated—particularly by the city's taxi drivers, who claim San Cristóbal as their patron saint—with religious ceremonies, feasts, processions, concerts, and a staggering number of fireworks. In one of the more interesting traditions of the *fiesta*, a procession of cars, trucks, and *combis* from all over Chiapas crawl up the road to Cerro San Cristóbal. At the top, drivers pop their hoods and open their doors so that the engine and controls can be blessed with holy water by a Catholic priest on behalf of San Cristóbal, patron saint of journeys, in hopes of avoiding accidents for another year on the perilous mountain roads.

⌐ SHOPPING

San Cristóbal is a financial crossroads for the indigenous peoples of the Chiapan highlands. The daily **market** overflows with fruit, vegetables, and assorted cheap goods. For souvenirs and jewelry, look to the market around **Iglesia y Ex-Convento de Santo Domingo** (open daily 8am-5pm) or the **Mercado de Artesanías y Dulces** (open daily 8am-7pm), on Insurgentes across from Madre Tierra. **Utrilla** and **Real de Guadalupe,** the two streets radiating from the northeastern corner of the *zócalo*, are dotted with colorful shops that sell amber and traditional attire. Tucked into the

Ex-Convento is **San Jolobil,** a cooperative "House of Weaving" made up of 800 weavers from Tzotzil and Tzeltal villages in the *chiapaneco* highlands, whose objective is to preserve and revitalize ancestral weaving techniques. Most top-quality *huipiles* cost more than your flight home, but San Jolobil is a good place to admire them. (☎/fax 678 2646. Open M-Sa 9am-2pm and 4-7pm. AmEx/MC/V.)

NIGHTLIFE

BARS

Cafe Bar la Revolución, on 20 de Noviembre, 2 blocks from the *zócalo*. This hopping spot has politically themed decor and live music. Beer 18 pesos. Mixed drinks 35 pesos. Live music daily 7:30-9:30pm. Open daily 11am-11:30pm.

La Paloma, Hidalgo 3 (☎678 1547). A quiet, intimate bar with candles and wicker furniture. Beer 20 pesos. Mixed drinks 35 pesos—try a Mayan Sacrifice. Live music M-Tu and Th-Su 9:30-10:30pm. Open daily 8am-midnight.

Latino's, Madero 23 (☎678 9927; latinos@sancristobal.com.mx), at Juárez. "Bar-club-restaurant" with food, 25-peso beers, and live music after 10:30pm. Cover 20 pesos. Open M-Sa 8pm-3am. MC/V.

CLUBS

Madre Tierra (p. 594). When the rest of the town goes home to sleep, the adventurous head to Madre Tierra. Live music (M-Sa after midnight) is as eclectic as the clientele. Beer 17 pesos. Happy hour 2-for-1 drinks 8-10pm. Open M-Sa 8pm-3am.

Blue Bar, Rosas 2 (☎678 2200), 1 block west and half a block south of the *zócalo*. Men get patted down by guards before entering this den of flashing lights and thumping beats. Live reggae 11:30pm and 1:30am. Cover Th-Sa 30 pesos. Open M-Sa 8pm-3am.

El Circo, on 20 de Noviembre 7, 1 block from the *zócalo*. A spirited crowd dances to a variety of music, from live salsa to 80s classics. Cover Th-Sa 25 pesos. Open M-Sa 8pm-3am.

Makia, Hidalgo 2 (☎678 2574), on the park. Young crowd sips drinks at candlelit tables and gets down to an eclectic mix of music under confetti lights. Beer 30 pesos. Mixed drinks 40 pesos. M-Th live music. Cover F-Sa 30 pesos. Open daily 5pm-3am.

DAYTRIPS FROM SAN CRISTÓBAL DE LAS CASAS

A host of indigenous villages lie within easy reach of San Cristóbal. Sunday morning is the best time to visit the markets of nearby villages, but you'll still have to compete with hordes of tour groups. All buses originate in San Cristóbal, so visiting more than one village in a single morning is difficult, though possible in the case of San Juan Chamula and Zinacantán. *Combis* leave from various stands in the vicinity of the market. Destination signs are rarely accurate; always ask drivers where they're going.

SAN JUAN CHAMULA. The town of San Juan Chamula ("the place of adobe houses" in Tzotzil; pop. 9000; elevation 2260m) is the largest and most touristed village near San Cristóbal. Home to 110 *parajes* (clusters of 15-20 families), it is known for its colors (black and blue), its *Carnaval*, and its unique indigenous-Catholic church. Chamulans expelled their last Catholic priest in 1867, and they are legendary for their resistance to the government's religious and secular authority—the last Catholic mass here was held in 1968. The bishop is allowed into the church only once a month to perform baptisms, and the government's medical clinic is used only after Mayan medicinal methods have failed. Villagers have great faith in the powers of local *ilol*, priests who function as medicine men. Before entering the lively church, which also functions as a hospital where both spirits and bodies are healed, you must obtain a permit (15 pesos) from the tourist office in the city hall in the *zócalo*. At the front of the church is a sculpture of St. John the Baptist, who, after the sun, is the second most powerful figure in Chamulan religion. Jesus Christ, who is believed never to have risen, resides in a coffin. Chamulans take their religion seriously, and any unfaithful residents who change religions (to increasingly popular Evangelical varieties, for example) are promptly expelled from the village. Over 38,000 people have been expelled since 1976.

> **! NO PICTURES, PLEASE.** The local Mayan practice a unique fusion of Catholicism and native religion. In this system of faith, it is commonly believed that cameras capture a piece of the spirit. While visiting these villages, do not take pictures in churches while devotees are present, and always ask before taking pictures of individuals; some may request a few pesos in return for a photo.

Multiple shrines in the residence of the current *mayordomo* (superintendant) honor each saint. Look for the leaf arches outside signaling the house's holy function. On Sundays, the mayor and town authorities line up in their white suits and red- and green-ribboned straw hats to listen to villagers' complaints and make rulings. The men in white wool vests who crowd around the mayor are the town's citizen policemen. Homes and chapels are generally not open to the public—join an organized tour for a peek into private Chamulan life.

The best time to visit Chamula is during **Carnaval,** the week before Ash Wednesday, a celebration that draws approximately 70,000 *indígenas* and 500 tourists each day of the festival. In addition to Chamula's *Carnaval*, the city celebrates the *fiestas* of **San Juan Bautista** (June 22-24), **San Sebastián** (Jan. 19-21), **San Mateo** (Sept. 21-22), and the **Virgen de Fátima** (Aug. 28). *(Combis to Chamula stop on Cárdenas, 1 block west and 1 block north of the market. 15min., every 15min. 5am-6pm, 7 pesos.)*

> **DRINK AWAY YOUR SINS.** When Coca-Cola first introduced its flagship beverage to the residents of San Juan Chamula, the drink's bubbly aftereffect was said to release a person's sins from the body. The beverage continues to be a staple in Chamulan religious practices.

SAN LORENZO ZINACANTÁN

Eight kilometers over the hill from Chamula lies the colorful community of Zinacantán (pop. 38,000), comprising a ceremonial center and its outlying hamlets. Village women wear ribbons in their braids and men flaunt dazzlingly red *chuj* (traditional vests). The village's flower industry has flourished of late, and Zinacantán has begun exporting its flowers internationally. The plastic-roofed structures that dot the hillsides are greenhouses. Removed from the religious tensions of Chamula, the *zinacantecas* hold mass on a regular basis. The village's handsome, whitewashed church dates from the 16th century and, along with the small white convent, is used for both Catholic and pre-Hispanic forms of worship. (Admission 10 pesos. Obtain a permit from the *caseta de turismo* in the *zócalo*.) As in Chamula, Jesus Christ is portrayed inside a coffin. Animal sculptures in the interior of the church attest to the pervasive presence of *indígena* religion, in which every family has its own animal soul. Festivals include

Fiesta de San Lorenzo (Aug. 1-19, peaking on Aug. 10), **Fiesta de San Sebastián** (Jan. 19-22), and *Semana Santa*. *(Combis to Zinacantán (20min., daily 6am-8pm, 12 pesos) leave from the lot on Edgar Robledo, across from the market.)*

HUÍTEPEC ECOLOGICAL RESERVE

The Huítepec Ecological Reserve, on the east face of the **Huítepec Volcano,** provides a chance to explore an evergreen cloud-forest ecosystem. Two trails wind around the park, which is home to over 100 species of birds and more than 300 species of plants. Those with medicinal properties or religious importance are marked by small signs. The shorter trail is an invigorating 2km hike that rises 240m. The longer 8km hike is led by a guide. For more information on the park and the tours offered, call or visit **ProNatura,** Pedro Moreno 1 at Benito Juárez, across from the Iglesia de San Francisco. *(The Reserve lies just off the road to Chamula, 3.5km from San Cristóbal, and can be reached by any combi headed in that direction. Ask the driver to let you off at the "Reserva Huítepec"; 10min., every 15min., 7 pesos. To return to San Cristóbal, go 500m downhill to a combi stop. ProNatura ☎ 678 0374 or 7698. Reserve open Tu-Su 9am-3pm. 20 pesos. Birdwatching tour 100 pesos. Plant-specific tours 40 pesos Tu-Su 7am.)*

ROMERILLO AND TENEJAPA

Marked by 32 blue-and-green wooden crosses, the **Cementerio de Romerillo,** on the way to Tenejapa (pop. 5000), sits atop the Chiapan highlands. This local cemetery comes alive during **Día de los Muertos** (Nov. 2). The planks on each mound of dirt are pieces of a relative's bed or door, and old shoes are scattered around for the spirits' use. The town of Tenejapa, 28km from San Cristóbal, is surrounded by mountains, canyons, and corn fields. Crosses representing the tree of life stand at crossroads, near adobe homes, and in front of **La Iglesia de San Ildefonso.** Women's *huipiles* (traditional Mayan textiles) are replete with traditional symbols, such as the sun, earth, frogs, flowers, and butterflies. Men wear black ponchos tied at the waist with a belt, red-and-white trousers, dark boots, and a purse worn diagonally across the chest. Religious and community leaders carry a staff of power and wear a long rosary necklace. Tenejapa's markets (open Th and Su mornings), the **Fiesta de San Alonzo** (Jan. 21), and the **Fiesta de Santiago** (July 25) attract crowds from near and far. *(Combis and taxis to Romerillo and Tenejapa leave from Utrilla 1 block west and 1 block north of the market. 45min., as they fill, 4 person min., 20 pesos.)*

GRUTAS DE SAN CRISTÓBAL

From the small entrance at the base of a steep, wooded hillside, a narrow fissure opens into a chain of caves that leads almost 3km into the heart of the rock. A modern concrete walkway, up to 10m above the cave floor at points, penetrates some 750m into the caverns. The dimly lit caves harbor a spectacular array of stalactites, stalagmites, columns, rushing streams, and formations said to resemble certain figures. Look out for Santa Claus. The park is relatively quiet and sweet-smelling, and a walking path and horse trails wind through the pine forest. Horses are available for rent across from the cave entrance (1 ride around the corral 10 pesos, 30min. rental 25 pesos, 1hr. 50 pesos, ride to San Cristóbal 120 pesos). The Grutas are a good place to get away from touristy San Cristóbal, though the requisite line of souvenir stands awaits you at the cave entrance. *Comedores* and *rosticerías* are also on site, but picnics are the best way to go here. There are numerous free barbecue pits for fires and outdoor cooking, but overnight camping is not permitted. *(Combis to the Grutas leave from Blvr. Sabines Gutiérrez No. 6, half a block to the right of the Cristóbal Colón station as you face it; every 10min., 8 pesos.* Camionetas *leave from the same spot; every 5-10min., 7 pesos. To return, hop on any* westbound *combi or* camioneta. *From the highway, the entrance is a 5min. walk through the park. Open daily 8am-5pm. 15 pesos. Vehicle entrance 10 pesos.)*

PALENQUE ☎916

In all of Mesoamerica, three sites are world-renowned for their expression of the beauty, power, and glory of the Mayan Classic period. Honduras has Copán, Guatemala has Tikal, and Mexico has Palenque. These impressive ruins straddle a magnificent 300m high natural *palenque* (palisade) in the foothills of the Chiapan highlands. Dense jungle meets the bases of Palenque's unique pyramids, and the sounds of birds, monkeys, and crashing waterfalls echo off the rolling hills. The town of Palenque (pop. 85,500) is not nearly as picturesque as the ruins, but it serves as an important crossroads for the thousands of travelers who come to visit the site, sample the waters of the famous *cascadas* of Agua Azul and Misol-Ha, make forays into the heart of the Lacandón jungle, and set off on excursions to Mayan sites in Guatemala.

▐ TRANSPORTATION

The ADO **bus station** and several local transportation hubs are all 5-8 blocks west of the *parque* on Juárez. To get to the *parque* from the ADO stations, turn right out of the station and follow Juárez to the left for six blocks. **ADO** (☎345 1344) runs first-class buses to: **Campeche** (6hr.; 8am, 9, 10pm; 226 pesos); **Cancún** (12hr., 8pm, 524 pesos); **Chetumal** (7½hr., 8pm, 302 pesos); **Mexico City** (12hr.; 6, 8, 9pm; 706 pesos); **Oaxaca** (13hr., 5:30pm, 524 pesos); **Playa del Carmen** (11hr., 8pm, 484 pesos); **Puebla** (10½hr., 7pm, 616 pesos); **Villahermosa** (2hr., 13 per day 7am-6:30pm, 94 pesos). **Cristóbal Colon**, out of the same station, runs buses to **San Cristóbal** (5hr., 6 per day 3am-11pm, 122 pesos), **Tapachula** (13hr., 8:45am, 334 pesos), and **Tuxtla Gutiérrez** (6½hr., 3am-11pm, 158 pesos). **Taxis** (☎345 0112) are 50 pesos to the ruins, El Panchán, and Mayabell, and 20 pesos within town. White van **combis** troll the main drag near the bus station and run between the town and the ruins for 10 pesos.

▐▐ ORIENTATION AND PRACTICAL INFORMATION

Palenque is in the northeastern corner of Chiapas, 274km from Tuxtla Gutiérrez. *Avenidas* run east-west, perpendicular to the north-south *calles*. The ruins are 8km southwest of the city.

Tourist Office: In the Casa de las Artesanías, at Juárez and Abasolo. Well-stocked with Chiapas maps and a helpful staff. Open M-Sa 9am-9pm, Su 9am-1pm.

Currency Exchange: Bancomer, Juárez 40 (☎345 0198). Open for exchange M-F 8:30am-4pm, Sa 10am-3pm. **Banamex,** Juárez 62 (☎345 0117). Open M-F 9am-4pm. Both have **24hr. ATMs.**

Luggage Storage: At the ADO and many 2nd-class stations. 4 pesos per hr. Open 24hr.

Emergency: ☎066.

Police: (☎345 1844), on Independencia in the Palacio Municipal.

Pharmacy: Farmacia Central (☎345 0393), on Juárez near Independencia. Open daily 7:30am-10:30pm.

Medical Services: Centro de Salud y Hospital General (☎345 1433), on Juárez near the ADO bus station, at the west end of town.

Fax Office: Buho's (☎345 0195), near the tourist office on Juárez. Open daily 8am-9pm. Several other fax services cluster near the tourist office on Juárez.

Internet Access: Internet Escorpión (☎345 1787), on Juárez near Independencia. 7 pesos per hr. Open daily 7am-10pm.

Post Office: (☎345 0148), on Independencia at Bravo, north of the *parque*. Open M-F 9am-4pm. **Postal Code:** 29960.

ACCOMMODATIONS

Accommodations in Palenque come in two styles: *cabañas* set deep within the jungle near the ruins and standard hotel rooms in town. Those near the ruins are rustic and lack many services, but are cheaper and more fun. In town, budget hotels cluster on 20 de Noviembre between Juárez and the parque. Prices may double during the high season at all the hotels (*Semana Santa*, July-Aug., and winter).

El Panchán (www.elpanchan.com), 2km from the entrance of the ruins. This oasis in the lush jungle is legendary among backpackers. Set alongside a trickling stream, the rustic *cabañas* keep the water out, but lack mosquito nets and occasionally electricity. Several options are under the same ownership. **Chato's Cabañas and Jaguar ❷** offers *cabañas* and rooms with private bath. Singles 180 pesos; doubles 220 pesos; triples 240 pesos. At **Jungle Palace ❶**, you can camp, hang your hammock (40 pesos), or sleep in a *cabaña* with shared bath. Singles 80 pesos; doubles 100 pesos. Other El Panchan hostels, including **Rashiktas ❶** (☎916 100 6908; www.rakshita.com), offer similar sleeping setups at the same prices. Cash only. **Margarita and Ed's ❷** (☎341 0063; edcabanas@yahoo.com) is a slightly more upscale option with the same jungle fever. Well-appointed rooms and *cabañas* with private bath. Singles and 2-bed *cabañas* 150 pesos; doubles 160-250 pesos, with A/C 300 pesos; triples 250-270; quads 380 pesos; quints 400 pesos. Cash only.

Canek Youth Hostel, 20 de Noviembre 43 (☎345 0150). An average, institutional-looking hostel with 12 small rooms. All have fan, decent bath, towels and soap, and mountain views. Check-out 10am. Dorms 60 pesos; singles 150 pesos; doubles 180 pesos. Cash only. ❶

Posada Charito, 20 de Noviembre 15 (☎345 0121), between Independencia and Aba-solo, half a block west of the *parque*. Budget hotel has large, clean rooms in painfully bright colors. Somewhat clean private baths. No hot water. Reception 24hr. Check-out 2pm. Singles 60-100 pesos; doubles 120-150 pesos; triples 180-200 pesos; quads 240-250 pesos. Prices vary by season. Cash only. ❶

Hotel Lacandonia (☎345 0057), on Allende above the pizzeria. Spacious rooms with private baths and Chiapan decorations are more luxurious than those at other similarly priced accommodations. Rooms from 300 pesos. Cash only. ❺

Mayabell Trailer Park and Camping, Carretera Palenque-Ruinas km 6 (☎348 4271; www.mayabell.com.mx), 500m from the ruins. The grassy grounds and upscale restau-rant attract loads of daytrippers, while the incredible nighttime quiet leaves the sounds of monkeys and birds ringing in your ears. Hammock rental 15 pesos, space 40 pesos. Tent 40 pesos. Trailer space 150 pesos. Car parking 20 pesos. Treehouse 100 pesos. Rooms have fan and private bath. Singles 400 pesos; doubles 400 pesos; triples 450 pesos. Hammock and room deposit 150 pesos or ID. Cash only. ❸

FOOD

Restaurants in Palenque are generally quite similar, with the telltale overpriced tourist menu. For produce, head to the **market**, on Juárez, seven blocks northeast of the *zócalo* (open daily 6am-3pm). **Súper Sánchez** is also near the town's center on Juárez right after the split with 5 de Mayo. (Open M-Sa 7am-9pm, Su 7am-2pm.) When lodging somewhere near the ruins, stock up beforehand to avoid tourist price hikes on food.

Cafe Don Mucho's, part of El Panchán (p. 601). The best dining option in the El Panchán complex, Don Mucho's is as much a part of the Palenque experience as the ruins themselves. Huge, vegetarian-friendly entrees (65 pesos) include bread and salad. All pasta, bread, and pizza are made on-site and bottled beers (17 pesos) are always cold. Nightly live music and fire-dancing 9pm-midnight. Next-door Internet cafe 15 pesos per hr., open 10am-10pm. Open daily 7:15am-midnight. Cash only. ❸

Restaurante las Tinajas, 20 de Noviembre 41, at Abasolo. Another location across the street. Serves heaping platters to crowds of locals and tourists alike. Try the hearty *sopes* (fried corn pancakes topped with various meats; 30 pesos), or the *picada de frijoles*, its veg-etarian sibling. Breakfast specials 28-43 pesos. Open daily 7am-11pm. Cash only. ❷

Restaurante Maya (☎345 0042), on Independencia at Hidalgo. Known as the "most ancient restaurant in Palenque," it is only 2050 years younger than the ruins. Crisp white tablecloths and prompt waiters complement big portions of classic Mexican dishes. Breakfasts 37-40 pesos. *Antojitos* 34-59 pesos. Meat entrees 60-100 pesos. Open daily 7am-11pm. MC/V. ❸

Maia's Cafe-Bar Restaurante, at Juárez and Independencia. Popular for its prime loca-tion and good food. Chicken tacos minus the grease 38 pesos. *Comida corrida* in the morning 35-55 pesos. Open daily 7am-11:30pm. Cash only. ❸

Pizzeria Palenque, Juárez 168 (☎345 0332), near Allende. A backpacker-heavy pizza parlor. Individual pies with a range of Mexican toppings 61-70 pesos. Open daily 1-11pm. Cash only. ❹

THE ARCHAEOLOGICAL SITE OF PALENQUE

Despite the notoriety of Chichén Itzá, Palenque is the crown jewel of Mexican Mayan ruins. The spectacular hillside setting and unique astronomical lookouts make it a pleasant place to spend the afternoon beating the heat and enjoying the multi-hued jungle. The ancient city of Palenque began as a small farming village in 100 BC, and grew steadily throughout the pre-Classic Period. Around AD 600, the

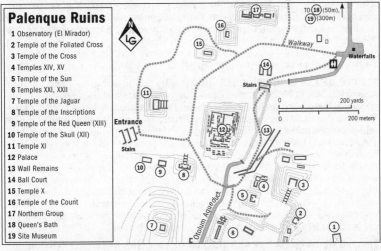

Palenque Ruins

1 Observatory (El Mirador)
2 Temple of the Foliated Cross
3 Temple of the Cross
4 Temples XIV, XV
5 Temple of the Sun
6 Temples XXI, XXII
7 Temple of the Jaguar
8 Temple of the Inscriptions
9 Temple of the Red Queen (XIII)
10 Temple of the Skull (XII)
11 Temple XI
12 Palace
13 Wall Remains
14 Ball Court
15 Temple X
16 Temple of the Count
17 Northern Group
18 Queen's Bath
19 Site Museum

city began to flourish, reaching its zenith over the next 200 years. An extensive trade network brought luxury goods such as obsidian, cinnabar, jadeite, and shells to the city. Palenque owes much of its success—modern and ancient—to the club-footed king Pacal ("Sun Shield" or "White Macaw" in Mayan), who inherited the throne from his mother, Zac-Kuk, in AD 615 at the age of 12. Pacal lived into his fifth *katun* (20-year period) and was succeeded in AD 683 by his elderly son Chan-Bahlum ("jaguar-serpent"). It was during the rule of these kings that most construction at Palenque took place. A century after Chan-Bahlum's death in AD 702, Palenque fell into oblivion, perhaps due to a siege at the hands of the rival Totonacs or another Mayan city. The museum suggests the intriguing possibility that Palenque was abandoned intentionally, because elders felt its time was over. The city was deserted around AD 850-900, and when Cortés arrived in the 16th century, he marched right through without noting its existence. Today, though they are impressive, the ruins of Palenque merely hint at the city's former majesty and only one quarter of the extensive sight is open to tourists.

The ruins of Palenque, 8km west of town, are accessible by *combis* (6am-6pm, 10 pesos) that depart from Hidalgo at Allende and from 5 de Mayo at Allende. One entrance is 300m from the site museum; the second is 2km farther. Walking to the ruins from Mayabell or El Panchan is a gradual 2km uphill walk, but there is a good sidewalk and the area is safe for tourists. Do not take the shortcuts to the back entrance from the campgrounds or the road, as they can be dangerous. *(Site and museum open daily 8am-4:30pm. The path from the main site to the museum, which passes the waterfalls, closes at 4pm. Bookstore and snack bar near museum open daily 9am-5pm. Park entrance 20 pesos. Ruins 45 pesos. Guided tours available at main entrance: tours in English up to 7 people 550 pesos, 7-14 people 700 pesos; tours in French or Italian up to 7 people 600 pesos; tours in Spanish up to 7 people 450 pesos, 7-14 people 550 pesos.)*

TOURS. Palenque is the best spot to organize a tour into the dense and ruin-rich Lacandón jungle area. Though the area is accessible on your own, it is one of the final strongholds of Zapatista rebels (p. 60), making travel a risky undertaking. Several tour operators make daytrips into the area to visit the famous Bonampak and Yaxchilan ruins, most of which include a boat ride along the Guatemala/Mexico border. Before signing on, make sure to clarify if meals, entrance fees, and road fees are included. **Viajes Misol-Ha,** Juárez 148, has several packages to the *cascadas* (100 pesos) and 12hr. trips to Yaxhilan/Bonampak from 500 pesos. (☎345 2271 or 1614; www.palenquemx.com/viajesmisolha.) **Servicios Turísticos de Palenque,** Av. Juárez and 5 de Mayo, offers similar packages (*cascadas* from 150 pesos; ruins from 550 pesos) as well as a van service to San Cristóbal (8hr.; 300 pesos) with stops at three *cascadas*. (☎345 2218 or 1340.)

TEMPLO DE LAS INSCRIPCIONES. Right of the main entrance is the tomb of **Alberto Ruz,** one of Mexico's most famous archaeologists and the discoverer of the temple, who insisted on being buried here. Past that tomb lies the Temple of the Inscriptions; its 69 steps represent King Pacal's 69 years of reign. Named for its tablets, which tell of the dynastic history of Palenque, the temple was the tomb of King Pacal and the first substantial burial place unearthed in the Americas. After finding six skeletons, Ruz dug into the interior crypt, removing over 400 tons of rubble by hand. There, he discovered the king's perfectly preserved sarcophagus, brimming with jade and other precious jewelry. The figure in the lower center of the tablet is Pacal, descending into the underworld with the *ceiba* tree directly over him. A hollow duct, designed to allow his spirit to exit the underworld and communicate with Palenque's priests, is on the right after the staircase. The temple is no longer open to the public and may not be climbed.

TEMPLO DE LA CALAVERA AND TEMPLO DE LA REINA ROJA. Excavations of the Temple of the Skull (XII) and the Temple of the Red Queen (XIII), constructed around the eighth century on top of older royal tombs, have unearthed burial chambers with human bone fragments and precious stones. The Temple of the Skull is so named due to a frightening stucco mask of a rabbit's skull on one of its north-facing pillars. Excavation of a sarcophagus in the Temple of the Red Queen revealed large amounts of cinnabar (a red mineral), jadeite, and malachite, and an interesting shell with a carved female figure. The discovery of a tiara and other jewelry suggests the importance of the figure, though her identity is not known.

EL PALACIO. In the center, across from the Temple of the Inscriptions, is the trapezoidal, postcard-perfect palace complex—a labyrinth of rooms, patios, and Palenque's signature four-story tower. The palace was most likely used for administrative and residential purposes, with royalty occupying the spacious quarters on the north side, and maids and guards in the cramped quarters on the south side. The large northeastern **Slaves' Courtyard** was probably used for administrative and political activities. The tower, unusual for the Maya, may have been used for astronomical observation. T-shaped ducts throughout cooled the air and doubled as representations of Ik, the god of breezes. The smaller galleries have carved panels and stucco masks. Visitors can climb down the staircase from the top of the platform to explore the dimly lit network of underground passageways, where it is likely that gubernatorial enthronement ceremonies took place. Don't miss the royal toilets, in the sunken courtyard below the tower. The four large rocks with small half-circle cutouts remain marked by years of royal pee.

PLAZA DEL SOL. The path between the palace and the Temple of Inscriptions crosses the recently reconstructed aqueduct before leading to Plaza of the Sun, or Crosses Group, which is usually crowded with tourists seeking good views. The Plaza, reconstructed and enhanced during the reign of Chan-Bahlum, is made up of the **Templo del Sol (Temple of the Sun),** the **Templo de la Cruz (Temple of the Cross),** **Temple of the Foliated Cross,** and the smaller **Temples XIV** and **XV.** The Temple of the Cross was named for a stucco relief of a cross discovered inside, which portrays a *ceiba* tree, the center of the Mayan universe. The outer layer of stucco has worn away, but the inner sanctum protects a large, sculpted tablet illustrating the enthronement of Chan-Bahlum, pictured to the right of the *ceiba* tree/cross, and reliefs on either side of the doors. The relief to the right represents God L, the lord of the underworld, furiously smoking a long ceremonial pipe and is one of the most recognized reliefs in all of Mayan history. Still partially buried, the Temple of the Foliated Cross lies across the Plaza from the Temple of the Sun. A carved interior panel also shows Chan-Bahlum being crowned, this time to the left of the Mayan foliated cross, which represents the corn plant. To the south of the Plaza, through the wall of trees, several unreconstructed temples surround the uncleared **Plaza Maudslay,** including **Temples XVII, XX, XXI,** and **XXII.** Downhill from Temple XIV, past the palace, lie the vestiges of a **ball court,** which was once equipped with wooden rings.

GRUPO NORTE. Across the path from the ball court is the **Templo del Conde** (Temple of the Count), named after the archaeologist Jean-Frédérick Waldeck (1766-1875), who referred to himself as a count and lived at the base of the Temple of the Cross. The temple contains three tombs and an inner sanctuary. The four other temples next to the Temple of the Count comprise the North Group. They were likely used for ceremonial purposes at first, but then gradually gave way to domestic residence. A small, steep path to the right of the North Group leads to the Queen's Bath and Montiepa.

QUEEN'S BATH AND MONTIEPA. After crossing the bridge, visitors will come across the Queen's Bath, a waterfall named for its once-exclusively female clientele. There are several small ruins (Grupos I and II, which were once residential areas) between the main plaza and back entrance, where the jungle has not been cleared. Swimming is no longer allowed. Palenque is full of paths leading to unrestored ruins and cascades. Bring bug repellent and a buddy if you want to explore.

⚐ DAYTRIP FROM PALENQUE

CASCADAS DE AGUA AZUL AND MISOL-HA

Tours leave from most hostels and hotels in town around 9am—you'll be picked up in a combi. 100-150 pesos gets you transportation and sometimes entrance fees (ask at the agency first). Brisas de Agua Azul buses, at Juárez and Av. Corregidora, 1 block east of the ADO station, will take you to the sites: Agua Azul (64km; 1¼hr.; 40 pesos plus 20-peso entrance fee; colectivo from crucero to entrance 4km, 10 pesos); Misol-Ha (21km; 20min.; 20 pesos plus 10-peso entrance fee; from crucero to entrance 1km).

 BEWARE. The access roads to both falls are notorious for tourist robberies and are generally not considered safe for walking.

These large *cascadas* (waterfalls) have seduced many a tourist. Agua Azul (Blue Water), 64km south of Palenque, is a breathtaking spectacle. The Río Yax-Há jumps down 500 individual falls, slipping in and out of rapids, whirlpools, and calmer pools. Currents are extremely dangerous, so swimming is only advisable in a few places. Obey the posted warning signs and ask an official before picking a swimming spot. *Comedores* and gift shops are located within a 20min. walk of the entrance. Rather than numerous small falls, Misol-Ha, 20km south of Palenque, is one giant drop. At its base is a pool for swimming. Bring a flashlight if you want to explore the cave behind the falls. Camping space and *cabañas* are available at all of the sites. After a hard rain, Agua Azul becomes *agua café* (brown water), and camping can be uncomfortable and even dangerous.

TAPACHULA   ☎962

Tapachula (pop. 300,000) bustles with sidewalk swap meets, stalls selling homemade root beer, and *marimba* music echoing into the night. Nearby mountains are home to the largest coffee growing communities in Chiapas and also provide the ideal backdrop for a range of activities for adventurous tourists looking to get off the beaten path. Largely uninterested in cultivating tourism, hot, noisy Tapachula serves more as a final stop in Mexico's southernmost reaches rather than a long-term hangout.

TRANSPORTATION. The **airport** is on the road to Puerto Madero, about 17km south of town. It's served by **Aeroméxico**, on Av. Central Ote. 4 (☎626 3282), and **Aviacsa**, Av. Central Sur 105 (☎626 0272). Tapachula's first-class **bus station** (☎626 2880 or 2881) is northwest of the *zócalo*, at Calle 17 Ote. and Av. 3 Nte. To get to the *zócalo* (15min. on foot; 20-peso taxi ride), take a left onto Calle. 17 Ote., walk two blocks, take a left on Av. Central, and continue south for six blocks. Take a right on Calle 5 Pte. and go three blocks west, to the northeast corner of the plaza. **Cristóbal Colón** heads to: **Cancún** (24hr., 928 pesos); **Chetumal** (18hr., 712 pesos); **Comitán** (5hr., 154 pesos); **Mexico City** (17hr., 5 per day 2:15-9:20pm, 822 pesos); **Oaxaca** (12hr., 7:15pm, 322 pesos); **Palenque** (10hr., 392 pesos); **San Cristóbal de las Casas** (7hr., 6 per day 7:30am-11:30pm, 206 pesos); **Tuxtla Gutiérrez** (7hr., 12 per day, 230 pesos). **Tica** runs buses to **Guatemala City** (5hr., 7am, 250 pesos), as does **Galgos Inter** (5hr.; 9:30am, 2:30pm; 250 pesos). The **RS station,** Calle 9 Pte. 63 (☎626 1161 or 3906), between Calles 14 and 16 Nte., sends buses to **Tuxtla Gutiérrez** (7½hr., 27 per day 4am-10pm, 102 pesos) via **Tonalá,** as well as to other destinations along the Chiapan coast.

ORIENTATION AND PRACTICAL INFORMATION. Tapachula is 16km from Talismán along the Guatemalan border and 303km west of Guatemala City. Tapachula's **zócalo** is on Calle 3 Pte. between Av. 6 and 8 Nte., northwest of the intersection of Av. and Calle Central. Avoid walking south of Calle 10 Pte. near the train tracks after dark; if you do happen to go, be sure and stay on Av. 4 Sur, the central avenue, and do not walk alone.

There is a **tourist information** module in the left side of the Casa de Cultura, next door to Iglesia de San Agustín. (☎626 1884 or 1485, ext. 116. Open M-F 8am-8pm, Sa 10am-2pm.) The **SECTUR** office, Av. 5 Nte. 5, between Calles Central Ote. and 1 Ote., also offers information. (☎628 7725. Open M-Sa 8am-8pm.) **Consulates** for some Central American countries are found throughout town: **Guatemala,** Av. 5 Nte. 5, 2nd fl., between Calle 1 and Calle Central Ote. (☎626 1252; open M-F 10am-3pm and 4pm-6pm); **El Salvador,** Av. 7 Sur 31, at Calle 2 Ote. (☎626 1253; open M-F 9am-4pm); **Honduras,** Av. 2 Sur 39, between Calle 2 and 4 Pte. (☎642 8150; open in summer M-F 10am-5pm, during the rest of the year M-F 9am-4pm). **Scotiabank,** on the east side of the *zócalo* at Calle 5 Nte., has a **24hr. ATM.** (☎626 1126. Open M-F 9am-5pm.) Other services include: **police,** Carretera Antiguo Aeropuerto km 2.5 (☎626 6538); **Red Cross** (☎626 1949), across from the post office; **Farmacias del Ahorro,** on Av. Central Pte at Av. 2 Nte. (☎628 8161; open 24hr.); **Hospital General** (☎628 1060), on the airport highway; **Internet** access at **Cyber Snoopy,** Av. 8 Nte. 7, near supermarket San Agustín (8 pesos per hr.; open daily 7am-11pm), and at **Cafe Tata,** Calle 17 Ote. 8, facing the bus station (10 pesos per hr.; open daily 10am-10pm); **fax** at **Telecomm,** next to the post office (☎/fax 626 1097; open M-F 8am-7:30pm, Sa 9am-5pm, Su 9am-1pm); and the **post office,** Calle 1 Ote. 32, between Av. 7 and 9 Nte. (☎626 2492; open M-F 8:30am-2:30pm, Sa 9am-1pm). **Postal Code:** 30700.

ACCOMMODATIONS AND FOOD. Budget rooms are a dime a dozen in Tapachula, especially near the market. Unfortunately, many rooms are as noisy, hot, and dirty as the rest of the city and few offer hot water. **Hostal del Ángel ❷,** Av.

8a Nte. 16, about half a block from the *zócalo*, is a pleasant hotel with clean, simple, spacious rooms surrounding a small, half-constructed courtyard with a cyber cafe in front. (☎625 0142. No hot water. Reception 8am-10pm. Singles 150 pesos, with TV and A/C 280 pesos; doubles 200/340 pesos. Cash only.) **Hotel Premier ❸,** Av. 8 Nte. 32, on the park, offers spotless rooms with fan, phone, cable TV, and purified water and an entertaining fish tank in the lobby. Laundry service and parking spaces are available. (☎626 4709. Singles 200 pesos, with A/C 300 pesos; doubles 250/350 pesos; each additional person 50 pesos. Cash only.) **Hotel Esperanza ❹,** Av. 17 Ote. 8 across from the bus station, is a clean but somewhat pricey hotel with A/C and cable TV that might be just the ticket if you are stuck overnight waiting for a bus. (☎625 9135. Singles 250 pesos; doubles 300 pesos; triples 350 pesos; suites 450 pesos; each additional person 80 pesos. Cash only.) **Hotel Casa Grande ❷,** 8 Av. Sur 28 on the corner of 2a. Pte., is a student-oriented hostel intended for long-term stays. The hostel has small but clean rooms, communal baths, a lovely garden, and a kitchen area. (☎626 6701. 100 pesos per person. Cash only.)

Taco and pastry stands fill the *zócalo* area. Several *comedores*, serving meals and *antojitos* for around 15-20 pesos, are located inside **Mercado Sebastian Escobar,** on 10 Av. Nte. between Calles 3 and 5 Pte. **San Agustín,** at the southwestern corner of the *zócalo*, has all your supermarket needs. (Open daily 6am-10pm.) Vegetarians will enjoy the fruit smoothies (26-32 pesos) and soy burgers (33 pesos) at **Naturalissimo ❸,** Av. Central Nte. 20, at Calle 1 Ote. (☎625 1727. *Comida corrida* 68 pesos. Open daily 7am-10pm. Cash only.) **Doña Leo ❸,** Portal Pérez C, in the archways on the southern side of the park, serves local specialties with salad and french fries for 50-70 pesos. *Caldos* (soups) cost 10-38 pesos. (☎626 4766. Open daily 7am-midnight. Cash only.)

> **CROSSING THE BORDER.** Before leaving Mexico, travelers must pay an **exit fee** of around US$20. If you flew into Mexico, this fee was included in your airfare. If you didn't fly in, go to any bank and ask to pay the DNE fee, and they will stamp your **immigration papers,** which you must then present, along with your **passport,** at the border immigration office. Citizens of the EU, Canada, and the US visiting Guatemala do not need a visa. Citizens from other countries need to get a visa from a Guatemalan consulate, such as the one in Tapachula. If you plan on staying longer than 90 days, check with an immigration office in Guatemala; otherwise, you might have to pay a fee when you leave. The easiest, safest, and most practical way to cross into Guatemala is to take a direct **bus** from Tapachula to Guatemala City. **Unión y Progreso** buses leave Tapachula from Calle 5 Pte., between Av. 12 and 14 Nte. (☎626 3379), for Talismán, passing by the ADO station on their way out of town (30min., every 15min., 10 pesos). They drop passengers a few blocks from the Mexican emigration office; follow the stream of *tricicleros* (passenger carts; 10 pesos). Present your passport and papers at the office and follow the crowd across the bridge. On the Guatemala side, get your passport stamped at a small blue building on the left. Beware of those who offer "help" getting your passport stamped, or anyone who asks for an entrance fee at this checkpoint—there is no fee to enter Guatemala here. It's best to change only a little bit of money with the men with credentials who are holding wads of *quetzales*. A **taxi** from Tapachula to Talismán can be obtained by calling the intercity taxi at ☎625 2030. If you choose to brave the crossing **on foot,** the closest crossing point from Tapachula is Talismán (16km), which has considerably less traffic than Ciudad Hidalgo (37km).

YUCATÁN PENINSULA

At the extreme southeastern edge of Mexico, tucked between the Gulf of Mexico and the Caribbean, imagination meets reality. Legends of Mayan civilizations, pirates, and Spanish *conquistadores* surround steamy jungles and centers of modern trade and sultry pleasures to create the ultimate travel experience.

The region's smallest state, colonial **Campeche** juxtaposes history and legend with modern petroleum plants. To the north, over two millennia of ruins in **Yucatán** give testament to savage pirate raids, brutal Spanish conquest, and ancient wars between Mayan dynasties. Colonial cathedrals in the Mérida metropolis and the Mayan pyramids of Chichén Itzá and Palenque embody the cultural roots of the *mestizo* nation. Finally, the Mayan Riviera on the Caribbean coast of sublime **Quintana Roo** exudes an unbridled hedonistic appeal. History takes a backseat to the allure of careless pleasures and natural treasures, including luscious jungles and crystalline waters along coral-rich barrier reefs. A unique bastion of debauchery, Cancún combines natural perfection with Vegas-like lawlessness, creating one of the world's top party destinations.

Small-town culture remains at the center of the Yucatán's appeal. Mayan is the primary local language, and indigenous religious practices persist as they have for centuries within the boundaries of Catholicism. Yucatec women still carry bowls of corn *masa* (dough) on their heads and wear lightweight, embroidered *huipiles* (traditional Mayan textiles), while modern Mayan men farm and fish for subsistence. Increasingly, however, the economic power of foreign tourism is leaving its mark on traditional Mexico, as young, educated workers flock to the cities to work in *gringo*-friendly restaurants, sell hammocks to beachside tourists, or act as archaeological guides. As indigenous culture and ancient Mayan villages become selling points for vacation packages, modern-day Mexico is caught between its proud cultural heritage and the increasing pressures of globalization.

HIGHLIGHTS OF THE YUCATÁN PENINSULA

GET WET in Tulum's eerily calm and crystal clear **underwater caverns** (p. 689).

STRIP DOWN with the young, beautiful, and very drunk on **Cancún's** world-famous beaches (p. 662).

GET FOOTLOOSE at one of **Mérida's** nightly streetside music festivals (p. 626).

TAKE THE STAIRS at the soaring pyramids of the ancient Mayan city of **Calakmul** for a views of uninterrupted jungle, now part of the extensive **Reserva de la Biosfera de Calakmul** (p. 617).

GET ACQUAINTED with the world's largest fish, the whale shark, off the coast of **Isla Holbox** (p. 666).

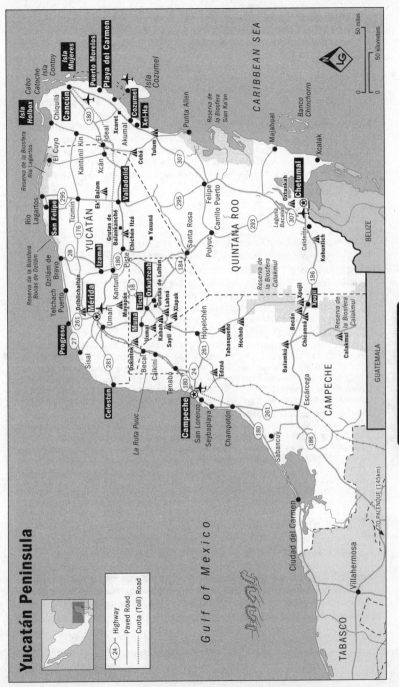

Yucatán Peninsula

24 — Highway
—— Paved Road
········· Cuota (Toll) Road

CAMPECHE

CAMPECHE ☎981

Campeche (pop. 220,000) is full of buried treasures. Around practically every corner in this peaceful city are beautiful colonial churches, foreboding stone embattlements, and hole-in-the-wall local watering holes. Old wood, stone, and stucco frame one of the peninsula's most scenic central parks, where shoe shiners and candy vendors find their daily share of shade. Pirates also thought the place to be full of treasure—their relentless raids on the commercial center prompted the construction of the city's most prominent features: a 17th-century cannon-lined wall and two hilltop fortresses. Campeche has fewer late-night parties than other Yucatán hot spots, but the city has a vitality that makes it worth a longer stay.

◗ TRANSPORTATION

Flights: Ingeniero Alberto Acuña Ongay (CPE; ☎816 5678), on Porfirio, 13km from the *centro.* Taxis to the *centro* 80 pesos. Served by **Aeroméxico** (☎816 6656).

Buses: Taxis from both bus stations to the *zócalo* 30 pesos. A confusing network of **local buses** (4.50 pesos) links Campeche's distant sectors to the old city. The market, where Gobernadores becomes the Circuito, is the hub for local routes. Buses can be flagged down along the Circuito, but do not regularly stop in the *centro.* Blue signs and crowds of people huddled in the shade mark the bus stops.

1st-class terminal: (☎981 9910), on Av. Central at Av. Colosio, 5km from the city center. **ADO** goes to: **Cancún** (7hr., 4 per day 7:15am-11:45pm, 346 pesos); **Chetumal** (7hr., noon, 262 pesos); **Ciudad del Carmen** (3hr., 15 per day, 144 pesos); **Mérida** (2½hr., every hr. 6:30am-7:30pm, 136 pesos); **Mexico City** (16hr.; 6:45, 10:10, 11:40pm; 892-1060 pesos); **Oaxaca** (M and F 9:55pm, 704 pesos); **Palenque** (6hr., 4 per day 12:30am-9:45pm, 226 pesos); **San Cristóbal de las Casas** (9-10hr., 9:45pm, 416 pesos); **Veracruz** (12hr.; 12:55, 8pm; 586-682 pesos); **Villahermosa** (7hr., 9 per day, 246-330 pesos); **Xpujil** (5hr., noon, 174 pesos).

2nd-class terminal: At Gobernadores and Chile, 500m from the old city. To reach the Parque Principal, catch a "Gobernadores" bus (4.50 pesos) across from the station and ask to be let off at the Baluarte de San Francisco. Turn right into the old city and walk 4 blocks on Calle 57 to the park. **ATS** and **Sur** go to: **Ciudad del Carmen** (3hr., 6 per day, 124 pesos); **Champotón** (every 30min., 30 pesos); **Mérida** (4hr., every 30min., 91 pesos); **Uxmal/Santa Elena** (3hr., 5 per day 6am-5pm, 71 pesos), stopping at every town on the way. **Unión de Transportistas de Camino Real** heads to destinations within the state of Campeche every 30min. Buses to **Edzná** (18 pesos), **Playa Seyba** (14 pesos), and **Sabancuy** (18 pesos) leave from the small building marked "Sur" in the rear of Parque Alameda, next to the market, across the Baluarte de San Francisco.

> **⚡TIP** **EASY RIDER.** Worried about booking that 18hr. bus trip? Worry no more. For peace of mind, all ADO tickets can be purchased online ahead of time at www.ticketbus.com.mx. For *de lujo* tickets, check out www.adogl.com.mx.

Taxis: (☎816 1113 or 6666). Taxis operate out of 4 stands: on Calle 8 at Calle 51, across from the post office; on Calle 55 at Circuito, near the market; and at both bus terminals. Local travel usually costs 25-30 pesos, or 30-35 pesos after dark.

Car Rental: Maya Rent-a-Car, Av. Ruiz Cortines 51 (☎816 0670), in the Hotel del Mar lobby. Open M-F 7am-6pm and 7-9pm.

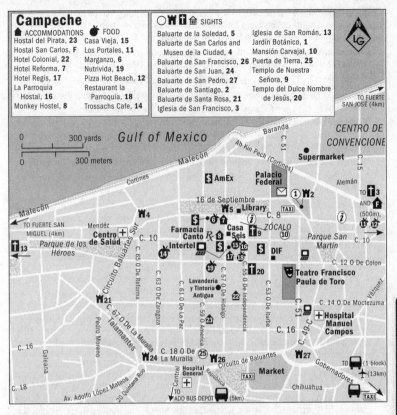

Campeche

ACCOMMODATIONS
Hostal del Pirata, **23**
Hostal San Carlos, **F**
Hotel Colonial, **22**
Hotel Reforma, **7**
Hotel Regis, **17**
La Parroquia
 Hostal, **16**
Monkey Hostel, **8**

FOOD
Casa Vieja, **15**
Los Portales, **11**
Marganzo, **6**
Nutrivida, **19**
Pizza Hot Beach, **12**
Restaurant la
 Parroquía, **18**
Trossachs Cafe, **14**

○ ♥ ¶ ⬤ 🏛 SIGHTS
Baluarte de la Soledad, **5**
Baluarte de San Carlos and
 Museo de la Ciudad, **4**
Baluarte de San Francisco, **26**
Baluarte de San Juan, **24**
Baluarte de San Pedro, **27**
Baluarte de Santiago, **2**
Baluarte de Santa Rosa, **21**
Iglesia de San Francisco, **3**

Iglesia de San Román, **13**
Jardín Botánico, **1**
Mansión Carvajal, **10**
Puerta de Tierra, **25**
Templo de Nuestra
 Señora, **9**
Templo del Dulce Nombre
 de Jesús, **20**

TO FUERTE SAN JOSÉ (4km)

ORIENTATION AND PRACTICAL INFORMATION

Campeche's historic *centro*, the old city, is based on an easy-to-follow numbered grid. North-south streets are odd numbered and increase to the west. East-west streets are even numbered and increase as they get farther from the coast. The *centro* is surrounded by a hexagonal series of roads known collectively as the **Circuito de Baluartes,** marked by seven lookout towers, or bulwarks. Within this area and the surrounding neighborhoods of San Francisco, Guadalupe, and San Ramón is some of Campeche's most beautiful colonial architecture. The *malecón* stretches along the Gulf of Mexico coastline.

Tourist Office: Calle 55 3 (☎811 3989 or 3990), between Calles 8 and 10, next to the cathedral. Houses a diorama of the old walled city and hands out pamphlets on area sights. Open daily 9am-9pm.

Banks: Santander Serfín (☎816 1055), on Calle 57 between Calles 10 and 12, just off the *zócalo.* Open M-F 9am-4pm, Sa 10am-2pm. **Banamex** (☎816 5252), at the corner of Calles 53 and 10. Open M-F 9am-4pm. Both have **24hr. ATMs.**

Luggage Storage: Guarda Plus, at the ADO station. 5-12 pesos per hr. Open 6am-10pm.

YUCATÁN PENINSULA

Bookstore: Calle 57 6 (☎816 1350), in the Casa de Cultura, across from the *zócalo*. A good selection of coffee table books in Spanish as well as maps and music from the area. Open M-F 9am-9pm, Sa 9am-2pm and 5-9pm.

Laundromat: Lavandería y Tintorería Antigua, Calle 57 28 (☎811 6900), between Calles 12 and 14. Same-day service 15 pesos per kg. Open M-Sa 8am-4pm.

Police: (☎812 7133), on Av. López Portillo at Prolongación Pedro Moreno Sascalum.

Red Cross: (☎815 2411), on Av. Las Palmas at Ah Kin Pech, 1km up the coast from the old city.

Pharmacy: Farmacia Canto, Av. López Mateos 365 (☎816 6204), at Lazareto. Another location (☎816 4100) at Calles 59 and 10, closer to the *zócalo*. **Free delivery** to nearby hotels. Open M-Sa 8am-10:30pm, Su 9am-9:30pm.

Medical Services: Hospital General (☎816 4233), on Central at Circuito Baluartes.

Fax Office: Telecomm (☎816 5210), in the Palacio Federal, opposite **Mexpost.** Open M-F 8:30am-7pm, Sa-Su 9am-1pm.

Internet Access: Calle 14 58 (☎816 5721), between Calles 49 and 51. A/C. 9 pesos per hr. Open daily 9am-11pm. **Intertel,** Calle 57 1 (☎816 7334), between Calles 10 and 12. 10 pesos per hr. Open M-Sa 9am-10pm, Su 9am-8pm.

Post Office: (☎816 2134), on 16 de Septiembre at Calle 53, in the Palacio Federal. Open M-F 8am-4pm, Sa 9am-1pm. **Mexpost** (☎811 1730) inside. **Postal Code:** 24001.

⌂ ACCOMMODATIONS

Campeche offers travelers ample opportunities to stay in colonial buildings, complete with soaring ceilings, old archways, and pastel facades, without going broke. Most quality budget accommodations are located in the *centro*. During July, August, and *Semana Santa*, hostels and hotels often fill up before sunset with Mexican and European tourists; call ahead for reservations.

Monkey Hostel (☎811 6605 or 800-CAMPECHE/2267-3243; www.hostal-campeche.com), at Calles 57 and 10, in the *zócalo*. The best location in town, Monkey Hostel has an unpretentious and friendly atmosphere that invites long visits and rooftop parties. Stay includes breakfast, kitchen access, linens, and purified water. Helpful staff can arrange tours to nearby sights. Bike rental 20 pesos per 2hr., each additional hr. 5 pesos. Laundry 40 pesos. Internet access 5 pesos per 30min. Reception 24hr. Check-out noon. Dorms 80 pesos; singles 180 pesos, with balcony 200 pesos. Cash only. ❶

Hostal del Pirata, Calle 59 47 (☎811 1757; piratehostel@hotmail.com), between Calles 14 and 16. This hostel sticks to its theme with pirate artifacts in every nook of the crumbling mansion. Quiet, fan-cooled dorms are spacious and sparkling clean. Outdoor kitchen and cafeteria with beer and soda for guest use. Bike rental 20 pesos per hr., 50 pesos per day. Dorms 95 pesos; partitioned doubles 180 pesos; private rooms 265 pesos. Cash only. ❶

La Parroquia Hostal, Calle 55 8 (☎816 2530; www.hostalparroquia.com), between Calles 10 and 12. This clean, attractive hostel in a colonial building is full-service, offering currency exchange, kitchen use, continental breakfast, lockers, and a great terrace overlooking the city. Bike rental 20 pesos per hr. Internet access 12 pesos per hr. Discounts at the 24hr. restaurant of the same name next door and the upscale Marganzo (p. 613) nearby. Dorms 90 pesos; private rooms 200 pesos. Cash only. ❶

Hotel Colonial, Calle 14 122 (☎816 2222), between Calles 55 and 57. Green rooms with bath, fan, and a retro look and feel. Common area has cable TV and a few chairs for lounging as well as purified water. A/C 90 pesos extra. Singles 175 pesos; doubles 240 pesos; triples 280 pesos; each additional person 35 pesos. Cash only. ❷

Hostal San Carlos, Calle 10 255 (☎816 5158; info@hostelcampeche.com.mx), at the intersection with Calle 49-B. Removed from the *centro* in the Barrio Guadalupe, the impeccably restored colonial house has decorative tile floors, furniture, and lighting. Linens and towels included. Internet, bike rental, and laundry available. Reception 24hr. Dorms 85 pesos. Cash only. ❶

Hotel Regis (☎816 3175), on Calle 12 between Calles 55 and 57. Large, white rooms with A/C, comfy beds, fan, checkered floors, and TV; some with balcony. The lobby courtyard has a small fridge and purified water. Singles 265 pesos; doubles 315 pesos; triples 365 pesos; each additional person 40 pesos. Cash only. ❹

Hotel Reforma, Calle 8 257 (☎816 4464), between Calles 57 and 59. Rooms with tiled floors and walls come with TV. Internet available. Reception 24hr. Check-out 1pm. Singles 120 pesos, with A/C 250 pesos; doubles 200/350 pesos. Cash only. ❷

◖ FOOD

Campechan cuisine is known for combining Yucatec specialties with European flavors and seafood. Sample *pan de cazón* (stacked tortillas filled with baby shark and refried beans, covered with an onion, tomato, and chile sauce) and *pámpano en escabeche* (fish broiled in olive oil and flavored with onion, garlic, chile, and orange juice). Don't be sucked into the overpriced restaurants in the *zócalo;* delicious, inexpensive food (7-28 pesos) can be found under the red *portales* (archways) in Parque San Martín, where you'll find several extremely popular restaurants, such as **Lonchería Conchita Cervera** ❶ and **El Portal de Oro** ❶ (open 6:30pm-1am). Campeche also has a **market,** on Circuito Baluartes, between Calles 53 and 55 near Baluarte de San Pedro (open M-Sa sunrise-sunset, Su sunrise-3pm), and a **supermarket,** San Francisco de Asís, in Plaza Comercial Ah Kin Pech, behind the post office. (☎816 7977. Open M-F and Su 7am-10pm, Sa 7am-11pm.)

▨ Marganzo (☎811 3898), on Calle 8 between Calles 57 and 59. With an ambiance as fresh and colorful as its food, Marganzo offers something for everyone's budget, though the *platos fuertes* tend toward the expensive side. *Tamales* (30 pesos), fish parmesan (88 pesos), and a suave guitar trio (Tu-Sa 8-10pm, Su afternoons) make this one of the best dining experiences in town. All meals come with tasty crab salad *bocatas* (sandwiches). Open daily 7am-11pm. MC/V. ❹

Los Portales (☎811 1491), on Calle 10 between Arista and Gómez Farías, off Parque San Francisco. At the end of the 1km walk from the *centro* you'll find cheap Campechan food and a small, quiet cobbled plaza beneath the clock tower. Traditional and vegetarian entrees 8-32 pesos. Open daily 6pm-1am. Cash only. ❷

Restaurant la Parroquia, Calle 55 8 (☎816 2530), between Calles 10 and 12. A popular, cavernous all-night eatery with round-the-clock TV. Low prices and heaping portions make up for the street noise. Steaming stacks of pancakes with honey, fresh fruit, and coffee, 40 pesos. 3-course *comida del día* 40 pesos. Open 24hr. Cash only. ❸

Pizza Hot Beach (☎811 3131), in Plaza Girasol. This well-known local eatery in a brand new location serves up huge, delicious pizzas, pasta, and sandwiches. Free delivery. Small pizza serves 2. Pizza 50-125 pesos. Open daily 9am-midnight. Cash only. ❸

Nutrivida, Calle 12 167 (☎816 1221), between Calles 57 and 59. Vegetarians, rejoice! Delicious, all-natural food, such as soy burgers (22 pesos), *chaya* (a native Yucatán plant, similar to spinach) *tamales* stuffed with soy (7 pesos), and homemade yogurt (8 pesos) served fast. Chicken or tuna salads 8-16 pesos. Open M-F 8am-2pm and 5:30-8:30pm, Sa 8am-2pm. Cash only. ❶

Trossachs Cafe, at Calles 12 and 63. A newly opened cafe in the front of a small family home. The coffee milkshake (18 pesos) draws students and mid-morning snackers. Open M-F 8am-11pm. Cash only. ❷

YUCATÁN PENINSULA

Casa Vieja, Calle 10 319, 2nd fl. (☎811 1311), between Calles 55 and 57. The view overlooking the *zócalo* and the collection of local folk art are worth the visit, even if the pricey food is hit or miss. Cuban plate 115 pesos. Pasta dishes from 75 pesos. Open daily 10am-11pm. MC/V. ❺

◎ SIGHTS

With ancient stone beautifully illuminated by the moonlight and street lamps, Campeche's historical treasures are best viewed by night. The city has seven *baluartes* (bulwarks), visible along Circuito Baluartes or from the bus by the same name. The only standing walls of the fortress are at **Puerta de Tierra** and **Baluarte de la Soledad,** which have museums and allow you to walk along their terraces.

The city has a popular **trolley system,** which tours the major sights and historic neighborhoods. The red "Tranvía" tours the *centro* and *malecón*, departing from Parque Principal (45min., every hr. 9am-1pm and 5-9pm). The green "El Guapo" and "Superguapo" (40min.) make short stops at either the Fuerte de San José (9am, 5pm; 70 pesos) or the Fuerte de San Miguel (every hr. 10am-1pm and 6-8pm, 70 pesos). Schedules and destinations are erratic, and trolleys often leave when they have the minimum 10 passengers; it's best to inquire with the driver about the route. Attendants ring a brass bell from the green kiosk in Parque Principal when they are about to depart. Tours are also available in English. Nearly all of Campeche's historical sights are within walking distance of the *centro*.

FUERTE DE SAN JOSÉ EL ALTO. Built in 1792, Campeche's smaller fort stands guard to the northeast of the city. The path leading to the operating drawbridge winds deliberately to prevent attacking pirates from using battering rams on the gate. Today, brutal weapons and models of dashing pirate ships dating from as early as the 14th century provide insight into the city's defensive past. Exhibits are in Spanish only. *(4km from the* centro *on the northern hills overlooking town. The "Bellavista" or "San José el Alto" buses, which pass in front of the post office, will drop you off halfway up the hill, a 3min. walk from the fort. Alternatively, the 4km walk is scenic and breezy. Head north along the* malecón *about 2.5km, then turn right at the PEMEX station and head up the steep hill another 1.5km. Open Tu-Su 9:30am-5:30pm. 27 pesos.)*

FUERTE DE SAN MIGUEL. Completed in 1801, this fort now houses the impressive **Museo Arqueológico de Campeche,** which has intriguing exhibits on the state's ruins and ancient Mayan city life, religion, war, power, trade, and beliefs about death and the afterlife. Don't miss the nice collection of jade masks from nearby sights like Edzná and Calakmul. On the top level, 20 cannons still stand guard. *(5km south of town, just before the town of Lerma. Take a 4.50-peso "Lerma" or "Playa Bonita" bus, both of which stop in front of the post office and will drop you off at the bottom of the steep, 600m hill leading to the fort. Open Tu-Sa 9am-5:30pm, Su 9am-noon. 34 pesos.)*

IGLESIA DE SAN ROMÁN. The church houses **El Cristo Negro** (The Black Christ), a 6 ft. ebony statue that arrived from Italy in 1575. The church, completed in 1570, was built for future protection and good luck after a locust plague struck the city. *(A few blocks southwest of the* centro *on Calle 10, past the long, narrow Parque de los Héroes. Open M-Sa 6am-noon, Su 6am-9pm. Sunday mass 7am, 1, 6pm.)*

JARDÍN BOTÁNICO XMUCH'HALTUN. Over 200 plant species thrive in the tiny open-air courtyard enclosed by trees, fountains, and the walls of the Baluarte de Santiago. *(At Calles 8 and 51. Open Tu-Su 9am-5pm. 20 pesos; Mexican citizens 10 pesos.)*

CASA SEIS. Part of the Casa de Cultura complex on the *zócalo*, Casa Seis is a beautifully restored 16th-century mansion with period-appropriate tiled floors and furniture. The staff rents walking audio tours of the historic *centro* for 100 pesos. (Calle 57 6. ☎816 1782; www.campechetravel.com. Open daily 9am-5pm. 5 pesos.)

IGLESIA DE SAN FRANCISCO Y ANTIGUO CONVENTO. This church, built in 1546 on an ancient Mayan foundation, marks the site of the first Mesoamerican Catholic mass in 1517 and the site of the baptism of Hernán Cortés's grandson. The three bells atop the Renaissance-style church toll for humility, obedience, and chastity. Ask the caretaker to open the gate to the roof for a view. *(On Alemán, about 1km northwest of the centro. Open daily 8am-noon.)*

TEMPLO DE NUESTRA SEÑORA DE LA PURÍSIMA CONCEPCIÓN. Francisco de Montejo initially ordered the construction of Campeche's cathedral in 1540, but the massive structure was not completed until 1705. The marble altar, stained-glass windows around the vaulted chapel, and Renaissance paintings are worth a look. *(In the zócalo. Open daily 6am-9pm. Daily mass 7pm. Free.)*

PARQUE ECOLÓGICO. This city park houses a zoo with native animals (crocodiles, turtles, monkeys, snakes) and picnic space. *(From Fuerte de San Miguel, turn right at the top of the hill. Open Tu-F 9am-1pm and Sa-Su 10am-4:30pm.)*

MANSIÓN CARVAJAL. Perhaps the most extravagant building in all of Campeche, this mansion stands as a striking reminder of the city's rich past as a center of commerce. Built in the 18th century by Rafael Carvajal Yturralde, who owned the most prosperous *hacienda* in the area, it features Moorish arches, Tuscan columns, wrought iron window coverings, and traditional black-and-white marble floors. Today, the government agency DIF (Integral Family Development) has its home here. *(Calle 10 14, between Calles 53 and 51. Open M-F 8am-3pm. Free.)*

BEACHES. Downtown Campeche lacks a conventional beach. For something refreshing, catch a "Lerma" or "Playa Bonita" bus to the beach of the same name 30min. away. *(Flag down a bus in front of the post office, every 20min., 5 pesos.)* Maintained by a wall with stairs leading to the water, the hard-packed, dirty sands of **Playa Bonita** fill up quickly in the summer. Entrance to the *balneario* of the same name is 5 pesos. *(Palapa rental 20 pesos. Open daily 9am-5pm.)* For a more beautiful beach without services, try **Playa Seyba,** 29km away.

ECO-ADVENTURES. Campeche's upstart tourist industry has created a few eco-adventure options near town. For information on tours and directions, call tour operators directly. **Turtlecamp Xpicob** offers interactive tours in turtle-rich mangrove swamps. *(Highway Mex. 180 at km 185. ☎812 5887.)* **Campamento Ecoturistico Yax-Ha** offers kayak and walking tours into the Yucatán bush. *(☎819 3470.)*

🎵 🎭 ENTERTAINMENT AND NIGHTLIFE

Traditional music fills the Campechan air almost every night. The city sponsors various outdoor events, such as the sound-and-light show at **Puerta de Tierra,** which tells the story of the *campechanos* staving off foolhardy pirates. Weather permitting, documentary film clips and eight actors keep the 80min. show exciting. (On Calles 59 and 18. 50 pesos. 8:30pm; July to mid-Aug. and *Semana Santa* M-Sa, the rest of the year Tu and F-Sa.) The state band, local trios, and dance groups perform in the **Parque Principal.** (Sa-Su 7:30pm.) The Casa de Cultura Seis, off the *zócalo*, holds **bingo** in the park. (Sa-Su 5-9pm. 1 peso per board.) More events are scheduled during high season (July-Aug. and Dec.); ask for a program at the tourist information center. On quieter nights, families, couples, and kids jog and ride bikes along the *malecón* or admire the musical fountain (daily performances at 7, 8, 9pm) next to the *zócalo* on Calle 8 by Calle 53. *Campechanos* celebrate the feast of **San Francisco,** the city's patron saint, beginning on October 4. Another popular festival, the **Feria de San Román** (Sept. 14-31), has been celebrated for over 400 years in the neighborhood of the same name.

Two bars compete for tourists' attention in the *centro.* **Iguana Azul,** Calle 55 11 x 10 y 12, has a pleasant vibe and serves huge specialty drinks for 35 pesos. (☎816 3978. Beer 16 pesos. Mixed drinks 35 pesos. Open daily 6:30pm-2am.) For a full night and a lively crowd, try **Captain Lafitte's,** complete with pirate waiters, indoor moats, and wooden boat decor. It opens at 7pm for fast food; the music and dancing kick in later. (Inside Hotel del Mar at Calle 59 and the shore. ☎816 2233. Sa live DJ. Open daily 7pm-2am.)

◤ DAYTRIP FROM CAMPECHE

EDZNÁ

Catch a bus in the lot across the park from the market on República. The building at the entrance is marked "SUR" and buses run from Campeche to Pich (40min., 13 per day, 18 pesos). Be sure to ask the driver when he will return (last bus 3:30pm). An ADO bus also makes the trip from Campeche (Tu-Su 7am, 12:30pm; round-trip 100 pesos). Site open daily 8am-4:30pm. 37 pesos. Bring bug repellent and water. Allow a minimum of 1½-2hr. to visit the site. Pack a lunch, as there are no on-site food vendors.

Once the most important city in western Campeche, Edzná provided a vital link between the Puuc region and more northerly sights. The word "Edzná" may relate to the Itzáes, a surname that now refers to a group of people native to southwestern Campeche who spread throughout the Yucatán during the late Classic and post-Classic periods. The site, settled in the middle of the pre-Classic period, covers 25 sq. km and once had a unique rainwater distribution system composed of an elaborate network of 29 canals, 27 reservoirs, and more than 70 *chultunes* (manmade water cisterns that channeled, drained, and stored rainwater). The crown jewel of the ruins, and the main reason to visit, is the **Edificio de Cinco Pisos** (Building of the Five Floors), which towers over the surrounding valley from atop the magnificent **Gran Acrópolis** (31m), a large base that supports several structures. Built in five stages, its 65 stairs—some adorned with hieroglyphics over 1300 years old—lead to tiers of columns crowned by a five-room temple that once housed a stela with an engraving of the corn god. The sun illuminated the stela twice yearly, signaling planting (May 2-3) and harvesting (August 9). From its heights, you can observe a dense, green jungle and a few small green mounds on the horizon, which are actually unexcavated ruins. Next to the Edificio is the architecturally intriguing **Templo del Norte,** remodeled at least four times over 1100 years. The alterations and superstitions of this stylistically varied temple are believed to correspond to the political circumstances in Edzná. The east side of the Gran Acrópolis faces the 135m wide stairway of **Nohoch-Ná** (Large House), which functioned as an administrative center as well as a stadium for events. Be sure to see the remains of the **ball court,** the loops of which are now missing, where the small size and sloped sides allow you to fully picture the game in action. The **Temple of Masks** has 3D stucco masks of the sun god in two stages, representing sunrise and sunset. The crossed or squinted eyes and flattened foreheads on the incredibly well-preserved masks are typical of the Maya and considered a sign of beauty. The **Small Acropolis** is the oldest group of buildings at the site, but the **Patio de los Embajadores** near its entrance is a modern addition. It took its name in honor of the many ambassadors who have visited the site since it began employing Guatemalan refugees to help with the reconstruction in 1986. The path to the right of the entrance provides a nice walk but ends in a small group of ruins that look minuscule by comparison.

XPUJIL
☎983

Blink as you cruise down Mex. 186 and you might miss Xpujil (pop. 1500), an ideal jump-off point for forays into the extensive and ruin-riddled Reserva de la Biosfera Calakmul. Second in size only to Sian Ka'an (p. 692), the reserve is one of the least explored regions of Mexico.

The farthest ruin from Xpujil, yet the most historically significant, is ⬛Calakmul, 120km from the town center. Discovered in 1931, the enormous pyramids of Calakmul signal a site of unrivaled political power, a power which often extended its circle of influence beyond Guatemala's Tikal. It is thought that Calakmul reached its height of power under the leadership of Great Jaguar Claw around AD 686. Great Jaguar Claw was responsible for the construction of much of the central plaza, which is home to the area's two 45m tall **pyramids,** known as Structure I and Structure II. The pyramids tower over the north end of the central plaza and are littered with the remains of fantastically detailed stelae—huge stone sculptures recounting the many battles, births, deaths, and weddings of the royal family. Great Jaguar Claw also led the town into battle with Tikal, at one point capturing powerful Tikal's leading lieutenant. Many of the other 120 stelae found on the site are dedicated to the great king. **Structure VII,** opposite Structure II in the central plaza, was built as a memorial tomb. The crypt revealed a huge number of jade masks and tools, which are now on display across the country. The ruins lie 120km from Xpujil town, reachable only by taxi. (Round-trip 700-800 pesos plus waiting. An additional 40 pesos is charged upon entering the Reserve at km 60. Ruins open daily 8am-5pm. 37 pesos.) Other nearby ruins include the ceremonial center of **Becan,** 8km east of Xpujil (open daily 8am-5pm; 37 pesos), and the ruins at **Xpujil** itself, 1km south of the bus stop in town (open daily 8am-5pm; 37 pesos).

The best accommodations and food in town can be found at the **Hotel and Restaurant Calakmul ❹,** a 10min. walk from the bus stop on the highway as you leave town towards Campeche. The legendary hotel is a meeting ground for incoming archeologists, as well as locals who are more than happy to share tales of tramping through the jungle in search of lost cities. Clean rooms in a modern building surround a grassy courtyard filled with flowers and a pet toucan. Somewhat primitive *cabañas* with shared bath, electricity, and mosquito nets are a better budget option. (☎871 6029 or 6006. *Cabañas* 250 pesos; rooms 470 pesos.)

Xpujil town has **no Internet, bank,** or **hospital** so come prepared with plenty of cash. Xpujil's **ADO bus station** (☎871 6027) is in the center of town at the crossroads of highways 186 and 261. *De paso* buses from **Chetumal** (2hr., 4 daily, 98 pesos) will stop to drop off and pick up passengers.

YUCATÁN

MÉRIDA
☎999

A teeming center of food and culture, Mérida (pop. 1 million) is the hub of the Yucatán Peninsula and a rich blend of indigenous history, colonial presence, and modern international flavor. Once known as the Mayan metropolis of T'ho ("Place of the Fifth Point" in Mayan), the city marked the center of the universe, the place where the four cardinal directions met. In 1542, the city was conquered and founded by Francisco de Montejo. Modern Mérida continues to serve as an important center of culture and business. In recent years it has gained popularity as a city where one can see not only international films and performances, but also local folk dancers, drawing visitors and immigrants from all over the world yet not succumbing to metropolitan indifference. The city's commercial centers burst with *jipis* (Panama hats) shipped from Campeche, *hamacas* from Tixcocob, and *henequén* (a hemp-like fiber) from all over the peninsula. The ever-crowded *zócalo* is the hub of the city and the site of frequent public *fiestas*, especially on Sundays, when families, musicians, dancers, and food vendors come out to enjoy the city at its most free and joyous.

CROSSTOWN TRAFFIC. Addresses in Mérida are given using an "x" to separate the main street from the cross streets and "y" ("and" in Spanish) to separate the two cross streets if the address falls in the middle of the block. Thus, "54 509 x 61 y 63" reads "Calle 54 509, between Calles 61 and 63."

⬛ TRANSPORTATION

INTERCITY TRANSPORTATION

Flights: Lic. Manuel Crecencio Rejon International Airport (MID), 7km southwest on Mex. 180. Taxis to the *centro* 110 pesos. Most airline offices are on Paseo Montejo and in Plaza Americana, the shopping center in the Hotel Fiesta Americana. MID services: **AeroCalifornia** (☎946 1682 or 920 3855); **Aerocaribe,** Paseo Montejo 500B x 45 y 47 (☎928 6790); **Aeroméxico,** Calle 56 N. 451 at Av. Colón, in the Plaza Americana (☎920 1260 or 800 021 4000; www.aeromexico.com); **American Airlines** (☎800 904 6000); **Aviacsa,** Paseo de Montejo 475 x 37 y 39 (☎925 6890 or 800 006 2200; www.aviacsa.com.mx); **Continental** (☎926 3100 or 800 523 3273; www.continental.com); **Mexicana,** Paseo de Montejo 493 x 43 y 45 (☎924 6633 or 800 502 2000; www.mexicana.com.mx).

Buses: Mérida's 2 main terminals are southwest of the *centro*. To reach the *zócalo* from either, walk north to Calle 63, then turn right and walk another 3 blocks from one or 4 blocks from the other.

1st-class terminal, Calle 70 555 x 71 (☎924 8391). Services: **Campeche** (every 30min. 6am-11:45pm, 136 pesos); **Cancún** (every hr. 6:30am-midnight, 250 pesos); **Chetumal** (4 per day 7:30am-11pm, 238 pesos); **Chichén Itzá** (6:30, 9:15am, 1pm; 88 pesos); **Mexico City** (8 per day 10am-10:15pm, 1124 pesos); **Palenque** (8:30am, 10, 11:30pm; 316 pesos); **Playa del Carmen** (10 per day, 5am-midnight, 258 pesos); **San Cristóbal de las Casas** (7:15pm, 434 pesos); **Tulum** (6:30, 10:40am, 12:40pm; 172 pesos); **Valladolid** (11 per day, 112 pesos); **Veracruz** (4 per day 10:30am-12:15am, 686 pesos); **Villahermosa** (10 per day, 370-446 pesos).

2nd-class terminal, Calle 69 544 x 68 y 70 (☎923 2287). Services: **Campeche** (11 per day, 92 pesos); **Cancún** (35 per day, 194 pesos); **Chichén Itzá** (6 per day, 54 pesos); **Playa del Carmen** (7 per day, 160-214 pesos); **Tulum** (8 per day, 121-186 pesos); **Valladolid** (6 per day, 74 pesos).

Autoprogreso station: Calle 62 x 65 y 67 (☎928 3965). Sends buses to **Progreso** (every 20min., 13 pesos).

Noreste station: Calle 50 531 x 67. Travels to **Celestún** (every hr. 5:15am-8:30pm, 41 pesos), **Izamal** (every 45min. 4:45am-9pm, 30 pesos), **Tizimín** (16 per day, 65-83 pesos), and other smaller towns.

LOCAL TRANSPORTATION

Public Transportation: Municipal buses run daily (6am-midnight, 5 pesos). Buses usually drop you within a few blocks of your destination. *Taxis colectivos* (more com-

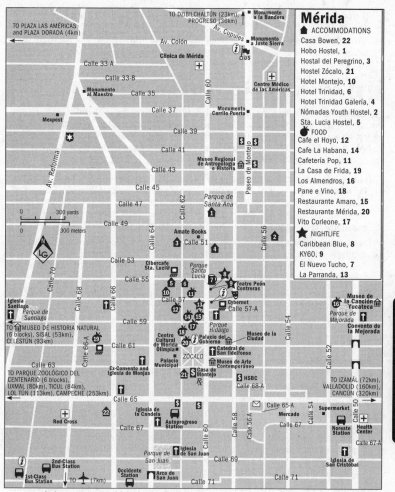

Mérida

▲ ACCOMMODATIONS
Casa Bowen, 22
Hobo Hostel, 1
Hostal del Peregrino, 3
Hostel Zócalo, 21
Hotel Montejo, 10
Hotel Trinidad, 6
Hotel Trinidad Galería, 4
Nómadas Youth Hostel, 2
Sta. Lucia Hostel, 5
❦ FOOD
Cafe el Hoyo, 12
Cafe La Habana, 14
Cafetería Pop, 11
La Casa de Frida, 19
Los Almendros, 16
Pane e Vino, 18
Restaurante Amaro, 15
Restaurante Mérida, 20
Vito Corleone, 17
★ NIGHTLIFE
Caribbean Blue, 8
KY60, 9
El Nuevo Tucho, 7
La Parranda, 13

YUCATÁN PENINSULA

monly known as *combis*) charge 5 pesos for any destination in the city; drop-offs are on a first-come, first-serve basis.

Taxis: They do not generally roam the streets, though it's becoming easier to hail one. A recent phenomenon is the scam-proof metered taxi, identified by the **"taxímetro"** sign on top, though they can sometimes be scarce in the *centro*. (☎928 3031 or 945 7500.) For a shorter wait, call one of the others at **Radio Taxis Grupo** (☎982 1504 or 1171). Stands are located along Paseo de Montejo, at the airport, or in the *zócalo*. Expect to pay 25-30 pesos for a trip within the *centro*.

Car Rental: Mexico Rent-a-Car, Calle 57A 491 (El Callejón del Congreso) x 58 y 60 (☎927 4916 or 923 3637). Another location on Calle 62 483A x 57 y 59. English, French, and Italian spoken. VW Beetles with unlimited km. High season 300 pesos per day; low season 260 pesos per day. Open M-Sa 8am-12:30pm and 6-8pm, Su

(Congreso location only) 8-10am. **World Rent-a-Car,** Calle 60 486C x 55 y 57 (☎924 0587; worldrentacar@hotmail.com). High season from 350 pesos per day; low season 295 pesos per day. Cars with automatic transmission and A/C from 580 pesos per day. Open daily 7am-9:30pm. **Tourist Car Rental,** Calle 60 421 x 45 y 47 (☎924 9471 or 924 9000). Also offers low rates.

■ ? ORIENTATION AND PRACTICAL INFORMATION

Mérida sits on the west side of Yucatán state, 30km south of the Gulf Coast. Even-numbered streets run north-south, with numbers increasing to the west; odd-numbered streets run east-west, increasing to the south. The *zócalo* is bordered by Calles 60, 61, 62, and 63. Most attractions and services are within easy walking distance from the *zócalo*, except the Paseo de Montejo, nine blocks northeast.

Tourist Information: In the **Palacio del Gobierno.** Open daily 8am-9pm. Also in the **Palacio Municipal** (☎930 3101). Open M-Sa 8am-8pm, Su 8am-2pm. Both distribute *Yucatán Today.* Also at the **Teatro Peón Contreras** (☎924 9290; open daily 8am-9pm), the **1st-class bus station** (open M-F 8am-8pm, Sa 8am-2pm), and near the **US consulate** (open daily 8am-8pm). Tourist info ☎942 0000, ext. 133.

Travel Agency: Yucatán Trails, Calle 62 482 x 57 y 59 (☎928 2582 or 5913; yucatantrails@hotmail.com). Canadian owner Denis Lafoy is a good source of information and hosts parties for travelers the 1st F of every month. Check the agency or *Yucatán Today* for details. Open M-F 9am-7pm, Sa 9am-1pm.

Consulate: US, Paseo de Montejo 453 (☎925 5011; fax 925 6219), at Colón. Open M-F 8am-1pm.

Banks: Banamex (☎924 1011), in Casa de Montejo on the *zócalo.* Has a **24hr. ATM.** through the courtyard. Open M-F 9am-4pm, Sa 10am-2pm. Other banks cluster on Paseo de Montejo and Calle 65.

American Express: Paseo de Montejo 492 x 41 y 43 (☎942 8200 or 8210). Open M-F 9am-2pm and 4-6pm, Sa 9am-1pm. Money exchange closes 1hr. earlier.

Luggage Storage: GuardaPlus, on Calle 70 x 69 y 71 serves 1st- and 2nd-class bus stations. 5-12 pesos per hr. Open 6am-10pm.

English-Language Bookstore: Librería Dante, Calle 59 x 60 y 62 (☎928 3674), and on the northwest corner of the *zócalo* (☎923 9060). Books related to the region, a few beach reads, and some English language magazines. Several other locations around town. Open daily 8am-8pm. For a wider selection, head to the Mérida branch of **Amate Books,** Calle 60 453A x 51 (☎924 2222; www.amatebooks.com). The newly opened shop hosts readings. Open T-Su 11am-2pm and 5-8:30pm.

Laundry: La Fe, Calle 61 518 x 62 y 64 (☎924 4531), 1 block west of the *zócalo.* Another on Calle 64 x 57 y 55. 50 pesos per 3kg. Open M-F 8am-7pm, Sa 8am-5pm.

Police: (☎925 2034 or 942 0070; tourist police 930 3200, ext. 40062), on Reforma (Calle 72) x 39 y 41, accessible by the "Reforma" bus.

Red Cross: Calle 68 533 x 65 y 67 (☎924 9813 or 983 0211).

24hr. Pharmacy: Farmacia Canto, Calle 60 513 x 63 y 65 (☎924 1490).

Medical Services: Centro Médico de las Américas, Calle 54 365 x Calle 33A (☎926 2111), for serious illnesses. **Clínica de Mérida,** Calle 32 242 x 27 y 29 (☎920 0411).

Internet Access: Cybernet, Calle 57A 491 (☎923 6492), at El Callejón de Congreso. 9 pesos per hr. Open M-Sa 9am-9:30pm. **Cibercafe Sta. Luci@** (☎928 1567), at Calles 62 and 55. 10 pesos per hr. Open daily 8am-midnight.

Fax Office: (☎920 2107), at Reforma (Calle 72) x 37, in the **Mexpost** office. Open M-F 8am-4pm, Sa 9am-1pm.

Post Office: Calle 65 x 56 y 56A (☎920 2102), in the Palacio Federal. Open M-F 8am-4:30pm. **Mexpost** next door. Open M-F 8am-4:30pm. **Postal Code:** 97000.

ACCOMMODATIONS

For those who love bargains and colonial architecture, choosing accommodations in Mérida will be a treat. Many of what were once elaborate, turn-of-the-century private mansions now offer affordable lodging near the main bus station and the *zócalo*. The hotels right outside the second-class bus station and a few blocks south of the *zócalo* have tempting offers, but the neighborhood is something of a red-light district and is not recommended for nighttime meandering. Even so, crime against tourists here is practically unheard of.

Nómadas Youth Hostel, Calle 62 433 x 51 (☎924 5223; www.nomadastravel.com). Mérida's oldest and most well-known hostel offers clean dorms with soaring ceilings, an outdoor kitchen, patios, live *trova* performances, and free daily salsa lessons. Trips to *cenotes*, Celestún, and other attractions can be arranged. Ask for a spot toward the back and near a fan. Continental breakfast included. Laundry sinks available. Separate girls bunk. Tent space 65 pesos; bunks 85 pesos. Private doubles 189 pesos, with bath 220 pesos. ISIC and HI discounts. Cash only. ❶

Sta. Lucia Hostel (HI), Calle 55 512 x 62 y 64 (☎928 9070; www.hostelstalucia.com). Mérida's newest hostel joins the already crowded hosteling scene with the HI stamp of approval. One crowded dorm room with weak fans and a few private A/C-equipped rooms share an immaculate bathroom and a pleasant kitchen/patio outdoor space. Breakfast, lockers, and Internet included. On-site tourist agent can help set up daytrips to nearby beaches and ruins. Dorm 85 pesos; private room with fan 130 pesos, with A/C 220 pesos. 10% HI discount. Cash only. ❶

Hostel Zócalo, Calle 63 x 60 y 62 (☎930 9562; hostal_zocalo@yahoo.com.mx). Perhaps the best located hostel in town, Zócalo, housed in an annex of the Montejo mansion next door, offers small dorm rooms with large, soft beds. Make supper in the communal kitchen and eat on a balcony overlooking the busy *zócalo*. No A/C. Breakfast and lockers included. Reception 24hr. Check-out noon. Beds 90 pesos; private rooms 130-300 pesos. Cash only. ❶

Hostal del Peregrino, Calle 51 488 x 54 y 56 (☎924 5491 or 162 5158; www.hostalperegrinobb.com). In a crumbling colonial mansion a few blocks from the city center, clean dorms with bright Mexican blankets make for a homey atmosphere. Pleasant rooftop patio, on-site tour agents, and a traditional open-air kitchen make up for the lack of ventilation. Private rooms are equipped with private baths, cable TV, and fans. Continental breakfast, Wi-Fi, and lockers included. Dorms with fan 130 pesos. Doubles 340 pesos, with A/C 390 pesos. Cash only. ❷

Hotel Trinidad, Calle 62 464 x 55 y 57 (☎923 2033; www.hotelestrinidad.com). Choose from colonial- or modern-style rooms at this friendly hotel that once appeared in *Art Forum* magazine. Rooftop hot tub, enormous TV with DVD and digital cable, plush mattresses, outdoor kitchen, and pool access at a neighboring hotel. Continental breakfast included. Singles and doubles with fan and shared bath 220 pesos, with private bath 320 pesos, with A/C 400 pesos. 20% student discount with valid ID on rooms without A/C. AmEx/MC/V. ❸

Hotel Trinidad Galería, Calle 60 456 x 51 (☎923 2463; www.hoteltrinidadgaleria.com). Dusty artwork decorates every nook and cranny of this quirky, overgrown colonial mansion. Clean old rooms are each devoted to a different art movement. 2nd fl. rooms have much better light and breeze. Couches and fountain with live turtles in the lobby. Large outdoor pool. Morning coffee included. Reception 8am-9pm. Singles and doubles 300 pesos, with A/C 400 pesos; triples 350 pesos. Cash only. ❹

Casa Bowen, Calle 66 521B x 65 y 67 (☎928 6109), between the main bus station and the *zócalo*. Rooms in this beautiful, slightly aging colonial mansion have fans and firm beds. Rooms in the adjoining building are not as attractive, but still comfortable. Reservations recommended July-Aug. Singles 180 pesos; doubles 250 pesos, with A/C 300 pesos; each additional person 50 pesos. Cash only. ❸

Hotel Montejo, Calle 57 507 x 62 y 64 (☎928 0390; www.hotelmontejo.com), 2 blocks north of the *zócalo*. Large wooden doors open into rooms with bath, fan, TV, window porticos, and high ceilings with wooden beams. Lush garden patio and restaurant available. Singles 280 pesos, with A/C 380 pesos; doubles 350/450 pesos; each additional person 60 pesos. MC/V. ❹

Hobo Hostel, Calle 60 432 x 49 y 47 (☎928 0880; www.hostelhobo.com). The well-used Spanish-style mansion is smaller and more removed than other hostels in the city. Dorm rooms have big, fluffy beds, overhead fans, and lockers. The large communal bath house is delightfully clean, but lacking in privacy. The central courtyard is a great place to lounge and catch up on your colonial Mexican history. No kitchen, but there is a communal fridge. Small coffee and toast breakfast included. Reception 24hr. Dorms 85 pesos; private rooms 200 pesos. Cash only. ❶

▐ FOOD

As the cultural and political capital of the Yucatán, Mérida's chefs work overtime introducing the uninitiated to the distinctive flavors of the area's Cuban-influenced Yucatec cuisine. Try *sopa de lima* (soup with freshly squeezed lime, chicken, and tortilla), *pollo pibil* (chicken with sour orange and herbs baked in banana leaves), *poc-chuc* (pork steak with pickled onions, doused in sour orange juice), *papadzules* (chopped hard-boiled eggs wrapped in corn tortillas served with pumpkin and tomato sauce), or *huevos motuleños* (refried beans, fried egg, chopped ham, and cheese on a crispy tortilla, garnished with tomato sauce, peas, and fried plantains). The cheapest food is at the **mercado,** particularly on the second floor of the restaurant complex on Calle 56A at Calle 67. (Complete Yucatec meals 30-40 pesos. Most stalls open M-Sa 6am-7pm, Su 6am-5pm.) The **Mercado de Santa Ana** at Calles 60 and 47 is smaller and much cleaner—the cleanest stalls will be the busiest. (Most stalls open M-Sa 6am-8pm, Su 8am-2pm.) A supermarket, **San Francisco de Asís,** Calle 65 x 54 y 52, is across from the market in a huge gray building. (☎924 3011. Open M-Sa 7am-9pm, Su 7am-5pm.)

> **TIP** **THE BIGGER THE SOMBRERO...** Though the streets of Mérida tend to be free of tourist gimmicks, the restaurants don't follow this rule. While in Mérida, the bigger and more extravagant the costume of the waiters, the bigger the prices on the menu.

▓ La Casa de Frida, Calle 61 526A x 66 y 66-A (☎928 2311). This beautiful addition to Mérida's restaurant scene offers interesting Mexican specialties like *chile en nogada* (*poblano* stuffed with ground meat and fruits, covered in a pecan cream sauce and pomegranate; 105 pesos) and creative vegetarian dishes (from 80 pesos). An attentive staff will make you feel relaxed among the cacti, twinkling lights, and Frida Kahlo reproductions. Entrees 65-130 pesos. Open Tu-Sa 6pm-midnight. Cash only. ❹

Cafe la Habana, Calle 59 511 x 62 (☎928 6502). This large cafe with A/C and a giant coffee roasting machine on display is at the heart of Mérida's vibrant cafe scene.

Always busy, it is a good place for coffee (from 14 pesos), people-watching, and checking email (12 pesos per hr.). Breakfast specials from 35 pesos. Open 24hr. MC/V. ❸

Restaurante Amaro, Calle 59 507 x 60 y 62 (☎928 2451). Popular with tourists seeking a night out in a calm setting. Attentive service and intimate candlelit tables in a quiet courtyard with live music and a variety of healthful Mexican dishes. Great vegetarian dishes like eggplant curry (62 pesos), *chaya* (leafy vegetable similar to spinach) crepes (69 pesos), and apple pie with wheat crust (30 pesos). Live regional *trova* guitar music 9pm. F 8:30pm tango show; cover 100 pesos. Open daily 11am-2am. MC/V. ❹

Cafetería Pop, Calle 57 501 x 60 y 62 (☎928 6163). Mérida's oldest cafe, this spotless, retro diner recently celebrated its 36th anniversary. Cheap, well-prepared food served by attentive waiters. Superior coffee (15 pesos) and scrumptious banana splits (45 pesos). Breakfast specials (28-48 pesos) served until noon. Other entrees (28-65 pesos) served noon-midnight. Open M-Sa 7am-midnight, Su 8am-midnight. MC/V. ❸

Pane e Vino, Calle 62 496 x 59 y 61 (☎928 6228; paneevino@operamail.com). For Italian treats and hearty salads, head to Pane e Vino. In the center of town just across from Teatro Mérida, the dimly lit restaurant and slow service caters to romantic vacationing couples. Big salad 50 pesos. Homemade gnocchi with fresh pesto 75 pesos. 10% service charge included on all meals. Open daily 9am-9pm. MC/V. ❹

Los Almendros (☎928 5459) and **Los Gran Almendros** (☎923 8135), both at Calle 50 493 x 57 y 59. Upscale, world-famous Yucatec food with picture menus make these the ideal places to splurge on local delicacies. *Poc-chuc* (grilled pork steak) or *pavo en relleno negro* (turkey with dark sauce; 90 pesos). Live *trova* at Los Almendros and instrumental music at Gran Almendros. Open daily 10am-11pm and daily 1-5pm, respectively. MC/V. ❺

Cafe el Hoyo, Calle 62 487 x 57 y 59 (☎928 1531). Catch up with Mérida's hip youth at the high tables in the red-painted courtyard. Game room off the side has classics like Clue® and an overgrown tree sprouting through the tables. Waffles all day from 50 pesos. Coffee frappes from 30 pesos. Also serves local beer (20 pesos) making it a popular F afternoon stop. Open M-Sa 9am-11:30pm. MC/V. ❸

Vito Corleone, Calle 59 508 x 60 y 62 (☎928 5777). Vito Corleone is the don of pizza in Mérida's downtown scene, making offers you can't refuse. Look for the huge hanging antique bicycle, the giant wood-fired oven, and the swarms of people spilling onto the street with steaming slices of favorites like margarita pizza (25 pesos for a small). Take-out and delivery also available. Open daily 10am-10:30pm. Cash only. ❷

Restaurante Mérida, Calle 62 498 x 59 y 61 (☎116 3489). Recommended by locals for cheap, dependable Yucatec cuisine. Entrees, like *cochinita pibil* (slow-roasted pork in citrus juice) and *pollo en escabeche* (marinated chicken), are a bargain at 35 pesos. Open daily 7:30am-1am. Cash only. ❷

🄖 SIGHTS

Mérida stands as a testament to the lengthy and often tumultuous history of the Yucatán. Surrounded by historic palaces, modern Oxxo stores, and a towering cathedral, the busy *zócalo* is the capital's social center. On Sundays, the surrounding streets are closed to traffic as vendors cram into stalls. Yucatec folk dancers perform in front of Palacio Municipal while crowds of people stroll along the cobblestone streets. If you can't make the Sunday festivities, don't fret. Mérida has daily cultural activities in the many plazas as well as a host of markets, theaters, and museums to explore. Free 1½hr. walking tours of the city begin at 9:30am in the information office at the Palacio Municipal.

MÉRIDA FOR POCKET CHANGE. Mérida is an easy place to live on the cheap. The best time to check out the sights is on Sunday, when you can rent a bike (10 pesos per hr.) and pedal from the central *zócalo* all the way out the Paseo Montejo, stopping to see the famously decorated city's many sculptures and murals. To cool off, hit one of the city's many cafes, such as Cafe el Hoyo for a local brew like the aptly named Cerveza Montejo.

■ **PALACIO DE GOBIERNO.** Built between 1879 and 1892, the Palacio fuses two architectural styles—Tuscan (main floor) and Dorian (upper floor). Giant murals by the famous Merideño muralist, Fernando Castro Pacheco (b. 1918), line the courtyard as well as the giant Versailles-like salon on the upper level. The murals, in somber tones, depict the violent history of the conquest and the subsequent *indigenismo* revival on the peninsula. Begun in the early 1970s, the murals took more than a decade to complete, yet are remarkably coherent in their style and story and offer one of the more dramatic and poetic retellings of Yucatec history. *(On the north side of the zócalo. Open daily 8am-10pm. Free.)*

■ **MUSEO REGIONAL DE ANTROPOLOGÍA E HISTORIA.** Mérida's most impressive museum is housed in the **Palacio Cantón,** a magnificent Italian Renaissance-style building. The collection includes Mayan head-flattening devices, jade tooth inserts, sacrificial offerings recovered from the *cenote sagrado* of Chichén Itzá, and a Chichén Itzá *chac-mool* (p. 646), in addition to intriguing exhibits on Mayan science, language, and distinctive ideals of beauty. The children's room has videos on modern tattooing techniques as well as Mayan language learning tools. Most exhibits are in Spanish and English. *(Paseo Montejo y Calle 43. ☎ 923 0557. Open Tu-Sa 8am-8pm, Su 8am-2pm. 37 pesos; Su Mexican citizens free.)*

CENTRO CULTURAL DE MÉRIDA OLIMPIA. The giant glass and steel building stands out from the other colonial buildings around the *zócalo.* A recently renovated exhibition hall with four galleries, the center hosts work by well-known local and international artists. The theater in the complex also has free performances: *trova,* the Yucatán's signature musical style, on Tuesdays; live bands on Wednesdays; classical music on Thursdays; and plays and dances on weekends. The downstairs planetarium is a popular spot for school children. A cinema shows international films nearly every day. Check the bulletin board near the entrance for a full schedule of events. *(Calles 62 y 61, just north of the municipal building. ☎ 942 0000; www.merida.gob.mex. Open Tu-Su 10am-8:30pm. Admission free; planetarium 30 pesos.)*

CATEDRAL DE SAN ILDELFONSO. Begun in 1563 and finished in 1598, the towering Catedral is the oldest on the continent and holds the world's largest indoor crucifix (20m). The cathedral's stone blocks were stolen from the Mayan temples of T'ho, and the interior was looted during the Mexican Revolution in 1915. *(On the east side of the zócalo. Open daily 6am-7pm. Daily mass 7am and 7pm. Free.)*

CASA DE MONTEJO. Probably begun in 1549 by Francisco de Montejo el Mozo, then the highest authority in Yucatán, the house was occupied by his descendents until the 1980s, when it was sold to Banamex. Built with stones from the Mayan temple T'ho, the 17th-century facade portrays warriors standing on the heads of their conquered. *(On the south side of the zócalo. Open M-F 9am-4pm, Sa 10am-2pm. Free.)*

MUSEO DE ARTE CONTEMPORÁNEO (MACAY). MACAY is renowned for its large collection of Mexican sculpture, as well as a few late murals by Fernando Castro

Pacheco. Much of the permanent collection is found in the nooks and crannies of the sunny central courtyard. Rotating exhibits by well-known Mexican painters are in the air-conditioned galleries on the upper level. The outside sculpture garden is worth a quick peek. *(Paseo Revolución x 58 y 60, on the east side of the zócalo, south of the Cathedral. ☎ 928 3258; www.macay.org. Open M and W-Su 10am-5:30pm. Free.)*

TEATRO PEÓN CONTRERAS. Named for the *merideño* poet José Peón Contreras (1843-1907), this beautiful, turn-of-the-century building is notable for its marble Rococo interior. The *teatro* has frequent concerts and shows; see the box office and the *Divertimento* booklet, found at the tourist office, for more information. *(Calle 57 x 60. ☎ 923 7354. www.culturayucatan.com.)*

UNIVERSIDAD AUTÓNOMA DE YUCATÁN. The headquarters of the state's national university, in a Hispano-Moorish complex dating from 1938, has screening rooms on the ground floor and a gallery with works by local artists and students. *(On Calle 57 x 60. Galería open M-F 9am-1pm and 5-9pm, Sa 10am-1pm, Su 10am-2pm. Movie schedule varies. Free.)*

PASEO DE MONTEJO. Aging French-style mansions, a large and impressive sculpture garden, and boutiques line the Paseo's brick sidewalks, culminating in the **Monumento a la Patria.** In faux-Mayan style, the stone monument—built by the Colombian artist Rómulo Rozo from 1945 to 1956—depicts Cinco de Mayo, scenes from the Mexican Revolution, and interpretations of the founding fathers of Mexico's constitution. On the other side of the monument, the *ceiba* (the Mayan tree of life) stretches above a pool of water, surrounded by conquistadors, the national symbol of an eagle devouring a snake, Mexican states' coats of arms, and butterflies in the four cardinal directions. For an interesting detour from the Paseo, veer left onto Colón to see historic mansions in varying stages of decay. On Sunday, half of the street is shut for the weekly city cycling circuit from 9am-12:30pm. Bike rentals are available at the Monumento a la Patria or in the *zócalo. (10 pesos per hr.)*

MUSEO DE LA CANCIÓN YUCATECA. A small museum home to sheet music, instruments, trophies, and portraits of the area's best singers and musicians. The center also hosts free concerts the last Wednesday of every month at 9pm. *(Calle 57 464 x 48. ☎ 923 7224. All exhibits in Spanish. Open M-F 9am-5pm, Sa-Su 9am-3pm. 10 pesos.)*

PARQUE ZOOLÓGICO DEL CENTENARIO. Check out tigers, bears, and hippos in a large park, complete with rides for kids, walking paths, and food stands. The zoo features a large aviary and fountains that visitors can walk through. These and other creatures make for a good show while wandering or riding the miniature train (10 pesos) that makes circuits of the park. *(On Calle 84 x 61 y 59, or at Calle 59 and Calle 86, Itzáces. Snag an "El Centenario" bus at Calle 64 x 61 y 63 and ask to be let off at the parque; 5 pesos. Park and zoo open 8am-6pm. Both free.)*

OTHER SIGHTS. The many churches, statues, and parks scattered throughout Mérida's *centro* invite exploration. Mérida has several remaining **arches,** built in the latter part of the 17th century, which used to mark the roads connecting the city with the rest of the state and established boundaries between the living quarters of European and indigenous peoples. The oldest is **San Juan,** Calle 64 x 71. **Iglesia Santiago,** on Calles 59 x 72, one of the oldest churches in Mexico, is worth a visit, as are **Iglesia de San Juan de Dios,** on Calle 64 x 69, and the **Franciscan Convento de la Mejorada,** at Calle 50 x 57 y 59, the cloisters of which have now been turned into the department of architecture for MACAY University. Other small museums include the **Museo de la Ciudad,** at Calle 61 x 58 y 60, a graphical exhibition on the city of Mérida, and the **Museo de Historia Natural,** at Calle 59 x 84 y 84A. *(Museo de la Ciudad* ☎923 6869. *Open Tu-F 8am-8pm, Sa-Su 8am-2pm. Free. Museo De Historia Natural* ☎924 0994. *Open Tu-Su 9am-4pm. 5 pesos.)*

▣ SHOPPING

Mérida offers the best shopping in the Yucatán, but nagging vendors and high-pressure salespeople are inescapable. The main **mercado** occupies the block southeast of the pink Palacio Federal, spreading outward from the corner of Calles 65 and 58. The second-floor **artisans' market,** part of the modern building behind and to the right of the Palacio Federal, sells *artesanías*, regional clothing, and the omnipresent hammock, made out of a traditional hemp-like fiber called *henequén* that is lighter and longer-lasting than cotton. Peruse white *huipiles* (traditional dresses and blouses; 250-350 pesos), *rebozos* (shawls; 220 pesos), and *guayaberas* (men's shirts; 150-250 pesos). Cheaper goods, such as *huaraches* (sandals), are sold on the first floor. While shopping in the crowded market, don't carry any valuables and keep your money in a safe place, like an under-the-shirt money belt.

> ❗ **CONSUMER BEWARE.** Though Mérida is one of the safest cities in Mexico, it's important to be on the defense against assaults on your wallet. In particular, be wary of the friendly, crafty multilinguals hanging out in the *zócalo* and in the market who claim to work for the tourist office. They will likely be passing out tourist information and offer to lead you to an "official" artisan market, where you will be charged two to three times the fair price for souvenirs while they receive a commission. Always ask for a receipt with the name and address of the store. Report fraud to the consumer protection agency (☎923 2323, Calle 59 x 54 y 56) or the government tourist office in the Palacio del Gobierno.

If you are worried about the prospect of hard-core bargaining, or if you just want to get an idea of the upper end of prices, you can try the government-run **Casa de las Artesanías del Estado de Yucatán,** Calle 63 503A x 64 y 66, where every item has a fixed price. (☎923 5392. Open daily 8am-8pm). Don't be fooled by imitations; look for the logo with two hands. Some of the boutiques around the *centro* offer slightly steeper prices than those you can bargain for in the *mercado*, but they are also air-conditioned, less stressful, and sometimes of higher quality. Although jewelry stores line the streets, the best prices are in the market or at the *zócalo* every Sunday, though you're more likely to get what you're paying for at more established stores. All genuine silver has ".925" stamped on it to verify it. **El Centro Joyero** (Calle 75 x 70 y 72) is another area to look.

▣ ▨ NIGHTLIFE AND ENTERTAINMENT

Though Mérida is full of relaxing, culturally interesting nightlife options, clubbing is better saved for another port. Mérida's nightlife happens in the streets where the city hosts almost nightly free music and cultural shows in its many *zócalos* and parks, each of which offers the chance to dance, drink, eat, and get a true taste of the *sabor* of the Yucatán. The free *Yucatán Today* magazine, found in the tourist office, has complete listings for events and shows. For a chilled out evening in a bar, try one of Mérida's many delicious, hard-to-find local beers, like the distinctive Montejo León and the darker Negra León. Local establishments give out free snacks with the purchase of a few beers.

Monday: Outdoor concerts with Yucatec dancing in the Palacio Municipal. 9pm.

Tuesday: 1940s-style big-band concerts in Santiago Park, at Calles 59 x 72. 9pm.

Wednesday: Miércoles de Espectáculo, a show in the **Centro Cultural,** on Calle 59 near Parque Centenario. 9pm.

▨ **Thursday: The Serenade,** at Calles 60 x 55, in Santa Lucía Park. The most historical event in Mérida, with well-known Mexican music, poetry, and folklore. 9pm.

Friday: University Serenade, at Calles 60 X 57, in the main university building. Theatrical performances at the **Centro Cultural** at 8pm. Also, on the 1st F of every month, Yucatán Trails throws a party for travelers (p. 620).

Saturday: Noche Mexicana, on Paseo Montejo between Calles 47 and 49. A night of national food, dance performances, and arts and crafts. 7-11pm. During ▨**En el Corazón de Mérida,** at the *zócalo* and at Calle 60 x 53 y 61, restaurants in the historic center move their tables into the streets under the stars.

Sunday: Mérida en Domingo. Art vendors, food stalls, and live music fight for space in the *zócalo* and surrounding streets. 9am-9pm.

BARS AND CLUBS

La Parranda, Calle 60 x 59 y 57, across from Parque Hidalgo. One of the central fixtures of Saturday night festivals, La Parranda is a tourist attraction all on its own. Beer is sold by the yard and salsa music circa 1990 is the house standard. Bottled beer 27 pesos. Open daily 11am-2am. MC/V.

KY60 (☎924 2289), on Calle 60 x 55 y 57. Part of the cluster of clubs on the same block that cater mostly to young locals looking for alternative music and late-night romance. The scene picks up around midnight. Cover men 130 pesos, women 70 pesos. Open F-Sa 10pm-3am.

Caribbean Blue (☎923 2279), next to KY60. Another venue for live music in a more formal setting. Music is usually Cuban or salsa. Cover 40 pesos. Open F-Su 10pm-3am.

El Nuevo Tucho, Calle 60 482 x 55 y 57 (☎924 2323). Entertains mostly Mexican customers with slapstick comedy troupes and live music. Free hors d'oeuvres for those ordering drinks. Live shows afternoons and evenings. Beer 29 pesos. Entrees 60-80 pesos. Open daily 11:30am-9:30pm. MC/V. ❹

▶ DAYTRIPS FROM MÉRIDA

DZIBILCHALTÚN

Buses leave from the Autoprogreso station (every 2hr. 7:20am-1:20pm, 7 pesos) and drop you off at the access road to the ruins, a 5min. walk from the entrance. Return bus schedule is 2½hr. later than the departure in the same place. Combis also run on an irregular schedule past the access road to the ruins (9 pesos). Taxis charge 350 pesos for a round-trip ride and 2hr. wait. Parking 10 pesos. Site open daily 8am-5pm; museum open Tu-Su 8am-4pm. 63 pesos; Mexican children under 13 free; Mexican students with ID free; Su free for Mexican citizens.

These ruins are worth a look, particularly because of ▨**El Museo del Pueblo Maya.** Peace, quiet, and the fact that the bus won't come for 2½hr. make for an ideal picnic spot. Situated 20km north of Mérida en route to the Gulf coast, Dzibilchaltún ("place where there is writing on stones" in Mayan) sprawls over 19 sq. km of jungle brush. The site flourished as a ceremonial and administrative center, with a peak of 40,000 inhabitants at one point, from approximately 500 BC until after the arrival of the Spanish in the 1540s, making it one of the longest continuously inhabited Mayan settlements. The carefully preserved site now houses a 300m "ecological path," with nearly 100 different species of birds and labeled plants, and the museum, which displays sculptures and ceramics from Dzibilchaltún and other Mayan sites, as well as more recent Catholic altars and contemporary Mayan handiwork. The museum is the first building to the left of the entrance. The path leading to the museum is lined with an all-star gallery of Mayan stelae with original sculptures from Chichén Itzá (p. 646) and Uxmal (p. 634).

From the museum, follow the path to **sacbé no. 1,** the raised causeway, and turn left. At the end of this road lies Dzibilchaltún's showpiece, the fully restored 5th-century **Templo de las Siete Muñecas** (Temple of the Seven Dolls), which covers 24,300 sq. m. The seven phallically enhanced clay "dolls" discovered in this temple at the four cardinal directions are on display in the museum. Shortly after sunrise during the spring and autumn equinoxes, a huge shadow mask of the rain god Chac appears as the sun's rays pierce the temple. The other end of the *sacbé* leads to a seemingly out-of-place chapel with a rounded roof that was a Mayan temple before being rebuilt by Franciscan missionaries. Just beyond the eastern edge of the quadrangle is **Cenote Xlacah** (Old People Cave), which served as a sacrificial well and water source, and is now a lily pad garden and mosquito breeding ground. Divers have recovered ceremonial artifacts and human bones from the depths of the 44m deep *cenote*, where you can now take a non-sacrificial dip. A path to the south leads past several smaller structures to the site's exit.

MAYAPÁN

Mayapán is 43km southeast of Mérida on Mex. 18 and 6km northwest of Tekit on the same road. It's the only site north of Mex. 184 and is not officially part of the Ruta Puuc; Ticul (p. 638) is the nearest base, a 1hr. drive away. Buses leave from the station in Mérida every hr. (18 pesos). Buses also pass by every hr. from Mérida on their way to Oxkutzcab (31 pesos). Open daily 8am-5pm. 30 pesos.

The ruins of Mayapán themselves are less impressive than its revered history as a central part of the late, great Mayapán alliance, but the on-site paintings are unique to the ruins circuit and worth the trip. From AD 1000 to 1200, the city was dominated by Chichén Itzá, which controlled the Mayapán League. After AD 1200, the beginning of its golden age, the 12,000 people of Mayapán overthrew Chichén Itzá and came to control the league. The 4 sq. km city was destroyed in 1441, when Ah Xupan of Uxmal rebelled against the Cocom dynasty in a fight to retrieve his daughter, a princess captured by Chichén Itzá's prince. Restoration began in 1948, producing several impressive structures. The principal pyramid is the **Pyramid of Kukulcán,** a smaller version of that at Chichén Itzá, with straight lines and little detail. The peak affords a view of the rest of the compact site. To the west are three stucco models with painted warriors; the round shape of the **Templo Redondo** stands out. **El Templo de Pescadores** has nicely preserved murals, and within the site are 32 *cenotes*, one of which is near the **Caracol.**

CELESTÚN   ☎998

Celestún (pop. 5500) is an ideal destination for those looking to escape the bustle of city life and avoid tourist towns filled with cruise ship vacationers. Seafood restaurants line the white beach, filled with bleached conch shells and fishermen rather than umbrellas. Celestún is also the most logical spot to enter the plankton-rich waters of the Ria Celestún Biosphere, home to over 200 species of migratory birds, including the flaming pink flamingo, regal ibis, and loudmouth cormorants as well as giant permits and bonefish. Bring your most potent bug repellent to ward off mosquitoes, which are striped like tigers and bite almost as hard.

⚏ ⚎ TRANSPORTATION AND PRACTICAL INFORMATION. Celestún lies 93km southwest of Mérida on the Gulf Coast. To get there by bus, go to the Noreste **bus station** in Mérida on Calle 67 x 50 y 52 (2hr., every hr., 38 pesos). By car, take **Mex. 281** into town where it becomes **Calle 11,** the main east-west street. Calle 11 passes the *zócalo* and hits the shore two blocks later. Odd numbers increase to the south, while even numbers increase to the west, toward the beach. The *zócalo* is bounded by **Calles 8, 10, 11,** and **13. Oriente** sends **buses** from a small booth at the corner of Calles 8 and 11 to **Mérida** (2hr., every hr. 5am-8pm, 41 pesos).

Other services include: **police,** on Calle 13 in the *zócalo* (☎999 155 4835; open 24hr.); **Farmacia Celestún,** Calle 11 94 x 8 y 10 (☎916 2106; open daily 8am-midnight); **Centro de Salud,** Calle 5 x 8 y 10 (☎916 2046; open daily 8am-8:30pm); **Telecomm,** on Calle 11 at the *zócalo* (☎916 2053; open M-F 9am-3pm); and **Internet** access at Hostel Ría Celestún (15 pesos per hr.). Bring a pocketful of cash as **there is no bank, ATM, or traveler's check exchange. Most services accept cash only.**

⚏ ACCOMMODATIONS. Mexican tourists and biologists flock to Celestún from mid-July through August, sending prices through the roof. Call ahead to make sure there's room. Most accommodations are on Calle 12. **Hostel Ría Celestún ❶,** Calle 12 104A x 13, has cool, simple, concrete bunker-style facilities with few windows and saggy beds, but a lovely garden. Hammocks, kitchen, snorkel gear, towels, TV/VCR, Internet (20 pesos per hr.), and bike rental (20 pesos per hr.) are all included. The owner can advise you on the area's sights. (☎916 2170. Dorms 70 pesos; private doubles 150 pesos. Prices rise about 50 pesos in high season. Cash only.) Right on the beach, **Hotel María del Carmen ❸,** Calle 12 111 x 13 y 15, is a 14-room complex. Spartan, golden-toned rooms have ocean views, balconies, and immaculate baths. Parking available. Try to get a room on the third level where sea breezes help out the struggling overhead fans. (☎916 2170. Singles and doubles 200-250 pesos, with A/C 300-350; each additional person 50 pesos. Cash only.) **Hotel Sol y Mar ❸,** Calle 12 104 x 11 y 13, is 1 block from the beach. Vacationing *merideños* love the spotless rooms with TV and fan. The colorful common area boasts a private bar, chirping birds, and a working fountain. (☎916 2166. Singles and doubles 250 pesos, with A/C 350 pesos; 1- and 2-bed suites with kitchen, refrigerator, and A/C 350 pesos; 3- and 4-bed suites 350 pesos, with A/C 450 pesos. Cash only.) Marco and the gang at **Restaurant and Camping El Muelle ❶,** on Calle 12 x 17 near the town pier, are hard at work transforming this popular nightlife spot into a backpacker's beach paradise. So far, three private *cabañas* and a shady camping area have been successfully readied. Clean communal baths and showers and kayak rental. (☎916 2170; boxmool@hotmail.com. Camping 100 pesos; *Cabañas* start at 300 pesos. Cash only.)

Those who don't come to Celestún for the flamingos come to eat the delectable seafood. Specialties include *jaiba* (blue crab), *pulpo* (octopus), and *caracol* (small conch) served fried, battered, or in a simple ceviche. Restaurants line Calle 12 and the beach, and *loncherías* cluster in the *zócalo* (most stalls open daily 6-11am and 6pm-10pm). **Restaurant la Playita ❹,** Calle 12 99 x 9 y 11, is a good place to park a towel and spend the day. This restaurant is fully equipped for beach fun with clean bathrooms and showers as well as a light seafood menu. Flavorful *jaiba frita* (fried blue crab) costs 70 pesos and ice cold beer runs 20 pesos. (☎916 2052. Open daily 10am-6:30pm. Cash only.) Popular, dutch-owned **El Lobo ❸,** on the corner of the *zócalo* between Calles 10 and 13, serves hot waffles with fresh fruit (37 pesos), pancakes (25 pesos), pizza (from 35 pesos), and assorted coffees from the second floor open-air balcony. (Open Tu-Su 8am-11am and 7pm-midnight. Cash only.) For true decadence, head to **La Palapa ⑤**, Calle 12 105 x 11 y 13, and try the outstanding and elegantly presented seafood (80-120 pesos) and *botanas* (snacks; 25-35 pesos) on the beach under the freshly painted giant *palapa*. (☎916 2063; www.hotelmanglares.com. Open daily 11am-6:30pm. AmEx/MC/V.)

◪ **SIGHTS.** Celestún's **estuary** is a major winter stop on the central migratory bird flyway. The best tour takes you south along the coast to **La Ría**, where you'll wind through a river tunnel of intertwining tree branches, pass the **petrified forests** of **Tampetén**, and observe the abandoned village of **Real de Salinas** for a breathtaking view of the salt fields. Heading north through La Ría, you'll reach the **Isla de Pájaros** (Island of Birds), an avian playground with hundreds of flamingos. The tour ends with a visit to a cold, freshwater *cenote*. To see more ruins, ask your boat captain to enter the inlet at **Punta Ninum.** Past the inlet, walk into the jungle and you will come to **Can Balam.** Two main tour operators offer different packages. The **co-op** of fishermen on the beach at the end of Calle 11 leaves right from the beach and allows you to see more of La Ría. (3hr.; 200 pesos per person, 6-person min.; request sights before paying. Tours daily 8am-4pm.) Tours given by **CULTUR** (the state government's tourist agency) leave from their center on Mex. 281, 2km before the town of Celestún. They offer two options: one stops at the flamingo colony, mangroves, and freshwater spring, while the other goes to the above places plus the petrified forest and salt flats. (1hr. 500 pesos; 2hr. 1000 pesos; 6-person max. Entrance 41 pesos per person. Tours daily 8am-6pm.)

If boating isn't your thing, the **bike ride** through the key is almost as stunning. Rent a bike and get advice on various routes from Marcos at Hostel Ría Celestún. Follow Av. al Puerto Abrigo south until you hit the entrance to the Charcos del Sal. Take a right at the small harbor. 4km down the dirt road (past a landfill) is Real de Salinas, an abandoned town that survived on the salt industry until the Revolution. Through the ruins and 2.8km farther down the road at Punta Lastre is a freshwater spring. On the way back, follow the trails on the west to find a private beach perfect for cooling off. A bike ride in the opposite direction, north along the shore, will take you to the tallest lighthouse on the peninsula, **Palmar Faro** (20km from the Celestún center), and to the peaceful **Maya Playa.** Bike rental (20 pesos per hr.) is available at Hostal Ría Celestún. (In town on Calle 12 104A. ☎916 2170.)

PROGRESO   ☎969

Only 30km north of Mérida on the northwestern Yucatec coast, Progreso (pop. 120,000) entices weary *merideños* seeking a convenient weekend retreat. For decades the seaside city, with a 6km pier stretching indefinitely out to the horizon, acted as land-locked Mérida's port, exporting Yucatec *henequén* (a hemp-like fiber). Today, a different kind of cargo passes through the harbor—a never-ending stream of cruise-ship tourists come ashore for fresh seafood and soothing, though not especially clean, beaches. Progreso's cool evenings and colorful vistas of sea and sky are a welcome break from big-city Mérida, but come Tuesday, when the cruise ships from Texas and Florida dock, chaos ensues.

▐ **TRANSPORTATION**

Autoprogreso **buses** travel to **Mérida** (☎955 3024; 50min., every 20min. 5:20am-10pm, 13 pesos). To get to the *zócalo* from the Progreso station, on Calle 29 between Calles 80 and 82, take a left out of the bus station onto Calle 29, then take a right onto Calle 80 and walk a block. To get to the beach, follow Calle 80 in the opposite direction. **Colectivos** leave for Mérida as they fill up from the northern side of the *zócalo*. (12 pesos. 8am-8pm.) *Colectivos* to nearby beaches like Chelem and Chicxulub leave from the corner of Calles 29 and 82 (8am-8pm).

⚙🛈 ORIENTATION AND PRACTICAL INFORMATION

Calle 19, Progreso's brick *malecón*, runs east-west along the beach. Odd-numbered roads run parallel to the *malecón*, increasing to the south. Even-numbered streets are north-south and increase to the west. Progreso's *zócalo* is bounded by **Calles 31** and **33** on the north and south and bisected by the main street, **Calle 80.**

> **Tourist Office:** (☎935 0104), on Calle 80 between Calles 25 and 27. To the right side of Progreso's Casa de la Cultura, north of the lighthouse. Has helpful maps of town and useful beach suggestions. Open M-F 8:30am-7pm, Sa 9am-2pm, Su 9am-1pm.
>
> **Bank: HSBC,** (☎935 0322), on Calle 80 between Calles 29 and 31. Has a **24hr. ATM.** Open M-Sa 8am-7pm.
>
> **Laundromat:** Calle 29 132 (☎935 0856), between Calles 76 and 78. Next-day service. Wash and dry 7 pesos per kg, 3kg min. Open M-Sa 9am-7pm.
>
> **Police:** (☎935 0026), in the Palacio Municipal on the west side of the *zócalo*. Open 24hr.
>
> **Pharmacy: Farmacia Canto** (☎935 1549), at Calles 29 and 80. Open daily July-Aug. 24hr., Sept.-Dec. and Jan.-June 7am-midnight.
>
> **Medical Services: Centro Médico Americano** (☎935 0951), at Calles 33 and 82. Open 24hr.
>
> **Internet Access: Inter Coffee del Sureste,** on Calle 80 between Calles 29 and 31. Enjoy the cranked-up A/C and fast connections. 8 pesos per hr. Open daily 9am-2am.
>
> **Fax Office: Telecomm,** next door to the post office. **Western Union** inside. Open M-F 8am-7pm, Sa-Su 9am-noon.
>
> **Post Office:** Calle 31 150 (☎935 0565), between Calle 78 and the *zócalo*. Open M-F 8:30am-3pm. **Postal Code:** 97320.

🛏 ACCOMMODATIONS

Hotel prices tend to soar in July and August—sometimes doubling on weekends—and vacancies may be hard to find. Plan ahead during the Easter rush as well. All hotels listed have hot water and fans. Camping on the beach, with several bath houses along the *malecón*, is also permitted and generally safe, though you will want to check in with police beforehand and distance yourself from the inebriates who may hang out by the pier.

> **Casa Isidora,** (☎935 4595; www.casaisidora.com), on Calle 21 between Calles 58 and 60. Farther from the *centro* than most hostels, Isidora makes up for it by offering a full service beach getaway. Constant entertainment with the swimming pool, bar, board games, and well-stocked book exchange. Rooms with fluffy white towels and big TVs. Breakfast and purified water included. Free Internet. Reservations recommended for summer. Doubles with fan 480 pesos, with A/C 580 pesos. AmEx/MC/V. ❺
>
> **Hotel Miramar,** Calle 27 124 (☎935 0552), between Calles 74 and 76. The 1st hotel to put down roots in Progreso is still a good value. Choose from spacious rooms or 4 well-ventilated fiberglass pods that probably looked cool in the 1950s. Singles 160 pesos; 1-bed doubles 220 pesos, 2-bed 260 pesos; rooms with A/C 310 pesos; each additional person 50 pesos. Prices rise 10% July-Aug. Cash only. ❸
>
> **Hotel Progreso,** Calle 29 142 (☎935 0039; hotel.progreso@hotmail.com), at Calle 78. The welcoming lobby with seashell and anchor decor and cold, purified water helps

make up for the low ceilings and cramped feel of some of the rooms. Immaculate rooms all have full-size beds, A/C, and cable TV. Singles 210 pesos; doubles 260 pesos; triples 310 pesos; quads 360 pesos. Cash only. ❸

Hotel San Miguel, Calle 78 148 (☎935 1357; sanmiguelhotel@hotmail.com), between Calles 29 and 31, down the street from Hotel Progreso. Offers large, clean rooms in citrus colors. Singles with fan 220 pesos; doubles with A/C 250 pesos. Cash only. ❹

🍴 FOOD

The *pescado frito* (fried fish) signs on nearly every corner attest to Progreso's obsession with cheap seafood, from the **market** on Calle 23 between Calles 80 and 78 to the small *loncherías* just behind the main drag. If you don't like your dinner caught in a net, pickings in Progreso are slim. The best option for vegetarians is the supermarket **San Francisco de Asís,** at Calle 80 144 between Calles 29 and 31. (☎955 3760. Open daily 7am-10pm.) The **Plaza del Mar** shopping center, on Calle 27 between Calles 76 and 78, hides an air-conditioned food court with a couple of affordable options, including pizza and Greek cuisine.

Restaurant los Cocos, between Calles 76 and 78, on the *malecón.* Choose your own fish from the day's catch and they'll fry it to golden-brown salty perfection (40 pesos), and have it served to you on the beach for an extra 5 pesos. Takeout also available. Entrees 90 pesos. Open daily 8am-7pm. Cash only. ❹

El Cordobés, Calle 80 150 (☎955 2621), at Calle 31. *Comida típica* comes with a great view of the park and the lovely Palacio Municipal as well as a laid-back attitude, which is a relief coming off the frenzied *malecón.* Get a heaping fruit salad for 38 pesos. Fish dishes from 75 pesos. Open daily 6am-midnight. Cash only. ❹

Flamingos (☎935 2122), on the *malecón* near Calle 72. You have your choice of seafood specialties, Chinese food (45-60 pesos), pastas (30-40 pesos), chicken dishes (45-60 pesos), and salads, though the fare may not be worth the price. However, access to clean bathrooms and showers for beachside patrons may make it worth the extra expense. Open daily 8am-1am. Cash only. ❸

🏖👁 BEACHES AND SIGHTS

Progreso's shallow waters, beach boardwalks, and *palapas* attract hordes of visitors in August but remain calm the rest of the year (except when cruise ships dock). The **Puerto de Altura** *muelle,* Mexico's longest pier, appears to extend infinitely from the beach west of the *malecón.* Because the peninsula's limestone shelf descends so gradually into the sea, the pier had to stretch 6km before reaching deep water. The beach east of the pier along the *malecón* is prime territory for food and art vendors as well as large families flirting with the gentle surf.

For a more remote beach experience, try the beaches at one of the many nearby fishing villages. **Chelem,** 9km west of town, or the even less inhabited **Chuburná,** 13km beyond Chelem, have lots of clean sand with few services and no strolling vendors. From Chuburná, you can also arrange for a birdwatching tour or rent a kayak to explore the north end of the Celestún Biosphere Reserve's lagoon, though tours are easier to arrange from Celestún. *Combis* leave for Chelem and Chuburná in front of the parking lot of the supermarket San Francisco on Calle 80. (Every 15min. or when full, until 8pm. 5.50 pesos.) *Combis* to Chuburná leave when full from the opposite side of the street, in front of HSBC (7 pesos). The wider, cleaner, closer beaches 3km to the east of town in **Chicxulub** are lined with the summer homes of Mérida's and Mexico City's well-to-do and provide for nice walks. (5min. *combi* ride from the northwest corner of Calles 82 and 29, near the bus station. 4 pesos.) Before heading to the beach, stop at **Uaymitun Reserve,** where a three-story observation tower allows you to look out over blue-green marshes home to thousands of pink flamingos. Before dawn and in the evening the flamingos come right up to the lookout to nest, and they spend the rest of the day further out on Laguna Ciénega. Binoculars are available for rent for 11.50 pesos. (Take a 4-peso *combi* to Chicxulub. At the *zócalo* in Chicxulub, find a Uaymitun-bound *combi* to continue to the observatory; 5 pesos. Open daily 8am-6pm.)

The largely unexplored Mayan city and salt distribution center of **X'cambó** ("Heavenly Crocodile" or "Trading Place") lies 10km east of Uaymitun and 26km east of Progreso, at the end of a 2km road that intersects the road to Telchac Puerto. The only way to get there from Progreso is by taxi (round-trip 300 pesos). The small, recently restored site consists of several structures and two **pyramids**— one of which supports two large, unidentified stucco masks. A Catholic church, still a place of pilgrimage and offering, was built into the side of one of the pyramids 50 years ago in honor of the Virgin of X'cambó. Small paths branch from the site to unexcavated ruins and tiny villages. (Open daily 9am-5pm. Free.)

LA RUTA PUUC AND ENVIRONS

Between Mérida and Campeche lies the hilly and fertile Puuc ("hills" in Mayan) region. In the heart of this remote area lie dozens of Mayan ruins, collectively known as La Ruta Puuc (The Puuc Route). In ancient times, between 300 BC and 1200 AD, the Mayan cities along La Ruta Puuc were linked by regular trade, a north-south *sacbé* (raised roadway), and a collective population of over 25,000 people. Today, the ruins are more visibly united by the salmon-pink limestone and the strikingly similar geometric decorative patterns.

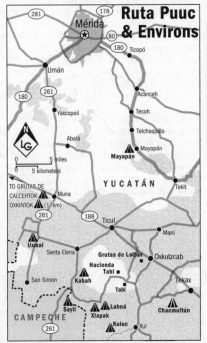

Though La Ruta Puuc refers to a very specific set of ruins (Uxmal, Kabah, Sayil, and Labná), the small farming towns and a few other nearby sights make worthwhile stopovers and are included in this section. The towns of Muna, Ticul, Oxkutzcab, and Santa Elena offer roofs, food, and friendly advice; choosing a place to stop during multi-day trips will hinge on the quality of accommodation you're looking for and the areas you plan to visit. Two to three days should provide ample time for exploration. Visitors from Mérida or Campeche take **Mex. 180** to **Mex. 184,** which runs east and forms the northern border of much of Puuc; together with **Mex. 261,** it frames most of the ruins. The sites

Oxkintok and **Las Grutas de Calcehtok,** not properly part of the Ruta, are 20km northwest of Muna, while the ruins of **Mayapán** lie 30km northeast of Muna.

Because of the large number of sites (and the relatively small size of some) scattered about the area, renting a car in Mérida is the easiest and most flexible way to see what you came for. The roads are generally safe and well-marked, and will bring you through jungle and indigenous villages on your way between sights. Travel agencies in both Mérida and Campeche offer organized tours, which are frequently whirlwind affairs. **Autotransportes del Sur** sends a "Ruta Puuc" bus from Mérida at 8am that will whisk you through Kabah, Sayil, Xlapak, Labná, and Uxmal—quickly enough to return by 4pm. The bus spends 30min. at the sites and 2hr. at Uxmal (87 pesos; admission to sites not included). No other buses travel the Sayil-Oxkutzkub road. Disorganized public transportation can be difficult and will undoubtedly lead to frustrating waits. Although *Let's Go* does not recommend hitchhiking, many travelers are successful at finding rides along the Sayil-Oxkutzkub road. Buses are most frequent in the mornings, but return trips are never guaranteed. Second-class buses do travel Mex. 261 frequently and will stop when flagged down. *Combis* run frequently between Oxkutzcab, Ticul, Santa Elena, and Muna, and will make any trip for the right price. To pursue this option, it is best, though not easiest, to catch *combis* from the *zócalo* in Muna.

▧ UXMAL

Uxmal (oosh-MAL; "thrice built" or "region of fruitful harvests" in Mayan) is sure to impress with huge palaces, exciting legends, and striking architecture set against the rolling green hills. Travelers can easily venture into the surrounding jungle to see structures yet to be excavated.

▤ TRANSPORTATION. Uxmal sits just off Mex. 261. Autotransportes del Sur runs from Mérida (1½hr., 6 per day, 45 pesos). The "Ruta Puuc" bus also stops here. From Campeche, take a "Camioneros de Campeche" bus to Mérida (3hr., 5 per day, 55 pesos) and ask to be dropped off at the ruins' access road. Last return bus 6pm. You may be able to catch a *combi* back to Santa Elena and surrounding villages with the hotel workers, but departure times are unpredictable.

▜▣ ACCOMMODATIONS AND FOOD. Uxmal is the only site on the Ruta Puuc with accommodations and food, and all the convenient rooms are in luxurious, multi-star hotels. Five kilometers north of the ruins on Mex. 261, **Rancho Uxmal ❹** has pink rooms and a swimming pool. (Rooms 250 pesos, with A/C 300 pesos.) The attached, *palapa*-covered **bar-restaurant ❸** serves breakfast for 30-50 pesos, and Yucatec favorites for 40-65 pesos. (☎977 6254. Open daily 8am-6pm.) Next door is **Cana Nah Restaurant ❹,** with better ambience and a larger pool, but generally the same menu. (☎910 3829. Entrees 50 pesos. Open daily 9:30am-6pm.) At the ruins, the air-conditioned **Restaurant Yax-beh ❹** makes sandwiches (45-50 pesos), spaghetti (80 pesos), and *comida típica*, all of which are decent but pricey. (Entrees 55-115 pesos. Open daily 8am-8:30pm. Cash only.)

◎ SIGHTS

In AD 200, Uxmal was a mere village with a system of *chultunes* (cisterns) to collect water for the dry months. Soon thereafter, Uxmal became the most prominent of the Ruta Puuc sites and its influence extended across the region. By AD 900, Uxmal had grown into a sizable town of 20,000 and dominated the fertile Santa Elena valley, and perhaps much farther, through what appears to have been a fairly violent process. The Xius, an immigrant group who probably came from Tikal or central Mexico, brought the cult of Quetzalcóatl in the 10th century, and merchants became the city's new rulers. Some evidence indicates an alliance with Chichén Itzá, but a wall built later around the inner city implies that Uxmal went on the defensive, possibly because that relationship had turned ugly. The city depopulated around the same time as the rest of the Puuc region—many archaeologists believe a series of droughts rendered the area uninhabitable, citing the *Chilam Balam*, Mayan texts from after the Spanish Conquest, which include both mythology and local history. *(Site and museum open daily 8am-5pm; shops close in winter 8pm, in summer 9pm. Light-and-sound show in summer 8pm, in winter 7pm. Show 30 pesos; English and French audio translations 25 pesos. Site, museum, and show combo 95 pesos. Parking 10 pesos. Spanish guides 400 pesos, other languages 450 pesos for 1-20 people. Video camera use 35 pesos. Free luggage storage. ATM in the museum complex.)*

CHULTUNE. On the walkway as you enter Uxmal is an example of a Puuc region *chultune*. This cistern, typical of the area, collected water for the city. Many Mayan sites depended on *cenotes* for collecting water, but groundwater in the Puuc region runs much deeper than in the rest of the peninsula, which forced residents to use *aguadas*, limestone-lined depressions, as reservoirs.

PIRAMIDE DEL MAGO. According to legend, the 35m "Pyramid of the Magician" was built overnight by a dwarf who hatched from a witch's egg and grew to maturity in a year. In response to a challenge by the king, who was angry over a previous defeat, the dwarf agreed to build the structure overnight. He completed the building and was named magician of the land. The pyramid, which contains five temples, was actually built in five stages between AD 600 and 900; the multiple stages of construction are apparent in the mix of stonework used and the differences between successive levels.

CUADRANGULO DE LOS PAJAROS. Immediately west of the pyramid lies the "Quadrangle of the Birds," named for the bird sculptures adorning the structures on its western side and the palm leaves (or feathers) on the roof. Buildings erected at different times enclose the north and south sides and center on an altar whose use is not known.

CUADRANGULO DE LAS MONJAS. Continuing to the west, Uxmal's famed nunnery lies in the large "Quadrangle of the Nuns." Circa AD 900, it was misnamed by the Spanish, who thought its many rooms resembled those of a convent. Each of the four buildings was built on a different level with distinctive decor. Some say the buildings represent the Mayan vision of the cosmos: the southern is the lowest and symbolizes the underworld; the northernmost is highest, the house of heaven; and the east and west buildings are on the same level, the middle world where the sun sets and rises daily. A column in the center stands as a symbolic *ceiba* tree, the center of the universe in Mayan cosmology. To the south lies the 34m long ball court, where only the western stone ring remains—a cement copy of the one in the museum. The court runs from north to south; the eastern side represents good and light, while the western side symbolizes evil and darkness.

EL CEMENTERIO. Emerging from the ball court, a path leads to a small, leafy plaza bounded by a pyramid to the north and a temple to the west. Stones that were once platforms at the foot of the pyramid bear haunting reliefs of skulls similar to those found at Chichén Itzá (p. 646). The platforms, known as *tzompantles*, likely relate to Uxmal's military victories and undertakings. To the west, *El Palomar* (Pigeon House), with a plain facade and cornice typical of older Puuc constructions, has three doors leading to the central patio.

PALACIO DEL GOBERNADOR. From the ball court, head south to the enormous Governor's Palace. Replete with strikingly well-preserved engravings and arches, it was one of the last buildings constructed, around AD 900. The attention to detail has led many to consider it the finest example of architecture at Uxmal. Intertwined stylized snakes, representing Quetzalcóatl, cover much of the frieze, along with Chac masks that create their own serpentine illusions. The center features the rain god Chac on his throne, in whose name many of Uxmal's most prominent structures were built. The building is thought to have served as the royal dwelling, as well as the meeting place for the town council.

CASA DE LAS TORTUGAS. Realistic, sculpted turtles adorn the upper frieze of the outwardly simple, two-story House of the Turtles; they may have symbolized rain, suggesting that the building was used for the worship of water.

GRAN PIRAMIDE. Also known as "The Dwarf's House," the Great Pyramid consists of nine square levels stretching 80m long and 30m high. According to legend, the spiteful ruler tried to undermine the dwarf-magician's less-traditional pyramid by complaining that its base was oval. He suggested settling their quarrel by seeing who could break a *cocoyol* (a small, hard-shelled fruit) on his head. The dwarf-magician cleverly slipped a turtle shell over his head and easily cracked the *cocoyol*, while the unfortunate king bashed in his own head. Atop the pyramid sits the **Macaw Temple,** with many engravings of the bird on its facade. The masks and artwork here have a more rounded look than other Uxmal art; they represent the 8th-century Codz-Poop ("rolled-up mat") style.

EL PALOMAR DOVECOTES. Just west of the Great Pyramid, these structures were designed in the same style as the nunnery. The name is derived from a series of roof-combs, which look like nesting sites, on the northern building. The protruding stones once supported stucco and stone figures now guarded in museums.

CASA DE LA VIEJA. To reach the "House of the Old Woman" from the entrance, follow the trail south to five buildings surrounding a small patio. Among these is the Casa, one of the oldest constructions in Uxmal, dating from between AD 670 and 770. It supposedly belonged to the witch who birthed the famed dwarf. **El Templo de los Falos** (the Temple of the Phalli), 500m farther south, was once adorned with phallic structures symbolizing earthly and human fertility.

KABAH

23km southeast of Uxmal, Kabah is bisected by Mex. 261 and is reachable by any 2nd-class bus between Mérida and Campeche; travel is easiest by the "Ruta Puuc" bus. Buses will only stop by request. Open daily 9am-5pm. 34 pesos. Video camera use 30 pesos.

Once the second largest city in northern Yucatán, Kabah ("Mighty Hand" in Mayan) was built by slaves during the Classic period (AD 700-1000). The highlight is the visual feast of the ⬛**Codz-Poop Temple** (Wall of Masks), the single most psychedelic piece of architecture on the Yucatán Peninsula. Two-hundred and fifty faces of Chac, the rain god, stare out fearsomely from the temple's western facade. The effect is diluted slightly because nearly all the noses are broken, but the spectacle is nonetheless alarming. Unlike other Puuc structures, characterized by plain columns and a superior decorative frieze, Codz-Poop stands out as an extreme example of the more ornate Puuc Classic Mosaic style. Chac's prominence relates to the importance of rain for the inhabitants of Kabah, where there is little to no rainfall for half of the year. Standing proudly behind the temple are two impressive statues whose facial scarring and claw-like hands indicate noble lineage. Continue east and you will come across the two-story **Palacio,** which contains 14 *chultunes* (cisterns), suggesting that it functioned as a residence for the elite. In contrast with the flamboyant facade of the Codz-Poop, the palace's groups of small columns, separated by simple panels, are more characteristic of the early Puuc or Classic Colonette style. A path (200m) beginning at the rear left corner of the Palacio will take you to **Las Columnas,** where the only columns are those set into the facade of the small rectangular building. The site is thought to have served as a court where justices settled disputes and gods comprised the jury. Across the street by the parking lot, a short dirt road leads to rubble (right), more rubble (left), and the famous **Kabah Arch** (straight). The arch marks the beginning of the ancient *sacbé* that ended with a twin arch in Uxmal. The archway is perfectly aligned with the north and south, testifying to the Maya's astronomical prowess.

> **🏴 TIP** **STYLE NUMBER 2.** The Codz-Poop style was developed late in the Classic Puuc period (AD 770-950). The exterior decorations, carved from thousands of pre-cut stones, were larger, more elaborate, and more durable than their stucco predecessors, due to new cement techniques developed to secure stones to the building. The name Codz-Poop, which means "rolled-up mat" in Mayan, is derived from the peculiar appearance of the repeated stone pattern.

SAYIL

Sayil lies 5km off Mex. 261 on the Sayil-Oxkutzcab road, a stop on the "Ruta Puuc" bus. A bus between Mérida and Campeche passes by the crucero 5km from the site (every hr.). Site open daily 8am-5pm. 34 pesos.

Sayil, located in a small fertile valley, at one time controlled over 70 sq. km of territory (possibly taking advantage of more distant patches of rich earth) and had a population of about 7000-8000. The site is a favorite of archaeologists for its long history and various styles of architecture. The **Palace of Sayil** stands out among the region's ruins as one of the only asymmetrical buildings. The unique three-story structure was constructed in several stages from around AD 650 to AD 900, and its facade remains a great example of the Classic Colonette style. It harbors 98 rooms, which served as housing, storage, and administrative space for 350 people. In the foundation are eight underground *chultunes*. Crowning the otherwise unadorned second level are friezes of Chac and the "Diving God" flanked by stylized serpents. The symbolism of these friezes is still being researched. Seven large human figures wearing ornate headdresses once decorated the third level of the palace. The *sacbé* across from the Palace leads to **El Mirador,** a lofty pyramidal temple topped by a once-painted and plastered roof-comb, typical of early Puuc architecture (though originally introduced in the Peten region of Guatemala). To the left, a 100m path leads through the jungle to the **Estela del Falo** (Stela of the Phallus), a tribute to Yum Keep, a Mayan fertility god. The peaceful feminine figure with the large phallus is worth a look, if only to lighten the mood. Among the buildings lying in pieces is **El Templo de las Cabezas** (The Temple of Heads), across the street and up a dirt path. The steep hike through a thriving colony of mosquitoes leads to a view of the top of Sayil's palace, which is best seen during the dry season.

LABNÁ

17km east of Mex. 261. No public buses make the trip; the "Ruta Puuc" bus or a private car are the best options. Site open daily 8am-5pm. 34 pesos.

YUCATÁN PENINSULA

The last of the Ruta Puuc ruins, Labná, the best example of the Puuc style, was constructed toward the end of the Late Classic period (AD 700-1000) when the Puuc cities were connected by *sacbé* (paved, elevated roads). A short, reconstructed section of the *sacbé* runs between Labná's most impressive sights: the palace and the Arch of Labná. The partially restored **palace** stretches along the northern side, to the left as you enter the site. Built in 12 stages, its 67 rooms, seven patios, and two levels lack architectural unity. On the second tier of the eastern portion is the image of Itzamná, the creator god, represented by a lizard in whose belly sits a human head. What Labná is famous for, though, is the picturesque **Arch of Labná,** which still has hints of its original red and green colors as well as ancient handprints on the inner walls. Archaeologists believe that the arch could have served as a ceremonial entry point for returning victorious warriors, as a vaulted passageway linking two ceremonial patios, or as an entrance for the upper class. The lattice designs and upper mosaic (in the form of two thatched houses) are considered a classic example of the Puuc style and are reminiscent of Maya-Toltec sites like Chichén Itzá (p. 646), whose residents conquered Puuc territories around AD 900. The observatory, **El Mirador,** stands atop a rocky pyramid, beyond the arch. The roof-comb of El Mirador was once magnificently decorated with stucco-modeled figurines of Mayan nobility. Back toward the palace, **El Templo de las Columnas** is off the *sacbé* to the right. The columns on the upper face, the middle layer, and the molding are great examples of the Classic Colonette style.

HACIENDA TABI

The hacienda is accessible only in the dry season with a reliable car. The way is well-marked heading south from the Grutas de Loltún; take the road that branches off to the right and follow the signs. The dirt road goes straight (4km) when the main road veers right. From Labná heading north, turn at the sign for the hacienda and go straight, passing three roads. Take a right at the 4th through the orchards. At the end, turn left and continue straight for 1km until the gate. The final 4km are unpaved. Open daily 9am-5pm. 20 pesos. The Hacienda, the upscale reconstructed main building, also has a B&B and camping space by reservation. (☎923 9454 or 996 8283; leta@fyc.org.mx. Camping 120 pesos per person; includes tent and sleeping bag. Doubles 540 pesos; includes fan, breakfast, and dinner. Cash only.)

A break from the Ruta Puuc ruins, this *hacienda*, built among waving grasses and hordes of yellow butterflies, is a monument to a less glorious part of Mexico's history. The building was once a sugar-producing facility that relied on Mayan and Chinese slave labor. A fire after the Caste War (1847-1901) destroyed a large part of the fields and the church, which was rebuilt in 1896. The **Casa Principal** was built in stages and finished in 1895 by its then-owner, Elogio Duarte Troncoso, a native of the Canary Islands. In 1910, the *hacienda* had 433 residents, who lived in huts near the processing facility. During the Revolution, the slaves were set free; most either moved to another plantation or dispersed to surrounding towns. Since 1993, the beautifully restored *hacienda* has been part of a state government reserve and lumbering has been prohibited, allowing for the growth of trees native to the area. The on-site museum, if open, will enrich the experience tremendously; if it's closed, try out your Spanish with one of the knowledgeable caretakers.

TICUL ☎997

Ticul (pop. 35,000) is a convenient, lively, and inexpensive base for exploring the Ruta Puuc sites of Uxmal, Kabah, Sayil, and Labná, as well as the Grutas de Loltún and the ruins of Mayapán (p. 628). In the streets around the large, bustling *zócalo*, you'll notice an excessive number of *zapaterías* (shoe stores)—

Ticul is the shoe-producing capital of southern Mexico. The town is home to the 17th-century Templo de San Antonio (open daily 8am-6pm) and hosts shoe fairs several times a year, where you'll see men carting tremendous stacks of shoe-boxes tied together with twine, with one box missing so they can see where they're going. On the outskirts of town, large *alfererias* (kilns) turn out enormous earthenware pots by the thousands for international distribution.

E TRANSPORTATION. Ticul's **bus station** (☎972 0162) is on Calle 24 x 25 y 25A, behind the church. Buses go to **Mérida** (every hr. 4:30am-9pm, 42 pesos), **Cancún** (8 per day, 1:30am-11:30pm, 204 pesos), **Tulum** (7am and 2:50pm, 150 pesos), and a few other destinations. **Combis** leave from Hotel San Miguel for **Muna** (12 pesos), **Santa Elena, Uxmal,** and **Kabah** (15 pesos) from Calle 30, between Calles 25 and 25A, and for **Oxkutzcab** from Calle 25A, between Calles 24 and 26 (every 20min., 10 pesos).

⚷ PRACTICAL INFORMATION. The main road, **Calle 23,** runs east-west with odd-numbered streets increasing to the south. Even-numbered streets run north-south, increasing to the west. The *zócalo* is east of Calle 26 between Calles 23 and 25; most activity is between it and Calle 30, three blocks west. There is a **Banamex** on Calle 26 199, between Calles 23 and 25, which **exchanges currency** and has a **24hr. ATM.** (☎972 1120. Open M-F 9am-4pm). Other services include: **police** on Calle 23, at the northeast corner of the *zócalo* (☎972 0210); **Farmacias Bazar,** Calle 25 201, at the corner of Calle 26A (☎972 1934; open 24hr.); **Centro de Salud,** Calle 27 226, between Calles 30 and 32 (open M-F 8am-4pm); **fax** at **Telecomm,** on Calle 24A between Calles 21 and 23, northeast of the *zócalo* (☎972 0146; open M-F 9am-3pm, Sa 9am-1pm); **Internet** access at **Flashnet,** on the eastern end of the *zócalo* (10 pesos per hr., open daily 9am-2am); and the **post office,** in the Palacio Municipal, on the northeastern side of the *zócalo*. (☎972 1120, open M-F 8am-2:30pm). **Postal Code:** 97861.

⚷◨ ACCOMMODATIONS AND FOOD. During the shoe fairs and in mid-July, cheaper hotels fill up with vacationing students, so it may be a good idea to reserve ahead before visiting Ticul. **Hotel Sierra Sosa ❸,** Calle 26 199A, between Calles 21 and 23 near the northwest corner of the *zócalo*, has clean baths, firm beds, strong fans, and TV. The small lobby is a meeting place for locals. (☎972 0008. Reception 8am-10pm. Check-out 1pm. Singles 170 pesos, with A/C 215 pesos; doubles 190/235 pesos; each additional person 25 pesos. Cash only.) **Hotel San Miguel ❷,** on Calle 28 half a block north of Calle 23, has clean rooms and no lobby. (☎972 0051. Reception 24hr. Singles 100 pesos; 1-bed doubles 130 pesos, with 2 beds 180 pesos. Cash only.) The nicest hotel in town, **Hotel Plaza ❺,** Calle 23 202 between Calles 26 and 26A, has rooms with large beds, private bath, and powerful A/C. Rooms overlooking the *zócalo* tend to be noisy. The pleasant garden patio restaurant serves breakfast 7-10am for 40 pesos. (☎972 0484; www.hotelplazayucatan.com. Doubles 460 pesos. MC/V.) **El Jardín Posada ❹,** Calle 27 216 between Calles 28 y 30, is set back from the street amid lush vegetation. Four attractive, spacious cabins come with A/C, living room, kitchenette, porch, and hammock. El Jardín also has a pool. (☎972 0401; www.posadajardin.com. Breakfast 40 pesos. Cabins 300-350 pesos. Cash only.) **Hotel San Antonio ❹,** Calle 25A 202 between Calles 26 and 26A, offers immaculate rooms with A/C, phone, and TV. (☎972 1893 or 1894. Reception 24hr. Check-out 1pm. Singles 234 pesos; doubles 292 pesos; triples and quads 351 pesos.)

After a hot day on the Ruta Puuc, Ticul is a great place to refuel and rehydrate. **Los Almendros ❹,** 1km from the *centro* off the Ticul-Chetumal highway (Calle 22B), was the first of a chain of restaurants now in Mérida (p. 617) and the birthplace of *poc-chuc* (pork cooked with onions, beans, tomatoes, and spicy *haban-*

ero peppers; 60 pesos). Los Almendros serves popular Yucatec cuisine, with dishes like *pollo pibil* (chicken marinated in bitter orange juice and baked in banana leaves; 50 pesos). The restaurant also has a pool. (☎972 0021. Open daily 9am-9pm. Cash only.) **Cocina Económica D'Rubí ❷,** Calle 25 216A between Calles 30 and 32, offers tourists two delicious, home-cooked daily specials that come with soup, side, and tortillas for 30 pesos. (☎972 0509. Open daily 9am-5pm. Cash only.) The only restaurant in town open for dinner is **Pizzeria la Gondola ❹,** Calle 23 208 at Calle 26A. La Gondola offers a taste of Italy with large pizzas for 75-90 pesos. (☎972 0112. Free delivery. Open daily 8am-1pm and 5:30pm-midnight. Cash only.) The **market,** off Calle 23, between Calles 28 and 30, has food stands, produce, and more. (Open daily 6am-2pm; busiest Tu, Th, and Sa.) **Super Solomon,** across from the market, has standard groceries. (Open daily 8am-10pm.) *Loncherías* along Calles 23 between Calles 26 and 30 serve up Ticul's cheapest food.

MUNA   ☎997

A mere 15km northeast of Uxmal, Muna (pop. 3500) is the best place for getting an early start at the ruins if you're coming from Mérida. It has recently grown into a convenient stop for tourists, with **Internet** access, above the PEMEX gas station in the town center (open daily 7am-10pm; 10 pesos per hr.), many **loncherías** (most open daily 6am-noon), **combis** (7 pesos to Uxmal), a **Copercaja currency exchange** booth, and basic services all located on the *zócalo*.

Two kilometers west of Muna on the Muna-Opichen highway you'll find **Conjunto Ecoturístico ❷,** a hotel/co-op/museum that offers *palapa* huts with fans and cool concrete floors and a large kitchen at your disposal. (☎999 970 2249 or 987 5585; www.mun-ha.com. 125 pesos per person.) **Hotel GL ❷,** Calle 26 200, is right before the *zócalo*, just off the highway on your right as you approach from Uxmal. This simple inn allows you to park outside your room, take a hot shower, sleep under a fan or A/C, and be on your way. Don't expect the highest standards of cleanliness. (☎991 0097. 1 person 130 pesos, with TV 150 pesos, with A/C 200 pesos; 2 people with fan 200 pesos; 3 people with A/C 300 pesos. Hammock space free. 10% student discount.) The best restaurant, **Lol-Pich ❸,** is 1km north on Mex. 261. A shady courtyard and small swimming pools as well as a forest of the namesake trees (pich) surround a small *palapa*-roofed seating area. Try the traditional entrees like *pollo pibil* (chicken marinated in bitter orange juice and baked in banana leaves) for 50 pesos. (☎999 221 0075. Open daily 10am-7pm. Cash only.)

SANTA ELENA   ☎997

This town, with 4300 Mayan residents, has the basics and then some, including a park and an 18th-century church (once the site of a Mayan pyramid) that boasts magnificent views from its roof (ask at the museum for the way up). The small local museum, on the top of the hill beside the church, showcases recently unearthed infant mummies dubbed "The Dwarves of Santa Elena" by the local newspaper. (Open daily 8am-7pm. 10 pesos.)

Santa Elena has a few appealing accommodations for travelers along Mex. 261. Be aware that American and Mexican student groups often fill up all the beds in town in late June and early July. **⧉Sacbé Bungalows ❶,** km 127, offers weary travelers a near-jungle experience with pristine and well-marked gardens as well as tidy *cabañas* with solar-heated showers, toilets, outdoor grills, and on-site breakfast (50 pesos). (☎985 858 1281 or 978 5158; www.sacbebunga-lows.com.mx. 2-bed bungalows 230-290 pesos; each additional person 50 pesos.) Closest to town, the **Flycatcher B&B ❺,** across highway 261 from the school, has four large suites with private baths and A/C. The extensive grounds have several marked hiking trails where you can spot wetland deer as well as jungle birds. (www.flycatcherinn.com. Rooms 500-700 pesos. Cash only.) Across the road and only 150m from Sacbé Bungalows lies **Hotel/Restaurant El Chac-Mool ❶**, which has hammock space in private *cabañas* (35 pesos) and four singles with fans and clean private baths. (Singles 200 pesos.) The adjacent **restaurant ❸** is the best in town, serving large helpings of eggs, tacos, chicken, sandwiches, and veggie options for 35-45 pesos. (☎978 5117. Open daily 10am-10pm. Cash only.) **La Central ❸**, off the *zócalo*, has traditional Yucatec meals for 40 pesos. (Open daily 11am-8pm.) Newly opened, **The Pickled Onion ❹**, 500m from town on the road to Kabah, is the last food stop before delving into the heart of La Ruta Puuc. Valerie, the friendly British-Canadian owner, will pack boxed lunches with advance notice (40 pesos). Dinner options include vegetarian treats such as *chaya* souffle (50 pesos) and meat and potato standards (65 pesos). (☎999 223 0708. Open M-Sa noon-8:30pm, Su 5-8:30pm. Cash only.)

Buses bound for Palenque via Campeche (7 per day 7:30am-7:30pm) from Mérida, as well as those headed the opposite way (7 per day 6am-8pm), pass town on **Mex. 261** at Calle 20 in front of the school. The "Ruta Puuc" bus stops between 9:15 and 9:30am along the highway at Calle 20, across the highway from the school. It then proceeds to the Ruta Puuc sites, ending up at Uxmal, but you'll need a lift or a **combi** to return to Santa Elena. To reach Grutas de Loltún, take a series of *combis* going to Ticul, through Oxkutzcab, and finally on to Loltún. Basic services include: **police** (☎978 5244), at the north end of the *zócalo*; **Farmacia Mirna**, one block south of the *zócalo* on Calle 20 (☎978 5048; open daily 8am-1pm and 5pm-10pm); and Dr. Luis Sansores Mian next door at the **Consultorio Médico.**

OXKUTZCAB   ☎997

Oxkutzcab (osh-kootz-KAB; pop. 30,000) lies farthest east along the Ruta. The town is much less touristed, so you'll get more for your money, but you will probably end up looking around forlornly, wondering where all the restaurants are. Oxkutzcab is known as the "Orchard of the State," and its central market is appropriately overflowing with fruits and vegetables. Climb the hill on Calle 54 to the Santa Isabel Church for a view of the entire city, or stop by the old railroad station, now the Casa de Cultura. Otherwise, there's not much else besides cheap lodging.

The accommodations listed below all are within walking distance of public transportation. **Hotel Rosalía ❶**, Calle 54 101 x 51 y 53, is a favorite among traveling vendors. Well-kept rooms with private bath, fan, and TV are 50m from the bus station and 100m from the *centro*. (☎975 0167. Singles 130 pesos; doubles with fan 160 pesos, with A/C 200 pesos; triples with A/C 330 pesos.) **Hospedaje Dorán ❶**, on the walkway behind the *loncherías* across from the market, isn't quite as nice. (Singles and 1-bed doubles 130 pesos; 2-bed doubles with TV 160 pesos.)

The Mayab **bus station** is on Calle 51 x 54 y 56, two blocks north of the *centro*. Buses go to: **Campeche** (6pm, 94 pesos); **Cancún** (8 per day 5am-midnight, 198 pesos); **Chetumal** (7 per day 4:20am-7pm, 146 pesos); **Mérida** (21 per day 5:30am-7:30pm, 48 pesos); **Muna** (21 per day 5:30am-7:30pm, 18 pesos); **Playa del Carmen** (8 per day, 170 pesos); **Ticul** (21 per day 5:30am-7:30pm, 10 pesos); **Tulum** (8 per day, 140 pesos). *Combis* across from the market leave for the Grutas de Loltún (8 pesos). The *zócalo* is bordered by **Calles 48, 50, 51,** and **53.** Local services include: **Banamex,** Calle 50 x 51 y 53 (**24hr. ATM;** open M-F 9am-4pm); **police** (☎975 0615); **Farmacia María del Carmen,** Calle 51 106 x 52 (☎975 0165; open 7am-11pm); **Hospital IMSS,** Calle 64 x 49 y 51 (☎975 0241), with 24hr. emergency service; **fax** at **Telecomm,** in the municipal building (☎975 0079; open M-F 9am-3pm, Sa 9am-noon); **Internet** access at **Interc@fe,** Calle 52, one block north of the *zócalo* (12 pesos per hr.; open M-Sa 8am-9pm, Su 9:30am-4:30pm); and the **post office,** on Calle 48 x 53 y 55. **Postal Code:** 97880.

GRUTAS DE LOLTÚN

Loltún is accessible by car on the Sayil-Oxkutzcab road. Alternatively, snag a combi to Oxkutzcab from Calle 25A between Calles 24 and 26 in Ticul (every 20min., 8 pesos). You'll be let off at Calles 23 and 26. Combis and colectivos leave across from Oxkutzcab's market for Loltún, on 20 de Noviembre. Ask to be dropped off at the caves (10min., 5 pesos). The caves are lit only during tours and you are not allowed to enter without a guide. Tours in English and Spanish daily 9:30, 11am, 12:30, 2, 3, 4pm. 54 pesos; guides expect tips of around 30 pesos per person. Parking 10 pesos.

The Grutas de Loltún comprise what is believed to be the largest cave system in Yucatán state. The word "loltún" ("stone flower" in Mayan) refers to the fascinating natural formations in the caves. The enormous caverns hold the earliest evidence of humans on the Yucatán, as well as fossils of extinct mastodons and saber-toothed tigers from the Ice Age. Around 2000 BC, the ancient indigenous people settled here to take advantage of the water and clay, leaving behind pottery, marine shells, carvings, and cave paintings. Thousands of years later, Mayan *campesinos* returned, seeking refuge from the Caste War. Important caverns include the **Galería de las Manos Negras** (known as the "Room of Inscriptions"), full of black-painted handprint murals representing the Mayan underworld; the **Na Cab** ("House of the Bees"), named for the many niches in the cavern wall that host beehives; and the **Maya Gallery,** which once contained an Olmec sculpture known as "La Cabeza de Loltún." Several caves contain hollow stalactites and columns—strike each one with the heel of your hand and listen as a soft booming sound reverberates throughout the caves. Archaeologists speculate that the Maya may have used these formations as a means of underground communication.

OXKINTOK

Oxkintok is 5km off Mex. 180, near the town of Maxcanú. Coming from Mérida, it is the 1st sight. Follow the well-marked road about 2km. Go right at the fork. The ruins lie about 3km farther. The last kilometer is unpaved. Open daily 8am-5pm. 34 pesos.

More than 40km northwest of Uxmal, Oxkintok (OSH-kin-tawk) was never a part of La Ruta Puuc in the days of the ancient Maya, but it was the largest city in the Puuc region during the early Classic period, possibly due to its involvement in the salt trade. The pinkish limestone and beautiful views overlooking the lonely green hills make it an attractive stop on the way to the other sights. The *centro* was constructed mostly between AD 400 and 600, and it was abandoned by 1050. Its architectural elements, symbolism, and materials have a Teotihuacán influence (p. 141), presumably acquired either by direct or indirect contact with other Mayan cultures who disseminated the style. The best views are to be found atop the **Ah-May Pyramid,** the tallest structure at 18m, and behind the **Palacio Chich,** in the Ah-Canul group. Next to Palacio Chich is the **Templo del Diablo** (Temple of the Devil), which displays a sculpture of a figure with raised arms and two curious holes bored in its forehead where horns would be. For a look at the mysterious inner workings of the Mayan underworld, bring along your flashlight and ask the guard to open up the three-story **Laberinto** (Labyrinth), where a tomb was found. Workers take you through the narrow corridors and subterranean rows that were likely a prison, an observatory, or a training camp for *sacerdotes* (priests).

GRUTAS DE CALCEHTOK

Follow the "Grutas" signs (the left fork) when approaching Oxkintok; the caves are 2km southwest of the ruins at the end of the paved road. A family from the ejido (coopera-tive) mans the entrance and will take you on a tour. The paseo turístico (4-person group 100 pesos) lasts less than 1hr. and goes to the Salón de Ceremonias. The adventure tour (5hr.) includes the Tumba del Rey (king's tomb) and 3 Mayan cemeter-ies. Wear old clothes and boots, as you will get filthy. Shoes with good traction are rec-ommended, as the cave is extremely slippery. Be careful about going in alone; it is easy to get lost in the cave system. Leaving a crumb trail is not recommended. Large groups should bring flashlights. Adventure tour prices negotiable. Open 8am-5pm.

From above, the cavern looks like it opens into a jungle, with a tropical ecosys-tem characterized by the honeybees, parrots, and leafy plants that fill the oasis. Once you descend the ladder, however, you will know that you have entered the *inframundo* (the unknown underworld). The view from inside the depression looking up, as light and jungle vines stream down, is breathtaking. A guide can take you deep inside the 10km long pitch-black caverns, his lamps illuminating thousands of unharmed and still growing stalactites, stalagmites, ancient pottery shards, and rock formations. A central stone slab is said to have been used for human sacrifice. During the Caste War 150 years ago, a group of 60 Maya sur-vived for months in the darkness of the *grutas* as a Spanish army waited out-side. The last person to live in the cave left in 1895; she had remained there since the time of the Caste War, having lost her parents inside. A Mayan priest was then brought to cleanse the cave of its *malos vientos* (bad spirits).

IZAMAL ☎988

Izamal (pop. 23,000), Mayan for "dew that falls from heaven," has been a site of spiritual pilgrimage for over a millennium and a half. Originally home to Izamná, a legendary Mayan demigod, the site is the resting place of the statue of the Vir-gen de Izamal. Over the years, the town has sported a variety of nicknames. The name "City of the Hills" refers to the town's many Mayan pyramids, remnants of the time when Izamal was the principal religious center of the Yucatec Maya. Iza-mal is also known as "The Yellow City" for the rich egg-yolk color and white trim of its main buildings and world-famous convent. "The City of Three Cultures," yet another of the town's nicknames, refers to the harmonious blend of Mayan pyramids, Spanish architecture, and *mestizo* character.

YUCATÁN PENINSULA

▐ TRANSPORTATION

The **bus station** (☎954 0107) is on Calle 32 between Calles 31 and 31A, behind the Palacio Municipal. Oriente and Autocentro **buses** go to **Cancún** (5½hr., 8 per day 6am-8pm, 106 pesos), **Mérida** (1½hr., every 30min. 5:30am-2am, 30 pesos), and **Valladolid** (2hr., 9 per day 6am-8pm, 41 pesos). For smaller towns in the area, catch a *combi* on Calle 31 next to the post office (6am-9pm). There are few taxis in town—a horse-drawn carriage is the closest option. Carriages line up in front of the bus station and take passengers to local hotels and sights for 10-15 pesos.

▐▐ ORIENTATION AND PRACTICAL INFORMATION

The road from Mérida, 50km to the west via Hoctún, becomes **Calle 31,** which runs east-west like the other odd-numbered streets. Calle 31 runs past the Convento de San Antonio, passing even-numbered north-south streets. Calles 30, 31, 31A, and the Palacio Municipal frame **Parque 5 de Mayo,** the town's *zócalo.* The larger **Parque Itzamná** is surrounded by buildings with arched entryways.

Tourist information: Palacio Municipal (☎954 0241, ext. 14), just west of the *zócalo* across from the Convento de San Antonio. The main office offers an invaluable walking map of the city. Open daily 9am-1pm and 5-8pm.

Bank: Banorte (☎954 0425), at Calles 31 and 28, just north of the Convento. **Exchanges currency** and has a **24hr. ATM.** Open M-F 9am-2pm.

Bookstore: Dr. Miguel Vera Lima, Izamal's historian, can be found at his office off Parque Itzamná. He sells books of fables and historical accounts.

Police: Calle 32 (☎954 0505), across from the bus station in the Palacio Municipal. Open 24hr. **Policía Turística** wear brown-and-tan uniforms and patrol the *zócalo*. Patrol daily 9am-2pm and 3-6pm.

Pharmacy: Farmacia Itzalana (☎954 0032), on the corner of Calles 31 and 32. Knock if closed.

Medical Services: IMSS (☎954 0241), southeast of the *zócalo* at Calles 37 and 24.

Fax Office: Telecomm, on Calle 32 in the Palacio Municipal. Open M-Sa 8am-7pm.

Internet Access: DirecWay (☎954 0950), at Calles 31 and 28, half a block east of Parque Itzamná. 20 pesos per hr.

Post Office: (☎954 0390), at Calles 31 and 30A. Has a card-operated **LADATEL** phone out front. Open M-F 8am-2:30pm. **Postal Code:** 97540.

ACCOMMODATIONS

Macan Ché Bed and Breakfast, Calle 22 305 (☎954 0287; www.macanche.com), between Calles 33 and 35, 8 blocks southeast of the *zócalo*. Take one of the carriages waiting on the north side of the Convento (5-10min., 10-15 pesos) or walk south 4 blocks on Calle 33 and turn right on Calle 22. The hotel is 200m behind a bougainvillea-covered wall. A private retreat for 12 lucky guests. Individually decorated rooms have themes like 'Santa Fe.' A hectare of cool gardens, a steam bath, and a natural rock-bottom pool are luxurious and relaxing. Breakfast included. Reception until 9pm. Check-out noon. Wi-Fi available under the *palapa*. Suites 350-700 pesos. Cash only. ❺

Posada Flory (☎954 0562), on Calle 30 at Calle 27. The place to go for some of the best hospitality in town. Flory herself, a 75-year-old encyclopedia of local history, will welcome you into 1 of her 10 uniquely decorated rooms, all with private bath, fan, and TV. A/C optional. Guests are welcome to use the living room and kitchen. Free purified water. Rooms 180-280 pesos. Cash only. ❷

Hotel San Miguel Arcangel, Calle 31A 308 (☎954 0109; www.sanmiguelhotel.com.mx), between Calles 30 and 30A. In the center of town, Hotel San Miguel is the most noticeable hotel in the area with its own private pyramid ruin. Doubles with A/C 540 pesos. ❺

FOOD

Don't plan on late-night wining and dining in the Yellow City: most restaurants close by early evening. For cheap eats, head to the Izamal **market,** on the corner of Calles 30 and 33, which offers up big portions of *tacos de venado* (deer tacos) and other regional specialties. (Open daily 6am-2pm and 5pm-8pm.) **Arborrotes El Angel,** on Calle 33 in the Parque Itzamná, sells the basics in a supermarket setting. Open daily 7:30am-9:30pm.

El Toro (☎967 3340), on Calle 33 between Calles 30 and 32. The generous servings of regional food at El Toro are delicious and a great value. Meals begin with a flavorful *puré de pepita* (puréed squash seeds with roasted tomato and cilantro), continue with regional dishes (65-90 pesos), and can be accompanied by an enormous glass of *horchata* (12 pesos) and tasty, handmade tortillas. Open M-Th 8am-11pm, F-Su 11am-1am. Cash only. ❹

Los Portales (☎954 0302), at the corner of Calles 30 and 31A next to the market. Kandi and company will fix you a plate of homecooked local specialties for rock-bottom prices in a super clean diner setting. Breakfast 20-30 pesos. Lunch and dinner entrees 35 pesos. Open daily 7am-7pm. Cash only. ❷

Restaurant Kinich-Kakmó, Calle 27 299 (☎954 0489), between Calles 28 and 30. Gorgeous, leafy setting. Serves Yucatec favorites (75 pesos) as well as the yummy, if meagerly portioned, vegetarian *papa dul* (squash salsa and hard boiled egg in hand-made rolled tortillas and topped with two sauces; 45 pesos). Open M, W, Su 11:30am-6pm; Tu and Th-Sa 11:30am-10pm. MC/V. ❹

Tumben-Lol, Calle 22 302 (☎954 0231), between Calles 31 and 33. Also serves Yucatec favorites, including their special *relleno negro de pavo enterrado* (turkey cooked in a dark, rich, spicy broth) for 70 pesos in an open air, bougainvillea-filled courtyard. Open daily 11:30am-6pm. Cash only. ❹

👁 SIGHTS

CONVENTO DE SAN ANTONIO DE PADUA. The huge, yellow convent consists of three main sections: the **church,** built in 1554; the **convent,** built in 1561; and the **atrium,** built in 1618. The atrium has 75 arches and is said to be second in size only to the Vatican. Several original 16th-century frescoes are painted on the facade and roof depicting the Virgin Mary, the arrival of the Spanish and the first missionaries, Franciscan priests, and a Spanish shield with the Castilla and León symbols. Inside the Baroque church is an ornate, wooden altar built in 1949 and covered in gold leaf by Tlaxcalan artisans. Through an opening in the altar, Izamal's famed statue of the Immaculate Conception, commissioned in 1558, is wheeled out for daily mass. Devotees make the pilgrimage to Izamal in her honor, as she is said to have the power to bestow miracles. She lives with her dresses and crowns in a room behind the altar. There were originally two statues, called Las Dos Hermanas; one was sent to Mérida and the other to Izamal. In 1829, Izamal's statue was destroyed in a fire, and Mérida's copy was brought here. Legend has it that the Izamal original was saved and taken to the nearby pyramid of Kinich-Kakmó. Every December 8, at the beginning of the town's 15-day *fiesta,* the two are said to spiritually switch places in **El Paso de las Dos Hermanas.** More stories are told at Izamal's small **community museum,** on Calle 31, on the north side of the Convent, which details Izamal's three histori-cal phases and has a model of the city in 500 BC. Four times a week, the con-vent is illuminated during **The Light of the Maya** light-and-sound show, which takes place in the atrium. You can visit the statue in Mexico's oldest **camarín** (alcove or resting place) by going through the door to the left of the main entrance to the church, passing the sacristy, and climbing the stairs. On your way down, visit the convent's small **museum,** which exhibits pictures and mementos of the Pope's visit to Izamal in August of 1993, when he held a mass and meeting specifically for the indigenous people in the area and bestowed upon the Virgin a necklace of pearls, as well as the honor of being queen and patroness of Yucatán. *(Mass daily 7am, 1, 7pm. Camarín open 8am-1pm. Convent museum open Tu-Su 9am-2pm and 4-7pm. 5 pesos. Community museum open Tu-W and F-Su 10am-1pm and 4:30-8:30pm. Free. Light show Tu and Th-Sa 8:30pm. 45 pesos.)*

PYRAMIDS. Five of the pyramids in Izamal are open to visitors and all are within walking distance of the *zócalo*. After ascending the 34m high pyramid of Kinich-Kakmó (dedicated to the fire and sun god, whose name means "fire parrot" or "sun face" in Mayan), visitors will truly appreciate Izamal's most dominating structure, which looks out over the city. The massive pyramid, measuring 200m by 180m, is the fifth largest in the country and the second largest in the Yucatán Peninsula. Kinich-Kakmó was built during the Early Classic period (AD 400-600) and formed the northern border of the ancient city's central plaza. (Entrance with resorted steps on Calle 27 between Calles 28 and 26.) Kinich-Kakmo was once outclassed by the imposing Pap-Hol-Chac ("Thunder House" or "Castle"), the largest pyramid in ancient Izamal. Pap-Hol-Chac was home to Mayan priests before its ruin and the subsequent construction of El Convento de San Antonio with its stones. Other pyramids dot Izamal, blending with the modern cityscape. Itzamatul ("He Who Receives or Possesses the Grace of the Sky") looms 22m high to the east and is the second largest pyramid in Izamal, offering excellent views of the city. (Entrance on Calle 26 between Calles 29 and 31). Habuc ("Dress of Water") is the most removed from the city center, on Calle 28, between Calles 35 and 37. Chal Tun Ha ("Eye of Water in Stone"), behind the Green River hotel on Calle 41, was recently restored. El Conejo, on Calle 22 between Calles 31 and 33, is also open to the public though appears to be little more than a pile of rocks to the untrained eye. Through the shop Hecho a Mano on 31A, you can catch a glimpse of Hum Pic Tok, a partially restored pyramid in the city center. The most centrally located pyramid, Kabul ("House of the Miraculous Hand"), is just north of the *zócalo* and is where the mask of Zamná was found. Unfortunately, surrounding homes and businesses make it almost impossible to reach, though there are plans to reopen the site in the future. *(All pyramids open daily 8am-5pm. No guides available at entrances. Free.)*

CHICHÉN ITZÁ ☎985

Gracing hundreds of glossy brochures and suffering the footfalls of thousands of tourists, the post-Classic Mayan ruins at Chichén Itzá seem like the equivalent of a Mayan Disney World. However, the hype is understandable. The religious and political center of ancient Mayan civilization, the impressive pyramid, which was once the site of human sacrifice as well as stunningly accurate astronomical calculations, was included in the 2007 list of the New Seven Wonders of the World. The town of Piste (pop. 3100), 2.5km away, offers a range of services but lacks the charm of other nearby colonial towns. The main reason to stay for a night in Piste would be to catch Chichén Itzá's light-and-sound show followed by an early morning scouting for spider monkeys amidst the rubble. Avoid visiting the ruins around noon, when the sun scorches and the tour buses roll in.

◰ TRANSPORTATION. The ruins of Chichén Itzá lie 1.5km from **Mex. 180** and 2.5km from the town of **Piste.** Mex. 180 runs west to Mérida (119km away) and east through Valladolid (42km) and Cancún (200km). The main access road is the well-marked cobblestone road from the eastern edge of Piste. Mex. 180 becomes **Calle 15,** the main drag in Piste. The main **bus** station (☎851 0052) in Piste lies on the eastern edge of town on Calle 15 next to the Piramide Inn. **ADO** sends buses to: **Cancún** (2½hr., 4:20pm, 142 pesos); **Mérida** (1½hr.; 2:10, 5pm; 80 pesos); **Playa del Carmen** (8am, 2:40, 4:15pm; 180 pesos); **Tulum** via **Valladolid** (2½hr.; 8:15am, 2:40, 4:15pm; 104 pesos). Second-class Oriente buses run to **Cancún** (every 30min. 8:30am-6:30pm, 94 pesos) and **Mérida** (every 45min. 7am-5:30pm, 54 pesos), stopping at all the towns in between. For **Valladolid,** take the second-class eastbound Cancún bus (20 pesos).

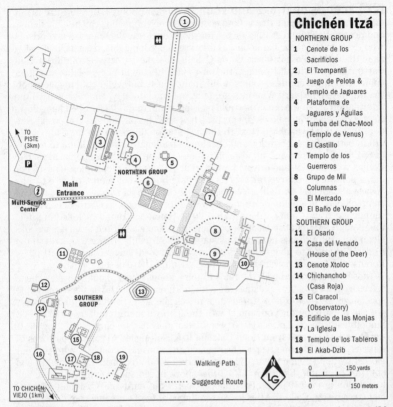

Chichén Itzá

NORTHERN GROUP
1 Cenote de los
   Sacrificios
2 El Tzompantli
3 Juego de Pelota &
   Templo de Jaguares
4 Plataforma de
   Jaguares y Águilas
5 Tumba del Chac-Mool
   (Templo de Venus)
6 El Castillo
7 Templo de los
   Guerreros
8 Grupo de Mil
   Columnas
9 El Mercado
10 El Baño de Vapor

SOUTHERN GROUP
11 El Osario
12 Casa del Venado
   (House of the Deer)
13 Cenote Xtoloc
14 Chichanchob
   (Casa Roja)
15 El Caracol
   (Observatory)
16 Edificio de las Monjas
17 La Iglesia
18 Templo de los Tableros
19 El Akab-Dzib

Walking Path
.... Suggested Route

0   150 yards
0   150 meters

YUCATÁN PENINSULA

Getting to the ruins is easy. To skip the 20min. walk from Piste, catch a **taxi** (30 pesos) or wait in the bus station for an eastbound bus (every 30min. until 5:30pm, 5 pesos). To get to Chichén Itzá from other towns, see bus listings for Mérida (p. 617), Cancún (p. 656), and Valladolid (p. 652). To return to Piste, wait in the bus parking lot until a taxi or bus swings by on its way to Mérida (every 30min.).

⑦ PRACTICAL INFORMATION. All services in Chichén Itzá are at the site's western entrance. (Open daily 8am-10pm.) Across from the ticket counter is a table where you can arrange for a guide. On the right is **luggage storage** (open daily 8am-6pm), past the ticket booth. **Restrooms, currency exchange,** an **ATM** (note that this is the only ATM in the Chichén Itzá/Piste area), a restaurant, an ice cream parlor, a gift shop (which accepts US$), a bookstore, a small museum, and parking (20 pesos) are available at the site.

You will have to visit Piste for most services, which include: **police,** at the Camandancia on the east side of the *zócalo* (open daily 8am-6pm); **Farmacia Isis,** on Calle 15, west of the *zócalo* (☎851 0216; open daily 7:30am-11pm); **Centro de Salud,** Calle 14 50, in the blue-green building west of the *zócalo* and 100m north of Mex. 180 (☎851 0005; open 24hr.); **Internet** access at **San Antonio,** across from the bus station (☎851 0089; 15 pesos per hr.; open daily 10am-9pm); **Caseta Telefónica,** across from the bus station (☎851 0088; open daily 10am-8:30pm); and **LADATEL** phones along Mex. 180.

⬛⬛ ACCOMMODATIONS AND FOOD. Although finding a bed in Piste is not difficult, finding lodging that is both economical and appealing can be a challenge, and nearby Valladolid is a better bet for the budget traveler. Beware taxi drivers who steer you to particular hotels, as they are likely doing this to get a commission from the owner. **Posada Olalde ❷**, on Calle 6 off Calle 15, across from Restaurant Carrousel down the dirt road, is the best place to stay in Piste. Olalde is a great value with large, spotless rooms in the main house and well-kept bungalows off the intimate courtyard. Víctor, a guide at the ruins by day, can give you all the information about the area you could possibly want. (☎851 0086. 1-bed bungalows 160 pesos; 2-bed bungalows 200 pesos; singles 180 pesos; doubles 250 pesos. Student discounts available.) Next to the bus station, **Pirámide Inn ❶**, Calle 15 30, offers bathrooms, electricity, and spacious, shady gardens in addition to a pool. (☎851 0115. Camp space 40 pesos per person. Some rental hammocks available. Rooms with fan, TV, and private bath start at 410 pesos for 2 people; 50 pesos per extra person. 5% charge for MC/V.) Extreme budget travelers are sure to like **Posada el Carrousel ❶**, Calle 15 41, 300m east of the town square, where they can camp or sleep in a hammock under a *palapa* for 40 pesos. El Carrousel has bathrooms, electricity, and gardens. (☎851 0078. Hammock rental included in price. Cash only.) **Posada Chac Mool ❸**, on Calle 15, 500m east of the town square, has clean but stuffy rooms near the bus station. The friendly owner who lives in the first room loves to give travelers the scoop on local happenings. (☎701 0270. Rooms with fan and private bath 200 pesos, with A/C 410 pesos. Cash only.)

Those too engrossed with the ruins to think about eating should consider themselves extremely lucky—pickings are slim in Chichén Itzá. The **on-site restaurant ❹** specializes in *comida non-típica:* high prices and small servings. You'll probably get the most bang for your buck with the 85-peso medium pizza. (☎851 0111. Smoothies 40 pesos. Entrees 50-85 pesos. Open daily 9:30am-6pm. MC/V.) **Las Mestizas ❹**, in Piste across from Hotel Chichén Itzá, is designed to cater to busloads of tourists, and the enormous space has capacity for you and a couple hundred of your closest pyramid-bound friends. Mestizas serves good breakfasts (25-50 pesos) and *comida regional*, like *cochinita pibel* (pork in red sauce wrapped in banana leaves), for around 50 pesos. (☎851 0069. Open T-Su 7am-10pm. Cash only.) **Restaurant Carrousel ❷**, Calle 15 41, is located in the *posada* of the same name. Tasty and inexpensive regional food abounds at this *palapa*-covered joint. *Chilaquiles con pollo* (tortilla casserole with cheese, onions, and chicken) are 20 pesos, as are enchiladas. (☎851 0078. Open daily 7:00am-11pm. Cash only.) Across the street and 100m west is **Los Pájaros ❸**, which serves equally good, cheap regional food under a small, smoke-filled *palapa*. Look for the roasting chickens and onions out front. (Entrees 25-40 pesos. Open daily 10am-10pm. Cash only.) You can save a few pesos by packing a lunch from one of the small **grocers** lining Calle 15 in Piste, near the *zócalo*.

🔵 THE ARCHAEOLOGICAL SITE OF CHICHÉN ITZÁ

The ruins lie a 20min. walk or a 30-peso taxi ride from Piste. Site open daily 8am-6pm. 95 pesos, students with valid ID 45 pesos, video camera use 35 pesos, Su free for Mexican citizens. A small museum presents the site's history, early writings about the ruins, some artifacts, and photos of its earlier conditions. Museum open daily 8am-6pm. Free. A light-and-sound show attempts to recreate the color and feel of Chichén Itzá in its heyday. Show daily in summer 8pm; in winter 7pm. 30 pesos, or free with admission; headphones with English translation 25 pesos. 2hr. guided tours begin at the entrance and cost 600 pesos for languages other than Spanish, including English, German, Italian, French, and Dutch; 500 pesos for Spanish; 60 pesos per person for groups of 8-10.

HISTORY. During the height of power in the 12th century AD, Chichén Itzá ("by the mouth of Itzá's well" in Mayan) was a huge political and religious center, with nearly 80,000 inhabitants, and the center of the powerful Mayapán League. Glorious Chichén Itzá, however, was not built overnight. Settlement of Chichén Itzá took place over three periods. The first two are known as the Maya Phase and are still visible today in the mostly unexcavated ruins of Chichén Viejo. The third phase, beginning around AD 1000, is known as the Toltec-Maya Phase, which left the most lasting constructions still seen today in Chichén Nuevo. It is believed that Puuc and Maya from Chiapas and Guatemala first settled the area around AD 700, building structures in the Chichén Viejo as well as a smattering of smaller structures in the Chichén Nuevo area. By AD 900, Chichén Itzá had become a larger and more powerful center of trade. Central construction in the Chichén Nuevo in the post-Classic style saw the building of the inner pyramid of El Castillo and the original Temple of Chac-mool. By AD 1100, Chichén Itzá was a major crossroads of trade and ideas, including the ever-expanding influence of the Toltecs from central Mexico. The Toltecs brought with them their own gods, including Quetzalcóatl, the serpent-god, and religious practices such as human sacrifice. It also saw the largest growth of the settlement and the building of major structures such as the current El Castillo and the ball court. However, by the mid-15th century, Chichén Itzá was abandoned—torn apart by constant warring with surrounding city-states and stripped of agricultural possibilities by the huge stress of supporting its large population. The site was abandoned in 1461. Although climbing on any of the structures is now prohibited, walking among the ruins of the once impressive city is still a perspective-altering experience.

JUEGO DE PELOTA (BALL COURT). The first stop for all tours, just northwest of El Castillo, the ball court rises as a monument to the great sport of the Maya. Though Chichén Itzá is home to more than seven ball courts of varying sizes, this playing field, bounded by high walls and impressive temples to the god of fertility, measures 146m by 37m, making it the largest in Mesoamerica. The surround sound effect of the court makes a few clapping tourists sound like a packed stadium. Check out the life-size reliefs on the southern wall showing the consequences (or honor) of winning—a man kneeling as blood-red serpents erupt from his neck. The elaborate game played here fascinated Cortés so much that he took two teams back to Europe in 1528 to perform before the royal court. The ball court continues to amaze modern Europeans, reputedly serving as the model for Harry Potter's famous Quidditch hoops.

EL TZOMPANTLI. A short distance from the ball court, underneath the shady trees to the south, is El Tzompantli (the Platform of the Skulls), which once exhibited the shrunken heads of prisoners and enemies. The eerie columns of bas-relief skulls lined up like gravestones on the lower platform walls conjure horrific images of skulls strung together to strike fear in the hearts of enemy prisoners. Nine skeletons were found beneath the mound that was used to perform ceremonies and cremations.

PLATAFORMA DE JAGUARES Y ÁGUILAS. Next to Tzompantli, the "Platform of Jaguars and Eagles" pays homage to the warriors, represented by jaguars and eagles, whose job it was to kidnap members of other tribes to sacrifice to the gods. On either side of the feathered serpent heads, reliefs of jaguars and eagles with human features clutch human hearts in their claws. A relief on the northwest corner of the structure still bears evidence of a bright color scheme with faint hints of red and green beeswax paints.

EL CASTILLO. Chichén's trademark, El Castillo (also known as Pyramid of Kukulcán) stands as tangible evidence of the astronomical mastery of the ancient Maya and is picture perfect in its newly restored state. The 91 steps on each of the four faces, plus the upper platform, total 365; 52 panels on nine terraced levels equal the number of years in a Mayan calendar cycle. A staircase divides each face of the nine terraces, yielding 18 sections representing the 18 Mayan *uinal* (months) in each turn of the Long Count dating system. The most impressive feature is the precise alignment of El Castillo's axes, which produces a biannual optical illusion. At sunrise during the spring and fall equinoxes, the rounded terraces cast a serpentine shadow down the side of the northern staircase. A light-and-shadow lunar serpent-god, identical to that of the equinoxes, creeps down the pyramid at the dawn of the full moon following each equinox.

TUMBA DEL CHAC-MOOL. Directly north of El Castillo is the Tumba del Chac-Mool (Temple of Venus), a square platform decorated with a feathered serpent holding a human head in its mouth. The temple's reliefs symbolize the planet Venus, as well as other stars and planets, and give information on their motions. The platform was most likely used for ceremonies. A statue of Chac reclining characteristically with his offering dish was found in the temple.

CENOTE DE LOS SACRIFICIOS (CENOTE OF THE SACRIFICES). This 60m-wide subterranean pool, 300m north of El Castillo and connected via a *sacbé* (raised paved roads), was Chichén Itzá's most important religious symbol. The rain god Chac was believed to dwell beneath the surface and requested frequent gifts of young virgin royal daughters in exchange for good rains. Elaborate rituals, beginning atop El Castillo and culminating in the sacrificial victim's 25m plunge to death, appeased the god during times of severe drought. Since 1907, over 30,000 sacrificial remains—including skulls, teeth, and jewelry—have been dredged from the 14m deep water, thanks to the work of American anthropologist and diplomat Edward H. Thompson (1856-1935), who at one time owned the entirety of the ruins. Unfortunately, much archaeological evidence was lost due to incautious dredging; for example, mud extracted from the *cenote* was used for the foundation of a neighboring *hacienda*.

TEMPLO DE LOS GUERREROS. On the left as you return from the *cenote*, and northeast of El Castillo, the "Temple of the Warriors" presents an array of carved columns that once supported a massive wood and thatch roof, but now stand like a great army at attention. On the temple itself, before two great feathered serpents and several sculpted animal gods, is one of Chichén's best-preserved *chac-mools* and a table where human hearts were ritually extracted. This building's ornamentation shows heavy Toltec influence: a nearly identical structure stands in Tula, the former Toltec capital to the west. The temple was built over the former Temple of Chac-mool. *(Climbing on the structure is prohibited.)*

GRUPO DE MIL COLUMNAS. Extending to the southeast of the Templo de los Guerreros, this "Group of a Thousand Columns" contains an elaborate drainage system that channeled rainfall away from what is believed to have been a civic or religious center. The columns bear inscriptions and carvings.

EL BAÑO DE VAPOR. The steambath is divided into three sections. In the interior, water was poured over hot rocks, creating steam to purify those in poor health or those involved with religious ceremonies. The steam-bath ritual is one of the oldest known traditions of the people of the region and can still be experienced by travelers headed to the mountainous Mayan regions to the south.

EL MERCADO. The final ruin before entering the older, central zone has taller, rounded columns and wider vaults that show the advances in architecture made over time. Mayan markets, as they still do today, operated largely on the barter system, often using cocoa beans as money.

CENOTE XTOLOC. To the east, off a small trail near the Market or off the first left from the main trail, is a *cenote* in a hollow beyond the ruined temple of the lizard-god Xtoloc. There is no path leading down the slope, and swimming is prohibited due to dangerous currents. The secular counterpart to the holy waters of the **Cenote de los Sacrificios,** this pool once provided all of Chichén with drinking water. To get behind the observatory, follow *sacbé* No. 5, which becomes a winding trail.

TUMBA DEL GRAN SACERDOTE/EL OSARIO. The High Priest's Grave is the first structure to the right of the path leading to the southern or central zones. The distinctive serpent heads mimic El Castillo, and a natural cave extends from the pyramid 15m into the earth. The human bones and votive offerings of gold, silver, and jewels found in this cave are thought to have belonged to the ancient high priests and members of seven distinct dynasties of Chichén Itzá.

EL CARACOL. Just beyond the **Casa del Venado** (House of the Deer) and **Chichan-chob** (Red House) lies the ancient observatory. One of the few circular structures built by the Maya, it consists of two rectangular platforms with large, west-facing staircases and two circular towers with spiral staircases that earned the building the name El Caracol (The Snail). The slits in the dome, functioning much like a sundial, can be aligned with the major celestial bodies and cardinal directions, and the red handprints above the doorway were supposedly made by the hands of sun god Kinich Ahau. Six protruding snake heads were used for burning incense. It is thought that the knowledge gained by astronomers at the observatory was put to use in the design and construction of El Castillo.

EDIFICIO DE LAS MONJAS. Built in six phases, these buildings were probably the residence of a high priest. To the Spanish, however, the stone rooms looked suspiciously like a convent—hence the ruins' name. Notches in the sides of the structure served as altars to various gods, but the predominant image is the face of Chac (the rain deity). Mayan glyphs are still visible above the entrance on the east side of the building. Also on the east side is the annex, which predates the rest of the convent. Above the doorway facing the small courtyard is a well preserved bas relief of a seated royal-divine figure. Many rooms in the convent have doorways that lead to dark corridors, which are home to bats, poisonous snakes, and frogs.

LA IGLESIA. This elaborate building, one of the oldest at the site, is diagonal to the convent and similarly misnamed. Its top-heavy walls are encrusted with intricate, hook-nosed masks of Chac. The "church" incorporates a variety of architectural styles: over the doorway are Mayan stone lintels, while the use of wood and inclined edges indicate a Toltec influence. Above the door, a crab, a turtle, an armadillo, and a snail represent the four Bacabs—brothers who, according to Mayan mythology, were placed at the four corners of the universe, the four cardinal directions, to hold up the sky.

TEMPLO DE LOS TABLEROS (TEMPLE OF THE PANELS). Just south of El Caracol, the "Temple of the Panels" has rows of columns and carved panels. Though difficult to decipher, the panels on the exterior walls contain emblems of warriors—jaguars, eagles, and serpents—in three rows. The upper part of the structure is believed to have been a site for fire-related ceremonies.

EL AKAB-DZIB. This complex, 60m east of the convent, earned its name for the "dark writing" found in its 17 rooms. The older parts of this structure are believed to be Chichén's most ancient buildings—the two central rooms date to the 2nd or 3rd century, while the annexes on either side and to the east were added later.

■ DAYTRIP FROM CHICHÉN ITZÁ

GRUTAS DE BALANKANCHÉ

6km east of Chichén Itzá, the caves are easily reached from Chichén or Piste by any eastbound bus on Mex. 180 (5 pesos). When boarding, be sure to tell the driver where you are headed. You can also take a taxi (30 pesos; round-trip 60 pesos, including wait). To get back, catch any westbound bus or colectivo, but be prepared to wait a while. Guided 30-45min. tours in English daily 11am, 1, 3pm; in Spanish 9am, noon, 2, 4pm. 54 pesos, 2-person min., 6-person max. Open daily 9am-5pm. Small museum free.

Descend into the ultra-humid corridors of the Mayan underworld at the inner caves of **Balankanché,** which were discovered in 1959 when a local tour guide noticed the passageway blocked with stones. Archaeologists believe the cave was a center for Maya-Toltec worship of the rain god Chac (Tlaloc) and the serpent-god Kukulcán (Quetzalcóatl) during the 10th and 11th centuries. For unknown reasons, subterranean worship in Balankanché stopped at the end of this period, and the offerings of pottery and sculpture rested undisturbed for nine centuries. Explorations have opened 450m of caves 25m deep, in which one could easily get lost if not for the light show that entertains and guides visitors. Pass by stalactites carved to resemble leaves, a huge column representing the sacred *ceiba* tree (the tree of life), and three groups of ancient ceramic vessels and stone sculptures. Hidden speakers tell the garbled story of the cave's past. The impressive stalactites and ceramics merit a visit, even if you have only a few extra hours on hand.

VALLADOLID ☎985

Tourists seem scarce in the subdued town of Valladolid (pop. 40,000), despite its location on the Mérida-Cancún route, its proximity to Chichén Itzá, and its numerous colonial churches and natural *cenotes*. The town is a quiet stop on the way to many of the major tourist attractions of the Yucatán and a blooming center of modern Mayan culture. In 1543, Spaniard Francisco de Montejo attacked the city, then the Mayan city of Zací (sah-KEY; "white falcon" in Mayan), which held out for several years before succumbing. Despite the imposing churches and grid-like streets that serve as reminders of Spanish dominion, the Maya were not so easily forgotten. In 1848, they rose up and took the city hostage for several months in what is now known as the Caste War. The Maya hold on to their past today: the language is still heard among Indian women weaving *huipiles*, between vendors on street corners selling locally made *huaraches*, and on the city's most colonial street, the Paso de los Frailes (Street of the Friars).

■ TRANSPORTATION

Traversed by **Mex. 180,** Valladolid sits in the heart of Yucatán state, between Mérida and Cancún. All **bus** lines operate out of a station (☎856 3448) in the *centro*, at Calles 39 and 46. To get to the *zócalo* from the station, take a left out of the main entrance and walk a block and a half east on Calle 39. If in doubt, look for the huge church bell towers. Buses go to: **Cancún** (2hr., 20 per day, 42-74 pesos); **Chichén Itzá**

(1hr., every 45 min. 7:15am-5:30pm, 20 pesos); **Chiquilá** (2½hr., 2:45am, 70 pesos); **Izamal** (1½hr.; 12:45, 3:50, 5pm; 41 pesos); **Mérida** (2½hr., every hr. from 12:15am, 74-112 pesos); **Playa del Carmen** (2½hr., 9 per day, 77-136 pesos); **Tizimín** (1hr., every hr., 19 pesos). **Bike** rentals are available at **Refaccionaria de Bicicletas Silva** and **Antonio "Negro" Aguilar** sports store (☎856 2125), both on Calle 44 between Calles 39 and 41. (7 pesos per hr. Both open M-Sa 8:30am-8pm, Su 9am-2pm.)

⚡🛈 ORIENTATION AND PRACTICAL INFORMATION

Even-numbered streets in Valladolid run north-south, increasing to the west. Odd-numbered streets run east-west, increasing to the south. The one notable exception is the Paso de los Frailes, which runs diagonally northeast to southwest, beginning at the intersection of Calles 41 and 46. Except for **Cenote X'keken** and the **Ek' Balam** ruins, everything lies within walking distance of the *zócalo*, circumscribed by Calles 39, 40, 41, and 42. Blocks are spaced out, so what appears to be a short jaunt might really be a long haul.

Tourist Office: (☎856 2063) in the Palacio Municipal, on the corner of Calles 40 and 41. Provides helpful maps and pamphlets. Open daily 9am-9pm.

Currency Exchange: Bancomer (☎856 2150), on the Calle 40 side of the *zócalo*. **24hr. ATM** next door. Open M-F 8:30am-4pm, Sa 10am-3pm. **Banamex** (open M-F 9am-4pm) and **HSBC** (open M-Sa 8am-7pm), on Calle 41 between Calles 42 and 44, offer the same services. HSBC also offers cash advances on credit cards.

Laundromat: Luyso, on the corner of Calles 40 and 33. Wash and dry 7 pesos per kg. Open M-Sa 8am-8pm, Su 8am-2pm. **Lavandería Tintorería el Gaucho,** Calle 42 165, between Calles 27 and 29. Full service 7 pesos per kg. Open M-Sa 8am-8pm.

Emergency: ☎066.

Police: (☎856 2100 or 3578) on Calle 41, 10 blocks east of the *zócalo*.

Red Cross: ☎856 2413.

24hr. Pharmacy: El Descuento (☎856 2615), on the corner of Calles 42 and 39 on the *zócalo*. Several other locations on the streets off the *zócalo*.

Hospital: (☎856 2883), on the corner of Calles 51 and 52.

Internet Access: Phonet, between Calles 39 and 41 on the *zócalo*. **Fax** available. Internet access 10 pesos per hr. Open daily 7am-midnight. **Ciber Atlantis,** on Calle 44 on the Parque La Candelaria. Open M-Su 10am-11pm. 8 pesos per hr.

Post Office: (☎856 2623), on Calle 40, in the *zócalo*. Open M-F 8:30am-3pm. **Postal Code:** 97780.

🏠 ACCOMMODATIONS

Penny-pinchers will want to stay away from the pricey hotels bordering the *zócalo*. Better bargains can be found one block west, especially on **Calle 44.**

Albergue/Hostel La Candelaria (HI) (☎856 2267; candelaria_hostel@hotmail.com), in peaceful Parque La Candelaria on the corner of Calles 35 and 44. A converted colonial mansion, La Candelaria tempts travelers to stay a few nights extra with its soothing, homey feel. Strong fans, full outdoor kitchen, hand-wash laundry areas, free lockers, leafy lunch patio, and TV room. Breakfast with fresh fruit included. Bunks 100 pesos, for HI members 90 pesos; private rooms 230 pesos. Cash only. ❶

Hotel Zací, Calle 44 191 (☎856 2167; www.hotelzaci.com), between Calles 37 and 39. A relaxing vacation from your vacation. Complete with phone, pool, cable TV, and on-site restaurant. Singles 245 pesos, with A/C 340 pesos; doubles 350/385 pesos. Cash only. ❺

Hotel Lili, Calle 44 192 (☎856 2163), between Calles 37 and 39, across from Hotel Zací. Hostel accommodations with shared bath. Singles 130 pesos; doubles 150 pesos. Nicer rooms with private bath also available: singles 160 pesos; doubles 180 pesos; each additional person 40 pesos. Cash only. ❶

Hotel María Guadalupe, Calle 44 198 (☎856 2068), between Calles 39 and 41. Rooms with clean bath, ceiling fan, and dark wood furniture. Rooms 220 pesos; each additional person 40 pesos. Cash only. ❸

🍴 FOOD

Comida yucateca, which blends European and Mexican flavors, tops every menu. Some favorites include *poc-chuc* (tender slices of pork marinated in a Yucatec sauce and covered with pickled onions), *panuchos* (tortillas filled with beans and topped with either chicken or pork, lettuce, tomato, and hot sauce), and *escabeche oriental de pavo* (a hearty turkey soup with pasta). *Xtabentún* is a delectable liqueur of anise and honey. To eat with the people, grab a *pibihua* (maize and bean rolls filled with beef and tomato salsa) from one of the many street vendors. Valladolid has a **municipal market,** four blocks northeast of the *zócalo*, bordered by Calles 30, 32, 35, and 37, which offers fresh fruit, meat, and vegetables for cheap. (Open daily 6am-1pm.) A supermarket, **Super Maz,** is on Calle 39 between Calles 48 and 50. (☎856 3774. Open daily 8am-10pm.)

🍴 **Bazar Municipal,** on Calle 39 at Calle 40, on the southeastern corner of the *zócalo*. A narrow courtyard crowded with cafes serving *comida típica*, pizza, and juice. *Comida corrida* (25 pesos) includes meat, beans, rice, tortillas, and a drink. Breakfast 20-25 pesos. Hours vary by restaurant, but most open daily 6am-midnight. Cash only. ❷

🍴 **Cafe Italia,** on the Parque Candelaria. Just like eating at home, if home happens to house a longtime professional Italian chef with a handbuilt, woodfired pizza oven. Fresh pasta with pesto 35 pesos. Woodfired pizzas 50-80 pesos. Open T-Su 8am-1pm and 6-10pm. Cash only. ❸

Las Campanas, Calle 42 199 (☎856 2365), on the southwestern corner of the *zócalo*. Though it might be a the biggest tourist trap in town, the stellar view of the cathedral and tasty *comida yucateca*, like *queso relleno* (wedge of cheese stuffed with meat, egg, and salsa; 55 pesos), make it a worthwhile pit stop to escape Valladolid's heat. Live music daily 9pm. Open daily 8am-1am. Cash only. ❹

Restaurante María de la Luz (☎856 2071), at the corner of Calles 42 and 39 on the west side of the *zócalo*, in the Hotel María de la Luz. Take in the life of the *zócalo* through the breezy French bay doors. Vegetarian and American dishes available. Hotel pool accessible to patrons. *Comida corrida* 50 pesos. Open daily 7am-10pm. MC/V. ❸

Restaurante Cenote Zací (☎856 2107), on Calle 36 between Calles 37 and 39. Underneath a giant *palapa* and atop a *cenote* surrounded by jungle trees, this restaurant has enough space and tables to feed busloads. Mediocre *comida yucateca* is redeemed by a free peek at the *cenote* and amusing song and dance shows. Sandwiches 30-35 pesos. Entrees 55-70 pesos. Open daily 8am-6pm. Cash only. ❹

🎵🎭 ENTERTAINMENT AND FESTIVALS

For a raving party scene, look elsewhere—Valladolid is a small, quiet city with few nightlife options. The *zócalo* is beautifully illuminated at night, and fills with strolling families, Mayan vendors, lively political orators, and guitar-strumming teens. Later at night, **Santos y Pecadores,** Calle 39 between Calles 38 and 40, is the only club in town that attracts a crowd. A young set parties to salsa and Spanish rock, romancing into the wee hours. (Open Th-Sa 9pm-late.) Several screens show Spanish-dubbed Hollywood films at **Cines Universal,** Calles 40 and 41. (☎856 2040. Shows daily 7 and 9pm; 40 pesos.) Valladolid hosts a number of cultural celebrations and parties in addition to the standard weekend activities. From January 22 to February 2, the **Virgen de la Candelaria** celebration brings bull fights and traditional music and dance to the fairgrounds.

👁 SIGHTS

While most visitors take the next bus to Mérida or Chichén Itzá, those seeking a dose of history, *cenotes*, and cathedrals have come to the right place. The natural Yucatec jungle is a steamy backdrop to the colonial city, creating a mix of natural and man-made beauty.

CATEDRAL DE SAN SERVASIO. According to legend, two criminals were pulled from the church and murdered by an angry mob. When the bishop found out, he had the church destroyed. It was rebuilt from 1720 to 1730 and is the only cathedral on the peninsula facing north instead of east. The massive colonial twin towers make it an unmistakable physical landmark. *(Over the zócalo on Calle 41. Open M-Sa 7am-1pm and 4-8:30pm, Su 6:30am-2pm and 4-10pm. Mass M-Sa 7pm; Su 7am, 1, 7pm. Free.)*

EL PASEO DE LOS FRAILES. This picturesque, colonial street with colorful, flat-front houses stands out in the otherwise plain city. The "Street of the Friars," dominated by pedestrians, provides the perfect setting for a morning or evening stroll. Many residents leave their doors open, but don't be too nosy peeking into courtyards. *(Calle 41A between Las Cinco Calles and San Bernardino.)*

MUSEO DE SAN ROQUE. This humble museum is a little more than a decade old. A relaxing courtyard and detailed information on Ek' Balam makes it a good pre-ruins stop. Avid craft shoppers can pick up tips on how to spot a fake. *(On the northwestern corner of Calles 41 and 38. All exhibits in Spanish. Open M-F 9am-9pm, Sa-Su 9am-8:30pm. Free.)*

CENOTE ZACÍ. In the middle of the city, Cenote Zací is a cavernous hollow full of protruding stalagmites, tropical gardens, and serene green-blue water. A small zoo surrounding the *cenote* houses a white falcon, the city's namesake. *(3 blocks east of the zócalo, on Calle 36 between Calles 37 and 39. No swimming allowed. Free view from the palapa restaurant on the edge. Open daily 8am-5pm. 15 pesos, children 10 pesos.)*

SAN BERNARDINO DE SIENA. Affiliated with the Ex-Convento de Sisal, the church was built over a *cenote* (visible from inside) in 1552 with stones from the main Mayan temple. It is the oldest ecclesiastical building in the Yucatán and bears a unique, square pattern. A large image of the Virgen de Guadalupe hangs on the altar in the back. Some of the paintings inside are original to the church. *(On Calle 41A, at the end of Paseo de los Frailes. Open M and W-Su 8am-noon. Free.)*

CASA DE LA CULTURA. This building, now the city's cultural center, was originally home to diplomats and later functioned as a school. Art exhibits are on display inside and an attendant in the front office can fill you in on upcoming traditional dance performances. If there is no show, you may be able to join a class (10 pesos per month). The region's traditional dance, the *jarana*, has several varieties, one involving braiding ribbons about a pole. Classes also cover dances from Jalisco and Veracruz. *(☎856 2063, ext. 1217. Next to the municipal building on the eastern side of the zócalo. Dance classes mostly in the late afternoon or evening. Admission free.)*

🔳 DAYTRIPS FROM VALLADOLID

🔲**CENOTE DZITNUP (X'KEKÉN).** The gorgeous *cenote*, ironically bearing a Mayan name that means dirty, allows you to escape underground in its refreshingly cool water. Visit before midday to catch a beam of light slicing through a circular hole in the roof, bathing the cavern in blue light. **Cenote Sambula** (25 pesos, children under 8 15 pesos) is only 200m away and offers beauty on a smaller scale. The well-lit Sambula has been used to film a number of commercials. *(6km west of town. To get there by car or bike, take Calle 39 to the highway toward Mérida. Make a left at the sign for Dzitnup and continue to the entrance plaza on your left. 20min. Alternatively, catch a dark blue colectivo taxi, 15 pesos, on Calle 38 between Calles 37 and 39. Open daily 8am-6pm. 25 pesos, children 15 pesos.)*

EK' BALAM. Ek' Balam ("Black Jaguar" in Mayan) was a Mayan city that flourished in the late Classical period, around AD 700-1000. The site covers 12 sq. km and was discovered a little more than 30 years ago, so excavation is still very much in progress. It contains several temples, a rare circular observatory, a ball court, and a *chac-mool* stone sacrificial table. Everything is organized around two plazas and divided by the ball court. Two walls surround the city—one for defense and one to keep the kids out of important religious buildings. The pyramid itself is one of the most massive in the Yucatán. At 30m high, it's not quite as tall as other Mayan pyramids, but its base is an astonishing 160m long. Note the two giant, unexcavated mounds flanking the pyramid—archaeologists expect to find more pyramids reaching 20-25m in height. The ruins are generally uncrowded and, as reconstruction continues, definitely merit a visit. Don't forget bug repellent! *(The ruins are 25km northeast of Valladolid. The Oriente bus, 40 pesos, leaves from the Calle 40 side of the main plaza at 9am and returns at 1pm. Taxis run 200-225 pesos round-trip, and the driver will generally wait up to 2hr. Taxis colectivos are a better deal at 30 pesos. Open daily 9am-5pm. 27 pesos; Su and holidays free for Mexican citizens.)*

QUINTANA ROO

CANCÚN ☎998

Built along the sparkling Caribbean coast, the once modest city of Cancún (pop. 500,000) has erupted into a metropolis whose alcohol-soaked, disco-shaken, sex-stirred insanity surpasses that of any other party destination in the Western Hemisphere. Ask university students who have "done" spring break Cancún and their eyes will inevitably glass over as they recall—or wish they could recall—night after night of drunken debauchery. Upside-down tequila shots and bikini contests, however, are not the only way to enjoy this former Mayan fishing village. Though Cancún is still recovering from the effects of Hurricane Wilma in 2005, cheap airfare and Cancún's central location on the peninsula make it a great starting point for budget-friendly excursions up and down the Mayan Riviera.

🔳 TRANSPORTATION

INTERCITY TRANSPORTATION

Flights: Aeropuerto Internacional de Cancún (CUN; ☎886 0028), south of the city on Mex. 307. Airlines include: **AeroCaribe** (☎884 2000); **Aeroméxico** (☎884 3571); **American** (☎800-904-6000); **Continental** (☎800-523-3273); **Delta** (☎800-902-2100); **Lan**

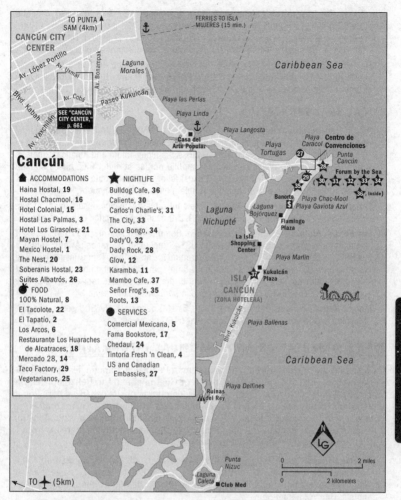

Cancún

⌂ ACCOMMODATIONS
Haina Hostal, **19**
Hostal Chacmool, **16**
Hotel Colonial, **15**
Hostal Las Palmas, **3**
Hotel Los Girasoles, **21**
Mayan Hostel, **7**
Mexico Hostel, **1**
The Nest, **20**
Soberanis Hostal, **23**
Suites Albatrós, **26**
🍴 FOOD
100% Natural, **8**
El Tacolote, **22**
El Tapatío, **2**
Los Arcos, **6**
Restaurante Los Huaraches
  de Alcatraces, **18**
Mercado 28, **14**
Taco Factory, **29**
Vegetarianos, **25**

★ NIGHTLIFE
Bulldog Cafe, **36**
Caliente, **30**
Carlos'n Charlie's, **31**
The City, **33**
Coco Bongo, **34**
Dady'O, **32**
Dady Rock, **28**
Glow, **12**
Karamba, **11**
Mambo Cafe, **37**
Señor Frog's, **35**
Roots, **13**
● SERVICES
Comercial Mexicana, **5**
Fama Bookstore, **17**
Chedaui, **24**
Tintoría Fresh 'n Clean, **4**
US and Canadian
  Embassies, **27**

Chile (☎886 0360); **LACSA** (☎887 3101); **Martinair** (☎886 0070); **Mexicana** (☎881 9090); and **US Airways** (☎800-003-0777). ADO runs a bus to the bus station (30min., 35 pesos). Private shuttles, SUVs, and taxis wait just outside customs (US$12-56).

TIP **WAIT!** Before leaving the airport, make sure to grab a copy of *Cancún Tips*. The magazine and accompanying coupon book is full of deals on bars, restaurants, and tours, and can help save a few pesos in Mexico's most expensive city. Available at the tourist office, airport, Plaza Caracol, and most hotels.

Buses: (☎884 1378; reservations 800 702 8000), on the corner of Uxmal and Tulum, facing Plaza Caribe. The 4 major companies are **ADO, Norte, Oriente,** and **Mayab.** Destinations include: **Campeche** (6hr., 4 per day 7:45am-10:30pm, 320 pesos); **Chetumal**

(11 per day, 216 pesos); **Chichén Itzá** (2½hr., several per day, 85-126 pesos); **Chiquilá** (3hr.; 7:50am, 12:40pm; 72 pesos); **Mérida** (every hr., 194 pesos); **Palenque** (14hr., 7:30pm, 498 pesos); **Playa del Carmen** (1hr., every 15min., 42 pesos); **Tulum** (every hr. 4am-11pm, 54 pesos); **Valladolid** (2hr., 7 per day 5am-5:30pm, 98 pesos).

Ferries: To get to Isla Mujeres, take a bus marked "Pto. Juárez" to 1 of 3 ferry depots north of town (**Punta Sam** for cars, **Gran Puerto** and **Puerto Juárez** for passengers; 15min.). Tour companies in the Zona Hotelera provide ferry service from 150 pesos.

LOCAL TRANSPORTATION

Public Transportation: Buses marked "Hoteles R1" (6.50 pesos) run every 5min. during the day and every 10-20min. at night between the bus station downtown and the end of the Zona at Club Med. They stop at blue bus signs along Tulum and Kukulcán; there is often live music, and buses can become mobile parties at night. Blue buses marked "Bus One" (with A/C and light jazz; 11 pesos) follow the same route as the Hoteles R1 buses. To get off either bus in the Zona Hotelera, give a hearty shout of "¡Señor!"

Taxis: Within the Zona Hotelera (ask at hotels for rates to specific destinations), downtown (around 20 pesos), and between (100-150 pesos). Set a price before getting in.

Car Rental: Alamo, at km 9.5 (☎886 0168). Summer high season US$75 per day not including insurance; summer low season US$43 including insurance. **Avicar,** Tulum 3 (☎887 2389 or 884 9635; www.avicar.com.mx). Cars with A/C and insurance. See website for rates and discounts. Open daily 8am-7pm. Other rental options are located along the Zona Hotelera, in the *centro*, and at the airport. Prices range US$35-55 per day, with A/C US$50-80. Look for coupons in *Cancún Tips* magazine.

Moped Rental: Vendors between km 3 and 5. 100 pesos per hr., 500 pesos per day. **Bicycles** and **in-line skates** 70 pesos per hr., 160 pesos per day.

✦⚡ 🛈 ORIENTATION AND PRACTICAL INFORMATION

Perched on the northeastern tip of the Yucatán Peninsula, Cancún lies 285km east of Mérida via Mex. 180, and 382km north of Chetumal and the Belize border via Mex. 307. Cancún is divided into two areas: **downtown**, or the *centro*, where you'll find bargains but no beaches, and the **Zona Hotelera**, with fewer bargains but oh-so-much beach. The Zona is a slender "7"-shaped strip of land, and addresses along its one main road are given by kilometer number. Kilometer numbers increase from 1 to 20 beginning at the outskirts of the *centro*.

Tourist Offices: Tulum 5 (☎887 4329; www.cancun.gob.mx), in City Hall on Ayuntamiento Benito Juárez. Ask for *Cancún Tips*, a free, English-language magazine with information, coupons, and maps. Also available at the airport, Plaza Caracol, and hotels. Open M-F 9am-5pm.

El Mochilero, (☎884 8490; elmochilerocancun@hotmail.com) located across the street from the bus terminal, caters to backpacker budgets and needs. Open daily 9am-5pm.

Consulates: Canada, km 8.5, Plaza Caracol, 3rd fl. (☎883 3360 or 3361, after-hours emergencies 800 514 0129; fax 883 3232). Open M-F 9am-5pm. **UK,** in Royal Sands Hotel (☎881 0100). Open M-F 9am-3pm. **US,** km 8.5, Plaza Caracol, 3rd fl. (☎883 0272, after-hours emergencies 999 947 2285 or 044 998 845). Open M-F 9am-1pm.

Currency Exchange and Banks: Bancomer, Tulum 20 (☎884 4400), at Calle Claveles. Open M-F 8:30am-4pm, Sa 10am-2pm. **Banamex,** Tulum 19 (☎881 6403). Open M-F 9am-4pm, Sa 10am-2pm. Both give cash advances and have **24hr. ATMs.** Independent **exchange booths** are plentiful in the *centro* and give better rates than vendors accepting dollars.

American Express: Tulum 208 (☎881 4000), 3 blocks south of Cobá. Open M-F 9am-6pm, Sa 9am-1pm. Another in the Zona Hotelera on the 1st fl. of Plaza Kukulcán at km 13 (☎885 3905). Open daily 10am-5pm.

Luggage Storage: Bus station, 2nd fl. 5-12 pesos per hr. Open daily 6am-9:30pm.

Bookstores: Fama, Tulum 105 (☎884 6541), between Claveles and Tulipanes. Small selection of English-language beach reading. Open M-Su 9am-9pm. The supermarket **Chedaui** (p. 660) also has a small selection of Spanish language books for those in desperate need of a good read.

Laundromat: Lavandería Alborada, Náder 5 (☎884 1584), behind the Ayuntamiento Benito Juárez. Self-service wash and dry 10 pesos. Open M-Sa 9am-8pm. **Tintorería Fresh 'n' Clean,** on Tulum next to Comercial Mexicana. Full-service: wash 10 pesos, dry 10 pesos. Self-service: 10 pesos per 3kg. Dry cleaning available. Open M-Sa 9am-8:30pm.

Emergency: ☎066.

Police: ☎884 1913, in city hall.

Red Cross: Yaxchilán 2 (☎884 1616).

24hr. Pharmacy: Farmacia París, Yaxchilán 32 (☎884 1049), at Rosas. Delivery available. Another at Cancún Center, right before the Convention Center.

Medical Services: Hospital Americano, Viento 15 (☎884 6133), 5 blocks south on Tulum after Cobá. For an **ambulance,** call **Total Assist,** Claveles 5 (☎884 8082), near Tulum.

Fax Office: Telecomm, (☎884 1529), on Xel-Ha at Sunyaxchén, next to the post office. Telegram service and **Internet** access. Open M-F 8am-7:30pm, Sa 9am-12:30pm.

Internet Access: Internet cafes are not hard to find, especially near the bus station on Tulum and Uxmal. Most hostels include free Internet and offer lower prices than independent cafes. **La Taberna,** Yaxchilán 23 (☎887 5433), is a sports bar, pool hall, cafe, and Internet cafe all rolled into one. 12 pesos per hr. Open daily 1pm-5am.

Post Office: (☎884 4544 or 892 4187), on Xel-Ha at Sunyaxchén. Open M-F 8am-6pm, Sa-Su 9am-12:30pm. **Postal Code:** 77601.

ACCOMMODATIONS

Trying to find cheap accommodations in the Zona Hotelera is not for the faint of heart. Budget travelers looking to have all the fun at a fraction of the cost will do better staying in the much calmer downtown area and partying in the Zona Hotelera, as public transportation between the two is cheap and frequent. Generally, the hotels on the lagoon side of the road and those before km 5 are cheapest. If you don't mind dipping into your retirement fund, any tourist agency can set you up at one of the behemoths in the Zona. Buses run less frequently during the early morning hours, however; it is advisable to travel in groups, especially post-clubbing. Prices generally rise during mid-summer and in the winter by 25%. Reservations are a good idea any time of the year.

Haina Hostal, Orquideas 13 (☎898 2081; www.hainahostal.com). Farther from the bus station than other hostels, but well worth the walk. Haina has spotless dorms with sturdy wooden bunks and cool lounging areas perfect for catching a *fútbol* match or a game of poker. Breakfast included. Free Internet and lockers. 50 peso deposit for linens and keys. Reception 24hr. 6-bed dorms 110 pesos. Cash only. ❶

The Weary Traveler: Mexico Hostel, Palmera 30 (☎887 0191; www.cancunhostels.com.mx), 4 blocks west of the bus station. This HI-approved hostel has a kitchen and a large common area for lounging. Breakfast and small dinner included. Linens and private lockers included. Lock deposit 50 pesos. Laundry 30 pesos. Free Internet. Reception 24hr. Check-out noon. Beds 100 pesos per night, with A/C 110 pesos. 10% discount for HI members. Cash only. ❶

Soberanis Hostal, Cobá 5 (☎884 4564), next to the supermarket at Tulum and Cobá. This well-maintained, 78-room hostel has dorms and private rooms to accommodate a wide range of budgets. 4-bed dorms have sturdy wooden bunks, private lockers, A/C, and bath in the room. Guests flock to the restaurant and open-air bar downstairs. 10% discount on tours booked through the tourist agency in the lobby. Breakfast included. Internet 15 pesos per hr. Reception 24hr. Check-out 1pm. Dorms 120 pesos; rooms from 595 pesos. 20% discount with ISIC or mention of Let's Go. MC/V. ❷

Hostal Las Palmas, Palmera 43 (☎884 2513; www.hotel-laspalmascancun.com), 3 blocks from the bus station on a quiet side street. A good deal in a convenient location. Dorms and private rooms with A/C and large, wooden bunks. One drawback is the lack of common area. Continental breakfast included. Internet 15 pesos per hr. Dorms 100 pesos; private rooms 250-360 pesos. Cash only. ❶

Hostal Chacmool Cancún, Gladiolas 18 (☎887 5873 or 884 1915; www.chac-mool.com.mx), on the Parque de las Palapas. There isn't much common space to hang out in, but the large dorm rooms with A/C and the lovely Parque de las Palapas more than make up for the deficit. The friendly owner can help arrange tours and snorkeling trips. Breakfast included. Laundry 30 pesos. 1hr. free Internet per day. Dorms 130 pesos; single 320 pesos, with bath 350 pesos. Cash or Paypal with MC/V only. ❺

Mayan Hostel, Margaritas 17 (☎892 0103; www.cancunhostel.com), 1 block from the bus station. The dorm rooms show their years of use, but a pleasant rooftop patio decorated with ceramics and tropical plants that overlooks a quiet park makes this a good option for those who want to stay close to the bus station. Guests do not receive a key and must be let in by the receptionist. Kitchen available. Locker and linens included. Free Internet. Reception 24hr. Dorms 110 pesos; 100 peso deposit. Cash only. ❶

The Nest, Alcatraces 49 (☎884 8967; mjkglobal@yahoo.com), at Claveles. This small hostel on a quiet, shady street feels worlds removed from the glitter of the disco circuit. One large dorm with powerful fans and private lockers. Gated garden with tables is a good escape from the heat. Full kitchen and small lounge. Breakfast included. Laundry 30 pesos. Internet 10 pesos per hr. Check-out 2pm. Dorms 115 pesos. Cash only. ❷

Suites Albatrós, Yaxchilán 154 (☎884 2242; www.albatroscancun.com). One of the best values in Cancún for a group. Share the jungle of a courtyard with the friendly owner's pet iguanas and carp. Apartment-like rooms have A/C, large beds and closets, and full kitchens. Rooms upstairs have balconies with laundry lines and sinks. Barbecue pits available. Make reservations at least 3 days in advance. Doubles 380 pesos; each additional person (up to 4) 50 pesos. Cash only. ❺

Hotel Los Girasoles, Piña 20 (☎887 3990; losgirasolescancun@hotmail.com), on a small side street. This family-run, well-lit hotel offers extremely clean rooms with A/C, kitchenettes, and cable TV. Rooms from 350 pesos, with kitchenette 400 pesos. Discounts in low season. Cash only. ❺

Hotel Colonial, Tulipanes 22 (☎884 1535; www.hotelcolonialcancun.com), off Tulum on the pedestrian mall. The Colonial's convenient *centro* location makes it a favorite among vacationers. Cramped rooms with TV face a lovely Spanish courtyard complete with tiled fountain. Internet 10 pesos per hr. Free parking. Doubles 350 pesos, with A/C 320 pesos. MC/V. ❺

◪ FOOD

Though the resort-heavy Zona Hotelera has a surprising number of affordable places serving tasty Mexican cuisine, chances of a good meal and good prices are better in the *centro*. The uninitiated should avoid the street vendors, who

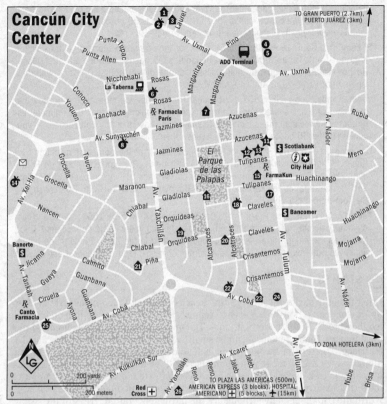

Cancún City Center

may or may not follow health codes. Those with stomachs of steel can eat with the locals at one of the countless stands in the **Parque de las Palapas,** three blocks from the bus station on Alcatraces. Two-course meals usually include *sopa* (soup) and fruit juice (35-50 pesos). A huge supermarket, **Comercial Mexicana,** is across from the ADO bus station on Tulum. (☎880 3330. Open daily 7am-midnight.) Smaller but more centrally located is **Chedaui,** Tulum 22, at the intersection with Cobá. (☎884 1155. Open daily 7am-11pm.)

Restaurante Los Huaraches de Alcatraces, Alcatraces 31 (☎884 2528), near El Parque de las Palapas. Locals love this cafeteria-style restaurant for its cheap and delicious regional food in the fan-filled dining room. Quesadilla fillings, such as squash blossoms, change daily (15-20 pesos). *Mole* made from scratch 50 pesos. Delivery available. Open Tu-Su 8am-7pm. Cash only. ❸

El Tapatío, Uxmal 30 (☎887 8317), at the corner of Uxmal and Palmera. Since 1981, the Camacho-Zepeda family has indoctrinated backpackers into the wonders of traditional Jalisco-style *pozole* (a chunky soup made with hominy kernels, radishes, lettuce, and meat; 55-65 pesos). Daily specials 50 pesos. Fruit smoothies 17-32 pesos. Open M-Sa 8am-1am, Su 9am-11pm. MC/V. ❹

100% Natural (☎884 3617; www.100natural.com.mx), near Yaxchilán and Sunyaxchén. The cook selects produce from beneath a central fountain at this open-air restaurant, where eclectic fare from *nopales* (vegetables made from the stems of prickly pears) to *bonito* flakes (dried fish) is followed by freshly baked goodies. Enjoy a fresh spinach, apple, and carrot *licuado* for 29 pesos. Salads 50 pesos. Live music weekend mornings. Delivery available. Open daily 7am-11pm. MC/V. ❹

El Tacolote, Cobá 19 (☎887 3045). Look for the *sombrero*-sporting yellow chicken logo out front. Tacos 8-56 pesos. Quesadillas 22 pesos. Seafood 90-125 pesos. Roving *mariachis* frequently make a stop during dinner hours. Delivery available. Open daily 11am-2am. AmEx/D/MC/V. ❹

Vegetarianos, Cobá 81 (☎887 1755), near Tankah. Opened more than a decade ago by a chef who has shared her secrets on Cancún's cooking channel, this intimate restaurant will give vegetarians a chance to sample the flavors of Mexican cuisine. All-you-can-eat buffet 55 pesos. *Licuados* 40 pesos. Open daily 8am-8pm. ❹

Los Arcos, (☎887 6673; www.losarcoscancun.com), at the corner of Yaxchilán and Rosas. A safe bet for filling meals and a stiff drink. The bar gets going on Friday nights when locals come to jam out to the classic rock DJ. Try the pasta with shrimp and marinara sauce for 79 pesos. 2-for-1 Happy hour daily 7-10pm. Open M-Th and Su 7pm-4am, F-Sa 7pm-5am. MC/V. ❺

Taco Factory, km 9.5, Plaza Party Center, Local 14 (☎883 1651; www.taco-factory.com), across the street from the Dady'O night club in the Punta Cancún area. Good for cheap, late-night munchies and people-watching in the Zona. Tacos made before your eyes with fresh tortillas. Quesadillas from 12 pesos. Tacos 20 pesos. Cash only. ❷

🔆 SIGHTS

Other than the packs of tourists at the beach or the bar, Cancún has little to offer by way of sights. For those eager to remind themselves they are indeed in Mexico, head to El Embarcadero at km 4. The massive port building is home to the local theater, **Teatro de Cancún,** and a small craft museum, **La Casa del Arte Popular Mexicano.** The theater has a rotating calendar of shows with something playing almost every night, mostly in Spanish. (☎849 4848; culturaytradicion@prodigy.net.mx. Tickets 200-300 pesos.) La Casa del Arte focuses primarily on Mexico's rich history of polychromatic folk art. The detailed displays make it well worth the trip. Especially striking are the intricately crafted "trees of life" (clay sculptures interpreting man's fall from the Garden of Eden) and the enormous snake-shaped rain stick. The gift shop is brimming with crafts bought directly from artisans all over Mexico. (☎849 4332 or 5583; www.museoartepopularmexicano.org. Open M-F 9am-7pm, Sa-Su 11am-7pm. 55 pesos; includes 20min. audio tour.) The small archaeological site of **El Rey,** on the lagoon at km 18, provides a glimpse into local history. The ruins were once part of a Mayan fishing community that inhabited what is now the Zona Hotelera from AD 150 to 1200. The centerpiece of the site is the king's pyramid, though it will only impress those who have yet to see any of the other spectacular Mayan ruins. Hundreds of iguanas that now find sanctuary here will keep you on your toes. (Open daily 8am-5pm. 34 pesos. Tours in English and Spanish 10am-3pm, 55 pesos.)

🏖 BEACHES

The world-famous beaches of Cancún are the town's biggest attraction. Don't fret about the wall of luxury hotels standing between you and the glorious surf—all beaches in Mexico are public property. There are regular public access points to the beaches along Kukulcán. Multi-hued turquoise waters caress the Caribbean coastline and gentle sea breezes stave off the heat of the day. Although you'll usually have plenty of sunburned company on the sands, Cancún's beaches are long enough (22km) and wide enough to accommodate meditating, napping, reading, swimming, and even a game of volleyball or soccer.

Stealing the show on the north side of the Zona Hotelera are **Playa Langosta** (at km 5) and **Playa Tortugas** (at km 6.5). The gradually sloping shores, small hotels, and clear waters make for better swimming than the beaches farther south. Less spectacular and also less crowded are **Playa las Perlas** (at km 2.5) and **Playa Linda** (at km 3.8) to the west. On the east side of the Zona Hotelera, **Playa Chac-Mool** starts just south of **Punta Cancún**. Heading south, you'll come across pleasant **Playa Marlín** (at km 12.8) and **Playa Delfines** (at km 17.8); normally quiet and uncommercial, these beaches are thick with locals on the weekends. Delfines and Marlin have the largest waves and also the highest salt content which makes underwater vision more difficult. At Delfines, umbrellas (100 pesos) and chairs (25 pesos) can be rented from the small shack near the life guard stand.

> **TAKE A HINT.** When swimming at any of the beaches along the Zona Hotelera, look for flags that indicate water conditions. Green and yellow flags mean "swim with caution." **Black flags mean "do not enter."**

Watersports enthusiasts are in luck: Cancún offers opportunities to participate in nearly every known aquatic sport. As in most resort areas, prices in Cancún are much higher than those in lower-profile neighboring communities. Many organized recreational activities can be arranged through the luxury hotels lining the beaches, or through private companies and tour guides. It is a good idea to have a sense of what you want to do and how much money you have to spend before starting to bargain with vendors, who have their own plans for your money. Expect to pay at least US$30 for the most basic snorkeling tours.

Aqua World, km 15.2 (☎848 8300; www.aquaworld.com.mx). A popular choice for exploring Cancún's aquatic paradise. Glass-bottom boat tours of Laguna Nichuplé (every hr. 9am-3pm, US$44) and jungle tours (last tour 2:30pm, US$55). Open daily 7am-10pm. MC/V.

Scuba Cancún, km 5 (☎849 7508 or 4736; www.scuba-cancun.com.mx). Well-established dive and watersport center offers scuba diving lessons (2hr.), using both training pool and ocean (US$88). Two-tank dive for certified divers US$68. Wet suit rental US$8. Snorkeling (daily 2 and 4:30pm) US$29. *Cenote* (cave) tour (Tu, Th, Sa 8am) US$79. Open daily 8:30am-8pm. MC/V.

TOP 10 MAYAN GODS

Most knowledge of the Mayan gods comes from the *Popul Vuh*, a 1550 compilation of creation myths. The original text was lost, but an 18th century translation survived, now kept in the Newberry Library in Chicago.

1. Itzamná: the god of creation, agriculture, writing, and healing. Alternate identities include serpent-god Kukulkan (an incarnation of the Aztec Queztacoatl), a night jaguar, and the sun god.

2. Chak: god of rain and harvest. Depicted with catfish whiskers, scales, and lightning bolt.

3. The Hero Twins: Hunahpu, identified by the black spot on his cheek and Xbanalque, who sports jaguar pelts. Pro-ballplayers who battled the underworld gods to avenge their father's death.

4. Ah Puch: "the flatulent one." Also the god of death. Associated with owls and represented with rotting skin and popped eyeballs.

5. Ix-Chel: the moon and fertility goddess. Her fling with Itzamná produced the bacabs, who hold up the four corners of the sky.

6. Vacub Caquix: the Seven Macaw. A deluded bird deity who thinks he's the sun god. The Hero Twins disabuse him of the idea.

7. Ek Chuah: god of both merchants and war. Coincidence?

8. Backlum Chaam: male sex god. Also one of the bacabs.

9. Acan: patron of intoxication and the honey brew, Balche.

10. Zipacna: Vacub Caquix's giant demon son. Kills 400 warriors in one sitting. Literally.

Blue Water Adventures, km 6.3 (☎849 4444; www.bluewateradventures.com.mx), at the marina. A range of aquatic adventures: snorkeling tours (3hr., US$42), jungle tours with snorkeling (2½hr.; US$45), and packaged daytrips to Isla Mujeres with time to shop (US$55, includes snorkeling and 2 meals). Open daily 8am-8pm. MC/V.

♫ ▣ ENTERTAINMENT AND SHOPPING

As night descends, Cancún morphs from a beachgoer's playground into the home of some of the biggest, hottest clubs in the Western Hemisphere. In the Zona, expect to see tipsy tourists parading, drink in hand, down Kukulcán. Crowds vary according to time and season. April hosts US college students, June welcomes high-school and college graduates, and late nights belong year-round to a stream of wealthy international tourists. Locals favor bars and discos in the *centro*, at the south end of Tulum near Cobá and at the north end of Yaxchilán near Sunyaxchén. Unlike much of Mexico, Cancún boasts a gay nightlife that is well incorporated into the large disco scene in the Zona, and the *centro* has a few proudly gay clubs as well. In the small parks in the *centro*, there are often live musicians and impromptu dance parties. Most establishments in Cancún open at 9pm, get going after midnight, and close when the crowds wane around dawn.

Cancún also has options for more relaxing entertainment. Movie theaters show many of the same films you would find in the US. Downtown, the **Plaza Kukulcán** and **Plaza las Américas** are two options; see www.cinepolis.com.mx for details.

SPORTS

Death comes every Wednesday at 3:30pm to the **Plaza de Toros** (☎884 8372 or 882 8248), on Bonampak at Sayil. Tickets for the bullfights (2hr.) are available at travel agencies on Tulum (300 pesos, under 5 free; group discounts available) or at the bullring on a fight day. Catch your favorite sports teams at the sports bar **Caliente**, in the Forum by the Sea in the Zona Hotelera, where you can enjoy drinks and snacks on red velvet seats. The huge screens broadcast coverage of every imaginable sporting event from the college level up and the bookies will happily help you place your bets. (☎883 4761 or 4762; www.caliente.com.mx. Open M-F 11am-1am, Sa-Su 10am-1am. AmEx/MC/V.)

SHOPPING

Cancún is best enjoyed on a loose budget. Popular international luxury brands on sale in Plazas Terramar, Caracol, Flamingo, Islas, and Kukulcán will swallow your dollars whole. Ravenous for crafts, dazed vacationers pour into the *centro* daily to shop at the tourist market, **Mercado 28,** on Av. Xel-Ha. Be ready to bargain, as the *mercado* has the heaviest concentration of doodads in Cancún. Popular items include *sombreros*, blankets, pottery, and leather goods. To get there from the Zona, take the R-2 bus marked Mercado 28 or the R-1 bus to the ADO terminal, from which it is a short 10min. walk. Parking available. (Open daily 9am-8pm.)

◖ NIGHTLIFE

Most bars in the *centro* are along Yaxchilán, near Uxmal, and on Tulipanes, off Tulum. In the Zona Hotelera, don't bother seeking out local bars—the party is at clubs and chains like Carlos'n Charlie's, T.G.I. Friday's, and Señor Frog's. Hotel **Happy hours** are usually between 5 and 7pm. Most of the glitziest clubs and discos are near the Zona's Punta Cancún, near Playa Caracol and Forum by the Sea. Cancún's glam clubs attract American youth eager for sinful pleasures. The dress code for discos is simple: less is more and tight is just right. Bikini tops often get women in for free; use your judgment in more laid-back clubs. US dollars rule in the Zona.

 MORE THAN A PINT, LESS THAN A 40. A good way to save a few pesos when out for a night at the bar or just kicking back with friends is to buy a *caguama* instead of a lone beer bottle. All major Mexican beer companies bottle *caguamas*, which contain a liter of beer, for around 40 pesos.

Coco Bongo, km 9.5 (☎883 5061; www.cocobongo.com.mx), in Forum by the Sea. Steamy, exhilarating, unstoppable. Vegas-style shows come to this always-popular club, where dancing to the eclectic rock, pop, and trance music is secondary to the main show. Cover M-F US$40, Sa-Su US$50; includes open bar. Shows 10:30pm. Open daily 10:30pm-late. AmEx/MC/V.

Roots, Tulipanes 26 (☎884 2437; roots@cancun.com), off Tulum. Caribbean-themed walls and eclectic artwork with a music motif set the stage in this superior jazz 'n' blues joint that opens to the pedestrian walkway. Live regional musicians Tu-Sa 10pm. Cover F-Sa 50 pesos; no cover if you sit on the patio. Open Tu-Sa 6pm-1am; kitchen closes at midnight. MC/V.

Carlos'n Charlie's, km 9.5 (☎883 1862), in the Forum by the Sea. Smaller than some of its locations in other Mexican cities, the Cancún Carlos'n Charlie's leaves the all-night dance parties to the big clubs. Sip drinks, nibble snacks, and watch the insanity pass on by. Beer 45 pesos. Margaritas 47 pesos. Open daily 10am-3am. AmEx/MC/V.

Señor Frog's, Blvr. Kukulcan, km 9.5 (☎883 1092; www.senorfrogs.com), across from Playa Chac Mool. Owned by the same company as Carlos'n Charlie's, Señor Frog's is a long-time Mexican chain and a popular mid-week hangout for tourists and locals alike. Beer 45 pesos. Open midnight-3am. Cash only.

Mambo Cafe, km 13.5 (☎840 6498 or 6499; www.mambocafe.com.mx), near the American Royal Resort, is the best place for true salsa nightlife. Frequented by locals and curious visitors eager to live out their dancing dreams. Come dressed for success (glitter and spangles are highly recommended). Free salsa classes Th 9-10pm. Cover F-Su men 100 pesos, women 70 pesos. Open Tu-Su 10pm-5am. Cash only.

Dady'O, km 9.5 (☎883 3333; www.dadyo.com.mx), in Forum by the Sea. The cave-like entrance lets you know you're headed into a disco inferno. The club opens onto a stage and dance floor streaked with lasers and pulsating with strobes, promising plenty of fun. Piercing booth upstairs. Bikini contests held regularly. Snacks 30-60 pesos. Cover US$15; with open bar US$35. Open daily 10pm-late. Cash only.

Dady Rock (☎883 3333). Brought to you by the same conglomerate that owns Dady'O and 7 other clubs in Punta Cancún, this club is distinctive for the variety of its music—anyone for techno pan pipes? Cover US$30; includes open bar. Open daily 6pm-late. Cash only.

The City, km 9 (☎848 8380; www.thecitycancun.com), next to Forum by the Sea. This multilevel megaplex can cram what seems like thousands of people through the door. Filled to capacity during spring break, The City can feel deserted other times of year. Live performances hosted by MTV during spring break; check website for performances throughout the year. Cover M and W-Su US$15, with open bar US$35; Tu US$15 with open bar. Open daily 10:30pm-5am. Cash only.

Bulldog Cafe (☎848 9800; www.bulldogcafe.com), in Forum by the Sea. Originally founded in Mexico City, the Bulldog Cafe attracts a mostly Spanish-speaking crowd with its *rock en español* and live performances by some of Latin America's biggest acts. Ladies drink for free. No cover. Open daily 10pm-5am. Cash only.

YUCATÁN PENINSULA

GLBT NIGHTLIFE

Though many of the clubs in the Zona combine straight and gay nightlife, the only explicitly gay nightlife is in the *centro*. The clubs listed below are straight-friendly and open to all.

> **SAFETY FIRST.** While the brave may leave the club at 5am feeling buzzed and ready for the bus ride back to the *centro*, the wise will travel in a group. Safety in numbers.

Glow, Tulipanes 30 (☎898 4522; www.glowcancun.com), next to Roots. Cancún's newest gay bar is handsomely decorated with stainless steel, chains, and miles of red velvet. Things heat up around 1:30am. Drinks from 50 pesos. Open Tu-Sa 11pm-6:30am. Cash only.

Karamba, Tulum 5 (☎884 0032; www.karambabar.com), on the corner of Azucenas. A spacious, multilevel gay bar and disco with pop-art murals and a wide variety of dance music. Nightly theme shows or contests at 1:30am. Cover 60 pesos. Open W-Su 10:30pm-5am. Cash only.

▶ DAYTRIP FROM CANCÚN

PUERTO MORELOS

Buses from Cancún to Playa del Carmen stop 2km west of Puerto Morelos (30min., every 10min. 5am-11pm, 17 pesos). To get to the zócalo, take a taxi from the taxi stand next to the bus terminal (20 pesos).

Even the gods would be content with the unspoiled coral reef and pristine white sand beach of Puerto Morelos (pop. 4500). The locals here do everything they can to preserve the serenity while trying to share it with a growing number of visitors. Waterskiing is forbidden, as are resort hotels and Cancún-style hedonism. Puerto Morelos has become a popular escape for tourists tired of city life and those in need of a little (or a lot) of relaxation. The most popular activity in Puerto Morelos—besides soaking up the rays—is heading out in a *lancha* to snorkel or scuba dive. Trips can be arranged at **Dive Puerto Morelos,** Rojo Gómez 14, two blocks north of the *zócalo*. The company also offers a full range of PADI certification courses. (☎206 9084; www.divepuertomorelos.com. 2hr. snorkeling trip 250 pesos, including 10min. boat ride, equipment rental, and marine park entrance fee; 4-person min. 2-tank dive 700 pesos, including equipment rental and park fee; 2-person min. Open daily 8am-2pm and 5-8pm. MC/V.)

> **! HEADS UP.** The reef around the town dock is not as clean or safe as that to the north, so avoid swimming in the wake of the fishing boats when possible and make sure you are visible while in the water.

For those interested in keeping two feet on the ground, **Mayan Adventour,** located in the stand on the west side of the *zócalo*, offers ATV tours to the nearby *cenotes*, or freshwater swimming holes. A few of these impressive *cenotes* are dry, and a number of the tours involve rappelling into a cave. (☎167 3991. 3½hr. tours include snacks and a full lunch. Tours leave daily at 9am and 1pm. Cash only.)

ISLA HOLBOX   ☎984

A barrier island marking the start of the Caribbean Sea and the end of the Gulf of Mexico, Isla Holbox (hohl-BOSH; pop. 1600) is Mexico's answer to the glam and glitter of Cancún. Stretching nearly 40km, the soft sand beaches are endless, the turquoise waters warm, and plentiful shells keep most beachgoers happy. For those into a little more action than relaxin',' the island is home to a host of seafaring outdoor activities ranging from catching the waves on a kite-board to swimming with the whale sharks. Come with cash if you intend to partake in any of the island's activities, as credit cards are rarely accepted on the island and there is no bank.

C TRANSPORTATION. To get to Isla Holbox, take the bus to Chiquilá (3hr., 72 pesos) from Cancún, then take the Hermanos ferry #9 (☎875 2010; 30min., 1 per hr. 6am-6pm, 40 pesos) or the Delfin fast boat, or *lancha* (15min., every 1½hr. 7:45am-6pm, 40 pesos). Return buses to Cancún leave at 7:30am and 1:30pm. Ferries and fast boats leave with ample time to catch the bus.

⛏ PRACTICAL INFORMATION. Isla Holbox is off the grid as far as local services go. There is **no bank, no ATM, no hospital, no police,** and **no cell service. Laundry** services are at **Lavandería Holbox,** Calle Tiburon Ballena. (☎875 2162. Wash and dry 35 pesos per 12 pieces. Open daily 8am-3pm and 5-8pm.) If you need to connect to the outside world, head to **El Parque,** on the town square, for fast Internet access (15 pesos per hr.) and long distance phone service (4 pesos per min. to the US and Canada, 6 pesos per min. to Europe).

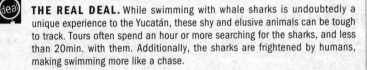

THE REAL DEAL. While swimming with whale sharks is undoubtedly a unique experience to the Yucatán, these shy and elusive animals can be tough to track. Tours often spend an hour or more searching for the sharks, and less than 20min. with them. Additionally, the sharks are frightened by humans, making swimming more like a chase.

⛏⛏ ACCOMMODATIONS AND FOOD. For those who want to stay in paradise a bit longer, cheap accommodations are tough to come by. **Posada Los Arcos ❹,** on the *zócalo,* is a long-time favorite among budget travelers. Slightly sagging mattresses and dim lighting attest to years of use, but each room comes with a private bath, refrigerator, overhead fan, and TV. (☎875 2043; www.holboxlosarcos.com. Rooms 150-350 pesos. Cash only.) **Hotel La Palapa ❺,** on the beach near the town pier, is as much a local establishment as its owner Lino. The well-kept rooms and bungalows, which opened in 1999, have shell-shaped showerheads, overhead fans, A/C, and handcrafted beach furniture on their decks. (☎875 2003; www.hotellapalapa.com. High-season singles and doubles 500 pesos; 3-bed bungalows 500 pesos. Low-season singles and doubles 700 pesos; 3-bed bungalows 900 pesos. Paypal or cash only.) Good seafood comes easily to the fishing village of Holbox. On the town square, funky **La Isla de Colibrí ❺** serves massive dishes amid folk art and Christmas lights. Try *camarones en salsa mango* (shrimp in mango salsa; 100 pesos) and finish the meal with a fresh fruit and yogurt bowl for 45 pesos. (☎875 2162. Open daily 8am-1pm and 4-10pm. Cash only.)

⛏ OUTDOOR ACTIVITIES. The largest tour company on the island is **Turística Miguel** (☎875 2028; www.holboxislandtours.com), on the corner of the *zócalo.* A seven-boat fleet takes tourists swimming with the **whale sharks** (June-Aug., 5hr., 800 pesos), snorkeling with the turtles at Cabo Catoche (June-Aug., 5hr., 800 pesos), **birdwatching** in the mangrove forests (6hr., 700 pesos), and **sport fishing** (1500-3000 pesos). Tours, which leave at 7am and return around lunchtime, include all the necessary equipment and typically provide a small breakfast and lunch. Turística Miguel also rents out golf carts, the island's primary mode of transportation. (100 pesos per hr.; full day 550 pesos.) Airborne activities can be arranged through Lino—as in Adrenalino—at Hotel La Palapa (p. 667). Laser

sailing (half-day 600 pesos, full-day 1000 pesos) and three-day kite surfing courses (1800 pesos) are taught by Lino himself, an Italian expat with 21 years on the island and an intense passion for the wind. **Windsurfing** is available upon request. (☎875 2003. Paypal or cash only.)

ISLA MUJERES   ☎998

In 1517, Francisco Hernández de Córdoba happened upon this tiny island only to find hundreds of small female statuettes scattered on the beaches and promptly named the island Isla Mujeres. Hernández had stumbled upon a sanctuary for Ixchel, the Mayan goddess of fertility, weaving, happiness, medicine, and the moon. For years, Isla Mujeres (pop. 8300) was a small fishing village with few visitors. It wasn't until the 1950s that vacationing Mexicans discovered the remote island. Americans, Australians, Canadians, and Europeans soon followed, transforming it into a hot spot for hippies and backpackers. While some locals still fish for a living, most now cater to daytrippers and those who use the island as a base for exploring the pristine waters around Isla Mujeres and Isla Contoy. Although the *centro* has become a full-fledged tourist haven, buildings do not crowd the beaches as they do in Cancún. One can easily find a piece of sand on one of the many beaches or get a glimpse of Caribbean life in the quiet southern *colonias*.

▐ TRANSPORTATION

Ferries are the only way to reach Isla Mujeres. They leave from Gran Puerto (3km north of downtown Cancún) and Puerto Juárez (200m beyond Gran Puerto), and are accessible by a "Puerto Juárez" bus, *microbús* (15min., 4.50 pesos), or taxi (from 16 pesos). Two companies run express ferries: **Maritimos Magaña** (☎877 0382; 20min., from Puerto Juárez every 30min. 6:30am-10:30pm; 35 pesos), and **UltraMar** (☎843 2011; 15min., every 30min. from Gran Puerto 5am-11:30pm, 35 pesos). Arrive early—ferries are notorious for leaving ahead of schedule when full. A car ferry runs to the island from Punta Sam (5km north of Puerto Juárez; 5 per day, 12.50 pesos per person, from 50 pesos per car; arrive 30min. early).

Walking is the best way to navigate the island's compact, cobblestone *centro*. For longer trips, red **taxis** (☎877 0066; 23-54 pesos) line up at the stand directly to the right as you come off the passenger dock, and zip to Playa Paraíso, Playa Lancheros, Tortugranja, Garrafón, and the Mayan sanctuary Ixchel. Prices to common destinations are listed at the taxi stand between the two ferry docks. You should have no problem catching one elsewhere. **Public buses** (4.50 pesos) pick up passengers from the ferry docks and only go as far as Playa Lancheros.

The best way to explore the ends of the island is to rent a moped, bike, or golf cart, all more common than cars. **Moped and golf cart** rentals available at **Pepe's Rentals,** Hidalgo 19, between Matamoros and Abasolo (☎/fax 877 0019; mopeds 80 pesos per hr., 300 pesos per day; golf carts 150/550 pesos; includes gasoline; open daily 9am-6pm; MC/V) and at **Moto Kan Kin,** Abasolo 15, between Hidalgo and Guerrero (☎877 0071; mopeds 100 pesos per hr., 250 pesos per day; open daily 9am-5pm; cash only). **Bicycles** can be rented from a number of vendors along **Rueda Medina** (80 pesos per hr.; cash only). Be sure to check the tire pressure and durability of the bike before handing over your money.

▣ ▐ ORIENTATION AND PRACTICAL INFORMATION

Isla Mujeres is a narrow landmass (7.5km by 1km) 11km northeast of Cancún, and the *centro* is laid out in a rough grid at the northwest corner of the island. Perpendicular to the dock is **Rueda Medina,** which runs the length of the island along the

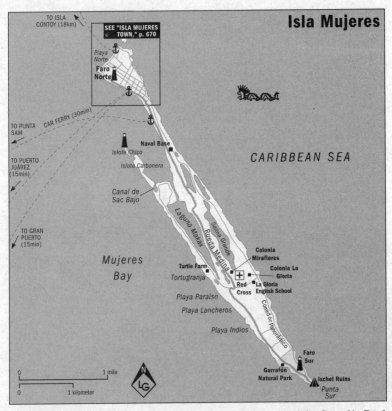

Isla Mujeres

TO ISLA CONTOY (18km)

SEE "ISLA MUJERES TOWN," p. 670

Playa Norte
Faro Norte

TO PUNTA SAM

CAR FERRY (30min)

TO PUERTO JUÁREZ (15min)

Naval Base
Islote Chico
Islote Carbonera

Canal de Sac Bajo

TO GRAN PUERTO (15min)

CARIBBEAN SEA

Laguna Makax

Salina Grande

Rueda Medina

Mujeres Bay

Turtle Farm
Tortugranja

Colonia Miraflores

Colonia La Gloria

Red Cross

La Gloria English School

Playa Paraíso

Playa Lancheros

Correo or Panorámico

Playa Indios

Faro Sur

Garrafón Natural Park

Ixchel Ruins

Punta Sur

0 ——— 1 mile
0 ——— 1 kilometer

N
LG

YUCATÁN PENINSULA

coastline, past the lagoon, Playa Paraíso, Playa Lancheros, and the Garrafón Reef. On the northeast coast, the Sea Wall Walk runs the length of the island, however this route is currently under construction and may not be accessible.

Tourist Office: (☎877 0307), on Rueda Medina. On the right side after the 1st left beyond the port. Open daily 9am-5pm. **Cooperativo Isla Mujeres** (☎877 1363), on Rueda Medina in the *palapa* near the PEMEX station, is a wealth of information about tours and local island happenings. Open M-Su 8am-8pm.

Currency Exchange: HSBC (☎877 0005), on Rueda Medina, on the right at the port's exit. Has **24hr. ATM.** Open M-Sa 8am-7pm. Another ATM is at Súper Xpress (p. 671).

Bookstore: Cosmic Cosas, Guerrero 70 (☎877 0555), inside the restaurant Mañana (p. 671). Buy, sell, and exchange books in various languages while snacking on delicious vegetarian-friendly foods. Open M-Sa 8am-10pm, closes 4pm in the low season.

Laundromat: Lavandería Tim Phó, Juárez 94 (☎877 0529), at Abasolo. Full service (2hr.) 55 pesos per 4kg. Open M-Sa 7am-9pm, Su 8am-2pm. **Lavandería Ángel** (☎877 1730), Hidalgo local A-3, near Chiles Locos. 40 pesos; 4kg min. Open M-Sa 8am-midnight.

Police: (☎877 0458), on Hidalgo at Morelos, in the Palacio Municipal. Open 24hr.

Red Cross: (☎877 0280), at the Colonia La Gloria, 3.5km south of town just before the Playa Lancheros roundabout.

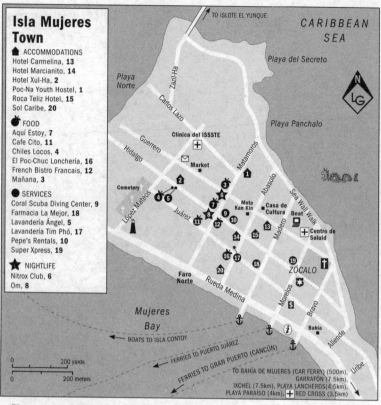

Isla Mujeres Town

🏠 ACCOMMODATIONS
Hotel Carmelina, **13**
Hotel Marcianito, **14**
Hotel Xul-Ha, **2**
Poc-Na Youth Hostel, **1**
Roca Teliz Hotel, **15**
Sol Caribe, **20**

🍎 FOOD
Aquí Estoy, **7**
Cafe Cito, **11**
Chiles Locos, **4**
El Poc-Chuc Lonchería, **16**
French Bistro Francais, **12**
Mañana, **3**

⚫ SERVICES
Coral Scuba Diving Center, **9**
Farmacia La Mejor, **18**
Lavandería Ángel, **5**
Lavandería Tim Phó, **17**
Pepe's Rentals, **10**
Super Xpress, **19**

⭐ NIGHTLIFE
Nitrox Club, **6**
Om, **8**

TO ISLOTE EL YUNQUE

CARIBBEAN SEA

Playa del Secreto

Playa Norte

Zazil-Ha

Carlos Lazo

Playa Panchalo

Clínica del ISSSTE ✚

Guerrero

Hidalgo

Market

Matamoros

Abasolo

Sea Wall Walk

Cemetery

López Mateos

Juárez

Moto Kan Kin

Casa de Cultura

Beat

Madero

✚ Centro de Saluid

Faro Norte

Rueda Medina

Morelos

ZÓCALO ✝

Bravo

Allende

Mujeres Bay

🛥 BOATS TO ISLA CONTOY

⚓ ⚓ ⚓ ℹ Bahia

FERRIES TO PUERTO JUÁREZ

FERRIES TO GRAN PUERTO (CANCÚN)

TO BAHÍA DE MUJERES (CAR FERRY) (500m),
GARRAFÓN (7.5km),
IXCHEL (7.5km), PLAYA LANCHEROS(4.5km),
PLAYA PARAÍSO (4km), ✚ RED CROSS (3.5km)

Uribe

0 |———————| 200 yards
0 |———————| 200 meters

Pharmacy: La Mejor, Madero 17 (☎877 0116), between Hidalgo and Juárez. Open M-Sa 9am-10:30pm, Su 9am-3:30pm.

Medical Services: Centro de Salud, Guerrero 5 (☎877 0117), at Morelos. The white building at the northwest corner of the *zócalo*. Open 24hr. **Doctor Antonio E. Salas** (☎877 0477), at the **Clínica del ISSSTE** on the corner of López Mateos and Carlos Lazo, speaks English and will make house calls. Clinic open M-F 8am-3pm.

Fax Office: Telecomm and Western Union, Guerrero 13 (☎877 0113), next to the post office. Open M-F 8am-7:30pm, Sa 9am-12:30pm.

Internet Access: Beat (☎877 1328), on Guerrero next to the health center. Fast connections with webcams. 15 pesos per hr. Open M-Sa 8am-10pm, Su 9am-4pm. **Dígame,** at Abasolo and Guerrero, has laptop connections in a well-appointed, candle-lit space. 15 pesos per hr. Open M-Sa 9am-10pm.

Post Office: (☎877 0085) Guerrero and López Mateos, at the northwest corner of town, 1 block from Playa Norte. Open M-F 9am-4pm. **Postal Code:** 77400.

🏠 ACCOMMODATIONS

During high season (July-Aug. and Dec.-Apr.), prices increase by about 100 pesos, and you should inquire ahead and make reservations. Free camping is permitted on the beach, but for safety reasons, it is best to check in with the police first.

▧ **Poc-Na Youth Hostel,** Matamoros 15 (☎877 0090; www.pocna.com), near Playa Panchalo. An all-inclusive resort disguised as a hostel, Poc-Na is a fixture on the island. Chill under the giant *palapas* (palm thatched umbrellas), tan on the private beach, fill up on cheap grub, then party at night. Also has 2 bars, volleyball courts, soccer fields, and ping pong tables. Can arrange snorkel tours. Restaurant open daily 8am-10:30pm. Breakfast included. Free lockers; you provide the lock. 30min. Internet free. Tent site 65 pesos; bunk beds 90-110 pesos; dorms with A/C 125 pesos; private rooms 240-320 pesos. Work opportunities available in exchange for room and board. Cash only. ❶

Hotel Marcianito, Abasolo 10 (☎877 0111). Recently remodeled, this great value has spotless rooms with lock boxes for valuables and overhead fans. Rooms on the 3rd fl. have ocean views. Doubles 300 pesos; triples 350 pesos. Cash only. ❸

Hotel Carmelina, Guerrero 4 (☎877 0006), between Abasolo and Madero. Carmelina has lively owners and bright colors to make up for hot nights. The breezy 3rd fl. is the coolest. Parking available. Reserve ahead Dec.-Jan. Doubles with fan 200 pesos, with refrigerator 220 pesos; triples with fan 380 pesos. Cash only. ❸

Hotel Xul-Ha, Hidalgo 23 (☎877 0075), between Matamoros and López Mateos. Set around a jungle-like courtyard, Xul-Ha is reminiscent of the Mayan ruins it is named after. Large rooms have ceiling fans and mirrors; some have balconies and refrigerators. TV in the small lobby. Rooms 230 pesos; with A/C and TV 250 pesos. Cash only. ❸

Roca Teliz Hotel, Hidalgo 93 (☎877 0407 or 0804). Centrally located behind a gift shop on a pedestrian-only street, this 10-room inn with a courtyard and fountain offers peace and quiet. High-season singles 200 pesos, with A/C 400 pesos; doubles 230/458 pesos. Low-season singles 150/350 pesos; doubles 180/408 pesos. MC/V. ❹

Sol Caribe, Abasolo 6 (☎877 1559). Those looking to save money on food will be pleased with the super clean, complete kitchens included in every room. Rooms have private bath, TV, and A/C. Singles 450 pesos; doubles 650 pesos. Cash only. ❺

◖ FOOD

Seafood abounds in Isla Mujeres, as do, strangely, crepes and waffles. *Ceviche de pulpo* (octopus) is a local delicacy. Restaurants along **Hidalgo** cater to tourists with extensive menus and perks like roving *mariachis*. These tend to be of the best quality; however, many of the menus are nearly identical and prices are gringo-adjusted. Plan ahead—many restaurant owners close between lunch and dinner for siesta. For cheap eats, head to the **municipal market,** on Guerrero between Matamoros and López Mateos, which is lined with food stalls. (Most stalls open daily 8am-4pm, longer during high season.) A supermarket, **Súper Xpress,** is at Morelos 5. (☎887 1094 or 1092. Open M-Sa 7am-10pm, Su 7am-9pm.)

▧ **Mañana,** Guerrero 70 (☎877 0555), on the corner of Matamoros and Guerrero. Hand-painted tables, indoor and outdoor seating, chill tunes, and friendly international owners make this a tourist favorite. Vegetarian-friendly meals like the handpressed veggie burger (70 pesos) come with a fresh salad. After lunch, grab a beach read from Cosmic Cosas. Open M-Sa high season 8am-10pm, low season 8am-4pm. Cash only. ❹

Aquí Estoy (☎877 1777), on Matamoros between Guerrero and Hidalgo. No seating. Pizzas with tasty toppings like goat cheese and pesto. Plenty of sauces and condiments. Slices and Mexican pizzas (tortillas with melted cheese and toppings) 13-24 pesos. Whole pizzas 75-110 pesos. Open M 1-9pm, Tu-F 4-10pm, Sa 1-10pm. Cash only. ❷

El Poc-Chuc Lonchería, Juárez 5, on the corner of Abasolo. Colorful murals of sharks and Mayan temples watch over as you dine on traditional Quintana Roo fare. **El Paisano,** across the street in the lattice-covered building, is owned and operated by the same family and offers similar high-quality island fare. 2 beers 25 pesos. Entrees 36-90 pesos. *Enchiladas en mole* 45 pesos. Poc-Chuc open M-Sa 8am-10pm. El Paisano open 10am-10pm. Cash only. ❸

French Bistro Francais, Matamoros 29 (☎143 2119), at Hidalgo. Hand-painted tiles and a parrot named Peety keep the place lively. Hearty meals are each served with 3 vegetable sides. French toast (45 pesos) and crepe specials (41 pesos) are popular morning picks, but the specialty is *coq au vin* (chicken in red wine; 97 pesos). Open daily Jan.-May and July-Dec. 8am-noon and 6-10pm. Cash only. ❹

Chiles Locos, Av. Hidalgo Local B-1 (☎877 1219), between López Mateos and Matamoros. A stand-out of Mexican cuisine along restaurant-packed Hidalgo. Chef Ziggy and wife Donna please customers with their signature *poblanos* stuffed with shrimp and cheese (95 pesos). They also serve a breakfast of eggs, crepes, and waffles (30-50 pesos). Happy hour with 2-for-1 drinks every evening. Open daily 7am-3pm and 5-11pm. Cash only. ❹

Cafe Cito, Matamoros 42 (☎877 0438), at Juárez. Sand and shells under the see-through tabletops let patrons pretend they never left the beach. Replenish body and soul with Mexican breakfasts (34-49 pesos), freshly made crepes (26-52 pesos), sandwiches (32-36 pesos), and fruit salads (20-32 pesos). Portions are small. Open M-Sa 7am-2pm, Su 8am-2pm. Cash only. ❸

🌀 SIGHTS

The Mayan ruins of **Ixchel**—a pilgrimage destination for women who sought help from the goddess of fertility—are on the southern tip of the island, accessible by taxi (54 pesos). Most of the site was reduced to rubble by Hurricane Gilbert in 1988, but a partially reconstructed one-room building and an awesome panorama of the Yucatán and the Caribbean await those who make the journey. You must enter the Garrafón sculpture park for access (30 pesos). **La Casa de Cultura,** Av. Guerrero and Abasolo (☎877 0639), offers afternoon courses (mostly for kids) in folkloric dance and music. It also houses the island's library and a few glass-encased Mayan artifacts. (Open M-F 9am-9pm.)

🌊 🏄 BEACHES AND OUTDOOR ACTIVITIES

The Caribbean beaches of Isla Mujeres offer more tranquility than the beaches in Cancún and are much easier to access. Hotels on the north end of the island tend to be hidden behind trees and far from the shore, leaving plenty of space for play or rest. The most popular and accessible beach is **Playa Norte,** on the north shore, where gentle breezes and waves lull sunbathers to sleep. The water is shallow, and you can wade out far from shore. Recline under the *palapas* (palm thatched umbrellas) in the hammocks of **La Barra de Kin,** a bar on the north side of the beach. On the southwest side of the island, **Playa Lancheros** and **Playa Paraíso** open onto Mujeres Bay, forming a smaller beachfront broken up by numerous boat docks. The south end of the island is now the property of **Garrafón,** an adventure park similar to, and with the same management as, Xel-ha and Xcaret (p. 693). Eastern shores of the island are much rockier and currents can be dangerous—**eastern beaches are not for swimming.**

The beautiful **Isla Contoy** (www.islacontoy.org), a wildlife sanctuary reef with over 100 bird species, lies 18km north of Isla Mujeres. Opportunities to commune with nature are abundant and include birdwatching tours, diving, snorkeling, and boat tours. Divers should ask to see the diving certificates of those they hire; and if they don't ask for yours as well, think again. The only licensed operator for the Isla Contoy is the **Cooperativo Isla Mujeres** (☎877 1363), on Rueda Medina in the *palapa* near the PEMEX station. Local captains take visitors snorkeling around Isla Mujeres (4hr.; tours daily 11am; 220 pesos, includes equipment, lunch, and park fees), snorkeling and birding at Isla Contoy (5hr.; tours daily 8 and 9am; 600 pesos, includes equipment, breakfast and lunch, and park fees), or fishing (5000 pesos for full-day private *lancha*, includes lunch and equipment). Most tours require a minimum of six people and are far less frequent during the low season. (Open M-Su 8am-8pm. Cash only.) The **Coral Scuba Diving Center,** Matamoros 13-A, is the oldest dive operation on the island and has cheap scuba diving packages. Trips include visits to the **Cave of Sleeping Sharks,** 70 ft. below the surface and three miles northeast of the island, where you can catch a glimpse of the man-eaters in their most vulnerable state. (☎877 0763 or 0572; www.coralscubadivecenter.com. 1-tank dive $29. Discover SCUBA lesson $59. MC/V.) **Bahía,** to the right of the dock on Rueda Medina, sells fishing, snorkeling, and diving gear. (☎877 0340. Open daily 9am-9pm.)

Like turtles? Head over to the **Tortugranja** (Turtle Farm), to the right at the Playa Lancheros roundabout, about 2km down the Playa Paraíso road. This biological research station breeds three species of sea turtles: Green, Hawksbill, and Lagerhead. Female turtles lay their eggs in the safety of the station's beach during the summer. When the eggs hatch, around September, the young are reared for a year before being released. You can see the adolescent turtles and native tropical fish in two tanks. The center welcomes volunteers for any amount of time to help monitor the beaches, tag turtles, and collect eggs at night from May to October. For volunteer information, speak to the director Luis Herrera. (☎877 0098 or 577 2794. Open daily 9am-5pm. 20 pesos.) Other aquatic delights include swimming with dolphins at **Dolphin Discovery,** at the end of the Playa Paraíso road. To get there, turn right at the Playa Lancheros roundabout and head 3km down the paved road. (☎849 4748 or 800 713 8862; www.dolphindiscovery.com. 30min. swim US$99. Reserve 1 day ahead. MC/V.) If you prefer your adventures in a strictly controlled environment, head to **Garrafón** park, where you'll fork over US$50 for access to a reef, climbing tower, hammocks, zip line, kayaks, a seaside pool, and much more. (Punta Sur. ☎877 1101; www.garrafon.com.)

🎵 NIGHTLIFE

Isla Mujeres offers a relaxing nightlife for those who want to escape the mega-clubs and throngs of drunken American teens in Cancún. The best nighttime activity is concentrated at the north end of Hidalgo. Around sunset, tourists and locals bounce from one bar to the next toasting with half-price Happy hour drinks. Backpackers hang all night long at the indoor and beach bars at **Poc-Na Youth Hostel** (p. 671). The indoor bar is open daily 8-

GIVING BACK

TEACH TO TOTS

The sound of happy chatter greets visitors to **La Gloria English School** on Isla Mujeres. Kids of all ages flock to the American-run school for daily English lessons emphasizing oral communication. The school addresses a pressing need in the island's changing social climate: as tourism increases, the ability to speak passable English is not just a convenience for the predominantly Mayan population, but a matter of economic survival.

Built and managed by the Washa family of Middleton, WI, La Gloria opened its doors in 2004 and has put down roots on the island, serving as an impromptu library and offering classes to all. Today, La Gloria also serves the community through clothing sales and an active volunteer program. Visitors to the island are welcomed to assist in classes (one week min. commitment), where they will act as secondary teachers, lending an extra ear, correcting mistakes, and interacting with the students in English. You can also help out by donating school supplies, as La Gloria gets much of its supplies through the kindness of tourists.

For information on volunteering, visit www.folges.org. La Gloria English School is at the top of the hill in Colonia La Gloria, about 3.5km south of town. Buses and taxis service the area. ☎888 0666. Mza. 156 Lote 20 Mujeres, Quintana Roo, Mexico, 77400.

11:30pm, and the beach bar gets going around midnight with 2-for-1 drink specials (40 pesos) and a DJ who spins an eclectic mix of hip hop and electronic to suit the international crowd. Music shuts down around 4am. **Om**, on Matamoros, stands out for its unique Indian decor and live salsa and jazz music. (Beers 25 pesos. Live music Th-Sa 10:30pm-1am. No cover. Open Tu-Su 7pm-late.) **Nitrox Club**, the bright red, unmarked building on the corner of Matamoros and Guerrero, is the local *discoteca*, suitable for all who feel the need to get down. Attracts a mostly local crowd with a few intrepid tourists thrown in the mix. (10 peso cover. Open F-Sa 11pm-7am.)

PLAYA DEL CARMEN ☎984

Smack in the middle of Quintana Roo's legendary Mayan Riviera, Playa del Carmen (pop. 150,000) has become a tourist destination in its own right in recent years. The city is the fastest-growing in Latin America, tempting travelers with pristine reef diving, untouched stretches of white sand beach, inland Mayan ruins, and fiery nightlife. Tourism has left its mark on the town in other ways, transforming the small seaside fishing village into a virtual smorgasbord of international flavors and architectures. The town's famous Quinta Avenida demonstrates just how rapidly styles come and go in Playa—new, slick storefronts go up everyday as the road pushes northward. Whether coming for a day or a week, Playa del Carmen is a required stop for every beach-happy traveler.

▐ TRANSPORTATION

Buses: From the station (☎873 0109 or 878 0309) at the corner of Quinta and Juárez, ADO sends 1st-class to: **Chetumal** (4½hr., 15 per day, 180 pesos); **Mérida** (5hr., 11 per day, 258 pesos); **Mexico City** (21hr.; 7:30am, 12:15, 7:17, 9:10pm; 1090 pesos); **Orizaba** (17hr., 7:15pm, 894 pesos); **Puebla** (23hr., 6:15pm, 1002 pesos); **San Andrés** (16hr.; 3:40, 10:20pm; 700 pesos); **Veracruz** (17hr.; 3:40, 10:20pm; 784 pesos); **Palenque** (15hr., 3:15, 5, 7pm, 456 pesos). Many lines offer service to **Tulum** (1hr., 22 per day, 34 pesos) with stops in **Xcaret, Xel-Ha**, and **Coba.** Daily service to the Cancún airport (1hr., every hr. 7am-7pm, 80 pesos).

Ferries: **UltraMar** (☎803 5581) and **Mexico Waterjets** (☎872 1508 or 1588; www.mexicowaterjets.com.mx) offer similar ferry service to Cozumel. Tickets can be bought from one of the many booths in front of the ferry terminal or bus station. Both companies take about 30-40min. to make the crossing and have boats leaving every hr. 5am-11pm. 110 pesos.

Taxis: Taxis line up on Juárez in front of the bus terminal and run to sights around Playa (40-60 pesos). Prices are negotiable; be sure to set a price before getting in the car.

Bike Rental: Isla Bicicleta, (☎879 4992; www.playadelcarmenbikes.com), at Calle 8 and Av. 10. Mountain bike rentals include locks, helmets, and baby seats if needed. 30 pesos per hr., 120 pesos per day, 700 pesos per week.

▟ ▌ ORIENTATION AND PRACTICAL INFORMATION

Playa is located on the Mayan Riviera, 68km south of Cancún and 63km north of Tulum. The ferry to Cozumel docks below the town's *zócalo*, a block south and a block west of the bus station. The heart of the tourist industry lies on the pedestrian walk, **Quinta Avenida,** to the north immediately out the doors of the bus station. **Juárez,** the town's other main drag, runs west from the beach to the Cancún-Chetumal road (highway 307), 1.5km away. Even-numbered east-west *calles* run northwards from Juárez; odd-numbered east-west *calles* run south from Juárez; north-south *avenidas* increase by five from the beach.

Tourist Office: (☎873 2804), on the corner of Juárez and Av. 15. English, French, and Italian spoken. Open M-F 9am-8:30pm, Sa-Su 9am-5pm.

Currency Exchange: HSBC (☎873 0272), on Juárez, 1 block west of the *zócalo*. Exchanges traveler's checks and has a **24hr. ATM**. Open M-F 8am-7pm, Sa 9am-4pm.

Bookstore: Mundo Librería (☎879 3004; www.smallworldbooks.org), on Calle 1 between Av. 20 and 25. Stocks a wide selection of new and used beach reads, atlases, and academic studies in English, German, and Spanish. Exchange available for used books only. Open M-Sa 9am-8pm. MC/V.

Laundromat: Lavandería Lua, on Calle 4 between Av. 10 and 15. Full-service 12 pesos per kg. 3 kg. min. Express 2hr. service 2 pesos more per kg. Open 8am-9pm.

Emergency: ☎066.

Police: (☎873 0191), on Juárez, 2 blocks from the plaza between Av. 15 and 20.

Red Cross: (☎873 1233), on Av. 25 at Juárez.

Pharmacy: Farmacia del Carmen (☎873 2330), on Juárez, opposite the bus station. Open daily 7am-11pm.

Medical Services: Centro de Salud (☎873 0314), on Juárez and Av. 15, across from the post office.

Internet Access: La Taberna Internet Cafe (☎803 0447 or 0448), on the corner of Calle 4 and Av. 10. 16 pesos per hr. Open daily 10am-4am. **El Point,** on Av. 10 between Calles 2 and 4. 16 pesos per hr. Open daily 8am-1am.

Post Office: (☎873 0300), on Juárez, 2 blocks from the plaza. Open M-F 9am-5pm, Sa 9am-1pm. **Postal Code:** 77710.

ACCOMMODATIONS

With Playa's stunning recent growth, both luxury and budget accommodations are proliferating. Hostels are the way to go if you are looking to spend less than 350 pesos per night, the going rate for the cheapest hotels. During high season (Dec. 21-Apr. 15 and July 15-Sept. 15), prices are especially high and reservations are necessary. Most establishments lie along Quinta or Juárez, near the beach.

Hostel Playa (☎803 3277; www.hostelplaya.com), on the corner of Calle 8 and Av. 25. 3 men's and 3 women's bedrooms encircle a spacious living area with books, games, hammocks, full kitchen, TV/DVD, and purified water. Party on the rooftop patio at midnight. Owners provide everything from coffee to bathroom scales to snorkel rentals. Dorms 100 pesos; doubles 250 pesos. Cash only. ❶

Posada Freud (☎873 0601; www.posadafreud.com), on Quinta between Calles 8 and 10. Palm trees and colorful hammocks draw travelers to Freud's 11 unique abodes with clean, beachy decor. The small on-site bar is perfectly situated for people-watching. Reception 24hr. Check-out noon. Reservations recommended. Rooms from US$37-70 depending on the season. 12-bed penthouse US$200. MC/V. ❺

Hostel El Palomar (☎873 0144 or 803 2606; www.elpalomarhostel.com), on Quinta between Juárez and Calle 2. The 2 spacious, single-sex dorms in this small hostel come with big wooden bunks, continental breakfast, kitchen use, and the best rooftop view of the ocean in Playa. The rooftop party gets going around 11pm. Free Internet. Reception 9am-10:30pm. Check-out 1pm. 16-bed dorms 120 pesos; 4-bed dorm 130 pesos; private rooms with double bed, shared bath, and small balcony 380 pesos. Cash only. ❶

Hostel Colores Mexicanos (☎873 0065; lucaemiliano@yahoo.com), on Av. 15 between Juárez and Calle 2. A good option for those seeking a quieter dorm atmosphere or for small groups. The well-lit courtyard has plenty of chairs and tables for impromptu picnics. Minimalist rooms include ceiling fans, lockers, private baths, and plenty of soap.

Linens included. Reception 9am-9pm. Check-out noon. 4-bed dorms 120 pesos; singles 200 pesos; doubles 400 pesos; each additional person 50 pesos. Cash only. ❷

Posada Papagayo (☎873 2497), on Av. 15 between Calles 4 and 6. A good option for those seeking more privacy than offered by a dorm. The breezy lounge area and green interior garden make up for the slightly stuffy rooms. Reception 24hr. Check-out noon. Singles and doubles 220 pesos; triples 280 pesos. Prices rise by up to 100 pesos in high season. Cash only. ❷

Urban Hostel (☎879 9342), on Av. 10 between Calles 4 and 6. 2 blocks from the beach. The cheapest hostel in Playa, Urban promotes the bohemian vibe with bunk beds under a giant *palapa* and ceiling fans. Kitchen available. Continental breakfast included. Small lockers; bring your own lock. Ring the bell for reception. Check-out noon. Dorms 100 pesos; private rooms with shared bath 200 pesos. Cash only. ❶

Posada Lily (☎871 3016). The flaming pink building on Juárez, 1 block west of the plaza. Noisy but convenient location near the bus station. Houses small, cushy beds in clean rooms with powerful fans. Parking available. Reception 8am-9pm. Check-out 1pm. No phone reservations. Singles with double bed 200 pesos; 2 double beds 250 pesos. Cash only. ❷

◗ FOOD

It can be hard to find a bargain among Quinta's flashy French and Italian restaurants that cater to a growing tourist population. For a sampling of the finest Playa has to offer, check out the Little Italy district, north of Av. Constituyentes near the beach. While Quinta is the place to splurge on a meal, inexpensive regional cuisine at the *loncherías* west of Av. 10 near Calle 6 will fill your belly without emptying your pocket. Breakfast vendors flood the *zócalo* early. For essential grocery goods, head to **Playa Mart,** on the northwestern corner of the *zócalo*. (☎803 1779. Open daily 8am-10pm.)

Java Joe's (☎876 2694; www.javajoes.net), on Calle 10 between Av. 5 and 10. A favorite of Playa's burgeoning expat community. Pick up tips from Java Joe himself while enjoying the infamous coffee (15 pesos) and bagel sandwiches (30-65 pesos) at tables that spill out into the street. Open daily 6:30am-11pm. Cash only. ❷

Media Luna (☎873 0526), on Quinta between Calles 12 and 14. This eatery with spacious seating has found its niche experimenting with international fusion foods. Vegetarians will be in heaven, and all but the most serious meat-lovers will be satisfied with the chicken dishes. Fruit platters with granola 55 pesos. Tropical fruit crepes 60 pesos. Creative salads 55-65 pesos. Open daily 8am-11:30pm. MC/V. ❹

Super Carnes HC de Monterrey/La Raza, Calle 1 190, between Av. 20 and 25. For the best *arracheras* (steak fajitas) in town, locals head to this restaurant/butcher shop with enormous portions and a casual atmosphere. Full meals, including potatoes, guacamole, and drinks for around 90 pesos. Meals for 3 people 130 pesos. Open daily noon-7pm. Cash only. ❹

Taquería Billy the Kid, on the corner of Av. 15 and Calle 4. Famous throughout the Mayan Riviera for the incredibly cheap tacos, Billy the Kid has a well-earned reputation and a devoted local following. Make sure to request the *cebolla cocida* (cooked onions) on your steak taco (4 pesos). Drinks 8 pesos. Open daily 5pm-4am. Cash only. ❶

Estas Son las Mañanitas (☎873 0114), on Quinta between Calles 4 and 6. Even picky locals recommend this blend of Mexican and Italian cuisine. Pizza from 89 pesos. Traditional Mexican dishes 69-175 pesos. Open daily 7am-11:30pm. AmEx/MC/V. ❺

Restaurant La Tarraya (☎873 2040), on the beach at the end of Calle 2. This budget-friendly bar-restaurant is perfect if you don't want to leave the beach. Fish filet *tikin xic* (freshly barbecued) 130 pesos per kg. Open daily noon-9pm. ❸

Playa del Carmen

ACCOMMODATIONS	● FOOD	★ NIGHTLIFE
Hostel Colores	Cafe Tropical, 8	Blue Parrot, 4
Mexicanos, 18	Hui Min, 17	Bourbon Street, 10
Hostel El Palomar, 19	Estas Son las	Coco Maya, 3
Hostel Playa, 9	Mañanitas, 14	Mambo, 11
Posada Freud, 7	Java Joe's, 5	Voga, 6
Posada Lily, 20	Media Luna, 2	Wana Bana, 1
Posada Papagayo, 13	Restaurante La	
Urban Hostel, 12	Tarraya, 16	
	Super Carnes HC	
	de Monterrey, 21	
	Taquería Billy	
	the Kid, 15	

Cafe Tropical (☎873 2111), on Quinta between Calles 8 and 10. Enjoy the generous portions of falafel, hummus, chicken, and seafood beneath a giant, shady *palapa*. Street-side tables are perfectly situated to watch the Quinta traffic. Smoothies 27 pesos. Omelettes with a rich variety of fillings 43 pesos. Big falafel sandwiches 49 pesos. Pad thai noodles 89 pesos. Open daily 7am-midnight. MC/V. ❹

Hui Min (☎113 3263), on Calle 2 between Av. 10 and 15. You can't beat the prices at this family-owned Chinese restaurant. A great place to fill your belly. Heaping spoonful of any rice or noodle dish 10 pesos. Plentiful platters 30 pesos. Spring rolls 10 pesos. Open daily 10am-11pm. Cash only. ❷

🏄 🏊 BEACHES AND WATERSPORTS

Lined with palm trees and skirted by the turquoise waters of the Caribbean, Playa's beaches are sandy, white, and oh-so-relaxing. They are relatively free of seaweed and coral, strewn instead with scantily-clad tourists and a small forest of umbrellas. In search of an aquatic escape? Vendors near the *zócalo* have a "special offer, just for you"—which may involve snorkeling, scuba diving, fishing, jetskiing, parasailing, or windsurfing. Some of the fancier hotels just south of the pier rent equipment, as do shacks a few hundred meters north. One reliable stand is **Jaime's Marina,** at Calle 10 on the beach in front of El Faro Hotel. (☎984 130 2034; www.jaimesmarina.bravehost.com. 2hr. sail/snorkel tours 350 pesos per person; 2-person min. Full-day private windsurfing lesson 600 pesos. Kayak rentals 200 pesos per hr. Skydiving 2250 pesos per person. Cash only.)

Less damaged by Hurricane Wilma in 2005 than other spots on the Mayan Riviera, Playa's off-shore reefs have become a hot spot, entrancing divers with bright coral reefs, ancient underwater formations, and plentiful schools of fish. **Abyss Dive Shop,** on Av. 1 between Calle 10 and 12, will fulfill all your diving and snorkeling needs. It services 13 different dive sites and caters to all skill levels. (☎873 2164; www.abyssdivecenter.com. "Discover" scuba trips US$80. Open-water courses US$350. 2-tank dive US$65, equipment US$15. Trips leave 9am, 2pm; 2-person min. Open M-Tu and Sa-Su 8:15am-6pm, W-F 8:15am-9pm. MC/V.) **Tank-Ha Dive Center,** on Av. 5 between Calles 8 and 10, is another reputable diving company. It owns a fleet of seven boats, offers the full range of PADI courses, and conducts dives in Dutch, English, French, German, Italian, and Spanish. (☎873 0302 or 879 3427; www.tankha.com. 1-tank dive US$40. 2-tank dive US$70. Trips leave 9am, 2pm; 2-person min. Multi-day dive packages receive 10-15% discount. 2-tank *cenote* dive US$110; 4 person max.; includes lunch and transportation to *cenotes.* Popular 2½hr. snorkel tour visits 2 reefs. 9:30am and 1:30pm. 4-person min. US$40. MC/V.)

■♫ NIGHTLIFE AND ENTERTAINMENT

Come nightfall, Quinta transforms from a busy thoroughfare of vendors into a glitzy nightspot. Sun-lovers recuperate from the day's rays by swaying in hammocks and jiving to live jazz and salsa. Though chains such as Carlos'n Charlie's and Señor Frogs near the ferry dock are popular with American teens grooving on American hip hop, Playa has plenty of alternatives with a more international flavor.

THE REAL DEAL. Though Cancún claims to have cornered the market on nightlife, Playa del Carmen is now nipping at its heels. Though you won't find the same smoke and light shows, Playa offers more budget-conscious night owls plenty of beachside options to dance until dawn.

Blue Parrot Inn (☎872 0083), on Calle 12 at the beach. Once on the list of the 10 best beach bars in the world, the Blue Parrot hasn't lost its tropical touch. Swings replace the conventional bar stools and the nightly ▩ **pyrotechnic-friendly fireshow** is the best attraction in town. It can also be viewed for free from the beach, though a small donation is requested for the dancers. M and Th 9-11pm women drink free. Cover 100 pesos. Kitchen open 5-11pm. Dance club open 10pm-4am. Cash only.

Mambo (☎803 2656 or 2657), on the corner of Calle 6 and Av. 0. Mambo reels in a crowd with its colorful atmosphere and salsa music. Dancers file in at 11:30pm and the band goes on at midnight. Get prepared with an 80-peso salsa lesson before the club opens at 11pm; details are at the club. Open W-Su 8pm-4am. Cash only.

Coco Maya, on Calle 12 next to the Blue Parrot Inn. The newest club in town, Coco Maya offers an alternative to the Blue Parrot for getting down into the wee hours. Nightly DJ spins hip hop and electronic while music videos are projected onto the surrounding walls. Beers 30 pesos. Mixed drinks 50 pesos. Open W-Sa 9pm-5am. Cash only.

Bourbon Street, on Quinta between Calles 6 and 8. Try to identify the famous musicians decorating the walls while listening to live rock and jazz. Beers 30 pesos. No cover. Open daily 9am-2am. Cash only.

Wana Bana (wanabanabar@yahoo.com.mx), on Quinta between Calles 30 and 32, is home to the burgeoning GBLT nightlife scene in Playa. The laid-back bar has special events such as karaoke and 70s-theme parties early in the night to draw crowds and make connections. No cover. Open daily 5pm-2am. Cash only.

Voga, on Calle 10 between Quinta and Av. 1, hosts electronic and techno DJs for GBLT and straight travelers alike. Cover 50 pesos. Open W-Sa 11pm-5am. Cash only.

COZUMEL   ☎987

The calm, tropical diving mecca of Cozumel—"land of the swallows" in Mayan—once served as the home base of Maya, Spaniards, and even pirates. French diver Jacques Cousteau called attention to the amazing coral formations and colorful marine life of Palancar Reef, the world's second largest barrier reef. Today, the island is popular among those who wish to explore Mexico's natural beauty without forgoing luxury and service. Much of the island remains undeveloped and ripe for exploration. Miles of empty white sand beaches, Mayan ruins, and crocodile-filled lagoons encourage travelers to look beyond the island's main city, San Miguel de Cozumel (pop. 80,000).

▐ TRANSPORTATION

Cozumel Airport (CML; ☎872 0485), 2km north of town, provides an alternative to land and water transportation to the island. Served by **Aerocaribe** (☎872 3456), **Continental** (☎872 0487), and **Mexicana** (☎872 2945). Catch a taxi (☎872 0041) as you come off the dock to the airport (51 pesos) or to Punta Moreno (200 pesos); set a price before the taxi departs.

Ferries: The most popular form of transportation to reach the island from Playa del Carmen. **UltraMar** (☎803 5581) and **Mexico Waterjets** (☎872 1508 or 1588; www.mexicowaterjets.com.mx) offer similar ferry service to Playa del Carmen. Tickets can be bought from one of the many booths in front of the ferry terminal. (Both companies 30-40min., every hr. 6am-10pm; 110 pesos.) **Trans de Caribe** sends car ferries from Punto Venados to Cozumel, 20 min. south of Playa del Carmen on the way to Tulum (☎872 7688 or 7671).

Car Rental: LE$$ Pay, Melgar 628 (☎872 4744 or 869 0030; www.lesspaycars.com.mx), about 1km south of town. VW Safaris 385 pesos per day. Jeeps 660 pesos per day. Mopeds 360 pesos per day. Discounts for multi-day rentals. Open daily 8am-8pm. AmEx/MC/V. **Hertz** (☎872 5979), on Av. Juárez between Av. 5 Nte. and 10

Isla Cozumel

Nte. 4-door economy with A/C US$35 per day. Jeeps US$50. Open daily 7am-8pm. MC/V.
Cuarto y Quinto Poder, Av. Salas 3 (☎869 1328), between Melgar and Av. 5. VW convertible US$36. Scooters 250-350 pesos per day. Prices include mileage but not gas. MC/V.

> **TIP** **CRUISE CONTROL.** Renting a car or moped is the best way to see the whole island of Cozumel. Buses are non-existent and taxis are pricey. Split the cost with a pal to be environmentally and economically conscious. Don't forget that you must show a valid driver's license and produce an accepted credit card to rent any motorized vehicle on the island.

ORIENTATION AND PRACTICAL INFORMATION

The island of Cozumel is 18km east of mainland Quintana Roo and 85km south of Isla Mujeres. At 53km long and 14km wide, Cozumel is Mexico's largest Caribbean island. **San Miguel de Cozumel,** home to the island's ferry docks, is on the western coast. Downtown, *Avenidas* run parallel to the sea and increase by fives. *Calles* are even north of Av. Juárez and odd south of Av. Juárez. The most popular beaches lie south of San Miguel on the western shore. Beaches on the eastern coast are much less developed; in fact, most of the interior of the island is unpopulated, creating plenty of opportunities for exploration by moped. The perimeter road makes a 75km loop along the sea, with several nice views and swim points. The free *Blue Guide to Cozumel,* available at tourist locations and hotels, has useful information and coupons.

Tourist Office: (☎869 0211 or 0212), on the 2nd fl. of Plaza del Sol, in the *zócalo*. Open M-F 9am-7pm, Sa 9am-1pm. Wooden stands on each corner of the Plaza del Sol can also provide helpful tips and maps of the island.

Consulate: US (☎872 4574, emergencies 872 0624 or 6152; usca@cozumel.net), on the 2nd fl. of Plaza Villa Mar shopping mall in the *zócalo*. Open M-F noon-2pm.

Banks: Banorte (☎872 0718), on Av. 5 Nte., between Juárez and Calle 2. Exchanges traveler's checks. Open M-F 9am-4pm, Sa 10am-2pm. **HSBC** (☎872 0182), in the plaza. Open M-Sa 8am-7pm. Both banks have a **24hr. ATM.**

Bookstore: Fama (☎872 5020), on Av. 5 between Juárez and Calle 2 Nte. CDs, books, magazines, and maps in English and Spanish. Open daily 9am-10pm.

Laundromat: Lavandería Margarita (☎872 2865), on Av. 20 Sur between Salas and Calle 3 Sur. Wash 15 pesos, dry 11 pesos per 10min. More for full-service. Open M-Sa 7am-9pm, Su 8am-5pm.

Emergency: ☎066.

Police: (☎872 0409), on Calle 11 Sur, in the Palacio Municipal.

Red Cross: (☎872 1058), on Av. 20 Sur at Salas. Open daily 7am-11pm.

Pharmacy: Farmacia Kiosco (☎872 2485), on the *zócalo* near Hotel López. Open M-Sa 8am-10pm, Su 9am-10pm.

Medical Services: Centro Médico de Cozumel, 1 Sur 101 (☎872 3545), at Av. 50. Open 24hr. For non-emergencies, there is a small **medical consult** next to Farmacias Similares, on the corner of Calle 1 Sur and Av. 15 Nte. A doctor is there most afternoons and evenings, but be prepared for a line. For diving or pressure-related emergencies, the island has a hyperbaric-chamber-equipped **DAN referral center** at 21 Calle 5 Sur (☎872 2387 or 1430; www.sssnetwork.com). Open 24hr.

Fax Office: Telecomm, (☎872 0056; fax 872 0376), in the same building as the post office. Western Union services available. Open M-F 8am-7:30pm, Sa-Su 9am-12:30pm.

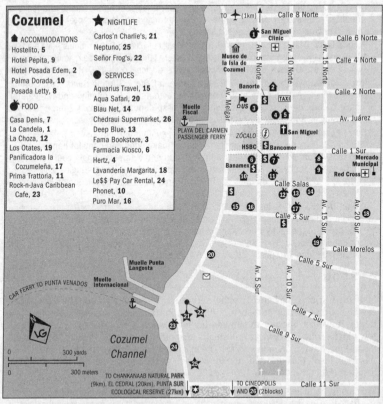

Cozumel

★ NIGHTLIFE

Carlos'n Charlie's, **21**
Neptuno, **25**
Señor Frog's, **22**

● SERVICES

Aquarius Travel, **15**
Aqua Safari, **20**
Blau Net, **14**
Chedraui Supermarket, **26**
Deep Blue, **13**
Fama Bookstore, **3**
Farmacia Kiosco, **6**
Hertz, **4**
Lavandería Margarita, **18**
Le$$ Pay Car Rental, **24**
Phonet, **10**
Puro Mar, **16**

♠ ACCOMMODATIONS

Hostelito, **5**
Hotel Pepita, **9**
Hotel Posada Edem, **2**
Palma Dorada, **10**
Posada Letty, **8**

♦ FOOD

Casa Denis, **7**
La Candela, **1**
La Choza, **12**
Los Otates, **19**
Panificadora la
    Cozumeleña, **17**
Prima Trattoria, **11**
Rock-n-Java Caribbean
    Cafe, **23**

Internet Access: Internet is all over the island. Most cafes charge about 10 pesos per hr. Look for hostels with free Internet for the best deal. **Blau Net,** 233 Av. Salas (☎872 7673), between Av. 10 and Av. 15, has fast service. 10 pesos per hr., 15 pesos for 2hr.

Post Office: (☎872 0106), off Melgar, just south of Calle 7 Sur along the sea. Open M-F 9am-5pm, Sa 9am-1pm. **Postal Code:** 77600.

ACCOMMODATIONS AND CAMPING

Since they cater primarily to foreign divers with cash to burn, hotels are generally more expensive in Cozumel than on the mainland and hostels are scarce. Sadly, the extra pesos do not guarantee higher quality. Consider asking to see the room before paying—quality may vary considerably by hotel. Try to grab a room before noon during high season. Free camping, particularly in secluded spots on the island's east side, may be the cheapest and most peaceful option, but be sure to check in with police first as camping is not permitted at certain times of year when the sea turtles come ashore.

※ Hostelito, Av. 10 42 (☎869 8157; www.hostelito.com), between Juárez and Calle 2 Nte. The only hostel on Cozumel holds up its end of the bargain with immaculate dorms and bathrooms with A/C, a large open-air kitchen, and free Wi-Fi. Reserve ahead during high season. Reception 9am-9pm. Check-out noon. Linens and lockers included. Towels 20 pesos. Some snorkel gear available for rental. Dorms 120 pesos; private rooms 350 pesos. Cash only. ●

Posada Letty, Calle 1 Sur 272 (☎872 0257). Well-kept blue-and-green rooms have big windows and beds. Feels more like a house than a hotel as the family pets roam around the courtyard. Singles 250 pesos; doubles 300 pesos; each additional person 50 pesos. Cash only. ❸

Hotel Pepita, Av. 15 120 (☎872 0098), between Calle 1 Sur and Salas. Costs a little extra, but the A/C, private bath, free coffee, astounding hospitality, and refrigerator make it worth the price. Remote control 100 peso deposit. Reception 24hr. Check-out 1pm. Singles and doubles 350 pesos; each additional person 50 pesos. Cash only. ❺

Hotel Posada Edem, Calle 2 124 (☎872 1166; gustarimo@hotmail.com), between Av. 5 and 10. Fish, turtles, and Plumita the parrot make good company for hanging out in the lobby. Functional pink rooms with fans surround a tropical jungle courtyard. Purified water in lobby. Wi-Fi. Reception 8am-7pm. Check-out noon. Singles 180 pesos, with A/C 280 pesos; doubles 220/280 pesos; each additional person 50 pesos. Prices drop in low season. Cash only. ❸

Palma Dorada Inn, Salas 44 (☎872 0330; palmadorada2@prodigy.net.mx), between Melgar and Av. 5. A large 3-star inn aimed at attracting divers with cheerful paintings of sea creatures, beachy decor, and plenty of greenery. Small continental breakfast included. Check-out 1pm. Rooms from 350 pesos, with A/C and balcony 500 pesos, with kitchenette from 750 pesos. MC/V with 6% charge. ❺

◨ FOOD

Like any Caribbean island, Cozumel serves up plenty of seafood. The high-priced eateries along Melgar and surrounding the Plaza del Sol target the resort-vacationer, however, and not the budget traveler. Moderately priced restaurants lie a few blocks from the *centro*, and small cafes offering *comida casera* (homemade meals) are hidden on side streets. The **market** at Salas between Av. 20 and 25 Sur has fresh meat, fish, and fruit; the *loncherías* next door are the cheapest. **Chedraui,** a supermarket, is at Melgar 1001. (☎872 5404. Open daily 7am-10pm.)

▨ Prima Trattoria (☎872 4242; www.primacozumel.com), on Av. Salas between Av. 5 and 10. Trattoria is the dressed-down version of the similarly-named Italian restaurant in the Wynston resort. Divers come in droves to feast on pasta so fresh that the hand-cranked pasta machine handle leaves a mark on the chef's palm. Lobster ravioli in tomato cream sauce 140 pesos. Whole-wheat pasta 15 pesos extra. Open daily 5-10:30pm. AmEx/MC/V. ❺

Los Otates (☎869 1059), on Av. 15 between Calles 3 Sur and 5 Sur. The most popular *taquería* on the island. Sit on the open-air patio and watch the taco masters churn out the house specialty, *tacos al pastor* (roasted pork tacos with pineapple and onions; 7 pesos). Open daily 6pm-4am. Cash only. ●

Rock-n-Java Caribbean Cafe, Melgar 602 (☎872 4405), near LE$$ Pay. Enjoy coffee (15 pesos), fruit-topped french toast (50 pesos), and homemade desserts, all with a view of the Caribbean. Salads 38-68 pesos. Massive sandwiches 48-70 pesos. Open M-F and Su 7am-10pm, Sa 7am-2pm. Cash only. ❸

La Candela (☎878 4471), at Av. 5 and Calle 6 Nte. Newly renovated, this no-frills eatery is such a hit with locals that they plan to extend services to include dinner in the next year. The menu is small but quality is high. Each of the 8 delicious daily specials (50-60 pesos) comes with rice, beans, potatoes, soup, and iced tea. Open daily 8am-6pm. Cash only. ❹

Panificadora la Cozumeleña (☎872 0189), on Av. 3 between Av. 15 and 10. For little more than pocket change, this bakery and coffee shop serves sweet treats (5-10 pesos), coffee brewed from Chiapas-grown and island-roasted beans (15 pesos), and piles of fluffy buttermilk pancakes (30 pesos). Open M-Sa 7am-11pm. Cash only. ●

La Choza (☎872 0958), on Av. 10 between Salas and Calle 3 Sur. Known for having the best *fajitas de camarón* (shrimp *fajitas;* 165 pesos) on the island, complete with fresh guacamole. All meals come with soup and 2 salsas. Vegetarian options like *sopa azteca* (tomato-based tortilla soup) 44 pesos. Open daily 7am-10:30pm. MC/V. ❺

Casa Denis (☎872 0067), on Calle 1 between Av. 5 and 10, across from the artisan market. Enjoy home-cooked recipes perfected since 1945 beneath photos of the family and of Che Guevara fishing with Fidel Castro. Breakfast 27-42 pesos. Mayan pork 105 pesos. *Comida regional* 100-340 pesos. Buffalo wings 40 pesos. Open M-Sa 8am-10pm, Su 5-11pm. Cash only. ❹

📷 OUTDOOR ACTIVITIES

DIVING. Many visitors make the trek to Cozumel with one goal: diving in the island's beautiful coral reefs. Part of the second largest reef system in the world, Cozumel first gained fame when Palancar Reef on the south end of the island made French diver Jacques Cousteau's list of the top 10 dive sights in the world. Though Hurricane Wilma seriously damaged many of the reefs in 2005, the delicate coral formations are once again beginning to proliferate. The best way to see the reefs is by organizing a diving trip with one of the many dive shops on the island. *(Look for shops affiliated with ANOAAT, Asociación Nacional de Operadores de Actividades Aquaticas Turísticas, or IANTD, International Association of Nitrox and Technical Divers. Never dive with a company who does not require proof of PADI certification. Dive shops should also provide transportation to and from dive sites, as many of the reefs are inaccessible without a boat. Deep Blue, Salas 200 near Av. 10, offers a complete range of PADI courses, such as the 3-day openwater course for US$400. Daily 2-tank day and night trips to Palancar, Paradise, and San Francisco reefs for US$68. Full equipment rental for US$18. ☎872 5653, US 214-343-3034; www.deepbluecozumel.com. Open daily 7am-9pm. MC/V. Aqua Safari, on Melgar at Calle 5 Sur, offers similar services. ☎872 0101; www.aquasafari.com. 2-tank dive leaves daily at 8:30am and 1:30pm and includes a small snack; US$60. Open M-F 7am-8pm, Sa-Su 7am-6:30pm. MC/V.)*

> **DON'T TOUCH THE CORAL.** We repeat: don't touch the coral! One stray kick of the flipper can destroy hundreds of years of growth. Beginners should stay at least 1m away from the coral at all times to prevent contact, and advanced divers should pay careful attention to their buoyancy control.

SNORKELING. Like diving, snorkeling Cozumel's reefs is on every traveler's list of things to do when visiting the Mayan Riviera. Snorkeling can be done from shore or through a guided boat tour. To snorkel on your own, head to **Chakanaab Natural Park** (p. 684) or the **Punta Sur Ecological Reserve** (p. 684). Alternatively, rent gear from one of the dive shops (50-100 pesos), rent a moped (p. 679), and head to one of the beaches south of town. **Playa San Francisco,** at km 14, and **Playa Palancar,** at km 20, both offer superb snorkeling with sights of barracuda, turtles, and coral reefs from shore as well as small restaurants and shady *palapas. (Boat tours can be arranged from any of the stalls lining the Muelle Fiscal. Most tours are around 2hr., are organized in groups of 12, include equipment rental, and cost around 250 pesos per person. Many dive shops also arrange snorkel tours, but often lump them together with diving. Try to get on a boat with only snorkelers to ensure better guides as well as more snorkeling-friendly reefs.)*

BEACHES. Beachcombers should not be disheartened by the slightly murky waters near San Miguel: the island's true treasures lie outside town on the eastern coast. Beaches to the south of San Miguel tend to be more commercial and host beach clubs like Playa Mía, Mr. Sancho's, and Paradise Beach, all popular with the cruise ship crowds who drop anchor in the harbor daily. **Playa Palancar,** 20km south of San Miguel, is a better option. The small **Palancar Beach Club** has a full dive and snorkel center, restaurant, showers, and quiet stretches of white sand. *(At km 20 on the Cozumel Carretera Sur. Open daily 9am-5pm. Cash only.)* Eastern beaches **Bonita** (km 38), **Punta Chiqueros, Punta Morena,** and **Mezcalitos** (at the end of the highway) are rougher but virtually undeveloped, leaving miles of sandy shoreline for those who prefer the company of sea gulls over tourists. All east coast beaches are accessible from Cozumel's main highway. Given the **strong currents and undertow** in the **Chen Río** and **Playa San Martin** areas, swimmers should exercise caution.

ABOVE-WATER ACTIVITIES. Though Cozumel is a shrine to underwater activities, those wishing to remain on the surface can also enjoy Cozumel's beaches and sea breezes. Surfing is an increasingly popular sport on the island. Hard-charging surfers head to **Mezcalitos** for beach breaks, while more adventurous and experienced surfers head to **Punta Morena,** where shallow coral reefs can sometimes cause injury. Though the only surf shop was washed away by Hurricane Wilma, plans are in the works to rebuild the **Punta Morena Beach and Surf Club,** at km 44, in early 2008. *(☎872 4058; puntamorena@hotmail.com. Open M-Sa 9am-5pm.)* Kiteboarding also draws crowds from November to April, when winds are the best. At **Puro Mar Bikini Shop,** 298 Av. 5, Adrian is the island's official source of kiteboarding information, gear, and classes. *(☎872 4483; www.cozumelkiteboarding.com. 3-4hr. lessons US$250; beginners need about 3 days to become self-sufficient. Open M-Sa 10am-7pm.)* Finally, even fishermen have a home in Cozumel. Many boats will take fly fishermen or deep sea fishermen out in groups of two to four people. **Aquarius Travel,** 2 Calle 3 Sur, leads full day fly-fishing tours for US$300. Gear rental is not included. *(☎869 1096; www.aquariusflatsfishing.com.)*

⬡ SIGHTS

The Federación de Parques y Museos de Cozumel (FPMC; www.cozumel-parks.com) operates the four big attractions on the island: Chankanaab Natural Park, Punta Sur Ecological Reserve, the San Gervais ruins, and the Museo de la Isla. Popular with families, Chankanaab Natural Park, a natural amusement park, protects a beautiful bay circled by a well-kept botanical garden, museum, dolphin pen (visitors can pay to swim with the near-domesticated mammals), and restaurants. The abundant fish and stunning coral formations in the bay, open to snorkelers and scuba divers, are the real attractions. *(Carretera Costera Sur km 9.5. Take Av. Melgar south out of town and look for signs. ☎872 0914. Open daily 7am-6pm. 176 pesos, children under 3 free. Snorkel equipment 100 pesos. MC/V.)*

At the southern tip of the island 27km from downtown, the **Punta Sur Ecological Reserve** wows visitors with boat rides through crocodile-infested lagoons and snorkeling trips along the turtle-populated Colombia reef. Also, check out the **Museum of Navigation** and the small **ruins** of a Mayan tomb. The ◨**lighthouse** at Punta Celerain within the reserve presents a thrilling view of the sand dunes on Cozumel's southern shores. *(☎872 0914. Carretera Costera Sur km 27. Open daily 9am-5pm. 110 pesos. Snorkeling equipment 100 pesos.)*

A former Mayan trading center, Cozumel is sprinkled with dozens of ruins. Unfortunately, none of them have survived the years of hurricanes and the encroaching jungle. The very small **El Cedral,** the oldest of the ruins on the island, dates back to the 9th century and lies in the town square of the small farming community of El Cedral. *(Follow the paved road to the east off the Carretera Sur at km 18 about*

2km. Free.) The only excavated and reconstructed ruins are at **San Gervasio,** which includes the remains of an observatory and several houses, temples, and arches that once made up the most prominent community in Cozumel. *(Take Juárez out of town. After 8km, a "San Gervasio" sign marks a gravel road branching to the left. Follow the road another 6km. ☎800 2215. Open daily 7am-4pm. 60 pesos.)*

The air-conditioned **Museo de la Isla de Cozumel,** on the waterfront between Calles 4 and 6, is small but worth a visit, if only to escape the stifling heat. Its four themed rooms are full of artifacts, photos, coral, and marine and jungle trivia. The Coral and Reefs room, with colorful exhibits and a wealth of information on Cozumel's marine treasures, may especially enrich the underwater experiences of prospective snorkelers and scuba divers. *(☎872 1434. Open daily 9am-5pm. 33 pesos.)*

🎵 NIGHTLIFE AND ENTERTAINMENT

Next to the endless revelry of Cancún and Playa del Carmen, Cozumel's nightlife can feel confined. Docked tourists get their jollies at chains like **Señor Frogs** and **Carlos'n Charlie's.** If you are in desperate need of a night of dancing, the local dance club is **Neptuno,** at Calle 11 Sur and Melgar. Multi-level dance floors, neon lasers, and throbbing electronic riffs keep locals and tourists happy. (☎872 1537. Beers 35 pesos. Cover 45 pesos. Open Tu-Sa 9pm-6am.)

Fortunately, Cozumel has a host of relaxing and enlightening evening activities to keep the non-daytrippers entertained. The week culminates with **live music performances** by local salsa and jazz bands every Sunday in the Plaza del Sol from 7-10pm, when locals and tourists mingle and dance beneath the town gazebo. **Cozumel Mini Golf,** on Av. 15 at Calle 1 Sur, offers adults the opportunity to drink and putt. The elaborate 18-hole course has tricky water spots and banked curves designed by the owner. (☎872 8570; www.czmgolf.com. Beer 20 pesos. 18 holes 70 pesos. Open daily 10am-10pm, last tee-off 9pm.)

If you're in town in the spring, don't miss the **Fiesta de Santa Cruz,** held in late April and early May in the inland farming community of El Cedral, to the southwest of San Miguel. This religious festival traces its roots 150 years back to the War of Castes, when Don Casimiro Cárdenas fled with his family from the mainland to the relative peace of Cozumel. One of the first pioneers in the area of El Cedral, Casimiro promised that, in return for divine protection, he and his descendants would pray devotedly to the Cross. The event is marked by dances, feasts, and parades. The island also has a small **Carnaval** celebration, usually in late February. Call the tourist office for more information.

TULUM ☎984

For a small town, Tulum (pop. 10,000) attracts an astonishing variety of travelers. Daytrippers from Cancún pass through just long enough to snap a few pictures of the impressive seaside ruins. Diving enthusiasts come from all over the globe to explore the second largest reef in the world and the network of over 700km of *cenotes* (underground fresh-water caves). Stressed-out city dwellers flock to the beachside *cabañas* to escape electricity, phones, and clothing. Finally, a youthful bohemian crowd parties their way up and down the shore come nighttime.

▐ TRANSPORTATION

Getting around Tulum can be time-consuming and expensive. Although numerous **taxis** are readily available in Pueblo Tulum, along Mex. 307, and at various *cabañas,* fares add up fast. Thirty-five pesos will take you from town to the closest *cabañas,* but fares rise quickly as you travel farther south. The best budget option for those with ambitious plans is to rent a **bicycle** and give your legs an old-fashioned workout. To get to any of the sights near Tulum (Tulum ruins, the *cenotes*, and Xel-Ha), wave down one of many white *colectivo* vans (10-20 pesos) that pass nearly every 10min. from 8am to 9pm.

Bus Stations: All buses leave from the main **ADO** station (☎871 2122), on the west side of Mex. 307, in the middle of the Pueblo. Buses head to: **Cancún** (2hr., every hr., 72 pesos); **Chetumal** (3½hr., 11 per day, 114-144 pesos); **Chichén Itzá** (3hr.; 9am, 2:30pm; 140 pesos); **Cobá** (1hr., 5 per day 7am-6pm, 30 pesos); **Mexico City** (22hr.; 8:30am, 1:10, 4:45pm; 1050 pesos); **Palenque** (12hr.; 4:15, 5:45pm; 424 pesos); **Playa del Carmen** (1hr., every hr., 34 pesos); **Mérida** (4hr., 10 per day, 176 pesos); **San Cristóbal de las Casas** (15hr.; 4:15, 5:45pm; 542 pesos); **Valladolid** (2hr., 8 per day, 47-60 pesos); Cancún airport (2hr., 8:20am and 5pm, 120 pesos). Buses going to and from Playa del Carmen stop at the Tulum archaeological crossing before heading into town and on the way out of town from the main terminal.

Car Rental: Many hotels along the Boca Paila road offer car rental, but be sure to reserve ahead. **Buster Rent a Car,** at Av. Tulum and Juniper Sur (☎871 2831; www.busterrentacar.com). Economy cars start at US$35 per day; insurance and mileage included. Look for discounts advertised on the web page. AmEx/MC/V.

Bike Rental: Iguana Bike Shop (☎119 0836; iguanabike@prodigy.net.mx), on Satelite Sur 1½ blocks from Av. Tulum. 80 pesos per day, includes lock, basket, lights, and insurance. Flyers around town give a 10% discount. Open daily 9am-7pm. Cash only.

✦🛈 ORIENTATION AND PRACTICAL INFORMATION

Located 50km southeast of Cobá and 127km south of Cancún, Tulum is the southernmost tourist attraction on the Caribbean coast of Quintana Roo, and the easternmost of the major Mayan archaeological sites along the Mayan Riviera. Tulum sprawls over three separate areas: the *zona arqueológica* near the ruin, the beach *cabañas* lining the coastal road Carretera Boca Paila, and Pueblo Tulum, which sprawls along Mex. 307 (Av. Tulum). Coming from the north, you will come first to the *zona arqueológica*, about 3km before town, where several restaurants, hotels, overpriced mini-marts, and a gas station take advantage of traffic to the ruins. One kilometer south is a well-marked turn-off to the left leading to food and accommodations at the beachside *cabañas* (about 2-3km from Mex. 307; take a left on Boca Paila for *cabañas* Diamante K and a right for all the others). Pueblo Tulum, another 1.5km farther to the south, offers a handful of roadside restaurants, hotels, and services. Addresses for places along the beach are listed in terms of their distance from the ruins.

Tourist Office: Though there is no official tourist office, **Weary Traveler Backpacker's Center** (☎871 2389 or 2390; www.intulum.com), in the Weary Traveler Hostel, offers invaluable maps of the area. Open 24hr. **Booths** in front of the parking lot of the Tulum ruins and in the artisan market provide general info. Open daily 8am-2pm. Additionally, the privately operated **www.todotulum.com** website offers helpful information on sights and hotels in the area.

Currency Exchange: HSBC (☎871 2201), 2 blocks north of the bus station on Av. Tulum. **24hr. ATM.** Open M-Sa 8am-7pm. Many *casas de cambio* line Av. Tulum.

Laundromat: Lava Easy (☎115 0684), 5 blocks north of the bus station on Av. Tulum between Satelite and Centauro Nte. Wash and dry 15 pesos per kg. Open M-Sa 8am-8pm.

Police: (☎871 2055; emergencies 871 2688), in the Delegación Municipal near Bital.

Pharmacy: Canto Farmacia (☎871 2319), on the west side of Mex. 307, on the same block as the bus station. Open daily 8am-11pm.

Medical Services: Centro de Salud (☎871 2050). Heading south from the bus station, take the 1st 2 lefts. Open daily 8am-8pm; 24hr. for emergencies.

Internet Access: Internet cafes cluster around the bus station on Av. Tulum. **Charlie's Town,** 1 block north of the bus station on Av. Tulum, offers fast service and Skype®. 9 pesos per hr. Open daily 10am-midnight.

Post Office: (☎119 0843), on Av. Tulum and Satelite Nte. Open M-F 9am-4pm. **Postal Code:** 77780.

ACCOMMODATIONS

The *cabañas* of Tulum offer a unique experience that shouldn't be missed, though it might require splurging for a night or two. Relatively cheap, right on the white beaches, with little or no electricity (bring a flashlight and some candles), Tulum is a great place to chill on pristine beaches in hammocks as you perfect your tan, with or without clothing. Bring mosquito netting (though the *cabañas* we list provide netting over beds) and repellent; the bugs can be nasty. During high season (mid-Dec. to Apr. and July-Aug.), arrive early in the morning or make reservations. Couples with small children may be uncomfortable with the "clothing optional" environment. Check with the hotel before booking; some explicitly do not allow children. Cheaper hostels are located downtown.

Hotel Cabañas Diamante K, km 2.5 on Boca Paila (☎998 185 8300 or 984 876 2115; www.diamantek.com). Diamante K caters to travelers in search of serious escape. Outdoor showers, hanging beds, and "natural A/C" make the transition from beach to *cabaña* almost seamless. At night, garden torches light the area and paths connect the *cabañas,* restaurant, bar, and beach. Electricity during meal times. Simple *cabañas* start at 500 pesos; suites up to 2500 pesos. Cash only. ❺

Rancho Tranquilo, Av. Tulum 86 (☎871 2784; www.ranchotranquilo.com.mx), about 500m south of the bus station. From the bus station, walk south on the same side of the road and cross the bridge. Rancho Tranquilo is another 100m marked by two big surfboards. A tropical paradise right off the main highway, Rancho Tranquilo caters to a range of travelers with dorms, private *palapas,* and suites with kitchen, A/C, and private baths. Carefully maintained garden and tiled barbecue pit. Breakfast and kitchen use included. Free Wi-Fi. Bus to the beach 10 pesos. Laundry 30 pesos. 6-bed dorm 120 pesos; rooms start at 300 pesos. Prices fall 50-70 pesos in low season. Cash only. ❶

The Weary Traveler Hostel (☎871 2389 or 2390; tourdesk@intulum.com), 1 block south of the ADO bus station. Like a very chilled-out summer camp. Join the gang for free daily rides to the beach and other sites, barbecues, and a chance to ride the "Party Bus." Breakfast included. Outdoor communal kitchen. Lockers and linens included. Free Internet. On-site bar (beer 15 pesos) provides the most happening nightlife in town. Su barbecue 6pm-midnight (50 pesos). Single beds in dorms 100 pesos, with A/C 130 pesos; private rooms 280 pesos. Cash only. ❶

El Crucero (☎871 2610; www.el-crucero.com), off Mex. 307 in the *zona arqueológica,* across from Hotel Acuario. Just a few paces from the ruins, El Crucero offers young travelers a clean bar-restaurant and helpful staff. Internet 10 pesos per hr. Reception 8am-9pm. Check-out 1pm. Dorms 100 pesos; rooms 400 pesos, with A/C 600 pesos. Prices fall about 100 pesos in low season. AmEx/MC/V. ❶

Hotel Latino (☎871 2674 or 108 2684; tulumhotellatino@hotmail.com), on Andromeda St. between Orion and Beta Sur. Take a right 2 blocks north of the bus station, and then your 1st left. A small but slick little hotel in the center of town. A/C, flat-screen TVs, Wi-Fi, small pool, hammocks, and free bicycle use. Rooms with double beds start at US$50, more in high season. Cash only. ❷

Cabañas Copal (from Canada and the US ☎877-532-6737, international 604 834 5153; www.cabanascopal.com), 5km south of the ruins on Boca Paila. Part of a trio of beachside hotels, Copal offers the ultimate beach vacation: cliff-top views of crashing waves, spa treatments, little electricity, and a "clothing optional" environment. Hot water, common phones, and Wi-Fi. Nearby mini-marts and restaurants. *Cabañas* with common bath and shower start at 300 pesos, with private bath from 500 pesos. Prices rise 100 pesos in high season. MC/V. ❺

L'Hotelito (☎984 1240), on Av. Tulum and Beta Nte. Clean but basic rooms in a thatch-roofed 2-story house. Rooms with fan and shared bath 350 pesos. 100 pesos less during low season. Cash only. ❺

☕ FOOD

Although points of interest in Tulum are rather spread out, hearty and inexpensive food is never far away. The *pueblo* has many cheap *loncherías* and markets close to the bus station, while the beachside *cabañas* offer satisfying, budget-friendly restaurants with international cuisine. There is also a supermarket, **Super Marcaribe,** four blocks north of the bus station (☎871 2226; open daily 7am-10:30pm), and a **Mini-Super El Pipazo,** south of Cabañas Copal, next to the Nohock Tunich Cabañas (☎871 2271; open daily 7:30am-9pm).

¡Qué Fresco! (US ☎415-387-9806; www.zamas.com) at Hotel Zamas on the Boca Paila road, 6km south of the ruins. A treat for the eye and the stomach—the bright, bold color scheme is complemented by cool, blue-green waves rushing by on both sides. Fresh Mexican options include vegetarian dishes (from 75 pesos). Peanut butter, honey, and banana sandwich 50 pesos. Hearty breakfasts from 50 pesos. Open daily 7:30am-11pm. Cash only. ❹

Don Cafeto, Av. Tulum (☎871 2207), 4 blocks north of the bus station. Serves both local specialties and American standards. Walk in and smell the blackened *poblanos* and roasting meat, but watch out—that bowl of marinated veggies they whisk to your table is *picante!* Breakfasts 35-60 pesos. Mexican specialties such as *mole poblano* 80 pesos. Decadent coffee milkshakes 50 pesos. Open daily 7am-11pm. MC/V. ❸

La Nave Pizzería, Av. Tulum 570 (☎871 2592). Thin-crust brick-oven pizzas (from 40 pesos) with fresh ingredients and toppings, and spinach or seafood ravioli (80-140 pesos) are made daily by the Italian owners. Portions are small, but meals are served with onion focaccia and homemade bread. Open M-Sa 7:30am-11pm. ❸

Casa Díaz, at Av. Tulum and Oriente Nte. Smoke from the grill wafts across the open-air room as plastic tables and chairs spill onto the sidewalk. *Tacos al pastor* 6 pesos. Drinks 8 pesos. Open daily 6pm-midnight. Cash only. ❶

📷 NIGHTLIFE

Tulum is no Acapulco. The nightlife is mostly limited to the younger set, but there's certainly fun to be had in the small number of local clubs. **Acabar,** on Av. Tulum, is the best bet for live music. Rotating acts throughout the week ranging from heavy rock to a roots/reggae night. (☎108 8748. Mojitos 40 pesos. Beer 20 pesos. Open W-Su 5pm-late. Cash only.) In a town with limited nightlife, **Mezzanine,** km 1.5 on Boca Paila, has a Friday night scene that is as close as it gets to a dance party. The chic wooden deck overlooks the ocean and cool mixed drinks (40 pesos) can be enjoyed from one of the many scattered bean bag chairs.(☎112 2840; www.mezzanine.com.mx. Cover 100 pesos after 9pm. Open daily 8am-10pm, F until 2:30am. Cash only.)

🏄 WATERSPORTS AND OUTDOOR ACTIVITIES

BEACHES. Like the rest of the beaches in the Mayan Riviera, Tulum's are picture-perfect, to the point of seeming almost unreal. The only thing lacking is the commercialism that has long dominated the scene in Cancún and recently swept through Playa del Carmen. Here, you'll find a handful of bathers free of worry and, occasionally, of clothing. All beaches are public and **Playa Maya** offers a bar and a small restaurant. Offshore, waves crash over the **barrier reef,** the largest in the Americas, which runs the full length of the Yucatán Peninsula and Belize; the segment near Tulum was less damaged by Hurricane Wilma in 2005 than areas to the north. Although the water is not as clear as at Xel-Ha or Akumal, the fish are just as plentiful. The popular **Kiteboarding School Tulum** on the beach in front of El Paraiso restaurant is another way to enjoy Tulum's beaches. *(To mingle with the fish, rent scuba and snorkeling equipment from Dive Tulum, at Cabañas Diamante K, which also offers trips to the reef and a nearby cenote. ☎871 2096; www.divetulum.com. Snorkeling equipment US$5 per day. Trips US$25. 1-tank dive US$35; 2-tank dive US$50. Open daily 9am-5pm. Another option is Punta Piedra, 5km south of the ruins, a bit past Cabañas Copal. Snorkeling equipment 50 pesos per day. All-inclusive 3hr. trips from their beach 250 pesos. Open daily 8am-7pm. Kiteboarding School Tulum; ☎745 4555, www.extremecontrol.net. Open daily 9am-5pm.)*

CENOTES. Tulum's hidden treasures are the numerous *cenotes* sunken into the surrounding jungle. Most *cenotes* are open from 8am to 4pm. Diving alone is not recommended, but organized groups routinely explore the calm and clear waters.

⊠Hidden Worlds Cenote Park, on Mex. 307 about 12km from Pueblo Tulum, is a good way to see a series of spectacular *cenotes* with interactive guides. The privately owned property has more than 25 *cenotes* and has installed lights in many of them to illuminate the dramatic formations. Cenote Tak Beh Ha ("place of hidden waters"), which gave the park its name, is a highlight of all the snorkeling tours. The newly opened Dreamgate *cenote* is for advanced cave divers only and is virtually unscathed by human hands. Tours also include a ride of the jungle on their "Jungle Mobile," a tractor-turned-truck that can leap over rocks. The new skycycle sails from the top of the jungle canopy all the way to a deep cenote. *(To get to Hidden Worlds from Tulum, take a north-bound colectivo on Mex. 307. 20min., every 10min., 15 pesos. ☎877 8535; www.hiddenworlds.com. 1hr. snorkeling tours US$25-40, including equipment; 5 times per day. Discounts for children under 12. 2-tank scuba dive US$75, including equipment and guide. Discounts for larger groups. Open daily 9am-5pm. MC/V.)*

Cenote Escondido and **Cenote Cristal** are both 3km south of the intersection of Mex. 307 and the road to Cobá (30 pesos). Here you will find fresh-water tropical fish and green underwater vegetation in cool, crystal-clear waters. After following the road to Cobá 1.6km west out of town, you will come

ON THE MENU

MEXICAN CURES FOR THE HANGOVER

Those endless nights soaked in tequila have finally caught up to you. The fun-filled haze has been replaced by a splitting headache, and you don't think you can get on the rickety bus to the next town. Fortunately, you are not alone. *Mexicanos* long before you have had to deal with the *resaca* (hangover) and have come up with a variety of spicy and pungent concoctions to help you out. Here are a few local remedies.

The **michelada** combines lemon juice, tabasco sauce, and light beer in a glass with a salted rim. Mexicans swear that the delicious brew will eliminate hangovers quickly and painlessly.

Don't forget the oregano, *chile picín,* and onions to top your **menudo,** a spicy stew of cow intestines served at cafes. The more pungent, the faster your head will clear.

Not to be confused with "barbecue," **barbacoa** is cow brains served with tortillas. Load on the coriander and onions. Turn the cow brains into a soup and you've got *birria,* with the same healing properties. For the best effects, top your *birria* with red salsa from the *chile de árbol.*

Popular in and around the Copper Canyons, *arí* is a pungent drink made from ant excretions. The excretions are collected from a tree, boiled down with garlic, tomatoes, and *chiles rojos,* and served chilled to grumpy partiers the morning after.

across the **Cenote Calaveras,** named for its squash-like shape, also called the Temple of Doom. Look for a path behind a newly constructed house on your right (admission 50 pesos). Continue on the main road 1.5km farther to the clearly marked mini-paradise **El Gran Cenote,** part of the second largest underground river in the world, the Osh-Beh-Ha, and regarded as the best spot in the area for snorkeling (50 pesos; divers 65 pesos). Its unforgettable beauty is like something out of a fairy tale—bats, birds, and butterflies flutter over the cold, clear blue waters filled with friendly fish and green lily pads. Discovered more recently than its neighbor is the often crowded **Cenote Dos Ojos,** which was featured in the 1999 IMAX film *Journey Into Amazing Caves.* Dos Ojos is a popular dive spot for the many organized groups that leave from Tulum and Playa del Carmen. You must be a certified open water diver to dive in the often crowded Dos Ojos (1-tank US$50, 2-tank US$90), but there are 450m of cavern to see with just snorkel gear and a flashlight. The dive center has also installed lights to illuminate the beautiful sights that made it to the IMAX screen. Several free *cenotes,* mainly of interest to those who don't mind the bugs, are hidden across the street from the ranches and hotels at the southern end of **Boca Paila** right before **Sian Ka'an;** an especially large one lies behind a wooden gate opposite **Rancho San Erik.** Ask for a map at Punta Piedra.

◙ THE ARCHAEOLOGICAL SITE OF TULUM

The ruins lie a brisk 10min. walk east of Mex. 307 from the zona arqueológica crossing. The amusement park-style train pulled by a tractor (20 pesos) covers the distance in slightly less time. Tickets are sold at a booth to the left of the parking lot and at the entrance to the ruins. Open daily 8am-6pm. 45 pesos, video camera use 30 pesos. Guided tours available in several languages (45min.; 1-4 people 350 pesos, 5-8 people 400 pesos, 9-12 people 450 pesos, 13-16 people 500 pesos); inquire at the information or ticket booth.

The ruins at Tulum, known as Záma to its ancient residents, are best known for their picturesque setting perched above the multi-hued waters of the Caribbean. Once an important trading port between the interior Yucatán communities and the rest of the Mayan world reaching to Honduras, Tulum was one of the last pre-Hispanic Mayan cities and reached its zenith during the late post-Classic Period (1250-1550). Surrounded by a series of impressively high walls, the fortified and fully functional city was spotted by the Spaniard Juan de Grijalva in 1518 while on a scouting expedition from Cuba and promptly gave the name Tulum, or "wall." In 1544, the city fell to Spanish conquistadors, but it continued to serve as a fort from which the Spanish fended off English, Dutch, and French pirates. In the early 1840s, the site was rediscovered by archaeologists Frederick Catherwood and John Stevens, though the location had some continued use by local Maya. As late as 1847, Tulum provided refuge for Maya rebels fleeing government forces during the Caste War. Today, the ruins are infested with mosquitoes and busloads of sunburnt tourists from Playa del Carmen, but it remains an impressive and worthwhile excursion into the Mundo Maya.

THE WALL. The impressive wall, made of small rocks wedged together, protecting the city's landward sides, is the first structure to greet visitors. The wall, originally 6m thick and 4m high, kept away aggressive neighbors from other Mayan city-states while a smaller inner wall served as a political-religious boundary, preventing all but the 150 or so priests and governors of Tulum from entering the inner precinct. It is also the oldest standing structure in Tulum, dating back to the Terminal Classic Period (AD 800-1000). Every evening, the rays of the setting sun illuminate the representations of the Mayan Descending God that cover the western walls. From the southernmost wall, once a lookout point, you can admire a view of the turquoise sea below.

LA CASA DEL NOROESTE AND LA CASA DEL CENOTE. Left of the entrance to La Casa del Noroeste (the House of the Northwest) lie a grave and the remains of the platforms that once supported the thatched-roof houses of important religious figures of Tulum. One step closer to the ocean, up the small hill, is La Casa del Cenote (the House of the Cave). Built atop a small limestone shelf over a deep blue *cenote*, the house feels like part of the encroaching jungle. The western corridor of the home was the final resting ground for many, indicating that the house may have played an important role as a family crypt for royal residents of Tulum.

TEMPLO DEL DIOS VIENTO. A few paces to the south of La Casa del Cenote, the Templo del Dios Viento (Temple of the Wind God) is perched precipitously on the northeastern side of the beach. The temple was ingeniously designed to act as a storm-warning system. Sure enough, before Hurricane Gilbert struck the site in 1988, the temple's cavernous airways dutifully whistled their alarm.

EL CASTILLO. The most prominent structure in Tulum, El Castillo (the Castle) looms to the east over the rocky seaside cliff, commanding a view of the entire walled city. The pyramid, built in three separate stages, may not have been intended as a pyramid at all: the current structure was probably only built around the 12th or 13th century. The two columns separating the three entrances are in the form of serpents and a figure of the Descending God is visible above the center entrance—though it is tough to get close enough to see it. Elsewhere, bee-like imagery alludes to the importance of honey in Caribbean trade. More recently, El Castillo served as a lighthouse, guiding returning fishermen through the gap in the barrier reef. In front of the temple is the large sacrificial stone where the Maya held public ceremonies and religious rituals. Behind El Castillo, overheated tourists can scale the steep steps for a refreshing dip in the ocean.

TEMPLO DEL DIOS DESCENDIENTE. This structure stands immediately below the castle on the north side of the main religious plaza. A barely visible, fading relief of a feathered, armed divinity diving from the sky gives the temple its name, the Temple of the Descending God. The figure, seen on many buildings and on many stelae in Tulum, is believed to represent the setting sun, an important god for a city named after the sun itself. The building was once adorned with polychromatic murals of events from the life of this winged figure.

LA CASA DE LAS COLUMNAS AND EL PALACIO REAL. In the plaza below the El Castillo/Templo de Dios Descendiente plaza, El Palacio Real (the Royal Palace) and other important residential houses rest with faded majesty. Characterized by the many columns at their entrances and topped by giant carvings of the serpent-god, these flat-roofed houses were the largest residential homes in Tulum.

TEMPLO DE LOS FRESCOS. This temple is Tulum's best example of post-Classic Mayan architecture. Built in three separate stages, the Temple of the Paintings is really one temple on top of a series of older temples. Visible from the north side, 600-year-old murals with a bit of the original red coloring depict deities intertwined with serpents, fruits, corncobs, and flowers—all images associated with the gods of agricultural and fertility. The stela outside the temple is the only one ever found at Tulum, and the oldest piece at the site, dating from AD 546.

▓ DAYTRIPS FROM TULUM

SIAN KA'AN BIOSPHERE RESERVE

Follow the coastal road 7km south of Tulum to the Mayan arch at the entrance. The Centro Ecológico Sian Ka'an (☎984 871 2499; www.cesiak.org), next to the zona arqueológica bus station, leads the best tours (kayak birding tour US$68 per full-day, US$45 per half-day), departing from Tulum. Open daily 9am-5pm. You can also call the offices of The Amigos de Sian Ka'an (☎984 114 0750; www.siankaan-tours.org.), a group of ecologists and scientists who work to maintain the reserve. Open M-F 9am-2pm and 4-7pm. Free.

Sian Ka'an ("Where the Sky is Born") comprises roughly 10% (over 5200 sq. km) of the state of Quintana Roo and is Mexico's largest coastal wetland reserve, encompassing tropical forests, *cenotes*, savannas, mangroves, lagoons, and 112km of coral reef. Protected by federal decree since January 20, 1986, the immense reserve was Mexico's first ▓**UNESCO Natural World Heritage site.** It is home to 1200 species of flora, 336 species of birds, 103 species of mammals, and 23 pre-Classic and Classic Mayan archaeological sites. The best way to see the immense reserve is by an organized boat tour. Expert guides can point out bonefish, barracuda, snowy egrets, spoonbilled herons, and even pink flamingos to those with untrained eyes. Those who like to go it alone drive or bicycle down the 57km unpaved road, but often end up staring at a wall of dense jungle and watching blue crabs scuttle across the road. To get an independent peek at all the reserve has to offer, check out the open-air *cenote* immediately to the right of the Mayan arch at the entrance. The refreshing water is home to many species of fish as well as a host of orchids. The small fishing village of **Punta Allen** lies at the southern end of the 57km road. Though the small town is well off the beaten path, a few homes offer rooms and can cook your catch. Adventurous fishermen and birdwatchers can arrange independent tours from the town dock. Punta Allen can be reached by taxi (300 pesos one way) or independent transportation.

XEL-HA

Xel-Ha lies 15km north of Tulum; ask any northbound bus or colectivo to drop you at Xel-Ha (15 pesos). Taxis charge 80-100 pesos. To get back at the end of the day, vigorously wave down a bus on its way to Tulum. Locals will usually be able to tell you when the next one is due to pass. ☎998 883 3143; www.xelha.com.mx. Open daily 9am-6pm. M-F US$27, Sa-Su US$20; all-inclusive snorkel gear, lockers, towels, and all-you-can-eat restaurants US$51. 10% discount for tickets purchased online.

Xel-Ha (SHELL-ha; "Where the Water is Born") was once a Mayan fishing village, but is now an interactive aquarium (read: amusement park) set in the Yucatec jungle. Nestled amid 84 hectares of jungles, caves, and coves, Xel-Ha allows visitors to take in the beauty of the area with convenience. Float in an inner tube or snorkel down the nearly 4m deep central river as it flows from a *cenote*. Admire parrot fish and meter-long jackfish. It is no wonder that an average of 1600 people or more enter the park daily; you can stop along the way for adrenaline rushes from rope swings and rock jumps. With dolphin swims (from US$115), rocky paths, hidden *cenotes*, beach chairs, and hammocks overlooking the river, it's easy to spend a whole day here, either alone or with friends. For relative peace during busy times, cross the inlet and explore the underwater caves, or stay dry and visit the sea turtle nesting camp (Apr.-Nov.) on the beach. Try to come early, as tourists begin to arrive by the busload around noon. If you choose not to purchase the all-inclusive admission, you can rent towels (US$3) and snorkel gear (US$10) at the shower area. Bring insect repellent; the mosquitoes can be ruthless.

Besides the water activities, there is a small archaeological site on the highway, 100m south of the park entrance. **El Templo de Los Pájaros** and **El Palacio,** small Classic and post-Classic ruins, are all that remain of the once powerful Mayan community. The former (the farther into the jungle) overlooks a peaceful, shady *cenote* where swimming and rope swinging are allowed.

COBÁ

These Mayan ruins are less than 50km northwest of Tulum. To get to the ruins from the Cobá bus station, walk south on the main street in town as far as the T-junction at the lake. Take a left on Voz Suave; the ruins are a 5min. walk. Buses do not return to Tulum until 4, 5, or 6pm, but taxis (300 pesos) wait hungrily outside; share the ride. Bring a water bottle, hat, and plenty of mosquito repellent. Ruins open daily 8am-5pm. 45 pesos. Parking 10 pesos; bicycle rental inside 25 pesos. Tour guides can be found at the entrance. A 45min. tour for 1-6 people starts at 250 pesos, but bargaining is certainly an option. Allow at least 2hr. to see most of the site.

Stretching over 70 sq. km deep within the jungle, the ruins of Cobá recall what was perhaps the largest of all Mayan cities, and certainly one of the most important during the Classic Period. Inhabited at various intervals for over a millennium, the city reached its economic, political, and religious climax in the late Classic Period (AD 600-800), when it flourished as a commercial crossroads for the entire Yucatán Peninsula, connecting distant Mayan cities through its vast network of *sacbé*, ancient Mayan roadways. By the post-Classic Period, around AD 1000, Cobá had mysteriously lost its power to the nearby cities of Tulum and Xcaret, though it seems to have regained some of its importance between AD 1200 and 1500. However, when the Spanish arrived, they found the city abandoned. It remained in obscurity until John Stevens and Frederick Catherwood documented it with notes and drawings in the mid-19th century. Today, the tranquil, shaded ruins, surrounded by several shallow lakes, receive far less attention than those at Chichén Itzá and Tulum. The government has put less money into the site, leaving an estimated 6500 buildings unexcavated. Nevertheless, work slowly continues at Cobá; each year brings to light new structures.

Through the gate, the site's main attractions lie in a Y-shaped formation. The **Grupo Cobá** dates from the Early Classic Period (AD 200-600) and is near the entrance, at the base of the "Y." **Templo de la Lluvia** (Temple of the Rain) looms an impressive 28m high. Different levels are evident for each of the seven 52-year periods, each under a new chief priest. Only the front face of the temple has been excavated, revealing a corbel-vaulted passageway that you can explore. In front of the structure is a stone sacrificial table for animal offerings to Chac, the rain god. A second passageway leads farther south and has red plant dye from the 5th century still visible on the walls; it leads visitors to **Plaza del Templo,** where assemblies were once held. Return to the main path for a look at the **ball court** with its intact stone arches. The ball game was part of a sacred ceremony in which the movement of the round rubber ball made from native rubber trees symbolized the sun and moon, and it is believed the Maya thought the game maintained cosmic order. As in Mexico's current beloved game, *fútbol*, players could not touch the ball with their hands. Varying sources say that either the winners were sacrificed as an honor, or that the losers were sacrificed as punishment.

One kilometer farther up the trunk of the "Y" and another kilometer up the right branch brings you to the **Grupo Macanxoc** and its eight stelae. On the way, a section of the well-engineered Mayan *sacbé* awaits. This particular road is 20m wide and 4m above the jungle floor, made to weather otherwise crippling tropical rainstorms. Measuring up to 20m wide, the *sacbé* at Cobá range in length from several meters to 100km. Believed by some to serve a ritualistic rather than practical function, some *sacbé* have been built up to 4m above the ground. The ornately carved stone slabs of the Grupo Macanxoc were memorials above the tombs of Mayan royals, but unfortunately, their pictorial secrets are now barely discernible. The one exception is the first, the impressive and well-preserved **Retrato del Rey,** which portrays a king with quetzal-feather headdress and bow and arrow.

Along the left-hand branch of the "Y" is the **Templo de las Pinturas** (Temple of the Paintings), named for the richly colored frescoes that once adorned the building. The group of 20 buildings to which the temple belongs was constructed in the post-Classic period (AD 1250-1550) from reused stones and building materials. Follow an unmarked trail northwest of the temple to the three stelae of **Chumuc Múl.** The first is the tomb of a victorious captain, and it depicts a kneeling Mayan ballplayer, forever preserved with his ball. The second stela shows a princess, and the third portrays a priest, whose seal is stamped on the slab with a jaguar's head, a common Mayan symbol of worship. Two-hundred meters farther lies **sacbé No. 1,** a road that led all the way to Chichén Itzá, 101km west. Runners were posted every 5km to deliver messages via a series of quick jogs. Images of the honeybee god around the site are a reminder of Cobá's past as an economic hub, as the Maya used honey (along with salt, coconuts, and jade) as a medium of exchange.

Several hundred meters farther, toward the pyramid Nohoch Múl, you'll come upon another ball court, **Temple 10,** and the well-preserved **Stela 20.** Finally, you will see towering **Nohoch Múl,** the tallest Mayan structure in all the Yucatán. A climb up this breathtaking, 42m high stone pyramid will make the entire visit worth your while. The pyramid's nine levels and 127 steps, where Mayan priests once led processions, display carvings of the "diving god" similar to those in Tulum.

> ❗ **PERILOUS PYRAMIDS.** When descending, be especially careful not to lose your footing—several people have slipped and died during the descent. One way to avoid falling is by sitting down and working your way to the ground using your hands for support.

On your way out, the large lake just outside the ruins has a few crocodiles. Local entrepreneurs have discovered that tourists are willing to pay 5 pesos to watch them being fed. The better (and only) place you should think about swimming after a hot day at the ruins is the *cenote* on the far side, which feeds the lake.

CHETUMAL ☎ 983

The capital city of Quintana Roo, Chetumal (pop. 140,000) is a hub of activity and prosperity in Mexico's youngest state. Founded in 1889 as a naval base, the port's early inhabitants made a living intercepting arms and illegally harvested wood intended for Mayan rebels during the Caste War. The nearby English colony of Belize proved to be a strong influence on the town and many of the early buildings are in the English colonial style—wooden saltbox numbers with stilts and porches. They all came splintering down in 1955 when Hurricane Janet raged through, changing the cityscape for good. Today, you'll find a wide boulevard filled with speeding cars, a lively shopping district, and nearby natural wonders like the Laguna de Siete Colores in Bacalar (p. 698).

⌐ TRANSPORTATION

Flights: Aeropuerto Internacional de Chetumal (CTM), Prolongación Av. Revolución 660 (☎832 0465), 3km west of the city. Serves **Fleet Mexicano,** including **Aerocaribe** and **Mexicana** (☎832 6675) as well as **Aviacsa** (☎832 7676), on Cárdenas at 5 de Mayo. Taxis to the *centro* cost 50 pesos.

Buses: ADO station (☎832 5110), Insurgentes at Belice. To reach the *centro* from the station, your best bet is a taxi (15 pesos). 1st-class buses go to: **Belize City** (3hr.; 11:45am, 3, 6pm; 100 pesos); **Campeche** (7hr., noon, 262 pesos); **Cancún** (5½hr., 23 per day, 228-274 pesos); **Flores/Tikal** (8hr., 6am, 2pm; 290 pesos); **Mérida** (6-7hr., 4 per day 7:30am-11:30pm, 250 pesos); **Mexico City** (22hr.; 11:30am, 4:30, 9pm; 962 pesos); **Ocosingo** (5 per day 1:30am-11pm, 378-436 pesos); **Palenque** (7½hr., 11pm, 356 pesos); **Playa del Carmen** (4½hr., 23 per day, 190-228 pesos); **San Cristóbal de las Casas** (478-568 pesos); **Tulum** (3½hr., 11 per day, 152 pesos); **Tuxtla Gutiérrez** (7:45, 9:55, 11pm, 501 pesos); **Villahermosa** (9hr., 8 per day, 259 pesos); **Xpujil** (2hr., 10 per day, 98 pesos). **Caribe** lines leave from the 2nd-class bus station, at Colón and Belice, to **Xcalac** (5:40am, 4:10pm; 56 pesos). **Mayab** goes to: **Bacalar** (1hr., 26 pesos); **Cancún** (7hr., 178 pesos); **Mérida** (8hr., 8, 11:30am, 11pm; 180 pesos); **Playa del Carmen** (6hr., 140 pesos); **Ticul** (6 per day, 154 pesos); **Tulum** (5hr., 114 pesos).

Combis: On Francisco Primo de Verdad, 2 blocks east of Héroes. *Combis* leave for **Bacalar** (45min., every 40min. 6am-8pm, 15 pesos), **La Unión** (2½hr., every hr. 6am-6pm, 30 pesos), and **Santa Elena** (every hr., 8 pesos).

Taxis: Abundant in the *centro.* Within the *centro,* prices are negotiable (most trips 10-15 pesos).

BORDER CROSSING. To enter **Belize** for 30 days, Canadian, EU, and US citizens need only a valid passport and a bus ticket. To enter **Guatemala,** Canadian, EU, and US citizens need a valid passport but not a visa. For those who do need a visa, the process is quick and costs US$15. For more information, contact each country's **consulate** in Chetumal: **Belize,** Carranza 562 (☎044 9838 7728; open M-F 9am-2pm and 5-8pm, Sa 9am-2pm); **Guatemala,** Chapultepec 354 (☎832 3045; open M-F 10am-2pm).

✳☑ ORIENTATION AND PRACTICAL INFORMATION

Tucked into the southeastern corner of the Yucatán Peninsula, Chetumal is just north of **Río Hondo,** the border between Mexico and Belize. The shopping district lines **Héroes,** starting at **Mercado Viejo** and extending 1km south to the bay, and is packed with duty free shops. At the southern end of Héroes lies **Bahía,** a four-lane avenue that follows the bay for several kilometers, flanked by statues, small plazas, and playgrounds. From here you can see part of Belize—the long, distant piece of land to the south.

Tourist Offices: Módulos de Información, in the *centro* in front of the Museo de la Cultura Maya. Another branch on Bahía between Reforma and Hidalgo near Maqueta de Payo Obisbo. Both open daily 9am-8pm. **Secretaria Estatal de Turismo,** Centenario 622 (☎835 0860), between Ignacio Somosot and Ciricote, 4km from the *centro.* Open M-F 8am-6pm.

Currency Exchange and Bank: Banks line Héroes. **Bancomer** (☎832 5300), on Juárez at Obregón. Good rates and **24hr. ATM.** Open M-F 8:30am-4pm, Sa 10am-3pm.

Laundromat: Lavandería Juárez, Av. Chapultepec, between Madero and Independencia.

Luggage storage: At the ADO bus station. Open 24hr. 10 pesos per hr.

Emergency: ☎066.

Police: (☎832 1500), on Insurgentes at Belice, next to the bus station.

Red Cross: (☎832 0571), on Chapultepec at Independencia.

Pharmacy: Farmacia Canto, Héroes 99 (☎832 0483). Open M-Sa 7am-11pm, Su 7am-10pm.

Hospital: Hospital General, Quintana Roo 399 (☎832 1932), at Siordia.

Fax Office: Telecomm (☎832 0651), by the post office. Open M-F 8am-6pm, Sa-Su 9am-12:30pm.

Internet Access: Webcenter Internet (☎832 8138), on Aguilar between Belice and Héroes. Before 3pm 8 pesos per hr., after 3pm 10 pesos per hr. Open daily 8am-2am. **Odissey,** Zaragoza 190 (☎833 0100), between 5 de Mayo and Héroes. 10 pesos per hr. Open daily 9am-10pm.

Post Office: Calles 2 (☎832 2578), 1 block east of Héroes. Open M-F 9am-4pm, Sa 9am-1pm. **Mexpost** inside. **Postal Code:** 77000.

▟ ACCOMMODATIONS

Chetumal's budget accommodations are far from fancy, but they score points for location and convenience. A stroll down Héroes, south of the market, will yield many options. Reservations are necessary from mid-July through August. For a more luxurious experience, look into staying at one of the lagoon-side ranches in nearby Bacalar (p. 698).

Hotel María Dolores, Obregón 206 (☎832 0508), half a block west of Héroes. A Donald Duck cartoon points the way to aqua-colored rooms with private bath and fan. No A/C. Free purified water. Parking available. Restaurant attached. Check-out 1pm. Singles 215 pesos; doubles 235-270 pesos; triples 305 pesos. Cash only. ❸

Hotel Ucum, Gandhi 167 (☎832 0711; www.hotelucumchetumal.com). Dark, clean rooms have tiled floors and modern baths. Coffee after 7am. Parking available. Check-out 1pm. Singles and doubles 200 pesos, with cable TV 230 pesos, with A/C 350 pesos; triples with fan 230 pesos; quads with fan 260 pesos. Cash only. ❸

COJUDEQ Youth Hostel (☎832 0525), on Calle Heróica Escuela Naval, half a block from Veracruz, behind the theater. Marked only by the small *chac-mool* statue lounging in the yard, Chetumal's only hostel is certainly budget. Tidy 4-bed dorms are a bit cramped, but clean. The not-so-private institutional bathrooms could be cleaner. Lockers available. Beds 50 pesos. Cash only. ❶

Hotel Posada Pantoja, Lucio Blanco 81 (☎832 1781), 4 blocks from Veracruz. What is lost in location is gained in comfort and service. Spacious, cheerful rooms with A/C, coffee, and cable TV. Rooms on the right, above the reception, are newer and more attractive. Singles 280 pesos; doubles 360 pesos; each additional person 60 pesos. ❹

▛ FOOD

Chetumal is an international crossroads, and its restaurants serve a spicy blend of Mexican and Belizean cuisine as well as some Chinese buffet-style food and Middle Eastern options. *Loncherías*, at the **Mercado Viejo** on Héroes and Aguilar, and at **Altamarino,** on Obregón, west of Héroes, are the best deals.

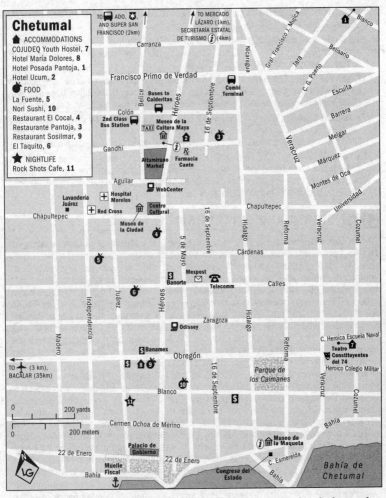

Chetumal

♠ ACCOMMODATIONS
COJUDEQ Youth Hostel, **7**
Hotel María Dolores, **8**
Hotel Posada Pantoja, **1**
Hotel Ucum, **2**

● FOOD
La Fuente, **5**
Nori Sushi, **10**
Restaurant El Cocal, **4**
Restaurante Pantoja, **3**
Restaurant Sosilmar, **9**
El Taquito, **6**

★ NIGHTLIFE
Rock Shots Cafe, **11**

Try to get a good sense of the sanitation situation in the kitchen before order-ing (open daily 6am-6pm). Stock up on vitals at the **Super San Francisco de Asís,** next to the bus station (open daily 7am-10pm).

Restaurant El Cocal (☎832 0882), in Hotel Los Cocos at the corner of Héroes and Héroes de Chapultepec. The terraced seating and neon-blue lighting as well as the strong A/C draws Chetumal's busy businessmen and well-dressed travelers for break-fast and dinner. Fruit and granola 40 pesos. Scrambled eggs with *frijoles*, tortillas, fruit, and coffee 50 pesos. MC/V. ❸

Restaurante Pantoja, Gandhi 181 (☎832 3957). A very popular family restaurant for locals and visitors alike. Delicious *comida casera del día* (homemade meals that rotate daily; 40 pesos) and great breakfasts (40 pesos) beat market prices. Open M-Sa 7am-7pm. Cash only. ❸

Nori Sushi Bar (☎ 129 2059; www.chetumal.com/sushibar), on Blanco between Héroes and 5 de Mayo. A sleek, small, and very white interior lends a posh vibe to the atmosphere. Maki rolls from 40 pesos. MC/V. ❸

El Taquito, Calles 220 (☎ 833 1602). Snack on tacos and *antojitos* under a fan-cooled *palapa* while your beef smokes on the spit. Tacos 8 pesos. Quesadillas 10 pesos. *Brocheta vegetariana* 35 pesos. Open M-Sa noon-5pm and 7pm-midnight. Cash only. ❷

Restaurant Sosilmar, Obregón 206 (☎ 832 6380), in front of the Hotel María Dolores. Tasty fish filets (60 pesos), *milanesa de puerco* (60 pesos), or *comida del día* (50 pesos) served amid green decor. Breakfasts 30-50 pesos. Open daily 8am-10:30pm. Cash only. ❹

La Fuente, Cárdenas 222 (☎ 832 5373). A 2-table dining area fronts the health-food store of the same name. Offers fresh juices and vegetarian *antojitos* and tells a thorough history of the soy bean. Sandwiches 12-18 pesos. Soy burgers 20 pesos. 3 tacos 21 pesos. Open M-F 8am-6pm, Sa 8am-3pm. Cash only. ❷

🎲 🎵 SIGHTS AND ENTERTAINMENT

At the northern end of the Altamarino market is the **Museo de la Cultura Maya,** on Héroes between Gandhi and Colón. This interactive museum explores the Maya's three-leveled cosmos—the earth, underworld, and heavens—with glyphic text, sculptures, stelae, and models of famous Mayan temples. Though the museum only has a small collection of artifacts, digital reproductions and detailed explanations give a cohesive overview of complex Mayan cosmology. (☎ 832 6838. Open Tu-Th 9am-7pm, F-Sa 9am-8pm, Su 9am-7pm. 50 pesos.) Stop in next door at one of the free art galleries, which showcase the work of regional artists. The **Museo de la Ciudad,** Héroes 68, in the Centro Cultural de las Bellas Artes south of the market, details the history of Chetumal and has art exhibits next door. Check with the office for other cultural events and shows. (Open Tu-Su 9am-7pm. 10 pesos.)

Though Chetumal has long stretches of coastline, none of them are suitable for swimming. The nearest **beach** is the *balneario* at Calderitas. Buses leave from Colón, between Héroes and Belice. (15min., every 30min. 7am-9pm, 5 pesos.) Although the shores are rocky and the water can be cloudy, the beach draws shoulder-to-shoulder crowds during summer and school holidays. Going left at the fork on Héroes (instead of right, toward Calderitas) and following the signs for 16km will bring you to **Oxtankah,** a set of ruins constructed sporadically over the course of many centuries, beginning in AD 200. In 1531, Spaniards arrived at the site and built a church before being forced to flee two years later. The few remains today showcase an intriguing mix of Mayan and Spanish architecture and history. (There is no public transportation to the site. For jungle adventures and other ecotourism excursions, contact **Sacbé Tours,** Av. Napoles 399. (☎/fax 833 2080, toll-free 800 036 4892; www.sacbetours.com.)

Chetumal's nightlife scene is mostly confined to window shopping at the duty free stores along Héroes. A small, brave, 20-something crowd gets down Cancún-style at **Rock Shots Cafe,** on Juárez between Blanco and Merino. (☎ 833 4720. Cover 40 pesos; Sa women free before midnight. Open Th-Su 11pm-4am.)

🔳 DAYTRIP FROM CHETUMAL

BACALAR

Buses leave from the station at the corner of Hidalgo and Verdad. (45min., every 40min. 6am-9pm, 15 pesos.) Last bus returns 8pm. The Bacalar ADO station is on Calle 5, one block south of the zócalo, and sells tickets for de paso buses to Mahahual and Cancún.

The road to Bacalar (36km from Chetumal; pop. 10,000) is peppered with vine-covered *cenotes* and fresh-water lagunas. Easily accessible *balnearios* (spas) equipped with *palapas*, parking, and restaurants just off the highway provide a chance to cool off in the turquoise waters and escape the hustle of Chetumal.

The town of Bacalar has access to the second largest lagoon in all of Mexico, **La Laguna de Siete Colores,** so named for the seven hues reflected in its depths. This beautiful spot, with its powdery white limestone beaches and warm fresh water, is popular with swimmers, kayakers, and sunbathers. The most obvious landmark in town is a large **fort,** which now houses an interesting museum and offers a good photo-op from its lookout tower. (Open M-Th 9am-7pm, F-Su 9am-8pm. 50 pesos.)

Behind the fort and 250m to the left lies the **Balneario Ejidal,** a complex of *palapas* and restaurants on an *ejido* (communal farm) where you can rent kayaks (100 pesos per hr.), take a *lancha* tour of the lagoon (1hr., 70 pesos per person), and swim to your heart's content. (Open daily 9am-5pm. Entrance 5 pesos. Parking 10 pesos. *Palapas* 20 pesos, Camping 50 pesos.) Across the narrow stretch of water from Balneario Ejidal is **Playa de las Piratas** and the channels where the sea dogs supposedly entered the lagoon. If you decide to paddle to Playa de las Piratas, be aware that the current goes toward the Playa, making for a hard return paddle.

The artist **Gilberto Silva** (☎ 834 2657) has a workshop and modest gallery in town on Calle 26, between Calles 5 and 7, next to the Casa de Cultura. It's worth a stop, even if just for a chat with the friendly man. In the studio, he makes exquisite carvings of Mayan monuments in limestone and then casts them in a mixture of local clay and minerals. His works are distributed as far as the Museum of Natural History in New York City, but he'll sell them to you for surprisingly affordable wholesale prices, starting at 250 pesos.

APPENDIX

SPANISH QUICK REFERENCE

PRONUNCIATION

Each vowel has only one pronunciation: A ("ah" in father); E ("eh" in pet); I ("ee" in eat); O ("oh" in oat); U ("oo" in boot); Y, by itself, is pronounced the same as Spanish I ("ee"). Most consonants are pronounced the same as in English. Important exceptions are: J, pronounced like the English "h" in "hello"; LL, pronounced like the English "y" in "yes"; and Ñ, pronounced like the "ny" in "canyon." R at the beginning of a word or RR anywhere in a word is trilled. B and V have similar pronunciations; at the beginning of a word they both sound like the English "b" (as in "boy"), while elsewhere they carry a softer sounding "b." H is always silent. G before E or I is pronounced like the "h" in "hen"; elsewhere it is pronounced like the "g" in "gate." D is pronounced softer, similar to the English "th." X has a bewildering variety of pronunciations: depending on dialect and word position, it can sound like English "h," "s," "sh," or "x."

Spanish words receive stress on the syllable marked with an accent (´). In the absence of an accent mark, words that end in vowels, "n," or "s" receive stress on the second to last syllable. For words ending in all other consonants, stress falls on the last syllable.

The Spanish language has masculine and feminine nouns, and gives a gender to all adjectives. Masculine words generally end with an "o": *él es un tonto* (he is a fool). Feminine words generally end with an "a": *ella es bella* (she is beautiful). Pay close attention—slight changes in word ending can cause drastic changes in meaning. For instance, when receiving directions, mind the distinction between *derecho* (straight) and *derecha* (right).

LET'S GO SPANISH PHRASEBOOK

ESSENTIAL PHRASES

ENGLISH	SPANISH	PRONUNCIATION
Hello.	Hola.	O-la
Goodbye.	Adiós.	ah-dee-OHS
Yes/No	Sí/No	SEE/NO
Please.	Por favor.	POHR fa-VOHR
Thank you.	Gracias.	GRAH-see-ahs
You're welcome.	De nada.	deh NAH-dah
Do you speak English?	¿Habla inglés?	AH-blah een-GLESS
I don't speak Spanish.	No hablo español.	NO AH-bloh ehs-pahn-YOHL
Excuse me.	Perdón/Disculpe.	pehr-THOHN/dee-SKOOL-peh
I don't know.	No sé.	NO SEH
Can you repeat that?	¿Puede repetirlo?/¿Mande?	PWEH-deh reh-peh-TEER-lo/MAHN-deh

SURVIVAL SPANISH

ENGLISH	SPANISH	ENGLISH	SPANISH
Good morning.	Buenos días.	How do you say (dodge-ball) in Spanish?	¿Cómo se dice (dodge-ball) en español?
Good afternoon.	Buenas tardes.	What (did you just say)?	¿Cómo?/¿Qué?/¿Mande?
Goodnight.	Buenas noches.	I don't understand.	No entiendo.
What is your name?	¿Cómo se llama?	Again, please.	Otra vez, por favor.
My name is (Pánfilo).	Me llamo (Pánfilo).	Could you speak more slowly?	¿Podría hablar más despacio?
What's up?	¿Qué tal?	Where is (the bath-room)?	¿Dónde está (el baño)?
See you later.	Nos vemos./Hasta luego.	Who?/What?	¿Quién?/¿Qué?
How are you?	¿Qué tal?/¿Comó está?	When?/Where?	¿Cuándo?/¿Dónde?
I'm sick/fine.	Estoy enfermo(a)/bien.	Why?	¿Por qué?
I am hot/cold.	Tengo calor/frío.	Because.	Porque.
I am hungry/thirsty.	Tengo hambre/sed.	Go on!/Come on!/Hurry up!	¡Ándale!
I want/would like...	Quiero/Quisiera...	Let's go!	¡Vámonos!
How much does it cost?	¿Cuánto cuesta?	Look!/Listen!	¡Mira!
That is very cheap/expensive.	Es muy barato/caro.	Stop!/That's enough!	¡Basta!
Is the store open/closed?	¿La tienda está abierta/cerrada?	Maybe.	Tal vez/Puede ser.

INTERPERSONAL INTERACTIONS

ENGLISH	SPANISH	ENGLISH	SPANISH
Where are you from?	¿De dónde viene usted?	Pleased to meet you.	Encantado(a)/Mucho gusto.
I am from (Europe).	Soy de (Europa).	Do you have a light?	¿Tiene fuego?
I'm (20) years old.	Tengo (veinte) años.	He/she seems cool.	Él/ella me cae bien.
Would you like to go out with me?	¿Quiere salir conmigo?	What's wrong?	¿Qué te pasa?
I have a boyfriend/girl-friend/spouse.	Tengo novio/novia/esposo(a).	I'm sorry.	Lo siento.
I'm gay/straight/bisex-ual.	Soy gay/no soy gay/soy bisexual.	Do you come here often?	¿Viene aquí a menudo?
I love you.	Te quiero.	This is my first time in Mexico.	Esta es mi primera vez en Mexico.
Why not?	¿Por qué no?	What a shame: you bought Lonely Planet!	¡Qué lástima: compraste Lonely Planet!

YOUR ARRIVAL

ENGLISH	SPANISH	ENGLISH	SPANISH
I am from (the US/Europe).	Soy de (los Estados Uni-dos/Europa).	What's the problem, sir/madam?	¿Cuál es el problema, señor/señora?
Here is my passport.	Aquí está mi pasaporte.	I lost my passport/lug-gage.	Se me perdió mi pasa-porte/equipaje.
I will be here for less than six months.	Estaré aquí por menos de seis meses.	I have nothing to declare.	No tengo nada para declarar.
I don't know where *that* came from.	No sé de dónde vino eso.	Please do not detain me.	Por favor no me detenga.

GETTING AROUND

ENGLISH	SPANISH	ENGLISH	SPANISH
How do you get to (the bus station)?	¿Cómo se puede llegar a (la estación de autobuses)?	Does this bus go to (Guanajuato)?	¿Esta autobús va a (Guanajuato)?
What bus line goes to..?	¿Cuál línea de buses tiene servicio a...?	Where does the bus leave from?	¿De dónde sale el bús?
When does the bus leave?	¿Cuándo sale el bús?	How long does the trip take?	¿Cuánto tiempo dura el viaje?
Can I buy a ticket?	¿Podría comprar un boleto?	I'm getting off at (Av. Juárez).	Me bajo en (Av. Juárez).
Where is (the center of town)?	¿Dónde está (el centro)?	Please let me off at (the zoo).	Por favor, déjeme en (el zoológico).
How near/far is...?	¿Qué tan cerca/lejos está...?	Where is (Constitución) street?	¿Dónde está la calle (Constitución)?
I'm in a hurry.	Estoy con prisa.	Continue forward.	Siga derecho.
I'm lost.	Estoy perdido(a).	On foot.	A pie.
I am going to the airport.	Voy al aeropuerto.	The flight is delayed/canceled.	El vuelo está atrasado/cancelado.
Where is the bathroom?	¿Dónde está el baño?	Is it safe to hitchhike?	¿Es seguro pedir aventón?
Where can I buy a cellphone?	¿Dónde puedo comprar un teléfono celular?	Where can I check email?	¿Dónde se puede chequear el correo electrónico?
Could you tell me what time it is?	¿Podría decirme qué hora es?	Are there student discounts available?	¿Hay descuentos para estudiantes?

ON THE ROAD

ENGLISH	SPANISH	ENGLISH	SPANISH
I would like to rent (a car).	Quisiera alquilar (un coche).	north	norte
How much does it cost per day/week?	¿Cuánto cuesta por día/semana?	south	sur
Does it have (heating/air-conditioning)?	¿Tiene (calefacción/aire acondicionado)?	public bus/van	bús
stop	pare	slow	despacio
lane (ends)	carril (termina)	yield	ceda
entrance	entrada	seatbelt	cinturón de seguridad
exit	salida	(maximum) speed	velocidad (máxima)
(narrow) bridge	puente (estrecho)	dangerous (curve)	(curva) peligrosa
narrow (lane)	(carril) estrecho	parking	estacionamiento, parking
toll (ahead)	peaje (adelante)	dead-end street	calle sin salida
authorized public buses only	transporte colectivo autorizado solamente	only (traffic only in the direction of the arrow)	solo
slippery when wet	resbala mojada	rest area	área de descansar
danger (ahead)	peligro (adelante)	do not park	no estacione
do not enter	no entre	do not turn right on red	no vire con luz roja

DIRECTIONS

ENGLISH	SPANISH	ENGLISH	SPANISH
(to the) right	(a la) derecha	near (to)	cerca (de)
(to the) left	(a la) izquierda	far (from)	lejos (de)
next to	al lado de/junto a	above	arriba

ENGLISH	SPANISH	ENGLISH	SPANISH
across from	en frente de/frente a	below	abajo
(Continue) straight.	(Siga) derecho.	block	cuadra/manzana
turn (command form)	doble	corner	esquina
traffic light	semáforo	street	calle/avenida

ACCOMMODATIONS

ENGLISH	SPANISH	ENGLISH	SPANISH
Is there a cheap hotel around here?	¿Hay un hotel económico por aquí?	Are there rooms with windows?	¿Hay habitaciones con ventanas?
Do you have rooms available?	¿Tiene habitaciones libres?	I am going to stay for (4) days.	Me voy a quedar (cuatro) días.
I would like to reserve a room.	Quisiera reservar una habitación.	Are there cheaper rooms?	¿Hay habitaciones más baratas?
Can I see a room?	¿Podría ver una habitación?	Do they come with private baths?	¿Vienen con baño privado?
Do you have any singles/doubles?	¿Tiene habitaciones simples/dobles?	I'll take it.	Lo acepto.
I need another key/towel/pillow.	Necesito otra llave/toalla/almohada.	There are cockroaches in my room.	Hay cucarachas en mi habitación.
The shower/sink/toilet is broken.	La ducha/pila/el servicio no funciona.	(The cockroaches) are biting me.	(Las cucarachas) me están mordiendo.
My bedsheets are dirty.	Mis sábanas están sucias.	Dance, cockroaches, dance!	¡Bailen, cucarachas, bailen!

EMERGENCY

ENGLISH	SPANISH	ENGLISH	SPANISH
Help!	¡Socorro!/¡Auxilio!/¡Ayúdeme!	Call the police!	¡Llame a la policía!
I am hurt.	Estoy herido(a).	Leave me alone!	¡Déjame en paz!
It's an emergency!	¡Es una emergencia!	Don't touch me!	¡No me toque!
Fire!	¡Fuego!/¡Incendio!	They robbed me!	¡Me han robado!
Call a clinic/ambulance/doctor/priest!	¡Llame a una clínica/una ambulancia/un médico/un padre!	They went that-a-way!	¡Se fueron por allá!
I need to contact my embassy.	Necesito comunicarme con mi embajada.	I will only speak in the presence of a lawyer.	Sólo hablaré con la presencia de un(a) abogado(a).

MEDICAL

ENGLISH	SPANISH	ENGLISH	SPANISH
I feel bad/worse/better/okay/fine.	Me siento mal/peor/mejor/más o menos/bien.	My (stomach) hurts.	Me duele (el estómago).
I have a headache/stomachache.	Tengo un dolor de cabeza/estómago.	It hurts here.	Me duele aquí.
I'm sick/ill.	Estoy enfermo(a).	I'm allergic to (nuts)	Soy alérgico(a) a (nueces)
Here is my prescription.	Aquí está mi receta médica.	I think I'm going to vomit.	Pienso que voy a vomitar.
What is this medicine for?	¿Para qué es esta medicina?	I have a cold/a fever/diarrhea/nausea.	Tengo gripe/una calentura/diarrea/náusea.
Where is the nearest hospital/doctor?	¿Dónde está el hospital/doctor más cercano?	I haven't been able to go to the bathroom in (4) days.	No he podido Ir al baño en (cuatro) días.

APPENDIX

EATING OUT

ENGLISH	SPANISH	ENGLISH	SPANISH
breakfast	desayuno	Where is a good restaurant?	¿Dónde está un restaurante bueno?
lunch	almuerzo	Can I see the menu?	¿Podría ver la carta/el menú?
dinner	comida/cena	Table for (one), please.	Mesa para (uno), por favor.
dessert	postre	Do you take credit cards?	¿Aceptan tarjetas de crédito?
drink (alcoholic)	bebida (trago)	I would like to order (the chicken).	Quisiera (el pollo).
cup	copa/taza	Do you have anything vegetarian/without meat?	¿Hay algún plato vegetariano/sin carne?
fork	tenedor	Do you have hot sauce?	¿Tiene salsa picante?
knife	cuchillo	This is too spicy.	Es demasiado picante.
napkin	servilleta	Disgusting!	¡Guácala!/¡Qué asco!
spoon	cuchara	Delicious!	¡Qué rico!
bon appétit	buen provecho	Check, please.	La cuenta, por favor.

MENU READER

SPANISH	ENGLISH	SPANISH	ENGLISH
a la brasa	roasted	frijoles	beans
a la plancha	grilled	leche	milk
al vapor	steamed	legumbres	legumes
aceite	oil	licuado	smoothie
aceituna	olive	lima	lime
agua (purificada)	water (purified)	limón	lemon
ajo	garlic	limonada	lemonade
almeja	clam	lomo	steak or chop
arroz (con leche)	rice (rice pudding)	maíz	corn
birria	cow brain soup, a hangover cure	mariscos	seafood
bistec	beefsteak	miel	honey
café	coffee	mole	dark chocolate chile sauce
caliente	hot	pan	bread
camarones	shrimp	papas (fritas)	potatoes (french fries)
carne	meat	parrillas	various grilled meats
cebolla	onion	pastes	meat pie
cemitas	sandwiches made with special long-lasting bread	pasteles	desserts/pies
cerveza	beer	pescado	fish
ceviche	raw marinated seafood	pimienta	pepper
charales	small fish, fried and eaten whole	plato	plate
chaya	plant similar to spinach native to the Yucatán	pollo	chicken

SPANISH	ENGLISH	SPANISH	ENGLISH
chorizo	spicy sausage	puerco/cerdo	pork
coco	coconut	pulque	alcohol made from maguey cactus
cordero	lamb	queso	cheese
(sin) crema	(without) cream	refresco	soda pop
dulces	sweets	verduras/vegetales	vegetables
dulce de leche	caramelized milk	sal	salt
empanada	dumpling filled with meat, cheese, or potatoes	sopes	thick tortillas, stuffed with different toppings
ensalada	salad	tragos	mixed drinks/liquor
entrada	appetizer	Xtabentún	anise and honey liqueur

NUMBERS, DAYS, AND MONTHS

ENGLISH	SPANISH	ENGLISH	SPANISH	ENGLISH	SPANISH
0	cero	30	treinta	weekend	fin de semana
1	uno	40	cuarenta	morning	mañana
2	dos	50	cincuenta	afternoon	tarde
3	tres	60	sesenta	night	noche
4	cuatro	70	setenta	day	día
5	cinco	80	ochenta	month	mes
6	seis	90	noventa	year	año
7	siete	100	cien	early	temprano
8	ocho	1000	mil	late	tarde
9	nueve	1000000	un millón	January	enero
10	diez	Monday	lunes	February	febrero
11	once	Tuesday	martes	March	marzo
12	doce	Wednesday	miércoles	April	abril
13	trece	Thursday	jueves	May	mayo
14	catorce	Friday	viernes	June	junio
15	quince	Saturday	sábado	July	julio
16	dieciseis	Sunday	domingo	August	agosto
17	diecisiete	day before yesterday	anteayer	September	septiembre
18	dieciocho	yesterday	ayer	October	octubre
19	diecinueve	last night	anoche	November	noviembre
20	veinte	today	hoy	December	diciembre
21	veintiuno	tomorrow	mañana	2008	dos mil ocho
22	veintidos	day after tomorrow	pasado mañana	2009	dos mil nueve

SPANISH GLOSSARY

aduana: customs
agencia de viaje: travel agency
aguardiente: strong liquor
aguas frescas: cold fresh juice/tea
aguas termales: hot springs
ahora: now
ahorita: in just a moment
aire acondicionado: air-conditioning (A/C)
al gusto: as you wish
alemán: German
almacén: (grocery) store
almuerzo: lunch, midday meal
altiplano: highland
amigo(a): friend
andén: platform
antro: club/disco/joint
antojitos: appetizers
arena: sand
arroz: rice
artesanía: arts and crafts
avenida: avenue
azúcar: sugar
bahía: bay
balneario: spa
bandido: bandit
baño: bathroom or natural spa
barato(a): cheap
barranca: canyon
barro: mud
barrio: neighborhood
bello(a): beautiful
biblioteca: library
biosfera: biosphere
birria: meat stew, usually goat or lamb
bistec: beefsteak
blanquillo: egg
bocaditos: appetizers, at a bar
bodega: convenience store or winery
boletería: ticket counter
boleto: ticket
bonito(a): pretty
borracho(a): drunk
bosque: forest
botanas: snacks, frequently at bars
bueno(a): good
buena suerte: good luck
burro: donkey
caballero: gentleman
caballo: horse
cabañas: cabins
cajeros: cashiers
cajeros automáticos: ATM
caldo: soup, broth, or stew
calle: street
cama: bed

cambio: change
caminata: hike
camino: path, track, road
camión: truck
camioneta: small, pickup-sized truck
campamento: campground
campesino(a): person from a rural area, peasant
campo: countryside
canotaje: rafting
cantina: bar/drinking establishment
capilla: chapel
carne asada: roasted meat
carnitas: diced, cooked pork
caro(a): expensive
carretera: highway
carro: car, or sometimes a train car
casa: house
casa de cambio: currency exchange establishment
casado(a): married
cascadas: waterfalls
catedral: cathedral
cenote: fresh-water well
centro: city center
cerca: near/nearby
cerro: hill
cerveza: beer
ceviche: raw seafood marinated in lemon juice, herbs, veggies
cevichería: ceviche restaurant
chico(a): boy (girl), little
chicharrón: bite-sized pieces of fried pork, pork rinds
chuleta de puerco: pork chop
cigarillo: cigarette
cine: cinema
ciudad: city
ciudadela: neighborhood in a large city
coche: car
cocodrilo: crocodile
colectivo: shared taxi
colina: hill
coliseo: coliseum, stadium
comedor: dining room
comida del día: daily special
comida corrida: fixed-price meal
comida típica: typical/traditional dishes
computador: computer
con: with
concha: shell
consulado: consulate
convento: convent
correo: mail, post office
correo electronico: email

cordillera: mountain range
corvina: sea bass
crucero: crossroads
Cruz Roja: Red Cross
cuadra: street block
cuarto: room
cuenta: bill, check
cuento: story, account
cueva: cave
cuota: toll
curandero: healer
damas: ladies
desayuno: breakfast
descompuesto: broken, out of order; spoiled food
desierto: desert
despacio: slow
de paso: in passing, usually refers to buses
de turno: a 24hr. rotating schedule for pharmacies
dinero: money
discoteca: dance club
dueño(a): owner
dulces: sweets
duna: dune
edificio: building
ejido: communal land
embajada: embassy
embarcadero: dock
emergencia: emergency
encomiendas: estates granted to Spanish settlers in Latin America
entrada: entrance
equipaje: luggage
estadio: stadium
este: east
estrella: star
extranjero: foreign, foreigner
farmacia: pharmacy
farmacia en turno: 24hr. pharmacy
feliz: happy
ferrocarril: railroad
fiesta: party, holiday
finca: farm
friaje: sudden cold wind
frijoles: beans
frontera: border
fumar: to smoke
fumaroles: holes in a volcanic region which emit hot vapors
fundo: large estate or tract of land
fútbol: soccer
ganga: bargain
gobierno: government
gordo(a): fat
gorra: cap

gratis: free
gringo(a): Caucasian
habitación: a room
hacer una caminata: take a hike
hacienda: ranch
helado: ice cream
hermano(a): brother (sister)
hervido(a): boiled
hielo: ice
hijo(a): son (daughter)
hombre: man
huevo: egg
iglesia: church
impuestos: taxes
impuesto valor añadido (IVA): value added tax (VAT)
indígena: indigenous person, refers to the native culture
ir de camping: to go camping
isla: island
jaiba: crab meat
jamón: ham
jarra: pitcher
jirón: street
jugo: juice
ladrón: thief
lago/laguna: lake
lancha: launch, small boat
langosta: lobster
langostino: jumbo shrimp
larga distancia: long distance
lavandería: laundromat
lejos: far
lento: slow
librería: bookstore
licuado: smoothie, shake
lista de correos: mail holding system in Latin America
llamada: call
loma: hill
lomo: chop, steak
lonchería: snack bar
loro: parrot
madre: mother
malo(a): bad
malecón: pier or seaside boardwalk
maletas: luggage, suitcases
manejar despacio: to drive slowly
manzana: apple
mar: sea
mariscos: seafood
matrimonial: double bed
menestras: lentils/beans
menú del día/menú: fixed daily meal often offered for a bargain price
mercado: market
merendero: outdoor bar/kiosk
merienda: snack
mestizaje: crossing of races

mestizo(a): a person of mixed European and indigenous descent
microbús: small, local bus
mirador: an observatory or lookout point
muelle: wharf
muerte: death
museo: museum
música folklórica: folk music
nada: nothing
naranja: orange
niño(a): child
norte (Nte.): north
nuez/nueces: nut/nuts
obra: work of art, play
obraje: primitive textile workshop
oeste: west
oficina de turismo: tourist office
oriente (Ote.): east
padre: father
palapa: palm-thatched umbrella
pampa: a treeless, grassland area
pan: bread
panadería: bakery
panga: motorboat
papagayo: parrot
parada: a stop (on a bus or train)
parilla: various cuts of grilled meat
paro: labor strike
parque: park
parroquia: parish
paseo turístico: tour covering a series of sites
pelea de gallos: cockfight
peligroso(a): dangerous
peninsulares: Spanish-born colonists
pescado: fish
picante: spicy
plátano: plantain
playa: beach
población: population, settlement
poniente (Pte.): west
policía: police
portales: archways
pueblito: small town
pueblo: town
puente: bridge
puerta: door
puerto: port
queso: cheese
rana: frog
recreo: place of amusement, bar-restaurant on the outskirts of a city

refrescos: refreshments, soft drinks
refugio: refuge
reloj: watch, clock
requesón: cottage cheese
río: river
ropa: clothes
sábanas: bedsheets
sabor: flavor
sala: living room
salida: exit
salto: waterfall
salsa: sauce
seguro(a): lock, insurance; adj.: safe
selva: jungle
semáforo: traffic light
semana: week
Semana Santa: Holy Week
sexo: sex
SIDA: AIDS
siesta: mid-afternoon nap; businesses often close at this time
sillar: flexible volcanic rock used in construction
sol: sun
solito(a): alone
solo carril: one-lane road or bridge
soltero(a): single (unmarried)
supermercado: supermarket
sur (S.): south
tarifa: fee
tapas: bite-size appetizers served in bars
telenovela: soap opera
termas: hot mineral springs
terminal terrestre: bus station
tienda: store
timbre: bell
tipo de cambio: exchange rate
tortuga: turtle
trago: mixed drink/shot of alcohol
triste: sad
turismo: tourism
turista: tourist; tourist diarrhea
valle: valley
vecindad: neighborhood
vegetariano(a): vegetarian
volcán: volcano
zócalo: central town plaza
zona: zone

CONVERSIONS

CLIMATE

	Average Temperature and Precipitation											
	January			April			July			October		
	°C	°F	mm	°C	°F	mm	°C	°F	mm	°C	°F	mm
Acapulco	21-31	70-88	10	22-32	71-89	5	24-32	75-90	208	24-32	75-90	145
Cancún	19-27	67-81	8	23-29	73-85	41	26-32	78-90	109	23-31	74-87	218
Guadalajara	7-24	44-75	18	12-30	53-86	8	17-27	62-80	249	13-27	56-80	48
Hermosillo	8-25	54-77	13	13-31	56-88	3	23-39	73-102	61	18-36	65-97	18
La Paz	12-23	54-74	5	14-30	58-86	0	23-36	73-96	10	20-32	68-90	15
Mazatlán	14-27	57-80	15	16-29	61-84	3	25-32	77-90	152	23-32	73-89	74
Mérida	17-29	63-84	25	21-35	69-95	23	22-34	72-93	163	21-31	69-88	94
Mexico City	6-21	43-70	10	11-26	52-79	28	12-23	53-73	183	10-22	50-72	61
Monterrey	9-19	48-67	15	18-30	65-86	33	23-34	74-94	58	18-28	64-83	76
Oaxaca	8-25	47-77	3	14-31	57-88	38	15-28	59-82	89	13-26	56-79	51
San Luis Potosí	6-20	42-68	8	13-29	55-85	13	14-26	58-79	48	11-24	52-75	28
Tijuana	8-20	46-68	73	11-23	51-73	27	17-29	62-84	2	14-27	57-80	15
Veracruz	18-24	64-75	23	23-28	73-83	23	23-31	74-87	376	22-29	72-85	135
Villahermosa	19-24	66-76	91	21-30	70-86	71	23-30	74-86	132	22-28	71-83	269

MEASUREMENTS

Mexico uses the metric system. The basic unit of length is the **meter (m)**, which is divided into 100 **centimeters (cm)**, or 1000 **millimeters (mm)**. One thousand meters make up one **kilometer (km)**. Fluids are measured in **liters (L)**, each divided into 1000 **milliliters (ml)**. A liter of pure water weighs one **kilogram (kg)**, divided into 1000 **grams (g)**, while 1000kg make up one metric **ton**.

1 in. = 25.4mm	1mm = 0.039 in.
1 ft. = 0.30m	1m = 3.28 ft.
1 yd. = 0.914m	1m = 1.09 yd.
1 mi. = 1.609km	1km = 0.62 mi.
1 oz. = 28.35g	1g = 0.035 oz.
1 lb. = 0.454kg	1kg = 2.205 lb.
1 fl. oz. = 29.57ml	1ml = 0.034 fl. oz.
1 gal. = 3.785L	1L = 0.264 gal.

DISTANCES (KM) AND TRAVEL TIMES (BY BUS)

	Acapulco	Chihuahua	Cancún	Cd. Juárez	Guadalajara	La Paz	Mazatlán	Mérida	Mexico City	Monterrey	Oaxaca	Puebla	Tuxtla Gutiérrez	San Luis Potosí	Tijuana	Veracruz
Acapulco		2440km	1946km	2815km	984km	4917km	1459km	1828km	411km	1402km	711km	537km	960km	828km	3228km	847km
Chihuahua	24hr.		3262km	375km	1552km	3237km	1031km	2945km	1496km	818km	2154km	1571km	2473km	1195km	1570km	1854km
Cancún	33hr.	47hr.		3600km	2442km	6499km	2963km	319km	1766km	2506km	1701km	1895km	1159km	2267km	4810km	1421km
Cd. Juárez	29hr.	5hr.	54hr.		1522km	3009km	1397km	3320km	1871km	1209km	2529km	2000km	2752km	1569km	1309km	2229km
Guadalajara	15hr.	17hr.	45hr.	25hr.		4159km	505km	2125km	676km	885km	1222km	805km	1608km	348km	2340km	1021km
La Paz	60hr.	46hr.	96hr.	41hr.	60hr.		3508km	6180km	4733km	4071km	5279km	4862km	5324km	4283km	1689km	5050km
Mazatlán	21hr.	15½hr.	53hr.	25hr.	8hr.	50hr.		2646km	1197km	928km	1743km	1326km	2105km	799km	1819km	1526km
Mérida	29hr.	42hr.	4hr.	47hr.	40½hr.	92hr.	40hr.		1449km	2189km	1408km	1791km	838km	1918km	4491km	1104km
Mexico City	6hr.	20hr.	26hr.	25hr.	10hr.	68hr.	18hr.	22hr.		989km	546km	129km	1030km	413km	3044km	345km
Monterrey	18hr.	12hr.	38hr.	17hr.	11hr.	60hr.	17hr.	32hr.	12hr.		1533km	1116km	1809km	537km	2382km	1085km
Oaxaca	9hr.	29hr.	29hr.	34hr.	17hr.	77hr.	27hr.	24½hr.	9hr.	21hr.		417km	542km	959km	3590km	450km
Puebla	7hr.	22hr.	24hr.	27hr.	12hr.	71hr.	20hr.	20hr.	2hr.	14hr.	4hr.		923km	542km	3285km	303km
Tuxtla Gutiérrez	14hr.	37hr.	19hr.	42hr.	28hr.	86hr.	17hr.	14½hr.	16hr.	28hr.	10hr.	14hr.		1590km	4193km	833km
San Luis Potosí	10hr.	14hr.	31hr.	18hr.	6hr.	60hr.	12hr.	27hr.	5hr.	7hr.	20hr.	16hr.	23hr.		2743km	846km
Tijuana	46hr.	22hr.	72hr.	17hr.	34hr.	22hr.	26hr.	66hr.	44hr.	36hr.	53hr.	46hr.	62hr.	36hr.		3354km
Veracruz	13hr.	28hr.	21hr.	33hr.	17hr.	76hr.	26hr.	13hr.	8hr.	17hr.	8hr.	4½hr.	13hr.	13hr.	52hr.	

INDEX